**FIFTH
EDITION**

SPECIAL
EDUCATION

CONTEMPORARY PERSPECTIVES
FOR SCHOOL PROFESSIONALS

MARILYN FRIEND

Professor Emerita, Department of Specialized Education Services
The University of North Carolina at Greensboro

New York, NY

Director and Portfolio Manager: Kevin M. Davis
Content Producer: Janelle Rogers
Development Editor: Alicia Reilly
Media Development Editor: Carolyn Schweitzer
Media Project Manager: Lauren Carlson
Portfolio Management Assistant: Anne McAlpine
Executive Field Marketing Manager: Krista Clark
Executive Product Marketing Manager: Christopher
    Barry
Procurement Specialist: Carol Melville
Cover Designer: Carie Keller

Cover Art: Getty Images/David Henderson
Full-Service Project Management: Thistle Hill
    Publishing Services
Composition: Cenveo® Publisher Services
Printer/Binder: LSC Communications/Kendallville
Cover Printer: Phoenix Color/Hagerstown
Text Font: 10/12 ITC Garamond Std

Credits and acknowledgments for material borrowed from other sources and reproduced, with permission, in this textbook appear on the appropriate pages within the text.

Every effort has been made to provide accurate and current Internet information in this book. However, the Internet and information posted on it are constantly changing, so it is inevitable that some of the Internet addresses listed in this textbook will change.

Photo credits are on page xxxiii and constitute a continuation of this copyright page.

Cataloging-in-Publication Data is available on file at the Library of Congress.

ISBN 10:   0-13-489500-2
ISBN 13: 978-0-13-489500-0

7 2021

About the Author

MARILYN FRIEND has been a professional educator for more than 40 years. She has worked as a general education teacher and a special education teacher, as well as a university professor, teacher educator, researcher, and staff developer. She is past president of the Council for Exceptional Children, the largest professional association for educators who work with students with disabilities and gifts/talents, and she was the 2016 recipient of the Teacher Education Division/Pearson Excellence in Special Education Teacher Education Award. Her specific areas of expertise include collaboration among school professionals, inclusive practices, co-teaching, and specialized instruction. What makes Dr. Friend unique is the balance among her professional activities: Although she recently retired as Chair and Professor of Special Education, Department of Specialized Education Services, The University of North Carolina at Greensboro, she has always maintained close contact with elementary, middle, and high school professionals, assisting educators in rural, suburban, and urban school districts to refine their practices for meeting diverse student needs. She has extensive accomplishments and experiences as both a scholar and as a knowledgeable practitioner and is widely recognized for her ability to translate research into effective classroom, school, and district/system practice.

Preface

THIS BOOK WAS ORIGINALLY WRITTEN FOR THE SAME REASON, I am sure, as many before it: As a university faculty member preparing teachers, I was dissatisfied with all the textbooks intended to introduce school professionals to special education. Some books were so technical that I doubted a preservice educator would retain the material included; others overly simplified this complex discipline. Yet others presented views that seemed out of touch with the realities of contemporary schooling. My goal in *Special Education: Contemporary Perspectives for School Professionals* was to write a text that would provide teacher candidates and other preprofessionals and early-career professionals—general educators, special educators, administrators, and related services providers—a solid grounding in contemporary special education concepts and practices. I wanted to produce an introductory book that clearly relied on the strong research base for this field and that not only aligned with current legislation but also placed that research and law within the very real and sometimes unclear and challenging world of students and educators, classrooms and schools, families and communities. Across five editions of this textbook, that goal has not changed. I hope this edition improves outcomes for students with disabilities and gifts/talents by substantially influencing the knowledge and skills of their teachers and other professionals who touch their lives at school.

New to This Edition

Special education changes rapidly, and in this fifth edition of *Special Education: Contemporary Perspectives for School Professionals*, great care has been taken to provide information that reflects the most current research and issues influencing the field. In addition, each chapter has been carefully reviewed, and updated references, examples, and strategies have been added. These are several of the most significant changes in this edition:

- *Integration of the most current legislation affecting education and special education.* The Every Student Succeeds Act (ESSA), the reauthorization of the Elementary and Secondary Education Act, now guides expectations, policy, and practice in U.S. schools, and its principles are reflected in this textbook. The most significant example relates to response to intervention (RTI): ESSA emphasizes the use of a multi-tiered system of support (MTSS), a tiered, schoolwide approach that incorporates both the academic emphasis of RTI as well as the elements of positive behavior supports. This broader conceptualization of support systems for students can have a strong influence on prevention of the need for special education as well as the assessment and eligibility process.

- *Updated diagnostic information.* Since the fourth edition, a major revision has been published of the *Diagnostic and Statistical Manual of Mental Disorders (DSM-5)* of the American Psychiatric Association. Although educational determination of the presence of a disability is separate from medical diagnosis, the *DSM-5* nonetheless selectively but significantly affects school practices. One clear example concerns autism. In *DSM-5*, the previously distinct subtype called Asperger syndrome was dropped because of a lack of evidence that clearly distinguished it from a more general diagnosis. This change is reflected in the fifth edition of *Special Education: Contemporary Perspectives for School Professionals*.

- *Videos that clarify concepts and illustrate the realities of students with disabilities, their families, and their teachers.* The availability of powerful video clips has greatly expanded in the years since the fourth edition, and this resource has been tapped for the fifth edition. A great deal of care has gone into selecting videos for these purposes: First, some videos are intended to succinctly summarize critical concepts related to special education or a specific disability or to summarize such information presented in text. Second, some videos depict children or youth with disabilities and/or their families, and these are included to make real what otherwise might be abstract understandings of them. Finally, several videos illustrate interventions or techniques effective when teaching students with disabilities, thus giving teacher candidates a glimpse into their future profession.

- *Issues facing the field of special education.* Perhaps because of the complexity of the needs that students with disabilities may have, the field continues to face ongoing and new issues. In this edition, such issues have been embedded in chapters where they are most relevant. For example, a discussion of the ongoing disproportionate representation of some students in special education is addressed in Chapter 3, updated information about co-teaching and other collaborative practices integral to special education is incorporated into Chapter 4, and the contentious topic of seclusion and restraint of students with challenging behaviors is addressed in Chapter 7.

- *The most recent research, data, and thinking about key topics in special education.* Up-to-date information is essential for today's professional educators, and this edition provides it. For example, all data related to the numbers of students receiving special education, their placements, their representation in various disability categories, and other facts about them have been updated. In addition, over 800 new references have been added, an indicator of the careful review of each concept presented and the search for the most contemporary thinking available about those concepts.

- *New stories about students with disabilities and their families.* Professionals who will work with students with disabilities need to understand the perspectives of students and families. Toward that end, new stories about students with disabilities and their experiences in public schools are included. This is most clearly seen in the chapter-opening vignettes; 14 of these have been replaced with new stories.

- *More examples of strategies and teaching techniques.* Although this book is not intended to comprehensively address teaching methods, each chapter includes research-based, specific strategies that address the learning and behavior needs of students with disabilities. Teacher candidates also are reminded throughout that many of the strategies presented in one chapter are easily and effectively used with students described in other chapters.

- *Instructional and assistive technology.* Technology seems to change almost on a daily basis, and the technology options included in the fifth edition have been carefully reviewed and revised to ensure that they reflect those new and improved options. At the same time, dated technology or options that are no longer available have been removed.

- *Time lines that provide snapshots of the history of important events.* Most professionals agree that teacher candidates should have a perspective on the development of the field of special education. However, they also note the need for such information to be presented in a succinct way. In the fifth edition, each chapter in which a historical view is appropriate includes an updated time line that captures key events in a way that can be quickly scanned and understood. This approach allows for considerable historical detail to be provided in an easily understood format.

- *Websites that lead readers to valuable resources.* The amount and quality of information available to educators through the Internet has exploded. In this new edition, every chapter includes new electronic sources of information, instructional strategies, and tools teachers will find valuable as they gather data, plan instruction, and learn about critical issues in the field. Those web-based resources also enable readers to extend their knowledge by exploring professional organizations representing individuals with disabilities and other special needs, investigating in more depth topics that could only be briefly introduced in the textbook, and discovering additional teaching strategies.

And those are just a few of the highlights. The fifth edition of *Special Education: Contemporary Perspectives for School Professionals* reflects along every dimension the most current information about special education.

Setting a Context

Two sets of experiences shaped my approach to writing this text. The first is my university work with preservice and practicing teachers in both general education and special education. I've had the privilege of taking a leadership role in developing two undergraduate special education teacher education programs: one that resulted in dual licensure and one that resulted in a special education major. I've also participated in creating several new graduate special education programs: alternative routes to licensure, master's degrees, and doctoral degrees. In addition, I've engaged in the collaborative, imaginative, and analytical work of revisioning special education teacher preparation to be responsive to the demands of this 21st century society. These experiences inform the goal I have for an introductory special education course: to inspire and foster enthusiasm and yet not shy away from the need to discuss the often complex and occasionally contentious issues that confront the field. We need school professionals who have foundational knowledge, extraordinary assessment and instructional skills, flexible thinking, and an understanding of and respect for the perspectives of colleagues and parents. Those elements are strongly represented in this text. I wanted to draw students into the material, to personalize it so that they feel the book is speaking to them and encouraging them to be the professionals needed for tomorrow's schools.

The second set of experiences reflected in this text is my work in schools. Observing, collaborating with, and teaching educators and administrators as they interact with pupils has taught me that children and youth can accomplish goals that sometimes are difficult even to imagine, as long as their teachers and other service providers believe in them and work together. I am firmly committed to inclusive practices—the way they can and should be. That is, I believe that all learners should be welcomed members of their learning communities. The goal is educating students in typical settings—but not abandoning effective practices or focusing on where students are seated to the exclusion of all other factors. Sometimes decisions for separate instructional settings have to be made, but in inclusive schools, they are cautious decisions that take into account both the costs and benefits to students and are revisited often. And so this textbook also reflects those beliefs: Early-career professionals should be optimistic about the potential of their students, but they also should be well schooled in the decision-making processes, settings, and instructional procedures that can best ensure that potential is realized.

The Plan of the Book

To introduce teacher candidates to a field as broad and complex as special education requires making decisions about what is most important to include, what just cannot be addressed, and what order to present and depth to provide on critical topics. The overall organization of *Special Education: Contemporary Perspectives for School Professionals* reflects those decisions. Core concepts related to the field of special education are introduced in Chapter 1, "Understanding Special

Education," and Chapter 2, "The Personnel and Procedures of Special Education." Chapter 3, "Multicultural Perspectives," explores several essential dimensions of diversity and multicultural issues as they relate to students with disabilities. Chapter 4, "Collaboration in Special Education," examines the increasingly central role that collaboration plays in the work of all of today's school professionals. Chapters 5 through 15 comprise the categorical segment of the text, each one devoted to a separate category of disability or special learning need (e.g., attention deficit–hyperactivity disorder and giftedness). Each of these chapters goes beyond the mere characterizing of students; the emphasis is on understanding and teaching them.

Topics Integrated into Every Chapter

Although some readers might prefer that the topic of parents be addressed in a single chapter, this approach belies the centrality of families in their children's education. Hence, the perspectives of *parents and families* are addressed in each chapter in a section designed to address issues pertaining to the overall chapter topic. Likewise, although it is not possible to provide extensive coverage of *instructional practices* in an introductory text, in each categorical chapter a section is devoted to providing examples of *research-based strategies and approaches* in order to give readers a sense of the ways they can have a positive impact on students. These strategies usually apply to several groups of students, but they are embedded where they seem most applicable. An additional example of an integrated topic is inclusion. Each categorical chapter explores *inclusive practices* related to particular groups of students—sometimes to highlight positive practices, sometimes to illustrate that more work is needed, and sometimes to examine the necessity of settings other than general education classrooms. One other topic is addressed in this manner: the *history of the field*. It worries me that in our zeal to prepare professionals who can meet the extraordinarily high expectations set for them today, we sometimes forget to give them a sense of the development of the field of special education and how today's practices are a result of that development. A brief examination of how the field of special education came to be what it is today seems appropriate, as does a similar analysis of the development of the disability specialty areas.

L WORLD EXPERIENCES

In addition to presenting the theories, concepts, and day-to-day realities of the field of special education, I've also attempted to bring to life the experiences and powerful stories of people with disabilities and their parents and families.

Chapter-Opening Vignettes

Chapter-opening vignettes describe the experiences of elementary, middle school, and high school students as they relate to the topics discussed in each chapter. These individuals' experiences are referenced at key points in the chapter as well. The vignettes can form the basis for applying information and strategies from the chapter, and they can be a launching point for discussions of issues influencing the field, including inclusive practices, collaboration, and response to intervention.

Students with Speech and Language Disorders

Firsthand Accounts

Firsthand Accounts allow teachers, other school professionals, students, and parents the chance to share, in their own words, their experiences and perspectives about life and learning related to special needs. Their words convey the core message of this book—that individuals with disabilities should be thought of in terms of their unique potential and abilities.

Back to the Cases

Each chapter concludes by asking readers to go **Back to the Cases** to apply what they have learned to the students they met at the beginning of the chapter. In some instances, questions are asked that require readers to analyze student characteristics and discuss how their success could be fostered. In others, situations educators are likely to encounter are outlined, and readers are asked how they would respond. In yet others, readers are asked to integrate learning across chapters to consider educational strategies for the highlighted students. This feature provides instructors with an effective summative activity for each chapter—one that can be completed by individual students or as a collaborative effort.

EVIDENCE-BASED PRACTICES

This text emphasizes contemporary information for practicing teachers: teaching approaches, strategies, ideas, and tips that are always based on empirically validated, peer-reviewed research findings. The goal is not to offer a comprehensive set of teaching methods but instead to demonstrate to novice educators how effective instructional practices can profoundly and positively influence student success.

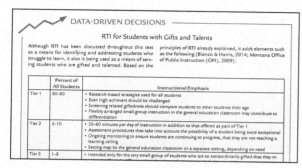

Data-Driven Decisions

Data-Driven Decisions focuses on the increasing importance in today's schools of data collection and use for instructional decision making. Topics addressed include formative assessment in classrooms, assessment for special education eligibility, data-based academic interventions, data tools on the web, data-based behavior interventions, collaborating around data, apps for gathering data, RTI and data, data to select technology, and many more.

INSTRUCTION IN **ACTION**
Numbered Heads Together

Numbered Heads Together is one example of a research-based cooperative learning approach that can be effective for teaching academic content and social interaction skills to students with emotional and behavior disabilities (Hunter & Haydon, 2013). Here are the steps to follow to implement Numbered Heads Together:

1. Assign students to heterogeneous groups of three or four. Students should be seated near one another.
2. Have students assign themselves numbers from 1 to 3 or 4.
3. Ask the class a question.
4. Have students "put their heads together" so that they can determine the correct answer or several answers, depending on the type of question that was asked. Students are instructed to be sure that every member of their group knows the answer(s).

5. Call the groups back together. Call a number (1 to 3 or 1 to 4), and have the students in the class with that number stand.
6. Call on one of the standing students to answer the question. If there is more than one correct answer, continue to call on students.
7. Ask the rest of the class to agree or disagree with the stated answer.
8. Award points or rewards. This can be done in several ways. Some teachers use a positive approach: As long as each student called on gets a correct answer, all teams are rewarded. Other teachers give each team one "pass" so that if a member does not answer correctly, the team still has an opportunity to be rewarded.

Source: Based on Maheady, L., Harper, G. F., & Mallette, B. (2001). Peer-mediated instruction and intervention and students with mild disabilities. Remedial and Special Education, 22(1), 4–14. Copyright 2001 by Pro-Ed, Inc.

Instruction in Action

Instruction in Action highlights teaching applications for specially designed instruction delivered by special education teachers or other professionals in various educational settings, including examples for individual or small-group situations. The feature provides sample lessons, tips, techniques, ideas, and approaches for working with students with special educational needs, whether in a separate setting or general education classroom.

POSITIVE • **BEHAVIOR** • SUPPORTS
Improving Behavior Through Social Skills Instruction

Most students with specific learning disabilities have difficulty navigating social interactions, which leads to behavior problems. Addressing this dimension of students' learning disabilities is critical for their success.

Types of Social Skills Problems

Skill deficit—the student has never learned the skill

Performance deficit—the student knows the skill but does not use it when appropriate

Self-control deficit—the student's lack of self-control results in problem behaviors, which interfere with learning and applying social skills (Kavale & Forness, 2012)

Example of Social Skills Instruction

Womack, Marchant, and Borders (2012) noted that social skills instruction delivered in isolation has seldom been shown to be effective. Instead, they recommend embedding social skills instruction in the classroom literature program

After the first book is read, the social skill addressed is explicitly introduced and steps for implementing it are taught and practiced.

Students are paired with a classmate to read one of the additional books and to role play the needed social skills, with teacher feedback provided.

Targeted students practice the social skills with classmates, but they also receive additional opportunities to apply the skills during small-group reading instruction.

Data are gathered prior to implementation and after teaching a social skill, including student knowledge and the skill and appropriate use of the skill.

Social skill instruction delivered in this manner is efficient in terms of time use and situates learning in the context of real life. It also fosters a high level of student engagement and builds student self-confidence. Finally, it incorporates peer-mediated instruction (including feedback and media-

Positive Behavior Supports

Positive Behavior Supports illustrates the contemporary emphasis on understanding the function of student problematic behavior and designing and implementing specific strategies in order to reduce inappropriate and increase appropriate behavior. In this feature, readers also will find discussions that deepen their understanding of the behavior challenges their students may present and resources to help respond to them.

PROFESSIONAL **EDGE**
Involving Students in the IEP Process

Most professionals agree that students should play an active role in developing their IEPs and participating in their implementation. Here are some ideas for involving students in the IEP process:

* Prepare to assist students by increasing your own understanding of student-led IEP meetings. One helpful resource is *Getting the Most Out of IEPs: An Educator's Guide to the Student-Directed Approach* (Thoma & Wehman, 2010).
* Provide students with materials that teach them about IEPs. One example is *Student-Led IEPs: A Guide for Student Involvement* (McGahee, Mason, Wallace, & Jones, 2001).
* Create an IEP scavenger hunt so that students gather information that will help them participate in the meeting.
* Have students read fiction books about individuals with disabilities to help them voice their own strengths and special needs.
* Involve students in the assessment, for example, by having them complete interest inventories.

* Have students send reminders to key participants, either by sending e-mails or composing letters, with assistance as needed.
* Involve students in meeting preparation, for example, by having them make name tags for participants.
* Ask students to write a paragraph about their strengths and needs.
* Assist students to draft IEP goals they consider important to their education.
* Ensure that students, even those who are young, attend all or part of the IEP meeting.
* Help students to rehearse parts of the IEP meeting they will lead.
* Teach students self-advocacy skills so that they can communicate their IEP goals to all their teachers.
* Involve students in monitoring their progress in achieving IEP goals, perhaps preparing first-person reports to share with parents.

Source: Based on Konrad, 2008.

Professional Edge

Professional Edge describes conceptual material, cutting-edge trends, and contemporary issues relevant to today's teachers. Included are new and sometimes controversial topics that experts in the field are talking about *right now*. It also provides a place in the textbook to provide critical "nuggets" of information that novice educators need (e.g., dealing with student death, responding to a student having a seizure).

ITTING-EDGE INFORMATION

The field of special education is multifaceted, fast moving, and continually influenced by new ideas. Teachers and other educational professionals are encouraged to maintain their connection and to find inspiration from this universe of information. In this fifth edition, careful attention has been paid to updating legislative and litigative information and presenting the most current statistics and other data related to the field.

Trends and Issues Affecting the Field of Emotional and Behavior Disorders

Many trends and issues related to the field of emotional and behavior disorders have been introduced elsewhere in this chapter. For example, you have learned about the controversy that exists about the definition of this disability and concerns about inclusive practices. However, if you asked experienced professionals to name the most important issues, they probably would include two topics as significant for the field: (a) the continuing difficulty that students and their families face in obtaining essential mental health services and (b) the controversy surrounding the use of seclusion and restraint with students with emotional and behavior disabilities.

Trends and Issues Sections

Trends and Issues sections conclude each chapter with a brief look at the most recent developments in the field, and the most interesting—and often still unresolved—questions and dilemmas.

TECHNOLOGY NOTES

Teacher Data Collection Technology Tools

Many free or low-cost tools are available to teachers to facilitate the data collection necessary as part of intervening to decide if a student's academics or behaviors are a serious concern. Several examples include the following:

Teacher's Assistant Pro
http://www.teachersassistantpro.com/
This iPad/iPhone app (free for limited access; low cost for unlimited access) is designed to enable teachers to easily track student behavior, whether accomplishments or problems. Teachers can create a file for each of their students, customize the types of behaviors they want to track, tally students' behaviors, and e-mail either recent or all records of student behaviors to parents or others.

Electronic Daily Behavior Report Card (e-DBRC)
http://edbrc.tamu.edu/
Developed by researchers at Texas A & M University, this tool is an electronic version of the classroom daily behavior report card that teachers for decades have used to communicate with parents concerning student behavior and to document a student's social and behavior skills. The app graphs student behavior, and a grade or rating is assigned for each day; it also easily allows data to be e-mailed and offers a way to help students analyze their own behavior.

Google Sheets
https://docs.google.com/spreadsheets/u/0/?pref=2&pli=1
One of the most versatile tools for data collection is a simple spreadsheet, such as the free Google Sheets. For example, on a spreadsheet, you can create a separate sheet for each student of concern in a single file, list behaviors being recorded horizontally across the top of the spreadsheet and dates of data collection vertically, with your tallies or other data in the cells. These data can then be transformed into charts, printed, or transmitted via e-mail.

Notemaster
http://www.kabukivision.com/
Notemaster is a generic note-taking app (a "lite" version is free) that teachers can use to create templates for tracking students' academic and social behavior. By creating skills checklists that can be infinitely duplicated, teachers can track student performance daily or track several students' behavior. The data records can be synced through Google Docs and then exported for reporting or e-mailing. As an alternative, you may already be using a notes app—such as OneNote or Evernote—that could be used in a similar fashion.

Technology Notes

Technology Notes showcases examples of the wide array of technology applications for teaching students with exceptional needs in special or general educational settings. The goal is to ensure that novice teachers understand that the lightning pace at which technological solutions are emerging holds immense promise for the achievement of students with disabilities and other special needs and to encourage readers to seek out even more information about technology for teaching students, gathering data, and collaborating with colleagues.

Did You Know?

Autistic savant refers to a person who has extraordinary skills that others do not have (although not all individuals who are savants have autism). Examples of these skills include mathematical calculations (e.g., figuring the day of the week for any date in history), memory feats (e.g., knowing every entry in a dictionary), and musical ability (e.g., playing any piece of music after hearing it just one time).

Did You Know?

Did You Know? highlights tidbits of information or resources related to selected chapter topics. These brief inserts point readers to additional resources, present research, or provide pertinent information intended to assist novices to better understand the text material.

AIDS TO UNDERSTANDING

Learning Outcomes and Summaries of Content

Learning Outcomes begin each chapter to focus reader thinking about the topics to be covered in the upcoming pages, and these are directly associated with the chapter's section headings. Each chapter ends with a **Summary** of the main ideas of the chapters, and these bring the chapter full circle by being organized based on the opening learning outcomes.

MyEducationLab™

Video Examples

In all chapters, embedded videos provide illustrations of special education principles or concepts in action. These video examples most often show students and teachers working in classrooms. They sometimes show students or teachers describing their thinking or experiences.

Self-Checks

Throughout the chapters, you will find MyEducationLab™: Self-Check quizzes. There are three to six of these quizzes in each chapter. They are meant to help you assess how well you have mastered the concepts covered in the section you just read. These self-checks are made up of self-grading multiple-choice items that not only provide feedback on whether you answered the questions correctly or incorrectly, but also provide you with rationales for both correct and incorrect answers.

MyEdLab **Self-Check 3.3**
MyEdLab **Application Exercise 3.3:** Factors Leading to Disproportionate Representation
MyEdLab **Application Exercise 3.4:** Interpreting Data

Application Exercises

Also at the end of each section, you can find one or two application exercises that can challenge you to use chapter content to reflect on teaching and learning in real classrooms. The questions you answer in these exercises are usually constructed-response items. Once you provide your own answers to the questions, you receive feedback in the form of model answers written by experts.

Advanced Data and Performance Reporting Aligned to National Standards

Advanced data and performance reporting helps educators quickly identify gaps in student learning and gauge and address individual and classroom performance. Educators easily see the connection between coursework, concept mastery, and national teaching standards with highly visual views of performance reports. Data and assessments align directly to national teaching standards, including **The Council for Exceptional Children (CEC)**, and support reporting for state and accreditation requirements.

Study Plan Specific to Your Text

MyEducationLab™ gives students the opportunity to test themselves on key concepts and skills, track their own progress through the course, and access personalized Study Plan activities.

The customized Study Plan is generated based on students' pretest results. Incorrect questions from the pretest indicate specific textbook learning outcomes with which the student is struggling. The customized Study Plan suggests specific enriching activities for particular learning outcomes, helping students focus.

Personalized Study Plan activities may include e-book reading assignments and review, practice, and enrichment activities.

After students complete the enrichment activities, they take a posttest to see the concepts they've mastered or areas where they still may need extra help.

MyEducationLab™ then reports the Study Plan results to the instructor. Based on these reports, the instructor can adapt course material to suit the needs of individual students or for the entire class.

Assignments and Activities

Designed to enhance students' understanding of concepts covered in class, these assignable exercises show concepts in action (through videos, cases, and/or student and teacher artifacts). They help students deepen content knowledge and synthesize and apply concepts and strategies they have read about in the book. (Correct answers for these assignments are available to the instructor only.)

Building Teaching Skills and Dispositions

These unique learning units help students practice and strengthen the skills that are essential to effective teaching. After examining the steps involved in a core teaching process, students are given an opportunity to practice applying this skill via videos, student and teacher artifacts, and/or case studies of authentic class-rooms. By providing multiple opportunities to practice a single teaching concept, each activity encourages a deeper understanding and application of concepts, as well as the use of critical thinking skills. After practice, students take a quiz that is transmitted to the instructor gradebook for performance reporting.

IRIS Center Resources

The IRIS Center at Vanderbilt University (http://iris.peabody.vanderbilt.edu), funded by the U.S. Department of Education's Office of Special Education Programs (OSEP), develops training enhancement materials for preservice and practicing teachers. The center works with experts from across the country to create challenge-based interactive modules, case study units, and podcasts that provide research-validated information about working with students in inclusive settings. In the MyEducationLab™ course, we have integrated this content where appropriate.

Teacher Talk

This feature emphasizes the power of teaching through videos of master teachers, who tell their own compelling stories of why they teach. Each of these featured teachers has been awarded the Council of Chief State School Officers Teachers of the Year award, the oldest and most prestigious award for teachers.

Course Resources

The Course Resources section of MyEducationLab™ is designed to help students put together an effective lesson plan, prepare for and begin a career, navigate the first year of teaching, and understand key educational standards, policies, and laws.

It includes the following:

- The **Lesson Plan Builder** is an effective and easy-to-use tool that students can use to create, update, and share quality lesson plans. The software also makes it easy to integrate state content standards into any lesson plan.

- **The Certification and Licensure** section is designed to help students pass licensure exams by giving them access to state test requirements, overviews of what the tests cover, and sample test items.

  The Certification and Licensure section includes the following:
  - **State Certification Test Requirements**: Here, students can click on a state and be taken to a list of state certification tests.
  - Students can click on the **Licensure Exams** they need to take in order to find
    - Basic information about each test
    - Descriptions of what is covered on each test
    - Sample test questions with explanations of correct answers
  - **National Evaluation Series**™ by Pearson: Here, students can see the tests in the National Evaluation Series (NES), learn what is covered on each exam, and access sample test items with descriptions and rationales of correct answers. Students can also purchase interactive online tutorials developed by Pearson Evaluation Systems and the Pearson Teacher Education and Development group.
  - **ETS Online Praxis**™ **Tutorials:** Here, students can purchase interactive online tutorials developed by ETS and by the Pearson Teacher Education and Development group. Tutorials are available for the Praxis I® exams and for select Praxis II® exams.
- The **Licensure and Standards** section provides access to current state and national standards.
- The **Preparing a Portfolio** section provides guidelines for creating a high-quality teaching portfolio.
- **Beginning Your Career** offers tips, advice, and other valuable information on:
  - *Résumé Writing and Interviewing:* Includes expert advice on how to write impressive résumés and prepare for job interviews.
  - *Your First Year of Teaching:* Provides practical tips to set up a first classroom, manage student behavior, and more easily organize for instruction and assessment.
  - *Law and Public Policies:* Details specific directives and requirements needed to understand the Elementary and Secondary Education Act and the Individuals with Disabilities Education Act.
- The **Multimedia Index** aggregates resources in MyEducationLab™ by asset type (e.g., video or artifact) for easy location and retrieval.

Visit www.myeducationlab.com for a demonstration of this exciting new online teaching resource.

Support Materials for Instructors

The following resources are available for instructors to download on www .pearsonhighered.com/educators. Instructors enter the author or title of this book, select this particular edition of the book, and then click on the "Resources" tab to log in and download textbook supplements.

Instructor's Resource Manual and Test Bank (0-13-444488-4)

The Instructor's Resource Manual and Test Bank provides a multitude of activities and ideas to help instructors teach their courses, whether traditional or online. Each chapter provides a teaching outline, learning activities and handouts, and a variety of test items.

PowerPoint™ Slides (0-13-448817-2)

The PowerPoint™ slides include key concept summarizations, diagrams, and other graphic aids to enhance learning. They are designed to help students understand, organize, and remember core concepts and theories.

TestGen (0-13-448818-0)

TestGen is a powerful test generator that instructors install on a computer and use in conjunction with the TestGen test bank file for the text. Assessments, including equations, graphs, and scientific notation, may be created for both print or testing online.

TestGen is available exclusively from Pearson Education publishers. Instructors install TestGen on a personal computer (Windows or Macintosh) and create tests for classroom testing and for other specialized delivery options, such as over a local area network or on the web. A test bank, which is also called a Test Item File (TIF), typically contains a large set of test items, organized by chapter and ready for use in creating a test, based on the associated textbook material.

The tests can be downloaded in the following formats:

TestGen Testbank file—PC

TestGen Testbank file—MAC

TestGen Testbank—Blackboard 9 TIF

TestGen Testbank—Blackboard CE/Vista (WebCT) TIF

Angel Test Bank (zip)

D2L Test Bank (zip)

Moodle Test Bank (zip)

Sakai Test Bank (zip)

Acknowledgments

Textbooks are not produced in isolation. They always involve expertise and input from a team that carries out myriad roles and responsibilities, from the announcement that it's time to work on a revision until and through the point in time that the book is produced. Through the entire revision process, collaboration is the norm. And so I want to be sure to give credit and deep thanks to all the many individuals who provided wonderful ideas as well as encouragement and support throughout the revision process. First, the marvelous professionals at Pearson who take a book from concept to reality should be acknowledged, especially Kevin Davis, Carolyn Schweitzer, Alicia Reilly, Janelle Rogers, and Anne McAlpine.

In a textbook revision, comments from reviewers are both welcomed and dreaded. They provide invaluable information leading to beneficial changes for readers, even if sometimes their insights involve spending hours reading to rethink a key topic or restructuring a chapter to more effectively discuss its material. They may never realize how influential their comments, concerns, and suggestions are in decisions about what to keep, what to add, what to delete, and how to improve content and features. Their reasoned and constructive input was instrumental in the preparation of this fifth edition of the book and in ensuring its accuracy and relevance. They are Judy Stuart (Furman University), Perianne R. Bates (Ohio University), and Cynthia Michlin (Arizona State University).

Yet another group of individuals must be mentioned among those who helped bring this project to fruition: the wonderful people who package the book and turn manuscript into a textbook. I would particularly like to thank the team members at Thistle Hill Publishing Services, Angela Urquhart and Andrea Archer, for their meticulous attention to detail.

A special acknowledgment is owed to Dr. Tammy Barron. With superb organization and attention to detail, she diligently worked to identify updated research and other reference materials that could be used to revise each chapter, checked all the web resources to ensure the links were active, and offered ideas for topics to enhance or simplify. I made this comment after she—as a doctoral student—assisted me in preparing the fourth edition, but it is still appropriate for the fifth: I suspect that before too long she'll be writing her own books—she's already a tremendously skilled professional.

Finally, these acknowledgments would not be complete without mentioning the other people in my life who support me no matter the projects that I am pursuing. My husband Bruce Brandon is the best cheerleader anyone could ever have: He acts as a sounding board for new ideas, reads and responds to drafts of manuscript, asks insightful questions, and searches the popular press for relevant articles. He also is infinitely patient with my need for hours of quiet writing time. He has said more often than any writing spouse deserves, "What can I do to help?" His love and patience mean everything to me. The rest of my family— my mom (Mary Ellen Penovich) and brother and sister-in-law (Dan and Cindy Penovich)—also offered encouragement and sympathy, as did my mother-in-law (Lorena Brandon). I appreciate their support and good-natured teasing about my need to try to save the world.

In memory of Howard B. Brandon

*Your kindness made the world a better place,
and your spirit will always be with us*

Brief Contents

Contents

3   Multicultural Perspectives   64

9 Students with Speech and Language Disorders   260

10 Students with Autism Spectrum Disorder   287

11 Students with Deafness and Hearing Loss   321

13 Students with Orthopedic Impairments, Traumatic Brain Injury, and Other Health Impairments   384

14 Students with Severe and Multiple Disabilities   419

Special Features

TECHNOLOGY NOTES

DATA-DRIVEN DECISIONS

Photo Credits

WavebreakMediaMicro/Fotolia, p. 1; Robin Nelson/ZUMAPRESS.com/Alamy Stock Photo, p. 4; Frank Leonardo/New York Post Archives /© NYP Holdings, Inc/Getty Images, p. 8; Spencer Grant/Age Fotostock/SuperStock, p. 14; Huntstock/Getty Images, p. 22; Vikki Martin/Alamy Stock Photo, p. 22; Peter Muller/Cultura/Getty Images, p. 24; Robin Nelson/PhotoEdit, p. 31; Christina Kennedy/PhotoEdit, p. 35; Courtesy of the subject, p. 38; Courtesy of the subject, p. 38; Courtesy of the subject, p. 38; Bill Aron/PhotoEdit, p. 47; Jules Selmes/Pearson Education, inc., p. 61; Sam Edwards/Caiaimage/OJO+/Getty Images, p. 64; Lisa F. Young/Fotolia, p. 70; Vladyslav Starozhylov/123RF, p. 82; Robin Nelson/PhotoEdit, p. 91; Ian Wedgewood/Pearson Education, inc., p. 93; Angela Hampton Picture Library/Alamy Stock Photo, p. 97; Shorrocks/Getty Images, p. 116; Mike Mols/Fotolia, p. 124; iStockPhoto, p. 139; tomazl/E+/Getty Images, p. 151; ZUMA Press Inc/Alamy Stock Photo, p. 157; Brad Wilson/The Image Bank/Getty Images, p. 160; ColorBlind Images/The Image Bank/Getty Images, p. 168; Voisin/Phanie/Science Source, p. 177; Nadezhda1906/Fotolia, p. 183; Aliaksei Lasevich/Alamy Stock Photo, p. 193; Ted Foxx/Alamy Stock Photo, p. 199; Pixelheadphoto/Fotolia, p. 205; Robin Nelson/PhotoEdit, p. 217; Stacy Walsh Rosenstock/Alamy Live News/Alamy Stock Photo, p. 225; Asiseeit/Getty Images, p. 229; David Grossman/Alamy Stock Photo, p. 232; Jim West/Alamy Stock Photo, p. 249; BL/BSIP SA/Alamy Stock Photo, p. 254; Ted Foxx/Alamy Stock Photo, p. 260; E. Dygas/Photodisc/Getty Images, p. 264; Alan Oddie/PhotoEdit, p. 273; dpa picture alliance archive/Alamy Stock Photo, p. 281; KidStock/Blend Images/Getty Images, p. 285; wallybird/Alamy Stock Photo, p. 287; Jules Selmes/Pearson Education, inc., p. 291; Robin Nelson/PhotoEdit, p. 298; Asiseeit/Getty Images, p. 305; Gail Shotlander/Moment Open/Getty Images, p. 309; AMELIE-BENOIST/BSIP/Alamy Stock Photo, p. 321; WavebreakMediaMicro/Fotolia, p. 326; Jacky Chapman/Janine Wiedel Photolibrary/Alamy Stock Photo, p. 335; Erika Schultz/The Seattle Times/AP Images, p. 343; ZUMA Press Inc/Alamy Stock Photo, p. 350; REUTERS/Alamy Stock Photo, p. 354; FatCamera/Getty Images, p. 363; Comstock/Stockbyte/Getty Images, p. 365; Roger Askew/Alamy Stock Photo, p. 371; Huntstock/Getty Images, p. 381; Brian Mitchell/Corbis Documentary/Getty Images, p. 384; Engelsmann/Agencja Fotograficzna Caro/Alamy Stock Photo, p. 388; Nikki Kahn/The Washington Post/Getty Images, p. 394; Annette Udvardi Coolidge/PhotoEdit, p. 402; George Dodson/PH College/Pearson Education, Inc., p. 408; Christopher Futcher/Getty Images, p. 411; Paul Doyle/Alamy Stock Photo, p. 419; Don Smetzer, p. 425; Shorrocks/Getty Images, p. 433; Robin Nelson/PhotoEdit, p. 437; Javier Larrea/age fotostock/Alamy Stock Photo, p. 445; Fstop123/Getty Images, p. 451; Stuart Monk/Hemera/Getty Images, p. 457; Jupiterimages/BananaStock/Getty Images, p. 457; Adrian Sherratt/Alamy Stock Photo, p. 460; The White House Photo Office, p. 460; Photo Researchers, Inc/Alamy Stock Photo, p. 460; Ian Lishman/Juice Images/Getty Images, p. 468; Rawpixel/123RF, p. 471; Rex Perry/The Tennessean/AP Images, p. 480

Understanding Special Education

Learning Outcomes

LO1.1 Articulate the foundational concepts that define special education.

LO1.2 Analyze how the history of special education, including key court cases, has shaped its development.

LO1.3 List the provisions in federal legislation that establish current special education and related policies and practices.

LO1.4 Describe the students who receive special education services.

LO1.5 Explain the role of parents and families in the education of children with disabilities.

LO1.6 Analyze critical topics currently influencing the field of special education and emphasized throughout this text.

EMMA

Emma is an eight-year-old student whose family considers her a sweet and funny child. She loves to go swimming and has a cat named Whisper who is always nearby. However, at school Emma faces a number of challenges. She has a mild intellectual disability (formerly called mental retardation) as well as attention deficit–hyperactivity disorder (ADHD), a moderate hearing loss, and delayed motor skills. Emma begins each day with her typical peers in Ms. Spellman's second-grade classroom, and she also joins them for science, music, and art as well as lunch and recess. However, because of the nature of her special needs, she is taught for 2.5 hours each day in a special education classroom. Her reading and math instruction there, delivered by special educator Ms. Wright, is aligned with the curriculum that all students access, but it emphasizes practical knowledge and functional skills she will need throughout her life. Emma also receives speech-language therapy, and the occupational therapist works with her on skills such as grasping a pencil and using scissors. In addition, a school district specialist for students who are deaf or hard of hearing consults with Ms. Wright once per week. Recently, Ms. Spellman and Ms. Wright have become concerned that Emma is often isolated when she is in general education settings. Most students ignore her, and she has not yet developed skills to join in their conversations and activities. The teachers are discussing several options to address this challenge, for example, creating a special "lunch bunch" program that would, with teacher guidance, help classmates better understand Emma and teach Emma how to engage in group interactions.

EVERETT

Everett is a seventh-grade student whose favorite baseball team is the Chicago Cubs, who has considerable artistic talent, and who would never stop playing computer games if his parents did not put a time limit on his computer use. Everett also has characteristics that can cause problems. He is insistent on precise daily routines for getting ready for school, beginning his schoolwork, moving from activity to activity during the day, and getting ready for bed. In fact, each day his teacher provides him with a schedule using pictures so he knows what will occur. However, any change in a routine—for example, if there is a special program at school—greatly upsets Everett. He may express his frustration by slapping himself or those around him, or he may scream loudly and refuse to move. Even though his teacher and parents know his behavior actually is a way for him to communicate that he is unhappy, his needs are so intense and his behavior can be so disruptive that he receives most of his instruction in a special education classroom for students with autism (also called autism spectrum disorder). A behavior specialist is assisting his teacher to find ways to help Everett communicate in a more constructive way, and a speech-language therapist also is working with him on communication strategies, including using sign language. In addition, Everett's school has a peer mentor program, and Everett has a friend Chris (another seventh-grade student) who sometimes sits with Everett at lunch, comes to the classroom to work with him, and helps him to develop social skills.

DANIEL

Daniel is a sophomore in high school, and he still struggles to understand why he has so much difficulty learning and how his learning disability affects who he is and how others respond to him. As he thinks about his first nine years of school, he cannot remember a time when school was fun. Even in kindergarten, he had difficulty learning his letters and numbers, and he quickly fell behind academically. Though he began receiving special education services in third grade, Daniel's reading comprehension is at about the fifth-grade level, and his math skills are at the seventh-grade level. Teachers generally have been supportive, but sometimes even when they mean well, their actions can be hurtful. Daniel remembers one teacher who usually reduced by half the amount of work he had to do—it made him feel as though he was too stupid to learn. For the past two years, Daniel has used recorded books downloaded to his iPod; this has been helpful, as has been accessing a computer when he takes tests. But he'd rather listen to music instead of boring social studies material, and he'd rather take tests like his friends do—not using the computer. As Daniel looks to the future, he is concerned. He cannot earn a regular diploma unless he passes high-stakes achievement tests in five courses. He'd like to go to the community college to become an airplane mechanic, but that would require having a diploma, and so the looming tests make him unsure whether he can pursue this goal. He considers himself fortunate to have many good friends who help him with schoolwork, but sometimes he is discouraged by the challenges he faces.

What brings you to the study of children and adults with disabilities and other special needs? Some people are interested because they have a child or family member with a disability, and their personal experiences attract them to the field. Others are drawn because of volunteer work sponsored by a high school club or a fraternity or sorority. Yet others, such as teachers, plan careers in which knowledge of individuals with disabilities and special education is essential. My own interest in pursuing a career working with individuals with disabilities came from several experiences, including volunteering during high school to join individuals with intellectual disabilities in recreational activities such as bowling and dancing; interacting with friends and neighbors whose families included members with disabilities; and meeting a little girl named Ranie, whom I helped in a religious instruction class when it became clear that she could smile but not read or write. In college, as a volunteer in a separate school for children with intellectual disabilities, I thought I could do a much better job than the teacher whose primary goal seemed to be occupying his students' days with craft activities, and I became convinced that special education would be a fascinating and enriching career in which I could truly make a difference.

In 2012, the most recent year for which data are available, approximately 6.7 million children and youth from birth to 21 years of age received special education services in U.S. schools (National Center for Education Statistics, 2015; U.S. Department of Education, 2014). Although these students have exceptional needs, it is more important to remember from the outset of your study of the infants, toddlers, children, youth, and young adults receiving special education that they are individuals for whom disability is only one small part of their identity. They are preschoolers with mischief in their eyes and insatiable curiosity; they are elementary students who enjoy learning in school and playing soccer and getting a cell phone; they are middle school students grappling with a larger school environment, who sometimes act like children and sometimes act too grown up and who want to fit in with their classmates; and they are high school students who experiment with clothes and hairstyles and piercings to establish their own identities, cannot live without Facebook, like or dislike certain teachers, and worry about what they will do after graduation. They are Emma and Everett and Daniel and other students just like them—or very different from them.

Whatever brings you to be reading this text—whether you are a special education teacher or related services provider candidate, a general education teacher trainee, the parent of a child with a disability, or someone who is merely interested in understanding this field—what is most critical is that you learn to look at all individuals, whether they are children or adults, in the context of their strengths and abilities, their value as individuals, and the contributions that they make to your life and that you make to theirs. Your perspective and how you learn to work with children and adults with disabilities as a professional can make all the difference in the world to the individuals about whom this text is written.

Concepts That Define Special Education

Students in school receive what is often referred to as *general education*. That is, they learn from the standard curriculum as taught by their teachers, without the need for extraordinary supports. For a small percentage of students, however, the typical programs and services of general education are not adequate. These students, carefully identified as having disabilities and educated in the most appropriate setting based on their individual needs, receive general education, but they *also* receive other programs and services referred to as *special education*. These students (along with other students with special needs) are the focus of this text.

When you think about special education, what images come to mind? A teacher working with a small group of students who struggle to read? A young man in a wheelchair in chemistry class? A classroom with two teachers, one general education and one special education? All of these images may be part of special education, but it is much more than that. As you explore this complex and rapidly changing field (e.g., Bateman, Lloyd, & Tankersley, 2015; Kauffman, 2015), you quickly will learn that it is characterized by a multitude of technical terms and acronyms. Your interest undoubtedly is in students and learning to work with them effectively, but it is equally important to understand the technical aspects of special education and what it offers to students and their families. Three key concepts form the foundation for all the special services that students with disabilities are entitled to receive through public schools. These terms are briefly introduced in the following sections, and you will learn more about them as you read the other chapters in this book.

Special Education

The first term to consider is the one that has already been introduced: *special education.* It has a precise definition that comes from the federal law that established it:

> The term "special education" means specially designed instruction, at no cost to parents, to meet the unique needs of a child with a disability, including:
> a. instruction conducted in the classroom, in the home, in hospitals and institutions, and in other settings; and
> b. instruction in physical education. (20 U.S.C. §1401[29])

That is, special education is the means through which children who have disabilities receive an education specifically designed to help them reach their learning potential. We will return later in this chapter to the topic of specially designed instruction as a key part of special education. Special education teachers have the primary responsibility for this specially designed instruction, but general education teachers, paraeducators, specialists, and other professionals also may contribute to providing special education. Emma, Everett, and Daniel, the students you read about at the beginning of the chapter, all receive specially designed instruction tailored to their needs. Perhaps most importantly, note that special education is *not* a place; it is the set of services students receive that may be provided in any school setting.

By providing special education, related services, and supplementary aids and services, professionals ensure that students with disabilities will reach their potential.

Related Services

The second component of special education services is called related services, and it is defined as follows:

> The term "related services" means transportation, and such developmental, corrective, and other supportive services (including speech/language pathology and audiology services, interpreting services, psychological services, physical and occupational therapy, recreation, including therapeutic recreation, social work services, school nurse services designed to enable a child with a disability to receive a free appropriate public education as described in the individualized education program of the child, counseling services, including rehabilitation counseling, orientation and mobility services, and medical services, except that such medical services shall be for diagnostic and evaluation purposes only) as may be required to assist a child with a disability to benefit from special education, and includes the early identification and assessment of disabling conditions in children. The term does not include a medical device that is surgically implanted, or the replacement of the device. (20 U.S.C. §1401[26])

You can see that this term encompasses many different types of supports for students with disabilities. These supports are not directly related to a student's instruction, but they are needed so that a student can access instruction. Related services for any single student could include a bus equipped with a wheelchair lift, individual counseling, and physical therapy. A team of professionals (discussed in Chapter 2) decides which related services are needed by each student with a disability. The speech-language therapy that Emma and Everett, introduced at the beginning of the chapter, receive is an example of a related service.

Supplementary Aids and Services

The third foundational concept essential to special education is supplementary aids and services, and it includes the following items:

> The term "supplementary aids and services" means aids, services, and other supports that are provided in regular education classes or other education-related settings to enable children with disabilities to be educated with nondisabled children to the maximum extent appropriate in accordance with section 1412 (a)(5). (20 U.S.C. §1401[29])

That is, supplementary aids and services are all the items that can help a student remain in a classroom with typical peers. One example of a supplementary aid or service is access to a computer with software that predicts what the student is likely to type next, thus reducing the amount of typing the student must do. Another example is preferential seating in the classroom (e.g., near the teacher or the whiteboard) for a student who has low vision or hearing loss. Take a moment to review Daniel's story at the beginning of the chapter. What supplementary aids and services does he receive?

As you probably have surmised, the three simple terms—special education that is specially designed instruction, related services, and supplementary aids and services—are anything but simple. In the remainder of this chapter and throughout this text, you will learn much more about them as well as many other terms related to special education. You also will learn more about your role, regardless of the profession for which you are preparing, in educating the students who are entitled to these services.

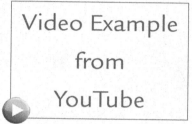

MyEdLab
Video Example 1.1
Watch this video, which gives you a glimpse into the day-to-day world of special education. (https://www.youtube.com/watch?v=b3X1S3T7udY)

MyEdLab **Self-Check 1.1**

MyEdLab **Application Exercise 1.1:** Meet a Paraprofessional

---

Development of the Special Education Field

In the preceding section, the fundamental concepts of special education were defined as they appear in federal law. However, that law did not suddenly come into existence. Special education evolved over time, as you can see in the time line in Figure 1.1, which highlights landmark events across the many dimensions of the field. Learning the story of its development can help you understand why special education is necessary and why it is so carefully regulated.

Early History

Although much of the earliest information about individuals with disabilities focused on adults, attention to children emerged in the 19th century as pioneering

FIGURE 1.1   **Timeline of the Development of Special Education Services**
This timeline shows some of the most significant events in the history of special education, illustrating how all the various disciplines represented in the field evolved concurrently and how current practices rely on past events.

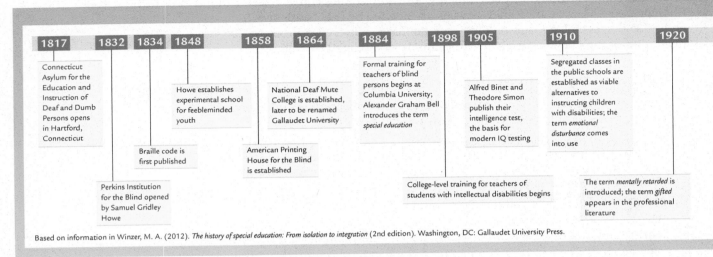

Based on information in Winzer, M. A. (2012). *The history of special education: From isolation to integration* (2nd edition). Washington, DC: Gallaudet University Press.

professionals took up their cause (Richards, 2014). For example, in 1800, French physician Jean-Marc-Gaspard Itard was hired to work with a 12-year-old child named Victor, who had been found wandering in the woods and was considered a feral child—that is, a human who was living much like an animal. In fact, he was called the "Wild Boy of Aveyron" (Harris, 2010; Scheerenberger, 1983). Victor was deaf and mute, and professionals disagreed about his potential, although he probably had an intellectual disability. Over the next five years, Itard worked with Victor to teach him functional skills (e.g., dressing, personal hygiene), social expectations, and speech, but progress was frustratingly slow. Itard initially considered his efforts with Victor a failure, but he later wrote that Victor could only be compared to himself, and by that measure, he had made great progress. In fact, Victor had learned the letters of the alphabet, the meanings of many words, and self-care. Through Itard's work with Victor, the notion that even children with significant needs could benefit from instruction and were worthy of attention was introduced (Kanner, 1964).

Another notable development in the field of special education came from France in the mid-19th-century work of Edouard Seguin and his physiological method (Seguin, 1866). Seguin, a student of Itard's, deeply believed that children who were blind, intellectually disabled, or emotionally disabled could be trained to become productive members of society. His method included creating a structured learning environment with attention to developing the senses, learning basic academic skills, and engaging in regular physical activity. Seguin brought several key concepts to the study of educating children with special needs, including the positive impact of rewards, the potentially negative impact of punishment, and the importance of structure and clear directions. These ideas are still essential to effective special education.

In the United States, the idea of providing care and support for children with disabilities emerged slowly during the 19th century. The first public school special class was established in Cleveland, Ohio, in 1875 (Steinbach, 1918), but it was disbanded shortly thereafter. Another was recorded in Providence, Rhode Island, in 1896, and others were established by the turn of the 20th century in cities such as Chicago, Boston, Philadelphia, and New York (Kode, 2002). However, several forces soon led to more rapid growth of special classes and became the basis for special education today.

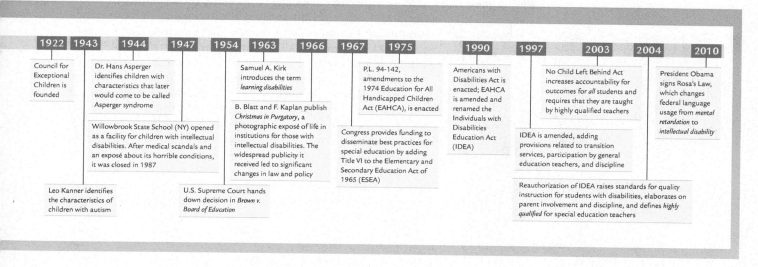

| 1922 | 1943 | 1944 | 1947 | 1954 | 1963 | 1966 | 1967 | 1975 | 1990 | 1997 | 2003 | 2004 | 2010 |

Council for Exceptional Children is founded

Dr. Hans Asperger identifies children with characteristics that later would come to be called Asperger syndrome

Willowbrook State School (NY) opened as a facility for children with intellectual disabilities. After medical scandals and an exposé about its horrible conditions, it was closed in 1987

Samuel A. Kirk introduces the term *learning disabilities*

B. Blatt and F. Kaplan publish *Christmas in Purgatory*, a photographic exposé of life in institutions for those with intellectual disabilities. The widespread publicity it received led to significant changes in law and policy

P.L. 94-142, amendments to the 1974 Education for All Handicapped Children Act (EAHCA), is enacted

Congress provides funding to disseminate best practices for special education by adding Title VI to the Elementary and Secondary Education Act of 1965 (ESEA)

Americans with Disabilities Act is enacted; EAHCA is amended and renamed the Individuals with Disabilities Education Act (IDEA)

No Child Left Behind Act increases accountability for outcomes for *all* students and requires that they are taught by highly qualified teachers

President Obama signs Rosa's Law, which changes federal language usage from *mental retardation* to *intellectual disability*

IDEA is amended, adding provisions related to transition services, participation by general education teachers, and discipline

Leo Kanner identifies the characteristics of children with autism

U.S. Supreme Court hands down decision in *Brown v. Board of Education*

Reauthorization of IDEA raises standards for quality instruction for students with disabilities, elaborates on parent involvement and discipline, and defines *highly qualified* for special education teachers

The Beginnings of Today's Education System

During the late 19th and early 20th centuries, urbanization, immigration, and industrialization flourished in the United States (Mondale & Patton, 2001). Large factories were being built in cities, and many people decided to give up the rural life of farming to seek employment in urban areas. Waves of immigrants joined them, and these individuals typically were unfamiliar with American culture and language. It was a stressful time in American society: Many middle-class people were fearful of the changes occurring, the living conditions for the new city dwellers often were squalid, and governments could not keep up with the demands for social services.

The impact of these societal tensions on people with disabilities was unfortunate and far-reaching. Prominent researchers began suggesting that individuals with intellectual and other disabilities were a threat to society and should not be allowed to have children. These professionals claimed that many immigrants fell into this group, that is, that they were "feebleminded" because they did not know English or American customs (Smith, 1985). Using this flawed rationale, the *eugenics movement* emerged in which many adults, including those with disabilities, were involuntarily sterilized in order to keep them from "diluting" what was considered the superior American race. Some 31 states passed laws to make the practice of sterilization legal when individuals were judged to be incompetent, and several of these laws were on the books until the 1970s (Fleischer & Zames, 2001). For example, in North Carolina, legislation was passed in 2012 to compensate 7,600 individuals (or their families) who were involuntarily sterilized between 1933 and 1977 (Severson, 2012), even though the required payments have not yet been completed (Hoban, 2015).

Although the eugenics movement and involuntary sterilization occurred in the past, historians argue that an emphasis on rejecting individuals for their differences instead of accepting them for who they are originated during this sad period in history and still dominates thinking in today's society. For schools, the events of this era both altered the face of education and planted the seeds of contemporary special education.

Compulsory public education began to grow during this same early 20th-century time period, partly as an economic response to the changing society

(Osgood, 2008). With few child labor laws in existence at this time, mandatory school attendance functioned to keep children out of the labor force; doing so ensured that jobs would be available for the rapidly growing pool of adult workers, both immigrants and those moving from farms to cities. Not surprisingly, schools were designed like the most innovative concept of the time, the assembly line. Just as cars and other products were created using piece-by-piece assembly in a standard way, so, too, were American citizens to be created by moving all children, the "raw material," from grade to grade as they received a standardized education.

As might be expected, it soon became apparent that student needs defied standardization. Some children who enrolled in school could not keep up academically with peers, were defiant or belligerent, or had physical disabilities (Osgood, 2010). Consistent with the prevailing belief that devalued anyone who failed to meet societal expectations of what is "normal," educators decided that these students should be removed from the assembly line of education and offered instruction better suited to their needs (Connecticut Special Education Association, 1936; Winzer, 2007).

With this thinking, separate special classes became increasingly common (Bennett, 1932; Pertsch, 1936). These classes were sometimes called *ungraded classes* because pupils across several grade levels were grouped and taught there (Groszmann, 1922). Further, as intelligence testing became popular during this same time period, educators came to trust that they had found a scientific basis for separating learners who would not succeed in typical classrooms (Mutua, Siders, & Bakken, 2011); that is, professionals believed that an intelligence quotient (IQ) score could be the basis for determining level of ability. Although not required by federal law, special education classes for students with intellectual disabilities, physical disabilities, and visual or hearing impairments became increasingly common through the first half of the 20th century.

To this point, students with significant disabilities have not been considered. That is for two reasons. First, many students with multiple special needs who today thrive because of advanced medical technology would not have survived during this era. For those who did, public school was not an option: These children were kept at home, educated by private agencies, or placed in institutions.

Until the second half of the 20th century, children with disabilities sometimes were sent to live in institutions and sometimes were denied any access to education. If in school, they were segregated in separate classrooms or schools.

Discrimination and a Call for Change

The expanding practice of educating students with disabilities in separate classes or schools continued unquestioned during the first half of the 20th century. However, shortly after the advent of the modern civil rights movement in education, with the 1954 *Brown v. Board of Education of Topeka, Kansas* decision clarifying that "separate cannot be equal," some professionals began questioning whether separate classes provided students with disabilities with an appropriate education.

Research and Rethinking of Assumptions

From the mid-1950s through the mid-1960s, researchers analyzed traditional special education in a series of studies collectively referred to as the *efficacy studies*. They compared the achievement and social adjustment of students with intellectual disabilities who were enrolled in special classes to that of students of similar abilities who remained in general education settings. The studies tended to find that students with intellectual disabilities in general education classes achieved more academically than those in special classes (e.g., Goldstein, Moss, & Jordan, 1965), probably because teachers' expectations of them were higher and because they were learning in the same curriculum as other students. In special classes, developing manual or job-related skills was emphasized, an approach reflecting the beliefs encouraged during the eugenics movement that such students were incapable of learning academic material.

By the mid-1960s, with the civil rights movement in the headlines, influential researcher Lloyd Dunn (1968) wrote a watershed essay entitled "Special Education for the Mildly Retarded: Is Much of It Justifiable?" Dunn questioned whether separate classes could provide an adequate education for students with disabilities, and he challenged educators to use emerging technology and research on effective teaching to educate students with disabilities along with their peers.

During the same time period, other professionals were looking beyond academic instruction to broader issues related to disabilities, especially the stigmatizing effect of labels (e.g., Goffman, 1963; Hobbs, 1975). For example, Mercer (1973) coined the phrase "the six-hour retarded child" to make the point that some students, often those from nondominant races or cultures or those who spoke a language other than English, were considered intellectually disabled while they were in school—but not in their neighborhoods. What became clear was that special education was not just a means of assisting children with disabilities; it also had become a means of discriminating against students who were perceived by educators—justifiably or not—as more challenging to teach (Codrington & Fairchild, 2012).

Litigation for the Rights of Students with Disabilities

During the same time that researchers were debating the quality and impact of special education on students, parent groups advocating for the rights of children with disabilities were becoming increasingly vocal (Winzer, 2012). Parents of children with significant disabilities rightly wanted to know why their sons and daughters could not be educated in the public school system—that is, why they were told to keep their children at home, put them in institutions, or send them to private agencies for their education. Other parents objected to the quality of their sons' and daughters' education. These parents began to win landmark court cases on their children's behalf. For example, in *Pennsylvania Association for Retarded Children v. The Commonwealth of Pennsylvania (PARC)* (1972), parents won the guarantee that education did not mean only traditional academic instruction and that children with intellectual disabilities could benefit from education tailored to their needs. Further, children could not be denied access to public schools, and they were entitled to a free public education. In *Mills v. Board of Education (Mills)* (1972), a class action lawsuit on behalf of the 18,000 children in the Washington, D.C., schools whose pupils included those with an entire range of disabilities, the court ordered the district to educate *all* students, including those with disabilities. It also clarified that specific procedures had to be followed to determine whether a student should receive special services and to resolve disagreements between parents and school personnel.

Other cases highlighted biases against certain students. In *Diana v. State Board of Education of California (Diana)* (1970), a Spanish-speaking child was placed in a class for students with mild intellectual disabilities after she scored low on an IQ test because it was administered in English. The public school system was ordered to test Spanish-speaking children in their native language. Finally, *Larry P. v. Riles (Larry P.)* (1972) concerned an African American student and discrimination in assessment. The court ruled that schools had to ensure that tests administered to students did not discriminate based on race. The *PARC, Mills, Diana,* and *Larry P.* cases together put a spotlight on the shortcomings and abuses of special education at that time and formed the framework for the legislation that today guides the field (Yell, 2006).

A Federal Response: Protecting Students with Disabilities

Litigation and legislation for children with disabilities intertwined during the 1960s and early 1970s. As federal court cases such as those just discussed were clarifying the rights of children with disabilities and their families, legislation was enacted to ensure that these rights were upheld.

Early Laws for Students with Disabilities

The first federal law to directly address the education of students with disabilities was the Elementary and Secondary Education Act of 1965 (P.L. 89-750). This law provided funding to states to assist them in creating and improving programs and services for these students (Yell, 2012). In 1974, Congress further focused its efforts by enacting the Education for All Handicapped Children Act, which increased federal special education funding and charged states with the task of creating full educational opportunities for students with disabilities. That law was amended for the first time in 1975, and that set of amendments, P.L. 94-142, the Education of the Handicapped Act, is considered the basis for all subsequent special education practice. This law captured many of the issues that were being addressed in the courts, funded efforts to find children with disabilities who were not in school, and mandated that states follow the law in order to receive federal funding (Yell, Katsiyannis, & Hazelkorn, 2007). The principles of this law are still in force today, and they are so essential to special education that they will be discussed in detail later in this chapter.

Refinements to the Law

Since 1975, federal special education law has been reauthorized several times (U.S. Department of Education, 2010; Yell, 2012). One significant set of changes occurred in 1986, when special education was expanded to include services to infants and young children. In 1990, the reauthorization renamed the law the Individuals with Disabilities Education Act (IDEA), the name by which it is currently known. This legislation also clarified the need for supports for students as they transitioned from high school to postschool educational or vocational options. In 1997, several significant additions were made when the law was again reauthorized: Procedures for addressing discipline for students with disabilities were included, parent participation was expanded, and the roles of general education teachers in educating students with disabilities were clarified. The most recent reauthorization in 2004 continued the pattern of refinement and revision: Provisions were added to ensure that IDEA is consistent with other federal general education laws and additional strategies were specified to resolve disputes with parents. As you read this text, you will learn more about these and other current provisions of IDEA.

Special Education as a Continuing Story

The passage of federal special education law in 1975 was revolutionary, and it has had many positive effects (Osgood, 2008). Many students who had been completely left out of the public school system now are guaranteed an education, decisions about students regarding special education have to be based on unbiased assessment information, and the rights of parents have been outlined and clear procedures put in place to ensure that any disagreements with school districts are addressed in an impartial way.

However, the passage of the law has not addressed all the issues of educating students with disabilities, and it has not ended debate about appropriate programs and services (e.g., Bateman, Lloyd, & Tankersley, 2015). The result has been additional litigation, usually brought by parents of children with disabilities who are dissatisfied with their children's special education. Several of the court cases that have shaped special education since P.L. 94-142 was passed are listed in Figure 1.2, and several of the key issues that still characterize the field are presented later in this chapter.

FIGURE 1.2   Supreme Court Cases That Have Shaped Special Education

These are significant Supreme Court cases addressing special education issues that have been particularly influential.

Court Case	Key Issue	Ruling
Board of Education of the Hendrick Hudson Central School District v. Rowley (1982)	Free Appropriate Public Education (FAPE)	• This decision, for the first time, defined what is meant by FAPE. It is considered met if the IEP, developed through the act's procedures, is reasonably calculated to enable the child to receive educational benefits.
Irving Independent School District v. Tatro (1984)	Related services	• Health services necessary to assist the student to benefit from special education, when they can be performed by a nonphysician, are considered a related service.
Honig v. Doe (1988)	Discipline	• Schools must abide by the stay-put provision (during administrative or court proceedings, the students must remain in their present placement). • Students cannot be excluded unilaterally for misbehavior related to their disability. • Excluding students from school for over 10 days constitutes a change of placement.
Cedar Rapids Community School District v. Garret F. (1999)	Related services	• Health services deemed necessary for a qualified child with a disability by the IEP team must be provided as long as a nonphysician can perform the services.
Schaffer v. Weast (2005)	Burden of proof	• Parents disputing proposed instructional plans for their children are responsible for proving why the plans are not adequate.
Winkelman v. Parma City School District (2007)		• Parents of children with disabilities are entitled to pursue their case in federal court without being represented by an attorney because they have a personal right under IDEA for their children to be appropriately educated. If they only held rights on behalf of their children, this would be prohibited.
Forest Grove School District v. T. A. (2009)		• In some situations, parents are entitled to be reimbursed for private school tuition, even when the child has never received special education services from a public school. Prior to this case, the interpretation of law was that public school services had to be accessed or tuition claims would not be considered.

Source: Based on Katsiyannis, A., Yell, M. L., & Bradley, R. (2001). Reflections on the 25th anniversary of the Individuals with Disabilities Education Act. *Remedial and Special Education, 22,* 324–334. Copyright © 2001 by Pro-Ed, Inc. Also based on Wright, P., & Wright, P. (2014, August). *Special education caselaw: Decisions from U.S. Supreme Court.* Retrieved from http://www.wrightslaw.com/caselaw.htm.

As the information in this section has illustrated, special education is a highly regulated and precise discipline that has evolved rapidly and continues to change. As you anticipate your work with students with disabilities, remember that information that was accurate just a few years ago may now be outdated. You will need to keep up with changes about the requirements of special education law and continually examine your knowledge and skills to ensure that they reflect contemporary thinking.

MyEdLab **Self-Check 1.2**

MyEdLab **Application Exercise 1.2:** An Overview of the History of Special Education

MyEdLab **Application Exercise 1.3:** Meet a Special Education Teacher

Laws Affecting Students with Disabilities

In the section you just finished reading, the federal law that governs special education was mentioned briefly. In this section, you'll continue to deepen your understanding of special education by learning more detail about that law as well as other federal laws that affect students with disabilities.

Individuals with Disabilities Education Act (IDEA) of 2004

Since the first special education law was passed in 1975, legislation has required the delivery of special education, related services, and supplementary aids and services, the concepts introduced at the beginning of this chapter. However, the delivery of those three services is based on core principles, also captured in the law. These principles are designed to ensure the educational rights of students with disabilities and their parents (Yell, 2012). They include zero reject, free appropriate public education (FAPE), least restrictive environment (LRE), nondiscriminatory evaluation, parent and family rights, and procedural safeguards.

Zero Reject

The principle of zero reject entitles all students with disabilities to a public education regardless of the nature or severity of their disabilities. To accomplish zero reject, each state has in place what is called a child find system, a set of procedures for alerting the public that services are available for students with disabilities and for distributing print and electronic materials, conducting screening, and completing other activities to ensure that students are identified. This principle of the law is directly related to the *PARC* and *Mills* cases discussed earlier in this chapter, in which parents won the right for their children to attend public schools.

Today, zero reject also addresses more than finding children with disabilities. It ensures that students with communicable diseases, such as AIDS, cannot be excluded from schools. It also guides school policies related to students with disabilities who commit serious offenses that might otherwise lead to long-term suspension or expulsion.

Free Appropriate Public Education

The education to which all students with disabilities are entitled must be a free appropriate public education (FAPE). That is, parents and family members cannot be asked to pay for special education services. In fact, if a decision is made that a student needs to be educated outside the student's own school district, the school district usually bears the cost for that placement, including the expense of transportation. Further, FAPE clarifies that the student's education must incorporate special education through specially designed instruction, related services, and supplementary aids and services. These elements are captured in the student's *individualized education program (IEP)*, a document described in detail in Chapter 2 (Etscheidt & Curran, 2010; Katsiyannis, Losinski, & Parks Ennis, 2015).

Least Restrictive Environment

The next principle of IDEA concerns how students receive FAPE. That is, students must be educated in the setting most like that of typical peers in which they can succeed when provided with the needed supports and services, or the least restrictive environment (LRE). It is presumed that the LRE for most students with disabilities is the general education setting, and educators must justify any instance in which a student with a disability is not educated there. However, the law spells out additional settings in which students may be educated, including general education with instruction in a special education setting for a small part of the day, a separate special education classroom where students spend most of the day, a separate school, and others (Marx et al., 2014).

Nondiscriminatory Evaluation

IDEA outlines the rights of students and their parents to ensure that any assessment completed as part of a special education decision-making process is unbiased, referred to as nondiscriminatory evaluation. Based on the *Diana* and *Larry P.* court cases already discussed, the law ensures the following:

- Tests are administered in the child's native language.
- Tests are appropriate for the child's age and characteristics.
- More than one test is used to assess the presence of a disability.
- A knowledgeable professional administers and interprets assessment results.
- Assessments occur in all areas of suspected disability (Yell & Drasgow, 2007).

Parent and Family Rights to Confidentiality

Information regarding a student's disability is highly confidential. IDEA clarifies that such information may be shared only with individuals who are working directly with the student. In fact, a log must be kept of anyone who accesses these student records. Further, parents have the right to request to see and obtain copies of all records kept regarding their child with a disability and to dispute information that they perceive is not accurate.

Procedural Safeguards

The final principle in IDEA concerns procedural safeguards (Osborne & Russo, 2014). Any decisions concerning a student with disabilities are made with parent input and in compliance with all aspects of the law. For example, parents must give written consent for their children to be assessed to determine if they have a disability. Similarly, parents must be invited to attend any meetings regarding their child, and they must give permission for the child to begin receiving special education. When parents and school personnel disagree on any aspect of special education, specific steps must be followed to attempt to resolve the dispute. The procedural safeguards that parents have will become clearer as you read about the people and procedures in special education in Chapter 2.

These six principles of IDEA guide educators to ensure that their students with disabilities receive the education to which they are entitled. Further, they are not just ideas that exist in the law. Instead, they are an integral part of day-to-day special education practices, and they are central to the roles and responsibilities of professionals who educate students with disabilities.

Other Legislation Related to Special Education

In addition to IDEA, a law that guarantees *educational rights*, special education is affected by laws that guarantee the *civil rights* of children and adults. These laws are Section 504 of the Rehabilitation Act of 1973 and the Americans with Disabilities Act of 1990.

Section 504 of the Rehabilitation Act of 1973

When Congress enacted the Rehabilitation Act of 1973 (P.L. 93-112), it created the first civil rights legislation in the United States specifically intended to protect individuals with disabilities. Section 504, the final section of this law, states that

> No qualified handicapped person shall, on the basis of handicap, be excluded from participation in, be denied the benefits of, or otherwise be subjected to discrimination under any program or activity which receives or benefits from Federal financial assistance. (Section 504, 29 U.S.C. §794[a])

This law broadly defines *disabilities* as impairments that significantly limit one or more major life activities, including walking, seeing, hearing, and learning. Further, it protects all people with disabilities, not only children, from discrimination in programs receiving federal funding, including all public schools (Guthrie, 2006). Some of the provisions framed in this law that affect children of school age were clarified in IDEA, but this law protects some students who are not eligible for the services outlined in that law (Zirkel, 2014). An example of a student served through Section 504 might be one who is an average learner but has Type I diabetes. Through Section 504, the school district would ensure that school professionals working with the student understand his needs and that the student has immediate access to snacks and water or other supports related to his medical condition. This student does not need the *educational* services of IDEA, but he is entitled to special accommodations that may not be available to other students.

Unlike IDEA, no federal funding is allocated to implement Section 504, so any services or supports provided to students through this law must be paid for by the local school district. Section 504 has many provisions, and you will learn more about them in Chapter 6 in the discussion of attention deficit–hyperactivity disorder (ADHD), another special need sometimes addressed using Section 504 provisions.

Americans with Disabilities Act of 1990

By far the most comprehensive legislation protecting the rights of individuals with disabilities, no matter their age, is the Americans with Disabilities Act of 1990 (ADA) (U.S. Department of Justice, 2009). This more recent legislation, which was amended and expanded in 2008, applies to both public and private sectors, including libraries, state and local governments, restaurants, hotels, theaters, transportation systems, and stores (Davis, 2015). With the exception of public school applications, ADA largely has replaced Section 504. In addition to the other provisions of this law, it directly addresses communication, and so it requires that closed captioning be provided to accommodate individuals who are deaf or hard of hearing. It is the ADA that ensures that buildings have access ramps and that most have elevators, that buses and trains can accommodate wheelchairs, and that employers may not refuse to hire a new employee because that individual has a disability. Mentioning ADA is an opportunity to remind you that many students' disabilities have a lifelong impact, such that these individuals may access certain supports and services even after they leave school. One difference is worth noting, however. Although professionals in schools are obligated to find students entitled to special education and deliver those services, the same requirement does not exist in ADA. Thus, persons who wish to receive services must actively seek them.

IDEA and related laws ensure that students with disabilities receive an appropriate education and that they can lead productive lives after their school years.

Taken together, IDEA, Section 504, and ADA ensure that people who have disabilities have the right to fully access throughout their lives all the programs, services, and activities available to other individuals. These laws also clearly establish that civil rights protections specifically include individuals with disabilities and that discrimination will not be tolerated.

MyEdLab **Self-Check 1.3**

MyEdLab **Application Exercise 1.4:** Least Restrictive Environment

Students Who Receive Special Education

Although the federal civil rights laws for people with disabilities just outlined use a very broad and functionally based definition of *disability*, IDEA, the law that directly addresses education, defines 13 specific categories of disability, and only students with these disabilities are eligible for special education services:

- Specific learning disability
- Speech or language impairment
- Intellectual disability
- Emotional disturbance
- Multiple disabilities (i.e., students who have more than one disability)
- Hearing impairment
- Orthopedic (or physical) impairment
- Other health impairment
- Visual impairment
- Autism
- Deaf/blindness (i.e., students who are both deaf and blind)
- Traumatic brain injury
- Developmental delay

If you scan the table of contents of this book or preview Chapters 5 through 14, you will see that each of these disabilities is discussed in detail, including the definitions as specified by the law, the characteristics of students with these disorders, perspectives of students' parents and families, and research-based instructional approaches best suited for teaching students with these special needs. And in Chapter 2 you will learn about the detailed set of idea-mandated procedures that are followed to determine whether a youngster has a disability and is eligible for special education.

Prevalence of Students with Disabilities

How many students with disabilities are there? The answer to that question at any point in time is referred to as the *prevalence* of students of disabilities, and information to determine prevalence is gathered each year by the U.S. Department of Education as part of IDEA. As you can see by reviewing Figure 1.3, in 2012–2013, 5.8 million school-age children and youth received special education, or approximately 8.4% of students ages 6 to 21 (U.S. Department of Education, 2015). Students with specific learning disabilities comprise the largest group of students, accounting for more than one-third (39.5%) of all those receiving special education. Students with speech or language impairments form the next largest group (17.9%) of all school-age students receiving special education.

The data in Figure 1.3 also demonstrate changes occurring in the students who are identified as having disabilities. During the decade between 1990–1991 and 2000–2001, the number of students identified as having disabilities grew nearly 38% while the overall school-age population (i.e., the total number of school-age students) grew approximately 15% (U.S. Department of Education, 1992b, 2002d, 2011a). Since 2000–2001, however, the pattern of overall rapid growth is no longer in place. Notice that the overall number of students identified with disabilities has grown just slightly. The number identified as having learning disabilities has declined over the past 10 years, and the same is true for students with intellectual disabilities and emotional disturbance. At the same time, the numbers of students identified as having autism or other health impairments (the category that includes many students with ADHD) have skyrocketed. No single explanation can be offered for the fluctuating prevalence rates. The decrease in the number of students with learning, intellectual, and emotional disabilities may be due in part to recent efforts to ensure that students receive early

FIGURE 1.3

Students Ages 6 Through 21 Served Under IDEA: Number by Disability Category[a]
(Percentage of total student population with disability)

Disability Category	1992–1993	2002–2003	2012–2013
Specific learning disability	2,438,147 (51.05)	2,822,648 (47.2)	2,268,098 (39.8)
Speech or language impairment	1,007,575 (21.09)	1,118,576 (18.7)	1,032,729 (18.1)
Intellectual disability	552,703 (11.57)	571,160 (9.56)	415,697 (7.3)
Emotional disturbance	413,691 (8.66)	483,544 (8.09)	358,389 (6.29)
Multiple disabilities	109,746 (2.29)	131,444 (2.2)	124,722 (2.1)
Hearing impairments	64,110 (1.34)	71,222 (1.19)	68,069 (1.19)
Orthopedic impairments	56,555 (1.18)	67,747 (1.13)	52,052 (0.91)
Other health impairments	83,178 (1.74)	448,312 (7.5)	757,904 (13.3)
Visual impairments	24,873 (0.52)	25,315 (0.42)	24,987 (0.43)
Autism	18,893 (0.39)	140,280 (2.34)	440,592 (7.7)
Deaf/blindness	1,315 (0.02)	1,605 (0.02)	1,281 (0.02)
Traumatic brain injury	5,291 (0.11)	22,478 (0.37)	25,020 (0.43)
Developmental delay[b]	0 (0)	66,164 (1.1)	122,901 (2.1)
All disabilities	4,775,534	5,971,495	5,693,441

[a]Data are for the 50 states and the District of Columbia.
[b]Optional reporting on developmental delay for students ages 3 through 7 was first allowed in the 1997–1998 school year. This category now applies to children only to age 9.

Sources: U.S. Department of Education. (1999). *17th annual report to Congress on the implementation of Individuals with Disabilities Education Act* (Vol. 1). Washington, DC: Author.
U.S. Department of Education. (2005). *27th annual report to Congress on the implementation of Individuals with Disabilities Education Act* (Vol. 1). Washington, DC: Author.
Institute on Disability, University of New Hampshire. (2013). *Annual disability statistics compendium* (Tables 11.1, 11.2, 11.3a, 11.3b, 11.3c). Durham, NH: Author. Retrieved from
http://disabilitycompendium.org/archives/2013-compendium-statistics.

and intensive interventions designed to prevent the need for special education services (e.g., Berkeley, Bender, Peaster, & Saunders, 2009). The rising number of students with autism is likely influenced by increasing awareness of and attention to this disability (e.g., Lord & Bishop, 2010).

What other factors do you think might be contributing to changes in the prevalence of students with various disabilities? Regardless of any influences, it is likely that all teachers, not just special educators, will instruct students with disabilities.

Special Education for Young Children

Although the focus of this text is on school-age students with disabilities (ages 5 to 21), IDEA also includes provisions for young children (ages birth to 5). For children birth to 2 years old, special education is not always required by federal law. However, all states now provide services to these infants and toddlers, and approximately 339,071 children nationwide receive them (U.S. Department of Education, 2015). For children ages 3 to 5, special education services have been mandated in IDEA since 1986, and in 2013, 745,336 children received these services (U.S. Department of Education, 2015). As you might guess, some young children who are identified as eligible to receive special education have significant special needs that were identified at a very early age, including physical and sensory disabilities, intellectual disabilities, or autism. However, many young children with disabilities who receive services have milder needs, typically related to language development or motor skills. Because it is often impossible to determine the exact nature of young children's special needs, they may receive services through the IDEA general disability label of *developmentally delayed*, a category that may be used for children up to 9 years of age.

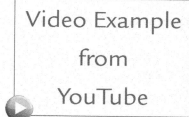

MyEdLab
Video Example 1.2

Video Example 1.2 provides a bit of advice from students with disabilities to all teachers. (https://www.youtube.com/watch?v=ITMLzXzgB_s)

Students with Special Needs Not Specifically Included in IDEA

As you read about the students who receive special education, have you stopped to think about the students whom you might have assumed would be mentioned but who have not been? Because special education as defined through IDEA is available only to the students with one or more of the 13 disabilities mentioned earlier, some students needing special supports receive them through other means.

Students Who Are Gifted or Talented

Thus far, students who are gifted or talented have not been discussed, even though these students clearly have special needs. IDEA does not provide for special education for these students. In fact, although 46 states define *giftedness*, only four states mandate education of these students while at the same time providing full funding for it; 10 states neither mandate nor fund gifted education; and the remainder of the states have some combination of mandates and partial funding (Davidson Institute for Talent Development, 2015). Further, in some states and districts, special and gifted education are part of a single governing agency, while in others this is not the case. Because this group of students has special needs, though not those associated with special education, in Chapter 15 you will read more about their characteristics and instructional approaches recommended for them.

It is important to note, too, that some students with disabilities also are gifted or talented, and these students are sometimes referred to as *twice exceptional* or as having *dual exceptionalities* (Barnard-Brak, Johnsen, Hannig, & Wei, 2015). These students need a combination of services: They are entitled to special education, related services, and supplementary aids and services to address their disabilities, but they also need gifted education with its enrichment and encouragement to develop their gifts and talents. These students also are discussed in Chapter 15.

Students with Attention Deficit–Hyperactivity Disorder

A second group of students not addressed directly in IDEA comprises students with attention deficit–hyperactivity disorder (ADHD) (Thomas, Sanders, Doust, Beller, & Glasziou, 2015). ADHD is not, by itself, a disability category. Many students with ADHD receive support through the broader provisions of Section 504, introduced earlier in this chapter, and this assistance is largely the responsibility of general education teachers. However, some students with ADHD may receive special education services when their disorder is significant enough that they are identified as *other health impaired (OHI)*. Because so many students now are categorized as having ADHD, some of whom are receiving special education, you will have the opportunity to learn more about this special need in Chapter 6.

Students at Risk for School Failure

One additional group of students not eligible for services through IDEA is important to mention: students who often are referred to as being *at risk* (Bergmann & Brough, 2013). These students may be homeless, abuse drugs or other substances, live in poverty, or have any of hundreds of other characteristics that can negatively affect their learning. Although students with disabilities also may have these risk factors, the presence of these risk factors alone does not constitute disability. These students need the attention of caring and skillful teachers who can set high expectations, teach in a way that maximizes student potential, and instill in students the love of learning. As you work in schools, you are likely to hear professionals mention that a particular student *should* be in special education but is not eligible. Often they are referring to a student at risk. Students at risk often need many types of supports and services, but they do not have disabilities and are not eligible for special education.

MyEdLab **Self-Check 1.4**

MyEdLab **Application Exercise 1.5:** Disability Categories: Prevalence v. Percentages

---

Parent and Family Roles in the Education of Children with Disabilities

Parents—including natural, adoptive, and foster parents; guardians; and other individuals acting in the parent role—are the strongest advocates that children with disabilities have (Harris, 2015). For example, as far back as 1874, a parent went to court to argue that her child with an intellectual disability had a right to be educated in a public school. The courts at that time believed that a free education for all children was not meant to include those thought to be "incapable" of being educated and ruled against her. Since that time, parents and other advocates have been instrumental in working for the rights of students with disabilities through organizations such as the Arc (formerly called the Association for Retarded Citizens), the United Cerebral Palsy Association (UCP), the Council for Exceptional Children (CEC), and hundreds of other disability-specific groups (e.g., the National Association for Down Syndrome). These parents have been instrumental in guaranteeing that their children receive a high-quality education. They have lobbied for strong legislation to protect the rights of their children, and they have taken their cause to court when they believed those rights were not being upheld.

Parents and Their Children with Disabilities

Entire books have been written, thousands of studies have been conducted, and whole courses have been taught on the relationships of parents and other family members with their children with disabilities. A fairly straightforward conclusion can be drawn from this significant work: Parents and family members see their children primarily as children for whom a disability is only one small part of who they are; they do not make a disability the overriding characteristic of their children. Robert and Timothy and their parents illustrate this point. Robert is highly gifted in a traditional way: He excels in school, and he is a talented pianist. Timothy is gifted, too. He is gregarious and usually surrounded by a set of friends; he is also a star on his Little League baseball team. Robert and Timothy are twins, and their parents have carefully helped each boy to reach his potential and to be proud of his accomplishments. Little attention is paid on a day-to-day basis to the fact that Timothy has an intellectual disability. After a visitor who did not know the boys had listened to Robert play a complex piece of piano music, she asked Timothy what he was really good at. Timothy demonstrated his strong, positive self-concept when he said, "Baseball. I play a million times better than Robert."

Although much has been written about the stress of raising a child with a disability (e.g., Graziano, McNamara, Geffken, & Reid, 2011), professionals increasingly are recognizing that parents and family members cherish their children with special needs. For example, Colavita, Luthra, and Perry (2014) analyzed survey responses of 141 parents of children (ages 3 to 19) with intellectual disabilities, including autism. They found that the parents described strengths of their children, including:

- Personality characteristics, such as being loving, happy, creative, courageous, and honest
- Social personality characteristics, such as being helpful and playful, having a sense of humor, and displaying friendliness
- Cognitive functioning, such as being motivated and having savant skills
- Coping abilities, such as being cooperative and resilient and responding to reinforcement
- Specific skills, such as having hobbies, navigating technology, and having self-help skills

To a professional educator, this understanding of positive perspectives is especially important because there is a tendency among school personnel to most often contact parents about problems or to focus on student deficits. If you reflect on the strengths of families of children with disabilities, you will find that you can build strong working relationships with them—relationships based on a multidimensional understanding of your students.

Parent Participation in Special Education

Parent participation is essential in special education. Research strongly supports the fact that when parents of students with disabilities actively participate in their children's schooling, achievement is higher and fewer behavior problems occur (Lalvani, 2012). However, it is well recognized that school–home partnerships have not always been easy to build.

Barriers to Parent Participation

Many factors contribute to some parents' reluctance to participate actively in their children's education. For example, time is a critical issue for many parents. Often both parents work, and one or both may have a second job; they may have other children who need attention and elderly parents to care for; and they have to manage the innumerable details of supporting their families. They simply may not be able to attend a meeting that school professionals schedule at 3:45 P.M. on Thursday or at 7:30 A.M. on Friday.

Many other barriers also exist for families from diverse backgrounds (Rodriguez, Blatz, & Elbaum, 2014). Some families face language barriers in interacting with school professionals; others may lack transportation. Some families, including those of migrant workers, move frequently; thus, developing a close working relationship with a teacher is unlikely. Some parents may be unfamiliar with the customs of U.S. schools or are uncomfortable with them. They also may find some teachers and administrators are insensitive to their needs.

Did You Know?
The Center for Parent Information and Resources (http://www.parentcenterhub.org/) is a federally funded hub for families with children with disabilities. The site addresses parent reactions when they learn their child has a disability, includes dozens of links to information parents might find helpful, and links parents with their local parent support organization.

Strategies to Encourage Parent Participation

Teachers are well intentioned. They want to welcome parents to school and encourage their participation. Muscott (2002) recommends that you follow these four principles to create school–home partnerships:

1. Use family-centered practices. Emphasize family strengths, not weaknesses, and family choice about services. Think about how you can support the entire family in your interactions, not only one child with special needs.
2. Respect the unique characteristics of each family. Often the most straightforward way to find out what a family needs is to ask. It may be tempting to think that you know what a family is like because you learned about their culture in a course or workshop, but remember that no single set of traits can be assigned to any family. Each is different.
3. Recognize that families have understandings of their children's special needs that may differ from yours. Whatever your role in the school, your job is not to convince family members that their child has a certain disability or to help them be "realistic." Rather, you are to provide exemplary services and offer assistance to the family, whatever their perception of their child.
4. Match your strategies and resources to family preferences. If you truly understand the first three principles, then this will seem logical. Giving a single parent with several children a book on interventions and advice for using them at home is a strategy that will likely fail. Asking that parent what her concerns and priorities are for her child and offering one specific idea for addressing them will likely be more effective.

Throughout this text, you will learn more about parents of children with disabilities and how you can effectively work with them.

Video Example
from
YouTube

MyEdLab
Video Example 1.3

Much more than words can convey, parents are your partners in educating your students, a point eloquently made as this parent describes her child, his challenges, and her experiences working with school personnel in Video Example 1.3.
(https://www.youtube.com/watch?v=FPxPPgVWbmY)

MyEdLab **Self-Check 1.5**

MyEdLab **Application Exercise 1.6:** Independent Living

MyEdLab **Application Exercise 1.7:** Parent Participation in Special Education.

Critical Topics Influencing Special Education

Although the core principles of special education have remained constant for more than four decades, you already have learned that special education is in many ways a constantly evolving field. Not surprisingly, the rapid pace of change is accompanied by emerging trends and debate over critical concerns. Four of the most significant topics include (a) inclusive practices as the guiding belief system for educating students with disabilities in the 21st century; (b) collaboration as a pivotal component of effective inclusive schooling; (c) rigorous and evidence-based instructional practices for all students, including those with disabilities; and (d) positive, systemic approaches for responding to student behavior. Some of these topics merit the attention of an entire later chapter (e.g., collaboration); others are mentioned in several chapters as appropriate (e.g., inclusive practices, instructional approaches, behavior techniques). All of them are integral to understanding current programs and services for students with disabilities and effectively educating them. Here, each of these issues is introduced as a way of clarifying the major themes that are foundational to this text and to your study of the field of special education.

Did You Know?

Students with disabilities more than other students are rejected by peers and have difficulties with social interactions; not surprisingly, they also are more likely to be victims of bullying (Young, Ne'eman, & Gelser, 2011).

Inclusive Practices and Access to the General Curriculum

No topic related to special education has had as wide an impact or has caused as much controversy as inclusion. Even though the term *inclusion* appears nowhere in federal legislation governing the education of students with disabilities, it has been the subject of endless discussion (Waitoller & Kozleski, 2015).

Formal and Informal Definitions

Inclusion, often called *inclusive practices*, is a belief system or philosophy. It is shared by every member of a school as a learning community—teachers, administrators, other staff members, students, and parents—about their responsibility to educate all students so that they reach their potential.

Although the physical location of students in schools and classrooms is one dimension of inclusiveness—the general education setting is strongly preferred—inclusion is not about where students sit as much as it is about how adults and classmates welcome all students to access learning and recognize that the diversity of learners in today's schools dictates that no single approach is appropriate for all (e.g., Braunsteiner & Mariano-Lapidus, 2014). Ultimately, inclusive practices encompass those students who are gifted and talented, those who are at risk for failure because of their life circumstances, those with disabilities, and those who are average learners. Likewise, it includes all the teachers and other staff members who work in today's schools.

Inclusion has a foundation in the history of special education: Soon after the passage of P.L. 94-142, the forerunner of IDEA, parents of children with significant intellectual disabilities began to express dissatisfaction at the separateness of their children's education (Itkonen, 2009; Winzer, 2012). Yes, their children were now clearly entitled to access public schools, but they often were housed in separate schools that had no typical learners, or they were placed in a separate wing of a school and treated as though they were not part of that school's community. These parents took their cause to court as a civil right rather than an educational issue (Fleischer & Zames, 2001). They argued that separate schools and classes caused their children to miss the full range of school experiences and that this practice was discriminatory. These parents wanted their children included with other students in school, and thus the concept of inclusion was introduced to the field of education. It was extended in 1986 when Madeline Will, then Assistant Secretary for Special Education and Rehabilitation in the U.S. Department of Education, proposed a *regular education initiative (REI),* urging general education and special education teachers to work together to educate *all* their students (Will, 1986). As a result, attention for more than three decades has focused on what constitutes inclusive practices, for whom inclusive practices are appropriate, and how the special needs of students with disabilities can be met within the general education context.

It should be mentioned that the formal definition of *inclusiveness* is often adjusted when placed in practice in schools. In fact, what is considered inclusion varies widely depending on the clarity of state and local policies related to this aspect of special education, the resources available to foster such practices, teacher and administrator understanding and commitment, and parent and community support (Friend, 2014; Tremblay, 2013). In some schools, inclusive practices are exemplary and mirror a formal definition, and teachers and specialists demonstrate daily how diverse groups of students can learn together and still have their special needs met. In other schools, the term *inclusion* is used, but the corresponding practices that contribute to its success may not be in place. A basic but important example of appropriate practices concerns disability etiquette.

PROFESSIONAL **EDGE**

Disability Etiquette

Here are some tips for ensuring that your interactions with students and colleagues with disabilities are respectful and appropriate:

- *Use person-first language.* Say "students with disabilities" or "John, who has a physical disability." Placing the disability first (e.g., "LD students," "special education kids," "IEP students," "SPED children") inappropriately emphasizes the disability instead of the person.
- *Avoid the term handicapped.* Some individuals consider this word derogatory, and except in a historical context, it is no longer used in federal special education laws or regulations. The terms *disability* and *special needs* are alternatives. Not even parking spaces should be labeled *handicapped*; they are *accessible.*
- *Avoid the language of pity.* Say "wheelchair user" instead of "wheelchair bound," and do not use words such as *victim, sufferer,* or *afflicted.*
- *Talk to the person.* Be sure to talk directly to the person (whether a student, colleague, or other), as illustrated in the photo, rather than to a paraeducator, interpreter, or assistant who is present.
- *Don't make assumptions.* Sometimes people assume that individuals who have significant physical disabilities or sensory disabilities (e.g., blindness or deafness) also have intellectual disabilities. It is better to err by presuming competence than lack of competence.
- *People with disabilities are individuals.* Every person with a disability is unique, with likes and dislikes, problems and joys. Remember that disability does not define the person.

Source: Excerpts from United Spinal Association. (2015). *Disability etiquette: Tips on interacting with people with disabilities.* Retrieved from http://www.unitedspinal.org/disability-etiquette/#basics. Copyright 2015 by United Spinal Association and Access Resources. Reprinted with permission.

The Debate About Inclusion

Views about inclusive practices vary widely. Some professionals argue that the only way a school can truly demonstrate an inclusive belief system is to place nearly every student in general education full time (Pierson & Howell, 2013; Sailor, 2015). They point out that public education has two curricula. The first curriculum is *explicit*; that is, it is the curriculum that guides the instruction of typical learners, and advocates argue that it cannot truly be accessed by students with disabilities unless they fully participate in general education. The second curriculum is *implicit* and includes social interactions and skills that are best learned with typical peers. Advocates stress that students with disabilities likewise must be with peers to access this curriculum (Gottfried, 2014). These professionals insist that competent and dedicated teachers, adequate supports and services, and a strong commitment can guarantee any student's success without the need for a separate location.

Other individuals have expressed significant concerns about the aspect of inclusive practices related to students being educated in general education classes with typical peers (e.g., Fuchs & Fuchs, 2015; Kauffman, 2015). Some parents fear that their children will be bullied or that they will learn inappropriate behaviors in general education settings. They express uncertainty about whether their children's special needs can be met adequately in a general education classroom. Some professionals also question whether the general education setting truly is the appropriate environment for some pupils, particularly when general education teachers also must meet the needs of 20, 30, or even more other students in the class; the pacing of instruction is brisk; and the availability of a special education teacher to provide support may be limited (Eisenman, Pleet, Wandry, & McGinley, 2011). These professionals suggest that many students need a smaller class size, a higher degree of structure, specialized instructional methods, and, for some, a curriculum that emphasizes life skills, that is, interventions that can be delivered most readily in a special education classroom for part or most of the school day.

Research on Inclusive Practices

Most professionals fall somewhere between these two opposing views in their thinking about inclusion. They strongly support inclusive practices and access to general education for most students. However, they acknowledge that careful attention must paid to administrative understanding and support, teacher preparation and commitment, and practical details (such as time for planning and schedules) in order to achieve success (e.g., Sullivan, Artiles, & Hernandez-Saca, 2015; Youngs, Jones, & Low, 2011). They also recognize that some students should receive some highly specialized instruction in a separate setting, usually for a small part of the school day (e.g., McLeskey & Waldron, 2011).

Research generally supports these ideas. For example, Huberman, Navo, and Parrish (2012) studied four school districts in which students with disabilities demonstrated unusually high academic outcomes. What the districts shared included a strong commitment to inclusive education, a highly collaborative school culture, and professional development for teachers and others on topics such as effective instructional practices. In another study, Cosier, Causton-Theoharis, and Theoharis (2014) analyzed reading and math achievement of students with various disabilities, ages six though nine, in relation to the number of hours spent in general education. Controlling for variables that could bias the results, they found a strong positive relationship: The more hours students spent in general education, the more positive their academic outcomes. The authors cautioned, however, that their results had to be placed in a context of fostering effective classroom instructional practices and administrative support.

The social dimension of inclusive practices also has been the focus of research. First, many students feel stigmatized when they spend part or all of the day in special education settings (Connor, 2006). Further, some high school students with significant disabilities have been found to have positive experiences when they receive at least some of their education with their peers, particularly in terms of their social relations and friendships with typical classmates (Carter, Moss, Hoffman, Chung, & Sisco, 2011). One other component of social inclusion also should be mentioned—students' relationships with their teachers. Crouch, Keys, & McMahon (2014) studied this issue with 133 students with disabilities who were transferring from a separate school to a total of 23 public schools. Querying the students and their new teachers, they found that students who had many positive and few negative social interactions with teachers felt a higher sense of belonging. They concluded that inclusiveness is possible but that this social aspect of it is critical for its success.

Inclusiveness—welcoming all students as members of their school communities—results in academic and social benefits for students with disabilities and ensures that they are prepared for their lives after their school years.

Inclusive Practices in This Text

This discussion of inclusion is intended to help you understand the approach that is taken in this book. The viewpoint is that inclusive schools are possible and necessary for 21st-century education. This does not mean that every student is educated with peers at all times, but it does mean that the responsibility of discovering effective means for all students to learn together is taken very seriously, and deviations from this approach are made with reluctance and only after careful deliberation.

When a decision is reached for any type of separate education, it is based on data about the student's academic, social, behavior, and other needs, and it is monitored carefully to ensure that the cost of this decision to the student is worth the benefit the student is receiving. Further, the decision is reviewed and revised based on changing needs rather than rigidly scheduled for an entire school year, and it is premised on the goal of reducing or eliminating the separate service as soon as possible.

Collaboration

Inclusive schooling seems like it should be a readily achievable goal; it is anything but that. Educating students with disabilities as true members of a learning community requires that some professionals set aside long-held beliefs and that they change their classroom practices. It also requires that administrators set high expectations for student outcomes and hold teachers accountable for instructing their students so that those expectations are realized. Such ingredients for inclusive schooling rely heavily on professionals and parents working closely with each other (Friend & Cook, 2017). Not surprisingly, collaboration has become a crucial dimension to the planning, delivery, and evaluation of inclusive special education and related services.

Collaboration Definition

Collaboration refers to the way in which professionals interact with each other and with parents or family members as they work together to educate students with disabilities. It concerns the quality of their professional relationships—for example, whether they work as partners in their efforts or whether one or another assumes control while others acquiesce. Collaboration never exists as a goal in and of itself: It is the means for achieving other goals.

Examples of situations calling for collaboration are almost limitless in today's schools (Friend & Cook, 2017). For example, professionals must work closely with parents and family members, and they may be asked to participate on teams that include teachers and other school personnel (e.g., a speech-language pathologist) as well as representatives from agencies outside the school (e.g., a social worker or representative from the juvenile justice system). In addition, general education and special education teachers or other professionals may work together in general education classrooms instructing all of their students by *co-teaching,* a special form of collaboration discussed in detail in Chapter 4. Which of these examples of collaboration might help Daniel, the student you met at the beginning of the chapter, to achieve his goal of earning a high school diploma?

Simply put, the days are gone when an individual could enter the field of education just to work with students. Now a significant part of school professionals' jobs, no matter the setting or type of position, pertains to interacting effectively with other adults. There is too much to know and too much work to be done to have each professional functioning in isolation—to succeed and help students succeed takes the partnership of collaboration.

Easier Said Than Done

Does collaboration seem to you to be so inherent to being an education professional that you are perhaps wondering why it even needs to be highlighted? That is because, although few educators would disagree about the importance of collaboration, its implementation is quite complex. For example, although most special educators take coursework in working with other professionals and parents, the same is not necessarily true for other teachers. When expected to work together, some professionals may lack the knowledge and skills for doing so effectively and efficiently.

Another dilemma relates to practical matters for teachers, such as the time available to meet. In fact, lack of shared time is generally the most often expressed concern of professionals expected to collaborate in the delivery of services to students with disabilities. This problem has many variations: Teachers may not have adequate time to meet with paraeducators, specialists such as speech-language therapists may not be available when teachers can meet with them, and so on.

One additional collaboration dilemma concerns administrative support. Unless principals and other school leaders actively foster a collaborative culture, set expectations for all staff members, and themselves become students of collaboration, a sense of community is unlikely to develop. And without that critical support, outcomes for students with disabilities may be disappointing.

Accessible and Effective Instruction

Although the social purposes of inclusive practices are important for students, both those with and without disabilities, and can have lifelong value, they are not enough. The goal of an inclusive education is for the approximately 80% of students with disabilities who do not have significant intellectual disabilities to achieve academically at a level similar to their peers and for the others to learn essential skills aligned with the general curriculum. Data suggest that although some progress has been made toward reaching this goal, an immense amount of work remains to be done. The following sections briefly summarize several aspects of the topic of instruction.; they are addressed in considerably more detail in later chapters.

Rigor and Accountability

Public education in the 21st century is distinguished by multiple reform initiatives calling for rigorous academic standards and high expectations for all students' achievement. For example, the Elementary and Secondary Education Act (ESEA) (also called the No Child Left Behind Act or NCLB), the general education law that shapes many contemporary education practices, includes these provisions:

- All students should be proficient in reading and math, including nearly all students with disabilities
- Nearly all students with disabilities are required by law to take the same standardized achievement tests as their peers without disabilities; only a few students with significant disabilities may take an alternate assessment,

and even this is to be aligned with the standards that other students must meet.

Rigor and accountability are extended through several provisions of IDEA:

- Special educators monitor and report their students' progress as often as other students receive progress reports or report cards, usually at least four times during the school year (Yell, 2012).
- All students with disabilities participate in assessments with necessary accommodations or through alternate assessments, as noted above (Yell, Katsiyannis, Collins, & Losinski, 2012); their scores are reported in the same way as those of other students.

Yet another indicator of the importance or rigor and accountability is the adoption in many states of the Common Core State Standards (CCSS) or similar standards (March & Peters, 2015). Although not mandated in any law, most states have decided that for their citizens to compete in the global society, they should learn from sophisticated problem-solving tasks, challenging reading assignments that require careful analysis, and writing experiences supported by evidence. Students with disabilities are expected to participate in this instruction (e.g., Spencer, 2015).

Evidence-Based Practices

Both IDEA and federal laws that address the education of all students require that educators use *evidence-based practices* (Council for Exceptional Children, 2006). This means that they must make decisions about what to teach their students and determine how effective that teaching/learning process has been based on data that they gather. They also must teach, using programs, interventions, strategies, and activities that have been demonstrated through research to be effective (Santangelo, Novosel, Cook, & Gapsis, 2015). Thus, evidence-based practices form a third critical aspect of accessible and effective instruction. Reading instruction provides a clear example of the use of practices based in research. Many perspectives have been offered on how children learn to read, but not all of them have a research base. For struggling readers, one strongly evidence-based approach is called *direct instruction (DI)*. First developed in the 1960s, DI has been demonstrated by decades of research to be effective in helping children, adolescents, and adults learn to read through a fast-paced, highly structured series of lessons (e.g., Flores et al., 2013; Magliaro, Lockee, & Burton, 2005). DI is considered an evidence-based practice, the first of many such practices you will read about as you progress through this text.

Two terms you may already know are directly related to evidence-based practices: universal design for learning (UDL) and differentiation. Universal design for learning (UDL), sometimes also referred to as *universal design for instruction (UDI)*, originated in the field of architecture, where professionals realized that when access to buildings for people with disabilities was arranged after the building was completed (i.e., retrofitting), the result was often unsatisfactory, such as a poorly placed elevator or an awkward or unsightly ramp. However, if access was integrated in the original building design, it could become a seamless part of the structure, often adding to its beauty and being enjoyed by many more people than those with disabilities. Applied to education, UDL says that teachers should design instruction from the beginning to meet a wide range of learner diversity rather than try to retrofit, or make adjustments, after they already have created their lessons (Maryland State Department of Education, 2011; Pisha & Stahl, 2005). If teachers do this, they usually find that most students can benefit from their efforts. UDL is not a replacement for the specialized instruction of special education, but when UDL is in place, students with disabilities, as well as others who need alternative educational approaches, benefit.

One way to operationalize UDL is through *differentiation*—the notion that changes can be made in many different aspects of the teaching/learning process to enable diverse student learning needs to be met (Herrelko, 2013). The concept of differentiation originated in the area of gifted education, but it also is employed by special education teachers in their separate classrooms as well as by general and special educators working in inclusive schools. Differentiation often includes changes made to the content being taught (e.g., more, less, alternative), the process being used to teach it (e.g., visuals versus words), and the ways students demonstrate they have learned it (e.g., a test versus a multimedia presentation). Like the broader concept of UDL, differentiation is not at all unique to special education, but it provides a basis for effective special education techniques.

Prevention Through Response to Intervention and a Multi-Tiered System of Support

Yet another key aspect of instruction is systematically adjusting it as a proactive, preventive approach. In response to intervention (RTI), when a teacher raises concern about a student's rate of learning, a data-based system of increasingly intensive interventions is put in place and carefully tracked to see if it might be possible to accelerate the student's learning in order to avoid the need for special education (Brennan, 2015). Using evidence-based practices, teachers, reading and math specialists, and other professionals make every effort to find the key to unlock the student's potential. If ongoing data collection indicates that the student is gradually catching up to peers, professionals know that the student does not have a disability. If in spite of their best efforts they find the student is not making enough progress to eventually catch up, then the professionals may begin the formal procedure of determining whether the student has a disability.

RTI was included in IDEA as an option for determining whether a student has a learning disability. However, a tiered approach now also has been applied to addressing serious student behavior issues (Saeki et al., 2011) and to generally providing effective remedial education services to at-risk learners. This broad system of proactively intervening for both academic and behavior concerns is referred to as a **multitiered system of support** (MTSS) (e.g., Forman & Crystal, 2015). Regardless of use and name, the overall goal is to try to effectively address student learning or behavior issues as soon as they occur, rather than delaying until formal assessment procedures indicate that a disability exists (Nelson, Oliver, Hebert, & Bohaty, 2015). In this way, it is anticipated that some students who might otherwise have been labeled as disabled will instead succeed without the need for that serious, potentially stigmatizing, and possibly inappropriate determination (Johnson, Pool, & Carter, 2012). RTI and MTSS have many important dimensions, and as you read this text, you will learn more about these promising approaches.

Assistive and Instructional Technology

A final dimension of accessible and effective instruction is the use of instructional and assistive technology, that is, the devices, equipment, and services that improve the learning and functional capabilities of students with disabilities (Meyen, 2015). Many students with disabilities use instructional and assistive technology to facilitate learning. Technology may be low-tech (e.g., a grip to help a student hold a pencil), mid-tech (e.g., an audio recorder used during a class lecture), or high-tech (e.g., an electronic communication board that "talks" for the student when various buttons are pushed). IDEA requires that students have access to the instructional and assistive technology they need. That is, student need must be

Instructional and Assistive Technology Options for Students with Disabilities

As you read this summary of some of the categories of assistive technology devices, try to determine into which category they fall.

Category	Explanation	Examples
Sensory enhancers	• Help students with vision or hearing loss access their environments	• Text magnifier • Scanner with speech synthesizer • Communication board
Keyboard adaptations and emulators	• Alternative to standard computer keyboard	• Joystick • Light pen • Touch screen • Touch-sensitive keyboard pad • Raised plastic dots attached to computer keys to aid in identifying them
Environmental controls and manipulators	• Modify operation of a device to facilitate use	• Switch controlled by breath • Telephone with voice dialing • TTY (text telephone)
Instructional uses of technology	• Software that facilitates learning	• Software to practice math facts • Computerized remedial reading instructional programs
Motivational devices	• Encourage students to interact with their environment	• Spinner operated with a large button switch • Stuffed animal that plays music when squeezed
Mobility devices	• Assist students to get around the school and participate in student activities	• Self-propelled walker • Manual or powered wheelchair • White-tipped cane used by individuals who are blind
Self-care aids	• Facilitate hygiene and other personal functions	• Adapted eating utensils • Toothbrush with easy-to-grip handle

assessed, appropriate devices need to be provided, and the student must be taught how to use them. With each passing year, the technology available to facilitate learning grows exponentially. As you work in schools, you probably will see students using a wide array of such technology, including options such as those mentioned in Technology Notes.

Positive Behavior Supports

Some students with disabilities have behaviors that are so disruptive or dysfunctional that they interfere with other students' learning. For example, a student who has difficulty transitioning from one activity to another, like Everett, the student with autism you met at the beginning of this chapter, might express his frustration by pushing classmates. Too often in the past, such behaviors were addressed through some type of negative consequence, such as taking away computer time or sending the student to the office.

Current practices are very different. Now, professionals use positive behavior supports (Cramer & Bennett, 2015; Swain-Bradway, Pinkney, & Flannery, 2015). First, they establish schoolwide and classroom standards for behavior so that students understand expectations. Then, if a problem occurs, they look at student behaviors in the context of the situation in which they occurred, carefully defining what is happening in order to design ways to reduce the negative behavior, increase desired behavior, and help the student have a better academic and social quality of life.

In the example of the student who pushes others, professionals would meet to analyze this serious problem, and once it was better understood, they might then try to prevent some of the student's frustration by ensuring that the work the student was assigned was not too difficult. They might also teach the student a better way to express frustration—perhaps by teaching him to say "Help me" and rewarding him for appropriate or acceptable behavior. They would work closely with the family, too, designing a behavior program with parents so that there could be consistency between the approaches used at school and home.

You will find that positive behavior supports can enhance your relationships with students and enable them to succeed in school. They are helpful for many students, and they are critical for students with emotional disabilities, some students with autism, and other students with extraordinary behavioral needs.

MyEdLab **Self-Check 1.6**

MyEdLab **Application Exercise 1.8:** The Key to It All

MyEdLab **Application Exercise 1.9:** Inclusive Education

MyEdLab **Application Exercise 1.10:** Evidence-Based Practices in Inclusion

---

Summary

LO1.1   Special education is a broad, complex, and rapidly changing field that exists to ensure that students with disabilities receive the education to which they are entitled. It has three parts: (a) special education that is specially designed instruction that meets the needs of students with disabilities, (b) related services, and (c) supplementary aids and services.

LO1.2   Special education today is the culmination of efforts by researchers, professionals, parents, and legislators that began prior to the 19th century. Services for children with disabilities grew significantly in the United States during the early part of the 20th century, but those services were questioned and changed as a civil rights issue and were shaped by key court cases. The result of advocacy on the part of students with disabilities was federal laws to protect their rights.

LO1.3   The Individuals with Disabilities Education Act (IDEA) is the federal law that prescribes the procedures and services required for students with disabilities. It encompasses six key principles: (a) zero reject, (b) free appropriate public education (FAPE), (c) least restrictive environment (LRE), (d) nondiscriminatory evaluation, (e) parent and family rights, and (f) procedural safeguards. Other laws affecting students with disabilities include Section 504 and the Americans with Disabilities Act.

LO1.4   IDEA specifies 13 disabilities that may qualify children, birth through 21 years of age, to receive special education, including specific learning disabilities, speech or language impairments, intellectual disabilities, emotional disturbance, other health impairments, autism, orthopedic impairments, hearing impairments, visual impairments, deaf/blindness, traumatic brain injury, multiple disabilities, and developmental delays. Other students with special needs include those who are gifted/talented, those who have ADHD, and those at risk.

LO1.5   The parents and families of students with disabilities have been their strongest advocates, and their efforts have greatly influenced the field. However, sometimes barriers must be overcome in order for parents to participate in their children's education.

LO1.6   Contemporary special education is characterized by inclusive practices, and such practices, despite continuing controversy, are central to this text. In inclusive schooling, collaboration defines the school culture, although its implementation sometimes is challenging. Inclusive schooling also includes highly effective instruction, including evidence-based practices, universal design for learning, and differentiation, as well as preventive models such as response to intervention and the individualized approaches of specially designed instruction and instructional and assistive technology. A final key topic in special education concerns student behaviors, and current approaches stress positive behavior supports (PBS).

RAEKWON

Fourth-grader Raekwon came to Larson Elementary School from a nearby community. At Larson, all students are screened at the beginning of the school year to determine their proficiency in critical reading skills. For example, entering fourth-grade students are expected to read appropriate passages at a rate of 94 words per minute with fewer than three errors. Raekwon read at 52 words per minute, and he did not comprehend what he had read. Although Raekwon's teacher uses a research-based reading program (called a *tier 1* intervention), Raekwon was immediately enrolled in a remedial reading program designed to improve his skills (called a *tier 2* intervention). This instruction is provided three times each week for 30 minutes, taught by a specially trained paraprofessional. His progress in this program will be carefully monitored to determine if it is effective in increasing his fluency and comprehension so that he eventually will approach the skill level of his classmates. If it is not producing this result, he will receive even more intensive instruction (called a *tier 3* intervention), delivered by the school's reading specialist, for five days per week. If even this reading intervention is not effective, a team of professionals and Raekwon's parents will consider whether he should be assessed to determine his eligibility for special education.

LILY

Lily is 11 years old and transitioning from elementary school to middle school. She has an intellectual disability and tends to have difficulty with social interactions; she also can disrupt a class with loud, angry outbursts when she does not want to participate in an assigned activity, dislikes teacher directions to her, or perceives her work is "for babies." However, since kindergarten she has spent nearly her entire school day in general education, assisted by a paraprofessional who has always been with her. At the annual review of Lily's IEP, her parents were surprised when the team recommended that Lily receive all of the following year's academic instruction in a special education setting. They noted how successful Lily's education had been to date; complimented teachers on their commitment to Lily's academic, social, and behavioral goals; and directly asked why the service arrangement at the elementary school could not be replicated in middle school. Lily's parents refused to sign the IEP, and they later commented that they felt like the educators had made a decision before the meeting. Lily's parents have asked for a meeting with the director of special education, but they also have made it clear that they will pursue this matter through the IDEA due process procedures if they are not satisfied with the outcome of that meeting.

WILLIAM

William is in tenth grade. He knows he is at a crossroads, but he is not sure about what to do with his life. Since third grade, he has been educated in a self-contained class for students with emotional and behavior disabilities; his opinion is that he never has been able to learn to control his anger, and that's why he's there. He despises being called a "retard" by other students—that is the name most kids use for students in any special education class. He has good friends who are already well-established gang members, and while so far he has not formally affiliated with the gang, he feels pressured by his friends to join while his grandmother, his legal guardian, urges him to stay in school and away from gang members. William has had several arrests for misdemeanor crimes, but those are in his juvenile record, and so they don't worry him too much. He comes to school about half the time, and his special education teacher, Mr. Powell, has encouraged him to enroll in the school's credit recovery program. Mr. Powell is convinced William is bright and has great potential and still has the option to graduate on time with his classmates. William knows Mr. Powell is making an extra effort to connect with him, arranging to meet him after school and to help him find job possibilities. But William just doesn't know which path he'll take.

In Chapter 1, you were introduced to the complex and exciting world of special education. You learned about the development of the field, laws that mandate services for students with disabilities, the students who receive those services, and key issues facing professionals. However, you probably were left with many questions about the details of special education, including the roles and responsibilities of the professionals who provide special education services to students, the required procedures educators follow to determine if a student can receive special education services, and the range of services a student with disabilities might receive. These questions are answered in this chapter.

Whether you plan to be a special education teacher or a general education teacher, a school administrator or a teaching assistant, or a professional providing a related service (e.g., counseling, psychological services, speech-language therapy), if you work in a public school setting, you undoubtedly will work closely with other professionals as well as parents and family members on behalf of students with disabilities. Further, you will participate in and perhaps lead meetings at which critical decisions are made regarding whether a student is eligible to receive special education services, what those services should include, whether to continue those services, and how to prepare a student to transition from school into adulthood. The greater your understanding of all the professionals involved in special education and the procedures that must be followed for students to receive those services, the better prepared you will be to make a positive contribution.

The Professionals Who Work in Special Education

If you think about the broad range of needs of students with disabilities, you will not be surprised to learn that many professionals are involved in providing special education and related services. Some of these individuals work directly with students, some are involved mostly in determining whether a student has a disability, and others offer indirect support.

Special Education Teachers

Special education teachers are the professionals who provide day-to-day instruction and other support for students with disabilities. If they serve students in more than one school—as may happen in rural areas or for students with hearing loss or vision impairments—they may be called itinerant special educators.

Special education teachers' roles and responsibilities vary considerably (Eisenman, Pleet, Wandry, & McGinley, 2011; Hillel Lavian, 2015; Mulrine & Huckvale, 2014; Weiss, Petrin, & Farmer, 2014). Depending on the specific state teacher licensure regulations, these teachers may work with students with only one type of disability (e.g., students with autism), or they may work with students with varying disabilities (e.g., students with mild disabilities, including those with learning disabilities, emotional disabilities, or mild intellectual disabilities). In addition to providing instruction that may be remedial (re-teaching), developmental (teaching based on the student's functional learning level), or strategic (teaching tool skills to help the student succeed), special education teachers typically may also prepare materials adapted to meet students' special needs, assess and report student progress in learning, support students academically and socially, and manage students' overall education programs. Increasingly, special education teachers consult with their general education colleagues to ensure student needs are met and teach in general education classrooms at least part of each day, but they also may work in special education settings such as resource rooms, self-contained classrooms, and separate schools, settings that are explained in more detail later in this chapter.

Did You Know?

Students with disabilities in high-poverty area schools are far more likely than students in other locales to be instructed by special education teachers with limited (and sometimes almost no) preparation for their roles (Mason-Williams, 2015).

Bilingual Special Educator

Students who have disabilities and whose first language is not English sometimes receive their special education services from a bilingual special education teacher—that is, a professional who is knowledgeable about both bilingual education and special education. Such a teacher usually has special training in (a) knowledge of language proficiency, (b) appropriate assessment tools and techniques, (c) cultural and linguistic diversity, (d) effective delivery of instruction, and (e) professionalism for working with colleagues, families, and community members (Klingner, Boelé, Linan-Thompson, & Rodriguez, 2014; Rodriquez, Carrasquillo, & Lee, 2014; Ochoa, Brandon, Cadiero-Kaplan, & Ramírez, 2014). Although bilingual special educators are not found in all school districts, where they are available they can provide the dual set of services that some students need (Delgado, 2010).

Early Childhood Special Educator

Professionals who work with infants, toddlers, and young children with disabilities (ages birth to five years) are called early childhood special educators or sometimes *early interventionists*. Generally, they are expected to have knowledge about a wide range of disabilities because distinguishing among young children's specific special needs—particularly for those with speech-language, intellectual, or behavior concerns—often is not possible. These professionals may visit children's homes; teach in a special class that may be housed at a special center or in an elementary school; or work with preschool, kindergarten, or Head Start teachers in general education settings.

Adapted Physical Educator

Some students cannot safely or successfully participate in a standard physical education program, often because of their physical needs, and they rely on a professional who can adapt exercises, games, and other activities (Columna, Lieberman, Lytle, & Arndt, 2014; Council for Exceptional Children, 2011). This professional, an adapted physical educator, sometimes works directly with students with disabilities, either during a general physical education class or in a separate special class. However, the adapted physical educator also may consult with other physical educators so that those professionals can appropriately address the needs of their students with disabilities. In some school districts, physical educators receive professional development and assist in providing this service to students with disabilities.

Related Services Professionals

You learned in Chapter 1 that the Individuals with Disabilities Education Act (IDEA) mandates both special education and related services. The following sections describe the professionals who are most likely to work with you who provide related services to students with disabilities.

Speech-Language Pathologist

Many students with disabilities have special needs related to speech or language, and the professionals who diagnose such needs, design interventions to address them, deliver the services, and monitor student progress are speech-language pathologists (e.g., Light & McNaughton, 2015; Wei, Wagner, Christiano, Shattuck, & Yu, 2014; Maul, 2015). These professionals also may be referred to as *speech-language therapists* or simply *speech therapists*.

For example, if a kindergarten student is having difficulty correctly making certain sounds (e.g., "thunny" for "sunny") or a sixth-grade student cannot form sentences, a speech-language pathologist is likely to provide speech-language therapy. However, speech-language pathologists also have other roles. They may assist students who are deaf or hard of hearing to learn American Sign Language or use their residual hearing to best advantage, and they may teach students who do not have the ability to speak other ways to communicate (e.g., using pictures or a computer system). They may assist students with significant disabilities to learn functional skills like swallowing and controlling tongue movements.

School Psychologist

School psychologists are professionals who are licensed to administer intelligence tests and other assessments used in determining whether a student is eligible to receive special education services; they also are responsible for communicating this information to parents (Graves, Proctor, & Aston, 2014; Kellems, Springer, Wilkins, & Anderson, 2015). In addition, school psychologists are experts in understanding students' social and emotional needs. They often work with other professionals and families to design interventions to help students learn social skills and appropriate behavior (Rodriguez, Campbell, Falcon, & Borgmeier, 2015). In some school districts, school psychologists work directly with students; in others, they consult with teachers and other professionals who implement the interventions they have recommended to assist particular students.

As a related services professional, a speech-language pathologist assists students to develop communication skills but, depending on needs, also may aid them with eating, drinking, and swallowing.

School Counselor

Most of the professionals described thus far work primarily with students experiencing difficulties in school and their parents. However, school counselors are professionals who work with all students, including those with disabilities, and they generally are considered the problem solvers of a school (Bureau of Labor Statistics, 2015; Deasy, Zaccagnini, Burton, & Koury, 2014). They may work with individual students to address personal problems; they may conduct lessons for an entire class of students to resolve issues in peer relationships; and they may assist students with disabilities in accessing appropriate high school courses, in locating the right college or university to attend, or in finding a part-time job. School counselors are found in nearly all high schools and middle schools; whether they are assigned to elementary schools depends on state and local practices.

School Social Worker

As you learn more about the field of special education and students with exceptional needs, you will find that in addition to the instruction and support offered by school personnel, an array of services is available outside of schools. School social workers are the professionals who coordinate the efforts of educators, families, and outside agency personnel to ensure that students receive all the supports they need (Beisse & Tyre, 2013; Stanley, 2012; Bureau of Labor Statistics, 2015). For example, a school social worker may contact a family when a student has been truant repeatedly, and if the problem persists, this professional will contact the appropriate social agency to ensure that the student's attendance improves. Social workers also might help a family in great need to access charitable organizations that can provide clothing and food or to arrange for counseling. Like school counselors, school social workers often have responsibilities for all the students in a school who need their services, not just those with disabilities.

School Nurse

The school nurse is another professional who usually is responsible for all the students in a school—one whose importance in special education procedures and services often is overlooked. The school nurse screens children in the areas of vision and hearing, ensures that all students' immunization records are on file, provides routine assistance for students who are ill, educates students about health topics, and manages the distribution of any medications students may take (Mcintosh, Thomas, & Maughan, 2015; Pufpaff, Mcintosh, Thomas, Elam, & Irwin, 2015). For students with disabilities, the school nurse may be a member of the team that makes a decision about eligibility for special education services, may be called on to interpret medical information, may serve as a liaison between the family physician and school personnel, may help to generate an emergency plan for addressing a students' health needs, and may educate staff about students' medical conditions and requirements.

Educational Interpreter

Some students who are deaf or significantly hard of hearing have an educational interpreter—a professional who listens to the words being spoken in school and then translates them into sign language (Huff, 2010). These professionals have to understand the field of deafness and the likely needs of students who are deaf. They also have to be familiar with all aspects of the entire school curriculum. Of course, interpreters provide this service to students accurately and unobtrusively within the general or special education setting as well as during activities such as physical education, art, and assemblies.

Occupational Therapist

An occupational therapist helps students gain independence in school and the community by teaching functional and other living skills such as grasping a pencil, cutting with scissors, buttoning and zipping clothes, and tying shoe laces (More, 2015). This individual also might help students learn to feed themselves, wash their faces, use a computer, or cook their own meals. They also are likely to assist students to learn problem-solving and decision-making skills. Occupational therapists often are called upon to determine whether students need adapted equipment (e.g., a spoon with a thick handle; a modified computer keyboard) and to instruct students on how to use such equipment.

Physical Therapist

If a student's disability affects the ability to move, a physical therapist might provide services (National Clearinghouse for Professions in Special Education, 2009). This professional deals with students' muscle strength and flexibility, mobility, posture, and positioning (e.g., helping a student sit up in a wheelchair or stand for a while each day to improve circulation). Physical therapists may help students maintain or improve the use of their large muscles, and they may work with students to increase balance and coordination, such as when students walk using crutches or braces. Physical therapists also may be involved in decisions about the type of wheelchair or other equipment that would best meet students' needs.

Others Who Work in Special Education

Although special education teachers and key related services personnel provide most of the interventions that students with disabilities receive, several other groups of individuals play pivotal roles in special education.

General Education Teacher

In the 21st century, any discussion of the professionals who work in special education would not be complete without highlighting the role of the general education teacher. More than ever before, students with disabilities receive part or all of their instruction in typical elementary, middle, and high school classrooms, which makes general education teachers integral members of the special education team (Grskovic & Trzcinka, 2011), often working directly with any particular students with disabilities for far more time than special educators. They are the professionals who are knowledgeable about the expectations of the curriculum for the grade level or course, who are usually responsible for implementing universal design for learning (UDL) practices that enable their diverse learners to succeed, and who manage the social environment of their classrooms. Collaboration between general education and special education teachers is critical for student learning. Think about how important a role Raekwon's general education teacher plays in implementing effective instructional practices, monitoring his progress, and—if he does have a disability—ensuring that his special needs are addressed in the classroom.

Paraeducator

Paraeducators—also called *paraprofessionals, teaching assistants, instructional assistants, one-to-one assistants,* and *aides* (although this last term is no longer preferred)—are educators who work under the direction of a teacher or another school professional to help in the delivery of services for students with disabilities (Brock & Carter, 2015; Brown & Stanton-Chapman, 2015). Paraeducators can be assigned a wide variety of tasks, depending on state regulations and local policies. They might tutor a student who is learning to read; accompany a student with an emotional disability from class to class to provide structure and prevent inappropriate behaviors; or serve as a student's personal assistant, pushing a student's wheelchair and helping the student with eating and other personal care activities. Paraeducators work under the direction of professionals who tell them what needs to be done and how to work with students. You will learn more about the roles and responsibilities of paraeducators and your interactions with them in Chapter 4.

Parents

Of all the individuals with whom you will interact on behalf of your students with disabilities, no one is more important than the students' parents or the individuals who serve in that role (e.g., grandmother or grandfather, guardian, foster parents) (Diliberto & Brewer, 2014). It is students' parents who have their best interests at heart in a way that no one else can, it is they who advocate for their children no matter the issue, and it is they who can tell you about your students' lives outside the world of school. One of the most important lessons you can learn as a professional educator is to listen carefully, without judgment, to your students' parents and take into account their perspectives on their children's strengths and needs. In the following Firsthand Account, you can read one parent's perspective on her role in the education of her son.

A "QUIRKY KID" GOES TO MIDDLE SCHOOL

SANDY AND JOHN *are proud of their son John, who is 12 years old and a sixth-grade student. Sandy shares the story of her son's early years and his new experiences—positive and negative—as a middle school student with autism.*

John stopped breathing right after he was born, and he was rushed to the neonatal intensive care unit (NICU). Then there were several other medical emergencies. When we finally brought him home, he was a very fussy baby and a very quirky kid. I would talk to the doctors, and they would tell me I was just a nervous first-time mom. But noise really bothered him, and he had food allergies and significantly delayed speech. He also hated grass–don't even think about sitting that child in the grass! I've got a picture of me with him at 7 or 8 months in the grass, and his legs are curled up around his neck! And every time we would go to the doctor's office, he would start screaming, and he would scream almost the whole time. I kept saying, "There is something wrong." The doctor kept saying, "No, he's a boy, he's an only child, his father was probably a late talker." He was finally diagnosed with PDD [pervasive developmental disability], a form of autism, but not until he was 5 years old.

John spends all day in general education, but it took a lot to get ready for middle school. During the summer, we walked through the building again and again so he'd know his way around. We practiced with the locker and the combination lock; that was a nightmare. But I didn't want him to have a key around his neck—that's just another target on him, telling everyone he's different. It's bad enough that he skips instead of walking sometimes, and that makes kids look at him.

This year there is co-teaching in language arts and math, but I don't know if that's enough. Science and social studies are very abstract, and he can get overwhelmed. Overall, though, it's going pretty well. His special education teacher is very energetic and does a great job. He calls me right away when there is a problem, and he puts out many fires before they become big problems. All the teachers have been really cooperative. Teachers need to be very structured but also flexible. This year, teachers cut back on some of the work, saying, "It's not worth stressing him out, battering him with too much information that he has stopped taking in anyway. We'll revisit later." In the past, some have said, "He needs to do all of it." Those teachers don't see him coming home and head-banging because he is so frustrated. Does he really need to do 50 problems? Isn't 25 enough? Fair isn't when everybody does the same work; it's when they get what they need.

When I think about the future, I could see John being one of those quirky college history professors. He loves history, although sometimes he can just pound you with all the facts he has memorized. I could also see him as a musician—he's in band and choir and does very well. But in middle school, it's so hard. He was playing the trumpet for band, but there were a couple of nasty boys who kept teasing him. So the teacher asked John to play the tuba to get him away from them. John was carrying this tuba on his back and got to the divided doorway in the hall, and he couldn't figure out how to get it through the door, how to turn it. The kids were saying, "Oh, c'mon. What's wrong with you?" A girl who is really his friend saw him and took the tuba to help, but the kids behind him were teasing, "Oh, look. You're letting a GIRL carry the tuba."

John is very hard on himself. The first thing he does when he gets home from school is strip out of his school clothes and watch TV. I let him do that for about 45 minutes so he can decompress. Then we're ready to move on. He also participates in an after-school social skills group that is really helpful.

What my husband and I want—really—is for John to be successful and happy. My husband plays golf, and we're trying to get John to enjoy that. He could play alone if he wanted, or with just one buddy—it's not overly social. John would like to be a baseball player. That would be OK because it's also a sport where there isn't lots of close contact. He knows all of the statistics about his favorite team.

Source: Courtesy of Sandra L. Gasior and John Gasior.

Additional Service Providers

This description of individuals who contribute to the work of special education still is not complete. Several other professionals—some with very specialized areas of expertise, whom you may meet only when a student has a particularly unique need—also may contribute to a student's education (e.g., National Clearinghouse for Professions in Special Education, 2009). Examples of these service providers include the following:

- *Rehabilitation counselor.* This professional helps students, often through special education transition planning, to find and keep appropriate employment upon high school completion. Rehabilitation counselors usually work in a community agency setting.

- *Art or music therapist.* This therapist assists students who are better able to understand their special needs or begin to cope with them through the use of art or music.
- *Orientation and mobility specialist.* This specialist assists students with visual impairment to gain independence by teaching them how to move about confidently in the classroom, the school, and the community.
- *Audiologist.* An audiologist, an expert in diagnosing problems related to hearing and the ear (e.g., loss of balance because of inner-ear problems), may provide services to assess hearing loss and determine whether it can be addressed with the use of a hearing aid or other device or strategies.
- *Inclusion facilitator.* This individual ensures that students with disabilities receive the supports and services they need to succeed in a general education setting. The inclusion facilitator also answers teachers' questions about working with specific students and helps teachers access resources to foster inclusive practices.
- *Language interpreter.* A language interpreter might be employed to facilitate communication with the student and his or her family in schools with many students whose native language is not English.
- *Special education administrator.* The special education administrator has the responsibility, in many school districts, of ensuring that all the policies and practices related to special education are carried out appropriately.
- *Technology specialist.* A technology specialist is responsible for evaluating whether a student with a disability needs technology support and, if so, what types of support. This is an emerging school position not yet found in all school districts.
- *Therapeutic recreation specialist.* This professional, often working through a community agency or hospital, assists students and families to use recreational activities to improve students' functioning and independence. This specialist may attend IEP meetings to explain services and support family priorities in this domain.
- *Psychometrist or educational diagnostician.* This professional, in some locales, completes the individual assessment of students for special education. The psychometrist or educational diagnostician is specifically trained to administer and interpret tests but does not have the broad set of skills of a school psychologist.
- *Support personnel.* Others in addition to those in traditional professions often contribute to special education services. One example is *bus drivers.* These individuals must have special training in order to transport students with disabilities, and they may be responsible for helping to load and unload students, addressing safety concerns and behavior issues, and implementing an evacuation plan in case of an emergency. Another example is *school resource officers* (SROs). These individuals, often police officers assigned to work in schools, may interact with students in cases of serious behavior incidents. Evidence suggests that for them to work effectively with students with disabilities, they should have training that is specific to this student group (Kleierleber, 2015).

MyEdLab **Self-Check 2.1**

MyEdLab **Application Exercise 2.1:** Roles of Educators

Determining Student Eligibility for Special Education Services

A small percentage of students with disabilities are identified when they are very young. These children often have significant physical or sensory (vision or hearing) disabilities, an intellectual disability, autism, or developmental delays. Lily, whose story you read at the beginning of the chapter, is an example of a student who began receiving special education services at a very young age. Most students, though, begin school just like their peers, and they are identified as having disabilities only after they experience extraordinary difficulties in school. As a school professional, you have a responsibility to thoroughly understand what happens from the time someone expresses concern about a student struggling in school through the steps of assessment and identification of the student as eligible for special education along with the procedures in place to review the education programs of students with disabilities. This process is outlined in Figure 2.1 and explained in more detail in following sections.

Initial Consideration of Student Problems

General education teachers are the professionals most likely to express concern about a student that begins the process of deciding whether that student is entitled to special education services. Usually, the teacher carefully thinks through what the problem might be, tries several strategies to address the problem, discusses the student informally with other teachers and administrators to help determine the seriousness of the situation, and contacts the parents to discover their view of what is occurring (Friend & Bursuck, 2015). The teacher also is likely to gather data to document that concern, including keeping samples of the student's work or creating a log of behavior incidents that occur in the classroom.

General Education Interventions

What if these informal approaches fail to address the teacher's concern for the student? In some states, the next step the teacher takes is to request that the case be reviewed by a team of professionals (Zirkel, 2012). Such a team has any of several different names, depending on state and local policy—teacher assistance team, intervention assistance team, *student assistance team,* and *instructional consultation team* are a few common ones. The professionals designated to serve on these teams also vary: Some teams are composed exclusively or primarily of general education teachers; some include at least one special education teacher; and some include those two professionals in addition to related services professionals, such as the school nurse and the speech-language pathologist. Regardless of the team's name or composition, its goals are to help the teacher problem solve regarding the student, to generate new ideas for helping the student, to consider various explanations for the noted problems, and to prevent—if possible—the need for special education (e.g., Hoover & Lowe, 2011). IDEA now permits school districts to use a portion of their special education funding to provide extra support for such struggling students with this goal of reducing special education referrals in mind (Yell & Walker, 2010).

These teams generally have very precise procedures that are set locally rather than at the state level. For example, the general education teacher usually completes a brief form that provides the team with information about the nature of the concern and the strategies already implemented to help the student. At the team meeting, a specific agenda is followed to discuss the problem, generate some new ideas for intervention, and help the teacher decide which ideas might be effectively implemented. The team also assigns responsibilities for gathering additional information as needed and assisting the teacher in documenting intervention effectiveness. A date is set to review whether the intervention is working and to decide

FIGURE 2.1   The Special Education Decision-Making Process

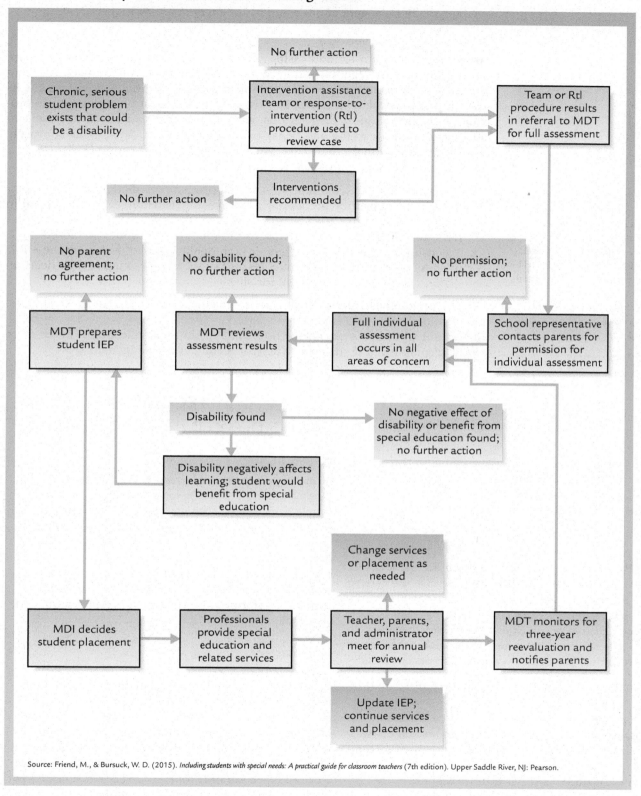

Source: Friend, M., & Bursuck, W. D. (2015). *Including students with special needs: A practical guide for classroom teachers* (7th edition). Upper Saddle River, NJ: Pearson.

what to do next. Raekwon, the fourth-grader you met at the beginning of the chapter, might be a student discussed by an intervention assistance team.

Response to Intervention

An alternative option for addressing serious student learning problems was approved in the 2004 reauthorization of IDEA. Originally intended to contribute to the early identification of possible learning disabilities, 17 states now mandate its use for that purpose (Hauerwas, Brown, & Scott, 2013), but nearly all states provide guidelines to local districts that want to use this data-based approach to address students' learning and behavior problems (Zirkel, 2011). This approach, briefly introduced in Chapter 1, is called response to intervention (RTI).

RTI has two main purposes (Kavale & Spaulding, 2008):

1. To ensure that students receive research-proven remediation and other supports as soon as they are identified as having academic difficulties, even in kindergarten, rather than waiting until an academic or behavior gap has grown significantly and, perhaps, to the point that it cannot be closed
2. To ensure that professionals gather high-quality data to document the effectiveness of those remedial strategies and supports and to guide their decision making about possible referral for special education services

The ongoing use of data to determine whether a student is responding to the interventions being implemented is referred to as continuous progress monitoring. In Technology Notes, you can see how this type of data collection is much more easily accomplished by using a variety of readily available technology.

Did You Know?

The traditional approach to identifying learning disabilities, which relies on a significant discrepancy existing between ability and achievement, has been criticized as a "wait to fail" approach. RTI is designed to address learning gaps as soon as they are recognized instead of waiting for them to become so great that they constitute a disability.

TECHNOLOGY NOTES

Teacher Data Collection Technology Tools

Many free or low-cost tools are available to teachers to facilitate the data collection necessary as part of intervening to decide if a student's academics or behaviors are a serious concern. Several examples include the following:

Teacher's Assistant Pro

http://www.teachersassistantpro.com/
This iPad/iPhone app (free for limited access; low cost for unlimited access) is designed to enable teachers to easily track student behavior, whether accomplishments or problems. Teachers can create a file for each of their students, customize the types of behaviors they want to track, tally students' behaviors, and e-mail either recent or all records of student behaviors to parents or others.

Electronic Daily Behavior Report Card (e-DBRC)

http://edbrc.tamu.edu/
Developed by researchers at Texas A & M University, this tool is an electronic version of the classroom daily behavior report card that teachers for decades have used to communicate with parents concerning student behavior and to document a student's social and behavior skills. The app graphs student behavior, and a grade or rating is assigned for each day; it also easily allows data to be e-mailed and offers a way to help students analyze their own behavior.

Google Sheets

https://docs.google.com/spreadsheets/u/0/?pref=2&pli=1
One of the most versatile tools for data collection is a simple spreadsheet, such as the free Google Sheets. For example, on a spreadsheet, you can create a separate sheet for each student of concern in a single file, list behaviors being recorded horizontally across the top of the spreadsheet and dates of data collection vertically, with your tallies or other data in the cells. These data can then be transformed into charts, printed, or transmitted via e-mail.

Notemaster

http://www.kabukivision.com/
Notemaster is a generic note-taking app (a "lite" version is free) that teachers can use to create templates for tracking students' academic and social behavior. By creating skills checklists that can be infinitely duplicated, teachers can track student performance daily or track several students' behavior. The data records can be synced through Google Docs and then exported for reporting or e-mailing. As an alternative, you may already be using a notes app—such as OneNote or Evernote—that could be used in a similar fashion.

RTI usually is based on what is called a three-tiered approach to intervention (Catts, Nielsen, Bridges, Liu, & Bontempo, 2015), sometimes called *tiered interventions* and sometimes given an alternative, locally selected name. The experience of Raekwon, introduced at the beginning of this chapter, illustrates this approach. Tier 1 is used most often with reading but is sometimes applied to math or behavior concerns, and it generally refers to using research-based approaches for all students so that high-quality instruction is ensured. Students for whom continuous progress monitoring indicates ongoing difficulty despite this instruction move to the next tier. Tier 2 generally involves small-group instruction several times each week using more intensive instructional strategies and other supports, such as peer tutoring or small-group remedial instruction. The small numbers of students who *still* do not respond positively to this more intense instruction after a specified period of time are identified for additional services. Tier 3 is the most intensive level, usually involving daily one-to-one instruction or small-group instruction outside the classroom. In some systems, tier 3 may include deciding that a student needs special education, a decision-making process that may incorporate some or all of the assessment procedures described later in this chapter. In other systems, tier 3 occurs prior to consideration for special education. Although RTI is sometimes thought of as a model for elementary schools, it is gradually also being implemented in middle and high schools.

Multi-Tiered Systems of Support

As RTI was implemented, professionals noted that students often had needs beyond academics—for example, social/emotional, behavioral—that would best be addressed as soon as recognized. An alternative framework emerged, called multitiered system of support (MTSS), that utilizes RTI principles and practices for academics but also extends them beyond the academic domain. MTSS also focuses on schoolwide improvement and the importance of ensuring that classroom, school, and district efforts to improve outcomes for all students are carefully articulated and aligned. It stresses collaboration between general education and special education professionals, and it recognizes the importance of professional development for building teachers' skills to deliver tiered interventions.

Although RTI is outlined in IDEA and is directly linked to assessment for special education, the *Every Student Succeeds Act*, passed in December 2015 as the reauthorization of the Elementary and Secondary Education Act (previously referred to as the *No Child Left Behind Act*), incorporates multi-tiered systems of support as a means for improving academic and behavioral outcomes for struggling students, including those with disabilities as well as those who live in poverty, English learners, and others. States and local school districts make decisions about the exact procedures to be followed and interventions to be used, although MTSS is mandated schoolwide for the lowest performing schools (U.S. Department of Education, 2015).

Note that response to intervention and multi-tiered systems of support are addressed in more detail in Chapter 5, since they have further applicability to students who may be identified as having learning disabilities. However, RTI and MTSS are educational practices you are very likely to encounter, regardless of your role or geographic location, and in the Instruction in Action, you can find resources to help you learn more about this data-driven way of thinking about student learning and behavior difficulties.

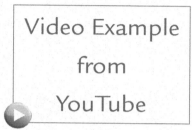

MyEdLab
Video Example 2.2

Video Example 2.2 is a summary of how the professionals in one high school are implementing RTI as a means of improving outcomes for its students. As you watch, consider these questions: How does this model demonstrate the flexibility that is integral to response to intervention? How does this high school's model differ from what might occur in an elementary school? What do you see as the advantages and disadvantages of this model?
(https://www.youtube.com/watch?/y=YtTKuBZ-nvY)

INSTRUCTION IN **ACTION**

Resources on Response to Intervention and Multi-Tiered Systems of Support

Although you will learn more about RTI and MTSS in Chapter 5, the following websites will help you begin to better understand their potential and provide you with tools for implementing both models.

- *RTI Wire* (http://www.jimwrightonline.com/php/rti/rti_wire.php) This website includes a brief explanation of RTI. It also includes dozens of links to materials related to using RTI, including interventions related to reading, math, and behavior; tools for recording data related to students' responses to specific instruction; and research-based interventions that might be part of an RTI model.
- *RTI Network* (http://www.rtinetwork.org/) On this website, you will find a wide array of tools for understanding and implementing both RTI and MTSS, including checklists of steps to follow, suggestions for data collection, and a blog so that you can connect with others. The site includes information for elementary school, middle school, and high school levels.
- *National Center on Response to Intervention* (RTI) (http://www.rti4success.org/). This U.S. Department of Education sponsored website has as its goal increasing the capacity of states and districts to effectively implement RTI and MTSS procedures. It includes many materials and a discussion forum, and it includes information on the implementation of RTI and MTSS with English language learners. This site also includes an expert discussion of the similarities and differences between the two models.
- *Intervention Central* (http://www.interventioncentral.org/) This website is dedicated to providing free RTI resources to teachers and other school personnel. Two examples of available tools are a behavior report card that can be customized based on student needs and a template for making graphs to summarize data gathered about individual students.
- *National Center on Intensive Intervention* (http://www.intensiveintervention.org/) The focus for this website is on the data-driven and deliberate process of individualizing instruction for struggling learners and intensifying it to improve their achievement. Resources include data collection charts and sample lesson plans.

Screening

In states that do not have a mandated intervention assistance team, RTI, or MTSS process, some type of screening still usually occurs when a student is experiencing extraordinary difficulties in school. The school psychologist, the counselor, the principal, or another professional has the responsibility of meeting with the general education teacher(s) to discuss the nature (what is the problem that is occurring?), severity (how intense is the problem?), and persistence (for how long has the problem existed?) of the student's difficulty. This professional also reviews existing information about the student, including report card grades, achievement test scores, examples of classroom work, attendance records, and any other documentation that can clarify the student's past and present performance and inform a decision about whether special education might need to be considered. An exception to screening (as well as the team and RTI and MTSS procedures already described) concerns parents: Generally, if a parent formally requests that a child be assessed to determine whether a disability exists, the following steps are implemented, often without the general education intervention or RTI or MTSS process being completed.

Special Education Referral and Assessment

If the intervention assistance team's discussion, response to intervention or multi-tiered systems of support procedures, or screening process leads to the consensus that a student's difficulties are serious enough that special education should be considered, the student is referred for a full assessment as required by IDEA before any services can be provided. At this point, a multidisciplinary team convenes for that purpose. The team may include some of the same team members as the general education intervention team (e.g., the school psychologist) but not others (e.g., the team usually includes the student's general education teacher but not several teachers from different grades or departments); parents also are members of this team. These members and their contributions are described in the section on individualized education programs (IEPs).

When an RTI or MTSS system is in place, data gathered about the student's academic performance may be integral to this process. These data also may, based on state policies, be used as the primary information in making a decision about the need for special education services, and so the steps described in the following section related to formal assessment may be modified or bypassed.

Parents' Rights

Before discussing the details of the special education eligibility determination process, it is important to elaborate on the discussion from Chapter 1 about the rights of parents on behalf of their children in all aspects of special education, beginning at the very first step of student assessment. Parents have these rights:

- To request and give permission for individual testing of their child. IDEA explicitly states that no individual assessment carried out to decide whether a student needs special education can occur without this approval. If the parents disagree with the evaluation results from school, they may seek an independent evaluation.
- To be meaningfully informed, in writing, about the procedures of special education and parent rights, including all procedural safeguards and the way to seek an evaluation of their child that is independent of the school district's evaluation.
- To have their child tested in the language the child knows best. This may include providing an interpreter for a student who is deaf or a test in braille for a student who is blind as well as the administration of tests in the child's primary language.
- To be full members of the team that decides what services a student should get, how often, and how much. Parents must voluntarily approve these decisions. In addition, they may request a review of the IEP at any time, and they may withdraw consent for special education services at any time.
- To have their child receive a free appropriate public education. *Free* is defined as at no cost to the parents or student, except for the usual fees associated with attending school. *Appropriate* means the student's educational plan must be tailored to the specific identified needs.
- To have their child educated in the least restrictive environment—that is, the setting most similar to general education in which their child can succeed with appropriate supports.
- To be notified in writing whenever the school proposes any of the following: a reevaluation, a change in the student's placement, a decision not to evaluate their child, or a decision not to change a disputed placement.
- To (a) informal dispute resolution, (b) mediation, and (c) an impartial hearing in instances in which a significant disagreement occurs, as long as the request is made within two years of the situation at issue. You will learn more about all of these procedures later in this chapter.
- To have access to their child's education records within 45 days of a formal request, to request changes in information they perceive to be inaccurate, and to give permission for anyone other than those working directly with the child to access records.
- To be kept informed of their child's progress at least as often as are parents of other students.

Does it seem as though parents are given many rights? In fact, they are, and that is deliberate. If you recall that in the past students were denied their educational rights, it is understandable that IDEA is crafted to ensure that such inequities cannot happen again.

Assessment Components

Once parents agree to an assessment of their child, professionals begin a process that may be fairly simple or extraordinarily complex. IDEA does not describe the specific domains in which students suspected of having disabilities should be assessed. However, the law does state that students must be evaluated to determine their strengths and also to explore any area of functioning in which a disability is suspected. For many students, then, the assessment addresses these areas (Bakken, Obiakor, & Rotatori, 2013):

- *Vision and hearing screening.* If not completed before a formal referral occurs, the school nurse usually checks to be sure that a student's learning difficulties are not the result of a vision or hearing problem. If screening indicates a need in this area, the student's family is referred to the appropriate medical specialist before other types of assessment are undertaken.
- *Intellectual ability.* A student's intellectual ability usually is assessed with an intelligence test, a type of assessment that can be given only by professionals with special training (i.e., a school psychologist or psychometrist). This measure informs the team about the student's capacity to learn.
- *Achievement.* An individual achievement test typically is administered by the school psychologist or psychometrist, a special education teacher, or another professional. This assessment component helps the team to determine the student's present level of learning. The results are used instead of scores that the student may have earned on a group achievement test because the former is likely to be a more accurate estimate of the student's learning than the latter. In RTI or MTSS systems, the data from the three tiers of intervention would be used for this purpose.
- *Social and behavioral functioning.* Another critical area is how students manage their interactions with peers and adults. Using checklists, questionnaires completed by teachers and parents, observations, and other approaches, the team considers whether a student's social skills or behaviors are part of a suspected disability.
- *Developmental history.* Professionals often are assisted in understanding a student's special needs by learning about the family background as well as any developmental delays, illnesses, or injuries the student experienced as a young child. This information often is obtained by a social worker who may visit the family in their home and request that they complete an inventory covering these topics.
- *Other areas as needed.* Depending on the difficulties the student is experiencing and the suspected areas of disability, other assessments also may be completed. For example, Jasmine's first language is French, and her speech is very difficult to understand. Her evaluation would include a specialized assessment completed by a speech-language pathologist. For any student who has been referred by general education teachers, those professionals' input is sought: They might contribute student work samples, complete a social skills inventory, report anecdotal observations, or recount discussions with parents.

Assessment Procedures

As you read the chapters in this text that describe the disabilities students may have, you will learn more about the specific types of assessments employed to determine whether the disability exists and the procedures used for each. For all assessments, though, IDEA clearly outlines general procedures that must be followed so that the evaluation is nondiscriminatory—that is, accurate and fair (Yell & Drasgow, 2013). First, any assessment instrument used must be *valid* (i.e., it must measure what it is supposed to measure) and *reliable* (i.e., it must have consistency), and it must be free of racial or cultural bias. Second, the instrument must be administered by a professional trained to do so, and that professional must carefully follow the test's directions. Third, any instrument used must take into account the possible impact of the suspected disability (Cumming, 2008). For example, if a student with limited fine-motor skills is asked to write a response, that response is unlikely to really represent what the student knows because the disability area (motor skill) interferes with the performance.

In addition, if a student's primary language is not English, testing must be completed in the language with which the student is most comfortable to ensure that a language difference is not inadvertently labeled a disability (Olvera & Gomez-Cerrillo, 2011; Scott, Boynton Hauerwas, & Brown, 2014). Further, no single test can be used to determine whether a student is eligible for special education. Multiple measures must be used to help the team decide on appropriate services, and several different professionals must be involved in assessment and decision making.

As you can see, many safeguards are in place regarding the assessment of students for possible special education eligibility. For each of the safeguards just described, what might happen to particular students if it is ignored?

Every student who may have a disability and receive special education services must first have a comprehensive and individual assessment to determine eligibility.

Decision Making for Special Education

After a student's comprehensive assessment has been completed, the multidisciplinary team meets to make three critical decisions: (a) whether the student has a disability, (b) whether the disability adversely affects educational performance, and (c) whether the student would benefit from special education.

For the first decision, the team members review all the data gathered to decide whether the student has one of the disabilities addressed by IDEA. The criteria for making this decision are set by each state based on the disability definitions included in IDEA, but the decision must be made based on the collective judgment of team members, considering all the information gathered and not relying solely on exact test scores. For example, suppose a team is deciding whether a student has an intellectual disability: In most states, the student's intelligence (IQ) test score needs to be below 70 and accompanied by significant difficulties in managing day-to-day tasks. However, a student with a test score of 68 who can make friends, play in the neighborhood, and ride a public bus alone to go shopping might not be identified as disabled. A judgment must be made. The team reviewing the assessment data also must take into account two other factors. If the student's school difficulties are the result of limited English proficiency or a lack of appropriate instruction (Yell & Drasgow, 2013), assistance is needed but a disability probably does not exist.

If the team determines the student has a disability, the second decision to be made is whether the disability is adversely affecting the student's education. This usually is the case—but not always. For example, Shana might have a medical condition that clearly represents a disability, but the condition is controlled with medication that has no significant side effects. Shana has a disability, and steps may need to be taken to ensure that she takes her medication during the school day, but she does not need special education.

The third decision made by the team is whether the student is eligible to receive special education and related services and can benefit from these services. Usually, if the student has a disability and it is affecting learning, services will be provided based on assessed need—special education, related services, and supplementary aids and services.

All of the decisions just outlined typically are made at a single meeting, and the student's parents participate in making these decisions (Wolfe & Durán, 2013; Wright, Wright, & O'Connor, 2010). In addition, they may contribute additional information or evaluation results concerning their child. Consistent with the protection of parent rights, if the student does not have a disability affecting learning or is not eligible for services, the team must notify the parents of this fact.

Preparing the IEP

If team members decide that a student is eligible for special education, they then prepare an individualized education program (IEP). This document summarizes all the information gathered concerning the student, sets the expectations of what the student will learn over the next year, and prescribes the types and amounts of special services the student will receive (Gibb & Dyches, 2016; Wright et al., 2010). The IEP is such a central part of a student's special education that an entire section later in this chapter is devoted to helping you understand what it includes.

Deciding About Placement

The final decision made by the multidisciplinary team is placement—that is, the setting in which the student will be educated. Placement ranges from full-time participation in general education, through a combination of general education and special education settings, to a full-time special setting, depending on the student's needs. The full range of special education placement options is outlined later in this chapter.

Monitoring for Students with Disabilities

If you refer back to Figure 2.1, you can see that the special education decision-making process does not end with the placement decision. IDEA also includes a clear set of procedures for monitoring student progress to ensure the student's program and placement remain appropriate.

Annual Review

The first strategy for monitoring progress is the annual review. At least once each year, but more often if necessary, professionals working with the student—often a general education and a special education teacher, a school district administrative representative, and possibly other service providers (e.g., a speech-language pathologist)—meet with parents to review the IEP (Wrightslaw, 2009; Yell, Katsiyannis, & Ryan, 2008). During the review, they update information about the student's learning, review the student's progress, and set goals for the upcoming year. After the new IEP is written, parents receive a copy of this document, which guides the student's education for the following year. If minor changes are needed in the IEP during the year, the law allows it to be amended rather than rewritten.

Three-Year Reevaluation

The second monitoring provision in IDEA takes into account the fact that students with disabilities change over time. At least every three years, and more often if the team decides it is necessary, the student with a disability is reassessed using many of the same procedures included in the initial assessment process. The purpose of this three-year reevaluation is to determine whether the student's program and services remain appropriate or whether they need to change, either to become more or less intensive. However, this reevaluation can be streamlined. If team members and parents decide that no purpose would be served in completing a new assessment, existing information can be used instead (Yell, 2006). This approach makes sense. For example, consider

David, a high school student with a moderate intellectual disability who is due for a reevaluation. He was assessed for the first time when he was 3 years old, and he went through this process again at ages 6, 9, and 12. He has learned a great deal, but his overall ability level has been consistent; the team's focus therefore has been shifting toward vocational skills. David's team members might understandably decide that they can use work samples, teacher-made assessments, and information provided by David and his parents to review his educational plan and create a new one instead of administering standardized tests yet again.

The role of parents in reevaluation is somewhat different than in the initial special education decision-making process. Parents have the right to be informed of the reevaluation, and they are encouraged to participate, but school districts are entitled to complete the reevaluation and prepare a new IEP even if parents choose not to participate. In practice, this means that school districts are not required to obtain written parent permission to complete this monitoring step.

MyEdLab **Self-Check 2.2**

MyEdLab **Application Exercise 2.2:** Referral and Assessment

---

Understanding the Individualized Education Program

The individualized education program (IEP), mentioned earlier in the chapter, captures all of the decisions made through the special education assessment, eligibility, and instructional planning procedures. Every student who receives special education services has a current IEP, and as you have learned, the IEP generally must be reviewed and updated annually. The IEP serves as a blueprint for the services that a student is to receive, and it clarifies the types and amounts of those supports (e.g., Cheatham, Hart, Malian, & McDonald, 2012; Kurch & Mastergeorge, 2010). The guidelines for who participates as members of the IEP team for each student and the elements that must be contained in an IEP are specified clearly in IDEA regulations (20 U.S.C. ß320.321).

Members of the IEP Team

The team that writes the first IEP for a student identified as having a disability often includes all the professionals who participated in assessing the student, and they collaborate so that everyone feels a sense of ownership for the student's education. Thus, IEP teams generally include the following members:

- *Parents.* Clearly, parents are the central members of the IEP team, both because it is their right and because they know their child better than anyone else does. Schools are responsible for ensuring that parents can truly be partners in developing their child's IEP (Lalvani, 2012; Lo, 2012). If parents need interpreting services because they are not proficient in English or because they are deaf, that service must be provided. Further, school personnel must explain the results of assessments and any other information pertaining to the student in terms that parents can readily understand. Some school districts help parents prepare for IEP meetings by sending them a set of questions to think about prior to the meeting.

- *Special education teacher.* At least one special education teacher is part of the IEP team because this professional often can best provide information on the day-to-day instructional needs and options for a student with a disability. This professional can offer ideas for ensuring appropriate curriculum access, identify supplementary aids and services the student may need in the general education setting, and suggest other strategies for individualizing the student's program.

- *General education teacher.* If the student for whom the IEP is being prepared will participate in general education, even on a limited basis, the team generally includes at least one general education teacher. General educators offer detailed knowledge of the curriculum and contribute a "reality check" on expectations in general education settings; they also may have significant responsibility for implementing parts of the IEP.

- *A school district representative.* As you might expect, providing special programs, services, and instructional and assistive technology to students with disabilities requires a commitment of financial resources from the school district. One person on the IEP team must function as the official school district representative to indicate that such a commitment is being made and that adequate resources will be dedicated to providing the services written into the IEP. A school principal may serve in this role. The school psychologist, special education coordinator, or another team member also may be designated as the district representative.

- *An individual who can interpret the results of any evaluations.* Someone on the IEP team must have the expertise to explain clearly for parents and other team members the results of the evaluations that have been completed. In many cases, the school psychologist or psychometrist has this responsibility.

- *Representatives from outside agencies providing transition services.* Once a student is 16 years of age or older, plans for the transition to postschool pursuits may include professionals from outside the school. For example, if William, the student who has an emotional disability and who was described in the beginning of the chapter, was entitled to services from the Department of Vocational Rehabilitation after high school, a representative from that agency might attend the IEP meeting to ensure clear communication among all team members about the services that could be provided.

- *The student.* Increasingly, educators are realizing that students with disabilities should have a voice in the process of planning for their education (Quann, Lyman, Crumlish, Hines, Williams, Pleet-Odle, & Eisenman, 2015). A range of options exists regarding student participation: Very young students sometimes do not attend their IEP meetings, or they attend for parts of their meetings. However, older students usually attend their IEP meetings and actively participate in them, even students with significant disabilities. Although not yet a common practice, some professionals are preparing students to lead their IEP meetings (Griffin, 2011). The Professional Edge feature provides ideas for increasing student involvement in the IEP process.

- *Other individuals with knowledge or expertise related to the student.* The regulations on who participates in IEP meetings leave open the possibility that one or more individuals beyond those listed previously should attend these meetings because they have valuable information to contribute. Paraeducators, especially those who work one to one with a particular student, may be included in this category.

- *Exceptions to IEP team composition.* If the parents and the school district agree that a particular team member's attendance is not necessary (e.g., a related service professional whose service will not be discussed), that team member can be excused from the IEP meeting. In other instances, team members may submit their information in writing instead of attending the meeting in person. In both of these examples, parents must agree in writing to excuse team members from attending.

Involving Students in the IEP Process

Most professionals agree that students should play an active role in developing their IEPs and participating in their implementation. Here are some ideas for involving students in the IEP process:

- Prepare to assist students by increasing your own understanding of student-led IEP meetings. One helpful resource is *Getting the Most Out of IEPs: An Educator's Guide to the Student-Directed Approach* (Thoma & Wehman, 2010).
- Provide students with materials that teach them about IEPs. One example is *Student-Led IEPs: A Guide for Student Involvement* (McGahee, Mason, Wallace, & Jones, 2001).
- Create an IEP scavenger hunt so that students gather information that will help them participate in the meeting.
- Have students read fiction books about individuals with disabilities to help them voice their own strengths and special needs.
- Involve students in the assessment, for example, by having them complete interest inventories.

- Have students send reminders to key participants, either by sending e-mails or composing letters, with assistance as needed.
- Involve students in meeting preparation, for example, by having them make name tags for participants.
- Ask students to write a paragraph about their strengths and needs.
- Assist students to draft IEP goals they consider important to their education.
- Ensure that students, even those who are young, attend all or part of the IEP meeting.
- Help students to rehearse parts of the IEP meeting they will lead.
- Teach students self-advocacy skills so that they can communicate their IEP goals to all their teachers.
- Involve students in monitoring their progress in achieving IEP goals, perhaps preparing first-person reports to share with parents.

Source: Based on Konrad, 2008.

Required Components of the IEP

Although the forms on which IEPs are written vary somewhat across states and local school districts, IDEA spells out clearly the components that must be included in every IEP (Winterman & Rosas, 2014). As you read the following sections, you may wish to have an IEP form from your state on hand so that you can see how the required components are addressed. (You should be able to download a sample from your state's Department of Education website.)

Present Level of Performance

A student's IEP must include accurate and current information about any domain in which a concern exists, including academic achievement, social functioning, behavior, communication skills, physical skills, vocational skills, and others as appropriate. Collectively, this information is referred to as the present level of academic achievement and functional performance (sometimes shortened to the acronym PLOP or, in some states, PLAFP). This IEP component often comprises individual and group achievement test scores, teacher ratings of student behaviors, and scores on assessments completed by specialists such as speech-language pathologists and occupational therapists. However, present level of performance has another required dimension: The IEP must address how the student's disability affects involvement and progress in the general education curriculum. This requirement helps to ensure that the IEP team sets high standards for students with disabilities—standards that, in most cases, should not be different from those for typical learners. For example, Carlos is a high school student with an emotional disability. He has difficulty controlling his anger, and he expresses this anger with loud profanities directed at his teachers. He often refuses to complete assignments. However, Carlos is a very bright young man, and when he is appropriately motivated, he easily masters the high school curriculum. Think about how this aspect of Carlos's disability could affect his involvement and progress in general education.

Annual Goals

The overall purpose of the IEP process is to ensure that every student with a disability has a carefully designed educational program and that progress within that program can be documented (Gibb & Dyches, 2016). Annual goals are statements of the major accomplishments expected for the student during the upcoming 12 months, and they must be able to be measured objectively. An example of an academic goal for Alice, a fifth-grade student who is hard of hearing and who currently reads at a beginning third-grade level, might be "By the end of the school year, given a literary passage written at the fifth-grade level, Alice will read fluently—110–120 words per minute—with at least 90% accuracy on 10 trials over a 5-week period." Notice that this goal is much more than a vague hope that Alice will improve in reading; instead, it specifies the skill (fluency), the type and level of material (literary passage, fifth-grade level), and the criteria for success (110–120 words per minute, 90% accuracy). This goal could easily be measured by timing Alice's reading and recording her fluency and the number of errors.

For Manuel, a ninth-grade student with an intellectual disability, a goal in the social domain might be "By the end of the school year, in academic classes and the cafeteria, Manuel, when verbally and visually prompted, will correctly label the basic emotions of others (anger, surprise, fear, joy, sadness) in 8 out of 10 trials by pointing to the correct visual image." How does this goal meet the requirements of being specific rather than vague? How can it be measured? Keep in mind, too, that goals also may address any other areas of need, including the communication and behavior domains and vocational and self-help skills.

One additional point should be clarified about annual goals: According to IDEA, goals are required only in areas of education affected by the disability. Thus, for many students, the IEP represents only part of their education—the areas in which they need specially designed instruction. David's IEP represents an example of this concept. He has a significant learning disability that affects reading. His IEP reflects his disability, and his goals were written to improve his reading skills across the curriculum. However, David's math skills are just about at grade level, and so his IEP does not address math.

Short-Term Objectives or Benchmarks

When IDEA was reauthorized in 2004, the requirement for short-term objectives was removed for all students except those few who take an alternate assessment. If your state implemented this change, annual goals provide a road map for the education of most students with disabilities. However, for all students with the most significant needs (e.g., students with multiple or severe disabilities), the law preserves short-term objectives (intermediate steps that lead toward accomplishment of the goal, used for discrete skills such as addition of two-digit numbers) or benchmarks (major milestones, used when specific skills cannot be specified, such as grade-level reading performance) (Gibb & Dyches, 2015; Kurz, Elliott, Wehby, & Smithson, 2010). Short-term objectives or benchmarks give parents and educators a way to gauge student progress toward reaching the goals set for them.

Special Education and Related Services

The components of the IEP build on one another. Present level of performance helps the team to decide appropriate goals (and, for some students, objectives or benchmarks), and the goals lead the team to decide which special education and related services a student needs. For example, Jordan may need small-group instruction supplemented with consultation between the special education teacher and the general education teacher. Richard might need a separate class and speech-language therapy. Emily might need transportation in a bus equipped with a wheelchair lift.

Supplementary Aids and Services

In addition to spelling out special education and related services, the IEP also must clearly outline the supplementary aids and services (SAS) needed to support the student in general education. Permitting a student to use a calculator in math class, to dictate answers to assignments instead of writing them, and to have modified assignments (e.g., 12 problems to complete instead of 20) are examples of supplementary aids and services. Another type of SAS is direct support, perhaps offered by a one-to-one paraprofessional or, for a student who is deaf, a sign language interpreter.

Assistive Technology

One important category of supplementary aids and services is *assistive technology*. If the team determines that assistive technology might help the student, the student's needs in that area must be assessed and the technology provided (Jones & Hinesmon-Matthews, 2014).

Participation with Peers Who Do Not Have Disabilities

The presumption in IDEA is that students with disabilities should, in most cases, be educated with their peers (Marx, Hart, Nelson, Love, Baxter, Gartin, & Schaefer Whitby, 2014). On the IEP, the team must clearly state the extent to which the student will *not* be in general education, including other activities in that setting (e.g., lunch, recess, and school assemblies), and that decision must be justified.

Accommodations for State and District Testing

Most students in public schools take annual achievement tests that measure their learning in core academic subjects. For each student with a disability, the IEP must indicate any accommodations that the student needs when taking these tests (Lane & Leventhal, 2015). For example, the student might need to take the test in a small group instead of with an entire general education class. Likewise, the student may need extended time to take the test.

Achievement tests are not appropriate for a few students with disabilities, and if this is the case, the IEP must include a statement of why the testing is not appropriate and how an alternate assessment of the student's progress will be made (Kearns, Towles-Reeves, Kleinert, Kleinert, & Thomas, 2011). Each state determines acceptable types of alternate assessments and the procedures for conducting them. For example, for students with multiple disabilities, a portfolio of work, gathered throughout the school year, may serve this purpose because it can demonstrate learning across time.

Dates and Places

This component of the IEP is straightforward: The IEP must indicate the date on which it becomes effective and for how long it lasts (i.e., no more than one year, but it may be less). The IEP also must specify how often services are to be provided and where they are to occur (e.g., in the general education setting or in a special education classroom). This latter IEP component is sometimes referred to as the *placement decision*.

Transition Service Needs and Transition Services to Be Provided

By the time a student with a disability is 16 years old, the team writing the IEP must address transition, specifying measurable postsecondary goals based on transition assessments for training, education, employment, and other relevant areas (Flannery, Lombardi, & Kato, 2015). Transition services on the IEP could include career exploration; participation in a vocational preparation program; training in life skills, such as keeping a budget and writing checks; experience in a work setting; or any other service or activity related to the student's postschool plans.

Did You Know?

Each state provides guidance to local school districts on the specific components of IEPs. If you'd like to view a sample IEP, the National Association of State Directors of Special Education (NASDSE) document on writing IEPs that are aligned with today's high achievement standards includes examples (http://www.nasdse.org/portals/0/standards-basediepexamples.pdf).

Video Example from YouTube

▶

MyEdLab
Video Example 2.3

This video, which was created to assist parents of children with disabilities to understand what occurs at an IEP meeting, can give you a general sense of what these meetings are like.
(https://www.youtube.com/watch?/v=0k0irMNfKmY)

Age of Majority

In many states, the rights that parents have on behalf of their children with disabilities may transfer to the children at the age of majority, usually 18 years old (National Center on Secondary Education and Transition and PACER Center, 2002). If this is the case, students must be informed at least a year before this transfer of rights as to what those rights are.

Measurement of Progress

In addition to all the information already described, the IEP includes one more essential element: a statement about how the student's progress in meeting goals and objectives will be measured, including the ways in which this information will be communicated to parents. Some students' progress might be measured by individual testing, and this information might be sent to parents as a supplement to the standard report card each time one is issued.

Other Considerations

The team preparing the IEP has one final responsibility: Members must consider special situations related to some students. For example, if a student has limited English proficiency, the team must incorporate language needs into the IEP. If the student is blind or visually impaired, provisions for instruction in braille must be part of the IEP, if it is needed. Similarly, for a student who is deaf or hard of hearing, the team must consider language and communication needs, including how the student will interact with school professionals and classmates using her usual method of communication, which might be sign language. Finally, if a student has significant behavior difficulties, the team must identify strategies for addressing them.

Although the process of creating an IEP can appear daunting, school districts have very clear guidelines to direct educators through the process. If you follow those procedures carefully, ask for assistance as you refine your skills, and rely on the input from your colleagues on the IEP team, you'll make important contributions to ensuring your students' success.

MyEdLab **Self-Check 2.3**

MyEdLab **Application Exercise 2.3:** IEP Components

Placement Options for Students with Disabilities

As you have learned, after the IEP has been prepared, the team responsible for the student's education must decide the setting in which the student can most successfully be educated. The required components of the IEP establish a clear expectation that most students will be educated completely, or to a significant extent, in general education settings. However, students' needs vary, and so a continuum of placement options must still be available so that all students receive an appropriate education (e.g., Kurth, Morningstar, & Kozleski, 2014). Figure 2.2 summarizes data on the proportion of all school-age students with disabilities in the United States placed in each educational setting option.

A student's placement can be changed at any time by the student's team and with parental permission, and it must be examined when the IEP review occurs.

FIGURE 2.2   **Educational Environments for Students with Disabilities**

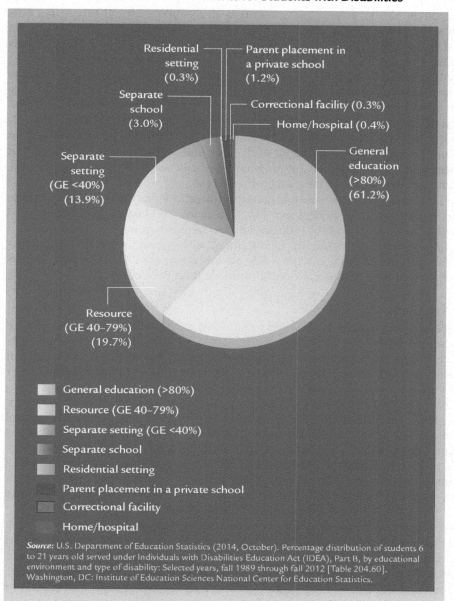

Source: U.S. Department of Education Statistics (2014, October). Percentage distribution of students 6 to 21 years old served under Individuals with Disabilities Education Act (IDEA), Part B, by educational environment and type of disability: Selected years, fall 1989 through fall 2012 [Table 204.60]. Washington, DC: Institute of Education Sciences National Center for Education Statistics.

In addition, if a student commits a zero-tolerance violation (e.g., bringing drugs or a weapon to school), he can be moved for up to 45 days to an interim alternative placement while decisions are made about how best to address this serious situation.

The Continuum of Special Education Placements

The range of options for educating students with disabilities is called a continuum of alternative placements because they range from least to most restrictive. The continuum includes the following settings: (a) general education, (b) resource class, (c) separate class, (d) separate school, (e) residential facility, and (f) home or hospital (U.S. Department of Education, 2015).

Did You Know?

Placement for students with disabilities was first addressed by Elizabeth Farrell. Born in 1870, she grew up to become a teacher in New York City. She created the earliest class placement option for students with intellectual disabilities, called *ungraded classes*, where children across several grade levels were taught practical skills using innovative methods. Farrell was the founder of the Council for Exceptional Children (Kode, 2002).

General Education

In 2012–2013, 62% of school-age students with disabilities spent more than 80% of their school time in general education settings (U.S. Department of Education, 2015). Dominic, a sixth-grader with autism, is an example of a student in this group. He spends the entire day with his classmates, except for the check-in session he has each day with Ms. Harrison, his special education teacher, during the 20-minute advisory period that is part of the school's schedule for all students. He also works twice each week with Mr. Wheaton, the speech-language pathologist, but this often occurs during the advisory period as well. Ms. Harrison spends approximately two class periods (English and math) in the general education classroom each day so that Dominic's IEP goals and objectives are addressed, but she does this by working not only with Dominic but with other students as well. Four other students in the classes also have IEPs.

For a student in high school, general education placement could include (a) one traditional class period per day in a resource class to learn study and organization strategies and (b) indirect support between general education teachers and the special education teacher. Many other types of instructional arrangements fall into this general category. Lily, whom you met at the beginning of this chapter, participates in general education more than 80% of the day.

Resource Class

Resource support usually is assigned to students who are placed in general education between 40% and 79% of the school day. Currently, 19% of students receiving special education services are placed in resource services (U.S. Department of Education, 2015). For example, Tanya has a severe hearing loss. Although her homeroom is a general education class with typical classmates, she spends two hours each day with her special education teacher in a resource class for intensive work on vocabulary development and comprehension of her middle school academic courses. She especially needs assistance learning the many abstract concepts taught in her social studies class. Paul also receives resource support. He has a moderate intellectual disability, and he receives his language arts and math instruction from a special education teacher. However, he is assigned to a general education third-grade classroom for science, social studies, and other classes, including art, music, and physical education.

You should be aware that the term *resource* as used here refers just to the amount of time spent outside general education, not the type of instruction that occurs. Resource programs vary widely in this regard. In some locales, resource services are supplemental to core instruction in general education. For example, an elementary, middle, or high school student may have one resource "class" per day during which assistance is provided in whatever academic area the student is experiencing difficulty, and it may include reteaching, help in completing projects or homework, or extended time for an assessment. In other locales, resource services take the place of general education instruction. That is, a student who has "resource math" receives math instruction from a special educator qualified to teach that subject and who gives the grade for that subject; the student does not participate in a general education math class.

Separate Class

When students are educated in a general education classroom located within a public school for less than 40% of the school day, they are considered to be placed in a separate class. Approximately 14% of students with disabilities receive their education in this setting (U.S. Department of Education, 2015). Jon, a fourth-grader, is an example of a student in this group. Jon has multiple disabilities, and when he experiences difficulty in communicating what he wants or becomes frustrated with his work, he often is very noisy and rather aggressive, hitting those around him and occasionally trying to bite them. His team has determined that he can be most successful in a small, highly structured classroom with a variety of supports and personnel in place to address his complex intellectual, physical, and behavioral needs. However, Jon's special education teacher ensures that he has contact with students without disabilities. Accompanied by a paraeducator, he usually joins his typical classmates for science, working on alternative goals that are aligned with the general science curriculum. That is, he may not do the exact same activities as other learners, but his goals are directly related to what the other students are studying.

Although separate classes also are still the placement of choice in some school districts for quite a few students with significant intellectual or emotional disabilities or multiple disabilities, this type of placement is being called into question by more and more professionals, as you will see when you learn more about these students in Chapters 7, 13, and 14. William, whom you read about at the beginning of this chapter, is educated in a separate setting. What might be opportunities for him to interact with typical peers?

Separate School

A small number of students with disabilities—approximately 3%—require such specialized services that they attend a public or private separate school (National Center for Education Statistics, 2015). One group that sometimes needs this restrictive placement is students with very serious emotional disabilities for whom a typical public school does not provide enough structure and safety (e.g., Wasburn-Moses, 2011). Another group comprises students with very complex disabilities who require many services that cannot be provided in typical schools. As you might guess, the decision to assign a student to a separate school is a very serious one because this placement usually limits the possibility of contact with typical peers and does not offer ready access to the general education curriculum. Nonetheless, for a small number of students, this setting does constitute the least restrictive environment.

Residential Facility

Just a few students with disabilities—far less than 1%—live in residential settings, where they go to school and live 24 hours a day (National Center for Education Statistics, 2015). In some states, students with visual impairments or those who are deaf or hard of hearing may be placed in such a school. Often, though, students in this placement have very complex needs, such as significant multiple disabilities that include difficult behavior. Sometimes students with emotional disabilities who need the safety and structure of full-time supervision likewise attend a residential facility.

Additional Placement Settings

A small number of students with disabilities are educated in other settings (National Center for Education Statistics, 2015). For example, approximately 1.2% of students attend a private school based on a parental, rather than a team, decision. An additional 0.3% of students are educated while they are in correctional facilities. Students in parent-determined schools may receive a variety of services based on the school's practices; students in correctional facilities may have a full-time special education teacher who provides services or may receive daily or weekly visits from an itinerant special educator.

Finally, 0.4% of students receive services in either a home or hospital setting, as may happen when a student is suspended or expelled, is receiving extensive medical treatment, or is so medically fragile that coming to school is not possible. For such students, a teacher usually visits the home or hospital setting for a few hours each week, bringing students' work, tutoring them, and providing other services as specified on the IEP.

Changes in Placement

It is important to understand that students' placements are not static. They change as students' needs change. For example, a student making excellent progress in a core content class taught by a special educator may be placed for the next semester in a general education classroom. A student experiencing serious behavior problems may be moved from a small amount of daily special education service in a separate setting to a self-contained setting. Such changes may be made as part of the annual review of the student's education, or they may occur at other times as needed. Any change in placement must be approved by parents and recorded on the IEP.

One special case of placement change occurs when a student with a disability has a major behavior incident, such as bringing a gun or drugs to school, or when the student has already been suspended from school for 10 days or is being considered for expulsion. These serious behavior infractions trigger a procedure called *manifestation determination*. The IEP team is charged with the responsibility

POSITIVE • **BEHAVIOR** • SUPPORTS

Classroom Practices That Foster Positive Behavior

Even if you are just beginning your professional journey as an educator, you should keep in mind that the classroom practices you implement will either encourage appropriate student behavior or contribute to misbehavior. Here are questions to keep in mind:

Physical Environment

- Are the walls, floors, and furniture clean and in good repair?
- Is the furniture adjusted to the proper size for students? Is it placed to decrease problems with traffic flow?
- Are rules, routines, and procedures posted so that they can be seen and read or understood?
- Are distracting or unnecessary items removed from view and reach?
- Are all materials organized and easily accessible?
- Do students have secure and adequate spaces for personal storage?
- Do instructional areas of the classroom have clear visual boundaries for students?

Scheduling

- Is the daily schedule of activities posted and reviewed regularly?
- Are the times for transitions and noninstructional activities posted and reviewed regularly?
- Is there a method for posting changes to the schedule?
- Does the schedule provide each student with independent work, one-to-one instruction, small- and large-group activities, socialization, and free time?
- Does each student spend most of the time engaged in active learning activities, with little or no unstructured downtime?
- Are students given opportunities to demonstrate or learn choice-making skills?

Instruction

- Are lesson objectives developed based on students' levels of functioning?
- Are assignments relevant and meaningful to students?
- Are materials based on students' needs?
- Are time frames adequate for the tasks planned?
- Are task directions clear and brief?
- Are oral directions paired with pictures, icons, or written words that students can read or understand?
- Is the pace of instruction appropriate for the needs of all students?
- Are provisions made for students who need more time?
- Are student checks for understanding conducted frequently?
- Is specific academic praise provided during instruction?
- Is corrective feedback provided promptly and positively during instruction?
- Is the goal of social acceptance by peers emphasized?
- Is there an emphasis on the development of student autonomy, individual responsibility, and interdependence with other students?
- Are mechanisms in place for regular communication between the teacher and families?
- Are skills taught in the settings and situations in which they are naturally needed?
- Are friendships promoted between students with and without disabilities?
- Are classroom assistants actively involved with students to promote independence and peer interactions?

Source: Adapted from *Positive behavior support project: A multi-tiered system of support.* Best Practice Classroom Management Checklist. Reprinted by permission.

of deciding whether or not the behavior the student has displayed is directly related to the disability. If it is, the team must create a specific plan to address the behavior, that is, to complete additional evaluations, to make changes in the student's placement or program, and/or to teach the student skills so as to avoid similar problems in the future. If the behavior is determined to not be related to the disability, the student is subject to the discipline procedures that would be followed for any student, except that the student must continue to receive a free appropriate public education (e.g., through home-based instruction).

Remember, even though a full continuum of alternative placement options exists for students with disabilities, more than half spend more than 80% of the school day in general education classrooms. That means that regardless of the professional role for which you are preparing, you will likely work with students in that setting and collaborate with others to successfully meet students' needs. In the Positive Behavior Supports feature, you can learn how to assess your own and others' classrooms in terms of their likelihood of facilitating appropriate student behavior and, thus, learning for the many diverse learners who will be educated there.

MyEdLab **Self-Check 2.4**

MyEdLab **Application Exercise 2.4:** The Continuum of Placement Options

MyEdLab **Application Exercise 2.5:** Maximizing Time in the General Education Classroom

---

Resolving Disagreements Regarding Special Education

Sometimes professionals and parents disagree about what special education programs and services should include, how much service should be provided, or where that service should take place (e.g., Feinberg, Moses, Engiles, Whitehorne, & Peter, 2014). When disagreements such as these occur, they must be resolved in a fair and timely manner. Your first approach in solving a disagreement should be to use positive communication strategies (Edwards & Fonte, 2012). However, when an informal approach is not successful, IDEA includes specific provisions for addressing disputes (Rock & Bateman, 2009), as long as this occurs within two years of the alleged violation.

Dispute Resolution

The first strategy for addressing complaints is to hold a resolution session (Center for Appropriate Dispute Resolution in Special Education, 2014b). This meeting must occur within 15 days of the notice of complaint having been received by the school district, and it must be attended by individuals who understand the situation, including a school district representative with decision-making authority. The intent is to try to resolve the issues without having to take any further steps. If this is accomplished, the parties sign an agreement that describes the resolution.

Mediation

In addition to the informal dispute-resolution meeting, IDEA requires that all states offer mediation, at no cost to parents, as another early formal step in resolving differences. In mediation, an impartial professional meets with each party (i.e., usually the parents and the school district representatives) to try to find a way for the dispute to be resolved (Center for Appropriate Dispute Resolution in Special Education, 2014a; Zirkel & McGuire, 2010). The mediator does not make a decision for the parties but helps them find a workable solution.

For example, the parents of a child with autism might be insisting that a specific training program they believe is best be used daily at school. School personnel might maintain that the program has some positive qualities but that it is too intensive and time consuming to be appropriate for the student. The mediator might be able to get the parties to agree to implement parts of the program at school and closely monitor the child's progress. If agreement is reached through mediation, a legally binding document specifying the resolution is signed by all parties and no additional action is needed.

Due Process Hearing

From the very beginning of the special education process of referral, eligibility, programming, and placement, parents, on behalf of their children, as well as school districts, have what is called the right to due process. Due process refers to a clear set of procedures for making all the critical decisions that are part of special education. All the steps outlined earlier in this chapter that must be taken before a student can receive special education services are part of due process. Typically, parents are more likely to exercise their due process rights than are school districts. Parents do so when they believe the school district is not providing their child with the education to which that child is entitled (Yell, 2015).

The vehicle through which due process rights are addressed is called a *due process hearing*. If informal attempts to resolve disputes (including mediation) fail, then this formal procedure must be followed. In a due process hearing, usually parents make a formal complaint against the school district, and an impartial hearing officer (often an attorney who has been trained for this role) is appointed by a state special education official. This individual acts in many ways like a judge, reading all the documents related to the issue, scheduling and presiding over the hearing, reviewing a transcript of the proceeding, and eventually issuing a written decision based on the evidence provided and the testimony of witnesses at the hearing. If either party disagrees with the decision of the hearing officer, the decision can be appealed to a state-level review hearing officer. This individual reviews all the documents from the initial hearing and writes a decision, either agreeing with the initial decision or overturning it. However, even this is not the end of the process. Either party can still take the issue to court, but only after all the steps outlined here have been completed.

Due process hearings usually are held because the needs of students with disabilities are complex and the types, intensity, and quality of services often can be subject to interpretation. Here is an example: The Greens have a daughter, Jessica, who has multiple disabilities. She has a significant intellectual disability, uses a wheelchair, and needs assistance with personal care. Her parents want her to be educated with her peers in middle school. The school district contends that a general education setting is not the least restrictive environment for Jessica and that her education should occur primarily in a self-contained special education class, with opportunities for interacting with typical classmates provided at lunch, assemblies, and in elective classes such as art. Who is right? What types of information do you think might be presented to help a hearing officer make a decision in such a case?

Many educators complete their careers without ever participating in a due process hearing. If the parents of one of your students disagree with a decision concerning their child, though, you may be asked to testify at a hearing. If this occurs, you usually will meet beforehand with the school district attorney, who will help you prepare. Your responsibility will be to answer clearly and honestly the questions you are asked, using objective information you have related to the student (e.g., samples of written work or records of communication with parents). Because a hearing involves conflict, participating in it can be stressful, but your contribution can be important in helping a hearing officer decide what is appropriate for the student.

Did You Know?

The National Center on Dispute Resolution in Special Education (CADRE) (www.directionservice .org/cadre/index.cfm) is funded by the U.S. Department of Education for the purpose of encouraging parents and educators to find collaborative solutions to their disagreements.

MyEdLab **Self-Check 2.5**

MyEdLab **Application Exercise 2.6:** Procedures for Resolving Disagreements

Issues Related to Special Education Professionals and Procedures

In Chapter 1, the point was made that special education is a dynamic field that is constantly evolving. This is certainly true of topics that have been addressed in this chapter. The next sections address two issues facing the field: (a) changing roles and responsibilities of special education teachers and (b) the impact of response to intervention and multi-tiered systems of support procedures on today's school practices.

Special Education Teacher Changing Roles and Responsibilities

Special educators have long been expected to be flexible and adept at managing a multifaceted job, and these professionals often report that they find their careers interesting, challenging, and rewarding. However, in the 21st century, even the most experienced and proficient special education teachers sometimes feel like they cannot keep up with their many roles and responsibilities (Bettini, Cheyney, Wang, & Leko, 2015; Hillel Lavian, 2015). A partial list of special education teacher responsibilities includes:

- Provide direct instruction to students with disabilities across a variety of grade levels and subject matter (academic and nonacademic)
- Develop positive working relationships with general educators, administrators, parents, and other special services providers (Youngs et al., 2011)
- Consult with general education teachers concerning students
- Co-teach with general education colleagues (Friend, 2015/2016)
- Supervise paraeducators working with individual students or on behalf of groups of students in general or special education settings (Causton & Tracy-Bronson, 2015)
- Collaborate with parents (Cook, Shepherd, Cook, & Cook, 2012)
- Keep up with paperwork, including progress monitoring, formative and summative data collection and interpretation, IEP development, and assessment reports
- Complete leadership responsibilities such as chairing a special education department, providing professional development to colleagues on key special education topics, or serving as a compliance monitor
- Participate in larger school initiatives such as professional learning communities (e.g., Blanton & Perez, 2011)
- Contribute to the implementation of RTI procedures (even though this is not a responsibility of special education), including delivering RTI programs to students who are not on the special educator's caseload (Mitchell, Deshler, & Lenz, 2012)

Special education teachers' roles and responsibilities include working with students with disabilities, collaborating with general education teachers and many others, and completing the considerable paperwork that documents services students receive.

At the same time, special educators typically are responsible for many of the same activities as other teachers, including chores such as hall duty and bus duty and contributions to school programs such as serving as the advisor for a club or sports team. They also are held to the same accountability standards. That is, they are evaluated on the extent to which their students achieve required academic standards.

Taken together, one clear challenge for the field of special education is ensuring that special education teachers' roles and responsibilities do not become so diverse that these professionals lose their primary focus, that is, the education of students with disabilities (Eisenman et al., 2011). The complexity of a special educator's job should not discourage you if you are a special education teacher candidate (Wasburn, Wasburn-Moses, & Davis, 2012), but it should alert you that you will need to discuss your responsibilities with your principal or other supervisor and to recognize that you are unlikely to have a job that is narrow in scope.

Response to Intervention and Multi-Tiered Systems of Support: Issues in Implementation

Response to intervention (RTI) and Multi-Tiered Systems of Support (MTSS) are preventing some students from needing special education services by providing them with appropriate instruction as soon as their learning, behavior, or social difficulties are noticed. However, a number of questions and concerns surround RTI and MTSS, and these may affect you. One issue concerns the problem-solving process that is central to these approaches: For RTI and MTSS to be effective, general education teachers must thoroughly understand them. They also must know and be able to implement research-based instructional and related practices and to document their impact on student learning and other outcomes (Johnson, Pool, & Carter, 2012).

A second issue concerns the appropriate roles of special educators in RTI and MTSS procedures. In some locales, these teachers help to explain RTI or MTSS to their colleagues, participate on teams making decisions about interventions for students, and deliver some of the intensive instruction to targeted students these approaches require. The dilemma that sometimes occurs relates to workload: How can special educators balance their desire to assist their colleagues and students who struggle (but who have not been identified as having disabilities) with their other responsibilities?

Yet another RTI issue relates to students with limited English proficiency (Ortiz et al., 2011; Scott, Boynton Hauerwas, & Brown, 2014), specifically, making sure that RTI does not inadvertently lead to these students being identified as having a disability. For example, some professionals have questioned whether enough is known about effective reading instruction for English language learners and whether current assessment procedures can distinguish between students acquiring language skills from those who possibly have disabilities (Haager, 2007). Such discussions are important reminders to professionals that no single procedure can provide all the answers to understanding student needs and that complex decision making is part of being a special educator.

RTI and, increasingly, MTSS are now widely used as a means to provide intensive academic and behavior interventions to struggling students from preschool through high school (Faggella-Luby & Wardwell, 2011; Fisher & Frey, 2013), and applications of them will be discussed in nearly every chapter in this text. However, while these models hold great promise, they are not simple and all-encompassing solutions to students' special needs (Saeki, Jimerson, Earhart, Hart, Renshaw, Singh, & Stewart, 2011; Turse & Albrecht, 2015).

MyEdLab **Self-Check 2.6**

MyEdLab **Application Exercise 2.7:** Current Issues in Special Education: RTI

Summary

LO2.1 Many individuals play key roles in special education. These include special education teachers, related services professionals, and others such as general education teachers, speech-language therapists, school psychologists, paraeducators, and parents.

LO2.2 Most students are identified as needing special education after they begin school. The process of determining whether a student has a disability may begin through a general education intervention team process, response to intervention (RTI) or multi-tiered systems of support (MTSS) procedure, screening, or a direct request for assessment, the latter typically initiated by a parent. If a disability is suspected, parent permission is obtained for a full, multidimensional assessment of the student's strengths and potential areas of disability, and if the student is eligible for special education, the team prepares the student's individualized education program (IEP) and decides on placement.

LO2.3 The IEP, reviewed annually, is the document that outlines the special education to be received by a student with a disability. It has a number of required components that clarify the student's present level of performance, annual goals, short-term objectives for a few students, special education and related services, participation in general education, accommodations for instruction and testing programs, dates for service, placement (i.e., where the student will be educated), transition services, and progress measures.

LO2.4 Although most students with disabilities receive much or all of their education in general education settings, resource rooms, separate classes, separate schools, residential schools, and home or hospital options also may be the least restrictive environment for some students.

LO2.5 If disagreements occur between parents and school professionals related to placement or any other part of special education, specific procedures are followed to resolve those disputes. First, dispute resolution and mediation are offered; these informal approaches can lead to agreement without more formal procedures. However, if agreement is not reached, a due process hearing occurs. If resolution is not accomplished through this hearing and its appeal, the dispute may be addressed in court.

LO2.6 The field of special education is undergoing rapid changes related to professionals and procedures. Two issues are (a) the changing roles and responsibilities of special education teachers and the impact these changes are having on their job; and (b) the pervasive influence of RTI and MTSS on contemporary school practices for struggling students, despite the fact that these approaches still are somewhat controversial.

Back to the Cases

Now that you've read about the personnel and procedures of special education, look back at the student stories at the beginning of this chapter. Then, answer the questions about each of their cases.

MyEdLab **Case Study 2.1**

RAEKWON. Because Raekwon's reading fluency and comprehension was significantly below that of his peers, he was identified almost as soon as he enrolled at Larson Elementary School as needing supplemental intensive interventions.

MyEdLab **Case Study 2.2**

LILY. When students with disabilities transition from one school level to the next (i.e., preschool to elementary, elementary to middle, middle to high), decisions about needs and services can be contentious.

MyEdLab **Case Study 2.3**

WILLIAM. Because of behavior problems, William was identified as having an emotional disability and has received services in a separate special education classroom for seven years. He has experienced teasing, and he dislikes being labeled as a student with a disability.

One of the greatest strengths of the United States is the diversity of its people, and this diversity is reflected in the students that populate today's schools. Racial and ethnic differences constitute one aspect of this diversity, and demographic trends suggest that such diversity has increased considerably in U.S. schools over the past several decades. For example, in 1972, a total of 22.2% of all public school students were students of color. In 2013 (most recent available data), this number had increased to 50% (Keaton, 2012; National Center for Education Statistics, 2016). Although this student diversity provides a rich educational resource, in too many instances it is still viewed as a barrier rather than an opportunity.

In Chapters 1 and 2, you learned many of the fundamental concepts that define the field of special education and that create a systematic and supportive system for educating students with disabilities. In this chapter, you will focus on diverse learners like Kuai, Makenson, Maria, and others in today's schools. In particular, you will consider how educators must take care to ensure that students whose language, learning styles, social interaction skills, and behavior may be somewhat different from those of other students (and teachers) are not inadvertently identified as disabled (Cavendish, Artiles, & Harry, 2015). In addition, you will explore the sometimes unique needs of students from diverse groups who have disabilities. As a professional educator, you have the responsibility of being alert for bias and for taking into account your students' characteristics based on their culture and experiences. Doing this requires that you think about your own background and experiences and how they have shaped your perceptions.

Understanding Culture

Have you ever stopped to consider the concept of *culture* and its impact on our daily lives? Culture is a complex system of underlying beliefs, attitudes, and actions that shapes the thoughts and behaviors of a group of people, distinguishing them from other groups (Nieto & Bode, 2012). Culture is influenced by the environment and is learned, shared, and constantly changing. We are all cultural beings, but if we have been exposed primarily to only one culture, it is difficult for us to view our own culture objectively or to see it as anything other than "simply the way things are." Pang (2001) has likened culture to the air—always there but not seen by those who live in it. Our culture provides the lens through which we view and interpret the world. It greatly influences our behaviors and our perceptions. Do you think Pang's observations are correct? Think of examples that support or refute her observation about culture.

Elements of Culture

Culture consists of a number of elements, including values and behavior patterns. Values are those cultural elements held in great esteem or considered to be important by a society. For example, the dominant culture, or the culture of those in power in the United States, values individualism and independence (Gross, 2015). However, other cultures, including some Native American cultures, place greater emphasis on functioning effectively as a part of a group. These values, in turn, shape behavior patterns, or customary ways of conducting oneself.

For example, children from the dominant American culture are encouraged from the time they are very young to become more and more independent, sleeping over at friends' homes, flying by themselves to visit relatives in another region of the country, and moving away to attend college. They also learn to value being rewarded for individual accomplishment (e.g., honor roll, medals and trophies

Video Example
from
YouTube

▶ MyEdLab
Video Example 3.1
This video introduces additional ways to think about culture and its importance to you as a professional educator.
(https://www.youtube.com/watch?v=nGTVjJuRaZ8)

for community sports achievement). In contrast, in a culture that values interdependence, far more attention is paid to teaching children about sharing, contributing to the group and helping others to do so, and seeking accomplishment by working with others rather than against them. These patterns are neither good nor bad; the two are simply different.

Language is another element of culture. To some degree, language influences thought. Further, the importance of a concept to a culture often is reflected in how that concept is developed in language (Kaplan, 2011). For example, in some languages, including the Alaskan Native language Inuit, many words are used to refer to the concept of snow because it is important to the culture (Jacot de Boinod, 2014). Similarly, the Somali language has many words for camel. Conversely, in the language of the Lakota, a Native American people who highly value peace and respect, no word exists to express the concept of war (Marshall & Marshall, 2005). What other examples of language as a critical element of culture can you identify?

Perspectives and worldviews also are important elements of culture (Lee & Foster, 2011). For example, Native Americans may have a different perspective on historical events, such as the 1800s westward expansion of the United States, than is typical of that of the dominant culture. This event may evoke in them feelings of sorrow or resentment. In contrast, for members of the dominant culture, it may bring to mind feelings of victory or accomplishment. Likewise, the views Native Americans may hold with respect to concepts such as the ownership of land and the relationship of humankind to the rest of nature also may vary from the views of the dominant culture. Members of the dominant culture embrace the notion of individual ownership of land, but this concept is foreign to traditional Native American cultures. Perspectives and worldviews such as these shape our interactions with others and with our environment.

Macroculture and Microculture

All members of a society, to some extent, share cultural aspects of that society. For example, in the United States, people embrace many democratic ideals. These overarching cultural aspects within a society are referred to as macroculture. Macroculture tends to unify the diverse members of a society and define them to others. For example, if you travel to another country, you probably first identify yourself to people you meet as an American. However, within the American macroculture, a number of subgroups form distinct microcultures—that is, groups that have distinguishing characteristics with respect to culture, such as language or dialect, values, behaviors, and worldviews. Such microcultures may be based on any of several factors, and many microcultures exist within a macroculture. For example, socioeconomic status (SES) is a term often used to refer to an individual's educational and income levels, and it may define some microcultures (e.g., working class or middle class). As illustrated in Figure 3.1, microcultures overlap each other, as well as with the macroculture, implying that they share some elements but also maintain distinctions.

As you think about the cultural characteristics associated with various microcultures, you should remember that many factors converge to influence the extent to which individual members of a microculture demonstrate those characteristics. For example, although two individuals may have a common racial or ethnic background, their socioeconomic differences may result in very different cultural profiles. Two individuals may even be demographically identical (e.g., same race or ethnicity, same sex, same SES background, same age), but because of different experiences or life circumstances, they may be very different with respect to cultural characteristics. For example, consider Jennifer and Stacey, who are both White, middle-class females in their twenties. Jennifer is the daughter of a military family, and she has lived in three different countries and two

Did You Know?
Cultural competence is a contemporary term for understanding and acting in a way that is respectful of diversity. This term is used in education, health care, business, and many other professions.

FIGURE 3.1   **Understanding Macroculture and Microculture**

Macroculture refers to an overarching set of cultural ideas. However, all the factors in the figure can contribute to microculture—that is, a subgroup that exists within the macroculture, such as being a southerner or a Protestant. One person typically belongs to several microcultures.

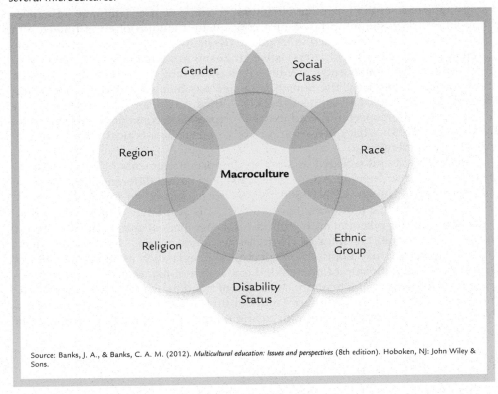

Source: Banks, J. A., & Banks, C. A. M. (2012). *Multicultural education: Issues and perspectives* (8th edition). Hoboken, NJ: John Wiley & Sons.

U.S. cities, fully participating in diverse cultures throughout her childhood. Stacey is from a small city in the Midwest, and her experiences with diverse individuals have been limited to interactions with classmates, church members, and neighbors. As a result of their life experiences, Jennifer and Stacey may have very different cultural perspectives. How might they differ in their beliefs? How might they be similar? This is why it is often unproductive to make broad assumptions about the cultural characteristics of an individual based solely on demographic factors.

Understanding the concepts of macroculture and microculture is integral to understanding diverse students (Ratner, 2012). Macroculture provides you with a broad awareness of students' likely cultural characteristics. Microculture enables you to recognize that no member of any culture fits a single profile of that culture and that your responsibility is to respond to the unique microcultural characteristics of students and their families. How do these concepts apply to Maria, the high school student you met at the beginning of this chapter?

Culture and Race

Race continues to be a dominant theme in U.S. culture (e.g., Alhumam, 2015). Because of the historical legacy of segregation in American society, in many instances members of certain racial groups have interacted primarily with other members of their racial group in home, school, and community settings. Although legally enforced segregation is no longer practiced, racial isolation is still common. School data highlight this point: Public schools in which at least 50% of the students are African American enroll 48% of all Black public school students; schools in which the majority of students are Hispanic enroll 57% of all Hispanic public school students (Aud, Fox, Kewal Ramani & National Center for Education Statistics, 2010). Further, the racial composition of schools also correlates with poverty levels. That is, in 2012–2013, higher percentages of Black (45%), Hispanic (45%), and American Indian/Alaska Native (36%) students attended high-poverty public schools than did Pacific Islander students (26%), students of two or more races (17%), Asian students (16%), and White students (8%) (Aud, Fox, & Kewal Ramani, 2015). And perhaps most importantly, students enrolled in the most racially segregated schools, including those who are White, generally have lower academic achievement outcomes than students attending more racially diverse schools (Bohrnstedt, Kitmitto, Ogut, Sherman, & Chan, 2015).

A number of factors contribute to the persisting racial isolation in schools. It is partly driven by socioeconomic disparities, as mentioned above. However, it is also influenced by our inclination as humans to seek interaction with those we feel are most like us. This has reinforced cultural differences between racial groups.

The relationship between race and culture is further complicated by other influencing factors. For example, some individuals identify themselves as being members of more than one racial group. According to data from the U.S. Census Bureau (2011), approximately 2.9% of the U.S. population do so, data echoed in the 4% of enrolled students identified in this way (Kena et al., 2015). Additionally, individuals vary with respect to the extent to which they adopt characteristics associated with a particular group or internalize values and standards associated with that group (Nieto & Bode, 2012).

Keep in mind that racially influenced cultural differences do exist, but they are the result of the interaction of many elements rather than genetics (Athanases, Wahleithner, & Bennett, 2012; Gunn, Bennett, & Morton, 2013). In other words, just as the concepts of macroculture and microculture illustrate how no individual can be understood based on a superficial understanding of that person's culture, you should not make assumptions about a student or family's culture on the basis of race.

MyEdLab **Self-Check 3.1**

MyEdLab **Application Exercise 3.1:** What Is My Culture?

Culture and Learning

Given how culture strongly influences thought and behavior, it is not hard to imagine that it plays a significant role in learning (e.g., Bal, Kozleski, Schrader, Rodriguez, & Pelton, 2014; Nieto, 2014). In fact, almost every aspect of the teaching and learning process is culturally influenced—from decisions about what is important to learn to decisions about how learning is best accomplished and assessed (e.g., Cooper, He, & Levin, 2011; Warikoo, 2015).

The Content of Instruction

If you think about the United States, can you identify the microculture that traditionally has controlled key government decisions? To help your thinking, recall pictures from the early to late 20th century that you have seen of Congress in session. Who is usually portrayed? Now think about education and its leaders—until relatively recently, what group would represent most of the superintendents of local school districts? Did you think of White males? In many aspects of U.S.

Culture influences how students think and act in school; it also influences how teachers perceive and respond to their students.

society, including education, the thinking of this group has been dominant. The implications of this fact are significant: Those who have made decisions about what knowledge is valid and important typically have been White males. Too often, the perspectives, experiences, and contributions of women, people of color, and people with disabilities have been marginalized. Because school knowledge often has been assumed to be objective and neutral (Banks & Banks, 2013), the issue of perspective seldom has been raised, and underlying assumptions or biases rarely questioned—until recently.

The **knowledge construction** process—that is, the way in which a particular framework is used to develop, approve, and disseminate new information—generally is not directly examined or studied in school. Thus, students and educators are vulnerable to whatever bias may exist in their curricula and instructional materials. Omissions or distortions can go unchallenged and become ingrained characteristics of the curriculum, proving difficult to eradicate. This circumstance can lead to curriculum content that is incomplete or inaccurate. An example from the recent past illustrates this point: Older textbooks on U.S. history rarely mentioned the roles of women, African Americans, or individuals with disabilities. Although this omission would be glaring in the 21st century, it took many years for it to be recognized, debated, and eventually addressed.

Cognitive Styles

Aside from the content of instruction, *how* students are taught and assessed also is culturally influenced (Shealey, Alvarez-McHatton, & Wilson, 2011; Yeatts & Strag, 2014). One example of this concept concerns cognitive style, that is, the inclination to take a particular approach or orientation to thinking and learning.

Field Independence

The cognitive styles of some cultural groups are described as field independent, or characterized by the inclination to be analytical in processing information. Students referred to as *field independent* tend to focus on specifics and are not as strongly influenced by surrounding context. These students often learn best when instruction is organized in discrete, incremental steps and geared toward independent work for which individual recognition is received (Klein, 2008; Rassaei, 2015). For example, consider the task of learning to write a business letter. A learner who has a field-independent cognitive style might benefit most from a step-by-step explanation of how to write each component of the letter (e.g., inside address, greeting, body), with clarifying examples provided. The teacher might then ask the student to practice individual components of the letter. Finally, the teacher might ask the student to write an example of a business letter independently.

Field Sensitivity

Unlike field-independent cognitive styles, field-sensitive cognitive styles are those that reflect a holistic approach to processing information. Field-sensitive students make use of the context of a learning situation and are said to "require the forest in order to see the trees." These students tend to focus on broader concepts before details, and they may learn best through hands-on, authentic tasks, rather than out of context through books, lectures, and worksheets. Additionally, these students may prefer working in groups instead of alone because they may value interdependence more than independence. Again using the example of letter writing, a learner who has a field-sensitive cognitive style might benefit by beginning with an authentic purpose for learning to write business letters (e.g., making a special request of the principal or inviting a guest speaker to class). Also beneficial would be exploring situations in which one would write business letters, with examples of business letters presented before individual components are discussed. Although the teacher would point out the standard components of the business letter, the teacher also could show an actual letter and relate it back to the discussion of why business letters are written. Practice in writing business letters might be provided by pairing or grouping students and having them write letters inviting the principal to a class activity—that is, for a real purpose.

As you look at these two approaches to learning, think about your responsibility to embrace both the field-independent and field-sensitive cognitive styles of your learners within a single lesson. What might be the challenges of accomplishing this? Along what other dimensions of learning might your diverse students vary?

Effects of Cultural Dissonance

As might be expected, traditional classrooms typically reflect the dominant culture. As a result, dissonance may be created between the cultural environment of the classroom and that of some diverse learners. Cultural dissonance refers to a significant discrepancy between two or more cultural frames of reference. When this happens, academic and behavior problems can result (Shealey et al., 2011). As you read the following sections, think about how this dissonance may be affecting Josef's performance in school.

Academic Challenges

In U.S. schools, many lessons focus on a skill presented in isolation and rely heavily on step-by-step analytical thinking, as was the case in the first business letter example. However, students who have field-sensitive cognitive styles may perform poorly in such lessons—not necessarily because of lack of ability, but rather because the instructional approach does not match well with their strengths. If such lessons are the rule rather than the exception, over time the academic performance of the field-sensitive learner may be artificially depressed (Wu, Morgan, & Farkas, 2014).

Behavior Challenges

Behavior patterns also are culturally influenced (Sailes, Cleveland, & Tyler, 2014). For example, some culturally and linguistically diverse students show greater movement, energy, and vitality as a natural course of interacting with others. Their conversations may have features associated with greater exuberance or verve (e.g., louder voices or dramatic gestures) than are typical in the dominant culture (Obiakor, Utley, Banks, & Algozzine, 2014), and they may prefer to work in a group, demonstrating the cultural value of *communalism*—that is, the valuing of the group over the individual. As you might suspect, teachers sometimes consider these behaviors inappropriate and disruptive. Consequently, students from cultural backgrounds that embrace these behaviors are at greater risk of being punished for them (Vincent, Randall, Cartledge, Tobin, & Swain-Bradway, 2011). For example, African American students are suspended at three times the rate of Caucasian students (Office of Civil Rights, 2014). The Positive Behavior Supports outlines additional cultural considerations related to student behavior.

POSITIVE • **BEHAVIOR** • SUPPORTS

Cultural Influences on Behavior

Teachers should consider cultural influences such as these in their interactions with diverse students (Grossman, 2003):

Interactional Styles

- *Degree of directness.* In some cultures, it is preferable to get right to the point in the most unequivocal manner possible, without considering how the listener might feel about what you have to say. In other cultures, preference is given to less direct communication styles, with more elaborate introductory or intervening discourse and greater deference to how the message is received by the listener.

- *Level of emotionality.* In some cultures, a dramatic display of emotions through voice volume and tone, gestures, and facial expressions is typical, while in others this is considered inappropriate.

- *Degree of movement and vocalizations.* In some cultures, it is common for more than one person to speak at a time. In other cultures, this practice is seen as rude. Likewise, in some cultures, a high level of physical activity and verbal exchange may be a natural accompaniment to cognitive activity (e.g., school seatwork), while in others this is not typical.

- *Display of consideration for others.* In some cultures, consideration for others is shown by refraining from behaviors that may offend them. In other cultures, consideration is more often shown by being tolerant of the behaviors of others that one might personally find unpleasant or offensive. For example, in some cultures, one may show consideration of others by not playing music loudly (because others may be disturbed by it). In other cultures, the tendency may be to learn to tolerate loud music if someone else is enjoying it.

- *Attitudes toward personal space.* In some cultures, speakers customarily remain at least 2 feet apart when speaking to one another. Failure to recognize this is often interpreted as a desire to seek intimacy or as a prelude to aggression. In other cultures, closer interactions are common and physically distancing oneself might be interpreted as aloofness.

Response to Authority Figures

- *Perceptions of authority figures.* In some cultures, students may view all adults as authority figures by virtue of their status as adults. In other cultures, position may be a primary determiner (e.g., teachers, police officers). In yet other cultures, designation as an authority figure must be earned by behavior.

- *Display of respect for authority figures.* In some cultures, students show respect for authority figures by not making eye contact; in other cultures, the opposite is true. Likewise, questioning authority figures is considered disrespectful in some cultures; in other cultures, this practice may be valued as an indicator of critical thinking.

- *Response to management styles.* In some cultures, having a permissive management style is viewed as a way to encourage the child's individuality and self-expression. In other cultures, such a management style indicates weakness or lack of concern.

What examples can you think of that illustrate how these cultural elements might be displayed in classroom behaviors? How can these factors affect your interactions with your students' parents?

Based on Grossman, H. (2003). *Classroom behavior management for diverse and inclusive schools* (3rd ed.). New York, NY: Rowman & Littlefield.

Aside from culturally influenced behavioral characteristics, behavior differences also can stem from frustration and feelings of alienation. When a student cannot see herself in the curriculum to which she is exposed, when the teacher's instructional approaches consistently conflict with the way she learns best, and when her behaviors are often misinterpreted negatively by others, this student may understandably feel misunderstood and behave in a way that reflects this (e.g., Brown-Wright, Tyler, Stevens-Watkins, Thomas, Mulder, Hughes, ... & Gadson, 2013). These behaviors are not evidence that something is wrong with the student; rather, they are a predictable human reaction to negative experiences.

MyEdLab **Self-Check 3.2**

MyEdLab **Application Exercise 3.2:** Culture and Learning

Diversity in Special and Gifted Education

Long before special education laws even existed, the percentage of students of color placed in special and gifted education varied significantly from the percentage of these students in the general population. This condition, referred to as disproportionate representation, has received significant attention over the past two decades, and the discussion of this issue is likely to continue for years to come (Bal, Sullivan, & Harper, 2014; Ford, 2014b). The following discussion clarifies important dimensions of disproportionate representation.

Representation in Special Education

Despite more than 30 years of effort to eliminate disproportionality, it continues to exist in special education (Skiba, Middelberg, & McClain, 2014). Specifically, African American students are nearly three times more likely than other students to be identified as intellectually disabled and more than twice as likely as other students to be labeled as having emotional or behavioral disabilities (U.S. Department of Education, 2011). For no other racial or ethnic group is disproportionate representation as severe, although other examples exist. For example, Native American students are nearly twice as likely as other students to be identified as learning disabled (Sullivan & Bal, 2013). In contrast, students from the Asian/Pacific Islander group have far less risk of being identified as learning disabled, intellectually disabled, or emotionally or behaviorally disabled than any other group of students.

Continuum of Placements

Federal data also are gathered on the educational environments that form the continuum of placements in which students with disabilities are served. Although the trend is improving, these data reveal that non-Caucasian students with disabilities, especially African Americans, are more likely to be served in special education placements that separate them from their nondisabled peers than students who are Caucasian (U.S. Department of Education, 2011). As you examine the detailed data in Figure 3.2, consider how the factors already presented in this chapter may affect this troubling pattern related to the environments in which students of different races and ethnicities receive special education.

Why Disproportionality Matters

Given that special education generally includes individualized instruction, greater per-pupil expenditures, and possible instruction in a small-group setting, you

Did You Know?

Since the 2004 reauthorization of the Individuals with Disabilities Education Act (IDEA), all states have been required to implement procedures to prevent disproportionate representation in special education, to closely monitor this issue, and to implement remedial procedures when a school district has significant disproportionality.

FIGURE 3.2   **Percentage of Students with Disabilities Ages 6 Through 21 Educated in Different Educational Environments, by Race/Ethnicity (Fall 2013)[a]**

Race	In General Education 80% or more of the day	In General Education 40–79% of the day	In General Education less than 40% of the day	Other Settings
White	65.1	18.7	10.9	5.4
Hispanic	60.6	19.6	16.2	3.6
African American	56.5	20.1	17.6	5.9
Native Hawaiian/Other Pacific Islander	49.7	30.3	16.4	3.6
American Indian/Alaska Native	61.9	23.9	11.2	3.0
Two Races	63.7	19.1	13.0	4.2

[a]Note that the reported data do not sum to 100% because of the small numbers of students educated in settings other than typical schools (e.g., separate schools); those data are not included here. Additional small errors are attributable to rounding.

Source: U.S. Department of Education. (2015). *Thirty-seventh annual report to Congress on the implementation of the Individuals with Disabilities Education Act, 2015* (p. 49). Washington, DC: Author.

might ask why disproportionate representation is viewed as problematic, at least from the standpoint of those who are overrepresented in such programs. If special education structure and support improve learning, then why would it not be considered a privilege to have greater access to it?

The stigmatization associated with labeling is one reason that disproportionate representation has become an issue. Labels such as *intellectually disabled* and *emotionally disturbed* have inherently negative connotations, and it is inappropriate to apply such labels to students who do not have disabilities merely as a means of giving them access to educational supports. Labels also can inadvertently encourage educators to lower expectations for the labeled students. In an attempt to address learning problems that teachers believe are intrinsic to certain students, they sometimes "teach down" to students who have disability labels (Cavendish, Artiles, & Harry, 2015). This practice can lead to a self-fulfilling prophecy, or the idea that students will do or become what is expected of them. Professionals can create or worsen learning problems in students who do not have disabilities by treating them as though they have intellectual limitations. Think about Maria, whom you met at the beginning of the chapter. How could this factor be affecting her reluctance to remain in school?

Related to the issue of labeling are the liabilities associated with instructional tracking. Students labeled as disabled often have reduced opportunities to interact with typical students. As suggested previously, this may be particularly true for students of color because they are more often placed in educational settings outside the general education classroom. Part of what students learn occurs through their interactions with peers, particularly in areas such as social skills development. If students are segregated in special education classrooms, they have fewer opportunities to see typical academic and social behaviors modeled by classmates. Additionally, research has suggested that grouping students homogeneously by ability may negatively affect the academic achievement of students assigned to low-ability groups (Harris, 2012).

Representation in Gifted Education

Racial and ethnic representation in gifted education is almost a mirror image of representation in special education (Ford, 2014a). That is, African American students tend to appear in gifted education in smaller numbers than would be expected (Subotnik, Olszewski-Kubilius, & Worrell, 2014). These students represent 19% of the school-age population, but they constitute only 10% of students served in gifted and talented education programs. Similar figures are found for Hispanic students, an issue which has become a topic of passionate debate and the basis for litigation (Ford, 2014a). In contrast, students who are Asian or Caucasian are overrepresented in these programs (e.g., Warne, Anderson, & Johnson, 2013). When you reflect on what you have learned about culture and learning, what could be the impact of this underrepresentation and overrepresentation?

Factors Contributing to Disproportionate Representation

No easy answers can be found to the question of what causes the disproportionate representation of students of color in special and gifted education programs and how to reduce it (Ford, 2014b). Two factors that clearly seem to contribute to the problem are poverty and systemic bias.

Poverty

Poverty is a critical variable that influences the occurrence of disabilities (e.g., Emerson, Shahtahmasebi, Lancaster, & Berridge, 2010), and it clearly is a factor likely influencing disproportionality. In 2013, 15.6 million children, that is, 22% of all children under the age of 18, lived in poverty. Nearly one-third of these children are under the age of 5. The percentage was highest for African American children (39%), followed by American Indian/Alaska Native children (36%) and Hispanic children (32%). The percentage for Caucasian children and Asian children was approximately 13% (National Center for Education Statistics, 2015). Poverty has been associated with factors such as increased childhood exposure to lead, increased prenatal exposure to toxins such as tobacco and alcohol, lack of prenatal care, and poor nutrition, all of which have been associated with increased disability rates.

Undoubtedly, the negative effects of poverty contribute to the disproportionate representation of students of color in special and gifted education (Artiles et al., 2010; Skiba et al., 2008). However, once socioeconomic differences are accounted for, disproportionality remains significant (e.g., Skiba, Middelberg, & McClain, 2014). This suggests that in addition to the effects of poverty, other variables contribute to disproportionate representation (Sullivan & Bal, 2013; Sullivan, Artiles, & Hernandez-Saca, 2015).

Systemic Bias

At least part of the problem of disproportionate representation can be attributed to systemic bias, or favoritism toward a particular group that occurs at multiple levels within a society or institution, making such favoritism an implicit part of it. This type of bias can occur in many ways within an educational system, as could be the case with Makenson, whose story was presented at the beginning of the chapter. Here are some examples of bias:

- *Curriculum and instruction.* As noted earlier, the content of the curriculum and the instructional approaches teachers use can predispose some students to failure. If only one worldview or cognitive orientation is embraced, some students will be placed at a disadvantage for learning and at greater risk for special education referral.
- *Teacher attitude.* Although the topic makes some professionals uncomfortable, teachers themselves can harbor attitudes and beliefs that do not facilitate the

Students of color, especially African American males, are more likely than White students to be identified as having certain disabilities, decisions sometimes influenced by systemic bias and the impact of students living in poverty.

education of culturally diverse students. Negative teacher attitudes and expectations toward students of color have been noted by a number of researchers (Dray & Wisneski, 2011; Skiba et al., 2014). Classroom observational studies have suggested that teachers tend to have more positive interactions with White students (e.g., praising them or calling on them) than is the case for students of color (Maholmes & Brown, 2002). Negative teacher attitudes also may be reflected in how discipline policies are implemented. Students of color have been found to be more likely than White students to receive harsher punishments for the same rule violations (e.g., Skiba, Chung, Trachok, Baker, Sheva, & Hughes, 2014).

- *Special education referral process.* The special education referral process also has been criticized for potential bias (National Alliance of Black School Educators, 2002). Once this process has been initiated, frequently it is assumed that any problems that exist are in the child. Professionals often do not critically examine how elements of the classroom environment, such as those discussed previously in this chapter, may contribute to the academic or social challenges faced by referred students.

Attention is focused as never before on how to reduce disproportionality, and through IDEA federal funds have been allocated to further study and address it. Among the recommendations for addressing disproportionality being implemented are these (Skiba, 2015; Skiba et al., 2008):

DATA-DRIVEN DECISIONS

Response to Intervention/Multi-Tiered Systems of Support as Solutions for Disproportionality

Although first proposed as an alternative means of identifying students who have learning disabilities, response to intervention (RTI) and more recently multi-tiered systems of support (MTSS), especially related to reading instruction, have been heralded as a means of reducing the overrepresentation of African American students and other at-risk groups in some special education categories (e.g., learning disabled, intellectually disabled), and data are key to accomplishing this goal (Turse & Albrecht, 2015).

At the Classroom Level

- All students in elementary school are screened at the start of each school year to see if they have age-appropriate reading skills (e.g., letter names and sounds, fluency as measured by correct words read per minute).
- Screening is repeated at mid-year and again later in the school year.
- For students receiving tier 2 or tier 3 intervention, teachers gather data to determine whether the interventions are having a positive impact. This process is called progress monitoring and is the basis for deciding whether different or more intensive strategies should be used.

At the School Level

- An RTI or MTSS team meets regularly to discuss students who are struggling and to make

decisions regarding interventions and referral to special education.
- In some schools, a data team provides feedback to each teacher on student performance. If a teacher appears to be struggling to address student needs, observation, professional development, and coaching may be offered.

At the District Level

- District general and special education administrators discuss with principals data from their schools, student progress, the number of special education referrals, and signs of issues related to disproportionality.
- The district must submit each year a report to the state's department of education that includes the number of students from each racial group identified to receive special education and the disability label assigned. This report may trigger mandatory corrective action.

Are these strategies working? Some successes have been reported (e.g., Albrecht, Skiba, Losen, Chung, & Middelberg, 2012), and many questions remain (e.g., Albrecht, Skiba, Losen, Chung, & Middelberg, 2012; Turse & Albrecht, 2015). What is clear is that attention is focused like never before on disproportionality, its devastating impact, and strategies to eliminate it.

- Better teacher preparation regarding cultural differences and potential biases
- Improved strategies for behavior management, because discipline is one of the major reasons students are referred for special education services
- Prevention and early intervention, such as those used in response to intervention (RTI) and multi-tiered systems of support (MTSS), topics addressed later in this chapter
- Increased attention to possible bias in the assessment process for determining special education eligibility
- Increased family involvement in decision making regarding strategies and interventions to address student needs

Each of these ideas requires focused and significant effort, and all of them demonstrate the complexity of this issue. Only through such efforts, however, is a more equitable education system likely to emerge—one that results in all students being represented proportionately in both special and gifted education. RTI and MTSS represent efforts being made to address these priorities, and this is the topic of Data-Driven Decisions.

MyEdLab **Self-Check 3.3**

MyEdLab **Application Exercise 3.3:** Factors Leading to Disproportionate Representation

MyEdLab **Application Exercise 3.4:** Interpreting Data

Recommended Practices for Diverse Students with Special Needs

Given the significant impact that culture plays in the educational process, increasing attention has been given to culturally responsive instruction (Utley & Obiakor, 2015). Although additional research is needed in this area, several promising practices have been identified with respect to the education of culturally diverse students, including those with disabilities. Two types of practices are important: Some of these practices relate to eliminating bias in the process by which students are determined to be eligible for special education, and others focus on the nature of instruction for diverse learners who have disabilities. Note that recommended practices related to students considered for gifted and talented programs are outlined in Chapter 15.

Promising Practices in Referral and Identification

As you have learned, the adverse effects of poverty on the learning process and the existence of cultural dissonance between teachers and students can complicate the identification process for culturally diverse students with disabilities (Sullivan & Bal, 2013). For example, students who are preoccupied with satisfying basic needs (e.g., hunger, safety, and a sense of belonging) may not perform well academically and hence may be at increased risk for special education referral, a likely scenario for Makenson, who was introduced at the beginning of the chapter. Similarly, students whose cognitive styles or behaviors are not understood or embraced by their teachers may be at increased risk for special education referral (Dedeoglu & Lamme, 2011). Several steps can be taken to ensure fairness in the identification process.

Redesigning the Prereferral and Intervention Process

As you learned in Chapter 2, before a referral for special education is officially made, the educators involved come together as a team to develop a deep understanding of the student's learning or behavior difficulties and to suggest strategies to address these difficulties. In the case of culturally diverse learners, a number of authors have suggested that during the traditional prereferral process or RTI or MTSS procedures, the team should carefully examine factors in the student's environment that may influence learning (Bal et al., 2014). For example, Garcia and Ortiz (1988) recommended systematic examination of these classroom and teacher variables, and they are still relevant for today's educators:

- The experience of the teacher in working effectively with students from diverse populations
- Evidence that the teacher is knowledgeable with respect to the student's culture
- The extent to which the curriculum incorporates aspects of the student's culture
- The extent to which instruction addresses the student's language characteristics
- The extent to which instruction reflects the student's cognitive style
- The overall quality of instruction and opportunity to learn

Other leaders in the field (e.g., Rueda, Klingner, Sager, & Velasco, 2008; Williams, 2015) add that professionals should not assume that any intervention process is sensitive to cultural factors that may affect student learning. They note the importance of placing test scores within the context of a student's language proficiency, length of residence in the United States, and the impact of any unusual stressors (e.g., homelessness). What other factors might teams consider in order to avoid unintended bias in their discussions of students?

Alternative Assessment Strategies

Beyond enhanced intervention prior to referral, others have recommended alternatives to traditional assessment procedures (Aganza, Godinez, Smith, Gonzalez, & Robinson-Zañartu, 2015). One suggestion has been to make the eligibility determination process less dependent on standardized, norm-referenced assessment instruments because they tend to emphasize verbal skills, analytical thinking, and field-independent cognitive styles—elements that may lead to lower scores for many culturally diverse students. For example, portfolio assessment, performance assessment, and curriculum-based assessment have been offered as effective ways to accurately assess diverse students' capabilities:

- In *portfolio assessment*, examples of students' everyday work are selected to document competence and progress in a certain area. For example, writing samples may be collected over time to show the development of writing skills.
- *Performance assessment* involves evaluating students' skills in a certain area through actual performance of an activity. For example, performance assessment could be used to evaluate scientific knowledge and problem-solving skills by having students perform an experiment.
- *Curriculum-based assessment* specifically targets components of the curriculum actually taught in the students' classroom (as opposed to commercially available standardized tests that may or may not be closely aligned with the school's curriculum). In some applications of curriculum-based assessment, students' performance is compared to that of classroom or school peers, not to a national sample, as is the case for most norm-referenced tests.

Although there is no guarantee that alternative assessment approaches are unbiased or even that these approaches are feasible on a large scale, they do have the potential to create a more culturally responsive process for accurately determining which students have disabilities and need special education. They also are consistent with the rationale for response to intervention, discussed in the next section.

Did You Know?

Whether English learners are overrepresented in special education is a topic of ongoing disagreement among professionals. Many indicate that ELs are disproportionally identified because of assessment biases, lack of cultural understanding, and systemic prejudice (Bal, Sullivan, & Harper, 2014).

Universal Screening and Early Intervention

Universal screening and intensive early intervention for young children also have been proposed as being potentially valuable. Through universal screening, all students' learning is periodically monitored so that any delays occurring are noticed sooner rather than later. In this model, students with learning problems receive high-quality interventions targeted to their areas of need in general education beginning early in kindergarten, and so factors that might negatively affect learning can be addressed before they lead to school failure. Only if these interventions fail is a student found eligible for special education. You will learn more detail about this aspect of RTI and MTSS in Chapter 5.

Obviously, one key to the successful implementation of universal screening and early intervention is the broad conceptualization of high-quality interventions. If only one cognitive style is emphasized in generating interventions, students who do not prefer this cognitive style will be at a disadvantage. In this case, the same bias and ultimate outcome could result.

Promising Practices in Instruction

A number of instructional strategies have been found helpful in the education of culturally and linguistically diverse learners with disabilities. These approaches—including differentiated instruction, universal design for learning, multicultural education, and sheltered English—are briefly described in the following sections. The approaches are complementary and often are combined to maximize instructional outcomes for culturally and linguistically diverse learners and diverse learners who also have disabilities (Lo, Correa, & Anderson, 2015; Voltz, Sims, Nelson, & Bivens, 2008).

Differentiated Instruction

Differentiated instruction focuses on designing and delivering effective learning experiences for students, regardless of their unique characteristics. It is intended to allow teachers to more effectively address the learning needs and preferences of individual students (Bender & Waller, 2011; Goddard, Goddard, & Kim, 2015).

Differentiated instruction is integral to teaching diverse students and includes strategies such as learning contracts and tiered lessons (Laud, 2011). Learning contracts allow teachers and students to work together in tailoring the what and how of instruction to student learning needs and preferences, an approach consistent with today's curriculum standards. For example, in an instructional unit on poetry that uses learning contracts, individual students may have the opportunity to identify the kind of poetry they wish to target for in-depth study, choose the strategies they would like to use to learn about the selected poetry (e.g., Internet research, analysis of the work of famous poets), and determine how they would like to demonstrate what they have learned (e.g., writing original poetry, delivering an oral presentation comparing the writing styles of famous poets). Tiered lessons allow teachers to differentiate instruction within a given skill area based on the prior knowledge and skill base that individual students bring to the learning task. For example, in a tiered lesson on telling time using a standard clock face, three tiers or groups may be used. One group may be doing cooperative learning activities focused on telling time to the nearest quarter hour; another to the nearest 5-minute interval; and yet a third to the nearest minute. How might differentiated instruction provide motivation for Maria to remain in school?

Universal Design for Learning

Like differentiated instruction, universal design for learning (UDL) should be a key dimension of working with diverse learners. In UDL, learning activities provide multiple means of representation or modes of presentation (e.g., auditory, visual, varying levels of complexity). Learning activities also must allow students to respond in various modes and should be designed to engage learners with varying interests and aptitudes (Ashton, 2015; Marino, Gotch, Israel, Vasquez, Basham, & Becht, 2014). Educators often use instructional or assistive technology in the implementation of universal design to make instruction accessible for a broader array of students (Hall, Cohen, Vue, & Ganley, 2014). For example, electronic books—electronic versions of texts that have been downloaded onto hand-held devices—may enable the use of software to translate these print materials into multiple languages. This can be particularly helpful for English language learners.

Multicultural Education

Multicultural education is an approach to education that includes perspectives from and content about diverse groups, embraces diverse cognitive styles, and promotes equity in a diverse society (Paris, 2012). The five major dimensions of multicultural education are as follows (Banks & Banks, 2013, 2014):

1. *Content integration* implies that the curriculum that students learn should include content about diverse populations and present information from diverse points of view. Instruction should include examples of key concepts and principles from a variety of cultures.
2. *Knowledge construction* focuses on how teachers explore with students the influences of culture on (a) the manner in which knowledge itself is constructed and (b) the manner in which decisions are made regarding what does and does not constitute valuable or important knowledge. The point is to determine how cultural assumptions and biases influence key instructional components.

INSTRUCTION IN **ACTION**

Multicultural Teaching: Bringing Learning to Life

Grade Level: 10–12

Time: Five class periods

Students: Several Spanish-English bilingual students, a few students with learning disabilities (LD), and a heterogeneous group of typical students

Objectives

1. Students will identify the main parts of the cardiovascular system and their functions.
2. Students will describe several heart diseases or conditions and their causes.
3. Students will learn a healthy dietary and exercise program.

Lesson Plan A

Suggested Procedures

1. Explain that the class will spend the next few days studying the cardiovascular system, related diseases, and disease prevention.
2. Assign pages in the textbook to read on the structure and function of the cardiovascular system and risk factors.
3. Review the major concepts in a reading assignment, asking questions frequently to check comprehension. Show a video on how the heart works. Encourage

students to take notes on the discussion of the textbook assignment and the video.
4. Assign pages in the textbook to read on heart attacks and heart disease.
5. Review the major concepts in the reading assignment; give a mini-lecture elaborating on what physicians do when someone has a heart attack.
6. Invite the school nurse as a guest speaker to talk about how exercise and diet can promote cardiovascular health.

Evaluation

Evaluate each student's mastery of the objectives using a quiz.

Resources

Video on how the heart works.

Lesson Plan B

Suggested Procedures

1. Invite students to share the experiences of family members or friends who have heart disease. Explain that the class will study the cardiovascular system, diseases, and disease prevention.
2. Divide the class into three groups based on students' reading levels. Have three sets of reading materials ready. One set, written at the lowest reading level,

describes heart diseases. A second set, written at an intermediate level, describes the circulatory system. A third set, written at a more difficult level, describes the parts of the heart. Distribute the appropriate reading materials to each group. Have students read and then quiz each other within their groups until all group members have mastered the material.

3. Regroup the students into four groups; each new group should have two or three members from each of the first groupings. Assign each new group one of the following problems or tasks to complete collaboratively:

   • Explain what types of exercise contribute to the health of the cardiovascular system. Suggest an exercise program for persons ages 15 to 25 that will promote cardiovascular health; give reasons for the suggestions.

   • Explain what cholesterol does to the cardiovascular system. Develop European American and Mexican menus that are low in cholesterol.

   • Develop a Spanish-English dictionary that will help Spanish-speaking people with limited English skills to communicate with an English-speaking doctor about common heart problems.

   • Determine and describe the functions an artificial heart must perform. Describe the conditions under which one might be helped by an artificial heart.

4. Have each group orally present its completed project to the class. Encourage students to use relevant diagrams, charts, and activities to engage classmates. Make copies of the students' exercise programs, menus, and dictionaries for the entire class.

5. Provide a study guide on the material students should know, as well as additional copies of the first reading assignments for students who wish to read what other groups read. Encourage the students to study together and to quiz each other on the study guide.

Evaluation

1. Evaluate students' comprehension of main ideas through group projects.

2. Evaluate students' mastery of the objectives using a quiz.

How Do the Revisions Improve the Lesson?

Learning Style

• Many students tend to learn better through cooperative learning (Lesson Plan B) than through individualistic learning (Lesson Plan A). Cooperative learning also fosters peer tutoring, which helps low-achieving students be successful.

• Many students learn better and achieve more when they actively participate during instruction (Lesson Plan B) rather than being passive recipients of information (Lesson Plan A).

Relevance

• Little attempt is made in Lesson Plan A to relate the curriculum to these particular students.

• Lesson Plan B includes several attempts: the introductory discussion, the use of the Spanish language in one project, the use of Mexican foods in a group project, and the invitation for students themselves to develop a diet and exercise program.

Skill Levels

• Lesson Plan A makes no provision for students' diverse skill levels.

• Lesson Plan B does this in two ways: First, reading assignments are made according to students' reading levels, although students later have to teach each other about what they read so no one misses content areas. Second, students are encouraged to study together with a study guide to direct work.

Language

• The Spanish-English dictionary assignment helps bilingual students learn English words. It can also sensitize English-speaking students to language barriers.

Boredom

• Lesson Plan B is more interesting than Lesson Plan A without sacrificing integrity. It also encourages more thinking. Students learn better when the lesson itself is enjoyable.

Source: Adapted from Grant, C. A., & Sleeter, C. E. (1998). *Turning on learning: Five approaches for multicultural teaching plans for race, class, gender, and disability.* Reprinted by permission of John Wiley & Sons, Inc.

3. *Prejudice reduction* refers to activities that are designed to examine and reduce bias in attitudes by using methods and materials that build positive perspectives.

4. *Equity pedagogy* refers to the use of instructional strategies that embrace the learning characteristics and cognitive styles of diverse populations. The goal is to modify teaching so that all students can achieve academic success.

5. An *empowering school culture* focuses on eradicating systemic factors such as the negative effects of grouping and tracking practices and disproportionality in achievement and placement in special education. Elements that contribute to this dimension include staff-student interactions, sports participation, labeling, and other practices.

If you think carefully about these dimensions of multicultural education, you should quickly recognize that teaching with a multicultural perspective is challenging and permeates every aspect of instruction. It has implications not only for *what* is taught but also *how* it is taught. Like differentiated instruction and universal design, it seeks to build on the strengths and prior knowledge students bring to the learning context. Further, it requires teachers to carefully examine their own beliefs and practices and to adjust them in order to be more responsive to their students' diverse needs. An example of a multicultural perspective is illustrated in the Instruction in Action, demonstrating how to make a specific lesson plan more culturally responsive.

Instruction for English Language Learners

As you have been reading this chapter, perhaps you have been wondering about students whose primary language is not English. These students are referred to as English language learners (ELLs) or sometimes English learners (ELs). With the growing number of English language learners in schools has come increased attention. In 2012–2013, 9.2% of public school students (4.4 million) were considered ELs, up slightly from 8.7% in 2002–2003. Of these, 71% spoke Spanish; 4% spoke a Chinese language; 4% spoke Vietnamese, and 2% spoke Haitian/French Creole (Migration Policy Institute, 2015). As many as 1 million of these students experience serious learning or emotional disabilities and may be eligible for special education (Hart, 2009).

As students who are English learners become increasingly language proficient, their needs and the programs that serve them may vary.

Given the current and growing number of English learners in schools, it probably is not surprising that state and local education agencies are required to establish English proficiency standards. Although no specific instructional methodology is endorsed, states receive financial assistance to support their efforts in helping English learners meet English proficiency standards. Some instructional methods commonly used with English language learners are discussed in the following sections.

Bilingual Education

For some students, the preferred strategy for reaching English proficiency standards is bilingual education, an approach that uses the student's dominant language along with English for instructional purposes (Valentino & Reardon, 2015). The most common model of bilingual education, the *transitional approach*, uses the student's native language for instruction only until the student has mastered English sufficiently to receive instruction in English only. Students typically exit these bilingual programs within two to five years. Maintenance bilingual approaches are designed to be longer term and to enhance the development of competence both in the native language and English.

English as a Second Language

In English as a second language (ESL) programs (sometimes called *English as a foreign language* or EFL), professionals teach English directly to individuals who speak another language. However, unlike bilingual programs, ESL programs do not use the student's native language to teach the curriculum but instead provide direct instruction on the English language, sometimes in a setting separate from general education but increasingly through ESL and general education teachers co-teaching, a topic addressed in Chapter 4 (Honigsfeld & Dove, 2012). In ESL programs, no conscious effort is made to maintain or facilitate the development of the student's native language.

Sheltered English

A third instructional approach for students who are not native English speakers uses controlled vocabulary and sentence structure, along with prompting, to facilitate comprehension in English language learners. In these sheltered English programs, teachers might use concrete objects and gestures to help convey meaning. Language demands also may be modified by adjusting the rate of speech and providing context clues (e.g., using pictures). As English language competence improves, prompts and controlled vocabulary are gradually removed (Dabach, 2014).

When you consider bilingual education, ESL, and sheltered English approaches, you can deduce that each has advantages and disadvantages. Which programs are used in the schools in your geographic region? As you discuss this topic with your classmates, keep in mind and add to your conversation the other cultural components introduced earlier in this chapter and analyze the advantages and disadvantages of each approach for students who are both English learners and students who have disabilities.

Putting It All Together

There is definitely a lot to think about in planning and delivering instruction for diverse students, including those with disabilities (Kummerer, 2010). With this in mind, several authors have integrated aspects of differentiated instruction, multicultural education, universal design, and sheltered English into a single framework. Voltz, Sims, Nelson, & Bivens (2006) developed the M^2ECCA framework, which applies the approaches just discussed to the critical aspects of instruction: methods, materials, environment, content, collaboration, and assessment.

- *Methods of instruction.* This is the how of instruction—that is, what teachers do to teach the lesson. Differentiated instruction, universal design, multicultural education, and sheltered English all address this component. The students' strengths, interests, experiential base, cognitive style, and facility with English must be considered in selecting the best approach.
- *Materials of instruction.* These are the tangible tools that are used in the instructional process. Differentiated instruction, universal design, and sheltered English all speak to accessibility of instructional materials. This factor includes the use of technology as well as the use of materials that reflect the skill level, learning preferences, and facility with English of the students with whom the materials are to be used. It also includes the notion that instructional materials should reflect all types of diversity, including cultural, ethnic, gender, and disability status.
- *Environment of the classroom.* The physical arrangement, along with other issues that affect the instructional climate (e.g., classroom and behavior management), contribute to this factor. For example, to promote an empowering school culture, multicultural education stresses the importance of creating an environment that values individual differences. This, in turn, creates a climate in which students are more likely to be accepting of differences made in assignments that are a natural outgrowth of differentiated instruction. Differentiated instruction recommends varying the physical arrangement of the class and the rules and routines used to accommodate differences in learning and interaction styles.
- *Content of instruction.* The curriculum is the next part of this model. Multicultural education seeks to enhance the curriculum by integrating content that reflects a variety of cultures, reduces bias, and explores the knowledge

construction process. Differentiated instruction, to some degree, also addresses curricular issues. While the basic curriculum itself is held constant in differentiated instruction, the pace at which learners proceed through the curriculum and the depth with which curricular content is explored may vary based on student needs.

- *Collaboration in instruction.* Interactions to promote student success occur among various professionals within schools (e.g., general education teachers, special education teachers, bilingual or ESL teachers, administrators), but they also include the interactions that occur between school professionals and parents as well as those between school professionals and professionals in non-school settings (e.g., social service agencies, government agencies). An example from differentiated instruction is co-teaching, an approach discussed in Chapter 4. Multicultural education and sheltered English likewise suggest the need for educators across disciplines to work together and for educators to reach out to families and members of the community in bridging any cultural gaps that may exist between teachers and their students.
- *Assessment process.* Assessment both begins and ends the instructional cycle, providing data on how far students have progressed in the curriculum and what their strengths and needs are. This, in turn, forms the foundation for new instruction. By using principles embodied in multicultural education and universal design, professionals maximize the effectiveness of assessment by reducing the extent to which factors such as cultural mismatches and residual effects of disabilities inappropriately influence students' ability to show what they know.

As you can see, the M^{2}ECCA framework integrates many of the principles of differentiated instruction, universal design, multicultural education, and sheltered English, and it has elements that might positively affect the education of Kuai, Makenson, and Maria. As a professional educator, you can use this framework to better understand and address the needs of all your diverse learners.

MyEdLab **Self-Check 3.4**

MyEdLab **Application Exercise 3.5:** Differentiating Instruction to Meet the Needs of Diverse Students

MyEdLab **Application Exercise 3.6:** Making Assessment Culturally Relevant

MyEdLab **Application Exercise 3.7:** Use of Native Languages and Culturally Relevant Materials

---

Parents and Families of Diverse Students with Disabilities

If the mother of one of your students sent you an e-mail each week thanking you for your efforts with her child, asking questions, and offering to volunteer in the class, how would you react? What if that same parent volunteered to bring snacks for a class party or for the yearbook staff? Or sent her child with a "Teachers Are the Best" coffee mug for you at the holidays? On the other hand, what would you think of a mother who never returned your phone calls (the only number you have for her is at her place of employment)? Who did not return permission forms for school activities? Who failed to come to IEP and other meetings? But then, what if you learned that this mother does not speak English fluently, does not have a cellphone, does not have transportation, and is caring for her elderly grandmother? The point is that biases can exist beyond the immediate classroom when professionals work with families.

Most educators would agree that educational programs are strengthened when families and school personnel work together effectively. Attention to the task of developing effective partnerships with families is important for all students, but it can be particularly critical with families whose cultures differ significantly from the culture of the school (Olivos, Gallagher, & Aguilar, 2010). Unfortunately, it is with this very population of families that schools have historically been most challenged in developing effective collaborative relationships (Mundt, Gregory, Melzi, & McWayne, 2015), as may be the case for Kuai's family, introduced at the beginning of the chapter.

PROFESSIONAL EDGE

Supporting Parents: From Possible Confusion to Clarification

You are learning a tremendous amount about response to intervention, multi-tiered systems of support, and special education, and it is likely you will receive additional professional development as an early career teacher. But think of the confusion parents may face if they are not familiar with these critical school procedures and services and cannot readily access detailed information about them. And imagine the possible reactions of parents who may not speak English and who may be unfamiliar with the U.S. school system in general. Here is a small sample of points of confusion and strategies to help to address them (e.g., Byrd, 2011; Lo, 2012; Jung, 2011).

Point of Possible Confusion Related to RTI, MTSS, and Special Education

1. Knowledge of the required processes
   Ex: Understanding of what is involved in a parent meeting for RTI or MTSS—that it's more than a teacher-parent conference
   Ex: Knowledge of the legal elements of special education decision making
2. Understanding of the vocabulary
   Ex: Terms such as *response to intervention, multi-tiered systems of support, progress monitoring, research-based practices*
   Ex: Terms such as *least restrictive environment, multidisciplinary team, assessment language,* specific disability category labels
3. Interactions with professionals
   Ex: Professional expertise of meeting participants and their contributions
   Ex: Professionals who will be directly involved in delivery of any services
   Ex: Need for premeeting communication as well as postmeeting communication
4. Meeting content and protocols
   Ex: Understanding the purpose of the meeting, the required parts of the meeting, the likely length of the meeting, and the steps taken after the meeting, as well as the data discussed, the time lines for interventions, and the data to be gathered
   Ex: The required participants, the mandated components of the meeting and their order, the necessity of assigning a disability label and its implication, the services that will be provided, the parents' role in the

meeting, including contributing ideas and disagreeing with proposed decisions

What other points of possible confusion can you identify for parents of the students from diverse backgrounds you may teach? What strategies should you implement to reduce the confusion?

Strategies for Clarification

- Create a simple brochure, translated into all languages of the school community, and provide it to parents prior to a meeting. For special education, use this brochure as a supplement to the legally mandated parent rights documents.
- Contact the parents to ask if there are questions. Encourage the parents to bring a friend or relative to any meetings.
- Make a list of the most common terms used, and prepare straightforward definitions of them; provide parents with this information.
- Have someone at meetings be a "jargon monitor," charged with carefully listening and watching parent reactions to check their understanding.
- Ask parents questions that require extended answers to check their understanding; avoid yes/no questions for this purpose.
- Establish the standard that individuals who attend meetings remain for the entire time rather than coming and going.
- Provide parents with a list of each person participating and their professional role.
- Provide contact information for at least one professional at the meeting.
- Meet and talk with parents prior to the meeting to be sure the parents understand what will occur.

Discuss with the parent prior to the meeting; try to clarify that parent input is desired and that questions are welcomed.

- Make sure that parents are seated next to the person they know best so that it is easier to ask a whispered question at the meeting.
- Ask the interpreter to provide a complete translation and not a summary of points made; check that the interpreter knows the terms that will be used.
- Make a personal contact with parents after the meeting to check for questions or misunderstandings.
- Provide a plan or IEP in parents' native language.

Parents of Diverse Learners and Participation in Their Children's Education

For some parents, participation in their child's education is relatively easy. They are available to come to meetings and conferences; they may volunteer at school; and they closely monitor their child's progress, helping with homework and asking about assignments and grades. But that is not the case for all parents. For example, think about Kuai's parents from the story you read at the beginning of the chapter. Imagine how confusing the U.S. educational system might be to them. And if it were determined that Kuai did have a disability, consider how the procedures, terminology, and expectations of the special education system would be perceived by them. Not surprisingly, parents of children from diverse backgrounds, especially those not fluent in English (Jung, 2011), often have limited meaningful participation in their children's education. It's not that they are not interested; it's that they do not have the tools they need. The Professional Edge addresses this topic, highlighting common dilemmas and offering ideas for addressing them.

Factors That Educators Directly Influence

Despite the recognized need for developing educational partnerships with culturally diverse families, educators may engage in a number of practices that are counterproductive to this goal. For example, educators may believe, sometimes without being aware of their perceptions, that families from middle- or high-socioeconomic backgrounds are more concerned about their children's learning and more interested in being involved in their education than are families from low-socioeconomic backgrounds (Gregg, Rugg, & Stoneman, 2012). Based on these preconceived notions, educators may devote greater efforts to working with some parents and family members than others and to value their input more. Some of the variance that may occur in how presumably concerned parents respond to school personnel versus how presumably unconcerned parents respond may be because, in part, of differences in how school personnel interact with them from the outset. A self-fulfilling prophecy can apply to families just as it can apply to students.

Another practice that sometimes thwarts efforts to develop collaborative partnerships with culturally diverse families is the use of a one-size-fits-all approach to family involvement (Gonzalez, Borders, Hines, Villalba, & Henderson, 2013; Yamamoto & Li, 2012). In such an approach, educators unilaterally expect families to interact with them in a prescribed way. Families whose cultural frameworks and life circumstances are similar to those of school personnel may be more likely to embrace these often unspoken expectations. However, as cultural dissonance increases, so does the likelihood that roles designated by school personnel for family members will be deemed untenable or unproductive by them. If families are uncomfortable with the school's view of family involvement, they may be inclined to avoid it. Unfortunately, their actions often are misinterpreted as a lack of interest or lack of caring.

In addition to showing overall respect for diverse cultural groups, teachers must remember that within any group, culturally influenced factors also can affect home–school interactions (e.g., Jung, Stang, Ferko, & Han, 2011). For example, conceptualizations of disability are culturally influenced, particularly with respect to areas such as learning disabilities, mild intellectual disabilities, autism, and emotional disabilities (Morrier, Hess, & Heflin, 2008; Scior, Addai-Davis, Kenyon, & Sheridan, 2013). However, conceptions of disability also vary according to group norms and expectations. In some instances, parents from diverse cultures may hold broader ideas about normalcy than is the case in the traditional school context. When the student performs adequately in nonschool settings, parents may reject the idea presented by educators that their child has a disability. This would not be an instance of denial but rather a reflection of dissonance between conceptualizations of disability.

Factors Beyond the Direct Influence of Educators

Other factors beyond the direct control of educators also can adversely affect interactions with culturally diverse families. For example, family members may harbor unhelpful preconceived notions about schools and school personnel (Nieto, 2014). If family members of culturally diverse students experienced school difficulties themselves, their attitudes toward their children's schooling may be influenced by their past negative experiences. Additionally, culturally diverse families may experience feelings of distrust for school personnel that result from the view that the school is merely an extension of a culture that they find oppressive and from which they feel alienated (Bower, Bowen, & Powers, 2011; Andrews, 2015). Parents from culturally diverse backgrounds also may be offended by the disproportionate representation of students of color in some areas of special education (Hernandez, Harry, Newman, & Cameto, 2008).

Other socioeconomic realities also can negatively affect the development of partnerships with culturally diverse families (Li, 2010). The fact that people of color are disproportionately represented among our nation's poor often means that these families spend a greater proportion of their time, energy, and efforts in meeting basic survival needs—a daily part of Makenson's life—than is the case for other families. Additionally, parents of students with disabilities must not only address the everyday stresses of parenting but also must manage stresses associated with having a child with special needs (Ghosh & Parish, 2013). In the case of culturally diverse parents of students with disabilities, these stresses are further compounded by being culturally different in a society that often views such differences negatively. Given the myriad sources of stress faced by many culturally diverse parents of students with disabilities, it seems reasonable that these parents may not always be physically, emotionally, or psychologically available to participate as vigorously in the education of their children as educators—or they themselves—might desire.

Developing Collaborative Relationships

Despite the special challenges associated with building partnerships with culturally diverse families, such partnerships can be developed successfully. Approaches that encourage educators to personalize interactions with families are helpful in this regard. One approach originally developed by Shea and Bauer (1993) includes five phases that involve asking parents to identify goals they have for collaborative relationships and activities that may be used productively to accomplish these goals. The five phases include the following:

1. *Intake and assessment.* During this phase, interactions occur between family members and educators to determine the needs of each participant regarding the educational relationship. This phase helps answer these questions: What needs of this family should be satisfied through the collaborative relationship? What needs of educators hopefully will be satisfied?
2. *Selection of goals.* During this phase, specific goals of the collaborative relationship are jointly developed on an individual family basis. These goals are derived from the stated needs of all parties and help to shape the nature of activities that will constitute family involvement.
3. *Planning and implementing activities.* This phase involves implementing the activities designed to accomplish the goals outlined in the previous phase.
4. *Evaluation of activities.* This phase includes input from families as well as educators. It helps to answer questions such as these: Are we following

through with our plan? Is our plan doing a good job of addressing our needs?

5. *Review.* This phase allows for a review of the process as well as the product of the collaborative relationship. It helps to answer questions such as these: To what extent have our needs changed? What changes need to be made in the process we use to collaborate?

An approach such as this allows parents to become more active partners in shaping the home–school relationship. It also provides a flexible framework in which the life circumstances and cultural characteristics of individual families can be readily accommodated. Meeting with family members in nonschool settings, such as a local library, place of worship, or fast-food restaurant, are examples of alternative sites that may be mutually agreed on by educators and individual families. Helping families access needed resources such as health care, English language classes, and parent training classes may be a unique way to develop collaborative partnerships designed around needs articulated by some families. How might such strategies encourage Kuai's parents to become active participants in his education?

The development of effective collaborative partnerships with families of culturally diverse learners is integral to the task of delivering appropriate educational services to this population of students. Families, regardless of their cultural or socioeconomic group, are concerned about the educational well-being of their children. It is up to every educator to find ways to connect with families and build effective educational partnerships with them.

MyEdLab **Self-Check 3.5**

MyEdLab **Application Exercise 3.8:** Mini Case Study

Issues and Trends Affecting Diverse Exceptional Learners

Diversity has many dimensions. Although this chapter has focused primarily on cultural and linguistic diversity and their effects on students' education, you should keep other critical factors in mind that may profoundly influence students' schooling experience. Two such factors are (a) a student's physical location (urban and rural) and (b) a student's sexual orientation.

Geography as an Element of Diversity

Have you ever considered how profoundly where students live could affect their education? Geography is directly related to resource allocation, availability of services, and living conditions, which may directly affect schooling options and student achievement.

Urban Education

The conditions of urban education disproportionately affect students of color because it is largely these students who populate urban classrooms: A large majority of the 100 largest school districts in the United States enroll under 50% students who are Caucasian. Thirty-five percent of these districts have student populations more than 75% non-Caucasian (Sable, Plotts, & Mitchell, 2010). The result is that a number of the issues highlighted elsewhere in this chapter may be concentrated in urban schools (e.g., Bohrnstedt et al., 2015).

Equity issues. A number of equity issues arise with respect to urban education. For example, student access to fully credentialed, experienced teachers is a chronic problem (Martinez-Garcia & Slate, 2012). In special education, large school districts are more likely than their smaller counterparts to cite the lack of qualified applicants as a significant barrier to filling special education positions (Rich, 2015). Although early-career teachers bring enthusiasm and the latest instructional knowledge and skills to their jobs, evidence suggests that these teachers are not as effective with students in urban areas as teachers with more experience (Martinez-Garcia & Slate, 2012).

Another equity issue concerns the schools themselves. The physical condition of urban schools often compares unfavorably to that of their suburban counterparts (Hudley, 2013). For example, inner-city schools tend to be older and more likely to be severely overcrowded than those in suburban and rural areas (Planty & DeVoe, 2005). This factor is significant because greater academic gains have been associated with long-term smaller class size, particularly for students from low-SES backgrounds (Krasnoff, 2015). And when a school's condition is a symptom of a high-poverty district, teachers there are less likely to feel supported by their administrators than teachers in other districts (Fall & Billingsley, 2011).

School choice programs. As you probably have seen in the popular media, the failure of some large urban school districts to improve student test scores has encouraged efforts to make radical changes in the governing and funding structures that support these districts or select schools within these districts. For example, charter schools, for-profit schools, and vouchers for private schools are receiving ongoing attention as ways to address what is sometimes perceived as the failure of urban schools. Public charter schools often are in urban areas where there are higher concentrations of students of color (Miron, 2011), and serious questions have been raised about the extent to which charter schools contribute to racial segregation and the exclusion of students with disabilities (e.g., Frankenberg, & Siegel-Hawley, 2012; Stern, Clonan, Jaffee, & Lee, 2015). Other charter schools are being established to serve only particular groups of students with disabilities (e.g., those with autism). Both situations can call into question the core principles of special education. Finally, some charter schools employ teachers with fewer years of teaching experience than do traditional public schools. How do you think school choice options could affect the education of diverse students and those with disabilities in the districts most affected by these practices?

Teachers and their preparation. The preparation teachers receive to work in diverse, urban environments is essential for student success and is an ongoing area of concern (Bales & Safford, 2011; Shealey et al., 2011). For example, teachers who work in these settings generally need to have strong pedagogical skills, but they also need to be adept at forming relationships with their students as well as maintaining a strong commitment to social justice (Tricarico, Jacobs, & Yendol-Hoppey, 2015). In some locales, teachers for urban settings are recruited from other countries, and these educators may face many challenges in their new careers (Dunn, 2011). When teachers are not carefully prepared to work with culturally and linguistically diverse learners, negative consequences, including disproportionality, may result.

The diversity of the teaching force also is important (Dedeoglu & Lamme, 2011). In some school districts, the number of teachers of color is painfully small. For example, whereas African American males are overrepresented in special education programs, they are severely underrepresented in the special education teaching force, comprising only 0.4% of elementary special education teachers and 2.2% of secondary special education teachers (Rice & Goessling, 2005).

Rural Education

Approximately 25% of U.S. students attend schools in rural areas (National Center for Education Statistics, 2013). Further, 6.1 million of these students live in poverty, an increase of 25% over the past 15 years (Rural Family Economic Success Action Network, 2016). The special issues related to education in rural areas have not received nearly the amount of attention as those for urban areas, but they can be just as significant.

Disability Identification and Access to Services. Interestingly, a recent report found that rural areas have rates of identification for students with disabilities that are higher than those of the United States as a whole (Strange, Johnson, Showalter, & Klein, 2012). However, this trend does not seem to be related to any type of negative stereotyping or funding issues; instead, it apparently reflects a willingness to identify students in order to provide assistance.

However, serious issues may occur related to the delivery of services to rural students, especially those who are identified as having disabilities (Miretzky & Stevens, 2012). For example, in some locales, interpreters for students who are deaf are simply not available, and students may end up with an interpreter accompanying them to class via Skype or another electronic format. For other services, including physical and occupational therapy and speech-language therapy, school districts may not find needed personnel at all. In yet other cases, students with specialized needs, such as visual impairments, may have to go to a residential school in order to receive their educational services because no options exist in the local schools.

Teaching Conditions. Teaching conditions in rural areas sometimes contribute to turnover in staff, which, in turn, may negatively affect student achievement (Johnson, Showalter, Klein, Lester, 2014). For example, rural teachers as a whole are paid less than teachers in suburban or urban settings (Schuette, 2015). In addition, they may be isolated in important ways (Lockette, 2010). One African American teacher described her students' curiosity and desire to touch her because they had never interacted with a person of her race. Another who works on an Indian reservation talks of the poverty of her students. Yet another describes the culture of the community and how it sometimes clashes with his own. For all these teachers, isolation also may be geographic, with long drives necessary to reach destinations such as grocery stores and auto services.

Sexual Orientation

One additional topic related to diversity that should be mentioned concerns students' sexual orientation. Students who are lesbian, gay, bisexual, or transgender (LGBT) comprise as much as 10% of a school's population (Young, 2011), and during their school years, a large majority of them will be verbally or physically harassed or physically assaulted because of their sexual orientation (Bullying Statistics, 2015).

For students who are LGBT and who also have disabilities, stigmatization is highly likely and may occur both because of sexual orientation and disability status (Duke, 2011; Morgan, Mancl, Kaffar, & Ferreira, 2011). These negative experiences often span settings, including school, the workplace, supported living programs, the general community, and the LGBT community. The problem is compounded by the fact that little attention has been directed toward addressing these students' needs, and special educators report being ill prepared to support them (Richmond, 2012). In too many schools, homosexuality is a forbidden topic in special education programs (Duke, 2011), and so students do not have the opportunity to observe positive LGBT role models; nor do they have opportunities to strengthen their self-identity. Some students with disabilities are even excluded from basic sex

Video Example
from
YouTube

MyEdLab
Video Example 3.3
This video includes brief interviews with teachers from rural areas discussing their experiences. (https://www.youtube.com/watch?v=hU2WhYccbTY)

education programs, and some educators may believe that students with disabilities (including those with intellectual disabilities and autism) are mostly asexual, which, of course, is not at all an accurate perception.

The risks for LGBT students, whether or not they have disabilities, are significant. Their fear at school of being bullied or ridiculed may affect their academic outcomes, behavior, and mental health (Centers for Disease Control and Prevention, 2014; Robinson & Espelage, 2011). When bullied because of sexual orientation, students are more likely to isolate themselves and abuse drugs or alcohol. If family and friends support them, they are much more likely to develop a positive self-concept; if rejected, they are highly likely to experience depression. Not surprisingly, these students also are two to three times more likely than other students to attempt suicide (Bishop & Casida, 2011).

Diversity has many dimensions, including race, culture, gender, sexual orientation, and religion.

All professionals—special educators, general educators, related services personnel, and administrators—have an obligation to proactively support these students by stopping jokes or slurs related to sexual orientation, establishing zero-tolerance policies related to bullying and other harassment of LGBT students, and by teaching accurate information about sexual orientation and tolerance of others. Most importantly, education professionals should listen—sincerely and respectfully—when students ask for assistance.

MyEdLab **Self-Check 3.6**

MyEdLab **Application Exercise 3.9:** Issues and Trends Affecting Diverse Exceptional Learners

Summary

LO3.1   Culture provides the lens through which people view and interpret the world. Although culture mediates every aspect of our lives, unless you encounter cultural dissonance, you are barely aware that it exists.

LO3.2   Cultural factors have a great impact on the learning process. If various cognitive styles are not considered in professionals' approach to instruction, students' learning may suffer.

LO3.3   The disproportionate representation of students of color in special and gifted education has been a lingering challenge to the field, especially for African American students. Poverty and systemic bias have been cited as probable contributors to this challenge.

LO3.4   A variety of practices related to assessment and instruction (e.g., assessment redesign and alternative assessment approaches; universal screening; differentiated instruction and universal design for learning; multicultural, bilingual, ESL, and sheltered English education) can be effective in addressing the needs of students from diverse groups, whether they have disabilities or not.

LO3.5   Promoting collaborative relationships with families is a critical factor in the educational success of culturally diverse students with disabilities. In order to facilitate such relationships, school personnel must be prepared to work with parents as individuals and learn about and respect cultural differences and provide supports for parents so that they can participate meaningfully in their children's education.

LO3.6   Although this chapter has focused primarily on cultural and linguistic diversity, other types of diversity also merit discussion, including diversity based on geography (urban, rural) and diversity based on other student characteristics such as sexual orientation.

Back to the Cases

Now that you've read about multicultural perspectives in special education, look back at the student stories at the beginning of this chapter. Then, answer the questions about each of their cases.

MyEdLab **Case Study 3.1**

KUAI. As a newcomer to the United States, Kuai is unfamiliar with the language, culture, and school expectations. His situation is complicated by the fact that he lives in a rural area with access to only very limited ESL services, complemented by the efforts of Mr. Levinson and Ms. Tobin, who are trying to help him but who are not knowledgeable in teaching an English language learner.

MyEdLab **Case Study 3.2**

MAKENSON. Makenson has had a difficult life, characterized by homelessness, transience, and poverty, and his teachers are seeing symptoms of the stress he experiences because of the uncertainties in his circumstances.

MyEdLab **Case Study 3.3**

MARIA. For her entire life, Maria has needed to operate in two languages and two cultures: the native language and culture of her home, and a different language and culture in school. Now she is exhibiting behaviors that endanger her success in the school culture.

4 Collaboration in Special Education

Learning Outcomes

LO4.1 Describe what *collaboration* is and why it is critical in providing special education services to students with disabilities.

LO4.2 Analyze how the essential components of collaboration—including beliefs, personal prerequisites, communication skills, interaction processes, programs or services, and context—contribute to its effectiveness in educational settings.

LO4.3 Outline collaborative practices on behalf of students with disabilities that are most common in today's schools, including teams, co-teaching, and consultation.

LO4.4 Discuss the role of collaboration in working with parents and family members.

LO4.5 Describe issues related to collaboration in special education.

as a team—that is, the meeting is the *what*. The factor that varies is the way in which the team approaches its work—that is, the *how* is either collaborative, as on the team that encourages ideas from all parties, or directive, as on the team that avoids certain topics.

Characteristics of Collaboration

You can further appreciate what collaboration is and what place it has in your professional role by learning about its characteristics (Friend & Cook, 2017). As you read this section, think about how a collaborative style can positively affect your interactions with colleagues and parents.

Collaboration Is Voluntary

No matter your role, you might be directed to work with a group of other professionals on a committee or team. You might even be told that you have been partnered to teach with a specific colleague. Neither of these situations feels particularly voluntary. That is partly correct: Being assigned to work in proximity with others is not voluntary, and it is inevitable and appropriate that in schools such decisions will be made, often by an administrator, without your input. However, the choice of whether you and your colleagues use the style of collaboration remains voluntary. On the committee or team, you and others choose whether to participate as little as possible, thinking of yourselves as a collection of individuals, or to engage fully, recognizing the increased potential of working together—that is, collaborating. Similarly, you and your teaching partner(s) choose whether to divide students and work separately or to blend your talents and create new, shared teaching possibilities. In both cases, proximity is mandated, but collaboration is chosen.

Collaboration Is Based on Parity

Parity refers to the concept that, in collaboration, the contributions of all participants are equally valued. For example, imagine that you are at a meeting about a student who has been hospitalized because of significant emotional and mental health issues. As an early-career professional with limited experience working with such students, you may be intimidated by other participants' casual use of medical terms, and you might believe that you have nothing to offer to the conversation. This would be a breakdown in parity. However, if you realize that you have a unique perspective on how to successfully reach the student in an education setting, you might make a contribution in that area. A sense of parity would exist.

Of course, parity has to be fostered for every person participating in an interaction. In interactions with parents, the vocabulary you use may affect parity. Similarly, if you repeatedly refer to formal reports and other paperwork that the parent does not have, parity may become a problem. How might parity apply to general education teachers in their interactions with you? What might cause a breakdown in parity? It is essential that you work to ensure parity in interactions with both parents and general education colleagues, as well as paraprofessionals and others with whom you interact.

Collaboration Requires a Mutual Goal

One of the greatest challenges of working with other adults in schools can be confirming a shared goal. If a special education teacher is meeting with a general education teacher because a student has been disruptive in class, the special education teacher might assume that the goal is to find out why the behavior problem has been escalating so that it can be addressed and the student maintained in the classroom. However, the general education teacher might have requested the meeting to suggest that the student spend more time away from the general education setting. Clearly, this interaction is not based on having a mutual goal. Alternatively, if the teachers decide that their purpose in meeting is to analyze the situation and decide whether to call the parents or request consultation from the school psychologist, they do have a mutual goal. Although it may seem obvious that professionals should ask each other explicitly about the goals of their interactions, often this does not occur. You are far more likely to succeed in collaboration if you make this simple effort.

Collaboration Involves Shared Responsibility for Key Decisions

When you collaborate, you and your colleagues share the critical decisions related to your goal, but the tasks required to reach that goal usually are assigned to individuals. For example, a special educator and a general education teacher sharing instruction might decide that the students' project will be to dramatize a scene from the literature being read. However, the general education teacher might assume the responsibility of preparing the evaluation rubric for this project while the special educator prepares an organizer to help some students remember all the parts to the assignment and the due dates. Note that in the hectic world of today's schools, not all work can be shared. In collaboration, then, shared responsibility for key decisions contributes to parity and mutual goals while allowing professionals to be efficient through a division of labor.

Collaboration Includes Shared Accountability for Outcomes

Sharing accountability follows directly from sharing responsibility for key decisions. If team members decide to try a behavior intervention plan for a student and it is highly effective, they should share the credit for its success. However, if the plan somehow backfires and causes even further problems, they should avoid trying to assign blame and instead collectively ask, "What should we do now?" In collaboration, shared accountability implies that all participants have contributed to planning and implementing a strategy and fully accept the outcomes of those decisions, whether they are positive or a cause for concern.

Collaboration Requires Sharing Resources

In collaboration, each participant must contribute some type of resource. Perhaps a special educator can offer materials that focus on the same curriculum goals but address them in a more explicit way or at a lower reading level. That professional also can share technical information about a student's physical, academic, or behavior needs. The general education teacher's contribution may be the time to implement the planned intervention and to monitor its impact. By sharing resources, everyone engaged in the collaboration shares ownership for the activity or intervention.

Collaboration Is Emergent

As you have probably surmised, collaboration depends on the development of trust, respect, and a sense of community among participants. However, traits such as these cannot exist, fully developed, at the outset of a working relationship, and so these characteristics of collaboration are referred to as *emergent*. That is, anyone who engages in collaboration begins with a small amount of these characteristics. Would you risk working closely with a colleague if you could not find at least a small amount of trust and respect for that person's

Achieving parity can be challenging when participants in collaboration have cultural differences.

knowledge and skills? However, these characteristics become stronger as participants' positive experience in collaboration grows (Conderman & Hedin, 2014). For example, at the beginning of the school year, Ms. Galliano, a new special education teacher, learned that she would work closely with Ms. Brighton, the speech-language pathologist, regarding services for Luis. Early in the year, both professionals worked diligently to be respectful, to get to know each other's strengths, and to clearly communicate concerning Luis's program. Later, though, as they became familiar with each other's style, after they jointly and successfully managed a difficult meeting with Luis's parents, and through many lunch periods spent discussing their instructional views, they came to realize that they could rely on each other. They both believed they had Luis's best interests at heart, even when they disagreed, and they both recognized that if a problem occurred, it could be resolved. Their collaborative relationship evolved based on their shared work until they sensed that they were a strong and productive educational team. Michelle and Kira, who you met at the beginning of the chapter, have gone through a similar process of developing trust and respect.

Of course, not all efforts that should be collaborative end up that way, and negative experiences, especially early in a partnership, can be difficult to overcome. For example, Mr. Vega, a high school science teacher, and Ms. Hall, a special educator, have been assigned to teach together. Mr. Vega states clearly that he does not need any "help" and tells Ms. Hall that he expects her to remain quiet while he teaches, offering that she has his permission to work with struggling students after his instruction has concluded. Even though Mr. Vega admits later that he misunderstood how they could work together and tries to foster a partnership, it takes a long time for Ms. Hall to trust Mr. Vega and believe that he is sincere in his changed view of their shared work.

Collaboration in the Context of IDEA

Although collaboration in the field of special education has existed informally almost since its inception, more than ever before, it is a direct or implied expectation in services for students with disabilities or other special needs. That is, in today's schools, there is recognition that everyone involved in designing, implementing, and monitoring the learning of these students has a contribution to make.

In fact, the current provisions of the Individuals with Disabilities Education Act (IDEA) contain the strongest expectations ever for collaboration in special education. As you learned in Chapter 2, collaboration among professionals and between professionals and parents is integral to nearly every dimension of the federal law, including the following:

- Participation of general education teachers on most IEP teams
- Increased parent involvement
- Required conflict resolution efforts when disagreements occur
- Emphasis on educating students in the least restrictive environment
- Consultative special education services

In addition, collaboration is essential even prior to the determination of the need for and delivery of special education services. It is essential for the effective implementation of a response to intervention (RTI) or multi-tiered systems of support (MTSS) process, the major point of Instruction in Action.

As you continue to learn about collaboration and its role in the delivery of special services to students with disabilities and those at risk for failure, keep in mind that collaboration has become increasingly integral to many aspects of society, including business and industry (Fullan & Quinn, 2016; Sanker, 2012). In fact, a recent advertisement in a business magazine proclaimed, "Collaborate or die!" Because schools tend to reflect the important trends that shape society

INSTRUCTION IN **ACTION**

Response to Intervention, Multi-Tiered Systems of Support, and Collaboration

Collaboration is integral to RTI and MTSS procedures. Here are examples of its use:

Tier 1

- Teachers provide high-quality instruction to all students. This suggests that universal design for learning, differentiated instruction, curriculum-based assessment, and positive behavior supports will be provided—all areas in which special educators have highly specialized knowledge to share with their general education colleagues.

Tier 2

- Professionals systematically engage in shared problem solving to design more intensive interventions for students who need them.
- Professional development, consultation, and other collaborative strategies are implemented to assist teachers to assess student needs, implement appropriate interventions, and evaluate student progress.
- As interventions are implemented, the problem-solving team collaborates to monitor their impact on student learning and behavior.
- Parents are included in the planning, implementation, and monitoring process.
- When tier 2 is divided into subtiers (i.e., multiple interventions), the problem-solving process is repeated, often involving more professionals in the collaboration.

Tier 3

- The problem-solving team works together to monitor even more carefully whether intensive interventions are having a positive impact on student learning and behavior.
- Based on data, the team decides whether interventions are effective and the next steps for the student. If the interventions are having a positive impact, monitoring continues or less intensive interventions may be needed. If the interventions are not successful, the team may decide to proceed with a special education decision-making process.
- The multidisciplinary team, which includes the members you read about in Chapter 2, conducts a comprehensive evaluation that includes RTI or MTSS data along with other measures, follows all requirements for parent participation, and collaborates to determine whether the student has a disability and is eligible to receive special education services.
- Unique to RTI and MTSS procedures, particularly for students with disabilities, the team may be responsible for determining whether standardized test information is needed in addition to the ongoing assessment information gathered during the tiers of interventions.

Source: Based on Mellard, D. (2005). *Understanding responsiveness to intervention in learning disabilities determination*. Nashville, TN: National Research Center on Learning Disabilities, Peabody College, Vanderbilt University.

(Friend & Cook, 2017), collaboration will remain a significant part of your role as a school professional.

MyEdLab **Self-Check 4.1**

MyEdLab **Application Exercise 4.1:** What Is Collaboration?

Essential Elements of Collaboration

As you interact with parents and family members, teachers, administrators, related services professionals, paraeducators, and others, it is not enough to simply hope that collaboration will evolve. You can express your own commitment to collaboration, and you can learn a set of skills that can make the goal of collaboration a reality. These interrelated elements of collaboration (Friend & Cook, 2017) are described next.

Personal Belief System

Having read to this point in the chapter, are you convinced that the effort that collaboration requires results in positive outcomes for both students and teachers? This consideration, your *personal belief system*, is the first element of collaboration. If you firmly believe that collaboration is worthwhile, you are ready to learn the more technical aspects of this style. If you are uncertain, then you are not likely to embrace collaboration, particularly when it is challenging to accomplish.

An example related to your experiences as a student can further illustrate this point. Do you believe that the work you do with others is better than the work you do alone? Before you quickly say yes, think about the last time you were assigned a group project in one of your courses. Did you mentally groan at the prospect? How might this indicate your readiness and willingness to collaborate? Among all the professionals with whom you will work in schools, the level of commitment to collaboration will vary greatly. Their perspectives, combined with your own viewpoint, will determine whether you will have many opportunities to participate in collaborative activities or whether you will complete much of your work without such support.

Communication Skills

When coupled with facial expressions, posture, and other nonverbal signals, the words we choose and the way we express them comprise our communication skills (Beebe & Masterson, 2012; Trenholm, 2014). Communication skills can be taught and learned readily, and entire university courses are devoted to this topic. More importantly, communication skills can have a huge effect on the development of collaboration, or they can inhibit it (Kozleski, Yu, Satter, Francis, & Haines, 2015; Walker, 2015).

When all is well and your interactions are positive, you do not necessarily need to have exemplary communication skills. Your colleagues know what you mean, and they do not take offense or read alternative meanings into your words. However, when controversial or awkward situations arise, excellent communication skills are not only helpful but essential (e.g., Conderman & Hedin, 2014). The problem is that if you do not practice these skills when it is easy to do so, you are unlikely to suddenly have them when the situation demands them. Think about the IEP meeting that Derek, introduced at the beginning of the chapter, was attending. How might the communication skills of each participant affect the outcome of the meeting?

Dozens of models of communication and sets of communication skills have been described in the professional literature, and presenting a comprehensive list of them is not possible here. However, the following concepts and strategies can be especially helpful to you as an educator and illustrate the importance of these skills for collaboration.

Effective Communication Strategies

To enhance your communication skills for collaboration, the place to begin is with listening (Ames, Maissen, Brockner, 2012; Hackman & Johnson, 2013). Even though your teachers have been instructing you on effective listening since you were an elementary school pupil, as a school professional you may find that listening is very challenging. You may be distracted because you are thinking about another student or an upcoming conference, you may be so tired that you have difficulty following the details of what the speaker is saying, or you may be confused by the information being presented. Suggestions for improving your listening skills by overcoming such common listening barriers include these:

- *Want to listen.* Remember, there is no such thing as disinterested people—only disinterested listeners.

- *Demonstrate listening behavior.* Be quiet and alert, sit straight, lean slightly forward and make eye contact as appropriate, and let your face radiate interest.
- *React positively.* The only time a person generally likes to be interrupted is when being "applauded" by nods, smiles, or comments. Be generous with your applause.
- *Empathize with the other person.* Try to put yourself in the other's place so that you can see that point of view.
- *Ask questions.* When you do not understand, when you need further clarification, or when you want to show you are listening, ask questions, but avoid questions that could embarrass or criticize the other person.
- *Leave your emotions behind (if you can).* Try to push your worries, your fears, and your problems away. They may prevent you from listening.
- *Get rid of distractions.* Put down any papers, electronic devices, and other items that may divert your attention.
- *Get the main points.* Focus on the main ideas. Examples, stories, and so on are important, but they usually are not the main points.
- *React to ideas, not to the person.* Do not allow your reaction to the person to influence your interpretation of what is being said. Good ideas can come from people whose skills or personality do not match yours.
- *Do not argue mentally.* When trying to understand the other person, arguing mentally while you are listening sets up a barrier between the two of you.
- *Use the difference in rate.* You can listen faster than anyone can talk (500 words/minute versus 100–150 words/minute, respectively). Think back over what the speaker has said to remember and reflect on the message.

Another example of effective communication skill occurs when you encourage others to continue speaking through the use of nonverbal signals (Beebe, Beebe, & Redmond, 2014). For example, if you effectively make eye contact, occasionally nod, and sit so that you are leaning forward slightly, the colleague who is explaining to you her frustration about a student's apparent lack of motivation to complete in-class or homework assignments is likely to sense that you understand and want to know more. By communicating with your body, you convey important messages without interrupting the speaker.

A third example of effective communication skill concerns describing students, situations, and events using nonevaluative language. For example, as you discuss Francis, it might be tempting to say something like this: "He's a problem. His behavior is too disrespectful to describe, and the rude comments he makes under his breath—but audible enough for everyone to hear—constantly cause a commotion." Notice how these descriptors of Francis are actually evaluations. Instead, suppose you say, "During the past week, Francis has been sent out of class four times by three different teachers, twice for using profanity, once for a comment he made to another student that made her cry, and once for repeatedly refusing out loud to begin work assigned in class." Now you have described accurately what Francis is doing without making judgments about it. Nonevaluative language clearly is preferred.

One final example of effective communication concerns the use of questions that encourage the other person to continue speaking. What is the difference in the way these questions are posed?

- What are his characteristics as a reader?
- Does he read at grade level? Does he understand what he reads? Does he attempt to sound out words that he does not know?

In the first question, the person responding would be free to discuss any of the student's characteristics. The response might include reading level, comprehension, and word attack skills, but it also might include information about the

MyEdLab
Video Example 4.1

Video Example 4.1 provides a concise summary of keys to effective communication, which you can use in nearly any situation you may encounter as a professional educator. (https://www.youtube.com/watch?v=v4OmXaihEp0.com)

Did You Know?

One of the most effective communication skills you can learn to use is silence. During awkward or difficult interactions, allowing a few seconds of silence can help you to listen more carefully and learn more information by encouraging others to continue speaking and providing you with those seconds to think about your response.

Did You Know?

If you would like to learn more about communication skills, many free materials are available. For example, if you go to http://www.free-management-ebooks.com/, click on the "eBooks" tab, and then select the topic of communication skills, you will find a summary of skills that can assist you in refining your communication skills.

student's fluency and reading interests. In the second example, each question could be answered with a simple yes or no, and the person asking the questions would be largely controlling the types of answers that would likely be given. In your interactions with colleagues and parents, one goal usually is to learn from them. If that is the case for this situation, the first type of question generally would be preferred to the second.

Communication Habits to Avoid

As you learn communication strategies that foster strong collaboration, you also should know that some communication habits have the potential to undermine your working relationships with colleagues and parents. For example, if a teacher rushes up to you outside the school office, hands you a crumpled piece of paper that looks like it was supposed to be student work, exclaims, "Look what Shannon did to her assignment!," and looks at you expectantly, what would your response be? It might be tempting to say, "I'll take care of it," or "She's having a bad day; you can send her down to my room, and I'll talk to her," or "What would you like me to do?" All of these responses are quick fixes that indicate you are the person who can remedy the problem—even though you really do not know enough about what happened to respond. Whenever someone is explaining what happened, your reaction should be to seek additional information. In this example, a much more appropriate response would be, "What happened?" With that information, you could gain a better understanding of the situation.

Another example of ineffective communication is the use of questions that actually state your opinions. For example, Mr. Dewey and Ms. Hector are discussing Jamia's behavior plan. Mr. Dewey says, "You're not thinking of using a point system, are you?" Careful consideration of Mr. Dewey's words indicates that he is probably trying to communicate that he is not in favor of a point system, but he uses a question that clearly includes the answer that he wants to hear instead of directly stating his opinion. A far better interaction would have been this: "I'm opposed to the use of a point system with Jamia because. . . . What is your opinion?" If you find that your communication with others is peppered with questions ending with phrases such as "aren't you?," "can't you?," and "will you?," this might be a communication skill you could improve. You will be perceived as far more respectful and honest if you own your opinions and encourage others to express theirs.

One final example of ineffective communication concerns the use of *jargon*. As you learn about the field of special education and become accustomed to the acronyms and expressions associated with it, you may forget when you speak to others, especially parents, that not everyone has this familiarity. If you say to a parent, "Your child's WJ and CBA data indicate problems in phonemic awareness, and RTI interventions such as AR have not been successful," you have said many words but probably communicated little. To communicate effectively, you need to adjust the words you use depending on the person to whom you are speaking. Remember, too, that the use of understandable language contributes to parity, discussed earlier in this chapter.

It is hoped that these few examples of effective and ineffective communication have piqued your interest in learning more. As you listen to professionals in schools, you can sharpen your own skills by focusing on how they use words that exemplify essential characteristics of collaboration—parity, trust, and respect. You can also notice how some communication seems to interfere with the development of collaboration.

Interaction Processes

An interaction process is a set of steps that are followed using effective communication in order to accomplish the mutual goal of collaboration. A number of interaction processes are common in schools, but the one most often used is some form of interpersonal problem solving (Newell, 2010; Newell & Stutman, 2012). In this process, professionals meet as a group to systematically identify and resolve student, service delivery, or other professional problems. For example, when you meet with the occupational therapist to devise an alternative way for a student to grip a pencil or crayon, or when you confer with parents to determine how to encourage a student to arrive on time at school for his first-block class, you are problem solving. Likewise, when you meet with a schoolwide team to discuss how to help a struggling student who does not have a disability be more successful in the classroom, you engage in problem solving (e.g., Newton, Horner, Todd, Algozzine, & Algozzine, 2012). If you think about all the roles and responsibilities you may have in school, you can see that most of them can be considered from a problem-solving perspective; this makes it essential that you know and can carry out this key process.

Several authors have proposed interpersonal problem-solving models (e.g., Dettmer, Knackendoffel, & Thurston, 2013; Friend & Cook, 2017; Martin & Dowson, 2009). However, all problem-solving models generally incorporate six steps:

1. Create a climate for problem solving.
2. Identify the problem.
3. Generate alternatives.
4. Assess the potential solutions.
5. Implement the intervention.
6. Evaluate the intervention outcome.

Each step is discussed in the following sections.

Create a Climate for Problem Solving

When you problem solve with others, you need to ensure that all participants are committed to the process. One way to accomplish this is to communicate optimism about success. Thus, if at the beginning of a meeting, a team member says, "Here we go again. I'm getting frustrated that we can't seem to find a way to help Mel learn to communicate his needs," you have a signal that commitment may be wavering. Your response might be, "I've been thinking, though. With all of us here today to discuss this and with the new ideas we've been researching, I think we have lots of new options to explore." You are trying to help set a positive context for the problem-solving process.

Identify the Problem

This problem-solving step is deceptively simple. The problem may seem obvious to you, and so you may think that your view of it is shared by all participants. However, when you work with a group, each person may have a different perspective of the problem. At a team meeting, for example, a general education teacher may perceive that the problem is a student's poor organization skills, while the special education teacher may believe the problem is the other teacher's reluctance to give the student extra time to organize his materials. At the same time, the psychologist may believe that the student possibly has a short-term memory problem. Because the problems you will discuss with others in your collaborative interactions usually are complex and do not have single, clear answers, it is imperative to spend enough time to ensure that all participants share the same understanding of the problem (Brightman, 2005; Newton, Horner, Todd, Algozzine, & Algozzine, 2012; Tren & Boles, 2011).

The complexity of accurately identifying problems can be compounded when the participants represent multiple cultures (Scott & Wildman, 2015); in such instances, clear communication is critical. One effective way of identifying problems is to determine, as objectively as possible, what the current situation is; to describe what the ideal situation would be; and then to describe the problem as a gap between these two circumstances.

Generate Alternatives

In this step, participants brainstorm ideas for addressing the problem that they have mutually identified. They are careful to avoid evaluating each other's ideas (e.g., "I don't think that will work"), instead trying to encourage the expression of as many ideas as possible. Although some options will be discarded later as unrealistic, during this part of problem solving the intent is to generate as many ideas as possible because the quantity of ideas generated tends to increase the overall quality of the solution eventually implemented. Michelle and Kira, whom you met at the beginning of the chapter, often brainstorm about ways to help make algebra concepts more "alive" for the students in the class they co-teach.

Assess the Potential Solutions and Select One or More for Implementation

Once a lengthy list of ideas has been compiled, participants eliminate those that are not feasible (e.g., providing a paraeducator for every general education teacher in the school) and those that are unlikely to be implemented or are mostly fanciful (e.g., attaching a student who seems to be in constant motion to his seat with Velcro strips sewn to his pants). Each of the remaining ideas is considered carefully (e.g., creating a teacher study group on differentiating instruction; providing teachers with a brief workshop on the student's communication device). Advantages and drawbacks of implementing the idea are noted as well, with a focus on identifying solutions that will reduce the gap between the current and ideal situations. Based on this discussion, the number of ideas is gradually reduced to a few. These are assessed for practical matters, such as cost, time involved, and consistency with student needs, and then one or two ideas are selected for implementation. The final part of this step includes making detailed plans for implementing the one or two selected ideas.

Implement the Intervention

The most straightforward step of problem solving occurs after all the efforts of completing the preceding steps. The intervention or strategy is implemented, and data are gathered so that effectiveness can be measured. One question during implementation usually concerns time: For how many days or sessions should an intervention be implemented before its outcome is assessed?

Evaluate the Intervention Outcome and Decide Next Steps

After a specified period of time, those involved in problem solving meet to decide whether the solution has been effective. If the intervention has been successful, it may be terminated or continued in its current form. If some difficulties have occurred, it may be modified. If the participants decide that serious problems exist, other ideas are likely to be tried, or the group may decide that the problem needs to be reconceptualized. Perhaps, if a student's behavior plan has corrected the behavior, the plan may be phased out. Or the special education teacher may have data to suggest that the plan is effective, but he finds that it takes up too much time during instruction. In this case, the team might try to streamline the plan or eliminate some parts of it. Finally, if the teacher reports that little or no improvement in behavior is occurring, even after systemic implementation over a reasonable period of time, the team might decide to try a completely different intervention.

Additional Considerations for Problem Solving

You might have the impression that problem solving occurs primarily when students have academic or behavior needs. Although this is an important part of the problem solving in which you will engage, it is not *all* of the problem solving. For example, you might problem solve to increase fathers' involvement at your school (e.g., Mueller & Buckley, 2014) or to increase all staff members' knowledge about assistive technology (e.g., Judge, Floyd, & Jeffs, 2008). You might also engage in a different type of problem solving—one that concerns students but is far more prescriptive. This often occurs in RTI or MTSS procedures, when specific assessed student learning needs are addressed by a predetermined set of programs or interventions (e.g., Barrio, Lindo, Combes, & Hovey, 2015).

As you prepare to become a school professional, you will find that you also need skills for carrying out additional interaction processes that foster collaboration. For example, you will probably practice interviewing parents and conducting conferences with them. You also will discuss how to resolve the conflicts and address the resistance that sometimes occurs in school settings concerning students with disabilities and their services. Finally, you will offer feedback to colleagues and paraeducators. All of these activities are processes because they have steps, but often they are specialized applications of problem solving.

Finally, just as you can learn to monitor and improve your communication skills, you can analyze and refine your skills for effectively problem solving with colleagues and others. Both sets of skills are critical: If you have good communication skills but cannot help move an interaction from beginning to end through a series of steps, frustration may occur. Likewise, if you know the steps of problem solving and can implement them from beginning to end but without constructive communication, participants may see the process as directive, not collaborative.

Programs and Services

The next element of collaboration is to design programs and services that foster it. Although as an early career educator you may not have significant input into the design of programs and services, your understanding of them can help you make an informed judgment about the potential for collaboration. Later in this chapter you will learn about three services that rely heavily on collaboration: teaming, co-teaching, and consultation.

Supportive Context

The fifth and final element that must be in place for collaboration to flourish is a supportive context. As you gain experience as a professional, you may be able to influence the extent to which collaboration is valued in your school and resources are dedicated to fostering it. However, the professional who is most responsible for creating a school culture that encourages collaboration is the principal (Ketterlin-Geller, Baumer, & Lichon, 2015). The principal can ensure that professionals' schedules are arranged to permit them to meet occasionally. This individual also can serve as a facilitator for problem solving. Perhaps most important, the principal can explicitly make collaboration a standard for all the professionals in the school, providing incentives for those working together and directly addressing those who are uncomfortable with the idea. Finally, the principal often can arrange for professional development to help staff members become more aware of the expectations of collaboration and more skillful in implementing collaborative practices (Nichols & Sheffield, 2014).

When you put all the elements of collaboration together, you can see that with commitment and understanding, collaboration is a powerful tool for educating students with disabilities. However, you also begin to recognize that it involves far more than simply having conversations with colleagues (Lingo,

Here are several electronic collaboration tools you might find useful in your work as an early-career special educator:

- Google Apps for Education (https://www.google.com/edu/)

  Nearly all professionals use Google for some purpose. For collaboration, options include the following:

  - Calendar

    Professionals who co-teach or otherwise need to share information on a schedule can create a shared calendar. For co-teachers, lessons are loaded into the description of an appointment, ensuring that the special educator has critical information and attachments and providing a means for adjustments to be made, even when face-to-face planning is not available.

  - Docs

    Files in this app can be edited live and shared with colleagues. Those working together also can chat about their work from within the document they are creating.

  - Hangouts

    When collaboration includes several individuals who may not be in one location, Hangouts offers a free video chat for up to 10 people. It also includes

an option for sharing documents and uploading photos during the interaction.

- Trello (https://trello.com/)

  Trello is a free collaboration tool designed specifically to assist teams of any size to manage their work. Each project (e.g., a student being discussed by an RTI team) is assigned to a "board," and team members add "cards," which are any items related to the project (e.g., student data, a summary of a phone call with a parent). Participants can add comments within Trello, thus fostering efficient communication.

- Padlet (https://padlet.com/)

  Another collaboration tool is an online bulletin board, and Padlet is an example. In this app, you can create a private site for collaboration, invite others to join the group, post information, incorporate a calendar, and complete many other activities. Anything posted can be printed and exported.

  This list of collaboration apps is far from complete (e.g., check out Slack, Voxer, and Yammer, among others). The message is that collaboration is no longer dependent on face-to-face interactions, and many busy professionals are maximizing their effectiveness by collaborating in the cloud.

●─○─○─

Barton-Arwood, & Jolivette, 2011). As professionals increasingly rely on their partnerships with others, they also are exploring alternative ways to collaborate, especially those now widely available electronically, the topic of Technology Notes.

MyEdLab **Self-Check 4.2**

MyEdLab **Application Exercise 4.2:** Successful Collaboration

Applications of Collaboration for Schools

Informal opportunities for collaboration occur in schools every day. An occupational therapist and a special educator discuss a problem and devise an accommodation for a student who is having trouble grasping small items. Five teachers explore the possibility of creating a page on the school website to highlight the service activities of all the students in the school. The examples are endless. However, formal structures that rely on collaboration also exist. The most common of these include teams, co-teaching, and consultation (Kauffman & Badar, 2014).

Teams

You learned in Chapter 2 that teams play an important role in special education. Through a prereferral, response-to-intervention, or multi-tiered systems of support process, a team designs interventions to help students succeed before considering whether special education services are needed (e.g., Nellis, 2012). A team completes the assessment of a student who might have a disability, determines eligibility for special education, prepares the IEP, and monitors the student's progress (Friend & Cook, 2017). Now it is time to think in more detail about the team itself and your role as a collaborative team member.

Understanding Team Concepts

A team in education consists of two or more interdependent individuals with unique skills and perspectives who interact directly to achieve their mutual goal of providing students with effective educational programs and services (Dettmer, Knackendoffel, & Thurston, 2013). You can see that some of the characteristics of collaboration are embedded in this team definition, including the existence of mutual goals. However, as the definition suggests, a team is much more.

For example, team members should clearly identify themselves as being part of a team. That is, they should have a sense of affiliation with the intervention assistance team, response to intervention team, or the IEP team, instead of feeling like a guest or as if the team's business is not truly their own. Team members also abide by a set of formal and informal rules. An example of the former is the procedure the team follows in discussing students. An example of the latter is the group's collective understanding about whether team meetings begin on time or whether being 10 minutes late is acceptable.

Team members also recognize that the success of their work is related directly to the success of the work of all team members (Johnson & Johnson, 2009). For example, after an IEP meeting in which Jay's need for instruction related to vocabulary development was carefully addressed, the special education teacher knows he can work with the speech-language pathologist, the paraeducator, and the parents to achieve the goals the team wrote. In addition, team members value their differences; they understand that the professional and personal diversity that they bring to the team enhances the opportunity for collaborative and creative problem solving.

Team Effectiveness

Think about the teams of which you have been a member through sports, community groups, or school. What made your team effective? For an educational team, effectiveness depends on several factors. First, team effectiveness can be judged by the quality of the outcomes the team produces (Nellis, 2012). By recommending strong, research-based interventions, was the team successful in reducing the number of students who needed to be referred for full assessment and possible special education placement? In how many instances was the team successful in resolving specific student problems in inclusive classrooms?

A second component of team effectiveness is the clarity of team goals (Erickson, Noonan, Carter, McGurn, & Purifoy, 2015; Fulk, 2011). If all members understand the goals of the group, the team's work will be efficient and student needs will be met; if this does not occur, much valuable time may be spent clarifying goals or resolving issues that arise because of the resulting confusion.

A third component concerns team members themselves: On effective teams, members feel that their own needs are being met; that is, even if teamwork is challenging, they believe that its benefits outweigh its costs (Friend & Cook, 2017). However, team members also must be accountable. They need to understand that their contributions, such as getting specific tasks finished on time, affect all team members and that the quality of their work may determine the quality of the team.

Teams—whether in education or in other professions—are most effective when they have strong goals, members committed to the team's purpose, clear procedures, and measurable outcomes.

Finally, teams are effective when members monitor their own behaviors, offering input but not monopolizing conversations, helping the process of teaming by making suggestions that can resolve emerging conflicts and encouraging quiet members to offer their comments. In other words, team effectiveness depends as much on the extent to which each member helps the team accomplish its business as it does on the expertise that each member brings to the teaming situation (Dettmer et al., 2013). How might this element of team effectiveness affect the outcome of Derek's IEP team meeting for Robert?

As an early-career professional, you might form a collaborative partnership with a *mentor*, whose responsibilities include answering questions, offering suggestions, and providing a supportive connection (Ingersoll & Strong, 2011).

Special Education Teams

In Chapter 2, you were introduced to the *multidisciplinary team,* the set of individuals who participate in the special education decision-making process. These professionals tend to coordinate their efforts but keep separate the responsibilities traditionally associated with their roles. This type of team is the minimum acceptable level of partnership for special education procedures, but it is not the only type of special education team (Friend & Cook, 2017). In some schools, team members communicate more and share more discussion about services to be offered, but each professional still delivers services separately. This type of team is referred to as *interdisciplinary*. In a few schools, an even more blended type of teaming is found: On a *transdisciplinary team,* members share their information, skills, and service delivery. For example, a general education teacher may implement strategies recommended by the speech-language pathologist. The special education teacher may work on cutting and buttoning skills based on consultation with the occupational therapist. The speech-language pathologist may incorporate a reading goal from the special education teacher into her work with a student. Transdisciplinary teams are the most collaborative special education teams, but they also are the most difficult type of team to create and sustain.

Co-Teaching

The rise in inclusive practices has brought about the need for service delivery options that allow students with disabilities to access their education with their peers in general education while also receiving specialized services (Friend, 2015/2016). One response to this need has been the development of co-teaching (Friend, 2014; Honigsfeld & Dove, 2010), the teaching approach that Michelle and Kira, whom you met at the beginning of this chapter, are participating in. Co-teaching is a service delivery model in which two educators—one typically a general education teacher and one a special education teacher or other specialist—combine their expertise to jointly teach a heterogeneous group of students, some of whom have disabilities or other special needs, in a single classroom for part or

SPEAKING FROM EXPERIENCE

IT'S ALL ABOUT THE KIDS

Steven Everage is a traditionally prepared teacher who majored in English and history after serving as a Marine Corps instructor. Stephanie Riley originally wanted to be a school psychologist. However, after completing her undergraduate degree in psychology and working as a teaching assistant, she decided she preferred working in the classroom and completed her master's degree in special education. Mr. Everage and Ms. Riley have worked together for two years, and most recently co-taught two sections of sixth-grade reading as well as two sections of sixth-grade language arts.

Steve: When we began, I was a brand new teacher. I wasn't supposed to have any co-taught classes, and at 10:30 the night before school started, my schedule was suddenly changed. That's when I found out I was co-teaching with Stephanie.

Stephanie: I was doing hall duty on the first day of school, and the counselor came up to me and said, "You're not going to co-teach with [Mr. Jones]; you're co-teaching with the new guy, Everage." And I said, "WHAT??!!!!"

Steve: So neither of us knew before school started that we were working together. And I had never had any experience with working with anyone else. In college, that was not something that was ever stressed. But I have a sister who is a teacher, and I called her, and she gave me a rundown on what to do and what not to do! She saved me.

Stephanie: I don't think I had ever even talked to Mr. Everage before we began that first day. So at the beginning, it was a little awkward.

Steve: But it didn't take long to get things going in the right direction.

Stephanie: For introductions, Steve said, "This is Ms. Riley and I'm Mr. Everage, and WE are your teachers!"

Steve: I do need to thank my sister for that one. She told me it was important for the kids to know right away that we were both teachers. And I found out quickly that we had similar personalities. We both have strong opinions, but we learned that no matter how we sometimes differed in our opinions, the kids always come first.

Stephanie: Yes, our philosophies of teaching are similar. It's all about the kids—all our decisions, all the instructional strategies we try, even taking a few extra students into our co-taught classes. We make mutual decisions, but that is our focus.

Steve: We really focus on differentiation. This year we have had reading levels that range from first grade to 10th grade. We really struggled at first to figure out how to wrap our heads around what we needed to do, and then we decided to differentiate everything. We use a lot of stations so the kids can work on the standards they need. That also gives us the opportunity to have flexible groups going on as well. We take each individual child and focus our teaching on what that child needs.

Stephanie: We really emphasize data. We used the high-stakes data from achievement testing, but we also do a lot of preassessing to decide how to teach. Looking at where students are to see what they need next; we don't treat the class as a single group.

Steve: Our students did well. Forty-nine percent of all the students in our school who scored proficient on the sixth-grade language arts test came from our classrooms. And our students' growth overall was nearly twice what was average for all the students in our school. We had some kids whose growth was five or six times what is average. We had a *really* good year.

Stephanie: Advice for teachers? Be open and flexible, and don't be selfish! I've had horrible co-teaching experiences where general education teachers wouldn't share . . . space, kids, control. You have to open yourself up to working together. Oh, my gosh, it helps tremendously.

Steve: To get the results you want, you truly have to be a team. It's both of us, not one person. You sometimes have to put your personal feelings aside and make sure you're putting the kids first. You have to learn to not worry, not be embarrassed about making mistakes; you have to rely on each other.

Stephanie: And it's okay to disagree. However, we have to go back and check on our focus, and if we stay focused on kids, it always comes out right.

Steve and Stephanie: (Finishing each other's words and laughing) We call each other our work wife and work husband! In many ways, that's really true. And the biggest challenge we face? It's having a substitute teacher because it doesn't work the same way.

Steve: But if that's our biggest problem, we think we're doing okay.

Source: Courtesy of Steven Everage and Stephanie Riley

FIGURE 4.1   Co-Teaching Approaches

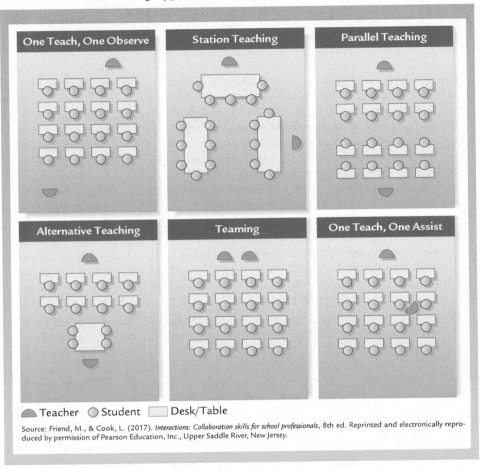

Source: Friend, M., & Cook, L. (2017). *Interactions: Collaboration skills for school professionals*, 8th ed. Reprinted and electronically reproduced by permission of Pearson Education, Inc., Upper Saddle River, New Jersey.

all of the school day. In Speaking from Experience, Steve and Stephanie discuss their co-teaching experience.

For co-teaching to be effective, the professionals must maximize the benefit of having two individuals with different types of expertise working together (Dieker & Rodriguez, 2013; Murawski, 2015). They accomplish this first through clear communication concerning their instructional philosophies, their own strengths and weaknesses as educators, their expectations for themselves and each other, and their preparation for assuming co-teaching roles. Then they decide how to best use their talents in the classroom. Some of the approaches co-teachers might use include (a) one teach, one observe; (b) parallel teaching; (c) station teaching; (d) alternative teaching; (e) teaming; and (f) one teach, one assist (Friend, 2014). Each approach is discussed in the following sections and depicted visually in Figure 4.1.

One Teach, One Observe

In the one teach, one observe co-teaching approach, one educator manages the instruction of the entire group of students while the other gathers data on one student, a small group of students, or even the entire class. Either teacher may observe, but often special educators know more ways to collect data on students and may need to share that skill with general education teachers. If professionals notice that a student seems to be having a great deal of difficulty transitioning from one activity to the next, they might observe so that they can address this problem. Or they might observe how students approach independent work tasks or for how long they work before becoming distracted. Professionals might also gather data related to a student about whom they are concerned in preparation for an intervention assistance team meeting.

Parallel Teaching

In some instances, two professionals may decide to split a group of students in half and simultaneously provide the same instruction. This would be appropriate if both teachers were highly qualified in the subject area, or this might occur during discussion so that all students would have more opportunities to participate. In an elementary math class, this approach might be used when some students can work without manipulatives for counting but other students still need them. With middle or high school students, this approach would be helpful for review sessions. With both teachers reviewing, they could more readily address student questions and monitor their mastery of the standards being taught. One consideration in using this approach is noise: If two teachers are conducting the same lesson simultaneously in a small classroom, the noise level can become too high. If this is a problem, the teachers might try seating the students on the floor on opposite sides of the classroom or, for middle or high school students, having the student groups face away from each other.

Station Teaching

In *station teaching*, the teachers divide instruction into two, three, or even more nonsequential components, and each is addressed in a separate area of the room. Each student participates in each station. For example, in an algebra class, one group of students might be working with the general education teacher as she introduces systems of equations, the second group might be working with the special educator to review last week's information, and the third group might be working on reports about famous mathematicians. All students would receive instruction at all three stations. In an elementary classroom, one group might work with the speech-language pathologist on vocabulary and sentences, the second group might discuss the current story with a general education teacher, and the third group might work independently on story writing. With younger students or students who have difficulty working independently, there might only be two stations, each with a teacher. Halfway through the instruction, the groups would simply switch. In a secondary setting, particularly if class periods are relatively short (e.g., 45 to 50 minutes), a station might last the entire class period. In that case, the lesson plan would have to span two or three days in order for all students to access all the stations.

Alternative Teaching

In some situations, pulling a small group of students to the side of the room for instruction is an appropriate strategy. When do you think this might occur? If you immediately think about this as a way of providing remedial instruction to students who did not understand a previous lesson, you are thinking like many teachers, and alternative teaching certainly may be implemented for this purpose. But for what else might you use this approach? What about *preteaching*—that is, helping students learn vocabulary words before they are introduced in large-group instruction? What about enrichment? What about teaching several students key concepts that they missed because they were absent? Many professionals appropriately worry that too much alternative teaching, especially for a remedial purpose, can give the impression of having a separate special education class operating within the walls of the general education classroom. This can be stigmatizing for students. However, if the purpose of the group varies and if the teachers take turns working with the small group, this can be a powerful use of two professionals in the classroom.

Teaming

When teachers have built a strong collaborative relationship and their styles are complementary, they may decide to use a teaming approach to co-teaching—fluidly sharing the instructional responsibilities of the entire student group:

- One teacher delivers a brief lecture while the other teacher models note-taking skills for students using the Smartboard™.
- One teacher explains a math procedure, and the other teacher interjects questions to ensure that all students understand.
- Two teachers decide to explain latitude and longitude to their students by coming dressed to illustrate the difference: One wears a shirt with vertical stripes, and the other wears a shirt with horizontal stripes.

Some teachers use this approach extensively and find it energizing. However, for some teachers, the informality and the spontaneity of this approach do not match their styles. Teaming has the potential to capture students' attention and so can be an effective way to co-teach, but because the opportunities for dividing students into a variety of groups is powerful, teaming generally should be combined with other approaches, not used exclusively.

One Teach, One Assist

In this co-teaching approach, one teacher manages the instruction of the entire student group while the other circulates through the classroom, providing assistance. For example, assisting is an accepted co-teaching practice when one teacher is monitoring to ensure all students are completing a math equation correctly. However, assisting has significant drawbacks as well. If teachers, especially special educators, spend too much time assisting, they probably will be bored and feel more like paraeducators than teachers. Also, one teacher assisting students may be a significant auditory or visual distraction for some students. Finally, if either teacher assists a great deal, some students will come to rely heavily on this always-available source of help instead of learning to work independently. This co-teaching model has been criticized for being used too frequently and with too little result, especially in secondary classrooms (e.g., Dieker & Rodriguez, 2013).

Selecting a Co-Teaching Approach

When teachers are new to co-teaching, they sometimes decide that they should select just one approach, avoiding use of the others. Generally, that is not recommended practice. Use of the co-teaching approaches should be based on several key factors: (a) the needs of the students, (b) factors related to teachers, (c) the specific curricular material to be taught, and (d) practical matters such as the classroom's physical space and the availability of shared planning time.

Student need is the primary consideration in deciding how to co-teach. If a new concept is being introduced, teachers may decide to create heterogeneous groups of students and to divide the content into three parts, implementing station teaching. Alternatively, they may decide to use parallel teaching so that all students work with a teacher but in smaller groups than would otherwise be possible. If a few students need assistance in learning vocabulary, alternative teaching might be preferred. And, of course, multiple approaches could be used in a single lesson, with the vocabulary introduced to some students as others check homework (i.e., alternative teaching) and then all students grouped for stations or parallel teaching.

Teachers' expertise and familiarity comprise the second factor affecting co-teaching approaches. Teachers new to co-teaching and relative strangers to each other might decide to employ station teaching or parallel teaching, as long as the approach is appropriate for meeting student needs. As co-teachers gain experience and deepen their professional relationship, teaming may be preferred for some instruction. And when co-teachers have reached maturity in their shared classroom, they may change approaches midlesson if they decide it would facilitate student learning. For example, they might decide to change from teaming to stations if part of the instruction is confusing to some students. Or they might decide to have some students begin a project while they meet with small groups (i.e., alternative teaching) to review critical concepts.

The third consideration in selecting a co-teaching approach is the planned instruction. If teachers wish to determine which students understand background information, one might ask questions while the other observes and records student responses (i.e., one teach, one observe). If a novel being introduced involves the introduction of vocabulary, discussion of literary devices, and provision of the historical context for the story, stations might be appropriate. When a lesson involves points of view related to a war or a controversial science issue, parallel teaching followed by student discussion or debate could be effective.

The final factor that influences the selection of a co-teaching approach relates to several practical matters. For example, if shared planning time is limited, co-teachers may try to identify patterns that can make them more efficient. To prepare for a Friday quiz, co-teachers may use parallel teaching every Thursday because they usually spend much of the class time reviewing critical concepts taught earlier in the week. If classroom space is very limited, co-teachers may decide that they can implement station teaching, but only if one group works on clipboards while seated on the floor. Such practical matters do not prevent co-teaching; instead, they are opportunities to use problem-solving skills.

Generally, then, which co-teaching approach or approaches to implement in a single lesson is a decision that professionals make—and sometime change—to best accomplish their goals. They are flexible in their lessons but relentless in their efforts to improve student outcomes.

Other Co-Teaching Considerations

Co-teaching is a particularly sophisticated type of collaboration that some have likened to a professional marriage. Just as in a personal relationship, great care

Video Example
from
YouTube

MyEdLab
Video Example 4.2

As you consider how to implement co-teaching approaches, you probably are realizing that the possibilities for co-teaching are endless. Video Example 4.2 gives you a glimpse into what is possible when two teachers blend their expertise to educate a diverse group of students. (https://www.youtube.com/watch?v=v8ple6CZX6PM.com)

INSTRUCTION IN **ACTION**

Getting Off to a Great Start with Co-Teaching

The following are some questions that effective co-teachers address to ensure the establishment of a strong partnership:

- Have we set up the classroom to communicate that it has two teachers—for example, two teachers' chairs and both names on the board?
- How have we discussed each person's perception of what co-teaching should look like and what the roles and responsibilities of each person should be?
- How have we made partnership integral to classroom materials—for example, both names on the course

syllabus and both names on the newsletter that is sent home to parents?
- What will we do on the first day so that students understand we have parity in the classroom—for example, how will we introduce yourselves and who will talk about which of the key first-day topics such as classroom expectations and procedures?
- How will we divide students on the first day so that they observe both of us engaged in teaching?

must be taken in a professional relationship to attend to details, to ensure that communication is clear and direct, to address problems when they are minor so they do not become significant, and to maximize the talents of both participants (Friend, 2014; Seglem & VanZant, 2010). Further, if one professional is a novice and the other is experienced, the co-teachers may have to be especially careful that they build a partnership that is satisfactory to both. In Instruction in Action, you will find a set of questions co-teachers can use to get their partnership started on a strong and collaborative foundation.

Consultation

A third application of collaboration occurs in consultation, "a voluntary process in which one professional assists another to address a problem concerning a third party," often a student (Friend & Cook, 2017, p. 187). In many ways, consultation is a specialized form of problem solving (Kampwirth & Powers, 2016).

In a consulting process, the consultant meets with the other professional, first working to establish a positive relationship. Across several meetings, they jointly identify the problem, brainstorm ideas for addressing it, and select options that seem likely to succeed. The professional receiving consultation support then implements the intervention and reports on its success. Together, the consultant and the other professional decide whether they need to continue to meet, either to revise the intervention or to continue monitoring its effectiveness. In some cases, the consulting relationship ends when the problem is resolved. However, if the consultant has ongoing responsibility for the student in question, consultation might occur for the entire school year. This might occur when specialists assist special educators and general educators to effectively instruct students with visual impairments or hearing loss. As you can see, the overall intent of consulting is to help a professional encountering a problem—often a teacher working to address a student need.

This example of an interaction between behavior specialist Mr. Corlone and beginning special educator Ms. Mitchell concerning Randy, a middle school student with autism, illustrates the important contribution of consultation to collaborative school services.

Mr. C: I've been looking forward to this second meeting so that we could really start to get at the dilemmas you're seeing for Randy in school.

Ms. M: Me, too. It was very helpful last time we met to discuss some of the details about Randy's background and how we would work together, but I'm anxious to address the problems.

Mr. C: Let's do it. What are the specific concerns that you have about Randy?

Ms. M: I don't even know where to begin. At the beginning of the year, Randy had a very difficult time adjusting to this school. He spent a great deal of time rocking and crying, and he refused to do almost everything. We got past all that, but now I see some of those same behaviors returning.

Mr. C: How so?

Ms. M: Yesterday was a good example. It was time for the students to stop their work to leave for lunch. I had used my usual strategy with Randy of alerting him ahead of time that a change was coming and of talking to him about the need to begin to put away his materials. He seemed fine at first, but suddenly he swept everything off his desk and began to rock and cry. I have no clue why.

Mr. C: What did you do?

Ms. M: I gave him a little time to calm down and then started over again. The second time the problems did not occur.

Mr. C: What ideas have you had about what might be happening?

Ms. M: ...

As you think about this interaction, consider multiple dimensions of collaboration. For example, at what point in the problem-solving process is this interaction occurring? What part of the consulting process has already been completed? How do you know? What should happen next in this conversation? If you were advising these professionals about effective communication skills, what would you say to help them enhance this consultative discussion?

For some school professionals, consultation is a typical and significant role responsibility (Dougherty, 2014; Erford, 2015; Rosenfield, 2012). For example, school psychologists and counselors often have time set aside in their schedules to meet with both special education and general education teachers to discuss how to meet student needs in the classroom. They might work directly with the student on occasion, but they rely on the teachers to implement most of the strategies and to monitor student responses. Special education teachers might or might not have consulting responsibilities. In New York and some other states, certain special educators are assigned to be *consultant teachers*. If you are a consulting teacher or in a similar role (e.g., an autism specialist), you might model effective ways of working with certain students, meet with teachers to discuss student issues, and observe in classrooms to determine student needs and progress. If you work as a resource or self-contained teacher, particularly in an inclusive school, you might receive or offer consultation, and it may be formal or informal, as is true for Makayla, whom you were introduced to at the beginning of this chapter (e.g., McKenney & Bristol, 2015; Meyers, Tobin, Huber, Conway, & Shelvin, 2015).

Have you noticed that all the examples of consultation in this section imply that the consultant works with other professionals but not with the student? Your observation is correct (Kampwirth & Powers, 2016). Consultation is an indirect service, not a direct service. Consultation is an effective means for professionals to collaborate when the student in question needs only minimal support. It also may be used as a transition strategy for a student who no longer needs intensive special education services. In some cases, as with a student with physical or sensory disabilities, consultation provides an opportunity for teachers to obtain the technical information they need, such as how to use a specialized computer keyboard or a communication device.

Consultation sometimes is appropriate for other situations, too. For example, a consultant might assist a classroom teacher regarding a student at risk to decide if the student should be referred to the response-to-intervention team. Consultation also can have a positive impact on the skills of the professionals who benefit from it. For example, when they learn a new strategy for teaching a student with a behavior disability, they might find that they can use it with other students as well.

As programs and services for students with disabilities have become more inclusive and as high standards and accountability have become central to education, collaborative options such as teaming, co-teaching, and consulting continue to expand (Cook & Friend, 2010; Thomson, 2013). However, these formal applications of collaboration can reach their potential for meeting student needs only if you and your colleagues understand how to develop them and carefully continue to refine them.

Did You Know?

The examples outlined in this chapter are just a sample of the types of collaboration you may experience as an educator. For example, as an early-career professional, you might form a collaborative partnership with a *mentor*, whose responsibilities include answering questions, offering suggestions, and providing a supportive connection (Ingersoll & Strong, 2012).

MyEdLab **Self-Check 4.3**

MyEdLab **Application Exercise 4.3:** Models of Co-Teaching

Collaboration with Parents and Families

You already are becoming aware that parents and families play a critical role in special education procedures, planning, and programming. The message that accompanies this awareness is that your job includes understanding parents and families in order to collaborate with them (Collier, Keefe, & Hirrel, 2015; Haro & Olivos, 2014). However, you also have explored in Chapter 3 some of the dilemmas of working with these families. With increasing diversity in U.S. society, it is risky to assume that you can truly understand families simply because you are a caring educator (Luet, 2015). Knowledge and skills must be a companion to your care.

Families and Collaboration

Many barriers to professional–parent collaboration can arise (Reiman, Beck, Coppola, & Engiles, 2010). Following are some of the most common (Friend & Bursuck, 2015):

- Parents may have had negative experiences when they were in school, so they may be reluctant to come to school and are uncomfortable interacting with school professionals.
- Some parents who live in poverty or who have come to the United States from another country may view educators as authority figures to whom they must listen. As a result, they may not share information or offer their point of view.
- Parents may encounter logistical problems in getting to school for meetings and conferences. Some lack transportation, some need child care, and some cannot leave their jobs to come to school during the times educators usually wish to meet.
- Some parents are confronted with language barriers in schools and misunderstandings that arise from cultural differences.
- Schools may not make parents feel welcome. Educators may ask them to wait for a lengthy period of time for a meeting to begin or may schedule meetings at inconvenient times, and they may inadvertently ignore or minimize concerns that parents raise concerning their children.
- If parents' beliefs or actions are in conflict with those of school professionals, some educators conclude the parents are not good parents or that they do not care, and so they may make only a minimal effort to interact with them.
- Some educators are intimidated by parents, particularly those who are knowledgeable about special education and who insist on particular programs or services or who have obtained legal counsel. As a result, they may limit communication with these parents.
- Communication from school to home may focus on negatives about the child rather than on balancing those negatives with positives.
- Professionals and parents may develop stereotypes of each other, and they may act on those stereotypes instead of on objective information.

The collaboration that occurs between family members and professionals can be instrumental in helping children to achieve their potential.

When you consider parent interactions with school professionals, would you add other items to the preceding list? Researchers have explored the participation of parents and students in special education procedures, including IEP meetings (Hernandez, Harry, Newman, & Cameto, 2008; Wagner, Newman, Cameto, Javitz, & Valdes, 2012). They have found that the extent to which parents are involved in their children's services and the extent to which they are satisfied with those services are related to factors such as these:

- *Socioeconomic status.* Families from the lowest income group generally have the least involvement in their children's services but a high degree of satisfaction with them.
- *Race/ethnicity and primary language.* Although data related to race and ethnicity can be difficult to interpret, parents whose primary language is English are more likely to be involved and more likely to indicate their children are not getting required services.
- *Student grade level.* Parents of children in elementary school are more involved and more positive about services than parents of children in upper grades.
- *Nature and severity of the disability.* Parents of children with significant disabilities are more involved in their children's services than other parents, but they also are less satisfied than other parents with those services.

Taken together, all of these factors should lead you to the conclusion that your responsibilities for working with parents must receive considerable attention, or positive results are unlikely.

Building Partnerships with Parents

If so many challenges exist, what can you do to encourage collaboration with parents? The first step is working to understand families' perspectives, and these perspectives may vary depending on how recently the child was identified as having a disability and parents' understanding of that information. In one study, researchers found that parents experienced three general phases related to their child's disability diagnosis (Miron, 2012):

- A reaction phase that included feelings of concern, confusion, and/or helplessness, which included the development of understanding based on key positive or negative interactions with professionals
- A transition phase in which parents grew in acceptance of and accommodation to their child's special needs and began advocating for their child
- An integration phase in which self-education, a range of supports, and relationships with service providers led to parents' assimilation of their changed lives because of having a child with a disability

How could the words you use and the beliefs you convey affect both parents' understanding of their child's special needs and their perception of educators' commitment to meeting those needs at each of these phases?

In addition to understanding parents' perspectives as just described, it also may be essential to recognize that collaboration is not the goal in all parent interactions. Although some parents will embrace collaboration and be actively involved in working closely with you on behalf of their child, for others the first step might be to create conditions that encourage meaningful parent *participation* (Kasahara & Turnbull, 2005). This might be accomplished by providing parents with information about what will occur at a team meeting prior to the meeting date. It could also involve having one person from the school meet separately with the parents prior to a team meeting so that the parents are prepared for what will occur in the larger group meeting. For a few parents, participation might be enhanced by making sure that supplies such as paper, pencils, and folders are available for parents' use; by providing them with samples of their child's work; or by offering to assist with transportation.

Did You Know?

Although family engagement is a strong indicator of school success for immigrant students, their parents may be unfamiliar with the expectation of school involvement, uncomfortable in school settings, or constrained by child care or work responsibilities (Fontil & Petrakos, 2015; Suarez-Orozco, Onaga, & de Lardemelle, 2010).

To foster participation that might lead to collaboration, you also need to address cultural differences (e.g., Gleason & Gerzon, 2014). Lynch (2011) suggests that educators remember three points: (a) Culture is dynamic, and so what you may know of a culture from prior experience may not be valid today; (b) although culture influences people, so do other factors, such as socioeconomic status; and (c) no cultural group is homogeneous. These statements, particularly in the context of the information presented in Chapter 3, can serve as reminders that as you strive to understand a certain culture and learn to respect its norms, you should avoid treating all members of that cultural group as though they are alike. Developing cultural sensitivity truly is learning to balance knowledge with openness.

Many other options exist for encouraging parent participation. As noted in the section on communication skills, you should avoid using jargon when interacting with parents. You also can help by asking parents questions about which they may have a unique and valuable perspective. For example, you might ask, "When you ask your child about his favorite part of the school day, what does he say?" or "What are the most important goals that you have for your child for the upcoming school year and after graduation?" When you ask questions that honestly invite parental input, participation is more likely to occur.

Ultimately, perhaps the most important way to increase parent participation is to recognize that unless you have a child with needs very similar to those of the parents with whom you are interacting, you cannot understand those parents' perspective, and you should not expect that you ever will, not in any complete sense. If you can remind yourself of this fact, you will probably remember that listening to the parents' point of view is the first step in fostering parent collaboration (Fishman & Nickerson, 2015).

Issues Related to Collaboration in Special Education

Although collaboration is integral to the roles of professional educators, many questions remain concerning its implementation and impact. Issues related to collaboration include the extent of its application in special educators' work with paraeducators, the limits to collaboration created by lack of time to meet with colleagues, and the research base for measuring collaboration's effectiveness.

Working with Paraeducators

Federal special education law acknowledges the importance of paraeducators to the education of students with special needs and notes that they should be trained to carry out their jobs (Webster, Blatchford, & Russell, 2013). In Chapter 2, the roles and responsibilities of paraprofessionals were outlined. However, another dimension in any discussion of paraeducators is the nature of their working relationships with professionals and parents and the place of collaboration in professionals' work with paraeducators (Stephens & Woodbury, 2011).

If you consider the responsibilities that paraprofessionals have in special education and general education settings, what would you say should be the relationship between them and the teachers and other specialists with whom they work? Is collaboration appropriate? The answer to this question is somewhat complicated.

Paraeducators are valuable members of the instructional teams for students, but these staff members do not have the same professional status or job responsibilities as the professionals (Giangreco, Suter, & Doyle, 2010). Even if paraeducators have teaching licensure, they are employed in a nonteaching capacity at a much lower pay scale and generally have responsibilities much more limited than those of professionals. And so, in some cases, collaboration is appropriate, but in others, it is not. For example, occasionally a paraeducator will refuse to carry out the directions of the teacher, possibly by "forgetting" them or asserting that they are not best for the student. Once in a while, a paraeducator will contact the parents and discuss school matters even though the teacher has specifically and appropriately requested that this not occur. How would you handle situations such as these? If the paraeducator is assigned to work under your direction, you are responsible for providing day-to-day supervision for that individual (Ashbaker & Morgan, 2012). This implies that you appropriately assign work to the paraeducator, meet to discuss plans and problems, and ask for input from others who also observe the paraeducator with students (Jones, Ratcliff, Sheehan, & Hunt, 2012). If a serious problem arises, you are faced with a supervisory matter, not a collaborative one, and you are obligated to meet with the paraeducator to discuss it. Because your principal or another administrator probably has the formal supervision responsibility (i.e., the authority to require changed behavior or to sanction the individual), if you cannot satisfactorily resolve the situation, you should involve your administrator, who will likely request that you keep a record of any negative incidents that occur.

Is it possible for special educators to collaborate with paraeducators? Yes, and most paraeducators are wonderful, caring, and skilled individuals who are true advocates for students and who recognize that teachers and other professionals direct their work (Stockall, 2014). Your collaboration with them is somewhat similar to the possibility of your principal collaborating with you. Just as your principal may truly collaborate during a meeting at which a student crisis is discussed, you understand that this does not mean that you and your principal should share all decision making and that your input always will be sought. The same notion holds for paraeducators. You can and should collaborate with your paraeducator as appropriate for the situation, such as to coordinate snack time or to discuss accommodations that might help a student during world history class. However, at times you will explain to the paraeducator what needs to be done, and it is appropriate to expect the paraeducator to follow your directions— possibly to use a specific computer program to help a student with word attack skills or to position a student in a particular way that encourages better posture and social interactions with other students.

Many professionals have strong working relationships with their paraprofessionals, and together they function as an instructional team (Theoharis & Causton, 2014). If you communicate clearly with paraprofessionals about their work, invite their feedback and insights, and resolve differences as soon as they arise, you will find that the balance of appropriate supervision and collaboration is easily achieved.

Time for Collaboration

If you ask any experienced school professional to name the greatest barrier to effective collaboration in schools, you will undoubtedly be told that it is lack of time for shared planning (Hunter, Jasper, & Williamson, 2014; Ploessi Rock, Schoenfeld, & Blanks, 2010). Makayla, the special educator introduced at the beginning of this chapter, knows this challenge well. Several issues are involved. First, activities carried out collaboratively take longer to plan and evaluate than activities carried out by individuals. If three people meet to discuss Colby's problems at his community-based job, it may require an hour to discuss and address. If you are working on the problem yourself, you will think about it as you do other tasks, decide on a course of action, and carry it out much more quickly.

The second aspect of time concerns the need for shared time (Friend, 2014; Murawski, 2012). In most schools, special education teachers, general education teachers, and other professionals all have planning time. The dilemma is that they do not have time *together* to discuss shared students. Thus, teams need adequate time to meet when all members can be present and focused on their tasks; co-teachers need opportunities to discuss lessons they have delivered, to plan future lessons, and to assess student progress; and consultants need time to interact with the other professionals. Too often, this time is found during lunch breaks, before or after school, or during evenings and weekends. Many dedicated educators contribute a significant amount of time beyond the school day in order to complete their work, but if they are expected to collaborate, at least some common planning time should be made available during the school day.

A third dilemma related to time concerns the willingness of each participant to collaborate (Friend, 2014). Even when shared planning time is scheduled, in some schools it is not used as intended. A special educator may decide that calling parents and completing IEPs have priority over planning with a general education colleague for the upcoming week. A general education teacher may excuse himself from a planning meeting after just a few minutes, noting that grades are due and no other time is available to finish calculating them. Although all professionals will sometimes find that there are just not enough hours in the day and that they have to make difficult decisions about how to use the available time, if collaboration is not a priority, its benefits are unlikely to be seen.

A final time issue concerns a chronic problem for busy educators: running late to arrive at planned times for collaboration. As you walk down the hall or across the courtyard for your meeting, what should you say to the colleague you encounter who says, "I'm so glad I ran into you. I really need to discuss something with you. It'll only take a couple of minutes." If a true emergency exists, of course you will send word to your waiting colleagues and attend to this matter. However, if you stop each time someone asks for your input, you might damage your collaborative relationships with those waiting for you. Your chronic tardiness could be seen as a lack of interest in and respect for the shared work.

Are you wondering how professionals in schools find time for collaboration? You will find several suggestions in the Professional Edge. Which seem feasible to you? As you talk to practicing teachers and other professionals, explore other ideas for creating time for collaboration by asking them how they manage this chronic challenge.

The Effectiveness of Collaboration

As you learned earlier in this chapter, collaboration does not have value unless it is a vehicle for achieving goals for students and their families (Cook & Friend, 2010). Thus, it is always a dimension of some other activity. This has made it difficult to study, and the majority of information about collaboration consists of stories of success, reports of perceptions, or advice for accomplishing it in schools (e.g., Tannock, 2009; van Garderen, Scheuermann, Jackson, & Hampton, 2009). Further, because collaborative activities tend to be complex—involving several individuals, each of whom has unique contributions to make—trying to study collaboration by comparing the activities of several groups is likewise challenging.

If you look for research that studies only collaboration, you will find that such studies often embed collaboration within broader efforts, such as school

PROFESSIONAL **EDGE**

Finding Time for Collaboration

Professionals have become very creative at finding ways to create time for collaboration. Here are a few of their ideas:

- Other professionals in the school, including principals, assistant principals, counselors, social workers, department chairpersons, psychologists, and ' supervisors, contribute a small amount of time (perhaps two class periods per month) covering class sessions and thus releasing teachers for planning.
- When substitute teachers are in a school, they typically are not entitled to the planning time of the teacher they are replacing. Instead, they provide coverage for a set of co-teachers during that time period.
- Co-teaching partners begin each class period with 3 or 4 minutes of instructionally appropriate, independent work time, during which students work alone or with a partner. While students work, the teachers complete informal planning.
- Principals and part of the school staff show instructionally relevant videos or other programs to groups of students so that other staff members can plan.

- When school-based staff development sessions are scheduled, they begin late or conclude early, with the gained time used for collaboration.
- Teachers come once each month after school for co-teaching planning sessions; they receive required staff development credit for doing so.
- When district staff development is scheduled, co-teachers may opt to attend a session that has no speaker or agenda except to provide an opportunity for planning.
- If educators can only arrange to meet before or after school for planning, they make their work more enjoyable by bringing favorite snacks or meeting at a coffee shop instead of staying at school.
- Professionals find funds for substitute teachers, possibly through grants or contributions from state or local foundations, parent-teacher organizations, or disability advocacy groups.

improvement (Isenberg & Walsh, 2015; Walsh, 2012) or inclusive practices (Huberman, Navo, & Parrish, 2012). You also might locate studies about the impact of communication skills on parents' or professionals' sense of collaboration (e.g., Williamson & McLeskey, 2011). Another group of studies may document the effectiveness of teaching a specific problem-solving process and implementing it to address student academic and behavior concerns (Newell, 2010).

Another way to explore the research related to collaboration is to examine studies about collaborative applications such as teaming, co-teaching, and consultation. More research exists in these areas, but it only indirectly addresses collaboration. For example, teams have been studied in business and education for many years. For schools, data have been gathered concerning the importance of strong team leadership, the impact of clear team procedures on team productivity, and the elements that create the sense of community that maximizes team effectiveness (e.g., Gülcan, 2014; Runhaar, ten Brinke, Kuijpers, Wesselink, & Mulder, 2014). However, how can collaboration be separated from these elements? Generally, it has not been studied as a discrete part of teams, but, rather, it has been assumed to be the result of other positive team features.

Collaboration in the context of consultation also should be considered. Consultation has a considerable research base, mostly in disciplines such as school psychology, counseling, and business; much less research exists related to teacher consultants. Researchers have explored consultants' communication skills, the impact they have on consultation outcomes, and the impact of various consultation models (e.g., Erchul & Martens, 2010). Research in this domain also has explored teacher and parent perceptions of consultation effectiveness and the extent to which consultants' recommendations are actually carried out (e.g., Coffee & Kratochwill, 2013). However, isolating and studying the impact of collaboration on the consultation process has been challenging, and too few studies related to this topic have been completed to reach valid conclusions.

A similar perspective can be offered on co-teaching. Many studies have been completed, but only a handful directly address the collaborative aspect of co-teaching (e.g., Hang & Rabren, 2009; Scruggs, Mastropieri, & McDuffie, 2007; Walsh, 2012). For example, Magiera and her colleagues (Magiera, Smith, Zigmond, & Gebaner, 2005) completed 49 observations of co-teaching in eight high schools. They found that both co-teachers spent considerable time monitoring student work and that special educators did not usually lead instruction. However, detailed analysis of one of the successful co-teaching partnerships indicated that co-planning and other collaborative activities were integral to positive student outcomes and teachers' satisfaction.

The still developing status of research related to collaboration does not mean that it is not important or that it should be considered a minor part of your roles and responsibilities. Although it has proven particularly challenging to document that collaboration is an evidence-based practice, it is still true that today's schools rely more than ever on strong collaborative relationships among professionals and others (Nieto, 2009). The data that have been gathered related to collaboration suggest it is a powerful approach when used appropriately (e.g., Caron & McLaughlin, 2002; Huberman et al., 2012).

Collaboration as a standard for school professionals is still maturing. It should not be surprising that the research basis for it is still emerging. What is important for all educators to remember is that they should stay abreast of developments related to collaboration, remain open to new ideas about it, and possibly even join with colleagues to read and learn more about it.

MyEdLab **Self-Check 4.5**

MyEdLab **Application Exercise 4.6:** The Role of Paraprofessionals in Collaboration

Summary

LO4.1   Collaboration is a style through which teachers and other professionals can conduct their interactions with each other and parents. It is based on voluntariness, parity, mutual goals, shared responsibility for key decisions, shared accountability for outcomes, shared resources, and the emergence of trust, respect, and a sense of community. Collaboration plays a prominent role in the delivery of services to students with disabilities and other special needs.

LO4.2   For collaboration to exist, professionals must believe it is valuable, use effective communication skills, follow clear processes (e.g., interpersonal problem solving), create programs and services that support it, and work with administrators to create a culture that fosters it.

LO4.3   In addition to informal collaboration, three formal applications are common in today's schools: (a) teaming, which occurs as part of RTI or MTSS when students are identified as struggling, as well as during the special education identification and program planning processes; (b) co-teaching, the service option in which special education is delivered in the general education setting through teacher partnership; and (c) consultation, through which one professional assists another to address a student concern or other related matter, with special educators sometimes the beneficiaries or providers of such service.

LO4.4   Although nearly all professionals would assert that collaboration with parents and family members is critical, accomplishing this can be challenging. Sometimes, a first step is increasing meaningful parent involvement, accomplished in part through genuine respect and attention to the potential challenges of cultural differences.

LO4.5   Several issues characterize collaboration, including the complexity of professionals working with paraeducators, the realistic barriers created when shared planning time is not available for collaboration, and the emerging but as of yet equivocal research base for collaborative practices.

Back to the Cases

Now that you've read about collaboration in special education, look back at the student stories at the beginning of this chapter. Then, answer the questions about each of their cases.

MyEdLab **Case Study 4.1**

MICHELLE. As you learned in the case study, Michelle has faced several challenges in forming a strong partnership with co-teacher Kira. Some have been related to her knowledge of algebra; some have been related to building trust and respect.

MyEdLab **Case Study 4.2**

DEREK. As Robert's teacher, Derek wants to be sure his educational program and services are effective. Think about his role with the behavior consultant as well as his participation on the IEP team from the perspective of collaboration.

MyEdLab **Case Study 4.3**

MAKAYLA. Makayla understands that collaboration may be integral to today's schools and considers herself well-prepared for this professional role, but she is also feeling overwhelmed by the number of collaborative obligations she has.

5

Students with Specific Learning Disabilities

NATHANIEL

Nathaniel's first-grade teacher, Ms. Ivers, was the first to notice that Nathaniel was not keeping up with his peers, despite the fact that he attended school regularly and fully participated in the reading program approved for this grade level. Data gathered on his reading performance confirmed her perception. During the late fall, and based on the recommendation of the school's response to intervention (RTI) problem-solving team, Nathaniel participated in a reading tutoring program three times per week, but frequently gathered data documented that this did not accelerate his learning. During early spring, he received 40 minutes per day of small-group, intensive reading instruction from the reading specialist, but the weekly checks on his progress suggested that even this intervention was not proving to be effective. Toward the end of first grade, the multidisciplinary team used the data during the RTI process and classroom work samples as well as the results of additional assessments to determine that Nathaniel had a learning disability in reading. Now, at the beginning of fourth grade, Nathaniel is described as a student of contradictions: When speaking in class, it is obvious that he is a bright young man who has many abilities and interests. However, when he attempts to read, he struggles with nearly every word and often does not comprehend what he has read. Writing is also difficult for Nathaniel. His fourth-grade teacher often asks him to explain what he has written because the words on the paper are jumbled and difficult to discern. To address his needs, Nathaniel receives supplemental reading instruction every day from the special education teacher, is provided extra time to complete written assignments, uses technology that helps him with grammar and spelling, and has permission to ask classmates for assistance. Socially, Nathaniel has many friends among his peers.

DELORES

So far, Delores has not had a very good middle school experience. For the first week of school, she had difficulty finding all her classrooms and twice couldn't get her locker to open. It was embarrassing to have to ask a teacher for help. Then yesterday, in the cafeteria, she tried to sit with some girls she knew from elementary school, but they spread out at the table and wouldn't let her join them. As she walked to her bus at the end of the day, a group of boys on one of the other buses started chanting as she walked by, "Retard, Retard! Do-Do-Delores!" No one stopped them, and they continued the bullying comments that evening on a social media site. Delores fervently wishes that she hadn't been named after her great grandmother, and she is unsure whether she can fit

in with her middle school peers. Delores attends a regular English class, but she was required to sign up for a remedial reading course because she reads at a late third-grade level; that means she does not get to take the art class she would have preferred. She also is enrolled in what's called "Sixth-Grade Math Fundamentals," but everyone knows it's math for struggling learners. Delores likes her special education teacher and her math teacher, but she is still uncertain about talking to them about the bullying from her peers. She tried to talk to her father about it, but he told Delores he knows she has limited ability, just like him, and that she should expect other kids to tease her. Delores wants to succeed in middle school, but she is so distracted by all the social interactions that it is difficult to focus on her schoolwork, and she is afraid she is making a bad impression on her teachers.

AUDELL

Audell is a 10th-grade student at Central High School. Diagnosed with a learning disability during third grade, he received much of his core language arts and math instruction in a special education classroom in elementary school. This pattern continued in sixth grade, but when Audell learned that he would not be allowed to start learning another language and that he would have to take a remedial reading class, he protested to his school counselor, complained to his parents, and eventually convinced his IEP team that he should participate in general education classes, with support in reading and writing provided during the 30-minute intervention period the school scheduled for all students. Now in high school, Audell is playing basketball and is popular with his peers. He is embarrassed about his reading skills, but he has created a strong support network. His special education teacher is always willing to help him complete a complex assignment, and he has two friends who don't make fun of him when he needs help with spelling on written assignments or help understanding material in his textbooks. His English teacher ensures that appropriate technology support is in place for reading and writing, and a counselor makes sure that he is enrolled in the classes needed to graduate on schedule. Most of all, his mother has been his champion and tutor. She patiently works with him on homework, edits his written assignments, advocates for him at IEP meetings, and encourages him to pursue his dreams. Those dreams include attending a Division II college on a basketball scholarship, which will require a great deal of focus and academic effort. But Audell is confident he can succeed and is increasingly comfortable advocating for himself in his high school classes.

Have you ever been in a class—perhaps advanced math or a foreign language—and suddenly realized that you had absolutely no understanding of the information being presented? Even after reviewing your notes and asking questions of classmates, you simply did not grasp the concepts. Maybe the experience left you questioning your abilities and feeling incapable of learning. Have you ever become disoriented while driving in an unfamiliar area? Not only did you not know how to get to your destination, but you also were not sure which direction was north or how to get back on your way. Friends may have found your situation funny, but your sense of discomfort was tinged with panic.

Neither of these experiences by itself indicates a learning disability (LD), but it can give you a small insight into what it is like to have a learning disability and how students with specific learning disabilities often experience frustration and a sense of failure, particularly in school. Their special needs may affect their ability to learn to read, to compute, to speak, to write, or any combination of these. These students may experience difficulty remembering, and they may show gaps in their social skills. Students with specific learning disabilities sometimes are puzzling to educators because they can be highly proficient in one area (e.g., math) but at the same time significantly delayed in another (e.g., reading).

Understanding Learning Disabilities

Compared to many other disability areas, the field of learning disabilities has had a relatively brief and intense evolution (Hallahan & Mercer, 2001). The work of medical professionals, psychologists, educators, and parents all contributed to the current understanding of this disorder.

Development of the Learning Disabilities Field

The history of learning disabilities, displayed in Figure 5.1, began long before the term was introduced. As early as the 19th century, researchers were interested in how injuries to the brain affected adults' functioning (Zumeta, Zirkel, & Danielson, 2014). In the 20th century, this line of research became more focused when Goldstein (1942) studied brain-injured soldiers returning from World War I (Smith, 1998). This work eventually was applied to the study of children who were presumed to be brain-injured from unknown causes because they experienced unexplained learning difficulties (Danforth, 2009). Researchers focused on trying to improve these students' learning, not by developing academic interventions, but instead by trying to develop their perceptual skills (e.g., balance, eye–hand coordination, ability to stay within the lines when tracing a line in a visual maze), working from the assumption that the emphasis on perception would eventually lead to improvements in learning (Frostig & Horne, 1964; Kephart, 1960; Strauss & Lehtinen, 1947).

FIGURE 5.1   **Timeline of the Development of the LD Field**

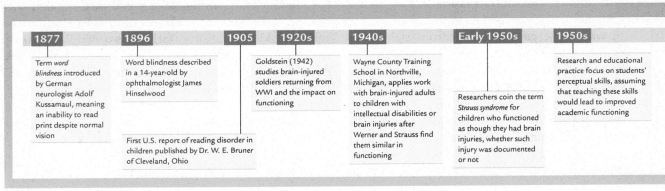

During the 1960s, learning disability was formally established by law as a category of disability (Lerner & Johns, 2015). At the same time, as researchers failed to demonstrate that teaching perceptual skills improved learning, the field shifted from this approach to direct instruction in academics (Hallahan & Kauffman, 1976). Since then, professionals have continued to build a legal and scientific understanding of learning disabilities and to explore alternative instructional methods for students with learning disabilities (e.g., Lovett, Lacerenza, De Palma, & Frijters, 2012; Peng & Fuchs, 2016; Suggate, 2016).

Definitions of Learning Disabilities

Although the term learning disabilities was coined 50 years ago and the study of learning disabilities has been pursued intensely ever since (Hale, Alfonso, Berninger, Bracken, Christo, Clark, . . . Yalof, 2010), considerable controversy still exists over what a learning disability really is. The definition that largely shapes students' programs and services is the federal definition included in the Individuals with Disabilities Education Act (IDEA). However, two other definitions are also influencing the field, and these are also explained in the following sections.

Federal Definition

The federal definition of learning disabilities articulated in P.L. 94-142 in 1975 has changed very little since then. According to IDEA,

> Specific learning disability means a disorder in one or more of the basic psychological processes involved in understanding or in using language, spoken or written, that may manifest itself in imperfect ability to listen, think, speak, read, write, spell, or do mathematical calculation, including conditions such as perceptual disabilities, brain injury, minimal brain dysfunction, dyslexia, and developmental aphasia. Specific learning disability does not include a learning problem that arises primarily as the result of visual, hearing, or motor disabilities, of an intellectual disability, of emotional disturbance, or of environmental, cultural, or economic disadvantage. (IDEA 20 U.S.C. §1401 [2004], 20 C.F.R. §300.8[c][10])

Because states are required to adhere to the provisions of the federal special education law, all of them use either this definition or a minor variation of it (Coomer, 2015). As you would expect, the definition focuses on school tasks and learner characteristics and needs, and it clearly explains that learning disabilities are distinct from other disabilities. It should also be noted that federal law uses the term *specific learning disability*, but some states and many authors use the simpler term *learning disability*. In this chapter, the terms are used interchangeably.

Did You Know?

If you are interested in learning more about how the field of learning disabilities evolved, try searching for information about some of these pioneers who made significant contributions to its development: Samuel Orton, Grace Fernald, Heinz Werner, Samuel Kirk, and William Cruickshank.

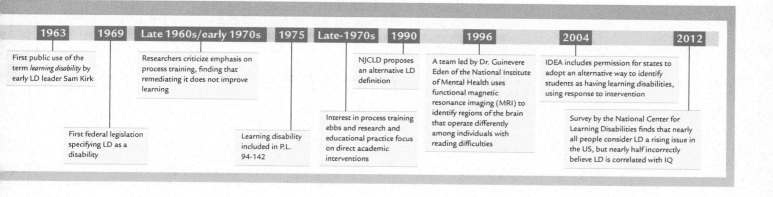

| 1963 | 1969 | Late 1960s/early 1970s | 1975 | Late-1970s | 1990 | 1996 | 2004 | 2012 |

First public use of the term *learning disability* by early LD leader Sam Kirk

Researchers criticize emphasis on process training, finding that remediating it does not improve learning

NJCLD proposes an alternative LD definition

A team led by Dr. Guinevere Eden of the National Institute of Mental Health uses functional magnetic resonance imaging (MRI) to identify regions of the brain that operate differently among individuals with reading difficulties

IDEA includes permission for states to adopt an alternative way to identify students as having learning disabilities, using response to intervention

First federal legislation specifying LD as a disability

Learning disability included in P.L. 94-142

Interest in process training ebbs and research and educational practice focus on direct academic interventions

Survey by the National Center for Learning Disabilities finds that nearly all people consider LD a rising issue in the US, but nearly half incorrectly believe LD is correlated with IQ

One aspect of this definition that sometimes can be confusing is the concept of psychological processes. The following are examples of psychological processes:

Attention, including the ability to select what to focus on and to sustain that focus

Auditory processing, including the ability to efficiently interpret auditory input and to distinguish among sounds

Visual processing, including the ability to accurately recognize and distinguish among shapes, letters, and numbers

Executive function, including the ability to be aware of one's thinking and to manage and direct it

Long-term memory, which is primarily the ability to retain information over time once it is learned

Working memory, which is primarily the ability to remember information while processing it (e.g., remembering what to write long enough to take notes)

Processing speed, that is, the length of time it takes for a student to take in, comprehend, interpret, and act on information received through any channel (e.g., visual, auditory)

These examples illustrate how language is central to a definition of learning disabilities and how students identified with this label may exhibit a wide range of learning strengths and deficits.

Alternative Definitions

The National Joint Committee on Learning Disabilities (NJCLD) includes representatives from 11 professional and parent organizations concerned about individuals with learning disabilities (National Joint Committee on Learning Disabilities, 2015). This group has expressed concern about the federal LD definition for several reasons, most of which are related to what the definition does not address: the heterogeneity of students with learning disabilities, the impact of learning disabilities on social perception, the lifespan impact of learning disabilities, and the possibility that learning disabilities can exist concomitantly with other disabilities.

Because of these perceived deficiencies in the federal definition, the NJCLD created its own definition of learning disabilities, which it suggests is more accurate and comprehensive:

> Learning disabilities is a general term that refers to a heterogeneous group of disorders manifested by significant difficulties in the acquisition and use of listening, speaking, reading, writing, reasoning, or mathematical abilities. These disorders are intrinsic to the individual, presumed to be due to central nervous system dysfunction, and may occur across the lifespan. Problems in self-regulatory behaviors, social perception, and social interaction may exist with learning disabilities but do not by themselves constitute a learning disability. Although learning disabilities may occur concomitantly with other handicapping conditions (for example, sensory impairment, mental retardation, serious emotional disturbance), or with extrinsic influences (such as cultural differences, insufficient or inappropriate instruction), they are not the result of those conditions or influences. (NJCLD, 1990)

The newest definition of learning disabilities comes from the American Psychiatric Association's (APA) *Diagnostic and Statistical Manual*, 5th edition (DSM-V) (2013). This definition, labeled *specific learning disorder*, may be used by educators, clinicians, or researchers, and it has a medical basis:

> A neurodevelopmental disorder of biological origin manifested in learning difficulties and problems in acquiring academic skills markedly below age level and manifested in the early school years, lasting for at least six months; not attributed

to intellectual disabilities, developmental disorders, or neurobiological or motor disorders. (adapted from *DSM-5*, pp. 68–70)

This definition calls for a diagnosis that indicates a severity level of mild, moderate, or severe. It also requires that the area of disorder be identified: impairment in reading, impairment in written expression, and/or impairment in mathematics. Note that one implication of this definition is that a student could be identified as having a specific learning disorder by a medical professional, even if the student has not been thus identified at school.

Essential Dimensions of a Definition of Learning Disabilities

The various definitions of learning disabilities may leave you wondering what is most important to understand about them. Although debates about the definitions are likely to continue, most professionals seem to agree that learning disabilities include these dimensions (Hale et al., 2010; Kavale & Forness, 2012; NJCLD, 2011; Scanlon, 2013):

- Learning disabilities comprise a heterogeneous group of disorders. Students with learning disabilities may have significant reading problems (dyslexia), difficulty in mathematics (dyscalculia), a disorder related to written language (dysgraphia), or difficulties with oral language. They may have difficulty with social perceptions, motor skills, or memory. Learning disabilities can affect young children, students in school, and adults. No single profile of a person with a learning disability can be accurate because of the interindividual differences in the disorder.
- Learning disabilities are intrinsic to the individual and have a neurobiological basis. Learning disabilities exist because of some type of dysfunction in the brain, not because of external factors such as limited experience or poor teaching.
- Learning disabilities are characterized by unexpected underachievement. That is, the disorder exists when a student's academic achievement is significantly below his or her intellectual potential, even after intensive, systematic interventions have been implemented to try to reduce the learning gap. This topic is addressed in more detail later in this chapter.
- Low achievement by itself does not constitute a learning disability; it must be accompanied by a disorder related to psychological processing.
- Learning disabilities are not a result of other disorders or problems, but individuals with learning disabilities may have other special needs as well. For example, being deaf cannot be considered to be the basis for having a learning disability. However, some students who are deaf also have learning disabilities. Similarly, individuals who have attention deficit–hyperactivity disorder (ADHD), the focus of Chapter 6, also may have a learning disability, but ADHD does not constitute a learning disability.

Prevalence of Learning Disabilities

According to annual data gathered as part of IDEA during the 2012–2013 school year, approximately 2.34 million students between ages 6 and 21 had learning disabilities (U.S. Department of Education, 2015). This category has the highest number of students with disabilities (39.8% of all students needing special education), about 3.4% of the entire school population.

Further exploration of prevalence data reveals several interesting facts. For example, from when the federal law was first passed in 1975 until the beginning of the 21st century, specific learning disability was the fastest-growing category of special education, growing from only 22% of all students receiving special education (Horn & Tynan, 2001) to nearly 50% in 2002 (U.S. Department of

Education, 2004). Since then, this trend has reversed itself; the number of identified students has steadily declined (U.S. Department of Education, 2015). An explanation of these data generally includes multiple factors, including (a) the use of the relatively new category of *developmentally delayed* for some young children who might previously have been labeled as LD and (b) efforts to provide early intervention through RTI positively affecting student learning, thus preventing the need for special education (Stuebing, Fletcher, Branum-Martin, & Francis, 2012).

The matter of gender can be raised as a prevalence issue, too. Researchers generally have found that the ratio of boys to girls identified as having learning disabilities is at least 2:1, or perhaps even 3:1 or 4:1 (Centers for Disease Control and Prevention, 2011; Cortiella & Horowitz, 2014). Many explanations have been offered for this phenomenon: Boys might be labeled as having learning disabilities more frequently because of medical factors, such as their greater vulnerability to prenatal and postnatal brain damage; maturational factors, including their documented slower rate of development; sociological factors, such as societal expectations for high achievement from males; and brain organization factors, including the greater likelihood in boys of genetically based impulsivity (Smith, 2004). In practice, girls identified as having learning disabilities as a group usually have more severe academic deficits than boys (Lerner & Johns, 2014).

Taken together, these prevalence data illustrate that learning disabilities represent a complex disorder affecting many students. They also demonstrate that the current federal definition of learning disabilities probably leads to inconsistency in identifying students as having this special need. In fact, dissatisfaction about who is eligible to receive services due to having this disability is largely what led to the development of response to intervention (RTI) procedures, addressed in more detail later in this chapter.

Causes of Learning Disabilities

As you might suspect from the preceding discussion about the development of the learning disabilities field and the definition of the disorder, in most cases the cause of a learning disability is simply not known, and it is highly unlikely that a single primary cause will ever be identified (Buttner & Hasselhorn, 2011; Brandenburg, Klesczewski, Fischback, Schuchardt, Buttner, Hasselhorn, 2014). Generally, though, the possible causes of learning disabilities can be divided into two categories: physiological causes, and curricular and environmental contributors (Eunice Kennedy Shriver National Institute of Child Health and Human Development, 2014).

Physiological Causes

Several possible physiological causes of learning disabilities have been identified by education professionals and medical researchers (Gilger & Wilkins, 2008). These include brain injury, heredity, and chemical imbalance.

First, as proposed from the earliest work in the learning disabilities field, brain injury probably causes some students' disorders. The injury may occur prenatally, as might happen when a mother consumes alcohol or drugs, contracts measles, or smokes cigarettes. An injury also might occur during the perinatal period, as when a baby is deprived of oxygen during birth. Brain injury also can occur postnatally because of a high fever, a head injury (e.g., falling from a bike or playground equipment), an illness (e.g., meningitis), or an accident (e.g., a near drowning). In the Technology Notes, you can learn more about recent advances in understanding the brain and learning disabilities.

Considerable evidence indicates that heredity is another physiological cause of learning disabilities (Haworth & Plomin, 2010; National Institute of Child

You've probably read or heard about studies that are exploring brain functioning and its relationship to reading skills. Although intriguing, much of the research at this point is suggestive rather than definitive. Here are some tidbits that may eventually provide educators with clear directions for helping struggling readers:

- On a visual word-rhyming task, struggling readers showed less activation in the parts of the brain associated with competent reading whether they had average to above average measured IQs (90 or higher) or lower IQs (75–90), indicating that poor readers have difficulties processing sounds regardless of their measured general ability level (Tanaka et al., 2011).
- As researchers are more able to identify specific profiles of students with dyslexia, interventions tailored to those profiles may be most effective in improving students' reading skills (Heim, Pape-Neumann, Van Ermingen-Marbach, Brinkhaus, & Grande, 2015).
- Studies of brain activity demonstrate the development of *executive function* (EF), that is, the ability to

purposefully guide mental processes and actions, and EF (e.g., attentional control, organization, planning) is related to competent reading (Corso, Cromley, Sperb, & Salles, 2016). For example, the ability of children to control their own behavior (which is an EF) is positively associated with word and nonword reading skills in early elementary school.
- Although some researchers have asserted that intensive phonics instruction results in positive development in the parts of the brain associated with competent reading, others have cautioned that the implication that the brain can be "repaired" is misleading (Strauss, Goodman, & Paulson, 2009).

Are you interested in this fascinating area of research? You can find additional information at these websites:

- http://brainlens.org/ (Laboratory for Educational Neuroscience at the University of California–San Francisco)
- http://cibsr.stanford.edu/ (Stanford University Center for Interdisciplinary Brain Sciences Research [CIBSR])

●●●

Health and Human Development, 2014a). Teachers have reported for years that many parents of children with learning disabilities comment, "He's just like his father [or mother]." Now research is supporting those claims. In fact, when one or both parents have a learning disability, their children may have as much as a 30–50% chance of also having that disorder (Castles, Datta, Gayan, & Olson, 1999). Critics of this research have noted that it does not consider possible environmental factors. That is, perhaps parents and their children share learning disabilities because of similar exposure to allergens or environmental toxins such as lead. However, studies of twins and siblings support the heritability of learning disabilities (Rosenberg, Pennington, Willcutt, & Olson, 2012). The reading level of one identical twin is very likely to predict the reading level of the other, even when they are reared apart, and this holds true when one has been identified as having a learning disability. In contrast, a nontwin sibling's reading level is much less likely to predict the reading level of the other sibling when they are reared separately. This line of research provides evidence of a genetic link.

A third physiological cause of learning disabilities sometimes mentioned is biochemical. For some children, learning disabilities seem to be related to significant attention problems, which may be the result of chemical imbalances in the brain. This topic is explored in more depth in Chapter 6 on students with attention deficit–hyperactivity disorder (ADHD).

You should be careful in attributing learning disabilities to physiological causes. Just because a child has a head injury does not mean that a learning disability is inevitable. Likewise, just because one child has a learning disability does not mean a sibling will have the disorder. Perhaps in the future, emerging medical technology will provide scientists and researchers with new tools for studying the relationship between the brain and individuals' patterns of learning. In the meantime, professionals should consider such information intriguing but somewhat speculative.

Curriculum and Environmental Contributors

For some children, learning disabilities are caused by the situations in which they live (National Institute of Child Health and Human Development, 2014b). For example, children who have poor nutrition may develop learning disabilities, as may those who live for an extended period of time in a highly adverse emotional climate. Some students have learning disabilities because of toxins in their environments, as might happen to children who develop lead poisoning because of the use of lead-based paint in older homes or from corroded water pipes. Yet other children may have too little stimulation (e.g., adults who fail to model language, lack of access to books, few experiences such as visits to the zoo) (National Joint Committee on Learning Disabilities, 2015). Some students may be inappropriately identified because their primary language is not English (e.g., Burr, Haas, & Ferriere, 2015). When you think about all these factors, can you identify a single group of youngsters who might be most expected to have learning disabilities because of environmental causes? If your response is children who live in poverty, you are correct (e.g., Anderson, Howland, & McCoach, 2015). These children also may be placed at greater risk of having learning disabilities because of poor medical care or low parent education level, sometimes resulting in less modeling of language and fewer early learning experiences (Skiba et al., 2008).

One other environmental cause of learning disabilities should be mentioned. Although in an ideal world this paragraph would not need to be written, some students have learning disabilities because of poor instruction (Haycock & Crawford, 2008). When teachers use preferred but ineffective instructional practices, do not consider the differences in students' maturational levels, and ignore students' specific learning needs, they can cause some students to display characteristics of learning disabilities. This cause of learning disabilities is one of the most controversial. IDEA specifically prohibits students who receive poor instruction from being identified as having this or any other disability on that basis. However, some professionals argue that if teaching has been so inadequate that a learning disability has been created in a student, then that student should receive the benefit of a specialized education to remediate the problem (Hale, 2015).

MyEdLab **Self-Check 5.1**

MyEdLab **Application Exercise 5.1:** Definitions

MyEdLab **Application Exercise 5.2:** Organizing Information about Causes

---

Characteristics of Individuals with Learning Disabilities

Individuals with learning disabilities are an extraordinarily heterogeneous group, with different areas of strengths and special needs in the cognitive, academic, social-emotional, and behavior domains. The following sections highlight some of the most common characteristics.

Cognitive Characteristics

Although students with learning disabilities typically have average or above-average intelligence, they usually display weaknesses in one or more areas of cognition, including attention, perception, memory, and thinking/processing.

Attention

Students with learning disabilities may have poor selective attention (Mattison & Mayes, 2012). One way to illustrate what this means is to think about the setting you are in as you read this paragraph. Stop to listen and look around. Is someone nearby typing on a computer or texting from a phone? Is there noise in the hallway or on the street? Is there a pile of reading material right beside you? Until you were directed to notice items such as these, you likely ignored them because your attention was devoted to reading your textbook. Students with learning disabilities may have extraordinary difficulty attending to only the important stimuli in their environments. The other reading material may be as captivating as the book in front of them; the plane overhead is as noticeable as the teacher's voice.

Perception

Many students with learning disabilities exhibit perceptual problems (Lerner & Johns, 2015; Silver & Silver, 2014). *Perception* does not pertain to whether a student sees or hears, but, rather, to how the student's brain interprets what is seen or heard and acts on it. For example, a student with a visual perception problem may see perfectly well the words on a page. However, when asked to read the words, she may skip some of them. Other symptoms of visual perception difficulties include spatial orientation and judgment (e.g., bumping into things; not knowing how to safely get from one point to another); the ability to distinguish right from left; labored handwriting; and overall clumsiness or awkwardness in walking, skipping, balancing, and other large-motor activities. Problems in auditory perception often include difficulties with perceiving sounds that are not attributable to a hearing loss. For example, some students may have trouble understanding whether the word spoken was *team* or *teen*, *odor* or *over*, *pet* or *bet*. Of course, the result can be misunderstood directions, poor communication, and awkwardness in social interactions.

Memory

In addition to problems related to attention and perception, students with learning disabilities may experience problems with memory (Compton, Fuchs, Fuchs, Lambert, & Hamlett, 2012; Berninger & Swanson, 2013). Everyone has two types of memory: short term and long term. **Short-term memory** is the mechanism by which a person holds information in the mind for a brief amount of time—less than a minute. Unless it is acted on in some way, it is gradually lost. One simple example is when you look up a phone number. You remember it long enough to dial it, but if you delay dialing, you probably have to look up the number again unless you have consciously taken steps to remember it (e.g., by repeating it several times). **Long-term memory** is the permanent storage mechanism in the brain, and information to be remembered generally has to be transferred from short-term to long-term memory. An example might be verses from a favorite childhood song: Even if you have not recalled them for many years, you can still sing the words as soon as you hear a title such as "If You're Happy and You Know It." Students with learning disabilities may have difficulty with either short-term memory or long-term memory, or both.

MyEdLab
Video Example 5.1

In this video, a student with a learning disability talks about how information in some subject areas is easier to remember than that in others and what he does to overcome problems with memory.

Information Processing

Finally, students' general information-processing or thinking skills may be deficient (e.g., Toll, Van der Ven, Kroesbergen, & Van Luit, 2011; Van der Molen,

Henry, & Van Luit, 2014). Students with learning disabilities may have difficulty with metacognition, or thinking about thinking. They may lack the ability to actively consider how new information they are learning relates to other information already stored or how to apply that knowledge in a novel learning situation. For example, as you read this chapter, you probably are actively relating the concepts to people you know who have learning disabilities or perhaps to knowledge you acquired in a course in psychology. You might also be using a strategy to help you remember information that may be on a test—for example, by repeating key ideas aloud. These are all metacognitive activities. Some students with learning disabilities seldom use such strategies to foster their learning without explicit training (discussed in a later section of this chapter).

Academic Characteristics

By far the most commonly noted characteristic of students with learning disabilities is their struggle with school learning (e.g., Gage, Lierheimer, & Goran, 2012). Their difficulties may occur in reading, spoken language, written language, mathematics, or any combination of these. Academic difficulties comprise the most likely reasons for classroom teachers to suspect a student has a learning disability, and such difficulties often are emphasized in the services provided by special education teachers.

Reading

Most students with learning disabilities experience significant problems in reading (Berninger & Swanson, 2013; Swanson & Vaughn, 2010), as is true for Nathaniel, introduced at the beginning of the chapter. For example, many students struggle with *phonological awareness*, which is the ability to make the connection between letters and the sounds they stand for. This skill is essential for developing reading proficiency. These students are not able to sound out words, and they often rely on visual cues or the context in which a word is used to determine what the word is.

Other students struggle with *oral fluency* (e.g., Graves, Duesbery, Pyle, Brandon, & McIntosh, 2011). They may read aloud in a word-by-word manner without appropriate inflection or rhythm, unable to relate the patterns of spoken language to the printed word. Students with weakness in this area often dread being asked to read aloud in class.

One other typical reading problem for students with learning disabilities is *comprehension* (Faggella-Luby, Drew, & Schumaker, 2015; Kennedy, Deshler, & Lloyd, 2015). Unlike the student previously described who labors to say each word, some students are able to read a passage so fluently that you might assume they are highly proficient readers. However, when they are asked questions about what they have read, these students may have little or no understanding of the words. Not surprisingly, students who have difficulty with phonological awareness and oral fluency also are likely to experience weakness in reading comprehension.

You might find that some people refer to reading problems of all sorts as *dyslexia* (e.g., Snowling & Melby-Lervåg, 2016). The Professional Edge clarifies the meaning of this term and strategies for addressing dyslexia.

Oral Language

Another academic area that can be a significant problem for students with learning disabilities is oral language. Problems usually fall into the areas of phonology, morphology, syntax, and pragmatics.

Students may have difficulties with *phonology*—that is, using the correct sounds to form words. They may struggle with *morphology*, the study of the smallest meaningful units of language (e.g., that *-ed* denotes past tense or that

Understanding Dyslexia

What Is Dyslexia?

- Dyslexia is a brain-based type of learning disability that specifically impairs a person's ability to read.
- People with dyslexia typically read at levels significantly lower than expected despite having normal intelligence.
- Common characteristics among people with dyslexia are difficulty with spelling, phonological processing (the manipulation of sounds), and/or rapid visual–verbal responding.
- Dyslexia can be inherited in some families, and recent studies have identified a number of genes that may predispose an individual to developing dyslexia.

What Is the Treatment?

- Early identification for students with dyslexia is particularly urgent given recent studies showing that effective language instruction appears to generate repair in underactivated sections of the brain responsible for this disorder (Ferrer, Shaywitz, Holahan, Marchione, Michaels, & Shaywitz, 2015).
- Many students with severe reading disabilities benefit from a beginning reading program that includes the following elements (Friend & Bursuck, 2016, p. 218):
  Direct instruction in language analysis. For example, students need to be taught skills in sound segmentation or in orally breaking down words into their component sounds.

A highly structured phonics program. This program should teach the alphabetic code directly and systematically using a simple-to-complex sequence of skills.
Writing and reading instruction in combination.
Intensive instruction. Reading instruction for at-risk students should include large amounts of practice in materials that contain words they are able to decode.
Teaching for automaticity. Students must be given enough practice so that they are able to read both accurately and fluently.

What Is the Prognosis?

- For those with dyslexia, the prognosis is mixed.
- Because dyslexia affects such a wide range of people and produces such different symptoms and varying degrees of severity, predictions are difficult to make.
- Outcomes generally are positive for individuals whose dyslexia is identified early, who have supportive family and friends and a strong self-image, and who are involved in a proper remediation program.

Source: National Institute of Neurological Disorders and Stroke. (2015, September). *Dyslexia information page.* Bethesda, MD. Retrieved from http://www.ninds.nih.gov/disorders/dyslexia/dyslexia.htm

pre- means "before"). Likewise, students may have problems with *syntax*, the rules of grammar, or with *semantics*, the meanings of words or phrases. Finally, *pragmatics*—the ability to successfully participate in interactions with others—may be a weakness.

If you think about all these elements of spoken language, you can begin to see how pervasive the effects of this type of learning disability can be. For example, a student with poor oral language skills may miss subtle meanings of words during conversations or fail to understand the punch line of a joke based on word meanings. Such a student also may have difficulty participating in conversations with classmates or adults and also may be identified as needing speech-language services when the problem is, in fact, a learning disability.

Written Language

For some students, learning disabilities are manifested in written language (Berninger, & May, 2011; Berninger & Niedo, 2014). For example, the motor coordination required for handwriting can be overwhelming for some students. As shown in the sample in Figure 5.2, it is nearly impossible to determine what these students have written even though the words form complete sentences and are spelled correctly.

For other students, the deficiency is spelling (Sayeski, 2011). Not only do these students labor to discern the sounds comprising words, but they also may be unable to distinguish between appropriate uses of homonyms (e.g., meet–meat; there–their) or to recognize when they have written a misspelled word (e.g., *seperate* instead of *separate*; *advise* instead of *advice*). Students also may have difficulty

FIGURE 5.2   **Writing Sample from a Middle School Student with Learning Disabilities**

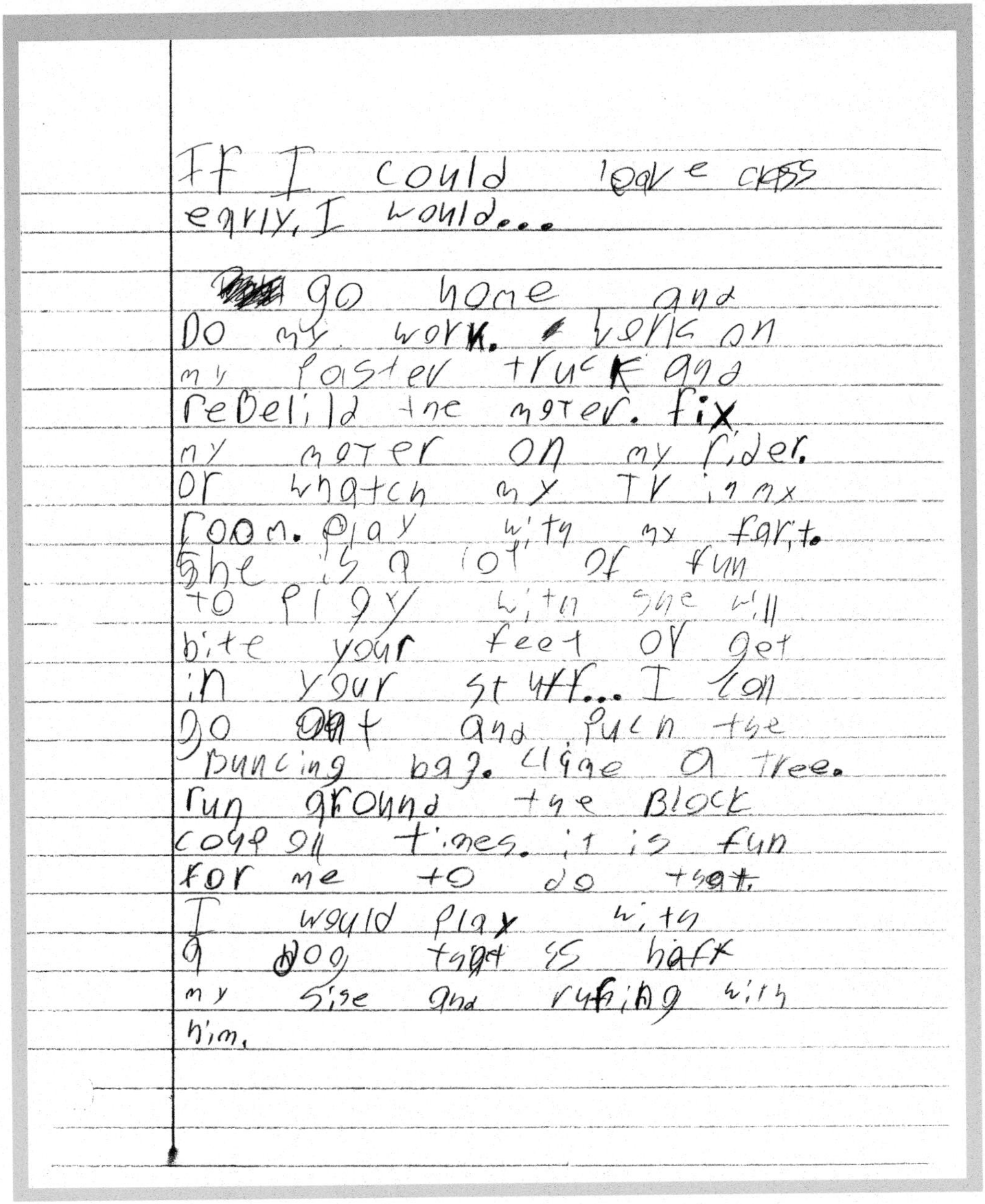

knowing when and how to punctuate the sentences they write, struggling not only with the appropriate application of periods and commas, but also with the use of apostrophes (e.g., *it's—it is* instead of *its*—possessive form). Finally, they may also be uncertain about capitalizing words (e.g., *My Brother likes mexican food*).

In an era when spelling, punctuation, and many other conventions of written language can be corrected with computer software and other electronic tools (e.g., Peterson-Karlan, 2011), perhaps the most serious issue for students with learning disabilities in written expression is composition skill (Hoover, Kubina, & Mason, 2012; Mason, 2013). In order to write effectively, students need to be able to organize their thoughts, present them in some type of logical order, and provide enough details to convey the intended message to readers (Carretti, Motta, & Re, 2016). These tasks can be exceedingly difficult for students with learning disabilities like Audell, who was described at the beginning of the chapter. When telling a story, they may make assumptions about what the reader knows (e.g., not explaining who a main character is but writing as though the reader is familiar with this character) or jump from topic to topic (e.g., mixing together information about the causes, battles, and outcomes of World War II instead of presenting them as categories of information). Because of their disability, these students sometimes struggle with using adjectives to enrich their writing (e.g., *The meal was good. We had lots of stuff* instead of *Thanksgiving dinner was delicious. We devoured turkey roasted to a golden brown, fluffy mashed potatoes, crunchy green bean casserole, and pecan pie.*). As these students move through school, they often find it difficult to succeed in the many school tasks that rely on clear written expression.

Mathematics

A final domain in which students with learning disabilities may experience difficulty is mathematics (Burns, Kanive, & DeGrande, 2012; Nelson, Burns, Kanive, & Ysseldyke, 2013), a disorder sometimes referred to as *dyscalculia*. This is true for Delores, introduced at the beginning of the chapter. Some students are not able to learn basic math facts or fundamental computational skills. Others cannot grasp the principles of estimation, mental calculation, and probability. Yet others find mastery of fractions or decimals difficult. For some students, learning various types of measurement or concepts related to time is extraordinarily challenging. Geometry is a weakness for others. One other area that may cause difficulty is problem solving. Whether because of the reading requirement or the inability to understand the mathematical concepts that underlie the problem, students may be unable to sort relevant from extraneous information, to recognize the correct computational procedure, or to determine whether the answer they obtain is reasonable (Fletcher & Navarrete, 2011). The Instruction in Action provides further information about students with learning disabilities and helping them to learn mathematics.

INSTRUCTION IN **ACTION**

Helping Students Succeed in Math

Students struggle in math for many reasons. Following are suggestions for helping students to succeed (Fletcher & Naverette, 2011; Wadlington & Wadlington, 2008):

Address Math Anxiety

- Create a safe classroom environment; never criticize or ridicule students struggling with math and expect the same respectful behavior of all students.
- Help a student become an expert in a specific part of math, for example, illustrating word problems.
- Share stories of famous people who have overcome their learning difficulties.
- Use cooperative math games to help students become more comfortable with the language and symbols of mathematics.

Use General Instructional Strategies That Foster Math Learning

- Seat students near the focus of instruction.
- Be well organized in teaching math concepts, and present them in a highly structured and logical order.
- Analyze math skills to be taught, breaking them into small steps and then teaching each step separately with

frequent reviews both during instruction and on subsequent days.
- Use manipulatives, even for older students.
- Provide repeated practice in foundational skills so that they are overlearned.
- Arrange math tutoring for some students, with a classmate, older peer, volunteer, or paraprofessional.

Teach Mathematical Communication

- Have students write in a math journal to help them become comfortable with math terms and ideas.
- Model new vocabulary, providing concrete examples.
- Have students create mathematical dictionaries that illustrate key terms and concepts.
- Stress meaning rather than rote memorization.
- If students struggle with reading, be sure math problems are read aloud or are audio-recorded.
- Assess student learning often, in both formal and informal ways. Use ongoing assessment data to reteach and group students for instruction.
- Analyze students' error patterns; they provide important information about what students do and do not understand.

Social and Emotional Characteristics

Understanding the social and emotional characteristics of students with learning disabilities is as important as appreciating their cognitive and academic traits. How students perceive themselves and others and how adept they are in social situations can significantly affect their learning success (Idan, & Margalit, 2014). Further, their accomplishments in life may depend on this ability to interact effectively with others. Two areas are particularly relevant: social perception and motivation.

Social Perception and Social Competence

Many students with learning disabilities may have some type of deficit in the area of social skills (Brooks, Floyd, Robins, & Chan, 2015; Smith & Wallace, 2011). When compared to peers without disabilities, these students tend to have lower self-esteem. They often are less accepted by their nondisabled peers than are other students, and they are more likely than typical peers to be bullied (Good, McIntosh, & Gietz, 2011). Delores, the middle school student discussed at the beginning of this chapter, experiences such difficulties.

Even when students with and without learning disabilities are directly queried about their social interactions repeatedly over several years, the former group has lower social status (Good, McIntosh, & Gietz, 2011), a fact that may be explained in two ways. First, among nondisabled peers who value school and proficiency at school-related tasks, students with learning disabilities may be viewed as less desirable classmates because of their academic struggles. Second, the status of students with learning disabilities may be related to their *social competence*—that is, their ability to accurately receive, interpret, and respond to the subtleties of interpersonal interactions (Leichtentritt & Shechtman, 2010; Milligan, Phillips, & Morgan, 2015). Seth exemplifies problems in social competence. He was seated on the floor of the office in his middle school with several of his peers, waiting to be seen by the principal about an altercation that had occurred during lunch. The boys were discussing a variety of topics, including who had won the cafeteria shoving match and who had bragging rights for the lowest grades on their recently issued report cards. In the middle of this conversation, Seth chimed in, "I'm going to see my grandma next weekend." Even though the other boys' topics of conversation may not have been those preferred by an adult, Seth's comment illustrates his obvious lack of awareness of the nuances and expectations of him in this social situation. The other boys immediately began making fun of him. As you might expect, students with learning disabilities who have poor social skills often are reported to have difficulty making and keeping friends, and they may feel lonely and depressed, especially through adolescence and adulthood (Feldman, Davidson, Ben-Naim, Maza, & Margalit, 2016; Sharabi & Margalit, 2011).

It is important to note, however, that some students with learning disabilities are well adjusted and liked by their peers and teachers, as is true of Nathaniel and Audell, students introduced at the beginning of the chapter (Estell, Jones, Pearl, & Van Acker, 2009). One explanation for this finding concerns the learning environment. When teachers value and respect students, focus on their abilities, and create a supportive social environment, students thrive. Conversely, when too much emphasis is placed on students' problems, students become negative about themselves and are viewed in this way by peers.

Another explanation is offered by those who hypothesize that students with learning disabilities and poor social competence form a distinct subgroup who have nonverbal learning disabilities (NLDs) (e.g., Cornoldi, Ficili, Giofrè, Mammarella, & Mirandola, 2011; Mammarella, Ghisi, Bomba, Bottesi, Caviola, Broggi, & Nacinovich, 2014). These students may read and speak fluently, but because of a dysfunction in the part of the brain that controls nonverbal reasoning, they are unable to accurately interpret nonverbal communication (e.g., facial expressions, posture, eye contact), and they fumble in social interactions. For example, a student with this disorder might not recognize that he is receiving "the look" from a teacher or a parent and thus may not change the behavior at issue. Likewise, this student might keep talking during a conversation, failing to understand the signals from others that they would like to talk, too.

Motivation

Many special education and general education teachers, especially those in middle and high schools, comment that students with learning disabilities are not motivated to learn, and research suggests that this is a common characteristic (Lichtinger & Kaplan, 2015; Melekoglu, 2011), although not universal, as demonstrated by the story about Audell's determination to successfully complete high

school at the beginning of the chapter. *Motivation* is the desire to engage in an activity. This desire can be intrinsic (e.g., out of curiosity, as when you complete a crossword puzzle simply to see if you can) or extrinsic (e.g., for payment, as when you agree to help a neighbor with chores to earn money for a planned vacation). Ideally, all students would be intrinsically motivated to learn, but many students with learning disabilities are not. This could be due to what is called their *locus of control*, which is their belief about whether their life experiences are determined by internal (e.g., personal effort and skill) or external (e.g., luck) factors. Students with learning disabilities often attribute academic success to external factors and failure to internal factors. For example, if a student with learning disabilities does well on a test, he may comment

that it is because of "good luck" or "an easy test." If the student does not pass it, he may say, "I'm dumb." You can easily see how this would eventually lead to a low level of motivation.

Learning disabilities affect students' academic performance, but they also may result in struggles with social interactions.

However, it is difficult to determine whether lack of motivation is a characteristic of some students with learning disabilities because of neurological dysfunction or whether it is an effect of students' school experiences. For example, some students demonstrate learned helplessness by giving up on a task before they even try (e.g., Hen & Goroshit, 2014). They may do this because they have failed at so many school tasks that they would rather not begin the work than fail again, or they may have discovered that if they say they cannot do a task, the teacher or a peer will help them do it.

Behavior Characteristics

If you think about the possible results of having deficits in academic subjects, selective attention, social competence, and motivation, you probably will conclude that a significant number of students with learning disabilities (although not all) also have behavior problems (Berry Kuchle, Zumeta Edmonds, Danielson, Peterson, & Riley-Tillman, 2015; Sebag, 2010). You are correct. However, whether the behaviors are part of the learning disability or a result of the frustration that many of these students experience is unclear. For some students, difficulties in communicating with others may lead to inappropriate behaviors. For others, the prospect of not being able to complete an academic task might cause them to act out in a sort of learner "road rage." Examples of behavior problems that have

MyEdLab
Video Example 5.2

Video Example 5.2 provides brief interviews with three students with LD, focused on friendship, which can help you to better understand how they perceive themselves and explain their disabilities to others. (https://www.youtube.com/watch?v=P0nX2q2Q_Fg)

been studied in students with learning disabilities include excessive out-of-seat behavior, talk-outs, and physical and verbal aggression.

One of the difficulties in discussing the behavior characteristics of students with learning disabilities is the fact that a significant number of these students have comorbid (i.e., occurring simultaneously) learning disabilities and attention deficit–hyperactivity disorder (ADHD). In fact, it is estimated that between 16% and 31% of students with LD also have ADHD (Wei, Yu, & Shaver, 2014). This comorbidity factor raises the possibility that the behavior problems of some students with learning disabilities are, in fact, symptoms of a second disorder. Details about the characteristics of students with ADHD are covered in Chapter 6. The Positive Behavior Supports provides one example of educators' efforts to help students with learning disabilities learn appropriate classroom behavior through an emphasis on social skills.

Of course, no student with a learning disability has all of the characteristics just described, and the impact of a problem in any of these areas depends on many factors, including student supports from family, teachers, and friends.

POSITIVE • **BEHAVIOR** • SUPPORTS

Improving Behavior Through Social Skills Instruction

Most students with specific learning disabilities have difficulty navigating social interactions, which leads to behavior problems. Addressing this dimension of students' learning disabilities is critical for their success.

Types of Social Skills Problems

Skill deficit—the student has never learned the skill

Performance deficit—the student knows the skill but does not use it when appropriate

Self-control deficit—the student's lack of self-control results in problem behaviors, which interfere with learning and applying social skills (Kavale & Forness, 2012)

Example of Social Skills Instruction

Womack, Marchant, and Borders (2012) noted that social skills instruction delivered in isolation has seldom been shown to be effective. Instead, they recommend embedding social skills instruction in the classroom literature program by following these general steps:

Identify a social skill needed by a student (e.g., taking turns, bullying)

Select several children's books that address that skill, using two to four books to address each skill, usually over a 2-week period.

After the first book is read, the social skill addressed is explicitly introduced and steps for implementing it are taught and practiced.

Students are paired with a classmate to read one of the additional books and to role play the needed social skills, with teacher feedback provided.

Targeted students practice the social skills with classmates, but they also receive additional opportunities to apply the skills during small-group reading instruction.

Data are gathered prior to implementation and after teaching a social skill, including student knowledge and the skill and appropriate use of the skill.

Social skill instruction delivered in this manner is efficient in terms of time use and situates learning in the context of real life. It also fosters a high level of student engagement and builds student self-confidence. Finally, it incorporates peer-mediated instruction (including feedback and mediation), which research suggests is an effective approach (e.g., Lo, Correa, & Anderson, 2014). How does this approach have the potential to address the three types of social skills deficits noted?

MyEdLab **Self-Check 5.2**

MyEdLab **Application Exercise 5.3:** Bridget

Identifying Learning Disabilities

In order for students to receive special education services to address their learning disabilities, they must be identified as being eligible for them. This involves assessments to determine the existence of learning disabilities. Based on the information derived from these assessments, the multidisciplinary team must decide that the disability exists and that students are eligible for services (if the disability negatively affects educational performance).

IDEA 2004 made dramatic changes to the basis on which students may be identified as having a learning disability, and three different criteria related to learning are now included. First, the law still permits traditional assessment procedures based on identifying discrepancies between ability and achievement, the procedure that has been in IDEA since it was first enacted. Second, students who are not making the progress necessary to meet expected achievement standards (i.e., when research-based interventions have not accelerated too-low achievement) also may be eligible. Third, students may be identified when they show a pattern of strengths and weaknesses that indicates the presence of a learning disability (e.g., a large discrepancy between achievement in two subject areas). The latter two options typically incorporate response to intervention (RTI) or multi-tiered system of support (MTSS) procedures, although at the present time, only RTI is explicitly sanctioned as a means of identifying students as having learning disabilities. The federal LD criteria are summarized in the Professional Edge and explained in more detail throughout this section.

Traditional Approach to Assessment for Learning Disabilities

In Chapter 2, you learned that all students who receive special education services first go through a careful process of assessment. For students with learning disabilities being assessed in the traditional way, this process includes both formal and informal assessments. These assessments are designed to create a picture of a student's learning capacity, academic achievement in reading and mathematics, social and emotional skills, and behavior patterns.

Formal Assessments

In many school districts, the formal assessments used to determine whether a student has a learning disability are either norm-referenced or criterion-referenced tests. Norm-referenced tests are those in which the student taking the test is being compared to a large number of students, or *norm group*. Examples of norm-referenced tests used to identify learning disabilities include intelligence tests, such as the Wechsler Intelligence Scale for Children–V (Wechsler, 2014), and achievement tests, such as the Woodcock–Johnson IV (Schrank, Mather, & McGrew, 2014a, 2014b; Schrank, McGrew, & Mather, 2014). Another example is the Learning Disabilities Diagnostic Inventory (LDDI) (Hammill & Bryant, 1998), which was designed specifically to assist professionals in identifying in school-age children intrinsic processing problems related to listening, speaking, reading, writing, mathematics, and reasoning. Unlike other assessments that compare the achievement of students to all other students, the LDDI compares the learning patterns of students only to those of students known to have learning disabilities.

Criterion-referenced tests are another type of formal assessment that may be used during this type of evaluation for learning disabilities. These tests are designed to determine whether a student has learned a specific body of information, so they represent an absolute standard rather than the comparative standard of norm-referenced tests. One example of a criterion-referenced test nearly everyone has experienced is a driver's test. This test is designed to determine whether you have learned enough to drive an automobile safely; comparing you to other

Learning Disability Criteria

Criteria for determining whether a student has a learning disability are multifaceted and complex. In addition to specification about the members of the team, the need to include observational data and multiple data sources, and the documentation required as part of the process, these are relevant excerpts from the IDEA regulations concerning the LD criteria.

Each state's criteria

Must not require the use of a severe discrepancy between intellectual ability and achievement for determining whether a child has a specific learning disability

Must permit the use of a process based on the child's response to scientific, research-based intervention; and

May permit the use of other alternative research-based procedures for determining whether a child has a specific learning disability (§300.307 Specific learning disabilities)

The team may determine that a child has a specific learning disability if

The child does not achieve adequately for the child's age or to meet State-approved grade-level standards in one or more of the following areas, when provided with learning experiences and instruction appropriate for the child's age or State-approved grade-level standards:

Oral expression.

Listening comprehension.

Written expression.

Basic reading skill.

Reading fluency skills.

Reading comprehension.

Mathematics calculation.

Mathematics problem solving.

The child does not make sufficient progress to meet age or State-approved grade-level standards in one or more of the areas identified in paragraph (a)(1) of this section when using a process based on the child's response to scientific, research-based intervention; or

The child exhibits a pattern of strengths and weaknesses in performance, achievement, or both, relative to age, State-approved grade-level standards, or intellectual development, that is determined by the group to be relevant to the identification of a specific learning disability, using appropriate assessments, and

The group determines that its findings are not primarily the result of—

A visual, hearing, or motor disability;

Intellectual disability;

Emotional disturbance;

Cultural factors;

Environmental or economic disadvantage; or

Limited English proficiency (§300.309 Determining the existence of a specific learning disability)

Source: U.S. Department of Education. (2006, August). *Individuals with disabilities education act, final regulations.* Retrieved from http://www.gpo.gov/fdsys/pkg/FR-2006-08-14/pdf/06-6656.pdf.

test-takers is not relevant. Examples of criterion-referenced tests to assess for learning disabilities include the Stanford Diagnostic Reading Test–4 (Karlsen & Gardner, 2005) and the Brigance Comprehensive Inventory of Basic Skills–II (e.g., Brigance, 2010).

Classroom Assessments

Classroom assessment information, usually considered informal, is the second type of data gathered to determine whether a student has a learning disability. Three types of classroom assessments are most often used: (a) curriculum-based measurement, (b) portfolio assessment, and (c) observation.

Curriculum-based measurement (CBM) is designed specifically to supplement information obtained from formal assessments by sampling a student's understanding of the classroom curriculum (e.g., Espin, Busch, Lembke, Hampton, Seo, & Zukowski, 2013). CBM may include having a student read short passages from books in the district language arts or English curriculum and answer comprehension questions. By comparing the student's reading rate (i.e., correct words read per minute) and comprehension to a sample of other students in the classroom or the district, a determination can be made about the student's learning progress.

Teachers may complete a portfolio assessment as another type of classroom assessment. A *portfolio* is a purposeful collection of a student's work that demonstrates the quality and progress of her learning. For a student being assessed for learning disabilities, a portfolio might include drafts and final versions of writing assignments or samples of assignments and problems solved in mathematics. The intent of a portfolio is to capture a snapshot of the student's performance in the reality of the classroom, and it usually supplements other data gathered in the assessment and identification process.

A third form of classroom assessment is observation. For a student to be identified as having a learning disability (regardless of the criteria being used for determination), federal law requires that he be observed in the general education classroom or, for young children, in a school-like environment, such as a preschool. Observation often involves getting a general sense of the student's academic and behavioral functioning in the classroom. It may also include tabulating information of interest—how often the student leaves his seat, how often the student blurts out answers instead of raising his hand, and how the frequency of such behaviors compares to that among other students in the class.

Criteria for Eligibility

In schools using a traditional approach to identifying learning disabilities, the multidisciplinary team convenes once assessment data have been gathered. Using all of the assessment information, the team then uses the following questions to determine if a student meets the eligibility criteria for having a learning disability:

1. *Does a significant gap exist between the student's ability and academic achievement?* In this traditional identification approach, the team typically compares the student's scores on an individual intelligence test with his scores on the individual norm-referenced or criterion-referenced achievement measures. Curriculum-based measures and portfolio information also are likely to be considered. For example, if a student's measured intellectual ability (i.e., IQ) is 100 but his equivalent reading score is 80, a decision might be made that a learning disability exists. However, if the intelligence score is 90 and the reading score is 88, no significant discrepancy and, hence, no learning disability exists. Any other related information (e.g., information from parents or teacher's records) also can be used in answering this question. Many school districts using this approach have specific guidelines for determining whether a gap is significant (e.g., using standard scores, the discrepancy between ability and achievement must be at least 18 points).

2. *Is the learning problem the result of a disorder in an area of basic psychological processing involved in understanding language?* These processes are included in the definition of *learning disabilities* that you learned earlier and in the description of student characteristics. As the team looks at all the assessment data, it must consider whether such processing problems are present.

3. *Can other possible causes of the learning problem be eliminated?* As noted earlier, the IDEA definition of a learning disability includes the provision that the disability cannot be the result of other factors, including environmental factors (e.g., an unsatisfactory home or school situation), poor teaching, poverty, and poor school attendance. Similarly, learning disabilities cannot be the result of other disabilities (e.g., intellectual disability, vision or hearing disability, behavior disability) or a language difference. This requirement to eliminate possible alternative explanations for a student's learning problems is called the *exclusionary clause.*

If the student's learning problems are serious enough, if the other criteria are met, and if the team determines that the student would benefit from special education, the student is eligible to receive services as having a learning disability.

RTI for Identifying Students Who Have Learning Disabilities

As introduced in Chapter 2, the traditional approach to identifying the presence of learning disabilities as just described has been criticized as a "wait to fail" model because students must progress far enough in school and experience significant academic frustration to even be considered as having learning disabilities (Lyon et al., 2001). Response to intervention (RTI) was added to IDEA 2004 specifically to address these concerns about the identification of students as having learning disabilities (Compton et al., 2012). Although RTI is permitted, but not required, in the law, some form of it is used in all 50 states (Coomer, 2015; Fuchs & Vaughn, 2012). Note that multi-tiered systems of support (MTSS) could be applicable in this discussion, too, but in current special education law only RTI is specified as an alternative approach to identifying learning disabilities.

RTI includes these principles, which illustrate how distinct it is from traditional assessment and identification procedures:

1. It replaces the ability–achievement discrepancy criteria with a simple, direct assessment of the extent of a student's underachievement. This eliminates the need to wait for a discrepancy between ability and achievement to emerge, and it fosters immediate, intensive interventions as soon as unexpected underachievement occurs.
2. RTI includes periodic assessment of all students, called universal screening, using high-quality measures, a practice considered especially critical in prekindergarten through second grade. Doing so provides clear documentation of efforts to identify and address student learning problems.
3. A strong emphasis exists in RTI to prevent whenever possible the identification of a student as having a learning disability. That is, the frequent data collection, use of scientifically based interventions, and deliberate use of increasingly intensive instruction are intended to ensure that many avenues for increasing student achievement have been systematically implemented before the team decides the student has a specific learning disability. This careful focus on data and the use of effective instructional strategies is the topic of Data-Driven Decisions.

DATA-DRIVEN DECISIONS

Options for Recording Data

Regardless of your planned professional role, you will be expected to gather and interpret data in order to determine what to teach, how to teach it, and whether your instruction has been effective. Numerous tools exist to help you in data collection, and many of them have been developed to help teachers use response to intervention procedures. Here are several you might find valuable:

ChartDog Graph Maker

http://www.interventioncentral.org/tools/chart_dog_graph_maker is a page on the Intervention Central website. It enables you to create and save charts for individual students on any skill or behavior you choose.

Curriculum-Based Measurement Warehouse

http://www.interventioncentral.org/cbm_warehouse is another Intervention Central webpage. It offers options for paper-and-pencil data collection. It has 14 preformatted and open-format templates with specific instructions for effectively using each one.

Graphing Made Easy

http://www.oswego.edu/~mcdougal/web_site_4_11_2005/index.html at the State University of New York at Oswego has a simple spreadsheet that can be used to record academic or behavior data as well as suggestions for customizing your charts.

If you would like to make your own data charts and then analyze the data, you will find helpful the set of tutorials at the UCEA Center for the Advanced Study of Technology Leadership in Education at the University of Kentucky (http://schooltechleadership.org/research/school-data-tutorials/data-collection-templates/). The brief video lessons cover data entry, column set-up, and data analysis.

Three-Tiered Models in Response to Intervention

The most common procedures being used to implement the RTI approach address reading problems, and they are outlined in three-tiered models of intervention (Björn, Aro, Koponen, Fuchs, & Fuchs, 2016). Nathaniel, whom you met at the beginning of the chapter, has experienced the three-tiered approach, which is pictured in Figure 5.3.

Here is an explanation of each tier:

Tier 1. Most students should succeed when they are taught to read using practices that have been demonstrated through research to be effective. All students participate in tier 1, and educators are responsible for implementing proven instructional methods, including differentiation, and closely monitoring the progress of students in the core reading curriculum.

Tier 2. For approximately 20% to 30% of students, tier 1 instruction is not enough. That is, the gap between their skills and what would be considered average progress is significant, and it is likely, based on the data, to get worse. Based on diagnostic data gathered, students in tier 2 receive supplemental instruction that might include structured tutoring by a trained assistant or teacher, additional opportunities to practice skills, and individually paced instruction. The interventions are research based, and they are in addition to the core reading instruction being delivered in the classroom.

Tier 3. If diagnostic data indicate that a student still is not making adequate progress in acquiring essential reading skills when tier 2 interventions are being implemented, even more intensive interventions are initiated. For the few students who need this intensive assistance (i.e., usually no more than 5% to 10% of all students), instruction usually is delivered by a reading specialist or even a special educator and often occurs outside the general education classroom. The instruction might include a specific reading program (e.g., Wilson Reading, Corrective

FIGURE 5.3   Response to Intervention: Pyramid of Interventions in Academic Systems

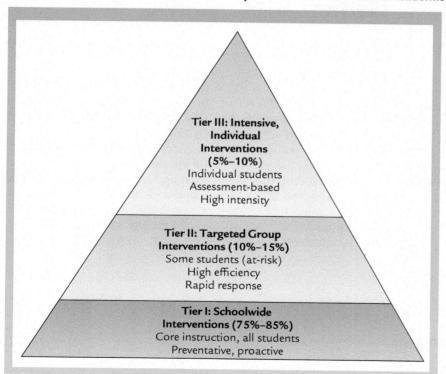

Tier III: Intensive, Individual Interventions (5%–10%)
Individual students
Assessment-based
High intensity

Tier II: Targeted Group Interventions (10%–15%)
Some students (at-risk)
High efficiency
Rapid response

Tier I: Schoolwide Interventions (75%–85%)
Core instruction, all students
Preventative, proactive

Reading), but it is primarily characterized by its intensity, its repeated opportunities for practice and review, its reliance on carefully analyzed and sequenced instruction, and its use of frequent data collection for continuous monitoring of progress. In some but not all applications, this tier is considered a special education service.

Criteria for Eligibility

When RTI is the approach used to assess students for the possible presence of learning disabilities, decision making is slightly different from that in traditional approaches. The multidisciplinary team still convenes and considers the available data, but its focus is on the following:

1. Even though research-based, individually designed, systematically delivered, and increasingly intensive interventions have been implemented, is the student still exhibiting significant gaps in learning compared to what would be expected? Is it likely that, despite the interventions, the gaps will stay the same or increase instead of decrease? Generally, even when RTI procedures are fully implemented, traditional achievement data, classroom observation data, other curriculum-based measures, and sometimes even measures of ability (all described in the preceding section) also may be considered in making a decision about eligibility. However, emphasis remains on the existence of a significant learning gap that, without additional support, will worsen over time.

2. If the team decides that the student is *nonresponsive to intervention*, the student may be determined to have a learning disability.

As RTI has become widely implemented, many questions have been raised related to its use as a means of identifying students as having specific learning disabilities and as a means of preventing the development of significant learning gaps. These topics are addressed later in this chapter.

Patterns of Strengths and Weaknesses

The third permitted means of determining the presence of a specific learning disability contains elements of the other two methods. That is, the team may decide that a pattern of strengths and weaknesses (PSW) indicates the presence of a learning disability. Depending on state policies and local procedures, different types of patterns may be examined. For example, the pattern may be based on discrepant achievement across academic areas as measured by norm- or criterion-referenced measures, such as those utilized in the traditional model. Thus, math achievement is at grade level or above, but reading achievement is significantly below grade level. However, the PSW could be within an area, as might occur when a student reads very accurately but without fluency or when a student reads very fluently but without comprehension.

The criteria for determining the presence of a specific learning disability and the procedures followed, including the types of data gathered, vary by state. For example, if your state has adopted MTSS as its framework, that term may be used instead of RTI. But keep in mind that RTI typically is embedded as part of MTSS, and so the steps followed to identify whether a student has a learning disability will be very similar. As you work in schools, you will undoubtedly learn the details of the specific learning disabilities (SLD) identification approach for your locale.

Did You Know?

Intervention Central (http://interventioncentral.org/) is a website that includes many free resources for teachers working with students struggling academically or behaviorally. It includes links to videos describing various aspects of the RTI and MTSS processes, examples of strategies for working with students, and curriculum-based measures for assessing students' foundational reading and math skills.

Video Example
from
YouTube

MyEdLab
Video Example 5.3
Who has a learning disability (LD)? You might be surprised at the people with LD showcased in this video. (https://www.youtube.com/watch?v=xoeZAXUZbqQ)

MyEdLab **Self-Check 5.3**

MyEdLab **Application Exercise 5.4:** Serge

MyEdLab **Application Exercise 5.5:** Curriculum-Based Measurement

Educating Students with Learning Disabilities

Students with learning disabilities are educated in a range of settings. However, strong emphasis is placed on ensuring that these students are held to the same academic expectations as are typical learners. Federal law outlines the basic requirements for how all students with disabilities receive their education. Within those guidelines, though, many options exist.

Early Childhood

Young children generally are not diagnosed as having learning disabilities for several reasons. First, the indicators of learning disabilities (e.g., problems related to reading, math, or oral and written language) typically are not apparent in preschool children. Second, because the possibility of misdiagnosis is so high, professionals are reluctant to risk the negative impact on child self-perception and teacher expectations that might occur if the learning disability label is applied in error. Overall, the considerable normal differences in rates of development among young children make formal identification inappropriate; what might appear to be a learning disability could easily turn out to be a developmental difference well within the normal range.

Programs for young children with *developmental delays* (the general term you have learned, often given when young children receive special services) usually address areas indirectly related to learning disabilities. For example, such programs focus on improving children's gross-motor skills (e.g., hopping) and fine-motor skills (e.g., using scissors or crayons), their expressive language skills (e.g., naming objects, asking questions to indicate need) and receptive language skills (e.g., following simple directions), their attention (e.g., persisting in a task for several minutes), and their social skills (e.g., taking turns, playing in a group). Interventions in all of these areas help create a solid foundation for later academic tasks, and students with significant delays in these areas may or may not later be identified as having learning disabilities.

Elementary and Secondary School Services

Ninety-eight percent of school-age students with learning disabilities receive their education in a typical public school setting (U.S. Department of Education, 2015). As you can see from the information presented in Figure 5.4, more than 66% of today's students with learning disabilities spend nearly their entire school day in general education settings with their peers. These statistics illustrate the strength of the trend toward inclusive practices introduced in Chapter 1. Only 20 years ago, just 22% of students with learning disabilities spent this much time in general education settings (U.S. Department of Education, 1993).

However, knowing the proportion of time that students spend in general education versus special education settings does not adequately convey what an individual student's services might involve. In schools using best practices, a student with SLD in general education—whether for a large or small part of the day—would use materials adjusted for his reading level and other special needs and access a computer and other appropriate assistive and instructional technology, as illustrated in the Technology Notes. Peer supports, such as peer tutoring or a buddy system, would be in place, and a special educator might co-teach in the classroom for part of the day (Friend, 2014).

In the resource setting (the typical arrangement when students leave the classroom for part of the day), the student would receive intensive, individually

FIGURE 5.4 Educational Placements of Students Ages 6 to 21 Who Have Learning Disabilities (in percentages)

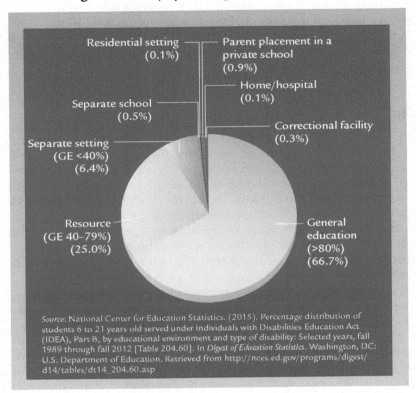

Residential setting (0.1%)

Parent placement in a private school (0.9%)

Home/hospital (0.1%)

Separate school (0.5%)

Correctional facility (0.3%)

Separate setting (GE <40%) (6.4%)

Resource (GE 40–79%) (25.0%)

General education (>80%) (66.7%)

Source: National Center for Education Statistics. (2015). Percentage distribution of students 6 to 21 years old served under Individuals with Disabilities Education Act (IDEA), Part B, by educational environment and type of disability: Selected years, fall 1989 through fall 2012 [Table 204.60]. In *Digest of Education Statistics*. Washington, DC: U.S. Department of Education. Retrieved from http://nces.ed.gov/programs/digest/d14/tables/dt14_204.60.asp

designed, and closely monitored instruction in any academic area affected by the learning disability. A student who is away from the general education classroom for more than 60% of school time is in a self-contained program in which most or all core academic instruction is delivered by a special education teacher who is highly qualified in the core content areas. However, students in such settings often join general education classmates for some instruction, as well as for related arts and electives such as art, music, and technology. In middle and high school settings, students may take exploratory classes, electives, or study skills courses with other students.

Inclusive Practices

As you know, decisions about where students receive their education are determined on the IDEA principle of *least restrictive environment* (LRE) and the specific needs identified in their IEPs. Within this context, the issue of whether inclusive practices are the best educational approach for students with learning disabilities was debated for many years (e.g., Carlberg & Kavale, 1980; DeSimone & Parmar, 2006; McPhail & Freeman, 2005; Volonino & Zigmond, 2007). In the early 21st century, it appears that fundamental questions about whether students with learning disabilities should receive at least some services with their peers have largely been answered, but many questions regarding the best combinations of support in general education settings and special education settings remain (McLeskey, Landers, Hoppey, & Williamson, 2011).

It is important to remember the premise of this text—that inclusion is about how the adults and students in any particular school think about teaching and learning for all the students who go there. Being inclusive does not mean that

•–•–• TECHNOLOGY NOTES

Tools for Students with Learning Disabilities

Technology provides many tools to help students with learning disabilities access the curriculum, take in information, organize their thinking, and demonstrate their learning. Here are several examples:

Text-to-Speech Software

- Both the Macintosh and Windows current operating systems include free text-to-speech functions. In the former system, it's included as part of system preferences/speech. In the latter, it's called *narrator* and is accessed through the Control Panel's Ease of Access icon.
- Natural Reader (http://www.naturalreaders.com/) has a free basic version for both Mac and Windows operating systems that converts virtually any computer text (e.g., word processing, e-mail) or scanned print text to voice, and it can then save the converted files into MP3 and other formats for later listening. An upgraded version with additional features such as word prediction and spell checking is available for a moderate cost.
- Adobe Acrobat Reader XI (http://get.adobe.com/reader/) is the free software most professionals have to open pdf files, and it includes a built-in text-to-speech reader for that file type. It is activated from the View button/Read Out Loud.

Apps to Facilitate Learning

- *Middle School Math Planet,* recommended for students in grades 6–9, is designed to help students build fluency in core math skills. Students can complete activities, or they can complete basic fact drills. Student data are kept within the program so that progress can be monitored.
- *Splash Math,* specifically recommended for students with learning disabilities or dyslexia, has grade-specific math activities, primarily basic functions, which are aligned with the Common Core State Standards. This app is appropriate for students in grades 1–5.
- *Clicker Docs,* for grades 6–12, is a word processing app that reads text aloud at each punctuation, offering alternative word choices for misspellings. Word banks tailored to student needs can be loaded into the app. This app helps students to learn how to edit their work with the feature that adjusts the text reading as punctuation is changed. This app also let students e-mail their work or upload it to Dropbox.
- *Mystery Word Town,* for elementary students, is a game app that incorporates practice on spelling words, and the difficulty level of the words can be adjusted based on student needs. One feature allows custom word lists to be created, and lists for several students can be kept on a single app.
- *SparkNotes,* intended for high school students, includes study guides for most of the literature read in those grades. The analyses offered can help students more deeply understand their reading assignments, although the publisher cautions that the app includes literature with themes that are not appropriate for young readers and notes that students should use this app as a supplement rather than a replacement for reading assigned material.

students never leave the general education setting. Instead, it means that consideration is given to how a student's needs can be met within the classroom context before resorting to instruction in a separate setting. If the latter is considered in the student's best interest, it is provided for as long as it is warranted. Within that framework, professionals in the field now are thinking about the outcomes for students who receive an inclusive education versus those who receive more traditional services. The data are mixed.

For example, Tremblay (2013) studied outcomes for elementary students with learning disabilities in co-taught/inclusive versus solo-taught separate special education settings. He found that the students in the co-taught setting outperformed peers in the separate setting on reading measures. They also had better school attendance. Rea, McLaughlin, and Walther-Thomas (2002) reported similar results for students in middle schools. They found that the students with learning disabilities in inclusive programs earned higher grades, scored at comparable or higher levels on achievement tests, and attended school more days when compared to students with learning disabilities in resource programs.

Not all the results are clearly positive, however. For example, McLeskey and Waldron (2011) reviewed research literature on two topics: (a) instructional practices that improve outcomes for students with SLD and (b) the implementation of such practices in general education settings. They concluded that, particularly for reading instruction, many students with SLD need at least a small amount of instruction in a separate setting. Dyson (2007) reported that parents of students with LD being educated in general education settings experience frustration and stress and find they have to frequently advocate for their children with school professionals. Ultimately, the outcomes for students with SLD depend largely on the quality of the instructional practices in general education classrooms, including implementing universal design for learning (UDL) and differentiation; the availability of supports such as assistive technology; and the provision of intense, separate instruction as it is needed (Sailor, 2015).

Transition and Adulthood

The outcomes for students with learning disabilities as they move into adulthood are as varied as the individuals who compose this group (Gerber, 2012). Some of these young adults successfully complete high school and move into postsecondary options—vocational training, college, and employment—with confidence and success. However, many young adults experience difficulties (e.g., Lee, Rojewski, Gregg, & Jeong, 2015). For example, Murray, Goldstein, Nourse, and Edgar (2000) followed the progress of two cohorts of high school graduates with and without learning disabilities for up to 10 years. They found that the graduates with learning disabilities were significantly less likely to have participated in any form of postsecondary education, and if they did participate, they were more likely than other students to have attended a training school or vocational program than a college or university. Rabren, Eaves, Dunn, & Darch (2013), analyzing survey data one year following high school graduation, found that students with high scores related to education/training (indicating participation in postsecondary education) were more satisfied overall with their lives than those with low education/training scores. Similarly, those with high scores related to their current employment were more satisfied with their lives than those with low scores.

Transition Planning

Why do many students with learning disabilities who are acknowledged to have at least average intelligence continue to have various difficulties as they become adults even though their aspirations are similar to those of students without disabilities (Cortiella, 2011)? Consider the traits and skills students need to go to college or to obtain and keep a job, including an ability to work independently and to seek assistance as needed; to be organized; to focus attention for long periods of time; to listen, speak, read, write, and compute effectively and efficiently; to problem solve; and to handle social situations with competence. These are the precise areas that characterize the challenges faced by many students with specific learning disabilities. And because these students may demonstrate a slower rate of career maturity, poor ability to advocate for themselves, and low self-esteem, they may have unrealistic job expectations in terms of how to juxtapose their strengths and weaknesses with vocational choices (Ju, Kortering, Osmanir, & Zhang, 2015). Think about Audell, the high school student introduced at the beginning of this chapter. How might his learning disabilities affect his postsecondary options, especially given his goal of obtaining a basketball scholarship?

Since transition planning was added to federal special education law in 1990, increased attention has been paid to issues such as those just outlined by preparing students with learning disabilities for life after high school. As you know, a transition plan includes a statement of needs that begins at age 16 and is updated annually. The statement pertains to the student's course of study and puts forth a specific plan with measurable goals and an explanation to the student of his rights.

However, the quality of transition plans and services is still not fully established (Carter, Lane, Cooney, Weir, Moss, & Machalicek, 2013; Cortiella & Horowitz, 2014). Researchers studying students in the transition process have reported disappointing results (Agran & Hughes, 2008; Hitchings et al., 2001): Of the students who had received special education services during their elementary or secondary school years, only one could recall participating in a meeting specifically to plan transition. Many of the students had difficulty explaining the nature of their disabilities and the impact their disabilities might have on career choice, and few reported taking an active role in transition planning.

Model Transition Practices

Model practices for transitioning for students with learning disabilities include a number of features, including these (Shaw, Dukes, & Madaus, 2012):

- Inclusion of career awareness and exploration activities beginning in the freshman year and continuing through high school
- Instruction related to skills needed for successful transition, including problem solving, organization, self-advocacy, and communication
- Transition planning activities for school professionals and community members regarding the next steps that might be needed to improve activities and services
- A structured process for addressing transition, completed across time, involving appropriate people and resources, and clearly documented

In addition, students and parents should be integrally involved in transition planning. Academics should be given priority; however, work experiences increasingly are being incorporated into student plans, and linkages should be created between students and their parents and postschool services, such as the Division for Vocational Rehabilitation.

When students with learning disabilities attend college, they can receive supports through the Americans with Disabilities Act (ADA), a law you learned about in Chapter 1.

MyEdLab **Self-Check 5.4**

MyEdLab **Application Exercise 5.6:** Encouraging Self-Advocacy

MyEdLab **Application Exercise 5.7:** Inclusive Practices

Recommended Educational Practices for Students with Learning Disabilities

For more than two decades, professionals have been investigating which techniques and methods are most effective for addressing the academic, cognitive, social, and behavioral needs of students with learning disabilities. A wealth of research information now is available to guide teachers' practices (e.g., Ciullo, Lembke, Carlisle, Thomas, Goodwin, & Judd, 2016; Gillespie & Graham, 2014; Jitendra, Burgess, & Gajria, 2011; Schumaker & Deshler, 2009; Solis, Ciullo, Vaughn, Pyle, Hassaram, & Leroux, 2012). These data indicate that two methods, used in combination, are highly effective for most students, regardless of their age or their specific type of learning disability: direct instruction (DI) and strategy instruction (SI).

Direct Instruction

Direct instruction (DI) is a comprehensive, teacher-led approach based on decades of research. Direct instruction emphasizes maximizing not only the quantity of instruction students receive but also the quality (National Institute for Direct Instruction, 2016; Rupley, Blair, & Nichols, 2009). This approach includes clear demonstrations of new information in small segments, practice that is teacher guided, and immediate feedback to students on their work. Direct instruction is based on these guiding principles:

1. Present lessons in a well-organized, sequenced manner.
2. Begin lessons with a short review of the previously learned skills that are necessary to begin the lesson.
3. Begin lessons with a short statement of goals. Provide clear, concise explanations and illustrations of what is to be learned.
4. Present new material in small steps with practice and demonstrations at each step. Provide initial guidance through practice activities.
5. Provide students with frequent opportunities to practice and generalize skills.
6. Ask questions to check students' understanding, and obtain responses from everyone (Mather & Goldstein, 2001, p. 146).

The Instruction in Action illustrates the use of direct instruction in a sample lesson plan.

INSTRUCTION IN **ACTION**

Using Direct Instruction

Direct instruction (DI) is one of the most recommended approaches for teaching students with learning disabilities. Here is a sample lesson plan based on DI principles.

Title of Lesson: Contractions (e.g., *he's, she's, it's, that's*)

Classroom Management: (1–2 minutes)

Grading Criteria: 15% reading sentences correctly, 35% generation of new sentences with learned contractions, 25% completed worksheet, and 25% slate writing activity.

Contingency: If the entire class's criterion level performance is at or better than 85% correct, students qualify for extra slate time (i.e., free choice to write or draw on their slates).

Specific Learning Outcomes: (1–2 minutes)

"Today, we are going to learn about contractions. You will learn to read a contraction alone and in a sentence. You will also learn to correctly write a contraction when given two words, and use the newly learned contraction in a sentence."

Anticipatory Set: (3 minutes)

Focus Statement. "Most often when we speak, we shorten a word or phrase by omitting one or more sounds. Listen to this sentence, 'It is raining.' Now listen again as I omit a sound, 'It's raining.' What two words did I shorten by omitting a sound?" (Students respond.) (Repeat with other examples such as "He's going to the store" and "She's at the mall.")

"When we shorten a word or phrase by omitting one or more sounds or letters, it is called a contraction."

Relevance of the Lesson. "It is important to learn how to read contractions because they are often used in storybooks, newspapers, magazines, and most material that you read. Also, you need to learn how to write contractions to use in your own writing."

Transfer of Past Learning. "We learn many new words in reading. A contraction is a special word because it is written differently than a regular word. Learning how to read and write contractions will make you a better reader and writer."

New Vocabulary Terms: (1–2 minutes)

Contraction—shortening of a word or phrase by omitting one or more letters or sounds.

Apostrophe—a mark that takes the place of the missing letter(s) in the contraction; it looks like a comma but is placed at the top of the line.

Teaching: (10–12 minutes)

1. Review decoding words in isolation and in sentences: *he, she, it, that, is*. Have students use words in their own sentences.

   Questions
   "What is this word?"
   "Read this sentence."
   "Use this word in your own sentence."

2. Define a contraction and an apostrophe.

   Questions
   "When a word or phrase is shortened by omitting one or more letters or sounds, it is called a _____."
   "What is the name of the visual mark used to take the place of the missing letters?"

3. Present examples and nonexamples of contractions, and have students identify them.

   Examples:
   he's, she's, it's, that's.
   Nonexamples:
   cat, drum, bell.

   Questions
   "Is this a contraction? Why or why not?"

4. Model the sequence of steps for forming contractions.

   Example: It is
   a. Write the two words together without a space between them.
   b. Erase the letter *i* in *is*, and put an apostrophe in its place.
   c. Read the new word by blending the sounds. Point out that the apostrophe doesn't make a sound.

   Have students read the word, spell it, and repeat the word again.

   d. Write sentences:
   It is hot today.
   It's hot today.
   "Do these two sentences mean the same thing? How do you know?"
   Have students read sentences with the teacher.
   Have students use the contraction in a new sentence.

   e. Repeat steps a–d with other examples (e.g., *he, she, that*) using simple sentences.

5. Do a discrimination test of irregular words and previously known words. Call on students as a group to read words by randomly pointing to each word several times.

6. Test individual students on reading contractions.

Guided and Independent Practice: (5–8 minutes)

1. Students first complete a worksheet with teacher direction and then do similar exercises independently. Students match the contraction with the two words that it is composed of.

2. The teacher provides guided and independent practice in writing the contractions on slates when the two words that make up the contraction are presented on the board.

3. Examples on board: *he is; she is; it is; that is*

4. Students will correctly write the contractions in newly generated sentences and share sentences with the class.

Closure: (3 minutes)

"Today, we learned about contractions and the apostrophe. We also learned that contractions have the same meaning as the two words that make them up. What is a contraction? What is an apostrophe? What word means the same as *it is*? What two words make up *he's*?"

Source: Jitendra, A. K., & Torgerson-Tubiello, R. (1997). Let's learn contractions! *Teaching Exceptional Children*, 29(4), 16–19. Copyright © 1997 by the Council for Exceptional Children. Reproduced by permission of the Council for Exceptional Children via Copyright Clearance Center.

Strategy Instruction

One of the overall goals for all students' education is independence. Because of students' learning disabilities, achieving academic independence can be particularly difficult. Some students cannot write essays because they do not know the components of an essay and what content goes in an introduction, body, and conclusion. Others do not comprehend their textbooks because they do not have a plan for processing and remembering the information presented. Yet others struggle to take notes because they cannot decide what information is essential or how to organize it. Strategy instruction (SI), a highly recommended method for students with learning disabilities, addresses these types of problems (Krawec & Montague, 2012). *Strategies* are techniques, principles, and rules that guide students to complete tasks independently (Friend & Bursuck, 2016).

Strategies outline the steps students can take to accomplish learning tasks and provide some type of memory assistance (often an acronym) so that students can easily recall them (e.g., Freeman-Green, O'Brien, Wood, & Hitt, 2015). Teachers usually introduce strategies by helping students realize an instructional dilemma (e.g., a challenge students encounter with word problems in math) and then explaining why the strategy will help them overcome the dilemma. In the Instruction in Action, you can see specific strategy examples.

INSTRUCTION IN **ACTION**

Sample Learning Strategies

Here are two examples of learning strategies to help students with learning disabilities succeed in a wide variety of tasks.

The AWARE Strategy for Note-Taking

The AWARE strategy is designed for high school and college students who need a systematic way to remember to take notes effectively during lectures and other instruction.

1. **A**rrange to take notes.
   Arrive early.
   Take a seat near the front or center.
   Obtain a pen and notebook.
   Note the date.
2. **W**rite quickly.
   Indent minor points.
   Record some words without vowels.
3. **A**pply cues.
   Attend to accents and organizational verbal cues.
   Record cued lecture ideas.
   Make checkmarks before cued ideas.
4. **R**eview notes as soon as possible.
5. **E**dit notes.
   Add information you forgot to record.

Add personal details.
Supplement notes with details from readings.

TREE for Writing

TREE is designed for elementary school students as a way to assist them in learning how to write persuasive essays.

1. **T**opic sentence
   Tell what you believe.
2. **R**easons
   Tell three or more reasons: Why do I believe this?
   Will my readers believe this?
3. **E**nding
   Wrap it up!
4. **E**xamine
   Ask myself: Do I have all my parts?

Keep in mind that students need to be taught how to use strategies. They should see the importance of the strategy, discuss it, watch you model it, and memorize it. You should provide ongoing support until students can use a strategy independently.

Source: Based on Hughes, C. A., & Suritsky, S. K. (1993). Notetaking skills and strategies for students with learning disabilities. *Preventing School Failure, 38*(1), 7–11; Harris, K. R., Graham, S., & Mason, L. H. (2003). Self-regulated strategy development in the classroom: Part of a balanced approach to writing instruction for students with disabilities. *Focus on Exceptional Children, 35*(7), 1–16.

Many research-based strategies have been described in the professional literature (e.g., Friend & Bursuck, 2016; Montague, Enders, & Dietz, 2011; Pfannenstiel, Bryant, Bryant, & Porterfield, 2015), from those for enhancing writing skills to those for learning social studies to those for solving algebraic equations. You are likely to find a strategy that can assist a student with learning disabilities regardless of her age or specific needs.

MyEdLab **Self-Check 5.5**

MyEdLab **Application Exercise 5.8:** Direct Instruction Reading Lesson

MyEdLab **Application Exercise 5.9:** Split-Page Note-Taking

Parent and Family Perspectives

Unlike the parents of students with significant sensory, cognitive, or physical disabilities, who may learn of their child's disabilities soon after birth, parents of children with learning disabilities often are not aware of their child's special needs until the child is enrolled in school and experiences frustration and failure in academic tasks. Parents may be surprised when they are informed about their child's disability, relieved to hear an explanation for their child's struggles to learn, or concerned about the time lost in finding effective interventions. As Mary, a college-educated professional and the mother of first-grader Guy, told school professionals as they conducted the initial eligibility and IEP meeting:

> Stop. Wait. You're saying my son has a disability—a disability. You've just changed my whole world and how I think about Guy. You can't just say, "He's learning disabled. Let's write a plan for his education." I need to think about this. I need to understand better what this means. It may be routine to you, but he's my son. I can't sit here right now and make decisions. It's his life we're talking about. I wouldn't sign a contract to buy a car without a lot of thought and some careful research. How can you expect me to sign these papers about Guy's life without even knowing what I'm signing? I need to know what this means and what I'm agreeing to before I can sign anything.

Although not all parents can express their sentiments in such an articulate manner, it is important to remember that the disability label often affects parents of students with learning disabilities in ways that school professionals cannot completely understand (Heiman, Zinck, & Heath, 2008). Many parents will have to redefine their image of their child. Some parents may blame school personnel for their child's problems, especially if the child is identified during middle or high school. Other parents may believe that they have failed their child and that they should have been able to prevent the disability. Parents may also inappropriately lower their expectations for their children's success in school (Shifrer, 2013). Special education teachers and other school professionals need to be aware that their attitudes toward parents, their communications with them, and their openness to parent and family perspectives can affect greatly the quality of the student's education and support received from home. In fact, one of the most common concerns expressed by parents of students with learning disabilities about school services is the frequency (e.g., too little) and focus (e.g., negative instead of positive) of communication from teachers and other professionals.

Parents as Partners

Many parents of students with learning disabilities take active roles in their children's education. For example, Duquette, Fullarton, Orders, & Robertson-Grewal (2011), in a qualitative study that examined the advocacy roles of parents of students with specific learning disabilities, found that parents—especially mothers—undertook a variety of advocacy roles for their children, working with school professionals or in opposition to them. Their efforts were based on their understanding that their children required support in order to succeed in school and that, as parents, they sometimes were their children's only advocate.

But parents sometimes report that their relationships with school professionals are not conducive to involvement. Rodriguez, Blatz, and Elbaum (2014) used focus groups and individual interviews with 96 parents of children with disabilities, including learning disabilities and others. Among other findings, parents' responses were almost equally divided between the perception that schools/teachers were receptive to parent input and the perception that they were not receptive. Parents also reported that the quality of their children's services was dependent on the specific teacher involved and that lack of communication was a barrier to parents' involvement in their children's education. In yet another study, Starr, Foy, Cramer, and Singh (2006) compared the experiences of parents of students with learning disabilities to those of parents of students with other, more apparent disabilities (e.g., Down syndrome). They found that the former group of parents generally was less satisfied than the latter group with their interactions with school professionals and the services their children received. The authors cautioned that their data suggest the importance of educating teachers about forming partnerships with parents and ensuring that promised supports and services are implemented. Clearly, working closely with parents should be a top priority for professionals who teach students with learning disabilities.

MyEdLab **Self-Check 5.6**

MyEdLab **Application Exercise 5.10:** Family Responses to Their Child's Learning Disability

---

Trends and Issues Affecting the Field of Learning Disabilities

Controversy has characterized the field of learning disabilities almost since its inception, and that trend continues today. In this era in which educational standards are as high as they have ever been and teacher accountability for student outcomes is a priority, it is not surprising that many aspects of learning disabilities continue to be examined under a critical lens.

Issues Related to Response to Intervention

Did You Know?

Signed into law by President Obama in December 2015, the Every Student Succeeds Act is the reauthorization of the Elementary and Secondary Education ACT (formerly called *No Child Left Behind*). This law incorporates multi-tiered systems of support (MTSS), a topic you can learn more about at this U.S. Department of Education website: http://www2.ed.gov/about/inits/ed/earlyliteracy/tools.html

Earlier in this chapter, you learned how response to intervention, sometimes embedded as part of a multi-tiered system of support, is being implemented as a procedure for identifying students as having learning disabilities in a way that is significantly different from traditional approaches. RTI has many benefits, including its reliance on data directly related to instruction and its potential for heading off serious learning problems through early intervention (e.g., Ritchey, Silverman, Montanaro, Speece, & Schatschneider, 2012; Zirkel, 2011a). A rapidly growing body of professional literature is exploring both the applications and the viability of RTI. Not surprisingly, a number of questions are being raised regarding its use.

First, fundamental questions have been raised about the demonstrated effectiveness of RTI in remediating students' learning problems. One carefully designed study sampled RTI implementation and outcomes for students in grades 1 through 3 in 146 school districts in 13 states (Balu, Zhu, Doolittle, Schiller, Jenkins, & Gersten, 2015). The researchers found that first-grade students who received reading interventions beginning in the fall had lower reading scores in the spring than similar students who did not receive interventions. For students in grades 2 and 3, interventions had no significant impact on spring reading outcomes. If RTI does not lead to improved student outcomes, should it be integral to addressing struggling learners? Is it a valid means for determining whether a student might have a learning disability?

Second, some professionals are concerned that RTI may not adequately and fairly address the diversity of students who may have learning disabilities (Cramer, 2015; Graves & McConnell, 2014). For example, students who are gifted and who also have learning disabilities may be able to compensate enough for their areas of deficiency that they will not be identified using an RTI model, even though a traditional approach would have highlighted a discrepancy between these students' potential and their achievement (Crepeau-Hobson & Bianco, 2011). A possible result is that RTI might underidentify students who are gifted and learning disabled. Conversely, concern has been raised regarding RTI for students who have been overrepresented in special education, including those from culturally diverse groups and those who live in poverty and other high-risk situations. For these students, a real risk of overidentification may exist (e.g., Artiles, Bal, & King Thorius, 2010; Denton, 2012; Skiba et al., 2008).

A third area of concern has to do with the specific procedures that make up response to intervention and the ways these procedures are implemented (e.g., Compton et al., 2012; Vujnovic, Fabiano, Morris, Norman, Hallmark, & Hartley, 2014). Some of the questions being raised are these:

- Which interventions are most likely to result in accelerated student learning?
- Should all students proceed through each tier of instruction, or are the needs of some students such that they should immediately receive the highly intensive instruction of tier 3?
- For how long should an intervention be implemented before it is determined to be ineffective?
- How often and for how long should students receive tier 2 and tier 3 interventions?
- Which research-based interventions should be used at each tier?

A fourth set of concerns pertains to the resources required to effectively and fully utilize RTI models. For example, implementing RTI requires that educators understand research-based interventions and strategies for data collection related to screening, diagnostics, and progress monitoring (e.g., Spear-Swerling & Cheesman, 2012). The implication is that considerable professional development is needed, and resources must be committed for that purpose. In addition, professionals need appropriate materials for assessment and instruction; again, resources must be allocated for the purchase of such items.

Yet another area of concern relates to the emerging implementation of RTI, sometimes in MTSS, in states and local school districts (Zirkel, 2011a, 2011b). Although intended to directly address problems in the identification of students as having learning disabilities, in many locales RTI has become a renewed and more data-driven way to provide high-quality instruction to any struggling learner, and it is being implemented to address behavior problems as well as academic deficits (e.g., Freeman, Miller, & Newcomer, 2015; Myers, Simonsen, & Sugai, 2011). This may be a positive step, but it calls into question whether RTI is truly being used as a means of determining the presence of learning disabilities. This point of view is bolstered by the fact that most states require at least some traditional assessment procedures to be followed, even when an RTI system is in place (Ahearn, 2008).

Response to intervention and multi-tiered systems of support have the potential to significantly change how students who struggle to learn receive their education. However, professionals generally agree that much work remains to be done related to research, state and local policies, and classroom practice. Whatever your planned role as a professional educator, you should anticipate that you will be affected by RTI/MTSS, and you should closely watch for developments related to its implementation.

Response to intervention (RTI), sometimes embedded as part of a multi-tiered system of support (MTSS), was added to IDEA as an option for identifying the presence of a learning disability, but it is now often used beyond that purpose, raising questions about its validity and appropriate use.

Transition to Post-Secondary Options for Students with Specific Learning Disabilities

Because students with specific learning disabilities also have average or above average abilities, you might expect that, given strong special education services through the school years, they would attend college and succeed in careers much like their peers without disabilities. That is not necessarily the case. For example, although the graduation rate for students with SLD has improved over the past several years, it is still considerably lower than the rate for students without disabilities (National Center for Education Statistics, 2016). Further, given the available data, concern continues to be voiced about the supports and services students with SLD are receiving that prepare them for college and subsequent careers (Bassett & Dunn, 2012). Although transition was introduced earlier in this chapter, this discussion focuses in more depth on issues related to it.

One area of concern relates to students' academic access. For example, in the classroom, students with SLD seldom use technology designed specifically to address their special needs (e.g., technology to provide access to print materials) (e.g., Adebisi, Liman, & Longpoe, 2015; Cortiella, 2011). Others have noted that there is a tradition of setting lower expectations for these students and thus excluding them from courses such as those necessary to anticipate a career in science, technology, engineering, or mathematics (Doren, Murray, & Gau, 2014; Dunn, Rabren, Taylor, & Dotson, 2012). An example is the practice of enrolling students with SLD in "basic" courses that follow the same curriculum but may simplify it. A related practice is grouping students who struggle to learn, both those with SLD and others, so that professionals sometimes find it nearly impossible to hold rigorous standards and instruct students at the pace needed. Without access to a variety of accommodations and clear expectations that students can succeed in the same courses as nondisabled peers, the postsecondary futures of students with SLD too often are limited.

Challenges exist beyond access to the content necessary for success. Two related sets of skills are essential for students as they leave high school: self-determination and self-advocacy (e.g., Field & Hoffman, 2012; Prater, Redman, Anderson, & Gibb, 2014). *Self-determination* refers to students' knowledge and skills to understand their strengths and weaknesses and to use that knowledge to set and pursue goals. *Self-advocacy* refers to students' skills for speaking on their own behalf and constructively communicating to others their needs.

Many examples of the importance of these skills can be presented, especially for a student such as Delores, introduced at the beginning of this chapter. First, if students do not assert their interests and career plans, they may permit others to make key decisions regarding their postsecondary education (Madaus, Faggella-Luby, & Dukes, 2011). Further, students need to be willing to identify themselves as having a disability. Some students are reluctant to do this on college applications because they fear it will affect their admission status; others have been inappropriately advised by school counselors to drop their learning disability designation prior to applying for college. In addition, students need to research and access the supports available to them from the college or university campus office designed to provide such assistance. These supports might include tutors, note-takers, and audiotaped textbooks. Finally, students need to be confident enough to articulate their needs to professors and negotiate accommodations, such as extended time for tests, so that they can compensate for their learning disabilities. Unless students learn and use strong self-advocacy skills, they are likely to drop out of college or to remain underemployed or unemployed (Madaus et al., 2011). If they have these skills, they are likely to complete college and enter the workforce much like other young adults (McCall, 2015).

MyEdLab
Video Example 5.4

How do the points described in this section apply to Bridget, the student with dyslexia who discusses her school experience and future goals in this video?

MyEdLab **Self-Check 5.7**

MyEdLab **Application Exercise 5.11:** Trends and Issues

MyEdLab **Application Exercise 5.12:** Progress Monitoring in RTI

Summary

LO5.1   The origin of the learning disabilities field can be traced to 19th-century research on the brain, but recognition of learning disabilities as a discrete disability category occurred in the 1960s. The definition of *specific learning disability* (SLD) that guides most school practices today originated in the first federal special education law in 1975. Students with learning disabilities, which may have physiological or environmental causes, comprise the largest group receiving special education.

LO5.2   Students with learning disabilities experience problems in psychological processing, and they may experience problems in cognition (e.g., perception or memory), one or more academic areas, social or emotional functioning, and behavior.

LO5.3   Three approaches may be used to determine whether a student has a specific learning disability: (a) a discrepancy between ability and achievement, (b) failure of a student's learning rate to improve when research-based interventions are used (a direct application of response to intervention or multi-tiered systems of support), and (c) patterns of strengths and weakness in learning.

LO5.4   Most students with learning disabilities receive their services in general education settings with some type of special education assistance there or in a separate setting. A few are educated in more restrictive settings such as separate classes or schools.

LO5.5   One recommended instructional practice for students with learning disabilities includes direct instruction, which is a highly structured, teacher-led approach for teaching students across academic areas. A second recommended practice is strategy instruction, which includes explicit steps, systematically taught, to guide students so that they can achieve independence in completing common academic tasks.

LO5.6   Some parents of students with specific learning disabilities are highly involved in their children's education. However, other parents, especially those from nondominant cultures and those who live in poverty, find that significant barriers to participation can occur.

LO5.7   Two important issues currently facing the learning disabilities field are (a) the validity of and appropriate uses for response to intervention and (b) transition needs and services for students with learning disabilities as they leave high school for postsecondary education or employment.

Back to the Cases

Now that you've read about specific learning disabilities, look back at the student stories at the beginning of this chapter. Then, answer the questions about each of their cases.

MyEdLab **Case Study 5.1**

NATHANIEL. Nathaniel is a student who received early and intensive intervention that is part of the response to intervention (RTI) procedures, but he still was identified as having a learning disability and now goes to a separate special education setting for reading instruction.

MyEdLab **Case Study 5.2**

DELORES. Delores is struggling for social acceptance in middle school, and she has become the victim of bullying.

MyEdLab **Case Study 5.3**

AUDELL. Audell is working hard to reach his goal of obtaining a basketball scholarship, and he has an extensive system of supports in place. But he still sometimes wonders whether he will actually succeed.

6

Students with Attention Deficit–Hyperactivity Disorder

Learning Outcomes

LO6.1 Define attention deficit–hyperactivity disorder (ADHD), explain its prevalence and causes, and outline its development as a recognized special need.

LO6.2 Describe characteristics of individuals with attention deficit–hyperactivity disorder.

LO6.3 Explain how ADHD is identified.

LO6.4 Outline how learners with attention deficit–hyperactivity disorder receive their education.

LO6.5 Describe recommended interventions and educational practices for students with ADHD.

LO6.6 Explain the perspectives and concerns that parents and families of students with attention deficit–hyperactivity disorder may have.

LO6.7 Identify trends and issues influencing the field of ADHD.

CEDRIC

Cedric has always been an active child. He has the dubious distinction of having been asked not to return to two different preschool programs because of his behavior; concerns were raised about his safety and that of other students after several incidents of running away from teachers, climbing on classroom furniture, and pushing and repeatedly hitting other children. One of the preschool teachers used the word *whirlwind* to describe Cedric. Cedric's parents report that he prefers games and activities that include lots of movement, and he most enjoys swimming at the neighborhood pool. Cedric's pediatrician diagnosed him with ADHD when he was 4 years old, and he has taken medication since that time. His mother also has attended a variety of parent education classes to learn how to better understand and respond to Cedric's attentional problems. At home he follows a highly structured routine each morning and evening, and he earns rewards (such as extra swimming time) for positive behavior. In first grade, Cedric has difficulty with the necessary classroom structure and procedures, as well as the expectation for focusing attention, remaining seated for some activities, and taking turns. Cedric's teacher often is surprised by what he has learned: She sometimes assumes that he is not listening because he so often is moving, but she is gradually recognizing this is not always the case. The school's intervention team has discussed Cedric's academic and behavior needs. For now, since he is making appropriate learning progress, they are focusing on helping his teacher address behavior concerns. Cedric says of his behavior, "Sometimes I just do things and can't stop," a description his teacher would consider very accurate. Cedric has a Section 504 plan that addresses his medication and behavior plan. He does not receive special education services, nor does that seem likely to happen at this point. Although he experiences difficulties, he does not have a disability as defined by the Individuals with Disabilities Education Act (IDEA).

CARLOS

Carlos is a sixth-grade student at Carter Middle School. He is from a bilingual home, and he speaks fluently in both Spanish and English, but he has had an IEP since he was in the second grade because of significant reading problems in both languages, and he participates in a remedial reading course co-taught by a reading specialist and his special education teacher. His teachers generally have commented that he is an exceptionally active student who seems to have difficulty attending to schoolwork. Last year, after several serious behavior incidents and multiple meetings called by Carlos's teachers and principal, his concerned mother consulted his pediatrician. Based on multiple assessments, Carlos was determined to have attention deficit–hyperactivity disorder (ADHD). The medication prescribed has helped Carlos in terms of focusing on schoolwork, but thus far it has not seemed to positively influence his performance in reading, and his behavioral difficulties seem to be accelerating. Students who might be positive role models tend to avoid Carlos, and so he is associating with students who often are disruptive in school and who are experimenting in the neighborhood with alcohol and cigarettes. The situation is somewhat complicated by the fact that Carlos, his mother, and his two siblings currently live with his maternal grandparents. Carlos's grandfather characterizes his behavior as stubbornness and punishes him. Carlos's mother does not believe this is appropriate, but she is hesitant to anger her father.

MARCUS

Marcus will graduate in one more year from M. L. King High School, and with this major milestone in sight, he knows he will make it. He believes he has had to work harder than most other students, not only to learn but also to do all the other things related to attending school. He includes on this list activities such as remembering to take books and assignments home; remembering to do homework, especially long-term projects; getting everything back to school; and turning in his assignments instead of leaving them in his locker. He writes *everything* down, and he also relies on a close friend to help him keep track of the details of being a high school student. At home Marcus tries to follow a routine and to go to bed at a reasonable time, but he keeps two alarm clocks set and places them across the room from his bed because he tends to oversleep. Marcus has encountered several teachers who were unwilling to accommodate his special needs, maintaining that he could pay attention if he tried. In those situations, Marcus has had some behavior issues, including storming out of a classroom and using profanity after arguing with one teacher. Most teachers have been understanding, though. He is especially grateful that his high school resource teacher, Mr. Lewis, encouraged him to think about his future. Because of his dual interests in working outdoors and outdoor sports, Marcus plans to attend a two-year community college program in turf-grass management technology while he decides whether to continue his education with a degree in business administration. Marcus knows that adults with attention problems often have difficulty selecting a major and sticking with the demands of postsecondary education, and he is determined to avoid these problems. Marcus is identified as having both a learning disability and a health impairment for his ADHD, but his parents, and now Marcus himself, are adamant that he can manage his special needs through structure and behavior supports rather than relying on medication as an intervention.

When you were in school, did you have classmates like Cedric, Carlos, and Marcus who could not seem to focus on their schoolwork, who were constantly getting out of their seats and distracting other students from learning? Even as a child, you realized that the active behaviors of those classmates were unusual. Have you ever had a friend who always was thinking about something other than the situation at hand? Did it seem that every time you asked that friend a question, you had to ask it again, even though you were sure he or she was paying attention to you? Perhaps you are one of the students who displayed such behaviors, and you are reading this paragraph thinking that you could have contributed your own story to begin this chapter.

Students who have attentional problems have received extensive consideration, especially during the past three decades, both among the scholars who have made great strides in understanding the nature of this disorder (e.g., Mary, et al., 2016; Wiggs, Elmore, Nigg, & Nikolas, 2016) and in the popular press through newspaper and magazine articles (e.g., Leonard, 2016; Scudder, Lipkin, & Finding, 2015). A positive result is that parents and professionals now better understand that attention deficit–hyperactivity disorder (ADHD) is a lifelong and chronic disorder. It can profoundly affect students' early childhood and school careers as well as their adjustment during adulthood (Howard et al., 2016; Matthies, Philipsen, & Svaldi, 2012; Schneider, Lam, & Mahone, 2016; National Institute of Mental Health, 2008).

It should be noted as you begin reading this chapter that ADHD is **not** a disability directly addressed by the Individuals with Disabilities Education Act (IDEA). That is, there is **no disability category in IDEA called *ADHD*.** In fact, many students with ADHD are served through Section 504 of the Vocational Act of 1973, a topic introduced in Chapter 1 and discussed in greater detail later in this chapter. However, if ADHD is significant, a student also may qualify for services as *other health impaired* (OHI), as Marcus did, even though ADHD is a disorder that is very different from the other chronic health conditions included in the OHI category (and discussed in Chapter 13). However, because ADHD is such a common disorder about which so much is known and because it is often comorbid with specific learning disabilities and emotional disabilities, it merits in-depth consideration, and so it is addressed in this text in its own chapter.

Understanding Attention Deficit–Hyperactivity Disorder

The fact that some children are so extraordinarily active that adults take notice and view them as having behavior problems has been recognized for many years. Today's thinking about these students and best practices for effectively working with them comes from decades of research and discussion.

Development of the ADHD Field

The first known formal description of ADHD was reported by British physician George Still in 1902, attributing some children's unexplained misbehavior and impulsivity to an unknown medical condition (Lange, Reichl, Lange, Tucha, & Tucha, 2010). Interest in understanding and treating attentional problems continued through the 20th century, with physicians and psychologists first studying children's *hyperactivity* (excessive movement) but shifting their research in the 1970s to children's *cognitive impulsivity*—that is, their difficulties focusing. This latter line of research eventually led to exploration of the brain's role in ADHD, and work in that area dominates the field today (e.g., Duerden, Tannock, &

Dockstader, 2012; Tamm & Juranek, 2012). Figure 6.1 concisely summarizes the history of the study of ADHD.

Terminology Related to ADHD

The language used to describe attentional problems has reflected the evolving thinking about their origins and characteristics. In the early part of the 20th century, children were called *hyperkinetic* and were referred to as having minimal brain dysfunction (MBD) (Lange et al., 2010). Later they were called *hyperactive* (Renshaw, 1974). In 1980, the *Diagnostic and Statistical Manual of Mental Disorders–III (DSM-III)* introduced the term attention deficit disorder (ADD) to describe this group of children, and it noted that the condition could exist with or without hyperactivity (American Psychiatric Association, 1980). Several years later that term was redefined to encompass both types of the disorder and was called attention deficit–hyperactivity disorder (ADHD). In yet another revision, the fourth edition of the *DSM (DSM-IV)* retained the ADHD term but reverted to distinguishing whether hyperactivity was present (American Psychiatric Association, 1994). Even though you might still hear some professionals and parents use the term ADD, the most recent and currently accurate term to describe this disorder is attention deficit–hyperactivity disorder (ADHD).

Definition of Attention Deficit–Hyperactivity Disorder

Because ADHD is not a category of disability in IDEA, it is not defined there. The definition instead is found in the *Diagnostic and Statistical Manual of Mental Disorders* of the American Psychiatric Association (5th edition) (DSM-V). Attention deficit–hyperactivity disorder (ADHD) is considered a distinct psychiatric disorder not explained as another mental disorder (e.g., schizophrenia), although it may exist concurrently with other disorders, such as autism. Individuals with ADHD display multiple symptoms across two or more settings; the symptoms began occurring prior to 12 years of age; and the disorder negatively affects social, emotional, or academic functioning. It is important to note that for a diagnosis of ADHD to be valid, a student must clearly demonstrate a pattern of behaviors consistent with the diagnosis, and those behaviors must occur over time and negatively affect the student's academic and/or social functioning. That is, ADHD symptoms are not related to a single stressful event nor are they triggered by particular activities (e.g., occurring only when expected to read for a long time), but they do cause the student to struggle to learn.

The definition of ADHD is clarified through a listing of the diagnostic criteria used to determine whether a child has ADHD. These include the following:

- For some students with ADHD, inattention is the primary symptom. These students may skip important parts of an assignment, may appear to be daydreaming during large-group instruction, cannot seem to get organized, and generally seem forgetful both in school and at home. This variation of the disorder is called ADHD—predominantly inattentive type.
- For another group of students with ADHD, the primary symptom is a combination of hyperactivity—high amounts of movement, and impulsivity—and inability to "put on the brakes" before acting. Students who have this type of ADHD tap their desks and wiggle in their seats, often run instead of walk, blurt out answers, appear to have an internal engine that does not stop, and may talk a lot. This form of the disorder is called ADHD—predominantly hyperactive–impulsive type.
- Some students with ADHD have symptoms suggesting that both inattention and hyperactivity–impulsivity are part of their disorder. These students are referred to as having ADHD—combined presentation.

FIGURE 6.1 Time Line: Development of the ADHD Field

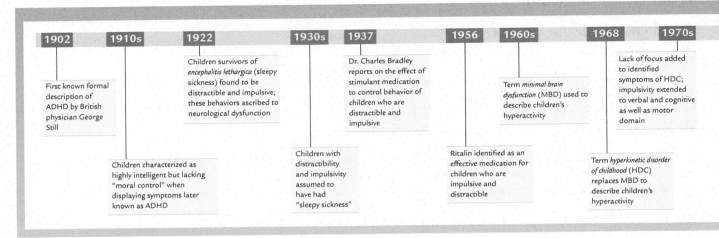

The terms for and descriptions of ADHD can be a bit confusing. This list summarizes the key elements of ADHD, which you, as an educator, should keep in mind:

1. ADHD is considered *neurobiological* (i.e., originating in the brain), and it is developmental, beginning during childhood. Although emphasis in the past was nearly exclusively on ADHD as it affected children and youth, the current diagnostic criteria include examples of how this disorder affects adults.
2. ADHD is a developmental impairment of executive function, that is, the ability to comprehend, monitor, and direct one's cognition in order to achieve goals. The term *self-regulation* often is associated with executive function.
3. ADHD is chronic, long-term, and not acutely acquired (i.e., not the immediate result of an accident or injury). It may exist in a mild, moderate, or severe level.
4. The primary trait of ADHD is an inability to attend beyond what is typical for peers of comparable age. Significant impulsivity also may be characteristic.
5. ADHD is not situational; that is, it affects the children and adults who have it across multiple settings. However, children's symptoms may be most apparent at school because of the structure and expectations there.
6. Students with ADHD are more likely to have a *production* deficit rather than an *acquisition* deficit. That is, they may take information in and sometimes surprise their teachers by what they know, as in the case of Cedric, who was described at the beginning of the chapter. Their greatest difficulty often lies in production—that is, in completing their work.
7. ADHD is not caused by environmental situations or other disabilities, but it may be present with them.

Did You Know?

ADHD is considered a mental health disorder. At the federal level, it is studied by the Centers for Disease Control and Prevention (http://www.cdc.gov/ncbddd/adhd/) as well as the U.S. Surgeon General and the National Institute of Mental Health (http://www.nimh.nih.gov/health/topics/attention-deficit-hyperactivity-disorder-adhd/index.shtml).

Prevalence of Attention Deficit–Hyperactivity Disorder

A discussion of the prevalence of ADHD is not straightforward. Some professionals maintain that ADHD simply does not exist—that it has been created by parents who want an explanation for their children's difficult behaviors and by pharmaceutical companies that want to sell medication for both children and adults with attentional problems (e.g., Saul, 2014; Smith, 2012). However, several major organizations, including the National Institutes of Health (NIH) and the American Medical Association (AMA), as well as the U.S. Surgeon General, have concluded that the disorder is real and that it occurs across the life span (Barkley et al., 2002; Centers for Disease Control and Prevention, 2016).

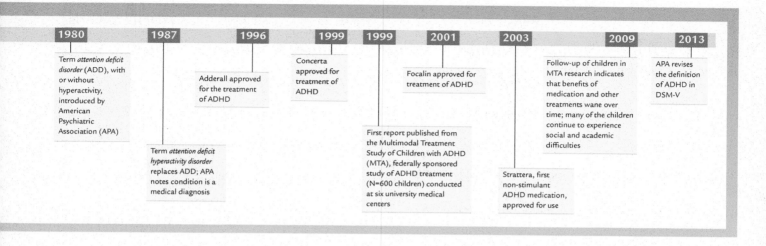

Currently, ADHD is one of the most common childhood psychiatric disorders, with parent reports indicating that one in 10 children between the ages of 4 and 17 have been diagnosed (Visser, Zablotsky, Holbrook, & Danileson, 2015). Other estimates are somewhat lower, around 5% (American Psychiatric Association, 2013). Further, it is estimated that between 2.5% and 4% of adults (American Psychiatric Association, 2013; National Institute of Mental Health, 2008) have this disorder.

Prevalence Based on Gender

Would you guess that boys or girls are most often identified as having ADHD? Early research suggested that boys might be up to nine times more likely than girls to have this disorder (Arnold, 1995), but more recent studies indicate that the ratio is closer to two or three to one (Centers for Disease Control and Prevention, 2016). Even these figures are tentative. Although girls and boys may exhibit the same symptoms of ADHD, girls may display lower levels of these symptoms (Owens, Cardoos, & Hinshaw, 2015) and so may not be identified as often. You can learn more about ADHD in girls in the Professional Edge.

Prevalence Based on Race and Poverty

One other dimension of ADHD's prevalence is important to consider: differences that may exist based on race/ethnicity and poverty. Some data indicate that ADHD occurs among children in various racial or ethnic groups (Toplak, et al., 2012), while other studies suggest that Caucasian students are more likely to be diagnosed than African American or Hispanic students (Morgan, Staff, Hillemeier, Farkas, & Maczuga, 2013). However, differences may exist in terms of treatment. For example, using data from a nationwide, multifaceted study, Graves and Serpell (2013) found that African American and Hispanic children were less likely than Caucasian children to receive medication for ADHD, even when factors such as income level and insurance were accounted for.

Causes of Attention Deficit–Hyperactivity Disorder

The causes of attention deficit–hyperactivity disorder have been debated for many years. In the past, some professionals claimed that ADHD was the result of permissive parenting, that children's apparently uncontrolled behavior occurred because no limits were placed on them. Other professionals proposed that ADHD was caused by diet—either food allergies or the consumption of too much sugar—or by other allergies. Although parenting skills certainly influence

The symptoms of ADHD in girls may be subtly different from those in boys. Nadeau and Quinn (2004) prepared the following checklist for girls to complete if they are concerned they may have ADHD. Nearly all girls will check some of the items, but a professional assessment might be warranted if many are checked.

ADHD Checklist for Girls

Please place a check mark beside each item that you feel describes you.

❏ 1. It's very hard for me to keep track of homework assignments and due dates.

❏ 2. No matter how hard I try to be on time, I am usually late.

❏ 3. I have trouble getting to sleep at night.

❏ 4. I have trouble getting up in the morning.

❏ 5. I jump from one topic to another in conversation.

❏ 6. I interrupt other people when they're talking, even though I try not to.

❏ 7. Even when I try to listen in class my thoughts start wandering.

❏ 8. I have difficulty remembering what I've read.

❏ 9. I can't seem to get started on school assignments until the last minute.

❏ 10. My room is very messy.

❏ 11. My friends say I'm "hyper."

❏ 12. My friends call me "spacey."

❏ 13. I forget to do things my parents ask me to do.

❏ 14. I frequently lose or misplace personal items.

❏ 15. My parents and teachers tell me I need to try harder in school.

❏ 16. I am distracted easily by sounds or by things I see.

❏ 17. My parents tell me that I overreact to things.

❏ 18. I feel anxious or worried a lot of the time.

❏ 19. I feel moody and depressed, even for no reason.

❏ 20. My moods and emotions are much more intense during the week before my period.

❏ 21. I am easily frustrated.

❏ 22. I'm pretty impatient and hate to wait.

❏ 23. I feel different from other girls.

❏ 24. I wish my parents understood how hard high school is for me.

❏ 25. I feel mentally exhausted when I get home from school.

❏ 26. It takes me longer to get assignments done compared to my classmates.

❏ 27. Even when I study hard I can't seem to remember things when I'm taking an exam.

❏ 28. It's so hard for me to stay organized.

❏ 29. I only make good grades in the classes that really interest me.

❏ 30. I have trouble completing papers and projects on time.

❏ 31. The only way I can really study for a test is to stay up late the night before.

❏ 32. I sometimes eat to calm down.

❏ 33. It seems like I'm always messing up.

❏ 34. I fidget or doodle in class because it's hard for me to sit still and listen.

❏ 35. I blurt things out without thinking.

Source: From Nadeau, K. G., & Quinn, P. (2004). *ADD (ADHD) self-report questionnaire for teenage girls.* Used with permission from ADDvance, www.addvance.com.

children's behaviors and a few children do have reactions to certain foods and other environmental elements, research on these factors indicates that neither is a primary cause of ADHD, nor is too much television watching or poor schooling (National Institute of Mental Health, 2009b). However, research into these and other causes of ADHD continues.

Perhaps you are wondering what *does* cause ADHD and why some students in almost every school have this disorder. Attention deficit–hyperactivity disorder is the result of a disorder of the brain, but other factors also probably contribute to the severity and persistence of the symptoms, including physiological and environmental factors.

Physiological Factors

Many medical and educational professionals have studied physiological causes of ADHD. One significant factor is *heredity*. Researchers have explored characteristics of the parents, siblings, and other close relatives of individuals with this disorder and often found that individuals with ADHD are much more likely than other individuals to have a family pattern of ADHD (e.g., Akutagava-Martins, Rohde, & Hutz, 2016). In fact, professionals agree that heredity is the greatest contributing factor to the development of ADHD (National Institute of Mental Health, 2009a; National Resource Center on ADHD, 2012).

Such studies can be flawed, though, because of environmental factors. For example, all members of a family may live in such a chaotic setting that they appear to have attentional problems. As an alternative, some researchers have studied fraternal and identical twins—those raised in the same household and those raised in two different households—as might happen with adoption. Using this approach, researchers can better separate the effects of heredity from those of environment. In this line of research, the most convincing studies are those of identical twins: They are highly likely to share the disorder, whether they have been raised in the same household or in different households (Greven, Rijsdijk, & Plomin, 2011; Pingault, et al., 2015).

Some of the most contemporary and exciting research related to ADHD concerns the differences in the brains of those with this disorder (e.g., Casey & Durston, 2014). For example, several studies have found that certain regions of the brains of individuals with ADHD are slightly smaller than is typical (Gilsbach, et al., 2012). Other differences can be understood by referring to the illustration of the brain in Figure 6.2.

Using magnetic resonance imaging (MRI) and other medical technology, scientists have found that several parts of the brain—the frontal lobe, the temporal lobe, the parietal lobe, the basal ganglia, and the cerebellum—often function differently in individuals with ADHD than in other people (Arnsten & Berridge, 2015; Berridge & Arnsten, 2015). Specifically, for children and adults with ADHD, the level of blood flow is lower than typical in those regions of the brain.

FIGURE 6.2   Regions of the Brain Related to ADHD

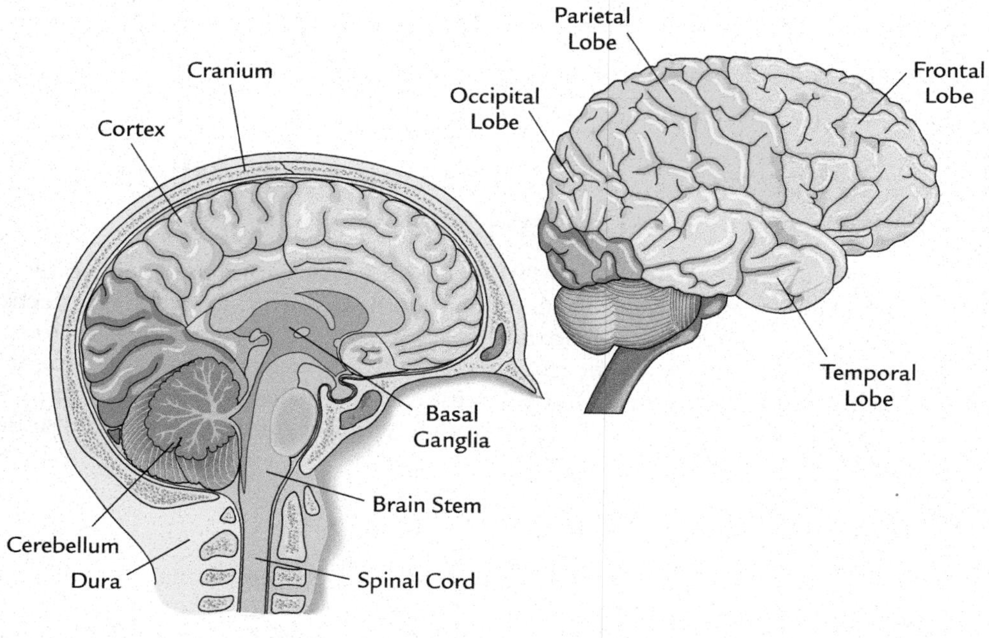

Source: Based on Figure 1 from B. J. Casey and Sarah Durston. (June, 2006). From behavior to cognition to the brain and back: What have we learned from functional imaging studies of attention deficit hyperactivity disorder? *American Journal of Psychiatry, 163*, 957–960.

ADHD is a complex disorder. Some students with ADHD have a Section 504 plan to address their needs, but others are eligible for special education services.

In addition, some researchers have found that some individuals with ADHD may show less electrical activity in certain brain regions than is typical (e.g., Tamm & Juranek, 2012). Of course, professionals who are studying these neurological causes of ADHD hope that their work will lead to more effective treatments, a topic addressed later in this chapter. This area of study is rapidly changing, and far more detailed and definitive information about the brain and ADHD probably will be learned in the next few years.

Environmental Factors

Most current work investigating ADHD emphasizes physiological causes, and environmental factors generally are seen as primarily contributing to the severity of the symptoms (e.g., Nikolas, Klump, & Burt, 2012). For example, if a young child with attention deficit–hyperactivity disorder is raised in a highly structured home in which clear rules are in place and appropriate behavior is emphasized, that child is likely to display a milder set of ADHD characteristics than is a similar child raised in a home with little structure.

However, researchers are finding that environmental factors might actually contribute to the development of ADHD for some children. In particular, a significant correlation seems to exist between children with high levels of lead in their blood during the first two or three years of life and ADHD (Nigg, Elmore, Natarajan, Friderici, & Nikolas, 2016). Similarly, maternal prenatal smoking and alcohol consumption have been found by some researchers to be correlated with an increase of ADHD in children (Knopik et al., 2016), although this finding is not universal (Obel et al., 2016).

> MyEdLab **Self-Check 6.1**
>
> MyEdLab **Application Exercise 6.1:** Types of ADHD
>
> MyEdLab **Application Exercise 6.2:** Interpreting Data

Characteristics of Individuals with Attention Deficit–Hyperactivity Disorder

Learning about the causes of ADHD provides you with a perspective on why some students experience difficulty in school. However, in order to effectively teach these students, you also need to recognize their typical characteristics. Although generalizing about students is risky, by learning about the cognitive, academic, social/emotional, and behavior characteristics of students with ADHD, you will be better prepared to appropriately understand, plan for, and address their needs.

Cognitive Characteristics

The cognitive characteristics of students with ADHD are thought to be directly related to the unusual features of their brains. Interestingly, the parts of the brain that are different in individuals with ADHD are those known to regulate attention. Barkley (2015) considered this fact as well as all the research describing the behavior of individuals with ADHD. Using this substantial set of information, he proposed that the primary deficit in individuals with ADHD is not really attention; rather, it is behavior inhibition and self-regulation problems related to these neurological factors (Barkley, 2015). In other words, it is not that students with ADHD cannot pay attention; it is that they cannot regulate where their attention is directed, how often it switches to other areas, or how to redirect their attention when it wanders. These problems with behavior inhibition set the stage for dilemmas related to the executive functions, as noted earlier, that are the mental activities that help them regulate their behaviors (Miller, Nevado-Montenegro, & Hinshaw, 2012). Executive functions can be grouped into these four mental activities that operate interactively (Barkley, 2006):

1. **Working memory** is the mental activity that enables students to remember events and use hindsight and foresight based on that memory. For example, if a student was corrected previously for leaving his seat during large-group instruction, a typical student would remember the teacher's words as he began to stand again—and probably would sit back down. However, a student with ADHD probably would not recall the teacher's instructions or consequences for the behavior and would get out of his seat again. In fact, this might happen repeatedly, which explains the often-heard comment that students with ADHD do not seem to learn from experience. Cedric, the elementary student discussed at the beginning of the chapter, might have difficulty in this area.

2. **Self-directed speech** is that little voice in your head that keeps you thinking about the topic at hand instead of allowing your thoughts to wander. This mental activity, sometimes called *self-talk*, is the mechanism students use to reflect on how they are doing, to problem solve, and to follow instructions. Although young children may vocalize their self-talk as they develop this skill, by the time children are school age, they usually carry out this mental activity privately. Carlos, the student introduced at the beginning of the chapter, probably has difficulty with self-directed speech.

3. **Control of emotions and motivation** involves setting aside frustration and other emotions to complete a task as well as generating emotions internally and taking the perspectives of others. For example, have you ever been faced with an extraordinarily frustrating task? It could have been academic, such as solving a complex math problem, or it could have been a daily activity, such as replacing the tiny screw that holds your eyeglasses together. To accomplish the task, you probably took a deep breath to calm down and persisted until you succeeded. Some students with ADHD are not able to manage their emotional responses, and so when faced with frustrating tasks, they may have temper tantrums or storm out of the room. The outbursts that Marcus, the high school student introduced at the beginning of the chapter, sometimes experiences are evidence of this problem.

4. **Reconstitution**, or *planning*, refers to the ability for both analysis and synthesis. *Analysis* is the skill of breaking down what is observed into component parts; *synthesis* is the skill of combining parts in order to perform new actions. Reconstitution enables educators to teach students key skills but not to have to directly teach every example of every skill: Students can put similar pieces together themselves. Thus, when students learn the parts of a sentence, they usually can write longer and shorter sentences, add adjectives to the nouns in their sentences, and recognize sentences in many contexts. Students with ADHD may, academically or behaviorally, have difficulty with this activity. They may not recognize the similarity of one academic task to another; they may not realize that the rules for conduct in the classroom are similar to the rules that one should follow in the lunchroom.

According to this conceptualization of ADHD, as most children develop and their behavioral inhibition increases, the executive functions increasingly control motor behavior; their self-regulation skills develop. That is, behavior becomes more planful and deliberate because children increasingly are able to implement the executive functions to think before they act, to remember consequences and thus change their behavior, to persist at a task even when it is difficult, and to realize on their own what behaviors might be considered appropriate in new situations. In children with ADHD, problems in behavioral inhibition contribute to problems in the development of executive functions. The result is poor motor control—distractibility and/or impulsivity.

ADHD is, in many ways, a problem of internal time management (Barkley, 2012). Students cannot slow down the sequences of internal mental activities that would let them better manage their behaviors. This model of ADHD has direct applicability for teachers. If you can identify the type of problems a student is having related to behavior inhibition and the executive functions, then you can implement teaching strategies to address the problem or work around it. Examples of strategies that can assist students to overcome problems related to executive function are included in Instruction in Action.

Before leaving the topic of cognitive functioning in students with ADHD, brief mention should be made of these students' intellectual abilities. If you review the diagnostic criteria for ADHD, you will see that no mention is made of a range of intellectual ability for students who have this special need. In fact, students who have ADHD may be gifted, average, or struggling learners (Weyandt & Gudmundsdottir, 2015). In addition, students with intellectual disabilities also may be identified as having ADHD (Ekstein, Glick, Weill, Kay, & Berger, 2011). ADHD is not directly related to intelligence (de Zeeuw et al., 2012).

INSTRUCTION IN **ACTION**

Executive Function and Strategies for Learning

Here are several specific strategies that professionals can use to address disorders related to executive function often characteristic of students with ADHD:

- *Calendar and Buddy Review:* If students are given a calendar for keeping track of homework each week, many frustrations can be relieved. Teachers may partner students to ensure that the correct information is written on each calendar and that the appropriate books are packed to go home. If students have difficulty writing, they can use their phones to take a photo of posted homework assignments.
- *Color-Coded Notes:* Different aspects of instructional content (e.g., vocabulary, key ideas, supporting details, tools) can be highlighted with different colors. This may help students who have difficulty organizing and understanding notes or text.
- *Organizational System:* Providing an organizational system—such as a notebook with color-coded dividers for different subjects, homework, and assignments—may enable the students with disorders related to executive function to experience more success.
- *Metacognitive Strategies:* Often students must be taught strategies to use when trying to learn new material, when studying, or when completing classwork. Metacognitive strategies help make the student aware of the

mental processes she is using to learn or to rehearse information.

- *Student Evaluation of Work Progress:* For the student who is often off task, some instruction may be beneficial to teach him to monitor when he is and is not doing what he is supposed to be doing. This awareness can be the first step in teaching the student what to do when he finds that he is not on task.
- *Graphic Organizers:* Graphic organizers are available for many different forms of content, problem-solving techniques, relationships, and information formats. They are excellent tools for lecture guides, study guides, and class activities because they help students understand how their ideas relate to one another. Technology options are available, too (e.g., the app Mindmeister).
- *Model Note Taking:* Students may benefit from the teacher demonstrating how to take notes on the board, including an explanation of abbreviations and symbols.
- *Student Evaluation of Overall Progress:* A student with executive control difficulties may benefit from learning how to accurately judge her progress in completing projects and other school activities. For example, working with the student to create a series of personal deadlines for completing sections of a report and then tracking progress teaches important planning skills.

Academic Characteristics

Because ADHD is not related to intellectual ability, it is not surprising that the academic characteristics of students with ADHD can vary tremendously. Some students with ADHD also are gifted or talented, and educators may find that they need both to challenge these students and to assist them to focus their unique abilities (Baldwin, Omdal, & Pereles, 2015; Foley-Nicpon, Assouline, & Fosenburg, 2015), using diverse instructional interventions and other supports to help them reach their potential.

Many students with ADHD can be successful in school, particularly if effective interventions are put in place, a point illustrated in Marcus's story at the beginning of the chapter. Taught by knowledgeable teachers and supported by family members and others, they achieve at or near grade level, complete high school and postsecondary education, and generally are able to overcome or compensate for the symptoms of ADHD that could have negatively affected their education.

However, success in school for students with ADHD is not assured. The majority of these students experience difficulty with the academic structure and demands of school, and they consistently achieve below their potential (Basch, 2011; Owens & Hinshaw, 2016). Not surprisingly, there appears to be a correlation between the severity of the symptoms of ADHD and achievement: The more severe the symptoms are, the greater the negative impact on school performance (Birchwood & Daley, 2012; Daley, Jacobsen, Lange, Sorensen, & Walldorf, 2015). For some students, their academic self-concept is an important contributing factor; that is, when they view themselves as being not very capable of succeeding at schoolwork, they are more likely to stop trying and to develop behaviors that lead to further academic failure (e.g., Craparo, Magnano, Gori, Passanisi, Lo Piccolo, & Pace, 2015; Martin, 2012). Conversely, if they are successful, they

---

TECHNOLOGY NOTES

Technology to Help with Daily Tasks

The time students spend learning how to use the many features of a smartphone or tablet device can lead to a lifetime of success, particularly for students in high school who have significant attentional problems. Consider how a smartphone could assist a student to do these tasks and functions:

- Set a repeating alarm as a reminder to take medication.
- Record the deadline for a long-term assignment as well as intermediate deadlines for each part of the assignment.
- Input a class schedule, including important details such as A days and B days, as are typical in some schools.
- Keep a list of important information such as the locker combination, teachers' names, and the school dress code.
- Enter the address of a friend's house in order to use the GPS function.
- List important school events such as football, basketball, and other games and their locations; school

holidays; dates for high-stakes testing or exams; and club meetings.
- Create a daily to-do list, and prioritize the tasks.
- Keep a copy of a recorded textbook or other assigned reading material available for listening as time allows.
- Set reminder alarms before important obligations or appointments.
- Use the calculator for math assignments (as permitted) or other daily tasks, such as computing the number of hours worked at a part-time job.
- Write memos or notes about items that need to be remembered.
- With an added keyboard or thumb typing, take notes in class.
- Activate the wireless feature to transmit a calendar, set of notes, or other information to be printed.

What uses do you make of your smartphone that might be valuable for students with ADHD? How would you go about helping such students to learn how to use a smartphone to get organized and remember important items?

develop a positive academic self-concept and are more likely to keep trying, even when schoolwork is difficult. Some students with ADHD can be helped in developing a positive academic self-concept through the use of technology. As outlined in the Technology Notes feature, readily available technology can help students be successful in organizing and completing school tasks.

Social and Emotional Characteristics

The social and emotional characteristics of students with ADHD have long been a concern for professionals who work with these students. Key domains needing intervention have included students' self-esteem and overall social functioning and the likelihood that they will experience depression.

Self-Esteem

Self-esteem refers to a person's overall regard for himself or herself as a person. If you have positive self-esteem, you perceive yourself as having many strengths; if you have negative self-esteem, you sense in yourself many weaknesses. Whether students with ADHD have positive or negative self-esteem is not clear. Some researchers (e.g., Capelatto, de Lima, Ciasca, & Salgado-Azoni, 2014; Varley, 2011) have found that students with ADHD have much lower self-esteem than typical peers of the same age. Others have found few differences. For example, in a large-scale study of elementary school students, Eisenberg and Schneider (2007) found that the self-perception of students with ADHD toward their math and reading achievement was similar to that for students without this disorder, the exception being that boys with ADHD were somewhat more negative about their math skills than were other boys. It should be noted, though, that parents and teachers were more negative about students, especially girls, with ADHD than about other students.

Social Functioning

In contrast to the somewhat contradictory data about self-esteem, information about the social functioning of students with attention deficit–hyperactivity disorder is clear. Students with ADHD often experience challenges in coping with social demands at school, at home, and in other settings (Eiraldi, Mautone, & Power, 2012; Chromik, Quintin, Lepage, Hustyi, Lightbody, & Reise, 2015). For example, these students might not recognize that they need to behave differently in different types of social situations (Kloo & Kain, 2016). They may not realize that there are particular ways to act when in school and talking to their teachers that are different from the ways they act when playing with their friends on the playground. Students with ADHD also are not particularly accurate at judging their own social abilities, tending to overestimate them (Al-Yagon, 2016).

Given these difficulties with social functioning, you can probably guess that students with ADHD are more likely than their peers to have problems in developing and maintaining friendships. In fact, adolescents with ADHD report that they have fewer close friendships than do those without ADHD (Kawabata, Tseng, & Gau, 2012). Students with ADHD also are more likely than other students to be seen as both victims of bullying and bullies themselves (Wiener & Mak, 2009). Their parents confirm this finding. Students with ADHD also are more likely than other children to be rejected by their peers (Mrug et al., 2012). These difficulties in forming and maintaining friendships and avoiding negative interactions with those perceived as friends are found for both boys and girls (McQuade & Hoza, 2015).

Behavior Characteristics

The frequency and severity of behavior problems for students with ADHD vary widely, a fact that you can easily understand by reviewing the diagnostic criteria for the disorder. Students who have the hyperactive–impulsive or combined type of ADHD usually have behavior problems that are immediately apparent to their teachers and other school personnel. Those who have inattentive ADHD may not have many outward behavior symptoms of their disorder, but they may be disruptive in the classroom when they try to find their misplaced materials or need ongoing teacher assistance to stay focused on their work.

Students with ADHD exhibit an array of disruptive behaviors well known to educators, including the following (National Institute of Mental Health, 2016; Reis, 2002):

- Failure to closely attend to details or making careless mistakes in schoolwork
- Inappropriately out of seat
- Failure to complete schoolwork
- Excessive talking
- Failure to listen when spoken to directly
- Running, climbing on furniture, or in older students, a frequent feeling of restlessness
- Difficulty organizing tasks and activities
- Avoidance of, dislike of, or reluctance to engage in tasks that require sustained effort, such as schoolwork or homework

Students with ADHD also may have difficulty working alone or in large groups (Zentall, Moon, Hall, & Grskovic, 2001). Teachers have reported feeling significantly less confident about teaching students with ADHD, particularly those with behavior problems, compared to teaching other students (DuPaul & Jimerson, 2014; Ohan, Visser, Strain, & Allen, 2011).

Did You Know?
ADHD is a disorder that occurs in children throughout the world. One recent review of studies conducted in every region of the world (Polanczyk, Salum, Sugaya, Caye, & Rohde, 2015) found the prevalence of ADHD in children and adolescents to be 3.4%.

Comorbidity with Other Disorders

Any discussion of the characteristics of students with ADHD would be incomplete without mention of comorbidity, or the simultaneous occurrence of two or more disabilities or disorders (American Psychiatric Association, 2013). Although estimates vary widely, one study found that approximately 26% of students who were identified as having learning disabilities also were diagnosed with ADHD (Forness & Kavale, 2001a). Marcus, the high school student introduced at the beginning of this chapter, has both a learning disability and ADHD. The number is even higher for students with emotional disabilities: Approximately 43% of these students also have ADHD. In addition, approximately 40% of students receiving special education services as other health impaired have been diagnosed as having ADHD, and some of these students also have a health impairment in addition to significant ADHD (U.S. Department of Education, 2015). ADHD also has been associated with intellectual disabilities, emotional disabilities, autism, and traumatic brain injury.

In addition to comorbidity with disabilities as defined in IDEA, researchers have studied the extent to which ADHD exists with psychiatric disorders (National Institute of Mental Health, 2009a). Estimates of this type of comorbidity range from 30% to 60% (U.S. Department of Education, 2008a). Approximately one-half or more of students with ADHD have disorders such as emotional impulsivity; disruptive behavior disorders, including oppositional defiant disorder (ODD); aggression; and anxiety (Pliszka, 2015). (The symptoms of these disorders are presented in Chapter 7.) These students also may have serious sleep disorders and may be at higher risk for substance abuse (including nicotine, alcohol, and caffeine) (e.g., Molina et al., 2013). These comorbidity statistics have several implications. First, the high rate at which ADHD occurs simultaneously with IDEA disabilities partly explains why so much overlap seems to occur in the characteristics of these groups. Second, the simultaneous occurrence of ADHD with other serious disorders should serve as a caution to educators that interventions that address only the visible symptoms of ADHD may not truly address all the critical areas of student need. Third, comorbidity data highlight the importance of recognizing that interventions outlined in one chapter of this textbook might be equally applicable to a student whose disability label is related to a different chapter (e.g., learning disabilities or autism spectrum disorder). Finally, a discussion of comorbidity serves as a reminder that school professionals should stay in close contact with parents and medical personnel regarding students with ADHD.

MyEdLab **Self-Check 6.2**

MyEdLab **Application Exercise 6.3:** Jake

Identifying Attention Deficit–Hyperactivity Disorder

Because attention deficit–hyperactivity disorder is primarily a psychiatric rather than an educational disorder, deciding whether a student has ADHD requires close collaboration among physicians, psychiatrists, and other medical personnel, as well as school professionals and parents. The procedures to determine whether the diagnosis can be made medically have been outlined by the American Academy of Pediatrics (2011), and the steps outlined in Chapter 2 must be followed to determine whether a student is eligible for services through IDEA. The following is a summary of how both sets of procedures typically are implemented.

Initial Referral

Some parents will already have discussed their child's behavior with their physician or pediatrician during the child's preschool years, and so some students will already have been diagnosed as having ADHD when they begin school, as was the case for Cedric. However, most referrals occur when children are faced with the structure and need for sustained attention required for success in elementary school. When children encounter difficulty in the school setting, some parents will ask their doctor if their child's behavior signals ADHD and request that an evaluation for this disorder be completed. General education or special education teachers also may suggest to parents that they discuss their child's behavior with a physician, but because teachers are not qualified to make a diagnosis, they may not in any way suggest that they suspect the child has ADHD. In addition to primary care or family practice physicians and pediatricians, pediatric neurologists, psychiatrists, and psychologists also may diagnose ADHD.

Assessment

No single test can reliably indicate whether a student has attention deficit–hyperactivity disorder. Therefore, an assessment for ADHD requires input from medical professionals, parents and family members, and school personnel.

Medical Assessment

In considering whether a child has ADHD, the physician first tries to eliminate other problems that might have similar symptoms. Thus, routine vision and hearing screening and a thorough physical examination typically are completed.

The doctor usually asks the parents about the pregnancy and developmental history of the child. In addition, parents are asked questions such as these:

- When did you first notice that your child seemed to have more behavior problems than other children? What types of problems is your child experiencing?
- How is your child doing in school?
- Is there a family history of ADHD, or did anyone in your family experience behavior problems during the school years?
- How does your child get along with other children? Siblings? How easily does your child make friends?
- In what situations do you observe your child experiencing behavior problems? Home? School? Church? Activities such as scouting, dance lessons, or music lessons? In a child care setting?
- What do you find are the most effective means for disciplining your child?
- What are your child's interests? Hobbies? In what areas does your child excel?

The intent of such questions is to determine whether the child meets the criteria for ADHD as described in *DSM-V*. However, because ADHD is so often comorbid with other disorders, medical personnel also will determine whether another disorder may be causing the ADHD symptoms or whether another disorder exists in addition to ADHD. To gain an even better understanding, the physician also may interview the child about his perception of the problems being experienced and what is causing them. The doctor supplements the information obtained from parents and the child with input from teachers and other school personnel.

Continuous Performance Tests

Some professionals who evaluate children for ADHD use as one measure continuous performance tests (CPTs), assessment instruments designed to require a student to sustain attention in order to respond correctly to the test items (Hall, Valentine, Groom, Walker, Sayal, Daley, & Hollis, 2015). These instruments usually take advantage of computer technology. For example, the *Conners' Continuous Performance Test–III* (Conners, 2014) requires the student taking it to watch the computer screen for a single letter to appear. If the letter is an *X*, the student does not press the space bar; the student does press the space bar for any other letter. A similar test is the *Integrated Visual and Auditory Continuous Performance Test + Plus* (IVA+Plus) (Sanford & Turner, 2006). Although continuous performance tests have appeal because they seem to directly assess the key characteristics seen in students with ADHD, to date research has not clearly supported their ability to differentiate between students with ADHD and those without (Huang-Pollock, Karalunas, Tam, & Moore, 2012). Moreover, CPTs cannot distinguish students who do not respond quickly because of ADHD from those who are slow at processing because of a learning disability. Given these problems, CPTs generally are not considered appropriate by themselves for making a diagnosis of ADHD, although information from them is sometimes used to supplement other assessment information.

Parent Assessment

Whenever children are being evaluated for ADHD, their parents provide critical information to inform medical and education professionals. In addition to questionnaires and interviews that are used to gather general information, parents usually complete a behavior rating scale. Examples of such scales are the *Conners' Parent Rating Scale–Revised* (CPRS-R) (Conners, 1997b) and the *Child Behavior Checklist for Ages 4–18, Parent Form* (CBCL/6–18-R) (Achenbach & Rescorla, 2007).

Teacher and School Assessment

After parents and close family members, teachers typically are the most significant adults in children's lives. Although some children as young as age 4 sometimes are identified as having ADHD (American Academy of Pediatrics, 2011), most are diagnosed when they are in elementary school, spending most of each day with one teacher (Kos, Richdale, & Hay, 2006). This teacher provides a valuable perspective on the child's functioning in the school environment and is usually asked to complete a behavior checklist similar to that for parents. Examples of such a checklist are the *Conners' Teacher Rating Scale–Revised* (Conners, 1997a) and the *Child Behavior Checklist, Teacher's Report Form* (Achenbach, 1991). When doctors receive completed copies of these checklists from both parents and teachers, they not only can use the information as one dimension of the diagnostic process, but they also can judge whether there are significant discrepancies between parents' and teachers' perceptions of the child.

Teachers also may provide other types of information regarding students who may have ADHD, including samples of students' work that illustrate attention to detail, ability to complete work, and ability to follow instructions. Teachers also may contribute anecdotal information that helps describe in detail what students are like while they are at school. Teachers may be asked to collect data about students' behaviors. For example, a teacher might record for a one-hour period how often a student inappropriately left her seat or tally how many times during a week a student had tantrums.

Additional Considerations for IDEA Eligibility

The information gathered by medical personnel can assist school professionals in making a decision about whether a student with ADHD is eligible for services through IDEA, but additional steps are needed. For example, a psychologist usually administers an individual intelligence test and an individual achievement test—assessments discussed in Chapter 5. Additional information also may be gathered about the student's behavior, often by having a psychologist, counselor, special educator, or other school professional observe the student in the general education classroom and other school locations. Once these data have been collected, the team meets to continue the special education decision-making process, about which you already have learned.

ADHD or Gifted

One additional topic should be mentioned in discussing the identification process: Some professionals note that students who are gifted and talented (a topic addressed in detail in Chapter 15) sometimes are misdiagnosed as having ADHD (e.g., Mullet & Rinn, 2015). In fact, many behaviors associated with ADHD also are associated with giftedness. Examples include poor sustained attention, impulsivity, higher than typical levels of activity and restlessness, and difficulty adhering to rules. However, distinctions do exist: While students with ADHD experience difficulty in attending in nearly all situations, those who are gifted are inattentive only in specific situations, such as when they are bored. Impulsivity characterizes students with ADHD, but for students who are gifted, it often is a signal that good judgment is lagging behind intellectual development. In addition, students with ADHD may not follow rules because of their inability to regulate their behaviors; those who are gifted may deliberately question rules and create their own.

The possibility for misdiagnosing students who are gifted as ADHD illustrates the importance of the assessment process. By observing students in several settings, listening carefully to parent and teacher perceptions of students, and gathering other detailed medical, family history, and achievement information, professionals can accurately identify students' needs and develop options to help them succeed.

Eligibility

Whether a student is determined to have ADHD is a decision made by a pediatrician or family physician. If a student does have ADHD, the doctor discusses with parents the options for treatment, including medication and behavior interventions.

The doctor and parents also develop a follow-up plan to monitor the child's progress. The school team decides whether the ADHD is adversely affecting the student's educational performance (U.S. Department of Education, 2011). If they determine this to be the case, they have the option of identifying the student as eligible for IDEA services as other health impaired (OHI). Remember, though, that not all students with ADHD are eligible. Many students with ADHD who receive medication can be successful in school when minor accommodations are made in their general education classrooms. Such students may be eligible for a Section 504 plan that outlines the needed classroom supports but does not include special education services.

A comparison of IDEA and Section 504 requirements is outlined in Figure 6.3. A third option is possible as well. As you learned earlier in this chapter, a significant number of students assessed for ADHD are found also to have learning, emotional, or other disabilities. These students are eligible for IDEA services because of their other disabilities, regardless of whether their ADHD is determined to be a disability.

ADHD is diagnosed by a pediatrician or other physician, with input from parents and teachers.

MyEdLab **Self-Check 6.3**

MyEdLab **Application Exercise 6.4:** Eric

Educating Students with Attention Deficit–Hyperactivity Disorder

How students with ADHD receive their education depends on many variables, including when they are diagnosed, whether they are eligible for special education services, and whether they have other disabilities.

Early Childhood

Although most students with ADHD are diagnosed after they enter elementary school, children as young as 2 years of age have been identified as having this disorder (Harvey, Youngwirth, & Thakar, 2009). Considerable difficulty exists in making an accurate diagnosis at an early age because formal assessment instruments generally are not designed for very young children, development may vary considerably among children, and some of the behaviors associated with ADHD may be appropriate in toddlers and preschoolers. Very young children who are diagnosed as having ADHD often have sleep problems, difficulty bonding, difficulty taking turns or sharing, more accidents than would be expected, an inability to remain still for even a few minutes, difficulty following directions, repeated instances of inappropriately intruding into others' space, and forgetfulness (Stormont & Stebbins, 2005).

For children who exhibit these symptoms to an excessive degree and who have been diagnosed with ADHD, early intervention is crucial. Young children with ADHD are at risk, like Cedric, for being expelled from daycare and preschool settings, the places they are most likely to receive their education prior to

FIGURE 6.3   Comparing Section 504 and IDEA

Component	Section 504	IDEA
Requirements of the law	• Any school receiving federal financial assistance must provide students covered an education comparable to that provided to other students.	• Students with disabilities must have available a free appropriate public education with special education related services and supplementary aids and services designed to address their individual needs.
Individuals protected	• All school-age children who have a physical or mental impairment that substantially limits a major life activity, have a record of such an impairment, or are regarded as having such an impairment. Major life activities include walking, seeing, hearing, speaking, breathing, learning, working, caring for oneself, and performing manual tasks.	• Children age 3 through 21 (or graduation) who have one of the 13 disabilities specified in the law and whose educational performance is adversely affected by the disability. States may also serve infants and toddlers ages birth through 2.
Funding	• Does not provide additional funds. IDEA funds generally may not be used to serve students protected only under Section 504.	• School districts receive additional federal funding for students identified as having disabilities.
Evaluations	• Parent notice (but not consent) is required for initial evaluation. Requires periodic reevaluations and reevaluation before a significant change in placement. Evaluation must occur at no expense to parents.	• Parent consent required before initial evaluation. Reevaluation required at least every three years. Provision for independent evaluations. Evaluation must occur at no expense to parents.
Placement	• Placement is general education classroom with supports in place to facilitate access to the educational experience. Parent participation not mentioned (but strongly advised).	• Placement must be in the least restrictive environment (LRE), which is most often the general education setting but also could be a part-time or full-time separate special education classroom, separate school, or specialized setting (e.g., residential, hospital). Parent participation required.
Documentation	• Section 504 plan that specifies accommodations to be provided and related details.	• Individualized education program (IEP) with components specified in the law.
Services	• Eliminates barriers that would prevent a student from full participation in programs and services available to all students.	• Special education, related services, and supplementary aids and services to enable student participation in all the programs and services as well as extracurricular activities (e.g., field trips) available to all students.
Due process	• Impartial hearing must be conducted when disagreements occur and cannot be resolved. Requires notice, the right to inspect records, the right to participate in a hearing and to be represented by counsel, and a review procedure. Complaints are filed with the Office of Civil Rights.	• Impartial hearing must be conducted when disagreements occur and cannot be resolved and mediation and conflict resolution are not successful. Due process procedures outlined in the law. Complaints are filed with the state.
Enforcement	• U.S. Office for Civil Rights, U.S. Department of Education.	• Office of Special Education and Rehabilitative Services promulgates IDEA regulations, U.S. Department of Education.

kindergarten. Further, without early intervention, their behaviors are likely to continue and escalate as they move to elementary school. Few studies of intervention effectiveness have been completed with young children. However, the most recent recommended practice is for behavioral interventions with parents to be the primary means of intervention, with medication used only if interventions are not successful (DuPaul & Kern, 2011).

Elementary and Secondary School Services

School-age students with ADHD receive their education based on their needs. Because ADHD is not by itself a disability in IDEA, the federal government does not gather and publish information regarding the locations where these students are educated. Even if students are eligible as other health impaired (OHI), because this disability category includes children with other disabilities, it is not possible to identify where students with ADHD receive their education using data from this disability group. Finally, students who have both ADHD and a learning or emotional disability are served in accordance with the least restrictive environment provision of IDEA, but the specific application of this dimension of the law for these students cannot be discerned from the annual reports issued about IDEA implementation.

Given the nature of ADHD, the fact that many students with ADHD receive accommodations through Section 504 plans, and the emphasis on inclusive practices for students with learning and emotional disabilities (who may also have ADHD), you can probably safely assume that most students with ADHD receive their education in a general education classroom (U.S. Department of Education, 2011). This means that general education teachers, with support from special education teachers and other school professionals, must focus their efforts on collaborating with parents to find effective means for helping students with ADHD to compensate for their special needs in order to succeed in their schoolwork (Marton, Wiener, Rogers, & Moore, 2015).

Transition and Adulthood

Although professionals used to believe that ADHD was a disorder that most students outgrew by adolescence, this view is no longer considered accurate (Buoli, Serati, & Cahn, 2016; Hinshaw et al., 2012). In fact, up to two-thirds of students diagnosed with ADHD during their school years continue to have the disorder in adulthood (Kolar, Keller, Golfinopoulos, Cumyn, , & Hechtman, 2008). Older students with ADHD show a decline in hyperactivity and inattention, but so do students who do not have ADHD, and so the gaps between the two groups remain.

A description of young adults with ADHD must be considered tentative because data regarding this disorder's impact after the school years are still emerging. Many adults with ADHD are disorganized and impulsive and have poor work skills. They tend to be anxious, disorderly, and impatient, and they may become bored easily. They often lose their belongings, and they may have difficulty forming relationships. Many adults with ADHD change jobs frequently and express dissatisfaction with their jobs (e.g., Jarrett, 2016; Painter, Prevatt, & Welles, 2008). However, many others complete college degrees or programs at technical schools, find employment in occupations where their characteristics do not leave them at a disadvantage (e.g., a doctor in an emergency room; a CEO with a skillful administrative assistant), and learn to compensate for their special needs.

Whether students with ADHD successfully transition into postschool options can depend heavily on their understanding of their disorder, their skills for advocating for themselves, the support they receive during high school, and their overall ability to cope with their symptoms. Having a supportive family is also crucial (McIntyre & Hennessy, 2012). Finally, adults with ADHD have a better chance of being satisfied with their lives if they have received supports for any comorbid conditions and, for many, if they take some type of medication (Davidson, 2008).

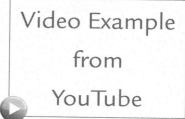

MyEdLab
Video Example 6.3

In Video Example 6.3, three young adults with ADHD recall their school experiences and current strategies for managing their disorder.
(https://www.youtube.com/watch?v=NL483G4xKu0)

MyEdLab **Self-Check 6.4**

MyEdLab **Application Exercise 6.5:** Accommodations

Recommended Educational Practices for Students with Attention Deficit–Hyperactivity Disorder

Recent progress in understanding the causes of ADHD, coupled with research on treatment effectiveness, provides a wealth of information for school professionals who work with students with this disorder. Perhaps the most comprehensive study ever undertaken of interventions for students with ADHD is the Multimodal Treatment Study of Children with ADHD (MTA), a federally funded research project conducted by 18 leading experts in the field of ADHD (National Institute of Mental Health, 2002), with follow-up studies of the participants still continuing. The following description of effective interventions draws heavily from that project and follow-up reports on the students who participated.

Medication

Although not universally supported and not recommended as the preferred treatment for children younger than age 6, according to the MTA and other professional recommendations (American Academy of Pediatrics, 2011), medication often is an effective short-term intervention for students with ADHD. As you begin to learn about this information, keep the following points in mind:

- *The use of medication is controversial.* Some parents and professionals believe that too many students are declared to have ADHD and given medication as a sort of quick fix for their challenging behaviors at school and at home (Connor, 2011; Stolzer, 2012). In contrast, data from the MTA study suggest that medication for this group of students can be highly effective in controlling symptoms (Biederman, 2003), although recent reports acknowledge that the appeal of medication diminishes over time (National Institute of Mental Health, 2009b), and many families decide to discontinue its use. Some parents also have expressed concern about the side effects of medication (e.g., loss of appetite) and the potential for later substance abuse. Researchers have found that side effects related to growth tend to be mild and seldom pose serious problems if medication is properly matched to the child and monitored closely (Kubiszyn, Mire, Dutt, Papathopoulos, & Burridge, 2012; Powell, Frydenberg, & Thomsen, 2015). Concerning substance abuse, results are mixed, with some research suggesting little or no relationship between use of medication for ADHD and substance abuse (e.g., Serra-Pinheiro et al., 2013), although others have noted that when ADHD exists with other disorders (such as learning disabilities or emotional disabilities), risk for substance abuse may increase (e.g., Molina et al., 2012). Children who take medication have a slight risk of other complications, and medications for ADHD contain warnings concerning these risks (National Institute of Mental Health, 2008).
- *The decision to prescribe medication only indirectly involves school professionals.* Clearly, school personnel observe their students daily and form opinions about the seriousness of their behaviors and what may help them, but school personnel *do not* have the expertise to recommend to parents that medication be considered. As you learned earlier in this chapter, pediatricians and other medical personnel usually ask for educators' input as they evaluate a student

for ADHD, and they also may request that teachers and other school personnel periodically report on the apparent effects of medication on a student's school performance. In fact, educators are explicitly prohibited from directly or indirectly telling parents that a student should take medication for ADHD.

- *Medication is helpful in ameliorating the symptoms of ADHD in 70% to 80% of the students for whom it is prescribed.* Nearly two-thirds of all students diagnosed as having ADHD take some type of medication at some point, the most common age range for this being between 11 and 17 years (Centers for Disease Control and Prevention, 2011a). Taking medication usually reduces significantly the amount of daydreaming or disruptive behaviors that students display. However, it is critical to recognize that students taking medication do not automatically improve in terms of academic achievement, as was the case for Carlos, introduced at the beginning of the chapter. Additional interventions, including educational and behavior strategies, usually are needed, thus making the expertise of teachers and other educators a critical companion to medication as an intervention. Further, when systematic behavior interventions are used in conjunction with medication, lower doses of medication may be effective (Smith & Shapiro, 2015).

Four different types of medication are commonly used to reduce the symptoms of ADHD. A large majority of students for whom medication is prescribed take stimulant medication (Palli, Kamble, Chen, & Aparasu, 2012), including Ritalin, a medication first introduced for students with ADHD in 1956 (Eli Lilly, 2003). Other stimulant medications include the trade names Dexedrine, Cylert, Adderall, and Focalin. An additional recently developed stimulant medication approved for school-age children and adults is Vyvanse. Nonstimulant medication also is available, typically Strattera, also approved for use with children as well as adults. Antidepressants and antihypertensives are occasionally prescribed. Antidepressant medications include Tofranil, Prozac, and Zoloft. Antihypertensive medications, also used to lower blood pressure, include Clonidine and Tenex. The chart in Figure 6.4 provides additional details about the names, side effects, benefits, and cautions concerning these and other medications that students with ADHD may be taking.

Factors to take into account when medication is being considered include these (e.g., DuPaul & Jimerson, 2014):

- The child's age
- Prior attempts at other interventions and their impact on the behaviors of concern
- Parent and child attitudes toward using medication
- Presence in the household of substance abusers (stimulant medications are controlled substances)
- Severity of symptoms
- Availability of adults in the household to supervise use of medications, ensuring that medications are taken regularly and as prescribed
- Participation in sports or the likelihood of enrollment in the military (in some cases, students can be banned from either of these activities if they are taking medication)

The controversy over the appropriateness of using medication for treating students with ADHD probably will remain for the foreseeable future. New types of medication are being identified, and researchers continue to learn more about the causes and preferred treatments for this disorder. As an educator, your responsibility is to have an accurate understanding of what medication can and cannot accomplish. Further, teachers must recognize their roles in enhancing the success of students taking medication for ADHD by designing effective instruction for them and collaborating with parents in monitoring students' progress

Did You Know?

Many alternative treatments have been proposed for ADHD. These include herbal formulas, vitamin regimens, special diets, and biofeedback. Although some alternative treatments show promise and may be used to supplement traditional treatments (Karpouzis & Bonello, 2012), none of these treatments are recommended by medical professionals in lieu of medical, behavioral, and educational options.

FIGURE 6.4 **Examples of Medications Prescribed for Students with ADHD**

Drug	Common Side Effects	Duration of Behavioral Effects	Comments
Concerta (methylphenidate)	Insomnia, decreased appetite, weight loss, headache, irritability, stomachache	About 12 hours	Works quickly, lasts 12 hours so no need to administer at school; however, it is not recommended when child has anxiety or motor tics
Ritalin (methylphenidate)	Insomnia, decreased appetite, weight loss, headache, irritability, stomachache	About 3 to 4 hours	Works quickly, effective in 70% of those for whom it is rescribed; however, it is not recommended when child has anxiety or motor tics
Ritalin-SR (methylphenidate)	Insomnia, decreased appetite, weight loss, headache, irritability, stomachache	About 7 hours	Long-lasting so no need to administer at school; however, it is not recommended when child has anxiety or motor tics
Focalin (dextro-methylphenidate)	Insomnia, decreased appetite, weight loss, headache, irritability, stomachache	About 4 to 5 hours	Works quickly and requires half the dose of comparable Ritalin; however, it has the same potential risks as Ritalin for a child with anxiety or motor tics
Dexedrine (dextroamphetamine)	Insomnia, decreased appetite, weight loss, headache, irritability, stomachache	About 3 to 5 hours (tablet); about 7 to 10 hours (spansule)	Works quickly and is long-lasting so no need to administer at school; however, it is not recommended when child has anxiety or motor tics
Adderall (mixed salts of a single-entity amphetamine product)	Insomnia, decreased appetite, weight loss, headache, irritability, stomachache	About 3 to 6 hours	Works quickly and may last somewhat longer than standard stimulants; however, it is not recommended when child has anxiety or motor tics
Adderall XR (mixed salts of a single-entity amphetamine product)	Insomnia, decreased appetite, weight loss, headache, irritability, stomachache	About 12 hours	Works quickly and is long-lasting so no need to administer at school; however, it is not recommended when child has anxiety or motor tics
Tofranil (imipramine, hydrochloride)	Dry mouth, decreased appetite, headache, stomachache, dizziness, constipation, mild tachycardia, tremor	12 to 24 hours	Lasts all day and may be helpful for a child with comorbid depression; however, it may take 2–4 weeks for a clinical response and cannot be suddenly discontinued
Metadate CD (methylphenidate)	Insomnia, decreased appetite, weight loss, headache, irritability, stomachache	About 8 to 10 hours	Useful for adolescents as no midday dose is required; however, it is not recommended when child has anxiety or motor tics
Catapres (clonidine, hydrochloride)	Sleepiness, hypotension, headache, dizziness, stomachache, nausea, dry mouth, localized skin reaction with patch	3 to 6 hours (oral form); 5 days (skin patch)	Useful when the child has comorbidity, a tic disorder, or severe hyperactivity/aggression; it cannot be started or discontinued suddenly
Strattera (atomoxetine HCl)	Decreased appetite, insomnia, nausea and vomiting, fatigue, dizziness, mood swings	About 8 to 10 hours	Not a controlled substance and works quickly; however, long-term effects for children are still being studied (e.g., suicidal thinking)
Vyvanse (Lisdexamfetamine)	Difficulty falling asleep or staying asleep, decreased appetite, uncontrollable shaking of a part of the body, dizziness, jitters, headache	12 hours or more (taken once daily)	Consistent effect for a long period of time, less affected by diet than other medications, and difficult to abuse; however, it takes effect slowly and may interact negatively with antidepressants

Sources: Based on Parker, H. C. (2003, April 3). *Medication chart to treat attention deficit disorders.* Retrieved from www.ldonline.org/ld_indepth/add_adhd/add_medication_chart.html; based on Atomoxetine HCl. Retrieved from http://healthyplace.com/medications/strattera.htm; based on Novartis Pharmaceuticals U.S. (2001, November 15). *FDA grants marketing approval for Focalin, The first chemically advanced form of Ritalin for ADHD—New drug for ADHD contains only the effective isomer of Ritalin;* National Center for Biotechnology Information. (2010). *Lisdexamfetamine.* Retrieved from http://www.ncbi.nlm.nih.gov/pubmedhealth/PMH0000397/

and any problems that arise when medication has been prescribed (Bussing et al., 2012a).

Parent and Professional Education

In addition to medication, researchers have found that effectively educating students with ADHD requires that their parents and teachers understand the disorder and develop effective strategies for responding to the symptoms children are likely to display (Bussing et al., 2012b).

Parent Education

Although parent and student education programs generally are not sufficient by themselves to address the symptoms of ADHD, in

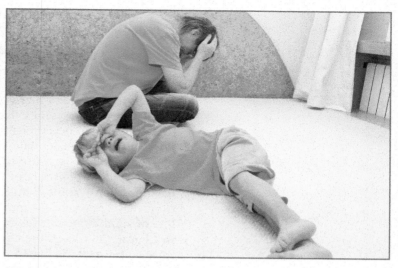

conjunction with other interventions they can help a family to better understand and respond to the child's special needs (Power et al., 2014). Regularly scheduled group parent education sessions should first address behavior management skills, including how to set consistent expectations and limits, create an effective discipline system that includes rewards and negative consequences, develop a strategy to address serious behavior problems, and identify the child's strengths to build positive self-esteem. In addition, parents need to learn techniques for stress and anger management to use with their child and in other aspects of their lives, strategies for assisting their child in making and keeping friends, and skills for working with school personnel on behalf of their child (Moghaddam, Assareh, Heidaripoor, Eslami Rad, & Pishjoo, 2013). Other topics for parent education include up-to-date information about ADHD and research-supported interventions, appropriate evaluation and treatment procedures, and advocacy skills, including knowledge of IDEA and Section 504 (Chako, Wymbs, & Flammer-Rivera, 2008).

Parents of children with ADHD face critical decisions about the best treatment options, especially regarding the potential benefits and problems with medication.

Professional Education

Although many teachers and other educators have accurate general knowledge about students with attention deficit–hyperactivity disorder, they also have many misconceptions (Canu & Mancil, 2012; Sciutto et al., 2016). They generally know the classic symptoms of ADHD but may not realize that students with ADHD often can perform better in a novel situation than in a familiar one or that students may respond in a more compliant way to their father's directions than to their mother's. Similarly, teachers often know more about the diagnosis and characteristics of ADHD than about effective interventions. Staff development sessions can increase professionals' knowledge of these students and how to reach them (Barnett, Corkum, & Elik, 2012). The researchers in the MTA study found that it also was beneficial to assist the teachers in developing effective home-school communication systems, using appropriate teaching techniques, establishing appropriate classroom rules and behavior management systems, responding quietly to student behavior disruptions or ignoring them when possible, and differentiating instruction (Roberts et al., 2015; Wells et al., 2000).

Environmental Supports

Most students with ADHD are fully capable of learning what is being taught in their classrooms. However, they need assistance to access that learning and to complete it. One way for professionals to provide that assistance is through environmental supports—that is, the arrangement of the learning setting so that it supports students with attentional disorders. Here are some examples of environmental supports for students with ADHD:

1. The classroom physical space should be organized and free of distractions. Students should be able to work without looking at or bumping into classmates. In a crowded classroom, the use of desk carrels may help. A desk carrel is a three-sided piece of cardboard, about 15 inches in height, that can be placed on a student's desk to shield her from other classroom activity. Desk carrels can be purchased or made.

2. Physical space considerations also should include the number and intrusiveness of decorations. Although decorations are not usually a problem in middle school and high school, some elementary teachers pride themselves on having brightly colored bulletin boards and intricate art projects suspended from the classroom ceiling. Such displays should be kept out of the direct line of sight of students with ADHD.

3. In Chapter 1, you learned about the importance of posting clear classroom rules and discussing expectations for students. This environmental support is particularly important for students with ADHD.

4. Teachers should post and follow classroom routines. If a change in the schedule is necessary, a student with ADHD should be warned of the change. The teacher should then plan to stay close to the student with ADHD because, even with a warning, the change may cause the student to have behavior difficulties.

5. Another type of environmental support concerns pacing of instruction. Teachers help students with ADHD when they mix difficult or tedious tasks with those that are more stimulating. Teachers also can build into their instruction opportunities for student movement. For example, in secondary classrooms, students who think they know an answer can be told to stand or to turn around in their seats. Younger students can transition between activities by clapping to music or marching around the classroom.

Environmental supports are very much part of universal design for learning. They do not harm any students, they enhance learning for many of them, and they can be incorporated into classroom procedures and activities at the elementary, middle, and high school levels.

Behavior Interventions

Because of problems with behavior inhibition, students with ADHD may display challenging behaviors. As you might expect, a cornerstone of effective education practices for these students is systematic behavior intervention.

Many of the behavior interventions that you learn in order to assist students with disabilities can be implemented for students with ADHD (e.g., Majeika et al., 2011). In addition, many students with ADHD can be taught to use self-monitoring as a means of understanding and then reducing inappropriate behavior, such as calling out answers, and increasing appropriate behavior, such as working on assignments until they are completed (e.g., Moodi, Alizadeh, Bonab, & Soleimani, 2015). This topic is addressed in Data-Driven Decisions.

Many other examples of behavior interventions, effective for students with ADHD as well as other students with behavior problems, can be identified. The following sections highlight several of these interventions (Burke & Loeber, 2015; DuPaul & Jimerson, 2014).

Rewards

Providing rewards for appropriate behaviors is a common behavior intervention. In one study (Wells et al., 2000), these common behaviors were identified as important for students: getting started; interacting with others in a polite way; following

DATA-DRIVEN DECISIONS

Students Gathering Data on Their Behavior

Students often can be taught to gather data about their own behavior, which then can be the basis for designing interventions to decrease inappropriate behavior and increase appropriate behavior (Wills & Mason, 2014). Steps to teaching a simple self-recording strategy are these:

- Analyze the student's ability to self-monitor and self-record, and think about the type(s) of behavior the student could self-monitor.
- Prepare needed materials, including some type of simple recording form as illustrated below.
- Discuss self-recording with the student to develop buy-in necessary for success; include the student in the decision about the clearly defined behavior to be recorded (e.g., calling out answers or on-task/off-task behavior).
- Explain the procedure to be followed, including when to use it and how to record behavior on the chart. One way to do this is to use an audible or vibrating repeating timer on a student tablet or phone; when it goes off, the student should record whether or not the behavior is occurring. Another strategy is to record every incident of a behavior, such as inappropriately getting out of her seat.
- Model the steps in the procedure, and then have the student practice them.
- Implement the procedure. At first, the teacher should closely monitor the accuracy of the student's self-recording. Gradually, such checks can be occasional.
- Reward the student for accurately recording behavior.

- Gradually phase out the need for this strategy as the student improves behaviors based on his awareness of them.

Other aspects of self-recording involve teaching students how to graph their behavior so they can follow their progress, teaching students to self-reward, and engaging students in setting goals related to their behavior. More information on working with students on gathering data is available at this website: http://www.behavioradvisor.com/SelfMonitoring.html.

Casey's Behavior Recording Chart for Class Discussion Time (10:30–11:00 a.m.)

	Out of seat without permission ☹	Raised my hand to answer when Ms. Armand asked a question ☺
Date:		
Date:		
Date:		
Date:		

Sample Recording Form Illustrating a Behavior to Decrease and a Behavior to Increase

classroom rules, including those about being quiet and remaining seated; completing assigned work; stopping when directed to prepare for the next activity or class; and following directions. For each student, a small subset of these behaviors was selected. Students were rewarded with points or tokens for performing the identified behaviors. They could then trade in their points or tokens for rewards. Over time, students had to display more correct behaviors for longer periods of time in order to earn rewards. A more recent study (Bubnik, Hawk, Pelham, Waxmonsky, & Rosch, 2015) demonstrated that rewards used in combination with medication can help students with ADHD attend in a way nearly comparable to their peers. Remember that if you use rewards, you should use them in combination with praise, and you should give them for behaviors that help students (e.g., completing work) instead of only for compliance (e.g., not getting out of their seats).

Low-Involvement Strategies

For some students with ADHD, if you can intervene to stop an inappropriate behavior when it is minor or just beginning, you can avoid the need for more intensive interventions. For example, if Calvin is beginning to talk to a classmate when there should be silence, making eye contact with him may cause him to stop speaking. If that is not effective, proximity control might work: Physically move toward Calvin and stand near his desk or table, placing your hand on his shoulder if necessary to gain his attention. For a few students, you may have private signals. If Calvin is getting too loud in a group discussion, two taps on his desk may serve as a reminder to use an "indoor" voice. Finally, if Calvin is struggling, you might create a break for him by asking him to help you with a chore. Although these low-involvement strategies may not be effective for all students, they can help reduce the amount of time you spend addressing student behavior, leaving more time for teaching and student learning.

Token Economy

Another behavior intervention that can assist students with ADHD and other behavior disorders is a token economy. Some students enjoy participating in this type of behavior management program because it involves all the students in the class. Others are likely to improve their behavior because of the positive peer pressure the system can foster. In a token system, you distribute to students physical tokens (e.g., stickers, poker chips, craft sticks) or points for appropriate behavior. The tokens can be redeemed for rewards that are "priced" based on their popularity. You can learn how to create such a classwide reward system by reviewing Positive Behavior Supports.

POSITIVE • **BEHAVIOR** • SUPPORTS

Using a Token Economy

A token economy is an in-class system for rewarding students for appropriate behavior. Here are the steps for creating a token economy, whether in a general education or a special education setting:

1. *Identify the behaviors for which students can earn credit.* You might select completing and turning in work, keeping hands to oneself, talking in a classroom voice, bringing to class all needed (and specified) learning supplies, returning homework, or exhibiting other behavior that can be clearly observed. Students can be involved in deciding what behavior(s) to include.

2. *Decide on the classroom "currency."* You could use points, tickets distributed during class, X's on a recording sheet, credits marked on an app (e.g., Class Dojo), play money, or any other system. In choosing a currency, keep in mind that you need to efficiently award it and monitor its use.

3. *Assign a value to each target behavior.* Simple behaviors should have a lower value. More difficult behaviors should have a higher value. In a very simple system, you would assign the same value (for example, one point) for each target behavior on a daily basis.

4. *Decide on the privileges or rewards students can earn.* Having variety in the possible "purchases" students can make helps maintain interest in the system (e.g., make-your-own-homework-assignment privilege; lunch with the teacher). Include on the reward list at least one item that costs the minimum amount of currency a student might earn (for example, one point) so that all students have the opportunity to participate in the economy.

5. *Assign purchase "prices" to the privileges and rewards.* In general, if a reward is readily available and not limited in quantity, its purchase price should be lower (e.g., sticker). Items that are tangible (and perhaps literally cost more), limited in supply, or time consuming should have a higher cost (e.g., lunch with a friend and the teacher).

6. *Explain the economy to students.* Demonstrate the economy with several examples to ensure that students understand it. You might give your system a name. For example, you could call it *Cougar Cash* or *Bulldog Bucks*, reflecting the name of the school mascot. When the economy is new, student participation should be carefully monitored to check that students are earning and receiving tokens and spending them as intended.

7. *Establish a systematic way for students to exchange their currency for privileges or rewards.* In most classrooms, it is effective to allow students to use their currency once a week or once every two weeks on a particular day. By having a consistent time and a system for the exchange, you avoid a constant stream of student requests for privileges or rewards and the aggravation of the constant monitoring this would require.

Keep token economies simple for young students and more complex for older students, and let students help select the rewards and assign values for them. You also may need to adjust the behaviors being targeted and the rewards being offered as time passes.

The examples presented here illustrate only a few of the many strategies available to special educators, general education teachers, and others who work with students with ADHD. You will learn about other behavior interventions that also are effective for students with ADHD in the Chapter 7 discussion of students with emotional disabilities.

Instructional Interventions

Instructional interventions are likely to be effective with many students with ADHD (Evans et al., 2016; Johnson, Reid, & Mason, 2012), and they should be designed to provide structure, a brisk pace, and variety. Here are several examples of such strategies:

- *When giving directions, be sure the instructions follow the three Cs: clear, concise, and complete.* After introducing the activity, say, "Take out one sheet of paper. Put on the heading. Write three sentences to describe the main character's feelings." Avoid saying things such as "OK. Let's get going. Take out some paper—does everyone have paper? Regular paper . . . no, regular with the holes punched. Got it? OK. Now put the heading on your paper, you know, name. . . . No, don't number your paper. Not for this. It's really nice outside—if we get finished early, we might end class out on the benches."
- *When giving directions, have students repeat the directions back to you.* Doing this will ensure that everyone hears the directions twice and more students will be likely to remember them.
- *When older students have a lengthy or complex assignment, break the assignment into several short tasks.* Consider giving students a deadline for each of the segments to help them stay organized.

INSTRUCTION IN **ACTION**
Teaching to Help Students with ADHD Succeed

Universal design for learning (UDL), introduced in Chapter 1, asserts that educators should anticipate the needs of all their students as they plan instruction. The following principles can help you implement UDL principals for students with ADHD and guide you in developing effective teaching strategies for them:

- Use more rewards for students with ADHD than may be necessary for other students. If consequences are necessary because of inappropriate behavior, they should occur immediately.
- Change the rewards used for students with ADHD more frequently than those for other students. For example, let students select a reward from a menu that includes 8 or 10 choices.
- Plan ahead. Especially when transitions are about to occur or on days when the schedule is disrupted, remind students of changes, ask them to review rules or procedures, and prompt them to recall rewards and consequences for classroom behavior.
- Students with ADHD often need more external cues to help them regulate their behavior. Reminders, pictures, signals, and other approaches are helpful.

- Any intervention that addresses behavior needs to be continued only if data suggest it is effective; most interventions should be modified as time goes by to sustain their usefulness.
- During instruction, use brief periods of large-group instruction characterized by a businesslike tone and fairly brisk pace. Change activities relatively often, alternating between those that are likely to require higher and lower levels of attention.

As you think about these principles, how might they affect how you manage your classroom? Which of the principles might be beneficial for nearly all learners with special needs? Which seem unique to students with ADHD? Think about what challenges might occur in using these principles and how you could overcome them.

Source: Based on Pfiffner, L. J. & DuPaul, G. J. (2015). Treatment of ADHD in school settings. In R. A. Barkley (Ed.), *Attention-deficit hyperactivity disorder: A handbook for diagnosis and treatment* (4th ed.). New York, NY: Guilford Press.

- *Use as much active responding during instruction as possible.* For example, use a strategy called "One Say, All Say": When one student gives a correct response, have all the students repeat it. If the student's response is not correct, call on other students until the correct response is given and then have classmates repeat it.

These examples barely introduce the range of interventions that should be used when teaching students with ADHD. Instruction in Action includes additional ideas for reaching these learners.

MyEdLab **Self-Check 6.5**

MyEdLab **Application Exercise 6.6:** Teaching Organizational Skills

MyEdLab **Application Exercise 6.7:** Classroom Structure and Self-Management

---

What Are the Perspectives of Parents and Families?

School professionals need to work effectively with parents on many issues related to students with ADHD. These include participating in assessment, coordinating interventions between school and medical professionals, monitoring medication (both its effect and whether it is being taken as prescribed), planning and implementing any needed behavior strategies, and managing homework.

Parenting Children with ADHD

Being the parent of a child with ADHD can be exhausting and extraordinarily stressful (McIntyre & Hennessy, 2012; Mikami, Chong, Saporito, & Jiwon Na, 2015). Even when these children are very young, they may not sleep as long or as often as other children, they may seem to move without stopping, and their behaviors may seem unfocused. One set of parents described their daughter's preschool escapades as including climbing into the cupboards over the kitchen counters, dangling from a shower curtain rod, and hiding in the oven during a game of hide and seek (McCluskey & McCluskey, 1999). As children with ADHD grow older, the problems do not necessarily end. Children's disruptive or inattentive behaviors may worsen with increased freedom (Evans, Sibley, & Serpell, 2009). Parents may be faced with decisions about whether to use medication to treat their children, and they need to build positive relationships with the teachers and other school personnel educating their children (Bussing, Koro-Ljungberg, Gurnani, Garvan, Mason, Noguchi, & Albarracin, 2015; Coletti et al., 2012).

Parents of children with ADHD also face the same dilemmas as those whose children have other special needs. They must adjust their understanding and expectations for how their child will develop, and they must redefine their own roles in their children's lives. In addition, they have to deal with the reactions of family members such as grandparents, as happened with Carlos, introduced at the beginning of the chapter. These parents may at times also feel like they are referees between the child with ADHD and the child's siblings.

At school, parents may face an array of challenges. In one study, parents of students with ADHD reported that their children were from three to seven times more likely than other children to be receiving special education, to have been expelled or suspended, and to have repeated a grade (LeFever, Villers, Morrow, & Vaughn, 2002). Other parents may find themselves involved at school because their children are either victims of bullying or engaged in bullying behavior (Mayes, Calhoun, Baweja, & Mahr, 2015). Not surprisingly, parents may come to view their children as being at high risk for school failure.

Supporting Students by Supporting Parents

General education teachers and other school professionals can take many practical steps to enhance their interactions with parents of students with ADHD. Here are several points to keep in mind to foster collaboration:

1. *Be realistic in your expectations of parents.* If a parent is struggling to keep a family together because of a child's disruptive behavior, suggesting complex interventions probably will not work. Instead, try suggesting only one or two simple ideas that can be implemented easily.
2. *Encourage the parents to be good role models for the student.* If you can compliment the parents on keeping a sense of humor, on responding calmly to the child, or on other positive behaviors, you may encourage the parents to keep using those helpful approaches.
3. *Help parents to be realistic in their expectations for their child.* Although parents certainly understand their children better than educators do, you can suggest limiting the amount of time students should spend on homework. Also be sure to tell parents about their children's successes.
4. *Make related resources available to parents.* Although school professionals do not identify students as ADHD, once a child has been diagnosed, parents may seek information, and educators can help them meet that need. By keeping a list of websites, contact information for local support groups, and copies of brochures and other information created in your school district, you can empower parents to find answers to their questions and concerns.

MyEdLab **Self-Check 6.6**

MyEdLab **Application Exercise 6.8:** He Just Needs a Little Discipline

---

Trends and Issues Affecting the ADHD Field

The field of ADHD has evolved very rapidly. Educators and parents alike have difficulty keeping up with the changes in thinking about the causes, prevalence, and interventions for students with this disorder. Three significant issues to consider are (a) the identification of and appropriate treatment for very young children with ADHD, (b) the identification and treatment of individuals with ADHD in high school and adulthood, and (c) the status of knowledge on effective treatment of ADHD.

Young Children with ADHD

Many young children are active and have a limited attention span, and this is typical development, not ADHD. However, many parents of children with ADHD will tell you that they knew that their child was different at a very early age, that his behaviors or inattention were extreme.

The largest study to date of young children with ADHD, the Preschool ADHD Treatment Study (PATS), was undertaken by Greenhill et al., 2006. One finding of this study is that preschoolers sometimes can benefit from stimulant medication such as Ritalin but that it should be given in low doses and each child's reaction should be closely monitored since 1 in 10 children may have side effects so serious that the medication should be stopped.

The Ethical and Professional Dilemma

One result of the increasing recognition of ADHD as a disorder that can exist even in very young children is heated discussion about the appropriateness of labeling and medication for them (as well as other students with ADHD). Should preschool children be given stimulant medication to address attentional problems? Some professionals have argued that medication should be considered a last resort (e.g., Rajwan, Chacko, & Moeller, 2012), prescribed only if interventions such as parent training and behavioral interventions are insufficient to improve the child's functioning. In contrast, others (e.g., de Luis-García et al, 2015; Vaughan, March, & Kratochvil, 2012) have found that appropriate medication significantly reduces the symptoms of ADHD in young children and so enables them to better benefit from early educational experiences. Discussion concerning the use of the ADHD label and the appropriateness of various interventions for young children who have the characteristics of this disorder is likely to be shaped over the next several years by additional studies of children first diagnosed with ADHD at a very young age.

ADHD in Adolescents and Adults

With increased understanding of the causes of ADHD and more attention paid to long-term prognosis of children identified with the disorder, interest is growing in exploring ADHD in adolescents and adults (Ramsay & Rostain, 2016). Moreover, the use of medication among adults with ADHD has grown dramatically over the past several years (Fredriksen & Peleikis, 2016).

Outcomes for Adults Diagnosed as Children

One area of interest involves what happens to children with ADHD when they grow up (e.g., Hinshaw et al., 2012; Lahey et al., 2016). To date, very few studies have carefully followed a group of students who received medication or another intervention as they left high school for postsecondary education or work. Some information is available, but it is based on individual reports. For adults who do not continue treatment, outcomes are not very positive (Babinski et al., 2011; Fletcher, 2014). These adults are at higher risk for substance abuse, for problems at work, and for family difficulties. They may have problems keeping a job, trouble keeping up with life routines, and difficulties with self-discipline. They also are more likely to engage in criminal activity than those without ADHD (e.g., Harzke et al., 2012). Of adults who do continue treatment, medication seems to be effective in the same way that it is for children (Retz et al., 2012). Few other interventions have been systematically explored, but often recommended is a combination of therapy to address how ADHD and any comorbid disorders are affecting the individual's life, education about the disorder, and information about tools that can be helpful, such as computer scheduling software and day planners.

Identification of ADHD in Adolescents and Adults

A second area of concern related to adolescents, adults, and ADHD is late identification (Dipeolu, Hargrave, & Storlie, 2015). Some adults recall the difficulties they experienced as children in school, and they seek assistance when they recognize similar problems in adulthood. While adolescents with ADHD are not as likely as their younger counterparts to be hyperactive, they are at high risk for school failure, for suspension, for retention, and for behavior problems such as defiance and noncompliance (Lahey et al., 2016; Stringaris & Goodman, 2009), and it is essential that they seek or continue treatment.

For an adult seeking identification, an extensive developmental, family, and school history will likely be taken, and the individual will be asked to respond to survey or interview questions concerning current functioning. If a decision is made that ADHD is present, a physician will prescribe medication and help the individual to access other support resources.

Did You Know?

Many students with ADHD received extended time to take tests, but research suggests that although they make more reading errors and have lower comprehension, they do not take more time to complete tests and do not have more text anxiety than peers (Lewandowski, Hendricks, & Gordon, 2015). A resulting recommendation is to teach these students to use extra time to check their answers.

MyEdLab
Video Example 6.4
Video Example 6.4 summarizes the reasons adults seek treatment for ADHD.
(https://www.youtube.com/watch?v=lzGQ4dkyl8U)

For an adolescent, identification follows the same procedures used for other school-age students. In addition, an increased emphasis on careful transition planning, considered in detail in Chapter 5, can be particularly helpful for these students. Because many adolescents with ADHD should be able to succeed in higher education, transition planning might include learning study and organizational strategies, self-advocacy skills, ways to access services for students with special needs at college, and time management.

The Knowledge Base on Treatment for ADHD

Earlier in this chapter, you read about treatments for addressing the needs of students with ADHD. However, clear evidence that any single approach is more effective than another or that particular combinations of treatments will lead to the best long-term outcomes still does not exist. For example, the National Institute of Mental Health (2009c) reported that in follow-up studies of the students from the original sample from the MTA research project, results were mixed:

- Nearly all the students in the original studies showed sustained improvement in functioning when follow-up data were gathered.
- No differences were found in symptoms or functioning among students who had been assigned to different treatment groups, leading researchers to conclude that neither type nor intensity of a one-year treatment approach can, at this point, predict long-term outcomes.
- Students still had academic and social problems, including more conduct problems, more depression, and more psychiatric hospitalizations than other students.
- Students who had responded well to treatment in the original study were functioning best at the eight-year follow-up.
- Sixty-one percent of students no longer were taking medication at the follow-up, and these students were functioning as well as those still taking medication. Researchers reported that different students seemed to respond differently to medication, with some students gradually improving in response to medication, some quickly improving and sustaining those improvements, and some improving but then losing that improvement.

One dilemma in attempting to study treatment effectiveness is the number of factors that can affect results. For example, some families may decide to give their children medication at a very early age and at the same time provide behavioral and other supports. Other families may decide to use the same interventions, but they do so when the child is older. Yet other families may emphasize behavioral and academic interventions and decide against the use of medication or use it for a very short period of time. Each of these scenarios may result in different outcomes, and these and other variations in treatment and child characteristics makes predicting the long-term benefit of treatments exceptionally challenging.

What is clear is that the symptoms of ADHD are persistent and require a long-term perspective on treatment. Both teachers and professionals must recognize that interventions effective for young children may need to be reevaluated and possibly changed as students approach adolescence. Further, the increasing academic and social demands students face as they progress through school should be kept in mind: Without paying careful attention to them, students may lose whatever gains they have made. Ultimately, as a teacher, you should stay abreast of the continuing development of knowledge concerning this complex but relatively common childhood disorder so that you are prepared to assist students to reach their potential.

MyEdLab **Self-Check 6.7**

MyEdLab **Application Exercise 6.9:** The Potential Importance of Preschool

Summary

LO6.1 ADHD is not a disability category in IDEA, but it is defined in the *DSM-V* (i.e., inattentiveness, hyperactivity, and impulsivity, or a combination of these) and affects 3% to 7% of the school-age population. ADHD generally is believed to be caused by neurobiological problems resulting in deficient behavior inhibition, but it also is influenced by environmental factors.

LO6.2 Students with ADHD vary widely in their cognitive, academic, social/emotional, and behavior characteristics, and some students with this disorder have comorbid learning, emotional, and other disabilities.

LO6.3 Because ADHD is a medical condition, a doctor must make the diagnosis based on a comprehensive evaluation of the student that includes input from school personnel and parents. To be considered for special education services (usually as other health impaired), students who are ADHD also must be assessed by a team of school professionals. Decisions made about these students must follow IDEA guidelines.

LO6.4 Many students with ADHD receive services through Section 504 plans, depending on their needs. If their disorder constitutes a disability addressed through IDEA or if they have a comorbid disability, they are most likely educated in general education settings, unless other disabilities necessitate services in a separate setting.

LO6.5 Medication is recommended for many students with ADHD; other interventions, often used in combination with medication, include parent and professional education, environmental supports, behavior interventions, and instructional strategies and techniques.

LO6.6 Parents of students with ADHD vary in their responses to their children and their perceptions of the effectiveness of interventions, and educators should work to ensure that parents can access appropriate resources and set appropriate expectations for their children.

LO6.7 Issues related to ADHD concern the prescribing of medication for very young children, the persistence of ADHD past the school years, and the uncertain knowledge base on effective treatments and interventions for students with ADHD.

Back to the Cases

Now that you've read about attention deficit–hyperactivity disorder, look back at the student stories at the beginning of this chapter. Then, answer the questions about each of their cases.

MyEdLab **Case Study 6.1**

CEDRIC. Cedric is a student who is not eligible for services through IDEA because ADHD is not negatively affecting his educational performance; instead, he has a Section 504 plan.

MyEdLab **Case Study 6.2**

CARLOS. Think about the multiple aspects of the difficulties Carlos is experiencing in his community and in school. The challenge educators face, given that they cannot change the circumstances outside of school, is finding the most effective ways to teach students like Carlos.

MyEdLab **Case Study 6.3**

MARCUS. Marcus has experienced both success and failure in his school career, but he seems to be thinking about the future in a positive and realistic way.

7

Students with Emotional and Behavior Disorders

CHARLOTTE

Although still 5 years old, Charlotte is identified as having an emotional disability. School professionals have had many conversations trying to understand Charlotte, pondering her mother's drug use, her uncertain living arrangements with a grandmother and aunt sometimes informally taking over custody, and her extreme and sometimes contradictory school behaviors. One recent afternoon Charlotte seemed completely unaware of her behaviors or expectations for school conduct. Redirected by Ms. Sandoval, her special education teacher, to complete her work, Charlotte screamed "No!," threw papers, books, and crayons around the classroom, and then climbed onto a bookcase to get access to the blinds on the windows, pulling them down on herself when she fell. She then raced to Ms. Sandoval's desk and, deliberately it seemed, broke off the memory stick in the computer that held all of Ms. Sandoval's instructional items. Ms. Sandoval called for assistance, but before the counselor and principal (both trained in crisis procedures, as is Ms. Sandoval) arrived, Charlotte had punched Ms. Sandoval and then had run from the classroom. She pushed through the door, heading toward the highway; fortunately, the counselor caught her before anything worse could happen. After Charlotte had calmed down, the counselor asked her to talk about what had happened. Charlotte looked at her blankly with no recollection of the tumultuous afternoon. Ms. Sandoval comments with chagrin, "I'm well-prepared as a teacher for students with emotional disabilities, but Charlotte—there are times when I'm at a loss about what to do to reach her, to keep her safe, to help her learn, both academically and behaviorally. I'm so worried that if we can't change her current path, she'll have even more serious problems as she gets older." Charlotte's IEP goals include participating in cooperative social play with peers, following directions given by adults, and transitioning from activity to activity. Academically, Charlotte is slightly below average.

GABRIEL

According to Gabriel's mother, Ms. Archer, his first six years of public school were mostly negative. He had no friends, poor grades, and little motivation. Even after he was identified as having an emotional disability, his special education and general education teachers expressed frustration that they could not seem to reach him; they referred to him as being "in a shell." Ms. Archer openly admits that even though she loves her son, in trying to be realistic, she views the future with a sense of doom, anticipating drug or alcohol use, or perhaps even suicide. Now, however, she is daring to be just a little optimistic. As Gabriel transitioned to middle school, his IEP team made the difficult decision that his needs were so significant that he should be educated in a therapeutic day school, and that is where he is enrolled. He now has frequent counseling sessions, smaller classes, and a highly structured school environment. The staff members at the school are highly trained and strongly committed to helping students with emotional disabilities succeed. The term they use to describe Gabriel is "blossoming." He is gaining confidence and making a few friends. Several adjustments in his medication have helped to address behavior outbursts. In fact, discussions are already occurring about Gabriel returning to his neighborhood school. Both Ms. Archer and the team are concerned, however. Will he be welcomed at his middle school? How can the progress made at this separate school be continued there?

STEVEN

Steven has had a difficult life. His father was killed before he was born, and his mother has serious alcohol and drug problems. He spent much of his childhood in six different foster homes. Of his three older siblings, two are in state prison. Steven was retained in first grade and again in fifth grade, and his clearest memories of elementary school include feeling dumb and fighting classmates who called him names. While in middle school, Steven was arrested for setting fires in neighbors' trash cans; after that he attended an alternative school for students with significant behavior and academic problems. According to Steven, the school was "like prison, with guards all over the place and someone always in your face." He completed his first year of high school in his neighborhood in a self-contained program for students with emotional disabilities, but he missed 30 days of school that year. Steven began his sophomore year but dropped out last month. Asked why, he describes high school as a waste of his time. He also admits that he had a shouting match with a security guard and was probably going to be suspended again anyway. Steven has been arrested twice since he began high school: once for stealing a car and once for drug possession. He has no specific plans for getting his high school diploma. When asked what type of job he would like to have, he brightens and says that he would like a job where he would sit at a desk and have a secretary to take his calls and greet his visitors.

Of all the school-age students who have disabilities, few can be as puzzling as those who have emotional and behavior disorders. As you can tell from the vignettes about Charlotte, Gabriel, and Steven, these students defy simple description, and at times it is difficult to understand how they can be grouped into a single disability category. When compared to other students with disabilities, these students are more likely to have attended multiple schools, and they are four times more likely to have been suspended or expelled from school (Smith, Katsiyannis, Losinski, & Ryan, 2014; Duchnowski et al., 2012). Their teachers often report feeling unprepared to work with them (Gable, Tonelson, Sheth, Wilson, & Park, 2012; Regan, 2009). These students pose unique challenges to school personnel because they often need structure and therapeutic intervention strategies that are difficult to provide. At the same time, successful outcomes for students with emotional and behavior disorders rely on those interventions (e.g., Hauth, Mastropieri, Scruggs, & Regan, 2013).

Understanding Emotional and Behavior Disorders

The study of emotional and behavior disorders has gone on for centuries. Contemporary practices for students in public schools have their foundation in the work of early physicians and psychologists and their efforts to treat adults with mental illness.

Development of the Field of Emotional and Behavior Disorders

Fascination with insanity and mental illness can be found throughout history (Cook, Tankersley, & Landrum, 2014), but it was not until the very late 19th century that emotional problems in children were considered a valid topic for study. G. Stanley Hall was one of the first psychologists to specialize in the study of these children, publishing a two-volume book on adolescent psychology in 1904.

Several factors made it challenging to study children with emotional and behavior disorders (Winzer, 1993). First, no consistent set of terms existed to describe these children. Their disorders were called such intimidating names as *dementia praecox, catatonia, paranoia, childhood schizophrenia,* and *juvenile insanity.* Second, in many cases, mental illness and intellectual disabilities were still confused and addressed as though they were a single disorder. Third, professionals were reluctant to openly admit that children could have mental illness because this view contradicted the long held perspective that only adults were affected. Mental illness also was still sometimes associated with evil or satanic possession, making it seem unethical to assign this diagnosis to children.

An understanding of emotional disabilities as they pertained to children gradually developed in the 20th century, and services to address these students' needs eventually emerged. Particularly since the passage of federal special education laws, professionals in the area of emotional and behavior disorders have been researching factors that cause these disorders, studying effective interventions, and striving to ensure that all students who have these disorders are identified and educated appropriately. These topics are addressed later in this chapter, and significant events in this field are presented in Figure 7.1.

Definitions of Emotional and Behavior Disorders

The very language used to describe the students about whom this chapter is written requires explanation. For example, the Individuals with Disabilities Education Act (IDEA) uses the term *emotional disturbance (ED)* to identify this

FIGURE 7.1   Time Line of the Development of the Emotional and Behavior Disorders Field

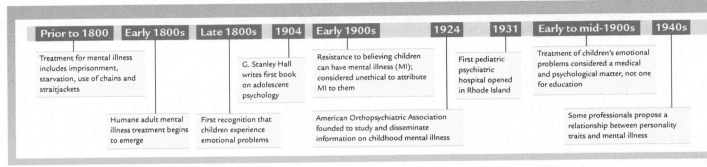

population. Many professionals in the field object to that term, noting that it carries a strong negative connotation. They advocate for the alternative—emotional and behavior disorder (EBD)—the term used throughout this chapter. However, other terms also are assigned to describe this group of students, including *emotionally disabled (ED), behavior disordered (BD), emotionally impaired (EI),* and *seriously emotionally disturbed (SED).* What terminology is used in your state to describe this disability?

Like the language used to describe students with emotional and behavior disorders, the definition of this disability category is somewhat controversial. The definition most often applied is the one found in IDEA. However, critics have pointed out major problems with that definition.

Federal Definition

As noted, the term used in IDEA for emotional and behavior disorders is emotional disturbance (ED), which the law defines as

> a condition exhibiting one or more of the following characteristics over a long period of time and to a marked degree that adversely affects a child's educational performance:
>
> a. An inability to learn that cannot be explained by intellectual, sensory, or health factors.
> b. An inability to build or maintain satisfactory interpersonal relationships with peers and teachers.
> c. Inappropriate types of behavior or feelings under normal circumstances.
> d. A general pervasive mood of unhappiness or depression.
> e. A tendency to develop physical symptoms or fears associated with personal or school problems.

The term includes *schizophrenia.* The term does not apply to children who are socially maladjusted, unless it is determined that they have an emotional disturbance (IDEA 20 U.S.C. §1401 [2004], 20 C.F.R. §300.8[c][4]).

For a student to qualify for services through this definition, three sets of factors must be taken into account: First, the student's problem has to occur for a long period of time, to a marked degree, negatively affecting educational performance. Second, only students meeting one or more of the five listed criteria are considered to have this disability. Third, like the definition of learning disabilities, this definition contains an exclusionary clause; that is, some students are explicitly prohibited from being identified as having emotional disturbance. Students who are socially maladjusted (i.e., those who intentionally act out or break rules) are not considered to have this disability unless they also meet one of the other criteria.

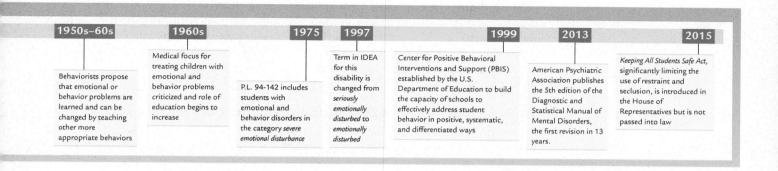

1950s–60s	1960s	1975	1997	1999	2013	2015
Behaviorists propose that emotional or behavior problems are learned and can be changed by teaching other more appropriate behaviors	Medical focus for treating children with emotional and behavior problems criticized and role of education begins to increase	P.L. 94-142 includes students with emotional and behavior disorders in the category *severe emotional disturbance*	Term in IDEA for this disability is changed from *seriously emotionally disturbed* to *emotionally disturbed*	Center for Positive Behavioral Interventions and Support (PBIS) established by the U.S. Department of Education to build the capacity of schools to effectively address student behavior in positive, systematic, and differentiated ways	American Psychiatric Association publishes the 5th edition of the Diagnostic and Statistical Manual of Mental Disorders, the first revision in 13 years.	*Keeping All Students Safe Act,* significantly limiting the use of restraint and seclusion, is introduced in the House of Representatives but is not passed into law

Criticism of the Federal Definition of Emotional Disturbance

Almost since the passage of P.L. 94-142, professionals have criticized the federal definition of emotional and behavior disorders. For example, a group of 30 professional organizations joined together as the National Coalition on Mental Health and Special Education to lobby for change to the definition, contending that the federal definition had several significant problems (Forness & Knitzer, 1992). First, they argued that the five criteria in the definition were not supported by research. Second, they noted that the reference to educational performance too narrowly focused on academic learning, excluding the important but indirect social curriculum of education.

A third criticism of the federal definition was particularly significant. The coalition maintained that the exclusionary clause concerning social maladjustment was unnecessarily confusing and that the intent was to exclude only juvenile delinquents, not all students with this disorder. They illustrated this point by describing students with conduct disorders, which are emotional and behavior problems involving aggression, destruction of property, lying or stealing, or serious rule violation (e.g., running away). The coalition reported that conduct disorder is the most common type of social maladjustment, that most states include social maladjustment in their educational definition of emotional disabilities, and that this group of students in fact makes up the largest single group of students included in this category. The coalition proposed the following alternative definition (Forness & Knitzer, 1992, p. 14):

> The term emotional or behavioral disorder means a disability characterized by behavioral or emotional responses in school so different from appropriate age, cultural, or ethnic norms that they adversely affect educational performance. Educational performance includes academic, social, vocational, and personal skills. Such a disability
>
>   **a.** is more than a temporary, expected response to stressful events in the environment;
>
>   **b.** is consistently exhibited in two different settings, at least one of which is school-related; and
>
>   **c.** is unresponsive to direct intervention in general education or the child's condition is such that general education interventions would be insufficient.
>
> Emotional and behavioral disorders can co-exist with other disabilities. This category may include children or youth with schizophrenic disorders, affective disorders, anxiety disorders, or other sustained disorders of conduct or adjustment when they adversely affect educational performance in accordance with section (i).

As you compare the two definitions, what do you notice? Do you think the coalition definition enhances your understanding of this disorder? Although the coalition was not successful in getting this definition incorporated into federal law, professionals who work in this field generally prefer the latter definition and use it to guide their work, contending that it does not violate the federal definition but rather provides a clearer basis for school practice.

Other Considerations in Defining Emotional and Behavior Disorders

One more topic should be mentioned before concluding this discussion. Because children's emotional and behavior disorders are a focus of treatment in the medical and mental health fields as well as the educational field, the disorders also have been defined by medical professionals. The *Diagnostic and Statistical Manual of Mental Disorders* (5th ed.) (*DSM-V*) (American Psychiatric Association, 2013), a publication you learned about in the Chapter 6 description of attention deficit–hyperactivity disorder (ADHD), contains a classification system and definitions of emotional disorders among children. This classification system, which refers to these conditions as mental disorders, includes disorders that you have probably heard of but that are not explicitly defined in special education law. Examples include disruptive, impulsive control, and conduct disorders such as oppositional defiant disorder (ODD), mood disorders such as persistent depressive disorder, and feeding and eating disorders such as anorexia nervosa. If you work with students with emotional disabilities, you may need to familiarize yourself with your students' medically diagnosed disorders so that you can better understand their instructional needs.

Prevalence of Emotional and Behavior Disorders

Controversy over the definition of emotional and behavior disorders and differences across school, medical, and mental health settings related to who is considered emotionally and behaviorally disordered contribute to uncertainty in estimating the prevalence of this disability among school-age children and young adults. According to the federally collected IDEA data (U.S. Department of Education, 2014), 358,389 students ages 6 to 21 received special education services as emotionally disturbed during the 2011–2012 school year, making this the fifth-largest disability category. This group of students comprised approximately 6.29% of all students receiving special education and 0.8% of all students in schools, a prevalence rate that is a moderate decline from a decade ago. As you learned in Chapter 3, African American students are overrepresented in this category of disability. They are more than twice as likely as students overall to receive special education services for an emotional or behavior disorder (Kauffman, 2014; U.S. Department of Education, 2014).

Data on prevalence from schools is only one source of information concerning this group of students. Prevalence estimates using data from mental health clinics, private practitioners, and other community sources indicate that many more children and youth in schools than are recognized have emotional and behavior disorders (Avenevoli, Swendsen, He, Burstein, & Merikangas, 2015; Slomski, 2012). In fact, it is estimated that one of every five children and adolescents has a mental health disorder requiring treatment (Merikangas et al., 2010) and that half of all adult mental illness began prior to age 14 (National Institute of Mental Health, 2009; Olfson, Blanco, Wang, Laje, & Correll, 2014). This difference in prevalence reports probably occurs because many children receive counseling or services in a community setting even though they do not meet IDEA eligibility criteria.

Video Example from YouTube

MyEdLab
Video Example 7.1

In this video, you can glimpse what it is like to be a child with a complex emotional disability and to be her parents. (https://www.youtube.com/watch?v=kMHnx2LDUfQ&list=PLLEBGGjoPD2D30nAXZyX4eOXApq5xlBG_&index=8)

Prevalence by Gender

As with both learning disabilities and ADHD, far more males than females are diagnosed at school as having emotional and behavior disorders. Although precise statistics are not available, researchers estimate that these disorders are found in boys three or more times more often than in girls (Duchnowski et al., 2012). Some professionals argue that these differences are inflated because of basic differences in teachers' reactions to students. They hypothesize that teachers are more likely to rate the same behavior displayed by boys and girls as more disturbing in boys. Further, they suggest that as boys move into adolescence, they tend to increase their acting-out behaviors while girls tend to turn inward (Skowron, Cipriano-Essel, Gatzke-Kopp, Teti, & Ammerman, 2014). The boys' behaviors are more disturbing to teachers, some hypothesize, and so boys are more likely to be identified as having these disorders.

Causes of Emotional and Behavior Disorders

Emotional and behavior disorders include a wide variety of complex problems, and seldom can any single, clear cause be identified for them. Two types of factors are most likely to contribute to the development of emotional and behavior disorders: biological factors and psychosocial factors.

Biological Factors

As is true for learning disabilities and attention deficit–hyperactivity disorder, research suggests that at least some emotional and behavior disorders are the result of a physiological problem. One consideration in this category is genetics and whether these disorders are inherited. In at least some instances, research supports this possibility (Beauchaine, 2015; van Beijsterveldt et al., 2013; Bartels, van de Aa, van Beijsterveldt, Middeldorp, & Boomsma, 2011). For example, some studies report that children with a parent who has schizophrenia, an adult mental illness, are much more likely than other children to develop this disorder (Van Haren, et al. 2012). Keep in mind, though, that evidence of such genetic connections is still the subject of debate (Barbosa-Leiker, Fleming, Hollins Martin, & Martin, 2015).

A second area examined as a biological influence is brain injury. Children whose mothers smoked or abused alcohol or drugs during pregnancy are more likely than other children to develop emotional and behavior disorders (e.g., Niarchou, Zammit, & Lewis, 2015). Brain injury also can be related to environmental toxins. Again, children diagnosed with lead poisoning or exposed over time to other chemicals in their homes and neighborhoods are at risk for developing these disorders. Poor nutrition is yet another factor that can affect neurological development and contribute to the development of emotional and behavior disorders. Finally, some children have neurologically based emotional disabilities as a result of an accident (e.g., falling from a bicycle) or illness (e.g., high fever).

Many stress factors in children's lives can increase their risk for developing emotional or behavioral disorders, including living in extreme poverty.

Psychosocial Factors

Children are influenced in their psychological and social development by the people around them, the events they experience, and their living conditions.

Collectively, these are considered psychosocial factors. The following psychosocial factors are associated with emotional and behavior disorders in children (Beauchaine, 2015; Skowron et al., 2014; Komro, Flay, & Biglan, 2011):

- *Chronic stress.* Some children grow up in home and community settings characterized by stress. Perhaps the child's parents fight frequently, sometimes physically assaulting each other. Perhaps the family does not have enough income for even a marginal existence, and so there are frequent moves to avoid eviction or periodic stays in a homeless shelter. Chronic stress also may come from the community—for example, when shootings, drug dealing, and gang activities are common occurrences.

- *Stressful life events.* A second group of psychosocial factors includes intense life events. Two of the most common examples are the death of a parent or primary caregiver and divorce. However, other stressful life events also can affect children. One common example is when children witness violence in homes or their communities.

- *Childhood maltreatment.* Reports on television and in newspapers are a constant reminder that child abuse is a very real health concern in the United States. According to the Children's Bureau (2016), in 2014 approximately 702,000 children were victims of abuse or neglect. Most professionals consider this figure to be a significant underestimate. In 91.6% of cases reporting abused or neglected children, the perpetrator is one or both of the parents (Children's Bureau, 2014), and alcohol or drug use is frequently involved. Children who are physically or psychologically abused are at greater risk of developing emotional or behavior disorders.

- *Additional family factors.* Other family problems also can influence children and possibly cause emotional and behavior disorders. For example, research suggests that when a parent is depressed, he or she may lack the motivation and energy to use effective child-rearing practices, and the children in the household thus will be at risk (Nelson et al., 2013). Peers may also play a role; if extreme sibling rivalry develops, emotional problems can result.

Making Sense of the Factors Contributing to Emotional and Behavior Disorders

Clearly, many different factors, alone or in combination with others, can lead to emotional and behavior disorders. The current thinking is that biological and psychosocial factors probably interact. That is, some children may have a genetic predisposition to have a disorder, and when they live in a situation that includes one or more of the other risk factors, they are more likely to develop a disorder. A related line of thinking addresses correlated constraints. It proposes that when children's lives are permeated with risk factors, those factors collectively promote maladaptive behavior patterns and subsequently constrain the development of positive adjustment (Hosp, Huddle, Ford, & Hensley, 2016).

However, you should keep in mind that children tend to have resilience; that is, they tend to be able to recover and not experience long-term harm from brief episodes of stress or single negative experiences (Zoloski & Bullock, 2012; Wu et al., 2013). And so many children, even those who might be at risk for developing emotional disabilities, do not experience these disorders. Resilience is explained more fully in the Professional Edge feature.

Did You Know?

Another risk factor, especially for aggressive behavior in children, is exposure to violence through media. As today's children watch violence on television, play video games that stress violence, listen to music with violence in the lyrics, and watch movies with violent themes, they are at risk for being desensitized to violence and, some research suggests, becoming increasingly aggressive, especially if other risk factors are present (American Academy of Family Physicians, 2015).

MyEdLab **Self-Check 7.1**

MyEdLab **Application Exercise 7.1:** Causes of Eric's Behavior

The Promise of Resiliency

Resiliency is the ability to bounce back from adversity, frustration, and misfortune. When schools, families, and communities help to build resiliency in children, those children are capable of becoming healthy, competent adults, in spite of the life stresses they may experience (Jennings, Frank, Snowberg, Coccia, & Greenberg, 2013; Longenecker, Zink, & Florence, 2012). Here are the seven C's of resilience (American Academy of Pediatrics, 2006; Healthy Children, 2015) and ways to foster them.

Competence (feeling able to effectively handle a situation)

- Teach students to focus on their strengths; celebrate their efforts
- Avoid comparing one student to another
- Empower students to make decisions

Confidence (belief in one own's abilities)

- Praise students honestly about specific accomplishments; avoid general, nonspecific praise
- Help students to take responsibility, but be realistic in setting those expectations so that success is likely

Connection (close ties to family, community, school)

- Ensure your classroom is a safe place for students (physically and emotionally)
- Help students to express all emotions in a constructive way
- Model how to address conflict

Character

- Frequently discuss with students how to make decisions about right versus wrong

- Use classroom situations to discuss how one person's behaviors can positively or negatively affect others
- Reinforce students for caring about others
- Deliberately work to build a sense of classroom community

Contribution (one's personal contribution makes the world better)

- Teach students about giving to others
- Model generosity through service projects and similar activities
- Create ways that students can contribute, whether at school or in the community

Coping (one's ability to manage and move past adversity)

- Teach students to talk to themselves in positive ways when faced with a challenging situation (i.e., teach self-management)
- If a student does something negative, help the student learn from the experience and problem solve about alternatives for the future
- Model effective coping strategies, and point out examples of effective coping to students

Control (Sense of having power to direct one's life)

- Teach how the choices students make affect their life experiences
- Teach and model persistence, and reward students for persisting in reaching their goals
- Involve students in setting classroom rules and enforcing them

Source: Used with permission of the American Academy of Pediatrics, *Building resilience in children and teens: Giving kids roots and wings*, 3rd Edition, by Kenneth R. Ginsburg, © 2015.

Characteristics of Individuals with Emotional and Behavior Disorders

The characteristics of students with emotional and behavior disorders vary so much that it is almost impossible to provide a comprehensive list. Instead, in this section, you will learn about some of the most common behavior and emotional, social, and cognitive, and academic qualities of these learners (Harrison, Vannest, Davis, & Reynolds, 2012).

Behavior Characteristics

The behaviors of students with emotional and behavior disorders often are not completely different from those of other students. Rather, they occur more often, with more intensity, for a longer time, and they have a significantly negative impact on student learning. Further, the behaviors of these students cover an entire spectrum. One of the most common ways of conceptualizing these behaviors is to think of them as being either internalizing or externalizing. Internalizing behaviors are those characterized as withdrawn or directed inward. Gabriel, the sixth-grader described at the beginning of this chapter, exhibits internalizing behaviors. Not surprisingly, because students with internalizing behaviors often do not disrupt the classroom, their needs can be overlooked by busy educators unless they are particularly vigilant.

Externalizing behaviors are those characterized as directed toward others; when students display these behaviors, they generally bother both teachers and other students. Charlotte and Steven, students whose stories began this chapter, both display externalizing behaviors. They are aggressive, and they could be described as acting out. As you might expect, students with externalizing behaviors are very likely to be identified by their teachers as needing assistance, and teachers' perceptions of these children can be negative (Murray & Zvoch, 2011).

Many examples of internalizing and externalizing behaviors can be identified. Figure 7.2 includes examples of both types of behaviors.

Thinking about students having internalizing or externalizing behaviors is a convenient way to illustrate the diversity inherent in emotional disabilities, but

FIGURE 7.2   **Examples of Internalizing and Externalizing Behaviors for Students with Emotional and Behavior Disorders**

Students with emotional and behavior disorders may display two types of behaviors that cause concern. *Internalizing behaviors* are characterized by withdrawal, and *externalizing behaviors* are characterized by acting out. Here are examples of both types of behavior.

Internalizing Behaviors

- Exhibits sad affect, depression, and feelings of worthlessness
- Cannot get mind off certain thoughts, ideas, or situations
- Cannot keep self from engaging in repetitive and/or useless actions
- Suddenly cries, cries frequently, or displays totally unexpected and atypical affect for the situation
- Complains of severe headaches or other somatic problems (stomachaches, nausea, dizziness, vomiting) as a result of fear or anxiety
- Talks of killing self—reports suicidal thoughts and/or is preoccupied with death
- Shows decreased interest in activities that were previously of interest
- Is excessively teased, verbally or physically abused, neglected, and/or avoided by peers
- Shows signs of physical, emotional, and/or sexual abuse

Externalizing Behaviors

- Displays recurring pattern of aggression toward objects or persons
- Argues excessively
- Forces the submission of others through physical and/or verbal means
- Is noncompliant with reasonable requests
- Exhibits persistent pattern of tantrums
- Exhibits persistent patterns of stealing, lying, and/or cheating
- Frequently exhibits lack of self-control and acting out behaviors
- Exhibits other specific behavior(s) that intrudes on other people, staff, self, or the physical environment to an extent that prevents the development or maintenance of satisfactory interpersonal relationships

such a simple framework can be misleading. In fact, a single student may display both types of behaviors. For example, Hector is a middle school student who usually keeps to himself. He may even be the victim of others' bullying. However, Hector may suddenly lash out at other students, hitting and cursing about what may seem to an observer to be a minor incident—for example, a classmate bumping into his desk.

Emotional Characteristics

Students' behaviors often are indicators of their emotions. Some students identified as having emotional disturbance experience anxiety as the result of excessive fears. They may be afraid of going to school, afraid of potential catastrophic events (e.g., hurricanes or terrorist attacks), or afraid of becoming ill. Fears such as these are intense and quite real to the students.

Other students with emotional and behavior disorders, like Charlotte, may feel anger. They may respond to your request for them to complete an assignment by refusing to work at all. They may perceive that a classmate who smiles at them is making fun of them. They may run from the classroom when corrected for using profanity. Often when students feel such anger, they display it through the externalizing behaviors of aggression (e.g., hitting, spitting, fighting).

Yet other students have very low self-esteem. They see only their negative characteristics instead of their positive traits, and they may describe themselves as worthless. When such feelings are chronic, these students may be identified as having depression, a mental illness that includes clusters of these symptoms persisting for more than two weeks (National Institute of Mental Health, 2012):

- Frequent sadness, tearfulness, crying
- Hopelessness
- Decreased interest in activities or an inability to enjoy previous favorite activities
- Persistent boredom, low energy
- Social isolation, poor communication
- Low self-esteem and guilt
- Extreme sensitivity to rejection or failure
- Increased irritability, anger, or hostility
- Difficulty with relationships
- Frequent complaints of physical illnesses, such as headaches and stomachaches
- Frequent absences from school or poor performance in school
- Poor concentration
- A major change in eating and/or sleeping patterns
- Talk of or efforts to run away from home
- Thoughts or expressions of suicide or self-destructive behavior

Approximately 5% of children and adolescents in the United States experience depression (Olfson, Blanco, Wang, Laje, & Correll, 2014). The risk of depression is approximately equal for boys and girls during childhood, but during adolescence, girls are twice as likely as boys to develop this disorder. If you understand the symptoms of depression in children and are vigilant as you interact with students, you can play an important role in urging parents to seek assistance for their children and in alerting counselors and other school professionals about students who may have this mental illness.

Sadly, when children's depression is untreated, it can lead to suicide, the third-leading cause of death among adolescents ages 15 to 19 and young adults ages 20 to 24 (National Institute of Mental Health, 2015). Most students who commit suicide give clear signals before they take their lives, and you should be alert to these warning signs. They are outlined in detail in the Professional Edge feature.

Youth Suicide—You Can Make the Difference

Youth suicide is preventable, if professionals, parents, and community members take seriously the warning signs such as the following:

- Belief that a person goes to a better place after dying
- Tendency to be impulsive (i.e., acting before thinking about consequences)
- Tendency to be a perfectionist
- Family history of suicide attempts
- Hopelessness, feeling that things will never get better

Verbal and Behavior Clues

Here are specific verbal and behavior clues that should cause you to seek assistance for a student identified as high risk for suicide:

Verbal Clues	Behavior Clues
"I shouldn't be here."	Talking or joking about suicide
"I'm going to run away."	Giving possessions away
"I wish I were dead."	Being preoccupied with death or violence in television, movies, drawings, books, playing, or music
"I'm going to kill myself."	Displaying risky behavior such as jumping from high places, running into traffic, and self-cutting
"I wish I could disappear forever."	Having several accidents resulting in injury, including close calls
"If a person did _____, would he or she die?"	Being obsessed with guns and knives
"The voices tell me to kill myself."	Previously having suicidal thoughts or attempts
"Maybe if I died, people would love me more."	
"I want to see what it feels like to die."	

Tips for School Professionals

Here are things that you can do if you suspect a student is at high risk for suicide:

- Know the warning signs.
- Know the school's responsibilities. The courts have held schools liable for not notifying parents in a timely fashion of a suicide threat or adequately supervising the suicidal student.
- Encourage students to confide in you. Encourage them to come to you if they or someone they know is considering suicide.
- Listen without being accusatory or judgmental and reassure students that help is available.
- Refer students immediately. You should escort a student you suspect is suicidal to the appropriate person, possibly the principal, psychologist, counselor, or social worker.
- Help to form a school crisis team and participate on it. If educators are prepared in advance, they are better able to respond to students' crises.
- Advocate for the child. Represent the student's interests until you are satisfied the student is safe.

Source: Based on Suicide Awareness Voices of Education (2003, August), *Suicide: Identifying high risk children and adolescents*. Retrieved from http://www.save.org/index.cfm?fuseaction=home.viewPage&page_ID=705E1907-C4DD-5D32-2C7087CE5924CCA4; and National Association of School Psychologists (2016), *Preventing youth suicide—Tips for parents and educators*. Retrieved from http://www.nasponline.org/resources-and-publications/resources/school-safety-and-crisis/preventing-youth-suicide/preventing-youth-suicide-tips-for-parents-and-educators

Social Characteristics

Students with emotional and behavior disorders experience significant challenges in establishing and maintaining social relationships with peers and adults. Some students have problems in their social interactions because they live in situations in which adults and other children model inappropriate social skills (Wagner, Kutash, Duchnowski, Epstein, & Sumi, 2005). For example, if the expectation in a student's home is that children should be quiet, that student may not know how to join peers in a game or activity or to ask a teacher for assistance. The message for educators is this: When students do not have the social skills necessary for them to interact effectively with peers and adults, they need to be taught those skills (Wilhite & Bullock, 2012).

Cognitive and Academic Characteristics

The first step in understanding the cognitive and academic characteristics of students with emotional and behavior disorders is to recognize the guidelines that are used in identifying these students. If a student's cognitive ability is below a certain level—usually an IQ of about 70—he generally will be considered to have an intellectual disability, and any behavior problems he displays will be thought of as secondary to or caused by his primary disability. The student generally will not be identified as having an emotional or behavior disorder. Thus, you might think that students with emotional and behavior disorders could have a cognitive ability from a low-average to a gifted range because there is no direct relationship between intelligence and emotional problems. Although this is true, most of these students have been found to have low-average to average intellectual ability (Lee, Rojewski, Gregg, Jeong, 2014; Sabornie, Evans, & Cullinan, 2006).

The academic difficulties that students with emotional and behavior disorders experience often are significant (Bountress, Chassin, & Lemery-Chalfant, 2016; Wiley, Siperstein, & Forness, 2011). They can range from low grade point averages to high risk for retention to high risk for dropping out of school (Mattison & Blader, 2013; Vannest, Temple-Harvey, & Mason, 2009). However, the picture is complex. For example, in one recent study, researchers found that students with emotional disabilities placed in self-contained classes at their schools demonstrated reading and math achievement at grade level, while those in a separate special school were significantly below grade level (Mattison, 2011).

The Question of Cause and Effect

Many professionals have considered this question: Do emotional and behavior disorders cause academic problems, or do students' chronic and significant academic problems cause emotional and behavior disorders? No clear answer to this question can be found. However, it is likely that both parts of the question contain some truth. Because of emotional difficulties, some students cannot adequately focus on schoolwork. At the same time, repeated failure in schoolwork contributes to some students' emotional and behavior disorders. What is most important for educators to keep in mind is that effective services for these students should address both academic and emotional and behavior needs.

Emotional and Behavior Disorders and Comorbidity

In Chapter 6 you learned that many students with ADHD also have other disabilities. The same point must be made for students whose primary disability is emotional disturbance. Many students who are identified as having an emotional or behavior disorder have comorbid, or additional, disabilities (Leyfer, Gallo, Cooper-Vince, & Pincus, 2013).

Some also have a learning disability, and others have ADHD. In addition, many of these students have more than one emotional or behavior disorder—for example, both depression and a disruptive behavior disorder. For school

Students with emotional and behavioral disorders often have comorbid disabilities such as ADHD or LD.

professionals, recognizing comorbid disorders is essential so that all the needed interventions can be implemented to help the student succeed.

MyEdLab **Self-Check 7.2**

MyEdLab **Application Exercise 7.2:** Mini Case Study

MyEdLab **Application Exercise 7.3:** Internalizing and Externalizing Behaviors

MyEdLab **Application Exercise 7.4:** Characteristics of Individuals with Emotional and Behavioral Disorders

---

Identifying Emotional and Behavior Disorders

Before special education services are considered for students with emotional and behavior disorders, professionals already have tried to assist them in many ways. General education teachers have implemented behavior reward systems and other strategies that have been successful with other students. In some schools, educators also have requested input from a prereferral team. In many school districts, response to intervention (RTI) or multi-tiered systems of support (MTSS) procedures are being implemented to address student behavior problems (Burke et al., 2012). If that is the case, a series of increasingly intensive, evidence-based interventions also probably have been tried. If none of these efforts is successful in addressing the student's needs, a referral is made to determine whether an emotional or behavior disorder exists, whether special education services are needed, and whether those services would benefit the student.

Assessment

Although the areas of assessment for emotional and behavior disorders are similar to those for learning disabilities and intellectual disabilities, the emphasis for the former is on emotional, behavior, and social concerns. As for all students, the assessment must address all pertinent aspects of student functioning, use multiple measures, and be nondiscriminatory.

Formal Assessments

Several types of formal assessments may be completed to help professionals decide whether a student has an emotional or behavior disorder. First, rating scales may be used to determine the nature and extent of a student's problems. For example, the *Scale for Assessing Emotional Disturbance* (2nd ed., SAED-2) (Epstein & Cullinan, 2010) is a norm-referenced instrument that teachers can complete in just a few minutes. It includes a subscale for each dimension of the federal definition: inability to learn, relationship problems, inappropriate behavior, unhappiness or depression, and physical symptoms or fears. An additional subscale addresses social maladjustment. Other rating scales that are to be completed by professionals and parents include the *Behavior Assessment System for Children* (BASC-2) (Reynolds & Kamphaus, 2004) and the *Behavior Rating Profile* (BRP-2) (Brown & Hammill, 1990).

In addition to assessments regarding emotional and behavior factors, cognitive ability and achievement levels also are measured. An intelligence test such as the *Wechsler Intelligence Scale for Children–IV* (WISC–V) (Wechsler, 2014) usually is administered to decide whether a student's cognitive level might be affecting her emotions and behavior. An achievement test such as the *Woodcock–Johnson Psychoeducational Battery–IV* (Tests of Achievement) (Schrank, Mather, & McGrew, 2014) helps the team decide the extent to which the emotional and behavior disorders are affecting the student's educational performance.

Classroom Assessments

An essential part of an assessment for emotional and behavior disorders is systematic observation in the classroom, lunchroom, physical education class, and other school and possibly home environments. Professionals need to see exactly what students do or do not do in a variety of activities and settings, they need to analyze what might trigger inappropriate behavior, and they need to consider the context in which the student is expected to function—the level of structure in the classroom, the number of adults with whom the student interacts, and so on. Rating scales measure what teachers, parents, and others perceive the student is doing. Observations of actual behavior provide confirmation of those perceptions and more detail about the student's strengths and problems.

Classroom assessments also can include curriculum-based measurements that demonstrate how the student is achieving in day-to-day schoolwork in core academic areas. This information supplements the standardized achievement data gathered as part of the formal assessment.

Other Assessment Strategies

Several other assessment strategies usually are included in deciding whether a student has an emotional or behavior disorder. A family history is obtained by interviewing parents and other key family members; this information can help to explain whether genetic and/or environmental factors might be affecting the student. The developmental history of the student in question, also obtained through parent interviews, provides professionals with information on whether the problem has been evident for some time or has recently emerged. For example, family members might be asked whether their child tended to dislike adult attention as an infant or toddler, whether the child began speaking at a later rather than an earlier age, and whether the child played with other children in age-appropriate ways.

In many cases, a psychologist or counselor also will interview the student who is being assessed. Using nonthreatening approaches, these professionals seek to hear from the student his perspective on what is occurring and the reasons for his problems. Think about this component of assessment. What information might be obtained directly from the student that would not otherwise be considered?

Medical Information. If a student is under the care of a physician or psychiatrist, school professionals, with parental permission, will request pertinent information from those medical professionals. For example, a student might be taking a medication related to depression, and school professionals need to know this information. Alternatively, a student might be receiving intensive therapy from a private clinic. Again, school professionals will obtain appropriate details so that they can be considered in their evaluation of the student.

Strengths-Based Assessment. Most of the assessments for emotional and behavior disorders are designed to discover details about the student's problems and to thoroughly explore the nature and severity of those problems. However, professionals also advocate assessing student strengths and assets. Strengths-based assessment refers to measuring students' social and emotional strengths, the characteristics that give them confidence, and the traits that help them cope with adversity. Epstein (2004) has developed a strengths-based assessment instrument, the *Behavioral and Emotional Rating Scale* (2nd ed., BERS), which gathers information on interpersonal strength, family involvement, intrapersonal strength, school functioning, and affective strength. Why is it particularly important to include strengths-based assessment information in the evaluation process for students with emotional and behavior disorders?

Eligibility

Once assessment data have been gathered, the multidisciplinary team, including the parents, meets to make the critical decisions regarding eligibility.

Eligibility Criteria

The team must address the following questions when deciding whether a student has an emotional or behavior disorder and should receive special education:

1. *Does the student have one or more of the characteristics in the definition of emotional disturbance?* If you refer back to the federal definition of this disability earlier in this chapter, you will see that the characteristics include unexplained difficulties in learning, unsatisfactory interpersonal relationships, a pervasive mood of unhappiness, and physical symptoms associated with personal or school problems. If a student is to receive special education, one or more of these characteristics must be documented through the information that has been gathered.

2. *Do the student's characteristics, as assessed, adversely affect educational performance?* Special education services are designed only for students whose education is being limited by their disabilities. Professionals look at cognitive ability and achievement data to make this decision. For students with emotional and behavior disorders, the concern is whether the emotional or behavioral difficulties prevent them from learning at a level consistent with their ability.

3. *Can social maladjustment be eliminated as the sole cause of the student's behavior problems?* As you have learned, the federal definition of emotional disturbance contains an exclusionary clause: If a student is socially maladjusted and no other emotional disability exists, she is not eligible for services. Recall, though, that many states do not use this clause in their definitions, and so for those states, this question would not be necessary.

If the multidisciplinary team answers yes to the preceding questions, the student is identified as having an emotional or behavior disorder and can begin to receive services if it is determined they would be beneficial. However, if the team's decision is that a disability does not exist or that the student is not eligible for special education services, the members might decide to recommend that a Section 504 plan be prepared to provide support to the student. Alternatively, they may assist the general education teachers working with the student to design interventions to address the emotional or behavior problems that prompted the initial referral.

> MyEdLab **Self-Check 7.3**
>
> MyEdLab **Application Exercise 7.5:** How Do You Know When It's an EBD?
>
> MyEdLab **Application Exercise 7.6:** Using Behavior Charts

Educating Learners with Emotional and Behavior Disorders

Because students with emotional and behavior disorders typically are capable of learning the same curriculum as their peers without disabilities, you might think that they are likely to be in general education settings. However, this often is not the case. These students are educated in the entire range of educational environments outlined in federal law—from general education through part-time special education to self-contained classes to separate educational facilities and homebound services (Villarreal, 2015). In fact, some data suggest that they are educated in separate settings more than most other students with disabilities (Wagner, Sumi, Woodbridge, Javitz, & Thornton, 2009).

Early Childhood

As you know, young children are not usually assigned specific disability labels. When the disability under consideration is an emotional or behavior disorder, the reluctance to assign a label is particularly strong, for several reasons. One is that when a child is young, judgments about the presence of emotional and behavior disorders are particularly difficult to make because of developmental differences. Another reason is that all the labels related to emotional and behavior disorders are viewed as having a strong negative stigma that professionals are uncomfortable assigning to young children.

Despite this uneasiness about labeling, however, professionals have for many years been concerned about the mental health of infants, toddlers, and preschoolers (Bagner, Garcia, & Hill, 2016; Bagner et al., 2015). This concern is based on two related factors. First, professionals are strongly committed to addressing the risk factors discussed earlier in this chapter for young children so that they are less likely to develop emotional and behavior disorders. In particular, professionals focus their efforts on educating young women about the risks associated with prenatal alcohol, nicotine, and drug use; teaching new mothers parenting skills; and improving parent–child relationships. Second, early interventionists know that young children who already are displaying behaviors known to be associated with later serious emotional and behavior disorders must receive intensive intervention at a very early age in order to change the course of their lives (Conroy et al., 2015; Hardy et al., 2015). Thus, they have developed a number of programs designed to help young children at risk for emotional and behavior disorders as well as their families.

Effective early intervention for children at risk of developing emotional and behavior disabilities includes several components (Conroy, Sutherland, Haydon, Stormont, & Harmon, 2009). These include the following:

- Precorrection (i.e., teaching appropriate behavior for particular situations before misbehavior has a chance to occur) combined with close supervision of students and monitoring of their behavior so that problems can be averted whenever possible
- Increased instructional pacing by increasing students' opportunities to respond during classroom instruction
- Increased rate of praise for students when they behave as expected
- Specific feedback to children about their behavior and error correction by teaching acceptable behavior
- Development and implementation of clear classroom rules
- Collaboration between professionals and parents
- Home–school communication

These elements are similar to those advocated for school-age groups, but they are not all necessarily emphasized in traditional early childhood programs. In addition, families often play a more central role in addressing their children's needs in these programs, and interventions are more likely to be designed for implementation across home and daycare/preschool settings.

Elementary and Secondary School Services

Students with emotional and behavior disorders in elementary, middle, and high school receive their education in all the settings described in IDEA. As Figure 7.3 shows, 44% of these students are in general education for 80% or more of

FIGURE 7.3   **Educational Placements of Students Ages 6 to 21 Who Have Emotional or Behavior Disorders (in percentages)**

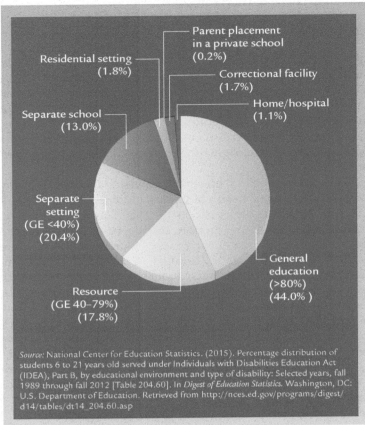

Source: National Center for Education Statistics. (2015). Percentage distribution of students 6 to 21 years old served under Individuals with Disabilities Education Act (IDEA), Part B, by educational environment and type of disability: Selected years, fall 1989 through fall 2012 [Table 204.60]. In *Digest of Education Statistics.* Washington, DC: U.S. Department of Education. Retrieved from http://nces.ed.gov/programs/digest/d14/tables/dt14_204.60.asp

the school day. Approximately 20.4% of them attend self-contained special education classes, and more than 18% are educated in separate schools or other facilities (U.S. Department of Education, 2015).

Placements for students with emotional and behavior disorders vary considerably across states (U.S. Department of Education, 2015). In Alabama, 70.5%, and in North Dakota, approximately 72.9% of these students are in general education settings at least 80% of the school day. In contrast, New Mexico places 39.5% of these students in a special education setting for most of the school day, and New York follows closely at 34.6%. Think about the practical and potential lifelong implications for students of these wide differences in placement decisions: If you were a student with an emotional or behavior disorder and you lived in Alabama, you would have a very good chance of being educated beside your peers without disabilities. However, if your family moved to California, you probably would spend much of the day in a special education classroom, interacting primarily with other students with emotional and behavior disorders, excluded from many of the typical social lessons learned in the general education environment. Do you think such differences should exist? Why or why not?

The types of services students receive may vary somewhat based on the setting in which they are educated. In a general education classroom, a student may be expected to meet most of the same expectations as other students, but the teacher probably will pay closer attention to effective instructional approaches and interventions that can reduce inappropriate behavior. In a resource room, students may receive instruction from a highly qualified special educator in a single academic subject such as reading or English, or they may get assistance with organizational skills, general learning and study strategies, and self-management techniques. The special educator in this setting also will manage various types of behavior intervention programs designed to help students display appropriate classroom behavior. In a self-contained special education classroom, a small group of students may spend the day with a single teacher or move as a group among several special education teachers, with limited amounts of time spent with peers either in academic or related arts classes. Students in a self-contained level of service often are working on highly structured behavior management systems that stress rewarding students for appropriate behavior. For example, leaving the classroom unaccompanied might be a reward earned by displaying appropriate in-class behavior.

For students needing an even more restrictive placement, alternatives may include day treatment or residential programs (Flower, McDaniel, & Jolivette, 2011; Ghuman & Sarles, 2013). Day treatment programs are special schools that include special education in small classes and place a strong emphasis on individualized instruction. They usually also include individual and group therapy, family counseling, vocational training, crisis intervention, positive skill building, and other services such as recreational, art, and music therapy. Residential programs, usually attended by students with the most serious or dangerous emotional problems, are just what the name suggests: Students live at these schools, attending classes and participating in therapeutic and recreational activities. The school services may look much like those in a day treatment program.

Inclusive Practices

Given the data about educational placements for students with emotional and behavior disorders, it is clear that inclusive practices are an issue for these students (e.g., Duchnowski & Kutash, 2011; Villareal, 2015). In fact, the debate about inclusion for students with emotional and behavior disorders has been particularly contentious. Among the areas of concern are the following:

1. *Curriculum*. With today's academic standards, general education classrooms establish high expectations for students. This pressure may cause students with emotional and behavior disorders to develop further problems. At the same time, these classrooms often do not emphasize social skills development, anger management, and other topics that may be crucial for students with emotional disabilities. Unless these concerns are directly addressed, students may be inadvertently set up for failure (Simpson & Mundschenk, 2012).

2. *Social rejection*. Students with emotional and behavior disorders often have difficulty making friends, or they make friends with students who have similar problems. Just as important, general education teachers are more negative about students with these disorders than about any other group of students with disabilities. They may not directly address these students' social and emotional needs (Evans, Weiss, & Cullinan, 2012), and they often do not have a sense of ownership for the students or feel responsible for their success or failure. This concern implies that teachers need professional development to learn how to support students in the social domain.

3. *Mental health treatment*. Students with emotional and behavior disorders often need comprehensive services that include a strong mental health component in addition to academic supports (Gudino, Lau, Yeh, McCabe, & Hough, 2009). Although general education classrooms address academic and social domains, they are not structured to incorporate mental health services, such as counseling. However, it should be noted that the provision of mental health treatment can be problematic in any school setting, whether inclusive or more restrictive (Bruhn, Woods-Groves, & Huddle, 2014).

Two important points should be made in thinking about the inclusion of students with emotional and behavior disorders. First, the concerns just mentioned are based on the assumption that inclusion is mostly about where students sit. The view of this text is that inclusion is about welcoming all students to their learning community—that is, their school. Thus, in inclusive schools, students with emotional disabilities might spend most (or all) of the day in a general education classroom, or a small part of the day, or they might have the option of leaving that classroom if it becomes too stressful. In addition, students without disabilities might tutor students with emotional and behavior disorders in the special education classroom, and they might also serve as buddies for these students. In other words, students can be included even if they do not sit in a general education classroom for the entire day.

Second, with careful planning and preparation, school professionals are succeeding in supporting some students with emotional and behavior disorders in their general education classrooms (e.g., Allday et al., 2012; Skerbetz & Kostewicz, 2015). One approach for doing this is through co-teaching (Conderman & Hedin, 2015). In another example, a group of researchers provided staff development for general education teachers, principals, and other staff on a specific behavioral intervention to support students with externalizing behaviors in general education settings (Benner, Nelson, Sanders, & Ralston, 2012). By providing this training and ongoing coaching on using the intervention, students' problem behaviors generally decreased and their on-task behaviors increased.

Thus, to say that inclusion for students with emotional and behavior problems is not possible is an overstatement: It is more accurate to say that it requires strong administrative support; a plan for implementation that addresses academic, behavioral, and emotional needs; attention to enhancing the knowledge and skills of general education teachers as well as other school professionals; and the option for alternatives for students who need them. How might these concepts apply to Charlotte, Gabriel, and Steven, the students whose stories appeared at the beginning of this chapter?

Transition and Adulthood

The outcomes for students with emotional and behavior disorders have been disappointing (Kern et al., 2015). For example, the most recent available data indicate that only 51% of students with these disorders graduate from high school with a standard diploma (U.S. Department of Education, 2015). Although some students later earn their high school diplomas through GED programs, those who do not are especially at risk for poor adult outcomes. In addition, students with emotional and behavior disorders have difficulty finding and keeping jobs (Villareal, 2015).

Improving outcomes for students with emotional and behavior disorders is quite feasible and may make life-changing differences for students like Steven, introduced at the beginning of the chapter. The key is to translate the knowledge base for effective interventions into widespread practice (e.g., Benner, Kutash, Nelson, & Fisher, 2013). For example, students with these disorders should be served through family-centered approaches that coordinate school and community assistance (Test, Fowler, White, Richter, & Walker, 2009). Better access to mental health services for students and their families is needed (Sukhera, Fisman, & Davidson, 2015). Focused transition programs with measurable goals that provide vocational training and on-the-job training also can help outcomes (Walsh, 2010), as can specific training for self-determination (Cuenca-Sanchez, Mastropieri, Scruggs, & Kidd, 2012). In addition, these students should be taught specific skills that will help them pursue postschool options. An example is anger management, a skill described in the Instruction in Action. Finally, better training for school professionals is necessary so that all the other elements of transition can be implemented.

Did You Know?

Researchers have found that adolescents with some emotional disabilities—including psychotic disorders and disruptive behavior disorders—are at high risk for being arrested between ages 12 and 24 (Constantine, Andel, Robst, & Givens, 2013). They call for early interventions and changes in social policy to change the trajectory for these students.

INSTRUCTION IN **ACTION**

Teaching Anger Management Skills

Research has demonstrated that students can be taught anger management strategies that help them to reduce their anger and to display anger more appropriately (e.g., Kellner, Bry, & Salvador, 2008; Moodi, Alizadeh, Bonab, & Soleimani, 2015). Anger management programs should be part of every teacher's resources. They include teaching students skills such as those listed below. Initial programs typically are followed by "booster" sessions to ensure that the skills become internalized.

- Recognize that anger is normal—everyone at some point gets angry. It is how a person responds to feelings of anger that are either constructive or destructive.
- Understand when anger is happening. Know personal physiological signs such as rapid breathing and tense muscles.

- Know what makes you angry (i.e., what your "triggers" are). Learn to avoid your triggers or to be alert to them so anger can be managed constructively.
- Use immediate strategies to calm down such as counting to 10 or taking several deep breaths. If possible, walk away and address the problem once you have calmed down.
- If you do not have the right words for your anger, draw a picture of it. Use the picture to talk to your teacher.
- Recognize and reward yourself for dealing with anger in a way that does not harm others and helps you.

You can learn more about this topic and find many related resources at the Anger Management website at http://www.angriesout.com/.

MyEdLab **Self-Check 7.4**

MyEdLab **Application Exercise 7.7:** How Students with EBDs Receive Their Education

---

Recommended Educational Practices for Students with Emotional and Behavior Disorders

Over the past 30 years, a strong base of research has developed that can guide school professionals in their work with students with emotional and behavior disorders. Effective practices include prevention, collaboration, procedures required by IDEA, and specific interventions.

The Importance of Prevention

Because of highly publicized incidents of school violence and research demonstrating poor outcomes for students with emotional and behavior disorders, the prevention of these disorders and related problems has in recent years become one of the highest priorities among school and community agencies concerned about children (Benningfield & Stephan, 2015; Chin, Dowdy, Jimerson, & Rime, 2012; Centers for Disease Control and Prevention, 2012).

Early Intervention

Prevention has several components. As you have read, one component is early intervention. Professionals agree that if early interventions could be implemented with young children who are at risk for developing behavior disorders, some children would not experience later problems. This type of early intervention may address young children's behavior (Basten et al., 2016). It also may address the development of their language and other communication skills because of

POSITIVE • **BEHAVIOR** • SUPPORTS

Key Components of Schoolwide Positive Behavior Support Programs

Schoolwide positive behavior support programs are based on the following principles:

- Universal expectations, that is, schoolwide participation with shared expectations in common areas such as hallways and the lunchroom and consistent expectations in the classroom
- Instruction for students on behavior expectations and rewards for meeting the expectations
- Emphasis on rewards or reinforcers for appropriate behavior and instruction to teach alternatives to inappropriate behavior
- Data-based decisions concerning student behavior

- Increasingly intensive behavior interventions for students who are not meeting behavior expectations
- A collaborative approach to addressing student behavior, usually with a team made up of representatives of grade levels or departments as well as special education and related services personnel, administrators, parents, and students

PBS usually includes tiers comparable to those used for academic response to intervention models. Figure 7.4 summarizes these tiers, gives examples of interventions at each tier, and specifies the proportion of students likely to be at each tier.

FIGURE 7.4

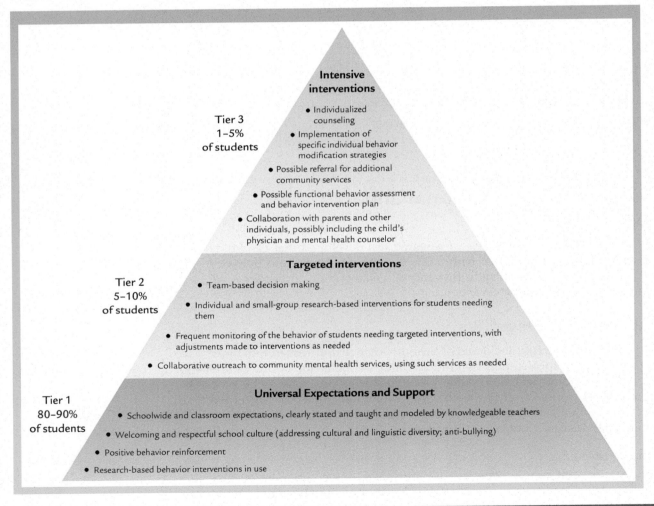

Tier 3
1–5%
of students

Intensive interventions

- Individualized counseling
- Implementation of specific individual behavior modification strategies
- Possible referral for additional community services
- Possible functional behavior assessment and behavior intervention plan
- Collaboration with parents and other individuals, possibly including the child's physician and mental health counselor

Tier 2
5–10%
of students

Targeted interventions

- Team-based decision making
- Individual and small-group research-based interventions for students needing them
- Frequent monitoring of the behavior of students needing targeted interventions, with adjustments made to interventions as needed
- Collaborative outreach to community mental health services, using such services as needed

Tier 1
80–90%
of students

Universal Expectations and Support

- Schoolwide and classroom expectations, clearly stated and taught and modeled by knowledgeable teachers
- Welcoming and respectful school culture (addressing cultural and linguistic diversity; anti-bullying)
- Positive behavior reinforcement
- Research-based behavior interventions in use

the evidence suggesting that one factor that may contribute to the development of emotional and behavior disorders is the frustration that results from poor communication skills (Ritzman & Sanger, 2007; What Works Clearinghouse, 2012).

Positive Behavior Supports

Another focus for prevention in elementary and secondary schools involves implementing schoolwide positive behavior supports (PBS) (Coffey & Horner, 2012; Freeman et al., 2016). In schools using PBS, in some instances part of a broader MTSS model, all students and teachers are clear about the expectations for behavior in all common use areas of the school—hallways, gym, cafeteria, and so on. Students are rewarded for knowing and following these rules. In addition, behavior expectations are set at the classroom level. That is, teachers arrange the physical space of the classroom, establish expectations with students, and arrange rewards tailored to the specific group of students. For students whose behavior is not addressed with these schoolwide and classroom strategies, often a team meets and creates an individualized behavior plan using the procedures for functional behavior assessment and behavior intervention plans outlined in the next section. As you can tell, PBS is based on prevention of behavior problems and increasingly intensive interventions, just as RTI is based on prevention of academic problems and increasingly intensive interventions. However, keep in mind that there is no provision in special education law for PBS to be applied to behavior. Details about the components of PBS are outlined in the Positive Behavior Supports.

Research on the effects of schoolwide PBS is encouraging (Chitiyo, May, & Chitiyo, 2012; McIntosh, Kim, Mercer, Strickland-Cohen, Horner, 2015). Professionals in schools using this approach report that they are more effective and that they are motivated to continue using PBS (Sadler & Sugai, 2009). PBS also has been demonstrated to have a positive impact on bullying, decreasing teacher reports of bullying and peer rejection (Bradshaw, Waasdorp, & Leaf, 2014). In middle school, this approach has led to fewer office discipline referrals, fewer suspensions, and an increase in math and reading achievement scores that could be directly attributed to fewer behavior problems (Lassen, Steele, & Sailor, 2006). Examples of the types of data gathered in a PBS system are summarized in Data-Driven Decisions. Why do you think that schoolwide PBS can have such positive effects?

The Effectiveness of Collaboration

A second element of effective practice for students with emotional and behavior disorders is *collaboration*, a topic that was introduced in Chapter 4. For students with emotional and behavior disorders, however, collaboration takes on an added dimension. Professionals have increasingly come to agree that because the needs of students with emotional and behavior disorders are so complex and addressed by so many different agencies and organizations, the only way to ensure effective services is to create systems for effective interagency collaboration—that is, collaboration that spans school and nonschool agencies (Poncin & Woolston, 2016; Povenmire-Kirk et al., 2015). These agencies might include the school, a community mental health agency, a family social services agency, the juvenile justice system, a state hospital or other residential facility, and so on.

Many examples of this type of interagency collaboration have now been documented, and collectively they are sometimes referred to as wraparound services (Fries, Carney, Blackman-Urteaga, & Savas, 2012). Most of these collaborations are based on a system of care (Stroul, 1996), an approach to interagency collaboration based on a coordinated network of service providers that is child

MyEdLab
Video Example 7.2
This video demonstrates both the schoolwide nature and positive approach of PBS in an elementary school.
(https://www.youtube.com/watch?v=nP1wcyekwxU)

Video Example from YouTube

MyEdLab
Video Example 7.3
This video demonstrates how PBS can be used in a high school setting.
(https://www.youtube.com/watch?v=vNMKZ99tIqE)

DATA-DRIVEN DECISIONS

Types of Data Professionals Collect

Data are as central to making decisions about student behavior as about their academic skills and progress. Once a behavior is clearly defined so that it can be observed consistently by you or another observer, these are examples of how related data may be gathered.

Data Collection Method	Explanation	Example
Narrative recording	Notes taken to describe a situation, often for initial understanding	When John was handed the math assignment, he put his head down, pulled his hoodie over his head, and refused to sit up after being directed three times to do so.
Antecedents-Behavior-Consequences (ABC)	Using a tablet or another recording format, this is a sort of diary of what happens immediately before the behavior, a description of the behavior, and what happens as a result of the behavior; it is repeated in cycles as needed	A: Karen asked to go to her locker and was told "no." B: Karen stomped back to her desk and sat down, rolling her eyes and audibly sighing. C: Teacher asked Karen to think about her behavior and make wise choices.
Event recording	A tally of each time a behavior occurs	A teacher tallied how many times James called out an answer during a 15-minute group discussion lesson.
Duration recording	A record of the length of time a behavior occurred	On her smartphone, a teacher timed how long Kathleen worked on her math assignment until she got distracted.

What are additional examples of appropriate uses of each of the methods (think across grade levels, subject areas, and types of student behavior disorders)? What would you do with the data once gathered? How could you create a graph or chart to summarize each type of data?

and family centered, community based, and sensitive to cultural diversity (Painter, 2012). The system of care approach is guided by these principles:

1. Children with emotional disabilities should have access to a comprehensive array of services that address their physical, emotional, social, and educational needs.
2. Children with emotional disabilities should receive individualized services in accordance with their unique needs and potential and guided by individualized service plans.
3. Children with emotional disabilities should receive services within the least restrictive, most normative environment that is clinically appropriate.
4. The families and surrogate families of children with emotional disabilities should be full participants in all aspects of the planning and delivery of services.
5. Children with emotional disabilities should receive services that are integrated with linkages between child-serving agencies and programs and mechanisms for planning, developing, and coordinating services.
6. Children with emotional disabilities should be provided with case management or a similar mechanism to ensure that multiple services are delivered in a coordinated and therapeutic manner and that they can move through the system of services in accordance with their changing needs.
7. Early identification and intervention for children with emotional disabilities should be promoted by the systems of care in order to enhance the likelihood of positive outcomes.
8. Children with emotional disabilities should be ensured a smooth transition to the adult service system as they reach maturity.

9. The rights of children with emotional disabilities should be protected, and effective advocacy efforts for children and youth with emotional disabilities should be promoted.

10. Children with emotional disabilities should receive services without regard to race/ethnicity, religion, national origin, sex, physical disability, or other characteristics, and services should be sensitive and responsive to cultural differences and special needs.

As you might expect, the outcomes of such shared work can vary significantly depending on the level of participation of each agency, the amount of coordination in their work, and the intensity of the interventions employed (Effland, Walton, & McIntyre, 2011; Poncin & Woolston, 2016). In essence, success of the system of care approach relies on the understanding that meaningful collaboration among families, professionals, and community services is the most effective way to address the multiple and complex needs of students with emotional and behavior disorders.

Requirements for Interventions in IDEA

IDEA requires that school professionals use very systematic procedures to document the behavior problems that students display, to analyze the reasons those behaviors occur, and to develop and systematically implement interventions intended to reduce inappropriate behaviors while increasing appropriate behaviors. Two specific procedures—functional behavior assessment (FBA) and the development of a behavior intervention plan (BIP)—are required for all students with disabilities who experience behavior problems, regardless of whether their identified disability involves emotional disturbance. For example, Renée is a student with autism. When she gets upset she tries to bite her teachers and herself. The team making educational decisions for Renée would need to complete a functional behavior assessment and a behavior intervention plan for her, even though she is not identified as having an emotional or behavior disorder. However, these procedures are particularly applicable to students with emotional and behavioral disorders.

The most effective services for students with emotional or behavioral disorders often involve ongoing collaboration among school, medical, mental health, and family social services professionals.

Functional Behavior Assessment

When a student misbehaves, school professionals are faced with the challenge of finding an effective way to respond. Functional behavior assessment (FBA) is a multidimensional and research-based problem-solving strategy for analyzing the student's behavior within the context of the setting in which it is occurring (Anderson, Rodriguez, & Campbell, 2015). The purpose is to decide the function of the behavior and to determine how to address it (Crone, Hawken, & Horner, 2015).

FBA is based on two assumptions. The first is that challenging behavior occurs in context; that is, it is influenced by the setting in which it occurs. Thus, the setting must be considered when you are trying to change a behavior. The second assumption underlying FBA is that challenging behavior serves a function for the student. Educators need to identify that function in order to change the behavior. Functional behavior assessment involves five steps:

1. *Identify the problem behavior.* Carefully describe the behaviors in observable ways, and prioritize them. For example, instead of stating that Tate sulks when work is assigned, the team would specify that four out of five times when

Tate is given a written assignment by the general education teacher, he puts his head down on his desk, covers his face, and does not respond to teacher requests that he begin his work.

2. *Describe in detail the settings in which the behavior occurs.* In the example of Tate, the setting of concern is the general education classroom. The team might further note that Tate is seated in the front of the room, that the class includes 27 other students, and that the desks are arranged in rows with aisles.

3. *Gather information about the behavior using interviews, rating scales, observation, review of student records, and other techniques.* One common observation technique is called an ABC approach, introduced in Data-Driven Decisions. ABC stands for *antecedents* (what comes immediately before the behavior that causes it to happen), *behaviors*, and *consequences* (what happens as a result of the behavior). For Tate, the antecedent is his teacher giving him an assignment. The behavior is what Tate does. The consequence is that his teacher asked him again to do the work. After several cycles of asking and refusing, the teacher sent Tate with a discipline referral to the office. One other element might be considered: setting events. These are things that may have happened earlier in the day that could be affecting the situation. For Tate, a setting event might be his working in the evenings at a fast-food restaurant and not getting enough sleep.

4. *Review the data.* The team would examine the observational data; they probably would also have information from the teacher, from Tate, and possibly from Tate's parents. They might compare what was observed to Tate's perception of his behavior and to his teacher's views.

5. *Form a hypothesis about the function of the behavior based on the data gathered.* If you were going to make an educated guess about what function Tate's behavior is serving, what would you say? One reasonable hypothesis is that Tate's behavior is his way of avoiding difficult assignments. By refusing to do the work, he gets sent to the office and does not have to complete the work. In other situations, behaviors could serve other functions (O'Neill, Albin, Storey, Horner, & Sprague, 2015), such as the following:

- For some students, behaving inappropriately is a way to get adults to pay attention to them, something they may crave.
- For other students, behaving inappropriately may be a means for ending a social interaction with a classmate.
- For yet other students, behaving inappropriately may help them to get items or activities that they want (e.g., having a tantrum results in being taken to the special education classroom, where the student is allowed to play with colored markers on the whiteboard while he "calms down").

What other functions can you think of that behaviors might address? If you think about Charlotte, Gabriel, and Steven, introduced at the beginning of the chapter, what functions might their behaviors have?

Behavior Intervention Plan

Based on the hypothesis the team makes, the next task is to create a behavior intervention plan (BIP), a set of strategies designed to address the function of the behavior in order to change it (Liaupsin, 2015). For Tate, the team decided to change the antecedent by arranging for Tate temporarily to be partnered with a classmate whenever lengthy written assignments were given. In addition, the team developed a *contract*. A contract is a research-based behavior intervention that clearly spells out expectations, rewards, and consequences for students, as illustrated in the Positive Behavior Supports feature. For Tate, the contract rewarded him for completing work. It also included an extended deadline so that he could work on such assignments in parts. The setting event of working in the evenings is one that the team decided it would not be able to address. Data were gathered to determine whether the assignment partner and contract with rewards and extended time were effective. In this case, the BIP was successful: It addressed the behavior so that learning could occur. If it had not been a success, the team would have been responsible for reanalyzing the information it had gathered about the problem, possibly looking for additional information, and designing another intervention. The new intervention also would be evaluated to check its effectiveness.

If you review all the Positive Behavior Supports features in the chapters that you have read as well as those in the chapters that follow this one, you will see that the strategies and interventions could be part of a BIP. In fact, the expectation today for students experiencing behavior problems is to teach them appropriate behaviors that will help them succeed not only in school but also later in life, clearly rewarding them for displaying those behaviors. Negative consequences,

POSITIVE • **BEHAVIOR** • SUPPORTS

Behavior Contracts

Behavior contracts, often used as one means of achieving IEP goals for students with serious behavior problems, can address a wide array of behaviors and can be used with elementary, middle school, and high school students. Figure 7.5 is one example of a behavior contract.

FIGURE 7.5

Behavior Contract

Effective dates: March 6, 2017–March 24, 2017

I, _____Tory_____, **agree to do the following:**
Begin assignments when they are given to me.
Ask for help by raising my hand if I am stuck.
Put completed assignments in the "Completed Work" tray.

I, _____Ms. Chavez_____, **agree to do the following:**
Check with Tory to be sure she understands the assignment.
Alert Tory when the time for completing an assignment is nearly up.
Give Tory 2 points for beginning her work, 1 point each time she asks for help by raising her hand, and 1 point for putting work in the "Complete Work" tray. Tory may accumulate up to 6 points per class period.

Reward

Each time Tory accumulates 10 points, she may spend them on 10 minutes of computer time.

Bonus

If Tory accumulates 25 points for two weeks in a row, she may assist Mr. Ames in the computer lab for one class period.

Penalty

If Tory does not attempt an assignment, she will be asked to complete it at home that evening.
If Tory calls out instead of raising her hand for help more than two times in a class period, this information will be shared with her mother.

Signatures

_____   _____
Tory Wheeler   **Ms. Chavez**

_____
Mrs. Wheeler

or punishment, although not eliminated completely, usually are employed only in partnership with positive behavior supports and only if no other effective approaches can be found.

Examples of Specific Interventions

In addition to interventions that are incorporated into the FBA and BIP procedures, general education teachers, special education teachers, and other professionals working with students with emotional and behavior disorders can use a wide variety of strategies to enhance student learning while fostering appropriate behaviors. For example, many students need assistance in recording their assignments, remembering when assignments are due, and dealing with the mechanics of completing them, including checking spelling and grammar. Others may benefit by learning how to use technology to self-monitor their learning behaviors, the topic of Technology Notes.

Peer-Mediated Instruction

The goal for many students with emotional and behavior disorders is to learn to participate in groups with other students without disruption. Some teachers use peer-mediated instruction, a collection of programs and interventions for which a long history of research has demonstrated success (e.g., Wexler, Reed, Pyle, Mitchell, & Barton, 2015), to accomplish this goal. Two examples of

TECHNOLOGY NOTES

Changing Behavior Using Handheld Devices

Self-monitoring is a research-based intervention for helping students with emotional disabilities to improve their behavior (e.g., Blood, Johnson, Ridenour, Simmons, & Crouch, 2011; Otero & Haut, 2016). It involves these three steps:

1. Teach the student to discriminate occurrences versus nonoccurrences of the target behavior (e.g., on task versus off task; attending versus not attending).
2. Teach the student to self-record the behavior (e.g., Am I on task? Am I attending?).
3. Teach the student to graph the behavior.

Although in the past, teaching self-monitoring generally involved written descriptions of the behavior and paper-and-pencil recording and graphing forms, technology now offers more efficient, effective, and motivating strategies to accomplish the same goals. Here are examples of how handheld devices are being used for this purpose:

- To monitor and increase on-task behavior during reading
- To monitor and improve appropriate behavior during small-group math instruction
- To complete daily tasks with less or no prompting needed
- To improve time management
- To take medication on the prescribed schedule

To use this technology, these are the steps:

1. Ensure that the student has the ability to use the electronic device selected, whether a tablet device, an iPod, a netbook, or another device.
2. Clearly identify the target behavior, preparing examples and nonexamples for the student, and determine the setting and length of time for monitoring.
3. Identify rewards the student will earn for accurate monitoring.
4. Obtain the student's buy-in.
5. Teach the student (a) how to use the device, (b) what behavior to record, and (c) what the reward system is and how it will be checked.
6. Periodically check the student's accuracy of recording and provide the earned reward, addressing any implementation problems that occur.
7. As the monitoring results in a change in behavior, adjust or phase out the self-monitoring procedure.

This approach to teaching self-monitoring has tremendous potential, for the following reasons:

- Handheld devices are inexpensive, especially when compared to laptop or desktop computers.
- The software for student data gathering is free or inexpensive.
- Use of a handheld device generally is motivating for the student.
- A handheld device generally is not stigmatizing.

INSTRUCTION IN **ACTION**

Numbered Heads Together

Numbered Heads Together is one example of a research-based cooperative learning approach that can be effective for teaching academic content and social interaction skills to students with emotional and behavior disabilities (Hunter & Haydon, 2013). Here are the steps to follow to implement Numbered Heads Together:

1. Assign students to heterogeneous groups of three or four. Students should be seated near one another.
2. Have students assign themselves numbers from 1 to 3 or 4.
3. Ask the class a question.
4. Have students "put their heads together" so that they can determine the correct answer or several answers, depending on the type of question that was asked. Students are instructed to be sure that every member of their group knows the answer(s).
5. Call the groups back together. Call a number (1 to 3 or 1 to 4), and have the students in the class with that number stand.
6. Call on one of the standing students to answer the question. If there is more than one correct answer, continue to call on students.
7. Ask the rest of the class to agree or disagree with the stated answer.
8. Award points or rewards. This can be done in several ways. Some teachers use a positive approach: As long as each student called on gets a correct answer, all teams are rewarded. Other teachers give each team one "pass" so that if a member does not answer correctly, the team still has an opportunity to be rewarded.

Source: Based on Maheady, L., Harper, G. F., & Mallette, B. (2001). Peer-mediated instruction and interventions and students with mild disabilities. *Remedial and Special Education*, 22(1), 4–14. Copyright © 2001 by Pro-Ed, Inc.

peer-mediated instruction are peer tutoring and cooperative learning. In peer tutoring, each student works with one other student to practice math facts, review vocabulary, or complete another instructional task. One student is the tutor, or the student responsible for acting as the peer teacher; the other student is the tutee, or the student answering the questions. In one successful peer-tutoring approach, called *reciprocal tutoring*, both students take both roles in a single tutoring session.

In cooperative learning, students work in groups of three or four. They have a specific task to complete, play assigned roles (e.g., note taker), and take accountability for the learning. One cooperative learning method, called "Numbered Heads Together," combines the skills and learning efforts of students with a bit of luck; it is described in the Instruction in Action feature.

For peer tutoring and cooperative learning to be effective with students with EBD, teachers must implement it carefully, following methods that have been demonstrated through research to produce positive outcomes. In addition, students should receive instruction in appropriate leadership, communication, decision-making, and trust-building skills. Finally, teachers or others implementing peer tutoring and cooperative learning should assess its impact on student achievement and monitor student behavior in these instructional arrangements (Lo, Mustian, Brophy, & White, 2011).

Teacher-Led Instruction

One final area of intervention should be mentioned. Students with emotional and behavior disorders clearly struggle with academic achievement, and evidence increasingly points to the importance of using specific programs and procedures to help them learn (e.g., Kelly & Shogren, 2014; Nikolaros, 2014). In addition, many of the strategies that make instruction effective for all students are particularly important for these students, including the following:

- Keep lesson objectives clear.
- Deliver lessons in a lively manner, and make sure that students are engaged by frequently using participation strategies.

- Use concrete vocabulary and clear, succinct sentences.
- Give all students immediate encouragement and specific feedback.
- Use meaningful materials, and provide examples to which students can relate.
- Have students recite in unison.
- Break down a large assignment into smaller ones. As students finish each mini-assignment, build in reinforcement for task completion.
- When students make mistakes, help them to learn from those mistakes. Be careful not to overcorrect, and praise any progress toward the desired behavior change.
- Follow low-interest activities with high-interest activities so that students get occasional breaks from difficult or less interesting activities.
- Build on student interests. Students often learn by relating material to real-life situations that they find interesting.
- Allow students to make choices. Let them decide between two tasks or select the order in which they complete assigned tasks.
- Employ appropriate technology applications that can engage student interest and increase motivation.
- Use hands-on, experiential learning activities to enable students to apply learning to the real world. This is one of a teacher's most powerful tools.

A discussion of instructing students with emotional and behavior disorders would not be complete without mentioning the importance of one additional topic: the qualities, abilities, and perspectives of the teacher. Perhaps more so than for any other group of students with special needs, teachers of students with emotional disabilities must have a strong sense of confidence in their ability to help these students and the capacity to care deeply even when students' behavior makes it difficult (e.g., Sullivan, Sutherland, Lotze, Helms, Wright, & Ulmer, 2015). That is, students with emotional disabilities need teachers with whom they can build strong positive relationships.

MyEdLab **Self-Check 7.5**

MyEdLab **Application Exercise 7.8:** Preschoolers Regulating Their Emotions

MyEdLab **Application Exercise 7.9:** Strategies That Work in the Classroom

---

Video Example
from
YouTube

MyEdLab
Video Example 7.4

This video extends the idea that families of children with emotional disabilities often feel "blamed and ashamed" in interviews with mothers. (https://www.youtube.com/watch?v=nlCPlrULSGA)

Perspectives of Parents and Families

Have you considered what it might be like to be the parent of a child with an emotional or behavior disorder? What do you think might be the greatest challenges you would face? The greatest joys? One report summarized in its title the experiences of these students and their families: "blamed and ashamed" (U.S. Department of Health and Human Services, 2003).

The Impact of Having a Child with an Emotional or Behavior Disorder

The parents and family members of students with emotional and behavior disorders face several unique challenges. First, families seeking mental health services for their children face the possibility of stigma (e.g., Mann & Heflinger, 2016). This may affect their willingness to label their child with an emotional or behavioral disorder. Stigma also may affect students (e.g., Rüsch et al., 2016), and the resulting stress may negatively affect their outcomes.

Second, students with emotional and behavior disorders are at high risk of having at least one parent who also has an emotional, behavior, or other psychosocial disorder (Mantymaa et al., 2012). For example, in a series of studies looking at predictors of such problems in over 2,300 children ages 9 to 17, Copeland, Shanahan, Costello, and Angold (2009) found that those at highest risk were likely to have parents or a step-parent who were diagnosed as having mental illness, abused drugs or alcohol, or engaged in criminal activity. These data suggest that working with these parents may, in some cases, be complicated by parents' needs and the extent to which they are being addressed. If a parent is abusing drugs or alcohol, she is less likely than another parent to be able to actively participate in her child's education and the decisions to be made regarding programs and services.

A third barrier for these families is the often negative interactions that occur regarding their children. Teachers frequently are frustrated with students with emotional and behavior disorders; this emotion may lead teachers to have an overall negative perception of the student and the family. Teachers may then contact the family to enlist its help in addressing school problems, too often asking the parents to punish the student for behavior problems at school and too seldom involving the parents in reward systems. The parents may not be able to carry out the requests made by the teachers, or the parents' efforts may not be successful. The result may be additional frustration on the parts of teachers and parents alike.

The negative interactions between school professionals and family members sometimes are highlighted during meetings. Parents may be anxious about working with school personnel, worried about the behaviors of their child, and concerned that any meeting will be an opportunity to learn about yet another issue related to their child that they may feel powerless to address (Jones, Dohrn, & Dunn, 2004). Parents' behaviors at meetings may be viewed as combative or disruptive. Unless school professionals recognize the reasons for these behaviors, they may form even more negative opinions about the student and family.

One other challenge faced by families of students with emotional and behavior disorders concerns advocacy (Kaff, Teagarden, & Zabel, 2014). Many disability groups are represented in schools and the community by advocacy groups that are led by parents. These groups often can collectively ensure that their children's rights are upheld and foster positive perceptions of their children's special needs by educating professionals, other parents, and students and by seeking positive publicity concerning individuals with disabilities. Although advocacy for children with emotional and behavioral disabilities is gradually increasing (e.g., Dikel, 2014), it is not common and generally does not exist among parents of students with emotional and behavior disorders (Knitzer, 2005).

Building Positive Relationships

More than anything else, families need professionals to genuinely care about their children. And so for educators working with families of students with emotional and behavior disorders, it is essential to diligently strive to form strong partnerships using a collaborative focus such as that outlined earlier in this chapter and to be flexible in terms of expectations for family involvement. Efforts also may involve parent education and support groups.

Parent Education

In some cases, schools can offer assistance to parents by teaching them strategies that might help them to address their children's behavior at home (Wagner, 2014). Parent education can also address topics such as how to help their children with homework, how school services for their children are structured, how to access community resources, and how to advocate for their children (Tahhan, St. Pierre, Stewart, Leschied, & Cook, 2010).

Of course, parent education programs that require struggling parents to come to school at times that are convenient only for teachers and administrators are not likely to be successful. A variety of options should be considered, including offering programs at times that are convenient for parents; locating programs in community centers, libraries, or other settings that are possibly more familiar and comfortable for parents than the school; and creating options such as packets of print or electronic materials that can be accessed by parents (e.g., information sent home; information on a school or teacher website; information that can be disseminated by school social workers through home visits).

Support Groups

For some families, one of the most helpful options is a support group that includes the parents of other students with emotional and behavior disabilities (Mendenhall, Arnold, & Fristad, 2016; National Dissemination Center for Children with Disabilities, 2010). In support groups, parents share information about local resources and services, trade ideas for addressing specific problems, and obtain the reassurance of knowing that they are not alone in dealing with day-to-day challenges. Although school professionals might arrange to start a support group, parents take the lead and give the group its identity and direction. More common than school-based support groups are those that exist in the local community. Teachers can help parents access this type of assistance by keeping at hand details about such groups or knowing who at school (such as the counselor or social worker) can provide the needed information.

MyEdLab **Self-Check 7.6**

MyEdLab **Application Exercise 7.10:** Perspectives of Parents and Families with EBDs

MyEdLab **Application Exercise 7.11:** Collaborative Relationships

---

Trends and Issues Affecting the Field of Emotional and Behavior Disorders

Many trends and issues related to the field of emotional and behavior disorders have been introduced elsewhere in this chapter. For example, you have learned about the controversy that exists about the definition of this disability and concerns about inclusive practices. However, if you asked experienced professionals to name the most important issues, they probably would include two topics as significant for the field: (a) the continuing difficulty that students and their families face in obtaining essential mental health services and (b) the controversy surrounding the use of seclusion and restraint with students with emotional and behavior disabilities.

The Problem of Access

The number of students with emotional and behavior disorders in the United States has risen during the past decade, and the nature and severity of these students' disorders have become more serious. For example, the rate of hospital stays for children with mood disorders increased 80% between 1997 and 2010 (Pfuntner, Wier, & Stocks, 2013). However, the first problem related to access concerns identification: Whether considering schools or community services, far fewer students receive treatment than the number of students who need it. In fact, it has been estimated that less than 20% of the approximately 14 million youth who have mental illness receive treatment and that 90% of those who commit suicide have an untreated emotional or behavior disorder (National Alliance on Mental Illness, 2010). Further, up to 70% of youth in correctional facilities have some type of mental disorder, and 20% of incarcerated youth have a very serious mental illness; few of these youth receive any type of treatment for their disorders (National Alliance on Mental Illness, 2013).

For some families, access requires unthinkable sacrifices. In order to access Medicaid services that can provide mental health interventions, families that make enough money to survive but too much to be eligible must relinquish custody of their children. In using what has been called a psychiatric lockout, parents hope their children will receive critical services by being in the custody of the state (Cohen, 2013).

Creating a Promising Future

To address the problem of access, professionals, parents, and community agency personnel are lobbying politicians to pass legislation to expand and strengthen services for students with emotional and behavior disorders and their families (e.g., American Academy of Pediatrics, 2016) by emphasizing better health care coverage that includes coverage for these disabilities and providing funding for families that cannot afford services. The importance of these efforts has been punctuated by several events of the 21st century that have been extraordinarily stressful for children, including catastrophic natural disasters, the unexpected death of a loved one such as from gun violence, and the absence of parents due to military ser-

vice (e.g., National Center for Child Traumatic Stress, 2016). Each of these, as well as other stressful events, has taken a toll on the emotional well-being of untold numbers of students.

Experts agree that a critical need exists to eliminate the stigma associated with mental illness and to implement programs that can prevent or mitigate the development of emotional and behavioral disorders in children.

For school professionals, emphasis is on recognizing students' emotional and behavioral disorders, responding to them appropriately, and providing access through the use of best practices (Losinski, Maag, & Katsiyannis, 2015; Riney & Bullock, 2012). Instead of punishing students for misbehaviors, educators need to understand that behaviors may be related to mental health issues and to identify and implement programs and interventions that have been demonstrated to help students with such problems. Administrators, teachers, other school professionals, and even school board members should understand and observe the results that can be obtained using positive behavior supports and counseling and similar services. They also need to emphasize the prevention of these disorders by using schoolwide systems, as outlined earlier in this chapter.

Use of Restraints and Seclusion

When students with emotional and behavior disorders exhibit behaviors likely to result in serious harm to themselves or others, emergency measures are sometimes employed. Two such measures are the use of (a) physical restraint and (b) seclusion. The value and appropriate use of both of these procedures are vigorously debated in the field.

Physical restraint occurs when a teacher or another professional restricts a student's freedom of movement, physical activity, or access to his body (Council for Children with Behavioral Disorders, 2009a). For example, Lucas believes he has been treated unfairly by his teacher. As the teacher tries to talk to him in a way designed to calm him, Lucas instead speaks in a louder and louder voice. He suddenly moves toward the teacher with fists up, screaming that he will show her what is fair, flipping desks over and swinging at other students. Another teacher, trained in a specific and safe procedure for restraining students in such situations, prevents him from harming himself or others.

Seclusion occurs when a student is involuntarily confined to a room, left alone, and prevented from leaving. For example, in one morning, Beverly has repeatedly bullied others in her class by hitting them, grabbing items on their desks, and threatening them with harm after school. After several other interventions, the teacher tells Beverly that she will be placed in seclusion if she continues this behavior. Beverly's response is to turn to the nearest classmate and hit him. Using restraint, Beverly is placed in a seclusion room. An assistant monitors her through a window in the door, at the same time preventing Beverly from leaving the room. Ten minutes after Beverly stops pounding on the door and after speaking with her teacher, she is released from the room to rejoin her peers.

Many concerns exist regarding the use of physical restraint and seclusion in schools. These are some of the issues:

- Thirty-five states now have policies related to restraint and seclusion for students with disabilities, but the quality of these policies varies widely. For example, only 22 states prohibit restraint except in cases of emergency (Butler, 2015). Appropriate policies regarding restraint and seclusion should address student safety and emergency procedures, parent notification, alternatives to these procedures, and requirements for debriefing and follow-up after they are employed.
- Although many professionals claim that physical restraint and seclusion can benefit students, little research exists to document the effects of them on students' behavior and learning (U.S. Senate Committee on Health, Education, Labor, and Pensions, 2014).
- Many professionals question whether restraint and seclusion should even have a place in school settings, noting that if they are used repeatedly, they may indicate a failure in instruction (Council for Children with Behavioral Disorders, 2009a, 2009b).

Restraint and seclusion is such a controversial topic that the U.S. Department of Education in 2012 produced a resource document concerning its use. The 15 principles to guide the use of restraint and seclusion outlined are included in the Professional Edge. As a professional educator, your responsibility is to stay informed about the emerging knowledge base on this topic and consider carefully the legal, educational, and ethical impact of using these procedures with students.

15 Principles to Guide the Use of Restraint and Seclusion

1. Every effort should be made to prevent the need for the use of restraint and for the use of seclusion.

2. Schools should never use mechanical restraints to restrict a child's freedom of movement, and schools should never use a drug or medication to control behavior or restrict freedom of movement (except as authorized by a licensed physician or other qualified health professional).

3. Physical restraint or seclusion should not be used except in situations where the child's behavior poses imminent danger of serious physical harm to self or others and other interventions are ineffective and should be discontinued as soon as imminent danger of serious physical harm to self or others has dissipated.

4. Policies restricting the use of restraint and seclusion should apply to all children, not just children with disabilities.

5. Any behavioral intervention must be consistent with the child's rights to be treated with dignity and to be free from abuse.

6. Restraint or seclusion should never be used as punishment or discipline (e.g., placing in seclusion for out-of-seat behavior), as a means of coercion or retaliation, or as a convenience.

7. Restraint or seclusion should never be used in a manner that restricts a child's breathing or harms the child.

8. The use of restraint or seclusion, particularly when there is repeated use for an individual child, multiple uses within the same classroom, or multiple uses by the same individual, should trigger a review and, if appropriate, revision of strategies currently in place to address dangerous behavior; if positive behavioral strategies are not in place, staff should consider developing them.

9. Behavioral strategies to address dangerous behavior that results in the use of restraint or seclusion should address the underlying cause or purpose of the dangerous behavior.

10. Teachers and other personnel should be trained regularly on the appropriate use of effective alternatives to physical restraint and seclusion, such as positive behavioral interventions and supports and, only for cases involving imminent danger of serious physical harm, on the safe use of physical restraint and seclusion.

11. Every instance in which restraint or seclusion is used should be carefully and continuously and visually monitored to ensure the appropriateness of its use and safety of the child, other children, teachers, and other personnel.

12. Parents should be informed of the policies on restraint and seclusion at their child's school or other educational setting, as well as applicable federal, state, or local laws.

13. Parents should be notified as soon as possible following each instance in which restraint or seclusion is used with their child.

14. Policies regarding the use of restraint and seclusion should be reviewed regularly and updated as appropriate.

15. Policies regarding the use of restraint and seclusion should provide that each incident involving the use of restraint or seclusion should be documented in writing and provide for the collection of specific data that would enable teachers, staff, and other personnel to understand and implement the preceding principles.

Source: U.S. Department of Education. (2012). *Restraint and seclusion: Resource document.* Retrieved from https://www2.ed.gov/policy/seclusion/restraints-and-seclusion-resources.pdf

---

MyEdLab **Self-Check 7.7**

MyEdLab **Application Exercise 7.12:** Trends and Issues in the Field of Emotional and Behavior Disorders

MyEdLab **Application Exercise 7.13:** The Controversial Use of Physical Restraint and Seclusion

Summary

LO7.1   The study of children with emotional and behavior disorders commenced at the beginning of the 20th century in the fields of medicine and psychology, and it continues today. The current definition of emotional and behavior disorders—called *emotional disturbance* in IDEA—and their prevalence continue to be debated, but professionals agree that both biological and psychosocial factors are contributing causes of these disabilities.

LO7.2 Students with emotional and behavior disorders display internalizing and externalizing behaviors, and their emotional difficulties often lead to problems in social relationships. Typically, these students have low-average to average ability, but their achievement is below expected levels.

LO7.3 Formal and informal assessment instruments and procedures used to identify whether students have emotional and behavior disorders include behavior checklists and related assessments; interviews with professionals, parents, and students; observations; ability and achievement testing; and medical information.

LO7.4 Many students with emotional disabilities spend a significant amount of time in special education settings, a fact supported by the widely acknowledged difficulty of implementing inclusive practices for these students.

LO7.5 Best practices for students with emotional and behavior disorders include prevention, particularly with early intervention; collaborative efforts on the part of school and community personnel; functional behavior assessments and behavior intervention plans; and classroom instruction designed to provide structure and engagement.

LO7.6 The parents and families of students with emotional and behavior disorders often feel isolated from others and struggle to find appropriate services to help their children.

LO7.7 Two of the most serious issues facing the field of emotional and behavior disorders today are (a) the lack of adequate mental health services for children and youth and (b) controversy surrounding the use of seclusion and restraint.

Back to the Cases

Now that you have read about emotional and behavior disorders, look back at the student stories at the beginning of this chapter. Then, answer the questions about each of their cases.

MyEdLab **Case Study 7.1**

CHARLOTTE. You are spending another sleepless night worrying about Charlotte and what you can do to help her. You finally crawl from bed to jot down a few notes in order to capture your thoughts.

MyEdLab **Case Study 7.2**

GABRIEL. Gabriel's team discussed at length the most appropriate and least restrictive environment (LRE) for him. With his mother's strong support, the team decided that, at least for the short term, he should attend a separate school.

MyEdLab **Case Study 7.3**

STEVEN. Steven has dropped out of school. Since he is old enough to leave school legally and has done so, the school is no longer responsible for him. Or is it?

8

Students with Intellectual and Developmental Disabilities

Learning Outcomes

LO8.1 Outline the development of the field of intellectual disabilities, define current terminology related to this disability, and explain the prevalence and causes of it.

LO8.2 Describe characteristics of individuals with intellectual disabilities.

LO8.3 Explain how intellectual disabilities are identified.

LO8.4 Outline how learners with intellectual disabilities receive their education.

LO8.5 Describe recommended educational practices for students with intellectual disabilities.

LO8.6 Explain the perspectives and concerns that parents and families of students with intellectual disabilities may have.

LO 8.7 Identify trends and issues influencing the field of intellectual disabilities.

SHANDRA

Shandra likes school—except, that is, for the parts that she does not like. She is enrolled in Ms. Nehring's third-grade class, where every morning begins with morning work such as math problems for practice or a reading or writing assignment. Because Shandra has a mild intellectual disability, the tasks she completes often are adjusted to better meet her needs. For example, her math problems may involve adding or subtracting two-digit numbers without regrouping as her peers focus on multiplication, and her reading work is based on stories at a kindergarten level. After morning work, Shandra leaves her classroom for 90 minutes, going to Mr. Kramer's special education class for reading instruction and once each week receiving speech-language therapy while there. However, Shandra learns with her typical classmates for the remainder of the day, including math, science, and social studies, as well as art, music, and physical education. She has two good friends with whom she always eats lunch. Shandra's peers have known her since kindergarten, and they are so accustomed to helping her to understand directions and follow them that they do this without any prompting from teachers. However, despite peer support and Ms. Nehring's best efforts, the part of school that Shandra does *not* like is social studies. She sometimes sighs loudly when it is time for this subject, and she occasionally refuses to participate in class discussion and projects. Ms. Nehring and Mr. Kramer are collaborating to address Shandra's increasingly resistant behavior; they do not want her to miss this key instruction and do not want her reaction to become a pattern or to become more problematic.

ANTHONY

Anthony is still a little overwhelmed at the middle school he attends as a sixth-grader, but even so, he likes it. In elementary school, he spent about half the day in the special education room with his teacher, Mr. Reynolds, and when he was in a general education class, he was accompanied to the room by either a paraeducator or a peer buddy. His school was also much smaller. In middle school, Anthony has a locker that he practiced learning to open over the summer, and he changes classes with other students, moving from one room to another, which he also practiced

before the school year began. He receives reading, English, math, and social studies instruction from two special educators. The teachers are careful to align their teaching with the district curriculum and state learning standards, but they emphasize the vocabulary, reading, math, and other skills Anthony and his classmates need for daily living. Anthony receives science instruction and his elective classes (e.g., art, music, technology, Spanish) in general education. Anthony is required to take a high-stakes test each year, just like most students, but his alternate assessment is based on a portfolio of samples of his work rather than a traditional paper-and-pencil test, and it is scored using a rubric. Anthony has Down syndrome; he also has several heart problems and already has had two surgeries to correct them. Anthony is very positive about his future, as is his family. He anticipates that he will work in the family's printing business once he finishes school.

ERNEST

Ernest is 20 years old, and in just a few weeks, he will graduate from Wild Creek High School. For the past two years, Ernest's educational goals have focused on his transition from high school to postschool options. He has learned many life skills such as using public transportation and asking for assistance when needed, he has participated in a vocational program with a community work component, and he has continued refining his academic skills. Ernest has a moderate intellectual disability, but its cause is unknown. Ernest is shy; he often has to be prompted to make eye contact with his teachers, classmates, and others he meets. However, he loves classic 1960s music, and so if such music is playing or someone mentions a song he knows, he becomes very animated. Ernest recently received great news: He has been admitted to a special program at a regional university, and so he'll be going to college. While enrolled in the two-year program, he will have an on-campus job, he will take some courses designed just for students with similar needs but also several standard university courses, and he will have a mentor, a typical undergraduate student enrolled in the university's therapeutic recreation program. Ernest is excited and a little scared about living away from home; his parents are scared, too, but they know this experience will help Ernest prepare for his adult life.

During most of the history of public schools, students with intellectual disabilities, previously called *mental retardation*, have been characterized primarily by the word *can't*—what they can't do, what they can't learn, what they can't participate in. For example, in my own late-1970s classroom for students with mild intellectual disabilities, no books were provided because of the strongly held belief that these students could not learn to read. As these students became adults, the emphasis on their limitations continued. Except for those individuals who blended into society and shed their disability labels, most people with intellectual disabilities lived with their parents, were placed in residential facilities, or resided under close supervision in group homes with several other adults with disabilities.

Although the past sometimes still influences professionals in today's schools, contemporary thinking about individuals with intellectual disabilities now is based on much higher expectations and a world of possibilities, not limitations, as Ernest and his parents are learning. This has meant rethinking beliefs about these students' academic potential and the priorities they may have for their lives beyond the school years. As you read this chapter, continue to think about your own beliefs about children and adults with intellectual disabilities, including the stigma associated with the now outdated term *mental retardation* and the influence your perceptions can have on these students' lives.

As you learn about this group of students, you may notice that the focus of this chapter is on students with mild or moderate intellectual disabilities. That is deliberate and based on the tremendous diversity of students who may have this disability. You will learn about students with autism who may have intellectual disabilities in Chapter 10, those with traumatic brain injury who may have intellectual disabilities in Chapter 13, and those with multiple and severe disabilities who also have intellectual disabilities in Chapter 14.

Understanding Intellectual Disabilities

Contemporary perspectives on intellectual disabilities are a response to past views and practices. By understanding how this field developed and was shaped by societal trends, you can better appreciate the significance of today's changing vocabulary and rising expectations for students with this disability.

Development of the Field of Intellectual Disabilities

Focused study of and interest in individuals with intellectual disabilities began in the early 19th century—earlier than the study of people with most other disabilities (Hickson, Blackman, & Reis, 1995). As the time line in Figure 8.1 illustrates, the field evolved for the next 100 years, with an optimistic emphasis on care and treatment and a belief that many individuals would be "cured."

The turmoil in American society at the beginning of the 20th century that you read about in Chapter 1 led to a radical shift in thinking about individuals with intellectual disabilities. Optimism was replaced by pessimism. Prominent physicians and psychologists theorized that intellectual disabilities—called *mental deficiency* at that time—were inherited, that they were accompanied by criminal tendencies, and that allowing people with these disabilities to have children would undermine the strength of American society (Kanner, 1964). As a result, professionals gradually abandoned efforts to educate these children and adults, and they became satisfied with providing custodial care for them, either in institutions or segregated special classes (Winzer, 2009). Most experts agree that the early 20th century was the lowest point in the modern history of education for individuals with intellectual disabilities (Wehmeyer & Patton, 2000).

FIGURE 8.1   Time Line of the Development of the Field of Intellectual Disabilities

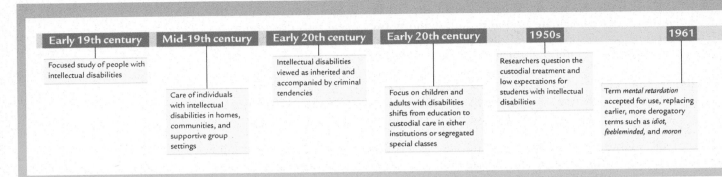

Until the latter part of the 20th century, many children with intellectual disabilities were sent to live in institutions. Today, professionals stress helping these students to reach their potential and to function successfully in their communities.

By the middle of the 20th century, beliefs were beginning to change (Grossberg, 2011), and for the next two decades, the efforts of researchers, social reformers, and parents guided the field toward major reform. The result of their diligence was the litigation that eventually formed the basis for Public Law (P.L.) 94-142, the federal special education law now called IDEA (the Individuals with Disabilities Education Act).

Definitions of Intellectual Disabilities

As is true for some other students with disabilities, the language that describes students with intellectual disabilities requires clarification. Although the term *mental retardation* (MR) was widely used from the middle of the 20th century until recently to describe the individuals who are the focus of this chapter, many parents and advocates urged a change in terminology because of the offensive connotations associated with MR (Patel, Greydanus, & Merrick, 2014; Lyle & Simplican, 2015). This advocacy effort was successful: On October 5, 2010, President Barrack Obama signed into law "Rosa's Law," a bill that immediately changed the term *mental retardation* in all federal applications to *intellectual disability* (Rosa's Law, 2009). Soon after, a comparable decision was made by the U.S. Supreme Court (*Hall v. Florida*, 2014). Another term you will see in this chapter and in your career as a professional educator is **developmental disabilities**, a broad term usually used in reference to chronic and significant impairments such as cerebral palsy and autism that result in intellectual disabilities (American Association on Intellectual and Developmental Disabilities, American Network of Community Options and Resources, National Association of Councils on Developmental Disabilities. The Arc, & United Cerebral Palsy, 2015). As you learned in Chapter 1, this term also is sometimes used instead of a more specific disability label for children ages 3 to 9 receiving special education services.

You may find that your state uses yet other terms to refer to students with intellectual disabilities. For example, you may hear the term **cognitive impairment** or **cognitive disability**, or *mental impairment, mental disability,* or *mental handicap.* Over the next several years, it is likely that such terms will gradually be

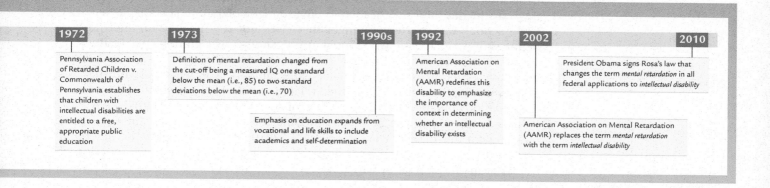

| 1972 | 1973 | 1990s | 1992 | 2002 | 2010 |

1972 Pennsylvania Association of Retarded Children v. Commonwealth of Pennsylvania establishes that children with intellectual disabilities are entitled to a free, appropriate public education

1973 Definition of mental retardation changed from the cut-off being a measured IQ one standard below the mean (i.e., 85) to two standard deviations below the mean (i.e., 70)

1990s Emphasis on education expands from vocational and life skills to include academics and self-determination

1992 American Association on Mental Retardation (AAMR) redefines this disability to emphasize the importance of context in determining whether an intellectual disability exists

2002 American Association on Mental Retardation (AAMR) replaces the term *mental retardation* with the term *intellectual disability*

2010 President Obama signs Rosa's law that changes the term *mental retardation* in all federal applications to *intellectual disability*

replaced with the contemporary terminology. These changes will reflect a positive step in transforming understanding of these students and their potential.

Federal Definition

The definition generally used by educators is the one in IDEA. This definition for intellectual disability is based on one developed in 1982 by the American Association on Mental Retardation (AAMR) (renamed in 2007 as the American Association on Intellectual and Developmental Disabilities, or AAIDD). It states that an intellectual disability is

> significantly subaverage general intellectual functioning, existing concurrently with deficits in adaptive behavior and manifested during the developmental period, that adversely affects a child's educational performance. (IDEA 20 U.S.C. §1401 [2004], 20 C.F.R. §300.8[c][6])

This definition illustrates the important fact that the intellectual disability designation is assigned only when a student demonstrates both low intellectual ability and significant problems with adaptive behavior—that is, the day-to-day skills that are necessary for independence (e.g., self-care, the use of money). The third part of the definition clarifies that the identification of intellectual disability is made only if the condition is present by the time the student is 18 years old—the generally accepted definition of the phrase "during the developmental period." If an adult was injured or experienced an illness that resulted in a significant reduction in intellectual ability, a term such as *cognitive impairment* might be used, but the term *intellectual disability* usually would not be applied.

American Association on Intellectual and Developmental Disabilities (AAIDD) Definition

In 1992, the AAMR revised its definition on which federal special education law was based. It reaffirmed the use of this new definition in 2002 and updated it yet again in 2010, even though the group has not yet been successful in changing the IDEA definition. This newer definition is similar to the original one, except that is clarifies the domains of adaptive skills, noting that they encompass (a) *conceptual* understandings related to literacy, numeracy and reasoning; *social* proficiency such as interacting appropriately with others and obeying laws; and (c) *practical* competencies related to self-care and functioning independently (Schalock et al., 2010).

The current AAIDD definition is also a refinement because it is expanded through a discussion of key assumptions that must be analyzed in judging whether an individual has an intellectual disability. One assumption relates to considering the context in which the person lives (Luckasson & Schalock, 2013; Schalock &

Luckasson, 2013; Shogren, Luckasson, & Schalock, 2014). For example, some students are eligible for special education as having an intellectual disability only while they are in the intensive academic environment of public schools. When they leave school and find employment that does not rely heavily on specific academic skills, the label may no longer apply. Another assumption specifically calls attention to cultural and linguistic diversity, acknowledging that various cultures may have different responses to and expectations for individuals with this disability. Assumptions are also outlined related to individual's strengths, even in the presence of limitation, the importance of focusing on supports that help individuals succeed, and the goal of improving the overall life functioning of individuals with this disability (Schalock et al., 2010). As you compare the older and newer definitions of intellectual disabilities, would you support the adoption of the latter in IDEA? Why or why not?

Diagnostic and Statistical Manual Definition

As you learned in Chapters 6 and 7, some diagnoses are medical in nature and are guided by the definitions in the *Diagnostic and Statistical Manual–5th edition* (DSM-V). For intellectual disabilities, this manual follows very closely the AAIDD definition; that is, it encompasses conceptual, social, and practical dimensions. Perhaps most significantly, DSM-V stresses the need for comprehensive assessment of this disorder; it specifies that a person's overall functioning level should be carefully evaluated rather than relying exclusively on the results of intelligence quotient (IQ) testing.

Prevalence of Intellectual Disabilities

During the 2011–2012 school year, 0.73% of all children ages 6 through 21, or 415,697 students, received special education because they were identified as having an intellectual disability (U.S. Department of Education, 2015). An additional 0.21%, or 122,901 students, in this age group were served with the general label *developmentally delayed*, the alternative federal disability category for students ages 3 through 9 that includes some students with intellectual disabilities. The percent of all students with this disability has continued a slight decline in recent years after a sharp decline from the late 1970s through the 1980s, most likely attributable to more accurate identification of students as having other disabilities (such as learning disabilities and autism) (Van Naarden et al., 2015).

Because the decision to identify an individual as having an intellectual disability involves professional judgment, no single prevalence estimate is considered definitive. For example, the American Association on Intellectual and Developmental Disabilities (Luckasson et al., 2002) estimates that 2.5% of the entire population has this disability. Among children, the Centers for Disease Control and Prevention (2015) estimates that 1.10% of children ages 3–17 have an intellectual disability, although the latter number has fluctuated considerably in recent years because of changes in the way these data are gathered. Collectively, prevalence data suggest that most professionals are likely to teach students with intellectual disabilities, and some evidence suggests this disability group is underidentified (e.g., Luckasson & Shalock, 2013; Shalock & Luckasson, 2013).

Other Prevalence Considerations

Little research has explored the prevalence of intellectual disabilities in boys versus girls or based on age. Generally, boys are thought to have intellectual disabilities at a slightly higher rate than girls (1.5:1). In addition, some specific syndromes that include intellectual disability (topics addressed later in this chapter) affect boys and girls at different rates (Koenig & Tsatsanis, 2005).

Video Example
from
YouTube

▶

MyEdLab
Video Example 8.1

These definitions of intellectual disabilities can seem technical and not related to your role as a professional educator. To better understand these students, think about what you would do if you had Mary, the student in this video, in your class.
(https://www.youtube.com/watch?v=PzPkt9vri3E)

The aspect of prevalence and intellectual disability that has received the most attention among educators is the disproportionate representation of African American students, especially boys, in this group (Ford, 2012; Zhang, Katsiyannis, Ju, & Roberts, 2014). As you learned in Chapter 3, the reasons for this situation include teacher expectations for student classroom behavior and academic performance, racial/ethnic bias, bias in assessment, and risk factors such as living in poverty. Presently, African American students are approximately 2.48 times more likely than other students to be identified as having an intellectual disability, based on their overall representation in the population (U.S. Department of Education, 2016). These data indicate that despite widespread attention to disproportionate representation, the issue still exists.

Causes of Intellectual Disability

For most students with intellectual disabilities, especially those with mild impairments, the cause of the disability cannot be determined. Shandra, the elementary student introduced at the beginning of this chapter, is in this group of students. For students with more significant intellectual disabilities, the causes usually are considered in terms of when they occurred: during the *prenatal* (before birth), the *perinatal* (during or immediately after birth), or the *postnatal* (after birth) period. The following examples illustrate these three time periods, the types of conditions that can lead to intellectual disability, and the extent to which scientific knowledge about this disability has progressed.

Prenatal Causes of Intellectual Disabilities

Intellectual disabilities sometimes are caused by factors at play before birth; these are referred to as prenatal causes, and the resulting conditions sometimes can be labeled as syndromes, that is, consistent clusters of characteristics. For example, they may be the result of chromosomal abnormalities such as Down syndrome, fragile X syndrome, Prader-Willi syndrome, and fetal alcohol spectrum disorders, each briefly described in the following sections.

Down Syndrome. Probably the most well-known of all the genetic disorders that can result in intellectual disabilities is Down syndrome (DS). One in every 792 children is born with DS (National Down Syndrome Society, 2016; de Graaf, Buckley, & Skotko, 2015), and this syndrome occurs in both sexes and across racial/ethnic groups. The cause of DS is clear: Individuals typically have 46 chromosomes—23 contributed each by one's mother and father. In nearly all individuals with Down syndrome, faulty cell division results in an extra chromosome being present in the 21st chromosome pair, and so the syndrome is sometimes called trisomy 21. It is this extra genetic material that causes children with this syndrome to have easily identified characteristics.

When these children are young, they often have poor muscle tone and may be called "floppy" babies. They also have eyes that slant upward and small ears, and their tongues may seem somewhat large for their mouths. More than half of these children have vision impairments or hearing loss, and approximately the same number have heart defects that may require medication or surgery (National Down Syndrome Society, 2016). Many also have respiratory and thyroid conditions. Students with this syndrome usually have mild or moderate intellectual disabilities. Anthony, the middle school student described at the beginning of this chapter, has Down syndrome.

Although Down syndrome can occur in any expectant mother, there is a correlation with age. Mothers who are 25 years old have a 1 in 1,300 chance of having a baby with Down syndrome. At age 35, this increases to 1 in 350, and mothers who are 42 years old have a 1 in 55 chance of having a baby with DS (National Institute of Child Health and Human Development, 2014).

Did You Know?

The National Association for Down Syndrome (NADS) (www.nads.org) provides counseling and support to families of children newly diagnosed with this syndrome. It also advocates for the rights of individuals with Down syndrome and provides news related to this disorder.

Fragile X Syndrome. The most common form of inherited intellectual disability is fragile X syndrome, sometimes called Martin-Bell syndrome. Both men and women may carry the disorder, but only mothers transmit the disorder to their children. This syndrome develops when a mutation occurs in one of the genes in the X chromosome. The mutation occurs in a gene segment that is repeated in most people about 30 times. In those with this disorder, the segment is repeated from 55 to 200 times, causing the gene to turn off—that is, to stop producing a chemical present in the cells of people who do not have this disorder (National Fragile X Foundation, 2016). Full fragile X syndrome (gene repeated more than 200 times) is seen in approximately 1 in every 4,000 males and 1 in every 8,000 females (National Institute of Child Health and Human Development, 2013), although far more individuals have what is called *permutation*—that is, gene repetition between 55 and 200 times (Genetics Home Reference, 2016a). When the full abnormal gene repetition occurs, it causes a deficiency of a protein that develops synapses between nerve cells and often leads to an intellectual disability. Males with this disorder usually have significant intellectual disabilities (Roberts et al., 2005; Schwarte, 2008); females usually have much milder impairments.

Individuals with fragile X syndrome tend to have long faces, large ears, and poor muscle tone, but generally they are healthy. They often display characteristics similar to those in students with attention deficit–hyperactivity disorder (ADHD), including distractibility, and they may share some characteristics with students who have autism, including hypersensitivity to certain stimuli (e.g., the sound of a doorbell, the feel of certain types of clothing) and a tendency to say or do the same thing over and over again (Vekeman et al., 2015; Berry-Kravis et al., 2010; Langthorne & McGill, 2012). Students with this syndrome also are likely to become anxious when routines are changed, may have emotional problems such as depression, and often have poor social skills.

Prader-Willi Syndrome. Yet another disorder resulting from prenatal factors is Prader-Willi syndrome, which is much less common than Down syndrome and fragile X syndrome, occurring in about 1 of every 12,000–15,000 babies (Prader-Willi Syndrome Association, 2015). It is caused by any of several types of mutation on chromosome 15 (e.g., the father's chromosome is missing in the child; the mother contributes both chromosome 15s instead of one coming from the father). It occurs equally in boys and girls and occurs in individuals from any race or ethnicity.

Children who have Prader-Willi syndrome may have mild or moderate intellectual disabilities, but some have abilities in the low-average to average range (Prader-Willi Syndrome Association, 2015). Research on the specific cognitive characteristics of these individuals is just beginning (e.g., Manning et al., 2016; de Souza et al., 2013).

These children typically are happy as toddlers, and their behavior is similar to that of their peers. As they reach school age, though, they begin to have significant behavior problems, including stubbornness, problems switching from one activity to another, and resistance to changes in routines (Chevalère et al., 2015). However, the primary characteristic of this disorder is an insatiable appetite and compulsive eating, and this symptom generally begins between the ages of 2 and 4. Students with this disorder may steal food or eat discarded food, and educators working with these students must ensure that all food is kept locked away. Obesity occurs in 95% of these students if food intake is not carefully controlled. Families who have children with Prader-Willi syndrome often are under a great deal of stress because of the need to provide constant control and extensive behavior interventions (Manning et al., 2016; Wulffaert, Scholte, & Van Berckelaer-Onnes, 2010).

The technical information in the preceding paragraphs may leave you thinking that most prenatally occurring intellectual disabilities are caused by chromosomal problems. This is not the case. There are many other prenatal causes of intellectual disabilities, including those described in the following sections.

Fetal Alcohol Spectrum Disorders (FASD). Many children have intellectual disabilities because of the harmful impact of maternal alcohol consumption. In fact, FASD is considered the leading cause of intellectual disabilities and the only one that clearly is preventable, with some experts estimating that as many as two-thirds of all students receiving special education for these disabilities may be affected by it.

The term fetal alcohol syndrome (FAS), first used in 1973, describes the most severe form of this disorder. The prevalence of FAS generally is believed to be significantly underreported and ranges from 0.5 to 2.0 cases per 1,000 babies born, with some regional variation in rate (May & Gossage, 2016). Less severe forms of FASD include alcohol-related neurodevelopmental disorder (ARND) and alcohol-related birth defects (ARBD), and the prevalence of these disorders is approximately 2 to 5 cases per 100 births (Centers for Disease Control and Prevention, 2016b; May et al., 2014). Keep in mind, though, that not every student with FASD has an intellectual disability.

Students with FAS usually are somewhat small and slower in their development than other children. Their eyes may be small, with drooping eyelids, the groove between the upper lip and nose may be absent, and the lower part of the face may seem flat. These students often have mild or moderate intellectual disabilities, and they also are likely to have a very short attention span as well as hyperactivity, learning disabilities, and poor coordination (Dybdahl & Ryan, 2009).

Phenylketonuria. Phenylketonuria (PKU) is an inherited metabolic disorder that affects 1 out of every 10,000–15,000 babies (Genetics Home Reference, 2016b). PKU occurs when the body is unable to produce an enzyme needed to process the amino acid *phenylalanine*, which is present in many high-protein foods, including meat and eggs. As a result, phenylalanine accumulates in the body, and it may cause an intellectual disability. Children inherit PKU only if both parents carry the defective gene that causes it, and it affects boys and girls equally. PKU is mentioned here because you have undoubtedly seen a warning about it: If you look at the small print on a can of diet soft drink, you will see a warning to "phenylketonurics" that the product contains phenylalanine, the chemical they cannot metabolize. All states now mandate that newborns be tested for PKU.

The treatment of PKU can begin even before a baby is born; when a mother known to carry this gene controls her dietary intake of phenylalanine, prenatal harmful effects can largely be avoided. Treatment for the child begins as soon as the disorder is detected, and it consists of a carefully planned diet low in foods containing phenylalanine (National Institutes of Health, 2012). For example, certain high-protein foods such as meat, fish, and poultry are not allowed. Although it was once believed that the special diet could be discontinued around age 6, lifelong control of diet is the current recommended practice (National Institutes of Health, 2012). When the diet is followed and chemical levels in the blood are carefully monitored, students with this disorder experience no significant effects on intellectual ability or learning.

Toxoplasmosis. Toxoplasmosis is an infection caused by a parasite, and more than 60 million people in the United States carry it (Centers for Disease Control and Prevention, 2013), including 10% to 15% of women of childbearing age (15 to 45 years old). It usually is harmless because the body's immune system prevents it from causing illness. However, an expectant mother who becomes infected with the parasite for the first time can pass it on to her unborn child. The baby

Video Example from YouTube

MyEdLab
Video Example 8.2

The four students in this video all have been affected by FASD. (https://www.youtube.com/watch?v=kfyYUq1yjTk)

may seem fine at birth, but an intellectual disability or blindness may develop later in life. It is important to know that this parasite is spread through a cat's fecal matter. Thus, expectant mothers are cautioned to have someone else clean the litter box.

Perinatal Causes of Intellectual Disability

In some instances, a problem that occurs during or immediately after the birth of a child leads to an intellectual disability. For example, premature babies weighing less than 3.3 pounds have a 10% to 20% risk of having an intellectual disability (Behrman & Butler, 2007). Birth injury is another category of causes of intellectual disabilities during the perinatal period. For example, if a baby is deprived of oxygen while being born or if the infant is hurt by the incorrect use of forceps or procedures followed during birth, an intellectual disability may result.

Postnatal Causes of Intellectual Disability

Children who are born without disabilities sometimes develop an intellectual disability as a result of an accident or illness that occurs during childhood. Examples include encephalitis, lead poisoning, and brain injury, described below.

Encephalitis. Inflammation of the brain, or encephalitis, can be caused by any viral infection. Vaccinations have reduced the chances of most children getting certain viral infections (e.g., measles, mumps, chicken pox), but this disease also can be carried by certain types of mosquitoes and animals that have rabies. In some cases, encephalitis results in intellectual disabilities.

Lead Poisoning. You already have learned that young children exposed to lead are at higher risk for developing learning disabilities, emotional and behavior disorders, and ADHD. Lead poisoning can lead to intellectual disabilities as well. It is estimated that 500,000 children ages 1 through 5 have raised levels of lead in their blood (Centers for Disease Control and Prevention, 2016a). Even though lead-based paint was banned in 1978, it is the primary source of childhood lead exposure and is found in more than 4 million buildings in which young children live. Like fetal alcohol syndrome, lead poisoning is a completely preventable cause of intellectual disabilities. Eradication of lead poisoning in children by 2020 is part of a set of federal priorities to improve the health of people in the United States.

Brain Injury. Although many children have accidents and experience no long-term negative effects, any event that causes injury to the brain can be a cause of intellectual disabilities. Examples include falls from bicycles or playground equipment, automobile accidents, near drowning, child abuse, and severe malnutrition. This topic is addressed further in Chapter 13.

Does it seem that the causes of intellectual disabilities are a little overwhelming? Remember that the preceding discussion includes only a few of all the causes and that advances in medical technology are providing additional information every year. These advances someday may help prevent some types of intellectual disabilities from ever occurring and may minimize the impact of those that cannot be prevented.

MyEdLab **Self-Check 8.1**

MyEdLab **Application Exercise 8.1:** Changing Terminology

MyEdLab **Application Exercise 8.2:** Overview of Causes

MyEdLab **Application Exercise 8.3:** Definitions and Causes of Intellectual Disabilities

Characteristics of Individuals with Intellectual Disabilities

As you read about the causes of intellectual disabilities, you learned some of the specific characteristics associated with individuals who have well-known syndromes and disorders. In this section, the emphasis is on a more general picture of the cognitive, academic, social, behavior, emotional, and physical/medical characteristics of this group of students.

Cognitive and Academic Characteristics

A student is identified as having an intellectual disability only if his IQ score places him at approximately 2 standard deviations or more below the mean or average score of 100. And even though IDEA does not draw these distinctions, in traditional classification systems individuals are grouped based on the extent of their intellectual impairment:

Mild intellectual disabilities	IQ = 55–69
Moderate intellectual disabilities	IQ = 40–54
Severe intellectual disabilities	IQ = 25–39
Profound intellectual disabilities	IQ = below 25

What does all this mean? Perhaps you have seen a diagram like the one presented in Figure 8.2—a *bell-shaped curve*. It demonstrates how these concepts relate to one another. The average IQ score is considered 100. Most people—approximately 68% of them—have an IQ score that falls between 1 standard deviation (i.e., 15 points) below the mean and 1 standard deviation above the mean, or between 85 and 115. As you can see from the figure, the IQ scores for students with intellectual disabilities fall significantly below this range.

Keep in mind that IQ scores are approximations that guide professionals in making decisions about students' needs, but the scores should not by themselves dictate decisions regarding students. A student with an IQ slightly above 70 could be identified as having an intellectual disability if he was experiencing many problems in adaptive skills. Likewise, a student with a score slightly below 70 might not be identified if she seemed to be functioning well.

FIGURE 8.2   **Bell-Shaped Curve for IQ Scores**

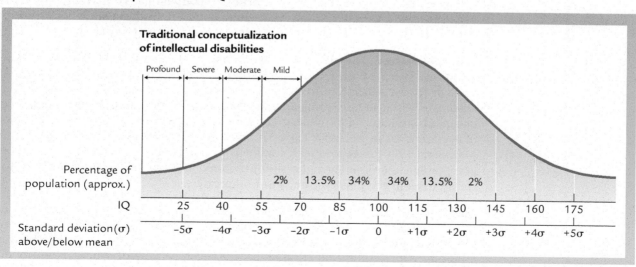

Although some variation of this classification system of mild, moderate, severe, and profound is used in most states, it has bothered professionals for many years because of its emphasis on limitations and its tendency to relate specific scores to highly stigmatizing labels. To address these and other significant shortcomings, the American Association on Intellectual and Developmental Disabilities (AAIDD) (Schalock et al., 2010) offers an alternative, multidimensional classification system that incorporates these major life elements:

- Intellectual abilities—This dimension captures the traditional means of classification, scores on intelligence tests.
- Adaptive behavior—This dimension is the second element of traditional models and considers an individual's ability to carry out typical, age-appropriate activities.
- Health—This dimension includes both physical well-being and mental health; it is not considered in the traditional classification system.
- Participation—This dimension encompasses the roles and interactions a person has across home, school, work, and community.
- Context—This dimension refers to the personal and environmental circumstances in which a person lives.

The goal of this model is to avoid a stigmatizing labeling system and instead to recognize that individuals with intellectual disabilities function differently depending on each of the dimensions and so need different levels and types of supports at various points in time. Although not commonly used in schools, this system enables professionals to look in a constructive way at arranging services so that individuals with intellectual disabilities can reach their potential.

Cognitive Functioning

The cognitive characteristics of students with intellectual disabilities have a significant impact on several dimensions of cognitive functioning (Bergeron & Floyd, 2006), including memory, generalization, metacognition, motivation, language, and academic skills.

Memory. In some respects, students with intellectual disabilities have cognitive functioning difficulties similar to those of other students about whom you have already learned. One example concerns working memory. Do you recall that students with ADHD have difficulty with working memory, or the ability to remember what needs to be done and how much time there is to do it? Students with intellectual disabilities also experience these problems. They are likely to forget what they are supposed to do, particularly if a task involves many steps. However, technology is helping to address this dilemma. The Technology Notes explains how a variety of tools are being used to help these students overcome limitations in working memory and other aspects of their special needs.

Generalization. The ability to learn a task or idea and then apply it in other situations is called generalization. When a student learns in language arts or English to use adjectives to make her writing more interesting and then uses adjectives when she is writing an essay in a social studies class, generalization has occurred. Students with intellectual disabilities have difficulty with generalization of academic tasks, behavior expectations, and social interactions. For example, if a student who tends to speak loudly is being taught to keep his voice at an acceptable classroom level, the skill may need to be taught in general education classrooms, in the music room, and in the cafeteria.

Metacognition. Another challenge for many students with intellectual disabilities is metacognition, or the ability to "think about thinking," which was introduced in Chapter 5 in the discussion of students with learning disabilities. Students with intellectual disabilities are most successful when they are not

●·●·● **TECHNOLOGY NOTES**
Technology to Accommodate Learning

Readily available technologies can help students with intellectual disabilities succeed both in school tasks and skills needed to achieve independence in jobs and their communities (Ayres, Mechling, & Sansosti, 2013). Here are examples:

- Cihak, Wright, McMahon, Smith, and Kraiss (2015) taught adolescents with mild to moderate intellectual disabilities to use three functional digital literacy skills, including (a) sending and receiving e-mail; (b) accessing, organizing, and saving information with social bookmarking from websites about careers; and (c) using cloud storage in order to retrieve, change, and upload documents. All the students learned the skills and reported valuing them. Given that nearly all adults use computers for both personal and employment purposes, the authors stressed the significance of providing these students such access.

- Yakubova and Bouck (2014) explored the use of scientific and graphing calculators with elementary students with mild intellectual disabilities for solving computational problems and word problems. The students were able to learn to use both types of calculators (although they had preferences for one over the other), and as a result of this learning they increased their accuracy in solving computational and word problems and decreased the amount of time it took them to do so.

- Smith, Ayres, Mechling, Alexander, Mataras, and Shepley (2015) used video prompting to teach three high school students with moderate intellectual disabilities office tasks that would help them to obtain jobs: (a) collating and stapling sets of papers; (b) organizing a binder; and (c) preparing letters for mailing. After students were introduced to one of the tasks, if they could not complete a step needed (e.g., putting a stamp on the envelope), they were shown a brief video of the necessary step. All students were able to learn the three tasks and generalize most of the steps to working with similar materials.

- Douglas, Ayres, and Langone (2015) found that shopping lists that included pictures, delivered to iPhones, increased students' effectiveness and efficiency in community grocery shopping. Further, some students learned the words on the list without explicit instruction.

●·●·●

expected to make judgments about what to do next; otherwise, they may struggle. For example, Anthony, the student you met at the beginning of the chapter, has learned how to move from class to class in his middle school. One day, however, his usual route was disrupted: A corridor was closed because of a broken water pipe. Although other students easily diverted to an alternative hallway, Anthony became confused and required assistance to find his way to his next class.

Motivation. Some students with intellectual disabilities share another characteristic with students with learning disabilities. They experience problems with motivation and learned helplessness—that is, the tendency to give up easily. For students with intellectual disabilities, however, learned helplessness may not be a result of frustration with the task at hand. It sometimes develops because professionals and classmates, in attempts to be helpful, are too eager to offer assistance. Some students soon learn that if they simply wait, someone will help out. Professionals are working to teach students with intellectual disabilities skills such as self-management so that they learn to begin and complete school tasks (e.g., Douglas, Ayres, & Langone, 2015; Wadsworth, Hansen, & Wills, 2015).

Language. As you might expect, many students with intellectual disabilities have delays in the development of language. For example, it may take longer for them to learn concepts such as *up/down* and *over/under*. These students also may struggle with words that are abstract in meaning and benefit when professionals can make those words more concrete. Here is an example: A middle school student with an intellectual disability was in a social studies class learning about democracy, a very abstract concept. By using discussions and examples, the student was able to learn what democracy means. When other students wrote essays on the subject, she compiled pictures and described them to her classmates.

For example, she held up a picture of a protest rally and explained that in a democracy people can say things that other people do not like and that the people saying the things cannot be put in jail for saying them. No one doubted that she grasped the essential meaning of democracy.

Academic Skills. Students with intellectual disabilities usually have to work harder and practice longer than other students in order to learn academic skills (Wei, Blackorby, & Schiller, 2011). They typically process information at a slower speed than other students. Because of these limitations, sometimes in the past assumptions were made about the so-called ceilings that these students would reach in learning. Now, however, professionals are balancing the realistic understanding that learning is difficult for these students with the conviction that they may learn more than anyone ever thought they could—if they are given the opportunity. For example, Allor, Gifford, Al Otaiba, Miller, and Cheatham (2013) found that students with intellectual disabilities who had not responded well to traditional reading instruction significantly improved their recognition of words and their skill for sounding out words. Another study (Dessemontet, Bless, & Morin, 2012) found that when students with intellectual disabilities are educated in general education classrooms with peers, they often make more progress in reading than similar students who are taught in separate special education classes.

Keep in mind that you may be expected to gather data related to students' cognitive and academic functioning and to monitor their progress in acquiring skills related to these domains. The Data-Driven Decisions feature describes strategies for gathering these data.

Social, Behavioral, and Emotional Characteristics

The social, behavioral, and emotional characteristics of students with intellectual disabilities can vary as much as those of students without disabilities. Stereotypes that assign specific characteristics to particular groups of children generally are not accurate unless a specific behavior is associated with a particular disorder, such as those you read about earlier in the chapter.

Social Characteristics

Many students with intellectual disabilities have difficulties in social relationships (Forts & Luckasson, 2011; Hughes et al., 2012), as does Shandra, the student you met at the beginning of this chapter. They tend to be less accepted by their peers and more likely to be rejected by them, although inclusive practices and specific interventions may help typical students to be more positive about their peers with disabilities (e.g., de Boer, Pijl, Minnaert, & Post, 2014), as can structured extracurricular activities (e.g., Eidelman, 2013). Several reasons can be offered for these difficulties in social relationships. First, many students with intellectual disabilities have immature behaviors that make other students want to avoid them. Second, their ways of dealing with social situations may be inappropriate (Shepherd, Hoban, & Dixon, 2014). For instance, a student with an intellectual disability may walk up to a group of students engaged in conversation and elbow his way in and speak too loudly; those students then may form a negative perception of him. Finally, students with intellectual disabilities may have difficulty picking up subtle social cues, and so they may misinterpret other students' actions.

Adaptive Behavior Characteristics

To be identified as having an intellectual disability, a student must display, in addition to limited intellectual ability, deficits in adaptive behavior. These are some of the skills that are included in the area of adaptive behavior:

- *Communication*—the ability to exchange thoughts, messages, or information with other people through speaking, sign language, or other means

DATA-DRIVEN DECISIONS

Tools for Data Collection

Teachers and other professionals increasingly are gathering student data on their phones and tablet devices. Here are several examples of apps you might find helpful, all inexpensive or free and most available on multiple operating systems (e.g., IOS, Android, Windows).

Google Sheets

A spreadsheet is one of the most versatile data collection tools teachers can find. Google Sheets, similar in many ways to Microsoft Office Excel, is free and can be used across settings. Some special educators create a separate sheet for each student on their caseload so that they can have all their data at their fingertips. Others create a separate spreadsheet for each student, or if they are co-teaching, they group students in each class. If your school participates in Google Classroom, you also have access to Google Sheets data collection templates.

Direct Assessment Tracking Application (D.A.T.A.)

This app enables you to measure how often and for how long events occur (e.g., for how long a student is off task; how many words the student reads correctly in 1 minute). You can track four different events simultaneously, count up or down, save data by student name, and gather data periodically by setting either a sound-based or vibrating timer. You also can add notes to the data sets you create, and you can e-mail your data from the device.

Teacher's Assistant Pro

This sophisticated app allows you to enter data for one, several, or all of your students, along with parent contact information, and this information can be imported to the device. Secondary teachers can enter students by class period. The app is a means to gather data on student actions and classroom achievements, and the data gathered can be transmitted to school administrators, parents, or yourself using e-mail, Dropbox, or text messaging. Photos can be included, and the data to be gathered can be completely customized. This app is especially helpful for tracking student behavior.

Super Duper Data Tracker

This app enables you to create multiple goals for all of your students and to monitor their progress in reaching those goals. Multiple types of responses are allowed (e.g., correct, incorrect, assisted response), and the app calculates the data (e.g., the student was able to identify the main idea in 48% of the examples). Notes can be added to the recorded data; data can be stored in the Cloud and e-mailed for individual students or a group of students; and the number of data sessions is unlimited.

- *Self-care*—the ability to tend to personal hygiene, eating, and other related tasks
- *Social skills*—the ability to interact appropriately with others
- *Home living*—the ability to manage the day-to-day tasks of living in an apartment or house
- *Leisure*—the ability to use free time productively
- *Health and safety*—the ability to take precautions and act in ways that do not endanger oneself or others
- *Self-direction*—the ability to make and implement decisions
- *Functional academics*—the reading, writing, math, and other skills needed for independence
- *Community use*—the ability to identify and access services and activities in the neighborhood or area
- *Work*—the ability to obtain and keep employment

In very young children, adaptive behavior may include learning to crawl and then walk and learning to speak. In elementary school, adaptive behavior includes taking turns, following directions, and moving safely around the school and its grounds. For middle and high school students, adaptive behavior includes going to the mall, dining out with friends, changing classes at school, and preparing for employment. Students with mild intellectual disabilities may experience

MyEdLab
Video Example 8.3

This video provides an overview of how to use Google Sheets data collection templates. (https://www.youtube.com/watch?v=BGl8eXiTWe4)

delays in a few areas of adaptive behavior. Students with more significant disabilities are likely to have difficulties in many of these domains.

Additional Behavior Characteristics

Some types of intellectual disabilities are related to specific behaviors. Prader-Willi syndrome, introduced earlier in this chapter and characterized by compulsive eating, is one example. However, many students with intellectual disabilities do not display extraordinary behaviors. Rather, they need rewards and consequences much like those needed by other students, perhaps with a greater emphasis on the use of tangible rewards (e.g., stickers, small prizes) used in a very systematic way. A few students may have self-injurious behaviors such as pulling their hair out or picking at their skin. When such behaviors are present, the services of a behavior specialist will likely be needed to design interventions to reduce or eliminate the behaviors.

Emotional Characteristics

A relatively new topic being explored in relation to school-age students with intellectual disabilities is these students' mental health (Kok, van der Waa, Klip, & Staal, 2016). Researchers have found that students with intellectual disabilities experience more loneliness than do students without disabilities (Sharabi, 2015), and these feelings may persist into adulthood (Gilmore & Cuskelly, 2014). Clearly, valuing individuals with intellectual disabilities includes understanding that they experience the same emotions as others and that they have mental health needs. The Professional Edge includes ideas on how professionals can foster friendships for these students.

Physical and Medical Characteristics

Most students with mild intellectual disabilities do not have any extraordinary medical conditions. However, some researchers have found them to be more likely than other students to be obese and not physically fit (Golubovic, Maksimovic, Golubovic, & Glumbic, 2012; Grondhuis & Aman, 2014).

PROFESSIONAL **EDGE**

Promoting Friendships

Teachers and other professionals play a pivotal role in fostering friendships between students with intellectual disabilities and their classmates (Rossetti, 2015). Using strategies such as these is beneficial for all students:

- Peer tutoring (addressed elsewhere in this chapter) and cooperative learning activities often promote friendship. Use the many resources available to teach students how to work together, and change groupings about once per month to ensure that all students have the chance to interact with one another.
- Deliberately create a classroom and school culture (no matter the setting) that values diversity and demands respect for each person. Posters and slogans contribute to this culture, but students should be directly taught to value each person as a unique individual.

- Seat students who may be isolated toward the front, and seat peers who tend to be supportive nearby.
- Make sure that you demonstrate respect as you interact with each student, genuinely welcoming all students, avoiding criticizing any student, and following all district guidelines and ethical practices concerning confidentiality.
- Use literature related to friendship as a teaching tool.
- Teach students the social skills they need to foster friendship.
- Arrange small-group interactions with you so that you can model social skills, provide practice for students, and facilitate students' interactions.
- Focus on the positive, providing rewards to students for respectful interactions with each other. However, you should also directly address instances of disrespectful interactions, probably enlisting parents to address the problem.

As a student's cognitive impairments become more pronounced, the likelihood of having serious physical problems and medical conditions needing intervention increases. Examples were provided earlier in the descriptions of specific causes of intellectual disabilities: For example, children with Down syndrome likely will have vision or hearing loss or heart problems requiring surgery. For educators, knowing about students' health and medical needs is important for several reasons. First, if a student's medical condition is fragile or changing, educators need to know whether an emergency might occur and how to respond. Second, if a student should be wearing glasses or using a hearing aid or another medical device, educators need to be prepared to monitor this. Finally, some students may miss significant amounts of school because of surgery or illness; in these cases, professionals are responsible for working with parents to minimize the impact on student learning.

MyEdLab **Self-Check 8.2**

MyEdLab **Application Exercise 8.4:** Who Is Star?

MyEdLab **Application Exercise 8.5:** Mini Case Study

Identifying Intellectual Disabilities

For students with intellectual disabilities to receive special education services, they must go through the formal process of identification. For some students, this will have occurred when they were very young, even infants, using assessment methods designed just for that age group. Other students are identified when they enter kindergarten and cannot manage the academic, social, and other expectations of the school setting, and yet others are identified sometime during the elementary school years.

Assessment

For students who may have intellectual disabilities, assessment focuses on intellectual functioning and adaptive skills, as stressed in the definitions presented earlier. However, medical and other information also is assessed as appropriate.

Assessment of Intellectual Functioning

You already have learned that one common test used to assess intellectual functioning in students being considered for special education services is the *Wechsler Intelligence Scale for Children* (WISC–V) (Wechsler, 2014). Another test sometimes used is the *Stanford–Binet Intelligence Scales* (5th ed.) (Roid, 2003). These tests tend to measure a student's overall abilities and predict school achievement. They are individually administered only by professionals who have been specially trained to do so.

You should keep in mind that no single test can measure all aspects of intelligence. Moreover, intelligence tests tend to ignore what some people consider key components of intelligence, such as creativity and humor. Most professionals also acknowledge that no single, universally accepted definition of *intelligence* exists. And so, although intelligence tests and the scores they produce are integral to the procedures of special education, they should be treated as valuable information, not as a prescription of a student's abilities and limitations.

Assessment of Adaptive Behavior

The assessment of adaptive behavior is completed through interviews or surveys with parents, teachers, and others and with direct observation of the student. The goal is to obtain an accurate description of how well the student is functioning across school, home, and community settings.

One assessment instrument used for determining adaptive functioning is the *AAIDD Diagnostic Adaptive Behavior Scale* (DABS) (Tassé et al., 2014). This instrument, developed for children and youth ages 4 to 21, is designed to assess a wide range of adaptive skills. Using a semistructured interview format, a professional who has been trained to administer it asks a person who knows the target student well the questions it contains (Tassé, Schalock, Balboni, Spreat, & Navas, 2016). The scale measures conceptual skills such as the ability to read essential information and to understand numbers and time. It also assesses social skills such as the ability to follow directions and rules and an individual's level of gullibility, as well as practical skills such as self-care and ability to access public transportation and appropriately use a phone.

Another measure of adaptive behavior is the *Vineland Adaptive Behavior Scales* (3rd ed.) (Sparrow, Cicchetti, & Saulnier, 2016). This instrument is based on interviewing, and it must be administered by a psychologist, social worker, or other appropriately trained professional. Other forms can be completed by parents/caregivers or teachers. The scales address communication, daily living, socialization, and motor skills across the student's life span, and they include an assessment of motor skills for children younger than 6 years old and an optional behavior assessment for children older than 5. On these and other adaptive behavior instruments, a student's current level of functioning is compared to that of typical children. The score provides an estimate of whether the student is functioning at the expected level, above the expected level, or below it.

Assessment of Medical Factors

For students with medical considerations, school team members may seek input from appropriate medical professionals concerning medications being taken, health risks for or limitations needed on physical activities, chronic conditions that school professionals should be aware of, and anticipated medical procedures that may affect school attendance or performance. These factors may be found to be integral to students' disabilities and services they may need at school.

Eligibility

The decision to identify a student as having an intellectual disability must be based on the assessment information that has been gathered. The essential questions that are asked include the following:

1. *Does the student's intelligence, as measured on a formal individual assessment, fall at least 2 standard deviations below the mean? That is, is the student's measured IQ approximately 70 or below?* The federal definition of intellectual disability refers to significantly subaverage intellectual functioning, and the IQ scores mentioned earlier represent the operational definition of that term. However, as noted earlier, no cutoff score is considered absolute, and students with scores slightly above 70 might still be considered in this disability category.

2. *Does the student display deficits in adaptive behavior?* For this decision, team members review data from the adaptive behavior scales used in the assessment as well as observational data and anecdotal information offered by teachers, parents, and others. In many ways, answering this question relies on making a judgment call. Although the scales provide scores that indicate a student's functioning level in the adaptive domain, the team must consider the school and home context and the student's overall success in each. If clear and persistent deficits are noted, the decision is straightforward. However, for some students whose skills are marginal, discussion might be needed about the scores obtained versus observed student functioning. As with intelligence measures, a test score is considered a guideline.

3. *Do the student's characteristics adversely affect educational performance?* Federal special education law is premised on the adverse effect of disabilities on student learning and behavior, and so the team must consider this question as well as the others.

If the multidisciplinary team finds that the student meets the criteria to be identified as having an intellectual disability and will benefit by receiving special education, the remaining special education procedures are followed, and an individualized education program (IEP) is prepared so that the student receives an appropriate education. Some of the options for that education are outlined in the following section.

MyEdLab **Self-Check 8.3**

MyEdLab **Application Exercise 8.6:** Tory's Psychoeducational Report

---

Did You Know?

Special Olympics (http://www.specialolympics.org/), founded by Eunice Kennedy Shriver, is a global organization with programs in 220 countries. Its goal is to foster inclusiveness for individuals with intellectual disabilities through the world of sports, giving them the opportunity to focus on their abilities. Many school districts participate in Special Olympics.

How Learners with Intellectual Disabilities Receive Their Education

Students with intellectual disabilities access the same sets of services in the same settings as other students with disabilities. However, because of the nature of their special needs and the importance of both early intervention and transition from school to adult life activities, their education often includes some specialized options.

Early Childhood

Young children who have clearly recognizable disorders that include an intellectual disability sometimes are identified as needing special services shortly after birth, and these babies may begin their education during the first few months of life. For these very young children, services often are based in the home and have an emphasis on helping family members learn how best to teach their children (Pretis, 2011). Both parents and early childhood professionals view this type of service as highly valuable in fostering children's development and learning and increasing parent confidence in working with their young children (Totsika, Hastings, Vagenas, & Emerson, 2014). This type of early intervention usually includes an early interventionist who consults with the family, but it also can involve a physical therapist, speech-language pathologist, and other specialists (e.g., Fey, Yoder, Warren, & Bredin-Oja, 2013; Guralnick, 2007). Services for these infants and toddlers may include medical and health professionals as well.

These young children move into preschool programs at age 3, where they may be joined by children who recently have been identified as having developmental delays or other disabilities. Preschool programs have been demonstrated to have strongly positive effects on the language skills, motor development, and preacademic skill development of children with intellectual disabilities (e.g., Guralnick, 2016). Both professionals and families strongly support such programs, and attention on them increasingly focuses on parent participation and inclusive education.

Elementary and Secondary School Services

Students with intellectual disabilities in elementary, middle, and high school are entitled to receive their education in the least restrictive environment just like other students with disabilities. However, if you review the information included

FIGURE 8.3   Educational Placements for Students Ages 6 to 21 Who Have Intellectual Disabilities (in percentages)

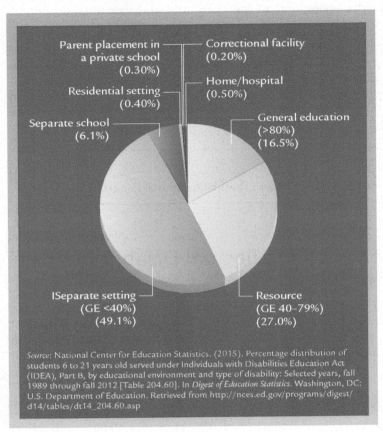

Parent placement in a private school (0.30%)

Correctional facility (0.20%)

Residential setting (0.40%)

Home/hospital (0.50%)

Separate school (6.1%)

General education (>80%) (16.5%)

ISeparate setting (GE <40%) (49.1%)

Resource (GE 40–79%) (27.0%)

Source: National Center for Education Statistics. (2015). Percentage distribution of students 6 to 21 years old served under Individuals with Disabilities Education Act (IDEA), Part B, by educational environment and type of disability: Selected years, fall 1989 through fall 2012 [Table 204.60]. In *Digest of Education Statistics.* Washington, DC: U.S. Department of Education. Retrieved from http://nces.ed.gov/programs/digest/d14/tables/dt14_204.60.asp

in Figure 8.3, you can see that only a small proportion of students identified with this disability spend more than 80% of their time in general education classrooms. In fact, the most common setting for these students is a special education classroom for more than 60% of the day.

When students with intellectual disabilities are in general education classrooms with their peers, the extent to which they participate in exactly the same activities and the amount of support they need depends on the student's level of functioning. In one first-grade classroom, Jasmine—who has a moderate intellectual disability—was participating in a review of consonant blends. The chart being used contained nearly two dozen blends, but when it was Jasmine's turn to pronounce a blend and include it in a word, she always was given the blend *fr*, which happened to be at the beginning of her family name, *Franklin*. No special accommodations were needed.

Some students need alternative activities based on the general education curriculum. For example, the students in a sixth-grade social studies class were studying cultures, and they had reached the study of ancient Egypt. As part of the unit, students were given the assignment of creating a magazine that ancient Egyptians would have wanted to read. Some students applied their new knowledge to produce magazines that contained references to Egyptian recreation, politics, and religion. Chase, a student with a moderate intellectual disability, created a picture magazine that incorporated artifacts from ancient Egypt for which he would see references in the normal course of life, including pharaohs and pyramids.

Other students with intellectual disabilities are supported in general education settings through the use of paraprofessionals (Giangreco, 2010; Stockall, 2014), but many students spend at least part of the day receiving specialized academic instruction in a special education setting. For example, in Ms. DeCuir's classroom of middle school students who take an alternate assessment, the goal of the math program, which is aligned to the standards all students must reach but is adjusted to be appropriate for these students, is to assist students to learn the skills they will need in order to shop, order in a restaurant, and possibly work in a fast-food restaurant. For some students, the concept of a budget and saving money also is a priority. This is part of a **life skills curriculum**, a plan for students' education that stresses skills they need throughout life. In several lessons, the middle school students review coins and paper currency using real coins and facsimiles of bills, and they practice at their own skill levels how to make change—an **applied academic skill**. On Friday, Ms. DeCuir plans to take the students to the Dollar Store so that they can make small purchases and put their skills into action. The outing will conclude with a stop at a fast-food restaurant where students will practice ordering food items based on how much money they have. The outing is part of **community-based instruction (CBI)**—that is, experience in applying skills learned in the classroom within the larger context of the community in which the students live. Notice how such activities also can build students' adaptive functioning, which is likely to result in increased independence as they move toward adulthood.

High school students are more likely than younger students to be educated primarily in special education settings, although in some communities inclusion is emphasized (Carter, Moss, Hoffman, Chung, & Sisco, 2011). Andrew, a student with a mild intellectual disability, exemplifies a blended approach to education. As a junior, he decided to take introductory Spanish. Although you might find his decision surprising, there is a reason. He lives in a community with many Spanish-speaking residents and wants to know about their language. No Spanish instruction was available in a special education class. With a strongly supportive Spanish teacher, Andrew learned basic Spanish. However, Andrew's English and math classes were taught by special education teachers. Three afternoons each week Andrew went to a local nursing home with his **job coach**, Ms. Hickman. There he learned how to change bed linens, check that supplies such as tissues and towels were available in each room, and assist residents with tasks such as eating. Ms. Hickman's role was to analyze the skills that Andrew needed, help him learn them, and ensure that he could carry out his responsibilities independently. Andrew hopes to enroll in a nurse's assistant program after leaving high school.

A few students with intellectual disabilities attend separate schools or live in residential facilities that include academic programs. Usually, these are students who have complex medical needs requiring the on-call availability of nursing or medical staff, or they are students who have very serious behavior problems in addition to intellectual disabilities. In some regions of the United States, separate schools for students with moderate intellectual disabilities that were built around the time the first federal special education law was passed are still in place. They are becoming less and less common, though, as access to the general education curriculum and emphasis on an academically and socially integrated education have become priorities.

When students with intellectual disabilities receive an appropriate education, most are able to live productive lives and hold full-time or part-time employment.

Inclusive Practices

Despite the fact that the parents of children with intellectual disabilities were leaders in the educational movement that greatly increased inclusive practices, the preceding discussion indicates that this goal has been only partially achieved. Why are so many students with intellectual disabilities still separated for instruction?

The answer to this question is complex. One factor affecting the education of these students is traditional thinking. Many educators still believe that the best instructional arrangement for these students, particularly as they move from elementary to middle and high school, is a special education classroom. Many high school special education teachers for students with mild to moderate intellectual disabilities have asked, "Why would I support putting my students into classrooms where they don't know what is being taught and can't keep up with the pace? They need the practical skills that I give them." Their concern for their students is understandable, and their advocacy for their education is important, especially given the current climate of accountability and the resulting pressure on secondary teachers to ensure that students are successful on high-stakes tests.

However, the belief that only special educators can give the students what they need and that the general curriculum is irrelevant for these students is troublesome; alternative ways of thinking can be found. For example, Clarke, Haydon, Bauer, and Epperly (2016) reported teaching five students with intellectual disabilities how to use response cards as a way of increasing their participation in general education science and social studies classes, and the intervention improved student performance and increased their on-task behavior. Another example comes from high schools that implement a peer-buddy program in which students without disabilities receive an elective credit to assist students with intellectual and other disabilities in their general education classes (Hughes & Carter, 2008). This highly successful arrangement has many benefits: Students with intellectual disabilities receive the support they need to succeed in general education classes, general education teachers are satisfied that the problem of not being able to get to all the students who need assistance is being addressed, and the peer-buddies are exploring career options related to special education. In other high schools, too, students with intellectual disabilities participate in general education academics and electives while receiving the supports they need (Yu, Newman, & Wagner, 2009), sometimes through the use of paraprofessionals and sometimes through co-teaching.

As academic standards continue to rise and pressure grows for educators to increase instructional rigor, more and more questions are being raised about appropriate educational options for students with intellectual disabilities, and some of the factors prompting these questions are reviewed in the section on issues later in this chapter. Few educators would argue about the need for a continuum of services for students with intellectual disabilities, but how decisions are made regarding where students are educated and how often and why those decisions are revisited have not been adequately addressed. Further, no one would argue about a continuing priority to carefully coordinate all the various special education, related, and community services these students require in order to create flexible models that address students' needs while providing them access to the general curriculum and extracurricular activities, and all the academic, emotional, behavioral, and social benefits resulting from that access.

Transition and Adulthood

As students with intellectual disabilities reach adolescence, emphasis usually shifts to helping them make a successful transition from school to adulthood.

Video Example
from
YouTube

MyEdLab
Video Example 8.4
The points about inclusive practices made in this section are clearly demonstrated in the young woman's straightforward advice to teachers about teaching students like her in this video. (https://www.youtube.com/watch?v=YOwDfnoek6E)

Some students will leave school at about age 18 with their peers. Others are entitled to receive services through age 21. For students with mild intellectual disabilities, transition may emphasize learning tasks that foster independence, including planning and using a household budget; searching for and finding employment; using resource tools such as electronic planners, apps to facilitate daily living, and Internet sources; and developing hobbies and recreational skills. For students with more significant intellectual disabilities, the same types of preparation may be emphasized but on a somewhat more limited basis. Instead of budgeting, for example, math activities may focus on making wise choices about using spending money. The vehicle through which this type of planning occurs is the transition plan that is required by federal special education law, and it is a collaborative effort on the part of parents, the student, and professionals (Landmark, Ju, & Zhang, 2010; Prince, Katsiyannis, & Farmer, 2013). The importance of transition planning for these students, including postsecondary opportunities and self-determination, introduced in Chapter 5 concerning students with learning disabilities, is addressed in detail in the final section of this chapter as an important trend for the field.

Remember that some students with intellectual disabilities will never again be identified as such once they leave school. They will blend into their communities, get by with assistance from family and friends, and lead happy and productive lives. Other students will need structured support throughout their lives. They may work in entry-level jobs in businesses (e.g., copy assistant in an office, assembly-line worker) or schools (e.g., housekeeping staff), or they may work in a specialized setting (e.g., a business that employs people with disabilities to assemble materials for other businesses). Many will live independently, but some will live with family or with other individuals with disabilities, with assistance provided. Most importantly, the plans these students and their families have for their futures should guide the types of transition services they receive (Kaehne & Beyer, 2014). How might you apply these ideas in thinking about transition for Ernest, the high school student you met at the beginning of this chapter?

MyEdLab **Self-Check 8.4**

MyEdLab **Application Exercise 8.7:** Life Skills and Applied Academics

MyEdLab **Application Exercise 8.8:** An Inclusive Preschool for Carlyn

---

Recommended Educational Practices for Students with Intellectual Disabilities

A number of instructional strategies that are effective for teaching students with intellectual disabilities already have been introduced in this chapter. Strategies such as planning for generalization and making abstract concepts more concrete are essential to these students' education. Likewise, some students need a life skills curriculum and functional academics. Others need to participate in the general education curriculum. All of these options illustrate the diversity of recommended instructional practices. Also important are strategies that have been introduced in other chapters—for example, direct instruction and behavior interventions such as clear rules, schoolwide behavior plans, and the use of contracts.

Here, the focus is on two additional strategies: task analysis and peer-mediated instruction. Both are important across elementary, middle, and high school settings and across special education and general education classrooms.

Task Analysis

In earlier chapters, you explored the concepts of universal design for learning (UDL) and differentiation. These concepts also can be applied to teaching students with intellectual disabilities. For example, you have learned that students with intellectual disabilities experience difficulty with metacognition. To succeed, they often need to have their assignments and activities clearly outlined and presented to them so that they do not have to make judgments about what to do next or whether other options should be considered. The instructional strategy for ensuring this type of very systematic learning—and one that enables you to make appropriate decisions about planning instruction—is called task analysis. Think about how complex most school tasks are. Working on the computer involves turning it on, finding and loading the correct program, launching that program, following directions to complete the work, saving it, printing it, exiting the program, and shutting down the computer. You may complete such a task with ease, but for many students with intellectual disabilities, such a task is daunting. In task analysis, the professional's responsibility is to break into small steps any task or activity—from following classroom rules to using musical instruments to completing a writing assignment—and then teach those steps to students. By guiding students such as Ernest, whom you met at the beginning of the chapter, to learn each small step of the process and then put the steps together, teachers can help these students master more and more complex tasks. The Instruction in Action feature outlines the steps for using task analysis and includes examples of its application.

INSTRUCTION IN **ACTION**

Using Task Analysis

Task analysis often is helpful in teaching academic, vocational, and social skills to students with intellectual disabilities. You teach each small step to the student, and then help the student to put the steps together, which is sometimes called *chaining* them.

- Chaining can be forward—you help the student to do the first step, then you do the rest; then you help the student to do the first two steps, and you do the rest; and so on.
- Chaining also can be backward—you complete all the steps except the last one, and the student does only that step; then you complete all the steps except the last two, and the student does those two steps; and so on.

Whether you choose forward or backward chaining to teach skills to students depends on the students' abilities and the type of task. For example, teaching classroom routines might be best taught using forward chaining. Teaching students to put the proper heading on their papers might best be accomplished through backward chaining.

The following examples illustrate the use of task analysis for two life skills, one for younger students and one for older students: tying shoes and getting ready for a foods class. Would you choose forward chaining or backward chaining for each?

Tying Shoes

1. Pinch the laces.
2. Pull the laces.
3. Hang the ends of the laces from the corresponding sides of the shoe.
4. Pick up the laces in the corresponding hands.
5. Lift the laces above the shoe.
6. Cross the right lace over the left one to form a tepee.
7. Bring the left lace toward you.
8. Pull the left lace through the tepee.
9. Pull the laces away from one another.
10. Bend the left lace to form a loop.
11. Pinch the loop with the left hand.
12. Bring the right lace over the fingers and around the loop.
13. Push the right lace through the hole.
14. Pull the loops away from one another.

Getting Ready for Foods Class

1. Put on your hair net.
2. Gather your books and items together.
3. Take those materials to the shelves in the back of the room.
4. Place your materials in the assigned section.
5. Go to the closet and select an apron.
6. Put on the apron.
7. Go to your desk and wait quietly for the instructor to start class.

Source: Courtesy of www.BehaviorAdvisor.com

Once task analysis has been completed, students with intellectual disabilities may need to practice the component steps for a task more than other students do. For academic work, a computer with drill-and-practice software (e.g., for math facts or for consonant sounds) will make the amount of practice available almost limitless. For activities such as following classroom routines or moving around the school, parents or family members, peers, paraprofessionals, or volunteers might be able to assist.

Peer-Mediated Instruction

Another way of making learning accessible to all students is to use *peer-mediated instruction*, in which peers teach peers. Doing so can involve cooperative-learning strategies that bring together student groups of three, four, or even more students (Jimenez, Browder, Spooner, & Dibiase, 2012). Another peer-mediated instructional approach is peer tutoring (Harris & Meltzer, 2015). Peer tutoring is an approach to instruction in which students are partnered, provided with instructional materials that they are to learn, and expected to help each other in accomplishing the learning goal.

There are several types of peer tutoring. One approach pairs older students who are struggling to learn with younger students. Another approach partners high-achieving students with struggling learners in their classrooms. An alternative approach is called *classwide peer tutoring (CWPT)*, and it assumes that peer tutoring should be reciprocal—that all participating students should have opportunities to be both the teacher and the learner (Maheady & Gard, 2010). Students with intellectual disabilities can successfully participate in these programs, which enhance their learning. Further, students without disabilities develop more positive views of their peers with special needs when peer tutoring is carefully implemented. You can learn the fundamentals of developing a peer-tutoring program in the Instruction in Action feature.

INSTRUCTION IN **ACTION**

Peer Tutoring

For students with intellectual disabilities, peer tutoring can be a means of facilitating inclusion, improving academic achievement, fostering positive relationships with classmates, and encouraging positive student behavior (Van Norman, 2007). These are the steps involved in setting up a peer-tutoring program (Fulk & King, 2001):

1. Explain the purpose of peer tutoring to students, and give a rationale for using it. Stress the idea of increased opportunities for practice and on-task behavior.
2. Stress collaboration and cooperation rather than competition.
3. Select the content and instructional materials for tutoring sessions.
4. Train students in the roles of tutor and tutee. Students need to learn specific procedures for
   - feedback for correct responses (for example, teach students to say, "That's correct. Good answer!").
   - error correction (for example, teach students to say, "That's not correct; the correct answer is. . . . I'll ask the question again. . . .").
   - score keeping (for example, have students use tally marks on a scorecard for correct answers).
5. Model appropriate behaviors for tutor and tutee. Demonstrate acceptable ways to give and accept corrective feedback.
6. Provide sample scripts for students to practice roles. Divide the class into practice pairs and teams.
7. Let pairs practice roles of tutor and tutee as you circulate, providing feedback and reinforcement of appropriate tutor and tutee behavior.
8. Conduct a follow-up discussion with the students regarding tutor and tutee behavior. Answer any student questions.
9. Repeat Steps 7 and 8, with students switching roles.

Once students know both the tutor and tutee roles, you can assign partners that may be kept for several weeks. Generally, peer tutoring is most effective with information that has clear correct or incorrect answers, particularly for younger students, and so you should select materials carefully for tutoring.

Source: Fulk, B. M., & King, K. (2001). Classwide peer tutoring at work. *Teaching Exceptional Children, 34*(2), 49–53. Copyright © 2001 by the Council for Exceptional Children. Reproduced with permission of Council for Exceptional Children via Copyright Clearance Center.

MyEdLab **Self-Check 8.5**

MyEdLab **Application Exercise 8.9:** Peer Tutoring

MyEdLab **Application Exercise 8.10:** Task Analysis

Perspectives of Parents and Families

Some parents of students with intellectual disabilities—parents whose children have disorders that can be identified medically—may learn about their children's likely needs even before they are born. Other parents—often those whose children have mild intellectual disabilities that are not the result of a specific cause—may suspect that their children are not keeping up developmentally with other youngsters, but they may not hear the phrase *intellectual disability* until their children begin school or even several years into school. No matter when parents and family members learn about their children's disabilities, the role of professionals is to foster collaboration by engaging parents as partners in planning for the children's education.

Most families of children with intellectual disabilities think of them in terms of their positive and not-so-positive traits and contributions, not as a disability label applied at school.

Parents' Reactions to Having a Child with an Intellectual Disability

Many authors have written about parents' responses to having a child with an intellectual disability. Some authors claim that parents may experience any or all of the classic stages of grief: denial, blame, fear, guilt, mourning, withdrawal, rejection, and acceptance (e.g., Prout & Prout, 2000). Others dismiss this set of responses as too simplistic to accurately capture the tremendous diversity of parent reactions and the factors that may influence reactions (e.g., International Association for the Scientific Study of Intellectual and Developmental Disabilities, Families Special Interest Research Group, 2014). For example, the amount of support offered by grandparents can affect parents' ability to respond to their children with intellectual disabilities (Mitchell, 2008). In cases in which grandparents can provide emotional support, assume some child care responsibilities, and help in day-to-day activities such as getting to medical appointments, the family benefits greatly.

Two additional examples of factors that affect parents' reactions to their children with intellectual disabilities are religious participation and culture (Blanks & Smith, 2009). Ault, Collins, and Carter (2013) surveyed parents about their religious participation and that of their children with disabilities. They found that these parents highly valued their faith and that both they and their children participated in congregational activities. The parents did report a need for even more support, although they appreciated a welcoming attitude among members of their faith community.

Cultural mores make the differences among families even clearer. Although Western culture views disability as a chronic physical phenomenon that needs fixing, some other cultures view disability as a spiritual phenomenon that is time limited and worthy of acceptance (Ly, 2008). In families that hold the latter set of

FIRSTHAND ACCOUNT

WELCOME TO HOLLAND

EMILY PERL KINGSLEY *is the mother of now-adult son, Jason, who has Down syndrome. She is an Emmy Award–winning writer for the children's program Sesame Street as well as the author of more than 20 children's books. She speaks frequently about her experiences as the mother of a child with a moderate intellectual disability. Her essay captures the feelings of many parents.*

I am often asked to describe the experience of raising a child with a disability—to try to help people who have not shared that unique experience to understand it, to imagine how it would feel. It's like this . . .

When you're going to have a baby, it's like planning a fabulous vacation trip—to Italy. You buy a bunch of guide books and make your wonderful plans. The Coliseum. The Michelangelo. David. The gondolas in Venice. You may learn some handy phrases in Italian. It's all very exciting.

After months of eager anticipation, the day finally arrives. You pack your bags and off you go. Several hours later, the plane lands. The stewardess comes in and says, "Welcome to Holland."

"Holland?!?" you say. "What do you mean Holland? I signed up for Italy! I'm supposed to be in Italy. All my life I've dreamed of going to Italy."

But there's been a change in the flight plan. They've landed in Holland and there you must stay.

The important thing is that they haven't taken you to a horrible, disgusting, filthy place, full of pestilence, famine, and disease. It's just a different place.

So you must go out and buy new guide books. And you must learn a whole new language. And you will meet a whole new group of people you would never have met.

It's just a different place. It's slower paced than Italy, less flashy than Italy. But after you've been there for a while and you catch your breath, you look around . . . and you begin to notice that Holland has windmills . . . and Holland has tulips. Holland even has Rembrandts.

But everyone you know is busy coming and going from Italy . . . and they're all bragging about what a wonderful time they had there. And for the rest of your life, you will say "Yes, that's where I was supposed to go. That's what I had planned."

And the pain of that will never, ever, ever, ever go away . . . because the loss of that dream is a very, very significant loss.

But . . . if you spend your life mourning the fact that you didn't get to Italy, you may never be free to enjoy the very special, the very lovely things . . . about Holland.

beliefs, discussions of adjustment may not even be appropriate. More important may be the issue of professionals' acceptance and responsiveness to the family's perspective (Johnson & McIntosh, 2009).

Ultimately, each family's reaction to having a child with an intellectual disability is unique, affected by many factors. The Firsthand Account poignantly illustrates this point.

Parent's Concerns

Although nearly all parents want their children with intellectual disabilities to have a normal life, the meaning of *normal* differs for families based on several factors (Cramm & Nieboer, 2012). One important consideration is the extent of the child's intellectual impairment. Children with mild impairments may be similar enough to their siblings that parents adjust their expectations but do not have extraordinary concerns. However, parents may have many questions about their children with moderate intellectual disabilities. Another factor affecting parents' concerns is age: Parents of young and school-age children are likely to worry about developmental and medical issues as well as behavior problems and their own ability to provide for their children's needs (Dempsey, Keen, Pennell, O'Reilly, & Neilands, 2009). Parents of adolescents express concern about those problems, too, but they also begin thinking about what their child will do and how their child will live after graduation. As the parents of children

9 Students with Speech and Language Disorders

Learning Outcomes

LO9.1 Outline the development of the speech and language disorders field, define speech and language disorders, and explain their prevalence and causes.

LO9.2 Describe characteristics of individuals with speech and language disorders.

LO9.3 Explain how speech and language disorders are identified.

LO9.4 Outline how learners with speech and language disorders receive their education.

LO9.5 Describe recommended educational practices for students with speech and language disorders.

LO9.6 Explain the perspectives and concerns that parents and families of students with speech and language disorders may have.

LO9.7 Identify trends and issues influencing the field of speech and language disorders.

JONAS

Jonas is in first grade. Looking at him, Jonas appears to be an average 6-year-old, full of energy, interested in everything, and rapidly learning. However, when Jonas speaks to his teacher or classmates, frustration followed by anger too often is the result. Jonas has received speech-language therapy since the age of 3 when his pediatrician finally agreed with his parents that his speech and language development problems were not about being a "late talker," and he was diagnosed as having developmental apraxia of speech, a disorder in which the pathway between the brain and the muscles of the mouth that are needed to produce clear speech is damaged. He receives special education services for his communication disorder. Jonas is eager to communicate, but his words are difficult to understand, and he often cannot produce sentences of more than a few words. For example, instead of saying "go together," he says "go-etter." When he is excited or anxious, his speech problems are more apparent, and the frustration and anger are the result of not being able to make himself understood. During preschool, Jonas received speech-language therapy three times each week; he now receives it twice each week, with his teacher and parents helping him practice at other times. A new concern also is emerging, which may possibly be related to Jonas's challenges in producing subtle but distinct sounds of language: He is also experiencing significant difficulty in reading.

SAVANNAH

Right before the beginning of fifth grade, Savannah was in a serious car accident that caused a traumatic brain injury as well as significant physical injuries. For that entire school year, Savannah received special education either at the hospital, at the rehabilitation center, or at her home. Savannah's physical injuries have long since healed, and outwardly she appears similar to her peers, but she still has significant cognitive and communication problems. For example, Savannah still encounters difficulty understanding the complex

directions that she now is expected to follow in middle school. Her special education teacher even referred her to the nurse to check for a possible hearing loss, since Savannah sometimes seemed not to recognize when she was spoken to. However, Savannah's neurologist clarified that this was actually a symptom of her receptive language problems. In casual and comfortable social situations, Savannah functions without a problem, but when under pressure to participate in class or during stressful academic activities, she is unlikely to be able to find the correct words. Savannah is receiving special education in language arts, and she works twice weekly with a speech-language therapist. Her teachers and parents know that Savannah's recovery is likely to take far longer than anyone had anticipated.

DAVID

David is an 11th-grade student at Walt Whitman High School. He is enrolled in a program with a vocational emphasis, learning important skills for getting and keeping a job when he leaves school at age 22. He spends part of the day in special education classes, part of the day in general education classes such as physical education, and part of the day in a vocational school, where he is learning skills to work as a data entry specialist. David has received speech-language services since he was a toddler, but the types of services have changed over time. When he was young, his speech-language therapist emphasized proper use of his lips and tongue to accurately produce sounds. Gradually, emphasis shifted to language skills such as vocabulary development. As he enters this final part of his schooling, the focus now is on assisting David to initiate conversations and ask questions and to understand idioms that he may encounter in the workplace (e.g., "That was a piece of cake." "Let's get this up and running."). Another priority is making sure that David appropriately makes eye contact with teachers, work supervisors, and peers. David's speech-language therapist consults with the professionals who are working with David so that they also emphasize these skills.

At some point in your life, you may have experienced a speech or language problem. Perhaps your parents have a recording of your preschool rendition of a favorite song in which you say "wabbit" for "rabbit" or "tate" for "cake." Everyone who hears the recording now chuckles at the mispronunciations that you have long since outgrown. More recently, you may have encountered a momentary problem in recalling a particular word you wished to write on your exam answer, probably because of fatigue or stress. You knew you knew the word, but you simply could not bring it to mind when you needed it.

These speech and language challenges that many individuals have faced are brief episodes—unsettling but temporary. As such, they provide no more than a glimpse of what it is really like to have a speech or language disorder. Imagine sitting in an elementary classroom and not being able to pronounce common words. Imagine being in high school and having difficulty grasping verbal directions and expressing your thoughts aloud. What might be the impact of these chronic problems on academic achievement? On interactions with peers and adults? On behavior? These are some of the topics considered in this chapter.

Understanding Speech and Language Disorders

Today's practices in the field of speech and language disorders are based on work that began nearly two centuries ago. This discipline has been influenced by research in medicine, psychology, and education, and it has progressed from simple approaches to complex understandings.

Development of the Study of Speech and Language Disorders

As you can see in the time line in Figure 9.1, some of the earliest work related to speech and language disorders was undertaken in Europe at the beginning of the 19th century on behalf of individuals who were deaf (Duchan, 2010). In the United States, the first textbook on speech disorders was published in 1802 by S. C. L. Potter. The rest of the 19th century was characterized by the use of unproven treatments—for example, improving speech by placing rolls of linen under the tongue.

Emergence of a Profession

Although much early work was completed by medical specialists, by the beginning of the 20th century it was clear that a new group of professionals called *speech clinicians* was emerging to address speech and language disorders. Most

FIGURE 9.1   Time Line of the Development of the Field of Speech and Language Disorders

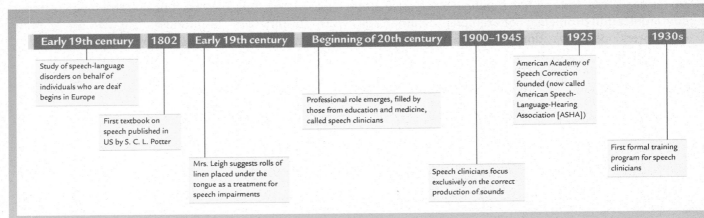

of the interventions these professionals provided for children with speech or language disorders took place in public schools (Duchan, 2011). However, the emphasis on speech-language therapy gradually shifted from exclusive attention to the correct production of speech sounds to the broader domain of children's overall ability to use language in order to communicate.

Contemporary Practices

Strongly influenced by the passage of federal special education law in 1975, the profession of speech-language therapy has continued to evolve. For example, in the past two decades, conceptualizations of speech and language disorders have expanded yet again to stress the role of communication. That is, professionals now acknowledge that not only is it important to recognize whether students can produce complete sentences using the correct tense, but it is also essential to think about what students are trying to express and to whom. This most recent thinking—including the communication context—is particularly significant for addressing the needs of students with disabilities.

Definition of Speech and Language Disorders

The number of terms and concepts associated with the field of speech and language disorders reflects the wide range of conditions it encompasses. In this chapter, the term speech and language disorders is used to refer to all the disorders that can occur within this disability category. However, you also may come across the term communication disorders. It, too, is a global term for all the conditions that make up this disability, but it sometimes is used to include difficulties with communication that arise from hearing loss, whereas the other term sometimes excludes those individuals.

In IDEA, the term speech or language impairment is used, and it is defined as

> a communication disorder such as stuttering, impaired articulation, language impairment, or a voice impairment that adversely affects a child's educational performance (IDEA 20 U.S.C. §1401 [2004], 20 C.F.R. §300.8[c][11])

This definition is far less detailed than the definitions of most of the other disabilities covered by IDEA, but it is deceptively simple. Combining speech and language problems into a single definition allows considerable variation to exist among states in terms of which students receive services and how they receive those services. In all states, students whose primary disability is a language disorder are served within this category. However, because IDEA includes speech services both within this category and as a related service, states vary in their regulations. In some states, students can have individualized education programs (IEPs)

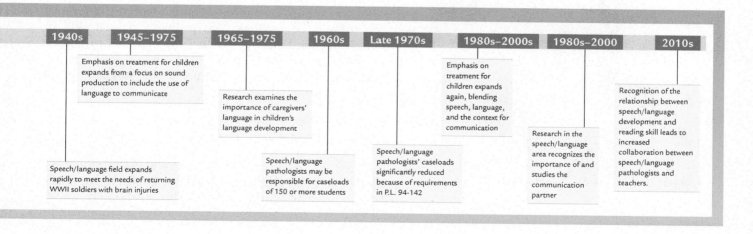

| 1940s | 1945–1975 | 1965–1975 | 1960s | Late 1970s | 1980s–2000s | 1980s–2000 | 2010s |

Emphasis on treatment for children expands from a focus on sound production to include the use of language to communicate

Research examines the importance of caregivers' language in children's language development

Emphasis on treatment for children expands again, blending speech, language, and the context for communication

Recognition of the relationship between speech/language development and reading skill leads to increased collaboration between speech/language pathologists and teachers.

Research in the speech/language area recognizes the importance of and studies the communication partner

Speech/language field expands rapidly to meet the needs of returning WWII soldiers with brain injuries

Speech/language pathologists may be responsible for caseloads of 150 or more students

Speech/language pathologists' caseloads significantly reduced because of requirements in P.L. 94-142 that are "speech only"; that is, the primary disability is considered the speech disorder, and special education services are offered for it even if those are the only services needed. In other states, students can only receive services for speech disorders as a related service—that is, only if the students have been identified as having other disabilities under IDEA. In those states, if speech therapy is the only special need, students are not eligible for special education.

Concepts to Describe Speech and Language Disorders

To appreciate the scope of special needs addressed in this disability category, more explanation is needed than is offered in the IDEA definition. A beginning point for exploring speech and language disorders is an overview of human communication.

Communication is the exchange of information and knowledge among participants (Zebron, Mhute, & Musingafi, 2015), and it is a basic and critical human need (Brady et al., 2016; Peets, 2009). Communication requires a *message* (the information or knowledge), a *sender* (the person who transmits the message), and a *receiver* (the person who applies meaning to the message). It also involves a *channel*, or a route through which the message travels. Finally, communication involves a sort of volleyball game, in which the sender and receiver send messages back and forth. For example, when a friend says to you "Are you ready to go?" while looking at his watch, standing in the doorway with his coat on, and fidgeting, the friend is the sender, you are the receiver, and the message concerns being late. The channel is both *verbal*—the words he spoke—and *nonverbal*—the glance at his watch and the posture of fidgeting while standing in the doorway. The back-and-forth of communication continues when you respond to your friend.

The first few years of life are the most critical for learning language.

Elements of Language

Language is the system of symbols, governed by complex rules, that individuals use for communication, and it is based on their culture (Newman, 2006). More than 6,900 languages are spoken throughout the world (Anderson, 2010), but not all languages rely on speaking. The clearest example of a nonspoken language is American Sign Language (ASL), the language used by some individuals who are deaf.

Language also must be thought of in terms of its application (Houwen, Visser, van der Putten, & Vlaskamp, 2016; Ryan, Gibbon, & O'Shea, 2016). Expressive language refers to the ability to produce language. Receptive language refers to the ability to comprehend language (Skwerer, Jordan, Brukilacchio, & Tager-Flusberg, 2015). If you have studied Spanish, Urdu, Mandarin, or any language that you did not speak as you were growing up, you are very familiar with the difference between these two concepts. You probably gained skill in comprehending the language when it was spoken to you or when you read it (receptive language) faster than you acquired the skills necessary to accurately speak the language or to write it (expressive language).

Language Disorders

When students have language disorders that cannot be explained by physical disabilities, intellectual disabilities, hearing loss, or other disabilities, they are referred to as having specific language impairments (SLIs) (Lukács, Ladányi, Fazekas, & Kemény, 2016; Mok, Pickles, Durkin, & Conti-Ramsden, 2014). For example, some students are not able to clearly distinguish among the words being spoken because they cannot discriminate among similar sounds. When a teacher, referring to a page in the social studies text, says "Let's look at the map," the student may focus her attention on the picture of a famous explorer (man) on the opposite page because she did not correctly hear the ending sound /p/. Some students make errors in forming words, perhaps saying "I getted three book at the library." Yet others experience challenges in forming sentences, saying "I overslept because I was late" instead of "I was late because I overslept." Some students have difficulty finding correct words or understanding the nuances of language (e.g., not understanding the expression *It's raining cats and dogs* or *You're trying to butter me up*), a problem being addressed with David, the high school student you met at the beginning of the chapter. Finally, some students experience difficulty participating in the social aspect of communication (Clarke et al., 2012; Norbury, 2014). They might monopolize a conversation, unaware that others would like to speak as well. Or they might start talking about a topic unrelated to the one currently being discussed, causing peers or adults to look at them questioningly.

The Professional Edge includes many additional examples of student behavior that might signal the presence of language disorders. As you look at the

Video Example
from
YouTube

MyEdLab
Video Example 9.1
This video, of a girl trying to explain a story she has read, illustrates both receptive and expressive language problems. What examples do you notice? (https://www.youtube.com/watch?v=UmLu8rzbHhE)

PROFESSIONAL **EDGE**

Recognizing Language Disorders

Are a student's difficulties symptoms of a language disorder? Here are some behaviors that might signal the need to seek input from a speech-language pathologist.

Receptive Language Problem Behaviors

- Responds inconsistently to sounds or speech
- Has difficulty understanding what gestures mean
- Often is unable to follow simple directions
- Repeats questions, apparently as a strategy for formulating an answer
- Subvocalizes what others say
- Has a short attention span even for preferred activities
- Sometimes looks "blank" when spoken to
- Often does not understand abstract concepts
- Seems not to comprehend the concept of taking turns during conversation
- Is easily distracted by extraneous sounds when receiving a communication
- Has problems understanding when a word has multiple meanings
- Has difficulty using phonics as a method for decoding words
- Often gives inappropriate answers
- Has difficulty learning new vocabulary
- Has difficulty with sequencing (e.g., events in a story, days of the week)

Expressive Language Problems

- Has difficulty formulating questions
- Struggles to learn songs and rhymes
- Often uses pronouns incorrectly (e.g., he, they, you)
- Seems unusually quiet
- Does not easily interact with classmates and other peers
- Has trouble with word finding (e.g., substituting the word "thing" or "stuff" for more precise words)
- Has an overall vocabulary level lower than that of peers
- Seldom contributes to class discussions
- Uses primarily very simple, short sentences
- Uses words incorrectly or leaves out key words or details
- Sometimes puts words in incorrect order in sentences
- Prefers more physical behavior to verbal expressive communication
- Rambles when telling a story or responding to questions, demonstrating a lack of structure and order to oral communication
- Uses an excessive number of "ums," pauses, and repetitions
- Relies heavily on words that describe concrete ideas rather than abstract ones
- Reluctant to ask for assistance when confused about classroom assignments or tasks
- Fails to recognize cues that signal to stop talking (e.g., a classmate's sigh or attempt to begin speaking)
- Significant memory problems

list, which behaviors might you expect to see in Savannah, the middle school student introduced at the beginning of the chapter?

Many other language disorders have been identified. For example, some students experience a language delay, that is, they acquire language at a slower rate than is typical (Paul & Roth, 2011; Wankoff, 2011). Other students, like Savannah, have aphasia, a loss of language after it has developed, as may happen after an accident or injury (e.g., Akbari, 2014; Kojima, Mimura, Auchi, Yoshino, & Kato, 2011). Yet other students may have central auditory processing disorders (CAPDs) (also called auditory processing disorders). They do not have hearing loss, but for some reason, their brains do not effectively interpret the auditory information that comes from their ears (Shive & Bellis, 2011), and so they may have difficulty in several related areas, including listening and speaking using the rules of the language. It should be noted that the existence of CAPDs remains controversial, with some professionals arguing that it is not a unique diagnosis and questioning its value in planning interventions (DeBonis, 2015).

Elements of Speech

Speech is the use of the oral channel for exchanging information and knowledge. Hundreds of muscles and structures can be involved in speech (Shames & Anderson, 2006), and some of these are highlighted in Figure 9.2.

First, breath has to be expelled from the lungs using the muscles of the rib cage and the diaphragm. This air has to be forced through the larynx (also called the *voice box*), which includes structures and muscles in the neck. Here the muscles control the amount of air flowing out at one time, causing the vocal

FIGURE 9.2   **The Human Structure for Speech Production**

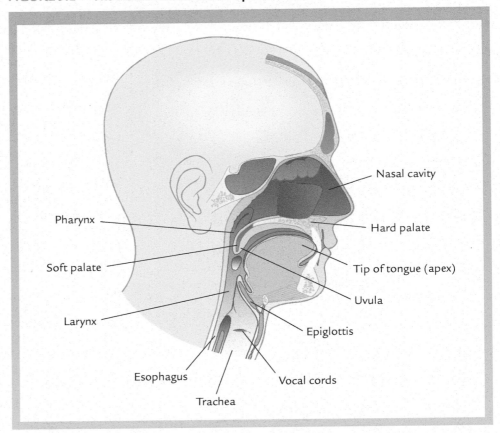

folds (also called the *vocal cords*) to *vibrate* and produce sound. Professional singers provide an example of how important this part of speech production can be. They have learned to control these muscles precisely so that they can make exactly the correct pitch at exactly the correct loudness. Finally, the structures and muscles in the head, including the lips, jaws, tongue, teeth, and soft palate, provide for the fine-tuning of speech. Think about what you do to form the sounds in these words: *bond, pond.* You rely mostly on your lips to form the sounds correctly. Here is another example. Say these words: *this, think.* These sounds require touching the tip of the tongue to the upper teeth. If you have ever been to the dentist for work that involved numbing your mouth, you know exactly how much clear speech relies on controlling your lips, teeth, and tongue.

Speech Disorders

As you might imagine, any problem related to the structures through which students produce speech can cause a speech disorder. These usually are categorized as relating to *voice* (e.g., loudness or overall quality of speech), *resonance* (e.g., the richness of a person's voice), *articulation* (i.e., accurate production of the sounds needed to form words), or *fluency* (i.e., speaking without hesitation). For example, Evelyn is a student with a voice disorder. When she speaks, she breathes very shallowly and her voice seldom reaches above a whisper. Brittany also has a voice disorder; if you heard her speak, you would describe her voice as having a harsh, rough quality. Some voice disorders are caused by physical disabilities such as cleft lip and palate, discussed later in the chapter.

Many young children experience articulation disorders, including omissions (*bo* for *boat*), substitutions (*wan* for *ran*), or additions (*ammaminal* for *animal*). These errors are considered disorders only when they persist beyond the typical developmental period, as illustrated in Figure 9.3.

The most common of fluency disorders is stuttering (Byrd, Logan, & Gillam, 2012). Stuttering occurs when a person's speech is broken by sound repetitions (e.g., *w-w-want*), prolonged sounds (e.g., *wwwant*), or unanticipated stoppages of sound. Some individuals who stutter also make unusual facial expressions or body movements as they struggle to speak. Interventions such as those outlined in the Professional Edge can have a strong positive impact when you work with students who have this disorder (e.g., Wolk & LaSalle, 2015; Snell et al., 2010).

FIGURE 9.3   Mastery of English Speech Sounds

Although most children master vowel sounds by 2 to 3 years of age, it takes several additional years to learn consonant sounds and blends and to use them in the beginning, middle, and end of words.

Student Age	Sounds Typically Measured
2	p, h, n, b, k
3	m, w, g, f, d
4	t, S ("sh"), j, ("y")
5	s, v, n, ("ng"), r, l, T ("ch"), z, D ("j")
6	q ("th" in "<u>th</u>in"), D ("th" in "<u>th</u>e"), ("zh" in "mea<u>s</u>ure")
8	Consonant blends and clusters

Source: Owens, R. E., Metz, D. E., & Farinella, K. A. (2015). *Introduction to communication disorders: A lifespan evidence-based approach.* Boston, MA: Pearson.

PROFESSIONAL EDGE

Interacting with Students Who Stutter

More than anything, students who stutter need a communication environment that is supportive. Professionals can help by following these guidelines:

- Don't tell the child "slow down" or "just relax."
- Don't interrupt or complete words for the child or talk for him or her.
- Help all members of the class learn to take turns talking and listening.
- Expect the same quality and quantity of work from the student who stutters as the one who doesn't.
- Speak with the student in an unhurried way, pausing frequently.

- Convey that you are listening to the content of the message, not how it is said.
- Have a one-on-one conversation with the student who stutters about needed accommodations in the classroom. Respect the student's needs, but do not enable.
- Don't make stuttering something to be ashamed of.
- Talk about stuttering just like any other matter.

You can watch a video about stuttering or download a handbook with additional valuable information about stuttering from the website of The Stuttering Foundation at http://www.stutteringhelp.org/Default.aspx?tabid=519.

Source: Reproduced by permission from *The Stuttering Foundation*. All Rights Reserved.

Video Example
from
YouTube

▶

MyEdLab
Video Example 9.2

To better understand this disorder, watch this video of a student who has received extensive speech therapy to improve his communication. What do you notice about the child's language? (https://www.youtube.com/watch?v=Te7N-tUdH-E)

One additional and complex speech disorder your students may experience is called *childhood apraxia of speech* (Ballard et al., 2015; Duffy, Strand, & Josephs, 2014). This disorder exists when a student has extraordinary difficulty in producing speech that other people manage easily. Jonas, whom you met at the beginning of the chapter, has this disorder. No matter how hard he may try, he cannot put together the movements and patterns required to speak. His lips, tongue, and other speech mechanisms seem to be unable to do what his brain is telling them to do. Students with apraxia usually understand language very well; the disorder is one of expression. As a result of apraxia of speech, some students' words are unintelligible. Many students with this disorder speak as little as possible, and so they often are perceived as being very shy or quiet and, possibly, struggling learners (Miron, 2012).

Prevalence of Speech and Language Disorders

According to recent figures from the U.S. Department of Education (2015), approximately 1.03 million students ages 6 to 21 received services for a speech or language disorder as their primary area of disability. This group constitutes approximately 1.7% of all school-age students and has fluctuated little over the past decade. However, these data do not provide a complete picture of the number of students who receive speech and language services because, as noted earlier, they do not include students whose needs are addressed by related services.

Distinguishing Between Speech and Language Prevalence Data

An additional dilemma exists in considering the prevalence of speech and language disorders. IDEA reports data only for the combined prevalence for these disorders, not for each separately. However, several studies have examined prevalence of speech and language disorders individually. Overall, researchers estimate that 5% of all children in first grade have a speech disorder and that nearly 6% of children in the primary grades have a language disorder not caused by a physical or sensory disability (National Institute on Deafness and Other Communication Disorders [NIDCD], 2016). Recognize, though, that even this information does not necessarily provide a clear picture of prevalence because some students have disorders that affect more than one area of speech or language, and many students have combinations of both speech and language disorders.

Other Prevalence Considerations

Several studies have examined whether speech and language disorders occur among boys and girls at approximately the same rate. Generally, boys are more likely than girls to be identified as having speech disorders in a ratio of approximately 2:1 (NIDCD, 2015). Boys are more likely than girls to be identified as having language disorders in a ratio of approximately 1.75:1. Prevalence related to race or ethnicity is difficult to estimate because of the many complicating factors that can arise in evaluating these students' speech and language skills, a topic addressed later in this chapter.

Causes of Speech and Language Disorders

Speech and language disorders are caused by many different factors. The following section highlights some of the most common biological and environmental causes.

Biological Causes

Some speech and language disorders are the result of problems related to the central nervous system or other systems within the body (e.g., Archibald, Joanisse, & Edmunds, 2011; Badcock, Bishop, Hardiman, Barry, & Watkins, 2012). Examples include intellectual disabilities, autism, or ADHD. Likewise, hearing loss or deafness and vision loss or blindness can be causes of speech and language disorders. When students have physical disabilities that include muscle weaknesses, as occurs in the disorder cerebral palsy (discussed in Chapter 13), they may not be capable of producing the sounds needed for speech and language. Emotional disabilities also can cause speech and language disorders. Think about a young child with an internalizing disorder, who is focused inward and who largely ignores other children and adults. The child's inattention to the speech and language occurring in the environment can lead to delays or disorders. Other biological causes may be related to heredity (e.g., Lewis et al., 2011; Peter et al., 2016).

One additional biological cause of speech and language disorders is referred to as *congenital*, meaning the disorder is present at birth as a result of a known or unknown cause. One example of a congenital disorder is cleft lip and/or palate, a relatively common birth defect in the United States, affecting one out of every 940 newborns (Centers for Disease Control and Prevention, 2016). A child born with a *cleft lip* has a separation between the two sides of the lip that often also involves the upper jaw. In a *cleft palate*, an opening exists in the roof of the mouth. Some children have cleft lips, some have cleft palates, and some have both conditions.

Environmental Causes

A second group of causes of speech and language disorders relates to a child's environment (e.g., Clarke et al., 2012). For example, some disorders occur because of repeated ear infections that interfere with hearing and eventually affect speech and language development (NIDCD, 2009; Racanello & McCabe, 2010). Another example of an environmental cause is neglect or abuse. Perhaps a young child is left alone much of the time without peer or adult language models. Alternatively, perhaps the child is punished for being noisy—for experimenting with speech sounds as all babies do or for talking as a toddler. In either case, a negative impact on speech and language development is likely.

An additional environmental factor that can lead to speech and language disorders is one that you have read about in other chapters—poverty (Nielsen & Friesen, 2012; Perkins, Finegood, & Swain, 2013). Children who live in poverty are more likely to be malnourished, possibly leading to brain damage and a variety of disabilities, including speech and language disorders. These children also are less likely than others to receive adequate medical care, and so illnesses such as ear infections and allergies are more likely to go untreated. Once again, speech and language disorders can be the outcome.

Making Sense of the Factors Contributing to Speech and Language Disorders

This discussion of causes of speech and language disorders could leave you with the impression that each cause is distinct and that identifying a cause is essential to intervention. This is not the case. As you learned in the discussions about learning disabilities, emotional and behavior disorders, and intellectual disabilities, in many cases the cause of a disability is unknown; the same is true for speech and language disorders. For example, a child's mother might have been a substance abuser, and during the birth process, a brief period of anoxia may have occurred. The child may have a slight hearing loss, a fact that goes undetected until the student reaches kindergarten. Although the child then receives services at school, the family is not able to provide reinforcement at home and so progress is slow. Often no single cause is identified, and in many cases, identifying a cause is not particularly helpful for planning the child's instruction.

MyEdLab **Self-Check 9.1**

MyEdLab **Application Exercise 9.1:** Analyzing Data: George's IEP

Characteristics of Individuals with Speech and Language Disorders

Students who have speech and language disorders are a diverse group, and any discussion of what they are like cannot completely describe them. However, in the following sections, some of the most common cognitive and academic, social and emotional, and behavior characteristics of these students are outlined.

Cognitive and Academic Characteristics

No generalizations can be made concerning the cognitive characteristics of students with speech and language disorders. These students may be academically gifted, they may be average in their cognitive ability, or they may struggle to learn and understand. In addition, many students who have intellectual disabilities also have speech and language disorders.

Academic Characteristics

Although the academic achievement of some students with speech and language disorders is comparable to that of their peers, these disorders often have a profound impact on students' ability to learn (e.g., Apel & Henbest, 2016; McLeod & Apel, 2015). From the day that children begin to comprehend language, it is an essential means through which they explore their world and come to understand it. When they enter school, the importance of language is magnified. Early school learning relies largely on the sharing of information using oral language. At the same time, students begin to learn how to use language for reading and writing. As students progress through school, they are expected to have an increasingly sophisticated vocabulary, spoken and written, in order to compose stories and essays and to comprehend complex written materials such as those found in textbooks. No matter what age, students also need speech and language skills for communication and learning in all their other subject areas as well as during nonacademic activities such as lunch and after-school programs.

Speech and Language Disorders and Reading

Most of the research on the influence of speech and language disorders on student learning focuses on reading, and the available information is sobering. Children who have significant speech or language delays are at high risk for reading difficulties (e.g., Nellis, Sickman, Newman, & Harman, 2014; Nippold, 2012), a problem that Jonas, the first-grade student you met at the beginning of this chapter, is experiencing. Further, children with speech and language disorders often are unable to benefit from the early literacy experiences that are common in kindergarten, and so they are at an academic disadvantage almost from the time they begin school.

The types of reading difficulties students encounter are directly related to their speech and language problems. Some students have difficulty learning to sound out words they read because they cannot distinguish among similar sounds. Others do not hear the rhythm of language in their heads as they read, and this interferes with comprehension. If you review all the elements of speech and language that have already been presented, you probably can list reading problems that are likely to be related to each (e.g., Archibald, Joanisse, & Edmunds, 2011).

Social and Emotional Characteristics

Many students with speech and language disorders struggle socially and emotionally (Gerber, Brice, Capone, Fujiki, & Timler, 2012; Havstam, Laakso, & Ringsberg, 2011). First, they must deal with their own self-concepts and their perceptions of how others interact with them. Students with fluency disorders, for example, may be the targets of peer teasing, as described by this student:

> I like participating in class, but when I'm answering questions (and stutter), I always hear whispers of people imitating my stuttering and giggling. Even when I'm not stuttering I can hear them imitate me in a stuttering voice. The other day this kid named Scott says, "It's funny when you stutter." When I tried to tell him to buzz off, he imitated me with every word, even though I hardly stuttered.

When students have negative experiences such as these, they may need assistance maintaining positive views of themselves.

In addition to teasing, students with speech or language impairments may experience difficulty in social situations in any number of ways, as is true of Jonas, whom you met at the beginning of this chapter. If they mispronounce words, others may have difficulty understanding them. If they cannot find the word they need during a conversation or if they do not use the conventions of grammar, they cannot fully participate in the interactions. In addition, some students face challenges because they do not understand how to participate in conversations, and so they may become socially isolated (Lee, Gibbon, & Spivey, 2016). The problem can be compounded by adults who form negative opinions about students with speech and language disorders and their ability to achieve (e.g., Overby, Carrell, & Bernthal, 2007).

Behavior Characteristics

Young children who cannot express their needs in words sometimes resort to inappropriate behaviors, as in the example of a toddler who bites a playmate in order to get a desired toy. A similar pattern can be seen among school-age students who have speech and language disorders. Some evidence is emerging to indicate that students with speech and language disabilities are at high risk for behavior problems and even for being identified as having emotional and behavior disorders (Benner, Ralston, & Feuerborn, 2012; Quattlebaum, Grier, & Klubnik, 2012). This relationship is explored in more detail in the Positive Behavior Supports.

POSITIVE • **BEHAVIOR** • SUPPORTS

Linking Speech and Language Disorders and Emotional and Behavior Disabilities

Researchers have clearly demonstrated that a link exists between emotional disabilities and speech and language disorders (Games, Curran, & Porter, 2012; Hopkins, Clegg, & Stackhouse, 2016; Schmitt, Justice, & O'Connell, 2014; Stiles, 2013). In a review of pertinent studies (Benner, Nelson, & Epstein, 2002), nearly nine 9 out of every 10 students with emotional disabilities in public schools also had language disorders. Among more specific findings were these:

- Students with language deficits are at substantially higher risk for antisocial behavior than students with speech disorders.
- Students with receptive language problems often are undiagnosed, and these students have higher rates of behavior problems than other students.
- The coexistence of language problems in students with emotional disabilities is 10 times higher than it is in the general population.
- Language disorders significantly and negatively affect interpersonal relationships, often leading to antisocial behavior.

It is not clear which problem comes first. That is, do the speech and language impairments cause the emotional problems, or do the emotional disabilities lead to the communication disorders? It really does not matter. Instead, this information suggests that educators should be alert for the simultaneous presence of both disabilities so that appropriate assessment, diagnosis, and intervention can be implemented as follows:

- Students with emotional and behavior disorders should be screened for the presence of language disorders. This type of screening sometimes is skipped with this group of students because of the immediate need to address their behaviors.
- Appropriate language interventions should be designed with input from speech-language pathologists for students needing these services.
- Screening and intervention should occur as early as possible. Students benefit from language instruction primarily when they are very young, and missing this opportunity is likely to lead to later emotional and behavior problems. A proactive approach emphasizing prevention is far superior to later attempts at remediation.

Speech and Language Disorders and Other Disabilities

You have already learned that the term *comorbidity* refers to the simultaneous existence of two or more disabilities. As mentioned earlier in this chapter, students with many different disabilities often have a comorbid speech or language disorder. In addition to students you have already learned about (i.e., those with learning disabilities, emotional disabilities, or intellectual disabilities), students with hearing loss, autism, physical or health disabilities, or multiple disabilities also may have a speech or language impairment.

Think about the issue of comorbidity as it is related to speech and language disorders. What might be the implications for students who have these disorders as well as another disability in terms of learning and behavior? Think, too, about the professionals who work with these students—whether they are general education teachers, special education teachers, or speech-language pathologists (SLPs). How would the presence of two disabilities affect their work with students?

> MyEdLab **Self-Check 9.2**
>
> MyEdLab **Application Exercise 9.2:** More Speech and Language Disorders

Identifying Speech and Language Disorders

The procedures used to evaluate students with possible speech or language disorders and to determine if they are eligible for special education services are similar to those for identifying other students with disabilities. Intellectual ability is assessed using formal testing instruments, and overall school achievement is considered.

Screening is completed to determine whether a vision or hearing loss is present. In this section, emphasis is placed on the evaluation strategies that directly address the speech or language disorder. Keep in mind that speech-language pathologists play a key role in assessing students with possible speech and language needs.

Assessment

A hallmark of assessment for speech and language disorders is the importance of integrating information obtained from formal assessments, data gathered from students' spontaneous conversations, and the contributions made by teachers and parents.

Speech Assessments

Several types of assessments may be completed to help professionals decide whether a student has a speech disorder. For many students, the speech-language pathologist administers a standardized test to determine whether a problem with articulation is present. An example of this type of instrument is the *Goldman–Fristoe Test of Articulation 3* (Goldman & Fristoe, 2015). Although tests used for this purpose vary, they all have the common goal of detecting errors in articulation that are not expected given the student's age. By asking a student to finish sentences or to name pictures that are part of the test, the speech-language pathologist can determine whether the student is omitting certain sounds, substituting one sound for another, adding sounds, or distorting the way a sound is made.

However, formal tests are not enough because they do not capture the way a student speaks in day-to-day activities. Speech-language pathologists also gather a spontaneous language sample that can help them to assess whether a student has an articulation disorder, a problem with voice or fluency, or a combination of disorders. They may ask a young student to talk about a toy or a game. They may engage an older student in a conversation about school, friends, or any other topic that seems likely to encourage the student to provide several paragraphs of conversation. In addition, the professional likely will ask parents to provide a history of the student's development related to speech and ask teachers to describe the student's strengths and problems.

Speech-language pathologists also examine the student's physical structures for producing speech. They may observe whether a student's teeth are aligned well enough for sounds to be produced correctly. They also may look for abnormalities in the student's hard palate (i.e., the roof of the mouth). Other items assessed include the student's ability to easily use the lips and tongue to produce speech sounds. Finally, the speech-language pathologist notes whether the student's breathing patterns are typical. How might each of these areas affect a student's ability to produce speech?

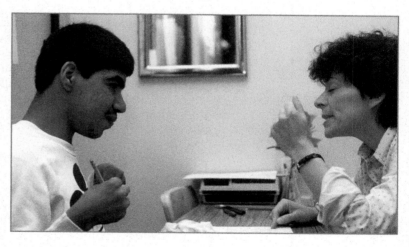

When students are English learners, professionals must take care that assessments reflect the students' abilities and skills rather than emerging English proficiency.

Language Assessments

Students with specific language impairments may experience difficulty in any of several areas, and the assessment must address each of these. Examples of language components that might be assessed include the following:

- Receptive and expressive vocabulary
- Ability to retrieve words as needed (sometimes called *word finding*)

Did You Know?

Because speech-language pathologists have extensive knowledge and skills for using communication to foster literacy skills, they sometimes are enlisted as part of response to intervention (RTI) or multi-tiered system of support (MTSS) procedures. Watson & Bellon-Harn (2014) outline ways that these professionals may co-teach with general education teachers or offer consultative services. The goal is to provide students with intensive intervention that may prevent the need for special education services.

- Comprehension and processing of sentences
- Correct use of the rules of grammar
- Comprehension of stories and other narratives
- Ability to produce language, whether to tell a story or to participate in a conversation

To gather information about these areas, the speech-language pathologist uses both formal and informal measures. Tests such as the *Comprehensive Assessment of Spoken Language* (CASL) (Carrow-Woolfolk, 1999) and the *Test of Adolescent and Adult Language 4* (TOAL-4) (Hammill, Brown, Larsen, & Wiederholt, 2007) are used to systematically assess the student's language production. Additionally, samples of the student's written schoolwork are reviewed, the student is observed in the classroom setting as well as in less structured environments (e.g., the lunchroom or playground), and parents and teachers are interviewed.

Assessment for Students Whose First Language Is Not English or Whose Use of English Is Nonstandard

One common dilemma faced by speech-language professionals is evaluating a student whose native language is not English or who speaks a variation of English that is considered nonstandard. In such a case, many precautions must be taken so that the assessment is accurate and fair (Paradis, Schneider, & Duncan, 2013; Peña, Gillam, & Bedore, 2014). For example, in the use of standardized tests, speech-language pathologists must ensure that the test was developed for use with the students to whom it is being administered (Shames & Anderson, 2006). They also must ensure that directions and other aspects of the test are not confusing to individuals who do not speak standard English; this may lead to incorrect responses, not because of language problems, but because of the style in which the directions are given.

Other general factors also must be reviewed in this type of assessment. The testing situation itself may be particularly stressful for a student who is not a native English speaker. The expectation for the student to participate in a conversation with the professional administering the assessment may violate some students' cultural norms (e.g., children should not speak at length to an adult who is an authority figure). What are other dilemmas that may arise in assessing students whose native language is not English or whose language is not standard English?

Eligibility

Along with data regarding cognitive ability, achievement, and other domains, the information about a student's speech and language skills is considered by a team that includes the parents, the student (if appropriate), general and special educators, an administrator, specialists such as the speech-language pathologist, and others as needed. They respond to these questions:

1. *Given the student's age, does the student have a significant delay or difference in speech or language that would be considered a speech or language impairment?* As noted in the preceding section, the professionals addressing this question must take into account whether the assessment data suggest a true disorder or a language difference because of native language or culture.
2. *Does the student's speech or language impairment adversely affect the student's educational performance?* As you know, this question must be asked because IDEA stipulates that special education services can be offered only if the disability negatively affects educational performance.
3. *Can the student benefit from special education intervention?* Although the answer to this question generally would be yes, if that has been the case for

the other questions, sometimes the issue is not completely clear. For example, it may be doubtful that special education services can address certain speech disorders, particularly for a student who is older—perhaps a high school student. Issues such as these must be considered.

Based on the answers to these questions, the multidisciplinary team determines whether the student needs special education. However as noted earlier, keep in mind the fact that in some states, students are eligible for services because of their speech or language disorders alone, whereas in other states, services in this area are provided only if students also have other disabilities. In the latter case, the student would have been evaluated for speech and language services to be provided as a related service, not as special education.

MyEdLab   **Self-Check 9.3**

MyEdLab   **Application Exercise 9.3:** Assessing Speech and Language Disorders

MyEdLab   **Application Exercise 9.4:** Diagnostic Checklist

How Learners with Speech and Language Disorders Receive Their Education

Students with speech and language disorders receive their education in the setting most appropriate for them based on their special needs. If the speech or language disorder is the primary disability, emphasis is placed on providing services in general education with peers. If other disabilities also exist, the team that makes the decision about placement will take these into account.

Early Childhood

Most young children are not given a specific disability designation because of the difficulty of completing an accurate assessment and the resulting risk of misidentification. However, the most critical time in life for speech and language development is early childhood, and much is known about typical speech and language development and problems that can occur for very young children (e.g., Lederberg, Schick, & Spencer, 2012). In fact, of the approximately 745,000 children ages 3 to 5 who received special education services through IDEA in 2013–2014, some 329,439 were identified as having speech or language impairments as the primary disability (U.S. Department of Education, 2015).

The Importance of Early Intervention

The rationale for providing intensive speech and language intervention for young children can be justified in several ways (Roberts & Kaiser, 2012). First, research suggests that when a problem exists, the earlier an intervention is begun and the longer it is implemented, the more likely the problem will be addressed effectively (Cohen-Mimran, Reznik-Nevet, & Korona-Gaon, 2016; Wilcox & Woods, 2011). Second, when early intervention is undertaken, services can be intense; that is, they can involve a speech-language pathologist, a teacher, and the child's family. By involving all the important adults in the intervention process, more services can be delivered and more positive results can be expected. The final justification also is related to the notion of intensity. Specifically, the progress that young children make in overcoming speech and language disorders will more likely be maintained if support is provided during these critical years across settings and across time. In recognition of this, there has been an increase in the extent to which speech-language therapists work with children between birth and age 3.

Approaches for Early Speech and Language Intervention

Traditionally, speech-language services were offered in a *pullout model*, even for very young children. That is, the speech-language pathologist would come to the home or preschool classroom to get the child to receive services; take the child to a separate room, classroom, or office; provide intervention individually or in a small group; and then return the child to the parent or classroom. This approach had the benefit of eliminating distractions for the child, but it removed the child from the natural setting in which speech and language occur and had the potential for stigmatizing the child.

Although a traditional approach sometimes is still appropriate, other options now often are implemented as well. For example, some young children receive their speech-language services in the context of the early childhood center, preschool setting, or kindergarten classroom. The advantage of this approach is that the speech-language pathologist can observe the child's ability to function in the natural environment.

One additional option is an approach that combines separate service, in-class service, and indirect service. In some cases, the speech-language pathologist periodically may work directly with a child in a separate setting, often to check on progress, to address particularly complex problems, and to make decisions about subsequent steps in intervention. However, at least some of the services are offered within the classroom context. The final component of this approach is consultation. The speech-language pathologist meets with the early childhood specialist or special educator to problem solve about the child's needs and to discuss interventions and how to ensure that the child's skill development continues even during the times between speech-language therapy sessions.

Elementary and Secondary School Services

Nearly all school-age students who have been identified as having speech or language disorders receive their education in a typical school setting. In fact, as you can see by reviewing Figure 9.4, approximately 87% of students with this disability are educated in general education classrooms more than 80% of the school day (U.S. Department of Education, 2015).

The way in which speech-language services are implemented depends on the nature of the student's disability. For example, many elementary students receive speech-language therapy services once or twice each week, usually for 30 minutes per session. In this model, the speech-language pathologist is likely to provide direct services in a separate setting. You may hear this service model referred to by children as "going to speech." When this approach is employed, the general education teacher and speech-language

FIGURE 9.4   Educational Placements of Students Ages 6 to 21 Who Have Speech or Language Impairments (in percentages)

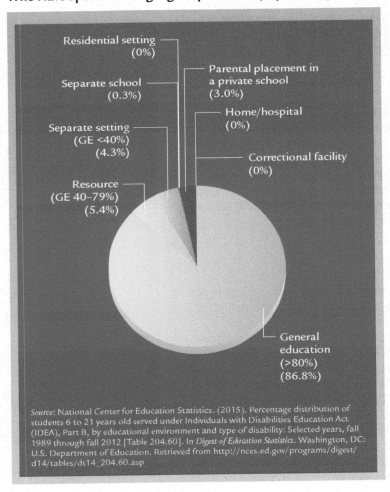

Residential setting (0%)

Separate school (0.3%)

Separate setting (GE <40%) (4.3%)

Resource (GE 40–79%) (5.4%)

Parental placement in a private school (3.0%)

Home/hospital (0%)

Correctional facility (0%)

General education (>80%) (86.8%)

Source: National Center for Education Statistics. (2015). Percentage distribution of students 6 to 21 years old served under Individuals with Disabilities Education Act (IDEA), Part B, by educational environment and type of disability: Selected years, fall 1989 through fall 2012 [Table 204.60]. In *Digest of Education Statistics*. Washington, DC: U.S. Department of Education. Retrieved from http://nces.ed.gov/programs/digest/d14/tables/dt14_204.60.asp

pathologist stay in touch so that the teacher knows which skills should be reinforced and the specialist knows what topics form the focus in the classroom language arts program as well as other areas of the curriculum. Keep in mind that in many school districts, speech-language pathologists work in two or more schools, and so their time to meet with teachers and to attend critical team meetings sometimes is limited.

For students who have disabilities in addition to speech or language disorders, as does David, who was introduced at the beginning of the chapter, services are part of their overall education program. Some of these students receive services in a pullout model similar to that previously described. For other students, a speech-language pathologist may provide services in the special education classroom. For example, if a student has a significant hearing loss that is affecting the clarity of her speech and receives special education services in a separate setting for 2 hours per day, the speech-language pathologist may provide services in the special education classroom. A similar approach may be employed for students with significant intellectual disabilities. Sometimes both in-class and pullout services are delivered.

Did You Know?

A review of 20 years of research on communication interventions for students with severe intellectual disabilities indicates that such efforts are worthwhile, leading to communication improvements for them (Snell et al., 2010).

Inclusive Practices

If you think about the nature of speech and language disorders and the impact they can have on all aspects of students' lives—their academic performance, their relationships with peers and teachers, and their interactions in the family and community—it really is not surprising that inclusive practices are readily supported for students with this disability. The most appropriate setting in which nearly all students can learn and practice speech and language skills is general education. One emerging role for professionals working there with students with speech and language disorders is co-teaching (Lindeman & Magiera, 2014; Vicker, 2009), a service delivery option you learned about in Chapter 4. When this inclusive approach is used, speech-language pathologists and general education teachers design and deliver language-based interventions to all the students in a class. For example, students may be divided into three groups. One group works with the general education teacher on a comprehension activity related to the story being read. The second group works with the speech-language pathologist on vocabulary related to the story. The third group works independently to write a different ending for the story or to draw pictures to illustrate their favorite scenes. Each group eventually completes all three activities. The Instruction in Action highlights how the trend over the past decade to provide more and more support for students with speech and language disorders in general education settings has positively affected those services.

Transition and Adulthood

Some of the needs of students with speech and language disorders who are transitioning from childhood to adulthood are similar to those of other students with disabilities. These needs include the ability to self-advocate, the importance of making wise choices regarding higher education and careers, and the skills to function successfully in a job and the community (Durkin, Conti-Ramsden, & Simkin, 2012). Some students also may need assistance in building self-esteem (Conti-Ramsden, Botting, & Durkin, 2008). Although fewer students receive speech-language services as they continue through school, some receive services until they graduate (Scott, 2014), as does David, the high school student introduced at the beginning of this chapter.

One indicator of the challenges faced by adolescents and young adults with speech and language disorders is found by looking at information about behavior. Experts estimate that the prevalence of language disorders among female

MyEdLab
Video Example 9.3
Another example of a student receiving services can be found in this video.
(https://www.youtube.com/watch?v=MxMYHbsY4X0)

INSTRUCTION IN **ACTION**

Traditional versus Classroom-Based Services for Students with Speech and Language Disorders

Speech-language services often are delivered in close collaboration with special educators, general education teachers, and parents. These are some of the most significant differences between the traditional and classroom-based approaches, although the precise roles of these professionals may vary somewhat state by state.

	Traditional Pullout Services	*Classroom-Based Services*
Intervention contexts	Isolates students from authentic contexts, presents intervention in a separate room	Includes students in authentic social situations, presents intervention in functional contexts (classroom, playground, lunchroom)
Role of the SLP	Serves as primary service provider, presents the intervention	Plans an intervention program (decides where, when, and who will facilitate language)
Relationship of the SLP to parents and teachers	Serves as the expert, engages teachers and parents as helpers	Collaborates with and values the expertise of parents and teachers, draws upon parents and teachers as change agents
Goals and objectives	Selects goals on the basis of test measures and language analyses, determines contents and tasks arbitrarily, without regard to curriculum	Bases goals on curricular content and tasks, individualizes expectations, determines need for adaptations or supports
Language focus	Addresses components of language removed from real discourse events	Focuses on language components as they relate to functioning in whole discourse events, integrates language parts
Assessment mechanisms	Relies on standardized measures, identifies students' weaknesses—what they can't do—compares students' performance to test norms	Assesses performance within curricular tasks, identifies abilities and influence of supports, determines functioning relative to curricular demands
Evaluation methods	Re-administers tests periodically, charts attainments of specific targets	Monitors outcomes continually, assesses functioning in context, analyzes products
Student roles	Places students in structured one-on-one interactions, leads to limited, passive roles	Draws upon an array of communicative events, permits active social roles and varied types of participation
Communicative options, demands	Limits or structures response options and participation in types of communication events	Requires flexible use of communication skills, leads to participation in a variety of "whole" communicative events

Source: Anderson, Noma B., & Shames, George H. *Human communication disorders: An introduction*, 7th Ed., © 2006. Adapted and electronically reproduced by permission of Pearson Education, Inc., Upper Saddle River, New Jersey.

juvenile delinquents is three times greater than in the rest of the population (Castrogiovanni, 2008). Further, most researchers agree that speech and language disorders are far more prevalent among juvenile offenders than among other young adults (Gregory & Bryan, 2015). As with young children, professionals clearly find that students who experience difficulty in communicating with words may turn to aggression or other inappropriate behavior as an alternative. This issue must be addressed, or students will be unlikely to make a smooth transition from school to adulthood (Durkin, Conti-Ramsden, & Simkin, 2012).

MyEdLab **Self-Check 9.4**

MyEdLab **Application Exercise 9.5:** Roles and Responsibilities of the Speech-Language Pathologist

MyEdLab **Application Exercise 9.6:** More with George

MyEdLab **Application Exercise 9.7:** Addressing Language Needs in the Classroom

Recommended Educational Practices for Students with Speech and Language Disorders

Students with speech and language disorders may benefit from the academic and behavior interventions that are effective for students with learning and behavior problems, but specialized interventions are needed as well. Some students receive articulation therapy, others are assisted to use their physical speech apparatus correctly, and yet others benefit from intensive programs that increase phonemic awareness. In the sections that follow, you can learn about two areas of particular interest: (1) the integration of speech and language services with literacy instruction and (2) augmentative and alternative communication.

Speech-Language Services and Literacy Instruction

Throughout this chapter, emphasis has been placed on how speech and language disorders can affect students' achievement and behavior. This relationship is widely recognized among school professionals (e.g., Snowling & Melby-Lervåg, 2016), and as a result, speech-language pathologists increasingly are partnering with general education teachers, special education teachers, bilingual educators, and others to ensure that all students receive the early communication assistance needed to develop crucial language and literacy skills (Cordewener, Bosman, & Verhoeven, 2012; Law, Plunkett, & Stringer, 2012; Nellis, Sickman, Newman, & Harman, 2014).

According to the American Speech-Language-Hearing Association (2016), speech-language pathologists can reinforce relationships between spoken language and preliteracy skills, provide interventions related to phonemic awareness and memory, analyze the language demands found in textbooks and other school materials and media, and analyze students' language so that interventions can be tailored to students' needs. Speech-language pathologists also can play roles in prevention, early intervention, assessment, therapy, program development, and documentation of outcomes. Finally, they can help to advocate for literacy programs at the local and state levels. How might some of these strategies assist Savannah, the middle school student you met in the beginning of this chapter?

A strong implication of this educational practice relates to collaboration (e.g., Woods, Wilcox, Friedman, & Murch, 2011). It is essential that school professionals recognize that their efforts are far more effective if they blend their expertise. This means that general and special education teachers need to keep speech-language pathologists informed about critical curriculum topics being addressed and problems that they observe in students. Conversely, speech-language pathologists must initiate conversations with teachers to discuss student needs and plan subsequent steps for interventions.

Communication Using Technology

Many students with speech and language disorders can be helped tremendously through technology (Drager, Reichle, & Pinkoski, 2010; Light & McNaughton, 2008). In addition to the app examples provided in the Technology Notes, computer hardware and software, tablet devices, smartphones, and options now available via the Internet can help students communicate effectively and practice the skills they are learning.

Augmentative and Alternative Communication

Augmentative and alternative communication (AAC) comprises strategies that compensate for an individual's communication limitations or disabilities. AAC

TECHNOLOGY NOTES

Enhancing Students' Speech and Language Skills

Many students with speech and language disorders, regardless of whether they have other disabilities as well, can learn new skills and practice emerging skills with the assistance of apps. Here are examples that only begin to illustrate the wide range of options available:

- *Dragon Dictation* is a voice recognition app. through which students can speak and instantly see their words. Students can use this app to compose sentences, paragraphs, and longer written assignments, but they also often find it helpful for e-mail, text messages, and social media. This app "learns" a user's voice, and so it becomes more accurate with repeated use.

- *Expressive Builder* was created to help students improve sentence formation as well as to improve their receptive and expressive language skills. Using this app, students can record in their own voice the sentences they create, they can use preloaded images to help them think of sentences, and professionals can add additional images to the app. This app also gives students three levels of hints to facilitate their language production.

- *Splingo's Language Universe* is an interactive game with four levels developed by speech-language pathologists to assist students in acquiring listening and language skills. Splingo is an alien with a sense of humor,

and he gives directions that involve interacting with images and animations (listening) in order to construct sentences (expressive language). The reward for students using this app is helping Splingo to build a spaceship to get to his home.

- *Articulation Station* is designed for students who have difficulty pronouncing consonant sounds. Practice focuses on target words and includes a variety of activities, although this app does require guidance by a professional or parent. Students apply their skills at the word, phrase, sentence, and story levels as they work on all 22 English consonant sounds. This app includes additional sub-apps that must be purchased and embedded to take full advantage of its features.

- *Abilipad* is an app that is a customizable keyboard that includes word prediction (in multiple languages) and text-to-speech features. It also can be used as an adaptive notepad. Keys can be assigned to be letters, words, sentences, or pictures, and individual keys can be combined to be larger (for students who need this adjustment). This app includes many other accessibility features, including changeable colors, adjustable font types and sizes, and the capacity to use images imported from other sources (e.g., images the student already is familiar with).

Video Example
from
YouTube

MyEdLab
Video Example 9.4
The impact this type of AAC can have on students and their families is clearly demonstrated in this video. (https://www.youtube.com/watch?v=8zuNsuHPRbY)

strategies usually are divided into two categories: (1) *unaided*, or those that do not require the use of special equipment or materials (e.g., sign language), and (2) *aided*, those that depend on some type of equipment or materials. Because sign language is addressed in Chapter 11, it is not considered here. Instead, the emphasis is on aided communication options. AAC can greatly benefit students with speech and language disorders (Raghavendra, Olsson, Sampson, McInerney, & Connell, 2012; Smith, 2015).

One example of an AAC device is a communication board. This device uses pictures, symbols, or printed words to facilitate student communication, and it can be low tech or high tech. For example, for a young student whose communication needs are fairly simple, a communication board might consist of small pictures arranged in rows and columns on a flat display. The student points to the picture that displays the desired message (e.g., "I want a drink" by pointing to a glass). Many far more sophisticated versions of communication boards exist as well (e.g., Jackson, Wahlquist, & Marquis, 2011). These boards may be computerized and include a synthesized speech component. Software also exists that professionals can use to tailor the images on a communication board to a student's precise needs, including highly technical academic topics. Also available are communication boards that appear on computer monitors and tablet computing devices (e.g., Xin & Leonard, 2015).

Word prediction software, available for computers, smartphones, and tablet devices, is another type of AAC tool. For students who have difficulty writing, this software guesses at the current word being typed and offers suggestions in a list. The student can select an option and avoid having to type the entire word, and the software ensures that words are spelled correctly. Word prediction software also serves to help composition skills. It predicts what the student's next words will be, and the student can either accept the prediction or substitute the intended word. This software opens many options for both academic success and social interactions with peers (King & Fahsl, 2012).

Augmentative and alternative communication (AAC) devices enable some students with disabilities to access learning, but they also promote both face-to-face and electronic social interactions.

Technology for Language Practice

Technology also assists students in skill development. Perhaps you have observed students in an elementary school using a computer program to practice their knowledge of letters and sounds. Alternatively, they may have been learning how to make new words by combining various letters. Such technology is commonplace and can be valuable for students who need extensive practice on basic speech and language skills. One example of such software is Fast ForWord (Scientific Learning), a set of programs for students in kindergarten through 12th grade that includes intensive skill development (from phonemic awareness to listening comprehension) using game-like exercises and immediate feedback.

Technology for students with speech and language disorders continues to advance. In some classrooms, the teacher wears a microphone and the students wear or sit near receivers so that they clearly hear the teacher's voice during instruction. This technology is referred to as a *soundfield amplification system* (da Cruz et al., 2016; Dockrell & Shield, 2012). Technology also is emerging to help students who stutter speak more slowly to avoid hesitations and to produce natural-sounding synthetic speech for those who cannot use their own voices. Certainly, one defining feature of schools of the very near future will be the extensive use of technology to help students communicate and learn. School professionals should stay abreast of developments in these areas, and if they are working with students using unfamiliar technology, they should seek input from specialists so that they can better interact with students and recognize if problems are occurring.

Did You Know?

Many individuals overcome stuttering difficulties to lead productive lives. The list of famous people includes Tiger Woods, James Earl Jones, Joe Biden, Johnny Damon, Bo Jackson, Herschel Walker, Mel Tillis, and Marilyn Monroe.

MyEdLab **Self-Check 9.5**

MyEdLab **Application Exercise 9.8:** Educational Considerations

MyEdLab **Application Exercise 9.9:** Expressive Language

Perspectives of Parents and Families

The importance of parents' participation in their young children's development is universally acknowledged, and it is the premise on which early intervention services for children with disabilities are based. When attention turns to children's speech and language development, parents' roles become, if anything, even more crucial (Moore et al., 2012; Venker et al., 2015). Children acquire speech and language skills by observing language models, by experimenting in communication with others, and by refining their language skills based on feedback from others.

Helping Parents to Develop Children's Language Skills

Have you ever observed parents with their young children? They talk to them, repeat their youngsters' words, and elaborate on their children's attempts to communicate (e.g., Child: "Me go." Parent: "Oh, do you want to go?"). Most parents intuitively interact with their young children in ways that encourage speech and language development. Even so, enhancing parents' awareness and understanding of speech and language development and helping them learn how to foster it can be very beneficial, especially for children with delays or disorders.

One example of educating parents comes from a summer "sound camp" for children with speech disorders (Al Otaiba & Smartt, 2003). Parents were taught about the concept of phonemic awareness and given simple activities to help their children practice at home the skills being learned at camp. When parents were asked about their perceptions of the camp and the parent education component of it, they reported that the camp was very helpful for their children. In addition, they commented that they had a much better understanding of the concepts related to speech and language development and that they could thus better help their children at home and advocate for them at school. The parents also appreciated learning how to teach their children—for example, using small steps and occasionally repeating or reviewing skills already learned. Other researchers have reported comparable results (Romski et al., 2011).

Diversity and Speech and Language Interventions

Because language is a core element in every culture, speaking with parents from diverse groups about students' speech and language needs can be particularly challenging (e.g., Baird, S., Kibler, & Palacios, 2015). For example, parents who do not speak English fluently may have difficulty helping their children to make sounds correctly and blend them into words. If English is not spoken in the home but school professionals are teaching it at school, students may not have enough opportunities to practice emerging skills and so may be at a disadvantage (Swanson, Hodson, & Schommer-Aikins, 2005). Based on what you have read in this chapter and your own experiences, what other issues can you identify that might occur with students with speech and language disorders whose parents are from nondominant cultures?

Other significant differences may exist between Western cultures and other cultures. Think about augmentative and alternative communication. Most school professionals applaud the emerging technologies that facilitate student communication, give students greater independence, and assist them in their learning (Pickl, 2011). School professionals not only encourage parent participation in choosing and using AAC devices but also rely on it. Not everyone shares this view, however. In some families, AAC may be seen as unnecessary or even detrimental because it can be intrusive in terms of family interactions. For example, some traditional Asian families may want AAC options that do not detract from the family's caregiving role. These families also may presume that AAC options are the responsibility of school professionals, not families. They may even delay approving of AAC devices for their children until they observe that such technology is accepted and used by other children.

MyEdLab **Self-Check 9.6**

MyEdLab **Application Exercise 9.10:** George Is a Second Grader

MyEdLab **Application Exercise 9.11:** Perspectives of Parents and Families of Children with Speech and Language Disorders

Trends and Issues Affecting the Field of Speech and Language Disorders

The complexity of the field of speech and language disorders guarantees that it is characterized by rapidly changing practice and controversy (e.g., Harris, Prater, Dyches, & Heath, 2009; Verdon, McLeod, & Wong, 2015). Two important topics for professionals who work with students with speech and language disorders are (a) identifying and addressing these disabilities in a multicultural society and (b) basing student interventions on evidence-based practices.

Differences versus Disorders in a Multicultural Society

Diversity is a defining characteristic of the U.S. population. Given this, school professionals who address students' speech and language needs must recognize how diversity affects their efforts.

Language Differences

Speech and language professionals are careful to distinguish between language differences—variations from standard speech and language that are considered normal—and language disorders—impairments that interfere with language comprehension and use (Bedore et al., 2012). One example of a language difference is an accent, a variation in the surface characteristics of language. If you have

PROFESSIONAL EDGE

Understanding Dialects

Many misconceptions exist regarding dialects (Newton, 2004). Here are some of the most common:

Myth: Other people have dialects, but not me.

Reality: No spoken language exists in a pure form, and so everyone speaks with some type of dialect.

Myth: People who speak a dialect usually are easily identified because their language is so different from what is "normal."

Reality: Some dialects may receive more attention than others (e.g., a southern drawl), but dialects may be subtle and often unnoticed.

Myth: Dialects refer to language spoken by people from poor, rural areas, or those considered undesirable.

Reality: Dialects exist across all peoples and cultures; they are not limited to specific cultures, groups, or income levels.

Myth: Dialects are flawed language, occurring when some people do not learn to "speak correctly."

Reality: Dialects are passed from generation to generation as children imitate the language of those in their community. A dialect is not a failed attempt of a language.

Myth: Dialects generally communicate negative social connotations.

Reality: How a dialect is perceived depends completely on the response of those who hear it. By itself, a dialect is neither negative nor positive.

As you work with students, you can help all of them to understand how language differences such as dialects are part of the diversity and richness of today's society. Here are some suggestions for helping students to understand dialects:

- Use literature written in various dialects (e.g., short stories, poems, dialogue). Students can read passages out loud, compare ways people talk with ways they write, and discuss spelling variations.
- Play music with lyrics in various dialects. Have students write out lyrics and discuss the language used (e.g., its authenticity).
- Recognize and respect student dialects by allowing their use without correction during classroom discussions, when they are writing in journals, or acting out plays with dialogue.
- Have students explore the grammatical rules of a dialect. They might try to create lessons for teaching the dialect to others or try translating a poem in standard English to a dialect.

friends from different parts of the country, you may comment that one of them has a Boston accent or a Southern accent. You are referring to the way they pronounce words or make particular sounds, but you are not implying that their language is disordered. If you know individuals who learned English after learning another language, you may notice that they, too, speak English with an accent.

A somewhat different example is a dialect, which refers to the structure of language and the rules that govern it. One dialect that has received considerable attention is African American Vernacular English (AAVE), sometimes called *Black-English* or *Ebonics* (e.g., Beneke & Cheatham, 2015; Wheeler, Cartwright, & Swords, 2012). It is spoken by many (but not all) working-class African American families, and it includes differences in some of the sounds made (*dis* for *this*) and words used (*Where is my paper at?* instead of *Where is my paper?*). The Professional Edge outlines myths and realities related to dialects and provides suggestions for addressing dialects in the classroom.

Keep in mind that dialects are differences, not disorders. In fact, in recent years, professionals have worked diligently to stop the practice of trying to change students' dialects. Instead, they have focused on helping students learn to *code-switch*, or to use standard English when it is important to do so and to use their dialect in the family, community, and other appropriate settings (Fisher & Lapp, 2013). The Instruction in Action explains more about code-switching.

INSTRUCTION IN **ACTION**

Breaking the Code on Code-Switching

Code-switching occurs when an individual switches from one language or dialect to another. It also can occur within a language, as when you speak differently (e.g., more formally, using or excluding particular words) to your grandmother than to your close friends. Here are three examples of code-switching:

Language Code-Switching

Students who are bilingual may switch between languages, either within a sentence or between sentences. Although this can indicate a problem in language proficiency, it may also have other purposes, such as the following (Sayer, 2008):

- A student whose first language is not English uses phrases or sentences in that language, especially to express complex ideas, emphasize a point, or convey nuances of emotion.
- A student speaks English to teachers but immediately switches to her first language in interactions with peers who also speak that language.

Dialectical Code-Switching

Dialects differ from standard patterns of English. African American vernacular English (AAVE) is one common dialect that has its own grammatical rules and patterns. Professionals recommend that teachers not treat this dialect as a set of errors but, rather, explicitly teach their students how to code-switch by showing them the differences, helping them to master these differences, and providing opportunities to practice code-switching (Wheeler, 2008). Here are examples:

- Subject-verb agreement (*John come [versus comes] to school every day.*)
- Possessives (*My brother [versus brother's] coat got torn.*)
- Past tense (*Joe finish [versus finished] his paper yesterday.*)

Digital Language Code-Switching

The abbreviated language forms students use for texting, e-mail, social networking, and instant messaging may show up in students' written work. As with dialects, it may be more effective to teach students to switch between text-speak and standard English than to convey to students that the former is inferior and incorrect. Here are examples:

- Use of phonetic or shortened spellings (e.g., *u, r, cuz*)
- Omission of capital letters at the beginning of sentences and in proper names
- Omission of apostrophes in contractions (e.g., *wont versus won't, cant versus can't*)

Which of these types of code-switching affect your own language use? Which might you encounter with your students? How could you teach code-switching to them?

Other Cultural Influences on Communication

Accent and dialect are not the only cultural factors that may affect language. Students who are English language learners may experience difficulty in learning how to begin or finish a conversation, may have to learn to take turns during conversations, may not understand subtle humor, and may struggle to pronounce some words correctly. Likewise, they may be reluctant to initiate conversations or to contribute to them.

The examples that have been provided in this section are intended only to illustrate some of the issues related to speech and language and diversity. Comparable comments could be made for the many other cultural groups that make up the population of this country. All school professionals need to be aware of their students' language differences and learn how to work appropriately with students who do not speak standard English. Further, they need to recognize the risk of mistaking a language difference for a language disorder and seek input from speech and language professionals when they have concerns regarding a particular student's speech and language skills.

Language differences, such as dialects, are not language disorders, and professionals know that students can learn to switch between formal and informal language patterns, depending on the situation.

The Use of Evidence-Based Practices

Throughout education, including special education and the field of speech and language services, a significant trend is the identification of *evidence-based practices* and their use in schools (Gerber, Brice, Capone, Fujiki, & Timler, 2012; Olswang, & Prelock, 2015). That is, speech-language therapists are emphasizing that the interventions used with students should be only those for which high-quality, multiple research studies have demonstrated effectiveness and a systematic use by clinicians has supported their use. The trend toward the use of evidence-based practices is a direct result of the accountability movement in today's schools.

The implications of using evidence-based practices in speech-language services are far reaching. Here are some examples:

- *Collection of data.* Speech-language therapists are expected more and more to gather systematic data that can be used to judge the effectiveness of their strategies for preventing the development of speech and language problems, their diagnostic procedures, and their methods for intervening to address student speech and language difficulties. Depending on student needs and your role, you could be asked to assist in this task.

- *Use of data for decision making.* Although decisions regarding speech and language services have always relied on data, the focus on evidence-based practices strengthens the expectation that interventions should be attempted or continued based on specific data related to the students with whom they are used and large-scale studies that document their impact (Baker & McLeod, 2011a; Snell et al., 2010). Conversely, strategies that are not supported by research or not demonstrated to be positively influencing students' skills should be discarded.

- *Professional education.* Clearly, speech-language therapists need to be educated about the importance of evidence-based practices and the ways in which they should guide practices in public schools. At the same time, teachers and other educators need to know why these practices should be central to speech-language therapists' work, how teachers can participate in further developing evidence-based practices, and what these practices imply for students and their families (Wilson, McNeill, & Gillon, 2015).

Knowledge about the effectiveness of various interventions for students with speech and language disorders undoubtedly will continue to expand (e.g., Vouloumanos & Waxman, 2014). These efforts can help ensure that the time available to improve outcomes for students will be spent as wisely as possible.

MyEdLab **Self-Check 9.7**

MyEdLab **Application Exercise 9.12:** Accent, Dialect, and Code-Switching

---

Summary

LO9.1   Speech and language disorders have been a professional area of study since the beginning of the 19th century. Although IDEA provides a simple definition of speech and language impairments, many specific disorders are encompassed by this disability category, including receptive and expressive language disorders and speech disorders. These disorders can result from biological or environmental factors.

LO9.2   Students with speech and language disorders vary widely in terms of their cognitive ability and academic achievement as well as in their social or emotional status and the likelihood of displaying behavior problems.

LO9.3   Speech-language pathologists are the specialists who evaluate students using formal and informal means to determine whether these disorders are present, but as for all students, a comprehensive evaluation is required, and a team determines eligibility for special education services.

LO9.4   Most students with speech and language disorders, often identified early in their school careers, receive their education in typical schools and participate in general education for nearly all the time.

LO9.5   Increasingly, interventions for students with speech or language disorders focus on blending the skills that speech-language pathologists can bring to the overall instructional program and the use of augmentative and alternative communication strategies, if needed.

LO9.6   The parents and families of students with speech and language disorders are as diverse as the students themselves, and their preferences and concerns may, in part, be culturally determined.

LO9.7   Issues facing the field of speech and language disorders include differentiating between language differences and language disabilities in an increasingly diverse student population and the importance of implementing evidence-based practices.

Back to the Cases

Now that you've read about speech and language disorders, look back at the student stories at the beginning of this chapter. Then, answer the questions about each of their cases.

MyEdLab **Case Study 9.1**

JONAS. Jonas often is frustrated when his attempts to communicate are not understood, and yesterday, after trying to explain himself multiple times, he hit a classmate who did not understand that he wanted to use the scissors the other student had. The teacher quickly intervened, but by then both children were crying—one because of the hit and Jonas because of his frustration. The team is meeting to discuss what to do to address this specific situation and to identify strategies to ensure that it does not happen again.

MyEdLab **Case Study 9.2**

SAVANNAH. Savannah is experiencing lingering effects related to her speech and language skills as a result of injuries she suffered in a car accident. She received hospital and home-based special education for an entire school year, but she still has difficulty communicating.

MyEdLab **Case Study 9.3**

DAVID. David is preparing to leave school for the world of work, where communication will be essential for success. As a student with a moderate intellectual disability, he may seek employment at a restaurant, a hotel, or a grocery store.

10 Students with Autism Spectrum Disorder

JUSTIN

Justin is a kindergarten student who was diagnosed with autism when he was just 2 years old. His parents were looking for an explanation for his language delays, his obsession with certain toys and activities, and his lack of eye contact and indifference to physical affection. Justin's grandmother, a special education teacher, suspected autism spectrum disorder, and she was correct. Fortunately, Justin receives intensive interventions in a preschool program, and the results have been remarkable in terms of his communication skills and ability to play with peers. Justin's overall intellectual and academic skills are slightly above average, and he participates in general education nearly all day, exceptions being 30 minutes each day of special education in a resource room with a focus on strengthening his language skills and working on his social skills, as well as 30 minutes twice each week of speech-language therapy. He also receives services (30 minutes each week) from the occupational therapist, but she comes to Justin's general education classroom for that purpose, teaching him and several other kindergarteners fine-motor skills. One recent setback is causing concern: Justin seems to have regressed in bathroom habits, with accidents happening when he fails to go to the restroom. His parents, kindergarten teacher, and special education teacher will meet soon with the school psychologist to discuss what might be causing this problem and to develop a plan for addressing it. His teachers suspect he gets so interested in what he is doing that he ignores his body's signals until it is too late.

PAULA

Paula is in eighth grade, and she receives special education services because she has an intellectual disability and autism. She was diagnosed at age 3, when she seemed to regress, no longer speaking the words she had learned and withdrawing from interactions with her brothers. Her parents have expressed concern that Paula's disabilities resulted from the vaccinations she received as an infant, but the pediatrician has assured them this is not the case. Paula has an extremely high need for structure. Her mother explains that a good day at home includes getting enough sleep (sometimes a problem) and then following a precise schedule in

precise order (e.g., having cereal and milk for breakfast, THEN making the bed, THEN getting dressed, and THEN going outside to play). A bad day is when, without enough sleep, there is a schedule change, whether it is that there is no milk, or the sheets need to be laundered, or it is raining so outdoor play is not possible. Tantrums, screaming, and hitting are likely in these situations. Understanding Paula's needs, the teacher during the school day follows a clear schedule that Paula has on her desk, and when there are variations (as when a special program is scheduled), staff members carefully prepare Paula for the change. Paula is learning basic reading and math skills from special education teachers, as well as skills for interactions with others. For example, Paula has a peer buddy who comes to the special education classroom to tutor her and share social times; one of Paula's IEP goals is to greet her buddy (and others) and initiate conversation with her.

CASEY

Casey, a 15-year-old boy, attends a large suburban high school. He is enrolled in a drama course, and some of the students in the course have befriended him, including Matt. On entering the classroom one day, Matt walked up to Casey and said, "What's up, dog?" a common greeting among the popular group at the high school. However, Casey did not understand and proceeded to become quite upset, repeatedly yelling "Don't call me *dog*!" Even though Matt tried to explain that it was a greeting, Casey did not understand. The special education teacher wrote a social story (explained later in this chapter) to help Casey understand that "What's up, dog?" is a greeting and does not mean that Matt is calling him a *dog*. It is just a funny way to be friendly and say "Hi." The social story was made with words and icons because Casey, as is common for students with autism, enjoys picture books. After the special educator introduced the story to him, he understood and even began using the expression himself. Casey's parents own a popular local restaurant, and they anticipate that Casey will work in the family business. They are working closely with school professionals to address situations that cause misunderstandings for Casey and to identify and teach him the skills he will need after he graduates.

If you watch the popular media for information about individuals with autism, you might wonder whether some professionals are making mistakes: In newspaper stories, magazine articles, movies, and novels, individuals with autism sometimes are portrayed as brilliant but eccentric, sometimes as significantly impaired, and sometimes as turned almost completely inward, as though incapable of dealing with the realities of day-to-day living. In fact, all of these descriptions could be based in truth. Autism, today often referred to as autism spectrum disorder (ASD), has been described as an enigma because individuals identified as having this disability may have widely different characteristics that set them apart from typical peers and from peers with other disabilities (Delmolino & Harris, 2012).

Understanding Autism Spectrum Disorder

The study of autism spectrum disorder is relatively new in the field of special education, as can be seen in the time line of its development in Figure 10.1. However, the evolution of understanding about this disability has been rapid (Matson & Goldin, 2013), and today's practices for students with autism spectrum disorder are informed by considerable and rapidly expanding research about students' characteristics and needs.

Development of the Field of Autism Spectrum Disorder

In 1943, psychologist Leo Kanner described a unique group of 11 children whose very unusual behaviors made them qualitatively different from children with other disabilities. According to Kanner (1943), these children's special needs were apparent in early childhood and included the following:

- An inability to relate typically to other people and situations
- Delayed speech and language development, failure to use developed language for communication purposes, and other speech and language abnormalities, such as extreme literalness
- Typical physical growth and development
- An obsessive insistence on environmental sameness
- An extreme fascination and preoccupation with objects
- Stereotypic or repetitive behavior and other forms of self-stimulation

The characteristics of autism as first described by Kanner more than half a century ago have been revised, refined, and broadened in recent years. Nonetheless, today's definitions and conceptualizations of autism continue to reflect many of Kanner's original observations.

Other developments in the field quickly followed, including the identification by Hans Asperger of a disorder potentially distinct from autism and familiar to many today as Asperger syndrome (Baron-Cohen, 2015). Also common was the belief, held by many professionals, that autism was caused by detached, non-nurturing mothers–sometimes called "refrigerator mothers" (Epstein, 2014). This misconception persisted until the 1980s when published studies of twins demonstrated a genetic basis for autism (Bergbaum & Ogilvie, 2016).

Refining Understanding

With continued research in the 1980s, the knowledge base about the wide range of disorders called autism quickly grew, as did interest in finding effective treatments (e.g., Wing, 1991). Autism was identified as a separate category of disability in the Individuals with Disabilities Education Act (IDEA) beginning in 1990.

Since that time, interest in, research about, and interventions for autism have exploded. This is partly due to a dramatic increase in the number of individuals

FIGURE 10.1   Time Line of the Development of the Field of Autism Spectrum Disorder

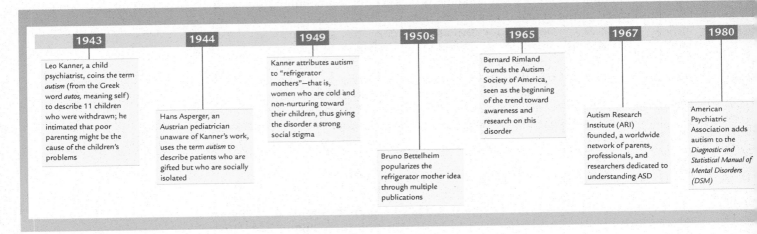

diagnosed with this disorder (Braun et al., 2015; Centers for Disease Control and Prevention, 2016). Research related to autism now is focused on identifying causes (e.g., Siu et al., 2016; Li, Zou, & Brown, 2012; Lo-Castro & Curatolo, 2014). Other efforts are focused on validating medical treatments (e.g. Berghaum & Ogilvie, 2016; McCormick, Hepburn, Young, & Rogers, 2015), identifying psychological therapies (e.g. Braida et al., 2015; Salazar et al., 2015), and evaluating educational interventions (e.g. Delmolino, Hansford, Bamon, Fiske, & LaRue, 2013; Rotheram-Fuller, & Hodas, 2015; Virues-Ortega, Rodriguez, & Yu, 2013). It is likely this work will eventually clarify the nuances of autism and the most effective approaches for students with this disorder.

Definitions of Autism Spectrum Disorder

As is true for many other disabilities, the language related to autism requires a brief explanation. The traditional term used for this group of students is *autism*, and that is the term used in IDEA and many state special education laws. The term *autism spectrum disorder (ASD)*, first used by Wing and Gould (1979), clarifies that this disorder occurs in many forms and cannot be described in any one way; ASD has rapidly become the term of choice among professionals in the field. In fact, as will be discussed later in this chapter, this term was recently adopted by the psychiatric community to replace several other terms formerly used to describe this disability.

Federal Definition

According to IDEA, autism is defined as follows:

i. Autism means a developmental disability significantly affecting verbal and nonverbal communication and social interaction, generally evident before age three, that adversely affects a child's educational performance. Other characteristics often associated with autism are engagement in repetitive activities and stereotyped movements, resistance to environmental change or change in daily routines, and unusual responses to sensory experiences.

ii. Autism does not apply if a child's educational performance is adversely affected primarily because the child has an emotional disturbance.

iii. A child who manifests the characteristics of autism after age three could be diagnosed as having autism if the criteria in paragraph (c)(1)(i) of this section are satisfied. (IDEA 20 U.S.C. §1401 [2004], 20 C.F.R. §300.8[c][1] [i–iii])

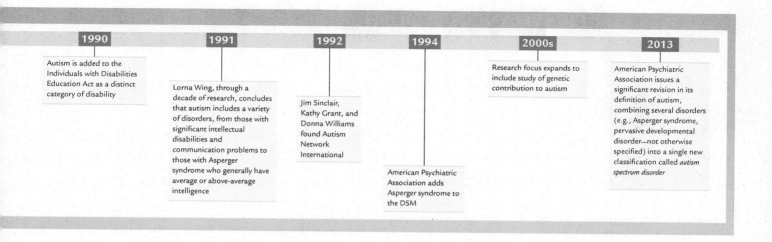

1990
Autism is added to the Individuals with Disabilities Education Act as a distinct category of disability

1991
Lorna Wing, through a decade of research, concludes that autism includes a variety of disorders, from those with significant intellectual disabilities and communication problems to those with Asperger syndrome who generally have average or above-average intelligence

1992
Jim Sinclair, Kathy Grant, and Donna Williams found Autism Network International

1994
American Psychiatric Association adds Asperger syndrome to the DSM

2000s
Research focus expands to include study of genetic contribution to autism

2013
American Psychiatric Association issues a significant revision in its definition of autism, combining several disorders (e.g., Asperger syndrome, pervasive developmental disorder—not otherwise specified) into a single new classification called *autism spectrum disorder*

This definition follows the pattern of IDEA, specifying some essential characteristics of students with the disorder, excluding other disabilities, and identifying the necessity of impact on educational performance. However, it does not provide much detail in terms of understanding the many types of students who might have this disorder.

Definition of the American Psychiatric Association

Because autism spectrum disorder generally is diagnosed by the medical community using criteria set forth in the *Diagnostic and Statistical Manual of Mental Disorders (DSM-V)* (American Psychiatric Association, 2013), it is important for educators to be aware of this definition as well as the one provided in IDEA. Although the previous version of the *DSM* included a broad category called pervasive developmental disorder (PDD) and within that category included autism disorder, Asperger disorder, and other related conditions, the current manual eliminated the narrow diagnostic labels and adopted the term **autism spectrum disorder (ASD)** to encompass all of them. The most significant criteria for ASD are significant difficulties in the domains of (a) social interactions or communication and (b) repetitive behavior and fixated or restricted interests.

This recent change in definition was a historic event for the field. The rationale for the change concerned the difficulty of distinguishing in the previous system among the various types of disorders (American Psychiatric Association, 2013). Concerns also have been raised, however. For example, some professionals believe that the new definition will significantly limit the number of individuals identified as having this disorder (Maenner et al., 2014), thus depriving them of needed supports and services (e.g., Posar, Resca, & Visconti, 2015). Others fear that the revised classification approach could dramatically affect the amount and types of research conducted on ASD (e.g., Carmack, 2014; Parsloe & Babrow, 2016).

Autism was included as a disability category for education in IDEA in 1990, but it also is a medical diagnosis described in the Diagnostic and Statistical Manual of Mental Disorders (DSM-V).

Did You Know?

Although the term *Asperger syndrome* is no longer part of the terminology for individuals with ASD, you probably will encounter the replacement phrase *students with high functioning ASD* (HFASD).

TEMPLE GRANDIN, A TRULY EXCEPTIONAL PERSON

TEMPLE GRANDIN *is one of the most famous individuals with autism. She is the author of several books about autism and has also written an autobiography. Now at Colorado State University, she is an associate professor who designs livestock facilities.*

Temple Grandin, Ph.D., is a truly accomplished professional. She is associate professor of animal science at Colorado State University. She is known worldwide for her work related to the humane handling of cattle at meat plants, work designed to reduce animal fear and pain. Nearly half of all cattle handling in the United States is based on equipment that she designed, and she has consulted on this topic with huge corporations such as

McDonald's and Burger King and others worldwide. In 2009, she was named a fellow of the *American Society of Agricultural and Biological Engineers.*

What makes Dr. Grandin's accomplishments even more remarkable is that she has autism. Born in 1947, she did not speak until she was 3 years old. At about that time, she was labeled *autistic,* and her parents were advised to place her in an institution. However, her mother enrolled her in a highly structured nursery school and also hired a nanny who spent many hours playing games with Dr. Grandin that emphasized taking turns. Dr. Grandin recalls middle school and high school as painful, full of teasing and name-calling. But he persisted, and after graduation, she began her college career in the field

of psychology, switching to animal science for her master's and doctoral degrees.

Dr. Grandin is a strong advocate for individuals with autism, and she has appeared on many network television shows and specials and has been featured in several major national magazines. She is also a best-selling author on this topic, and HBO has made a movie of her life. She believes that too many people believe that individuals with autism cannot achieve success, and she is committed to changing that perception.

An Emmy award winning movie, *Temple Grandin,* was made about this remarkable woman in 2010. You also can read more about her life and accomplishments at http://www.grandin.com/.

Video Example from YouTube

MyEdLab
Video Example 10.1

You can watch Dr. Grandin describe her life with ASD in this video. (https://www.youtube.com/watch?v=1qPFAT4p8Lc)

Making Sense of the Definitions

During this time of transition in the field of ASD, you may hear a variety of perspectives on which students have this disorder, the definitions and language used to describe them, and the priorities in terms of providing special education and other services to such students. To guide your understanding, keep in mind that IDEA's definitions are the ones generally used in public schools. However, the *DSM-V* definition can inform you about the medical community's perspective of these students. Ultimately, the most important way to make sense of formal definitions is to understand that individuals with ASD are first and foremost real people who lead real lives. You can read a brief biography of one well-known individual with ASD, Temple Grandin, in the Firsthand Account.

Prevalence of Autism Spectrum Disorder

The estimated prevalence of autism spectrum disorder varies widely and is the subject of ongoing debate (e.g., Christensen et al., 2016). The U.S. Department of Education (2015) reports the prevalence of autism as 0.7% of *all* students ages 6 to 21 (called the resident population), that is, approximately 455,000 students. However, that estimate is based on school data, which are usually incomplete. The Centers for Disease Control and Prevention (CDC) (2015a), through the Autism and Developmental Disabilities Monitoring (ADDM) network, estimates the prevalence as 1 in 68 children. The CDC also notes that boys are 4.5 times more likely than girls to have ASD (i.e., it occurs in 1 out of 42 boys and in 1 out of 189 girls).

Prevalence of ASD also may be affected by the *DSM-V* definitional change. Some professionals hypothesize that it will underrepresent people who truly do have ASD, while others propose it may inflate the numbers. For example, a study by Maenner et al. (2014) applied the *DSM-V* criteria to previous prevalence data and concluded a drop in the rate of diagnosis would occur.

Other Prevalence Considerations

Similar to other disability categories, questions often are raised about whether students from various racial or ethnic backgrounds are more or less likely to be identified as having ASD. The most recent IDEA data suggest some differences do exist (U.S. Department of Education, 2015): Keeping in mind that a risk ratio of 1 means that students are represented in a disability category exactly in the proportion as they are represented in the population, students who are Native Hawaiian/Other Pacific Islander have a risk ratio for autism of 1.25; Caucasian students have a risk ratio of 1.21. In contrast, Hispanic students have a risk ratio of 0.75, and those who are American Indian/Native Alaskan have a risk ratio of 0.88. That is, the first two groups of students are somewhat more likely to be identified, and the latter two groups somewhat less likely.

Racial, ethnic, and other differences extend to the domain of treatment as well. When researchers explore whether children diagnosed as autistic receive intensive early interventions, considered critical for achieving positive outcomes, they find that Caucasian children and children in high socioeconomic groups are more likely than other children to access such services (e.g., Irvin, McBee, Boyd, Hume, & Odom, 2012; Magaña, Parish, & Son, 2015).

Causes of Autism Spectrum Disorder

As with many disabilities, the specific causes of autism spectrum disorder are not completely understood. Professionals generally agree that symptoms of this disability are triggered by genetic differences or other malfunctions in the brain (e.g., Frazier et al., 2014), although environmental factors may contribute to the disorder (e.g., Kocovska, Fernell, Billstedt, Minnis, & Gillberg, 2012). Research on the causes of ASD is leading to rapid changes in the field. To learn about how to find the most current information, access the resources summarized in the Professional Edge.

Biological Factors

Researchers currently are focusing on genetic factors related to autism spectrum disorder, speculating that DNA likely is responsible for causing developmental dysfunction in the brains of individuals with this disability. Simple logic based on this hypothesis is that parents with autism spectrum disorder are likely to have a child with ASD. However, such cases are very rare. Extensive genetic research has shown that many genes may contribute to the development of ASD and various specific characteristics of this disorder (Gong, Yan, Xie, Liu, & Sun, 2012; Lo-Castro & Curatolo, 2014), but the degree of exhibited symptoms varies across family structure (e.g., Smith et al., 2009). For example, the father of a child identified with an autism spectrum disorder might have subtle characteristics (e.g., relatively intense concentration when working on a favorite project) compared with others, or odd social skills, but function in an acceptable manner in his social life. Some evidence also suggests a high frequency of autism spectrum disorder among siblings when compared to other disabilities (Yoo, 2015), although this is not a universal finding (De la Marche et al., 2012). Viewed collectively, research to date suggests that no single genetic factor is responsible for causing autism spectrum disorder, but instead that multiple genetic factors seem to intricately connect to form a wide range of developmental malfunctions.

Many topics related to autism spectrum disorder are changing rapidly. More students are being identified with ASD, medical studies are increasing knowledge about the causes of this disability, and research is under way to identify treatments and interventions that would be most beneficial to students. If you are interested in keeping up with research related to autism, here are resources to use:

- The Autism Centers of Excellence (ACE) Program (https://www.nichd.nih.gov/research/supported/Pages/ace.aspx) is supported by the National Institutes of Health and was created in 2007 to bring together several initiatives related to autism research. ACE's purpose is to conduct research on the causes of autism, and studies underway address genetics, environmental contributions, and immunological factors. The ACE program also is charged with examining the diagnosis of autism, including early detection, the characteristics of individuals with autism with an emphasis on behavior and communication, and treatments. A final area

of emphasis is intervention, including effective medical treatments. The Autism Research Institute (ARI) (http://www.autism.com) was founded by the father of autism research, Dr. Bernard Rimland, in 1967. This institute, based at the Cleveland Clinic, contributes funding to research on autism, and it provides summaries of the research being conducted. It emphasizes research through the life span, including studies of adults with ASD. At its website, you also can find information immediately helpful to teachers. For example, the site recently posted a video about accommodations that should be considered when working with students with ASD.

- The Organization for Autism Research (OAR) (http://www.researchautism.org/), founded in 2001, is focused on applied research, that is, research that has immediate implications for practice. This organization funds small research projects, but it also includes summaries of the results of its projects, information about other research, and classroom practice ideas.

Autism Spectrum Disorder and the Brain

If genes are the primary cause of autism spectrum disorder, what symptoms are found in the brain? Recent technology, such as magnetic resonance imaging (MRI), enables researchers to obtain accurate information about the brain, and a number of brain functions that may trigger autistic symptoms have been observed. For example, individuals with autism spectrum disorder have been found to have abnormalities in the cerebellum, the part of the brain that controls motor coordination, balance, and cognition (e.g., Salazar et al., 2015). Similarly, research has surveyed the frontal and temporal lobes: The frontal lobe manages social and cognitive functions (Klin, Jones, Schultz, & Volkmar, 2003; Pierce & Courchesne, 2001), whereas the temporal lobe is involved in understanding facial expressions and in social cues and memory (e.g., Dougherty, Evans, Myers, Moore, & Michael, 2016; Rahko et al., 2016; Itier & Taylor, 2004). Researchers generally have found that in these and other parts of the brain, individuals with autism spectrum disorder may have fewer cells, higher cell density, or less volume than in typical individuals, and their brain development is likely to be atypical (e.g., Lainhart, 2015).

Environmental Factors

Although the early belief that autism spectrum disorder was caused almost exclusively by environmental factors such as maternal neglect has long been proven untrue, most professionals agree that these factors can influence the number and intensity of symptoms (Vijayakumar & Judy, 2016). For example, the quality of care by family members and professionals plays an important role in the development of children with autism spectrum disorder (Burrell & Borrego, 2012; Ludlow, Skelly, & Rohleder, 2012; Mandy & Lai, 2016). A positive, structured environment can significantly improve behavior problems often displayed by these children and youth. In many cases, positive supports, unconditional family love, and similar factors probably have a positive effect on how the symptoms of autism spectrum disorder occur.

Autism and Immunizations

One of the most controversial causal issues related to autism spectrum disorder is immunization, especially that given for measles, mumps, and rubella (MMR). However, findings to date have largely discredited this view (Centers for Disease Control and Prevention, 2015b). For example, the Institute of Medicine 2013, part of the U.S. Department of Health and Human Services, did a thorough review of all available scientific evidence related to eight vaccines typically administered to young children (measles-mumps-rubella/MMR, varicella for chickenpox, influenza, hepatitis A, hepatitis B, human papillomavirus/HPV, meningococcal, and diphtheria-toxoid/tetanus toxoid/acellular pertussis containing). The conclusion issued was that vaccines generally are very safe and that serious side effects are very rare. In particular, no causal link was found between the MMR vaccine and ASD. This finding was echoed in a report by the American Academy of Pediatrics (2013), and it also is consistent with a retraction that was issued by the authors of a key study on this topic that had reported a clear link and fueled the debate on the danger of immunizations.

Despite the absence of evidence of a link between vaccinations and the onset of autism, you probably will meet professionals and parents who continue to believe a relationship exists. For example, in one study, researchers surveyed parents of children who had been diagnosed with autism, asking them whether they had changed or discontinued vaccinations for their children after the diagnosis (Bazzano, Zeldin, Schuster, Barrett, & Lehrer, 2012). Half of the parents had done so, still associating immunizations with an autism diagnosis.

MyEdLab **Self-Check 10.1**

MyEdLab **Application Exercise 10.1:** Defining and Understanding Autism Spectrum Disorder

Characteristics of Individuals with Autism Spectrum Disorder

Beginning at an early age and typically continuing throughout the life span, individuals with autism spectrum disorder have difficulty relating appropriately to others. They usually have a wide range of language and communication disorders. Many have an obsessive insistence on environmental sameness and are well known for their atypical and often difficult-to-understand behaviors, including stereotypic, repetitive, and self-stimulatory responses (e.g., Houwen, Visser, van der Putten, & Vlaskamp, 2016; Moulton, Barton, Robins, Abrams, & Fein, 2016). However, each student with these disabilities may have a unique combination of strengths and needs.

Cognitive and Academic Characteristics

Children and youth with ASD often have irregular patterns of cognitive and educational strengths and deficits, with the majority of individuals with ASD having some level of intellectual disability, although some have average to above-average ability (Gillberg, Helles, Billstedt, & Gillberg, 2016). Further, most individuals with autism have a comorbid psychiatric disorder, often depression or ADHD, and these individuals generally have poorer outcomes that those who do not have comorbid diagnoses.

Although children and youth with autism share some characteristics with students with other disabilities, their unique features set them apart and sometimes create significant challenges for those who serve them. These distinguishing characteristics include overreliance on rote memory, problems with theory of mind, and problem-solving challenges.

Rote Memory

Rote memory is the ability to easily remember things without necessarily knowing what they mean. Have you ever memorized a phrase in a different language or a mathematical formula so that you could say it or write it when you needed to—even if you did not understand what it meant? Those are examples of rote memory. Although rote memory usually would be considered an asset, it can be a great liability for students with autism spectrum disorder. Because they often have well-developed rote memory skills, students with these disabilities can give the impression that they understand certain concepts when in fact they do not (Gabig, 2008). For example, a student with autism may hear certain words or phrases in conversation and then use them in a rote manner that mimics comprehension. This parroting gives the inaccurate impression that the student has well-developed, higher-level comprehension skills.

Rote memory may be a disadvantage for students with autism spectrum disorder in another way, too. Adults often assume that having strong rote memory skills means that students can remember, at any time, pieces of information or events. But this is not true for many individuals with autism spectrum disorder. Although chunks of information are stored in memory, students with this exceptionality may have trouble retrieving them. Often, a question worded in a specific manner must be used to prompt retrieval from memory. For example, Devon, a 12-year-old boy with autism, has memorized all of the menu items at a fast-food restaurant. However, unless the server asks "May I take your order?" Devon cannot recall what he wants to order and may repeat all the items on the menu. The server's words need to be precise in order for Devon to access the information he has memorized.

Theory of Mind

One of the core cognitive deficits of autism spectrum disorder concerns theory of mind. This relatively new explanation of autism is based on the belief that people with this disorder do not truly understand that others have their own thoughts and points of view and that people with autism face challenges in understanding others' beliefs and emotions (Boucher, 2012; Hutchins et al., 2016). Difficulties with theory of mind can be seen when individuals with autism spectrum disorder have difficulty explaining their own behaviors, recognizing that others may not know answers to their questions, predicting others' emotions or behaviors, comprehending others' perspectives, understanding how behavior affects others' thoughts and feelings, participating in conversations, and distinguishing fact from fiction (Gupta, 2015; Miller, 2012; Myles & Southwick, 2005).

Although theory of mind has been explored in studying the development of all children (e.g., Miller, 2012), professionals are finding that deficits in this domain often distinguish individuals with autism spectrum disorder from individuals with other disabilities. For example, Robert, a high school sophomore with ASD, could not understand why he was in trouble for loudly announcing that his history teacher had bad breath. In his mind, he was only telling the truth and could not comprehend the impact of his words on his teacher or classmates.

Problem Solving

Many students with ASD have access to only one problem-solving strategy for a particular situation and use it consistently, regardless of whether it is successful and even if the situation changes. Difficulty retrieving information or strategies may make problem solving even more challenging (Alderson-Day, 2011). For example, when Alex could not find his toothbrush, he discontinued brushing his teeth. It did not occur to him to ask his mother to purchase a new toothbrush or to help him to find the old one. Although learners with autism spectrum disorder may be able to recite several problem-solving strategies and verbally report that they can be generalized, often they are not able to recall any of these strategies when needed. That is, Paula, who was introduced at the beginning of the chapter, has learned that if she is not sure how to find her classroom, she can ask another student or an adult, or look to see if she is near the office and ask someone there. When she suddenly becomes disoriented, though, she cannot remember what to do and begins screaming and thus still needs to be accompanied from class to class.

Problem solving becomes even more difficult if abstract concepts or interpersonal interactions are involved (Goddard, Howlin, Dritschel, & Patel, 2007). The problem-solving deficits of some students, especially those with average or above average intellectual ability, may not be recognized easily, thus making the situation even more complex. Their pedantic style, advanced vocabulary, and grammatically perfect responses often mask their skill levels. For these reasons, by the time they realize that a problem exists, they often are so confused or angry that their reactions are inappropriate, sometimes involving tantrums or withdrawal.

Social and Emotional Characteristics

The social and emotional challenges that students with autism spectrum disorder encounter are directly related to their other special needs. In particular, language disorders, unconventional language use, and immaturity often characterize these students (e.g., Ellis, 2016).

Language Disorders

Many students with autism spectrum disorder have extraordinary difficulties related to language (DiStefano, Shih, Kaiser, Landa, & Kasari, 2016), and these differences sometimes can be identified as early as their first birthday (Lazenby et al., 2016; Veness et al., 2012). This, in turn, has a significant negative impact on their abilities to interact successfully with others. For example, they may experience delays in developing language. In addition, they may fail to use language to communicate, or they may lack the desire to interact with others.

Several examples of language disorders can clarify how important this area is for students with autism spectrum disorder. Students may have problems with proxemics—that is, knowing the socially acceptable distance to maintain between people during conversation. These students may stand closer to or farther away from another person than is customary. They also may stare intensely at another person while interacting, making that person very uncomfortable. In contrast, some students may fail to make any eye contact at all, looking to the side or up or down during conversation. This makes it difficult for the other person to judge whether the student is engaged in the topic being discussed. In addition, students may fail to understand or respond to others' gestures and facial expressions during communication. As a result, they may not notice that the other person is bored or that the person wants to ask a question.

Other Language Problems

Students at the higher end of the autism spectrum often have unusual traits in their language skills (e.g., Lane, Lieberman-Betz, & Gast, 2016; Wing, 1981). For example, Louise, a 6-year-old with Asperger syndrome, told her mother that

Did You Know?

Neurodiversity is the concept that autism, as well as other disabilities, are normal variations of functioning of the human mind, not pathological conditions or deficits. The neurodiversity movement calls for appropriate supports and inclusiveness for all individuals and may refer to those without ASD or other disabilities as *neurotypicals*.

she "waved" her clothes on the bathroom floor. She was using the word *waved* instead of *left*. Her reason was that you "wave when you leave."

Many students with ASD cannot comprehend language related to abstract ideas such as democracy and justice. They also may struggle with understanding and correctly using figures of speech such as metaphors, idioms, parables, and allegories and grasping the meaning and intent of rhetorical questions. For example, when Rick was told, "Put your best foot forward," he looked down and asked which foot was his best foot!

Immaturity

When you think of an individual whom you consider mature, what characteristics come to mind? Maturity is often assessed by actions in social situations. To be socially adept, people must be able to perceive and understand social cues such as frowns, smiles, boredom, and other expressions of emotion. They must be able to think clearly about their own behaviors and the

behaviors of others. Some students with ASD may have good structural language skills, such as clear pronunciation and correct syntax, but otherwise poor communication abilities. For example, some students may repeat the same phrase over and over, talk with exaggerated inflections or in a monotone and droning style, discuss at length a single topic that is of little interest to others, or experience difficulty in sustaining a conversation unless it focuses exclusively on a particular narrowly defined topic. These communication problems are not surprising, given that effective communication requires that individuals have mutually shared topics to communicate about and are willing to listen as well as to talk.

The unique pattern of strengths and weaknesses that characterize each student with autism spectrum disorder is the basis for designing effective interventions for that student.

Communicative Intent

One characteristic that is somewhat unique to individuals with autism spectrum disorder concerns problems with communicative intent. That is, these students often do not communicate in order to obtain the attention of others, and they may not communicate for social purposes (Meadan, Halle, & Kelly, 2012). How might this characteristic apply to Justin, whom you met at the beginning of the chapter? Approximately 50% of individuals with autism are nonverbal; that is, they have few or no verbal language skills.

Those who do have verbal skills often engage in echolalia, repeating words and phrases that have been uttered by someone else with little or no understanding of their conventional meanings. Students also may have problems with pronoun reversals, using *you* for *I* and vice versa. They also may lack voice tone or inflection. Individuals with autism may have prosody problems—use of a monotone or sing-song tone of voice, regardless of the intended message (Chevallier, Noveck, Happe, & Wilson, 2009). Because of the many language disorders and communication challenges experienced by students with autism, they often make statements that do not make sense or give inappropriate responses to others' questions. They also experience frustration when their communication does not accomplish its purpose. As a result, these students often seem extraordinarily naïve or immature.

Behavior Characteristics

A final domain to consider in characterizing students with autism spectrum disorder is behavior. Some of the challenges these students may have include self-stimulatory behaviors, difficulty with generalizations, and sensory responses.

Self-Stimulatory Behaviors

Self-stimulatory behaviors may involve rocking, hand flapping, and any other repetitive, stereotyped behavior patterns that appear to have no apparent function (Centers for Disease Control and Prevention, 2015a; Rodgers, Riby, Janes, Connolly, & McConachie, 2012), although they sometimes are associated with stress. These behaviors, common for students with autism, tend to stigmatize them, interfering not only with social acceptance and integration but also with learning (McCormick, Hepburn, Young, & Rogers, 2015). Other similar behavioral challenges, such as self-injurious behaviors (e.g., self-biting, head banging), also can be serious issues; however, such behaviors are relatively uncommon.

When a student's behavior is uncontrolled and continued to an exceptional degree, it is referred to as perseveration, and this is one of the most common ASD characteristics. Perseveration may relate to an object, as when a student is obsessively interested in a toy; an action, as when a student rocks for an extended period of time; or a verbal pattern, as when a student asks the same question many times. Professionals working with students with ASD often implement structured behavioral programs to reduce these behaviors (e.g. Fiske et al., 2015).

Generalization Difficulties

A major challenge facing educators and others who work with students with autism spectrum disorder relates to students' difficulty in transferring information to new settings, individuals, and conditions. As a result, a student who is able to perform a written task in one classroom cannot be assumed to be able to perform the same task correctly in another classroom. To address generalization, professionals must spend considerable time developing strategies for enabling students to use information and skills flexibly. These strategies may include practicing skills in community and general education classroom settings, receiving support from peers, and learning to self-monitor (Smith, Ayres, Alexander, Ledford, Shepley, & Shepley, 2016).

Sensory Issues

Students with autism spectrum disorder experience a myriad of sensory processing issues (McCormick, Hepburn, Young, & Rogers, 2015; Woodard et al., 2012). That is, they have difficulty with the (a) tactile, (b) vestibular, (c) proprioception, (d) visual, (e) auditory, (f) gustatory, and (g) olfactory senses. Figure 10.2 provides an overview of each of the sensory systems, including its location and function.

The figure also provides examples of how students with autism may experience difficulties related to the senses. For example, you may know a person with autism who can hear sounds that are not discernible to those without autism or who finds the feeling of a tag inside a shirt very painful. Because the visual area tends to be a strength for students with autism spectrum disorder, visual supports often are used to assist in learning (Kaldy, Giserman, Carter, & Blaser, 2016; Meadan, Ostrosky, Triplett, Michna, & Fettig, 2011).

Sensory difficulties affect all areas of learning (e.g., McPartland, Bernier, & South, 2015). Many students with autism spectrum disorder receive occupational therapy to address these issues and to receive the maximum benefit from instruction. All professionals who work with students with autism spectrum disorder should be aware of the impact of sensory issues on behavior and achievement (e.g., Mays, Beal-Alvarez, & Jolivette, 2011).

FIGURE 10.2   **Understanding Sensory Systems and Autism**

Students with autism may experience difficulties with each of the seven sensory systems, described below, with examples given of the types of problems that may occur.

System	Location	Function	Example of Sensory Problems
Tactile (touch)	• Skin—density of cell distribution varies throughout the body. Areas of greatest density include mouth, hands, and genitals.	• Provides information about the environment and object qualities (e.g., touch, pressure, texture, hard, soft, sharp, dull, heat, cold, pain).	• Feel of fabric texture on skin may be painful; student may not feel heat or cold and so is more at risk for injuries.
Vestibular (balance)	• Inner ear—stimulated by head movements and input from other senses, especially vision.	• Provides information about where our body is in space and whether we or our surroundings are moving. Tells about speed and direction of movement.	• Student may lose balance more easily than classmates or experience difficulty in some games or activities (e.g., jumping rope, playing basketball).
Proprioception (body awareness)	• Muscles and joints—activated by muscle contractions and movement.	• Provides information about where a certain body part is and how it is moving.	• Student may seem clumsy, bumping into desks in narrow aisles or knocking crayons off a table.
Visual (sight)	• Retina of the eye—stimulated by light.	• Provides information about objects and persons. Helps us define boundaries as we move through time and space.	• Student may be very sensitive to bright lights such as those found in classrooms.
Auditory (hearing)	• Inner ear—stimulated by air or sound waves.	• Provides information about sounds in the environment (loud, soft, high, low, near, far).	• Certain sounds (e.g., fire alarm) may be too loud for the student; student may focus on sounds others do not attend to (e.g., electrical hum from classroom equipment).
Gustatory (taste)	• Chemical receptors in the tongue—closely associated with the olfactory (smell) system.	• Provides information about different types of taste (e.g., sweet, sour, bitter, salty, spicy).	• Student may refuse to eat anything except certain preferred foods.
Olfactory (smell)	• Chemical receptors in the nasal structure—closely associated with the gustatory system.	• Provides information about different types of smell (e.g., musty, acrid, putrid, flowery, pungent).	• Student may have a strong reaction to certain scents (e.g., perfume, materials used in a science experiment).

Source: Myles, B. S., Cook, K. T., Miller, N. E., Rinner, L., & Robbins, L. A. (2001). *Asperger syndrome and sensory issues: Practical solutions for making sense of the world* (p. 5). Autism Asperger Publishing. Reprinted with permission from Autism Asperger Publishing Co.

MyEdLab **Self-Check 10.2**

MyEdLab **Application Exercise 10.2:** Characteristics of Autism

MyEdLab **Application Exercise 10.3:** Teachers' Perspectives of Students with ASD

Identifying Autism Spectrum Disorder

The definition of autism in IDEA is very general, and so it is common for this disorder to be diagnosed using the more detailed criteria in *DSM-V* (American Psychiatric Association, 2013). Even so, identifying these students is rather complex because the symptoms occur in so many different ways and in so many degrees of intensity (e.g., Matson, Beighley, & Turygin, 2012). As for all students, a team, including the parents, must participate in the assessment and eligibility determination similar to those outlined in chapters you have already read. Finally, the child's developmental history is reviewed, and observations of behavior are assessed.

Assessment Related to Characteristics of Autism

Deciding whether a student has the characteristics of an autism spectrum disorder involves both formal and informal assessment. Psychologists and psychiatrists may use standardized instruments that are designed just for this purpose. One example is the *Autism Diagnostic Interview–Revised* (ADI–R) (Le Couteur, Lord, & Rutter, 2003). However, teachers and other professionals also may be asked to complete rating scales designed to screen students for the disability. Two examples of these rating scales are the *Modified Checklist for Autism in Toddlers-Revised* (M-CHAT) (Robins, Fein, & Barton, 2009) and the *Asperger Syndrome Diagnostic Scale* (ASDS) (Myles, Bock, & Simpson, 2001).

One additional evaluation informs professionals about whether a student has an autism spectrum disorder: sensory assessment. Usually administered by a trained professional, an instrument such as the *Sensory Profile-2* (Dunn, 2014) can be used to pinpoint specific sensory problems such as the ones about which you have already read.

Cognitive Ability, Academic Achievement, and Adaptive Skills

Part of the assessment for autism spectrum disorder is similar to the assessments completed for students who may have other disabilities. That is, individual intelligence tests are administered, as are both formal and informal assessments of academic achievement using standardized achievement tests and curriculum-based measures. Language assessment often is part of this process because, as already noted, most students with autism spectrum disorder have language-related delays or problems. In addition, students' adaptive behaviors are measured, including tasks related to self-help (e.g., dressing, brushing teeth) and functioning in the community (e.g., ordering in a fast-food restaurant, riding a bus).

Developmental Measures

Because autism spectrum disorder is considered a developmental disability, comprehensive assessment also must explore developmental characteristics. Using an instrument such as the *Psychoeducational Profile* (3rd ed.) (PEP-3) (Schopler, Lansing, Reichler, & Marcus, 2005), a professional can ask parents about their child's fine- and gross-motor skill development, language development, and related areas. For older students, questions may be asked concerning vocational skills, independent functioning, leisure activities, functional communication, and interpersonal behavior.

Behavior Assessment

Students with autism spectrum disorder nearly always have behavior challenges. These behaviors usually are assessed by asking parents, teachers, and others who interact with the student to complete a behavior checklist, a procedure you learned about in Chapter 7 regarding students with emotional disabilities.

In addition, a functional behavior analysis also may be helpful for determining the relationships between behavior and the environment for students with autism. As you may recall, the functional behavior analysis usually involves investigating antecedent events and their consequences based on a previously developed hypothesis about what is causing a behavior. Through this process, environmental, social, and communicative factors that might trigger problem

DATA-DRIVEN DECISIONS

Tools for Gathering Data about Students with ASD

Because ASD is diagnosed and monitored based on constellations of behaviors, having a wide array of data collection tools is critical for professionals working with these students. In addition to data collection options presented in other chapters, here are two websites that specifically address data collection for students with ASD as well as examples of the recording forms you will find on each website.

Practical Autism Resources

(http://www.practicalautismresources.com/forms-and-organizers)

Examples of Forms

- *Compliance:* Does the student do as requested? With or without prompting? How many prompts?
- *Independence:* Which steps of the skills being taught is the student able to complete without adult guidance?
- *Imitation:* If given a direction, does the student comply with it? How much support is needed for the student

to complete the direction (e.g., physical prompting, verbal prompting)?
- *Work behaviors:* Does the student get out the assigned work? Begin it? Persist? Complete it?

Project Start

(https://www.gvsu.edu/autismcenter/individual-student-data-collection-forms-217.htm)

- *Social interactions:* Did the student initiate an interaction with a peer? Did a peer initiate an interaction with the student?
- *Engagement:* For what amount of time or proportion of the instruction is the student engaged in the activity as directed by the teacher?
- *Independence:* Which steps of a multistep task can the student complete without prompting? With prompting (specify the number of prompts)?

behaviors are revealed and interventions can then be planned (Leader & Mannion, 2016). Think about how this type of assessment would be useful in understanding the challenges faced by a student like Paula, introduced in the opening of the chapter, both for initial assessment as well as intervention planning. Examples of data collection tools that might be used for both this type of functional behavior assessment and monitoring of the effectiveness of interventions are presented in Data-Driven Decisions.

Eligibility

After assessment data are gathered, the team of educators, medical professionals, parents, and related services personnel address the questions that guide special education decision making:

- Does a disability exist?
- Does it have a negative impact on educational performance?
- Is the student eligible for special education services?
- Will the student benefit from those services?

Two points should be stressed related to the determination of eligibility in the disability category of ASD. First, as for all students with disabilities, the most important part of the identification process is not what label is assigned but what services are provided to meet the student's needs. Continuous data collection, monitoring, and analysis through assessments and flexible interventions are essential to effectively educate such a student. Second, receiving a diagnosis of autism, especially if that decision occurs after a child has entered school, is particularly stressful for parents. Stories from parents often use expressions like "devastating," "numb," "run over by a truck," and "alone." Of course, others would add "relieved" and "affirmed" at having a label for their child's disorder. As you have learned, nearly all parents of children with disabilities experience a range of emotions upon learning of their child's special needs. For parents of children with ASD, the stress can be compounded by the sometimes sensationalized media coverage of this topic, the attention given to it by celebrities, and the sometimes very complex process of identifying and obtaining the appropriate services. Educators should be aware of the potential impact of this disability diagnosis and be prepared to offer the strong support that some parents are likely to need.

MyEdLab **Self-Check 10.3**

MyEdLab **Application Exercise 10.4:** Organizing Assessment Terminology

MyEdLab **Application Exercise 10.5:** Identifying Autism Spectrum Disorder

---

How Learners with Autism Spectrum Disorder Receive Their Education

Because children and youth with autism spectrum disorder differ greatly in their skill levels, their educational options vary as well. Generally, however, early and intensive education provides the best outcome.

Early Childhood

The National Research Council (2001) studied educational programs that provide early intervention services to young children with autism, and programs today still often have these characteristics (e.g., Frey, Small, Feil, Seeley, Walker, & Forness, 2015; Rollins, Campbell, Hoffman, & Self, 2016). The study found many instructional approaches and many variations regarding the setting in which the program was offered. For example, one program used the home as the instructional setting, and one used a school-only model. The programs shared the following features:

- Intervention prior to age 3
- Twenty to 45 hours of intervention per week
- Active family involvement
- Highly trained staff providing services to children with autism and their families
- Ongoing assessment of children's progress
- A systematically implemented curriculum
- A highly supportive teaching and learning environment
- A focus on communication goals and other developmental areas
- Plans to help students apply skills they learn in a variety of settings and to maintain their skills over time
- Individualized interventions for each student
- Plans to assist the young child and family transition from early childhood services to school-age programs

Since that report, researchers have continued to investigate these and other interventions for young children with autism spectrum disorder (e.g., Pasco & Tohill, 2015; Porter, 2012; Schertz, Odom, Baggett, & Sideris, 2012). Emphasis usually is on providing highly intensive interventions in a variety of settings with a high degree of family involvement so as to optimize student social and learning outcomes later in life.

FIGURE 10.3   **Educational Placements for Students Ages 6 to 21 Who Have Autism Spectrum Disorder (in Percentages)**

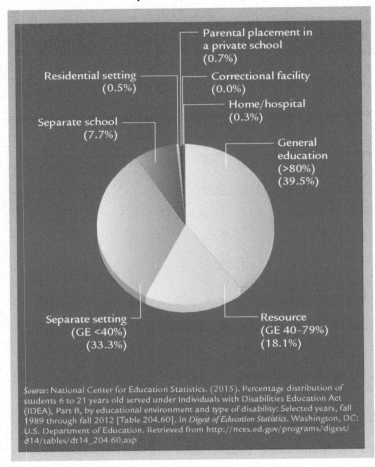

Parental placement in a private school (0.7%)

Residential setting (0.5%)

Correctional facility (0.0%)

Home/hospital (0.3%)

Separate school (7.7%)

General education (>80%) (39.5%)

Separate setting (GE <40%) (33.3%)

Resource (GE 40–79%) (18.1%)

Source: National Center for Education Statistics. (2015). Percentage distribution of students 6 to 21 years old served under Individuals with Disabilities Education Act (IDEA), Part B, by educational environment and type of disability: Selected years, fall 1989 through fall 2012 [Table 204.60]. In *Digest of Education Statistics*. Washington, DC: U.S. Department of Education. Retrieved from http://nces.ed.gov/programs/digest/d14/tables/dt14_204.60.asp

You might be thinking that many of these intervention approaches are not unique to just students with autism. Which of the items on the preceding list would apply to high-quality services for all young children with disabilities?

Elementary and Secondary School Services

According to current statistics, approximately 43% of students with autism spectrum disorder are educated primarily in a setting away from the general education classroom (U.S. Department of Education, 2015). Figure 10.3 illustrates the range of settings in which these students are served.

It should be noted that these placement data vary considerably by state. For example, fewer than 10% of students with ASD in Washington, DC, are primarily in general education settings, while in Iowa, the comparable number is greater than 60% (Kurth, 2015). Three states (Wyoming, West Virginia, New Mexico) have no students placed in settings such as separate schools or residential facilities, but 31% of students with ASD are placed in such settings.

Inclusive Practices

Although no single approach is always correct when deciding how students with disabilities should receive an education, a trend is emerging to support students with autism spectrum disorder in the general education setting more often than was common in the past (Crosland & Dunlap, 2012; Kleinert et al., 2015; Mesibov, Howley, & Naftel, 2016; Sainato, Morrison, Jung, Axe, & Nixon, 2015). For students to succeed in general education environments, however, some challenges must be addressed, including these (Majoko, 2016):

- Social isolation, often self-imposed
- Repetitive behavior and obsessions with specific objects or topics
- Focus on a narrow range of topics and inability to recognize that others may not share those interests
- Difficulty in transitioning from one activity to another in a timely manner
- Inability to recognize the feelings of classmates

These challenges should not lead to the conclusion that inclusive practices are not possible for students with ASD. One model available to guide professionals is the autism inclusion collaboration model.

Exploring the Autism Inclusion Collaboration Model

The *autism inclusion collaboration model* is designed to support general educators in their work with students with autism through collaboration with special educators and ancillary staff. The model has the following four components (Simpson, de Boer-Ott, & Smith-Myles, 2003):

- *Environmental and curricular modifications and general education classroom support.* For children and youth with autism, a variety of modifications and supports are particularly important because of these students' unique needs. The supports may include availability of appropriately trained support personnel, reduced class size, access to collaborative problem-solving relationships, adequate teacher planning time, professional development, and availability of paraprofessionals.
- *Attitudinal and social support.* Administrators, general and special education teachers, students with ASD, and their nondisabled peers must all understand and support each other in the educational system. Success depends on many types of collaboration.
- *Coordinated team commitment.* This component includes opportunities for planning and carrying out programs across all environments. It also recognizes that education professionals need support to ensure that students' needs are met in all environments. For example, if a student needs a visual schedule (explained later in this chapter), a special educator might be responsible for making that schedule available either on small cards or a tablet device that can be carried from the classroom to the lunchroom to the gym.
- *Home–school collaboration.* For successful inclusion, educators and parents must work together in a strong partnership to ensure that a comprehensive program is implemented for the student with autism spectrum disorder and that the skills the student learns at school are generalized at home and in the community.

Adequate supports—for students with ASD; the general education teachers who become their primary teachers; and the special educators, paraprofessionals, and others who may provide services for the students—are essential, but when educated in general education classrooms, these students can learn from their peers and readily access the general curriculum. In the Firsthand Account, you can read about Christopher, an elementary student who is demonstrating the possibilities of an inclusive education.

Collaboration on behalf of students with ASD may include school professionals, parents, community agency representatives, and specialists.

Transition and Adulthood

Adolescents and young adults with ASD often have difficulty learning skills that their nondisabled peers have learned with little or no formal instruction (Hendricks & Wehman, 2009; Matson, Hattier, & Belva, 2012). For example, students with autism may not know how to approach another student to have a conversation or otherwise interact. Similarly, think of how often and for how many purposes you use social media. A recent study examined the types of media that adolescents with ASD preferred (Mazurek, Shattuck, Wagner, & Cooper, 2012). The researchers found that these students frequently used screen media but that usually they used nonsocial media such as television and solo video games instead of social media.

Challenges often continue into adulthood (e.g., Howlin & Taylor, 2015). If youth with ASD plan to attend college, they need to be able to proficiently

FIRSTHAND ACCOUNT

MY BIGGEST DREAM FOR HIM IS TO JUST BE HAPPY

CATRINA HALEY *is Christopher's mom. She has experienced the joys and the challenges of being the parent of a child with autism spectrum disorder, and her story holds tremendous value in helping professionals understand their students with this disorder.*

I was 31 years old when I had Christopher, so I'm a late mom. I was married and it was my first child, his first child. After early problems, my pregnancy was very typical and I was very careful about everything. Christopher was born via C-section after 13 hours of labor. I bring all this up because my son has autism, and so in my mind I've played it over and over: Did I do anything wrong? You think of all these things that would/could have been. But I have come to a place now where the reason doesn't matter.

Christopher was very typical, crawled at 4 months, walked at 8 months, eating baby food and then finger food. But as time went on when he was about 2, 2½, I said, "Okay, he's not talking. Something is up. Why isn't he talking?" And I would take him to the pediatrician and he would say, "Give it three more months, give it six months, and if he isn't talking then, we'll start some speech therapy or look into some other options." He ended up starting speech therapy at around age 3. He learned sign language, so he would put his fingers together to sign for *more* or *thank you*. And I'm thinking, "If this kid can pick up sign language, I know there's something going on, there's some kind of cognitive development, but he's just not coming out with it verbally." He started in a preschool program when he was 3 and didn't say a word all year. Then his teacher called me and said, "He

just started naming all these people in the class and then he started naming the alphabet!" All this time when he wasn't talking, I would still read to him and point out numbers and other things like colors and shapes, but we had no idea that he was picking up because he wasn't talking. Another day, my son had a ruler, and he just said "1, 2, 3, 4 . . ."—he counted to 12. It's so funny to think people who have typically developing children—the things they take for granted. When Chris began speaking, he might say something Monday and may not say anything else until the next Monday.

The school system people believed he had a mild intellectual disability because when he was tested, the tester would say, "What color is that?" Then the tester noted that he wasn't talking—he was just looking at it and looking at her—so she decided he didn't know it and that's how he got labeled ID. I KNEW he's not that way; even as a toddler, if I asked him to bring me the baby wipes and a diaper, he'd get them and bring them to me, he just wouldn't say anything. So intellectual disability just didn't register.

Shortly before he talked at school, I came home from work one day and he was jumping on my mom's bed, just jumping up and down, having the time of his life, and I came in the room and he said, "Mommy!" I nearly fainted, because that was the first time he said "Mommy"—at 4 years old. And I just grabbed him in my arms and held him. It was just the moment that I had longed for and dreamed of, because at that time I didn't know what his voice sounded like.

Christopher was diagnosed with autism when he was 5, mostly because of his echolalia. He's now in third grade, and he is in general

education except for reading instruction. There are lots of stories. The principal told me this one: Last year, the incoming kindergarteners were registering, and one of them was running in the hallway. Christopher was coming out of the cafeteria and he stopped and he said, "Hey! No running in the hallway, kids!" Christopher is very literal; the rules are the rules, and there is no deviation to the left and the right. It's all very black and white; there is no gray.

You know what I went through, it's stages of grief, because in a way it's like, a death almost, a death of a dream. I was going to do all these things and first getting the MMR (measles-mumps-rubella vaccine) diagnosis was devastating, I can't tell you how many tears I cried, and then I got over that. I just dove head first into, "What is this? What do we do about it? How can I help my child achieve the best outcome for his life?"

Now Christopher talks a lot better, and his exchange is a little better, like if you say, "How was your day?" he'll say, "Good." "What did you learn?" "Science." It's always his response. And then some days he'll say, "Mommy did you have a great day?" And I say, "Yes, I did—how was your day?" "It was good." But the exchange only goes so far—we can't continue this conversation for 15 minutes . . . but I'm grateful for what I get.

My biggest dream for Chris is to have a happy life. Sometimes I want to cry: The other day I saw these three little kids chasing each other around the yard, just running in circles, and I thought, wow, they're just enjoying their life. My son is not that kid to run around with other kids. But my child is my child. My biggest dream is for him to just be happy, wherever he is in life. I just want him to know joy.

Source: Courtesy of Catrina Haley

FIGURE 10.4 Essential Components of Community Living

Families and professionals should consider all the following areas to assist students with autism to successfully transition from school to postschool opportunities (Stewart, 2001).

- Family and individual goals and preferences
- Residential preferences or plans
- Communication needs support plan
- Health and medical needs and services
- Community supports specific to purpose and place
- Community access and participation plans
- Environmental and physical supports (setting specific)
- Family and individual social supports (formal, informal, natural)
- Transportation plan (linked to purposes)
- Education plan
- Recreation and leisure plans
- Transition plan
- Employment plan
- Funding sources
- Person or agency coordinating
- Team members' roles and responsibilities

Source: Adapted from Stewart, R. (2001). Essential components of community living: A life span approach. *Indiana Resource Center for Autism Reporter, 5*(1), 18–27. Reprinted by permission.

advocate for themselves and communicate effectively (Barnhill, 2016; Ashby & Causton-Theoharis, 2012). If they plan to find employment, they must learn the skills that will make them marketable (e.g., Seaman & Cannella-Malone, 2016). Thus, careful planning for the transition to adulthood is necessary for these students, and this planning should occur across all domains. Depending on students' abilities and needs, areas of importance may include

- Self-help skills such as eating, dressing, personal hygiene, and grooming
- Play, leisure, and recreation skills
- Social skills
- Sexuality
- Home management skills such as bill paying, grocery shopping, and cleaning
- Vocational skills
- Skills for participating in postsecondary education, including living independently
- Skills for making personal decisions (i.e., self-determination) and accessing community opportunities

Stewart (2001) calls these topics *community membership skills*, and she emphasizes that they should be taught long before the student's formal transition steps begin at age 16. One model of life span issues for community membership is included in Figure 10.4. Which of these skills seem especially important for Casey, whom you met at the beginning of the chapter?

MyEdLab **Self-Check 10.4**

MyEdLab **Application Exercise 10.6:** Moving On

MyEdLab **Application Exercise 10.7:** Schoolwide Positive Behavior Support

Recommended Educational Practices for Students with Autism Spectrum Disorder

For many years, little research on effective interventions for students with ASD was available. Now that is changing (e.g., Höher Camargo, Rispoli, Ganz, Hong, Davis, & Mason, 2016; Koegel, Matos-Freden, Lang, & Koegel, 2012; Odom & Wong, 2015). Generally, recommended practices include early intervention, intensive instruction, planned but brief instructional periods, parent involvement, and sufficient one-to-one or small-group instruction to meet students' goals. All of these practices are designed to address the social, behavior, and sensory challenges of these students, and many of the practices benefit other students with disabilities as well. Similarly, many of the academic interventions introduced for students with learning disabilities, emotional disabilities, intellectual disabilities, and communication disorders can enhance learning for students with autism spectrum disorder.

The following sections highlight a sample of available interventions, but keep in mind that there are many others.

Environmental Supports

Environmental supports are changes in a student's surroundings that are considered key to effective instructional programming. Some of the most common environmental supports include visual supports, a home base, and assistive technology.

Visual Supports

Students with autism spectrum disorder generally benefit from visually presented information. One example for younger students involves labeling items (e.g., *desk, door, table*) in the general or special education classroom in order to help expand these students' vocabularies. Another example is a *visual schedule*, which presents a list of activities using a combination of icons, photographs, words, or clock faces to help students anticipate upcoming events and activities, develop an understanding of time, and predict change.

Task cards are similar. They help many students with ASD recall academic content, routines, or social skills. Typically presented on business-card-size paper, the task card lists the steps the student must follow in a series of directive statements, expressed in concise language. For adolescents, task cards can provide an overview of the routines and teacher expectations in each class. For younger children, a task card may outline four conversation starters that can be used with peers during lunch. Examples of visual schedules and task cards that special education teachers or general education teachers might use are included in the Instruction in Action.

The *travel card* is yet another type of visual support for students with autism spectrum disorder in middle or high school settings (Carpenter, 2001). This type of card provides an efficient and effective means for dealing with the complex scheduling and shortage of time for personalized communication that characterize secondary schools. As you read about travel cards in the Instruction in Action, think about how they would be helpful to parents, teachers, and students.

Educators use many additional informal visual supports. For example, if a student is working in a small group and is supposed to complete three math

---

INSTRUCTION IN **ACTION**

Visual Schedules and Task Cards

Students with ASD often benefit by having tasks, schedules, and activities clearly explained to them ahead of time. Using words, pictures, or a combination of both, professionals can prepare students for the school day, help them know what happens next, clarify expectations, and foster independence. Two examples of visual supports are given here. Try making a simple visual support for one of the students described at the beginning of the chapter or another student with whom you are familiar.

Today Is Monday, March 27, 2017

Attendance	8:15
Math	8:20–9:00
Reading and Centers	9:00–10:00
Spelling	10:00–10:15
Writing	10:15–10:45
Assembly*	10:45–11:30
Lunch and Recess	11:30–12:15
Music	12:30–1:15
Science	1:15–1:50
Read Aloud	1:50–2:20
Journal	2:20–2:25
Get Ready to Go	2:25
Bell Rings	2:30

*Sometimes the schedule changes

Get Ready for Lunch

1. Put books in desk   _____
2. Put math papers in blue folder   _____
3. Put pencils in pencil case   _____
4. Get lunch from backpack   _____
5. Sit at desk   _____
6. Look at teacher and wait   _____
7. When the teacher calls my name, _____
   give her this paper and get in line

Source: Moore, S. T. (2002). *Asperger syndrome and the elementary school experience: Practical solutions for academic and social difficulties.* Autism Asperger Publishing. Reprinted by permission of Autism Asperger Publishing Co.

---

problems before receiving the reward of working on the computer, the teacher may draw on a sheet of paper or a small whiteboard three simple pictures of a pencil. Each time the student successfully completes a problem, the teacher crosses off one of the drawn pencils. This lets the student know how much more work is required and does so in a way that does not require lengthy verbal explanations.

Home Base

Home base is a place students can go to when they are beginning to feel anxious or upset and need to calm themselves (Myles & Adreon, 2001; Myles & Southwick, 2005). For example, students with autism spectrum disorder can go to a home base to (a) plan or review the day's events; (b) escape the stress of the classroom; (c) prevent a "meltdown"; or (d) regain control if a tantrum, rage, or meltdown has occurred. A resource classroom or counselor's office may be used as the home base. When a student feels the need to leave the classroom, whether general education or special education, she can take assignments to the home base and work in that less stressful environment.

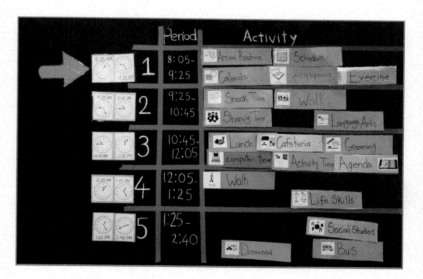

Students with ASD are assisted in understanding their school day through the use of visual schedules and other visual supports.

INSTRUCTION IN **ACTION**

Travel Card

As students move from elementary school to middle school and then high school, ensuring clear communication becomes more difficult. More teachers work with the students, the schools are larger, and maintaining close communication with parents can become more challenging. A travel card is designed to support middle and high school students with ASD by

- Increasing appropriate student behavior across environments
- Facilitating collaboration among teachers
- Increasing awareness among teachers of the academic, behavior, and social goals on which the student is working
- Improving home–school communication

- As you can see by looking at the accompanying figure, the travel card lists four or five of a student's target behaviors across the top and the classes the student attends along the left side. Classes include reading, science, social studies, and others. At the end of each period, the teacher indicates whether the student performed the desired behaviors by marking a 1 (yes), 0 (no), or NA (not applicable) on the card. At the end of the day, the positive notations are tallied and graphed. Points are accumulated toward a menu of rewards that have been negotiated by the student and the professionals responsible for the travel card.

	Did student follow class rules?	Did student participate in class?	Did student complete assignments?	Did student turn in homework?	Teacher's initials
Reading					
Science					
Social Studies					
Study Skills					
English					
Spanish					
Bonus Points	Went to nurse after getting off bus?			Has assignment book?	
Total	+	0			

Travel Card
Carmen

Date_____

Key   + = Yes   0 = No   NA = Not applicable

Teacher Comments/Suggestions/Announcements:

Source: Travel card from Myles, Brenda S., & Adreon, D. (2001). *Asperger syndrome and adolescence: Practical solutions for school success.* Autism Asperger Publishing. Reprinted by permission of Autism Asperger Publishing Co.

School personnel frequently schedule the school day of students with autism spectrum disorder so that they begin at the home base and have frequent stops there throughout the day. This creates a consistent student–teacher relationship and specifies a place to go when the need arises. It also can help students participate in general education by providing them with breaks from the social stress and stimulation of the classroom.

Through video modeling, professionals can take advantage of the strong visual learning preferences of many students with autism spectrum disorder and at the same time provide very concrete and specific skill instruction. This readily available technology is being used to teach skills such as these (Axe & Evans, 2012; Mason, Davis, Ayres, Davis, & Mason, 2016; Wynkoop, 2016):

- Appropriate classroom behavior (and reduction of inappropriate behavior)
- Verbal skills
- On-task and other learning behaviors
- Peer interactions
- Job-related skills

Several approaches to video modeling have been developed, usually based on who is selected to demonstrate on a video recording the skill being taught. These are the most common options (Cardon, 2016; Wynkoop, 2016):

- Adult models, usually someone familiar to the student such as a parent or teacher
- Peer model, usually someone of the same age and gender as the student, or perhaps a classmate or sibling

TECHNOLOGY NOTES
Teaching by Showing . . . for Real

- Self, when the student is "caught on camera" appropriately demonstrating the skill being taught and is then shown that video in order to increase his use of the skill
- Point-of-view, in which the image shown is what would be seen if the participant were actually engaged in the behavior. For example, a camera might be held over the shoulder of a peer stuffing an envelope, which would show the student with autism what he would see when completing the task
- Mixed model, using more than one of the above approaches

Students often view such videos on a computer, but they also can be placed on smartphones or tablets so that students can view them as they move from place to place. Teachers usually combine this learning experience with other techniques, including behavior plans that provide reinforcement.

The effectiveness of video modeling is well established, but as technology continues to evolve, new variations on this powerful instructional technique are likely to emerge. How might video modeling be implemented with Justin, Paula, and Casey, introduced at the beginning of the chapter?

Assistive Technology

You have learned about the importance of assistive technology for many students with disabilities, and you probably can surmise that students with autism spectrum disorder access technology, too. These students may use items that other students with disabilities use, such as adapted eating utensils, talking calculators, pencil grips, voice output devices, audible word-scanning devices, and talking word processors with text.

Yet another effective use of technology for students with autism is video-based intervention (VBI) (Rayner, 2015). For example, Axe & Evans (2012) showed adults with various facial expressions (e.g., bored, in pain). Other adult models then demonstrated appropriate responses. Children with autism in this research project learned the facial expressions and how to respond to them, correctly identifying and responding across different people and settings. Others have implemented VBI approaches to teach social skills (e.g., MacPherson, Charlop, & Miltenberger, 2015; Palmen, Didden, & Lang, 2012), self-help skills (e.g., Domire & Wolfe, 2014), and a variety of academic skills (e.g., Morlock, Reynolds, Fisher, & Comer, 2015; Yakubova, Hughes, & Hornberger, 2015). You can read more about this innovative assistive technology in the Technology Notes.

Instructional Practices

Many instructional strategies have been demonstrated to be effective with students with autism spectrum disorder (e.g., Asaro-Saddler, 2016). Three illustrative examples are priming, discrete trial intervention, and prompting.

Priming

Priming occurs when a parent, paraprofessional, teacher, or trusted peer previews with a student actual materials that will be used in a lesson or activity the day, the evening, the morning, or, occasionally, moments before that lesson or activity occurs. This is done as a means of reducing stress and anxiety by increasing student familiarity with the materials (Cihak, Smith, Cornett, & Coleman, 2012; Gengoux, 2015). Priming is most effective when it is built into the student's routine. It should occur in a relaxed environment and be facilitated by a primer who is both patient and encouraging. Finally, priming sessions should be short, providing a brief overview of the day's tasks in 10 or 15 minutes (Myles & Adreon, 2001).

Discrete Trial Interventions

Unlike most of the practices outlined so far that might easily be implemented by general education teachers, special education teachers, or others working with students with autism spectrum disorder, discrete trial interventions (DTI) (sometimes called discrete trial teaching or, in its most formal form, discrete trial training) is a group of approaches that require a significant time commitment and specialized training (Gongola & Sweeney, 2012; Plaisance, Lerman, Laudont, & Wu, 2016). This intervention is often implemented for preschool children, with trained parents and others possibly participating. This practice follows a basic pattern in which the teacher gives a prompt (i.e., cue) to which the student attends, a command for the student to perform, and finally a reward to the student for the desired behavior (Lovaas, 1987).

For example, the student could be given a prompt such as "Look at me" or a nonverbal cue such as pointing to the teacher's eyes. Once this command is given, the teacher waits for the student to focus attention as directed. In some instances, the teacher may need to guide the child physically through the desired behavior, such as lifting the child's chin so her eyes focus on the teacher when the command "Look at me" is given. In addition, the teacher may decide to reward behavior similar to or leading toward the desired behavior, a technique referred to as *shaping the behavior*. For example, when the command "Look at me" is given, a reward would be given if the student lifted her head briefly, even if she did not maintain eye contact. Of course, the goal is for students to be able to use the skills they learn in the discrete trial training across settings and situations.

A promising variation of discrete trial intervention has been reported by Radley, Dart, Furlow, and Ness (2015). They taught typical elementary students the principles of DTI, and those students worked with peers with ASD in learning academic skills. The students were able to learn and effectively use the DTI protocol, thus opening the possibility of implementing this intervention with older students and in a school environment.

Prompting

As you just learned, a prompt is a cue designed to get a student to perform a specific behavior, and it is effective in promoting student achievement. Prompts frequently are used by professionals working with students with ASD, and prompts vary based on their intrusiveness. For example, a physical prompt is very intrusive, with the teacher physically engaging the student (e.g., moving the student's hand to the pencil or turning the student's head toward the task). Somewhat less intrusive are gestures, such as pointing or signing, guiding the student where to look or move. Verbal questions or statements are even less intrusive prompts, involving no physical assistance at all. Finally, a written prompt, such as a cue card or keyword taped to the student's desk, is the least intrusive prompt. Prompts help students to learn without repeatedly making mistakes.

Prompts are helpful when teaching students with ASD a wide variety of skills, and in some instances they are employed for *errorless learning*. That is, the teacher will give a command to the student but then immediately, before the student can respond, prompt the student to give the correct response. The goal is to ensure the student always responds correctly, avoiding the problem of learning any task incorrectly. As the teacher observes that the student can carry out the task correctly, prompts are gradually removed.

Think about the value in using prompts as part of teaching students with ASD. How might you use them if you were working with students like Justin, Paula, or Casey, the students introduced at the beginning of the chapter?

Social Skills Supports

Perhaps the most important area of intervention for students with autism spectrum disorder is social skills (Channon, Collins, Swain, Young, & Fitzpatrick, 2012; Höher Camargo et al., 2016). Social skills interventions generally are positive behavior supports designed to enhance opportunities for social interaction, reduce problem behaviors, and build new competencies that have a positive impact on quality of life (Bondy & Weiss, 2013; Leaf et al., 2012). Specific issues that can be addressed include understanding the thoughts and feelings of others, following social rules, and learning self-monitoring.

Instruction

Unlike many typical learners, students with autism spectrum disorder must be directly taught the social skills they need to be successful. One example of an intervention for this purpose is the *power card strategy*, a visually based technique that uses a student's special interests to facilitate understanding of social situations, routines, and the meaning of language (Daubert, Hornstein,

POSITIVE • **BEHAVIOR** • SUPPORTS

Power Card: Teaching Appropriate Behavior Using Special Interests

Professionals sometimes use the special interests of students with autism to help them learn appropriate ways to behave in particular situations. For example, the following story was written for Cheyenne, a student who was fascinated with Elvis Presley. Then it was summarized, incorporating an appropriate picture, onto a power card that Cheyenne could keep on her desk or carry in her backpack.

Elvis and His Fans

Elvis Presley loves being the king of rock-and-roll, but sometimes it is difficult for him to be nice to everyone. At the end of a long day in the recording studio or after a concert, he is often tired, and it is difficult for him to be nice to fans and friends. Elvis has learned, however, that it is important to smile at people he meets and say nice things to everyone,

even when he is tired. He has learned that if he can't say something nice, it is better to just smile and say nothing at all. He stops and thinks about comments he makes before he says anything.

Just like Elvis, it is important for young people to think before they talk. It would make Elvis proud when you remember to do the following:

1. Think before you say anything. Say it in your head first before saying it out loud.
2. If you can't think of anything nice to say, don't say anything.
3. You do not have to say every thought out loud that you think.

When kids who love Elvis remember these three things, Elvis says, "Thank you, thank you very much!"

& Tincani, 2015; Gagnon, 2001). This intervention contains two components: a script and a power card. A teacher, therapist, or parent develops a brief script, written at the child's comprehension level, detailing the problem situation or target behavior. It includes a description of the behavior and describes how the child's special interest has addressed that social challenge. The power card, which is the size of a business card or trading card, contains a picture of the special interest and a summary of the solution. The power card can be carried; attached to the inside of a book, notebook, or locker; or placed on the corner of a child's desk. The Positive Behavior Supports provides an example of this technique.

Social Stories

A social story is an individualized text or story that describes a specific social situation from the student's perspective. The description may include where and why the situation occurs, how others feel or react, or what prompts their feelings and reactions (O'Handley, Radley, & Whipple, 2015; Rhodes, 2014). Social stories may be written documents, or they can be paired with pictures, audio recordings, or videos. They may be created by any professional or the parent, often with student input. Casey, the student you met at the beginning of the chapter, was provided with a social story to help him understand his peers' meaning in calling him a dog. Social stories are widely used to teach students with ASD, although one recent review called into question the strength of the evidence base for them (Leaf et al., 2015).

SOCCSS

Students with ASD sometimes do not understand social situations or do not have skills to resolve a social problem. The SOCCSS intervention (Roosa, 1995) is a teacher-directed strategy that helps students understand cause and effect and realize that they can influence the outcomes of many situations with the decisions they make. The letters in the SOCCS acronym stand for these steps:

- **S**ituation: The first step is to have the student identify (or help the student identify) the who, what, where, and when components of the event that occurred.
- **O**ptions: Next, the student brainstorms, with help as needed, options for responding to the situation. All student responses are recorded, whether they seem appropriate or not.
- **C**onsequences: For each option listed, the student identifies at least one consequence. This sometimes is the most difficult part of the process.
- **C**hoices: The student rates the option as positive or negative, based on the consequences of each.
- **S**trategies: After choosing an option, the teacher assists the student to form a plan for using that option the next time the situation arises.
- **S**imulation: This step is designed to provide practice for the student, who could draw the strategy being implemented, role play it, or imagine using it.

SOCCSS can be used with an individual student or as a group activity, depending on the situation and students' needs. Although this strategy is designed to be interpretive, it also can be used as an instructional strategy. That is, teachers can identify problems students are likely to encounter and address them using SOCCSS so that students have a plan prior to a situation occurring. A sample SOCCSS intervention that describes a problem being encountered by Danielle is included in the Positive Behavior Supports. How would you help this student to complete the worksheet?

POSITIVE • **BEHAVIOR** • SUPPORTS

SOCCSS in Practice

A form such as the one below is helpful for recording information as you implement the SOCCSS strategy with students with ASD. With your classmates, complete this form, and discuss the reasons for your responses.

SOCCSS **Worksheet**			
Situation			
Who		What	
When		Why	
Options		Consequences	Choices
Strategies			
Simulation Type		Simulation Outcomes	
Follow-Up			

Situation

Who: Danielle and classmates Susan, Evie, Jessica

What: Danielle wants to be friends with Susan, Evie, and Jessica. When they speak to her, she does not speak in return.

When: Before school, during lunch, after school

Where: On the school bus, school hallways, lunchroom

Why: Danielle thinks the comments made by her classmates are just words; because they are not about anything Danielle considers important, it does not seem necessary to respond

---

MyEdLab **Self-Check 10.5**

MyEdLab **Application Exercise 10.8:** Importance of Language and Social Skills

MyEdLab **Application Exercise 10.9:** Educational Approaches

Perspectives of Parents and Families

Parents of children with autism spectrum disorder usually are the first to recognize that their youngsters are responding differently to the world than are typically developing children. Some parents have reported that as an infant, their child was perfectly content to lie quietly in the crib staring at toys. The infant appeared to be a "good baby." One mother was convinced that her toddler was gifted because before the age of 2, he recognized all of the letters of the alphabet and could read several sight words. However, the child seldom initiated interactions with those in his environment.

Many parents of children with autism spectrum disorder begin to suspect that something is different in their child's development sometime around the child's first birthday. For example, the child may become attached to an object such as a stuffed animal and have an uncontrollable tantrum when the object is not in sight, or the child may show no interest in play, preferring to watch videos for hours on end. Although pediatricians are more aware than ever before of the possibility of ASD in young children and know that diagnosis is possible at 18 to 24 months of age, they may at first assure worried parents that there is little to be concerned about (Johnson, Burkett, Reinhold, & Bultas, 2016). For parents, though, nagging doubts usually persist.

Family Needs for Information and Support

Following diagnosis, parents may become frustrated because even though they have a name for their child's unique differences, they have little idea what to do about them. Many families of children with autism have found that early intervention, often with an intensive one-to-one home program, enables their children to make progress in the areas of behavior, communication, socialization, and self-help. This was definitely the case for Justin, who you met at the beginning of the chapter. This type of program, although beneficial to many children with ASD, may require a time commitment of up to 30 or 40 hours each week and can be emotionally and financially taxing for families.

Parents of children with autism spectrum disorder may find themselves required to play demanding roles in the lives of their children (e.g., Stoner & Stoner, 2016). In order to provide appropriate education, parents need to be familiar with the latest research on autism, understand special education law, and know how to be effective advocates for their children (e.g., Longtin & Principe, 2016).

Many parents have learned how to collaborate effectively with the professionals who provide services to their children and are valuable members of the school's educational team. These parents understand the value of knowing the characteristics of autism and effective educational practices. Parents of children with this disorder also need skills related to resolving differences within a constructive atmosphere and providing support for the professionals who work with their children (e.g., Rubenstein, Schelling, Wilczynski, & Hooks, 2015).

Like parents of children with other disabilities, parents of children with autism spectrum disorder often feel concern about their children's welfare in the years ahead, their children's ability to function independently at some point, and the community's acceptance of their children. Mothers of children with autism also report more stress in their lives than do mothers of children with other disabilities (Ekas & Whitman, 2011).

Parents of children with autism spectrum disorder benefit from the availability of both formal and informal social support, but such support must be individualized to meet the needs of each family. Potential sources of support include teachers, IEP team members, pediatricians and other health professionals, and other families of children with autism. Families often find that attending a local support group provides much needed information and support (Papageorgiou & Kalyva, 2010).

A review of qualitative research by Ooi, Ong, Jacob, and Khan (2016) affirmed the complexity of parenting a child with autism. In examining 50 articles that tapped the perspectives of nearly 1700 parents, the authors found that a diagnosis of autism strongly affected

Video Example
from
YouTube

MyEdLab
Video Example 10.4
This video, in which the father of a young man with ASD talks about his experience, illustrates why parents need to be familiar with the latest research and laws related to special education. (https://www.youtube.com/watch?v=WvH1sDn3v3I)

- Parents, including their emotional response to the diagnosis, challenges in raising a child with this disability, and the effect on their own careers, health, and leisure activities; however, some parents also reported joy and love for their children
- The rest of the family, including both supportive and nonsupportive reactions from extended family members and a strengthening or weakening of the parents' marriage
- Social interactions, including the benefits of being able to access support groups but the frequent social stigma when out in public
- Health and education services, including the benefits of specialized care for their children, the value of working with skilled and caring professionals, and the frustration of inconsistent care and therapies viewed as not providing benefit

In another study (Myers, Mackintosh, & Goin-Kochel, 2009), parents discussed their experiences. Those who were positive made comments such as this:

> Our son is our light and our joy. He has taught us to enjoy the little things . . . a pretty day, a beautiful flower . . . and he has taught us to let the bad things go . . . those days that just need to end. We are closer as a family, and we find as many ways as we can to live in the moment and be happy. Our life goals have changed since he was born, but they're really great goals.

On the other hand, parents who have a negative perspective offered this type of observation:

> Although I love my son, his struggle with autism has affected our entire family. My parents are supportive, but my husband's parents . . . not so much. I think they're a little afraid. I worry when we are out in public that he will have a meltdown. It embarrasses our other children, and sometimes we just pick him up and head for home; we retreat behind our closed doors. Sometimes I don't know if I will have the stamina to help him all the way through life.

The Roles of Siblings

Siblings often play important yet demanding roles in the lives of their brothers or sisters with autism spectrum disorder. For example, they may positively influence the development of their siblings' social and communication skills (Banda, 2015; Ben-Itzchak, Zukerman, & Zachor, 2016). In some families, they may be required to take on additional responsibilities in the home and serve as care providers in the absence of a parent. Despite having demands placed on them, siblings' knowledge of the disability may be limited. They should have access to resources appropriate to their developmental levels and be as well educated as their parents in the area of autism (Ferraioli, Hansford, & Harris, 2012). Many nondiagnosed siblings feel that they frequently are ignored in day-to-day family life. They may exhibit more difficulties in emotional, behavioral, and social adjustments and with peer interactions (McHale, Updegraff, & Feinberg, 2016), although many establish strong, positive relationships with their sibling with autism spectrum disorder. It is vital that parents help siblings pursue their own interests and spend time with them away from the sibling with autism.

MyEdLab **Self-Check 10.6**

MyEdLab **Application Exercise 10.10:** Importance of Communication

Trends and Issues Affecting the Field of Autism Spectrum Disorder

The field of autism spectrum disorder is still relatively young, yet it is faced with several significant issues. Among them are those related to more accurate information on assessment, diagnosis, and prevalence; the need for additional research to identify effective interventions; and the need for teachers prepared specifically to effectively educate these students.

Assessment, Diagnosis, and Prevalence

Consensus exists among professionals that early diagnosis of autism is critical so that appropriate interventions can be started while they have the greatest likelihood of improving a child's functioning. However, many challenges exist. For example, because of normal variations in many dimensions of child development, autism cannot be reliably diagnosed prior to 12 months (Zwaigenbaum et al., 2015). Further, many parents of very young children who eventually are diagnosed as having autism spectrum disorder still may initially be told that nothing is amiss.

Another factor often mentioned in the early identification of children with ASD is socioeconomic status. That is, children in families with higher incomes usually are identified as having ASD at younger ages than those in families who live in poverty (e.g., Daniels & Mandell, 2014). Children in the latter families are placed at a tremendous disadvantage in terms of accessing the services that would benefit them (e.g., early childhood programs available only if a diagnosis of autism has been made).

Yet another issue related to diagnosis is the need for a comprehensive research agenda leading to a greater understanding of the neurological, behavioral, and developmental characteristics of autism spectrum disorder. This, in turn, might help professionals identify key indicators of autism much earlier in a child's life. For example, although genes clearly play a role in the development of autism (Elamin & AL-Ayadhi, 2015), more than 100 genetic contributors have been identified, and their relative importance is not clear (Zwaigenbaum et al., 2015). The changes in the *DSM-V* are a reflection of the uncertainty that still exists regarding the identification of individuals with autism. Remember that one reason for combining several disorders into a single category was to focus on the behavioral similarities among individuals with ASD while avoiding controversy about which individuals meet the criteria for the previously delineated specific forms of the disorder.

A directly related matter is prevalence. Is it true that 1 in 68 children age 8 or younger have this disorder? Or is the number reported as part of IDEA—closer to 1 in 3,000 school-age children—more accurate? Do these significant variations in prevalence estimates for autism spectrum disorder matter? Yes. Resources often are allocated to study a disorder and to provide innovative treatments based on its prevalence, and so more accurate prevalence estimates of autism, especially those published by federal agencies such as the National Institutes of Health, might lead to more resource allocation.

Evidence-Based Interventions

Just as for other disability areas, concern exists in the field of ASD to find effective and research-based approaches for teaching students (Koegel, Matos-Freden, Lang, & Koegel, 2012). However, students with ASD are so unique that making global statements about effective practices can be risky (Lubas, Mitchell, & De Leo, 2016). Thus, professionals often have to rely on a combination of their knowledge of their students' strengths and needs and an array of evidence-based interventions, making careful selections and often adjusting the intervention to better suit the student. The potential problem with this approach is negatively affecting intervention effectiveness because of changes made to it.

Another issue related to interventions occurs when some professionals who work with individuals with ASD advocate for particular approaches with good intentions grounded in personal experience rather than in research. In fact, too many debates about the effectiveness of interventions for students with autism spectrum disorder seem to rely more on emotion than on data. Some of the interventions that have been recommended for which researchers have not been able to independently replicate the claims of those advocating the treatments include the following (Howlin, 2011; Schectman, 2007): auditory integration training, facilitated communication, use of secretin (i.e., a hormone aiding digestion that sometimes is given therapeutically to children), use of vitamin B6 and magnesium, dietary interventions (e.g., eliminating gluten and casein), chelation therapy (a detoxification procedure designed to address the concern that mercury poisoning is the cause of autism), and hyperbaric oxygen therapy (breathing extra oxygen in a pressurized chamber). A Web search would yield many sites related to these unproven approaches.

To address treatments such as these, studies that compare their impact on students need to be undertaken, and the results shared with practitioners and parents. In the meantime, you may find that parents insist on the effectiveness of particular treatments or interventions, and you should be prepared to seek out accurate information about them, taking care to use trustworthy sources. You also may need to consider the complex ethical issues that may be raised: You should not advocate such treatments, and although you can discuss your concerns with parents, you may not be able to convince them of your views.

Did You Know?

At the website for Research Autism (http://researchautism.net/), if you click on the tab for interventions you can find the evidence base (or lack of an evidence base) for hundreds of interventions and treatments for individuals with ASD.

Training and Support

Before autism was included as a separate disability category in IDEA in 1990, students with this disorder often received services from professionals prepared to work with students with severe and multiple disabilities or intellectual disabilities. Since 1990, the number of students identified with ASD has grown quickly, and the availability of teachers has not kept pace with this growth (Shyman, 2012). For example, teachers have to become familiar with multiple and rapidly changing theories and approaches, and they have to be able to apply these across students and settings. They also need to clearly understand highly technical behavioral techniques, they have to know how to select and use appropriate assistive technology, and they must have considerable knowledge of language acquisition and use and understand how to foster language development in their students. In addition, they have to be adept at creating needed adaptations in the environment, gathering data, and working collaboratively with parents, paraprofessionals, and colleagues.

Another teacher preparation need concerns professionals already working in schools. As more students with ASD spend increasing amounts of time in the general education setting, special educators need the skills to directly and indirectly support students there, and general educators need to welcome these students and understand principles and practices for effectively teaching these students (e.g., Chung et al., 2015; Iadarola et al., 2015). Clearly, the need for school personnel to be appropriately prepared for the inevitable increase of students identified through IDEA as having this disability is considerable and likely will grow for the next several years.

MyEdLab **Self-Check 10.7**

MyEdLab **Application Exercise 10.11:** Teacher Preparation

MyEdLab **Application Exercise 10.12:** Trends and Issues Affecting the Field of Autism Spectrum Disorder

Summary

LO10.1 The study of autism spectrum disorder is relatively young, having begun with Kanner's work, published in 1944. Today, this disorder is understood to have a biological rather than an environmental basis. Autism has multiple definitions. It is addressed in IDEA, and this is the definition used by most school professionals. However, *autism* also is defined in more detail in the 5th edition of the *Diagnostic and Statistical Manual (DSM-V)*, where it is labeled *autism spectrum disorder*.

LO10.2 Students with autism spectrum disorder may experience difficulties in cognitive and academic functioning, social and emotional abilities, and appropriate behavior. They also may experience a variety of sensory challenges.

LO10.3 These students usually are identified at a young age, with input from education and medical professionals, family members, and others.

LO10.4 Students with autism are entitled to the same special education services and supports as other children with disabilities, although they are less likely than many other students to be placed in general education for most of the school day.

LO10.5 Interventions for students with autism spectrum disorder can be grouped into these categories: environmental supports, assistive technology, instructional supports, and social skills supports.

LO10.6 Parents of children with autism spectrum disorder often need information about working with their children and finding support for themselves. Siblings, too, may need assistance.

LO10.7 Issues facing the field of autism include the need for better assessment and identification procedures, including more accurate prevalence estimates; more and better quality research on the effectiveness of interventions; and additional resources for preparing professionals to work with these students.

Back to the Cases

Now that you've read about Autism Spectrum Disorder, look back at the student stories at the beginning of this chapter. Then, answer the questions about each of their cases.

MyEdLab **Case Study 10.1**

JUSTIN. As a kindergarten student, Justin must learn how to be part of a group, how to interact with peers, and how to meet the academic and behavioral expectations of the classroom.

MyEdLab **Case Study 10.2**

PAULA. Paula has a number of challenging behaviors, and she becomes very upset at any change in routine. Think about Paula and what you know about behavior (you might review Chapter 7 as well as this chapter).

MyEdLab **Case Study 10.3**

CASEY. One focus in this chapter was the methods and strategies to help students with ASD learn, practice, and generalize socially appropriate behaviors across school settings. You have been asked to help Casey's teachers decide how to teach him their expectations in their classes.

Students with Deafness and Hearing Loss

Learning Outcomes

LO11.1 Outline the development of the field of deaf education, define *deafness* and *hearing loss*, outline their prevalence, and explain their causes and types.

LO11.2 Describe characteristics of individuals who are deaf or hard of hearing, including the impact of hearing loss on language and academic skills, social interaction opportunities, and career attainment.

LO11.3 Discuss how hearing loss is identified.

LO11.4 Identify the educational settings in which students who are deaf or hard of hearing receive services, and analyze the advantages and disadvantages for them in general education classrooms.

LO11.5 Explore recommended educational practices for students who are deaf or hard of hearing.

LO11.6 Consider the perspectives of the parents and families of a child who is deaf or hard of hearing.

LO11.7 Identify trends influencing the field of deaf education.

LILY

Lily is an 8-year-old second-grader. She was adopted from China when she was a baby. Lily has been wearing hearing aids since the adoption. She received a cochlear implant a month before her 3rd birthday. Her hearing loss is profound without her hearing aid and cochlear implant. With her hearing aid, her hearing loss is moderate to severe in her left ear. With her cochlear implant, she has a 20 dB hearing loss, which is considered normal hearing, although she is not able to access all sounds. Her primary mode of communication is speech, but she also uses sign, speech reading, and context clues to fill in the blanks of what she misses.

Lily attended the state school for children who are deaf or blind for preschool. Since kindergarten she has attended her neighborhood school, participating fully in general education, with full-time services from an interpreter/tutor who also provides additional instruction in vocabulary for 20 minutes two times a week. Lily receives consultative services from an itinerant teacher of students who are deaf or hard of hearing and also receives speech-language therapy three times a week for 30 minutes. Two of those sessions focus on speech goals and one is dedicated to language goals. The audiologist provides auditory training once a week for 30 minutes. Finally, the special education resource teacher also provides math help twice a week for 15 minutes.

Lily is above grade level in reading and at grade level in math; uses her listening skills, speech reading, and interpreter to understand what is happening in the classroom; and enjoys school and has many friends. If she doesn't understand something, she asks for clarification. Vocabulary, especially words with multiple meanings (e.g., *run, power*) and figurative language (e.g., "catch you later"), is an area of difficulty for Lily.

ZACHARY

Zachary is a seventh-grade student at Morehead Middle School. He has a moderate hearing loss as a result of an illness he contracted at the age of 18 months. He is also identified as having an intellectual disability. Zachary spends each morning in his special education classroom, where Mr. Reynolds, his special education teacher, helps him and his classmates with their reading, language arts, and math skills. In the afternoon, Zachary participates in the science class with his peers without disabilities, accompanied by a teaching assistant who supports the science teacher by assisting Zachary and three other students with disabilities in the class. Zachary also participates with his classmates in other classes, such as occupational exploration. Zachary communicates using some signs, some spoken words, and some gestures. His individualized education program (IEP) goals for this year include not only reading and math goals but also asking for assistance before becoming frustrated as well as participating appropriately in small-group activities with his peers. Mr. Reynolds is concerned about Zachary. Twice recently, the science teacher asked the assistant to escort Zachary from the room after he became very upset when he did not understand the teacher's directions. Mr. Reynolds is planning to meet with the teacher and the school psychologist after school tomorrow to discuss exactly what happened and then to consider whether Zachary might benefit from a behavior intervention plan.

BRIAN

Brian is a senior in high school, and he can best be described as a young man on a mission. He has already been admitted to a state university, where he plans to major in biology so that he can pursue a medical degree. He hopes to have a career as a researcher, possibly in a teaching hospital. He considers his greatest challenge to be writing; he relies heavily on his mom to edit his written assignments, and he has already met with staff members at the university writing center. Brian's special education teacher, general education teachers, and parents have no doubt he will achieve his career goal. Brian's moderate bilateral hearing loss probably has a genetic component; he has several relatives who have moderate to profound hearing loss. Perhaps because of this fact and because his aunt is very active in a local Deaf group while his parents are both hearing but proficient in American Sign Language, Brian seems to live comfortably in both the hearing and Deaf communities. He has friends who are Deaf and friends who hear; he attends Deaf events, but he also enjoys all the typical social activities that are part of being in high school. Brian has a sign language interpreter at school, but that is not a perfect solution. In some classes, he could probably succeed by speech reading and using an amplification system but, in his advanced math and sciences classes, he struggles to understand his teachers and sometimes cannot keep up with the lecture and discussions, even when notes are provided to him. But with his usual optimism, Brian explains he is glad he learned this in high school so that he can ask for appropriate supports when he gets to college.

I magine how your life might be different if you faced situations such as these on a daily basis:

- Being unable to use the drive-through at a restaurant because it requires the use of a speakerphone
- Needing to rely on another person, an interpreter, to talk to teachers, friends, and others, hoping that person understands the nuances of what you are saying
- Thinking that you have vacuumed the entire room before realizing the plug was pulled out

As you walk across campus, drive around town, or go shopping, you see many people talking on their cell phones or using earbuds to listen to music. We live in a sound-oriented society, and it is through sound that extensive amounts of information are conveyed, either deliberately or incidentally, through conversation. Family members discuss the events of the day, work through problems, and talk about upcoming activities, all within the earshot of children. By listening to these conversations and interacting through language with parents, neighbors, and others, children acquire and refine their communication skills, learn concepts, and develop social skills. Individuals who are deaf or hard of hearing often are cut off from such direct and incidental communication experiences. This not only affects their ability to develop communication and language skills but also negatively affects their experiential background as well as their knowledge of the world (Stewart & Kluwin, 2001; Weinberg, 2011).

Understanding Deafness and Hearing Loss

The long history of specialized education for students who are deaf or hard of hearing, illustrated in Figure 11.1, still strongly influences contemporary understanding of these individuals and how they are educated. However, evolving priorities in federal special education law and advances in technology are now changing professionals' perspectives of these students and their characteristics and needs.

Development of the Field of Deaf Education

Many professionals agree that the earliest special education in the United States began when Thomas Hopkins Gallaudet opened the American Asylum for the Education of the Deaf and Dumb (now the American School for the Deaf) on April 15, 1817, in Hartford, Connecticut (Winzer, 1993). This model, a residential school away from populated areas, became a national standard and, until the middle of the 20th century, often was the only option available to these children (Stewart & Kluwin, 2001). At that point, attitudes toward individuals with hearing loss began to shift, especially after the number of children who were deaf or hard of hearing increased significantly as a result of the rubella (i.e., measles) epidemic of that era, and residential schools were inundated. As a result, more local schools were forced to begin providing education to students who could not be accommodated in residential settings.

Another significant aspect of the history of the field of hearing loss is communication method. During the late 19th century, debate erupted about whether students who were deaf or hard of hearing should use sign language or oral language. The latter view prevailed, and it profoundly influenced the American field of deaf education for many years (Edwards, 2012). Students in the residential schools were prohibited from signing; it was believed that if students signed, they would not learn to speak. Many students who had never heard or used oral

FIGURE 11.1   Time Line for the Development of the Field of Deafness

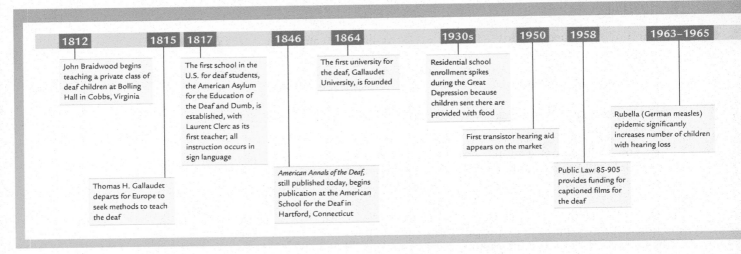

language were very frustrated, as were their teachers. Although this extreme view was eventually modified, controversy about communication methods is still today characteristic of the field of deaf education.

When Public Law (P.L.) 94-142 (now the Individuals with Disabilities Education Act, or IDEA) was passed in 1975, a wider variety of educational options for children with hearing loss became available for the first time. Since then, emphasis has centered on determining the appropriate and least restrictive settings for educating these students and researching the most effective communication methods (Berndsen & Luckner, 2012; Guardino & Cannon, 2015). Consequently, most residential schools for the deaf, once these students' most likely educational option, have experienced a decline in enrollment, and many have closed.

Definitions of Deafness and Hearing Loss

Did you know that disagreement exists about what it means to be deaf or hard of hearing? The three most frequently discussed views of deafness suggest that it is (a) a disability, impairment, disorder, or ailment; (b) a logistical problem, especially in terms of contact with the hearing community; or (c) a social community/culture in its own right (DesJardin, 2006; Higgins & Lieberman, 2016). Although each perspective is discussed in more detail later in the chapter, now is a good time for you to think about how deafness may be perceived from each viewpoint.

Many terms are used to describe an individual who has a hearing loss, which is the general term used in this chapter to collectively label various types of hearing disorders. People may describe themselves as being deaf, Deaf, hard of hearing, hearing impaired, or having a hearing disorder. Initially, you might think that deafness would be a simple concept describing a condition that could be diagnosed through administration of a hearing test. However, the psychological, cultural, and educational issues that are unique to individuals who have a hearing loss make it more difficult to define; it is not a simple matter of saying that an individual has a particular percentage of a hearing loss. Examples of considerations include the age of onset of the hearing loss, the cause of the hearing loss, the age at which intervention began, the family response, the hearing status of the family, the presence of additional disabilities, and the type of education program attended.

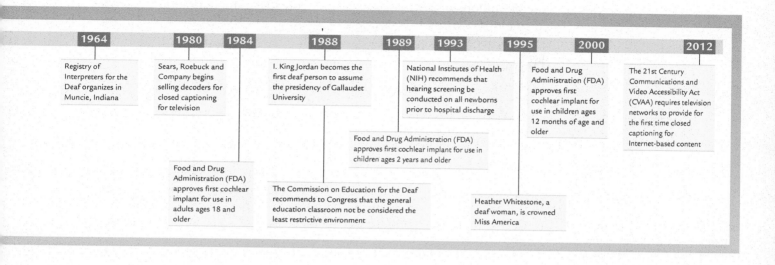

1964 Registry of Interpreters for the Deaf organizes in Muncie, Indiana

1980 Sears, Roebuck and Company begins selling decoders for closed captioning for television

1984 Food and Drug Administration (FDA) approves first cochlear implant for use in adults ages 18 and older

1988 I. King Jordan becomes the first deaf person to assume the presidency of Gallaudet University

The Commission on Education for the Deaf recommends to Congress that the general education classroom not be considered the least restrictive environment

1989 Food and Drug Administration (FDA) approves first cochlear implant for use in children ages 2 years and older

1993 National Institutes of Health (NIH) recommends that hearing screening be conducted on all newborns prior to hospital discharge

1995 Heather Whitestone, a deaf woman, is crowned Miss America

2000 Food and Drug Administration (FDA) approves first cochlear implant for use in children ages 12 months of age and older

2012 The 21st Century Communications and Video Accessibility Act (CVAA) requires television networks to provide for the first time closed captioning for Internet-based content

Federal Definitions

A starting point for technical definitions is the federal special education law. It uses two terms related to hearing loss: hearing impairment and deafness:

> Hearing impairment means an impairment in hearing, whether permanent or fluctuating, that adversely affects a child's educational performance but that is not included under the definition of deafness in this section. (IDEA 20 U.S.C. §1401 [2004], 20 C.F.R. §300.8[c][5])

> Deafness means a hearing impairment that is so severe that the child is impaired in processing linguistic information through hearing, with or without amplification, [and] that adversely affects a child's educational performance. (IDEA 20 U.S.C. §1401 [2004], 20 C.F.R. §300.8[c][3])

Some of the technical aspects of these definitions (e.g., fluctuating hearing loss) are addressed later in the chapter. What you can see is that these definitions are based on the first perspective mentioned—the one focusing on disability or impairment. Note that, as for all disabilities, the hearing loss must negatively affect educational performance. Finally, you might wonder about one related term discussed in Chapter 1: *deaf–blindness*. Students who have both of those disabilities have extraordinary special needs and are described in Chapter 14.

Additional Information on Definitions

The federal definitions related to hearing loss are not particularly controversial, but they are somewhat incomplete. Although still not representing consensus among all those in the field, the National Center for Education Statistics (2002) has extended the federal definitions:

> *Hearing impairment*—An impairment in hearing, whether permanent or fluctuating, that adversely affects a child's educational performance, in the most severe case because the child is impaired in processing linguistic information through hearing. (p. 546)

> *Deafness*—Having a hearing impairment which is so severe that the student is impaired in processing linguistic information through hearing (with or without amplification) and which adversely affects educational performance. (p. 546)

> *Hard of hearing*—Having a hearing impairment, whether permanent or fluctuating, which adversely affects the student's educational performance, but which is not included under the definition of "deaf." (p. 546)

If you compare the two sets of definitions, you will notice that, although the definitions of *deafness* are virtually identical, the definition of *hearing impairment* is clarified in the second set and a definition for hard of hearing is added.

Deaf Culture

In considering definitions, it is also important to recognize use of the term *Deaf* with a capital *D*. This term is used to refer to members of the Deaf community who embrace Deaf culture, a linguistic minority culture within a larger community (O'Brien & Placier, 2015). Membership in the Deaf community varies from place to place. Interestingly, it is not achieved through birth or right but is ascribed to an individual once a set of criteria is met. Factors often mentioned as important for Deaf culture identity include (a) being deaf; (b) using American Sign Language (ASL) as a primary means of communicating, which is a visual-gesturing language that has its own rules of grammar distinct from English; and (c) attending a residential school for the deaf (Pray & Jordan, 2012).

The fundamental value of Deaf culture is the assertion that Deaf people are whole people with ways of understanding, making sense of the world, and interacting (Manchaiah, Stein, Danermark, & Germundsson, 2015). This model is preferred to models of Deaf people as deficient. Deafness is not perceived as a disability—that is, it is not a condition that needs to be "fixed." Instead, deafness is viewed as an identity with its own rich history, traditions, and language (Eckert & Rowley, 2013; Obasi, 2014). The Deaf community often organizes local, regional, state, national, and international events such as conferences, athletic competitions, art shows, plays, and pageants.

Prevalence of Hearing Loss

No single set of data can adequately convey the prevalence of hearing loss. For example, the National Institute on Deafness and Other Communication Disorders (NIDCD) (2016) reports that more than 34 million persons in the United States have a hearing loss. As you might suspect, the highest prevalence is among individuals who are 65 years of age and older. For students in public schools, the Centers for Disease Control and Prevention (2015) reports that as many as 16.9% of children ages 6 to 19 have some degree of hearing loss, usually slight and often the result of ear infections, but that approximately 1.5 out of every 1,000 school-age children have an educationally significant hearing loss. Included in this group are children who are deaf and hard of hearing, as well as those who have a hearing loss in one ear, called a *unilateral hearing loss*. The U.S. Department of Education (2016) reports that approximately slightly less than 2% of all school-age students with disabilities ages 6 to 21 in U.S. schools are served under the disability category of hearing impairment. This represents a total of 69,220 students in public schools.

MyEdLab
Video Example 11.1
Video Example 11.1 gives you a glimpse into the Deaf culture through a discussion between Deaf students and their teacher. (https://www.youtube.com/watch?v=F5W604uSkrk)

Many, but not all, students with hearing loss also have other disabilities.

Hearing Loss and Other Disabilities

Research suggests that approximately 40% of all students who are deaf or hard of hearing have one or more additional, educationally significant disabilities, similar to Zachary, whom you met at the beginning of this chapter (Gallaudet Research Institute, 2011). The most frequently reported conditions include intellectual disabilities, learning disabilities, attention deficit–hyperactivity disorder (ADHD), and other health impairments. These students also may have cerebral palsy, a physical disability described in Chapter 13. Students with a hearing loss as well as an additional disability are unique (Vernon & Rhodes, 2009), and decision making regarding their education should emphasize looking at their strengths and preferences as a basis for instructional planning and meaningfully engaging families as participants in that planning (Guardino, 2008; Musyoka, Gentry, & Bartlett, 2016).

Causes of Hearing Loss

A hearing loss can occur before or after birth. A loss that is present at birth is referred to as a congenital hearing loss. One that develops after birth is referred to as an acquired, or adventitious, hearing loss. Most education professionals are less interested in whether a hearing loss is congenital or acquired than they are in whether the loss was prelingual, prior to speech and language development, or postlingual, after speech and language have developed. Generally, professionals agree that the longer children have had normal hearing, the greater the chance that they will maintain the knowledge and ability to use the language and communication skills they have developed (Schwartz, 2007).

Prelingual Causes of Hearing Loss

Do you remember reading about genetic causes of other disabilities, including intellectual disabilities? In the field of deaf education, more than half of all hearing losses in children are believed to have genetic causes (Centers for Disease Control and Prevention, 2016; Frangulov, Rehm, & Kenna, 2004). A genetic hearing loss is one caused by the presence of an abnormal gene within one or more chromosomes. Either one or both of the parents may have passed on this abnormal gene, or it may have developed as the result of a spontaneous mutation or change during fetal development (Morton & Nance, 2006).

Approximately 95% of children who are deaf or hard of hearing have hearing parents because most genetic hearing loss is the result of a recessive genetic trait rather than a dominant genetic trait (Shearer, Hildebrand, Sloan, & Smith, 2011). That is, both parents must have the trait before it can be transmitted, and even then the probability of the child being deaf is only one in four. Similarly, most deaf parents have hearing children.

Prelingual causes of hearing loss that are not hereditary include prenatal infections, illnesses, or conditions occurring at the time of birth or shortly thereafter. Examples include these:

- Intrauterine infections, including rubella (i.e., German measles) and herpes simplex virus
- Prematurity
- Toxemia during pregnancy, a condition that includes dangerously high blood pressure in the mother
- Anoxia (i.e., lack of oxygen) before, during, or after birth
- Malformation of ear structures

Postlingual Causes of Hearing Loss

A postlingual hearing loss usually happens as the result of a disease or an injury. Examples of conditions that can cause acquired hearing loss in children and youth include the following:

- Otitis media—ear infections that often are caused when bacteria related to a child's cold or other illness get inside the ear and produce fluids and mucus

FIGURE 11.2 **Diagram of the Human Ear**

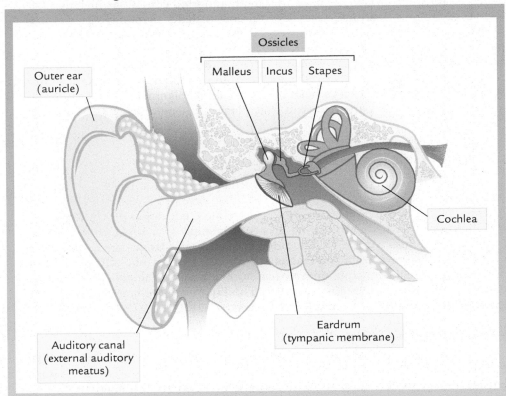

that are trapped there; these infections affect three out of four children by the time they are 3 years old

- Childhood diseases, including measles, chicken pox, influenza (i.e., flu), mumps
- Encephalitis—an inflammation of the brain caused by a virus that, in severe cases, is accompanied by high fever, severe headache, nausea and vomiting, stiff neck, double vision, drowsiness, and disorientation
- Head injury
- Repeated exposure to loud noise

Many of these causes have been introduced in other chapters, and they demonstrate how single illnesses or injuries can result in several types of disabilities.

Types of Hearing Loss

To understand types of hearing loss, it is first helpful to briefly review the structure of the ear. The simple diagram in Figure 11.2 summarizes this structure.

The next step in exploring hearing loss is to analyze the process of hearing. Hearing occurs when sound waves enter the outer ear and travel through the auditory canal to the *eardrum*, where tiny bones vibrate to amplify the sound and send it into the inner ear. There, the cochlea, a fluid-filled hearing organ that contains thousands of tiny cells with hairlike projections, experiences wavelike motions. These movements prompt the hair cells—the sensory organs that allow us to hear—to send messages to the brain, where they are translated into what we recognize as sound.

Once you can envision the hearing process, you can understand types of hearing loss, which can be classified into three basic types, depending on the location of the impairment within the ear: conductive hearing loss, sensorineural hearing loss, and mixed hearing loss.

Video Example

from

YouTube

MyEdLab
Video Example 11.2

This video demonstrates the process of hearing.
(https://www.youtube.com/
watch?v=az-5MSiXMGU)

1. *Conductive hearing loss.* A conductive hearing loss occurs when a problem of the outer or middle ear prevents sound from being conducted to the inner ear. This type of hearing loss can exist if part of the external or middle ear is not fully developed or if it develops abnormally. A conductive hearing loss also can be caused by disease within the external ear or the middle ear that leaves fluid or causes wax buildup, leading to improper movement of the eardrum or ossicles, the three small bones in the middle ear. Conductive hearing losses often can be improved (e.g., amplification through hearing aids). Brian, one of the students you met in the chapter opening, has conductive hearing loss.

2. *Sensorineural hearing loss.* A sensorineural hearing loss is caused by a problem in the inner ear or along the nerve pathway to the brain stem. As a result, the sound that travels to the inner ear and brain stem is not delivered at all or is much softer or distorted. Zachary, whom you read about in the beginning of the chapter, has this type of hearing loss.

3. *Mixed hearing loss.* A mixed hearing loss involves both a conductive and a sensorineural loss.

Two important additional factors in the discussion of types of hearing loss concern whether the hearing loss is bilateral or unilateral and whether the hearing loss fluctuates. A bilateral hearing loss is a loss in both ears; a unilateral hearing loss refers to a loss in only one ear. An individual with a unilateral hearing loss may experience difficulty localizing sound and listening in noisy settings. An individual with a fluctuating hearing loss may function differently from day to day because of periodic ear infections or a buildup of fluid or earwax.

Degree of Hearing Loss

One additional concept usually considered when discussing causes of hearing loss is the degree of loss—that is, the quantity and quality of sound that individuals with a hearing loss are able to process that affects their ability to understand and produce spoken language. Hearing loss is measured in decibels (dB), a measure of the intensity or loudness of sound. Whispering is about 20 to 25 dB; normal conversation is about 60 dB; a child screaming is about 90 dB. More important than the cause or type of hearing loss is the amount of residual hearing that an individual has and can use. The degree of hearing loss usually is explained by the use of seven classifications that can be arranged along a continuum that runs from normal hearing to a profound hearing loss, as you can see by examining Figure 11.3.

Mitchell and Karchmer (2004) report that approximately 60% of children receiving special education services have mild to moderate hearing loss and that

FIGURE 11.3   **Classification of Hearing Loss**

Hearing is measured in *decibels* (dB), that is, the loudness of sounds. This chart summarizes benchmarks of loudness and levels of hearing loss.

Average Hearing Level (decibels, dB)	Example	Description
1–15 dB	Quiet whisper, breathing	Normal hearing
16–25 dB	Rustling leaves	Slight hearing loss
26–40 dB	Babbling brook	Mild hearing loss
41–55 dB	Talking in the background, sounds of birds	Moderate hearing loss
56–70 dB	Noise in a busy neighborhood, normal conversation	Moderately severe hearing loss
71–90 dB	Electric pencil sharpener, telephone dial tone	Severe hearing loss
91 dB and above	Car horn, rock band	Profound hearing loss

Did You Know?

Many organizations provide information and resources for understanding deafness and Deaf culture. You might want to explore these:

- The Alexander Graham Bell Association for the Deaf and Hard of Hearing (www.agbell.org) is an international organization and resource center on hearing loss and spoken language approaches and related issues.
- Deaf Linx (www.deaflinx.com) is a website established to provide factual information and resources in support of a Deaf-friendly world.
- The National Association of the Deaf (NAD) (http://www.nad.org/) is a civil rights organization advocating for individuals with hearing loss across the life span. It holds American Sign Language as a core value.

the remainder have severe or profound hearing loss. However, you should keep in mind that this is a very general classification system. The ability to use residual hearing varies from individual to individual and is affected by additional variables, such as age of identification, use of amplification, the auditory environment, and cultural identity.

MyEdLab **Self-Check 11.1**

MyEdLab **Application Exercise 11.1:** Definition and Classification

MyEdLab **Application Exercise 11.2:** Ashley's Hearing Impairment

Characteristics of Individuals Who Are Deaf or Hard of Hearing

As you might expect, the population of individuals who are deaf or hard of hearing is very diverse. Some individuals with a hearing loss use American Sign Language (ASL) and identify with the Deaf community. Other people who are deaf or hard of hearing use both sign language and spoken language to communicate, and they have friends who are deaf, hard of hearing, and hearing, as is the case for Brian, the student you met at the beginning of this chapter. In addition, some individuals who are deaf or hard of hearing prefer to communicate using speech, are able to use their residual hearing, and function primarily in the general hearing society.

Hearing Loss and Child Development

A hearing loss may alter a student's development in two specific ways: (a) in the area of communication, which in turn influences many other areas of development, and (b) in the area of experiential learning.

Impact on Communication

The first point to remember in a discussion on the importance of communication is that children who are deaf or hard of hearing and have parents with a hearing loss differ in many respects from children who are deaf or hard of hearing and have hearing parents. Parents who are deaf or hard of hearing themselves often are able to communicate with their children sooner and with greater facility than hearing parents (Lu, Jones, & Morgan, 2016). As a result, research suggests that children who are deaf with parents who are deaf develop ASL skills at a similar rate as the spoken English skills of same-age hearing peers (Mayberry, 2010).

Like breathing, food, water, and sleep, communication is a basic human need. Communication is fundamental to everything we do every day: It defines and gives meaning to our emotions, beliefs, hopes, imaginations, and life experiences. Human infants are uniquely born with the ability to interact with their caregivers. Communication between infants and their caregivers is essential for two reasons. First, communication develops emotional bonds between children and their caregivers. Second, children acquire language as a result of early conversations with their caregivers. Through these interactions, children learn the underlying rules of the language used by the adults in their lives (Schirmer, 2001).

For children who are deaf or hard of hearing, the quality and quantity of interactions and communication partners tend to differ significantly from those of other children (McGowan, Nittrouer, & Chenausky, 2008; Traci & Koester, 2011). As noted earlier, most children who are deaf or hard of hearing are born to hearing parents who generally use spoken language as their primary means of communicating with others. In addition, because hearing loss is a low-incidence disability—that is, one that is relatively uncommon—most parents have never come into contact with a person who is deaf or hard of hearing. Consequently, they have a limited understanding of what it is like to have a hearing loss. Further, families with a child who has a hearing loss face the additional burden of having to decide what communication approach they will use with their child. Take the time to review the options in Figure 11.4, and you will see why this is often a difficult decision for families.

Experiential Learning

The second way that a hearing loss may alter an individual's development concerns the reduction in quantity and quality of direct and vicarious experiences. Learning is experiential in nature. We learn the characteristics of a concept as a result of numerous experiences with it. As a child's world of experience expands, deeper understandings are constructed. For example, think about your own ability to manage and use money. You began by being able to identify coins and bills. Education and experience helped you develop the skills to make purchases and count your change. Through additional training and practice, you learned how to use a checking account and an ATM. Figure 11.5 illustrates the potential differences in communication patterns, as well as overall opportunities for direct and incidental learning, that may exist for individuals who are hearing as compared to individuals who are deaf or hard of hearing (Scheetz, 2001).

Life experiences and concepts are stored and organized in memory structures called *schemata*. A schema (the singular of *schemata*) is a framework that enables us to organize a large amount of information into a unit of knowledge (Walsh & Gluck, 2015). For example, each of us has schemata for topics such as clothing, sports, insects, and music. Yet it is likely that we have slightly different schemata for the same concepts based on our individual interests and experiences. The more knowledge we acquire, the more elaborate our schemata become, and having more knowledge helps us organize information into accessible pathways. Conversely, the lack of experiences and/or the inability to access enough information creates gaps in pathways, making access more difficult. As a result of the gaps in experiential background, students who are deaf or hard of hearing may lack the schemata needed for following some abstract conversations, being able to comprehend what is happening in a story, understanding current events, or solving multistep problems (Stewart & Kluwin, 2001).

As you can see, children with hearing loss often do not bring to their educational experience the same extensive language, conceptual, and experiential knowledge that their hearing peers do. These deficits profoundly influence the characteristics of these learners and greatly affect most aspects of their educational process.

Cognitive Characteristics

Early research on the cognitive skills of individuals who were deaf or hard of hearing routinely found them to lag behind their hearing peers. The tests used in those studies often required comprehension of English and spoken language. Thus, many researchers were confusing cognitive ability with language ability. More recently, a variety of tests of cognitive ability have been developed that include nonverbal performance measures, such as tracing from a starting point to a stopping point on an increasingly complex maze and identifying the correct geometric form to put next in a sequence. The results of these studies indicate that a hearing loss in and of itself imposes no limitations on the cognitive capabilities of an individual (Maller & Braden, 2011; Moores, 2001); that is, the distribution of intelligence is the same for hearing and deaf/hard-of-hearing groups.

FIGURE 11.4 Communication Options for Individuals Who Are Deaf or Hard of Hearing

	Spoken English	Cued Speech	Signing Exact English (SEE2)	Signed English	Contact Signing/Pidgin Sign English (PSE)	American Sign Language (ASL)
Description	Individual taught to use residual hearing as effectively as possible through the use of hearing aids, cochlear implants, FM systems, or other assistive listening devices, while simultaneously developing speech skills.	Sound-based visual communication system using eight hand shapes in four different locations ("cues") in combination with the natural mouth movements of speech; supplements speech reading and aided residual hearing.	An invented system developed to visually represent morphemes of English. Used while simultaneously speaking. Approximately 65% of SEE signs are borrowed from ASL. Others are adapted using initialized forms (e.g., b hand shape for band). Also, prefixes (e.g., *im, dis*) and suffixes (*s, ed, ing*) are added. For example, the word *unbelievable* would be signed UN-BELIEVE-ABLE.	Users speak and sign at the same time, using English word order. Some signs borrowed from ASL while others borrowed from SEE. A more simple sign system than SEE2 because there are only 14 grammatical markers used (i.e., affixes). Does not have firm rules about signing literally or conceptually.	Viewed as a "bridge" between native ASL users and native English speakers. ASL signs usually used in English word order. Certain elements of English, such as function words, articles, pronouns, and prepositions, omitted to speed up communication.	A visual-gestural language recognized as a true language in its own right. Does not follow the grammatical structure of English; it has its own grammar and syntax. You cannot sign ASL and speak simultaneously. The grammar of ASL is expressed through body movement and facial expression. Used extensively within the Deaf community, a group that views itself as having a separate culture and identity from mainstream hearing society.
Potential Strengths	Speech is the primary mode of communication worldwide for social exchanges and provides the basis for the development of literacy skills.	System can be learned quickly, about 20 hours, although proficiency takes longer. English grammar is learned; and reading and writing skills develop approximately at the same rate as hearing peers.	Considered easier to learn than ASL for hearing individuals because it follows English word order.	Considered easier to learn for individuals who have already internalized English. Shows the use of verb tense markers, articles, and prepositions of English.	Like ASL, this is a visual-conceptual system of communication. Individuals can voice and sign simultaneously, but it is not always used that way.	A beautiful language. Many deaf people consider ASL to be the most natural and accessible language for them because of its visual properties.
Potential Limitations	Learning spoken English can be frustrating for those who do not benefit from amplification or were identified late. If this approach is not successful, individuals may have limited ways to communicate with others and experience language development delays, adversely affecting learning and social-emotional development.	Not used as commonly as other approaches; consequently, the number of people who cue is very limited. It is not truly a communication system since it is used to enhance receptive language skills; generally, individuals do not cue to express themselves.	Not a true language. Often described by native ASL users as artificial and cumbersome. Takes longer to convey messages. SEE2 is signed literally, not conceptually like ASL.	Not a true language. Cannot show every aspect of spoken English since there is no sign equivalent for many affixes. No community of adult users exists.	Not a true language—it is not ASL, nor is it English. Varies widely depending on communication partners' linguistic background and competence.	Can be challenging to make the transition from ASL to English as the first language to English as the second language through reading and writing. Can be difficult to develop speech and audition skills. A shortage of native ASL users makes it difficult for some schools to implement a true bilingual/bicultural program.

FIGURE 11.5 **Typical Communication and Experiential Input: Students Who Are Deaf or Hard of Hearing versus Students Who Are Hearing**

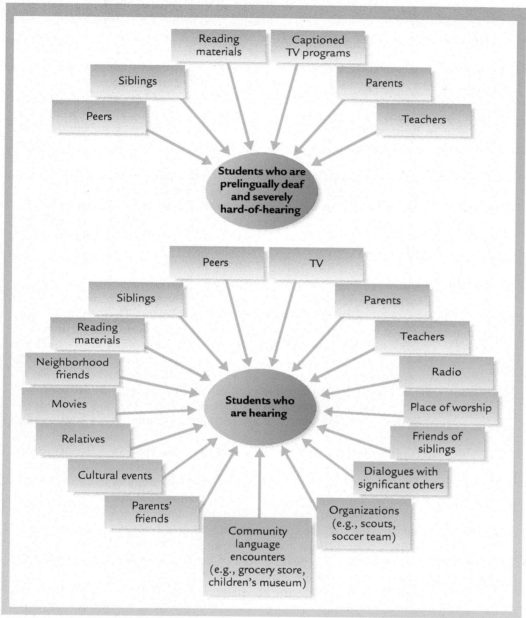

Academic Characteristics

The discussion earlier in this section regarding the presence or absence of early communication has important consequences for children's development of academic skills (Scott, 2011). That is, a hearing loss presents a potential barrier to communication, which in turn influences most areas of development, including those related to academic achievement (e.g., Qi & Mitchell, 2012). This central point is explained later in greater detail.

Language

Language is central to everything that we do because it is the means for communicating with others, thinking, and learning (Schirmer, 2001; Robertson, 2014).

Even though children who are deaf or hard of hearing have the same ability to learn language as their hearing peers, to achieve their linguistic potential they need to interact with adults and other children who consistently talk and/or sign with them. The experience of seeing, hearing, and forming words stimulates brain development in ways that help the child communicate more effectively (Diamond & Hopson, 1998). Consequently, a clear relationship exists between children's progress in language learning and the amount of conversation they have with sophisticated language users (DesJardin et al., 2014; Hart & Risley, 1999).

Communicating with others enables children to plan, explore, problem solve, question, and discuss. Unfortunately, many children and adolescents who are deaf or hard of hearing do not engage in conversations with family members, peers, or professionals (Tye-Murray, 1994). When they do have conversations, those interactions often are controlled by adults and consist of question-and-answer interchanges that are linguistically simple, concrete, and literal (Wood & Wood, 1997). This pattern of limited conversations can have negative long-term effects on the ability of individuals who are deaf or hard of hearing to acquire reading skills, access the curriculum, relate cause and effect, solve problems, and make thoughtful decisions about behaviors (Luckner, Bruce, & Ferrell, 2015).

Reading

Because hearing is not needed to read, you might assume that reading would not be a problem for students who are deaf or hard of hearing. That is not the case, primarily because of the communication and language development connection between hearing loss and reading (Luckner, Slike, & Johnson, 2012). Acquisition of a first language and ongoing language development throughout early childhood and elementary school are necessary for individuals to become skilled readers (Webb, Lederberg, Branum-Martin, & Connor, 2015; Goldin-Meadow & Mayberry, 2001). Sadly, many students who are deaf or hard of hearing are learning to read at the same time that they are learning to communicate and use language, and difficulties result.

Research on the performance of students who are deaf or hard of hearing using standardized tests of reading comprehension suggests that, on average, they encounter great difficulty in processing standard English in print but that their more effective interventions are having a positive impact. For example, although Traxler (2000) found that the median grade level for reading comprehension for these students as they were leaving high school was just below the fourth-grade level, Easterbrooks and Beal-Alvarez (2012) reported that 35–36% of high school students who are deaf or hard of hearing scored proficient on high-stakes testing in reading comprehension.

One additional factor makes the acquisition of reading skills difficult for students who are deaf or hard of hearing. Many children with a hearing loss do not have books read to them by adults, which has been determined to be an essential component in literacy development (Aram, Most, & Simon, 2008). Adults often do not read books to children who are deaf or hard of hearing because they feel uncomfortable signing, have a limited sign vocabulary, or they find it difficult to find a comfortable way to seat the child and hold the book to accomplish satisfactory visual contact.

Although the majority of students who are deaf or hard of hearing struggle to become fluent readers, some of these students perform on grade level when compared to their hearing peers (Easterbrooks, 2010, Lederberg, Miller, Easterbrooks, & Connor, 2014). The factors suggested to explain these students' success include the quality and quantity of interactions with significant others, parent participation in their education, supportive early educational environments, and high-quality educational programs (Donne & Zigmond, 2008; Luckner & Urbach, 2012; van Staden, 2013).

Written Language

Like reading, writing can pose challenges for students who are deaf or hard of hearing. In fact, research suggests that the problems faced by these students in mastering written English are even more formidable than those they encounter in developing reading skills (Moores, 2001; Williams & Mayer, 2015).

The problems that students who are deaf or hard of hearing often experience with writing have to do with the fact that writing is considered a secondary form of linguistic expression, and thus it is highly dependent on a foundation of a primary language system, such as speech or sign. Additionally, many students who are deaf or hard of hearing struggle with the mechanical as well as the organizational aspects of writing. In general, researchers find that these students continue to make slow improvement in written language throughout their educational programs (e.g., Arfé, 2015; Woblers, 2008).

However, as noted in the research on reading, students who are deaf and hard of hearing comprise a highly heterogeneous group. Many students have become successful writers (Aram, Most, & Simon, 2008; Wolbers, Dostal, & Bowers, 2012), and some even have become award-winning journalists (e.g., Kisor, 1990). One approach that can contribute to student success is simultaneous instruction in both American Sign Language (ASL), the language immediately accessible by students but that does not have a written form, and English (Dostal & Wolbers, 2014).

Mathematics

In general, students who are deaf or hard of hearing achieve at a higher grade level in mathematics than in reading or writing, although their achievement level generally still is problematic (e.g., Hrastinski & Wilbur, 2016; Kritzer, 2009). For example, Traxler (2000) reported that the median grade level in mathematics for 18-year-old students who were deaf or hard of hearing was just below a sixth-grade level for computation and a fifth-grade level for problem solving. As you might suspect, the same factors that affect reading proficiency contribute to their performance in mathematics, and these include their experiential deficits; difficulty with language, especially the highly specialized language and symbols of mathematics; and traditional instructional practices that emphasize rote memorization and an emphasis on computation rather than applied problem solving (Pagliaro, 2006).

The challenges of acquiring language can affect all aspects of the education of a student with a hearing loss, but some students—especially those who are identified as babies and have early intervention—achieve comparably to their hearing peers.

Social and Emotional Characteristics

The manner in which each of us understands others, our culture, and ourselves is strongly affected by direct interactions as well as incidental learning. For many children and youth who are deaf or hard of hearing, both of these areas are often compromised. For example, their impoverished diet of early conversations often continues into the preschool years, where they have fewer interactions as well as less exposure to social language (e.g., pragmatics, such as appropriate turn taking) and emotional language (e.g., vocabulary words such as *delightful* or *cruel*). This lack of interaction and limited opportunities to observe proficient users of social skills negatively affects the social and emotional development of these students.

As a result of these challenges, children and youth who are deaf or hard of hearing tend to have fewer friends, parents who have more restrictive rules for behavior, and parents who are unable to communicate expectations about social interactions (Marschark, 2007). When parents and adults cannot fluently communicate with the child who is deaf or hard of hearing, they are unable to explain the causes of other people's social and emotional behavior and cannot provide feedback about the child's behavior. Similarly, when other adults are unable to communicate well with these children, they tend to solve the children's problems for them rather than explain what to do, offer assistance, or give feedback. Thus, the linguistic and cognitive complexity of children's tasks may be reduced.

Socialization in educational settings is an area of particular concern for students who are deaf or hard of hearing. Some proponents of educating these students in general education settings contend that this is the best environment for developing social skills because the students have opportunities to interact with peers who are both hearing and deaf or hard of hearing. However, research has demonstrated that students who are deaf or hard of hearing are unlikely to form positive relationships with hearing peers unless efforts are made by professionals to bridge the communication barrier and to structure situations where positive interactions can occur (e.g., Ayantoye & Luckner, 2016).

Behavior Characteristics

To behave in socially appropriate ways, children and youth have to consider alternatives in social situations. Students who are deaf or hard of hearing often lag behind their hearing peers in recognizing the reasons for other people's behaviors, in part because they are less likely to receive or overhear explanations for those behaviors. As a result, they may not understand why people act or react the way that they do (Marschark, 2007). In addition, most of us learn to understand our emotions and the subtle differences between emotions (e.g., anger, frustration, disappointment) by interacting with others who explain how they are feeling or who describe how we might be feeling. Again, as a result of limited conversational partners, many students who are deaf or hard of hearing have a limited vocabulary of emotional language that helps them understand their own feelings or those of others (e.g., Wiefferink, Rieffe, Ketelaar, De Raeve, & Frijns, 2013). One successful approach for addressing the behavior problems that students who are deaf or hard of hearing may experience is called PATHS. The Positive Behavior Supports feature describes this approach.

MyEdLab **Self-Check 11.2**

MyEdLab **Application Exercise 11.3:** The Impact of Hearing Loss: Mini Case Study

---

Identifying a Hearing Loss

For a student to receive services as deaf or hard of hearing through IDEA, the formal procedure for assessment, identification, and eligibility must be followed, as it is for all students who might be eligible. The central concern is the student's capabilities and limitations related to hearing. However, as demonstrated in the following discussion, other areas of assessment also must be addressed.

Audiological Evaluation

A hearing loss is identified through the process of a hearing screening and/or an audiological evaluation. Hearing screenings are first conducted on newborns before they leave the hospital, a topic discussed later in the chapter.

The purposes of an audiological evaluation, a specialized series of hearing tests, are to determine if a hearing loss exists and to quantify and qualify hearing in terms of the degree of hearing loss, the type of hearing loss, and the

POSITIVE • **BEHAVIOR** • SUPPORTS

Promoting Alternative Thinking Strategies

The Promoting Alternative Thinking Strategies (PATHS) curriculum (Curtis & Norgate, 2007; Kusché & Greenberg, 1993) is a comprehensive program for promoting emotional and social competencies and reducing aggression and behavior problems in elementary school students. PATHS consists of approximately 130 lessons initially developed for students who are deaf or hard of hearing but also used with other students.

The PATHS curriculum, typically taught three times per week for 20–30 minutes per session, provides teachers with systematic, developmentally based lessons, materials, and instructions for teaching students emotional literacy, self-control, social competence, positive peer relations, and interpersonal problem-solving skills. PATHS lessons include instruction in many areas:

- Identifying and labeling feelings
- Expressing feelings
- Assessing the intensity of feelings
- Managing feelings
- Understanding the difference between feelings and behaviors
- Delaying gratification
- Controlling impulses
- Reducing stress

- Practicing self-talk
- Reading and interpreting social cues
- Understanding the perspectives of others
- Using steps for problem solving and decision making
- Having a positive attitude toward life
- Developing self-awareness
- Learning nonverbal and verbal communication skills

Research examining the effectiveness of using the PATHS Curriculum with students who are deaf or hard of hearing has demonstrated significant improvements for program youth compared to control youth in the following areas:

- Self-control
- Ability to tolerate frustration
- Social problem solving
- Recognition and understanding of emotions
- Social/emotional adjustment

As you review the topics included in PATHS, which do you think might be most appropriate for all students versus those who are deaf or hard of hearing? How could such a program be incorporated into general and special education programs?

---

configuration of the hearing loss. Degree and type of hearing loss have already been discussed. To determine the *configuration* of the hearing loss, the audiologist looks at qualitative attributes such as bilateral versus unilateral hearing loss, high-frequency versus low-frequency hearing loss, and flat versus sloping and stable versus fluctuating hearing loss. The audiologic evaluation consists of a battery of tests, including the following:

- A case history
- A physical examination of the outer ear, the ear canal, and the eardrum
- A pure-tone audiometry test of hearing that is recorded on a graph, called an audiogram
- Tests of middle-ear function

After the test battery has been completed, the audiologist reviews each component to obtain a profile of hearing abilities and needs.

Audiological evaluations also are carried out to periodically check the status of an individual's hearing loss. Specifically, professionals are interested in finding answers to questions such as these:

- Has the hearing loss improved as a result of medical intervention?
- Does the hearing loss fluctuate?
- Is the hearing loss progressively getting worse?

Simultaneously, it also is important to monitor whether students are benefiting from the use of amplification (e.g., cochlear implant, personal hearing aids, or assistive listening devices). Professionals want answers to these questions:

- Does the amplification work correctly?
- Does the hearing aid fit well?

- Is the power setting on the hearing aid set properly?
- Does the cochlear implant need to be reprogrammed?

Other Assessments

Although hearing is the primary consideration for eligibility for services in this disability category, other areas are not ignored. For example, the multidisciplinary team checks the student's vision and requests information about the student's overall health. An intelligence test is administered, as is an individual achievement test. These assessment procedures enable the team to determine whether the student is achieving at an expected level. Remember that measuring intelligence for students who have significant hearing loss usually involves the use of special tests that do not depend on the student's language skills. These students also complete an assessment of their specific communication skills, and teachers and parents may be asked to complete inventories regarding students' social and emotional functioning as well as their school and home behavior. For older students, an assessment related to transition goals is included.

Determination of Eligibility

The multidisciplinary team considers all the information gathered about the student in deciding whether the hearing loss constitutes a disability that requires providing special education services. Although federal law does not specify a minimum threshold of hearing loss that would make a student eligible for services and some states do not set forth more specific guidelines, the following student characteristics, measured through formal tests, are often considered:

- Inability to recognize most words spoken at a conversational level in a quiet room without the use of assistive devices
- A significant receptive or expressive language delay
- Impairment of speech articulation, voice, or fluency
- A significant discrepancy between verbal and nonverbal performance on an intelligence test
- Significant delay in the development of reading skills because of language deficit or overall significantly lower than expected academic achievement
- Inattention or serious behavior problems related to the hearing loss

If the multidisciplinary team determines that special education is appropriate, members then prepare the IEP and make decisions about communication methods and the need for language support (e.g., the need for interpreter services). Then the team members determine the educational setting in which the student's needs can best be met.

MyEdLab **Self-Check 11.3**

MyEdLab **Application Exercise 11.4:** Identifying a Hearing Loss

---

How Learners Who Are Deaf or Hard of Hearing Receive Their Education

The overriding concern in determining the appropriate and least restrictive educational environment for children who are deaf or hard of hearing was addressed by the U.S. Department of Education in 1992. In a document titled "Deaf Students

---

Video Example
from
YouTube

▶

MyEdLab
Video Example 11.3

Does loud music (and other loud noise) affect hearing? Yes, and this is affecting many young people, a point clearly made in this video. (https://www.youtube.com/watch?v=7OacRCJaH7U)

Education Services Policy Guidance," five considerations were listed for determining appropriate educational placements and IEP development for students who are deaf or hard of hearing:

1. Preferred communication needs of the child and family
2. Linguistic needs
3. Severity of hearing loss and potential for using residual hearing
4. Academic level
5. Social, emotional, and cultural needs, including opportunities for peer interactions and communication (U.S. Department of Education, 1992)

Though more than two decades have passed since this document was disseminated, these factors are used to help shape today's educational options for students who are deaf or hard of hearing.

Early Childhood

Early childhood services can begin as soon as a baby has been identified as having a hearing loss (Marchbank, 2011; Muse et al., 2013). Services usually are provided by a state's department of health or department of education. The goals of early intervention include these:

1. To help the family understand hearing loss and gain confidence as parents of children who are deaf or hard of hearing
2. To help the young child who is deaf or hard of hearing learn to communicate, to use any available hearing, and to interact socially
3. To help the young child become a fully participating member of the family (Boys Town National Research Hospital, n.d.)

An early intervention specialist for these children has knowledge about hearing loss and its effect on development. The family works closely with the specialist to identify needs, set priorities, help locate resources, and get questions answered. The specialist schedules regular visits to the family's home or another natural environment such as a day care setting or to a place where the child spends a majority of time.

The early intervention specialist also serves as the central point of contact between the family and the school program and/or other professionals. The specialist works with the family to identify and meet the child's needs by coordinating both formal and informal supports (e.g., Moeller, Carr, Seaver, Stredler-Brown, & Holzinger, 2013). An example of a formal support is the coordination of the multidisciplinary team to work with the family to determine strengths, needs, and resources. Examples of informal support include helping families participate in a parent group; organizing social gatherings and play groups; and introducing the family to deaf adults or to organizations such as the American Society for Deaf Children (ASDC), Hands and Voices, and Hearing Loss Association of America (HLAA).

Elementary and Secondary School Services

Elementary and secondary school services for students who are deaf or hard of hearing tend to occur in a variety of educational placements. As shown by the data presented in Figure 11.6, a large majority of these students are enrolled in typical public schools, but just slightly more than half participate in general education nearly all day (National Center for Education Statistics, 2015). Many receive resource or self-contained classroom special education support.

The placements that most school districts and states provide for students who are deaf or hard of hearing usually include those described in the following sections.

FIGURE 11.6   Educational Placements of Students Ages 6 to 21 Who Are Deaf or Hard of Hearing (in percentages)

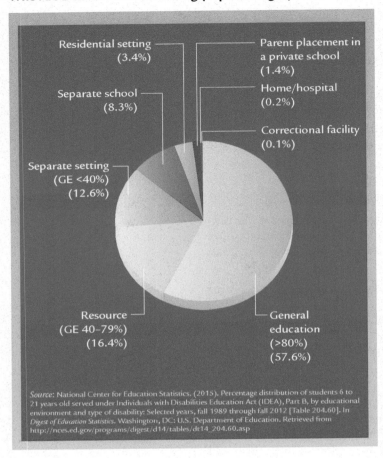

Residential setting (3.4%)

Separate school (8.3%)

Separate setting (GE <40%) (12.6%)

Resource (GE 40–79%) (16.4%)

General education (>80%) (57.6%)

Parent placement in a private school (1.4%)

Home/hospital (0.2%)

Correctional facility (0.1%)

Source: National Center for Education Statistics. (2015). Percentage distribution of students 6 to 21 years old served under Individuals with Disabilities Education Act (IDEA), Part B, by educational environment and type of disability: Selected years, fall 1989 through fall 2012 [Table 204.60]. In *Digest of Education Statistics*. Washington, DC: U.S. Department of Education. Retrieved from http://nces.ed.gov/programs/digest/d14/tables/dt14_204.60.asp

General Education Classroom

Students who are deaf or hard of hearing may receive their entire educational program with their hearing peers. They may be accompanied by an interpreter (i.e., a person who helps someone with hearing loss to communicate by translating what is said into signs or words with cues) in order for the students to meet their communication needs. Alternatively, they may use technology for this purpose as explained in the Technology Notes.

Generally, a teacher of students who are deaf or hard of hearing monitors the academic and social progress of these students and consults with general education teachers to make appropriate accommodations (Berndsen & Luckner, 2012; Mascia-Reed, 2010). In some areas, this consultation model is used when one teacher for students who are deaf or hard of hearing is responsible for students in several schools (Compton, Appenzeller, Kemmery, & Gardiner-Walsh, 2015).

General Education Classroom with Supplementary Instruction

Students who are deaf or hard of hearing may receive the majority of their instruction from general education teachers and also be provided direct instruction, additional practice, tutoring, or specialized skills instruction by a teacher of students who are deaf or hard of hearing and/or a speech-language pathologist. These services often are arranged during a specific block of time each week, and the instruction can occur in the general education classroom or in a resource room. This service relies on effective collaboration among all the professionals working on behalf of the student.

Separate Class for Students Who Are Deaf or Hard of Hearing

Slightly fewer than one in five students who are deaf or hard of hearing receive most or all of their instruction from a teacher of students who are deaf or hard of hearing in a special education classroom. These students are most likely to interact with their hearing peers during lunch, recess, art, library, physical education, extracurricular activities, and other school functions.

Other Settings

Approximately 12% of students who are deaf or hard of hearing attend a special school that serves only students with significant hearing loss (National Center for Education Statistics, 2015). Teachers of students who are deaf or hard of hearing provide instruction. These schools may be either public or private day schools, to which students commute from home each day, or public or private residential schools at which students live during the week. A few students—those with serious health problems, for example—may be served in home or hospital settings.

Inclusive Practices

The meaning of the least restrictive environment (LRE) for students who are deaf or hard of hearing is a source of ongoing debate. Supporters of inclusion contend

TECHNOLOGY NOTES
Technology for Classroom Support

Technology to support students who are deaf or hard of hearing continues to evolve (Collins, Goyne, & McCabe, 2013). Here are examples your students might access.

C-print

C-print is a computer-aided, speech-to-print transcription system developed as a classroom support service for students who are deaf or hard of hearing in general education classrooms. It is also used in some workplace settings.

- A typist called the *C-print captionist* types the teacher's lecture as well as students' comments into a laptop computer that has word-processing and abbreviation software.
- The typed information is simultaneously displayed on a second laptop computer or monitor for students who are deaf or hard of hearing to read during the lecture or discussion.
- The captionist uses a computerized abbreviation system to type the words of the teacher and students as they are spoken. The text display of the message appears approximately 3 seconds after the words are spoken and remains on the screen for approximately 1 minute.
- The text files are saved and can be used by students, tutors, and instructors after class by reading them on a monitor or from a printed copy (National Technical Institute for the Deaf, 2013).

Research indicates that many students who are deaf or hard of hearing prefer C-print to using an interpreter and that the C-print real-time display enables them to achieve a high level of comprehension of lecture material (e.g., Stinson & McKee, 2000). Limitations of C-print include the lag time between what is said and what appears on the screen, the captionist's possible difficulty in capturing other students' comments, and C-print's inability to capture visual material, such as illustrations and mathematical formulae.

FM System

FM systems have been described as being like miniature radio stations. To use one, the teacher wears a microphone that wirelessly transmits sounds via harmless radio waves. The student receives the sounds via an FM receiver, and, depending on the type, the receiver may be on the student's desk, worn behind the student's ear, or integrated into the student's hearing aids. This technology sometimes is adequate for a student with a mild hearing loss, and it can enhance the sound heard for a student who also uses hearing aids. Although FM systems have been available for many years, their popularity is returning because of the miniaturization of both the transmitting microphone and the receiver.

Sign Language Software

Vcom3D (http://www.vcom3d.com/signsmith.php) has developed animated GIFs (graphical interchange formats) and movies of signs that focus on vocabulary and concepts covered in the curriculum of early education classes (i.e., prekindergarten through third grade). In addition, Vcom3D has developed an interactive three-dimensional (3D) sign language dictionary of science terms and definitions to support access to standards-based science content for elementary- and middle-grade students. Each product uses animated 3D characters, called *signing avatars*. The characters can produce movements of the fingers and hands, facial gestures, body movements, and co-signs, in which two different words or ideas are signed at the same time. The characters can be programmed to communicate in either ASL or signed English.

that students who are deaf or hard of hearing should be integrated into general education settings and that all or most of their services can be provided in general education classrooms. They maintain that general education is the least restrictive environment for most of these students (e.g., Eriks-Brophy & Whittingham, 2013; Lindeman & Magiera, 2014; Nowell & Innes, 1997). Although there are many advantages to educating students who are deaf or hard of hearing in an inclusive environment, a variety of challenges exist as well, including issues related to the development of communication competence, the availability of social interactions, exposure to role models, and other areas already outlined (e.g., Fitzpatrick & Olds, 2015; Xie, Potmešil, & Peters, 2014). The Professional Edge lists some of the potential benefits and barriers to providing services in general education for students who are deaf or hard of hearing. However, keep in mind that implementing inclusive practices does not necessarily mean full-time participation in general education.

Potential Benefits and Barriers of Inclusive Practices for Students Who Are Deaf or Hard of Hearing

Professionals and parents continue to discuss the benefits and barriers to the participation of students who are deaf or hard of hearing in general education classrooms. Here are some of the points they make.

Potential Benefits

1. Students can live at home with their families.
2. Students are exposed to and required to communicate and interact with skilled language users.
3. Students have social interactions with students who live in the same community and thus provide opportunities for continual social contacts.
4. Students can observe, imitate, and receive feedback from age-appropriate peers about acceptable and unacceptable behaviors.
5. Students are taught the general education curriculum and are expected to participate in the standard learning tasks and assessments.
6. Students who are hearing have a variety of opportunities to interact with their classmates who have a hearing loss.
7. By living, learning, and socializing in settings with hearing people, students who are deaf or hard of hearing are ready to live and work in the community after graduation.

Potential Barriers

1. General education teachers may not want to teach students who are deaf or hard of hearing.
2. General education teachers and teachers of students who are deaf or hard of hearing may not have the necessary interpersonal communication and planning skills needed to work together to address student needs.
3. Most general education teachers have little experience working with students who are deaf or hard of hearing. Consequently, they may lack the ability to directly communicate with these students and may not know how to or want to use an interpreter.
4. Educational interpreters may not have the skills needed to model language or express content material (Schick, Williams, & Bolster, 1999), thus placing students at an academic disadvantage.
5. Students' access to the information transmitted during classroom discourse can be reduced significantly because of the rapid discussion rate, continuous turn taking, simultaneous speaking and high number of speakers, and quick topic changes.
6. Students may experience feelings of loneliness and isolation if they are unable to participate in social activities with peers because of communication difficulties.
7. Students may lack opportunities to interact with successful deaf adults as well as to gain access to the Deaf community.

Professionals developing educational plans and considering appropriate settings for students who are deaf or hard of hearing should ask these questions:

- Is this student developing age-appropriate communication skills?
- Is this student making satisfactory academic progress?
- Does this student have friends?
- Does this student have access to all components of the educational process, including lunch, recess, and extracurricular social and athletic activities?

If the answer to any of these questions is no, then it may be necessary to explore ways of providing increased support for the student or different placement options while still ensuring interactions with hearing peers.

Did You Know?

Most people who are deaf or hard of hearing are not good lip readers because only 30% of all spoken sounds are visible on the lips.

Transition and Adulthood

Successful adults who are deaf or hard of hearing can be found in almost every profession (Schroedel & Geyer, 2000), and a variety of stories about their lives have been published (e.g., Shea, 2013; Walker, 2001). Even though many students who are deaf or hard of hearing find high school to be academically challenging, they are significantly more successful at completing high school when compared to students who do not have disabilities and to other students with disabilities (Wagner, Newman, Cameto, & Levine, 2005). What might explain this? One possibility is that, in school, students who are deaf or hard of hearing can find adults and other students with whom they are able to communicate and socialize. Another factor is parent support. For example, a study by Michael, Most, and Cinamon (2013) found that parental support was directly related to career self-efficacy both for students with hearing loss and typical learners.

Students who are deaf or hard of hearing often successfully complete high school, transition to postsecondary education, and become successful in a wide range of professions.

However, the picture of students with hearing loss in postsecondary education is not all positive. Although significantly more students who are deaf or hard of hearing attend two- and four-year postsecondary education programs when compared to students with other types of disabilities or students without disabilities (Wagner, Newman, Cameto, & Levine, 2005), most of these students drop out prior to receiving a degree (English, 1997; Kelly, 2014). One reason for this unfortunate outcome may be related to these students' proficiency in academic language (Convertino, Marschark, Sapere, Sarchet, & Zupan, 2009), a continuation of the language challenges encountered throughout their academic careers. A reasonable conclusion to draw from this information is that many adults who are deaf or hard of hearing are not educated to the level of their capability, and so they may be at a disadvantage in addressing the demands of adulthood.

For students who are deaf or hard of hearing, the transition planning process and the transition component of the IEP should be considered capacity-building activities that bring together the resources of the students, families, professionals, adult service agencies, and community members and organizations. Sample activities to promote the process of transition for students who are deaf or hard of hearing, as suggested by Luckner (2002), are as follows:

- Teach a unit on and reinforce responsible and independent behaviors
- Take career field trips
- Read books with students about the work that people do
- Have students complete interest inventories to help them think about career options
- Set up job-shadowing opportunities for students
- Provide self-determination and self-advocacy training

Students who are deaf or hard of hearing have great potential—potential that too often goes untapped. Their prospects for successful adult lives are enhanced when educators realize the scope of their possible needs and enlist the widest array of resources to help them accomplish their dreams (Luckner & Sebald, 2013).

Video Example
from
YouTube

MyEdLab
Video Example 11.4

In this video, Jackie shares her growing-up experiences as a Deaf individual. Her story is a reminder that professionals' responsibility is to prepare students for their lives after the school years. (https://www.youtube.com/watch?v=vIcditMTKx4)

MyEdLab **Self-Check 11.4**

MyEdLab **Application Exercise 11.5:** Inclusive Classroom Practices

MyEdLab **Application Exercise 11.6:** Attitudes for Success in an Inclusive Classroom

DATA-DRIVEN DECISIONS

Filling in the Data Gap

Practices in the field of education of students who are deaf or hard of hearing have been guided more by emotional beliefs than evidence (Spencer & Marschark, 2010). The two most obvious examples are communication approaches and placement. The professional literature is replete with proponents of two communication approaches: auditory/oral approaches and the bilingual–bicultural approach (discussed later in this chapter). Yet to date, limited evidence supports either one of them with regard to educational outcomes (Swanwick & Marschark, 2011). Similarly, some professionals strongly advocate for inclusion while others vehemently support separate schools for students who are deaf or hard of hearing. Again, few data demonstrate that either placement is predictive of better educational outcomes (Stinson & Kluwin, 2011).

What we do know for certain is that the population of students who are deaf or hard of hearing is very heterogeneous. They have diverse educational and social needs, and those needs may change during the span of their educational careers. As a result, professionals need to collect data on a regular basis and share those data with other team members, including the student and the family, to make decisions about improving the quality of services provided to students. These are examples of data to gather:

Communication Approaches

Communication approaches can be conceptualized along a continuum for both receptive communication and expressive communication (e.g., DesJardin, 2006), from fully visual/sign mostly to visual/sign mostly to auditory/oral to fully auditory/oral.

From as early as possible, and at regular intervals, professionals and families should collect data and make informed decisions about each student's receptive and expressive communication preferences and select a communication approach that is effective for that individual.

Services and Placement

Ongoing data collection to monitor skills important for students' school success and to ensure that they have access to the academic content and social environment also is very important. In addition to the statewide annual assessments, standardized tests, and curriculum-based measurements, professionals can use informal assessments such as the *Classroom Participation Questionnaire–Revised Deaf/Hard of Hearing Students* (Antia, Sabers, & Stinson, 2007) and the *PARC: Placement and Readiness Checklists for Students Who Are Deaf and Hard of Hearing* (Johnson & Seaton, 2012).

Recommended Educational Practices for Students Who Are Deaf or Hard of Hearing

The past decade has seen increased attention on the use of a strong evidence base as a means of selecting instructional strategies for students. Unfortunately, the field of deaf education lacks much research to guide it, the topic of the Data-Driven Decisions. The information presented in this section is based on the research that does exist, as well as the literature on best practices. It describes examples of approaches that promote the academic and social development of these students.

Integrated Vocabulary and Concept Development

Many students who are deaf or hard of hearing have limited and/or delayed receptive and expressive vocabulary, and this negatively affects comprehension (Easterbrooks et al., 2015; Sarchet, Marschark, Borgna, Convertino, Sapere, & Dirmyer, 2014), especially as concepts and vocabulary become more abstract. Thus, to make academic progress in the content areas of the curriculum, these students require additional support. That support can come in a variety of forms. One approach that was beneficial for students in a study reported by Luckner and Muir (2001) was the use of preteaching and postteaching activities to supplement daily lessons and help make the content accessible. Preteaching essential vocabulary and concepts assisted the students in establishing the knowledge base needed to understand new information. Postteaching was used to review key concepts, clarify misconceptions, organize information, and expand students' knowledge of the content or skills emphasized during the lesson.

Experiential Ladder of Learning

How did you learn to ride a bike? To operate a computer? To tell someone that you cared about him or her? To cook a meal? Most of these skills are acquired through direct experience. Central to learning is the quantity and quality of experiences that we have in childhood and throughout life. Those experiences help shape our intelligence, character, and interests. Because many students who are deaf or hard of hearing grow up in homes where they are overprotected, they may miss mediated experiences (Marschark, 2007). In view of the limitations placed by a hearing loss on vicarious learning, it is important to structure authentic experiences for children and youth who are deaf or hard of hearing.

Bruner, Oliver, and Greenfield (1966) suggested that humans represent the experience of the world through three modes: (a) *symbolic* (words, language), (b) *iconic* (pictures, charts, graphs), and (c) *enactive* (experiences). Depth and breadth of knowledge about individual concepts and procedures comes from learning that involves all three modes. A useful framework for planning units of study and learning activities, suggested by Luckner (2002), is the *experiential ladder of learning*. It is presented in Figure 11.7. The ladder offers alternatives to using lecture, discussion, or assigned reading for assisting students to understand concepts and course content.

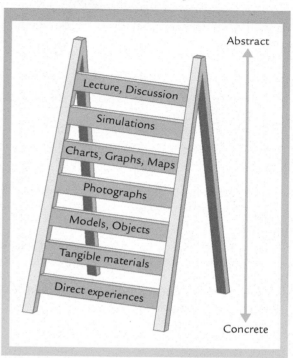

FIGURE 11.7   The Experiential Ladder of Learning

This organizer can help educators plan lessons that emphasize visual and hands-on learning.

Visual Teaching Strategies

Given the auditory limitations that accompany a hearing loss, many researchers and educators have suggested that educators establish a visually rich learning environment for students who are deaf or hard of hearing (e.g., Luckner, Bowen, & Carter, 2001). Professionals in these environments use (a) sign, finger-spelling, and speech reading (i.e., watching another person's face and mouth as she forms words); (b) equipment such as interactive whiteboards, document cameras, bulletin boards, computers, and televisions; and (c) materials including pictures, illustrations, artifacts, computer graphics, and films with captions.

Although there has been an increase in the use of interpreters and ASL features in educational settings, signing, like speech, provides a transient signal. The signal moves—it is there and then it is gone. Visual teaching strategies can be more permanent and can be used to help students focus on important information, see how concepts are connected, and integrate prior knowledge with new knowledge. Examples of visual aids that can be used in the classroom to enhance the communication and learning processes include classroom rule charts, job and choice menus, transition time cards and charts, task organizers, daily schedules, and the Internet. In addition, visual representations of knowledge—referred to by a variety of names, including *graphic organizers, semantic maps, webs, semantic organizers, story maps*, and *Venn diagrams*—can be used to provide a framework to make thought and organization processes visible. These visual teaching techniques allow professionals to omit extraneous information while emphasizing important concepts and demonstrating their connections to each other. Also, these visual representations of information are easier for students to remember than extended text.

INSTRUCTION IN ACTION

Accommodations for Students Who Are Deaf or Hard of Hearing

Many students who are deaf or hard of hearing can be supported in general education classrooms using accommodations such as these:

Environmental

- Seat the student in the best place to enhance attending and participation.
- Give the student a swivel chair on casters.
- Use a semicircular seating arrangement.
- Reduce noise and reverberation with the use of carpeting and draperies.
- Use flashing lights along with bells for signaling events in the class schedule and safety alarms (e.g., fire, tornado).

Input

- Use hearing assistance technology (HAT)—a personal frequency-modulated (FM) system or a classroom amplification system.
- Improve classroom acoustics (e.g., reduce background noise and reverberation).
- Stand in a place from which the student can read your lips.
- Face the student when talking.
- Use an interactive whiteboard or document camera.
- Employ an educational interpreter.
- Co-teach: general education teacher with a teacher of students who are deaf or hard of hearing.
- Provide a copy of your notes to the student.
- Supplement the lesson with visual materials (e.g., real objects, pictures, graphic organizers, photographs, charts, videos).
- Provide manipulatives for multisensory, hands-on instruction or activities.
- Provide a note taker for the student.
- Cue the student visually to indicate that someone is talking during class discussions or intercom messages.
- Repeat information that has been expressed by a person who is out of view or delivered over the intercom.
- Use captioned videos and television programs.
- Demonstrate directions to clarify what to do.
- Check for understanding by having the student restate the directions.

Output

- Allow more time for students to complete assignments.
- Allow the student to make models, role-play, develop skits, and create art projects to demonstrate understanding of the information.
- Allow a written or drawn response to serve as an alternative to an oral presentation.
- Allow the student to use a computer or word processor.

Social

- Teach hearing students to sign.
- Make available books about hearing loss and deafness.
- Invite adults who are deaf to share their stories at school.
- Structure activities and experiences so that students who are deaf and hearing students work together.
- Teach units on social topics (e.g., friendship, avoiding fights, emotions, stealing, dating, dealing with divorce).
- Provide direct instruction on specific social skills (e.g., starting conversations, giving compliments, responding to criticism).

Behavioral

- Place general rules and behavior expectations on charts displayed in the room, on a sheet of paper placed on the student's desk, or on the student's tablet or phone.
- Provide regular feedback and check often for progress on meeting behavior expectations.
- Develop a home–school contract with the student's family, whereby the student receives a specified reinforcer at home when he demonstrates a specific behavior in school.
- Use corrective feedback (e.g., "I would like you to take out a book and read when you finish your work, rather than talk to the person sitting next to you.")
- Increase the frequency of descriptive praise (e.g., "You really paid attention and stayed in your seat for the past 15 minutes.").
- Limit the number of distractions by establishing an isolated work/study area.
- Teach the student anger control strategies.

Evaluation

- Have test items signed to the student, and allow the student to respond in sign.
- Allow tests to be taken with the teacher of students who are deaf or with a paraprofessional.
- Provide extra time to complete tests and quizzes.
- Modify the vocabulary used in test items to match the student's abilities.
- Give shorter tests on a more frequent basis.
- Provide graphic cues (e.g., arrows, stop signs) on answer forms.
- Give alternative forms of the same test.
- Teach test-taking skills.

Grading

- Write descriptive comments, and give examples regarding student performance.
- Use a checklist of competencies associated with the course, and evaluate it according to mastery of the competencies.

Accommodations for Students Who Are Deaf or Hard of Hearing

Because most general education teachers have limited training or experience in working with students who are deaf or hard of hearing, they depend heavily on teachers of students who are deaf or hard of hearing to help them identify and implement ways to make the curriculum and social interactions accessible, as well as to ensure that the processes of assessment and grading are valid and reliable. The decisions about what specific accommodations to use depend on the goals for the student, the needs of the individual student, and the instructional style of the teacher. The Instruction in Action highlights some of the potential accommodations for students who are deaf or hard of hearing (Antia, Jones, Reed, & Kreimeyer, 2009). As you can see by examining the list, many of the accommodations for students who are deaf or hard of hearing also may be appropriate for students with other special needs.

MyEdLab **Self-Check 11.5**

MyEdLab **Application Exercise 11.7:** Interactive Whiteboard

MyEdLab **Application Exercise 11.8:** Recommended Educational Practices for Students Who Are Deaf or Hard of Hearing

---

Perspectives of Parents and Families

When hearing parents learn that their child has a hearing loss, they face a variety of challenges (Jackson, Wegner, & Turnbull, 2010), including understanding the impact of a hearing loss, finding appropriate services and support, and developing communication strategies (e.g., Poeppelmeyer & Reichert, 2015). Parents also have to deal with the reactions of family and friends. Whether the family chooses to use an oral approach, a sign language system based on the English language, or American Sign Language to communicate with their child, they have to make significant changes in how they interact with her. They must choose either to learn and use sign or to use amplification, optimizing residual hearing and speaking directly to the child.

In contrast, many parents who are deaf or hard of hearing themselves and involved in the Deaf community would prefer to have a child who is deaf or hard of hearing (e.g., Hinsliff & McKie, 2008; Patterson, 2015). Like most parents, parents who are deaf look forward to having a child who is a reflection of themselves. They bring their baby home to an environment where they will all share the same mode of communication—ASL or one set up to provide visual cues to environmental signals, such as doorbells and text telephones that flash lights rather than make noise. These parents are able to communicate with their child immediately, and the child is able to access incidental interactions that occur among family members because ASL is being used around them. Yet, as previously noted, less than 10% of children who are deaf or hard of hearing have parents who both have a hearing loss (NIDCD, 2016).

Thus, parents often feel alone and in need of support as they adjust to their child's special needs. At the same time, they want information in order to make the right decisions for him and to become advocates for the services he needs immediately as well as in the years to come. That support and information can be provided by an early intervention specialist, other parents who have gone through similar experiences, and parent organizations.

The Voices of Parents

As part of a larger study focusing on successful students who were deaf or hard of hearing, Luckner and Muir (2001) interviewed 19 parents to explore their perceptions of the factors that contributed to their child's success. They reported the following factors:

- Skilled and caring professionals
- Family support
- Early identification and early intervention
- Involvement in extracurricular activities
- The value of reading
- Perseverance

Parents were also asked, "What advice do you have to help other students who are deaf to become successful?" The following quotes exemplify what many parents shared (pp. 439–440):

- "Don't let deafness hold you back."
- "You just have to keep your child's best interests at heart."
- "Before you make any decision about how you're going to educate or how you're going to allow your deaf child to live, you make sure you get as much information as you possibly can."
- "I would go back and do less worrying and relax a little bit more and have a little bit more fun with him."

As a school professional, a key to working with parents of students who are deaf or hard of hearing is to remember that unless you have a significant hearing loss or are the parent of such a child, you do not understand their experience. You should look to the parents to help develop your own understanding of the child, the family, and their hopes and needs.

MyEdLab **Self-Check 11.6**

MyEdLab **Application Exercise 11.9:** A Mother's Perspective

MyEdLab **Application Exercise 11.10:** Perspectives of Parents and Families

---

Did You Know?

No universal sign language exists; hundred of versions of sign language are used across the world. However, Gestuno is a sign language system that is used at international gatherings of deaf people.

Trends and Issues Affecting the Field of Deaf Education

The field of deaf education is being affected by advances in science and technology and also shifts in thinking about appropriate communication options for students who are deaf or hard of hearing (Miller, 2015). Three trends illustrate these changes: (a) universal newborn hearing screening, (b) the increasing use of cochlear implants, and (c) the bilingual–bicultural approach for educating these students.

Universal Newborn Hearing Screening

Professionals in the field of deaf education have known of the advantages of identifying a child's hearing loss at an early age for more than half a century. Recent research has substantiated this perception by demonstrating that children identified with congenital hearing loss prior to 6 months of age acquire age-appropriate language skills by 36 months of age (e.g., Harris, 2010; Stika et al., 2015).

Yet, until recently, most children with a congenital hearing loss were not identified until they were nearly 2 years of age—old enough to take a formal hearing test. Now hospitals and agencies use two simple, inexpensive tests to screen babies for hearing loss. Both tests are safe, comfortable, and pose no risks to the infant. Many professionals refer to the screening programs by the name *Early Hearing Detection and Intervention (EHDI)*. This is an appropriate title because detecting a hearing loss is only the first step. Collectively, this notion of screening infants for hearing loss is referred to as universal newborn hearing screening. Currently, every state and territory in the United States has EHDI laws or voluntary compliance regarding screening the hearing of newborns, and, as a result, more than 97% of infants born in the United States have had their hearing screened before being discharged from the hospital (Centers for Disease Control and Prevention, 2015). Many children with significant hearing loss are identified within the first few months of their lives because of this screening, and this increases the likelihood that they will receive appropriate very early intervention (e.g., Muse et al., 2013).

Cochlear Implants

A cochlear implant is an electronic device that directly stimulates the hearing nerve in the cochlea, or the inner ear. This stimulation is designed to allow individuals with severe to profound hearing loss to perceive sound, as is true for Lily, whom you met at the beginning of the chapter. A cochlear implant consists of three parts. The *receiver* is the part that is surgically implanted. It looks like a magnetic disk and is about the size of a quarter. It is placed under the skin behind one ear. Tiny wires that extend from it, called *electrodes*, are surgically inserted into the cochlea. A small headpiece is worn just behind the ear, and it contains the microphone, which picks up sound in the environment, and the transmitter, which sends sound through the system. The speech processor is worn on the body, either behind the ear or on a belt. It is attached to the transmitter by a special cord. The cochlear implant converts sound energy into electrical signals. The signals are delivered to the electrodes in the cochlea, which in turn stimulate the auditory nerve fibers. The resulting information is sent to the brain. Figure 11.8 includes a diagram of a cochlear implant.

FIGURE 11.8   Diagram of a Cochlear Implant

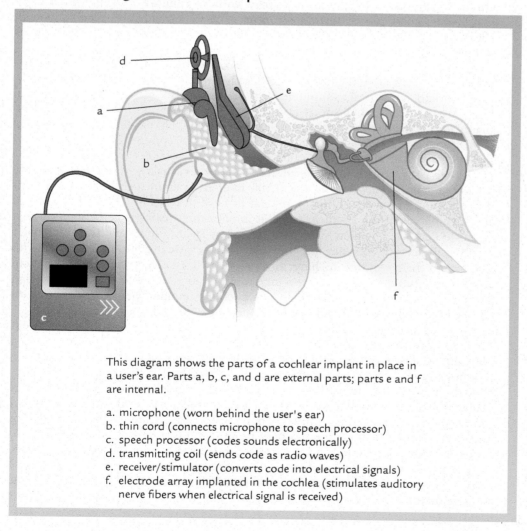

This diagram shows the parts of a cochlear implant in place in a user's ear. Parts a, b, c, and d are external parts; parts e and f are internal.

a. microphone (worn behind the user's ear)
b. thin cord (connects microphone to speech processor)
c. speech processor (codes sounds electronically)
d. transmitting coil (sends code as radio waves)
e. receiver/stimulator (converts code into electrical signals)
f. electrode array implanted in the cochlea (stimulates auditory nerve fibers when electrical signal is received)

The U.S. Food and Drug Administration (FDA) first approved cochlear implant devices for adults in 1985 and for children in 1990. Current FDA guidelines permit cochlear implantation in children with profound deafness as young as 12 months of age and in children with severe to profound hearing loss at age 2 years and older, and this is becoming a common procedure for students with hearing loss. Children even younger than 12 months of age occasionally receive a cochlear implant (American Speech-Language-Hearing Association, 2004). Not all children with a significant hearing loss are candidates for the use of this technology; professionals and families collaborate to determine whether a child is medically qualified and whether the development of oral communication skills is a priority.

For some children, a cochlear implant at a very young age can lead to enhanced language development and improved communication skills.

One of the primary reasons for choosing a cochlear implant is for the individual to develop spoken language and listening skills (Bat-Chava, Martin, & Imperatore, 2014); however, children still may use alternative communication strategies. For example, some children may employ simultaneous communication in which sign language and spoken language are used at the same time. Other children may use *cued speech*, explained earlier in Figure 11.4, in which eight hand-based cues, placed in four locations around the face, are combined with spoken language to help distinguish among similar sounds (e.g., /b/ and /p/) as speech is read.

Keep in mind, too, that controversy about cochlear implants exists. For example, questions arise regarding whether children who have had a cochlear implant should learn oral communication alone or also manual communication (e.g., Moores, 2009). Questions also have arisen about the use of cochlear implants for children with additional disabilities (Wakil, Fitzpatrick, Olds, Schramm, & Whittingham, 2014) and about the effectiveness of children receiving an additional cochlear implant as they enter adolescence (Desai & Patel, 2014).

Other issues relate to Deaf culture. Some individuals who strongly identify with Deaf culture view having a cochlear implant as an intrusive and inappropriate intervention for people who are deaf or hard of hearing. They point out that the very nature of the cochlear implant implies that deafness is a condition that needs to be "cured," a view strongly opposed by Deaf individuals. They also point out that the use of cochlear implants may threaten Deaf culture, as parents who encourage their children to have an implant will, in effect, be excluding them from that culture. Individuals who take a moderate view note that this is not an "either–or" matter—that individuals with cochlear implants may still identify with and participate in Deaf culture (Pray & Jordan, 2010).

Finally, you should be aware that problems can arise related to cochlear implants. Some individuals have contracted infections after the surgery, and a few individuals have lost what remaining hearing they had (U.S. Food and Drug Administration, 2014). The cochlear implant may fail or need repair, and individuals may have to adjust their lifestyles (e.g., avoiding some sports) to avoid damaging the implant. However, even though these risks and the other controversy surrounding cochlear implants may be considered deterrents to receiving them, children will likely increasingly be implanted because the research indicates that early implantation reduces or prevents the language and speech delays that often exist for children with severe to profound hearing losses and improves social interactions (e.g., Harris, 2015; Martin, Bat-Chava, Lalwani, & Waltzman, 2011).

Video Example

from

YouTube

MyEdLab
Video Example 11.5

The student in this video explains how having a cochlear implant has affected her life and her participation in Deaf culture. (https://www.youtube.com/watch?v=1k4e7EQHLRo&list=PLZY4zB2KVz8OCd2xqt1Ei2y8UNDV6HF1u)

FIGURE 11.9   **Examples of American Sign Language Signs**

These ASL signs can be helpful for school professionals working with students who are deaf or hard of hearing.

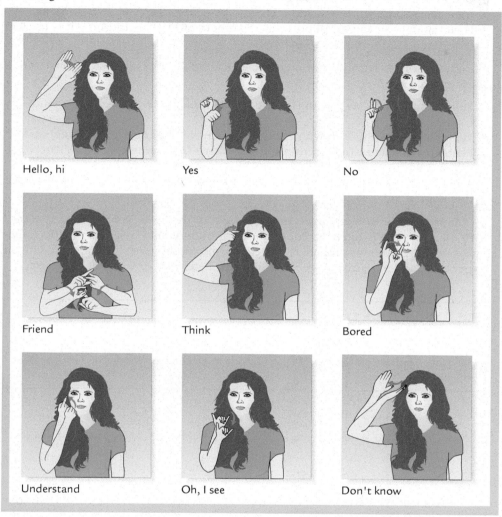

Bilingual–Bicultural Approach

In the past decade, a variety of residential schools and charter schools have adopted a bilingual–bicultural (Bi–Bi) approach to educating students who are deaf or hard of hearing. This means that ASL is the primary language of instruction and that English is taught as a second language through reading and writing print. The goal of bilingual–bicultural programs is for students to learn two languages (ASL and English) and to be able to function in two cultures (Deaf and hearing). Figure 11.9 provides a sample of some common ASL signs, but because ASL includes facial expressions and a unique grammatical structure, these examples cannot capture the richness of this distinct language.

Bilingual—bicultural programs support instruction in Deaf culture—that is, the history, contributions, values, and customs of the Deaf community. Supporters of Bi–Bi contend that when children who are deaf are able to establish a strong visual first language, ASL, they then have the tools they need for thinking and learning and to develop a healthy sense of self through connections with other deaf people. The principles of the Bi–Bi approach for students who are deaf or hard of hearing include these (Laurent Clerc National Deaf Education Center, 2015; Nussbaum, Scott, & Simms, 2012):

- Respect for the language of the student (ASL)
- Incorporating Deaf heritage information into teaching
- Using ASL to increase understanding of content information
- Increasing the complexity and metalinguistic knowledge of ASL students
- Developing a strong metalinguistic awareness of English and how it is used in different settings and situations

Professionals who do not support using the Bi–Bi approach often express these concerns:

- Limited attention is given to the development of speech and auditory training.
- Most parents of children who are deaf or hard of hearing are not fluent in ASL.
- Problems in successfully transitioning students from conversing in ASL to reading and writing in English have not been thoroughly explained.
- To date, little published research has clearly demonstrated the effectiveness of this approach.

As is true about many aspects of the field of deafness, spirited discussion of a Bi–Bi approach is likely to continue. Until high-quality research clearly establishes whether this approach is effective, opinions—albeit opinions based on experience and expertise—are most likely to determine the extent of its use.

MyEdLab **Self-Check 11.7**

MyEdLab **Application Exercise 11.11:** Advantages of Newborn Hearing Screening

MyEdLab **Application Exercise 11.12:** Trends and Issues Affecting the Field of Deaf Education

---

Summary

LO11.1 Concern for the education of individuals who are deaf or hard of hearing has existed for centuries in the United States. For today's students, hearing loss is defined in federal special education law and is considered a low-incidence disability.

LO11.2 Children and youth who are deaf or hard of hearing represent a very diverse group of individuals. Some use speech, some use sign, and some use both speech and sign to communicate. However, a hearing loss often affects the development of communication skills, which in turn often negatively affects language development, academic progress, socialization, and career attainment.

LO11.3 Assessment for eligibility for special education services for students with hearing loss focuses, of course, on the extent of the loss and the impact that it has on education, but it also incorporates ability, achievement, and social/emotional/behavioral domains.

LO11.4 Most students who are deaf or hard of hearing receive all or part of their education in general education settings, and this approach has many advantages. However, because of the diverse needs and preferences of students who are deaf or hard of hearing and their families, a variety of educational placement options must be available for them.

LO11.5 Recommended instructional practices for students who are deaf or hard of hearing focus on ways to increase students' vocabulary, concept knowledge, and experiential backgrounds.

LO11.6 The majority of students who are deaf or hard of hearing are born into hearing families, who must make a variety of difficult choices about how to communicate with and educate their child.

LO11.7 Issues and trends currently affecting the field of deaf education include newborn hearing screening, cochlear implants, and bilingual–bicultural educational approaches.

Back to the Cases

Now that you've read about students who are deaf or hard of hearing, look back at the student stories at the beginning of this chapter. Then, answer the questions about each of their cases.

MyEdLab **Case Study 11.1**

LILY. Since adoption, Lily has experienced strong family support and involvement in her habilitation and education. In addition, professionals have provided consistent collaborative services. Reflect on the information in this chapter, and consider how the collaborative interactions may change as Lily progresses in her academic career.

MyEdLab **Case Study 11.2**

ZACHARY. After meeting with the science teacher and school psychologist, Mr. Reynolds began to think that Zachary's change of behavior centers around the fact that the science concepts currently being taught are too abstract for Zachary and that he feels frustrated about not understanding the content.

MyEdLab **Case Study 11.3**

BRIAN. Brian is a senior in high school who has achieved a great deal thus far in his academic career, but it has not come without struggles. He is looking ahead to a bright future. Brian has already been admitted to a state university, where he plans to major in biology so that he can pursue a medical degree. He hopes to have a career as a researcher, possibly in a teaching hospital.

Based on the information presented in this chapter, consider what challenges Brian may encounter and how he and his IEP can help him prepare for college.

12 Students with Visual Impairments

JAYDEN

Jayden is a first-grade student who is rather shy, struggles academically, and tends to remain isolated even when his classmates are engaged in small-group activities. He spends part of the day with typical peers but also receives daily instruction from a teacher of students with visual impairments (TVI). Jayden has a cortical visual impairment (CVI), a complex disorder likely caused by a lack of oxygen that occurred during his birth; he also has moderate cerebral palsy and a mild intellectual disability, both attributed to the same cause. There is no single way to describe Jayden's visual loss because his condition can vary, depending on the visual situation he is in (e.g., looking at print material at his desk versus interacting with peers and his teacher during circle time), the amount of light available (he generally can see more when there is less light rather than bright light), whether there is movement related to the situation (he sees more when items are moving), and even whether he is having a "good" visual day or a "bad" one. Jayden's eyes appear normal; his vision loss is because of a neurological problem rather than any injury or deformity in his eyes. Jayden tends to see best through his peripheral vision, and so his general education teacher, Ms. Rosales, has learned that when Jayden looks away, it usually means he is focusing on the materials he has. Jayden's teacher for students with visual impairments works closely with Ms. Rosales to ensure that all the accommodations he needs are available when he is in that setting. She is also helping Ms. Rosales to coach Jayden as he learns social skills. In the special education setting, Jayden receives core instruction in language arts and math using the specialized techniques and accommodations that he needs. His TVI also monitors his vision use, helps him to learn to use his residual vision most effectively, and consults with the others involved in his education, including the occupational therapist and physical therapist.

ANNA MARIE

Anna Marie has a small amount of vision in a limited field in one eye and is blind in the other eye. She lives in a rural area. In elementary school, she was bused to a special class for students with visual impairments in a neighboring district, but she wanted to go to school with her friends, and so she began sixth grade at Madison Middle School. Her special education teacher, Ms. Barich, does not have a background in working with students like Anna Marie; her teaching license is in the area of mild disabilities. Ms. Barich had a long list of questions for the vision specialist who consulted with her right before school began, but even so, the beginning of the school year was rather difficult. First, Anna Marie was not prepared for the challenges of moving from class to class for most of the day; assigning a peer buddy helped with that problem. Second, Anna Marie's general education teachers had many questions about working with her: "If she cannot complete a lab because she cannot safely use the equipment, how should she be graded?" "In math, nearly everything is written on the board; how will she be able to keep up?" "If she composes in braille, how will I grade her work?" Ms. Barich has tried to be sure that all the teachers' questions are addressed while also working with Anna Marie to advocate for herself by asking for assistance when she needs help but being as independent as possible. Ms. Barich recently commented to a colleague that Anna Marie has caused her to look at the entire educational process in a new way—one that requires access without relying on sight.

ETHAN

Ethan is entering 10th grade as a student whose work is about average. His teachers find him to be hardworking, and they anticipate that he will reach whatever goals he sets. His favorite courses are those in science, and his current plan is to attend college and major in biology or chemistry because he is interested in the field of forensic science. His parents will take him to visit two colleges this year so that he can think carefully about whether this career is one he is likely to enjoy. That is important because Ethan has been blind since birth, and it takes careful preparation for him to fully participate in some academic settings, including science labs. One other problem he has encountered is textbook availability. His braille books do not always arrive on time, and this puts him at a disadvantage in his classes, even though his teachers are understanding. Ethan has a reputation with his peers of being funny, a little outspoken, and confident of his abilities, and his friends make sure that a couple of school bullies do not pick on him. Ethan thanks his parents for not overprotecting him, encouraging him to try things (like bike riding and distance running) that other parents of a child who is blind might have discouraged. Ethan will attend a summer camp designed specifically for students with vision loss; the camp helps students to improve their orientation and mobility skills, enabling them to move through their schools and communities with confidence and independence. He hopes to attend the same camp for the next two summers as well.

You probably have had the experience of being at home when the electricity goes off at night during a storm. You moved cautiously, occasionally bumping into furniture as you tried to find a candle and matches or a flashlight. Your usually familiar home was turned temporarily into something of an obstacle course. You also probably have experienced the disorienting effect of driving a car in dense fog or a bad storm when you could see only a small portion of the otherwise familiar road and scenery at any given time. Even though traffic was moving slowly, objects appeared to move very quickly into and out of view.

Experiences such as these may provide an analogy for what blindness or visual impairment can be like, but they are not entirely accurate. These experiences are temporary, unlike most visual impairments, which last throughout a person's life. Also, blindness is not about seeing blackness, as the examples convey; it is about seeing nothingness, as though you shut your eyes and try to see the back of your head. In addition, you have had the benefit of a wealth of visual experiences that help you understand your environment and that assist you during times when your vision is temporarily restricted or unavailable. Finally, and perhaps most importantly, you have not learned skills to compensate for a lack of vision or reduced vision.

Students with visual impairments compose a very diverse group, as you can understand from the stories about Jayden, Anna Marie, and Ethan. Their vision loss may vary from mild to severe, but in addition, they may or may not have additional disabilities that affect learning. As you learn about these students and their needs, keep in mind that their uniqueness makes generalizing about them difficult. As you meet students with visual impairments during your career, the input of specialists in this area will be invaluable in helping you understand and teach these students.

Understanding Visual Impairments

Some background information can help you to begin to understand the unique field of educating students with visual impairments. A brief look at its history demonstrates how thinking has changed regarding these students, while current approaches to defining visual impairment and estimating its prevalence provide a snapshot of the current status of the field. In addition, by learning about the structure and function of the eye, you can better understand some of the most common causes of visual impairment in school-age children.

FIGURE 12.1   Time Line of the Development of the Field of Visual Impairments

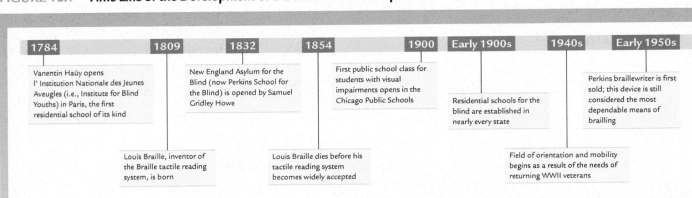

1784 Vanentin Haüy opens l' Institution Nationale des Jeunes Aveugles (i.e., Institute for Blind Youths) in Paris, the first residential school of its kind

1809 Louis Braille, inventor of the Braille tactile reading system, is born

1832 New England Asylum for the Blind (now Perkins School for the Blind) is opened by Samuel Gridley Howe

1854 Louis Braille dies before his tactile reading system becomes widely accepted

1900 First public school class for students with visual impairments opens in the Chicago Public Schools

Early 1900s Residential schools for the blind are established in nearly every state

1940s Field of orientation and mobility begins as a result of the needs of returning WWII veterans

Early 1950s Perkins braillewriter is first sold; this device is still considered the most dependable means of brailling

Development of the Visual Impairment Field

For centuries, professionals have recognized that individuals with visual impairments need specialized schooling. However, the way that instruction is provided has evolved significantly.

Early Thinking and Services

As shown on the time line in Figure 12.1, the history of visual impairments began in France. There, Louis Braille, born in 1809 and blinded at the age of 3 by an accident in his father's workshop, developed the dot-based system of reading and writing known today simply by his last name, *braille*. It was not until after Braille's death in 1854 that his system became widely accepted.

Residential Schools in the United States

Services for children with visual impairments began to develop in the United States during this same time period. In 1832, the New England Asylum for the Blind (now Perkins School for the Blind) was opened, led by noted philanthropist Samuel Gridley Howe (Hall, 2012). Howe believed that educational programs should follow three principles: (a) pay attention to each student's individual needs; (b) provide a curriculum similar to that for sighted students; and (c) expect students to integrate into their communities. Even though Howe was a pioneer in the residential school movement in the United States, he also was one of its earliest critics, publicly opposing the segregation of these students and advocating for public day school education for them (Roberts, 1986).

The Emergence of Public School Programs

In 1900, the first part-time class for students with visual impairments was established on an experimental basis in the Chicago Public Schools. Students spent most of the day in general education classes and received instruction in braille and typing from a special teacher. These new classes were designed specifically for students with low vision who were not blind; the intent was to rely on oral instruction as a means of preserving their residual sight, an approach referred to as *sight saving*.

The next significant change came in the 1950s when a dramatic increase occurred in the number of babies who were visually impaired because of a condition called *retrolental fibroplasia* (RLF). This condition developed when premature babies were placed in newly available incubators and given uncontrolled amounts of oxygen to assist their breathing. The high oxygen levels caused

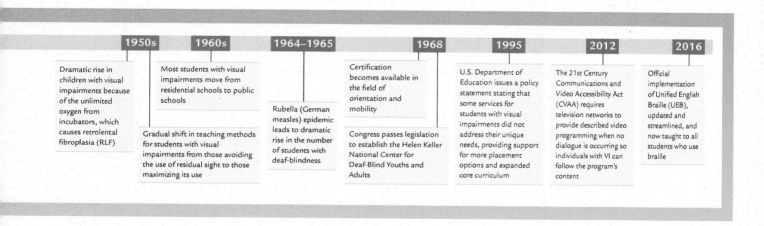

1950s
Dramatic rise in children with visual impairments because of the unlimited oxygen from incubators, which causes retrolental fibroplasia (RLF)

1960s
Most students with visual impairments move from residential schools to public schools

Gradual shift in teaching methods for students with visual impairments from those avoiding the use of residual sight to those maximizing its use

1964–1965
Rubella (German measles) epidemic leads to dramatic rise in the number of students with deaf-blindness

1968
Certification becomes available in the field of orientation and mobility

Congress passes legislation to establish the Helen Keller National Center for Deaf-Blind Youths and Adults

1995
U.S. Department of Education issues a policy statement stating that some services for students with visual impairments did not address their unique needs, providing support for more placement options and expanded core curriculum

2012
The 21st Century Communications and Video Accessibility Act (CVAA) requires television networks to provide described video programming when no dialogue is occurring so individuals with VI can follow the program's content

2016
Official implementation of Unified English Braille (UEB), updated and streamlined, and now taught to all students who use braille

underdeveloped blood vessels to grow into the retinas of the eyes, often leading to severe visual impairment. This disease, now called retinopathy of prematurity (ROP), still causes significant visual impairments that require medical treatment in many premature infants. Of these, 400 to 600 each year become legally blind from ROP (National Eye Institute, 2014).

The sheer number of students with visual impairments at that time gave parents the impetus and support they needed to advocate for establishing programs for these students in their local schools, and this created a revolution in their education. By the mid-1960s, schooling for students with visual impairments had largely moved from residential to local schools (Hatlen, 2000), a trend that continues today (U.S. Department of Education, 2015).

Other Historical Developments

Two other major historical developments shaped the provision of educational services to students with visual impairments in the latter half of the 20th century. The first development was a radical shift in the methods used to teach students who were partially sighted. In contrast to the earlier practice of sight saving for these students, research indicated that using residual vision could actually improve visual efficiency (Ashcroft, Halliday, & Barraga, 1965; Barraga, 1964; Holmes, 1967), and so sight-saving classes were disbanded in favor of programs that emphasized using available vision.

The second development was a sudden increase in the number of students with visual impairments who had additional disabilities—the result of a rubella epidemic in 1964 and 1965 that left 30,000 infants born with deaf–blindness and other health conditions (Hatlen, 2000). Advancements in medical interventions for premature infants has increased their survival rate dramatically, but these infants often have multiple disabilities, including visual impairments (Gulati et al., 2014; O'Connor, Wilson, & Fielder, 2007). Today, it is estimated that half or more of students with visual impairments have additional disabilities (e.g., Alimovic, 2013; Dammeyer, 2013).

Definitions of Visual Impairment

A variety of terms are used to describe visual impairment. Functional definitions are most often used in schools because they describe the impact of the vision loss on the student. Clinical definitions describe the clarity of a person's vision, and these definitions generally relate to legal matters and entitlement to special services beyond public schooling.

Functional Definitions

The term visual impairment is perhaps the most commonly accepted term to describe any level of decreased vision (American Foundation for the Blind, 2016b), from a mild loss that has little impact on daily life to total loss. However, the term *visual impairment* is global, and two subcategories generally are recognized within it: low vision and blindness:

1. People with low vision (also called moderate to severe visual impairment) have some vision, but they have difficulty accomplishing typical visual tasks. Using compensatory strategies, technology, and environmental modifications, these individuals can enhance their ability to accomplish these tasks. Students with low vision may need to use large print for reading, strong magnifying devices, and other adaptations. Some students in this group also

MyEdLab
Video Example 12.1

Before you begin reading about the definition of visual impairment and the characteristics of students, this video of a young man with deteriorating vision will provide a context for thinking about the information in this section.
(https://www.youtube.com/watch?v=PPGTfUr6O8o)

may learn to read braille and use tactile and auditory approaches to complete tasks. For example, they might learn to listen to books on tape to supplement print or braille reading.

2. Blindness (also called profound visual impairment) refers to having no vision or only light perception, or the ability to determine the presence or absence of light. Students who are blind complete most or all tasks primarily using touch and hearing. They learn to read and write in braille and use many day-to-day adaptive techniques (e.g., folding money in ways to denote various denominations). The terms functionally blind and educationally blind are used sometimes in schools to further describe these students.

Two other general terms are used to describe visual impairment: *congenital and adventitious.* Congenital visual impairment refers to a condition that is present at or near the time of birth, while an adventitious visual impairment is a condition that is acquired after birth, either in childhood or at some later point in life (Huebner, 2000). As you might expect, the age when a visual impairment occurs often has implications for education. Students with congenital visual impairments need access to alternative instructional approaches from the earliest age. For example, they develop an understanding of their environment by smelling, touching, and moving. Students with adventitious visual impairments may use their prior visual experiences for continued learning and for understanding alternative approaches to tasks. For example, these students may know the layout of the school grounds from when they could see it, and this helps to facilitate learning to move around those grounds with a long cane.

IDEA Definition

The Individuals with Disabilities Education Act (IDEA) uses a functional definition of *visual impairment*:

> Visual impairment including blindness means an impairment in vision that, even with correction, adversely affects a child's educational performance. The term includes both partial sight and blindness. (IDEA 20 U.S.C. §1401 [2004], 20 C.F.R. §300.8[c][13])

This definition stresses the point already introduced: Students' visual impairments cover an entire range, from mild to blindness. It also includes the provision that is common to all IDEA definitions: a negative impact on educational performance.

One more point should be mentioned regarding terminology. Although the federal government generally has chosen to use the term *disabilities* throughout IDEA and the Americans with Disabilities Act (ADA), the term *visual disabilities* rarely is used among professionals who work in educational settings with students with visual impairments. Professionals in the field generally use the term *visually impaired*, and so that term is used in this chapter.

Clinical Definitions

Clinical definitions of blindness rarely are used for determining eligibility for special education (although such clinical information is gathered as part of the assessment process), but they are used to qualify persons for Social Security benefits, federal tax exemptions, and other services. These definitions are based on clinical measures of visual acuity, the clarity or sharpness of vision, and visual field, the range in which objects can be seen centrally or peripherally.

Legal blindness refers to the condition in which central visual acuity is 20/200 or less in the better eye with corrective glasses or central visual acuity is more than 20/200 if a visual field defect exists so that it is 20 degrees or less in each eye (Koestler, 1976). Think back to your most recent eye exam. On a standard eye chart, the large letter at the top is used to determine if a person has 20/200 vision. If a person cannot identify that letter, then he is considered legally blind. A central field of 20 degrees can be simulated (roughly) by getting a large piece of poster board, cutting a hole in the middle about the size of a typical dinner plate, and then holding the poster board at arm's length. If a person sees only what is in the center hole of the poster board or less, regardless of visual acuity, the person also would be considered legally blind based on visual field restrictions. Remember, though, that a person who cannot read the top letter of an eye chart or who has a restricted visual field still may use vision for reading and other daily tasks, and so the legal definition of *blindness* is not especially helpful in determining educational needs. From the discussion of functional definitions, students who were legally blind might have moderate, severe, or profound visual impairments.

Low vision typically is defined as visual acuity of 20/70 to 20/200 in the better eye with correction or a visual field of 20 to 40 degrees or less in the better eye with correction (American Foundation for the Blind, 2016b). Some states use a visual acuity of 20/70 (or sometimes 20/60 or better) to provide a minimal level of acuity restriction for the purposes of qualifying for special services. Students who have a visual acuity between 20/70 and 20/200 typically would be considered to have mild or moderate functional visual impairments.

Prevalence

Visual impairment is considered a low-incidence disability because it occurs infrequently in the general population and in less than 0.5% of all children with disabilities (U.S. Department of Education, 2015). This means that compared to other categories of disabling conditions, the number of students with visual impairments is relatively low.

A precise prevalence figure for students with visual impairments in the United States is difficult to confirm because no single complete registry of students with visual impairments exists. For example, according to the U.S. Department of Education (2015), a total of 25,567 students with visual impairments and 1,243 students with deaf–blindness between the ages of 6 and 21 years received special education services during the 2012–2013 school year. However, these figures dramatically underestimate the total number of students with visual impairments because students who are visually impaired and have other disabilities often are reported in another category. This occurs because of the IDEA definition of *visual impairment* and its requirement of an unduplicated count—that is, any one student can be counted in only one disability category (Hatlen & Spungin, 2008).

Other Prevalence Information

Approximately 14 million individuals age 12 or older in the United States have some type of vision impairment; of those, approximately 11 million do or could function effectively with corrective lenses (Vitale, Cotch, & Sperduto, 2006). The American Printing House for the Blind (APH) (2016) reports that there are 60,393 legally blind children between the ages of 0 and 21. However, these figures also underestimate the number of students who receive special education services because only legally blind students can be registered with the APH, although it does include students who have additional disabilities.

Causes of Visual Impairment

Visual impairments result when problems exist in the structure or functioning of the eye, when the eye is damaged through illness or injury, or when a neurological problem prevents communication between the brain and the eye. The first step in understanding these causes of visual impairment is to briefly review the structure and functioning of the eye (Ward, 2000), which Figure 12.2 will help you understand.

FIGURE 12.2   Diagram of the Human Eye

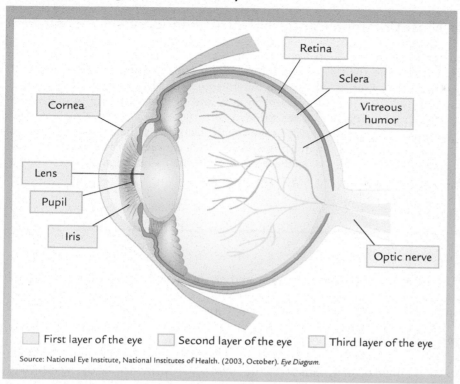

First layer of the eye   Second layer of the eye   Third layer of the eye

Source: National Eye Institute, National Institutes of Health. (2003, October). *Eye Diagram.*

Structure of the Eye and How It Works

The eyeball is an incredibly complex organ that is composed of three layers. The first layer is protective and includes the cornea, the transparent structure that both protects and has a major role in the process of bending the light rays entering the eye—a process called refraction. This layer also includes the white portion of the eye, called the sclera, which helps the eye maintain its shape.

The second layer of the eyeball is called the uveal tract. It includes the iris, the colored portion of the eye with a hole in the middle called the pupil. Behind the iris and pupil is the lens, the part of the eye that changes shape to focus light at the appropriate place at the back of the eye. The middle layer also includes the parts of the eye that nourish it and carry its blood flow.

The third and innermost layer of the eye is known as the retina. The retina is the light-sensitive membrane that covers the back wall of the eyeball. It connects the rest of the eye to the optic nerve, which allows the brain to process the visual information it receives. Various parts of the retina help people do close, detailed work; see colors; and see in low light and detect motion. And finally, the space between the lens and retina is filled with a transparent gel called **vitreous humor** that keeps the eyeball from collapsing.

Each eyeball lies in a pear-shaped, bony cavity known as the *eye socket*, and it is attached by six muscles. Two corresponding sets of muscles allow both eyes to move in a coordinated fashion, some contracting while others relax. Other structures outside the eyeball include the eyelids and tear ducts, which work together to protect the eyeball.

Now you can understand the very complex process of what happens when a person sees. Light rays enter the eye, traveling through the cornea where they are refracted. They continue traveling through the aqueous humor to the iris, which ensures that only the appropriate amount of light goes to the interior part of the eye. At this point, the lens bends the rays again to make finer adjustments. They

Five Most Common Causes of U.S. Childhood Visual Impairment

What causes visual impairments? As you can tell from the following list of the five most common causes in children, the answer typically relates to complex medical conditions (Vermont Association for the Blind and Visually Impaired, 2016):

- *Cortical visual impairment.* Damage in the brain in the area related to vision that causes individuals to have unusual and sometimes unpredictable visual responses to people, materials, and various environments
- *Retinopathy of prematurity.* A disease that occurs in premature babies in which damage is caused to the retina when abnormal blood vessels form there

- *Optic-nerve hypoplasia.* A condition in which the optic nerve, often in both eyes, fails to develop fully
- *Albinism.* An inherited condition that includes a lack of pigment in eyes and/or skin, resulting in underdeveloped retinas
- *Optic nerve atrophy.* Damage, sometimes progressive, to the optic nerve, which carries information from the eye to the brain, usually as the result of disease in one or both eyes.

---

land on the retina, where they come together, focused. They are then turned into electrical signals that travel along the optic nerve to the brain. The brain's interpretation of those electrical signals is what we know as sight.

Additional Examples of Visual Impairments

As well as the medical causes you just reviewed, a visual impairment can result from any number of problems with the anatomical structure of the eye or with the process of transmitting light rays to the brain and interpreting their meaning. Here are a few additional examples of conditions that can affect vision:

- *Strabismus.* The muscles of the eyes do not hold both eyes in proper alignment.
- *Amblyopia.* One eye does not develop vision or loses vision because of non-use, possibly caused by strabismus.
- *Cataract.* The lens is cloudy and cannot transmit light rays properly to the retina.
- *Glaucoma.* Damage to the optic nerve is caused when the aqueous humor does not flow properly.

Did You Know?

On the website of the National Eye Institute, which is part of the National Institutes of Health (NIH), you can explore simulations of various eye disorders and find detailed information about many aspects of vision and vision loss (https://nei.nih.gov/health/examples/#3).

These conditions represent only a small portion of the hundreds of causes of visual impairments. If you are responsible for teaching a student with a visual impairment, you will undoubtedly learn more about his specific visual condition and needs.

MyEdLab **Self-Check 12.1**

MyEdLab **Application Exercise 12.1:** What Does "Visual Impairment" Mean?

MyEdLab **Application Exercise 12.2:** Causes of Visual Impairments

---

Characteristics of Individuals with Visual Impairments

Think about how vision allows even the youngest children to move around freely in the environment, to find toys and friends with whom to play, and to observe and imitate their parents in routine activities. Children with visual impairments miss such incidental learning, which may have a significant impact on their development, learning, social skills, and behavior.

Cognitive Characteristics

Visual impairment directly influences development and learning in a variety of significant ways. Lowenfeld (1973) described the impact of blindness or low vision on cognitive development by identifying basic limitations on the child in the following three areas:

1. *Range and variety of experiences.* When a child has a visual impairment, experiences must be gained by using the remaining senses, especially touch and hearing. However, these senses do not compensate entirely for the quick and holistic information provided by vision (e.g., size, color, and spatial relationships). Unlike vision, exploring objects by touch is a part-to-whole process, and the person must be in contact with the object being explored. Some objects are too far away (e.g., stars, horizon), too large (e.g., mountains, skyscrapers), too fragile (e.g., snowflakes, small insects), or unsafe (e.g., fire, moving vehicles) to be examined tactilely.

2. *Ability to move around (i.e., mobility).* Vision allows for early and free movement within the environment, but blindness or severe visual impairment restricts such movement (Houwen, Visscher, Lemmick, & Hartman, 2009; Lieberman, Haegele, Columna, & Conroy, 2014). This restriction limits the person's opportunities for experiences and also affects social relationships. Children with visual impairments, unlike other children, must learn to travel safely and efficiently in the environment using a variety of orientation and mobility skills (i.e., competencies for traveling safely and efficiently through one's environment) and tools, such as the long cane (McAllister & Gray, 2007; Sapp, 2011).

3. *Interaction with the environment.* Because vision allows for quick gathering of information at a distance, people with typical vision have immediate and direct control of the environment. For example, if you walk into a crowded party, you can quickly scan the room, find someone or someplace to go to, and then move freely to that location. People who are blind or severely visually impaired do not have this same control of the environment. Even with effective mobility skills, they still have some level of detachment from the environment.

When the absence of experiences such as those just described is combined with the lack of opportunity to observe and imitate other children and adults, the effect on all areas of development can be significant (Cho & Palmer, 2008). For example, children with typical vision play interactive games before 10 months of age, but those with visual impairments do so 2 months later (Ferrell, 2000; Pogrund & Fazzi, 2002). Think about how this information applies to Ethan, whom you met at the beginning of the chapter. Analyze how his experiences have facilitated his academic and social development.

As a group, students with visual impairments exhibit a wide range of cognitive and intellectual abilities. Some students with visual impairments fall into the gifted range, and many students have average intellectual abilities. Others experience some level of intellectual disability, particularly if they have more than one identified disability. That is, among students with multiple and severe disabilities (the focus of Chapter 14), the incidence of visual impairment is quite high.

Many students with visual impairments also have other disabilities.

Academic Characteristics

The impact that visual impairments have on cognitive development likewise affects the development of academic skills (McLinden & Douglas, 2014), particularly in the areas of reading and writing (Bosman, Gompel, Vervloed, & van Bon, 2006; Savaiano & Hatton, 2013). For example, when you read or write, you rely, without realizing it, on your ability to distinguish the fine details of letters and words—something most students with visual impairments cannot do because of problems with acuity. These students instead use a variety of alternative media and tools for reading and writing, depending on their individual needs. They may use braille or an alternative form of print (Barclay, Herlich, & Sacks, 2010). About half the students with visual impairments who do not have additional disabilities develop reading and other academic skills commensurate with their peers with typical vision (Eisenbraun et al., 2009; Swenson, 2008; Wei, Blackorby, & Schiller, 2011), although learning vocabulary may be a challenge (Swenson, 2011). For students with multiple disabilities, especially intellectual disabilities, academic instruction may emphasize functional skills rather than the traditional curriculum (e.g., Ali, MacFarland, & Umbreit, 2011; Durando, 2008).

Braille Literacy Skills

Students who are functionally blind typically learn to read and write braille, as do some students with low vision. *Alphabetic braille*, also called Grade 1 braille, is an efficient and practical means of written communication based on the 26 letters of the alphabet, as shown in Figure 12.3. Capital letters are designated

FIGURE 12.3   **Braille Alphabet and Example of Its Use with Contractions**

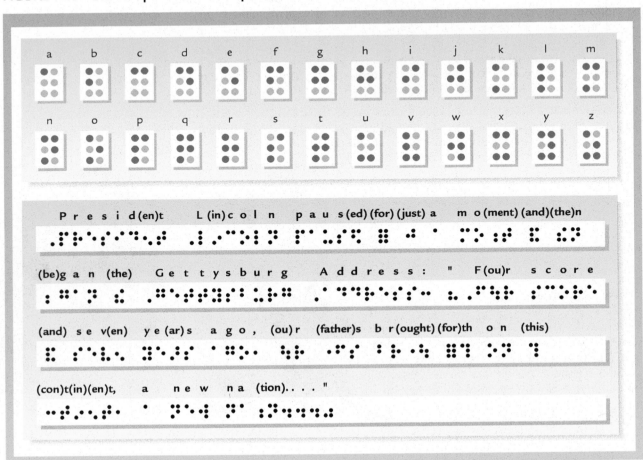

with a dot in the lower right-hand position preceding the letter to be capitalized. Another sign (the upper and lower dots on the right-hand side of the cell) designates italicized words. Also, various configurations are assigned to punctuation marks.

In addition to the 26 letters of the alphabet and the various punctuation marks, *literary braille*, also called Grade 2 braille, includes many contractions and short forms for words. Like print English, though, needs have changed, and beginning in 2016 unified English braille (UEB) was implemented in the United States as the literary braille standard. UEB added some contractions and deleted others, added some symbols that were not available in the previous version (e.g., <, >), and streamlined how web addresses and some other contemporary communications are brailled (Braille Authority of North America, 2013).

In addition to Grade 1 braille and UEB, other forms of braille exist as well. For example, the Nemeth code, developed in 1972 by blind mathematician Dr. Jonathan Nemeth, contains symbols that enable braille users to write and read problems in advanced mathematics such as algebra, geometry, and calculus. Other braille codes are used to represent science, music, and computer symbols.

Students learn to read braille by moving the fingers of both hands smoothly across the lines of braille words from left to right. Students learn to write first with a *braillewriter*—a mechanical device with six keys corresponding to each dot in the braille cell—generally starting in preschool or kindergarten. The writer presses various combinations of these six keys simultaneously to write the various configurations in each cell. Other keys allow the writer to space, backspace, and change lines. Some students use mechanical braillewriters, but electronic braillewriters are becoming increasingly commonplace in schools.

To teach braille, visual impairment (VI) specialists (i.e., teachers specially trained to work with students with visual impairments, also called teachers of students with visual impairments or, TVIs) work with young children to ensure that they have a wide range of experiences and develop the unique perceptual and hand movement skills needed for braille reading. Then, typically in kindergarten, TVIs provide direct instruction in braille literacy skills, often using an approach and materials that parallel those used by general education teachers (Crawford & Elliott, 2007). Some of this instruction may occur in the general education classroom setting, and so it requires appropriately adapted reading materials and close collaboration between the VI specialist and the general education teacher. Braille reading rates tend to be approximately half print reading rates. Although current research on braille reading is sparse, a rate of about 60 words per minute is considered appropriate for students in sixth grade; 100 to 125 words per minute is considered typical for students in high school (Piscitello, 2007). In contrast, adolescents who read print average 140 to 150 words per minute.

Because of the braille–print typical reading rate difference, students with vision impairments need additional tools for gathering information (e.g., Ely et al., 2006). For example, they may listen to audio-recorded books using sources such as those illustrated in the Technology Notes. Alternatively, they may use a live reader or access options on a computer.

Students who are functionally blind acquire braille literacy skills in much the same way that other students acquire print literacy skills.

For many individuals who are visually impaired, alternatives to using braille include recorded books and other learning materials. Here are examples of organizations that provide these services.

Learning Ally

Started in 1948 by the New York Public Library's Women's Auxiliary for World War II veterans who had lost their sight and until recently called Recording for the Blind & Dyslexic (RFB&D), Learning Ally (2016) currently has more than 6,000 volunteers who have uploaded some 80,000 digital recordings of textbooks and literature titles. It serves more than 200,000 members (kindergarten through adult) worldwide.

Visit the Learning Ally website (http://www.learningally.org/) to learn more about this organization and the work it does.

National Library Services for the Blind and Physically Handicapped (NLS)

Established more than 80 years ago, this federally funded program, which is part of the Library of Congress, provides braille and recorded materials for individuals who are blind or who cannot read because of other physical limitations. It was established originally for adults, expanded to include children in 1952, and expanded yet again in 1966 for individuals with other physical disabilities. This program offers full-length books and magazines that are distributed to a cooperating network of regional and local libraries and circulated to eligible borrowers using postage-free mail. Many materials also are available on the Internet through Web-Braille. Since 1966, the program has also included music.

Any resident of the United States, as well as any U.S. citizen living abroad, can access NLS materials. Of the more than 400,000 items available (e.g., books, magazines, music scores), the most popular are best-selling books, other fiction, biographies, and how-to books. Some titles are available in Spanish. Approximately 70 periodicals are also offered. The brailling and recording of the materials is completed mostly by volunteers. You can learn more about the NLS at http://www.loc.gov/nls/.

Bookshare

Bookshare™ provides the world's largest online library of accessible reading materials for people with visual impairments and other print disabilities, with the total number of titles now at 434,205. Members have unlimited access to digitally recorded books, magazines, and newspapers that can be downloaded and accessed through readily available text-to-speech software on computers, e-readers, and smartphones. Through a grant award from the U.S. Department of Education, materials from Bookshare can be obtained free of charge for eligible students in public schools. Learn more details at http://www.bookshare.org/.

Print Literacy Skills

Many students with low vision can use compensatory strategies and tools so that print is their primary literacy medium. Some students will use large-print materials (Douglas, McLinden, McCall, Pavey, Ware, & Farrell, 2011), but then they can read only when such materials are available in print or on the computer. Instead, most students are taught to use optical low-vision devices. For example, a magnifier, either handheld or spectacle mounted, makes reading print possible for some students. This option provides maximum flexibility because a magnifier is portable and can be used in almost any situation. Some magnifiers even have built-in light sources.

Electronic devices also can enlarge materials. The most common is a video magnifier. This device has a video camera that projects an enlarged image of the reading material to a screen (either near the student or at a distance). The user moves the material back and forth below the camera to follow the lines of text, thereby creating a moving image on the screen. The user can control the size of the letters on the screen and can select either black letters on a white background or vice versa, depending on which format can be seen more easily.

An alternative to devices like a video magnifier is the app called KNFB reader (KNFB, 2016). The user downloads the app to an iOS or Android device and then holds the device over print material. The device, which becomes the equivalent of a talking digital camera, snaps a picture of it; then within a few seconds, the print is read aloud in synthetic speech. This technology provides access to print even to students who are blind. Think of how such a reading option could assist a student like Anna Marie, whom you met at the beginning of this chapter.

Students with low vision share with students who are blind the need for acquiring additional tools to facilitate schoolwork and written communication. They may learn keyboarding skills, skills to use speech output devices and screen enlargement programs on the computer, and other access technologies—that is, high- and

TECHNOLOGY NOTES

Access Through Computers for Students with Visual Impairments

A variety of tools provide students with visual impairments access to the wealth of digital information available on computers, DVDs, e-readers, tablet devices, and the Internet. In fact, you may find that many students' needs can be met using the accessibility extensions available with Google classroom and other products. The key is to match the student's sensory capabilities with specific access tools, whether focusing on auditory, visual, or tactile options or a combination of these.

Auditory Tools

- *Synthetic speech.* Using a combination of screen-reading software and a speech synthesizer, a student who is visually impaired can access what is presented on the computer screen. The screen reader converts the characters or words into spoken language, whereas the synthesizer produces the sound. The user can control the speed of the speech as well as navigate the screen. An example of a commonly used and sophisticated screen reader is JAWS (Job Access with Speech) from Freedom Scientific.

- *Optical character recognition (OCR) with speech and scanner.* OCR devices convert printed text into electronic files and serve as reading machines for users who are visually impaired. These devices use scanners to input text and OCR software to convert the text into electronic formats that the user can then access in a variety of formats, such as braille and synthetic speech. An example of this software is OpenBook from Freedom Scientific.

Visual Tools

- *Screen-enlargement software.* Screen-enlargement software increases the sizes of images on computer screens. This option generally is available on all of today's computers and may not require special software.

Tactile Tools

- *Braille translation software.* This software converts print into braille (forward translation) and braille into print (backward translation), enabling students to output braille translations of text from the computer and print versions of their written braille work.

- *Braille printer.* An electronic braille printer (also called an *embosser*) connects to a computer and embosses braille on paper to provide hard copy. It functions like a standard printer.

- *Refreshable braille displays.* This output device is connected to a computer, often in front of or under the keyboard, and the characters on it can be felt in braille. The braille display consists of pins arranged in the shape of braille cells that raise and lower to form braille characters. Software converts the characters from the computer into the braille on the refreshable display.

- *Electronic braillewriter.* This device produces braille but also has special features, such as synthetic speech, braille and print translation, automatic erase and correction, and a memory for storing files. It can also interface with a computer, printer, and other devices. One example often used in schools is the BrailleNote Apex by Humanware.

- *Tactile graphics maker.* This device enables the automatic production of tactile graphics material using heat-sensitive paper.

low-tech options to help access computers and other sources of information. The Technology Notes provides additional information on the range of technological options to assist students with low vision as well as those who are blind. Finally, some students with low vision learn to read and write braille as a supplement to or replacement for print, an approach referred to as using *dual media*.

Social and Emotional Characteristics

Think for a few moments of the social skills that you use on a daily basis. Did someone teach you how to look at the people to whom you are speaking, how to wave good-bye when you depart, how to take turns when having a conversation, and how to use facial expressions to communicate nonverbally? In each of these situations, the answer is probably no. We typically develop social behaviors by observing social events and customs and imitating them (Zebehazy & Smith, 2011). Refinement occurs through repeated use of social behaviors and, if needed, indirect feedback from socially competent persons. Because a visual impairment restricts incidental learning through observation and imitation, students with visual impairments often have difficulties demonstrating socially appropriate behaviors (Correa-Torres, 2008; Ozkubat & Ozdemir, 2014).

The dilemma of developing social interaction skills extends to other types of interactions. Think, for example, about your own use of social media and other electronic avenues for social interactions (e.g., phone) and the role it plays in your day-to-day interactions with others. Think, too, about how you became proficient in using your devices by experimenting with buttons and menus and having friends show you tricks and techniques. Although youth with visual impairments are very frequent users of social media sites, they tend to be followers; that is, they usually access such sites to keep in touch with friends but not to grow their circle of contacts (Hewett, Douglas, Ramli, & Keil, 2012). Further, they are likely to need much more direct instruction than other students to effectively use this technology (Runyan, 2013).

Given the impact of a visual impairment on the development of social skills, students with visual impairments—like Jayden, whom you met at the beginning of this chapter—must receive direct and systematic instruction in areas such as these (Ophir-Cohen, Ashkenazy, Cohen, & Tirosh, 2005; Sacks & Silberman, 2000):

- Developing friendships
- Promoting risk taking and decision making
- Maintaining eye contact and facial orientation
- Demonstrating confident body postures
- Using appropriate gestures and facial expressions
- Using appropriate voice tone and inflection
- Expressing feelings
- Timing messages during communication
- Demonstrating appropriate assertiveness

Regardless of your planned professional role, the importance of teaching social skills to students with visual impairments should be a priority. Without explicit instruction, many students with this disability will struggle throughout their lives to establish friendships; interact appropriately with family members, friends, and others; and succeed in the workplace.

Behavior Characteristics

Visual impairment alone, of course, does not cause a student to have significant behavior disorders, although it does generally have some subtle influences on behavior. For example, students with visual impairments may be socially immature, more isolated, and less assertive than other children (Zebehazy & Smith, 2011), characteristics already noted earlier in this chapter and that may continue through-out childhood and adolescence. Additionally, students with visual impairments sometimes are viewed as less capable of taking care of their daily needs, and so others tend to do things for them (Shapiro, Moffett, Lieberman, & Dummer, 2005). When this happens, students can become even more passive.

Some students with visual impairments demonstrate stereotypic behaviors, or repeated behaviors that serve no apparent constructive function. Examples include eye pressing, finger flicking, head or body rocking, and twirling (Desrochers, Oshlag, & Kennelly, 2014). A variety of theories exist as to why students with visual impairments sometimes develop stereotypic behaviors (Brambring & Asbrock, 2010). They may occur because of restricted activity and movement in the environ-ment, social deprivation, or the absence of sensory stimulation. Usually, profes-sionals try to reduce or eliminate these behaviors by helping the student increase activity or by using behavior change strategies such as those mentioned through-out this text (e.g., rewards and teaching alternative, more positive behaviors).

MyEdLab **Self-Check 12.2**

MyEdLab **Application Exercise 12.3:** Psychological and Behavioral Characteristics

---

Identifying Visual Impairment

The initial identification of a congenital visual impairment generally occurs by an eye care specialist early in a child's life. When an ophthalmologist, a physician specializing in the care of the eyes, or an optometrist, a profes-sional trained to identify eye problems and to prescribe corrective lenses, detects a visual impairment that cannot be corrected by regular eyeglasses, that professional generally advises the parents to contact their local school regarding special education services. Other young children may be initially identified through child-find activities sponsored by local, regional, or state educational agencies (Barton, 2011). For a student with an adventitious visual impairment, initial identification may occur when the student's classroom per-formance or visual behaviors change, through regular vision screenings offered by local school districts, or by an ophthalmologist or optometrist. Once an initial identification has been made, a determination must be made as to whether the eye condition adversely affects the student's learning. This process involves a comprehensive educational assessment, followed by a determination of eligibility.

Assessment

According to regulations in IDEA, students who may have a disability must be assessed in areas related to the suspected disability. A unique focus in assessing students with visual impairments is to determine the extent, if any, to which an eye condition affects learning. Because psychologists and other professionals who usually carry out assessment procedures typically are not experts in visual impairment, the assessment team should include the VI specialist. This individual often serves as the coordinator of the assessment team and plays a central role in interpreting the student's needs and planning the student's education (American Foundation for the Blind, 2016a). For example, the VI specialist can help other team members know what accommodations are needed so that the assessment is accurate. Some students might need braille materials, others large-type materials, and yet others extended testing time.

Depending on the individual student's characteristics and likely needs, these are some of the specialized assessments for students being considered for special education as visually impaired:

- A functional vision assessment that directly evaluates the student's efficiency in using her vision across a variety of settings and tasks (e.g., up close and at a distance).
- A learning media assessment that examines a student's overall approach to using sensory information for learning (e.g., visual, tactile, and auditory) and identifies the kinds of literacy media (e.g., braille, large type, or regular type with low-vision devices) that a student needs in school (Koenig & Holbrook, 1995; McKenzie, 2007).
- A clinical low-vision evaluation that involves deciding whether the student could benefit from optical devices, nonoptical devices, or other adaptations.

As with all other students, assessments are also completed to determine the student's strengths and challenges in other domains, including cognitive ability, academic achievement, and social and behavioral functioning (American Foundation for the Blind, 2016c).

You might be interested to know that some professionals are proposing that response to intervention, typically used primarily with students with learning or behavior problems, also could be used for students with visual impairment, both as part of the assessment process and as a strategy for monitoring student learning progress and identifying other disabilities, such as a learning disability. This topic is explored in the Data-Driven Decisions.

Eligibility

After completing the comprehensive educational assessment, the team shares the findings and determines whether a student has a visual impairment that adversely affects learning. At this point, the team examines the assessment results in light of the criteria established by its state to determine whether the student is eligible

DATA-DRIVEN DECISIONS

Response to Intervention for Students with Visual Impairments

Response to intervention generally has been applied to sighted students experiencing academic problems and who are suspected of having a learning disability. However, Kamei-Hannan, Holbrook, and Ricci (2012) argue that the same principles and practices should be applied for students with visual impairments. Examples of application include these:

- *Universal screening* is designed to ensure students are making adequate progress in acquiring reading skills. Because students with visual impairments often experience significant problems in reading by Grade 3, they should be part of this screening so that interventions can be started as soon as a problem is detected and data can be gathered regarding whether a learning disability potentially exists (e.g., Jones, Smith, Hensley-Maloney, & Gansle, 2015).
- *Multitiered interventions* provide increasingly intensive intervention for struggling students. For students with

visual impairments, tier 1 consists of high-quality instruction using print, braille, or both in general and special education settings. Tier 2 involves more intensive instruction carefully matched to assessed needs. Tier 3 is even more intensive, and it might include collaboration by a TVI, general education teacher, reading specialist, and others.

- *Progress monitoring* is critical, creating a direct bridge between a student's learning and planned instructional strategies. For students with visual impairments, such monitoring can help professionals tailor instruction to assessed needs and make adjustments frequently.
- *Research-based interventions* ensure that students are taught using strategies demonstrated to be effective. In the field of visual impairments, research on recommended strategies sometimes is lacking. This RTI dimension argues for increased attention to research for this field.

to receive special education services as a student with a visual impairment. In many states, functional characteristics alone are used to determine eligibility. In other states, both functional and clinical criteria must be satisfied. If you check the website of your state's department of education, you can find these criteria.

MyEdLab **Self-Check 12.3**

MyEdLab **Application Exercise 12.4:** Identifying Visual Impairments

MyEdLab **Application Exercise 12.5:** Assessment

How Learners with Visual Impairments Receive Their Education

Students with visual impairments are educated in a variety of educational settings, ranging from home environments to general classrooms to specialized schools. The complexity of individual student needs, coupled with the low incidence of visual impairments, presents challenges to administrators and educators in providing each student with an appropriate education.

Early Childhood

Young children with visual impairments usually receive educational services in two types of programs. For infants and toddlers (through age 2), the most common type of service delivery is similar to the type you have learned about for other young children: a home-based program. Home-based services focus on working with families to optimize their children's development (e.g., Smyth, Spicer, & Morgese, 2014). Early interventionists often model appropriate strategies for working with young children, answer parents' questions, and provide resources. Such programs are offered by a variety of agencies—local school districts, special regional state education agencies, and private agencies—depending on the state or local organizational structure.

Many—but not all—students with visual impairments receive their education in a typical classroom; the IEP team makes this decision based on students' unique needs.

For preschool students with visual impairments (those ages 3 to 5), a center-based preschool is a common service delivery option. The focus of center-based programs is on direct and consistent teaching of specific developmental skills (e.g., fine-motor, gross-motor, and language) (Brambring, 2007; Celeste, 2007; Clark & McDonnell, 2008). Again, these programs may be offered through public school districts, private agencies, and other organizations, and they may be special programs for students with visual impairments, general programs for young children with special needs, or, increasingly, inclusive settings that provide early education to students with disabilities and nondisabled peers (Watson & McCathren, 2009).

Elementary and Secondary School Services

Students with visual impairments generally receive elementary and secondary school services in one or a combination of the following options: consultant model, itinerant services, resource model, or specialized school settings. A summary of their participation across educational environments is presented in Figure 12.4.

FIGURE 12.4   Educational Placements for Students Ages 6 to 21 Who Have Visual Impairments (in percentages)

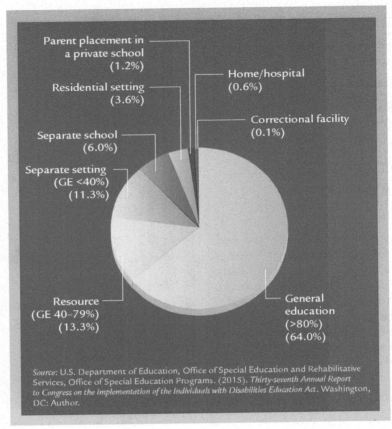

Parent placement in a private school (1.2%)

Home/hospital (0.6%)

Residential setting (3.6%)

Correctional facility (0.1%)

Separate school (6.0%)

Separate setting (GE <40%) (11.3%)

Resource (GE 40–79%) (13.3%)

General education (>80%) (64.0%)

Source: U.S. Department of Education, Office of Special Education and Rehabilitative Services, Office of Special Education Programs. (2015). *Thirty-seventh Annual Report to Congress on the implementation of the Individuals with Disabilities Education Act*. Washington, DC: Author.

Consultant Model

The consultant model is most appropriate for students who require few or no direct services related to their visual impairments. These students are involved in all activities of the general classroom, and the general education teacher provides primary direct instruction. The VI specialist collaborates closely with the general education teacher to plan appropriate adaptations and modifications of learning activities (e.g., describing pictures, pairing a student with a partner for a science experiment) and to provide adapted learning materials (e.g., large type, tactile maps) (Roe, Rogers, Donaldson, Gordon, & Meager, 2014). This approach also may be used to address the vision needs of students with additional disabilities, such as learning disabilities and intellectual disabilities.

Itinerant Teaching Model

The itinerant teaching model is perhaps the most widely used option for delivering specialized services to students with visual impairments. In this model, students attend their local schools, and general education teachers provide most of the instruction. A TVI travels from school to school to provide specialized instructional programs. The skills taught by an itinerant teacher specifically target areas of the curriculum that are unique to students with visual impairments, such as braille reading and writing skills, technology skills, independent living skills, and career education skills (Correa-Torres & Johnson, 2004). Also, the TVI provides specialized assessments, consults with classroom teachers and others on the educational team, and provides adapted classroom materials. The critical distinction between the itinerant model and the consultant model is that the TVI is providing consistent, direct instruction as an itinerant teacher; this does not occur under the consultation model. In reality, VI specialists often serve as both consultants and itinerant teachers.

The itinerant teaching model works well for students who have mild to moderate needs for instruction in specialized skills and generally are independent in the classroom. In addition to the services provided by itinerant TVIs, orientation and mobility specialists also work on an itinerant basis teaching students to travel safely in the school and community.

Resource Model

The resource model is ideal for students with visual impairments who have more extensive needs than can be met with the itinerant teaching model. In the resource model, a classroom is designated in the school district to serve elementary or secondary students. It is equipped with special materials, resources, and technology, and it is staffed full time by a TVI. Students participate in general classroom instruction to the extent determined appropriate by the educational team, with support available throughout the day from the TVI. In addition, students needing more intensive support go to the resource room for that specialized instruction. This is the approach the team decided was best for Jayden, introduced at the beginning of the chapter.

Although students in this type of program may not attend their neighborhood schools, the resource model provides options for students who have instructional needs that can be met only through consistent, often daily, service delivered by a highly trained VI specialist. For example, students who are beginning to learn braille reading and writing skills need to receive an hour or more of instruction per day simply to address their literacy needs (Koenig & Holbrook, 2000). A similar intensity level likewise is necessary for older students who have acquired visual impairments and must learn an alternative to print reading.

Special Classes and Schools

Some students with visual impairments need more than a resource program. They may be educated in full-time special classes offered in local school districts, special day schools, or private schools and specialized schools with residential options (often referred to as *residential schools for the blind*). Day classes or day schools are available primarily in large cities. Most states have a residential school for students with visual impairments.

Students in specialized schools have intensive needs that cannot be addressed appropriately through other program options. These students receive all of their instruction from teachers who are specifically prepared to teach students with visual impairments. Specialized instruction is offered throughout the day and, in the case of students in residential schools, during the mornings and evenings as well. Although the environment of the specialized school is typical of most schools, its setting and resources are specifically geared to the needs of students with visual impairments, including accessible computers and other forms of assistive technology, library and media resources, tactile teaching aids and devices, and adapted physical education equipment.

One concern often leveled at specialized schools is that they provide an isolated, segregated environment. This is rarely true today. Most specialized schools offer a range of options for providing inclusion in the city, town, or neighborhood through community-based instruction as well as local events, clubs, and other activities. Also, many specialized schools may offer options for students to attend some classes in the local school district with the assistance of an itinerant teacher who is on the special school faculty.

Did You Know?

Have you wondered whether students with visual impairments are likely to have guide dogs? Probably not. Because of the level of maturity, discipline, and commitment needed, only older adolescents and adults usually have these service animals. However, some children may be paired with specially trained dogs who are pets, thus preparing them for later use of a guide dog.

Many specialized schools are developing new options for addressing the needs of students with visual impairments. Most adhere to a so-called revolving door approach, encouraging placements for students of one or a few years at a residential school to gain needed compensatory and disability-specific skills while recommending attendance at a local school during the rest of their academic careers (Pogrund, Darst, S., & Boland, 2013). Also, many schools are offering targeted summer school programs or intensive, short-term instruction during the school year for students enrolled in local school programs. This is the type of program that Ethan, whom you met at the beginning of the chapter, plans to attend. For example, students might attend an intensive, short-term session for two weeks at a specialized school to learn technology skills that will allow more efficient access to information when they return to their local schools.

Inclusive Practices

Most students with visual impairments are educated in neighborhood schools with peers without disabilities (U.S. Department of Education, 2015). However, two factors must be considered. First, a general education setting is appropriate for many, but not all, students with visual impairments, and, as for all students with disabilities, its appropriateness must be determined by a team and on an individual basis. Second, specific and planned interventions from a professionally prepared TVI and other specialists is of paramount importance (Sharma, Moore, & Furlonger, 2010). These specialists must carry out a range of activities to ensure that appropriate accommodations and modifications are made in the learning environment and instructional materials and that supplemental instruction is provided as needed (Bardin & Lewis, 2008; Sapp & Hatlen, 2010). If participation in a general classroom setting is deemed most appropriate, as is the case for Anna Marie, introduced at the beginning of the chapter, the TVI works collaboratively with the educational team to accomplish the following:

1. Ensure that all educational materials are provided in appropriate media (e.g., large print, regular print with use of optical devices, braille, recordings); new technologies are making it relatively easy for general educators to complete some of these tasks themselves, sometimes more quickly than they could be completed by the VI specialist.
2. Ensure that the student is instructed in the use of appropriate devices and technology and that these devices are available in the learning environment.
3. Provide specialized instruction related to compensating for the visual impairment.
4. Recommend seating requirements and other environmental modifications (e.g., lighting control, glare reduction, reading boards).
5. Ensure that teachers and other professionals who provide direct instruction understand the unique needs of students with visual impairments.
6. Recommend modifications, if appropriate, in assignments or testing procedures.
7. Collaborate with members of the educational team on methods and techniques for including students with visual impairments in routine learning experiences.
8. Provide opportunities for students without disabilities to better understand visual impairment (Spungin & Ferrell, 1999).

The Instruction in Action provides a summary of the common accommodations and modifications made by TVIs to enable students with visual impairments to benefit from instruction in general education settings.

In considering which setting is the most appropriate placement for a student, the educational team must consider the individual student's needs (American Foundation for the Blind, 2012a). Sometimes a short-term placement in a more specialized setting may offer a better match for a student's learning needs at a

INSTRUCTION IN **ACTION**

Accommodating Instruction for Students with Visual Impairments

Many relatively simple strategies, put in place based on need, can facilitate the educational success of students with visual impairments (American Foundation for the Blind, 2016a; Holbrook, 2015; Luckner Bruce, & Ferrell, 2015). Here are examples:

Environment (e.g., Dell, Newton, & Petroff, 2016)

- Preferential seating (bus, classroom, cafeteria, other areas) or opportunity to move during instruction so as to be close to materials
- Instruction for student on the presence of stairs or other possible safety concerns and other aspects of the physical school campus (e.g., distances to specific locations)
- Special lighting and attention to items such as reducing glare
- Room arrangement (definition of areas; location of supplies, materials, personal belongings)

Curriculum, Instructional Methods, Materials (e.g., Zebehazy & Wilton, 2014)

- Need for preteaching and reteaching; for example, allowing the student to handle the pertinent materials the day before a demonstration lesson is taught

- Use of highlighted visual material, copies of notes or presentation slides, and other visual aids
- Use of technology supports
- Use of braille materials, large print, and/or audio recordings
- Oral or pictorial directions
- Physical prompting of student through steps of an activity or permission for student to touch teacher hands or materials to facilitate understanding
- Oral or audio-recorded responses and assignments
- Brightly colored markers, crayons, and pencils

Social Interactions and Behavioral Supports (e.g., Pevsner, Sanspree, & Allison, 2012; Swenson, 2012)

- Use of small groups for instruction
- Use of peer assistance, instruction in self-advocacy
- Breaks during instruction if fatigue is occurring
- Reduced assignments if frustration or fatigue is a problem
- Flexibility in scheduling for direct vision services and related services support

---

given period in his school career. Then, after the student attains appropriate compensatory skills, placement in an inclusive setting may be a valuable and lifelong option. For other students, less intensive support is adequate.

Transition and Adulthood

Children with visual impairments have limited opportunities to learn about jobs and workers through observation and incidental experiences (e.g., Green, 2010). Therefore, the transition to adulthood for these students actually must begin in preschool with a systematic and organized career education program. This effort must continue throughout the school years with a coordinated transition-planning process beginning in high school (Reed & Curtis, 2011).

Students with visual impairments have a very high graduation rate (76.8%), higher than that for students in any other disability category (U.S. Department of Education, 2015). However, adults with visual impairments still experience a high level of unemployment (approximately 60%) (Erickson, Lee, von Schrader, 2015). These two disparate facts demonstrate that students' educational success does not ensure later success in employment, and so improving and strengthening career education programs and transition services clearly must be a priority. Further, the skills addressed through such programs change with increasing age and skill development levels. Wolffe (2000) has identified general career education competencies for students across grade levels. For example, in preschool,

Video Example
from
YouTube

MyEdLab
Video Example 12.2

One support for inclusive education that cannot be underestimated is technology. In this video, watch comedian Tommy Edison demonstrate one of his favorite apps, and think about how this easily available tool can foster students' independence and participation in a general education setting. (https://www.youtube.com/watch?v=NeB0B8rAc8)

students should learn to listen, follow directions, and play. In elementary school, they should acquire the skills to follow complex directions, organize their work, and assume responsibilities such as chores. In middle school, these students should increase the number and type of responsibilities they assume and learn about work options and their work preferences. Finally, in high school, students should demonstrate well-developed work behaviors, participate in work experiences, and plan for their life after high school. As with all students who have identified disabilities, the formal transition planning process for students with visual impairments should begin as early as age 16 with a formal *individualized transition plan* (ITP). For these students, additional members of the team who assist with developing the transition plan may include representatives from the state's commission or department of services for persons who are blind or the state's rehabilitation agency. That is, many states have rehabilitation services that are specialized for persons with visual impairments, and professionals from these agencies should participate in developing the transition plans for these students. After graduation from high school, some students may continue in a postsecondary program at a residential school for the blind to gain additional skills needed either for employment or to enter a vocational school or a community or four-year college. Other students may enter a vocational rehabilitation program, either one specifically designed for persons with visual impairments or one designed for all persons with disabilities. There they learn specific vocational skills or receive on-the-job training and support. The elements of a student's postsecondary program, if desired by the student, are specified in a document called the *individual plan for employment* (VisionAware, 2012). This document is not part of IDEA, but in many ways it is like a postschool transition plan. It delineates the postschool goals of vocational rehabilitation services, outlines the training and other supports that are to be offered, and specifies the time frame for these services.

The career options for persons with visual impairments are extensive. With appropriate accommodations on the part of the employer and preparation on the part of the individual, almost all jobs available for persons with typical vision are also available to those with visual impairments. The role of the educational team is to help the student explore her individual interests and abilities, provide adequate career education during the school years, ensure a coordinated and effective transition plan, and facilitate the transition to adult services and adult life. How might these ideas be applied as professionals help Ethan, whom you met at the beginning of the chapter, plan for his life after school?

MyEdLab **Self-Check 12.4**

MyEdLab **Application Exercise 12.6:** Accommodations in the Physical Environment

MyEdLab **Application Exercise 12.7:** Social Skills

MyEdLab **Application Exercise 12.8:** Educational Materials

Recommended Educational Practices for Students with Visual Impairments

Best practices for students with visual impairments center around what, how, and where disability-specific skill instruction is provided for them. As an overview, the areas in which students need specialized instruction constitute *what* is taught, and the principles of special methods offer a framework for *how* instruction is provided. Finally, determining an appropriate educational placement to address each student's identified needs addresses *where* instruction takes place.

Instruction in the Expanded Core Curriculum

Professionals recognize that students with vision impairments have two sets of curricular needs. First, they must access the existing core curriculum, as required of all students and including, for example, language arts, math, and science. Of course, for most students, this includes reaching the high standards mandated in current federal education legislation. Second, they must access the expanded core curriculum that uniquely addresses visual impairment—for example, compensatory skills, social interaction skills, and career education skills (Allman & Lewis, 2014). The elements of the expanded core curriculum and specific examples in each skill area are provided in Figure 12.5.

VI specialists, especially those who provide support and instruction to students in inclusive settings, may struggle over the dilemma of what to teach in the limited amount of time available. The pressing demands of the day may force the teacher to focus on tutoring or other activities related to maintaining progress in the general classroom. Despite this challenge, professionals have affirmed that direct teaching of the disability-specific skills of the expanded core curriculum is essential for success in school and adult life and therefore should be considered a cornerstone of best professional practices (Sapp & Hatlen, 2010).

FIGURE 12.5   **Areas of the Expanded Core Curriculum and Examples of Specific Skills**

Expanded core area	Explanation	Examples
Compensatory access skills	Foundational skills for access to all areas of the core curriculum in a manner equal to that of his or her sighted peers.	Concept development, communication modes (calendar systems, braille, print), organizational skills, needed accommodations
Social interaction skills	Needed sequential teaching and modeling because individuals with visual impairments cannot learn these skills incidentally.	Social concepts, physical skills, social integration, parallel and group play, eye contact, tone of voice
Recreational and leisure skills	Development of tools for lifelong enjoyment.	Hobbies, sports, games, orientation, physical fitness
Assistive technology and technology skills	Tools for access to enhanced communication and learning as well as the general learning environment.	Media literacy, technical concepts, selection of appropriate assistive devices, media needs, accessibility of information
Orientation and mobility skills	Fundamental skills in order to travel as independently as possible, enjoying and learning to the greatest extent possible from the environment through which they are passing.	Body image, travel, spatial awareness, safety, directionality
Independent living skills	All the tasks and functions that people perform, according to their abilities, to live as independently as possible.	Hygiene, food preparation or retrieval, money management, time monitoring, dressing
Career education	Explicit information about the world of work that others learn through incidental visual experiences.	Exploring interests, areas of strength, job awareness, planning, preparation, placement, work ethic
Sensory efficiency skills	Efficient and effective use of remaining functional vision and tactile and auditory senses.	Visual, auditory, and tactile learning: environmental cues and awareness, personal attributes, sensory attributes, use of low vision devices
Self-determination skills	Knowledge and skills for taking charge of one's life.	Sense of self, decision making, problem solving, goal setting, personal advocacy, self-control, and

Principles of Special Methods

How students with visual impairments are taught should reflect their unique learning needs (Lohmeier, 2009; Zabala & Carl, 2010). For example, general education teachers often rely heavily on demonstration and modeling to deliver instruction, which clearly is not particularly helpful for students with visual impairments. Some 40 years ago, Lowenfeld (1973) described three principles of special methods that help to overcome the limitations imposed by visual impairment. These principles—the need for concrete experiences, the need for unifying experiences, and the need for learning by doing—still guide the field today.

Need for Concrete Experiences

First, teachers should provide early and ongoing opportunities for students to learn about their environments through tactile exploration of real objects and situations as well as through other available senses (Trief, Bruce, & Cascella, 2010). For students with low vision, such experiences should be supplemented, but not replaced, by visual exploration. When actual objects are not available, models may be useful.

Need for Unifying Experiences

Because a visual impairment limits the ability to perceive the wholeness of objects and events, teachers should provide opportunities for students to integrate parts into wholes. Developing study units in which connections among academic subjects and real-life experiences can be enhanced (e.g., studying community workers in social studies by visiting those workers in their workplaces) is an important way to provide unifying experiences.

Need for Learning by Doing

Finally, teachers should provide opportunities for students with visual impairments to learn skills by actually doing and practicing those skills. For example, one can easily see the value of teaching a student to weigh items in a balance scale by handling the scale to understand its parts and function, placing items of equal weight and unequal weight on the scale, handling standardized weights used with the scale, and distinguishing weight by using such weights on one side of the scale with an object placed on the other side. However, one can quickly understand the absurdity of providing a verbal description of a balance scale without the experience to make it meaningful. Most of the areas of the expanded core curriculum lend themselves very readily to a learning-by-doing approach.

All students, regardless of whether they are visually impaired, would benefit from instruction based on these three principles of special methods, and using methods such as these is integral to the concept of universal design for learning (UDL) that has been mentioned throughout this text. However, for students with visual impairments, the use of a concrete, activity-oriented approach is a necessity and must be an integral part of teachers' plans for differentiation (Jones & Hensley-Maloney, 2015).

Video Example from YouTube

MyEdLab
Video Example 12.3

Video Example 12.3 illustrates the use of a concrete, activity-oriented approach for students with visual impairments.
(https://www.youtube.com/watch?v=dPC_--R-Ma0)

MyEdLab **Self-Check 12.5**

MyEdLab **Application Exercise 12.9:** Orientation and Mobility

MyEdLab **Application Exercise 12.10:** Instructional Methods

MyEdLab **Application Exercise 12.11:** Independent Living Skills

---

Perspectives of Parents and Families

Students with visual impairments and their families are as diverse as all children and parents. To understand their perspectives, you must take the time to listen

FIRSTHAND ACCOUNT

GROWING UP AND HAVING GOALS

BILLY, a 10th-grade student, has an inherited disorder called Norrie disease, which is carried by females; he has been blind since birth and has a moderate hearing loss. The disease runs in his family; his maternal grandparents are blind, as are two cousins. But to Billy, a lack of vision in no way limits his experiences or life ambitions. Billy, his mom Ms. Pickens, and his TVI Ms. Deere, a former nurse with four years of K–12 teaching experience, participated in this conversation:

Billy: I want to go to UNC Chapel Hill, and I want to study journalism. My best subject is English. I want to write books for both children and adults, fiction books and nonfiction books. I started writing my first book a couple of summers ago. Here is how it started:

One thing I've always had trouble with is in math—coordinate planes and stuff like that. So my dad was using states as an example. He was giving me maps and talking about the Great Plains, but I really wasn't understanding it. So he said it would be better if we would go out there. So first we went to the Grand Canyon. And then we went to lots of other places. We went to Ohio, and at the National Football League Hall of Fame my dad read everything to me. And now I've been to 49 states, and I'm going to Hawaii this summer. So now I'm writing this book, and it's called, *The World as I See It,* and it's about my adventures and my trips.

I've done lots of other things. I was a Boy Scout, and I used to go on campouts. In summer camp, I earned a Polar Bear patch. We had to go down to the lake and jump in at 6:30 in the morning! I also went on a ski trip—it was my first time ever skiing. They put the skis on me, and they led me down this slope, and after I got help the first couple of times, I was doing it all by myself. I didn't even fall! I was also selected to go to a leadership institute for two days, but I got a really terrible cold and I couldn't go.

Back to school, math is the most challenging subject—it really keeps me going, keeps me working.

Ms. Deere: I go to Algebra with Billy because when he brailles his work, I have to write above it so his teacher can get immediate feedback; it is a priority in there. I don't co-teach—I'm just there to interpret the braille because it's Nemeth code. Also, Billy uses an audio graphing calculator, and he's had to learn how to use it, so I help with that.

We also work on the calculator in the resource room, and we focus on compensatory skills and technology use. Billy also receives instruction for orientation and mobility and some occupational therapy services, all in the resource room. And for summers, I really push students going to camps where they learn many skills. Billy is going for a month this summer. It's not for academics; it will help him get ready for life after high school . . . and they have so much fun!

Billy: It's divided. One week I'm going to learn cooking, one week is job training, one week is learning how to be independent, and one week is for technology.

Ms. Pickens: When I think of the ups and downs of schools, I've seen both ends. One TVI was good with one-to-one in her classroom, but she didn't communicate with the teachers, and I had to step in because of the communication breakdown. And sometimes she would push Billy too hard; I want him to be independent, but for some things he needed more guidance. But I'll tell you that Ms. Deere, she communicates with the teachers and with me, and she's an advocate for Billy, and she has no problem saying to me, "Mama, back off!" Sometimes I have to catch myself when I'm answering questions for him; I turn around and say, "OK, Billy, you answer that question. You have a brain and you can think!" He's growing up.

Billy: I'm learning how to use a GPS system called Trekker. I take it to landmarks and record them, like to the mobile units behind the school. And then I say the room number I'm supposed to go to, and it gives me directions on how to get there. I can record other places, too, like the store I go to.

Teachers should never try to do stuff for a person. It will cripple them. They should make the person think for themselves. And they should never lump you into a category with all blind children, because everyone is individual—they learn differently.

Source: Courtesy of Debra Pickens and Deborah Deere.

to their words and, to the greatest extent possible, try to understand their dreams and concerns from their individual points of view (Rainey, Elsman, Nispen, Leeuwen, & Rens, 2016). Keep in mind, too, that the individual circumstances of each family, the characteristics of the child, the support received from family and friends, cultural beliefs and customs, and a multitude of other factors influence and continually shape their feelings and perspectives. The Firsthand Account provides one example of this diversity: Billy has an inherited disorder and has been blind since birth. He, his mother, and his TVI share information about his day-to-day life, his school experiences, and his plans for the future.

Parent Perspectives

Parents of children with visual impairments face many challenges, and educators should be sensitive to these and be prepared to provide guidance as appropriate and information to help them in decision making. These are some of the areas in which parents have reported that they have concerns (de Klerk & Greeff, 2011; Leyser & Heinze, 2001):

- *Concerns and situations that caused stress:* The future, providing for their child's needs, finances, adequate services, effects on siblings, social concerns, and limited information and assistance available to help parents
- *Impact of the child's disability on family and changes over time:* Becoming happier over time, changing attitudes toward persons with visual impairments, becoming more compassionate, stronger family relationships, increased worrying, and need to plan more for the future
- *Strategies and supports that assisted parents in coping with concerns:* Actively helping their child, reading information, discussions with professionals, enjoying recreation and leisure activities, and praying
- *Factors contributing to parents' resilience:* Religious faith and family closeness, pursuit of inclusiveness of the child, in part by accepting assistance, and the development of a sense of accomplishment for managing their family's life circumstances

Additionally, parents have commented on their experiences with schools and inclusive practices. The parents generally are supportive but express concern about their child's social isolation, limited opportunities for participation in extracurricular and community activities, and classroom teachers' lack of knowledge about visual impairments or unwillingness to make needed accommodations.

Viewed collectively, the perceptions of parents of students with visual impairments represent themes mentioned throughout this text: Parents want what they view as best for their children, and what is best depends on their children's characteristics and needs. And, ultimately, parents are willing to do whatever is necessary to ensure successful outcomes for their children.

MyEdLab **Self-Check 12.6**

MyEdLab **Application Exercise 12.12:** Kyle's Family

MyEdLab **Application Exercise 12.13:** Perspectives of Parents and Families of the Visually Impaired

---

Trends and Issues Affecting the Field of Visual Impairment

More than 200 years of program development, trial and error, research, and legislative mandates have transformed educational services for students with visual impairments from those that started exclusively in residential schools to those that now are based largely in neighborhood schools. The population of students has also changed from one in which visual impairment was a sole disability to one in which more than half of all students with visual impairments have additional disabilities. As the field continues to develop, professionals face a growing number of issues to address and trends to facilitate, including the personnel shortage and the limited range of placement options for students with visual impairments.

Shortage of Fully Prepared Personnel

Perhaps now more than at any time in history, the field of visual impairment is facing a particularly severe shortage of qualified personnel to deliver special education services to students (Gale, Trief, & Lengel, 2010; U.S. Department of Education, 2015), despite several nationwide projects and initiatives to address the problem (e.g., Mason, Davidson, & McNerney, 2000; Summers, Leigh, & Arnold, 2006). Studies have indicated that only about 40 programs are available nationwide to prepare vision specialists (National Association of Blind Teachers, 2012), and of these, some do not have even one full-time faculty member. Similarly, just 17 programs prepare orientation and mobility instructors, and only 10 programs prepare specialists to work with students who are deaf–blind (Smith & Kelly, 2007).

Personnel issues in the field of visual impairments are compounded by other factors (e.g., Correa-Torres & Durando, 2011; Zhou, Smith, Parker, & Griffin-Shirley, 2011). For example, because visual impairment is a low-incidence disability, university programs tend to enroll small numbers of teacher candidates. Economic pressures result when teacher education courses have low enrollments and do not produce very many credit hours; some programs are being forced to reduce or close preparation programs in this area, thus making the personnel shortage even worse. In addition, the number of professionals reported as needed is probably an underestimate because some school districts with students needing services know that they simply will not be able to find the appropriate specialists and so do not even list such positions as unfilled. Finally, anticipated retirements among professionals in the field may make the problem of finding qualified personnel even more severe.

Think about the implications of this information: If insufficient numbers of teachers are providing services to students with visual impairments, then existing teachers have much higher caseloads than the recommended 8:1 student–teacher ratio. In fact, in a survey of itinerant teachers in North America, an average caseload size of 22 students was found among respondents (Griffin-Shirley et al., 2003). Further, if some vacancies are left unfilled, students are left without adequate specialized support. At least some students with visual impairments are not receiving appropriate educations under IDEA, though the true magnitude of the impact is not fully known.

The field is taking direct steps in response to the personnel shortage. University programs have started offering distance-based personnel preparation programs using web-based instruction, interactive television, and other approaches. Some states have initiated approaches for entering the profession with other than a university-based education, although such options have not met with widespread approval among professionals in the field. Also, some states are developing innovative programs, collaborating even across states and regions to address this sobering personnel shortage.

Did You Know?

Although Kelly and Smith (2011) found 256 articles about assistive technology for individuals with visual impairments, only two of the studies provided evidence-based results. The authors concluded that a high need exists to demonstrate the effectiveness of assistive technology options, rather than relying on descriptions and anecdotes.

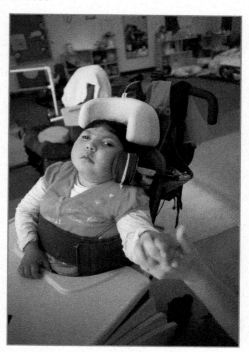

Innovative teacher preparation options, including distance education, are necessary because of the persistent shortage of teachers of students with visual impairments (TVIs).

Limited Continuum of Placement Options

A second significant issue facing the field is a limitation in the continuum of educational placement options for students with visual impairments that exists in most parts of the United States. Although best educational practices, federal law, and federal policy uphold the need for multiple options based on student needs, such placements tend to exist only in large cities and metropolitan areas. In many cases, services in suburban and rural areas are limited to consultant or itinerant teaching in local school programs or specialized schools, as you learned when you read about Anna Marie at the beginning of this chapter. These options do not benefit students who require support throughout the day, such as that provided by resource classes. In some communities, the only viable option is to seek placement in a residential specialized school.

Unfortunately, the field has made slow progress in exploring innovative options for providing a full array of services to students with visual impairments who live in rural areas and other geographic areas facing this challenge. In some cases, school districts have hired paraeducators to provide ongoing services when a TVI is not available (Lewis & McKenzie, 2010). However, as described earlier, these personnel often are not qualified to teach students and may even hamper students' progress toward independence (Harris, 2011). The shortage of teachers makes this problem worse. Now that agreement has been established and accepted on principles of best practice, professionals in the field of visual impairment are turning their attention to the critical issue of expanding the range of placement options for students with visual impairments.

MyEdLab **Self-Check 12.7**

MyEdLab **Application Exercise 12.14:** Trends and Issues Affecting the Field of Visual Impairment

Summary

LO12.1 The field of educating students with visual impairments has a long history that has progressed from the founding of residential schools in most of the United States to the current practice of educating most students in general education classrooms. Educational definitions of *visual impairment*, which affects approximately 5 out of every 100 students with disabilities, focus on eye conditions that have an adverse effect on progress in school and include students who are functionally blind and those with low vision.

LO12.2 Development, learning, behavior, and social and emotional domains are affected significantly by a visual impairment, and, as a result, students with this disability have educational needs that are unique.

LO12.3 Students with visual impairments generally are identified early in life by an eye care practitioner, but eligibility for special education services must be established through individualized assessments that determine the impact of the visual impairment on learning.

LO12.4 Educational placements for students with visual impairments are the same as those for other students with disabilities, although separate school and specialized residential options are more often considered than for most students with disabilities.

LO12.5 Best practices for students with visual impairments include the provision of instruction in the expanded core curriculum, use of disability-specific principles of special methods, and decisions on appropriate educational placements.

LO12.6 The views of students with visual impairments and their parents vary based on the nature of the visual impairment, the presence of additional disabilities, and the appropriateness of educational placements.

LO12.7 The field of educating students with visual impairments is facing a severe personnel shortage and a limited range of placement options. These factors have the potential to hamper appropriate services for these students.

Back to the Cases

Now that you've read about visual impairment, look back at the student stories at the beginning of this chapter. Then, answer the questions about each of their cases.

MyEdLab **Case Study 12.1**

JAYDEN. Jayden is a young student, and the programs and services he accesses in his first few school years may have a profound impact on his entire life. Imagine that you are part of the team writing his IEP. Consider all of the domains in which he may have needs (cognitive, academic, social/emotional, behavioral).

MyEdLab **Case Study 12.2**

ANNA MARIE. Anna Marie is attending the middle school in her neighborhood, and her day-to-day services will be provided by general educators and a special educator who is not specially trained in the area of visual impairments. Imagine that you are Ms. Barich, the special educator (or one of Anna Marie's general education teachers), and outline a plan for appropriately meeting Anna Marie's needs.

MyEdLab **Case Study 12.3**

ETHAN. Ethan, who has been blind since birth, is entering the 10th grade as an average student. His teachers find him to be hardworking, and they anticipate that he will reach whatever goals he sets. His parents have been supportive and have encouraged independence, which has provided Ethan with confidence and self-assurance. In the next phase of his educational career, Ethan will be asked to accomplish much.

13

Students with Orthopedic Impairments, Traumatic Brain Injury, and Other Health Impairments

Learning Outcomes

LO13.1 Outline the development of understanding of and services for orthopedic impairments, traumatic brain injury, and other health impairments, collectively referred to as physical and health disabilities, and explain the prevalence of these disabilities.

LO13.2 Describe characteristics of individuals with physical and health disabilities.

LO13.3 Explain how physical and health disabilities are identified.

LO13.4 Outline how students with physical and health disabilities receive their education.

LO13.5 Describe recommended educational practices for students with physical and health disabilities.

LO13.6 Explain the perspectives and concerns that parents and families of students with orthopedic impairments, other health impairments, and traumatic brain injury may have.

LO13.7 Identify trends and issues influencing the field of physical and health disabilities.

RYAN

Ryan began kindergarten right on schedule at age 5, and he enjoyed school, made new friends, and learned beginning reading and math skills along with his classmates. In April of Ryan's kindergarten year, however, his mother and teacher noticed that he seemed to tire easily. He also had several bouts with unexplained fever. Worried, his mother took him to the family pediatrician. After a series of tests and a referral to a specialist called a *pediatric oncologist*, Ryan was diagnosed with leukemia. Chemotherapy was started soon after that, and Ryan missed the final three weeks of kindergarten. Now beginning first grade, Ryan has completed his first round of chemotherapy, but he will undergo another cycle of this treatment soon. He attends school for the entire day, but he does not participate in physical education and also has permission to go to the nurse's office for a nap if he is tired. His mother sends him to school with snacks that he eats as he wishes; with little appetite, his doctors are concerned about increasing his caloric intake. Ryan is now bald, so he always wears a baseball cap. His friends at school are jealous since they are not permitted such headwear; one classmate asked if he could wear a cap if he got his dad to shave his head. Ryan's reading skills have not kept pace with those of his classmates, and Ms. Turner, a resource teacher, spends an hour each day in Ryan's classroom, assisting him and two other students with disabilities to improve their skills. Ms. Turner and Ms. Campbell, Ryan's first-grade teacher, are keeping in very close contact with Ryan's mother because his condition and needs can change rapidly.

KRYSTLE

Krystle is a seventh-grade student who struggles with her schoolwork and sees a mental health counselor once each week after school because of problems with self-esteem and depression. Krystle is a twin who was born 2.5 months premature. She experienced severe breathing problems and lived for the first three months of her life in the neonatal intensive care unit. Probably as a result of her perinatal problems, she has cerebral palsy. Krystle has received speech therapy, physical therapy, and occupational therapy since she was 3 years old. She did not walk until age 4, and she now uses leg braces and a walker to move around school. Although many people have been supportive of Krystle, she also has had some very negative experiences, including a situation in which a classmate several times deliberately tripped her and then made fun of her, mocking her sometimes difficult-to-understand speech. Krystle could participate in some activities in her physical education class, but for safety reasons, she needs to wear a helmet. She is so embarrassed by the helmet that she instead does not participate. Krystle still receives speech-language services as well as physical and occupational therapy, and she receives intensive reading instruction from a resource teacher and attends a co-taught math class. To her best friend Kaitlin, Krystle sometimes talks about what the future holds for her, whether she will ever have a boyfriend, what it will be like in high school, and what her options might be for a career. She knows her twin brother, who does not have any disability, will help her any way he can, but Krystle most of all wants to be able to be independent.

JEFFREY

Jeffrey is 18 years old and a high school senior. He is looking forward to graduation and is eager to go to college. However, about 10 months ago, Jeffrey's plans changed radically. Until then, he and his family had assumed he would attend college on a football scholarship. He had been on the varsity team since his 10th-grade year, and his coach frequently commented on his skill and determination, a combination sure to lead to success. Jeffrey had been contacted by several good schools, his grade point average was strong, and he had performed well on the SAT. That all changed during the first home game of the season. When tackled, Jeffrey remembers thinking, "Uh-oh. That was serious," and then remembers nothing else for two weeks. Jeffrey's neck had been broken, leaving him a quadriplegic, that is, with no ability to move either his arms or legs. After a lengthy hospitalization and a month in a rehabilitation facility, partnered with unwavering support from family and friends, Jeffrey regained his strength. With special education services, he has been able to complete his remaining courses, and he has learned to use a variety of assistive technology devices so that he can "type" by voice and operate lights and other devices using the small amount of control he has in his left ring finger. What has been a more difficult part of the recovery has been regaining confidence, and Jeffrey has received extensive counseling. One day his blog entry read, "Why did this happen to me? I had everything going for me, and I didn't do anything to deserve this. It's not fair; I'll never be a whole person again. Some of my friends won't even talk to me now." However, Jeffrey slowly has realized that he now has new friends, and he will soon graduate with his classmates. One of his graduation surprises is a service dog. Thunder is trained to open doors, retrieve items that fall, and even to put Jeffrey's arm back on the wheelchair armrest when it slips off. Jeffrey and Thunder plan to spend the summer getting to know each other. Jeffrey's parents, although concerned, are committed to helping him achieve his goal of going away to college. They are counting on Thunder and a personal assistant to provide the supports Jeffrey needs.

ost people know someone who has a physical or health disability. Perhaps as you were growing up, a friend was injured in a car accident and became physically impaired, or you had a classmate who had juvenile diabetes. Do your own experiences suggest to you that you already know quite a bit about people with physical and health disabilities? If so, caution is in order. Some students with health or physical conditions do not need special education at all—their special needs do not affect their education. Some students, though, have health or physical disabilities that are significant and that do affect their education—for example, those whose health needs result in frequent hospitalizations or those whose ability to learn is affected by their physical needs. This group also includes students who may have illnesses or disorders that you cannot see but whose disabilities still affect their strength, their memory and ability to complete schoolwork, and their behavior. The focus of this chapter is on students who have physical and health disabilities, specifically, orthopedic impairments, other health impairments (except ADHD, which was addressed in Chapter 6), and traumatic brain injury, who need special education. They are so unique that making general statements about them, while necessary in this overview, includes the risk of creating inaccurate impressions.

Understanding Physical and Health Disabilities

Interest in the characteristics and needs of people with physical and health disabilities certainly is not new, but early work emphasized medical needs and options for care. As you can see by reviewing the time line in Figure 13.1, only during the past century did education gradually become a priority.

Development of the Field of Physical and Health Disabilities

Accounts of people with physical and health disabilities have existed since ancient times, but it was not until the late 1600s that physicians and other prominent professionals advocated for the treatment of these disorders. Even in the 19th century, medicine was advancing, but options for assistance were still very limited (Winzer, 1993). The most common recommendation to parents of children with these disabilities was institutionalization. Families who kept their children at home did not have access to programs or services, and whether a child thrived often depended on the family's support network and community assistance (Longmore & Umansky, 2001).

Video Example
from
YouTube

▶

MyEdLab
Video Example 13.1
This video introduces you to a young lady whose sentiments are likely similar to those of many students with physical and health disabilities whom you may teach. (https://www.youtube.com/watch?v=CL8GMxRW_5Y)

FIGURE 13.1   **Time Line of the Development of the Field of Physical and Health Disabilities**

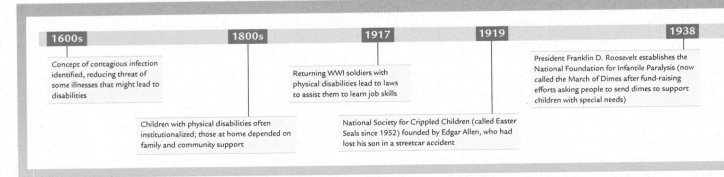

1600s
Concept of contagious infection identified, reducing threat of some illnesses that might lead to disabilities

1800s
Children with physical disabilities often institutionalized; those at home depended on family and community support

1917
Returning WWI soldiers with physical disabilities lead to laws to assist them to learn job skills

National Society for Crippled Children (called Easter Seals since 1952) founded by Edgar Allen, who had lost his son in a streetcar accident

1919

1938
President Franklin D. Roosevelt establishes the National Foundation for Infantile Paralysis (now called the March of Dimes after fund-raising efforts asking people to send dimes to support children with special needs)

Increasing Attention for an Ignored Group

Early in the 20th century, the needs of war veterans forced increasing attention on people with physical and health disabilities, and this attention contributed to a gradual increase in concern about children. Two organizations still active today that you probably are familiar with were founded during this era: Easter Seals and the March of Dimes. Organizations such as these helped keep attention focused on the needs of children with physical and health disabilities. Eventually, with key legal cases from the late 1960s and 1970s and the passage of the federal special education law (now called the Individuals with Disabilities Education Act, or IDEA) in 1975, these children claimed their rights along with other children with disabilities.

In the years since IDEA was first implemented, two court cases have been particularly significant for students with physical and health disabilities. First, in *Irving Independent School District v. Tatro* (468 U.S. 883), an 8-year-old girl with spina bifida (a condition discussed later in this chapter) needed clean intermittent catheterization (CIC) every 3 or 4 hours to help her relieve her bladder, and she could not attend school if this procedure was not performed. Her parents believed the school district was responsible for providing this service, but the district considered it a medical procedure not covered by IDEA. The U.S. Supreme Court supported the parents' view, identifying this procedure as a *related service*—that is, one needed by the child in order to attend school (unlike procedures needed just once a day that could be performed during nonschool hours). The court ruled that because the procedure could be performed by a school nurse or anyone else who attended a brief training session, it was not a *medical service*—that is, one that had to be completed by a physician (Vitello, 1986)—and thus, school personnel were directed to provide this support.

The second court case, *Cedar Rapids Community School District v. Garrett F.* (19 S. Ct. 992), further clarified schools' responsibilities for providing health-related services (Katsiyannis & Yell, 1999). Garrett F. was paralyzed from the neck down at age 4 as a result of a motorcycle accident, and his parents had ensured that his many physical needs were met in the classroom by providing a nurse for him. However, when Garrett was in fifth grade, his parents requested that the school district take over paying for this intensive support. The school district maintained that this was a medical service not required through IDEA. The U.S. Supreme Court ruled against the school district, stating that the only services considered medical were those that could only be performed by a physician. It established that the nursing care needed by Garrett was a related service under IDEA and that schools were obligated to provide it if required for students to attend school.

These two cases made it clearer than ever before that students with physical and health disabilities have as much right as other students to access education. This is the case even if their needs require professionals to offer highly specialized services.

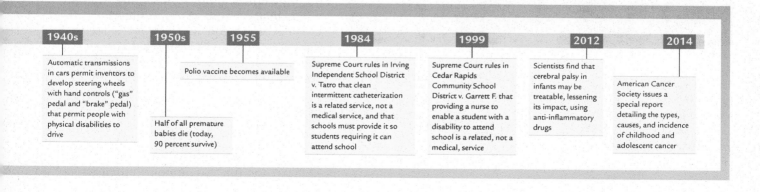

1940s	1950s	1955	1984	1999	2012	2014
Automatic transmissions in cars permit inventors to develop steering wheels with hand controls ("gas" pedal and "brake" pedal) that permit people with physical disabilities to drive	Half of all premature babies die (today, 90 percent survive)	Polio vaccine becomes available	Supreme Court rules in Irving Independent School District v. Tatro that clean intermittent catheterization is a related service, not a medical service, and that schools must provide it so students requiring it can attend school	Supreme Court rules in Cedar Rapids Community School District v. Garrett F. that providing a nurse to enable a student with a disability to attend school is a related, not a medical, service	Scientists find that cerebral palsy in infants may be treatable, lessening its impact, using anti-inflammatory drugs	American Cancer Society issues a special report detailing the types, causes, and incidence of childhood and adolescent cancer

FIGURE 13.2   **Prevalence of Physical and Health Disabilities**

Students ages 6 through 21 served under IDEA, Part B, by disability category.

	Number of Students Identified				
	1995–1996	*2004–2005*	*2010–2011*	*2014–2015*	*Percentage Change*
Orthopedic impairments	63,158	63,127	55,704	46,268	−26%
Traumatic brain injury	9,469	23,509	24,594	25,419	268%
Other health impairments	133,354	561,028	703,912	857,544	643%

Source: Figures are from Data Accountability Center. (2012). *Part B data and notes*. Washington, DC: U.S. Department of Education; and U.S. Department of Education (1997). *Nineteenth annual report to Congress on the implementation of IDEA.*

Looking at the Big Picture

Before exploring specific examples of the orthopedic impairments, traumatic brain injuries, and other health impairments that school-age students may have, it may be helpful to step back for a moment to keep the following information in perspective. First, review the information on the prevalence of these disorders in Figure 13.2.

Two points should be apparent. First, considering that approximately 6.4 million U.S. students ages 6 to 21 are eligible for special education (U.S. Department of Education, 2015), the total number of students in these groups is small. If you are a general education teacher, you probably will teach students with one or more of these illnesses or conditions but probably not every year. If you are a special services provider, you are more likely to work with students in these groups, but unless you specialize in this area, you, too, may find that these students are only periodically among those you serve. Second, the data indicate clear trends related to these disability categories. *Other health impairment* (OHI) has grown steadily over the past 15 years, possibly because of an increasing number of students identified as having attention deficit–hyperactivity disorder (ADHD) being included in this category. *Orthopedic impairment* (OI) has shown a slight but steady decline, and traumatic brain injury (TBI) has remained relatively stable. These trends reflect the evolving nature of the field of special education.

Most importantly, remember that students with these disabilities have many different needs, and their illnesses and conditions can have many different influences on their learning. Your first need in teaching them is to educate yourself about their unique strengths and challenges. Your responsibility is to find out what you need to know to work with them effectively and to ensure that they participate as fully as possible in school experiences (Halfon, Houtrow, Larson, & Newacheck, 2012; Strickland et al., 2015; Vaz et al., 2015).

Stephen Hawking, an eminent British theoretical physicist, was diagnosed more than 40 years ago with a neuromuscular disorder. He illustrates how important it is to avoid judging an individual's capabilities on the basis of their physical status.

Key Concepts for Understanding Physical and Health Disabilities

As you learn about students with physical and health disabilities, several concepts can help your understanding. First, the conditions and disorders described in the following sections can be thought of in terms of how they affect the individual student. Some conditions are chronic; that is, they exist all the time, typically change very little, and currently have no known cure. Cerebral palsy is one example. Others are acute; they are serious but can be treated and possibly cured. Childhood cancer falls into this group. A third group of disorders is progressive; they get worse over time and may lead to death. Muscular dystrophy is an example of a progressive disorder. Finally, some conditions and disorders are episodic; they occur with intensity but at times are dormant. Epilepsy is an episodic disorder. As you read about the many disorders described in the following pages, see if you can identify into which group each might be placed.

A second set of concepts related to these disabilities pertains to causes. Some physical and health disabilities are *congenital*, or present at birth. These disorders may occur because of a genetic problem or heredity, or they may be the result of an environmental influence during pregnancy (e.g., drug or alcohol use by the mother, injury to the mother or child). In many cases of congenital disabilities, the cause simply is not known. Other physical and health disabilities are *acquired*. They occur during or shortly after birth (perinatal causes, as was true for Krystle, whom you met at the beginning of this chapter), possibly because of trauma during delivery, or later as a result of an accident, illness, injury, or environmental factor (e.g., a severe allergy).

Finally, as you read this chapter, keep in mind that for some students with physical and health disabilities, no need exists for special education services because the condition is mild or readily treated with medication. These students may receive support through a Section 504 plan, a topic addressed in Chapter 6. For other students, their education can be successful only if special education and significant accommodations are made.

Understanding Orthopedic Impairments

Orthopedic impairments are conditions that affect movement—that is, an individual's gross-motor control or mobility (e.g., walking, standing) and fine-motor control (e.g., writing, holding or manipulating small objects using the hands, oral–motor skills). These disabilities may be mild, moderate, or severe, but in this discussion, the focus is on physical disabilities that have a significant effect on students' lives and educational needs. Krystle, one of the students introduced at the beginning of the chapter, has a physical disability.

Federal Definition

Although in IDEA this disability category is termed *orthopedic impairments*, most educators refer to students as having *physical disabilities*. Throughout this chapter, the latter term is used as a synonym for the former. According to the IDEA definition, an orthopedic impairment is

> a severe . . . impairment that adversely affects a child's educational performance. The term includes impairments caused by congenital anomaly (e.g., clubfoot, absence of some member, etc.), impairments caused by disease (e.g., poliomyelitis, bone tuberculosis, etc.), and impairments from other causes (e.g., cerebral palsy, amputations, and fractures or burns that cause contractures). (IDEA 20 U.S.C. §1401 [2004], 20 C.F.R. §300.8[c][8])

You can tell by the definition that this disability category includes students with many types of disorders. Some of those disabilities (e.g., those with a neurological basis, such as cerebral palsy) are described in terms of the parts of the body that are affected (e.g., Garfinkle, Wintermark, Shevell, & Oskoui, 2016; Best, Heller, & Bigge, 2010). Specifically, monoplegia is the term used when only one limb is involved. Hemiplegia occurs when the arm, leg, and trunk of the body on

FIGURE 13.3   **Types of Paralysis**

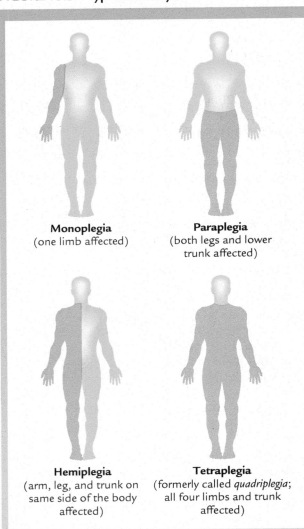

Monoplegia
(one limb affected)

Paraplegia
(both legs and lower trunk affected)

Hemiplegia
(arm, leg, and trunk on same side of the body affected)

Tetraplegia
(formerly called *quadriplegia*; all four limbs and trunk affected)

the same side are affected. Paraplegia occurs when only the legs are affected. Tetraplegia (formerly called *quadriplegia*) involves both arms and both legs, the trunk of the body, and the neck. Diplegia occurs when both legs or both arms are involved. This information is illustrated in Figure 13.3.

At the same time, some physical disabilities do not fall into this categorization scheme. As you read about each disorder, think about why this approach is helpful for thinking about some students but is not relevant for others.

Neurological Disorders

One group of physical disabilities comprises neurological disorders. These conditions occur because of a problem in the central nervous system—that is, the brain, the spinal cord, and their nerve endings. Examples of neurologically based physical disabilities include cerebral palsy, spina bifida, and spinal cord injury.

Cerebral palsy. The term cerebral palsy literally means "paralysis of the brain." This disability is a group of conditions involving muscle control, posture, and movement that is not progressive, meaning that it does not get worse over time. The problem that occurs for students with cerebral palsy is not in the muscles themselves. It is in the brain's ability to consistently tell the muscles what to do (Capio, Sit, Abernethy, & Masters, 2012). The most common type of cerebral palsy in children, affecting approximately 80% of those with this neurological condition, is called spastic cerebral palsy in which students' muscles are stiff (a condition referred to as *hypertonia*) and their movements are awkward (Centers for Disease Control and Prevention [CDC], 2016f). In athetoid cerebral palsy, students cannot control their muscles, and so they may have sudden and unexpected twisting motions or other movements. Other types of cerebral palsy are also diagnosed, and some students have complex disorders that include several types of this disorder.

When cerebral palsy is present at birth, its causes are usually unknown. However, any factor that can damage the developing baby's brain can increase the risk. For example, a genetic abnormality affecting the brain may result in cerebral palsy. Likewise, premature babies are at risk, as are those who have other medical conditions (e.g., heart problems, kidney problems) (Adams-Chapman, 2009). Newborns whose mothers abused alcohol or drugs, smoked cigarettes, contracted rubella or other serious infections, or experienced serious malnutrition during pregnancy also are at increased risk. After birth, children may develop cerebral palsy as a result of asphyxia—for example, by choking on toys or food or nearly drowning. Cerebral palsy also can occur when a child has been abused. Finally, severe infections such as meningitis can lead to cerebral palsy.

Because cerebral palsy involves a malfunction in the brain, students with this condition often have other disabilities as well (Gabis, Tsubary, Leon, Ashkenasi, & Shefer, 2015). These students may have vision or hearing loss, learning or intellectual disabilities, receptive and expressive communication disorders, or seizure disorders. Their physical limitations also may affect their ability to complete daily activities that you take for granted, including swallowing, controlling the bladder and bowels, and even breathing. But keep in mind that these students are unique (Davis et al., 2009): A student who has significant cerebral palsy may be academically gifted. Professionals need to be sure that they do not let the overall physical limitations of these students influence their perceptions of the students' abilities.

The total number of children with cerebral palsy can only be estimated because these students may be counted for IDEA purposes in the very broad category of *orthopedic impairment*. Alternatively, they may be included as having an intellectual disability, traumatic brain injury, or multiple disabilities, or they may not need special education services at all. Professionals estimate that 10,000 babies are born each year with cerebral palsy and that at age 8, approximately 1 of every 323 children has some form of this disorder (CDC, 2016g).

Spina bifida. When some children are born, the bones of the spinal column are not closed properly. This condition is called spina bifida (literally meaning "a split or divided spine"), and it also is a physical disability with a neurological basis (National Institutes of Health [NIH], 2015). Mild forms of spina bifida generally do not lead to significant disabilities. However, the most severe form, called myelomeningocele, occurs when the spinal cord and its covering protrude from the opening in the spine. This type of spina bifida is nearly always severe. Students with this condition usually are paralyzed in their lower bodies and legs. They often have *hydrocephalus* (an accumulation of cerebrospinal fluid in the brain), a condition that can be relieved by inserting a *shunt,* a small plastic tube that drains the fluid (Marlin, 2004). They also are likely to have various seizure disorders as well as bladder and bowel problems. Infants with severe spina bifida usually undergo surgery shortly after birth to close the opening in the spine, but this does not eliminate the effects of the condition.

Professionals agree that 70% or more of the cases of spina bifida are preventable (Spina Bifida Association of America, 2012). In particular, studies have suggested that women of childbearing age who eat a diet rich in folic acid are at much less risk for having a baby with spina bifida than are other women; it is estimated that 1,300 potential cases of spina bifida are *prevented* each year because of increased attention on the importance of folic acid (Williams et al., 2015). Since 1996, the Food and Drug Administration (FDA) has recommended that breads and similar foods be fortified with folic acid (Kurtzweil, 1999). These public health actions have had a positive effect: The incidence of spina bifida has fallen significantly since then (Shin et al., 2010). Currently, approximately 1,500 babies are born each year with this disorder, with the highest rate among Hispanic mothers (Centers for Disease Control and Prevention, 2015b). The hope is that with continued education of women across all socioeconomic and ethnic groups and ongoing folic acid research, this number will drop even more.

Spinal cord injury. Spinal cord injuries, affecting some 282,000 people annually (National Spinal Cord Injury Statistical Center, 2016), are an increasingly common source of neurological physical disabilities, particularly among adolescents. These injuries occur when there is a break, severe bruise, or other damage to the spinal cord that affects motor and sensory functions. It is through the spinal cord that most messages are carried from the brain to various parts of the body and from various parts of the body back to the brain. With a spinal cord injury, the brain cannot communicate with the body, and the result is paralysis. The type and extent of paralysis is determined by where the injury occurs; the higher up the spinal cord toward the neck, the more extensive the paralysis will be. Jeffrey, the student you met at the beginning of this chapter, experienced a sports-related spinal cord injury.

The causes of spinal cord injuries are ones that may have affected you, a family member, or a friend. They include automobile accidents (approximately 38% of cases), acts of violence (13.5%), falls (30.5%), sports injuries (9%), and other injuries (4%) (National Spinal Cord Injury Statistical Center, 2016). Among the injuries from violence, most result from gunshot and knife wounds, and the victims are likely to be from racial or ethnic minority groups. Among the injuries caused by sports, two-thirds are diving accidents.

Other data on spinal cord injuries are also important (National Spinal Cord Injury Statistical Center, 2016). Approximately 80% of all spinal cord injuries happen to males and only 20% to females. The age range of those who have suffered these injuries has been changing; over the past several years, the average age of injury has increased from 19 to 28 years old and now is estimated at 42 years old. These injuries are almost entirely preventable. Wearing a seatbelt, avoiding diving in shallow water, and using protective gear during sports are only three examples of how the incidence of spinal cord injuries can be greatly reduced.

Musculoskeletal Disorders

A second group of students with physical disabilities have musculoskeletal disorders (United States Bone and Joint Initiative, 2014); that is, their disabilities are the result of problems related to the skeleton or muscles. Although many disorders in this group may be temporary (e.g., bone fractures, muscular infections), some are chronic and likely to require special education. Two examples of the latter disorders are Duchenne muscular dystrophy and juvenile idiopathic arthritis.

Duchenne muscular dystrophy. Muscular dystrophy is actually an entire group of genetic disabilities, but the most common and most severe form of it is called Duchenne muscular dystrophy, named for the French neurologist Guillaume Benjamin Amand Duchenne, who first described it in the 1860s (Muscular Dystrophy Association, 2011). Duchenne muscular dystrophy occurs when a protein called *dystrophin*, used by the body to keep muscles working properly, is missing or significantly deficient. The first symptoms of muscular dystrophy usually occur when children are toddlers. They may seem awkward, and they may walk later than their peers. By the elementary years, these children's muscles begin to deteriorate, and usually by age 11 or 12, they need a wheelchair for mobility. The deterioration of muscles continues through adolescence, eventually affecting the lungs and heart. Individuals with a severe form of this disorder typically die by the time they are in their late teens or early twenties; those with a milder form have a normal life span (National Institute of Neurological Disorders and Stroke [NINDS], 2016a).

Duchenne muscular dystrophy is a genetic disorder that occurs almost always in boys (National Center for Biotechnology Information [NCBI], 2012). It is carried on the X chromosome, and if a woman transmits the chromosome to her son, that child has a 50% chance of having the disease. Because fathers give their sons a Y chromosome, they cannot transmit the disease. If a girl inherits the defective X chromosome, she becomes a carrier of the disorder, but she usually does not develop muscular dystrophy. Approximately 1 in every 3,500 to 5,000 boys has muscular dystrophy; that means about 15,000 school-age children have Duchenne or a milder form of this disorder (Centers for Disease Control and Prevention, 2016c).

Juvenile idiopathic arthritis. Arthritis is characterized by inflammation of the joints, and it exists in more than 100 forms, making it the most common chronic health condition in all people over the age of 15 (NCBI, 2011). Juvenile idiopathic arthritis (JIA) is an umbrella term for chronic forms of this disease diagnosed

Did You Know?

Some students receive nutrition through a gastronomy tube (sometimes call a G-tube or a feeding tube), usually with the assistance of a teacher, occupational therapist, or para-educator. You can learn more about G-tubes and see examples at http://www.feedingtubeawareness.org/.

when symptoms last for more than six weeks in children who are 16 years of age or less. The symptoms of the disorder are redness, swelling, and soreness in one joint or several joints. Students with JIA may limp in the morning, they may sometimes have limited mobility, and they may develop eye inflammations. The symptoms vary from student to student, and some students may have periods when no symptoms are present at all. Some students may not need any special services at all, some may have Section 504 plans, and some may need special education.

The exact cause of juvenile idiopathic arthritis is not known. It is an *autoimmune disorder*, in which the body mistakenly responds to some of its own cells as though they are foreign and should be fought off (NCBI, 2011). The symptoms of JIA occur when the immune system attacks these healthy cells. Researchers speculate that juvenile idiopathic arthritis may have a genetic basis that is triggered by a factor in the environment, perhaps a virus. Approximately 6.6–15 per 100,000 children under age 18 have JIA, although no single national database exists to track these children (Centers for Disease Control and Prevention, 2015e). Professionals estimate that between 70,000 and 100,000 children now have the condition. This disorder is found more often among girls than boys, in a ratio of approximately 2:1. Some children outgrow JIA, but most continue to have some types of symptoms throughout their lives.

Understanding Traumatic Brain Injury

A second group of students with physical and health disabilities have a brain injury. The IDEA definition of this disorder refers to it as traumatic brain injury (TBI), the result of a sudden and significant insult to the brain. You will find, though, that brain injury caused by other factors such as near drowning, diseases, or electrical shock is sometimes referred to as acquired brain injury (ABI) (Brain Injury Association of America, 2015), and this group of injuries is not directly addressed in IDEA.

Federal Definition

According to IDEA, *traumatic brain injury* is defined as

> an acquired injury to the brain caused by an external physical force, resulting in total or partial functional disability or psychosocial impairment, or both, that adversely affects a child's educational performance. The term applies to open or closed head injuries resulting in impairments in one or more areas, such as cognition; language; memory; attention; reasoning; abstract thinking; judgment; problem solving; sensory, perceptual, and motor abilities; psychosocial behavior; physical functions; information processing; and speech. The term does not apply to brain injuries that are congenital or degenerative, or to brain injuries induced by birth trauma. (IDEA 20 U.S.C. §1401 [2004], 20 C.F.R. §300.8[c][12])

This disability category was added to IDEA in 1990. Nearly all students who are identified as having traumatic brain injuries will have been hospitalized, making medical information integral to understanding these students.

Types of Traumatic Brain Injury

In some cases, traumatic brain injury is caused by a direct blow to the head, as might happen during a sports activity or in a fall. Other causes include physical violence and automobile accidents. When the brain is injured by bouncing around inside the skull but there is no physical damage to the skull itself, the injury is referred to as a closed head injury. When the skull is fractured and the membrane surrounding the brain is penetrated, resulting in the brain being directly injured, the injury is referred to as an open head injury (also, penetrating head injury or skull fracture) (NINDS, 2012).

Sometimes a mild brain injury is referred to as a *concussion*; this type of injury accounts for the majority of brain injuries. Usually, a child who receives a concussion does not lose consciousness. However, as you may know, a concussion is a serious injury that requires medical attention. Professionals fear that many children's injuries are never brought to anyone's attention and that some children who would benefit from treatment do not receive it (e.g., Arbogast et al., 2016; Kroshus, Garnett, Hawrilenko, Baugh, & Calzo, 2015).

The Effects of Traumatic Brain Injury

Nearly any domain of functioning can be affected by traumatic brain injury (e.g., Chesire, Buckley, & Canto, 2011; Gorman et al., 2016; Ransom et al., 2015). These are some of the areas that may be significantly affected when students experience traumatic brain injuries:

- *Cognitive skills.* Students may experience difficulty with reasoning, problem solving, memory, and organization.
- *Processing ability.* A traumatic brain injury can affect the speed at which a student can interpret information received through all the senses. For example, if someone is speaking to a student while music is playing, this may cause confusion and frustration.
- *Language.* Depending on the part of the brain that is injured, some students may experience speech and language disorders. In particular, they may have difficulty comprehending language and speaking fluently.
- *Academic achievement.* Many students with traumatic brain injuries regress in their levels of achievement and may struggle to regain lost skills and learn new ones.
- *Emotions.* Students who have experienced traumatic brain injuries often are characterized as having a changed personality. They may have difficulty controlling their emotions, and they may become frustrated, angry, or upset with an intensity that surprises their teachers and other professionals and often leads students to experience difficulties with peers (Yeates et al., 2007).
- *Behavior.* Students with traumatic brain injuries may have behavior problems similar to those of other students (e.g., refusing to work, leaving the classroom without permission, hitting others), but their problems may be more intense and more difficult to address because of the other cognitive difficulties caused by the injury (e.g., Davies, Jones, & Rafoth, 2010; Finnanger et al., 2015).

Prevalence and Causes

The statistics on traumatic brain injury are sobering. This condition is the most common cause of disability and death among individuals in the United States under the age of 21, resulting in 62,000 hospitalizations and 564,000 emergency room visits each year (CDC, 2016d). The two age groups at highest risk for TBI are children ages birth to 4 and young adults ages 15 to 19; and boys are about twice as likely as girls to experience a brain injury, especially when the TBI is the result of a sports injury. The causes of TBI are, for the most part, preventable. The most common cause in children up to age 14, accounting for approximately half of all TBI, is falling (e.g., from a bicycle when not wearing protective headgear or from playground equipment). TBI also occurs in automobile and motorcycle accidents, especially when children are not wearing seatbelts or are not otherwise properly restrained or protected. Assaults (e.g., firearms use) also are a cause of TBI. One final cause is referred to as struck by/against and includes

Students with traumatic brain injury may move from a hospital to a rehabilitation facility and then back to school. Their needs vary greatly and can change rapidly, so professional collaboration is especially important.

child abuse, especially shaken baby syndrome; this cause accounts for 25% of TBI in children.

Understanding Other Health Impairments

Some students have disabilities that cannot be seen but relate to health conditions. In IDEA, students with these disabilities are categorized as having other health impairment, the term *other* separating this group from students with intellectual or other disabilities that also may affect health.

Federal Definition

The IDEA definition for this disability category is as follows:

> Other health impairment means having limited strength, vitality or alertness, including a heightened alertness to environmental stimuli, that results in limited alertness with respect to the educational environment, that—
>
> i. Is due to chronic or acute health problems such as asthma, attention deficit disorder or attention deficit–hyperactivity disorder, diabetes, epilepsy, a heart condition, hemophilia, lead poisoning, leukemia, nephritis, rheumatic fever, and sickle cell anemia; and
> ii. Adversely affects a child's educational performance. (IDEA 20 U.S.C. §1401 [2004], 20 C.F.R. §300.8[c][9])

Examples of Health Impairments

Hundreds of health impairments that may affect children have been identified, but only a small sample of these disorders can be addressed here. Keep in mind, too, that students with attention deficit–hyperactivity disorder (ADHD) may receive special education services through this disability category, and so some of the students labeled with this disability were discussed in Chapter 6. Other types of health impairments are described in the following sections.

Asthma. The most common chronic illness among children is asthma, a lung disease that causes episodes of extreme difficulty in breathing (Akinbami, Simon, & Rossen, 2016). For some children, asthma may be fairly benign; for example, they have coughing spells when they laugh too hard. For other students, the condition is much more serious. When exposed to certain triggers, these students' airways swell and they produce mucus that makes it difficult for them to breathe (National Heart, Lung, and Blood Institute, 2014). These students may require emergency medical intervention. Asthma has a clear hereditary basis—if one parent has asthma, his or her child is likely to also have this disease. However, it often is triggered by allergens, including tree and grass pollen, dust, molds, animal dander, and food allergies to eggs, seafood, and other items, as well as by strenuous physical activity (Greiling, Boss, & Wheeler, 2005). Fortunately, for most students asthma usually can be controlled through medication and attention to environmental triggers (e.g., Burbank et al., 2015; Postma, Evans-Agnew, & Capouya, 2015).

Asthma affects approximately 6.3 million children (birth to age 18) in the United States (Centers for Disease Control and Prevention, 2016a; Chrisler & Child, 2012), 8.6% of all children. Further, the number of cases of asthma has been rising dramatically (Akinbami, Simon, & Rossen, 2016), and the severity has been increasing. Experts in this field advise parents to protect their children from known triggers such as tobacco smoke, outdoor allergens, and certain foods (e.g., nuts) as one means of addressing this problem (Cates, 2009). Only students who have severe asthma are likely to be entitled to special education services.

Epilepsy. A second example of a health impairment, one that is the result of a central nervous system problem, is epilepsy, sometimes called a seizure disorder.

Epilepsy is a neurological condition in which damage to the brain leads to periodic sudden, uncontrolled bursts of electrical activity that may be seen as seizures (Reilly & Ballantine, 2011).

Epilepsy occurs in two major categories: partial and generalized (Weinstein, 2002). Partial seizures occur when the electrical discharge affects only part of the brain. Partial seizures may involve involuntary twitching of muscles or rapid eye blinks. In *simple partial seizures*, the child may be aware of what is occurring but unable to stop it. In *complex partial seizures*, the child may make odd movements or even scream or run, or the seizures may occur as the child sleeps. In all cases of this type of seizure, the child will not remember what happened (Epilepsy Foundation, 2014b).

You may be more familiar with generalized seizures (Epilepsy Foundation, 2014c), the most well-known of which is the tonic-clonic seizure (formerly called a *grand mal seizure*). Sometimes this type of seizure is preceded by an *aura*, or warning, in which the child senses an odd smell, taste, or sound. Usually the student then stiffens, loses consciousness, and falls (the tonic phase), and then the student's arms and legs jerk (clonic phase) or contract. This type of seizure lasts several minutes but usually does not require medical intervention.

A second type of generalized seizure is referred to as an absence seizure (pronounced "ab-sawnce" and formerly call a *petit mal seizure*) (Epilepsy Foundation, 2014a). This type of seizure usually lasts for only a few seconds, and educators may mistake it for daydreaming or an attentional problem. Some students can have as many as 100 absence seizures per day. This type of seizure disorder usually disappears by adolescence, but students with this type of epilepsy may develop other types of seizures.

Two other types of generalized seizures also occur. The first is *atonic and tonic seizures* (also called "drop attack" seizures), in which the student suddenly falls to the floor, either because muscles have stiffened or because they have completely lost muscle tone; the student remains conscious during this type of seizure. The final type of generalized seizure is called *myoclonic*, in which there are sudden, brief muscle jerks, often affecting the neck, shoulders, and upper arms. These seizures range from mild to severe and occur most often in clusters and in the morning. You can read more about how to respond if a student has a seizure in the Professional Edge.

In half or more of all cases of epilepsy, no specific cause can be identified (National Institute of Neurological Disorders and Stroke, 2016b). When a cause is known, only rarely is it related to a genetic disorder. Instead, it is likely to be the result of a head injury, as caused by an automobile accident, a fall, or extreme child abuse (e.g., shaken baby syndrome). High fevers, poisoning, and brain tumors also can cause epilepsy. When a student has epilepsy, environmental factors can contribute to a seizure occurring. For example, sleep deprivation can serve as a trigger, as can flashing lights and loud or monotonous noise.

As is the case with other physical disabilities, assigning prevalence is difficult because no central registry exists. The Epilepsy Foundation (2014b) estimates that 300,000 U.S. school-age children through the age of 14 have epilepsy. The foundation also reports that African Americans and students from socially disadvantaged groups are at higher risk for this disorder than are Caucasians, and males are slightly more likely than females to develop epilepsy. Epilepsy also is comorbid with other disorders. For example, half the children who have both cerebral palsy and an intellectual disability also have epilepsy.

HIV and AIDS. HIV and AIDS were unknown in humans until the second half of the 20th century. HIV stands for *human immunodeficiency virus,* a virus that can take over a cell's own genetic material and then produce more diseased cells. This virus attacks the body's own immune system, making individuals with HIV more susceptible to illnesses. AIDS stands for acquired immune deficiency syndrome, and it is a collection of illnesses, including some cancers, that only individuals who have HIV can contract. HIV is transmitted through contact with

PROFESSIONAL **EDGE**

First Aid for Seizures

Everyone should know how to respond if someone (child or adult) is having a seizure. The first aid procedures recommended by the Epilepsy Foundation of America (2014c) are presented in detail below.

First Aid for Generalized Tonic-Clonic (Grand Mal) Seizures

- Keep calm and reassure other people who may be nearby.
- Don't hold the person down or try to stop his movements.
- Time the seizure with your watch.
- Clear the area around the person of anything hard or sharp.
- Loosen ties or anything around the neck that may make breathing difficult.
- Put something flat and soft, such as a folded jacket, under the head.
- Turn the person gently onto one side. This will help keep the airway clear. Do not try to force the mouth open with any hard implement or with your fingers. It is not true that a person having a seizure can swallow his tongue. Efforts to hold the tongue down can injure the teeth or jaw.
- Don't attempt artificial respiration, except in the unlikely event that the person does not start breathing again after the seizure has stopped.
- Stay with the person until the seizure ends naturally and the person is ready to resume activities.

- Be friendly and reassuring as consciousness returns; the person may need to rest or sleep.
- Call an ambulance if a seizure lasts more than 5 minutes, if another seizure begins, if it is unknown whether the individual is being treated for seizures, if the seizure happens in water, if the person requests this assistance, or if the person is pregnant, injured, or diabetic.

First Aid for Nonconvulsive Seizures

You don't have to do anything if a person has brief periods of staring or shaking of the limbs. If someone has the kind of seizure that produces a dazed state and automatic behavior, then do the following:

- Watch the person carefully, and explain to others what is happening. Often people who don't recognize this kind of behavior as a seizure think that the dazed person is drunk or on drugs.
- Speak quietly and calmly in a friendly way.
- Guide the person gently away from any danger, such as a steep flight of steps. Don't grab hold of her, however, unless some immediate danger threatens. People having this kind of seizure are on "automatic pilot" as far as their movements are concerned. Instinct may make them struggle or lash out at the person who is trying to hold them.
- Stay with the person until full consciousness returns.

Source: Based on Epilepsy Foundation (2014a, c). *First aid for seizures, First aid for generalized tonic clonic (grand mal) seizures*, and *First aid for absence seizures*. Retrieved from http://www.epilepsyfoundation.org/aboutepilepsy/firstaid/index.cfm, http://www.epilepsy.com/learn/treating-seizures-and-epilepsy/first-aid/tonic-clonic-seizures, and http://www.epilepsy.com/learn/treating-seizures-and-epilepsy/first-aid/absence-seizures

---

infected blood or other body fluids, as occurs with unprotected sexual contact and sharing of needles. Most students who have AIDS became infected during their mothers' pregnancies, and mothers abusing drugs and those with HIV who have complications during delivery are most likely to transmit the disease to their babies (Centers for Disease Control and Prevention, 2015c). However, an increasing number of youth are becoming infected through their own unprotected sexual activity, especially through male-to-male sex (Centers for Disease Control and Prevention, 2016b).

Precise data on the prevalence of HIV and AIDS are difficult to obtain. According to the Centers for Disease Control and Prevention (2015c), in 2014, some 1,863 new cases of HIV/AIDS were reported for children and adolescents through age 19. However, it is estimated that nearly half of the adolescents infected with HIV but who have not yet developed AIDS are unaware that they have the disease (Centers for Disease Control and Prevention, 2016b).

Although great strides are being made in treatments for HIV and AIDS, no cure exists. Students with AIDS may have to take medications in school, and they may have increasing absences if their health deteriorates. They may or may not require special education. One fact to keep in mind is that confidentiality policies about HIV and AIDS vary from locale to locale, and *professionals may not be*

Video Example
from
YouTube

MyEdLab
Video Example 13.2

Video Example 13.2 presents an overview of the first aid procedures recommended by the Epilepsy Foundation of America. (https://www.youtube.com/watch?v=fvlzKoP10iQ)

entitled to know that a student has this disorder (Sileo, 2005). For that reason, it is imperative that all school professionals use what are called *universal precautions* in addressing an illness or injury that may include blood or other body substances. You can read more about this important topic in the Professional Edge.

Cancer. Cancer, an uncontrolled division of abnormal cells, is relatively rare among children, but it does occur, and it remains the leading cause of death from disease for this group. The two most common types, accounting for more than half of all cases, are leukemia (i.e., blood cell cancers) and brain tumors (National Cancer Institute, 2014). Prior to the early 1960s, the mortality rate for some forms of pediatric cancer, including leukemia, was 100% (Brown & Madan-Swain, 1993). By the late 1970s, the situation had changed significantly such that the survival rate for all childhood cancers had risen to 55%. In the 21st century, the survival rate has climbed to over 70% (National Cancer Institute, 2014).

Students who are diagnosed and treated for cancer are at risk for a variety of learning problems (Hay, Nabors, Sullivan, & Zygmund, 2015), just like Ryan, the student introduced at the beginning of the chapter. Radiation may lead to problems in cognitive functioning. Students have been identified as having difficulties in mathematics, attention, and memory as well as behavior problems and social skills deficits. Some students in this group first may be identified as other health impaired because of the cancer. Later, they may be identified as learning disabled, intellectually disabled, or behavior and emotionally disabled because of the lasting effects of their illness.

Approximately 10,380 children in the United States were diagnosed with cancer in 2015 (CDC, 2015). Diagnoses for some cancers have risen slightly over the past 30 years, but those for leukemia have dropped.

PROFESSIONAL **EDGE**

Universal Precautions for School Professionals

No matter what your role in the school and no matter who your students are likely to be, you should be aware of the following *universal precautions* for dealing with blood and other body fluids that may carry blood-borne pathogens—that is, microorganisms (e.g., HIV/AIDS, hepatitis B, hepatitis C) that can be transmitted when blood or another body fluid from an infected individual comes into contact with an open cut, a skin abrasion, acne, or the mucous membranes of the mouth, eyes, and nose and cause disease and illness (Edens, Murdick, & Gartin, 2003):

- Wear disposable gloves and other protective equipment (e.g., a protective jacket or face mask) when performing tasks that involve risk of exposure, such as assisting a student with personal hygiene or responding to a student injury.
- In an accident or situation in which no gloves are available, place another barrier (e.g., an article of clothing) between yourself and the blood or body fluid.
- Notify a custodian if there is a blood spill. Custodial staff should use a hospital disinfectant or bleach solution to clean up blood spills and to disinfect potentially contaminated surfaces.

- Pick up potentially contaminated sharp objects (e.g., needles, knives, broken glass) with a tool such as pliers or tweezers. Never pick up such objects with your hands.
- Discard any articles contaminated with blood or body fluids in a leak-resistant and puncture-proof container.
- When you are ready to remove your gloves, turn them inside out as you do so to avoid contact with blood.
- Discard gloves in a leak-resistant container.
- Use soap and warm water to thoroughly wash hands and any skin that may have been contaminated. Flush with water if the eyes, nose, or mouth has come into contact with blood.
- If you had significant contact with a student's blood, seek medical attention.

School districts generally have specific policies in place for universal precautions and instruct new staff members on those procedures. If you have questions, your school nurse or principal should be able to answer them.

Source: Adapted from Grosse, S. J. (1999). *Educating children and youth to prevent contagious disease* [ERIC Digest]. ERIC Clearinghouse on Teaching and Teacher Education.

What do you think is the most common cause of cancer? If you said it is unknown, you are correct. A few conditions have genetic links, but many suspected causes have not been verified. Among the areas studied and to date *not* found to cause cancer are these: ultrasound use during pregnancy, low-level radon exposure, magnetic field exposure from power lines, maternal cigarette smoking, and exposure to specific viruses (National Cancer Institute, 2014). Research continues to focus on prenatal factors and environmental factors that could make children susceptible to cancer.

Sickle cell disease. One health impairment about which considerable information is available is sickle cell disease, a disorder that affects the part of the red blood cells that carries oxygen from the lungs to other parts of the body (National Center on Birth Defects and Developmental Disabilities, 2015). Normally, red blood cells are round and soft, and they can fit through small blood vessels. In sickle cell disease, these cells become sickle shaped and inflexible, and they block small blood vessels. This causes the flow of oxygen to be slowed or stopped. When this happens, individuals with this disease experience pain (the most common symptom), their bodies can be damaged (e.g., kidneys, lungs, bones), and they may become anemic. Educators may need to help students avoid extreme heat and cold, drink enough fluids, and use relaxation strategies to help avoid or cope with pain (Knight-Madden, Lewis, Tyson, Reid, & MooSang, 2011).

Students with a severe form of sickle cell disease may miss school frequently. They also may experience problems in learning and memory as well as in the behavior and social domains (Crosby et al., 2015; Dale, Cochran, Roy, Jernigan, & Buchanan, 2011). These students may have sudden crises, and educators who work with them need to be alert to the need to contact parents so that medical attention can be sought. Keep in mind, though, that most students with this disorder lead full and productive lives, and with early identification many of the potential complications of the disease can be prevented. Some students may not need any special services, others may have Section 504 plans, and those whose education is adversely affected may receive special education.

Sickle cell disease affects one in every 365 African American newborns (CDC, 2016e). One in 13 individuals of African descent carries the recessive gene for this disorder, but most never develop symptoms. However, sickle cell disease also affects Hispanic Americans, occurring in about 1 in every 16,300 births for that group.

Diabetes. One additional health impairment to mention is diabetes, a metabolic disorder in which the body cannot properly break down sugars and store them (CDC, 2015d). Because of this problem, children with the disorder must carefully monitor their diets and also receive injections of insulin. Approximately 208,000 children and young adults under the age of 20 have diabetes (CDC, 2014).

There are two types of diabetes. The first is type I diabetes, which most often is diagnosed during adolescence. The period following diagnosis can be particularly difficult for students: They have to change their eating habits, they may be embarrassed or upset by the diagnosis, they have to learn to monitor their blood sugar levels and find a time and place to do so, and they may have to face teasing from peers. Students who have juvenile diabetes often can be successful without any specific school intervention. However, they may need a Section 504 plan to accommodate their needs (e.g., procedures to monitor their glucose and for insulin injection; procedures for responding to high or low blood sugar). Some students need assistance only at particular times. For example, Ginger plays on the girls' junior varsity basketball team. During practices and games, her coach monitors her carefully to be sure she drinks enough fluids and does not ignore warning signals that she needs to rest. Approximately 18,000 children are diagnosed as having juvenile diabetes each year (CDC, 2014). If you work with students with diabetes, your school nurse can be an important source of information for helping these students to manage their disease.

Type II diabetes, which is preventable, has quadrupled among children over the past 30 years (Centers for Disease Control and Prevention, 2015d), with some 3,600 cases diagnosed each year. Consider this information: More than one-third of U.S. children ages 6 to 19 are either overweight or obese. This is more than double the rate from 20 years ago (Centers for Disease Control and Prevention, 2015a). Not surprisingly, the alarming increase in type II diabetes is causing health and school professionals to focus their attention on helping students and their families to understand the importance of healthy eating habits and adequate physical activity (Allen, 2012; Anderson, Newby, Kehm, Barland, & Hearst, 2015). It also is prompting these professionals to provide healthier foods at school and to limit students' access to soft drinks and other high-calorie food from vending machines (Schanzenbach, 2009; Tucker & Lanningham-Foster, 2015). Not all of these students may be entitled to special education, but the number who need these services is likely to continue to grow.

MyEdLab **Self-Check 13.1**

MyEdLab **Application Exercise 13.1:** Introducing Dr. Maxine Harper

MyEdLab **Application Exercise 13.2:** School Nurse

Characteristics of Individuals with Orthopedic Impairments, Traumatic Brain Injury, and Other Health Impairments

It is difficult to apply generalities to students who have physical and health disabilities because their strengths and needs can range immensely within a single domain as well as across domains. Some information about these students' characteristics was embedded in the descriptions of their disorders, but additional details can help you to understand how you can best meet their needs.

Cognitive and Academic Characteristics

Students with physical and health disabilities have cognitive and academic abilities that range from extraordinary giftedness and special talents to significant intellectual disability. Students' abilities in this domain often are related to the nature of the disorder, the severity of the disorder, and the effects of treating the disorder (e.g., Crosby et al., 2015; Daly, Kral, & Brown, 2008; Kennedy, 2008; Vu, Babikian, & Asarnow, 2011). For example, Edgar was in a farming accident in which he lost one arm just above the elbow and three fingers on his remaining hand. He also experienced serious internal injuries that required hospitalization. After being released from the hospital, he spent time in a rehabilitation facility while he adjusted to his injuries and was assessed for a prosthetic arm. Edgar was a high-achieving student before his accident, and he probably will continue at this level when he returns to school. In contrast, Marcy has cerebral palsy that has caused her to have diplegia. She has epilepsy as well, but it is usually controlled through medication. Marcy also has a moderate intellectual disability, which is not particularly surprising, given that she has two other conditions that are directly related to neurological functioning. Her curricular objectives are adjusted to take into account her current learning level.

As a professional educator, your responsibility is to get to know the cognitive and academic characteristics of your students with physical and health disabilities. Even more important, it is essential that you not presume that students who have limited ability to move or difficulty communicating also have limited intellectual ability—a common error, even in the 21st century. How might this apply to Jeffrey, introduced at the beginning of the chapter?

Behavior, Emotional, and Social Characteristics

Although students with physical and health disabilities do not always have special needs in the behavioral, emotional, and social domains, these areas can be particularly important for them. The reasons for this become clear when you understand all the information you have just read about the various conditions.

Behavior Characteristics

Some physical and health disabilities are associated with the presence of behavior problems. Perhaps the clearest example occurs among students with traumatic brain injuries (Aldrich & Obrzut, 2012). These students often cannot make judgments about appropriate behaviors, and they become anxious and frustrated when they are not told exactly what to do. They need exceptionally clear rules to follow, and they need reminders about those rules because they may have problems with memory. In addition, students with traumatic brain injuries may require very specific behavior intervention plans that have extensive rewards built in for appropriate behaviors. These students also may become aggressive as a means of expressing their frustrations. They need consistency, a topic addressed in the Positive Behavior Supports.

POSITIVE • BEHAVIOR • SUPPORTS

Addressing Behavior for Students with Traumatic Brain Injuries

Students with traumatic brain injuries often develop serious behavior problems. Here are some essential elements related to consistency and communication for addressing these students' behavior needs (Kay, Spaulding, & Smerdon, 2004):

Consistency Within the School

- All of the professionals at the school should be aware of the student's strengths and needs.
- Professionals should develop a highly detailed behavioral care plan consistently implemented across settings. Example: Brian responds best when given a choice in activities. School staff members all use this information. The media teacher asks Brian to choose from among three library books, and the language arts teacher has Brian decide whether to create a poster about the short story just read or to digitally record a summary of it.

Communication Within the School

- All the professionals working with the student should meet regularly to share information and report progress and problems.
- Formal communication should be supplemented with an informal dialogue about day-to-day events.
- If anyone at school notices a change in the student's behavior, a meeting should be called to discuss what is occurring and how to respond.

Consistency Between School and Home

- Different responses to the same behavior may confuse a student.

Example: Teachers respond to a student's frustration-based crying by matter of factly saying to him, "Take a break" and leaving him alone for 3 minutes. His parents respond by holding him and distracting him with a toy or game. The inconsistency may result in increased rather than decreased behavior problems.

Communication Between School and Home

- Clear communication between school professionals and parents is imperative.
- A daily behavior log can be exchanged in which parents and educators jot down notes about student successes and questions or concerns.
- Written communication can be supplemented with phone calls and e-mails.
- More formal interactions may occur when parents meet with school representatives because their child's conditions and needs may be changing rapidly and they need to update the professionals. Depending on the situation, the student also may attend all or parts of these meetings.

Communication Among Community Professionals, School, and Family

- Open lines of communication among medical and community services professionals, the school, and the family ensure that all the professionals working with the student across all settings are consistent in their approach.
- Multiple, fragmented, and inconsistent interventions can significantly limit student recovery and may even create additional behavior problems.

However, students with traumatic brain injuries represent only one group with behavior problems. Many students who have health disorders, including sickle cell disease and asthma, also may display inappropriate behaviors. Some of these behaviors relate to students' discomfort or irritability resulting from their disorders. Alternatively, some inappropriate behaviors represent the frustration of students who have limited ways to communicate. As you have learned in earlier chapters, teachers need to be aware of and respond to behavior as communication, and they should address the underlying issue, not only the behavior as a symptom of the issue.

Emotional Characteristics

One characteristic of students with physical and health disabilities is poor self-esteem (e.g., Cheong, Lang, Hemphill, & Johnston, 2016; Schinkel, 2010). Students who have cerebral palsy, spina bifida, or asthma may ask why they had to be born with their condition, and they may think of themselves as being less valuable than others (e.g., LeBovidge, Lavigne, Donenberg, & Miller, 2003). Students who experience a spinal cord injury, cancer, traumatic brain injury, or another sudden-onset condition may experience a wide range of emotional problems, including anger at their situation; rejection of the support offered by families, friends, and educators; and poor images of themselves as valuable people.

Professionals working with students with physical and health disabilities may encounter a perplexing problem: It may be difficult to assess the emotional strengths and needs of students with limited abilities to communicate. As for all needs related to communication, the use of assistive technology and input sought from parents and school staff working closely with students can help ensure that this critical dimension of growth is not overlooked.

Students with physical and health impairments, as well as those with traumatic brain injury, should access the full range of school activities unless their conditions make it impossible.

Social Characteristics

Students with physical and health disabilities also frequently need interventions related to interacting with their peers (e.g., Stewart et al., 2012; van Schie et al., 2013). For some students, this need relates to explaining their conditions to peers and responding when others tease or bully them. However, for others, the need is for social skills training to learn or relearn how to communicate with their classmates. For example, a student with muscular dystrophy may need to learn how to join games or discussions with classmates within the context of his changing physical abilities. Students with traumatic brain injuries may have to learn how to interact without becoming aggressive.

Perhaps the most critical element of these students' social relationships is having access to them. Teachers and other professionals, including counselors and social workers, play a central role in facilitating interactions among students with physical and health disabilities and their peers (Harrison, 2007). These professionals may need to create opportunities for students to interact in meaningful and positive ways, to use student grouping and cooperative class activities for this purpose, and to model for students how to interact appropriately.

Physical and Medical Characteristics

Some mention must be made of the physical characteristics of students in these groups. Many students with physical and health disabilities are more knowledgeable about hospitals, medications, and emergency procedures than adults. Some must take medication during school hours, and some must monitor the foods they eat and the activities in which they participate. No single statement can be made about their physical and medical needs except to mention that this domain is the one that probably is the basis for special education eligibility. Given this, professionals working with students in these groups should learn as much as they can about each student's conditions, risks, and needs.

MyEdLab **Self-Check 13.2**

MyEdLab **Application Exercise 13.3:** Definition and Characteristics of TBI

MyEdLab **Application Exercise 13.4:** Psychological and Behavioral Characteristics

---

Identifying Physical and Health Disabilities

For students with physical and health disabilities, the decision about eligibility for special education may be made at a very early age or during the school years. A medical assessment that is completed outside the school setting usually is a primary consideration for a student in this group.

Assessment

Most of the assessment procedures for students with physical and health procedures are identical to those for other students with potential disabilities. However, their physical functioning also must be evaluated.

Assessment of Medical Condition and Physical Functioning

Each disorder or condition that was briefly described in an earlier section of this chapter usually is diagnosed by a pediatrician or pediatric specialist using many different types of procedures. For example, blood tests are used to determine whether a child has sickle cell disease, juvenile diabetes, HIV or AIDS, or cancer. A student who may have a brain tumor or traumatic brain injury is likely to have a CAT scan (i.e., a specialized, three-dimensional X-ray) or an MRI (i.e., a procedure in which magnetic field and radio signals are used to construct images of the brain). A student with a spinal cord injury, cerebral palsy, or another physical disability probably was assessed by a medical professional using a standardized instrument to determine how much the student could move and how well. School professionals who may contribute to this type of assessment include physical therapists and occupational therapists.

Assessment of Intellectual Functioning, Academic Achievement, Language, and Related Areas

You already have learned about the procedures used to assess a student's ability, achievement, language, and communication skills. These formal assessments (e.g., IQ tests, achievement tests, inventories) and informal assessments (e.g., observations of the student, interviews and checklists completed by parents and teachers, curriculum-based assessments) also are used to assess a student with an orthopedic impairment, traumatic brain injury, or other health impairment. These assessments are important because they provide information on whether the student is struggling to learn—one of the conditions that must be met in order for the student to be eligible for special education services. However, for some students, measuring cognitive capability and achievement can be difficult because of the nature of the physical disability. If a student experiences difficulty communicating and also has limited movement ability, special care has to be taken so that ability is not underestimated.

Assessment of Behavior

You also have learned about the methods for assessing student behavior, and again, these measures often are used with students with physical and health disabilities. Parents and teachers may be asked to rate a student's behaviors, and if the student has an intellectual disability, an assessment of adaptive behavior is also likely.

Eligibility

The critical question for eligibility of a student with physical or health disabilities concerns whether the student's disability has a significant negative effect on educational performance. If it does, the student is eligible for special education services, and an IEP will be prepared and services implemented. If it does not, the team considers other options. For some students in this group, including students with ADHD and physical conditions that result in limited energy but no other direct educational impact, a Section 504 plan may be sufficient. For yet other students (e.g., some students with asthma), the decision may be made that no services are warranted.

MyEdLab **Self-Check 13.3**

MyEdLab **Application Exercise 13.5:** Identifying Physical and Health Disabilities

---

Video Example

from

YouTube

MyEdLab
Video Example 13.3

As you read about these placements in the following sections, think about what the education of the young man shown in this video might have been like in the past versus what it would be like today. (https://www.youtube.com/watch?v=9wl1LeQ_yWM)

How Learners with Physical and Health Disabilities Receive Their Education

In the past, students with physical and health disabilities identified as needing special education were likely to be educated primarily in a separate classroom or school so that their medical and physical needs could be met more easily. Today, it is clear that decisions should never be made based on the disability identified; instead, decisions should be based on the team's assessment of the specific educational needs of the student. As a result, students with physical and health disabilities now appropriately access a full range of placements.

Early Childhood

Students with significant physical and health disabilities may begin to receive special education services when they are still infants, following referral for services by social workers or early interventionists assigned to work with hospital personnel. At such an early age, most services are offered in the home, with early intervention specialists, physical and occupational therapists, and other professionals as needed coordinating their efforts to work with the family. During this time and continuing through the in-home, center-based, or preschool program that a student accesses upon turning age 3, services clearly are intended to help the child, but the relationship with family members also is essential (e.g., Alsem et al., 2016; Ziviani, Feeney, & Khan, 2011). Many parents during this time are seeking information and services, trying to learn about their children's special needs, coping with possible increased medical expenses and difficulties in arranging child care, and wondering if other families have had similar experiences. Early intervention professionals can be instrumental in helping family members to locate and access the resources that they need.

Elementary and Secondary School Services

When students with physical and health disabilities reach school age, several factors determine how they receive services. The presumption of IDEA is that the general education setting is preferred, and so a primary concern is how students' needs—including the academic, physical, and behavioral domains—can be supported to ensure students' success. As shown in Figure 13.4, slightly more than half of all students with physical disabilities and health impairments are educated primarily in general education classrooms; slightly fewer students with traumatic brain injury are placed in that setting. Many students in all three groups still spend a significant amount of time in special education classrooms, in residential facilities, and at home or in hospitals.

Some students with physical and health disabilities appropriately receive services in a resource room or separate setting for part of the school day, usually because the nature of their needs requires it. For example, a student who is learning how to chew and swallow food may need privacy while learning this essential skill because it is difficult to master and involves a high degree of concentration. Practice may occur during lunch, but additional assistance may be provided in the special education setting.

In some communities, students with significant physical disabilities, often also with significant intellectual disabilities, are educated in separate classes or separate schools. Often these are students with significant intellectual disabilities as well as physical disabilities. Many reasons—some valid, some not—are given for these decisions on placement. Some professionals still believe that these students should learn daily living skills from an alternative curriculum beginning at an early age in a special education classroom. Some mention easier accessibility to nursing assistance, the availability of specialized equipment and related services personnel, and the sense of family or community. Even when students are placed in these

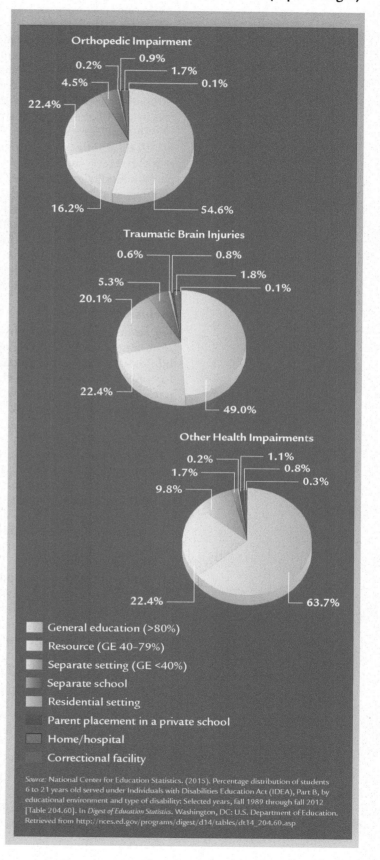

FIGURE 13.4   **Educational Placements of Students Ages 6 to 21 Who Have Physical and Health Disabilities (in percentages)**

Orthopedic Impairment

0.2%   0.9%
4.5%   1.7%
22.4%   0.1%
16.2%   54.6%

Traumatic Brain Injuries

0.6%   0.8%
5.3%   1.8%
20.1%   0.1%
22.4%   49.0%

Other Health Impairments

0.2%   1.1%
1.7%   0.8%
9.8%   0.3%
22.4%   63.7%

- General education (>80%)
- Resource (GE 40–79%)
- Separate setting (GE <40%)
- Separate school
- Residential setting
- Parent placement in a private school
- Home/hospital
- Correctional facility

Source: National Center for Education Statistics. (2015). Percentage distribution of students 6 to 21 years old served under Individuals with Disabilities Education Act (IDEA), Part B, by educational environment and type of disability: Selected years, fall 1989 through fall 2012 [Table 204.60]. In *Digest of Education Statistics*. Washington, DC: U.S. Department of Education. Retrieved from http://nces.ed.gov/programs/digest/d14/tables/dt14_204.60.asp

settings, school professionals have an obligation to ensure that these students have opportunities to participate in general education whenever possible—in core content classes, in related arts classes (e.g., music and technology), and in extracurricular activities.

However, in more and more communities, students with physical and health disabilities are placed in general education classrooms. Support is provided in a separate setting only if the team decides that a student's educational and behavioral needs cannot be met completely in the general education setting, even with extensive supports. This is the decision that was reached for Ryan, whom you met at the beginning of this chapter.

One placement option for a small number of students with physical and health disabilities is a hospital school program. This type of placement typically is reserved for students who need repeated treatments or surgeries or who miss many school days because of illness. In a small community, a hospital school program may be part of the responsibility assigned to a special education teacher. This professional serves as a liaison between the teachers at school and the student, teaching the student either in the hospital room or, if the student is at home for an extended period of time, in that location. In a larger community, a hospital school program may have several staff members—teachers and related services providers—who teach their pupils in a classroom in the hospital, in a student's hospital room, or in the student's home.

Inclusive Practices

For some students with physical and health disabilities, no discussion of inclusion is needed at all. Their special needs relate to their health or physical capabilities, and few other accommodations are needed, except perhaps the need for physical access to the classroom and instructional materials, provision of a paraprofessional to assist with personal care at certain times of the day, or flexibility because of absences. There is no reason to segregate these students from their peers.

The issue of inclusion is more likely to be raised regarding students who have significant or multiple disabilities, especially those with physical, medical, and intellectual disabilities. For these students, the team must address the same questions that have been raised in regard to other students with disabilities: What are the goals and objectives for the student within the context of the curriculum that all students follow? To what extent can appropriate supports and services be provided in the general education setting to ensure that the student progresses on IEP goals and objectives? Do any of the student's needs make education in the general education setting inappropriate (e.g., aggressive behavior or issues related to medical needs, such as unusual allergies)? One other factor to consider in making a placement decision is student voice. The Instruction in Action highlights the opinions of students and their families regarding their needs in inclusive settings. In many cases, effective use of universal design for learning, particularly through the use of technology and instructional differentiation, can make access to general education quite feasible.

Transition and Adulthood

The decisions that students with physical and health disabilities and their families face as they look toward the transition from school to postschool can be particularly complex (e.g., Osgood, Foster, & Courtney, 2010; Stumbo, Martin, & Hedrick, 2009). They must consider whether postsecondary education is the best option, address practical matters such as transportation and living arrangements, and think about career choices. They also must think about and access all the agencies that might provide support in adulthood and all the professionals who should be part of the transition-planning process for these students. What decisions might

INSTRUCTION IN **ACTION**

Students with Physical and Health Disabilities in General Education Classes

Students with physical and health disabilities and their parents report that the following supports are needed to foster student success in general education settings (Mukherjee & Lightfoot, 2000):

- *Clear information for teachers concerning the student's health and physical problems.* When such information was not provided, support varied considerably, with some teachers refusing to allow students to use the restroom as needed and others refusing to believe that a student felt ill.

- *A system for sending work home.* Students often had difficulty keeping up with assignments and other homework because of frequent absences.

- *A system for helping students catch up when they returned to school.* Students did not want to be on their own. They also asked teachers to keep in touch during long absences because this decreased the students' sense of isolation.

- *Adaptations for physical education and extracurricular opportunities (e.g., clubs).* Students wanted teachers to take seriously their desire to participate in all school activities.

- *Discussion of the condition.* Students requested that teachers check with them as to whether to discuss their medical condition with others, especially in their presence.

- *Attention to social interactions.* Students appreciated it when teachers made sure that a friend could stay with them while others completed an activity beyond their abilities.

- *Supportive climate.* Students wanted to be able to discuss with teachers their worries about their physical and health disorders and were appreciative when teachers listened and offered support.

These findings demonstrate how important it is for educators to be sensitive to student preferences and to be aware of how their own actions can either support students or interfere with their participation in instruction and school activities.

Jeffrey and his family, introduced at the beginning of the chapter, face once he graduates from high school? Think about him as you read the following sections.

Postsecondary Education

One consideration for students with physical and health disabilities concerns whether postsecondary education is the right choice (Burwell, Wessel, & Mulvihill, 2015; Stumbo, Martin, & Hedrick, 2009). For some students, this decision relates more to their academic abilities and interests than to their special needs. For others, though, factors such as stamina, the need for surgeries and other hospital procedures, resistance to illness, and other issues related to their illnesses or conditions must be considered. For these students, online learning may be a possibility. For a few students, yet another factor may be important. One young man with physical disabilities who had just completed high school made this comment: "I began school before I was 2 years old, and so I had been in school for four years before any of the other kids started. I already have more than sixteen years of education, and I need a break before I go to college—it's time for everyone else to do that other four years, but not me."

Practical Matters of Adulthood

Regardless of whether students and their families decide that a college or university is the best choice, other very practical matters sometimes have to be considered (Kraska, Zinner, & Abebe, 2007; Lindsay, 2016). For students who cannot drive, how will their transportation needs be met as they move toward adulthood? For students with significant physical limitations, what type of personal assistance will be necessary? How can it be made affordable? Living arrangements also can be a concern. Is a supported living arrangement—perhaps an apartment shared with another person with physical limitations plus an attendant—the best choice? What options are available in the local community? Financial concerns also may need to be raised. What options exist through insurance or Social Security benefits to cover medical needs such as hospitalization, medication, and equipment? What about needed assistive technology?

Many individuals with physical and health disabilities live in complete or near independence as adults. The options for achieving this independence have been enhanced tremendously by technology. The Technology Notes provides a wide range of resources to illustrate how children and adults find and use assistive technology.

Career Choice

Students with physical and health disabilities have many, many career choices, but they may need more help than other students in thinking carefully about their options. For example, a military career may not be possible for a student with sickle cell disease or severe asthma. A sales position that requires long days and extended travel may not be a choice for a student who is a recent cancer survivor. School professionals who help students make career choices should focus on students' abilities—what they *can* do. What are their strengths and interests? For students with these and intellectual disabilities, another option may be supported employment in which the individual learns job skills with careful coaching from a school professional or a coworker. You will learn more about supported employment in Chapter 14 when you read about students with severe and multiple disabilities.

TECHNOLOGY NOTES
Making the Impossible Possible

Many of the examples of instructional and assistive technology you've learned about elsewhere in this book also might be used by students with physical or health disabilities. Here is a list of additional websites that provide a wealth of information about assistive technology for these students:

- Alliance for Technology Access (ATA) (http://www.washington.edu/doit/alliance-technology-access-ata) ATA has as its mission increasing the technology use of children and adults with disabilities and other functional limitations. At its website, you can find a variety of information to help you further understand the use of assistive technology, including the following:
  - A link to a video that shows examples of assistive technology
  - Stories highlighting the successful use of technology
  - A link to sign up to receive ATA's newsletter with updates about technology and breakthrough programs and practices
- Abledata (http://www.abledata.com/) Abledata is a national database that includes detailed descriptions of more than 40,000 assistive technology products. It also has a searchable list of literature related to assistive technology. Because Abledata does not sell any products or produce any products, it offers objective information about products listed.
- Dreamms for Kids (http://www.dreamms.org/) Dreamms (Developmental Research for the Effective Advancement of Memory and Motor Skills) for Kids is a nonprofit organization dedicated to the use of assistive technology for children. The site includes a link to a clear explanation of assistive technology, many

links to information about assistive technology, and information about laws that govern the provision of assistive technology.
- Cerebral Palsy and Technology (http://www.computers-technology-cerebralpalsy.com/index.html) This website offers straightforward information and examples about technology to assist children and adults with cerebral palsy. The site is divided into sections on communication, mobility, and links to technology products and information. Within each section are descriptions, photos, and other information to explain the use of technology.

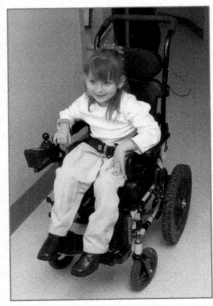

MyEdLab   **Self-Check 13.4**

MyEdLab   **Application Exercise 13.6:** Progress in General Education

MyEdLab   **Application Exercise 13.7:** Matt and Ashleigh

Recommended Educational Practices for Students with Physical and Health Disabilities

For students who have orthopedic impairment, traumatic brain injury, or other health impairments and also experience learning or intellectual disabilities, emotional or behavior disorders, or attention deficit–hyperactivity disorder, the instructional strategies that you have already learned about are appropriate. However, while you are implementing these instructional approaches, you also have to take into account two issues for these groups of students: (a) accessibility, so that they can benefit from your instruction, and (b) factors that are directly related to students' physical and health needs.

Access to Education

When typical learners and those with high-incidence disabilities come to school each day, they race or saunter through the classroom door, put their books and materials away, slip into their seats, chat with their friends, and begin their written or reading assignments. For students with physical and health disabilities, every one of these small activities may need an accommodation. That is, students in these groups usually need assistance in accessing their education (Myers, 2007). Part of this accessibility is related to physical accessibility—wheelchair ramps, elevators, wide doorways—but this type of access generally is straightforward. The access that is more challenging to accomplish, but critical, is access to instruction.

Aids for Posture and Mobility

Is there a position that you like to be in when you study? Seated at a desk with your materials around you? Sprawled on your bed? Propped up in a lounge chair? Students with physical disabilities may not be able to make choices such as these, at least not without assistance. Further, their posture and the position in which they sit or sometimes lie can have an impact on their ability to breathe as well as their comfort and their long-term health. Sometimes these students need to be physically moved into the positions that are recommended for them.

A second concern is how students move around the classroom and school. Wheelchairs have been mentioned to provide mobility for students (e.g., Wiart, 2011), but these are not the only options. Some students may have IEPs calling for instruction in mobility skills. In these cases, mobility equipment—such as gait trainers and adaptive walkers that help students maintain their balance and support their weight—are used to teach standing and walking skills (e.g., Cherng, Liu, Lau, & Hong, 2007). Yet others need braces and similar devices, collectively called orthoses, which stabilize their legs so that they can walk. You can read more about aids for posture and mobility by reading the Instruction in Action. No matter what devices are used, students must learn how to use them effectively.

Aids for Communication

Like students with communication disorders, some students with physical and health disabilities require assistance to communicate with their teachers and peers. Some use communication devices and other technology to convey their thoughts and needs. However, if students do not have the use of their hands

INSTRUCTION IN **ACTION**

Positioning, Seating, and Mobility

Students with physical and health disabilities may require special attention to positioning, seating, and mobility in order to stay healthy and learn effectively (Best, Heller, & Bigge, 2010).

Positioning

Positioning refers to keeping a student's body supported so that posture is maintained in a healthy way. For example, some students may slump over the side of the wheelchair if they are tired. Others may not be able to sit on the floor unless supported by a bolster. Yet others may need to change their position (e.g., sitting versus standing, sitting versus lying on their sides) several times during the day.

Positioning can help students to maintain muscle tone and posture, especially those whose conditions include a neurological element. For example, if Joan, who has cerebral palsy, is seated correctly in her wheelchair, it prevents her muscles from further tightening. Positioning also can help students use their upper bodies (i.e., the head, arms, hands) more effectively. If they are supported so that their bodies are stable, writing or pressing a switch will be accomplished much more easily. Finally, positioning makes the student feel safe and secure.

Seating

A student should be seated in a wheelchair with the same good posture that you probably heard about while you were growing up: pelvis in a neutral position, back straight, chin slightly tucked in. In addition, the feet need to be supported so that they are level. Foot support helps with overall body stability, and a safety factor comes into play, too.

If a student cannot hold his body in a healthy position while seated in the wheelchair, assistance is provided. Wedges may be placed around the student, a tray placed high enough so that it can be used to support the upper body, and straps or headrests may be included. If seating is not managed properly, the consequences for the student can be serious—a rounded back, sliding out of the wheelchair and risking injury, or having the head or body lean uncomfortably.

Mobility

Students with physical and health disabilities use many different types of aids for mobility. Some students will use a manual wheelchair that is lightweight and durable. However, the energy required to move such a wheelchair may be beyond a student's ability. An alternative is a wheelchair that is electric and motorized. Such a chair can be operated with a joystick or simple controls.

Some students use a walker, a rigid frame with wheels. It may be designed to provide support from the front, so that the student is pushing it. However, some walkers support from behind, helping the student to stand straight. Younger students also may use a travel stroller that is pushed by an adult. This stroller is similar to the type used for infants and toddlers but is designed with more support. Finally, some students may use a tricycle or go-cart, particularly during play periods. These mobility options help some students to participate in typical, age-appropriate activities.

---

to type or to point to pictures on a communication device, they have to look for other options. Some communication devices are made with larger sections that are edged with raised rims; for students who can touch the board but have some limitation in fine-motor control, this provides assistance in reaching and touching the correct icon or picture. Some students may not be able to use their hands at all. Such a student might wear a pointing wand attached to his head to touch items on the board. For all professionals working with students using aids to communicate, some adjustment during instruction might be needed. For example, some students may need additional time to respond to teacher questions. Others may need the teacher to ask questions that require primarily yes/no or one-word answers to facilitate communication, particularly during group instruction.

Some students communicate with multiple types of technology. Garry has cerebral palsy and epilepsy. He can speak, but he is difficult to understand. He cannot control his arms, hands, and fingers well enough to type or write. However, Garry is an above-average student. At school, he uses a communication board to talk to his classmates and teachers. He also uses voice recognition software to write papers and assignments. He uses the same software to communicate via e-mail with his cousins and grandmother who live in another state. The assistive technology that Garry is learning gives him communication access.

Aids for Learning

Whether students with physical and health disabilities learn easily or struggle, they may need special consideration related to schoolwork (e.g., Hart Barnett & Gay, 2015; van Rooijen et al., 2012). For example, some strategies accommodate student absences and fatigue. You might need to let students make up missed schoolwork without a penalty for lateness. You also might need to assist them in learning concepts and skills they missed while they were absent.

In general education classrooms, you might find that many of the instructional strategies presented throughout this text will be helpful. In addition, some students with physical and health disabilities may benefit from *curriculum overlapping.* In this approach, students participate in the same activities as typical classmates, but their goals are somewhat different. For example, as students work in cooperative groups to learn about causes of the Vietnam conflict, a student with physical and intellectual disabilities may be working toward the goal of responding to classmates when asked a question. You will learn about other approaches for fostering access to learning in Chapter 14 in the discussion of students with multiple and severe disabilities.

Another type of access to instruction may relate to assistive technology. Some students may need materials to be adapted so that they can be used. For example, the small counters being used by some students may need to be much larger for a student with limited motor control to be able to move them around. A beaker in the science class may need a handle so that the student can grasp it. Think about lessons you are likely to teach. What other accommodations might be needed to help students access learning?

Many students with the disabilities addressed in this chapter receive a range of related services (e.g., occupational and physical therapy, speech-language therapy) in addition to special education.

Related Services

Access to education for some students relates to procedures that enable them to attend school. In addition to clean intermittent catheterization, as resolved in the *Tatro* case discussed earlier in this chapter, some students may not be able to chew or swallow food and so may receive nourishment through a tube that leads directly to the stomach. The procedure, called *tube feeding,* may be carried out by a speech-language pathologist, a special education teacher, a paraprofessional, or a school nurse. Yet another student may need a constant supply of oxygen, and school professionals may need to ensure that the oxygen equipment is operating properly. Only a few students are medically fragile, and they may attend school accompanied by a nurse who can respond to medical emergencies.

Keep in mind that related services also pertain to other areas. For example, some students need specialized transportation, and this must be provided. An example is a student whose school bus must be equipped with a wheelchair lift. Other students with physical and health disabilities may need services from a speech-language pathologist, a physical therapist, an occupational therapist, or an adaptive physical educator, as did Krystle, whom you met at the beginning of the chapter. These professionals help students access education by addressing their communication needs, their large- and small-motor needs, and their needs for recreation and physical skill building, often within the context of the general education classroom.

> **Video Example**
> **from**
> **YouTube**
>
> MyEdLab
> **Video Example 13.4**
> Video Example 13.4 provides an overview of what physical therapy involves and presents snippets of therapy sessions with children. (https://www.youtube.com/watch?v=bn9Ibg7zCHw)

Factors Related to the Illness, Injury, Condition, or Disorder

The specific physical and health needs that students have also affect their access to education. Two areas for attention are school reentry and responses to crises or episodes related to students' disabilities.

School Reentry

Many students with physical and health disabilities miss a lot of school. They may be especially susceptible to illnesses and infections, they may require prolonged hospital stays, or they may have to make many trips to the doctor's office. The more school students miss, the more difficult it is for them to feel connected to their learning, their classmates, and their teachers. They often have to adjust to changes that occurred while they were absent and to their own changing physical status and emotional needs (Brier, Schwartz, & Kazak, 2015). For students with traumatic brain injuries, an additional consideration is that their personalities, behaviors, and learning abilities may have changed significantly as a result of their injuries, and school professionals and classmates should be prepared for those changes.

School reentry usually involves a representative from the medical community, school personnel who specialize in some of the services that the student may need (e.g., the related services previously explained), other members of the IEP team (e.g., an administrator, special and general educators), and the parents (Harris, 2009; Trask & Peterson, 2016). Parents often play a central role in the school reentry process. Because they are their child's best advocates, parents bring information from the medical community to school professionals and carry school information back to physicians and other medical personnel. Parents also ensure that lines of communication stay open, that any problems encountered are resolved quickly, and that their returning children are welcomed by peers and teachers. You can read more about school reentry and parent roles in the Professional Edge.

You will find that some school districts have clearly outlined procedures and checklists that are followed for school reentry. Others manage this process on a case-by-case basis. As a school professional, your responsibility is to make the contributions that you can, depending on your role, and to help the parents and student make the transition as smoothly as possible (Moore, Kaffenberger, Oh, Goldberg, & Hudspeth, 2009; Trask & Peterson, 2016).

Responding to Emergencies

Students with physical and health disabilities sometimes experience crises, episodes, and emergencies at school, and school professionals need to know how to respond. Using universal precautions and responding to student seizures (both explained earlier in this chapter) are two examples of responses that are well prescribed and should be in place in every school. In addition, parents can provide additional information about their children and answer questions you may have. However, you also should check with a school district representative. Some districts have policies about how teachers and other school professionals are to respond to certain situations, and you should be aware of and follow those policies.

Professionals who work with students with physical and health disabilities also should think about the possibility of a student death. What might you need to do to help your other students and colleagues cope with a classmate's death? How might you respond, and what assistance might you need for your students and yourself? These are topics addressed in the Professional Edge.

MyEdLab **Self-Check 13.5**

MyEdLab **Application Exercise 13.8:** PDAs

MyEdLab **Application Exercise 13.9:** Adaptive Devices

MyEdLab **Application Exercise 13.10:** Recommended Educational Practices

PROFESSIONAL EDGE

Returning to School

When a student is returning to school after a traumatic brain injury, professionals, health care providers, and family members should work together to ease what sometimes can be a challenging transition.

Collaboration Model

1. With parent permission, the hospital notifies a designated school district representative (e.g., special education director, special education teacher) about a student's status and upcoming discharge; this individual coordinates the student's return.
2. Medical and school professionals meet with family members to discuss needed supports and, in many cases, prepare an IEP.
3. The hospital sends the school representative relevant reports immediately upon the student's discharge.
4. The student returns to school immediately after discharge, possibly with a plan in place for the transition (e.g., a shortened school day at first).

Peer Education

1. If parents agree, a representative from the hospital or school district may visit a student's class(es) to directly address possible misunderstandings and rumors. Such a visit is completed before the student returns.
2. Information shared could include a developmentally appropriate explanation of what happened to the student, a video of the student greeting classmates from the hospital, a demonstration of specialized equipment the student will use, and suggestions on how classmates can assist and support the student.

General Classroom Strategies

1. Be sure that the expectations you set for the student are appropriate for the student's current level of functioning. Be clear about those expectations with the student, classmates, and family members.
2. Emphasize the positive (e.g., what the student does appropriately) rather than the negative (e.g., behavior issues). Be constructive and specific when redirecting the student by explaining what you want the student to do.
3. Frequently monitor the student's level of understanding and adjust assignments, communication, and other instructional elements as needed.
4. Be prepared for and accept inconsistencies in the student's academic, behavioral, social, and emotional levels of performance.
5. Communicate frequently with parents.
6. Provide accommodations specific to the student, based on identified and possibly changing needs, including those related to schedule (e.g., ensuring that there are clear routines), the instructional environment (e.g., reducing distractions), organization (e.g., giving detailed directions for assignments, possibly in oral, pictorial, and written form), curriculum and testing (e.g., adjusting homework amount and grading scale; changing testing format), behavior (e.g., avoiding overcorrecting and power struggles), and general support (e.g., providing a second set of textbooks to be kept at home; facilitating peer interactions).

Source: Gilette Children's Specialty Healthcare. (2007). *Returning to school after a traumatic brain injury: A guide for teachers.* St. Paul, MN: Author. Retrieved from http://www.gillettechildrens.org/fileUpload%5CReturning%20to%20School %20After%20a%20Traumatic%20Brain%20Injury.pdf. Wehman, P., & Targett, P. (2010). *Returning to school after traumatic brain injury.* Washington, DC: Model Systems Knowledge Translation Center, National Institute on Disability, Independent Living, and Rehabilitation Research. Retrieved from http://www.msktc.org/lib/docs/Factsheets/TBI_School_after_TBI.pdf

Perspectives of Parents and Families

Parents of children with physical and health disabilities usually have become experts on their children's special needs. They often have spent hours, days, and weeks beside their children's hospital beds; they have rushed their children to emergency rooms; and they have taken notes, visited websites, read books, attended support groups, and otherwise educated themselves about their children's conditions and their rights.

Parent Experiences

When parents find out that their child has a potentially life-threatening condition, a life-changing chronic disorder, or a serious injury, they first deal with the immediate

Some children come to school with life-threatening conditions; others experience sudden illnesses or accidents. Educators know intellectually that sometimes students die, but few consider this sad topic in terms of how to react.

Helping Students

When a classmate dies, students may express their feelings in many ways, including anger, withdrawal, aggression, anxiety, fear, guilt, or physical symptoms. Here are a few suggestions for helping students cope with the death of a classmate:

- Be honest in explaining to students what happened, keeping in mind their developmental stages and ability to understand. Sometimes, especially for younger students, it might be better to say that "Joe was very sick and the doctors could not make him better" than to discuss abstract concepts about death.
- Understand that students may express grief in many different ways and for different lengths of time. Some students may joke about death; that is sometimes their means of coping with something difficult to understand. Some students may be very sad or angry for a brief time, then seem to have recovered, and then show symptoms of grief again. Such a cycle may be repeated a number of times.
- Find a way for students to express their grief and their thoughts about their classmate. Students may wish to draw what they're thinking. They may want to make cards to give to the classmate's family, and they may

wish to talk about their classmate. Teachers should create a safe environment for these activities.
- Students also may have questions and misunderstandings about the classmate's death. These should be addressed in a straightforward way.
- A school counselor may be able to assist in helping you respond to classmates' grief.
- Keep in touch with parents, alerting them to the classmate's death and communicating with them about your plan for helping their child through this difficult experience.

Helping Yourself

Teachers need to grieve, too. Here are some considerations for you:

- Acknowledge that your grief will not likely follow precise stages or last for only a specified period of time.
- Learn about the tasks of grieving—understanding, grieving, commemorating—that are occurring.
- Use experiences with loss—not just death—to know what you need.
- Develop rituals to say goodbye to the student, such as creating a memory book.
- Ask colleagues for assistance.
- Be aware of your personal signs of stress; don't ignore them.
- Give yourself time and permission to grieve.
- Create a period for rest and renewal.

Source: From Munson, L. J., & Hunt, N. (2005). Teachers grieve! What can we do for our colleagues and ourselves when a student dies? *Teaching Exceptional Children, 37*(4), 48–51. Reproduced with permission of Council for Exceptional Children via Copyright Clearance Center.

Video Example
from
YouTube

▶ MyEdLab
Video Example 13.5
The impact of TBI on children and their parents is captured in this video. (https://www.youtube.com/watch?v=lBOo2a2BWMI)

matter at hand—survival. This is a stressful time (Huang, Kellett, & St John, 2010). Parents in this situation have reported that they focus on getting the care that is needed, making it through one day at a time, and not thinking too much about the future (Crow, Kohler, Cooper, & Atkins, 2010; Darcy, Knutsson, Huus, & Enskar, 2014).

As their child's condition stabilizes and the prognosis is clear—and perhaps as they also become accustomed to the procedures and routines of having a child with a physical or health disability—the parents' attention often turns toward educating themselves and beginning to advocate for their child (Kennedy, 2011; Popp, Conway, & Pantaleao, 2015). They also may question why their family was given this challenge. As time goes by, and depending on the severity of the disability, they may begin to explore education and career options for their child and perhaps even advocate on behalf of all families whose children have similar conditions. Of course, these reactions and families' specific actions and priorities may be heavily influenced by culture and education.

Siblings also may be affected by a brother or sister with a physical or health disability (e.g., Zegaczewski, Chang, Coddington, & Berg, 2016). Although research does not indicate that siblings perceive the other child as a stressor, at times the child with special needs requires full parental attention, which means time is taken away from the other children (Kao, Romero-Bosch, Plante, & Lobato, 2012). Siblings also may not understand why the illness or condition occurred, and they may imagine that they are to blame or that the disorder is contagious when, in fact, it is not. Interestingly, siblings usually recognize the positive effects of having a brother or sister with a disability as well as the challenges.

Advice to School Professionals

Lee and Guck (2000) offer extensive advice to professionals working with the families of children with physical and health disabilities. Among their suggestions are these:

- Help parents to develop an optimistic but realistic view of their child's illness.
- Encourage parents to maintain involvement with relatives and neighbors as well as immediate family.
- Help parents to ask questions of and continue communication with medical personnel.
- Know helpful materials that parents can access related to their child's condition.
- Ensure that the child's return to school is based on a comprehensive plan that is closely monitored. (p. 272)

MyEdLab **Self-Check 13.6**

MyEdLab **Application Exercise 13.11:** Abigail's Parents

Trends and Issues Affecting the Fields of Orthopedic Impairments, Traumatic Brain Injury, and Other Health Impairments

Advances in medical and computer technology have had a far-reaching impact on the field of physical and health disabilities. However, these developments also have raised questions: How prepared are teachers to work with students with physical and health disabilities? How available is technology to students who are not affluent?

Professionals Prepared to Work with Students with Physical Disabilities

Both general education teachers and special education teachers have expressed concern about their preparation to adequately teach students with physical disabilities. Heller and Swinehart-Jones (2003) are particularly concerned about the latter group of teachers because they often have the responsibility of providing information to the former group. Professionals need to understand students' functional limitations in several areas (e.g., motor, health), related psychosocial and environmental factors (e.g., motivation, social competence), and the details of students' physical impairments (e.g., neurological) (Ruppar, Roberts, & Olson, 2015). They likewise need expertise in these six domains: (a) physical and health monitoring, (b) adapted assessment, (c) modifications and assistive technology, (d) specialized instruction, (e) disability-specific curricula, and (f) ensuring an affective and learning environment. Teacher educators acknowledge that ongoing professional development is needed in order for these special educators to acquire and maintain the many skills required for them to effectively address their students' needs (Brown, Stephenson, & Carter, 2014).

Access to Technology

Technology of all sorts—including the examples you have read about in this chapter and the high- and low-technology examples from other chapters—significantly enhances the lives of individuals with physical and health disabilities. In some cases, technology is essential for enabling these individuals to learn effectively in school and to live independently as adults (e.g., Coleman & Cramer, 2015; Van Laarhoven, & Conderman, 2011). However, have you ever stopped to ask yourself who has access to technology such as computers and specialized devices and how these items are funded?

Part of the answer lies in the provisions of IDEA—the law requires that assistive technology for education be provided when needed. However, most professionals believe that many students and adults lack access to all the technologies they need (Abbott, Brown, Evett, & Standen, 2014; Coleman, 2011). Two groups that are not necessarily distinct from one another illustrate the problem: students who live in rural areas and those who live in poverty. Students who live in rural areas may have less access to computers, few options for transportation, an increased likelihood of being served by personnel who are not fully qualified (and who may lack skills for obtaining technology), and more barriers for mobility (e.g., lack of sidewalks, absence of curb cuts). Students who live in poverty,

DATA-DRIVEN DECISIONS

How Assistive Technology Decisions Are Made

Each student who uses assistive technology is unique, and there are thousands and thousands of technology options that could be selected to address specific needs. How do professionals and parents ensure that students access effective assistive technology? The process is heavily data driven, and includes these general steps:

1. *Identify what the problem is.* What is it that the student needs to do and cannot and that cannot be addressed through other strategies? Write? Communicate with others? Grasp small items such as scissors? Use the computer?
2. *Gather data regarding current functioning.* Teachers, related services professionals, parents, and the student often contribute information about the student's needs across a variety of settings, including the classroom, the home environment, and others. Data may be gathered through observation, review of existing information (e.g., on the IEP), or interviews.
3. *Generate possible solutions.* Often drawing on the expertise of an assistive technology (AT) specialist, the team brainstorms about devices and other tools that could address the student's need. Once a list is created, team members weigh the advantages and disadvantages of each option (Does it adequately

address the need? Will the student use it? What is the cost?).
4. *Complete a technology tryout.* Prior to a long-term decision and depending on the AT selected, a student may borrow a device from the school district or another agency to see if it addresses the identified needs and if it is one the student can readily use, functions reliably, and is acceptable to the student and family. During this phase, several devices may be used, and data are gathered about the effectiveness of each.
5. *Make a long-term technology decision.* Based on data gathered during the tryout phase, the desired AT is provided to the student and a plan is made regarding its use (including maintenance and a time line for reevaluation). Of course, such information is captured on the IEP for students served through IDEA.

If you would like to learn more about the process for selecting AT for students with disabilities, you might want to visit the website of the Wisconsin Assistive Technology Initiative (WATI) and review their publication *Assessing Students' Needs for Assistive Technology* (ASNAT) (http://www.wati.org/content/supports/free/pdf/ASNAT5thEditionJun09.pdf).

whether in rural, suburban, or urban areas, may encounter many similar barriers, and they may not even be aware of some of the technology options that exist (e.g., Berliner, 2009).

Access to technology is an ethical dilemma that school professionals face every day, even when professionals use a process such as the one described in Data-Driven Decisions to determine what technology a student should access. Other factors also influence decisions. For example, IDEA may fund a communication board that a student uses at school but may not fund a similar device for home. In some communities, extraordinary justification is required before technology can be accessed because, even if mandated by law, it takes resources from other programs and services. When technology involves an item that is tailored to a student's needs (e.g., a motorized wheelchair), consideration has to be given to replacement cost when the item no longer fits, and money has to be set aside for repairs. As an educator, you may find yourself participating in discussions of this important topic.

MyEdLab **Self-Check 13.7**

MyEdLab **Application Exercise 13.12:** Trends and Issues Affecting the Field of Physical and Health Disabilities

---

Summary

LO13.1 Individuals with physical and health disabilities have been known throughout history, but their treatment has been based on changing beliefs, from pessimism and isolation to optimism and opportunity. Students receiving special education because of physical or health disabilities include those with physical disabilities, called *orthopedic impairments* in IDEA (e.g., students with cerebral palsy, spina bifida, spinal cord injuries, muscular dystrophy, arthritis); those with *traumatic brain injuries*; and those with *other health impairments* (e.g., students with asthma, epilepsy, HIV or AIDS, cancer, sickle cell disease, diabetes).

LO13.2 Students with physical and health disabilities vary tremendously in cognitive ability, social and emotional needs, and behavior. What they have in common are medical or physical needs that may affect all other areas of their education.

LO13.3 Many students with physical and health disabilities are identified before they reach school age. Identification includes assessment of all critical areas, including information about any medical or health conditions.

LO13.4 Students with physical and health disorders receive their education based on the decisions made for them by the team preparing the IEP. They often receive early intervention, and in elementary and secondary schools they may spend little time in a separate setting or nearly all their time there. Inclusive practices apply to these students as to all others receiving special education. As students transition to adulthood, they often need assistance in considering postsecondary education, dealing with practical matters such as transportation, and selecting careers.

LO13.5 Recommended educational practices for these students include ensuring access through aids for mobility and posture, communication, and learning as well as addressing highly specialized needs such as school reentry and responses to emergencies.

LO13.6 The parents and families of students with physical and health disabilities often have dealt with medical and health crises, and they may have questions and concerns regarding access to services, the financial stress of having a child with physical or health needs, and options for their child's future.

LO13.7 Trends and issues facing the field of physical and health disabilities include ensuring that teachers preparing to teach students with physical and health disabilities have adequate knowledge and skills and the rapidly evolving options of technology and their availability to students.

Back to the Cases

Now that you've read about physical disabilities and other health impairments, look back at the student stories at the beginning of this chapter. Then, answer the questions about each of their cases.

MyEdLab **Case Study 13.1**

RYAN. Ryan probably faces a challenging school year as he enters first grade and continues treatment for leukemia. As Ryan's mother has become more knowledgeable about his disorder and the course of treatment that he will need, she has begun to worry. She is concerned that Ryan will get further and further behind academically, to the point that he will never catch up. Therefore, she has gone to the school and asked for Ryan to spend half of each school day in the special education classroom. She agrees that inclusion is a good idea, but for her son she believes that the small, structured environment and one-to-one or small-group specialized instruction possible in the special education classroom is the best option. As you reflect upon the best educational environment for Ryan, imagine you are part of the team determining how to best serve Ryan's needs.

MyEdLab **Case Study 13.2**

KRYSTLE. You will be attending Krystle's IEP meeting, and you've already been alerted that many different opinions exist among members of the IEP team on priorities for Krystle's education for the upcoming year. Some members are most concerned about Krystle's academic achievement and the fact that she seems to be falling further behind with each passing day, despite intensive reading instruction in the special education classroom. Others are voicing grave concern about Krystle's mental health and social functioning, emphasizing that unless she becomes comfortable with her strengths, challenges, and self-identity, she is unlikely to accelerate her learning rate.

MyEdLab **Case Study 13.3**

JEFFREY. Jeffrey is adjusting to many life changes. He wants to keep a positive attitude, but sometimes he is overwhelmed by the challenges he faces. Think about the impact of Jeffrey's injury on his academic achievement, social interactions, behavior, and outlook for the future.

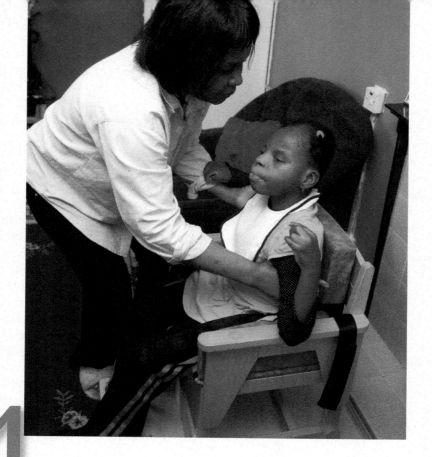

14

Students with Severe and Multiple Disabilities

ISABELLA

Isabella's parents had so looked forward to her birth; they had tried unsuccessfully for several years to have a child. However, when Isabella was born, life immediately got a little more complicated than they had prepared for. Isabella had a rare condition, completely undetected prenatally, called *occipital encephalocele*, a gap in her skull through which protruded a small sac filled with brain tissue. She was airlifted to a children's hospital and underwent, at just 3 days old, her first surgery. For the first three years of her life, Isabella spent many months in the hospital because of her special needs. She has a seizure disorder, a moderate intellectual disability, microcephaly (a significantly smaller than average head circumference), mild cerebral palsy, and low vision, and she is susceptible to respiratory infections. She began receiving special education services when she was 6 months old, and now she is completing her kindergarten year at Meadowbrook Elementary. She receives about half of her instruction in a special education classroom, where she is learning pre-literacy and early math skills, but for the remainder of the day, she participates in the kindergarten class, accompanied by a one-to-one paraprofessional. Isabella knows simple sign language, uses a communication device, and just recently accomplished potty training. She loves music and will complete almost any task in order to hear a few minutes of her favorite tunes. She has made it clear that she wants pierced ears like several of her classmates, and she imitates the behavior—good and not so good— of her friends in general education. She recently was part of a school music program, and, surrounded by her typical peers, she "played" the musical triangle, including a solo. Isabella's dad leaned over to the parent next to him, a complete stranger, and whispered, "That's my daughter. I'm so very proud of her."

JACKSON

Jackson is 14 years old and a seventh-grade student whose list of special needs is lengthy. He has a severe intellectual disability and is nonverbal. He also has seizures and a hearing loss, and he displays characteristics of autism (e.g., stereotypic behaviors). In elementary school, Jackson spent about half his school day in general education, but this year he is being educated mostly in a special education classroom with typical peer helpers working with him. This change was made with reluctance but out of necessity: Jackson has grown rapidly and is very strong, and when upset or overwhelmed, which is much more likely to happen in the general education classroom than special education setting, it can be challenging to keep him and his classmates safe. The special education classroom has a teacher and several assistants, and carefully structured procedures and activities can much more readily be arranged there. He

does participate in a music class, a favorite subject, with peers. Jackson's individualized education program (IEP) goals include indicating his preference when given a choice between two activities, using his communication device, moving independently between the special education classroom and the cafeteria, recognizing his name in printed form, and following one-step directions. The goals are designed to help him become more independent and to prepare him for eventual employment, though that is likely to be in a supported environment. Jackson's mother, Ms. Scanlan, notes that one of her greatest joys is when Jackson laughs; she says it is music. She also notes that raising Jackson has been challenging but rewarding. Her husband left when Jackson was just 2 years old, and it has taken the support of family, friends, and paid assistants to keep Jackson at home. Ms. Scanlan comments that she believes Jackson's purpose on earth is to help others learn to be tolerant, but she worries that she may soon need to consider placing Jackson in a residential facility because of his size, strength, and increasingly aggressive behavior. For now, though, she focuses on his love of *I Love Lucy* episodes and the love his two siblings clearly have for him.

CASSIE

Cassie is 16 years old. She has long blond hair that she likes to streak with purple. Like many girls her age, Cassie enjoys spending time with boys and actively seeks their attention by sitting next to them in class. She also likes to shop, watch music videos (especially those with a lot of visual effects and dancing), and take pictures of herself and others. She wants a job that involves photography when she graduates from high school. Cassie is a junior and participates in assemblies and other school events. Cassie also has severe and multiple disabilities. She has cerebral palsy that primarily affects her lower body, making it difficult for her to walk. She uses a wheelchair to get from one class to another and sometimes relies on a walker. For example, in her art class, Cassie uses her walker while working so that she can more easily reach and use her materials. Cassie also has a significant hearing loss. She relies on her vision to keep aware of what is going on around her. Because of Cassie's severe cognitive delay, she needs accommodations to facilitate learning. For example, during her Spanish class, students are learning new vocabulary and how to speak, read, and write those words in sentences. Cassie works with a peer buddy in class to learn pictorial vocabulary in English that her peer then translates into Spanish and uses in sentences. Because Cassie does not speak, she communicates through alternative means. She sometimes gestures, she knows several signs, and she also uses a picture board, pointing to pictures to communicate (e.g., a photo of a glass of water to indicate that she wants a drink).

Students with severe and multiple disabilities are children who, despite the complexity of their special needs, are quite capable of learning and want to be as much like their peers without disabilities as possible. Most of these students struggle to communicate to make their needs and thoughts known and find learning abstract material quite difficult. However, given the right amount and types of supports, these students can acquire important skills that will greatly improve their daily lives and interactions with others.

Keep in mind that the characteristics and needs of the students described overlap somewhat with those of students discussed in earlier chapters; you will notice references to those students as you read. This chapter considers students who have severe or profound intellectual disabilities, those who are both deaf and blind, and those who have two or more disabilities, usually from among these categories: autism, intellectual disability, communication disorders, vision or hearing loss, physical disabilities, traumatic brain injury, or other health impairments.

Understanding Severe or Multiple Disabilities

Many misconceptions exist concerning students with severe and multiple disabilities. This is due in large part to the small number of these students and to the fact that, until relatively recently, they generally did not attend neighborhood schools.

Development of the Field of Severe and Multiple Disabilities

Many of the historical developments in the field of severe and multiple disabilities have paralleled those in other disability areas. For example, you learned that during the 19th century, children with intellectual disabilities or hearing loss often were institutionalized. The same was true for children with multiple or severe disabilities. The focus of these early institutions was education and rehabilitation, but by the late 1800s, the goal changed from education to custodial care (Gardner, 1993). This trend continued until the mid-1900s, when families and professionals in the field began to advocate for the closure of institutions. Today, the vast majority of individuals with severe and multiple disabilities do not live in institutions but rather in supportive small-group homes or with their families (Mansell & Beadle-Brown, 2010). These and other key events in the history of severe and multiple disabilities are summarized in Figure 14.1.

It is important to remember that many children who thrive today because of advanced medical technology might not have survived to school age during the first half of the 20th century. During that time, many children with severe disabilities were simply kept at home by their families; they learned basic life skills by helping out at home and relying on those around them to teach and support them. However, outside support for children with severe disabilities was beginning to emerge. For example, the National Society for Crippled Children (now Easter Seals) was established in 1919, and private schools gradually became available for children with significant disabilities in some parts of the United States. Public schools, however, did not offer education to these students.

A Changing Climate and Advocacy

Landmark decisions during the late 1960s and early 1970s paved the way for the federal special education laws that now assure all students the right to education, regardless of the severity or complexity of their disabilities. Initially, students with severe and multiple types of disabilities were placed in special schools and educated apart from their peers, but increasingly they are receiving educational services in general education schools and classrooms. For example, in fall 1990, just 6.6% of students with multiple disabilities were educated primarily in general

Did You Know?

Disability Is Natural (https://www.disabilityisnatural.com) is a user-friendly website that provides a contemporary way of thinking about individuals with significant disabilities. Think especially about the apple analogy on its home page.

Did You Know?

One of the most famous individuals with multiple disabilities was Helen Keller (1880–1968). Both deaf and blind, she was taught by Anne Sullivan and became the first deaf–blind individual to earn a bachelor of arts degree. Keller was a world traveler, political activist, lecturer, and author of 12 books.

FIGURE 14.1 **Time Line of the Development of the Severe and Multiple Disabilities Field**

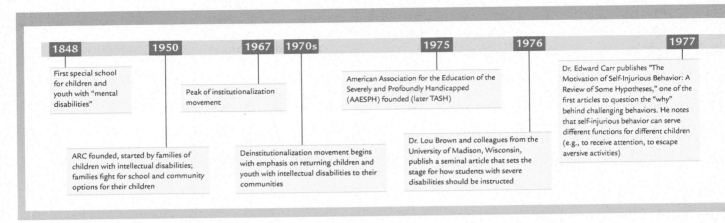

education, but by fall 2012, this percentage had risen to 12.9% (U.S. Department of Education, 1993, 2015).

In 1975, a small group of professionals and advocates formed the American Association for the Education of the Severely and Profoundly Handicapped (AAESPH), an organization whose purpose was to draw national attention to the status of individuals having severe and profound disabilities. In 1980, it was renamed The Association for the Severely Handicapped, or TASH, and today, to reflect the wishes of those it represents, the acronym *TASH* is used as the name of the organization. References to *severe* and *handicaps* have been dropped. TASH (http://tash.org) continues to represent the interests of those with the most challenging disabilities and leads the field in advocating for full rights, inclusion, and empowerment of this group of individuals.

Definitions of Severe and Multiple Disabilities

Students with severe disabilities quite simply are, first and foremost, students. Although they may have a wide range of significant special needs, their disabilities do not prevent them from having most of the same desires as others their age. These students' similarities with their peers should be emphasized and considered well before the focus is shifted to their disabilities and the descriptors that are attached to them. For example, Isabella may have several severe disabilities that interfere with her learning, but instead of focusing on these challenges, emphasis shifts to her love of music and its motivating potential to help her achieve. However, in order to be eligible to receive special education services, these students must, like all other students with disabilities, meet specific eligibility criteria as specified in the Individuals with Disabilities Education Act (IDEA).

Federal Definitions

Students with severe and multiple disabilities are described in several categories in IDEA; no single category exists that is labeled *severe and multiple disabilities*. First, this group includes students with severe and profound intellectual disabilities, terms introduced in Chapter 8 and for which no separate federal definition or category exists.

Second, this group comprises students who are both deaf and blind. In IDEA, these students are given a separate category because of the extraordinary nature of their needs, and this category is defined as follows:

> Deaf-blindness means concomitant hearing and visual impairments, the combination of which causes such severe communication and other developmental

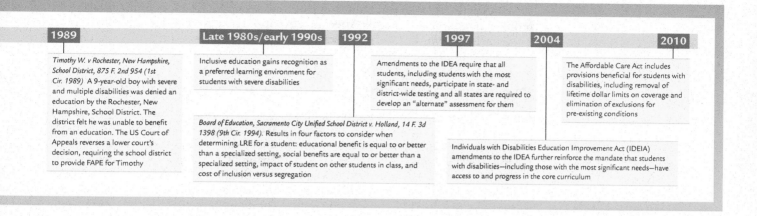

1989

Timothy W. v Rochester, New Hampshire, School District, 875 F. 2nd 954 (1st Cir. 1989) A 9-year-old boy with severe and multiple disabilities was denied an education by the Rochester, New Hampshire, School District. The district felt he was unable to benefit from an education. The US Court of Appeals reverses a lower court's decision, requiring the school district to provide FAPE for Timothy

Late 1980s/early 1990s

Inclusive education gains recognition as a preferred learning environment for students with severe disabilities

Board of Education, Sacramento City Unified School District v. Holland, 14 F. 3d 1398 (9th Cir. 1994). Results in four factors to consider when determining LRE for a student: educational benefit is equal to or better than a specialized setting, social benefits are equal to or better than a specialized setting, impact of student on other students in class, and cost of inclusion versus segregation

1992

1997

Amendments to the IDEA require that all students, including students with the most significant needs, participate in state- and district-wide testing and all states are required to develop an "alternate" assessment for them

Individuals with Disabilities Education Improvement Act (IDEIA) amendments to the IDEA further reinforce the mandate that students with disabilities—including those with the most significant needs—have access to and progress in the core curriculum

2004

2010

The Affordable Care Act includes provisions beneficial for students with disabilities, including removal of lifetime dollar limits on coverage and elimination of exclusions for pre-existing conditions

and educational needs that they cannot be accommodated in special education programs solely for children with deafness or children with blindness. (IDEA 20 U.S.C. §1401 [2004], 20 C.F.R. §300.8[c][2])

A third group of students is also included in this chapter. They have multiple disabilities, defined in IDEA as follows:

> Multiple disabilities means concomitant impairments (such as intellectual impairment-blindness, intellectual impairment-orthopedic impairment, etc.), the combination of which causes such severe educational needs that they cannot be accommodated in special education programs solely for one of the impairments. The term does not include deaf-blindness. (IDEA 20 U.S.C. §1401 [2004], 20 C.F.R. §300.8[c][7])

These disability definitions are consistent with the others included in IDEA. They stress the impairments that students have, and they emphasize that the disabilities must have a negative educational effect for students to receive services.

TASH Definition

Many professionals find the definitions provided in IDEA inadequate. These definitions tend to focus on deficits and lead professionals to emphasize students' challenges. This in turn can lead to negative portrayals of these students as individuals with severe and multiple disabilities who have limited skills and abilities, and therefore, as people who cannot learn. These views are inaccurate and serve to further perpetuate harmful and nonconstructive stereotypes (McDonnell, Hardman, & McDonnell, 2003). As you can see from reading about Cassie in the beginning of the chapter, such an approach would be quite limiting. Cassie's biography demonstrates that she has interests, strengths, and desires, in addition to special needs. The point is this: Students with significant disabilities can and do learn many skills (e.g., Browder et al., 2012; Westling, Salzberg Collins, Morgan, & Knight, 2014). Consistent with this change in emphasis, TASH defines persons with severe disabilities as

> individuals with disabilities of all ages, races, creeds, national origins, genders and sexual orientation who require ongoing support in one or more major life activities in order to participate in an integrated community and enjoy a quality of life similar to that available to all citizens. Support may be required for life activities such as mobility, communication, self-care, and learning as necessary for community living, employment, and self-sufficiency. (TASH, 2000)

This definition emphasizes that persons with severe disabilities can represent all types of individuals from all walks of life. For the purpose of this chapter, students with severe and multiple disabilities are defined as individuals who require ongoing and highly specialized support to participate fully in typical home, school, work, and community activities, regardless of the specific disability label(s) applied to them.

Prevalence of Students with Severe and Multiple Disabilities

The population of students having severe and multiple disabilities represents a low-incidence category constituting approximately 0.1% to 1% of the general school-age population and approximately 2% of the total population of students having special education needs (U.S. Department of Education, 2015). Consequently, based on natural proportion, it is not likely that more than one student with severe and multiple disabilities would be enrolled in any given general education classroom. Although relatively few students have this identification, their needs are significant, and they may require substantial supports and services to benefit from their special education programs.

Causes of Severe and Multiple Disabilities

Several causes of severe and multiple disabilities are known. These known causes can be divided into three categories, determined primarily by when they occur. Some disabilities originate prenatally, some occur perinatally, and some happen postnatally (Bilder et al., 2013). The causes of severe and multiple disabilities are similar to those for intellectual impairment, as discussed in Chapter 8. In case you need to review these causes, they are summarized in Figure 14.2. Keep in mind, though, that in many cases, a specific cause for the disabilities is not known.

The severity and complexity of the resulting disability varies depending on the genetic abnormality, the amount of actual damage done to the brain, and the cultural and physical environments in which the child is raised. In general, the more severe the genetic abnormality or the more pervasive the damage to neural

FIGURE 14.2   **Causes of Severe and Multiple Disabilities**

Many of the causes of severe and multiple disabilities, summarized below, are similar to those you learned about in Chapter 8 for intellectual impairment. Often, a specific cause for the disability cannot be identified.

Prenatal (before birth)	Perinatal (during birth)	Postnatal (after birth)
Chromosomal abnormalities	Lack of oxygen supply to the baby's brain (e.g., prolonged labor, disconnect of umbilical cord, cord wrapped around child's neck)	Infections (e.g., meningitis, encephalitis)
Viral infections (e.g., rubella, German measles)		Traumatic brain injury (e.g., fall, car accident, near-drowning, child abuse)
Drug/alcohol intake, especially during early months of pregnancy	Physical injury to the brain during birth	Lead poisoning
Malnutrition	Contracted infections during birth (e.g., syphilis)	Reaction to medication
Physical trauma to the mother		Environmental conditions (e.g., exposure to toxins)

Source: U.S. Department of Education. (1993). *Fifteenth annual report to Congress on the implementation of the Individuals with Disabilities Education Act.* U.S. Department of Education. (2003).

cells in the brain, the more severe the impact will be. However, a supportive environment that includes expectations for the child to learn can have a positive impact on overall development. Children who are not developing normally or whose normal development has been interrupted by an accident or a viral or bacterial infection typically struggle to learn incidentally (i.e., through observation) and require more direct intervention to understand their world. Some families are able to provide the needed stimulation and structured guidance to help their children acquire information, but others are not able to offer this type of assistance. As a result, two children with the exact same diagnosis may appear quite different in skill level and behavior.

Labels and Their Limitations

Labels are very common in special education and are used to categorize groups of students who presumably share a set of characteristics. The medical profes-

sional also labels conditions children have as a means of efficiently communicating about the disability, as was true for Isabella, whom you met at the beginning of the chapter. However, labels are rarely informative when it comes to determining educational intervention. The phrase *severe and multiple disabilities*, although convenient to use for collectively discussing students with significant special needs, does not provide a meaningful description of particular students. The same problem exists when a student is referred to as intellectually disabled, or any other categorical label, or when the student is described on the basis of a medical diagnosis.

Labels do not explain the most important aspects of a student. They do not help a teacher or an educational team determine the most effective ways to communicate with a student or how best to help a student learn; nor do they describe the individual strengths and goals of a student. Labels oversimplify the complexity of individual students and detract from viewing them as complete individuals, with likes and dislikes (Guon, Wilfond, Farlow, Brazg, & Janvier, 2014; Polloway, Smith, & Patton, 2015).

If you look past labels and limitations, you find that students with severe and multiple disabilities are mostly like other students—individuals who have much to offer.

MyEdLab **Self-Check 14.1**

MyEdLab **Application Exercise 14.1**: Multiple Disabilities and Deaf-Blindness

---

Characteristics of Individuals with Severe and Multiple Disabilities

Understanding the characteristics of students with severe and multiple disabilities is important. First, exploring their characteristics can highlight ways in which you can work effectively with students. In addition, by thinking about these students' characteristics, you can see how they are in many ways similar to students who have milder disabilities and students who are typical learners.

Video Example
from
YouTube

MyEdLab
Video Example 14.1

As you read the information that follows, think about the students in this video and how they illustrate—or not—the characteristics discussed. (https://www.youtube.com/watch?v=6FTESY7VApo)

Cognitive Characteristics

When students with severe and multiple disabilities are tested using typical standardized assessments such as intelligence quotient (IQ) tests, they typically will score within the severe or profound range of cognitive delay due to the heavy emphasis on verbal skills and the unfamiliar and out-of-context environment. While IQ scores in the range of 85 to 115 are considered average and characterize more than two-thirds of all students, IQ scores for students with severe and multiple disabilities tend to fall within the following ranges: 25 to 40 for students with severe intellectual disabilities and 0 to 25 for those with profound levels of intellectual disabilities (Grossman, 1983). While testing of this sort is usually done to provide evidence for eligibility to receive special education services, these assessments are not particularly helpful in determining who the student is, what skills are most critical to teach, or how best to provide instruction. Additional assessment information is needed. For example, some students may not be able to respond to a question about a complex concept such as death or dying, but they can identify a picture of dead plants among pictures of live ones because of a particular interest in this area. That is, additional effort must be taken to tap into these students' creativity and understanding.

Educational Implications

Because these students experience significant cognitive limitations, they need more time to learn new things and many opportunities to practice new skills. For example, John is learning to point to pictures to communicate interests and preferences, as well as to demonstrate knowledge. The more opportunities throughout the day in which John can use pictures to communicate these needs, the more quickly he is likely to learn this skill. In this example, John is learning more than just communication skills: He is learning a *strategy* of using pictures to communicate. An advantage of teaching strategies is that the student can use this skill to communicate a variety of things (e.g., interests, preferences, knowledge, joy, frustration, agreement, disagreement). Further, because communication is needed continuously throughout the day, numerous opportunities arise for practice. Another example of teaching a larger strategy is teaching students to follow step-by-step pictorial directions when they are completing multistep tasks. The larger skill is following directions—if students can learn to use such a format, then the number of tasks they can complete with greater independence increases. And since students are likely to experience many multistep tasks throughout the day, many teaching opportunities occur. Although students with severe and multiple disabilities learn at a slower rate, they can and do learn. Professionals' task is to select important and meaningful skills that can be taught under typical conditions throughout the school day.

Because of cognitive delays, students with severe and multiple disabilities usually have difficulty understanding abstract concepts. To address this issue, information needs to be presented in concrete ways. For instance, during a lesson on fractions, Sandra's teacher uses pictures of pizza slices to help her understand the concepts of *larger* and *more*, instead of the specific fractional pieces. As another example, to understand the passage of time, a relatively abstract concept, students may need pictorial representations showing how trees grow from seedlings to large trees or how babies become toddlers.

Finally, like many learners, these students experience difficulty generalizing information or skills learned to different settings, tasks, materials, and people. Although Sandra, who is learning about *less* and *more* during a class lesson on fractions, may learn to identify which of several pieces of the pizza is bigger or more, she may not generalize this knowledge when asked to give her classmate the container holding more liquid as part of a science experiment. To address these needs, educators use approaches such as the following (e.g., Downing, 2008; Russel, Allday, & Duhon, 2015; Ryndak et al., 2014):

- Teach a specific skill in a direct and systematic way by breaking it into very small steps as part of meaningful activities.
- Prompt students; that is, provide assistance to them using words, demonstrations, and even physical guiding, such as placing a hand under the student's hand to teach the use of a switch.
- Immediately reward correct responses.
- Teach within the natural context.
- Teach across as many settings, tasks, and people as possible so that the students can use what they learn in any appropriate situation.

Academic Characteristics

Even though less emphasis traditionally has been placed on academics for children with severe and multiple disabilities, they can and do learn important skills in this domain (e.g., Kliewer, Biklen, & Petersen, 2015). However, the depth of what they learn is likely to be different from that of their peers without disabilities. In science, a student may learn that electrical outlets are needed to operate certain appliances while other students are working to understand ohms, watts, and voltage. The key to designing academic instruction for students with severe and multiple disabilities is setting aside biases about their learning capability while recognizing the importance of making learning relevant and meaningful. Paraprofessionals often play a key role in facilitating the learning of these students. You can learn more about what they should—and should not—do in the Positive Behavior Supports.

Literacy

Students with severe and multiple disabilities often have been thought of as being incapable of acquiring literacy skills and, therefore, were provided with limited, if any, literacy instruction (Browder, Wakeman, Spooner, Ahlgrim-Delzell, & Algozzine, 2006; Cologon, 2013). However, these students should learn as many literacy and literacy-related skills as possible. For example, Browder, Lee, and Mims (2011) taught three teachers scripts to use to increase the comprehension and engagement of their three students with multiple disabilities during story lessons. All three students improved in both engagement and comprehension. In another study, Browder and her colleagues (Browder, Mims, Spooner, Ahlgrim-Delzell, & Lee, 2008) taught students with profound and multiple disabilities to respond to simple questions during shared stories by touching the objects related to the stories.

The focus in instruction such as this is on how best to ensure meaningful access. Some students may learn to recognize certain letters, such as the letters in their names; familiar and frequently used words (e.g., *girls, boys, lunch*); and favorite words (e.g., *Taco Bell, TV, ball*). Students may use pictures to help them recognize words and may write or sequence their thoughts using pictured information. For students with limited or no vision, objects or parts of objects can be attached to pages in specially designed books to help them understand what is read to them. A simplified text also can be added in both braille and print (Downing, 2005b; Lewis & Tolla, 2003).

Motivation plays a key role in teaching literacy skills to students with severe and multiple disabilities, and so building learning activities based on student interests is important (Koegel, Openden, Fredeen, & Koegel, 2006). For example, Mandy had a strong fascination with the aquarium in her first-grade class. At every opportunity, she went to the aquarium to stare at the fish. Mandy was nonverbal and did not know the letters of the alphabet, and so picture and word cards were created to take advantage of her interest. When Mandy went to the tank, she

Did You Know?

Guon, Wilfond, Farlow, Brazg & Janvier (2014) asked parents of children prenatally diagnosed as likely to have severe disabilities or die soon after birth about their prenatal experiences, their hopes, and their experiences with their children. Based on moral beliefs, beliefs about children, and religious beliefs, they found that these parents continued their pregnancies despite pressures to terminate and that many of them had, by the time of their child's birth, already chosen a plan for interventions.

POSITIVE • **BEHAVIOR** • SUPPORTS

Paraprofessionals as Facilitators of Education

Paraprofessionals are essential personnel in the education of students with significant disabilities (e.g., Brock & Carter, 2013; Carter, Moss, Hoffman, Chung, & Sisco, 2011; Giangreco, Doyle, & Suter, 2012). Their work with students, in both special education and general education settings, helps to minimize student disruptive and inappropriate behavior and maximize learning. Here are examples of recommended and discouraged or prohibited roles for paraeducators:

Paraeducators may

- Lead small-group instruction (i.e., review or practice) that includes both students with significant disabilities and typical peers
- Help the student to practice skills noted on the IEP as directed by the teacher (e.g., counting to 10, knowing common prepositions such as *over* and *under*; making a choice between two items)
- Implement behavior interventions as directed by the teacher (e.g., provide a reward when the student complies with a request)
- Facilitate interactions between a student and typical peers
- Assist the student with personal care activities such as using the bathroom and eating
- Move the student from place to place (e.g., push the wheelchair, move the student from the wheelchair to the floor for group time)

- Record student learning and behavior as directed by the teacher (e.g., the number of letters recognized, the percent of times the student makes eye contact when requested)

Paraeducators should not

- Provide initial instruction or primary instruction to the student, including finding new ideas and trying them out (e.g., ideas found through Internet research)
- Decide independently of the teacher whether or not a specific behavior intervention is working and whether or not to continue it (e.g., giving the student a break from the classroom by taking the student out of the class)
- Communicate with parents to discuss a student's problem behaviors or instructional challenges
- Stay so close to the student, including during lunch, recess, or assemblies, that other students and teachers tend to stay away
- Help the student when a peer can provide the assistance or the student can complete the task independently

Note that professionals should ensure that paraprofessionals have received adequate training to work with students with complex needs, that they understand teacher roles versus their roles, and that they are comfortable in asking for guidance as needed.

---

was asked to read the words on the cards (*fish, orange, black, white, striped*) and to find the fish in the tank that each word described. This activity addressed her IEP goal of learning vocabulary within the context of her interests.

Oral Language

Communicating orally may be particularly difficult for students with severe and multiple disabilities because of intellectual and physical challenges (De Bortoli, Balandin, Foreman, Arthur-Kelly, & Mathisen, 2012; Foreman, Arthur-Kelly, Bennett, Neilands, & Colyvas, 2014). Students may not rely on speech to communicate their needs, or their speech may be difficult to understand. Students may use a few words that are intelligible, especially to family members and friends, but many students will use other forms of nonverbal communication—facial expressions, body gestures, manual signs, pictures, and objects (Downing, 2005a; Ferm, Ahlsen, & Bjorck-Akesson, 2012). For example, Hatias, who is essentially nonverbal, was outside with his high school earth science classmates, monitoring the growth of their plants. To express his desire to get the large watering can, he tried to verbalize the word *can* while pointing to the shed where it was kept, vocalized several words that were unintelligible, signed *water*, and used gestures to indicate *big*. He increasingly exaggerated his communication until his message was understood. The use of multiple modes of communication is a frequent and positive approach when speech is not present or not effective by itself.

Receptive language also may be compromised for these students. They may have extreme difficulty processing oral language, and they often benefit when teachers, parents, and classmates present oral information in small segments,

Many students with severe and multiple disabilities find it difficult to communicate using speech. These students can benefit significantly from the use of augmentative communication devices (Light & McNaughton, 2014; McNaughton & Light, 2013).

Augmentative communication devices (ACDs) are adapted aids that provide students with alternatives to speech to convey their messages; you were introduced to a few examples of these devices in Chapter 9 on communication disorders. Here are some points to keep in mind about ACD and students with severe or multiple disabilities:

- ACDs can range from highly technological (computerized systems) to very light- or low-technological accommodations, such as picture boards and books.
- These devices can be developed to meet the unique needs of students with severe and multiple disabilities, providing graphic symbols, voice output, or written display as needed.
- ACDs for students with severe and multiple disabilities typically are easy to use, depict a visual symbol, and offer a relatively small number of individual messages.

- Because students need to communicate in all environments, ACDs also must be readily available and easily portable. One student may have several different devices to use for different purposes and in different situations.

One example of an ACD on a tablet device is displayed below.

clarifying their words with gestures, pictures, and objects (Beukelman & Mirenda, 2005; Downing, 2005a). In the Technology Notes, you can read about some of the alternative communication options available for these students, including Cassie, who was introduced at the beginning of the chapter.

Mathematics

If you were teaching students who could learn only the most essential math skills, which skills would you emphasize? Why? Students with severe and multiple disabilities demonstrate mathematic skills in various ways (Browder et al., 2012; Saunders, Bethune, Spooner, & Browder, 2013). Some students learn to recognize or match numbers. They may learn one-to-one correspondence through such activities as handing out materials and setting the table. All students, including those with severe and multiple disabilities, learn math more readily when they can see its application in their daily lives. For example, students may learn to recognize numbers in order to use a calculator or perform steps in a numbered task. Students may learn to identify certain times of day (e.g., 8:00 to start school, 10:00 for recess, 12:00 for lunch, and 3:00 to go home) by reading the daily schedule and matching it to clock time. Another example involves learning the concepts of *more* and *less* as they relate to money for making purchases.

Learning mathematics skills that have direct application to everyday activities can have a substantial impact on a student's quality of life and so should be an integral component of any meaningful curriculum (Browder et al., 2012; Westling & Fox, 2009). A recommended practice is to use math content standards for a specific grade level and identify the basic skills within these standards that are meaningful to students with significant disabilities (Browder et al., 2012; Collins, Kleinert, & Land, 2006). For instance, in an algebra class, students may learn to identify the single-digit numbers and letters in the equation and use pictures of preferred items to learn the amounts of the numbers.

INSTRUCTION IN **ACTION**

When You Can't Plan Ahead: Quick Tips for Educators in General Education Classrooms

When planning has not been possible or plans go awry, educators should be prepared to make adaptations on short notice, even if they are not as extensive as they would otherwise be.

Here are examples of materials teachers and paraprofessionals keep on hand for this purpose (Downing & Demchak, 2008):

- Index cards
- Felt-tip markers of different colors
- Consumable pictures grouped by category
- Highlighters of different colors
- A glue stick
- Sticky notes in various colors
- Blank white labels
- Scissors
- Extra batteries for switches and switch-activated devices

With these materials, sufficient accommodations can quickly be made as the general education teacher is giving directions to the class. For example, a special educator had adapted materials for a fifth-grader with severe disabilities so that she could participate in a creative writing activity that involved students writing their autobiographies. Because the student she was supporting did not speak or write, the special educator had obtained photographs from the student's family. The student was to sequence these in a specific order to "write" about herself. However, the general education teacher decided to postpone this activity for a later date and instead directed the class to write about whether or not they would want to join the circus. This assignment was related to a story that the class had just finished and a recent field trip. Using some brochures from the field trip, pictures from her picture library, and a glue stick, the special educator had the student determine which pictures were associated with a circus (learning vocabulary). The pictures were labeled and color-coded using highlighters. The student then was given choices of what she preferred: a picture of a circus performer or a picture of a completely unrelated field (e.g., police officer, cook). She was asked simple yes–no questions regarding why she liked a particular picture (occupation), which the teacher recorded next to the pictures. Although the special educator was not as prepared as she would have been if the lesson had been discussed in detail in advance, this simple adaptation using materials that accompanied the student created meaningful participation and an appropriate learning task for her.

As you can imagine, meeting the academic needs of students with severe and multiple disabilities requires careful planning and, when this occurs in general education, sophisticated collaboration between general and special educators. But sometimes, even with planning, back-up options are needed. The Instruction in Action provides reality-based options for these instructional situations.

Social and Emotional Characteristics

Students with severe and multiple disabilities typically display social and emotional skills that lag far behind those of other students their age. Limitations in communication skills and language development contribute to these challenges. For example, children typically use language to indicate interests in others' activities or to express their ideas about a current topic or project. These skills tend to develop naturally as children begin to understand the purpose of language through their day-to-day interactions with and observations of parents, family members, and friends. However, students with severe and multiple disabilities are not as likely to acquire these skills on their own. Instead, they usually require direct instruction in how and when to use language or alternative forms of communication to initiate and respond to others (e.g., Davis, Fredrick, Alberto, & Gama, 2012; Tullis, Cannella-Malone, & Payne, 2015). In addition, what they eventually learn is not likely to be at the same level of sophistication as their typically developing peers.

Despite difficulties in developing communication and social skills, students in this group still desire and benefit from social relationships. Friendships are particularly critical for these students, and friendships between children with and without severe disabilities are not unusual (e.g., Carter et al., 2015;

Shokoohi-Yekta & Hendrickson, 2010). Although some professionals question the ability of students with severe and multiple disabilities to truly make friends, considerable research indicates this is a real possibility and provides information on the means to facilitate it (Carter et al., 2016; Naraian, 2010).

Behavior Characteristics

Students with severe and multiple disabilities share behavioral characteristics common among students without disabilities. For example, some students may be outgoing and very animated while others may be reserved and shy. These students may also display behavioral characteristics that are less common. For example, students with physical and sensory impairments may engage in behaviors that seem highly unconventional and inappropriate (Oliver, Petty, Ruddick, & Bacarese-Hamilton, 2012). But understanding the disability helps to better understand the different behaviors the student may display. Thomas, a young man of 16 who is deaf and blind, illustrates this concept. Thomas has very limited communication ability and is quite isolated from the world, and so he amuses himself with the stereotypic behaviors of spinning around in tight circles and tapping his forehead with the back of his hand. Without understanding the complexity of Thomas's disabilities and his difficulty in obtaining sensory input, one might misjudge him and consider his behavior strange. However, when compared to others his age who also engage in self-stimulatory types of behaviors (e.g., doodling, pen clicking, paperclip tapping, hair twirling), the reason for the behavior becomes more apparent. Unfortunately, due to his visual impairment, Thomas cannot observe these more accepted forms of self-stimulatory behavior performed by others his age, and so he created his own.

Challenging Behaviors

Students with severe and multiple disabilities also can engage in behaviors that are disruptive to others, destructive of property, or harmful to themselves or others (Bethune & Wood, 2013; Oliver, Petty, Ruddick, & Bacarese-Hamilton, 2012; Westling, 2015). These behaviors can range in severity and intensity from minor off-task behaviors to loud crying and screaming or hitting others or themselves. For example, Aaron is an 8-year-old with a severe intellectual disability who does not speak and at times struggles to understand the expectations of others. He dislikes tasks that are repetitive in nature (e.g., writing his name over and over again), that require him to sit and listen for long periods of time, and that involve handling sticky or gooey materials (e.g., paints and glue). When asked to do such tasks, Aaron tears the paper, throws the pencil, and sometimes hits his head with his hand. Such behaviors are clearly not appropriate and can be challenging for teachers, parents, and others on the team to address, but they can understand these challenging behaviors, and Aaron can learn alternative behaviors. Aaron engages in these behaviors to communicate his dislike of such activities. Once the purpose behind the challenging behavior is understood, educators can implement strategies to reduce these behaviors while simultaneously teaching appropriate behaviors. Therefore, understanding the meaning behind these behaviors and providing the student with alternative means of meeting his needs is a critical consideration in addressing such occurrences. For the previous example of Aaron, can you imagine what he was trying to convey through his seemingly aggressive behavior? What might you do to prevent this type of behavior?

MyEdLab **Self-Check 14.2**

MyEdLab **Application Exercise 14.2:** We Are *Not* All the Same

Assessment of Students with Severe and Multiple Disabilities

Determining eligibility for services is not the primary reason for assessing students who have severe and multiple disabilities. Typically, identification occurs at birth, during infancy, or after some specific trauma, and the need for special education services is obvious (La Paro, Olsen, & Pianta, 2002). Rather than using tests to determine eligibility, assessment focuses on developing quality educational programs for these students (e.g., Browder, 2012).

Assessment for Instruction

Assessment should help educators understand how their students learn and what motivates them. Knowing this information can help teachers select the most appropriate teaching strategies for each student (Horrocks & Morgan, 2011; Jimenez, Mims, & Browder, 2012). As you might imagine, students with severe and multiple disabilities do not perform well in formal assessment situations. They often do not understand what is expected or why it is important to respond as desired. As a result, alternatives to formal and norm-referenced assessments generally are recommended. You can read about the advantages and disadvantages of different types of assessment for students with severe and multiple disabilities in the following sections.

Standardized Assessment

As you know, *norm-referenced assessments* are standardized tests that delineate specific skills that most students should demonstrate at certain ages or stages of development. Students typically are assessed in an artificial environment (e.g., the office of the psychologist or psychometrist), and they may not understand why they should do as requested. This type of testing is especially difficult for students with severe or multiple disabilities (Browder & Spooner, 2011; Ryndak, Jackson, & White, 2013). For instance, Brian is 11 years old and has developed several important skills, including grasping objects of interest (a red marker), following directions when getting ready to eat, and looking for a favorite magazine when it is out of sight. However, in a formal testing situation, he does not always grasp items presented to him (e.g., blocks, beads), may not follow simple directions to stack blocks or put objects into a container, and does not search for a toy that has been hidden from view. The lack of context or meaning interferes with Brian's ability to adequately demonstrate his knowledge. Consequently, Brian scores poorly on this test, ending up with an IQ score of 25 and a developmental age of 1 year or younger. This score does not reflect what Brian is capable of accomplishing.

Standardized assessments are problematic for students with severe and multiple disabilities for an additional reason: The results of such tests fail to help teachers decide what to teach or how (Brown, Snell, & Lehr, 2006; Heward, 2006). Because students with severe and multiple disabilities experience significant cognitive and language impairments, they are likely to score very low in every area being tested (Campbell, Reilly, & Henley, 2008; Westling & Fox, 2009). This can make it difficult to determine what skills are critical to learn. Some teachers may believe that they should teach students the items failed on a given test without considering student age, interests, and skill relevance. Doing so can lead to instruction in age-inappropriate and nonfunctional skills, such as teenagers being taught to engage in activities typical of a preschool or kindergarten classroom (e.g., coloring, playing with blocks), not in activities that will help them as adults.

Finally, low test scores can lead some to conclude that students with significant disabilities are not capable of learning higher-order skills. For example, Samantha, an adolescent with severe cognitive delay, may not be able to discriminate between coins and dollar bills. Based on this finding, one might conclude that Samantha could not learn how to make purchases or manage a checking account. However, with the appropriate supports, she can learn that in order to get a desired item, she must give the cashier money. The amount of money in her wallet can be predetermined, or she can be given only dollar bills so that she learns to wait for change before taking her purchase. If modified and supported correctly, the activity does not require Samantha to have a full understanding of the value of the individual coins and bills; she needs to comprehend only cause and effect. What other activities could Samantha also engage in, even though she does not have typical prerequisite skills?

Authentic Forms of Assessment

Authentic assessment enables students—including those with severe and multiple disabilities—to more accurately demonstrate their skills and abilities (e.g., Jaeger, 2012). Authentic assessment is an ongoing assessment process that occurs within the student's natural environment and includes observation of a student's performance as well as the necessary supports for the student.

Person-Centered Approach

A key characteristic of authentic assessment is making decisions about what to assess based on input from family members, friends, teachers, paraprofessionals, and others who know the student's abilities, strengths, and goals. In particular, those closest to the student—usually family members—are asked what they believe the student should learn so that the assessment considers the student's personal, cultural, and religious beliefs. This person-centered approach focuses the student's assessment and education plan on his unique characteristics and interests (Stewart, 2011; Wells & Sheehey, 2012) and not on any predetermined set of skills, such as those on a formal assessment. Once the team has this information, professionals and family members can use it to guide their observations of the student. The observational data are more meaningful than traditional test data in setting appropriate goals for the student.

Functional–Ecological Assessment

Another form of authentic assessment is a functional–ecological assessment, which provides a means of organizing information from written observation notes and video or digital recordings (Downing, 2008; Siegel-Causey & Allinder, 2005). A functional–ecological assessment analyzes the typical demands of the environment (e.g., what steps others typically engage in to complete activities) and the natural cues in the environment that exist to prompt the expected behavior. The student's performance is noted (what she can and cannot do), and the discrepancy between what is expected and how the student performs is analyzed.

Planning educational services for a student with severe or multiple disabilities is a team effort that draws on multiple perspectives and types of expertise.

As part of this type of assessment, professionals note how they can help the student complete a task, which helps them plan how to teach the student specific skills. The Instruction in Action provides an example of functional–ecological assessment of a spelling lesson. The outcome of such assessment is to discover skills that the student needs to learn and adaptations that need to occur to help the student be actively involved and successful in meaningful and frequently occurring activities. Results from this type of assessment, instead of an IQ score or a developmental level, lead to ideas for direct intervention. Think about Jackson, introduced at the beginning of this chapter. What might a functional–ecological assessment include for participation in his music class?

Portfolio Assessment

In addition to observational information, authentic assessment also includes examples of student work, such as an adapted geometry assignment in which the student matches by shape and color. Explanations of the adaptations used and how the student was supported accompany the samples. Videotaped segments or digital video recordings of the student learning in different activities and situations can be collected to document learning style. Such examples of student performance are maintained in a student portfolio that clearly creates a record to show a student's progress over time (Anderson, Farley, & Tindal, 2013; Kleinert, Harrison, Mills, Dueppen, & Trailor, 2014; Tindal, Yovanoff, & Geller, 2010).

INSTRUCTION IN **ACTION**

Functional–Ecological Assessment of Learning Environments

Setting: Third-grade classroom
Activity: Writing assignment using spelling words

Key

+ Does all parts of step independently
0 Doesn't complete step or does it incorrectly
P Does some parts of the step

Nondisabled Peer Inventory	Natural Cues	Student Performance	Discrepancy Analysis	Plan to Intervene (what to teach, accommodations, partial participation)
Get out paper and pencil.	Teacher instruction; other students doing this.	0	Still working on previous assignment (math); did not appear to hear teacher instruction. Does not have the physical ability to do this.	Reduce number of problems so assignments can be completed within typical time frame. Teach student how to use daily schedule to prepare him for upcoming events. Teach him to request help getting materials.
Put name on paper.	Teacher instruction; blank paper and pencil on desk.	0	Can grasp pencils/pens but cannot write name. Learning to recognize some letters. Cannot keep up with fast pace.	Provide different way to write using labels or name stamp; present two different names and have him select his name and indicate where it should be put on paper.
Write spelling words in sentences.	Teacher direction and example on the board. Past experience doing this.	0	Does not write.	Modify task demand. For example, student finds the picture that matches the word and indicates the line that is blank within a pre-written sentence that also contains pictures. A peer or adult support pastes in the picture.
Turn paper in when finished and get out book to read.	Teacher instruction; students finishing and handing in their papers and getting books to read. Finished with assignment.	P	Cannot physically do this. Doesn't understand the need to go on to another task.	Peer in front of student will ask him if he wants help turning in his paper. Teach student to use a device to respond or make this request. Teach him to check his daily schedule to see what's next. Offer choices of books to read.

Student portfolios can be an effective supplement to standardized educational assessments for students with severe and multiple disabilities. Student artifacts can be aligned with grade-level content standards to demonstrate student progress and accountability.

Authentic assessment—with a focus on person-centered planning, functional–ecological assessment, and portfolio assessment—provides teachers with accurate information about students' abilities and guides the development of meaningfully individualized programs. Further, such assessment provides clear information for future teachers to use as the students transition from grade to grade. Given the value of these approaches for students with severe and multiple disabilities, what might be the benefit of using authentic assessment for students without disabilities?

MyEdLab **Self-Check 14.3**

MyEdLab **Application Exercise 14.3:** Portfolios

MyEdLab **Application Exercise 14.4:** Assessment of Students with Severe and Multiple Disabilities

---

How Learners with Severe and Multiple Disabilities Receive Their Education

Several options exist for educating students with severe and multiple disabilities. These options vary depending on the age of the student, the geographical area in which the student lives, and the preference of family members. As you have learned, IDEA clearly states that students with disabilities should be educated with their peers without disabilities to the maximum extent possible.

Early Childhood

The importance of early intervention for children with severe and multiple disabilities cannot be stated strongly enough. These children, because of the complexity of their disabilities, enter preschool without the basic skills that most children acquire without effort. Their communication skills may be severely delayed. Some children may be learning to walk, and others may exhibit difficulties with sitting, crawling, or standing (e.g., Purvis et al., 2013; Salisbury & Copeland, 2013). Many children without disabilities enter preschool with basic literacy skills, and they can sit quietly listening to stories, understand those stories, and respond to questions. Children with severe and multiple disabilities typically display few literacy skills and thus enter preschool considerably more disadvantaged than their peers without disabilities.

Young children with severe and multiple disabilities may have had limited opportunities to interact with other children their age; given this, they may demonstrate minimal social skills (Hanline & Correa-Torres, 2012). Picture 3-year-old Belinda, who is blind and nonverbal. She also has difficulty moving her body and holding objects, and she has a severe intellectual disability. Belinda has not been able to learn much about objects in her life because she cannot see them at a distance; even when they are within her reach, she has great difficulty grasping and exploring them. She does not understand basic concepts because she cannot learn incidentally and is unable to ask questions about things she encounters. Belinda relies on the interactions of her peers without disabilities to keep her motivated to learn. Since it is difficult for Belinda to initiate interactions, her peers have been taught to approach her, place toys in her hands, and talk to her about them. They have learned to offer her two play items to touch and choose

FIGURE 14.3   Educational Placement of Students Ages 6 to 21 Who Have Severe and Multiple Disabilities (in percentages)

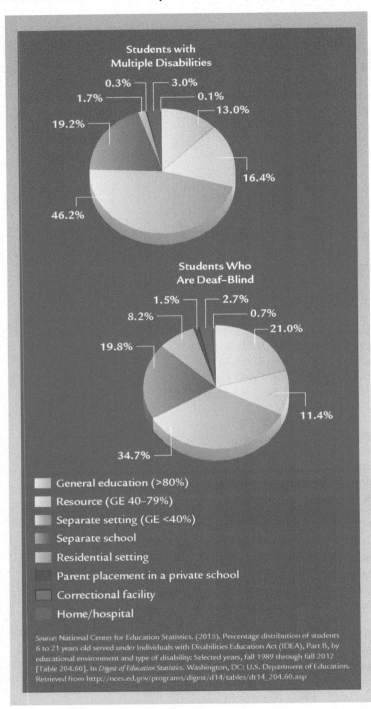

Students with Multiple Disabilities

0.3% — 3.0%
1.7% — 0.1%
19.2% — 13.0%
46.2%
16.4%

Students Who Are Deaf–Blind

1.5% — 2.7%
8.2% — 0.7%
19.8% — 21.0%
34.7%
11.4%

- General education (>80%)
- Resource (GE 40–79%)
- Separate setting (GE <40%)
- Separate school
- Residential setting
- Parent placement in a private school
- Correctional facility
- Home/hospital

Source: National Center for Education Statistics. (2015). Percentage distribution of students 6 to 21 years old served under Individuals with Disabilities Education Act (IDEA), Part B, by educational environment and type of disability: Selected years, fall 1989 through fall 2012 [Table 204.60]. In *Digest of Education Statistics*. Washington, DC: U.S. Department of Education. Retrieved from http://nces.ed.gov/programs/digest/d14/tables/dt14_204.60.asp

from. Belinda responds well to her peers' efforts to engage her, and they have the opportunity to learn about differences in a very positive way.

Unfortunately, most preschool children with severe and multiple disabilities have limited access to peers without disabilities. Although young children with disabilities have access to free and appropriate public education, those without disabilities do not have this legal guarantee. Therefore, the majority of typical preschoolers either stay at home or attend a private preschool. Finding ways to educate young children with severe disabilities with their nondisabled peers is an ongoing challenge that requires planning, education for professionals, and creativity (Barned, Knapp, & Neuharth-Pritchett, 2011; Hanline & Correa-Torres, 2012). For example, instead of placing children with severe disabilities in specialized settings during their preschool years, in some communities, needed support is provided to the child in more typical settings, such as Head Start programs and private preschools.

Elementary and Secondary Education

Many students with severe and multiple disabilities receive their education in segregated programs with an emphasis on life skills, a fact illustrated in the data presented in Figure 14.3.

However, this trend is changing. Consistent with IDEA, students with severe and multiple disabilities, like other students with milder disabilities, must have access to the core curriculum (Spooner & Browder, 2015). Further, the literature is clear regarding the benefits of placing these students in general education classes with their peers without disabilities (Brock, Biggs, Carter, Cattey, & Raley, 2016; Carter, Moss, Hoffman, Chung, & Sisco, 2011; Kurth, Lyon, & Shogren, 2015). Practices that foster success for other students with disabilities are effective for students with severe and multiple disabilities, too. Universal design for learning (UDL), cooperative learning and other peer-mediated instructional approaches, active and hands-on learning, and instructional differentiation are helping to open doors for students traditionally excluded from the general education environment (e.g., Hartmann, 2015). In many schools, these students are spending at least a significant part of their day in a general education setting.

Regardless of the program in which students participate, professionals agree that students with severe and multiple disabilities should be assigned to the same grade level as their chronological peers, not a grade level according to ability. The logic for this should be clear: These students are not going to catch up in any traditional sense, and so assisting them to learn as much as possible while moving through the years of their public school education is the preferred strategy.

The alternative might result in students who are 15, 16, or 17 years old and still assigned to elementary school.

Within an age-appropriate placement, specific accommodations are made across subject matter to enable students to access and participate in the core curriculum as much as possible (e.g., Downing & Eichinger, 2011). For example, during a study of the planets, one fourth-grader with severe and multiple disabilities—Stephen—may not be learning all the facts about the planets that his classmates are learning, but he is practicing finding certain colors by pointing, counting the planets to eight, and recognizing which of three different numbers is the numeral *8.* He also may be learning to distinguish a circle (the shape of a planet) from a square or another shape.

Pictorial and other supports can assist students who experience difficulty communicating to express their needs, often reducing their frustration and preventing behavior issues.

As students move from elementary school through middle school and into high school, the type of setting in which they are educated often changes. Even students who were members of general education classrooms in elementary school are likely to attend self-contained special classes or separate schools for their secondary education. The logic for this approach concerns the difficulty of the curriculum and teachers' and parents' concerns that these students' time is better spent learning functional skills. However, learning with nondisabled peers is as important for secondary-age students with severe and multiple disabilities as it is for younger students (Carter et al., 2015), resulting in a wide array of benefits as noted in the next section.

Inclusive Practices

You have already learned that students with severe and multiple disabilities, to a large extent, have remained segregated from their peers. However, across all school levels, inclusive practices have benefits for these students as well as for their peers and teachers (Kurth, Lyon, & Shogren, 2015; Rossetti, 2011). Benefits for students with severe and multiple disabilities include improvements in academic skills, social skills, motor skills (e.g., walking), communication skills, and appropriate behavior skills (Carter et al., 2015; Hudson, Browder, & Wood, 2013; Hunt, Soto, Maier, & Doering, 2003; Kleinert et al., 2015). The many benefits of inclusive practices extend to students without disabilities. Peck, Staub, Gallucci, and Schwartz (2004) analyzed responses from 389 parents of children with no disabilities who had classmates with severe disabilities. Parents reported that their children were more accepting and understanding of individual differences. In another study, Carter and Kennedy (2006) found that when at-risk students supported students with severe disabilities in a classwide peer-tutoring program, their academic skills increased.

> **Video Example**
> **from**
> **YouTube**
>
> MyEdLab
> **Video Example 14.2**
>
> The positive potential of inclusive practices is clearly illustrated in this video.
> (https://www.youtube.com/watch?v=4o__NMJuILM)

Partial Participation

When students are not able to fully perform an activity or project on their own, they often succeed with partial participation. This term refers to engaging in some parts of an activity with supports as needed. For example, when Isabella's class is engaged in learning to add two-digit numbers, the teacher asks her to find a particular one-digit number from among three different numbers in front of her. She does this twice and then uses Isabella's correct answers to form two-digit numbers that she uses in her demonstration to the entire class. Isabella is learning to identify single-digit numbers in the same lesson on addition that the teacher gives to the rest of the class. While they practice adding the two-digit numbers, Isabella works on counting small items to find the answer to addition of two of the single-digit numbers she identified.

Assistive technology, such as the use of switches, can play a major role in allowing students to partially participate in a variety of meaningful and age-appropriate activities. For instance, during 11th-grade English class, Lindsey, who cannot speak and has severe physical and intellectual disabilities, uses a simple switch to activate a random spinner that can point to class members' names or questions on a study guide. Her teacher calls on her whenever she intends to randomly call on a student in the class or to choose a question at random to quiz the class. In using the spinner, Lindsey partially participates in her English class and meets her IEP goal of activating the switch and responding to the direction of her teacher. The Technology Notes includes additional examples of switches and their uses with students with significant disabilities.

Paraprofessional Support

Paraprofessionals have come to play a critical role in the inclusion of students with severe and multiple disabilities in general education classrooms. These

TECHNOLOGY NOTES

Using Switches to Foster Participation and Independence

Simple technological devices such as switches allow students with physical and cognitive limitations to play a more active role in numerous academic and nonacademic activities.

- Switches offer students control over physical items that would typically be much too difficult for them to use.
- Using a switch, the student can watch and listen to a story on a computer and keep the story moving by activating the switch.
- A student without the physical means to cut can use a switch connected to battery-operated scissors to cut out shapes or pictures to be used in an assignment. A peer or adult holds the scissors and guides it, while the student with severe disabilities accesses the switch to provide the power.
- A student can also use a switch to turn on a media projector or other equipment used by the teacher during classroom instruction. For example, as directed by a teacher during a science demonstration, a student can activate a switch to power a fan that represents wind power. A control unit bypasses the normal electrical route of plugging a device into an outlet and makes it switch-dependent instead. As a result, almost anything that is electrical or battery operated can be used with a switch to place greater control in the hands of the student with limited physical and cognitive skills and to add to the learning of the entire class.

Switches come in a variety of different forms to meet the needs of students with severe physical limitations (see the photos):

- A flat-plate switch can be touched with any part of the body over which the student has control (e.g., hand, elbow, knee, foot, head).
- A Mercury or gravity switch can be used to encourage a student to move a certain body part, such as an arm, the head, or a leg, in a controlled fashion to activate a given device.
- A puff switch works when the student blows a puff of air.
- A toggle switch requires any movement from any direction to activate a device.
- A light or vibratory switch adds an additional sensory input to encourage the student to activate it.

Determining the best switch or switches to use for an individual student is a team effort and depends on the student's physical abilities, demands of the task, physical situation, and positioning needs of the student. Occupational and physical therapists can be particularly helpful in determining the type(s) of switches to use and the best position for the student.

Button switch   *Sip and puff switch*

individuals often provide the necessary added support for a student to ensure meaningful access to the core curriculum and to provide individualized instruction. These students may need extra adult support on a fairly regular basis, but a problem exists when paraprofessionals are left without instruction or supervision. Paraprofessionals tend to be the least-trained members of the team, yet they are asked to assist students with the most challenging educational and behavioral needs. These individuals need to receive ongoing training and monitoring by general and special educators as they appropriately support different students with severe and multiple disabilities in a variety of classrooms and grade levels.

Increasingly, experts in the field have begun to question the potential overreliance on paraprofessionals to maintain inclusive programs for students with severe and multiple disabilities (Feldman, Carter, Asmus, & Brock, 2016; Giangreco, 2010). Without appropriate training, paraprofessionals may not implement programs effectively and may hinder students' progress by remaining too close to them, overassisting and interfering with their interactions with other students. In fact, researchers are increasingly looking at how peers can provide more natural support to relieve an overreliance on paraprofessionals (Brock, Biggs, Carter, Cattey, & Raley, 2016).

General and special educators need to collaborate in their work with and supervision of paraeducators. Determining when, where, and how to assign these school staff members ensures high-quality support for students. Paraeducators supporting students with severe and multiple disabilities in general education classrooms should follow guidelines such as these:

- Interact with all students in the room, based on teacher directions.
- Teach small groups of children.
- Facilitate interactions among all students.
- Avoid hovering around the student with significant needs.
- Share information with general and special educators regarding the student's performance.
- Collect data on IEP objectives. Ask for guidance to do this properly.

Transition and Adulthood

Upon graduating from high school, students with severe and multiple disabilities should have adult options similar to those of their peers without disabilities. Unfortunately, fears and low expectations combine to limit adult goals for these students (Carter, Austin, & Trainor, 2011; Sarkar, 2015). However, families and educators are beginning to consider new options, such as home ownership with support, active participation in typical activities in the community, and postsecondary options. Whether these dreams can become reality often depends on the quality of the transition planning that occurs for these students and is required in IDEA, just as for all other students with disabilities (Carter, Austin, & Trainor, 2012; Van Laarhoven-Myers, Van Laarhoven, Smith, Johnson, & Olson, 2016).

Some students with severe and multiple disabilities leave school to work in a job in the competitive marketplace. They may work at a store bagging groceries or stocking shelves; as an office assistant, delivering mail, duplicating materials, and shredding unneeded documents; or in the kitchen at a hotel restaurant, filling and emptying the dishwasher. They also may share an apartment with a person without disabilities who offers valuable support. Other students are not employed; instead, they may live in a separate residential setting, attend a special adult day activity center, or work in a sheltered workshop, where they complete repetitive or made-up tasks for little or no pay. Whether students achieve the former or are limited to the latter often largely depends on the quality of the transition assistance they receive while they are in school.

Supported Employment

Clearly, the preferred and more progressive trend is to support individuals to work in real jobs that meet specific needs in the workforce, whether it is through employment in hotels, retail stores, restaurants, or offices (e.g., Wehman, Chan, Ditchman, & Kang, 2014). Supported employment is the practice of assisting adults with disabilities to obtain jobs in the competitive market and providing them with the necessary physical, instructional, and social support to ensure success for the employee and satisfaction for the employer. One strategy for supported employment involves coworkers helping to teach young adults the skills required in their jobs and helping them practice until they are proficient in carrying out their job responsibilities (Cimera, 2007; Hartman, 2009). This type of support is referred to as a natural support. Nearly everyone uses such supports, at least temporarily, when they begin a new job. For students with severe and multiple disabilities, this type of support is particularly helpful. If students need additional support, specialists called *job coaches* sometimes accompany them to their workplaces to do just what the job title implies: coach students as they master the requirements of the job and make sure that the job is completed satisfactorily. The goal is to gradually remove this intrusive support, but this may not always be possible or appropriate.

Community-Based Instruction

To ease the transition from school to work, students with severe and multiple disabilities need to experience instruction in the community where they can sample different types of jobs and become accustomed to accessing community facilities. Such instruction, referred to as *community-based instruction* (CBI), is highly individualized, reflecting the interests of students while helping them to explore new possibilities (Carter, Trainor, Ditchman, Swedeen, & Owens, 2009; Pickens & Dymond, 2014). Students in high school may take some classes with their peers and then spend one or two periods each day in the community, either working at a particular job or learning to access community resources (e.g., use a grocery store, post office, laundromat). Because students with severe and multiple disabilities have considerable difficulty generalizing skills learned in one environment to another, teaching students within the natural environment of the community (whether a vocational or recreational setting) reduces this problem with transfer of skills (Westling & Fox, 2009).

Keep in mind that students with severe and multiple disabilities usually attend school until they are 22 years old, an option included in IDEA. In addition, they are able to access financial support after they leave school for vocational training, housing, and other needs. Because of their extraordinary needs, they usually require some type of support for their entire lives. However, their school experiences should help to prepare them for a life with as much independence as possible.

MyEdLab **Self-Check 14.4**

MyEdLab **Application Exercise 14.5:** Technology for Inclusion

MyEdLab **Application Exercise 14.6:** How Learners with Severe and Multiple Disabilities Receive Their Education

---

Recommended Educational Practices for Students with Severe and Multiple Disabilities

For students with severe and multiple disabilities to receive the most appropriate education, professionals must use the practices that can have the greatest positive impact for them. A sample of recommended educational practices includes a meaningful and individualized curriculum, collaborative approaches for educating students, positive behavior supports, and inclusive education.

Meaningful and Individualized Curriculum

Because of the tremendous diversity among students with severe and multiple disabilities, they cannot be expected to fit into preexisting curricula. Instead, the team members responsible for designing students' education must work together to determine what will best meet the specific needs of different students.

Meaningful curriculum is relevant curriculum provided for each student according to interests, personal goals, and limitations in reaching those goals. The curriculum also must be age appropriate and not reflect the activities of much younger children. Using age-appropriate activities, expectations for performance will be modified to address the skill level and needs of the student.

Students who have been identified as having severe disabilities too often spend a significant amount of time in a life skills curriculum that consists primarily of nonacademic skill instruction such as grooming skills (e.g., handwashing, toothbrushing), socialization skills (waving "hi" to someone, making eye contact), food preparation skills, dressing skills, and home care. Although these skills are important, they can be addressed as they occur naturally throughout the day, not as isolated lessons. For example, dressing skills can be targeted when young children take off their shoes for playing in sand or when they don painting shirts for art. For older students, these skills can be addressed during physical education class when other students are also changing their clothes. Meaningful curriculum implies that these students access the core curriculum as mandated by law, albeit with adaptations and accommodations—based on their unique needs—that enable them to benefit from it.

Making the Core Curriculum Meaningful

Without exposure to a curriculum that may at first appear beyond the ability level of students with severe and multiple disabilities, these students are penalized in their education. Here is an example of making the curriculum meaningful: Nine-year-old Trevor participates in daily journal writing in his third-grade class by choosing from several different photographs and sequencing them in such a way that they tell about his weekend. After affixing the photos to his paper, Trevor chooses his name from among three different names written on sticky labels and attaches it to his paper. Trevor is learning to write using photographs to express himself, and he is also learning to recognize his name and add that to all of his work. When he is finished with his journal entry, his classmate Peter writes the words beneath Trevor's picture so that the meaning is clear, and then Peter reads the story back to Trevor.

Depending on the student's individually determined goals and objectives, the educational team members work together to analyze the activities of the curriculum and to determine ways to make the material meaningful for the student, often using ideas like those presented in the Instruction in Action.

Collaborative Approaches for Education

Collaboration has been stressed as important for many aspects of special education. For students with severe and multiple disabilities, collaboration with families and collaboration among the professionals and staff providing services on a day-to-day basis are both imperative.

Video Example
from
YouTube

MyEdLab
Video Example 14.3
Think about what meaningful curriculum means as you watch this video and listen to the teacher describe her students and the expectations set for them. What is your view of a meaningful curriculum for her students? (https://www.youtube.com/watch?v=kGPgv8V-cQE)

In the not-so-distant past, students with severe disabilities were considered unable to benefit from grade-level curriculum (Orelove, 1991). More recent thinking reflects higher expectations, with energies being used to determine how best to ensure access (e.g., Spooner & Browder, 2015).

Teaching the Big Ideas

One strategy is to identify the big ideas of the lesson and related vocabulary to make the information relevant to the student. Students with severe and multiple disabilities may not learn exactly the same information at the same level of understanding, but they can learn valuable skills during the same lesson.

For example, think about Cassie, introduced at the beginning of the chapter. In her English class, students are reading Mark Twain's *Huckleberry Finn* to understand the satire in the writing, given the political issues of the day. While Cassie may not be expected to understand Twain's satire, she is expected to understand some of the story line and several vocabulary words. Working with a peer tutor, Cassie learns vocabulary words such as *boy*, *Black*, *White*, *friend*, *paint*, *work*, *bad*, *good*, and *like*. While the class is discussing racial issues and the literary conventions that Twain uses when he addresses these topics, Cassie is using pictured information to understand the differences in skin colors and to learn the signs for *White*, *Black*, *boy*, *men*, *bad*, and *good*. The peer tutor acts out some of the big ideas that address the Black/White issues, using the signs and pictures to support the concepts. Cassie uses a pictorial adaptation of the book that is written at approximately a first-grade level and so is acquiring basic reading and vocabulary skills to aid her communication efforts. To keep her actively involved in the group discussion, the teacher asks her a simple question (*Which one is the White boy?*). Cassie differentiates between two or three pictorial options, and the teacher uses her answer to ask the entire class a more in-depth question (e.g., *What type of character is Huck Finn?*).

Teachers decide what the big ideas are and what vocabulary can be used to describe these ideas, gather the needed materials, and decide how to use the materials, incorporating them into the whole-class lesson. Finally, they decide how the students will demonstrate acquisition of the targeted skills.

Applying the Big Idea Approach

When you are teaching a high school lesson on World War II, the big idea is that war is fighting and fighting hurts people. This can be related to fighting that can occur between students and the importance of talking things through versus fighting. Vocabulary to be taught would include *fight*, *hurt*, *people* (or *men* and *women*), *talking*, *airplanes*, *bad*, and *good*. Pictures are pulled from the textbook as well as other books and from the Internet. Unrelated pictures are also used as distracters so that the student must demonstrate the ability to differentiate between the pictorial information based on the information presented. While the class discusses certain turning points of the war, the adult support (paraprofessional or special educator) asks the student to identify the target vocabulary from two or three pictorial options. The lead teacher routinely asks the student a simple question (e.g., *Which picture is of men negotiating or talking?* or *Which picture shows the use of airplanes in warfare?*). The adult support repeats and simplifies the question, stressing the key vocabulary words and assisting the student to make the appropriate selection. The lead teacher then praises the student and asks a nearby classmate to read the question on the back of the picture selected. This question in turn leads the class into more discussion of critical points. In this way, students of quite different ability levels have the same access to the core curriculum, but with very different outcomes.

Active Family Involvement

A critical aspect of educational programming necessarily involves family members and significant others. Those who know the student the best—the family—have the information needed to guide the team in the development of an effective and individualized program. Unique cultural considerations, beliefs, and religious preferences are best obtained from the family. In addition, family members know their child's unique styles of communication (e.g., that rocking her head from side to side means that Brittany wishes to get out of the wheelchair) and what seems to be most effective in helping their child to understand others. Family members know what has and has not worked for their child, and they can be strong advocates for ensuring the most appropriate program that meets their child's needs (e.g., Hubert, 2011).

Collaboration on the Team

Because students with severe and multiple disabilities often have complex needs, it is impossible for one person to know everything necessary to best address those needs. Instead, the most effective approach is to call on the collective knowledge and expertise that various team members bring to the educational planning process (Hunt et al., 2003; Ruppar & Gaffney, 2011). Family members, of course, are central team members, providing relevant and meaningful assessment information that helps to identify critical educational goals. Special educators have expertise in the area of individualizing instruction (e.g., curricular modifications), and related services professionals (e.g., speech pathologists, physical and occupational therapists) can provide more in-depth knowledge in their areas of specialization (e.g., suggestions regarding communication devices, positioning equipment, use of assistive technology).

Finally, the general education teacher brings to the team expert knowledge of the core curriculum. This person also provides information about how the day is organized, which helps to identify natural opportunities for peer interaction (e.g., during cooperative groups) and can help to highlight potentially difficult times (e.g., periods that require extensive sitting, listening, or note taking) so that additional support can be put in place (e.g., use of a paraprofessional). Collaborative planning is critical for bringing together everyone's expertise in support of an effective program for a student (Friend & Cook, 2017).

Positive Behavior Supports

As you learned in the discussion of the characteristics of students with severe and multiple disabilities, these students often have great difficulty communicating. This challenge can produce a great deal of frustration, leaving the student to convey intent through unconventional and undesired behaviors (Kim, Blair, & Lim, 2014; MacLean & Dornbush, 2012). Imagine how you would react if you could no longer express yourself through speech or other means and could not tell others about your feelings, needs, and desires. How would you want others to respond? Understanding the limitations that students with severe disabilities must cope with on a daily basis can help others respond in a positive and supportive manner versus a critical and punitive one.

Positive behavior supports for students with severe and multiple disabilities are not significantly different from those for other students. However, particularly careful attention is needed because of the complexity of these students' needs. A functional behavior analysis should be completed and a behavior intervention plan designed, implemented, and evaluated. Within the plan, the goal should be to enable students to get their needs met in appropriate ways (Bethune, & Wood, 2013; Mueller, Nkosi, & Hine, 2011).

Isabella, who was introduced at the beginning of the chapter, exemplifies the importance of using positive behavior supports with students with severe and multiple disabilities. By providing her with opportunities to be rewarded with her favorite music, she is learning appropriate behaviors that enable her to succeed in the general education classroom. The focus of a behavior support plan for a student like Isabella is to modify the environment as needed while simultaneously teaching prosocial and other adaptive skills. For example, if a difficult task is likely to elicit challenging behaviors, then efforts should be made to modify the task by either making it easier or breaking it into small and discrete skills and providing pictorial cues to help the student understand what he is to do. Similarly, by teaching positive and adaptive skills, the student can get her needs met in a socially acceptable manner. When challenging behaviors are associated with difficult tasks, the student might be taught either to ask for help as a way to lessen the frustration associated with the task or to ask to take a break as a way of temporarily avoiding the task altogether.

Did You Know?

Many students with severe and multiple disabilities use augmentative and alternative communication. You can learn more about this topic at the website of the International Society for Augmentative and Alternative Communication (ISAAC) (www.isaac-online.org), which lists resources, publications, and events and includes an idea exchange.

The way the student with severe or multiple disabilities asks for help or communicates these needs will vary. Some students may have adequate verbal language, and thus the focus of the intervention will be on teaching them to make requests at appropriate times. For students without verbal speech, alternative forms of communication—such as gestures, pictures, objects, and augmentative communication devices—may be used.

Inclusive Education

If you remember that inclusion is an increasingly research-based practice with numerous benefits for students, you can understand its importance for students with the most significant disabilities and the reasons why it is so stressed in this chapter. That is, inclusive education for students with severe disabilities does not refer only to the physical placement of students in age-appropriate general education classrooms. It also holds the expectation of systematic instruction, numerous support services, curricular adaptations, and differentiated outcomes. It also encompasses the firm commitment by all staff members in a school to share the responsibility for educating all students because it is their efforts that make the difference. Think about how each of the students introduced at the beginning of this chapter—Isabella, Jackson, and Cassie—are meeting success as educators address their IEP goals and objectives in the general education setting.

Remember, when students with significant disabilities participate in inclusive schooling, benefits accrue to teachers and other students as well (Cameron & Cook, 2013; Kurth, Lyon, & Shogren, 2015). Teachers gain the ability to learn together about the curriculum and individualizing instruction. More support is available to all students in a given classroom as special educators and related services provide support to all children. Students without disabilities (and their families) gain a greater understanding and acceptance of those who have disabilities and learn ways of providing natural supports in a variety of contexts (Olson, Leko, & Roberts, 2016).

MyEdLab **Self-Check 14.5**

MyEdLab **Application Exercise 14.7:** Teaching Students with Deaf-Blindness

---

Video Example
from
YouTube

▶ MyEdLab
Video Example 14.4

Video Example 14.4 highlights the love that parents have for their children with severe disabilities. (https://www.youtube.com/watch?v=FPxPPgVWbmY)

Perspectives of Parents and Families

As you might imagine, families' perceptions regarding their children with severe or multiple disabilities vary considerably. Some families view having a child with severe disabilities as a gift, but others may express more negative perceptions (e.g., Jackson & Roper, 2014; Turnbull, Turnbull, Erwin, & Soodak, 2006). Regardless, just as most parents have an unconditional love for their children, so, too, do parents of children with severe disabilities.

Family Members' Views of Their Children

Most parents eagerly seek out and highlight their children's gifts and talents. We all have experienced proud parents who eagerly share photos, newspaper clippings, or report cards that highlight their child's accomplishments. Families of children with severe and multiple disabilities also are able to quickly identify and share their children's gifts, as did Isabella's father in the story that opened this chapter. However, sometimes it is difficult for families of children with severe and multiple disabilities to see their positive attributes. Such a family may only see what the child cannot do. Such a narrow view of the child may in turn limit the opportunities the family provides. For example, if parents think their child cannot make choices, then the family will not include the child in the decision-making process.

Other factors influence how families come to perceive and thus accept a child with severe and multiple disabilities. The extent to which the family has the financial resources to pay for medical and other expenses associated with the disabilities can influence how it views the child. Similarly, access to extended family to help provide support can matter. Finally, the severity of a disability, the presence of challenging behavior, the quality of the child's educational program, and other external factors all can influence the family's perceptions. Clearly, this is a complex issue that requires that educators approach families as unique, bringing with them their own values, beliefs, and experiences that guide their perceptions and their behaviors (e.g., Bezdek, Summers, & Turnbull, 2010).

Considering Cultural Diversity

The way we are raised—specifically, the values and beliefs of our family, culture, religion, and community—influences our perceptions, including our views toward disabilities (Zheng, Maude, Brotherson, Summers, Palmer, & Erwin, 2015; Ravindran & Myers, 2012). Mainstream U.S. culture historically has viewed disabilities from a deficit orientation (Bottcher, 2012; Jones, 2012). However, not all families approach disabilities with a deficit approach, and this directly affects their children and their education. Specifically, families of different cultures may define disabilities differently (e.g., Al Khateeb, Al Hadidi, & Al Khatib, 2015; Long, Kao, Plante, Seifer, & Lobato, 2015). For example, some families see the birth of a child with a disability as a "gift from God," but families from other cultural and religious backgrounds may see the child's birth as punishment for some past indiscretion (Chen, Downing, Peckham-Hardin, 2002; McCabe, 2008). One view results in a goal of "fixing" the disability, the second results in a celebration, and the third results in feelings of shame and guilt.

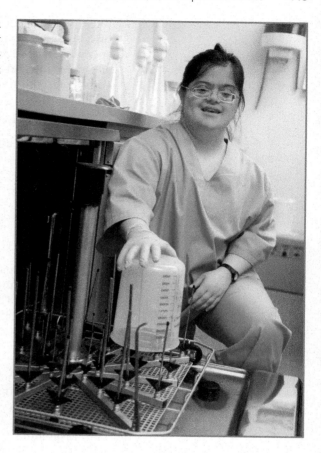

Parents of children with severe and multiple disabilities have the same goals as other parents—that their children lead happy, productive lives.

Similarly, in mainstream U.S. culture, educational programs for students with severe and multiple disabilities tend to focus on promoting independence and self-sufficiency (Erwin et al., 2016). For example, self-care, home care, academic skills, community access, vocational skills, and independent-living skills are typical targets. However, not all families share these values. Some traditional Latino families place less emphasis on acquiring self-help skills (Zuniga, 1998). Their children may enter school still reliant on others to help with feeding, dressing, and toileting. If educators fail to take the time to understand the family context, they may mistakenly conclude that the student is less capable than she really is. Also, because students with severe and multiple disabilities often experience deficits in these areas, the teacher is likely to identify instruction in self-help skills as a priority, even though family members may view the acquisition of academic, social, and communication skills as having greater importance.

Here is another example: In traditional Asian families, a child with a significant disability may be considered a source of shame, and caregiving often falls primarily on the mother. The child may, in essence, be hidden from others. For these families, community-based instruction and job training may be a lower priority than for families of European descent. In these situations, it is important for special educators to be aware of cultural factors that influence what families view as important and to work with families to develop educational plans that are consistent with those goals.

MyEdLab **Self-Check 14.6**

MyEdLab **Application Exercise 14.8:** Cultural Perspectives

Trends and Issues Affecting the Field of Severe and Multiple Disabilities

From the previous information provided on students having severe and multiple disabilities, you may be able to discern that several critical issues face professionals in this field. The practice of educating these students with their nondisabled peers is very much a trend as well as a critical issue. Two issues yet to be considered are accountability in assessment and integrated related service delivery.

Accountability of Academic Performance for All Students

Schools increasingly are being held accountable to ensure that all students learn and acquire basic skills and knowledge. Statewide tests are used to gauge schools' abilities to meet this charge. Since the 1997 reauthorization of IDEA, students with disabilities have been required to be included in any statewide testing process. This requirement was reaffirmed with the 2001 and 2015 reauthorizations of the Elementary and Secondary Education Act.

The Status of Alternate Assessment

Although most students with disabilities can participate in standard statewide tests with the use of proper accommodations (e.g., large print, extended time), these tests are not appropriate for students with the most significant needs (Anderson, Farley, & Tindal, 2015). Instead, IDEA requires that each state have an alternative assessment process to ensure that schools are meeting the needs of this group of students. That is, states must consider not only how to assess students but also what to assess. Specifically, the assessment must be directly linked to age-appropriate, grade-level content standards that apply to all students, but it also must incorporate a more functional set of learning outcomes. As for other students, the data from these assessments must be reported each year.

Approaches to alternate assessment are evolving rapidly. They generally blend the expectation that all students access the academic curriculum to the extent they can with the need to incorporate functional skills (Browder et al., 2004). Three approaches generally are used for assessment: (a) portfolio assessment and (b) authentic/performance assessment, both introduced earlier in this chapter, and (c) checklists and rating scales (Goldstein & Behuniak, 2011; Taylor & Pastor, 2013). These are explained in more detail in Data-Driven Decisions.

Concern continues to exist about alternate assessments (Goldstein & Behuniak, 2011; Schafer & Lissitz, 2009). Questions are being asked about which approaches provide the most accurate snapshot of a students' achievement, which approaches create that snapshot consistently across time, and which approaches are efficient enough that they can be implemented by educators without detracting from students' education.

DATA-DRIVEN DECISIONS

Approaches to Alternate Assessment

These are the alternate assessment approaches most often used to ensure that students with significant disabilities are included in achievement assessment systems. They are based on the curriculum in place for all students, although they may represent a subset of those standards. No more than 1% of all students are eligible to be assessed using these methods.

Portfolio Assessment

- A collection of samples of student work
- Often multiple samples that demonstrate growth/progress (e.g., number writing beginning with 0–2 and eventually increasing to 0–9)
- Based on the state's standards and directly related to the goals and objectives on a student's IEP

Performance Assessment

- Teacher/tester administered tasks given to the student based on the standards in the curriculum; often, the tasks are the same for all students, although they may be specified based on the student's IEP

- Real-time or video/audio assessment procedure with a rating of proficiency
- Used for tasks or behaviors that are not easily captured in another format such as a portfolio (e.g., problem solving or choice making)

Checklist/Rating Scale Assessment

- Teacher-completed analysis of the student's level of performance, typically applying standardized scale used for all students
- Rating scale is based on the standards in the core academic areas

In the near future, computer-based options for alternate assessment are likely to replace some current assessment practices for students with severe and multiple disabilities. An example of this has occurred in New York: Language arts and math alternate assessments now are computer based, while other assessments (e.g., science and social studies) use a portfolio approach.

Integrated Delivery of Related Services

A recommended practice in the area of severe and multiple disabilities is the integration of related and other services within the student's natural learning environment (Frattura & Capper, 2006; Hartmann, 2015; Kozleski, Yu, Satter, Francis, & Haines, 2015). This approach exists in contrast to *isolated service delivery*, a traditional approach in which specialists remove the student from a classroom and provide the service in a specialized environment, which tends to fragment understanding of the student into various deficit parts and does not lead to the development of a holistic program. Further, removing the student from a classroom means that he is missing valuable instructional time. Not only does the student miss instruction, but he also must generalize what was worked on in isolation with a specialist in a unique setting to the natural environment where it is most needed. These concepts apply whether the student is being educated in a special education or a general education classroom. For example, 15-year-old Derrick really enjoys his music class, where he has many opportunities to interact with his classmates. However, twice each week, the speech-language pathologist pulls him from this class to work on articulation goals in her office. Derrick misses out on the social interactions with his nondisabled peers as well as what the class is practicing for an upcoming recital. Although he likes the speech-language pathologist, he is not very responsive during this speech therapy time and obviously does not like working on pronouncing words that are difficult for him—words that he usually does not use when speaking to friends. At the same time, his music teacher and his peers are not learning ways of helping him to articulate his words because they never witness the techniques that the speech-language pathologist recommends.

Back to the Cases

Now that you've read about severe and multiple disabilities, look back at the student stories at the beginning of this chapter. Then, answer the questions about each of their cases.

MyEdLab **Case Study 14.1**

ISABELLA. Yesterday you were walking down the hall at your school when you overheard a conversation about Isabella between two people who are active in the parent–teacher organization. The gist of their discussion was questioning the expenditure of public funds to buy a state-of-the-art communication device for her. You heard one comment that kept you awake last night: "Why spend all that money on someone who will never be very communicative or lead an independent life with a job?" You decide to prepare a response for this parent so that you can use it when you see her again.

MyEdLab **Case Study 14.2**

JACKSON. As noted earlier in the chapter, Jackson is 14 years old, is nonverbal, and has a severe intellectual disability and multiple disabilities. Currently, he is educated mostly in a special education classroom with typical peer helpers working with him. Jackson's mother, Ms. Scanlan, worries that she may soon need to consider placing Jackson in a residential facility because of his size, strength, and increasingly aggressive behavior. Create a solid transition plan for Jackson, with the understanding of the importance of collaboration when addressing behavioral concerns, defining roles, and understanding responsibilities.

MyEdLab **Case Study 14.3**

CASSIE. The description of Cassie at the beginning of the chapter might be a description of any high school girl whose favorite pastimes are boys, shopping, music, and participation in school events. Cassie has benefited socially as well as academically from studying in an integrated setting. Now, as an 11th-grader, she is beginning to think about her postsecondary future and a job in the photography field. As a member of the IEP team, develop a transition plan for Cassie.

15

Students Who Are Gifted and Talented

HARRISON

Harrison's parents realized he was gifted when he was just 2 years old when one day they listened, astonished, as he picked up a recently delivered advertisement and began reading it aloud. They enrolled him in a preschool program and nurtured his talents at home, deciding to homeschool him when he turned 5. Harrison and his parents liked this arrangement, and his knowledge and skills grew exponentially. This year, however, Harrison is enrolled in his local elementary school in Ms. McClean's third-grade class, a change because of his parents' recent divorce. Twice each week a district teacher for students who are gifted and talented offers an enrichment program for Harrison and other students who are eligible for the GATE (gifted and talented education) program, but Harrison is already saying that he is bored with third grade and with GATE. Unaccustomed to the routines and procedures of elementary school, he sometimes refuses to put away materials when asked, and he often expresses surprise at what his classmates do not know. Ms. McClean is concerned at how often he is overheard saying to another student, "That's easy—you should know how to do it." Academically, Harrison is so far ahead of his peers that discussions are already being held about him skipping a grade next year, but in the meantime, Ms. McClean is trying to challenge him while also helping him to learn the expectations of a public school classroom.

KIMBERLY

Kimberly wakes up every school day with a knot in her stomach. She thinks a lot about what is going on and tries to analyze what is occurring, but she does not see any way to change things. When she recalls elementary school, her memories are filled with friendly teachers, interesting activities, and pride in her rapidly growing knowledge and skills. Now, though, she dreads school. She already knows most of what is being taught, and she feels as if doing assignments is surrendering when she would prefer to rebel. In addition, if she does well on the work, it humiliates her classmates because many of them do not learn easily, and it humiliates her because they tease her about being too smart. To her, being called "Einstein" is the ultimate insult. Kimberly's father has been threatening to take away her after-school computer privileges if her grades do not

improve, but she just cannot seem to make that happen. Her parents act as though she is doing this deliberately to hurt them. She would never, ever do that, but she still just cannot seem to do what they ask. Her grades are not so bad that she won't be promoted to eighth grade, but she clearly will not make the honor roll, and that upsets her parents, too. Kimberly is tired of being nagged by teachers and parents, tired of not wanting to achieve, and tired of worrying about everything.

GRAYSON

Grayson is a 10th-grade student who has had a unique educational journey. In first grade, he was identified as gifted because he already could read at a fourth-grade level and displayed math skills nearly as advanced. However, Grayson tended to be very rigid in his interactions with others, insisting that rules in games be followed precisely and becoming extraordinarily upset if those rules were not followed. He also struggled to work with his peers; he did not seem to realize that they did not always want to do just what he wanted. When Grayson's behavior problems kept escalating, he was evaluated for special education services and was determined to be eligible as having autism, specifically Asperger syndrome. The team decided that he would probably do best in a general education class with supports for his abilities but without participating directly in the gifted program, the thinking being that the program was raising his anxiety and contributing to the behavior problems. However, by the end of middle school, that decision was revisited, partly because Grayson's voracious appetite for learning was outpacing the support his teachers felt they could give him. Now in high school, he is officially considered "twice exceptional"—that is, he is gifted and also has a disability. He participates in advanced classes, but he still has difficulty making friends, at least partly because he frequently comments in class that he's bored and that, while other students might need to learn what is being taught, he already knows it. He is very interested in mathematics and already plans a career in that field. He is much less interested in English and does only enough schoolwork to earn average grades in that area. His special education teacher and the counselor are working with him intensely on social skills and his transition plan.

When you were in school, did you have classmates whose academic abilities were astounding? Whose scores on tests always made those of the rest of the class appear mediocre? Perhaps you knew someone who did not excel academically but who had extraordinary ability in dance, music, drama, or art. You might also have had a friend who kept her abilities well hidden, a friend who was a strong leader away from school but quiet and unmotivated in the classroom, perhaps like Kimberly, whom you met at the beginning of the chapter. All of these descriptions apply to students who are gifted and talented—students who clearly have extraordinary abilities or who seem to have great potential to develop their abilities.

Are you wondering why these students are addressed in a text about students with disabilities? After all, they are **not** a group with the protection of federal special education law. There are several reasons: First, if you think of this text in terms of the broader concept of *exceptionality*, then it is easy to understand that students who are gifted and talented are as exceptional as the other students discussed. Second, as you will learn as you read this chapter, some students with disabilities also have gifts and talents, and so their particularly unique needs should be considered, and that topic is included in this chapter. Finally, a number of the concepts already addressed in this text are directly applicable to this student group. As you read this chapter, however, do keep in mind that students who are gifted and talented are not protected in the same ways as students who are receiving special education and that no federal mandate requires services for them.

Understanding Giftedness

The study of giftedness has been marked by an evolution in definitions, programs and services, and professional interest. Today, new conceptualizations of giftedness are bringing renewed attention to the needs of students who have extraordinary abilities.

Development of the Field of Giftedness

Societal interest in extraordinary ability has existed for centuries (Jolly, 2005). As shown in Figure 15.1, it was the work of Lewis Terman and his colleagues (Jolly, 2008; Terman & Oden, 1959) that laid the groundwork for efforts in U.S. schools to identify and nurture students who are gifted. In a longitudinal study begun in 1921 and continuing until 2020, Terman and his successors have debunked myths about social and emotional abnormalities of students who are gifted. Their research has shown that a large number of these individuals have accomplished significant achievements but not eminence and has suggested that success generally is associated with a lifelong high degree of motivation or persistence.

Other researchers during the first half of the 20th century (e.g., Havighurst, Stivers, & DeHaan, 1955; Hollingworth, 1926, 1942; Passow, Goldberg, Tannenbaum, & French, 1955; Witty, 1951) also provided insights into the characteristics of students who are highly gifted. They suggested that giftedness should be defined more broadly than what can be measured on an intelligence test and led efforts to develop specialized programs for these students.

Emergence of a Profession

The 1959 launch of the Soviet space capsule *Sputnik* was perceived by many Americans—especially those in the scientific, engineering, and mathematical fields—as an embarrassing educational failure. As a result, a flurry of publications offered guidance to teachers on how to teach and counsel gifted students, but gifted education remained optional in public schools. Despite the narrow focus of this era, understanding of giftedness eventually broadened beyond high intelligence and

FIGURE 15.1   Time Line of the Development of the Field of Gifted Education

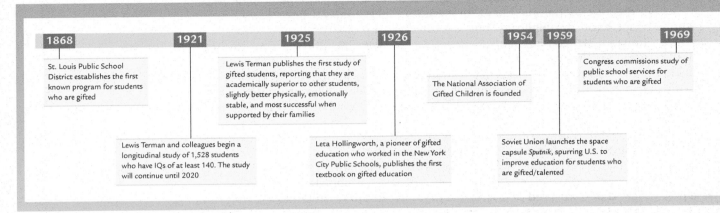

extraordinary academic skills, extending to areas such as athletic and musical ability.

Throughout the 1970s and 1980s, programs for students who were gifted grew and prospered, supported increasingly by state educational funding. This era in the field of gifted education culminated in 1988 when Congress passed the Jacob K. Javits Gifted and Talented Students Education Act. This law focused on identifying and serving students who were gifted and from culturally diverse groups, those living in poverty, and those with disabilities. However, no funding accompanied the law until 1994.

Recent Changes in the Field

In the 1990s, federal support for gifted education emphasized serving educationally disadvantaged students (Brulles, Castellano, & Laing, 2010; Castellano & Díaz, 2002). For example, publication of *National Excellence: A Case for Developing America's Talent* (U.S. Department of Education, 1993), a report that updated the definition of *giftedness*, noted the importance of nurturing gifts and talents in all students, and renewed attention on the need to identify and serve students from diverse groups.

As the field of gifted education has matured in the 21st century, it has been characterized by an increase of collaborative services and inclusion of students in general education settings (e.g., Brulles, & Winebrenner, 2012; Renzulli 2016; Subotnik, Olszewski-Kubilius, & Worrell, 2011). Current trends in education have raised issues for gifted education similar to those raised for special education, such as the possible negative impact of high-stakes testing on students who are gifted and talented (Moon, 2009). In addition, efforts to expand enrichment to whole schools have become part of school reform (e.g., Renzulli & D'Souza, 2014; Renzulli & Reis, 2012; VanTassel-Baska, 2015). This concept is illustrated by the curriculum options presented in Instruction in Action.

Definition of Giftedness

Throughout this text, you have been introduced to definitions of various exceptionalities with quotes from IDEA and authoritative professional organizations. For *giftedness,* no single authoritative definition can be cited; IDEA does not address it. States define giftedness depending on priorities and needs. However, one definition often used is a 1978 variation of the definition that appeared in the *Marland Report* (Stephens & Karnes, 2000):

> The term "gifted and talented children" means children and, whenever applicable, youth, who are identified at the preschool, elementary, or secondary level as possessing demonstrated or potential abilities that give evidence of high performance

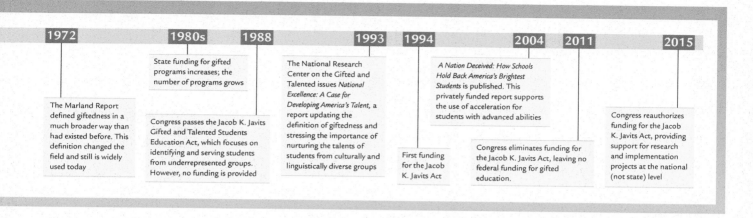

capability in areas such as intellectual, creative, specific academic or leadership ability or in the performing and visual arts and who by reason thereof require services or activities not ordinarily provided by the school. (P.L. 95–561, Title IX, [a])

This definition also clarified that giftedness includes these areas:

- General intellectual ability
- Specific academic aptitude
- Creative or productive thinking
- Leadership ability
- Visual and performing arts

The most recent federal definition of giftedness is included in the Jacob K. Javits Gifted and Talented Students Education Act of 1988, which was last reauthorized in 2001 as part of the Elementary and Secondary Education Act, then called the *No Child Left Behind Act*:

Children and youth with outstanding talent who perform or show the potential for performing at remarkably high levels of accomplishment when compared with others of their age, experience, or environment. These children and youth exhibit high performance capability in intellectual, creative, and/or artistic areas, possess an unusual leadership capacity, or excel in specific academic fields. They require services or activities not ordinarily provided by the schools. Outstanding talents are present in children and youth from all cultural groups, across all economic strata, and in all areas of human endeavor. (P. L. 100–297 §4130)

Another source for definitions of giftedness is the field, including professional organizations. For example, a third definition of giftedness is offered by the National Association for Gifted Children (NAGC) (2010):

Gifted individuals are those who demonstrate outstanding levels of aptitude (defined as an exceptional ability to reason and learn) or competence (documented performance or achievement in top 10% or rarer) in one or more domains. Domains include any structured area of activity with its own symbol system (e.g., mathematics, music, language) and/or set of sensorimotor skills (e.g., painting, dance, sports).

As you look at the older but still widely used *Marland* definition, the more recent Javits definition, and the broad NAGC definition, what differences do you see? Which definition best suits Harrison, Kimberly, and Grayson, the students described at the beginning of this chapter? In many ways, the definitions capture the evolution of thinking about giftedness: the shift from using the term *gifted* to using the term *talented*, the recognition that extraordinary ability may exist in one or several areas, and the acknowledgment that giftedness exists across the diversity of today's students.

Did You Know?

Carman (2013) reviewed 104 studies (in 38 journals) of students who are gifted and talented, analyzing researchers' definitions of giftedness. She found wide variations among the definitions used and concluded that because no uniform definition of giftedness exists, results from research are less generalizable than they otherwise would be, thus interfering with the development of a strong knowledge base.

INSTRUCTION IN ACTION

Instructional Activities Based on Specific Aptitudes

These are ideas for teaching students with talents in particular areas. Many of the ideas represent exemplary teaching ideas that can be implemented in some form for all learners.

Reading

- Select biographies and books in the content areas (including subjects dealing with multicultural issues) for supplemental reading.
- Provide literature that is broad based in form (myths, nonfiction, biography, poetry, etc.), is rich in language, and provides role models for emulation.
- Use children's literature that involves finding solutions to scientific, environmental, and mathematical problems or mysteries.

Writing

- Use a writing program that encourages incorporation of ideas from literature into stories.
- Encourage extracurricular experiences that are language based (e.g., yearbook).
- Encourage personal journal writing.

Verbal Expression

- Include experiences in foreign language in the curriculum.
- Help students develop word relationship skills (e.g., analogies, antonyms, homonyms).
- Provide opportunities for students to speak in public settings.
- Teach oral presentation and debating skills.

Math

- Focus on developing spatial skills and concepts through geometry and other media.
- Focus on logic problems that require deductive thinking skills and inference.
- Emphasize mathematical concepts more and computational skills less.
- Emphasize applications of mathematics in the real world through creation of special projects.
- Focus on the use of probability, estimation, statistics, and computer technology.
- Apply mathematical concepts across the curriculum—for example, have students assess the mathematical challenges of planning a Civil War battle.

Science

- Provide reading material that suggests experiments students can try, and provide a balance between text and activities.
- Help students develop a scientific hobby, such as bird watching, gardening, or electronics.
- Provide opportunities for naturalistic observation, for example, at a local pond.
- Provide basic tools such as a magnifying glass, binoculars, and a camera.

Social Studies

- Encourage an understanding of cultures.
- Study the development of cities.
- Encourage the development of geography skills and map making.
- Encourage the development of cultural literacy based on important historical events in U.S. history and world history.
- Help students develop an understanding of global interdependence.

Creativity/Aesthetics

- Provide opportunities for art appreciation.
- Provide music opportunities.
- Provide dramatic instruction.
- Provide opportunities for dance and movement.
- Consider providing an artist mentor.
- Provide unstructured activities, allowing students to choose the medium of expression.

Leadership and Social Skills

- Encourage work with student government, the safety patrol, and other school organizations and community groups, such as Scouts, book clubs, or church.
- Assist students in selecting biographies and autobiographies about high achievers.
- Provide monitored opportunities for involvement in volunteer and social service work in the community or at school.

Source: Based on Van Tassel-Baska, J. (1998). *Excellence in educating the gifted* (3rd ed.). Denver, CO: Love.

Generally, then, and based on these definitions, **giftedness** is evidence of advanced development across intellectual areas, within a specific academic or arts-related area, or unusual organizational power to bring about desired results. **Talent** sometimes is defined as extraordinary ability in a specific area, but it also now sometimes is used interchangeably with *giftedness*.

Contemporary thinking about giftedness recognizes that it has many dimensions in addition to academic achievement and is not a static student characteristic.

Alternative Conceptualizations of Giftedness

Many other conceptualizations of giftedness have been developed by professionals in this field. For example, Renzulli proposed that giftedness includes three related dimensions: (a) above-average ability; (b) task commitment or motivation; and (c) creativity, or the capacity for innovation, originality, expressiveness, and imagination and the ability to manipulate ideas in fluent, flexible, elaborate, and original ways (Renzulli & Reis, 2014). Renzulli's model has been foundational for professionals seeking ways to broaden the concept of giftedness and expand opportunities for students from diverse groups. Tomlinson and Jarvis (2014) contribute the notion that giftedness is not static but rather influenced greatly by opportunity and environment. She argues that schools should maximize every student's potential, a topic addressed in more detail later in this chapter.

Yet another conceptualization of giftedness is based on Gardner's work in the area of multiple intelligences (Gardner, 1993; Kornilov, Tan, Elliott, Sternberg, & Grigorenko, 2012; Mourgues, Tan, Hein, Elliott, & Grigorenko, 2016). Gardner argues that intelligence cannot be reduced to a single dimension reported by a test score. He notes that at least nine types of intelligence can be identified and that students may excel in any one or several of these: verbal/linguistic, visual/spatial, logical/mathematical, bodily/kinesthetic, musical, intrapersonal, interpersonal, naturalist, and existential. The Professional Edge provides more information about each of these intelligences. Gardner notes that many students have relative strengths; that is, in a self-comparison, they have more ability in some intelligences than in other intelligences. However, he defines *giftedness* as an absolute strength or having significantly more ability in any or all of the intelligences when compared to other individuals.

A Final Word on Definitions

Taken together, the definitions can be a little confusing. If you think about the purpose of defining an exceptionality such as giftedness, though, you can make sense of them. Definitions are important because they help professionals pinpoint

Teaching to Diverse Student Needs Through Multiple Intelligences (MI)

Over the past three decades, some professionals have reconceptualized intelligence from the traditional notion to one that emphasizes its multidimensional nature (Gardner, 1993; Sternberg, 2015). One strategy for reaching the range of diverse needs in many of today's classrooms—from those of students who struggle to those of students who are talented—is to arrange instruction to take into account nine intelligences:

1. *Verbal/linguistic.* The ability to use words effectively in prose, poetry, formal speech, informal conversation, and other forms, as well as the ability to understand others' words.
2. *Visual/spatial.* The ability to visualize forms, shapes, patterns, and designs, regardless of whether they exist in concrete form, as well as the ability to discern position in space and directionality.
3. *Logical/mathematical.* The ability to understand through the use of patterns as well as symbolic representations and the ability to apply reasoning.
4. *Bodily/kinesthetic.* The ability to use the body effectively through athletics, dance, movement, and other activities, as well as the ability to use the body skillfully (e.g., for delicate or intricate tasks, as a surgeon or sculptor must use her hands).
5. *Musical.* The ability to perceive, analyze, create, and perform through music, including culminating in practicing professionals such as composers, critics, and musicians.
6. *Intrapersonal.* The ability to analyze and understand oneself and to be able to take actions based on that understanding.

7. *Interpersonal.* The ability to observe, grasp, and act on the moods, emotions, perceptions, and other aspects of relationships with people.
8. *Naturalist.* The ability to understand, respond to, and explain phenomena encountered in nature, as illustrated by the work performed by professionals such as farmers, hunters, and veterinarians.
9. *Existentialist.* The ability to look at the "big picture" of human existence, often expressed through a high level of interest in philosophical questions.

The following websites can help you explore this fascinating and useful way of thinking about teaching and learning and the almost infinite options for differentiating instruction:

- Edutopia *http://www.edutopia.org/multiple-intelligences-research*

This site includes information about each of the intelligences, distinguishes them from learning styles, and clarifies the status of research on this approach to conceptualizing intelligence.

- John Hopkins University Professional Development New Horizons: Multiple Intelligences *http://education.jhu.edu/PD/newhorizons/strategies/topics/mi/*

This website outlines multiple intelligences and provides links to implementing teaching strategies related to them, including applications to English learners. It also includes information about MI as applied in the arts.

---

who they are studying in their research, and they help clarify who is entitled to special programs and services. When viewed this way, then, the definitions just outlined collectively represent an accurate picture of thinking about giftedness. They recognize the traditional perspective of high academic ability, but they also stress the importance of nurturing the talents of a diverse group of students.

Prevalence

Because so many definitions of giftedness have been offered, so little agreement exists on exactly what giftedness and talents are, and so much of gifted education is focused at the state and local rather than the federal level, estimates of the prevalence of students who are gifted and talented vary considerably. For example, a recent national study of programs for students who are gifted and talented reported that the percentage of students identified at the elementary level ranged from 1% to 50%, while at the middle and high school levels participants reported that between 1% and 10% of students are so identified (Callahan, Moon & Oh, 2014). The National Association for Gifted Children (NAGC) (2016a, 2016b) suggests that the prevalence is between 6% and 10%, or between 3 and 5 million students. But an example of how state policies can affect prevalence figures can be noted: In Connecticut, no more than 5% of students may be identified as gifted, and in Maine the cap is 3% to 5%.

Prevalence, Race, and Gender

In several chapters of this book, you have read that students from minority groups are overrepresented as having disabilities. Here, the opposite is true. Although specific statistics are difficult to find because no single federal agency gathers the data, professionals unanimously acknowledge that students from minority groups are significantly underrepresented in programs for those who are gifted and talented (Ford, Moore, & Scott, 2011; Gallagher, 2015). For example, Ford (2015) examined procedures followed for identifying students as gifted in an "equality" district (treat all students the same) versus an "equity" district (treat students based on their backgrounds and needs). Although the two districts' racial composition was approximately the same (African American and Hispanic populations), the latter district identified far fewer diverse students than did the former district. A nationwide concerted effort is under way to ensure that students from minority groups are not overlooked for gifted education (Esquierdo & Arreguín-Anderson, 2012; Yoon & Gentry, 2009).

Girls are another group underrepresented among students identified as gifted and talented (Kerr, Vuyk, & Rea, 2012; Smith-Doerr, 2012). This fact can be illustrated by examining specific content areas. For example, girls are less likely than boys to be identified as mathematically gifted (e.g., Olszewski-Kubilius, & Lee, 2011; Robinson, Lubienski, Copur, 2011). When they are identified, they are less likely to develop their talent by enrolling in related advanced courses in math or science during high school (Heilbronner, 2009). Although the reasons for these differences are not entirely clear, contributing factors may include parents' beliefs and treatment of their daughters and teachers' biases about boys excelling in math and science while girls excel in English (Petersen, 2013). The Professional Edge explores issues regarding giftedness in girls.

Determining Factors

Giftedness generally is considered to be the result of a combination of genetic and environmental factors (Thompson & Oehlert, 2010). The interaction can be highlighted by a single fact about giftedness: Although firstborn children are most likely among all children in a family to be gifted, if one child is gifted, chances are that other children in the family will be gifted, too. Firstborn children often receive considerable adult attention, and this environmental factor can help to maximize their potential. However, the fact that other children in the same family often are gifted suggests that heredity also may play a role.

> Video Example
>
> from
>
> YouTube
>
> MyEdLab
> **Video Example 15.1**
>
> Are you ready to meet students who are gifted and talented? This video provides a glimpse into their experiences in school. (https://www.youtube.com/watch?v=xVQBXr2I8Zs)

MyEdLab **Self-Check 15.1**

MyEdLab **Application Exercise 15.1:** Where Does Your State Stand?

MyEdLab **Application Exercise 15.2:** Understanding Giftedness

---

Characteristics of Individuals Who Are Gifted and Talented

Programs and services for students who are gifted and talented are based on studies of these students' characteristics, including cognitive, academic, and social/emotional (e.g., Housand, 2016a; Pfeiffer, 2012; Reis & Sullivan, 2009). As you read about each characteristic, think about students with whom you have

Girls who are gifted often face unique challenges in developing their potential. First, they may face external barriers, such as these:

- Parents who send subtle but conflicting messages, setting expectations for high achievement but also preferring appropriately feminine, demure behavior
- Bias in school, particularly in math and science classes
- Advertising that presents stereotyped and unrealistic images of ideal women that focus on physical appearance

In addition, girls also may face internal barriers:

- A loss of self-confidence as they grow older
- A sense that being gifted is a social disadvantage in interactions with peers
- Perfectionism that leads to setting unreasonable goals and unhealthy work habits in trying to achieve them

The combination of external and internal barriers often leads to underachievement. An example can be drawn from schools: In too many cases, bright boys who are highly verbal, who like to debate, and who frequently express curiosity are considered precocious, while girls with the same traits are considered aggressive. Other research has found that boys vocally dominate classrooms and receive more attention than girls.

Here are profiles of three women who rose above challenges to become eminent in their fields.

Dr. Maya Angelou was a poet, educator, author, and civil rights activist who influenced people all over the world with the beauty and wisdom of her words.

Judge Sonia Sotomayor is the third woman and the first Hispanic in history appointed to the U.S. Supreme Court. Although she grew up in public housing projects and her father died when she was 9 years old, with her mother's support she attended Princeton University and later Yale Law School.

Dr. Barbara McClintock was an American geneticist. In 1983, she became the first woman ever to receive an unshared Nobel Prize for her discovery of genetic transposition.

Sources: Based on TwiceGifted.net (2004). *Gender issues: Gifted girls*, Retrieved from www.twicegifted.net/gender.htm; and Reis, S. M. (2002), Social and emotional issues faced by gifted girls in elementary and secondary school, *SENG Newsletter*, 2(3), 1–5.

worked, either as a student or as a preservice professional. Have you known a student who displayed any of these characteristics?

Cognitive Characteristics

Students who are gifted often display advanced behaviors in the cognitive domain from an early age, and when they are nurtured, these characteristics continue to develop. As you read about these students' cognitive traits, keep these ideas in mind:

1. Not all students who are gifted display all of the characteristics or at the same level.
2. These characteristics may be viewed as developmental in the sense that some students may display them at early stages of development while others may not display them until later stages.
3. Many students who are gifted have particular clusters of these characteristics.
4. These characteristics may be evident only when students are engaged in an area of interest and aptitude.

Ability to Manipulate Abstract Symbol Systems

A student who is gifted may understand language and mathematics at an earlier age than is typical and may have unusual abilities for solving puzzles. These skills often continue to evolve throughout childhood and into adulthood. Prodigies such as Bobby Fisher, who benefited from mentoring at the Manhattan Chess Club, and Wolfgang Mozart, who inherited a genetic predisposition for music from Leopold Mozart, are examples of people for whom talent and a supportive environment resulted in eminence, or adult achievement of a high level in a particular field after years of productivity.

Power of Concentration

A student who is gifted and absorbed by a particular project or topic may be somewhat like an absent-minded professor. Both display a high degree of concentration and an ability to focus on a problem for a considerable period of time. For example, Julia became interested in horticulture at the age of 7. She found books about plants at her local library and spent most of her free time reading and studying about them. By the age of 11, she knew the names and growing conditions of all of the trees, shrubs, and flowers in her community.

Unusually Well Developed Memory

Memory, the ability to retain and recall past experience, is essential for acquiring knowledge and skills. Even from an early age, many students who are gifted have a phenomenal memory for information they have seen only once. One young boy at age 3 had memorized all the license plates, house numbers, and telephone numbers in his neighborhood. Another young girl at age 4 could recite Clement Moore's *A Visit from St. Nick* in its entirety after only one practice session.

Although memory is a central aspect of intelligence, it can be trivialized into spelling contest activity and other demonstrations and feats that have few long-term implications and little usefulness. However, the ability to recall military events, battle strategies, and their historical significance is an example of acquired information that can be used to understand and connect to other disciplines.

Early Language Interest and Development

Students who are gifted often exhibit precocious language development and an early strong interest in reading. Although early reading for all young children is more common today than it was several decades ago—probably because of the influence of smaller families, educational television, access to electronic media, and other societal changes—it is still moderately predictive of later advanced reading behavior (Olson, Evans, & Keckler, 2006).

Curiosity

Students who are gifted usually display curiosity—a strong need to know and to understand how the world works. From early childhood on, they crave making sense of the world. Adults who treat their questions with respect and provide information appropriate to the needs of these students will help build in them a personality orientation that seeks to discover the world. Harrison, whom you met at the beginning of the chapter, displays this characteristic.

Curious children ask questions frequently, and often these questions are on adult subjects that are fundamental to the large issues of life, such as "How was the world created?" and "Why do people die?" This type of questioning illustrates the advanced level of thought in which such students engage, an important indication of advanced development.

Preference for Independent Work

Students who are gifted often prefer working alone, figuring things out for themselves. This trait reflects their enjoyment in constructing an internal schema to solve problems rather than a tendency toward antisocial behavior. After eighth grade, Robert attended a special summer program at a major university and told the instructor that his goal was to complete algebra and trigonometry so that he could take Advanced Placement (AP) calculus in the fall. The instructor replied that all Robert needed to do was finish two math books, whereupon Robert said, "Give me the books." He reached his goal, and he began high school enrolled in the calculus class.

Multiple Interests

Students who are gifted have large storehouses of information and good memory skills. This combination often leads to these children having a wide range of interests. For example, Latasha was a 5-year-old child in first grade who appeared highly able, and the teacher decided to mention to her the concept of birds as linear descendants of dinosaurs. Even so, the girl's response, "Oh, you mean like *Archaeopteryx*," came as a surprise to the teacher. When asked about her favorite books, Latasha spoke of an interest in science fiction and in H. G. Wells's *War of the Worlds*, which she had read four times. Latasha's story illustrates that having multiple interests may be missed or go unappreciated in students who are gifted if the activities used with them do not allow for open exploration in a variety of areas. Further, multiple interests also can create frustration when a student is required to focus on a single and unpreferred area of study.

Ability to Generate Original Ideas

Students who are gifted can generate novel ideas alone or in collaboration with others. For example, John was a published poet in fourth grade partly because of his teacher's encouragement and partly by virtue of the writing talent search in his large school system. In another example, Lien, identified with a learning disability, and Phillip, identified as having an emotional disability, collaborated successfully as gifted 10-year-olds on building a model city, complete with electricity.

Academic Characteristics

The academic abilities of students who are gifted and talented often reflect their intellectual skills. Figure 15.2 presents some of the most common academic characteristics of these students, although unless students are academically gifted across all areas, they may not have all the characteristics listed.

Grayson is an example of a student who does not have broad academic talents. He excels in mathematics but not in English. Not surprisingly, he and other students who are similar to him, especially if they also have special needs, may be unmotivated in studying nonpreferred subjects (Olszewski-Kubilius, Subotnik, & Worrell, 2015). Positive Behavior Supports looks more closely at this topic.

Did You Know?

Some parents and educators think that students who are gifted and talented are just like other children—except for their special abilities. This is not the case. Students who are gifted and talented sometimes may seem like many individuals—that is, like an elementary student when riding a bike, like a teenager when reading, and like an adult when debating about an issue of interest. This notion is referred to as *asynchronous development*.

FIGURE 15.2   **Academic Characteristics of Students Who Are Gifted and Talented**

Reading Behaviors
- Has early knowledge of the alphabet
- Often reads early or unlocks the reading process quickly and sometimes idiosyncratically
- Reads with expression
- Has a high interest in reading; reads voraciously

Writing Behaviors
- Displays early ability to make written sound–symbol correspondence
- Exhibits fluency and elaboration in story writing
- Uses advanced sentence structure and patterns
- May show an interest in adult topics for writing, such as the state of the environment, death, war, and so on
- Writes on a topic or story for an extended period of time
- Generates many writing ideas, often of a divergent nature
- Uses precise, descriptive language to evoke an image

Speaking Behaviors
- Learns to speak early
- Has a high-receptive vocabulary
- Uses advanced sentence structure
- Uses similes, metaphors, and analogies in daily conversation
- Exhibits highly verbal behavior in speech (e.g., talks a lot, speaks rapidly, articulates well)
- Enjoys acting out story events and situations

Mathematical Behaviors
- Has early curiosity and understanding about the quantitative aspects of things
- Is able to think logically and symbolically about quantitative and spatial relationships
- Perceives and generalizes about mathematical patterns, structures, relations, and operations
- Reasons analytically, deductively, and inductively
- Abbreviates mathematical reasoning to find rational, economical solutions
- Displays flexibility and reversibility of mental processes in mathematical activity
- Remembers mathematical symbols, relationships, proofs, methods of solution, and so forth
- Transfers learning to novel situations and solutions
- Displays energy and persistence in solving mathematical problems
- Has a mathematical perception of the world

Social and Emotional Characteristics

Students who are gifted and talented often display social and emotional characteristics that are somewhat different from those discussed in relation to other students. As you read about these characteristics, think about how they might affect these students' interactions with classmates, teachers, and others.

Sense of Justice

Many students who are gifted display a strong sense of justice in their relationships. At later ages, they generally are attracted to causes that promote social equality and activities that reflect their concern for a humane world. For example, at age 6, Renee wanted to protest the nuclear waste dump disposal procedures in her community. She created signs, organized her friends, and held a kids' march.

Altruism and Idealism

Consistent with their sense of social justice, students who are gifted also often display a helping attitude toward others. For example, they may want to volunteer at a hospital or a senior center in the community, taking on a caregiving

POSITIVE • **BEHAVIOR** • SUPPORTS

Tackling the Challenge of Underachievement

Underachievement in academic settings is a major problem among some students who are gifted. Underachievement usually is the result of a lack of motivation (e.g., Liem & Chua, 2016), which may be caused by any of the following:

- General boredom
- Depression
- Impact of another disability (e.g., ADHD or a learning disability)
- Fear of failure
- Lack of challenging work
- Lack of meaningful work
- Lack of study skills
- Lack of family support for learning

Teachers can use these strategies to help to address motivation problems among students who are gifted:

- Counseling students individually on issues that may be affecting their achievement
- Using mastery learning strategies based on assessing student skills in order to assign work at appropriate levels; this approach needs strong teacher oversight to monitor for potential learning problems
- Conferencing with parents on how the motivation problem is displayed in school with dialogue on how to collaborate between home and school for improvement
- Teaching students metacognitive strategies directly related to planning, monitoring, and assessing learning progress

- Setting motivation "traps" by designing high-interest activities that will draw students into learning activities (e.g., having them write letters to their heroes or design advertising for a popular movie)
- Employing a tutorial model of instruction to assess the nature and extent of the problem
- Clustering students with motivation problems for instruction
- Encouraging student inquiry, hands-on work, and discussion activities
- Allowing students variety and choice in classroom and homework activities
- Providing extra encouragement based on praising specific accomplishments when performance standards are met
- Asking students to consider seriously the implications of not succeeding in their classes using items such as these:

  a. If I do poorly in this class, then _____;
  b. This class is important because _____; and
  c. The thing that I am most interested in learning more about is _____.

(Siegle & McCoach, 2005, p. 24)

Keep in mind that to the extent you consistently communicate to students, including those who are gifted, that you believe in their ability to achieve even when they appear uninterested, you can help them to reach their potential. How could you apply these ideas to Kimberly, the student introduced at the beginning of the chapter?

---

attitude. This altruism—unselfish concern for the welfare of others—and idealism—the act of envisioning things in an ideal form—frequently lead to student involvement in service organizations or leisure activities that can consume large amounts of energy but become a basis for later career decisions. One risk can be identified with these characteristics, however. Although students with special gifts and talents sometimes appropriately are asked to assist classmates, they should not spend so much time assisting classmates that their own learning is affected.

Sense of Humor

Have you ever known someone who could easily recognize or appreciate the inconsistencies and incongruities of everyday experience? Students who are gifted often have this ability, and it gives them a keen sense of humor (Bergen, 2009). However, humor also may signal difficulties. It sometimes is used to bully others or to defuse painful experiences such as being the victim of teasing or bullying (Peters & Bain, 2011). It also can be used for self-deprecation and self-defense, leading some students who are gifted to become known as class clowns or stand-up comics. Humor also may mask a sense of alienation. For all these reasons, humor from these students should be analyzed carefully.

Emotional Intensity

Just as students who are gifted are more able cognitively, they frequently experience emotional reactions at a deeper level than their peers, showing a capacity for emotional intensity, or the ability to focus emotions for long periods on a single subject or idea (Fonseca, 2016; Stutler, 2011). For example, the death of a pet caused prolonged grieving for Dylan. His emotional intensity was later apparent in his support for animal rights and his volunteer work at a local animal shelter. This characteristic, though, sometimes can make students who are gifted targets of bullying. Think of how Kimberly, the middle school student described at the beginning of the chapter, is reacting to what some might consider typical transition stresses as she moves from elementary to middle school.

Perfectionism

Students who are gifted may display characteristics of perfectionism, or striving for a self-imposed advanced goal or unrealistic standard (e.g., Mofield & Peters, 2015). These students focus undue energy on doing everything exactly so, and they dislike it if they or others make mistakes. For example, Sally became incensed when she received a score of 98% on her paper because of a punctuation error. She immediately asked the teacher if she could redo the paper.

As you encourage students to do their work, you should be aware of the risk of crossing a line that causes them to internalize unhealthy perfectionist tendencies (e.g., Fletcher & Neumeister, 2012). A realistic acceptance of error in people, in the world, and in oneself should temper the judgments students are likely to make. Growth should be toward excellence, not perfection.

High Level of Energy

Students who are gifted often display high energy in the conduct of play and work; this high energy can be observed in their ability to accomplish a great deal in a short time. For example, in fourth grade, Lenore decided on her own to work on homonyms one weekend after having been introduced to them in school on Friday. Through careful dictionary work, she discovered more than 450 homonyms and proudly brought her list to school on Monday.

As you learned in Chapter 6, some teachers can misinterpret the high energy level that students who are gifted bring to school tasks as hyperactivity. Using students' energy for productive purposes requires channeling it into meaningful tasks and encouraging persistence in working toward short- and long-term goals, which in turn will enhance students' motivation and success (Rubenstein, Siegle, Reis, McCoach, & Burton, 2012).

Strong Attachments and Commitments

Students who are gifted and talented often form strong attachments to one or two friends who may be a few years older or to an adult figure. As adults, they may develop equally strong attachments to their work. Laurel's life patterns illustrate this point. At age 12, she had maintained only two strong friendships, but those friendships were begun before she entered school and continued into adulthood. In her career as a teacher, she works tirelessly. She comments that it is not really like a job because she loves what she does. Teachers and mentors often are valuable for students who display strong attachments. They provide positive role models and can guide students in career choices.

Aesthetic Sensitivity

Some students who are gifted have extraordinary aesthetic sensitivity, which is a keen perception of the characteristics and complexity of the arts and the interrelationships of the arts with other domains. For example, Leonard has been composing music since he was in elementary school. Now in high school, he also writes lyrics. His next planned project is to produce a musical, and he plans to

MyEdLab
Video Example 15.2

As you think about all the characteristics of students who are gifted and talented, keep in mind that exploring them separately is less powerful than seeing them merged into an integrated understanding of these students. Which of the characteristics fit the student featured in this video? Which do not? If you were teaching this student, how would you encourage her to reach her potential?

choreograph it himself. He is planning the performance for the residents of a local elder care facility as well as the district's elementary schools. Leonard is not talented in just one area; he has the capacity to blend an understanding of several arts in a way that few can accomplish.

MyEdLab **Self-Check 15.2**

MyEdLab **Application Exercise 15.3:** What Is "Giftedness?"

Identifying Students Who Are Gifted and Talented

The procedures required by federal special education law for identifying students with disabilities do not apply in the area of giftedness; rather, each state sets its own criteria for identifying these students (National Association for Gifted Children and The Council of State Directors of Programs for the Gifted, 2015). Some states use traditional definitions of giftedness and limit the number of eligible students to a small percentage. Others use more contemporary definitions and offer services to many students.

Considerations for Identifying Giftedness

Before looking at best practices for identifying students as gifted and talented, some issues should be addressed. First, for a student to be identified as gifted, in some districts a teacher must recognize the needs of the student and refer that student as a candidate for services. Even this initial step can be problematic. For example, Bianco, Harris, Garrison-Wade, and Leech (2011) found that when teachers were presented with identical descriptions of students, except that for some teachers the student was identified as male and for others as female, the educators were far more likely to refer the male versus the female student for gifted services. This raises the question of whether bias sometimes may be operating before any type of identification process is undertaken.

Second, look at the types of instruments shown in Figure 15.3 that generally are used in traditional and nontraditional assessments to identify students as gifted. The instruments can influence whether giftedness is found. For example, some students do not do well on traditional tests but excel if they perform

FIGURE 15.3   **Assessment Tools Often Used to Identify Students as Gifted and Talented**

Traditional	Contemporary
Intelligence tests	Nonverbal ability tests
Achievement tests	Creativity tests
Aptitude tests (domain specific)	Student portfolios or performance by audition
Grades	Performance-based assessment
Teacher recommendations	Parent, peer, or community recommendations

(e.g., problem solving, composing music). One result of this recognition is that in recent years, the use of both performance-based and portfolio approaches has gained favor and both are included in several states' and school districts' identification guidelines (Kaufman, Plucker, & Russell, 2012; Pfeiffer, 2015).

Yet another assessment issue concerns students who are gifted across many areas versus those with talents in specific areas (Kornilov, Tan, Elliott, Sternberg, & Grigorenko, 2012; Schroth & Helfer, 2008). The latter group of students is much larger than the former, and assessment procedures need to take this fact into account. If assessment only identifies students with general giftedness, many students with special abilities may be missed. This also is the point at which assessment and programs intersect. If programs are designed only for the first group of students, the potential of students who need specialized opportunities in a specific area cannot be realized.

Underlying Principles of Effective Assessment

Regardless of the definition of giftedness used in a school district, several principles should guide student assessment (Brown et al., 2016).

Two-Stage Assessment Process

An assessment for gifted education should rely on a two-stage process. First, students should be screened using a traditional achievement or aptitude test. Many students may score near perfect on such a test. These students then may participate in *off-level testing*; that is, they take a more advanced test in order to obtain a better description of their abilities. Examples of instruments used for this type of assessment are the School and College Ability Test (SCAT) and the Sequential Tests of Educational Progress (Benbow & Stanley, 1996).

Measures to Match Programs

As you might guess, the use of measures that are relevant to gifted program emphasis is also a crucial consideration. If the program emphasis is writing, a writing sample should be included in the identification process. If the program emphasis is science, an assessment related to science concepts or perhaps a science project portfolio should be incorporated into the assessment procedures. Kimberly, the middle school student introduced at the beginning of the chapter, probably would benefit from this approach to assessment.

Other Considerations

Assessment for giftedness and talents also must consider several other factors. For example, checklists that are domain specific, describing abilities or interests in a particular area, such as mathematics or music, can help professionals pinpoint student strengths. In addition, most professionals agree that high ability alone does not constitute giftedness. Motivation, personality, persistence, and concentration also are essential. Assessment procedures need to take those factors into account.

Equity

Once assessment information has been gathered, *equity* becomes a concern. Rather than rely only on cutoff scores or particular sets of information, professionals need to rely on their judgment of individual student profiles to make decisions about eligibility for programs and services. This principle is important for two reasons. First, it is consistent with the understanding that giftedness has many dimensions. Second, it addresses concerns about students who have potential that has not been developed (Erwin & Worrell, 2012; Ritchotte, Rubenstein, & Murry, 2015).

Authentic Assessment

Another dimension to identifying students who are gifted and talented empha-sizes authentic assessment, or assessment that more clearly resembles the actual curriculum and instruction that students experience in schools, including writing essays, debating, and creating portfolios (Callahan, Moon, Oh, Azano, & Hailey, 2014; VanTassel-Baska, 2014). Instead of relying solely on intelligence and achievement test scores for identification, multiple criteria are used. Authentic assessment helps address the serious matter noted earlier of recognizing gifts and talents in minority students and girls. Two examples of second-stage authentic assessment practices are dynamic assessment and assessment of spatial ability.

Dynamic Assessment

The authentic assessment of giftedness involves tapping into fluid rather than static abilities (Popa & Pauc, 2015). Dynamic assessment, which is ongoing iden-tification of student learning needs and ability, is one approach used to assess

cognitive abilities that often are not apparent when most forms of standardized tests are used. Dynamic assessment usually consists of testing students, teaching skills to them, and then testing them again. The measure of gift-edness is how much students improve based on the skill instruction. This is a promising approach because disadvantaged learners who may be overlooked on traditional tests perform well on this type of assessment (e.g., Missett & Brunner, 2013).

Spatial Ability

Spatial ability is the capability to mentally visualize and manipulate objects. As with dynamic assessment, an assessment approach with a strong spatial component can greatly reduce the disparities between scores from students of various socioeconomic sta-tus (SES) levels and racial or ethnic groups (e.g., Kalbfleisch & Gillmarten, 2013). Examples of instruments that assess spatial ability include the Matrix Analysis Test, the Ravens Matrices, and the Universal Nonverbal Intelligence Test (2nd edition) (UNIT 2) (Bracken & McCallum, 2016).

Authentic assessment can assist professionals in identifying students whose potential might otherwise be overlooked.

Eligibility

The specific ways eligibility decisions are made for students who are gifted and tal-ented vary widely across states and school districts. Often, an eligibility committee is formed at the school level. It may include a specialist in gifted education, an administrator, and at least one teacher with experience in teaching students who are gifted and talented. Committee members review student profiles and make final decisions about students eligible for program placement. However, in other districts, decisions about participation may be made at the district level.

Response to Intervention and Students Who Are Gifted and Talented

In some school districts, an entirely different approach to considering students' gift-edness is being employed. That is, although response to intervention (RTI) and multi-tiered systems of support (MTSS) generally have been implemented in order to address the needs of students who are not achieving at the level or at the rate expected of them, they also are being used to ensure that students who have gifts and talents

Did You Know?

Students who have disabilities who also are gifted and talented participate in a dual identification process. Their disabilities must be identified using the IDEA process described in previous chapters, but they also must meet local or state requirements to be eligible for gifted services. Regardless of the type of gifted services provided, all the mandates of IDEA (e.g., accommodations, related services such as speech-language therapy, specially designed instruction) must be provided.

DATA-DRIVEN DECISIONS

RTI for Students with Gifts and Talents

Although RTI has been discussed throughout this text as a means for identifying and addressing students who struggle to learn, it also is being used as a means of serving students who are gifted and talented. Based on the principles of RTI already explained, it adds elements such as the following (Bianco & Harris, 2014; Montana Office of Public Instruction (OPI), 2009):

	Percent of All Students	Instructional Emphasis
Tier 1	80–90	• Research-based strategies used for all students • Even high achievers should be challenged • Screening related giftedness should compare students to other students their age • Flexibly arranged small-group instruction in the general education classroom may contribute to differentiation
Tier 2	5–10	• 20–60 minutes per day of instruction in addition to that offered as part of Tier 1 • Assessment procedures that take into account the possibility of a student being twice exceptional • Ongoing monitoring to ensure students are continuing to progress, that they are not reaching a learning ceiling • Setting may be the general education classroom or a separate setting, depending on need
Tier 3	1–8	• Intended only for the very small group of students who are so extraordinarily gifted that they require significantly different educational experiences to reach their potential • Strategies may include acceleration, curriculum compacting, dual enrollment, and other approaches that take the student away from typical educational practices • Core curriculum may be replaced with more advanced options • Assessment is ongoing to ensure the student is making progress

If you'd like to read more about the types of instructional interventions, the manual published by the Montana Department of Education (OPI) (2009) is helpful: http://opi.mt.gov/pub/RTI/Resources/RTI_Gifted_Talented.pdf

are appropriately challenged so that they learn in a way that is commensurate with their abilities. The Data-Driven Decisions feature explains more about this approach.

MyEdLab   **Self-Check 15.3**

MyEdLab   **Application Exercise 15.4:** Underrepresentation

MyEdLab   **Application Exercise 15.5:** Performance Assessment

How Learners Who Are Gifted and Talented Receive Their Education

Students who are gifted and talented receive their education in a variety of settings. No data are available to indicate the amount of time they spend in a particular setting, and decisions about placement often depend on the breadth and level of a student's abilities as well as on the program options generally available based on local and state policies.

Early Childhood Education

With the exception of children who are prodigies—that is, those who have abilities so remarkable that they come to the attention of researchers and the media at an early age—relatively little attention has been paid to young children who are gifted and talented (Obi, Obiakor, Drennon-Gala, Banks, & Green, 2016). In fact, in most school districts, students are not identified to receive services as gifted until they are in the middle elementary grades. However, some professionals are urging that this custom be rethought and that young children be identified to receive services (e.g., Pfeiffer, 2012). For example, in one early study (Fowler, Ogston, Roberts-Fiati, & Swenson, 1995), enrichment was offered to children ages 2 to 3. While it would be expected that approximately 5% of children of university faculty members would be identified as gifted, in this study 68% of those children were later identified. Among parents who had not completed high school, far less than 1% might be expected to be identified as gifted. In this study, 31% were later identified. This research suggests that early intervention could be a key component for encouraging students' gifts and talents, and similar research continues to emerge.

The Debate on Early Intervention

The thought of providing programs and services for young children who are gifted and talented raises many points of view. Advocates argue that the developmental benefits for all young children would likewise be available to young children who are gifted and talented if they received specialized instruction at the preschool level. They also note that even if programs began in kindergarten or first grade instead of later, children would be afforded greater benefits. Advocates also suggest that students in this age group tend to be particularly lonely because they have few age-mates who share their abilities, unlike older students who can access a greater range of peers in special programs and classes.

Those opposed to early gifted education programs state that all children should receive early intervention and that a special program for children who are gifted cannot be justified when every child would benefit from an enriched early childhood intervention. They also question the potential drain on financial resources from such programs, particularly in light of the budget constraints that most school districts are experiencing. Finally, critics express concern at the potential negative consequences of labeling young children, possibly segregating them and sending messages to them and others that they should not be part of typical early intervention programs.

Elementary and Secondary Education

When children who are gifted or talented enter the public schools, several placement options may exist to meet their needs. These include within-class grouping, full-time and part-time special programs, separate schools, and homeschooling.

Grouping

In most elementary and middle schools, students who are gifted and talented are educated with their typical peers. A variation is to place students in skill groups for part or all of the school day (e.g., for reading instruction or math instruction). Ability grouping is a characteristic of any program in which school personnel use test scores or school performance to assign (for all or part of the school day) same-grade students to groups or classes with markedly different levels of academic preparation. The most common type of group assigns several students who are gifted to a single, otherwise heterogeneously grouped class.

Within-class grouping is part of the concept of universal design for learning (UDL), and it can be effective at all levels of schooling and for students with many types of special needs. At the elementary level, it creates opportunities for students who already have mastered material being addressed be able to work on alternative and challenging assignments with peers. For students struggling to learn, it allows time for more practice or review. At the secondary level, it allows the teacher to plan to meet the tremendous range of student ability that may exist even in honors or Advanced Placement courses. Examples of how within-class grouping works include these: In one class, students were grouped by reading skill. They all read folktales, but each group was assigned folktales at the appropriate level. In an English class, groups were assigned different topics for their papers, thus permitting some students to pursue complex topics with added depth and breadth.

Full-Time and Part-Time Separate Classes

At the elementary level, some school districts offer completely separate classes for students who are gifted. This practice is based on evidence that many teachers struggle to differentiate for the students in their classes, spending the vast majority of the time on whole-group activities aimed at meeting the needs of average students. Another common approach is to group students for a specified period of time each week, perhaps for 2 hours each Tuesday and Friday morning. This arrangement sets aside time to nurture student talents. Of course, in most high schools, separate classes already exist through special programs such as Advanced Placement (AP), International Baccalaureate (IB), and dual enrollment (DE)—programs addressed in more detail later in this chapter.

Students who are gifted and talented may be educated with peers in general education, in part-time special classes, or in separate programs or schools.

Special Schools

Although far from common, a few residential public high schools have been developed for students who are gifted (e.g., Jones, 2011; Rollins & Cross, 2014). Moreover, governors' schools—special regional schools created and funded by the state (e.g., a state school for the arts; a state school for science, technology, engineering, and math, or STEM)—are popular options when they exist, particularly since they usually offer academic-year as well as summer opportunities. Other specialized day schools, both public and private, have emerged in response to the needs of these learners and the doctrine of parental choice. These schools, usually available only to the most highly gifted students, serve as immersion programs. They enable students to explore their areas of interest, develop their own skills, and accomplish their goals in a strongly supportive environment.

Homeschooling

One additional emerging educational option for students who are gifted and talented is homeschooling (Goodwin & Gustavson, 2012; Jolly, Matthews, & Nester, 2013). This option is one that parents may select when they have strong concerns about the quality and availability of options in local schooling or when they have a child who is so gifted or talented that attention to that child's abilities makes traditional schooling impossible (e.g., a skater who needs to practice during school hours).

Inclusive Practices

Clearly, students who are gifted and talented should be part of an *inclusive* school community, in the way that the term has been defined for this text. However, some professionals in the field of gifted education are skeptical that these students receive the education they need when they spend their days with peers in general education. Concerns include teachers' inability or unwillingness to provide differentiated instruction for what often is a tremendously broad range of student needs, and their tendency to focus their efforts on pupils who are struggling to keep up with grade-level expectations. An unfortunate result can be day-to-day boredom and lack of motivation for high-ability students, and even more important, a failure to maximize these students' potential (e.g., Hertberg-Davis, 2009).

One elementary and middle school model proposed to partially address the challenges of inclusive schooling for students who are gifted and talented is the *schoolwide cluster grouping model* (Brulles & Winebrenner, 2012). In this model, every classroom has students who are gifted or very high achieving along with learners who struggle, but no classroom has both those with the highest ability and those who struggle the most. The intent is to preserve heterogeneity in each classroom while relieving teachers of the daunting task of appropriately instructing students at both educational extremes.

In some ways, it helps to think of students who are gifted and talented just like you think of other students with exceptional needs. No single answer is always correct. When principles of universal design for learning are established, differentiation is commonplace, and professionals thoughtfully and inclusively group students, the needs of many students can be met in the classroom, at least much of the time. For students whose needs are extraordinary, additional options may be appropriate, as they are for students with disabilities. You can apply these concepts by discussing the best educational options for the students you met at the beginning of this chapter: Harrison, Kimberly, and Grayson.

Transition and Adulthood

Some people mistakenly assume that adolescents who are gifted and talented avoid the stresses and uncertainties that usually accompany the teenage years. After all, they are academically high achievers, or they have the potential to be high achievers, or they are obviously talented in an area such as art, music, drama, or sports and so have a direction for their lives—right? Evidence suggests that for many students, this is not the case. These students experience the same changes and challenges that all adolescents face—seeking personal relationships, developing a sense of ethics, and thinking about complex issues such as poverty and social justice. They, like their peers, have to struggle to develop their identities and to make choices about their futures.

Special Challenges

In addition to typical adolescent problems, students who are gifted and talented also may experience difficulties such as these (Buescher & Higham, 2001):

- *Ownership of their abilities.* These students know they have special abilities, yet they may also express disbelief about them. They may feel like impostors, waiting for someone to tell them that they are not that special after all.
- *Dissonance.* These students often have set very high standards for themselves. When they do not always achieve those standards, they may be dissatisfied with the gap between what they expected of themselves and what they have accomplished, even if others do not ever think a gap existed.
- *Competing expectations.* Adolescents who are gifted and talented often receive advice from parents, teachers, friends, grandparents, counselors, university representatives, and others. They may feel pulled in many directions, wanting to please everyone but also themselves.
- *Premature identity.* Because of all the pressures they may experience, some adolescents take on an adult identity too soon. They may make career choices prematurely, decide on educational options before they should, and then experience frustration with their choices.

All these dilemmas, combined with these students' tendencies to be extraordinarily sensitive to the people and world around them, can lead to increased risk for problems with motivation and a high degree of anxiety.

Supporting Adolescents Who Are Gifted and Talented

The outlook for students who are gifted and talented when they leave high school is not necessarily negative, but it is complex. These students need to work closely with counselors, mentors, and understanding teachers who can help them process the feelings they experience and carefully think through the important decisions they must make (Bailey, 2011; Wood & Gavin, 2009). Educators can assist these students by helping them to set priorities and avoid overcommitment, understand their own strengths and weaknesses, reframe mistakes as learning experiences, and identify sources of stress so that they can be addressed. In addition, schools should make it possible for these students to discuss their needs without fear of being ridiculed and without the risk of sensing that their concerns are being devalued (e.g., "What do you have to worry about? You have everything going for you!").

MyEdLab **Self-Check 15.4**

MyEdLab **Application Exercise 15.6:** Brianna's Accommodations

MyEdLab **Application Exercise 15.7:** How Early Should Education for Gifted Students Start?

Recommended Educational Practices for Students Who Are Gifted and Talented

In planning instructional programs for students who are gifted or talented, the following principles, referred to as a CLEAR curriculum model, are essential (Gubbins, Callahan, & Renzulli, 2014):

1. **(C)**ontinual formative assessment in order to ensure that students are grasping essential concepts but are not dwelling on material already mastered
2. Clear **(L)**earning goals that give a focus to the instructional program
3. Data-driven learning **(E)**xperiences employing evidence-based practices and adjusting instruction based on student needs
4. **(A)**uthentic products, that is, student projects and assignments with specific purposes rather than those that are contrived
5. A **(R)**ich curriculum that incorporates a wide range of materials and experiences.

When these principles guide students' instruction, the students' achievement is significantly higher than that of comparable students who are not enrolled in programs emphasizing these standards. Several specific practices based on these principles are recommended for effectively educating these students, including curriculum compacting, acceleration, enrichment, differentiation, and interventions tailored for diverse populations.

Curriculum Compacting

Some students who are gifted and talented already are familiar with most of the concepts being taught in their classrooms, or they can master the concepts in a fraction of the time that it takes their classmates. If these students' needs are not addressed, they can become frustrated. A solution to this problem is curriculum compacting, in which the goals of an instructional unit are identified, student refers to an instructional approach that assumes that students need many different avenues to reach their learning potential (Kanevsky, 2011; Tomlinson, 2014). It can address the content students are learning, the assessment tools through which learning is measured, the tasks students complete, and the instructional strategies employed (e.g., Schmitt & Goebel, 2015).

Curriculum design is one major component of differentiation for students who are gifted (Brown & Abernethy, 2009). What is important for these students to know and to be able to do at what stages of development? How do planned learning experiences focus on meaningful experiences that provide (a) *depth,* exploration of a topic or concept beyond what is normally addressed; and (b) complexity, exploration of multiple perspectives, issues, variables, and relationships, at an appropriate pace? Related to curriculum design is materials selection. In classrooms serving these students, materials should go beyond a single textbook, also including advanced readings that present interesting and challenging ideas, treat knowledge as tentative and open ended, and provide a conceptual depth that allows students to make interdisciplinary connections.

Above all, keep in mind that differentiation can benefit all the students in a classroom. When teachers use large-group, small-group, individual, and student–teacher conference grouping strategies and take into account student interests, cultural uniqueness, and learning styles, their classrooms can become exciting places where all students are meaningfully engaged in learning. Differentiation is the foundation of inclusive education practices—those that truly address the entire diversity of the student population.

Problem-Based Learning

Differentiation encompasses instruction that is inquiry based, is open ended, and employs flexible grouping practices. It enables teachers to prioritize key skills for struggling learners while at the same time nurturing the talents of those with extraordinary abilities. One example of differentiation, often recommended as part of contemporary education such as the Common Core State Standards, is *problem-based learning (PBL),* in which students encounter a real-world problem designed by the teacher to address key concepts (e.g., Buerk, 2016; Saunders-Stewart, Gyles, & Shore, 2012). The students explore the problem, gather research data about it, and design interventions to solve it. Particularly for students who are gifted, the instructional techniques needed by the teacher include high-level questioning skills, listening skills, conferencing skills, and tutoring in order to guide the process. PBL also incorporates flexible team grouping and whole-class discussion. Problem resolution usually involves student-initiated projects and presentations, guided by the teacher. You can learn more about problem-based learning, an approach highlighted for students who are gifted but applicable to all students, in the Instruction in Action feature.

In classrooms using problem-based learning, performance-based assessment is typical. Having students create products or critique their work provides a detailed picture of individual progress toward specific education goals. In fact, for students who are gifted and talented, the quality of performance on such measures may be a better indicator than paper-and-pencil measures of skills and concepts deeply mastered.

Interventions for Diverse Populations

General interventions that have been documented as successful with learners identified as gifted and economically disadvantaged include early attention to needs, family involvement, use of effective instructional and leadership strategies in the school, experiential learning approaches, encouragement of self-expression, community involvement, counseling efforts, and building on strengths (Figg, Rogers, McCormick, & Low, 2012; Lakin, 2016). As you have learned

INSTRUCTION IN **ACTION**

Problem-Based Learning

In problem-based learning, students are given realistic problems that are open ended and challenging. The problems do not have single correct answers. Students systematically problem solve using a wide variety of resources to find solutions. In a health class, one teacher proposed these problems to students:

Group 1: As a sports nutritionist, create a menu plan for a week for a female athlete who weighs 130 pounds; is 5 feet, 5 inches tall; and plays on a soccer team.

Group 2: As a diet expert, create a menu plan for a week for a fifteen-year-old boy who wants to build muscle and put on weight before football season.

This approach to instruction can help all students to make connections between what they are learning and school and real-world situations and is consistent with the contemporary education standards, but it is particularly effective with students who are gifted and talented because it encourages creativity, enables them to research problems in depth, and fosters skills for working independently of the teacher. The diagram summarizes the steps used in problem-based learning. How might you use such an approach as you work with students?

Source: From *Differentiated Instructional Strategies: One Size Doesn't Fit All* by Gregory, Gayle H. & Chapman, Carolyn. Copyright 2002. Reproduced with permissions of Sage Publications Inc. in the format textbook and other book via Copyright Clearance Center.

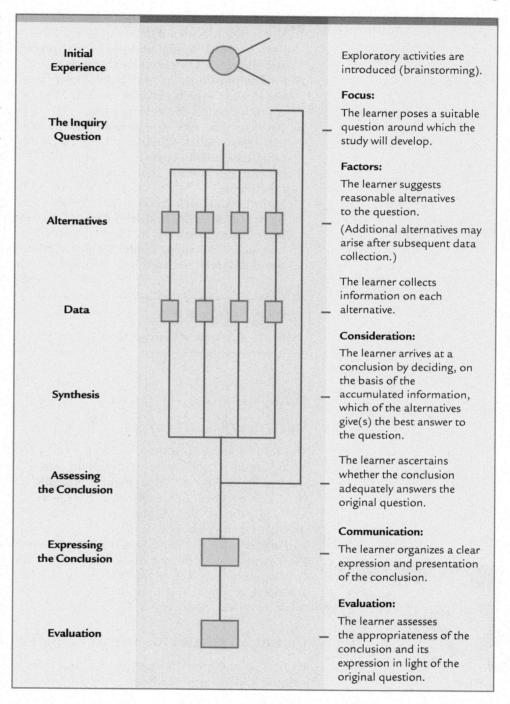

Initial Experience

Exploratory activities are introduced (brainstorming).

Focus:

The Inquiry Question

The learner poses a suitable question around which the study will develop.

Factors:

Alternatives

The learner suggests reasonable alternatives to the question.

(Additional alternatives may arise after subsequent data collection.)

Data

The learner collects information on each alternative.

Consideration:

Synthesis

The learner arrives at a conclusion by deciding, on the basis of the accumulated information, which of the alternatives give(s) the best answer to the question.

Assessing the Conclusion

The learner ascertains whether the conclusion adequately answers the original question.

Communication:

Expressing the Conclusion

The learner organizes a clear expression and presentation of the conclusion.

Evaluation:

Evaluation

The learner assesses the appropriateness of the conclusion and its expression in light of the original question.

throughout this text, it is also important to be sensitive to cultural values. For example, some students who live in poverty may mask their giftedness because of issues related to social acceptance. The following guidelines have been found effective in teaching students from nondominant cultures who are gifted and talented (e.g., Rubenstein, Siegle, Reis, McCoach, & Burton, 2012):

1. Provide separate instructional opportunities for students with the same developmental profiles. Students from diverse groups need to have opportunities to interact with students who are similar to themselves (Kaplan, 2011). Students should be grouped by critical variables—for example, by gender or social background.
2. Use technology to aid in transmission of learning. Applications of technology have evolved rapidly and hold great promise for students with disabilities and those from nondominant groups.
3. Provide small-group and individual counseling, mentorships, and internships, all of which make possible individual attention to affective as well as cognitive issues of development.
4. Focus on the arts as a therapeutic intervention as well as a creative and expressive outlet. Whether it be in art, music, drama, or dance and whether targeted students have high academic ability or a particular talent, the arts provide an outlet that fosters creativity and encourages higher-level functioning.
5. Use materials rich in ideas and imagination coupled with an emphasis on higher-level skills. Both self-concept and motivation are jeopardized when students overuse basic materials, as sometimes happens for English language learners. Challenging content with attention to ideas and creative opportunities is essential to avoid boredom and withdrawal.

MyEdLab **Self-Check 15.5**

MyEdLab **Application Exercise 15.8:** Instructional Strategies

---

Perspectives of Parents and Families of Students Who Are Gifted and Talented

The role of families in the development of giftedness and talent has been well documented in the literature (Garn, Matthews, & Jolly, 2012; Rubenstein, Schelling, Wilczynski, & Hooks, 2015). Parents typically have been key influences in their children's progress in specific talent areas as well as in generally nurturing the learning process (Reis & Morales-Taylor, 2016). Parents of these students often decide to make personal sacrifices to further their children's skills—for example, moving to place the child in a better school or with a master teacher or coach. Even parents who do not make such efforts still nurture their children's talent development. Families of high-achieving students who are gifted often are characterized as intact, and they tend to place high values on education and hard work (Schilling, Sparfeldt, & Rost, 2006).

Parent Strategies for Encouraging Their Children

Parents of children who are gifted often want advice on ways to nurture their children's abilities in the home. Some important approaches include these:

- Reading to the child at all ages
- Providing educational puzzles and games
- Holding dinner table discussions on issues of the day
- Having the child interact with adult friends, who may serve as role models or mentors
- Providing trips to the local library for books and research

MyEdLab
Video Example 15.4

Think about the parent in Video Example 15.4 and how her advocacy for her daughter might be admirable but at the same time a bit intimidating for school professionals.

- Traveling to interesting places and even having the child plan the trip
- Viewing films and special television programs together and discussing them
- Encouraging the child to be creative and expressive in the arts areas in which she shows a sustained interest

With the advent of so many educational alternatives outside schools for students who are gifted, parents have been forced to become analysts of educational services, often having to make choices among attractive options. For example, one option parents may consider is homeschooling, introduced earlier in this chapter. Usually the decision to homeschool emerges out of both a strong parental value system about the importance of individualized education and the characteristics of a child who is gifted that may suggest unevenness in ability and development. Frequent concerns of homeschooling parents of children who are gifted include what to do at home, how to select challenging educational content, how to keep a child who is gifted motivated and committed to learning, and when to opt for a more formal educational setting for their child.

Parent support frequently is cited by eminent individuals as having been critical to their success. Author Robert Penn Warren credited his literary talent to his father's reading him the classics until he went off to college. Robert Root Bernstein, a Nobel Prize–winning chemist, cited his mother's interest in his science projects as crucial to spurring him on to compete for a Westinghouse scholarship. These are but two of many examples of the positive outcomes of parent encouragement for children who are gifted and talented, and they suggest that, as for other students, working closely with parents is central to educational success (Fiebig & Beauregard, 2010).

MyEdLab **Self-Check 15.6**

MyEdLab **Application Exercise 15.9:** Advocacy

Trends and Issues Affecting Students Who Are Gifted and Talented

Many contemporary issues in gifted education have been hinted at elsewhere in this chapter. As you read the synopsis of several of these issues in the following sections, consider these questions: What are the implications of these topics for me as a professional educator? How might these topics affect the students with whom I may work?

Talent Development

The case could be made that all of education is about talent development—that is, nurturing one, several, or many abilities of students, a view of schooling at its best. For students who are gifted and talented, though, this topic has recently become a focus (e.g., Olszewski-Kubilius & Thomson, 2015). Whole schools have been founded and many schools reorganized around the talent development concept. Specialized searches for finding precocious talent in children identify and serve more than 200,000 students per year through national searches. Talent development efforts in the arts, especially through private lessons and tutorials, continue to thrive, as do those related to STEM. Parents, too, are integral to this trend; they are seeking opportunities for their children and ensuring that their potential is reached.

Did You Know?

If you are seeking additional information about students who are gifted and talented, including those who are twice exceptional, these websites contain a wealth of information:

CEC-TAG (http://cectag.com/), The Association of the Gifted, a division of the Council for Exceptional Children, advocates for students with gifts and talents and on its website publishes an array of useful resources.

NAGC (http://www.nagc.org/), the National Association for Gifted Children, is a professional organization dedicated to a diverse conceptualization of giftedness and the development of policies and practices supporting that view.

SENG (http://sengifted.org/), Supporting Emotional Needs of the Gifted, prioritizes helping families and communities in their work with individuals who are gifted and talented.

Talent development is premised on the belief that many individuals may possess special abilities, even if they do not have overall high abilities. The trend toward talent development is likely to continue because it addresses in an equitable way the increasing diversity of today's students.

Identification and Programming for Underrepresented Groups

No one would question that giftedness and talent exist in all segments of the population, yet students from minority groups and those who live in poverty remain underrepresented (Castellano & Frazier, 2011; Siegle et al., 2016). This situation exists despite more than 30 years of efforts to address this problem. In the 1990s, major national emphasis was given to this area through a priority assignment when federal funding in the Javits Act was allocated to explore this issue. Today, nearly every publication related to gifted education acknowledges the need to maintain focus on identifying students from underrepresented groups (e.g., Coleman & Shah-Coltrane, 2015; Peters & Gentry, 2012).

Students Who Are Twice Exceptional

Students with disabilities who also are gifted and talented sometimes are referred to as *twice exceptional*, and they are receiving more attention than ever before (Coleman & Gallagher, 2015). Students who have learning disabilities, ADHD, autism spectrum disorder, a vision or hearing loss, emotional disabilities, physical or health disabilities, or other special needs often are inadvertently excluded from programs serving those who are gifted, even though they may qualify when appropriate accommodations are made during the assessment process (e.g., Amend & Peters, 2015; Assouline & Whiteman, 2011; Foley-Nicpon, Assouline, & Fosenburg, 2015). In the Professional Edge, you can read more about students who are twice exceptional—and ideas for successfully instructing them.

Effective Differentiation

Although presented as a recommended practice, differentiation also is an issue in the field of gifted education because it has been perceived by educators in very different ways. One common misunderstanding of the term implies that students who are gifted receive a totally different program from other students. That is, average students take subject matter courses while students who are gifted learn higher-order skills, with the strong implications that students who are gifted do not need content and that other learners do not need higher-level skills. Obviously, this is not true, yet the debate continues. For some researchers, the heart of differentiated practice rests with students engaging in independent project work (Ozturk & Debelak, 2008). For others, differentiation is best satisfied through individualized approaches within the general education classroom (Cavilla, 2014; Tomlinson & Jarvis, 2014). For still others, differentiation requires an integrative and comprehensive set of experiences conducted in a separate setting with intellectual peers (Meier, Vogl, & Preckel, 2014; Robinson, 2003).

Some students who are extraordinarily gifted benefit by acceleration, which sometimes includes enrolling in college courses at a very early age.

When students have special gifts and talents as well as disabilities, finding effective ways to teach them can be a challenge. Here is a summary of characteristics of twice exceptional students (Colorado Department of Education, 2009):

Strengths	Challenges
• Superior vocabulary	• Easily frustrated
• Highly creative	• Stubborn
• Resourceful	• Manipulative
• Curious	• Opinionated
• Imaginative	• Argumentative
• Questioning	• Problems in written expression
• Problem-solving ability	• Highly sensitive to criticism
• Sophisticated sense of humor	• Inconsistent academic performance
• Wide range of interests	
• Advanced ideas and opinions	• Lack of organization and study skills
• Special talent or consuming interest	• Difficulty with social interactions

Teaching strategies for working with these students include the following:

1. Use key learning principles that apply to all students.
   - Build on student knowledge.
   - Nurture students' deep understanding of factual knowledge in order to prepare them for further and richer inquiry.
   - Help students to learn metacognitive strategies, that is, to have an awareness of their own learning and how it occurs.

2. Vary student instructional activities across these four factors, based on student needs:
   - *Time.* Use dynamic assessment to judge student work, often providing extended periods so that they can complete projects.
   - *Structure.* Identify big ideas that you would like students to learn so that you can prioritize activities. Relate new learning to knowledge and skills that students already possess (e.g., by using visual organizers to point out connections to students). Arrange the classroom so that there are quiet areas, areas for discussion, and areas with comfortable furniture.
   - *Support.* Create a classroom climate that is respectful and welcoming of all students. Provide the assistance students need (but not more than they need) in order to succeed. Advocate for students, and encourage them to become self-advocates.
   - *Complexity.* Employ strategies related to the other three dimensions in order to keep complexity as high as possible, avoiding the temptation to simplify and ensuring that students' learning is deep, authentic, and generalizable.

You can learn more about students who are twice exceptional at the 2eNewletter website: *http://www.2enewsletter .com/index.html*

Sources: Based on Coleman, M. R. (2005). Academic strategies that work for gifted students with learning disabilities. *Teaching Exceptional Children,* 38(1), 28–32; and Colorado Department of Education. (2009). *Twice-exceptional students: Gifted students with disabilities, an introductory resource book* (2nd edition). Retrieved from http://www.cde.state.co.us/sites/default/files/documents/gt/download/pdf/twiceexceptionalresourcehandbook.pdf

Each of these points of view has some validity, and the challenge facing school professionals is to recognize and act on all of them. One reason for these various points of view relates to the students who are being considered. If the programs respond primarily to precocity—that is, demonstrating early development or maturity in such ways as early language development, rapid learning ability, or unusual attention span—then advanced content is the logical form of differentiation. However, if professionals emphasize complexity of thought as a student characteristic, then a differentiated set of experiences that provides real-world problems to solve becomes the appropriate differentiated response.

Another source of disagreement on this issue relates to the level at which differentiation should occur. For some educators, the focus is on the individual student, with the program always responding to the interests and abilities present at a given point in time. For other educators, differentiation occurs through changes in curriculum goals and outcomes for groups of learners. For still other educators, it is implemented in a more general way through mentorships or chess clubs, for example. Perhaps a next step for the study of differentiation is one that simultaneously considers it from all these perspectives.

Alternative Program Models

In addition to the options available through university coursework and weekend or summer university programs for students who are gifted and talented, several other education options are becoming more common. These include technology-based options and opportunities external to schools.

Technology-Based Options

Some students participate in acceleration through technology as a delivery system for a high-powered curriculum (Housand, 2016b). Stanford University's Education Program for Gifted Youth (EPGY) (2016) is a prime example. Begun in 1963 when computers were a brand new idea, this program has kept as its goal making available to students who are gifted and talented advanced learning opportunities through distance education. More than 1 million students and families have accessed this program. Other similar innovative uses of technology for gifted programming are also growing. What might be the advantages and disadvantages of this option for students with special gifts and talents?

Opportunities External to Schools

Although local schools play critical roles in educating students, schools can be even more effective when they are coupled with outside community resources that supplement learning. One program model includes Saturday or summer enrichment programs (e.g., Kaul, Johnsen, Saxon, & Witte, 2016). These programs allow students who are gifted to use their leisure time pursuing a topic of academic interest, such as poetry, chemistry, or architecture, under the direction of a highly qualified instructor. Because such programs usually charge tuition, though, they may not be feasible for students who live in poverty. An example that is specific to university programming includes a talent search, usually targeted to academically able middle school students who qualify based on SAT scores (Muratori & Brody, 2012). Many of these programs, which are offered during the summer and include a residential component, provide accelerated content that is equivalent to high school coursework.

Other external activities that involve the community include mentorships and internships. The former involves selecting a mentor, an individual who serves as a role model to a student and establishes a one-to-one relationship (Pfeiffer & Shaughnessy, 2015). This connection helps a student understand how an adult experiences and processes the world; the relationship typically is built on some area of mutual interest. Internships and job-shadowing opportunities involve placements in community settings, usually for a period from two weeks to a full semester. The purpose is to help the student explore the real world and to see the work habits and task demands that accompany certain professions. Both of these alternatives are highly relevant for students who are gifted, particularly those who feel very different from the norm and may have time available as a result of program or content acceleration to explore different work environments and career options.

MyEdLab **Self-Check 15.7**

MyEdLab **Application Exercise 15.10:** Trends and Issues Affecting the Field of Gifted Education

Summary

LO15.1 The past century has seen many developments in the field of gifted education, although giftedness is not addressed in IDEA. Estimates of the prevalence of students who are gifted and talented vary dramatically based on state definitions and priorities, but professionals generally agree that the interaction of genetic predisposition and environmental support determines whether students develop giftedness.

LO15.2 Students who are gifted have common cognitive, academic, and social/emotional characteristics, including the ability to manipulate abstract symbol systems, intense power of concentration, and early language interest and development; specific behaviors in reading, writing, speaking, and mathematics; a strong sense of justice, altruism, and idealism; a sense of humor; emotional intensity; and strong attachments and commitments.

LO15.3 Although identification criteria and procedures vary by state and locality, most professionals use a two-stage assessment process. Best practices also recommend the use of authentic assessment, including dynamic assessment, and nonverbal spatial ability assessments.

LO15.4 Students who are gifted and talented receive services based on local policies. Options include grouping, part-time and full-time separate classes, specialized schools, and homeschooling.

LO15.5 Recommended practices for students who are gifted and talented include curriculum compacting, acceleration, enrichment, differentiation, and specific strategies for diverse student groups.

LO15.6 Parents need to be aware of the characteristics and needs of their children who are gifted and talented, and the options and opportunities available both within and outside school.

LO15.7 Examples of trends and issues affecting gifted education include talent development, identification of and programming for underrepresented groups, debates about effective differentiation, and alternative program models.

Back to the Cases

Now that you've read about students who are gifted and talented, look back at the student stories at the beginning of this chapter. Then, answer the questions about each of their cases.

MyEdLab Case Study 15.1

HARRISON. Harrison's story raises many questions about students who are gifted and the services they should receive. Analyze Harrison based on the information provided, and explain the characteristics of giftedness that are apparent. Consider his educational needs and the ways his teachers can help Harrison reach his full potential.

MyEdLab Case Study 15.2

KIMBERLY. Kimberly is struggling in many ways. She is unsure of her abilities, unsure of how to respond to the adults in her life, and unsure of her commitment to achievement in school. One of her teachers has recommended her for a program for girls who are gifted and talented, which she would attend during the coming summer.

MyEdLab Case Study 15.3

GRAYSON. It is important that you understand the conditions under which a student may be entitled to be eligible for services due to having a disability and being gifted. As a member of the IEP team discussing Grayson, it is also important to carefully determine how to best support a student such as Grayson, given the complex needs of students who are twice exceptional.

Appendix

CEC Knowledge and Skill Standards Common Core

Standard I: Foundations

ICC1K1: Models, theories, and philosophies, and research methods that provide the basis for special education practice.

ICC1K2: Laws, policies, and ethical principles regarding behavior management planning and implementation.

ICC1K3: Relationship of special education to the organization and function of educational agencies.

ICC1K4: Rights and responsibilities of students, parents, teachers, and other professionals, and schools related to exceptional learning needs.

ICC1K5: Issues in definition and identification of individuals with exceptional learning needs, including those from culturally and linguistically diverse backgrounds.

ICC1K6: Issues, assurances, and due process rights related to assessment, eligibility, and placement within a continuum of services.

ICC1K7: Family systems and the role of families in the educational process.

ICC1K8: Historical points of view and contributions of culturally diverse groups.

ICC1K9: Impact of the dominant culture on shaping schools and the individuals who study and work in them.

ICC1K10: Potential impact of differences in values, languages, and customs that can exist between the home and school.

ICC1S1: Articulate personal philosophy of special education.

Standard II: Development and Characteristics of Learners

ICC2K1: Typical and atypical human growth and development.

ICC2K2: Educational implications of characteristics of various exceptionalities.

ICC2K3: Characteristics and effects of the cultural and environmental milieu of the individual with exceptional learning needs and the family.

ICC2K4: Family systems and the role of families in supporting development.

ICC2K5: Similarities and differences of individuals with and without exceptional learning needs.

ICC2K6: Similarities and differences among individuals with exceptional learning needs.

ICC2K7: Effects of various medications on individuals with exceptional learning needs.

Standard III: Individual Learning Differences

ICC3K1: Effects an exceptional condition(s) can have on an individual's life.

ICC3K2: Impact of learner's academic and social abilities, attitudes, interests, and values on instruction and career development.

ICC3K3: Variations in beliefs, traditions, and values across and within cultures and their effects on relationships among individuals with exceptional learning needs, family, and schooling.

ICC3K4: Cultural perspectives influencing the relationships among families, schools, and communities as related to instruction.

ICC3K5: Differing ways of learning of individuals with exceptional learning needs including those from culturally diverse backgrounds and strategies for addressing these differences.

Standard IV: Instructional Strategies

ICC4K1:   Evidence-based practices validated for specific characteristics of learners and settings.

ICC4S1:   Use strategies to facilitate integration into various settings.

ICC4S2:   Teach individuals to use self-assessment, problem-solving, and other cognitive strategies to meet their needs.

ICC4S3:   Select, adapt, and use instructional strategies and materials according to characteristics of the individual with exceptional learning needs.

ICC4S4:   Use strategies to facilitate maintenance and generalization of skills across learning environments.

ICC4S5:   Use procedures to increase the individual's self-awareness, self-management, self-control, self-reliance, and self-esteem.

ICC4S6:   Use strategies that promote successful transitions for individuals with exceptional learning needs.

Standard V: Learning Environments and Social Interactions

ICC5K1:   Demands of learning environments.

ICC5K2:   Basic classroom management theories and strategies for individuals with exceptional learning needs.

ICC5K3:   Effective management of teaching and learning.

ICC5K4:   Teacher attitudes and behaviors that influence behavior of individuals with exceptional learning needs.

ICC5K5:   Social skills needed for educational and other environments.

ICC5K6:   Strategies for crisis prevention and intervention.

ICC5K7:   Strategies for preparing individuals to live harmoniously and productively in a culturally diverse world.

ICC5K8:   Ways to create learning environments that allow individuals to retain and appreciate their own and each other's respective language and cultural heritage.

ICC5K9:   Ways specific cultures are negatively stereotyped.

ICC5K10: Strategies used by diverse populations to cope with a legacy of former and continuing racism.

ICC5S1:   Create a safe, equitable, positive, and supporting learning environment in which diversities are valued.

ICC5S2:   Identify realistic expectations for personal and social behavior in various settings.

ICC5S3:   Identify supports needed for integration into various program placements.

ICC5S4:   Design learning environments that encourage active participation in individual and group settings.

ICC5S5:   Modify the learning environment to manage behaviors.

ICC5S6:   Use performance data and information from all stakeholders to make or suggest modifications in learning environments.

ICC5S7:   Establish and maintain rapport with individuals with and without exceptional learning needs.

ICC5S8:   Teach self-advocacy.

ICC5S9:   Create an environment that encourages self-advocacy and increased independence.

ICC5S10: Use effective and varied behavior management strategies.

ICC5S11: Use the least intensive behavior management strategy consistent with the needs of the individual with exceptional learning needs.

ICC5S12: Design and manage daily routines.

ICC5S13: Organize, develop, and sustain learning environments that support positive intracultural and intercultural experiences.

ICC5S14: Mediate controversial intercultural issues among students within the learning environment in ways that enhance any culture, group, or person.

ICC5S15: Structure, direct, and support the activities of paraeducators, volunteers, and tutors.

ICC5S16: Use universal precautions.

Standard VI: Communication

ICC6K1: Effects of cultural and linguistic differences on growth and development.

ICC6K2: Characteristics of one's own culture and use of language and the ways in which these can differ from other cultures and uses of languages.

ICC6K3: Ways of behaving and communicating among cultures that can lead to misinterpretation and misunderstanding.

ICC6K4: Augmentative and assistive communication strategies.

ICC6S1: Use strategies to support and enhance communication skills of individuals with exceptional learning needs.

ICC6S2: Use communication strategies and resources to facilitate understanding of subject matter for students whose primary language is not the dominant language.

Standard VII: Instructional Planning

ICC7K1: Theories and research that form the basis of curriculum development and instructional practice.

ICC7K2: Scope and sequences of general and special curricula.

ICC7K3: National, state or provincial, and local curricula standards.

ICC7K4: Technology for planning and managing the teaching and learning environment.

ICC7K5: Roles and responsibilities of the paraeducator related to instruction, intervention, and direct service.

ICC7S1: Identify and prioritize areas of the general curriculum and accommodations for individuals with exceptional learning needs.

ICC7S2: Develop and implement comprehensive, longitudinal individualized programs in collaboration with team members.

ICC7S3: Involve the individual and family in setting instructional goals and monitoring progress.

ICC7S4: Use functional assessments to develop intervention plans.

ICC7S5: Use task analysis.

ICC7S6: Sequence, implement, and evaluate individualized learning objectives.

ICC7S7: Integrate affective, social, and life skills with academic curricula.

ICC7S8: Develop and select instructional content, resources, and strategies that respond to cultural, linguistic, and gender differences.

ICC7S9: Incorporate and implement instructional and assistive technology into the educational program.

ICC7S10: Prepare lesson plans.

ICC7S11: Prepare and organize materials to implement daily lesson plans.

ICC7S12: Use instructional time effectively.

ICC7S13: Make responsive adjustments to instruction based on continued observations.

ICC7S14: Prepare individuals to exhibit self-enhancing behavior in response to societal attitudes and actions.

ICC7S15: Evaluate and modify instructional practices in response to ongoing assessment data.

Standard VIII: Assessment

ICC8K1:   Basic terminology used in assessment.

ICC8K2:   Legal provisions and ethical principles regarding assessment of individuals.

ICC8K3:   Screening, prereferral, referral, and classification procedures.

ICC8K4:   Use and limitations of assessment instruments.

ICC8K5:   National, state or provincial, and local accommodations and modifications.

ICC8S1:   Gather relevant background information.

ICC8S2:   Administer nonbiased formal and informal assessments.

ICC8S3:   Use technology to conduct assessments.

ICC8S4:   Develop or modify individualized assessment strategies.

ICC8S5:   Interpret information from formal and informal assessments.

ICC8S6:   Use assessment information in making eligibility, program, and placement decisions for individuals with exceptional learning needs, including those from culturally and/or linguistically diverse backgrounds.

ICC8S7:   Report assessment results to all stakeholders using effective communication skills.

ICC8S8:   Evaluate instruction and monitor progress of individuals with exceptional learning needs.

ICC8S9:   Develop or modify individualized assessment strategies.

ICC8S10:   Create and maintain records.

Standard IX: Professional and Ethical Practice

ICC9K1:   Personal cultural biases and differences that affect one's teaching.

ICC9K2:   Importance of the teacher serving as a model for individuals with exceptional learning needs.

ICC9K3:   Continuum of lifelong professional development.

ICC9K4:   Methods to remain current regarding research-validated practice.

ICC9S1:   Practice within the CEC Code of Ethics and other standards of the profession.

ICC9S2:   Uphold high standards of competence and integrity and exercise sound judgment in the practice of the professional.

ICC9S3:   Act ethically in advocating for appropriate services.

ICC9S4:   Conduct professional activities in compliance with applicable laws and policies.

ICC9S5:   Demonstrate commitment to developing the highest education and quality-of-life potential of individuals with exceptional learning needs.

ICC9S6:   Demonstrate sensitivity for the culture, language, religion, gender, disability, socioeconomic status, and sexual orientation of individuals.

ICC9S7:   Practice within one's skill limit and obtain assistance as needed.

ICC9S8:   Use verbal, nonverbal, and written language effectively.

ICC9S9:   Conduct self-evaluation of instruction.

ICC9S10:   Access information on exceptionalities.

ICC9S11:   Reflect on one's practice to improve instruction and guide professional growth.

ICC9S12:   Engage in professional activities that benefit individuals with exceptional learning needs, their families, and one's colleagues.

ICC9S13:   Demonstrate commitment to engage evidence-based practice.

Standard X: Collaboration

ICC10K1:   Models and strategies of consultation and collaboration.

ICC10K2:   Roles of individuals with exceptional learning needs, families, and school and community personnel in planning of an individualized program.

ICC10K3: Concerns of families of individuals with exceptional learning needs and strategies to help address these concerns.

ICC10K4: Culturally responsive factors that promote effective communication and collaboration with individuals with exceptional learning needs, families, school personnel, and community members.

ICC10S1: Maintain confidential communication about individuals with exceptional learning needs.

ICC10S2: Collaborate with families and others in assessment of individuals with exceptional learning needs.

ICC10S3: Foster respectful and beneficial relationships between families and professionals.

ICC10S4: Assist individuals with exceptional learning needs and their families in becoming active participants in the educational team.

ICC10S5: Plan and conduct collaborative conferences with individuals with exceptional learning needs and their families.

ICC10S6: Collaborate with school personnel and community members in integrating individuals with exceptional learning needs into various settings.

ICC10S7: Use group problem-solving skills to develop, implement, and evaluate collaborative activities.

ICC10S8: Model techniques and coach others in the use of instructional methods and accommodations.

ICC10S9: Communicate with school personnel about the characteristics and needs of individuals with exceptional learning needs.

ICC10S10: Communicate effectively with families of individuals with exceptional learning needs from diverse backgrounds.

ICC10S11: Observe, evaluate, and provide feedback to paraeducators.

From The Council for Exceptional Children. (2009). *CEC What Every Special Educator Must Know* (6th ed.). Reprinted with permission.

Glossary

ability grouping   Characteristic of any program in which school personnel use test scores or school performance to assign same-grade students at similar levels to groups or classes with markedly different levels of academic preparation.

absence seizure   Type of generalized seizure usually lasting for only a few seconds and sometimes mistaken for daydreaming or inattention; formerly called petit mal seizure.

acceleration   Practice of advancing learners through levels of curriculum according to individual achievement and performance.

accent   A normal variation in the surface characteristics of a language.

access technology   High-tech and low-tech devices and software that allow persons with impairments to gain access to computers and other forms of information.

acquired brain injury   Injury that occurs after birth as a result of accidents, illness, injuries, or environmental factors (e.g., severe allergies).

acquired immune deficiency syndrome (AIDS)   Collection of illnesses, including some cancers, that only individuals who have human immunodeficiency virus (HIV) can contract; most children become infected during mothers' pregnancies.

adapted physical educator   Physical education instructor who has received training in modifying games, exercises, and other activities to accommodate the needs of students with disabilities. Adapted physical educators may work directly with students or with other physical educators in an advisory capacity.

adaptive behavior   Day-to-day knowledge and skills necessary for independence, including communication, self-care, social skills, home living, leisure, and self-direction. Deficits in adaptive behavior comprise one component of identifying students with mental retardation.

additions   Articulation disorder in which a person inserts extra sounds in words spoken.

adventitious hearing loss   Hearing loss that develops after birth; also called acquired hearing loss.

adventitious visual impairment   A visual condition that is acquired after birth.

aesthetic sensitivity   A keen perception of the characteristics and complexity of the arts and the interrelationships of the arts with other domains.

altruism   Unselfish concern for the welfare of others, a characteristic of many students who are gifted and talented.

American Association on Intellectual and Developmental Disabilities (AAIDD)   Oldest interdisciplinary organization providing leadership to the field of mental retardation, particularly in the areas of definitions and classification systems (formerly called American Association on Mental Retardation or AAMR).

American Sign Language (ASL)   Visual-gesturing language that has its own rules of grammar distinct from English; used primarily by culturally Deaf people.

Americans with Disabilities Act (ADA) of 1990   Federal law protecting the civil rights of individuals with disabilities that applies to public and private sectors and addressing matters such as transportation, public accommodations, and telecommunications.

annual goals   IEP component that consists of statements of the major accomplishments expected for the student during the upcoming twelve months; must be able to be objectively measured.

annual review   Required meeting of parents and school professionals, occurring at least once each year, to review a student's IEP and set goals for the next year.

applied academic skill   Skill taught to students that has immediate applicability to day-to-day life. An example is making change for a dollar.

articulation disorder   Speech disorder involving the abnormal production of sounds, including additions, omissions, substitutions, and distortions.

assistive technology   Devices and services that improve the functional capabilities of students with disabilities.

asthma   Lung disease that causes episodes of extreme difficulty in breathing; most common chronic illness among children.

athetoid cerebral palsy   Type of cerebral palsy in which individuals cannot control their muscles and so may have sudden and unexpected twisting motions or other movements.

attention deficit disorder (ADD)   1980 term to describe individuals with the disorder now called attention deficit–hyperactivity disorder; it noted the condition could exist with or without hyperactivity.

attention deficit–hyperactivity disorder (ADHD)   Psychiatric disorder with symptoms occurring before age seven that includes a pervasive and significant pattern of inattention, impulsivity, and/or hyperactivity–impulsivity.

audiogram   Graph on which a person's ability to hear different pitches (frequencies) at different volumes (intensities) of sound is recorded.

audiological evaluation   Specialized series of hearing tests to determine if a hearing loss exists as well as to quantify and qualify hearing in terms of the degree of hearing loss, the type of hearing loss, and the configuration of the hearing loss.

augmentative and alternative communication (AAC)   Strategies for compensating for an individual's communication limitations or disabilities.

augmentative communication devices (ACDs)   Adapted high- or light-technological aids that provide students with alternatives to speech to convey their messages.

authentic assessment   Ongoing assessment process that occurs within the student's natural environment and includes observation of a student's performance as well as the necessary supports for the student. Authentic assessment also includes work samples that the student has produced.

autism spectrum disorders   Contemporary term used to speak collectively about autism.

behavior inhibition   The ability to regulate one's attention and how often it switches, and the behavior that accompanies this ability; students with ADHD have difficulties with behavior inhibition.

behavior intervention plan (BIP)   Set of strategies designed to address the function of a student's behavior in order to change it.

benchmark   A type of short-term objective included on the IEP.

bilateral hearing loss   Hearing loss in both ears.

bilingual–bicultural (Bi–Bi) approach   Teaching students ASL as the primary language of instruction and English as a second language for reading and writing print; its goal is for students to function in both the Deaf and hearing cultures.

bilingual education   An approach that is often used with English language learners (ELLs) in which the student's dominant language is used along with English for instructional purposes.

bilingual special education teacher   Professional who is knowledgeable about both bilingual education and special education.

blindness   Disability in which an individual has no vision or has only the ability to detect the presence or absence of light.

Brown v. Board of Education of Topeka, Kansas   Supreme court case that clarified that "separate cannot be equal," leading to racial desegregation of public schools.

cerebral palsy (CP)   Group of nonprogressive conditions involving muscle control, posture, and movement; literally means brain paralysis.

child find   State systems that support zero reject goal by alerting the public that services are available for students with disabilities and otherwise ensuring that students are identified.

clean intermittent catheterization (CIC)   Health service procedure that enables individuals to relieve their bladders.

cleft lip and/or palate   Fourth most common birth defect; a separation between the two sides of the lip that often involves the upper jaw and palate such that an opening exists in the roof of the mouth.

clinical low-vision evaluation   Examination performed by an optometrist or ophthalmologist who specializes in low vision to determine whether an individual with a visual impairment would benefit from the use of optical devices, nonoptical devices, or other strategies to enhance visual functioning.

closed head injury   Injury in which the brain is damaged by bouncing around inside the skull without physical damage occurring to the skull itself.

cochlea   Part of the inner ear that is shaped like a snail shell and contains thousands of tiny hair cells that vibrate in response to sound. These vibrations are converted into electrical signals that are carried to the brain by the auditory nerve to be interpreted and given meaning. Damage to these hair cells can be a cause of sensorineural deafness.

cochlear implant   Electronic device surgically implanted to stimulate nerve endings in the inner ear (cochlea) in order to receive and process sound and speech.

cognitive disability   Term sometimes used synonymously with mental retardation, although it also may include other conditions (e.g., autism).

cognitive impairment   Term sometimes used synonymously with mental retardation and often considered a newer, less stigmatizing description of this disability.

cognitive style   Inclination to take a particular approach or orientation to thinking and learning.

collaboration   Style for direct interaction between at least two co-equal parties voluntarily engaged in shared decision making as they work toward a common goal.

communication   The exchange of information and knowledge among participants that is a basic human need. It requires a message, a sender, a receiver, and a channel.

communication disorder   Term sometimes used synonymously with speech and language disorders, but also likely to be used in discussing individuals who have hearing loss.

communication skills   Words chosen and the way they are expressed, coupled with facial expressions, posture, and other nonverbal signals.

communicative intent   Characteristic of many students with autism in which they do not seek to obtain the attention of others and do not communicate for social purposes.

community-based instruction (CBI)   Highly individualized instruction in the community where students can sample different types of jobs and become accustomed to accessing community facilities. This

instruction reflects the interests of students, while helping them to explore new possibilities.

comorbidity   The simultaneous occurrence of two disabilities, disorders, or conditions.

complexity   A feature of curriculum that requires exploration of multiple perspectives, issues, variables, and relationships.

conduct disorder   The most common type of social maladjustment, described in the *Diagnostic and Statistical Manual of Mental Disorders*, that includes aggression, destruction of property, lying or stealing, or serious rule violation (e.g., running away).

conductive hearing loss   Hearing loss caused by the failure of sound waves to reach the inner ear through the normal air conduction channels of the outer and middle ear. In children, conductive loss often is medically correctable.

congenital hearing loss   Hearing loss that is present at birth.

congenital visual impairment   Visual condition that is present before or at birth.

consultation   Voluntary process in which one professional assists another to address a problem concerning a third party; in schools, consultants often are psychologists or other specialists, consultees often are teachers, and clients usually are students.

continuous performance tests (CPTs)   Assessment instruments designed to require a student to sustain attention in order to respond correctly to test items.

continuous progress monitoring   Data gathered as an ongoing part of instruction, often part of response to intervention (RTI).

control of emotions and motivation   Mental activity that involves setting aside frustration or other emotions in order to complete a task.

cornea   The transparent outermost layer of the eye that both protects it and has a major role in the process of refraction.

correlated constraints   When children's lives are permeated with several risk factors, those factors constrain the development of positive adjustment.

co-teaching   Service delivery model in which two educators, one typically a general education teacher and one a special education teacher or other specialist, combine their expertise to jointly teach a heterogeneous group of students, some of whom have disabilities or other special needs, in a single classroom for part or all of the school day.

creativity   Capacity for innovation, originality, expressiveness, and imagination and the ability to manipulate ideas in fluent, flexible, elaborate, and original ways.

criterion-referenced test   Assessment designed to determine whether a student has learned a specific body of information against an absolute standard rather than a comparative standard.

cultural dissonance   Significant discrepancy between two or more cultural frames of reference.

culture   Complex system of underlying beliefs and attitudes that shapes the thoughts and behaviors of a group of people.

curriculum-based measurement (CBM)   Approach to assessment that measures achievement by sampling a student's understanding of the classroom curriculum.

curriculum compacting   Educational practice in which the goals of an instructional unit are identified, student mastery of all or part of the goals is documented, and alternative instruction is provided as appropriate.

curriculum flexibility   A combination of learning options responsive to learner needs and contextual demands; options include acceleration through grade skipping, scaling of objectives, enrichment options, and out-of-school options.

day treatment programs   Special schools for students with emotional or behavioral disabilities where instruction is individualized or occurs in small classes. The educational program includes individual and group therapy, family counseling, vocational training, crisis intervention, positive skill building, and other services such as recreational, art, and music therapy.

Deaf community   The lives and activities of a group of people who have shared experiences relating to deafness and who use American Sign Language as their primary means of communication.

Deaf culture   The history, contributions, values, and customs of the Deaf community.

Deafness   A hearing impairment that is so severe that the child is impaired in processing linguistic information through hearing, with or without amplification, [and] that adversely affects a child's educational performance.

decibel   Logarithmic measure of the intensity or loudness of sound; commonly expressed as dB.

depression   Mental illness with symptoms that include chronic and significant feelings of sadness and hopelessness, and may include thoughts of death.

dialect   The structure of language and the rules that govern it.

Diana v. State Board of Education of California   1970 court case that highlighted bias against certain students as it occurred in assessment for placement in special education programs; resulted in the public school system's being required to test Spanish-speaking children in their native language.

differentiation   Modifying curriculum and other services to meet specific needs of individual learners.

diplegia   Paralysis of both arms or both legs.

direct instruction (DI)   A comprehensive, highly structured, teacher-led instructional approach that emphasizes maximizing not only the quantity of instruction students receive but also the quality.

discrete trial interventions   A group of approaches that require a significant time commitment and specialized training and that are often implemented with preschool children with autism spectrum disorder. Such interventions follow a basic pattern in which the teacher gives a prompt or cue to which the student attends, a command for the student to perform, and finally a reward to the student for the desired behavior.

disproportionate representation   Instances in which a particular group is represented significantly more or less than would be expected based on the percentages of those who comprise that group in the general population.

domain-specific   An ability or intense interest in a particular area of inquiry such as mathematics or music.

dominant culture   Culture of those in power.

Down syndrome   Genetic cause of mental retardation in which an extra chromosome is present in the twenty-first chromosome pair. Individuals with Down syndrome are usually short in stature, have straight hair and slanting eyelids, and may have hearing disabilities or heart conditions.

Duchenne muscular dystrophy   One type of a group of progressive genetic disorders involving a deficiency in the protein dystrophin that results in muscle degeneration; death usually occurs early in adulthood.

due process   Procedures specified in IDEA for making all the critical decisions that are part of special education.

dynamic assessment   Ongoing identification of student learning needs and ability.

dysgraphia   An impairment in the ability to produce written language.

dyslexia   An impairment in the ability to read or comprehend written language.

early childhood special educator   Professional who works with children with disabilities ages birth to five years old, including kindergarten; also called early interventionist.

echolalia   Behavior of some individuals with disabilities in which they repeat words and phrases that have been uttered by someone else with little or no understanding of their conventional meanings.

educational interpreter   Professional who translates spoken words into sign language for students who are deaf or significantly hard of hearing.

eminence   Adult achievement of a high level in a particular field after years of productivity.

emotional and behavior disorders (EBD)   Term preferred by professionals to describe emotional disabilities.

emotional disturbance (ED)   Term used in IDEA to describe the disability that students with emotional and behavior disorders have.

emotional intensity   Capacity to focus emotions for long periods on a single subject or idea.

English as a second language (ESL)   Practice of directly teaching English to individuals who speak another language.

English language learners (ELLs)   Students who are learning English as a second language.

English learners (ELs)   Students whose primary language is not English.

enrichment   Extending normal curriculum with different examples and associations that build complex ideas on the basis of the general curriculum.

environmental supports   Changes to students' surroundings that help them function successfully.

epilepsy   Neurological condition in which damage to the brain leads to sudden, uncontrolled bursts of electrical activity that may be seen as seizures.

executive functions   The mental activities that help individuals regulate their behaviors.

expanded core curriculum   Curriculum encompassing the range of skills that address disability-specific needs of students' visual impairments, including communication skills, social skills, daily living skills, and orientation and mobility skills.

expressive language   An individual's ability to produce language.

externalizing behaviors   Behavior excesses displayed by students with emotional and behavior disorders in which actions are directed at others (e.g., hitting, shouting).

fetal alcohol syndrome (FAS)   Prenatal, preventable cause of mild to moderate mental retardation resulting from maternal alcohol consumption. FAS is considered the leading cause of mental retardation.

field independent   Inclination to be analytical in processing information, such that consideration of surrounding context is not requisite to understanding.

field sensitive   Inclination to take a holistic approach to processing information, such that consideration of contextual variables becomes paramount to developing understanding.

fluctuating hearing loss   Hearing loss that varies from day to day. Some days a student may hear better or worse depending on a variety of factors (e.g., colds and allergies).

fluency disorder   Speech disorder in which hesitations during speech interfere with communication.

fragile X syndrome   Most common form of inherited mental retardation, transmitted from mother to child and causing a mutation in one of the genes in the X chromosome. Also called Martin-Bell syndrome.

free appropriate public education (FAPE)   Core principle in IDEA specifying that students with disabilities are entitled to receive an education designed to address their special needs, at no cost to parents.

functional behavior assessment (FBA)   Multidimensional problem solving strategy required in IDEA for students experiencing serious behavior problems. It includes analyzing a student's behavior within the context of the setting in which it is occurring for the purpose of deciding the function the behavior is serving and a way to address it.

functional–ecological assessment Form of authentic assessment that analyzes the typical demands of the environment (what steps others typically engage in to complete activities), identifies natural cues in the environment that exist to prompt expected behavior, documents student performance during meaningful activities, and specifies the discrepancy between expected behavior and student performance. Supports provided to the student are documented and initial considerations are explored that would facilitate more competent performance in meaningful activities.

functional vision assessment Evaluation process to determine whether a student with a visual impairment can use vision for accomplishing daily tasks and to ascertain the student's potential to increase the use of vision.

generalization Ability to learn a task or idea and then apply it in other situations.

generalized seizure Seizure that involves the entire body and may be one of two types: tonic-clonic or absence.

genetic hearing loss Hearing loss caused by the presence of an abnormal gene within one or more chromosomes.

hard of hearing Hearing loss, whether permanent or fluctuating, that adversely affects a student's educational performance but that is not included under the definition of "deaf."

hearing impairment (HI) Term that refers to any degree of hearing loss, from mild to profound, encompassing the terms *deaf* or *hard of hearing*. This term is losing acceptance by deaf persons because the word *impaired* has a negative connotation.

hearing loss General term used when a distinction among various types of hearing impairments is not critical to make.

hemiplegia Type of paralysis involving the arm, leg, and trunk of the body on the same side.

idealism Act of envisioning things in an ideal form; pursuit of one's ideals.

inclusion Belief system shared by every member of a school as a learning community, often based on a mission statement or vision, emphasizing the commitment to educate *all* students so they can reach their potential.

indirect versus direct service Intervention offered to students by special service providers versus intervention arranged among special service providers and general educators, but implemented by general educators or other school staff. Consultation is an example of an indirect service.

individualized education program (IEP) Document prepared by the multidisciplinary team or annual review team that specifies a student's level of functioning and needs; the instructional goals and objectives for the student and how they will be evaluated; the nature and extent of special education, related services, and supplementary aids and services the student will receive; and the initiation date and duration of the services. Each student's IEP is updated annually.

Individuals with Disabilities Education Act (IDEA) Federal law, first enacted in 1975, that protects the educational rights of infants, toddlers, children, and youth with disabilities (ages birth to twenty-one).

integrated related service delivery Practice of specialists in various disciplines (e.g., occupational therapists, physical therapists, adaptive physical educators) bringing their knowledge, skills, and expertise into students' typical learning environment to assist in the learning process versus removing students to special environments.

intellectual disabilities (ID) Contemporary term often used in place of the term *mental retardation*.

interaction process Sets of steps professionals use in order to collaborate; interpersonal problem solving is the most often used interaction process.

internalizing behaviors Behavior excesses displayed by students with emotional and behavior disorders in which actions are directed inward (e.g., extreme shyness, hypochondria).

interpersonal problem solving Interaction process in which a group of professionals identifies the problem, generates alternative solutions, implements the agreed-on intervention, and evaluates its outcomes.

interpreter Individual who helps people who are deaf or hard of hearing communicate by translating what a hearing person says into signs, spoken words with cues, or some other way of communicating. The interpreter also translates what the deaf person signs or cues into spoken words.

iris Colored portion of the eye with a hole in the middle that is called the pupil.

job coach Professional who helps individuals with disabilities to learn behaviors for succeeding in the workplace.

juvenile diabetes Metabolic disorder in which the body cannot properly break down sugars and store them.

knowledge construction Process by which a particular framework is used to develop, evaluate, and disseminate new information.

language Culturally based system of symbols, governed by complex rules, that individuals use for communication.

language difference Variations from standard speech that are considered normal; dialects are an example of a language difference.

language disorder Impairments that interfere with language comprehension and use.

***Larry P. v. Riles* (1972)** Federal court case that established that, because of their bias, IQ tests could not be used to identify African American students as having mental retardation.

learned helplessness Condition in which an individual who experiences repeated failure expects more failure and loses motivation.

learning disabilities (LD) Condition in which a student has a dysfunction in processing information typically found in language-based activities, resulting in interference with learning. Students with LD have average or above average intelligence but experience significant problems in learning how to read, write, and/or compute.

learning media assessment Evaluation process that gathers a variety of information to determine the primary and secondary learning media and literacy needs for students with visual impairments; often addresses a student's use of sensory channels and needs for general learning media.

least restrictive environment (LRE) Setting most like the one in which other students are educated in which a student with a disability can succeed. The presumption in current law is that the LRE for most students is general education.

legal blindness Disability in which distance visual acuity is 20/200 or less in the better eye with the best correction or in which the visual field is restricted to 20 degrees or less; this clinical measurement typically is used for legal purposes and entitlements.

lens The part of the eye that changes shape to focus light at the appropriate place at the back of the eye.

life skills curriculum A curriculum or learning system that stresses concepts and skills that students with mental retardation or other disabilities need to function independently.

long-term memory The brain's mechanism for permanently storing information it takes in.

low vision Visual impairment that exists after correction, but one in which the potential exists for the use of vision, with or without low-vision devices, to accomplish daily tasks.

low-vision devices Optical and nonoptical devices and strategies that allow an individual with low vision to accomplish near and distant tasks.

macroculture Overarching cultural structure of a society represented by the cultural aspects that all members of that society share.

meaningful curriculum Chronologically age-appropriate, relevant curriculum provided for each student according to interests, personal goals, and limitations in reaching those goals.

mediation Process in which a neutral professional assists parents and school district personnel in resolving disputes concerning any aspect of a student's special education.

mental disorder Terminology to describe emotional and behavior disorders as presented in the *Diagnostic and Statistical Manual of Mental Disorders*. These disorders may or may not be included in the IDEA definition of emotional disturbance.

mentor Qualified individual who works with students in areas of interest or ability, guiding the students' development and achievement.

metacognition Thinking about thinking, such as the ability to organize thinking before acting or the ability to relate information just learned to other information already stored in the brain.

microculture Subculture within a larger society that demonstrates some cultural characteristics that differ from the larger society.

Mills v. Board of Education **(1972)** Federal court case based on a class-action lawsuit establishing that all children with disabilities in Washington, D.C., are entitled to public education.

mixed hearing loss Hearing loss that is both sensorineural and conductive. A child with mixed loss has problems hearing muffled or quiet sounds. Mixed losses may fluctuate.

monoplegia Type of paralysis involving only one limb.

mood disorder An emotional disorder, described in the *Diagnostic and Statistical Manual of Mental Disorders*, that includes problems with affect. Depression is an example of a mood disorder.

multicultural education An approach to education that includes perspectives from and content about diverse groups, embraces diverse cognitive styles, and promotes equity in a diverse society.

multidisciplinary team Team of teachers, specialists, administrators, and parents who assess a student's individual needs, determine eligibility for special education, and develop the IEP.

musculoskeletal disorders Physical disabilities that are the result of problems related to the skeleton or muscles.

mutual goal Shared goal that is the basis for collaboration; should clearly be stated to achieve collaboration.

myelomeningocele Type of spina bifida that occurs when the spinal cord and its covering protrude from the opening in the spine.

National Joint Committee on Learning Disabilities (NJCLD) Group of representatives from ten professional and parent organizations concerned about and working on behalf of individuals with learning disabilities.

natural supports Existing resources in any environment (e.g., classmates, co-workers) that can provide support to an individual with severe and multiple disabilities.

neurological disorder Disorder that occurs because of a problem in the central nervous system, that is, the brain, spinal cord, or nerve endings.

nondiscriminatory evaluation Core principle in IDEA establishing that no instruments and procedures used to assess students for special education services shall be biased.

nonverbal communication Use of nonspeech modes to convey a message; for example, facial expressions, body gestures, manual signs, pictures, and objects.

nonverbal learning disability Subgroup of students with learning disabilities who cannot interpret nonverbal communication, such as facial expressions, posture, and eye contact.

norm-referenced test Assessment in which the student taking the test is being compared to a large number of students, or norm group.

occupational therapist Professional who assists students with disabilities in developing self-help, functional, and other skills of daily living, such as grasping a tool, buttoning, and tying.

omission Articulation disorder in which some of the sounds of a word are omitted.

open head injury Injury in which the brain is damaged when the skull is fractured and the membrane surrounding the brain is penetrated.

ophthalmologist Physician specializing in the care of the eyes and visual system, and in the prevention of eye disease and injury.

oppositional defiant disorder (ODD) A disruptive behavior disorder, as described in the *Diagnostic and Statistical Manual of Mental Disorders*, that is identified when students are defiant with adults and vindictive or blaming with peers to an excessive degree over a long period of time.

optic nerve The structure that transmits images from the eye to the brain.

optometrist Professional trained to identify eye problems and to prescribe corrective lenses.

orientation and mobility skills Competencies used by persons with visual impairments to travel safely and efficiently in the environment.

orthopedic impairment (OI) IDEA term that refers to students with physical disabilities.

orthoses Braces and other devices used to stabilize legs and support the weight of an individual with a physical disability so that the person can walk or maintain balance.

ossicles Linkage of the three tiniest bones in the body (malleus, incus, and stapes sometimes respectively called hammer, anvil, and stirrup) providing the mechanical coupling between the ear drum and the cochlea.

other health impairment IDEA term for students having medical conditions that result in limited strength, vitality, or alertness.

P.L. 94-142 Education of the Handicapped Act of 1975, later renamed Education of All Handicapped Children Act and currently called the Individuals with Disabilities Education Act, protecting the educational rights of students with disabilities.

paraeducator Individual employed as a noncertified staff member to assist certified staff in carrying out education programs and otherwise helping in the instruction of students with disabilities; also called a *paraprofessional*.

paraplegia Paralysis involving both legs.

parity Collaboration concept that participants' contributions are equally valued whether those contributions are great or small.

partial participation Term given to students' levels of participation in an activity when they are unable to fully perform an activity on their own but can engage in some parts of the activity with supports as needed.

partial seizure Type of seizure in which the electrical discharge affects only part of the brain; symptoms may involve twitching or rapid eye blinks.

peer tutoring Approach to peer-mediated instruction in which students are partnered, provided with instructional materials that they are to learn, and expected to help each other in accomplishing the learning goal.

Pennsylvania Association for Retarded Children v. The Commonwealth of Pennsylvania 1972 landmark case in which parents of children with significant intellectual disabilities won the guarantee to not only traditional academic instruction but also to education tailored to those children's special needs.

perfectionism Striving for a self-imposed advanced goal or unrealistic standard; characteristics and behaviors include compulsive work habits, extensive attention to detail, rigid routine, and unrealistically high standards for self and others.

person-centered approach Form of authentic assessment that focuses on the unique characteristics and interests of the student and not on any predetermined set of skills, as usually occurs on a formal assessment.

phenylketonuria (PKU) Inherited metabolic disorder that occurs when the body is unable to produce the chemicals needed to convert other, toxic chemicals into harmless products. Treatment generally includes a lifelong dietary regimen.

physical restraint Emergency intervention, generally implemented only when a student presents immediate serious threat of danger to self or others and personnel are appropriately trained, in which a teacher or another professional restricts a students' freedom of movement, physical activity, or access to his body.

physical therapist Professional who assists students with disabilities in developing muscle strength and flexibility and mobility, posture, and positioning skills.

positive behavior supports (PBS) A functional and data-based approach to responding to student behaviors with an emphasis on skill development.

Prader-Willi syndrome Form of inherited mental retardation caused by any of several types of mutation on chromosome 15.

precocity Demonstrating early development or maturity in ways such as early language development, ability to ask complex questions, rapid learning, extensive vocabulary, or unusual attention span.

present level of educational performance Required IEP component comprising information about a student's current level of academic achievement, social skills, behavior, communication skills, and other functioning areas.

priming Intervention in which a parent, teacher, other professional, or trusted peer previews with a student the actual materials that will be used in a lesson the day, morning, or evening before the activity occurs in order to prepare the student for that instruction.

procedural safeguards Specified in IDEA, provisions requiring that any educational decisions made about a student with disabilities be made with parental input and in compliance with the law.

prompt Cue designed to get a student to perform a specific behavior.

prosody Tone and inflection used when speaking; an area of difficulty for many students with autism spectrum disorders.

proxemics Study of acceptable spatial distances between people of various cultures and backgrounds; an area of difficulty for many students with autism spectrum disorders.

psychological processes Function of the brain, measured indirectly, through which it takes information in, interprets it, and acts on it.

psychosocial factors Influences on student's psychological and social development that include the people around them, the events they experience, and their living conditions.

pupil Opening in the center of the iris whose size determines the amount of light that enters the eye.

receptive language An individual's ability to comprehend language.

reconstitution Mental activity that involves the ability to break down what is observed or learned and to combine parts in order to perform new actions.

refraction Process of bending light rays that is part of vision.

related services Services required through IDEA for students with disabilities that enable them to benefit from special education. May include transportation, speech/language therapy, and adaptive physical education, among others.

residential program Service delivery option for students with extremely serious or complicated disabilities when education in a less restrictive setting is determined by the IEP team not to be possible. In residential programs, students live at the school, attending classes and participating in therapeutic and recreational activities.

resilience Ability to recover and not experience long-term harm from episodes of stress or single negative experiences.

response to intervention (RTI) Approach (first authorized in IDEA 2004) to identifying students as having learning disabilities based on the extent to which their learning accelerates or fails to accelerate when provided with increasingly intense instructional interventions.

retina Innermost layer of the eye consisting of the light-sensitive membrane that covers the back wall of the eyeball connecting the rest of the eye to the optic nerve.

retinopathy of prematurity Disease usually occurring in premature babies in which abnormal blood vessels grow in the retina, causing visual impairment.

rote memory Ability to easily remember things without necessarily knowing what they mean.

school counselor Professional who works with all students, including those with disabilities, to solve problems related to the social or affective domains.

school nurse Professional responsible for all students in a school, including those with disabilities, who conducts vision and hearing screenings, ensures all immunization records are on file, provides routine assistance for ill students, manages the distribution of medications students may take, and contributes information to other professionals about students' medical conditions.

school social worker Professional who coordinates the efforts of educators, families, and outside agency personnel to ensure that students receive all the supports they need.

sclera White portion of the eye that helps it maintain its shape.

seclusion Intervention, generally implemented only when other behavior strategies have not been successful and only with clear safety procedures in place, in which a student is involuntarily confined to a room, left alone, and prevented from leaving.

Section 504 of the Rehabilitation Act of 1973 Federal civil rights law protecting individuals with functional disabilities. Provides protection for some students not eligible for services through IDEA.

seizure disorder Neurological condition in which damage to the brain leads to sudden, uncontrolled bursts of electrical activity that may be seen as seizures; Epilepsy.

self-directed speech Mental activity that enables individuals to reflect on how they are doing, to problem solve, and to follow instructions; also called self-talk.

self-fulfilling prophecy The idea that professionals and others create disabilities or learning problems in students who are nondisabled by treating them as though they are disabled.

self-stimulatory behavior Repetitive, stereotyped behavior that has no apparent function; examples include rocking and hand flapping.

sensorineural hearing loss Permanent hearing loss caused by failure or damage of auditory fibers in the inner ear (cochlea) and/or damage to the neural system.

shared accountability Collaboration concept in which participants jointly accept the outcomes of their decisions, positive or negative.

shared resources Collaboration concept in which each participant contributes something in order to foster shared ownership of the goal that is the purpose of the collaboration.

shared responsibility Collaboration concept in which participants jointly make critical decisions, but they often divide the labor for achieving them.

sheltered English An instructional approach that uses linguistic scaffolding to facilitate comprehension.

short-term memory Brain's mechanism for temporarily storing information it takes in; if information in short-term memory is not saved in long-term memory, it is lost.

short-term objective Description of a step followed in order to achieve an annual goal on an IEP; sometimes called a benchmark.

sickle cell disease Medical disorder that affects the part of the red blood cells that carries oxygen from the lungs to other parts of the body; the most common symptom is pain.

social story Individualized text or story that describes a specific social situation from the student's perspective; its purpose is to help the student know how to respond appropriately to the described situation.

socially maladjusted Term that describes students who intentionally act out or break rules. Students who are socially maladjusted are excluded from the IDEA definition for *emotional disturbance,* a disability category.

socioeconomic status (SES) A measure of an individual's educational and income level.

spastic cerebral palsy Most common type of cerebral palsy in children, affecting approximately two-thirds of those with this neurological condition; muscles are stiff and movements are awkward.

special education Specialized instruction that students with disabilities are entitled to receive as articulated in IDEA.

special education teacher Professional who provides day-to-day instruction and other support for students with disabilities.

specific language impairment (SLI) Language disorder that cannot be explained by a physical disability, mental retardation, hearing loss, or another disability.

speech Use of the oral channel for exchanging information and knowledge.

speech and language disorders Collective term for all the disorders that can occur within the IDEA category called *speech or language impairment.*

speech disorder Problem with articulation, voice, or fluency.

speech language impairment Term used in IDEA to refer to speech and language disorders.

speech reading Interpretation of lip and facial movements in order to understand speech; also called lip reading. Used by people with hearing loss who communicate orally and by some people who become deaf or hard of hearing later in life.

spina bifida Neurological physical disability in which the bones of the spine do not close properly.

spinal cord injury Group of neurological physical disabilities that occur when there is a break, severe bruise, or other damage to the spinal cord that affects motor and sensory functions.

stereotypic behavior Repeated behaviors that serve no constructive function; examples include flapping the hands and rocking.

stimulant medication The most commonly prescribed medication for students with ADHD; examples include Ritalin, Dexedrine, Cylert, Adderall, and Focalin.

strategy instruction Method of teaching students techniques, principles, or rules applicable in many learning situations that guide them to complete tasks independently.

strengths-based assessment Measurement of students' social and emotional strengths, the characteristics that give them confidence, and traits that help them cope with adversity.

stuttering Most common fluency disorder occurring when a person's speech is broken by sound repetitions, prolonged sounds, or unanticipated stoppages of sound.

substitutions Articulation disorder in which one sound is used when another is correct (e.g., wan for ran).

supplementary aids and services (SAS) A range of supports provided in general education classes or other education-related settings that enable students with disabilities to be educated with children who are not disabled to the maximum extent appropriate.

supported employment Practice of assisting adults with disabilities to obtain jobs in the competitive market (not a sheltered workshop) and providing the necessary physical, instructional, and social support to ensure success for the employee.

systemic bias Favoritism toward a particular group that occurs at multiple levels within a society or institution; such favoritism becomes an implicit part of the functioning of that society or institution.

TASH Formerly The Association for Persons with Severe Handicaps. International advocacy organization for people with disabilities, which actively promotes the full inclusion and participation of persons with disabilities in all aspects of life.

task analysis Instructional process for ensuring systematic learning by breaking lengthy or complex tasks into distinct small steps and teaching those steps to students, separately at first and gradually in combination.

teacher assistance team (TAT) See *intervention assistance team.*

team Two or more interdependent individuals with unique skills and perspectives who interact directly to achieve their mutual goals of providing students with effective educational programs and services.

tetraplegia Paralysis involving both arms, both legs, the trunk of the body, and the neck; formerly called quadriplegia.

theory of mind Recent theory of autism spectrum disorder emphasizing that individuals with this disability truly do not understand that other people have their own thoughts or points of view.

three-tiered approach Multitiered, sequential system of support used in addressing the needs of students who experience academic difficulties. Each tier- or level- of instructional support is increasingly intense and individualized. Tier 3 often precedes recommendation for special education services.

three-year reevaluation Triannual process of reassessing the needs of a student with a disability; carried out by a multidisciplinary team.

tonic-clonic seizure Most well known of generalized seizures; person first stiffens, loses consciousness, and falls; then arms and legs jerk or contract; formerly called grand mal seizure.

toxoplasmosis Infection caused by a parasite carried by more than sixty million individuals; dangerous usually only to expectant women, who can pass it on to their unborn children, causing them to develop mental retardation or blindness.

traumatic brain injury (TBI) Acquired injury to the brain caused by an external physical force, resulting in total or partial functional disability or psychosocial impairment.

trisomy 21 Term used for Down syndrome; the twenty-first chromosome pair has an extra chromosome, or three (tri) parts.

unilateral hearing loss Hearing loss in only one ear; now believed to adversely affect the educational process in a significant percentage of students who have it.

universal design for learning (UDL) Based on concepts from architecture and product development, an approach for teaching and learning emphasizing the need to address in instructional planning the entire diversity of student needs.

universal newborn hearing screening Program for testing babies' hearing soon after they are born.

uveal tract Second layer of the eye that provides nutrition to it.

values Cultural elements held in great esteem or considered to be of great importance by a society.

visual acuity Clarity or sharpness of vision.

visual field Range in which an individual can see objects centrally or peripherally.

visual impairment Any level of vision loss that has an impact on an individual's ability to complete daily tasks; this term is often used to include both blindness and low vision.

visual impairment (VI) specialist Individual with extensive knowledge of visual impairments who usually takes a lead role in the assessment of students with visual impairments, who manages and delivers special education services to these students, and who provides consultation to other school professionals on students with visual impairments.

voice disorder Condition in which an individual has difficulty with pitch, intensity, vocal quality, or resonance.

working memory Mental activity that enables students to remember tasks, to determine the amount of time they have to complete the tasks, and to learn from past mistakes.

wraparound services An individually designed set of services involving multiple school and community agencies intended to provide the supports necessary for students with emotional or behavior disorders and their families in order to keep students in their homes.

zero reject Core principle of IDEA specifying that no student with a disability, regardless of its nature or severity, can be denied an education.

References

Chapter 1

Artiles, A. J., Harris-Murri, N., & Rostenberg, D. (2006). Inclusion as social justice: Critical notes on discourses, assumptions, and the road ahead. *Theory into Practice, 45*, 260–268.

Artiles, A. J., Kozleski, E. B., Trent, S. C., Osher, D., & Ortiz, A. (2010). Justifying and explaining disproportionality, 1968–2008: A critique of underlying views of culture. *Exceptional Children, 76*, 279–299.

Barnard-Brak, L., Johnsen, S. K., Hannig, A. P., & Wei, T. (2015). The incidence of potentially gifted students within a special education population. *Roeper Review: A Journal on Gifted Education, 37*(2), 74–83.

Bateman, B., Lloyd, J. W., & Tankersley, M. (2015). *Enduring issues in special education: Personal perspectives.* New York, NY: Routledge.

Bennett, A. (1932). *Subnormal children in elementary grades.* New York, NY: Columbia University, Teacher's College, Bureau of Publications.

Bergmann, S., & Brough, J. (2012). *Reducing the risk, increasing the promise: Strategies for student success.* New York, NY: Routledge.

Berkeley, S., Bender, W. N., Peaster, L. G., & Saunders, L. (2009). Implementation of response to intervention: A snapshot of progress. *Journal of Learning Disabilities, 42*, 85–95.

Brandon, R. R., & Brown, M. R. (2009). African-American families in the special education process: Increasing their level of involvement. *Intervention in School and Clinic, 45*, 85–90.

Braunsteiner, M., & Mariano-Lapidus, S. (2014). A perspective of inclusion: Challenges for the future. *Global Education Review, 1*(1), 32–43.

Brennan, D. D. (2015). Creating a climate for achievement. *Educational Leadership, 72*(5), 56–59.

Browder, D. M., Lee, A., & Mims, P. (2011). Using shared stories and individual response modes to promote comprehension and engagement in literacy for students with multiple, severe disabilities. *Education and Training in Autism and Developmental Disabilities, 46*, 339–351.

Carter, E. W., Moss, C. K., Hoffman, A., Chung, Y., & Sisco, L. (2011). Efficacy and social validity of peer support arrangements for adolescents with disabilities. *Exceptional Children, 78*, 107–125.

Chitiyo, M., & Wheeler, J. J. (2009). Challenges faced by school teachers in implementing positive behavior support in their school systems. *Remedial and Special Education, 30*, 58–63.

Codrington, J., & Fairchild, H. H. (2012, February). *Special education and the mis-education of African American children: A call to action* [position paper]. Ft. Washington, MD: Association of Black Psychologists.

Colavita, V. A., Luthra, N., & Perry, A. (2014). Strengths and challenges of children with a developmental disability: A qualitative analysis of parent perceptions. *Journal on Developmental Disabilities, 20*(3), 80–87.

Connecticut Special Education Association. (1936). *Development and progress of special classes for mentally deficient children in Connecticut.* New Haven, CT: Author.

Connor, D. J. (2006). Michael's story: "I get into so much trouble just by walking": Narrative knowing and life at the intersections of learning disability, race, and class. *Equity and Excellence in Education, 39*, 154–165.

Cooper-Duffy, K., Szedia, P., & Hyer, G. (2010). Teaching literacy to students with significant cognitive disabilities. *Teaching Exceptional Children, 42*(3), 30–39.

Cosier, M, Causton-Theoharis, J., & Theoharis, G. (2014). Does access matter? Time in general education and achievement for students with disabilities. *Remedial and Special Education, 34*, 323–332.

Council for Exceptional Children. (2006). *Evidence-based practice—Wanted, needed, and hard to get.* Arlington, VA: Author. Retrieved from www.cec.sped.org/AM/Template.cfm?Section=Home&TEMPLATE=/CM/ContentDisplay.cfm&CONTENTID=6465.

Cramer, E. D., & Bennett, K. D. (2015). Implementing culturally responsive positive behavior interventions and supports in middle school classrooms. *Middle School Journal, 46*(3), 18–24.

Crouch, R., Keys, C. B., & McMahon, S. D. (2014). Student–teacher relationships matter for school inclusion: School belonging, disability, and school transitions. *Journal of Prevention & Intervention in the Community, 42*(1), 20–30.

Damore, S. J., & Murray, C. (2009). Urban elementary school teachers' perspectives regarding collaborative teaching practices. *Remedial and Special Education, 30*, 234–244.

Davidson Institute for Talent Development. (2009, April). *Gifted education policies.* Retrieved from http://www.davidsongifted.org/db/StatePolicy.aspx

Davidson Institute for Talent Development. (2015). *Gifted education policies.* Reno, NV: Author. Retrieved from http://www.davidsongifted.org/db/StatePolicy.aspx.

Davis, L. J. (2015). *Enabling acts: The hidden story of how the Americans with Disabilities Act gave the largest US minority its rights.* Boston, MA: Beacon Press.

Duhaney, L. (2003). A practical approach to managing the behaviors of students with ADD. *Intervention in School and Clinic, 38*, 267–279.

Dunn, L.M. (1968). Special education for the mildly retarded—is much of it justifiable? *Exceptional Children, 35*, 5–22.

Dyson, L. L. (2005). Kindergarten children's understanding of attitudes toward people with disabilities. *Topics in Early Childhood Special Education, 25*, 95–105.

Eisenman, L. T., Pleet, A. M., Wandry, D., & McGinley, V. (2011). Voices of special education teachers in an inclusive high school: Redefining responsibilities. *Remedial and Special Education, 32*, 91–104.

Erwin, E. J., & Soodak, L. C. (2008). The evolving relationship between families of children with disabilities and professionals. In T. C. Jiménez, & V. L. Graf (Eds.), *Education for all: Critical issues in the education of children and youth with disabilities* (pp. 35–69). San Francisco, CA: Jossey-Bass.

Etscheidt, S., & Curran, C. M. (2010). Peer-reviewed research and individualized education programs (IEPS): An examination of intent and impact. *Exceptionality, 18*, 138–150.

Fleischer, D. Z., & Zames, F. (2001). *The disability rights movement: From charity to confrontation* (pp. 88–109). Philadelphia, PA: Temple University Press.

Flores, M. M., Nelson, C., Hinton, V., Franklin, T. M., Strozier, S. D., Terry, L., & Franklin, S. (2013). Teaching reading comprehension and language skills to students with autism spectrum disorders and developmental disabilities using direct instruction. *Education and Training in Autism and Developmental Disabilities, 48*(1), 41–48.

Forman, S. G., & Crystal, C. D. (2015). Systems consultation for multi-tiered systems of supports (MTSS): Implementation issues. *Journal of Educational & Psychological Consultation, 25*, 276–285.

Friend, M. (2008). *Co-teach! A handbook for creating and sustaining effective classroom partnerships in inclusive schools.* Greensboro, NC: Marilyn Friend, Inc.

Friend, M. (2013). Inclusive practices. In J. A. Banks (Ed.), *Encyclopedia of diversity in education* (pp. 1144–1147). Thousand Oaks, CA: Sage.

Friend, M. (2014). *Co-Teach! Building and sustaining effective classroom partnerships in inclusive schools* (2nd ed.). Greensboro, NC: Marilyn Friend, Inc.

Friend, M., & Cook, L. (2013). *Interactions: Collaboration skills for school professionals* (7th ed.). Upper Saddle River, NJ: Pearson/Merrill.

Friend, M., & Cook, L. (2017). *Interactions: Collaboration skills for school professionals* (8th ed.). Upper Saddle River, NJ: Pearson.

Fuchs, D., & Fuchs, L. S. (2015). Rethinking service delivery for students with significant learning problems: Developing and implementing intensive instruction. *Remedial and Special Education, 36*, 105–111.

Fuchs, D., Fuchs, L. S., & Stecker, P. M. (2010). The "blurring" of special education in a new continuum of general education placements and services. *Exceptional Children, 76*, 301–324.

Goffman, E. (1963). *Stigma*. Upper Saddle River, NJ: Prentice Hall.

Goldstein, H., Moss, J. W., & Jordan, L. J. (1965). *The efficacy of special class training on the development of mentally retarded children* (U.S. Office of Education Cooperative Research Program Project No. 619). Urbana: University of Illinois Institute for Research on Exceptional Children. (ERIC Document Reproduction Service No. ED002907).

Gottfried, M. A. (2014). Classmates with disabilities and students' noncognitive outcomes. *Educational Evaluation and Policy Analysis, 36*, 20–43.

Graziano, P. A., McNamara, J. P., Geffken, G. R., & Reid, A. (2011). Severity of children's ADHD symptoms and parenting stress: A multiple mediation model of self-regulation. *Journal of Abnormal Child Psychology, 39*, 1073–1083.

Groszmann, M. P. E. (1922). Special and ungraded classes. *Journal of Education, 95*(4), 102–103.

Guthrie, P. (2006). *Section 504 and ADA promoting student access: A resource guide for educators* (3rd ed.). Fort Valley, GA: Council of Administrators of Special Education.

Harlacher, J. E., Nelson Walker, N. J., & Sanford, A. K. (2010). The "I" in RTI: Research-based factors for intensifying instruction. *Teaching Exceptional Children, 42*(6), 30–39.

Harris, J. C. (2010). *Intellectual disability: A guide for families and professionals.* New York, NY: Oxford University Press.

Harris, K. I. (2015). The unexpected journey shared by families: Using literature to support and understand families raising a child with disabilities. *Early Childhood Education Journal, 43*, 473–484.

Hazelkorn, M., Packard, A. L., & Douvanis, G. (2008). Alternative dispute resolution in special education: A view from the field. *Journal of Special Education Leadership, 21*(1), 32–38.

Herrelko, J. M. (2013). A four-tier differentiation model: Engage all students in the learning process. *Teacher Education and Practice, 26*, 415–430.

Hoban, R. (2015, May 29). Eugenics compensation amendment continues to leave some victims out. *North Carolina Health News.* Retrieved from http://www.northcarolinahealthnews.org/2015/05/29/eugenics-compensation-amendment-continues-to-leave-some-victims-out/.

Hobbs, N. (1975). *The futures of children.* San Francisco, CA: Jossey-Bass.

Holzbauer, J. J. (2008). Disability harassment observed by teachers in special education. *Journal of Disability Policy Studies, 19*, 162–171.

Hoover, J. J., & Love, E. (2011). Supporting school-based response to intervention: A practitioner's model. *Teaching Exceptional Children, 43*(3), 40–49.

Huberman, M., Navo, M., & Parrish, T. (2012). Effective practices in high performing districts serving students in special education. *Journal of Special Education Leadership, 25*(2), 59–71.

Hyatt, K. J. (2007). The new IDEA: Changes, concerns, and questions. *Intervention in School and Clinic, 42*, 131–136.

Hyatt, K. J., & Filler, J. (2011). LRE re-examined: Misinterpretations and unintended consequences. *International Journal of Inclusive Education, 15*, 1031–1045.

Idol, L. (2006). Toward inclusion of special education students in general education: A program evaluation of eight schools. *Remedial and Special Education, 27*, 77–94.

Itkonen, T. (2009). Stories of hope and decline: Interest group effectiveness in national special education policy. *Educational Policy, 23*(1), 43–65.

Johnson, E. S., Pool, J. L., & Carter, D. R. (2012). Lessons learned from a tiered service delivery implementation project. *Intervention in School and Clinic, 47*, 139–143.

Jones, P., Fauske, J. R., & Carr, J. F. (2011). *Leading for inclusion: How schools can build on the strengths of all learners.* New York, NY: Teachers College Press.

Kanner, L. (1964). *A history of the care and study of the mentally retarded* (pp. 9–44). Springfield, IL: Charles C. Thomas.

Katsiyannis, A., Losinski, M., & Parks Ennis, R. (2015). Retrospective testimony and the IEP: Implications of R.E., M.E., et al. *v.* New York City Department of Education. *Preventing School Failure, 59*, 58–62.

Katsiyannis, A., Yell, M. L., & Bradley, R. (2001). Reflections on the 25th anniversary of the Individuals with Disabilities Education Act. *Remedial and Special Education, 22*, 324–334.

Kauffman, J. M. (2015). Opinion on recent developments and the future of special education. *Remedial and Special Education, 36*, 9–13.

Key, D. L. (2000). *Team teaching: Integration of inclusion and regular students.* (ED447140). Retrieved from www.edrs.com/members/sp.cfm?AN=ED447140

King-Sears, M. E. (2008). Facts and fallacies: Differentiation and the general education curriculum for students with special education needs. *Support for Learning, 23*(2), 55–62.

Kode, K. (2002). *Elizabeth Farrell and the history of special education.* Arlington, VA: Council for Exceptional Children.

Kretlow, A. G., & Blatz, S. L. (2011). The ABCs of evidence-based practice for teachers. *Teaching Exceptional Children, 43*(5), 8–19.

Lalvani, P. (2012). Parents' participation in special education in the context of implicit educational ideologies and socioeconomic status. *Education and Training in Autism and Developmental Disabilities, 47*, 474–486.

Leggett, D. G., Shea, I. I., & Wilson, J. A. (2010). Advocating for twice-exceptional students: An ethical obligation. *Research in the Schools, 17*(2), 1–10.

Lingo, A. S., Barton-Arwood, S. M., & Jolivette, K. (2011). Teachers working together: Improving learning outcomes in the inclusive classroom—Practical strategies and examples. *Teaching Exceptional Children, 43*(3), 6–13.

Litvack, M. S., Ritchie, K. C., & Shore, B. M. (2011). High- and average-achieving students' perceptions of disabilities and of students with disabilities in inclusive classrooms. *Exceptional Children, 77*, 474–488.

Lord, C., & Bishop, S. L. (2010). Autism spectrum disorders: Diagnosis, prevalence, and services for children and families. *Sharing Child and Youth Development Knowledge, 24*(2), 1–27.

Magliaro, S. G., Lockee, B. B., & Burton, J. K. (2005). Direct instruction revisited: A key model for instructional technology. *Educational Technology Research and Development, 53*(4), 41–55.

March, J. K., & Peters, K. H. (2015). Telling the Truth about the Common Core. *Phi Delta Kappan, 96*(8), 63–65.

Marx, T. A., Hart, J. L., Nelson, L., Love, J., Baxter, C. M., Gartin, B., & Schaefer Whitby, P. J. (2014). Guiding IEP teams on meeting the least restrictive environment mandate. *Intervention in School and Clinic, 50*, 45–50.

Maryland State Department of Education. (2011). *A route for every learner: Universal design for learning (UDL) as a framework for supporting learning and improving achievement for all learners in Maryland, prekindergarten through higher education.* Baltimore: Maryland State Department of Education.

McLaughlin, M. J. (2010). Evolving interpretations of educational equity and students with disabilities. *Exceptional Children, 76*, 265-278.

McLeskey, J. & Waldron, N. L. (2011). Educational programs for elementary students with learning disabilities: Can they be both effective and inclusive? *Learning Disabilities Research & Practice, 26*, 48-57.

McLeskey, J., & Waldron, N. L. (2007). Comprehensive school reform and inclusive schools. *Theory into Practice, 45*, 269-278.

McLeskey, J., & Waldron, N. L. (2011). Educational programs for elementary students with learning disabilities: Can they be both effective and inclusive? *Learning Disabilities Research & Practice, 26*, 48-57.

Mercer, J. (1973). *Labeling the mentally retarded.* Berkeley: University of California Press.

Meyen, E. (2015). Significant advancements in technology to improve instruction for all students: Including those with disabilities. *Remedial and Special Education, 36*, 67-71.

Mondale, S., & Patton, S. B. (2001). *School: The story of American public education.* Boston, MA: Beacon Press.

Morrissey, K. L., Bohanon, H., & Fenning, P. (2010). Positive behavior support: Teaching and acknowledging expected behaviors in an urban high school. *Teaching Exceptional Children, 42*(5), 26-35.

Muscott, H. S. (2002). Exceptional partnerships: Listening to the voices of families. *Preventing School Failure, 46(2)*, 66-69.

Mutua, K., Siders, J., & Bakken, J. P. (2011). History of intellectual disabilities. In Rotatori, A. F., Obiakor, F. E., & Bakken, J. P. (Eds.), *History of special education* [Advances in Special Education, Volume 21]. Bingley, UK: Emerald Group Publishing Limited.

National Center for Education Statistics. (2015). Children 3-21 years old served under Individuals with Disabilities Education Act (IDEA), Part B, by type of disability: Selected year, 1976-77 through 2011-12 [Table 204.30]. *Digest of Education Statistics 2013.* Washington, DC: Author.

National Center on Response to Intervention. (2010, March). *Essential components of RTI—A closer look at response to intervention.* Washington, DC: National Center on Response to Intervention.

Nelson, J. R., Oliver, R. M., Hebert, M. A., & Bohaty, J. (2015). Use of self-monitoring to maintain program fidelity of multi-tiered interventions. *Remedial and Special Education, 36*, 14-19.

Nichols, J., Dowdy, A., & Nichols, C. (2010). Co-teaching: An educational promise for children with disabilities or a quick fix to meet the mandates of No Child Left Behind? *Education, 130*, 647-651.

O'Connor, C., Hill, L. D., & Robinson, S. R. (2009). Who's at risk in school and what's race to go do with it? *Review of Research in Education, 33*, 1-34.

Osborne, A. G., & Russo, C. J. (2014). *Special education and the law: A guide for practitioners* (3rd ed.). Thousand Oaks, CA: Corwin.

Osgood, R. L. (2008). *The history of special education: A struggle for equality in American public schools.* Westport, CT: Greenwood-Praeger.

Osgood, R. L. (2010). Laggards, morons, human clinkers, and other peculiar kids: Progressivism and student difference in shaping public education in the United States. *Philosophical Studies in Education, 41*, 1-10.

Pertsch, C. F. (1936). *A comparative study of the progress of subnormal pupils in the grades and in special classes.* New York, NY: Columbia University, Teacher's College, Bureau of Publications.

Pierson, M. R., & Howell, E. J. (2013). Two high schools and the road to full inclusion: A comparison study. *Improving Schools, 16*, 223-231.

Pisha, B., & Stahl, S. (2005). The promise of new learning environments for students with disabilities. *Intervention in School and Clinic, 41*, 67-75.

Richards, P. L. (2014). Thomas Cameron's "Pure and Guileless Life," 1806-1870 [Chapter 2]. In S. Burch & M. Rembis (Eds.), *Disability histories* (pp. 35-57). Urbana, IL: University of Illinois Press.

Rieke, R. L., Lazarus, S. S., Thurlow, M. L., & Dominguez, L. M. (2013). *2012 survey of states: Successes and challenges during a time of change.* Minneapolis, MN: National Center on Educational Outcomes.

Rodgers, C. (2007). *Parenting and inclusive education: Discovering difference, experiencing difficulty.* New York, NY: Palgrave MacMillan.

Rodriguez, R. J., Blatz, E. T., & Elbaum, B. (2014). Strategies to involve families of Latino students with disabilities: When parent initiative is not enough. *Intervention in School and Clinic, 49*, 263-270.

Rozalski, M., Katsiyannis, A., Ryan, J., Collins, T., & Stewart, A. (2010). Americans with Disabilities Act Amendments of 2008. *Journal of Disability Policy Studies, 21*, 22-28.

Rueda, R., Klingner, J. K., Sager, N., & Velasco, A. (2008). Reducing disproportionate representation in special education: Overview, explanations, and solutions. In T. C. Jiménez & V. L. Graf (Eds.), *Education for all: Critical issues in the education of children and youth with disabilities* (pp. 131-166). San Francisco, CA: Jossey-Bass.

Saeki, E., Jimerson, S. R., Earhart, J., Hart, S. R., Renshaw, T., Singh, R. D., & Stewart, K. (2011). Response to intervention (RtI) in the social, emotional, and behavioral domains: Current challenges and emerging possibilities. *Contemporary School Psychology, 15*, 43-52.

Sailor, W. (2015). Advances in schoolwide inclusive school reform. *Remedial and Special Education, 36*, 94-99.

Salend, S. J. (2006). Explaining your inclusion program to families. *Teaching Exceptional Children, 38*, 6-11.

Salend, S. J., & Garrick-Duhaney, L. M. (2011). Historical and philosophical changes in the education of students with exceptionalities. In A. F. Rotatori, F. E. Obiakow, & J. P. Bakken (Eds.), *History of special education* (Advances in Special Education, Volume 21). Bingley, UK: Emerald.

Sanford, C., Newman, L., Wagner, M., Cameto, R., Knokey, A., & Shaver, D. (2011). *The post-high school outcomes of young adults with disabilities up to 6 years after high school: Key findings from the National Longitudinal Transition Study-2 (NLTS2)* (NCSER 2011-3004). Menlo Park, CA: SRI International.

Santangelo, T., Novosel, L. C., Cook, B. G., & Gapsis, M. (2015). Using the 6S pyramid to identify research-based instructional practices for students with learning disabilities. *Learning Disabilities Research & Practice, 30*, 91-101.

Scheerenberger, R. C. (1983). *A history of mental retardation.* Baltimore, MD: Paul H. Brookes.

Scruggs, T. E., Mastropieri, M. A., & McDuffie, K. A. (2007). Co-teaching in inclusive classrooms: A metasynthesis of qualitative research. *Exceptional Children, 73*, 392-416.

Seguin, E. (1866). *Idiocy and its treatment by the physiological method* [1971 reprinting by A. M. Kelly Open Library]. New York, NY: Wm. Wood and Company.

Severson, K. (2012, June 12). Payments for victims of eugenics are shelved. *New York Times.* Retrieved from http://www.nytimes.com/2012/06/21/us/north-carolina-eugenics-compensation-program-shelved.html?ref=kimseverson&_r=0

Silverman, S. K., Hazelwood, C., & Cronin, P. (2009). *Universal education: Principles and practices for advancing achievement of students with disabilities.* Columbus: Ohio Department of Education, Office for Exceptional Children. Retrieved from http://education.ohio.gov/GD/Document Management/DocumentDownload.aspx?DocumentID=73339

Sindelar, P. T., Shearer, D. K., Yendol-Hoppey, D., & Liebert, T. W. (2006). The sustainability of inclusive school reform. *Exceptional Children, 72*, 317-331.

Smith, J. D. (1985). *Minds made feeble: The myth and legacy of the Kallikaks.* New York, NY: Aspen.

Spencer, S. A. (2015). *Making the Common Core writing standards accessible through Universal Design for Learning*. Thousand Oaks, CA: Corwin Press.

Steinbach, C. (1918, September–June). Report of the special class department, Cleveland, OH. Proceedings and addresses of the forty-second annual session of the American Association for the Study of the Feeble-Minded held at Buffalo, NY. *Journal of Psycho-Asthenics, 23*, 104–109.

Sullivan, A. L. (2011). Disproportionality in special education identification and placement of English language learners. *Exceptional Children, 77*, 317–334.

Sullivan, A. L., & Artiles, A. J. (2011). Theorizing racial inequity in special education: Applying structural inequity theory to disproportionality. *Urban Education, 46*, 1526–1552.

Sullivan, A. L., Artiles, A. J., & Hernandez-Saca, D. I. (2015). Addressing special education inequity through systemic change: Contributions of ecologically based organizational consultation. *Journal of Educational & Psychological Consultation, 25*, 129–147.

Swain-Bradway, J., Pinkney, C., & Flannery, K. B. (2015). Implementing schoolwide positive behavior interventions and supports in high schools: Contextual factors and stages of implementation. *Teaching Exceptional Children, 47*(5), 245–255.

Taunt, H. M., & Hastings, R. P. (2002). Positive impact of children with developmental disabilities on their families: A preliminary study. *Education and Training in Mental Retardation and Developmental Disabilities, 37*, 410–420.

Taylor, K. R. (2010, October). Inclusion and the law. *Principal Leadership, 11*(2), 8–10.

Thomas, R., Sanders, S., Doust, J., Beller, E., & Glasziou, P. (2015). Prevalence of attention-deficit/ hyperactivity disorder: A systematic review and meta-analysis. *Pediatrics, 135*, e994–e1001.

Tremblay, P. (2013). Comparative outcomes of two instructional models for students with learning disabilities: Inclusion with co-teaching and solo-taught special education. *Journal of Research in Special Educational Needs, 13*, 251–258.

U.S. Department of Education, Office of Planning, Evaluation, and Policy Development. (2010, March). *ESEA blueprint for reform*. Washington, DC: Author.

U.S. Department of Education, Office of Special Education and Rehabilitative Services, Office of Special Education Programs. (2015). *37th Annual Report to Congress on the Implementation of the Individuals with Disabilities Education Act*. Washington, DC: Author.

U.S. Department of Education, Office of Special Education and Rehabilitative Services. (2010). *Thirty-five years of progress in educating children with disabilities through IDEA*. Washington, DC: Author.

U.S. Department of Education, Office of Special Education Programs. (2011a, July). *Children with disabilities receiving special education under Part B of the Individuals with Disabilities Education Act, 2010* [Data Analysis Systems (DANS), OMB #1820-0043]. Washington, DC: Author.

U.S. Department of Education, Office of Special Education Programs. (2011b, July). *Infants and toddlers receiving early intervention services in accordance with Part C of the Individuals with Disabilities Education Act, 2010* [Data Analysis Systems (DANS), OMB #1820-0557]. Washington, DC: Author.

U.S. Department of Education. (1992). *Digest of education statistics 1992*. Washington, DC: National for Education Statistics. Retrieved from http://nces.ed.gov/pubs92/92097.pdf

U.S. Department of Education. (2002). *24th annual report to Congress on the implementation of the Individuals with Disabilities Education Act*. Washington, DC: Author. Retrieved from http://www2.ed.gov/about/reports/annual/osep/2002/toc-execsum.pdf

U.S. Department of Education. (2011). *30th annual report to Congress on the implementation of the Individuals with Disabilities Education Act*. Washington, DC: Author. Retrieved from http://www2.ed.gov/about/reports/annual/osep/2008/parts-b-c/30th-idea-arc.pdf

U.S. Department of Education. (2014). *36th Annual Report to Congress on the implementation of the Individuals with Disabilities Education Act*. Washington, DC: Author.

U.S. Department of Justice. (2009). *A guide to disability rights law*. Washington, DC: Author. Retrieved from https://www.ada.gov/cguide.htm.

United Spinal Association. (2008). *Disability etiquette: Tips on interacting with people with disabilities*. Jackson Heights, NY: Author. Retrieved from http://www.unitedspinal.org/pdf/DisabilityEtiquette.pdf

Waitoller, F. R., & Kozleski, E. B. (2015). No stone left unturned: Exploring the convergence of new capitalism in inclusive education in the U.S. *Education Policy Analysis Archives, 23*(37), 1–33. [ERIC Document Reproduction Service No. EJ1062332]

Waldron, N. L., McLeskey, M., & Redd, L. (2011). Setting the direction: The role of the principal in developing an effective, inclusive school. *Journal of Special Education Leadership, 24*, 51–60.

Will, M. C. (1986). Educating children with learning problems: A shared responsibility. *Exceptional Children, 52*, 411–416.

Winzer, M. A. (1993). *The history of special education: From isolation to integration*. Washington, DC: Gallaudet University Press.

Winzer, M. A. (2007). Confronting difference: An excursion through the history of special education. In L. Florian (Ed.), *The SAGE handbook of special education* (pp. 21–33). Thousand Oaks, CA: Sage.

Winzer, M. A. (2012). *The history of special education: From isolation to integration*. Washington, DC: Gallaudet University Press.

Wolraich, M. L., & DuPaul, G. J. (2010). *ADHD diagnosis and management: A practical guide for the clinic and the classroom*. Baltimore, MD: Brookes.

Wright, P. W. D., & Wright, P. D. (2005). *Wrightslaw: IDEA 2004*. Hartfield, VA: Harbor House Law Press.

Yell, M. L. (2006). *The law and special education* (2nd ed.). Upper Saddle River, NJ: Merrill.

Yell, M. L. (2012). *Law and special education* (3rd ed.). Upper Saddle River, NJ: Pearson Education.

Yell, M. L., & Drasgow, E. (2007). Assessment for eligibility under IDEIA and the 2006 regulations. *Assessment for Effective Intervention, 32*, 202–213.

Yell, M. L., Katsiyannis, A., & Hazelkorn, M. (2007). Reflections on the 25th anniversary of the U.S. Supreme Court's decision in Board of Education v. Rowley. *Focus on Exceptional Children, 39*(9), 1–12.

Yell, M. L., Katsiyannis, A., Collins, J. C., & Losinski, M. (2012). Exit exams, high-stakes testing, and students with disabilities: A persistent challenge. *Intervention in School and Clinic, 48*, 60–64.

Young, J., Ne'eman, A., & Gelser, S. (2011). *Bullying and students with disabilities* [briefing paper]. Washington, DC: National Council on Disability. Retrieved from http://www.ncd.gov/publications/2011/March92011

Youngs, P., Jones, N., & Low, M. (2011). How beginning special and general education elementary teachers negotiate role expectations and access professional resources. *Teachers College Record, 113*, 1506–1540.

Zirkel, P. A. (2009c). Section 504: Student eligibility-update. *Clearing House, 82*, 209–211.

Zirkel, P. A. (2014). Legal issues under IDEA. In L. A. Wilkinson, & L. A. Wilkinson (Eds.), *Autism spectrum disorder in children and adolescents: Evidence-based assessment and intervention in schools* (pp. 243–257). Washington, DC: American Psychological Association.

Chapter 2

Angell, M. E., Stoner, J. B., & Sheldon, D. L. (2009). Trust in education: Professionals' perspectives of mothers of children with disabilities. *Remedial and Special Education, 30*, 160–176.

Bakken, J. P., Obiakor, F. E., & Rotatori, A. F. (2013). *Learning disabilities: Identification, assessment, and instruction of students with LD*. Bingley, UK: Emerald Emerald Group Publishing Limited.

Barnard-Brak, L., & Lechtenberger, D. (2010). Student IEP participation and academic achievement across time. *Remedial and Special Education, 31*, 343–349.

Bateman, D. F., & Jones, M. (2010). Due process hearing case study. *Teaching Exceptional Children, 42*(6), 71–73.

Bausch, M. E., Quinn, B., Chung, Y., Ault, M., & Behrmann, M. M. (2009). Assistive technology in the individualized education plan: Analysis of policies across ten states. *Journal of Special Education Leadership, 22*(1), 9–23.

Beisse, K., & Tyre, A. (2013). Caregiver involvement in the education of youth in foster care: An exploratory study. *School Social Work Journal, 37*(2), 1–20.

Bettini, E. A., Cheyney, K., Wang, J., & Leko, C. (2015). Job design: An administrator's guide to supporting and retaining special educators. *Intervention in School and Clinic, 50*(4), 221–225.

Blanton, L. P., & Perez, Y. (2011). Exploring the relationship between special education teachers and professional learning communities: Implications of research for administrators. *Journal of Special Education Leadership, 24*(1), 6–16.

Brock, M. E., & Carter, E. W. (2015). Effects of a professional development package to prepare special education paraprofessionals to implement evidence-based practice. *Journal of Special Education, 49*, 39–51.

Brown, T. S., & Stanton-Chapman, T. L. (2015). Experiences of paraprofessionals in U.S. preschool special education and general education classrooms. *Journal of Research in Special Educational Needs*. Advance online publication. doi: 10.1111/1471-3802.12095.

Brownell, M. T., Sindelar, P. T., Kiely, M., & Danielson, L. C. (2010). Special education teacher quality and preparation: Exposing foundations, constructing a new model. *Exceptional Children, 76*, 357–377.

Bureau of Labor Statistics. (2015, December). *Occupational handbook: Special education teachers*. Washington, DC: U.S. Department of Labor, Office of Occupational Statistics and Employment Projections. Retrieved from http://www.bls.gov/ooh/Education-Training-and-Library/Special-education-teachers.htm#tab-7.

Capizzi, A. M. (2008). From assessment to annual goal: Engaging a decision-making process in writing measurable IEPs. *Teaching Exceptional Children, 41*(1), 18–25.

Catts, H. W., Nielsen, D. C., Bridges, M. S., Liu, Y. S., & Bontempo, D. E. (2015). Early identification of reading disabilities within an RTI framework. *Journal of Learning Disabilities, 48*, 281–297.

Causton, J., & Tracy-Bronson, C. (2015). *The educator's handbook for inclusive school practices*. Baltimore, MD: Brookes.

Center for Appropriate Dispute Resolution in Special Education. (CADRE). (2014a). *IDEA Special Education Mediation. A Guide for Parents of Children & Youth (Ages 3–21)*. Center for Appropriate Dispute Resolution in Special Education (CADRE).

Center for Appropriate Dispute Resolution in Special Education. (CADRE). (2014b). *IDEA Special Education Resolution Meetings. A Guide for Parents of Children & Youth (Ages 3–21)*. Center for Appropriate Dispute Resolution in Special Education (CADRE). Retrieved from http://www.eric.ed.gov/contentdelivery/servlet/ERICServlet?accno=ED555850.

Cheatham, G. A., Hart, J. E., Malian, I., & McDonald, J. (2012). Six things to never say or hear during an IEP meeting: Educators as advocates for families. *Teaching Exceptional Children, 44*(3), 50–57.

Columna, L., Lieberman, L. J., Lytle, R., & Arndt, K. (2014) Special education terminology every physical education teacher should know. *Journal of Physical Education, Recreation & Dance, 85*(5), 38–45.

Cook, B. G., Shepherd, K. G., Cook, S. C., & Cook, L. (2012). Facilitating the effective implementation of evidence-based practices through teacher-parent collaboration. *TEACHING Exceptional Children, 44*(3), 22–30.

Council for Exceptional Children. (2011). *Adapted physical education teacher*. Retrieved from http://www.cec.sped.org/AM/Template.cfm?Section=Job_Profiles&Template=/CM/ContentDisplay.cfm&ContentID=1313

Cumming, J. J. (2008). Legal and educational perspectives of equity in assessment. *Assessment in Education: Principles, Policy & Practice, 15*, 123–125.

Deasy, G., Zaccagnini, C., Burton, J. I., & Koury, K. A. (2014). Working with children who have exceptionalities. In G. T. Eliason, T. Eliason, J. L. Samide, J. Patrick, G. T. Eliason, T. Eliason, … J. Patrick (Eds.), *Career development across the lifespan: Counseling for community, schools, higher education, and beyond* (pp. 349–367). Charlotte, NC: Information Age Publishing.

Delgado, R. (2010). "Poco a poquito se van apagando": Teachers' experiences educating Latino English language learners with disabilities. *Journal of Latinos and Education, 9*, 150–157.

Diliberto, J. A., & Brewer, D. (2014). Six tips for successful IEP meetings. *Teaching Exceptional Children, 47*(2), 128–135.

Edwards, C. C., & Fonte, A. D. (2012). The 5-point plan: Fostering successful partnerships with families of students with disabilities. *Teaching Exceptional Children, 44*(3), 6–13.

Eisenman, L. T., Pleet, A. M., Wandry, D., & McGinley, V. (2011). Voices of special education teachers in an inclusive high school: Redefining responsibilities. *Remedial and Special Education, 32*, 91–104.

Elliott, S. N., Kratochwill, T. R., McKevitt, B. C., & Malecki, C. (2009). The effects and perceived consequences of testing accommodations on math and science performance assessments. *School Psychology Quarterly, 24*, 224–239.

Etscheidt, S. (2007). The excusal provision of the IDEA 2004: Streamlining procedural compliance or prejudicing rights of students with disabilities? *Preventing School Failure, 51*(4), 13–18.

Faggella-Luby, M., & Wardwell, M. (2011). RTI in a middle school: Findings and practical implications of a tier 2 reading comprehension study. *Learning Disability Quarterly, 34*(1), 35–49.

Feinberg, E., Moses, P., Engiles, A., Whitehorne, A., Peter, M., & Center for Appropriate Dispute Resolution in Special Education. (2014). In the best interests of the child: Individualized education program (IEP) meetings when parents are in conflict. *Center for Appropriate Dispute Resolution in Special Education (CADRE)*.

Feuerborn, L. L., Sarin, K., & Tyre, A. D. (2011). Response to intervention in secondary schools. *Principal Leadership, 11*(8), 50–54.

Fisher, D., & Frey, N. (2013). Implementing RTI in a high school: A case study. *Journal of Learning Disabilities, 46*(2), 99–114.

Flannery, K. B., Lombardi, A., & Kato, M. M. (2015). The impact of professional development on the quality of the transition components of IEPs. *Career Development and Transition for Exceptional Individuals, 38*(1), 14–24.

Friend, M. (2015/2016, December–January). Welcome to co-teach 2.0. *Educational Leadership, 73*(4), 16–22.

Friend, M., & Bursuck, W. (2012). *Including students with special needs: A practical guide for classroom teachers* (6th ed.). Upper Saddle River, NJ: Pearson/Merrill.

Friend, M., & Bursuck, W. D. (2015). *Including students with special needs: A practical guide for classroom teachers* (7th ed.). Upper Saddle River, NJ: Pearson.

Giangreco, M. F., Prelock, P. A., & Turnbull, H. (2010). An issue hiding in plain sight: When are speech-language pathologists special educators rather than related services providers? *Language, Speech, and Hearing Services in Schools, 41*, 531–538.

Gibb, G. S., & Dyches, T. T. (2007). *Guide to writing quality individualized education programs*. Boston, MA: Allyn and Bacon.

Gibb, G. S., & Dyches, T. T. (2016). *IEPs: Writing quality individualized education programs* (3rd ed.). Upper Saddle River, NJ: Pearson.

Graves, S. J., Proctor, S. L., & Aston, C. (2014). Professional roles and practices of school psychologists in urban schools. *Psychology in the Schools, 51,* 384–394.

Griffin, M. M. (2011). Promoting IEP participation: Effects of interventions, considerations for CLD students. *Career Development for Exceptional Individuals, 34,* 153–164.

Grskovic, J. A., & Trzcinka, S. M. (2011). Essential standards for preparing secondary content teachers to effectively teach students with mild disabilities in included settings. *American Secondary Education, 39,* 94–106.

Haager, D. (2007). Promises and cautions regarding using response to intervention with English language learners. *Learning Disability Quarterly, 30,* 213–218.

Hauerwas, L.B., Brown, R., & Scott, A.S. (2013). Specific learning disability and response to intervention: State-level guidance. *Exceptional Children, 80,* 101–20.

Hillel Lavian, R. (2015). Masters of weaving: The complex role of special education teachers. *Teachers and Teaching: Theory and Practice, 21,* 103–126.

Hoover, J. J. (2011). Making informed instructional adjustments in RTI models: Essentials for practitioners. *Intervention in School and Clinic, 47,* 82–90.

Hoover, J. J., & Lowe, E. (2011). Supporting school-based response to intervention: A practitioner's model. *Teaching Exceptional Children, 43*(3), 40–48.

Huff, C. (2010). Determining a student's readiness to successfully use interpreting services. *Odyssey: New Directions in Deaf Education, 11*(1), 30–34.

Johnson, E. S., Pool, J. L., & Carter, D. R. (2012). Lessons learned from a tiered service delivery implementation project. *Intervention in School and Clinic, 47,* 139–143.

Jones, V. L., & Hinesmon-Matthews, L. J. (2014). Effective assistive technology consideration and implications for diverse students. *Computers in the Schools, 31,* 220–232.

Kavale, K. A., & Spaulding, L. S. (2008). Is response to intervention good policy for specific learning disability? *Learning Disabilities Research and Practice, 23,* 169–179.

Kearns, J., Towles-Reeves, E., Kleinert, H. L., Kleinert, J., & Thomas, M. (2011). Characteristics of implications for students participating in alternate assessments based on alternate academic achievement standards. *Journal of Special Education, 45,* 3–14.

Keierleber, M. (2015, November). Why so few school cops are trained to work with kids. *The Atlantic.* Retrieved from http://www.theatlantic.com/education/archive/2015/11/why-do-most-school-cops-have-no-student-training-requirements/414286/.

Kellems, R. O., & Morningstar, M. E. (2010). Tips for transition. *Teaching Exceptional Children, 43*(2), 60–68.

Kellems, R. O., Springer, B., Wilkins, M. K., & Anderson, C. (2015). Collaboration in transition assessment: School psychologists and special educators working together to improve outcomes for students with disabilities. *Preventing School Failure, 8,* 1–7.

Klingner, J. K., Boelé, A., Linan-Thompson, S., &Rodriguez, D. (2014). Essential components of special education for English language learners with learning disabilities: Position statement of the Division for Learning Disabilities of the Council for Exceptional Children. *Learning Disabilities Research & Practice, 29,* 93–96.

Kode, K. (2002). *Elizabeth Farrell and the history of special education.* Arlington, VA: Council for Exceptional Children.

Konrad, M. (2008). Involve students in the IEP process. *Intervention in School and Clinic, 43,* 236–239.

Kurch, J., & Mastergeorge, A. M. (2010). Individual education plan goals and services for adolescents with autism: Impact of age and educational setting. *Journal of Special Education, 44,* 146–160.

Kurth, J. A., Morningstar, M. E., & Kozleski, E. B. (2014). The persistence of highly restrictive special education placements for students with low-incidence disabilities. *Research and Practice for Persons with Severe Disabilities, 39,* 227–239.

Kurz, A., Elliott, S., Wehby, J., & Smithson, J. (2010). Alignment of the intended, planned, and enacted curriculum in general and special education and its relation to student achievement. *Journal of Special Education, 44,* 131–145.

Lalvani, P. (2012). Parents' participation in special education in the context of implicit educational ideologies and socioeconomic status. *Education and Training in Autism and Developmental Disabilities, 47,* 474–486.

Lane, S., & Leventhal, B. (2015). Psychometric challenges in assessing English language learners and students with disabilities. *Review of Research in Education, 39,* 165–214.

Light, J., & McNaughton, D. (2015). Designing AAC research and intervention to improve outcomes for individuals with complex communication needs. *AAC: Augmentative and Alternative Communication, 31,* 85–96.

Lo, L. (2012). Demystifying the IEP process for diverse parents of children with disabilities. *Teaching Exceptional Children, 44*(3), 14–20.

Marx, T. A., Hart, J. L., Nelson, L., Love, J., Baxter, C. M., Gartin, B., & Schaefer Whitby, P. J. (2014). Guiding IEP teams on meeting the least restrictive environment mandate. *Intervention in School and Clinic, 50,* 45–50.

Mason-Williams, L. (2015). Unequal opportunities: A profile of the distribution of special education teachers. *Exceptional Children, 81,* 247–262.

Maughan, E., & Adams, R. (2011). Educators' and parents' perception of what school nurses do: The influence of school nurse/student ratios. *Journal of School Nursing, 27,* 355–363.

Maul, C. A. (November 01, 2015). Working with culturally and linguistically diverse students and their families: Perceptions and practices of school speech-language therapists in the United States. *International Journal of Language & Communication Disorders, 50,* 750–762.

McConnellogue, S. (2011). Professional roles and responsibilities in meeting the needs of children with speech, language and communication needs: Joint working between educational psychologists and speech and language therapists. *Educational Psychology in Practice, 27,* 53–64.

McGahee, M., Mason, C., Wallace, & Jones, B. (2001). *Student-led IEPs: A guide for student involvement.* Arlington, VA: Council for Exceptional Children. Retrieved from http://files.eric.ed.gov/fulltext/ED455623.pdf.

McGrath, M. Z., Johns, B. H., & Mathur, S. R. (2010). Empowered or overpowered? Strategies for working effectively with paraprofessionals. *Beyond Behavior, 19*(2), 2–6.

McIntosh, C. E., Thomas, C. M., & Maughan, E. (2015). Introduction to the special issue: Increasing the collaboration between school nurses and school personnel. *Psychology in the Schools, 52,* 631–634.

Miller, J. A., & Short, R. (2011). Introduction to the special issue: School psychology education and training in the United States–Crucial issues and challenges. *Psychology in the Schools, 48,* 869–871.

Mitchell, B. B., Deshler, D. D., & Lenz, B. B. (2012). Examining the role of the special educator in a response to intervention model. *Learning Disabilities: A Contemporary Journal, 10*(2), 53–74.

More, D. H. (2015). Fact sheet: The role of occupational therapy with children and youth. Bethseda, MD: American Occupational Therapy Association. Retrieved from http://www.aota.org/-/media/Corporate/Files/AboutOT/Professionals/ WhatIsOT/CY/Fact-Sheets/Children%20 and%20Youth%20fact%20sheet.pdf.

Mueller, T. G., & Carranza, F. (2011). An examination of special education due process hearings. *Journal of Disability Policy Studies, 22*, 131–139.

Mulrine, C. F., & Huckvale, M. U. (2014). Secondary special education teachers as teacher leaders: Redefining their role. *Kappa Delta Pi Record, 50*(2), 61–64.

National Center for Education Statistics. (2015). *The condition of education 2013-Section 1: Participation in education: Children and youth with disabilities.* Washington, DC: U.S. Department of Education, Institute of Education Sciences. Retrieved from http://nces.ed.gov/programs/coe/indicator_cgg.asp.

National Center on Secondary Education and Transition and PACER Center. (2002, May). *Age of majority: Preparing your child for making good choices* [parent brief]. Retrieved from http://ici.umn.edu/ncset/new.html

National Clearinghouse for Careers in Special Education. (2009). *Physical therapist* [brochure]. Arlington, VA: Council for Exceptional Children. Retrieved from http://www.personnelcenter.org/phy_ther.cfm

Newman, L., Wagner, M., Huang, T., Shaver, D., Knokey, A.-M., Yu, J., . . . Cameto, R. (2011). *Secondary school programs and performance of students with disabilities: A special topic report of findings from the National Longitudinal Transition Study–2 (NLTS2)* (NCSER 2012-3000). Washington, DC: U.S. Department of Education, National Center for Special Education Research.

Ochoa, A. M., Brandon, R. R., Cadiero-Kaplan, K., & Ramírez, P. C. (2014). Bridging bilingual and special education: Opportunities for transformative change in teacher preparation programs. *Association of Mexican American Educators Journal, 8*(1), 72–82.

Olvera, P., & Gomez-Cerrillo, L. (2011). A bilingual (English and Spanish) psychoeducational assessment model grounded in Cattell-Horn Carroll (CHC) theory: A cross battery approach. *Contemporary School Psychology, 15*, 117–127.

Ong-Dean, C., Daly, A. J., & Park, V. (2011). Privileged advocates: Disability and education policy in the USA. *Policy Futures in Education, 9*, 392–405.

Ortiz, A. A., Robertson, P. M., Wilkinson, C. Y., Liu, Y., McGhee, B. D., & Kushner, M. I. (2011). The role of bilingual education teachers in preventing inappropriate referrals of ELLs to special education: Implications for response to intervention. *Bilingual Research Journal, 34*, 316–333.

Parnell, A. R. (2011). Physical and occupational therapists. In C. G. Simpson, J. P. Bakken, C. G. Simpson, & J. P. Bakken (Eds.), *Collaboration: A multidisciplinary approach to educating students with disabilities* (pp. 281–307). Waco, TX: Prufrock Press.

Pierangelo, R., & Guiliani, G. (2008). *Understanding assessment in the special education process.* Thousand Oaks, CA: Corwin.

Pufpaff, L. A., Mcintosh, C. E., Thomas, C., Elam, M., & Irwin, M. K. (2015). Meeting the health care needs of students with severe disabilities in the school setting: Collaboration between school nurses and special education teachers. *Psychology in the Schools, 52*, 683–701.

Pugach, M. C., & Winn, J. A. (2011). Research on co-teaching and teaming: An untapped resource for induction. *Journal of Special Education Leadership, 24*(1), 36–46.

Quann, M., Lyman, J., Crumlish, J., Hines, S., Williams, L., Pleet-Odle, A., & Eisenman, L. (2015). The HAWK Highway: A vertical model for student IEP participation. *Intervention in School and Clinic, 50*, 297–303.

Raue, K., & Lewis, L. (2011). *Students with disabilities at degree-granting postsecondary institutions* (NCES 2011-018). Washington, DC: U.S. Department of Education, National Center for Education Statistics, U.S. Government Printing Office.

Reiman, J. W., Beck, L., Coppola, T., & Engiles, A. (2010, April). *Parents' experiences with the IEP process: Considerations for improving practice.* Eugene, OR: Center for Appropriate Dispute Resolution in Special Education (CADRE).

Reynolds, B. H. (2008). Are principals ready to welcome children with disabilities? *Principal, 88*(2), 16–19.

Rock, M. L., & Bateman, D. (2009). Using due process opinions as an opportunity to improve educational practice. *Intervention in School and Clinic, 45*, 52–62.

Rodriguez, B. J., Campbell, A., Falcon, S. F., & Borgmeier, C. (2015). Examination of critical features and lessons learned for implementation of a tier 2 intervention system for social behavior. *Journal of Educational & Psychological Consultation, 25*, 224–251.

Rodriguez, D. (2005). A conceptual framework of bilingual special education teacher programs. In J. Cohen, K. T. McAlister, K. Rolstad, & J. MacSwain (Eds.), *ISB4: Proceedings of the 4th International Symposium on Bilingualism.* Somerville, MA: Cascadilla Press. Retrieved from www.lingref.com/isb/4/152ISB4.PDF

Rodriguez, D., Carrasquillo, A., & Lee, K. S. (2014). *The bilingual advantage: Promoting academic development, biliteracy, and native language in the classroom.* New York, NY: Teachers College Press.

Saeki, E., Jimerson, S. R., Earhart, J., Hart, S. R., Renshaw, T., Singh, R. D., & Stewart, K. (2011). Response to intervention (RTI) in the social, emotional, and behavioral domains: Current challenges and emerging possibilities. *Contemporary School Psychology, 15*, 43–52.

Scott, A. N., Boynton Hauerwas, L., & Brown, R. D. (2014). State policy and guidance for identifying learning disabilities in culturally and linguistically diverse students. *Learning Disability Quarterly, 37*(3), 172–185.

Serres, S. A., & Nelson, J. A. (2011). Professional school counselor. In C. G. Simpson, & J. P. Bakken (Eds.), *Collaboration: A multidisciplinary approach to educating students with disabilities* (pp. 237–252). Waco, TX: Prufrock Press.

Stanley, S. G. (2011). Visiting teachers and students with developmental disabilities. *Children & Schools, 33*, 168–175.

Stanley, S. G. (2012). Children with disabilities in foster care: The role of the school social worker in the context of special education. *Children & Schools, 34*, 190–192.

Staples, K. E., & Diliberto, J. A. (2010). Guidelines for successful parent involvement: Working with parents of students with disabilities. *Teaching Exceptional Children, 42*(6), 58–63.

Thoma, C. A., & Wehman, P. (2010). *Getting the most out of IEPs: An educator's guide to the student-directed approach.* Baltimore, MD: Brookes.

Turse, K. A., & Albrecht, S. F. (2015). The ABCs of RTI: An introduction to the building blocks of response to intervention. *Preventing School Failure, 59*(2), 83–89.

U.S. Department of Education. (2011). *30th annual report to Congress on the implementation of the Individuals with Disabilities Education Act, 2008.* Washington, DC: Author.

U.S. Department of Education. (2015). *37th annual report to Congress on the implementation of the Individuals with Disabilities Education Act, 2015.* Washington, DC: Office of Special Education and Rehabilitative Services, Office of Special Education Programs. Retrieved from http://www.ed.gov/about/reports/annual/osep.

U.S. Department of Education. (2015, December). *Every Student Succeeds Act: A new education law.* Washington, DC: Author. Retrieved from http://www.ed.gov/essa.

Vanderheyden, A. M. (2011). Technical adequacy of response to intervention decisions. *Exceptional Children, 77*, 335–350.

Vessey, J. A., & O'Neill, K. M. (2011). Helping students with disabilities better address teasing and bullying situations: A MASNRN study. *Journal of School Nursing, 27*, 139–148.

Wasburn, M. H., Wasburn-Moses, L., & Davis, D. R. (2012). Mentoring special educators: The roles of National Board certified teachers. *Remedial and Special Education, 33*, 59–66.

Wasburn-Moses, L. (2011). An investigation of alternative schools in one state: Implications for students with disabilities. *Journal of Special Education, 44*, 247–255.

Wei, X., Wagner, M., Christiano, E. A., Shattuck, P., & Yu, J. W. (2014). Special education services received by students with autism spectrum disorders from preschool through high school. *Journal of Special Education, 48*, 167–179.

Weiss, M.P., Petrin, R.A., & Farmer, T.W. (2014). Responsibilities of special educators in rural schools: A latent class analysis. *Exceptionality, 22*(2), 69–90.

What Works Clearinghouse. (2009). *Assisting students struggling with reading: Response to intervention (RTI) and multitier intervention in the primary grades: IES practice guide.* Washington, DC: Institute of Education Sciences (ED), National Center for Education Evaluation and Regional Assistance. Retrieved from http://www.eric.ed.gov/ERICWebPortal/contentdelivery/servlet/ERICServlet?accno=ED504264

White, R. B., Polly, D., & Audette, R. H. (2012). A case analysis of an elementary school's implementation of response to intervention. *Journal of Research in Childhood Education, 26*, 73–90.

Winn, S., & Hay, I. (2009). Transition from school for youths with a disability: Issues and challenges. *Disability & Society, 24*, 103–115.

Winterman, K. G., & Rosas, C. E. (2014). *The IEP checklist: Your guide to creating meaningful and compliant IEPs.* Baltimore, MD: Brookes.

Wolfe, K., & Durán, L. K. (2013). Culturally and linguistically diverse parents' perceptions of the IEP process. *Multiple Voices for Ethnically Diverse Exceptional Learners, 13*(2), 4–18.

Wright, P. W. D., Wright, P. D., & O'Connor, S. W. (2010). *Wrightslaw: All about IEPs.* Hartfield, VA: Harbor House Law Press.

Wrightslaw. (2009, April). *IEP FAQs: Can an IEP meeting be postponed?* Retrieved from http://www.wrightslaw.com/blog/?p=164

Yell, M. L. & Drasgow, E. (2013). Less to more restrictive settings: Policy and planning considerations. In D. D. Reed, F. D. DiGennaro Reed, & J. Luiselli (Eds.), *Handbook of crises intervention and developmental disabilities* (pp. 281–298). New York, NY: Springer.

Yell, M. L. (2006). *The law and special education* (2nd ed.). Upper Saddle River, NJ: Merrill.

Yell, M. L. (2012). *The law and special education* (3rd ed.). Upper Saddle River, NJ: Pearson.

Yell, M. L. (2015). *Law and special education* (4th ed.). Upper Saddle River, NJ: Pearson.

Yell, M. L., & Drasgow, E. (2007). Assessment for eligibility under IDEIA and the 2006 regulations. *Assessment for Effective Intervention, 32*, 202–211.

Yell, M. L., & Walker, D. W. (2010). The legal basis of response to intervention: Analysis and implications. *Exceptionality, 18*, 124–137.

Yell, M. L., Katsiyannis, A., & Ryan, J. B. (2008). Ensure compliance with the Individuals with Disabilities Education Improvement Act of 2004. *Intervention in School and Clinic, 44*(1), 45–51.

Yell, M., Katsiyannis, A., Ryan, J. B., & McDuffie, K. A. (2009). Schaffer v. Weast: The Supreme Court on the burden of proof in special education due process hearings. *Intervention in School and Clinic, 44*, 241–245.

Youngs, P., Jones, N., & Low, M. (2011). How beginning special and general education elementary teachers negotiate role expectations and access professional resources. *Teachers College Record, 113*, 1506–1540.

Zirkel, P. A. (2011). What does the law say? *Teaching Exceptional Children, 43*(3), 65–67.

Zirkel, P. A. (2012). State laws and guidelines for RTI: Additional implementation features. *Communiqué Online.* Retrieved from http://www.nasponline.org/publications/cq/39/7/professional-practice-state-laws.aspx

Zirkel, P. A., & McGuire, B. L. (2010). A roadmap to legal dispute resolution for students with disabilities. *Journal of Special Education Leadership, 23*(2), 100–112.

Chapter 3

Achilles, C. M., Finn, F. K., & Pate-Bain, H. (2002). Measuring class size: Let me count the ways. *Educational Leadership, 59*, 24–26.

Aganza, J. S., Godinez, A., Smith, D., Gonzalez, L. G., & Robinson-Zañartu, C. (2015). Using cultural assets to enhance assessment of Latino students. *Contemporary School Psychology, 19*(1), 30–45.

Ahram, R., Fergus, E., & Noguera, P. (2011). Addressing racial/ethnic disproportionality in special education: Case studies of suburban school districts. *Teachers College Record, 113*, 2233–2266.

Albrecht, S. F., Skiba, R. J., Losen, D. J., Chung, C. G., & Middelberg, L. (2012). Federal policy on disproportionality in special education: Is it moving us forward? *Journal of Disability Policy Studies, 23*, 14–25.

Alhumam, I. (2015). Reflections on racism in American schools. *Journal of Education and Practice, 6*, 160–161.

Anderson, J. A., Howland, A. A., & McCoach, D. B. (2015). Parental characteristics and resiliency in identification rates for special education. *Preventing School Failure, 59*, 63–72.

Andrews, S. W. (2015). Parents as partners: Creating a culture of respect and collaboration with parents. *NAMTA Journal, 40*, 129–137.

Artiles, A. J. (2003). Special education's changing identity: Paradoxes and dilemmas in views of culture and space. *Harvard Educational Review, 73*, 164–202.

Artiles, A. J., Bal, A., & King Thorius, K. A. (2010). Back to the future: A critique of response to intervention's social justice views. *Theory into Practice, 49*, 250–257.

Artiles, A. J., Kozleski, E. B., Trent, S. C., Osher, D., & Ortiz, A. (2010). Justifying and explaining disproportionality, 1968–2008: A critique of underlying views of culture. *Exceptional Children, 76*, 279–299.

Ashton, T. M. (2015). Unique universal design for learning. In W. W. Murawski & K. L. Scott (Eds.), *What really works in secondary education* (pp. 170–182). Thousand Oaks, CA: Corwin.

Athanases, S. Z., Wahleithner, J. M., & Bennett, L. H. (2012). Learning to attend to culturally and linguistically diverse learners through teacher inquiry in teacher education. *Teachers College Record, 114*(7), 1–50.

Atwater, S. A. C. (2008). Waking up to difference: Teachers, color-blindness, and the effects on students of color. *Journal of Instructional Psychology, 35*, 246–253.

Aud, S., Fox, M., and KewalRamani, A. (2015). Status and *trends in the education of racial and ethnic groups.* U.S. Department of Education, National Center for Education Statistics. Washington, DC: U.S. Government Printing Office.

Aud, S., Fox, M., KewalRamani, & National Center for Education Statistics. (2010). *Status and trends in the education of racial and ethnic groups* [NCES 20110-015]. Washington, DC: U.S. Department of Education, National Center for Education Statistics.

Aud, S., Hussar, W., Johnson, F., Kena, G., Roth, E., Manning, E., . . . Zhang, J. (2012). *The condition of education 2012* [NCES 2012-045]. Washington, DC: U.S. Department of Education, National Center for Education Statistics.

Baer, R. M., Daviso, A., Queen, R., & Flexer, R. W. (2011). Disproportionality in transition services: A descriptive study. *Education and Training in Autism and Developmental Disabilities, 46*, 172–185.

Bal, A., Kozleski, E. B., Schrader, E. M., Rodriguez, E. M., & Pelton, S. (2014). Systemic transformation in school: Using learning lab to design culturally responsive school-wide positive behavioral supports. *Remedial and Special Education, 35*, 327–339.

Bal, A., Sullivan, A. L., & Harper, J. (2014). A situated analysis of special education disproportionality for systemic transformation in an urban school district. *Remedial and Special Education, 35*, 3–14.

Bales, B. L., & Saffold, F. (2011). A new era in the preparation of teachers for urban schools: Linking multiculturalism, disciplinary-based content, and pedagogy. *Urban Education, 46*, 953–974.

Banks, J. A. (2006). *Cultural diversity and education: Foundations, curriculum and teaching* (5th ed.). Boston, MA: Pearson/Allyn & Bacon.

Banks, J. A., & Banks, C. A. M. (2013). *Multicultural education: Issues and perspectives* (8th ed.). Hoboken, NJ: John Wiley & Sons.

Basham, J. D., Israel, M., Graden, J., Poth, R., & Winston, M. (2010). A comprehensive approach to RTI: Embedding universal design for learning and technology. *Learning Disability Quarterly, 33*, 243–255.

Bender, W. N., & Waller, L. (2011). *The teaching revolution: RTI, technology, and differentiation transform teaching for the 21st century*. Thousand Oaks, CA: Corwin.

Bennett, C. I. (2003). *Comprehensive multicultural education: Theory and practice* (5th ed.). Boston, MA: Pearson/Allyn & Bacon.

Biddle, B., & Berliner, D. C. (2002). Small class size and its effects. *Educational Leadership, 59*(5), 12–23.

Bishop, H. N., & Casida, H. (2011). Preventing bullying and harassment of sexual minority students in schools. *Clearing House, 84*(4), 134–138.

Bohrnstedt, G., Kitmitto, S., Ogut, B., Sherman, D., and Chan, D. (2015). *School composition and the black–white achievement gap* (NCES 2015–018). Washington, DC: U.S. Department of Education, National Center for Education Statistics. Retrieved from http://nces.ed.gov/pubsearch.

Bower, H. A., Bowen, N. K., & Powers, J. D. (2011). Family-faculty trust as measured with the elementary school success profile. *Children & Schools, 33*, 158–167.

Brown-Wright, L., & Tyler, K. (2010). The effects of home-school dissonance on African American male high school students. *Journal of Negro Education, 79*, 125–136.

Brown-Wright, L., Tyler, K. M., Stevens-Watkins, D., Thomas, D., Mulder, S., Hughes, T., … & Gadson, N. (2013). Investigating the link between home–school dissonance and academic cheating among high school students. *Urban Education, 48*, 314–334.

Bullying statistics. (2015). *Gay bullying statistics*. Retrieved from http://www.bullyingstatistics.org/content/gay-bullying-statistics.html.

Byrd, E. (2011). Educating and involving parents in the response to intervention process: The school's important role. *Teaching Exceptional Children, 43*(3), 32–39.

Cartledge, G., & Kourea, L. (2008). Culturally responsive classrooms for culturally diverse students with and at risk for disabilities. *Exceptional Children, 74*, 351–371.

Casteel, C. A. (1998). Teacher–student interactions and race in integrated classrooms. *Journal of Educational Research, 92*, 115–120.

Cavendish, W., Artiles, A. J., & Harry, B. (2015). Tracking inequality 60 years after Brown: Does policy legitimize the racialization of disability? *Multiple Voices, 14*(2), 30–40.

Centers for Disease Control and Prevention. (2014, November). *Lesbian, gay, bisexual, and transgender health*. Washington, DC: Author. Retrieved from http://www.cdc.gov/lgbthealth/youth.htm.

Cooper, J. E., He, Y., & Levin, B. B. (2011). *Developing critical cultural competence: A guide for 21st-century educators*. Thousand Oaks, CA: Corwin.

Dabach, D. B. (2014). "I am not a shelter!": Stigma and social boundaries in teachers' accounts of students' experience in separate "sheltered" English learner classrooms. *Journal of Education for Students Placed at Risk, 19*, 98–124.

Dedeoglu, H., & Lamme, L. L. (2011). Selected demographics, attitudes, and beliefs about diversity of preservice teachers. *Education and Urban Society, 43*, 468–485.

del Carmen Salazar, M. (2008). English or nothing: The impact of rigid language policies on the inclusion of humanizing practices in a high school ESL program. *Equity & Excellence in Education, 41*, 341–356.

Donovan, M. S., & Cross, C. T. (Eds.). (2002b). *Minority students in special and gifted education*. Washington, DC: National Academies Press.

Dray, B. J., & Wisneski, D. (2011). Mindful reflection as a process for developing culturally responsive practices. *Teaching Exceptional Children, 44*(1), 28–36.

Duke, T. S. (2011). Lesbian, gay, bisexual, and transgender youth with disabilities: A meta-synthesis. *Journal of LGBT Youth, 8*, 1–52.

Dunn, A. (2011). Global village versus culture shock: The recruitment and preparation of foreign teachers for U.S. urban schools. *Urban Education, 46*, 1379–1410.

Emerson, E., Shahtahmasebi, S., Lancaster, G., & Berridge, D. (2010). Poverty transitions among families supporting a child with intellectual disability. *Journal of Intellectual & Developmental Disability, 35*, 224–234.

Fall, A., & Billingsley, B. S. (2011). Disparities in work conditions among early career special educators in high- and low-poverty districts. *Remedial and Special Education, 32*, 64–78.

Ferri, B. A., & Connor, D. J. (2010). "I was the special ed. girl": Urban working-class young women of colour. *Gender and Education, 22*(1), 105–121.

Ford, D. Y. (2014a). Segregation and the underrepresentation of Blacks and Hispanics in gifted education: Social inequality and deficit paradigms. *Roeper Review, 36*, 143–154.

Ford, D. Y. (2014b). Why education must be multicultural: Addressing a few misperceptions with counterarguments. *Gifted Child Today, 37*(1), 59–62.

Ford, D. Y., Moore, J., & Scott, M. (2011). Key theories and frameworks for improving the recruitment and retention of African American students in gifted education. *Journal of Negro Education, 80*, 239–253.

Ford, D., Grantham, T. C., & Whiting, G. W. (2008). Culturally and linguistically diverse students in gifted education: Recruitment and retention issues. *Exceptional Children, 74*, 289–306.

Fore, E., Burke, M. D., & Martin, C. (2006). Curriculum-based measurement: An emerging alternative to traditional assessment for African American children and youth. *Journal of Negro Education, 75*(1), 16–24.

Frankenberg, E., & Siegel-Hawley, G. (2012). Not just urban policy: Suburbs, segregation, and charter schools. *AASA Journal of Scholarship & Practice, 8*(4), 3–13.

Fritzen, A. (2011). Teaching as sheltering: A metaphorical analysis of sheltered instruction for English language learners. *Curriculum Inquiry, 41*, 185–211.

Garcia, S. B., & Ortiz, A. A. (1988). *Preventing inappropriate referrals of language minority students to special education* [occasional papers in bilingual education]. Silver Spring, MD: National Clearinghouse for Bilingual Education. Retrieved from http://files.eric.ed.gov/fulltext/ED309591.pdf.

Ghosh, S., & Parish, S. (2013). Prevalence and economic well-being of families raising multiple children with disabilities. *Children and Youth Services Review, 35*, 1431–1439.

Goddard, R. D., Tschannen-Moran, M., & Hoy, W. K. (2001). A multilevel examination of the distribution and effects of teacher trust in students and parents in urban elementary schools. *The Elementary School Journal, 102*, 3–17.

Goddard, Y., Goddard, R., & Kim, M. (2015). School instructional climate and student achievement: An examination of group norms for differentiated instruction. *American Journal of Education, 122*, 111–131.

Gonzalez, L. M., Borders, L. D., Hines, E. M., Villalba, J. A., & Henderson, A. (2013). Parental involvement in children's education: Considerations for school counselors working with Latino immigrant families. *Professional School Counseling, 16*, 185–193.

Graham, A., & Anderson, K. A. (2008). "I have to be three steps ahead": Academically gifted African American male students in an urban high school on the tension between an ethnic and academic identity. *Urban Review: Issues and Ideas in Public Education, 40*, 472–499.

Grant, C. A., & Sleeter, C. E. (2009). *Turning on learning: Five approaches for multicultural teaching plans for race, class, gender, and disability* (5th ed.). Hoboken, NJ: Wiley.

Green, T. D., McIntosh, A. S., Cook-Morales, V. J., & Robinson-Zanartu, C. (2005). From old schools to tomorrow's schools: Psychoeducational assessment of African American students. *Remedial and Special Education, 26*, 82–92.

Gregg, K., Rugg, M., & Stoneman, Z. (2012). Building on the hopes and dreams of Latino families with young children: Findings from family member focus groups. *Early Childhood Education Journal, 40*, 87–96.

Gross, Z. (2015). How can we overcome the dichotomy that Western culture has created between the concepts of independence and dependence? *Educational Philosophy and Theory, 47*, 1160–1165.

Grossman, H. (2003). *Classroom behavior management for diverse and inclusive schools* (3rd ed.). New York, NY: Rowman & Littlefield.

Guerra, P. L., & Nelson, S. W. (2009). Changing professional practice requires changing beliefs. *Phi Delta Kappan, 90*, 354–359.

Gunn, A. A., Bennett, S. V., & Morton, M. L. (2013). Culturally responsive literacy pedagogy: Using children's literature to discuss topics of religious diversity. *Florida Reading Journal, 49*(1), 17–24.

Hall, T. E., Cohen, N., Vue, G., & Ganley, P. (2014). Addressing learning disabilities with UDL and technology strategic reader. *Learning Disability Quarterly, 38*, 72–83.

Harris, D. M. (2012). Postscript: Urban schools, accountability, and equity–insights regarding NCLB and reform. *Education and Urban Society, 44*, 203–210.

Harry, B. (2002). Trends and issues in serving culturally diverse families of children with disabilities. *Journal of Special Education, 36*, 131–138.

Harry, B., & Klingner, J. (2007). Discarding the deficit model. *Educational Leadership, 64*(5), 16–21.

Hart, J. E. (2009). Strategies for culturally and linguistically diverse students with special needs. *Preventing School Failure, 53*, 197–208.

Hernandez, J. E., Harry, B., Newman, L., & Cameto, R. (2008). Survey of family involvement in and satisfaction with the Los Angeles Unified School District special education processes. *Journal of Special Education Leadership, 21*(2), 84–93.

Honigsfeld, A., & Dove, M. G. (2012). *Co-teaching and other collaborative practices in the EFL/ESL classroom: Rationale, research, reflections, and recommendations.* Charlotte, NC: Information Age.

Hudley, C. (2013, May). Education and urban schools. *The SES Indicator.* Washington, DC: American Psychological Association. Retrieved from http://www.apa.org/pi/ses/resources/indicator/2013/05/urban-schools.aspx.

Jacot de Boinod, A. (2014, April). *Cultural vocabularies: How many words do the Inuits have for snow?* New York, NY: The Guardian. Retrieved from http://www.theguardian.com/education/2014/apr/29/what-vocabularies-tell-us-about-culture.

Johnson, J., Showalter, D., Klein, R., & Lester, C. (2014). *Why rural matters 2013–2014: The condition of rural education in the 50 states.* Washington, DC: Rural School and Community Trust. Retrieved from http://www.ruraledu.org/user_uploads/file/2013-14-Why-Rural-Matters.pdf.

Jung, A. W. (2011). Individualized education programs (IEPs) and barriers for parents from culturally and linguistically diverse backgrounds. *Multicultural Education, 19*(3), 21–25.

Jung, A., Stang, K., Ferko, D., & Han, S. (2011). A commentary on cultural influences impacting the education of Korean American adolescents. *American Secondary Education, 40*, 31–38.

Kaplan, L. (2003). Inuit snow terms: How many and what does it mean? In F. Trudel (Ed.), *Building capacity in arctic societies: Dynamics and shifting perspectives.* [Proceedings from the 2nd IPSSAS Seminar]. Iqaluit, Nunavut, Canada: International Ph.D. School for Studies of Arctic Societies. Retrieved from http://www.uaf.edu/anlc/snow.html#citation

Kaplan, R. B. (2011). Cultural thought patterns. In T. Silva & P. K. Matsuda, *Landmark essays on ESL writing* (Vol. 17) (pp. 11–25). New York, NY: Routledge.

Keaton, P. (2012, April). *Numbers and types of public elementary and secondary schools from the common core of data: School year 2010–11—First look* [NCES 2012-325]. Washington, DC: U.S. Department of Education, National Center for Education Statistics.

Kena, G., Musu-Gillette, L., Robinson, J., Wang, X., Rathbun, A., Zhang, J., ... Dunlop Velez, E. (2015). *The condition of education 2015.* Washington, DC: U.S. Department of Education, National Center for Education Statistics. Retrieved from http://nces.ed.gov/pubs2015/2015144.pdf.

Klein, A. M. (2008, Winter). Sensitivity to the learning needs of newcomers in foreign language settings. *Multicultural Education, 6*(2), 41–44.

Krasnoff, B. (2015). *What the research says about class size, professional development, and recruitment, induction, and retention of highly qualified teachers: A compendium of the evidence on Title II, Part A, program-funded strategies.* Portland, OR: Northwest Comprehensive Center, Education Northwest. Retrieved from http://www.eric.ed.gov/contentdelivery/servlet/ERICServlet?accno=ED558138.

Kummerer, S. (2010). Language intervention for Hispanic children with language-learning disabilities: Evidence-based practice. *Intervention in School and Clinic, 45*, 192–200.

Laud, E. (2011). *Using formative assessment to differentiate mathematics instruction, grades 4–10: Seven practices to maximize learning.* Thousand Oaks, CA: Corwin.

Lee, S., & Foster, J. (2011). Exploring multiple views of history: Investigating the civil rights movement through an oral history project. *Multicultural Education, 19*(1), 14–19.

Li, J. (2010). "My home and my school": Examining immigrant adolescent narratives from the critical sociocultural perspective. *Race, Ethnicity and Education, 13*, 119–137.

Lo, L. (2012). Demystifying the IEP process for diverse parents of children with disabilities. *Teaching Exceptional Children, 44*(3), 14–20.

Lo, Y. Y., Correa, V. I., & Anderson, A. L. (2015). Culturally responsive social skill instruction for Latino male students. *Journal of Positive Behavior Interventions, 17*, 15–27.

Lo, Y., Mustian, A. L., Brophy, A., & White, R. B. (2011). Peer-mediated social skill instruction for African American males with or at risk for mild disabilities. *Exceptionality, 19*, 191–209.

Lockette, T. (2010). Three from the country. *Teaching Tolerance,* (38), 20–24.

Losen, D. J. (2011). *School discipline: What the research tells us—myths and facts* [NEPC discipline resource sheet]. Washington, DC: National Education Policy Center. (Eric Document Reproduction Service No. ED524712)

Maholmes, V., & Brown, F. E. (2002). Over-representation of African-American students in special education: The role of a developmental framework in shaping teachers' interpretations of African-American students' behavior. *Trotter Review: Race, Ethnicity, and Public Education, 14*(1), 45–59.

Marino, M. T., Gotch, C. M., Israel, M., Vasquez, E., Basham, J. D., & Becht, K. (2014). UDL in the middle school science classroom: Can video games and alternative text heighten engagement and learning for students with learning disabilities? *Learning Disability Quarterly, 37*, 87–99.

Marshall, J. M., & Marshall, J. (2005). *Walking with grandfather: The wisdom of Lakota elders.* Boulder, CO: Sounds True.

Martinez-Garcia, C., & Slate, J. R. (2012). Elementary school campuses and new teachers: A multiyear study. *Education and Urban Society, 44*, 83–96.

Messinger-Willman, J., & Marino, M. T. (2010). Universal design for learning and assistive technology: Leadership considerations for promoting inclusive education in today's secondary schools. *NASSP Bulletin, 94*(1), 5–16.

Michael-Chadwell, S. (2010). Examining the underrepresentation of underserved students in gifted programs from a transformational leadership vantage point. *Journal for the Education of the Gifted, 34*, 99–130.

Migraton Policy Institute. (2015). *Top languages spoken by English language learners nationally and by state* (ELL information center fact sheet series no. 4). Washington, DC: National Center on Immigrant Integration Policy. Retrieved from file://C:/Users/Marilyn%20Friend/Downloads/ELLFact%20Sheet-No4.pdf.

Miretzky, D., & Stevens, S. (2012). How does location impact meaning and opportunity? Rural schools and the NCATE diversity standard. *Teachers College Record, 114*(5), 1–36.

Miron, G. (2011). *Review of "Charter schools: A report on rethinking the federal role in education."* Boulder, CO: National Education Policy Center. Retrieved from http://nepc.colorado.edu/thinktank/review-charter-federal.

Miron, G., Urschel, J. L., Mathis, W, J., & Tornquist, E. (2010). *Schools without diversity: Education management organizations, charter schools and the demographic stratification of the American school system.* Boulder, CO and Tempe, AZ: Education and the Public Interest Center & Education Policy Research Unit. Retrieved from http://epicpolicy.org/publication/schools-without-diversity

Morgan, J. J., Mancl, D. B., Kaffar, B. J., & Ferreira, D. (2011). Creating safe environments for students with disabilities who identify as lesbian, gay, bisexual, or transgender. *Intervention in School and Clinic, 47,* 3–13.

Morrier, M. J., & Hess, K. L. (2012). Ethnic differences in autism eligibility in the United States public schools. *Journal of Special Education, 46,* 49–63.

Morrier, M. J., Hess, K. L., & Heflin, L. J. (2008). Ethnic disproportionality in students with autism spectrum disorders. *Multicultural Education, 16*(1), 31–38.

Moule, J. (2009). Understanding unconscious bias and unintentional racism. *Phi Delta Kappan, 90,* 320–326.

Muller, E. (2011). *Recruiting and retaining qualified special education personnel: Approaches from eight state education agencies.* Alexandria, VA: National Association of State Directors of Special Education, Project Forum. Retrieved from http://www.projectforum.org/docs/RecruitingandRetainingSpEdPersonnelApproachesfromEightSEAs.pdf

Mundt, K., Gregory, A., Melzi, G., & McWayne, C. M. (2015). The influence of ethnic match on Latino school-based family engagement. *Hispanic Journal of Behavioral Sciences, 37,* 170–185.

National Alliance of Black School Educators. (2002). *Addressing overrepresentation of African American students in special education: The prereferral intervention process.* Arlington, VA: Council for Exceptional Education.

National Center for Education Statistics. (2007). *The condition of education: Contexts of elementary and secondary education-charter schools* [Indicator32]. Washington, DC: U.S. Department of Education, Institute of Education Sciences. Retrieved from http://nces.ed.gov/programs/coe/2007/section4/indicator32.asp

National Center for Education Statistics. (2013, May). *The status of rural education.* Washington, DC: U.S. Department of Education. Retrieved from http://nces.ed.gov/programs/coe/indicator_tla.asp

National Center for Education Statistics. (2015). Fast facts: English language learners. In *The Condition of Education 2015* (NCES 2015-144). Washington, DC: U.S. Department of Education. Retrieved from https://nces.ed.gov/fastfacts/display.asp?id=96.

National Center for Education Statistics. (2015, May). Children living in poverty. In *The condition of education.* Washington, DC: U.S. Department of Education. Retrieved from http://nces.ed.gov/programs/coe/indicator_cce.asp.

National Center for Education Statistics. (2016, May). *Racial/ethnic enrollment in public schools.* In *The Condition of Education 2016.* Washington, DC: U.S. Department of Education. Retrieved from http://nces.ed.gov/programs/coe/pdf/coe_cge.pdf.

Nieto, S. (2014). *Finding joy in teaching students of diverse backgrounds: Culturally responsive and socially just practices in U.S. classrooms.* Portsmouth, NH: Heinemann.

Nieto, S., & Bode, P. (2012). *Affirming diversity: The sociopolitical context of multicultural education* (6th ed.). Boston, MA: Allyn & Bacon.

Obiakor, F. E., Utley, C. A., Banks, T., & Algozzine, B. (2014). What are emerging trends and future directions in effective inclusive schools for students with high incidence disabilities? In J. McLeskey, N. L., Waldron, F. Spooner, & B. Algozzine (Eds.), *Handbook of effective inclusive schools: Research and practice* (pp. 464–476). New York, NY: Routledge.

Office of Civil Rights. (2014, March). *Data snapshot: School discipline* (Issue Brief No. 1). Washington, DC: U.S. Department of Education. Retrieved from http://ocrdata.ed.gov/Downloads/CRDC-School-Discipline-Snapshot.pdf.

Olivos, E. M. (2009). Collaboration with Latino families: A critical perspective of home-school interactions. *Intervention in School and Clinic, 45,* 109–115.

Olivos, E. M., Gallagher, R. J., & Aguilar, J. (2010). Fostering collaboration with culturally and linguistically diverse families of children with moderate to severe disabilities. *Journal of Educational & Psychological Consultation, 20,* 28–40.

Olszewski-Kubilius, P., & Thomson, D. L. (2010). Culturally and linguistically diverse students in gifted education: Recruitment and retention. *Gifted Child Today, 33*(4), 58–64.

Oswald, D. P., Coutinho, M. J., & Best, A. M. (2000). *Community and school predictors of overrepresentation of minority children in special education.* Paper presented at the Civil Rights Project Conference on Minority Issues in Special Education: Harvard University, Cambridge, MA.

Pang, V. P. (2001). *Multicultural education: A caring-centered, reflective approach.* Boston, MA: McGraw-Hill.

Paris, D. (2012). Culturally sustaining pedagogy: A needed change in stance, terminology, and practice. *Educational Researcher, 41,* 93–97.

Planty, J., & DeVoe, J. (2005). *An examination of the conditions of school facilities attended by 10th-grade students in 2002* [NCES 2006302]. Washington, DC: U.S. Department of Education, National Center for Education Statistics.

Plunkett, S. W., Behnke, A. O., Sands, T., & Choi, B. Y. (2009). Adolescents' reports of parental engagement and academic achievement in immigrant families. *Journal of Youth and Adolescence, 38,* 257–268.

Rassaei, E. (2015). Recasts, field dependence/independence, cognitive style, and L2 development. *Language Teaching Research, 19,* 499–518.

Ratner, C. (2012). *Macro cultural psychology: A political philosophy of mind.* New York, NY: Oxford University Press.

Rice, C. J., & Goessling, D. P. (2005). Recruiting and retaining male special education teachers. *Remedial and Special Education, 26,* 347–356.

Rich, M. (2015, August). Across the country, a scramble is on to find teachers. *New York Times.* Retrieved from http://www.nytimes.com/2015/08/10/us/teacher-shortages-spur-a-nationwide-hiring-scramble-credentials-optional.html?_r=0.

Richmond, P. (2012). *Almost invisible: Representation of LGBT students in special education settings* (Master's thesis). Seattle WA: University of Washington. Retrieved from https://digital.lib.washington.edu/researchworks/bitstream/handle/1773/22439/Richmond_washington_0250O_11276.pdf?sequence=1.

Robertson, K. (2008). *Preparing ELLs to be 21st-century learners.* Retrieved from http://www.colorincolorado.org/article/21431/

Robinson, J. P., & Espelage, D. L. (2011). Inequities in educational and psychological outcomes between LGBTQ and straight students in middle and high school. *Educational Researcher, 40,* 315–330.

Rueda, R., Klingner, J. K., Sager, N., & Velasco, A. (2008). Reducing disproportionate representation in special education: Overview, explanations, and solutions. In T. C. Jiménez & V. L. Graf (Eds.), *Education for all: Critical issues in the education of children and youth with disabilities* (pp. 131–166). San Francisco, CA: Jossey-Bass.

Ruiz Soto, A. G., Hooker, S., & Batalova, J. (2015). *Top languages spoken by English language learners nationally and by state.* Washington, DC: Migration Policy Institute. Retrieved from file:///C:/Users/marilynfriend/Downloads/ELLFact%20Sheet-No4%20(1).pdf

Rural Family Economic Success Action Network. (2016, January). Rural counts: 6.1 million kids in poverty. Washington, DC: Annie E. Casey Foundation and Aspen Institute Community Strategies Group. Retrieved from http://rufes.org/2014/10/06/rural-child-poverty/.

Sable, J., Plotts, C., & Mitchell, L. (2010). *Characteristics of the 100 largest public elementary and secondary school districts in the United States: 2008–09* (NCES 2011-301). Washington, DC: U.S. Department of Education, National Center for Education Statistics.

Sailes, J., Cleveland, R., & Tyler, T. (2014). "P" soup: Creating healthy school environments through culture audits. *Childhood Education, 90*(1), 29–35.

Friend, M. (2007). The co-teaching partnership. *Educational Leadership*, *64*(5), 58–62.

Friend, M. (2014). *Co-teach! A handbook for creating and sustaining effective classroom partnerships in inclusive schools.* (2nd ed.) Greensboro, NC: Marilyn Friend, Inc.

Friend, M. (2015/2016, December–January). Welcome to co-teach 2.0. *Educational Leadership, 73*(4), 16–22.

Friend, M., & Bursuck, W. (2012). *Including students with special needs: A practical guide for classroom teachers* (6th ed.). Upper Saddle River, NJ: Merrill/Pearson.

Friend, M., & Cook, L. (2013). *Interactions: Collaboration skills for school professionals* (7th ed.). Upper Saddle River, NJ: Pearson/Merrill.

Friend, M., & Bursuck, W. D. (2015). *Including students with special needs: A practical guide for classroom teachers* (7th ed.). Upper Saddle River, NJ: Pearson.

Friend, M., & Cook, L. (2017). *Interactions: Collaboration skills for school professionals* (8th ed.). Upper Saddle River, NJ: Pearson.

Friend, M., Cook, L., Hurley-Chamberlain, D., & Shamberger, C. (2010). Co-teaching: An illustration of the complexity of collaboration in special education. *Journal of Educational & Psychological Consultation, 20*, 9–27.

Fulk, B. M. (2011). Effective communication in collaboration and consultation. In C. G. Simpson, J. P. Bakken, C. G. Simpson, J. P. Bakken (Eds.), *Collaboration: A multidisciplinary approach to educating students with disabilities* (pp. 19–30). Waco, TX: Prufrock Press.

Fullan, M. (2008). *The six secrets of change: What the best leaders do to help their organizations survive and thrive.* San Francisco, CA: Jossey-Bass.

Fullan, M., & Quinn, J. (2016). *Coherence: The right drivers in action for schools, districts, and systems.* Thousand Oaks, CA: Corwin Press.

Gülcan, M. G. (2014). Comparison of teachers' understanding of team work according to various variables. *Educational Research and Reviews, 9*(2), 59–66.

Gaumer Erickson, A. S., Noonan, P. M., Supon Carter, K., McGurn, L., & Purifoy, E. (2015). The Team Functioning Scale: Evaluating and improving effectiveness of school teams. *International Journal of Educational Research, 69*, 1–11.

Giangreco, M. F., Suter, J. C., & Doyle, M. (2010). Paraprofessionals in inclusive schools: A review of recent research. *Journal of Educational & Psychological Consultation, 20*, 41–57.

Gleason, S. C., & Gerzon, N. (2014). High-achieving schools put equity front and center. *Journal of Staff Development, 35*(1), 24–26.

Gurgur, H., & Uzuner, Y. (2010). A phenomenological analysis of the views on co-teaching applications in the inclusion classroom. *Educational Sciences: Theory and Practice, 10*, 311–331.

Hackman, M. Z., & Johnson, C. E. (2013). *Leadership: A communication perspective* (6th ed.). Long Grove, IL: Waveland Press.

Hallinger, P., & Heck, R. H. (2010). Leadership for learning: Does collaborative leadership make a difference in school improvement. *Educational Management Administration, and Leadership, 38*, 654–678.

Hamilton-Jones, B., & Vail, C. O. (2013). Preparing special educators for collaboration in the classroom: Pre-service teachers' beliefs and perspectives. *International Journal of Special Education, 28*(1), 56–68.

Hang, Q., & Rabren, K. (2009). An examination of co-teaching: Perspectives and efficacy indicators. *Remedial and Special Education, 30*, 259–268.

Haro, Z. L., & Olivos, E. M. (2014). Book review: The broken compass: Parental involvement with children's education. *Journal of Family Diversity in Education, 1*, 121–124.

Harry, B. (2008). Collaboration with culturally and linguistically diverse families: Ideal versus reality. *Exceptional Children, 74, 372–388.*

Hernandez, J. E., Harry, B., Newman, L., & Cameto, R. (2008). Survey of family involvement in and satisfaction with the Los Angeles Unified School District special education processes. *Journal of Special Education Leadership, 21*(2), 84–93.

Honigsfeld, A., & Dove, M. G. (2010). *Collaboration and co-teaching: Strategies for English learners.* Thousand Oaks, CA: Corwin.

Huberman, M., Navo, M., & Parrish, T. (2012). Effective practices in high performing districts serving students in special education. *Journal of Special Education Leadership, 25*(2), 59–71.

Hunter, W., Jasper, A. D., & Williamson, R. L. (2014). Utilizing middle school common planning time to support inclusive environments. *Intervention in School and Clinic, 50*, 114–120.

Ingersoll, R. M., & Strong, M. (2011). The impact of induction and mentoring programs for beginning teachers: A critical review of the research. *Review of Educational Research, 81*, 201–233.

Ingersoll, R., & Strong, M. (2012). What the research tells us about the impact of induction and mentoring programs for beginning teachers. *Yearbook of the National Society for the Study of Education, 111*, 466–490.

Isenberg, E., & Walsh, E. (2015). Accounting for co-teaching: A guide for policymakers and developers of value-added models. *Journal of Research on Educational Effectiveness, 8*, 112–119.

Johnson, D. R., & Johnson, F. P. (2009). *Joining together: Group theory and group skills* (10th ed.). Boston, MA: Pearson/Allyn & Bacon.

Johnson, D. W. (2009). *Reaching out: Interpersonal effectiveness and self-actualization* (9th ed.). Boston, MA: Pearson/Allyn & Bacon.

Jolly, A., & Evans, S. (2005). Teacher assistants move to the front of the class: Job embedded learning pays off in student achievement. *Journal of Staff Development, 26*(3), 8–13.

Jones, C. R., Ratcliff, N. J., Sheehan, H., & Hunt, G. H. (2012). An analysis of teachers' and paraeducators' roles and responsibilities with implications for professional development. *Early Childhood Education Journal, 40*, 19–24.

Judge, S., Floyd, K. M., & Jeffs, T. (2008). Using an assistive technology toolkit to promote inclusion. *Early Childhood Education Journal, 36*, 121–126.

Kampwirth, T. J., & Powers, K. M. (2012). *Collaborative consultation in the schools: Effective practices for students with learning and behavior problems* (4th ed.). Boston, MA: Pearson/Allyn & Bacon.

Kampwirth, T. J., & Powers, K. M. (2016). *Collaborative consultation in the schools: Effective practices for students with learning and behavior problems* (5th ed.). Upper Saddle River, NJ: Pearson.

Kasahara, M., & Turnbull, A. P. (2005). Meaning of family-professional partnerships: Japanese mothers, perspectives. *Exceptional Children, 71*, 249–265.

Kauffman, J. M., & Badar, J. (2014). Better thinking and clearer communication will help special education. *Exceptionality, 22*(1), 17–32.

Kennedy, A., Deuel, A., Nelson, T. H., & Slavit, D. (2011). Distributed leadership in professional learning communities. *Phi Delta Kappan, 92*(8), 20–24.

Ketterlin-Geller, L. R., Baumer, P., & Lichon, K. (2015). Administrators as advocates for teacher collaboration. *Intervention in School and Clinic, 51*(1), 51–57.

Khorsheed, K. (2007). Four places to dig deep to find more time for teacher collaboration. *Journal of Staff Development, 28*(2), 43–45.

Kovaleski, J. F., & Glew, M. C. (2006). Bringing instructional support teams to scale: Implication of the Pennsylvania experience. *Remedial and Special Education, 27*, 16–25.

Kozleski, E. B., Yu, T., Satter, A. L., Francis, G. L., & Haines, S. J. (2015). A never ending journey: Inclusive education is a principle of practice, not an end game. *Research and Practice for Persons with Severe Disabilities, 40*, 211–226.

Lamar-Dukes, P., & Dukes, C. (2005). Consider the roles and responsibilities of the inclusion support teacher. *Intervention in School and Clinic, 41*, 55–61.

Lingo, A. S., Barton-Arwood, S. M., & Jolivette, K. (2011). Teachers working together. *TEACHING Exceptional Children, 43*(3), 6–13.

Little, M. E., & Dieker, L. (2009). Co-teaching: Two are better than one. *Principal Leadership, 9*(8) 43–46.

Lortie, D. C. (1975). *Schoolteacher: A sociological study.* Chicago, IL: University of Chicago Press.

Luet, K. M. (2015). Disengaging parents in urban schooling. *Educational Policy* (first published online). doi: 0895904815616481.

Lynch, E. W. (2011). Conceptual framework: From culture shock to cultural learning in E. W. Lynch & M. J. Hansen (Eds.), *Developing cross-cultural competency* (4th ed.). Baltimore, MD: Brookes.

Magiera, K., Smith, C., Zigmond, N., & Gebaner, K. (2005). Benefits of co-teaching in secondary mathematics classes. *Teaching Exceptional Children, 37*(3), 20–24.

Malone, D., & Gallagher, P. A. (2010). Special education teachers, attitudes and perceptions of teamwork. *Remedial and Special Education, 31,* 330–342.

Martin, A. J., & Dowson, M. (2009). Interpersonal relationships, motivation, engagement, and achievement: Yields for theory, current issues, and educational practice. *Review of educational research, 79,* 327–365.

Mastropieri, M. A., Scruggs, T. E., Graetz, J., Norland, J., Gardizi, W., & McDuffie, K. (2005). Case studies in co-teaching in the content areas: Successes, failures, and challenges. *Intervention in School and Clinic, 40,* 260–270.

McGrath, M. Z., Johns, B. H., & Mathur, S. R. (2010). Empowered or overpowered? Strategies for working effectively with paraprofessionals. *Beyond Behavior, 19*(2), 2–6.

McKenney, E. W., & Bristol, R. M. (2015). Supporting intensive interventions for students with autism spectrum disorder: Performance feedback and discrete trial teaching. *School Psychology Quarterly, 30,* 8–22.

McKenzie, A. R., & Lewis, S. (2008). The role and training of paraprofessionals who work with students who are visually impaired. *Journal of Visual Impairment & Blindness, 102,* 459–471.

Menninger, W. C. (1950). Mental health in our schools. *Educational Leadership, 7*(8) 520.

Meyers, A. B., Tobin, R. M., Huber, B. J., Conway, D. E., & Shelvin, K. H. (2015). Interdisciplinary collaboration supporting social-emotional learning in rural school systems. *Journal of Educational & Psychological Consultation, 25,* 109–128.

Miron, C. (2012). The parent experience: When a child is diagnosed with childhood apraxia of speech. *Communication Disorders Quarterly, 33,* 96–110.

Mueller, T. G., & Buckley, P. C. (2014). The odd man out: How fathers navigate the special education system. *Remedial and Special Education, 35,* 40–49.

Murawski, W. W. (2012). Ten tips for using co-planning time more efficiently. *Teaching Exceptional Children, 44*(4), 8–15.

Murawski, W. W. (2015). Creative co-teaching. In W. W. Murawski & K. L. Scott (Eds.), *What really works in secondary education* (pp. 201–215). Thousand Oaks, CA: Corwin Press.

Murray, M. M., & Curran, E. M. (2008). Learning together with parents of children with disabilities: Bringing parent-professional partnership education to a new level. *Teacher Education and Special Education, 31,* 59–63.

Nardon, L., Steers, R. M., & Sanchez-Runde, C. J. (2011). Seeking common ground: Strategies for enhancing multicultural communication. *Organizational Dynamics, 40,* 85–95.

Nellis, L. M. (2012). Maximizing the effectiveness of building teams in response to intervention implementation. *Psychology in the Schools, 49,* 245–256.

Newell, M. L. (2010). The implementation of problem-solving consultation: An analysis of problem conceptualization in a multiracial context. *Journal of Educational and Psychological Consultation, 20,* 83–105.

Newell, S. E. and Stutman, R. K. (2012). The episodic nature of social confrontation. In Anderson, J. A. (Ed.), *Communication yearbook 14* (pp. 359–392). New York, NY: Routledge.

Newton, J. S., Horner, R. H., Todd, A. W., Algozzine, R. F., & Algozzine, K. M. (2012). A pilot study of a problem-solving model for team decision making. *Education and Treatment of Children, 35*(1), 25–49.

Nichols, S. C., & Sheffield, A. N. (2014, March). Is there an elephant in the room? Considerations that administrators tend to forget when facilitating inclusive practices among general and special education teachers. *National Forum of Applied Educational Research Journal, 27*(1–2), 31–44.

Nieto, S. (2009). From surviving to thriving. *Educational Leadership, 66*(5), 8–13.

Nowell, B. L., & Salem, D. A. (2007). The impact of special education mediation on parent–school relationships: Parents' perspective. *Remedial and Special Education, 28,* 304–315.

Olivos, E. M., Gallagher, R. J., & Aguilar, J. (2010). Fostering collaboration with culturally and linguistically diverse families of children with moderate to severe disabilities. *Journal of Educational & Psychological Consultation, 20,* 28–40.

Olson, B. J., Parayitam, S., & Bao, Y. (2007). Strategic decision making: The effects of cognitive diversity, conflict, and trust on decision outcomes. *Journal of Management, 33,* 196–222.

Penuel, W., Riel, M., Krause, A., & Frank, K. (2009). Analyzing teachers' professional interactions in a school as social capital: A social network approach. *Teachers College Record, 11,* 124–163.

Pierangelo, R., & Guiliani, G. (2008). *Understanding assessment in the special education process.* Thousand Oaks, CA: Corwin.

Ploessl, D. M., Rock, M. L., Schoenfeld, N., & Blanks, B. (2010). On the same page: Practical techniques to enhance co-teaching interactions. *Intervention in School and Clinic, 45,* 158–168.

Reiman, J. W., Beck, L., Coppola, T., & Engiles, A. (2010). Parents' experiences with the IEP process: Considerations for improving practice. Eugene, OR: *Center for Appropriate Dispute Resolution in Special Education (CADRE).* Retrieved from http://www.directionservice.org/cadre/pdf/Parent-IEP%20Process.pdf.

Roach, A. T., & Elliott, S. N. (2009). Consultation to support inclusive accountability and standards-based reform: Facilitating access, equity, and empowerment. *Journal of Educational & Psychological Consultation, 19,* 61–81.

Rosenfield, S. (Ed.). (2012). *Becoming a school consultant: Lessons learned.* New York, NY: Routledge.

Rosenholtz, S. J. (1989). Workplace conditions that affect teacher quality and commitment: Implications for teacher induction programs. *Elementary School Journal, 89,* 421–439.

Runhaar, P., ten Brinke, D., Kuijpers, M., Wesselink, R., & Mulder, M. (2014). Exploring the links between interdependence, team learning and a shared understanding among team members: The case of teachers facing an educational innovation. *Human Resource Development International, 17,* 67–87.

Sanker, D. (2012). *Collaborate: The art of we.* San Francisco, CA: Jossey-Bass.

Santangelo, T. (2009). Collaborative problem solving effectively implemented but not sustained: A case for aligning the sun, the moon and the stars. *Exceptional Children, 75*(2), 185–209.

Sarason, S. B. (1982). *The culture of the school and the problem of change* (2nd ed.). Boston, MA: Allyn & Bacon.

Scott, C. P. R., & Wildman, J. L. (2015). Culture, communication, and conflict: A review of the virtual global team literature. In J. L. Wildman & R. L. Griffith (Eds.), *Leading global teams* (pp. 13–32). New York, NY: Springer Science+Business.

Scruggs, T. E., Mastropieri, M. A., & McDuffie, K. A. (2007). Co-teaching in inclusive classrooms: A metasynthesis of qualitative research. *Exceptional Children, 73,* 392–416.

Seglem, R., & VanZant, M. (2010). Privileging students' voices: A co-teaching philosophy that evokes excellence in "all" learners. *English Journal, 100*(2), 41–47.

Sheridan, S. M., Warnes, E. D., Woods, K. E., Blevins, C. A., Magee, K. L., & Ellis, C. (2009). An exploratory evaluation of conjoint behavioral consultation to promote collaboration among family, school, and pediatric systems: A role for pediatric school psychologists. *Journal of Educational & Psychological Consultation, 19*, 106–129.

Shyman, E. (2010). Identifying predictors of emotional exhaustion among special education paraeducators: A preliminary investigation. *Psychology in the Schools, 47*, 828–841.

Silverman, S. K., Hazelwood, C., & Cronin, P. (2009). *Universal education: Principles and practices for advancing achievement of students with disabilities.* Columbus: Ohio Department of Education, Office for Exceptional Children.

Sims, E. (2008). Sharing command of the co-teaching ship: How to play nicely with others. *English Journal, 97*(5), 58–63.

Stephens, T. L., & Woodbury, C. (2011). Paraeducators. In C. G. Simpson & J. P. Bakken (Eds.), *Collaboration: A multidisciplinary approach to educating students with disabilities* (pp. 71–85). Waco, TX: Prufrock Press.

Stockall, N. S. (2014). When an aide really becomes an aid: Providing professional development for special education paraprofessionals. *Teaching Exceptional Children, 46*(6), 197–205.

Suarez-Orozco, C., Onaga, M., & de Lardemelle, C. (2010). Promoting academic engagement among immigrant adolescents through school-family-community collaboration. *Professional School Counseling, 14*(1), 15–26.

Summers, J. A., Hoffman, L., Marquis, J., Turnbull, A., Poston, D., & Nelson, L. L. (2005). Measuring the quality of family-professional partnerships in special education services. *Exceptional Children, 72*, 63–81.

Tannock, M. T. (2009). Tangible and intangible elements of collaborative teaching. *Intervention in School and Clinic, 44*, 173–178.

Theoharis, G., & Causton, J. (2014). Leading inclusive reform for students with disabilities: A school- and systemwide approach. *Theory into Practice, 53*, 82–97.

Thomson, C. (2013). Collaborative consultation to promote inclusion: Voices from the classroom. *International Journal of Inclusive Education, 17*, 882–894.

Tren, V., & Boles, K. C. (2011). *Rating your teacher team: Five conditions for effective teams.* Thousand Oaks, CA: Corwin Press.

Trenholm, S. (2011). *Thinking through communication: An introduction to the study of human communication* (6th ed.). Boston, MA: Pearson/Allyn & Bacon.

Trenholm, S. (2014). *Thinking through communication: An introduction to the study of human communication* (7th edition). Upper Saddle River, NJ: Pearson.

van Garderen, D., Scheuermann, A., Jackson, C., & Hampton, D. (2009). Supporting the collaboration of special educators and general educators to teach students who struggle with mathematics: An overview of the research. *Psychology in the Schools, 46*, 56–78.

Wagner, M., Newman, L., Cameto, R., Javitz, H., & Valdes, K. (2012). A national picture of parent and youth participation in IEP and transition planning meetings. *Journal of Disability Policy Studies, 23*, 140–155.

Walker, A. (2015). Clones, drones and dragons: Ongoing uncertainties around school leader development. *School Leadership & Management, 35*, 300–320.

Walsh, J. M. (2012). Co-teaching as a school system strategy for continuous improvement. *Preventing School Failure, 56*(1), 29–36.

Wasburn-Moses, L. (2009). An exploration of pre-service teachers' expectations for their future roles. *Teacher Education and Special Education, 32*, 5–16.

Webster, R., Blatchford, P., & Russell, A. (2013). Challenging and changing how schools use teaching assistants: Findings from the effective deployment of teaching assistants project. *School Leadership & Management, 33*, 78–96.

Welch, M., & Tulbert, B. (2000). Practitioners, perspectives of collaboration: A social validation and factor analysis. *Journal of Educational & Psychological Consultation, 11*, 357–378.

Williamson, P., & McLeskey, J. (2011). An investigation into the nature of inclusion problem-solving teams. *Teacher Educator, 46*, 316–334.

Chapter 5

Adebisi, R. O., Liman, N. A., & Longpoe, P. K. (2015). Using assistive technology in teaching children with learning disabilities in the 21st century. *Journal of Education and Practice, 6*(24), 14–20.

Agran, M., & Hughes, C. (2008). Asking student input: Students' opinion regarding their individualized education program involvement. *Career Development for Exceptional Individuals, 31*, 69–76.

Ahearn, E. M. (2008). *State eligibility requirements for specific learning disabilities* [in Forum brief policy analysis]. Retrieved from http://projectforum.org/docs/StateEligibilityRequirementsforSpecificLearningDisabilities.pdf

Al-Yagon, M. (2011). Fathers' emotional resources and children's socio-emotional and behavioral adjustment among children with learning disabilities. *Journal of Child and Family Studies, 20*, 569–584.

Anctil, T. M., Ishikawa, M. E., & Tao Scott, A. (2008). Academic identity development through self-determination: Successful college students with learning disabilities. *Career Development for Exceptional Individuals, 31*, 164–174.

Anderson, J. A., Howland, A. A., & McCoach, D. B. (2015). Parental characteristics and resiliency in identification rates for special education. *Preventing School Failure, 59*, 63–72.

Artiles, A. J., Bal, A., & King Thorius, K. A. (2010). Back to the future: A critique of response to intervention's social justice views. *Theory into Practice, 49*, 250–257.

Balu, R., Zhu, P., Doolittle, F., Schiller, E., Jenkins, J., Gersten, R. (2015). *Evaluation of response to intervention practices for elementary school reading.* Washington, DC: U.S. Department of Education, Institute of Education Sciences.

Banda, D. R., Matuszny, R. M., & Therrien, W. J. (2009). Enhancing motivation to complete math tasks using the high-preference strategy. *Intervention in School and Clinic, 44*, 146–150.

Bassett, D., & Dunn, C. (2012). Introduction to the special issue on transition and students with learning disabilities and emotional-behavior disorders. *Intervention in School and Clinic, 48*, 3–5.

Bear, G. G., Kortering, L. J., & Braziel, P. (2006). School completers and non-completers with learning disabilities: Similarities in academic achievement and perceptions of self and teachers. *Remedial and Special Education, 27*, 293–300.

Berkeley, S., Bender, W. N., Peaster, L. G., & Saunders, L. (2009). Implementation of response to intervention: A snapshot of progress. *Journal of Learning Disabilities, 42*, 85–95.

Berninger, V. W., & May, M. (2011). Evidence-based diagnosis and treatment for specific learning disabilities involving impairments in written and/or oral language. *Journal of Learning Disabilities, 44*, 167–183.

Berninger, V. W., & Niedo, J. (2014). Individualizing instruction for students with oral and written language difficulties. In J. T. Mascolo, V. C. Alfonso, D. P. Flanagan, J. T. Mascolo, V. C. Alfonso, & D. P. Flanagan (Eds.), *Essentials of planning, selecting, and tailoring interventions for unique learners* (pp. 231–264). Hoboken, NJ: John Wiley & Sons.

Berninger, V., & Swanson, H. L. (2013). Diagnosing and treating specific learning disabilities in reference to the brain's working memory system (Chapter 17). In H. Lee Swanson, Karen Harris, & Steve Graham (Eds.), *Handbook of learning disabilities* (2nd ed.) (pp. 307–325). New York: Guilford.

Berry Kuchle, L., Zumeta Edmonds, R., Danielson, L. C., Peterson, A., & Riley-Tillman, T. C. (2015). The next big idea: A framework for integrated academic and behavioral intensive intervention. *Learning Disabilities Research & Practice, 30,* 150–158.

Björn, P. M., Aro, M. T., Koponen, T. K., Fuchs, L. S., & Fuchs, D. H. (2016). The many faces of special education within RTI frameworks in the United States and Finland. *Learning Disability Quarterly, 39,* 58–66.

Brandenburg, J., Klesczewski, J., Fischbach, A., Schuchardt, K., Buttner, G., & Hasselhorn, M. (2014). Working memory in children with learning disabilities in reading versus spelling: Searching for overlapping and specific cognitive factors. *Journal of Learning Disabilities, 48,* 622–634.

Brigance, A. (1999). *Brigance comprehensive inventory of basic skills–Revised.* North Billerica, MA: Curriculum Associates.

Brigance, A. H. (2010). *Comprehensive Inventory of Basic Skills-II.* North Billerica, MA: Curriculum Associates.

Brooks, B. A., Floyd, F., Robins, D. L., & Chan, W. Y. (2015). Extracurricular activities and the development of social skills in children with intellectual and specific learning disabilities. *Journal of Intellectual Disability Research, 59,* 678–687.

Burden, R. (2008). Is dyslexia associated with negative feelings of self-worth? A review and implications for future research. *Dyslexia, 14,* 188–196.

Burns, M. K., Kanive, R., & DeGrande, M. (2012). Effect of a computer-delivered math fact intervention as a supplemental intervention for math in third and fourth grades. *Remedial and Special Education, 33,* 184–191.

Burr, E., Haas, E., & Ferriere, K. (2015). *Identifying and supporting English learner students with learning disabilities: Key issues in the literature and state practice* [REL 2015-086]. Washington, DC: Regional Educational Laboratory West, Institute for Education Sciences. Retrieved from http://www.eric.ed.gov/contentdelivery/servlet/ERICServlet?accno=ED558163.

Buttner, G., & Hasselhorn, M. (2011). Learning disabilities: Debates on definitions, causes, subtypes, and responses. *International Journal of Disability, Development and Education, 58*(1), 75–87.

Carlberg, C., & Kavale, K. (1980). The efficacy of special versus regular class placement for exceptional children: A meta-analysis. *Journal of Special Education, 14,* 295–309.

Carretti, B., Motta, E., & Re, A. M. (2016). Oral and written expression in children with reading comprehension difficulties. *Journal of Learning Disabilities, 49,* 65–76.

Carter, E. W., Lane, K. L., Cooney, M., Weir, K., Moss, C. K., & Machalicek, W. (2013). Parent assessments of self-determination importance and performance for students with autism or intellectual disability. *American Journal on Intellectual and Developmental Disabilities, 118,* 16–31.

Carter, E. W., Lane, K. L., Pierson, M. R., & Glaeser, B. (2006). Self-determination skills and opportunities of transition-age youth with emotional disturbance and learning disabilities. *Exceptional Children, 72,* 333–346.

Cartwright, K. B. (2012). Insights from cognitive neuroscience: The importance of executive function for early reading development and education. *Early Education and Development, 23,* 24–36.

Castles, A., Datta, H., Gayan, J., & Olson, R. K. (1999). Varieties of developmental reading disorder: Genetic and environmental influences. *Journal of Experimental Child Psychology, 72,* 73–94.

Centers for Disease Control and Prevention. (2011). *Attention-deficit/hyperactivity disorder (ADHD): Data and statistics.* Atlanta, GA: Author. Retrieved from http://www.cdc.gov/ncbddd/adhd/data.html

Cincinnati Public Schools. (2006). *Pyramid of interventions: Quick guide.* Cincinnati, OH: Author. Retrieved from http://www.cps-k12.org/general/Pyramid/QuickGuide.pdf

Ciullo, S., Lembke, E. S., Carlisle, A., Thomas, C. N., Goodwin, M., & Judd, L. (2016). Implementation of evidence-based literacy practices in middle school response to intervention: An observation study. *Learning Disability Quarterly, 39,* 44–57.

Collett-Klingenberg, L. L. (1998). The reality of best practices in transition: A case study. *Exceptional Children, 65,* 67–78.

Compton, D. L., Fuchs, L. S., Fuchs, D., Lambert, W., & Hamlett, C. (2012). The cognitive and academic profiles of reading and mathematics learning disabilities. *Journal of Learning Disabilities, 45,* 79–95.

Compton, D. L., Gilbert, J. K., Jenkins, J. R., Fuchs, D., Fuchs, L. S., Cho, E., . . . Bouton, B. (2012). Accelerating chronically unresponsive children to tier 3 instruction: What level of data is necessary to ensure selection accuracy? *Journal of Learning Disabilities, 45,* 204–216.

Coomer, L. F. (2015). *Definitions and criteria used by state education departments for identifying specific learning disabilities* (Master's thesis). Retrieved from http://digitalcommons.wku.edu/theses/1515.

Cornoldi, C., Ficili, P., Giofrè, D., Mammarella, I. C., & Mirandola, C. (2011). Imaginative representation of two- and three-dimensional matrices in children with nonverbal learning disabilities. *Imagination, Cognition and Personality, 31*(1–2), 53–62.

Corso, H. V., Cromley, J. G., Sperb, T., & Salles, J. F. (2016, February 4). Modeling the relationship among reading comprehension, intelligence, socioeconomic status, and neuropsychological functions: The mediating role of executive functions. *Psychology & Neuroscience,* doi:10.1037/pne0000036.

Cortiella, C. & Horowitz, S. H. (2014). *The state of learning disabilities: Facts, trends and emerging issues.* New York, NY: National Center for Learning Disabilities.

Cortiella, C. (2011). *The state of learning disabilities.* New York, NY: National Center for Learning Disabilities. Retrieved from http://www.ncld.org/types-learning-disabilities/what-is-ld/state-of-learning-disabilities

Cramer, L. (2015). Inequities of intervention among culturally and linguistically diverse students. *Perspectives on Urban Education, 12*(1). Retrieved from http://www.urbanedjournal.org/archive/volume-12-issue-1-spring-2015/inequities-intervention-among-culturally-and-linguistically-di.

Crepeau-Hobson, F., & Bianco, M. (2011). Identification of gifted students with learning disabilities in a response-to-intervention era. *Psychology in the Schools, 48,* 102–109.

Danforth, S. (2009). *The incomplete child: An intellectual history of learning disabilities.* New York, NY: Peter Lang Publishing.

Denton, C. A. (2012). Response to intervention for reading difficulties in the primary grades: Some answers and lingering questions. *Journal of Learning Disabilities, 45,* 232–243.

DeSimone, J. R., & Parmar, R. S. (2006). Middle school mathematics teachers' beliefs about inclusion of students with learning disabilities. *Learning Disabilities Research and Practice, 21,* 98–110.

Doren, B., Murray, C., & Gau, J. M. (2014). Salient predictors of school dropout among secondary students with learning disabilities. *Learning Disabilities Research & Practice, 29,* 150–159.

Dunn, C., Rabren, K., Taylor, S., & Dotson, C. (2012). Assisting students with high-incidence disabilities to pursue careers in science, technology, engineering, and mathematics. *Intervention in School and Clinic, 48,* 47–54.

Duquette, C., Fullarton, S., Orders, S., & Robertson-Grewal, K. (2011). Insider, outsider, ally, or adversary: Parents of youth with learning disabilities engage in educational advocacy. *International Journal of Special Education, 26,* 124–141.

Dyson, L. L. (2007). The unexpected effects of inclusion on the families of students with learning disabilities: A focus-group study. *Learning Disabilities: A Multidisciplinary Journal, 14,* 185–194.

Espin, C. A., Busch, T. W., Lembke, E. S., Hampton, D. D., Seo, K., & Zukowski, B. A. (2013). Curriculum-based measurement in science learning vocabulary-matching as an indicator of performance and progress. *Assessment for Effective Intervention, 38*, 203–213.

Espin, C., Wallace, T., Campbell, H., Lembke, E. S., Long, J. D., & Ticha, R. (2008). Curriculum-based measurement in writing: Predicting the success of high-school students on state standards tests. *Exceptional Children, 74*, 174–193.

Estell, D. B., Jones, M. H., Pearl, R., & Van Acker, R. (2009). Best friendships of students with and without learning disabilities across late elementary school. *Exceptional Children, 76*, 110–124.

Estell, D. B., Jones, M. H., Pearl, R., Van Acker, R., Farmer, T. W., & Rodkin, P. C. (2008). Peer groups, popularity, and social preference: Trajectories of social functioning among students with and without learning disabilities. *Journal of Learning Disabilities, 41*, 5–14.

Faggella-Luby, M. N., & Deshler, D. D. (2008). Reading comprehension in adolescents with LD: What we know, what we need to learn. *Learning Disabilities: Research & Practice, 23*, 70–78.

Faggella-Luby, M. N., Drew, S. V., & Schumaker, J. B. (2015). Not such a simple story: Contradictory evidence from a review of story structure research for students at-risk. *Learning Disabilities Research & Practice, 30*, 61–75.

Falk-Ross, F., Watman, L., Kokesh, K., Iverson, M., Williams, E., & Wallace, A. (2009). Natural complements: Collaborative approaches for educators to support students with learning disabilities and literacy difficulties. *Reading and Writing Quarterly, 25*, 104–117.

Feldman, D. B., Davidson, O. B., Ben-Naim, S., Maza, E., & Margalit, M. (2016, January 26). Hope as a mediator of loneliness and academic self-efficacy among students with and without learning disabilities during the transition to college. *Learning Disabilities Research & Practice.* doi: 10.1111/ldrp.12094.

Ferrer, E., Shaywitz, B. A., Holahan, J. M., Marchione, K. E., Michaels, R., & Shaywitz, S. E. (2015). Achievement gap in reading is present as early as first grade and persists through adolescence. *Journal of Pediatrics, 167*, 1121–1125.

Ferri, B. A., & Connor, D. J. (2010). "I was the special ed. girl": Urban working-class young women of colour. *Gender and Education, 22*, 105–121.

Field, S. L., & Hoffman, A. S. (2012). Fostering self-determination through building productive relationships in the classroom. *Intervention in School and Clinic, 48*, 6–14.

Fletcher, J. M. (2005). Predicting math outcomes: Reading predictors and co-morbidity. *Journal of Learning Disabilities, 38*, 308–312.

Fletcher, J. M., Lyon, G. R., Fuchs, L., & Barnes, M. A. (2007). *Learning disabilities.* New York, NY: Guilford Press.

Fletcher, T. V., & Navarrete, L. A. (2011). Learning disabilities or difference: A critical look at issues associated with the misidentification and placement of Hispanic students in special education programs. *Rural Special Education Quarterly, 30*(1), 30–38.

Flores, M. (2009). Teaching subtraction with regrouping to students experiencing difficulty in mathematics. *Preventing School Failure, 53*, 145–152.

Fontana, J. L., Scruggs, T., & Mastropieri, M. A. (2007). Mnemonic strategy instruction in inclusive secondary social studies classes. *Remedial and Special Education, 28*, 345–555.

Forness, S. R., & Kavale, K. A. (2001). ADHD and a return to the medical model of special education. *Education and Treatment of Children, 24*, 224–247.

Freeman, R., Miller, D., & Newcomer, L. (2015). Integration of academic and behavioral MTSS at the district level using implementation science. *Learning Disabilities: A Contemporary Journal, 13*(1), 59–72.

Freeman-Green, S. M., O'Brien, C., Wood, C. L., & Hitt, S. B. (2015). Effects of the SOLVE strategy on the mathematical problem solving skills of secondary students with learning disabilities. *Learning Disabilities Research & Practice, 30*, 76–90.

Friend, M. (2014). *Co-teach! A handbook for creating and sustaining effective classroom partnerships in inclusive schools.* (2nd ed.) Greensboro, NC: Marilyn Friend, Inc.

Friend, M., & Bursuck, W. (2012). *Including students with special needs: A practical guide for classroom teachers* (6th ed.). Upper Saddle River, NJ: Merrill/Pearson.

Friend, M., & Shamberger, C. (2008). Inclusion. In T. L. Good (Ed.), *Twenty-first century education: A reference handbook* (Volume II, Part XI, Ch.64; pp. 124–131). Thousand Oaks, CA: Sage.

Friend, M., & Bursuck, W. D. (2016). *Including students with special needs: A practical guide for classroom teachers* (7th ed.). Upper Saddle River, NJ: Pearson.

Frostig, M., & Horne, D. (1964). *The Frostig program for the development of visual perception: Teacher's guide.* Chicago, IL: Follett.

Fuchs, D., Compton, D. L., Fuchs, L. S., Bryant, J., & Davis, G. N. (2008). Making "secondary intervention" work in a three-tier responsiveness-to-intervention model: Findings from the first-grade longitudinal reading study of the National Research Center on Learning Disabilities. *Reading and Writing: An Interdisciplinary Journal, 21*, 413–436.

Fuchs, L. S., & Vaughn, S. (2012). Responsiveness-to-intervention: A decade later. *Journal of Learning Disabilities, 45*, 195–203.

Gage, N. A., Lierheimer, K. S., & Goran, L. G. (2012). Characteristics of students with high-incidence disabilities broadly defined. *Journal of Disability Policy Studies, 23*, 168–178.

Galway, T. M., & Metsala, J. L. (2011). Social cognition and its relation to psychosocial adjustment in children with nonverbal learning disabilities. *Journal of Learning Disabilities, 44*, 33–49.

Gardner, T. J. (2011). Disabilities in written expression. *Teaching Children Mathematics, 18*(1), 46–54.

Gerber, P. J. (2012). The impact of learning disabilities on adulthood: A review of the evidenced-based literature for research and practice in adult education. *Journal of Learning Disabilities, 45*, 31–46.

Gilger, J. W., & Wilkins, M. A. (2008). A typical neurodevelopmental variation as a basis for learning disorders. In M. Mody & E. R. Silliman (Eds.), *Brain, behavior, and learning in language and reading disorders* (pp. 4–40). New York, NY: Guilford.

Gillespie, A., & Graham, S. (2014). A meta-analysis of writing interventions for students with learning disabilities. *Exceptional Children, 80*, 454–473.

Goldstein, K. (1942). *Aftereffects of brain injuries in war.* New York, NY: Grune & Stratton.

Good, C. P., McIntosh, K., & Gietz, C. (2011). Integrating bullying prevention into schoolwide positive behavior support. *Teaching Exceptional Children, 44*(1), 48–56.

Goodman, J. I., Hazelkorn, M., Bucholz, J. L., Duffy, M. L., & Kitta, Y. (2011). Inclusion and graduation rates: What are the outcomes? *Journal of Disability Policy Studies, 21*, 241–252.

Goran, L. A., & Gage, N. A. (2011). A comparative analysis of language, suspension, and academic performance of students with emotional disturbance and students with learning disabilities. *Education & Treatment of Children, 34*, 469–488.

Graves, A. W., Duesbery, L., Pyle, N. B., Brandon, R. R., & McIntosh, A. S. (2011). Two studies of Tier II literacy development: Throwing sixth graders a lifeline. *Elementary School Journal, 111*, 641–661.

Graves, E., & McConnell, T. (2014). Response to intervention: Providing reading intervention to low income and minority students. *Educational Forum, 78*, 88–97.

Graves, S., & Mitchell, A. (2011). Is the moratorium over? African American psychology professionals' views on intelligence testing in response to changes to federal policy. *Journal of Black Psychology, 37*, 407–425.

Gregg, M., & Nelson, J. M. (2012). Meta-analysis on the effectiveness of extra time as a test accommodation for transitioning adolescents with learning disabilities: More questions than answers. *Journal of Learning Disabilities, 45,* 128–138.

Gumpel, T. P. (2007). Are social competence difficulties by performance or acquisition deficits? The importance of self-regulatory mechanisms. *Psychology in the Schools, 44,* 351–372.

Hadders-Algra, M. (2011). Challenges and limitations in early intervention. *Developmental Medicine & Child Neurology, 53* (Suppl 4), 52–55.

Hale, C. (2015). Legendary LD: Learning disabilities, creativity, and social class. *Disability Studies Quarterly, 35*(1). Retrieved from http://dsq-sds.org/article/view/3806.

Hale, J., Alfonso, V., Berninger, V., Bracken, B., Christo, C., Clark, E. ... Yalof, J. (2010). Critical issues in response-to-intervention, comprehensive evaluation, and specific learning disabilities identification and intervention: An expert white paper consensus. *Learning Disability Quarterly, 33,* 223–236.

Hallahan, D. P., & Kauffman, J. M. (1976*). Introduction to learning disabilities: A psycho-behavioral approach.* Upper Saddle River, NJ: Pearson.

Hallahan, D. P., & Mercer, C. D. (2001, August). *Learning disabilities: Historical perspectives.* Paper presented at the Learning Disabilities Summit: Building a Foundation for the Future, Washington, DC. (ERIC Documentation Reproduction Service No. ED458756)

Hammill, D. D. (1993). A brief look at the learning disabilities movement in the United States. *Journal of Learning Disabilities, 26,* 295–310.

Hammill, D. D., & Bryant, B. (1998). *Learning disabilities diagnostic inventory.* Austin, TX: Pro-Ed.

Haworth, C. A., & Plomin, R. (2010). Quantitative genetics in the era of molecular genetics: Learning abilities and disabilities as an example. *Journal of the American Academy of Child & Adolescent Psychiatry, 49,* 783–793.

Haworth, C. A., Kovas, Y., Harlaar, N., Hayiou-Thomas, M. E., Petrill, S. A., Dale, P. S., & Plomin, R. (2009). Generalist genes and learning disabilities: A multivariate genetic analysis of low performance in reading, mathematics, language and general cognitive ability in a sample of 8000 12-year-old twins. *Journal of Child Psychology and Psychiatry, 50,* 1318–1325.

Haycock, K., & Crawford, C. (2008). Closing the teacher quality gap. *Educational Leadership, 65*(7), 14–19.

Heim, S., Pape-Neumann, J., Van Ermingen-Marbach, M., Brinkhaus, M., & Grande, M. (2015). Shared vs. specific brain activation changes in dyslexia after training of phonology, attention, or reading. *Brain Structure & Function, 220,* 2191–2207.

Heiman, T., Zinck, L. C., & Heath, N. L. (2008). Parents and youth with learning disabilities: Perceptions of relationships and communication. *Journal of Learning Disabilities, 41,* 524–534.

Hen, M., & Goroshit, M. (2014). Academic procrastination, emotional intelligence, academic self-efficacy, and GPA: A comparison between students with and without learning disabilities. *Journal of Learning Disabilities, 47,* 116–124.

Hitchings, W. E., Luzzo, D. A., Ristow, R., Horvath, M., Retish, P., & Tanners, A. (2001). The career development needs of college students with learning disabilities: In their own words. *Learning Disabilities Research and Practice, 16,* 8–17.

Hoeft, F., Hernandez, A., McMillon, G., Taylor-Hill, H., Martindale, J. L., Meyler, A., . . . Gabrieli, J. D. E. (2006). Neural basis of dyslexia: A comparison between dyslexic children and non-dyslexic children equated for reading ability. *Journal of Neuroscience, 26,* 10700–10708.

Hoover, T. M., Kubina, R. M., & Mason, L. H. (2012). Effects of self-regulated strategy development for POW+TREE on high school students with learning disabilities. *Exceptionality, 20*(1), 20–38.

Horn, W. F., & Tynan, D. (2001). Time to make special education "special" again. In C. E. Finn, A. J. Rotherham, & C. R. Hokanson (Eds.), *Rethinking special education for a new century.* Washington, DC: Thomas B. Fordham Foundation and Progressive Policy Institute.

Hughes, M. T., Schumm, J. S., & Vaughn, S. (1999). Home literacy activities: Perceptions and practices of Hispanic parents of children with learning disabilities. *Learning Disability Quarterly, 22,* 224–235.

Idan, O., & Margalit, M. (2014). Socioemotional self-perceptions, family climate, and hopeful thinking among students with learning disabilities and typically achieving students from the same classes. *Journal of Learning Disabilities, 47,* 136–152.

Idol, L. (2006). Toward inclusion of special education students in general education: A program evaluation of eight schools. *Remedial and Special Education, 27,* 77–94.

Jitendra, A. K., & Torgerson-Tubiello, R. (1997). Let's learn contractions! *Teaching Exceptional Children, 29*(4), 16–19.

Jitendra, A. K., Burgess, C., & Gajria, M. (2011). Cognitive strategy instruction for improving expository text comprehension of students with learning disabilities: The quality of evidence. *Exceptional Children, 77,* 135–159.

Jochum, J., Curran, C., & Reetz, L. (1998). Creating individual educational portfolios in written language. *Reading and Writing Quarterly: Overcoming Learning Difficulties, 14,* 283–306.

Ju, S., Kortering, L., Osmanir, K., & Zhang, D. (2015). Vocational rehabilitation transition outcomes: A look at one state's evidence. *Journal of Rehabilitation, 81*(2), 47.

Karlsen, B., & Gardner, E. (1995). *Stanford diagnostic reading test* (4th ed.). Orlando, FL: Harcourt Educational Measurement.

Karlsen, B., Gardner, E. F. (2005). *Stanford Diagnostic Reading Test* (4th ed.) (SDRT-4).

Kavale, K. A. & Forness, S. R. (2012). *The nature of learning disabilities: Critical elements of diagnosis and classification.* Hoboken, NJ: Taylor and Francis.

Kavale, K. A., & Forness, S. R. (2000). What definitions of learning disability say and don't say. *Journal of Learning Disabilities, 33,* 239–256.

Kavale, K. A., & Mostert, M. P. (2004). Social skills interventions for individuals with learning disabilities. *Learning Disability Quarterly, 27,* 31–43.

Kavale, K. A., & Spaulding, L. S. (2008). Is response to intervention good policy for specific learning disability? *Learning Disabilities Research and Practice, 23,* 169–179.

Kavale, K. A., Spaulding, L. S., & Beam, A. P. (2009). A time to define: Making the specific learning disability definition prescribe specific learning disability. *Learning Disability Quarterly, 32,* 39–48.

Kennedy, M. J., Deshler, D. D., & Lloyd, J. W. (2015). Effects of multimedia vocabulary instruction on adolescents with learning disabilities. *Journal of Learning Disabilities, 48,* 22–38.

Kephart, N. C. (1960). *The slow learner in the classroom.* Columbus, OH: Merrill.

Kim, W., Linan-Thompson, S., & Misquitta, R. (2012). Critical factors in reading comprehension instruction for students with learning disabilities: A research synthesis. *Learning Disabilities Research & Practice, 27,* 66–78.

Kortering, J. L., & Christenson, S. (2009). Engaging students in school and learning: The real deal for school completion. *Exceptionality, 17*(1), 5–15.

Kovas, Y., Haworth, C., Dale, P. S., & Plomin, R. (2007). The genetic and environmental origins of learning abilities and disabilities in the early school years. *Monographs of the Society for Research in Child Development, 72*(3), 1–160.

Krawec, J., & Montague, M. (2012, Spring). *Cognitive strategy instruction* [Current Practice Alerts, Issue 19]. Arlington, VA: Division for Learning Disabilities, Council for Exceptional Children.

Lackaye, T. D., & Margalit, M. (2006). Comparisons of achievement, effort, and self-perceptions among students with learning disabilities and their peers from different achievement groups. *Journal of Learning Disabilities, 39,* 432–446.

Lee, I. H., Rojewski, J. W., Gregg, N., & Jeong, S. (2015). Postsecondary education persistence of adolescents with specific learning disabilities or emotional/behavioral disorders. *Journal of Special Education, 49,* 77–88.

Leichtentritt, J., & Shechtman, Z. (2010). Children with and without learning disabilities: A comparison of processes and outcomes following group counseling. *Journal of Learning Disabilities, 43,* 169–179.

Lerner, J. W., & Johns, B. (2012). *Learning disabilities and related mild disabilities: Characteristics, teaching strategies, and new directions* (12th ed.). Belmont, CA: Wadsworth.

Lerner, J. W., & Johns, B. (2015). *Learning disabilities and related disabilities: Strategies for success* (13th ed.). Stamford, CT: Cengage.

Lerner, J., & Kline, F. (2006). *Learning disabilities and related disorders: Characteristics and teaching strategies* (10th ed.). Boston, MA: Houghton Mifflin.

Lichtinger, E., & Kaplan, A. (2015). Employing a case study approach to capture motivation and self-regulation of young students with learning disabilities in authentic educational contexts. *Metacognition and Learning, 10,* 119–149.

Lindstrom, L., Doren, B., Metheny, J., Johnson, P., & Zane, C. (2007). Transition to employment: Role of the family in career development. *Exceptional Children, 73,* 348–366.

Lo, Y., Correa, V., & Anderson, A. (2015). Culturally responsive social skill instruction for Latino male students. *Journal of Positive Behavior Interventions, 17,* 15–27.

Lo, Y., Mustian, A. L., Brophy, A., & White, R. B. (2011). Peer-mediated social skill instruction for African American males with or at risk for mild disabilities. *Exceptionality, 19,* 191–209.

Lovett, M. W., Lacerenza, L., De Palma, M., & Frijters, J. C. (2012). Evaluating the efficacy of remediation for struggling readers in high school. *Journal of Learning Disabilities, 45,* 151–169.

Lyon, G. R., Fletcher, J. M., Shaywitz, S. E., Shaywitz, B. A., Torgesen, J. K., Wood, F. B., . . . Olson, R. (2001). Rethinking learning disabilities. In C. E. Finn, A. J. Rotherham, & C. R. Hokanson (Eds.), *Rethinking special education for a new century* (pp. 259–287). Washington, DC: Thomas B. Fordham Foundation and Progressive Policy Institute.

Madaus, J. W. (2008). Employment self-disclosure rates and rationales of university graduates with learning disabilities. *Journal of Learning Disabilities, 41,* 291–299.

Madaus, J. W., Faggella-Luby, M. N., & Dukes, L. (2011). The role of non-academic factors in the academic success of college students with learning disabilities. *Learning Disabilities: A Multidisciplinary Journal, 17*(2), 77–82.

Mammarella, I. C., Ghisi, M., Bomba, M., Bottesi, G., Caviola, S., Broggi, F., & Nacinovich, R. (2014). Anxiety and depression in children with nonverbal learning disabilities, reading disabilities, or typical development. *Journal of Learning Disabilities, 49,* 130–139.

Mason, L. H. (2013). Best practices and current trends in written instruction for students with learning disabilities. *Learning Disabilities: Practice Concerns and Students with LD, 25,* 45–63.

Mather, N., & Goldstein, S. (2001). The learning environment. In *Learning disabilities and challenging behaviors: A guide to intervention and classroom management* (pp. 138–161). Baltimore, MD: Paul H. Brookes.

Mattison, R. E., & Mayes, S. (2012). Relationships between learning disability, executive function, and psychopathology in children with ADHD. *Journal of Attention Disorders, 16,* 138–146.

Mayes, S. D., Calhoun, S. L., & Crowell, E. W. (2000). Learning disabilities and ADHD: Overlapping spectrum disorders. *Journal of Learning Disabilities, 33,* 417–424.

McCall, Z. A. (2015). The transition experiences, activities, and supports of four college students with disabilities. *Career Development and Transition for Exceptional Individuals, 38,* 162–172.

McCurdy, M., Skinner, C., Watson, S., & Shriver, M. (2008). Examining the effects of a comprehensive writing program on the writing performance of middle school students with learning disabilities in written expression. *School Psychology Quarterly, 23,* 571–586.

McLeskey, J., & Waldron, N. L. (2011). Educational programs for elementary students with learning disabilities: Can they be both effective and inclusive? *Learning Disabilities Research & Practice, 26,* 48–57.

McLeskey, J., Landers, E., Hoppey, D., & Williamson, P. (2011). Learning disabilities and the LRE mandate: An examination of national and state trends. *Learning Disabilities Research & Practice, 26,* 60–66.

McPhail, J. C., & Freeman, J. G. (2005). Beyond prejudice: Thinking toward genuine inclusion. *Learning Disabilities Research and Practice, 20,* 254–267.

Melekoglu, M. A. (2011). Impact of motivation to read on reading gains for struggling readers with and without learning disabilities. *Learning Disability Quarterly, 34,* 248–261.

Milligan, K., Phillips, M., & Morgan, A. S. (2015). Tailoring social competence interventions for children with learning disabilities. *Journal of Child and Family Studies, 25,* 856–869.

Montague, M. (2008). Self-regulation strategies to improve mathematical problem solving for students with learning disabilities. *Learning Disability Quarterly, 31,* 37–44.

Montague, M., Enders, C., & Dietz, S. (2011). Effects of cognitive strategy instruction on math problem solving of middle school students with learning disabilities. *Learning Disability Quarterly, 34,* 262–272.

Mulligan, G., Halle, T., & Kinukawa, A. (2012). *Reading, mathematics, and science achievement of language-minority students in grade 8* [Issue Brief. NCES 2012-028]. Washington, DC: National Center For Education Statistics.

Murray, D., Goldstein, D. E., Nourse, S., & Edgar, E. (2000). The postsecondary school attendance and completion rates of high school graduates with learning disabilities. *Learning Disabilities Research and Practice, 15,* 119–127.

Myers, D. M., Simonsen, B., & Sugai, G. (2011). Increasing teachers' use of praise with a response-to-intervention approach. *Education & Treatment of Children, 34*(1), 35–59.

National Center for Education Statistics. (2015). Percentage distribution of students 6 to 21 years old served under Individuals with Disabilities Education Act (IDEA), Part B, by educational environment and type of disability: Selected years, fall 1989 through fall 2012 [Table 204.60]. In *Digest of Education Statistics.* Washington, DC: U.S. Department of Education. Retrieved from http://nces.ed.gov/programs/digest/d14/tables/dt14_204.60.asp.

National Center for Education Statistics. (2016, May). *Children and youth with disabilities.* Washington, DC: U.S. Department of Education. Retrieved from http://nces.ed.gov/programs/coe/indicator_cgg.asp.

National Institute for Direct Instruction. (2012). *About direct instruction (DI).* Retrieved from http://www.nifdi.org/15/about-di

National Institute for Direct Instruction. (2016). Basic philosophy of direct instruction. Retrieved from http://www.nifdi.org/what-is-di/basic-philosophy.

National Institute of Child Health and Human Development. (2007). *Down syndrome.* Washington, DC: National Institutes of Health. Retrieved from http://www.nichd.nih.gov/health/topics/Down_Syndrome.cfm

National Institute of Child Health and Human Development. (2014a, February). Learning disabilities: Condition information. Bethesda, MD: Author. Retrieved from https://www.nichd.nih.gov/health/topics/learning/conditioninfo/Pages/default.aspx.

National Institute of Child Health and Human Development. (2014b, February). *What causes learning disabilities?* Washington, DC: National Institutes of Health. Retrieved from https://www.nichd.nih.gov/health/topics/learning/conditioninfo/Pages/causes.aspx.

National Institute of Neurological Disorders and Stroke. (2009, March). *Dyslexia information page*. Bethesda, MD: Author. Retrieved from http://www.ninds.nih.gov/disorders/dyslexia/dyslexia.htm

National Joint Committee on Learning Disabilities. (1990, January). *Learning disabilities: Issues on definition*. Rockville, MD: Author. Retrieved from www.ldonline.org/njcld/defn_91.html

National Joint Committee on Learning Disabilities. (2007). Learning disabilities and young children: Identification and intervention. *Learning Disability Quarterly, 30,* 63–72.

National Joint Committee on Learning Disabilities. (2009, June). *NJCLD factsheet*. Retrieved from http://www.ncld.org/content/view/500/389/

National Joint Committee on Learning Disabilities. (2011). Learning disabilities: Implications for policy regarding research and practice: A report by the National Joint Committee on Learning Disabilities 2011. *Learning Disability Quarterly, 34,* 237–241.

National Joint Committee on Learning Disabilities. (2015). *LD on-line: National Joint Committee on Learning Disabilities*. Retrieved from http://www.ldonline.org/about/partners/njcld.

Nelson, P. M., Burns, M. K., Kanive, R., & Ysseldyke, J. E. (2013). Comparison of a math fact rehearsal and a mnemonic strategy approach for improving math fact fluency. *Journal of School Psychology, 51,* 659–667.

Ortiz, A. A., Robertson, P. M., Wilkinson, C. Y., Liu, Y., McGhee, B. D., & Kushner, M. I. (2011). The role of bilingual education teachers in preventing inappropriate referrals of ELLs to special education: Implications for response to intervention. *Bilingual Research Journal, 34,* 316–333.

Pastor, P. N., & Reuben, C. A. (2008). *Diagnosed attention deficit hyperactivity disorder and learning disability: United States, 2004–2006*. Atlanta, GA: National Center for Health Statistics, Vital Health Statistics. Retrieved from http://www.cdc.gov/nchs/fastats/adhd.htm

Peng, P., & Fuchs, D. (2016). A meta-analysis of working memory deficits in children with learning difficulties: Is there a difference between verbal domain and numerical domain? *Journal of Learning Disabilities, 49,* 3–20.

Peterson-Karlan, G. R. (2011). Technology to support writing by students with learning and academic disabilities: Recent research trends and findings. *Assistive Technology Outcomes and Benefits, 7*(1), 39–62.

Peterson-Karlan, G. R. (2011). Technology to support writing by students with learning and academic disabilities: Recent research trends and findings. *Assistive Technology Outcomes and Benefits, 7*(1), 39–62.

Petryshen, T. L., & Pauls, D. L. (2009). The genetics of reading disability. *Current Psychiatry Reports, 11,* 149–155.

Pfannenstiel, K. H., Bryant, D. P., Bryant, B. R., & Porterfield, J. A. (2015). Cognitive strategy instruction for teaching word problems to primary-level struggling students. *Intervention in School and Clinic, 50,* 291–296.

Prater, M. A., Redman, A. S., Anderson, D., & Gibb, G. S. (2014). Teaching adolescent students with learning disabilities to self-advocate for accommodations. *Intervention in School and Clinic, 49,* 298–305.

Rabren, K., Eaves, R. C., Dunn, C., & Darch, C. (2013). Students with learning disabilities' satisfaction, employment, and postsecondary education outcomes. *Journal of Education and Learning, 2*(2), 14–22.

Rea, P. J., McLaughlin, V. L., & Walther-Thomas, C. (2002). Outcomes for students with learning disabilities in inclusive and pullout programs. *Exceptional Children, 68,* 203–222.

Reschly, D. J., & Hosp, J. L. (2004). State SLD identification policies and practices. *Learning Disability Quarterly, 27,* 197–213.

Ritchey, K. D., Silverman, R. D., Montanaro, E. A., Speece, D. L., & Schatschneider, C. (2012). Effects of a tier 2 supplemental reading intervention for at-risk fourth-grade students. *Exceptional Children, 78,* 318–334.

Rodriguez, R. J., Blatz, E. T., & Elbaum, B. (2014). Parents' views of schools' involvement efforts. *Exceptional Children, 81,* 79–95.

Rosenberg, J., Pennington, B. F., Willcutt, E. G., & Olson, R. K. (2012). Gene by environment interactions influencing reading disability and the inattentive symptom dimension of attention deficit/hyperactivity disorder. *Journal of Child Psychology and Psychiatry, 53,* 243–251.

Rupley, W. H., Blair, T. R., & Nichols, W. D. (2009). Effective reading instruction for struggling readers: The role of direct/explicit teaching. *Reading and Writing Quarterly, 25,* 125–138.

Sailor, W. (2015). Advances in schoolwide inclusive school reform. *Remedial and Special Education, 36*(2), 94–99.

Sanetti, L. H., & Collier-Meek, M. A. (2015). Data-driven delivery of implementation supports in a multi-tiered framework: A pilot study. *Psychology in the Schools, 52,* 815–828.

Sapon-Shevin, M. (2003). Inclusion: A matter of social justice. *Educational Leadership, 61*(2), 25–28.

Sayeski, K. L. (2011). Effective spelling instruction for students with learning disabilities. *Intervention in School & Clinic, 47,* 75–81.

Scanlon, D. (2013). Specific learning disability and its newest definition: Which is comprehensive? and which is insufficient? *Journal of Learning Disabilities, 46,* 26–33.

Schiff, R., Bauminger, N., & Toledo, I. (2009). Analogical problem solving in children with verbal and nonverbal learning disabilities. *Journal of Learning Disabilities, 42,* 3–13.

Schrank, F. A., Mather, N., & McGrew, K. S. (2014a). *Woodcock-Johnson IV Tests of Achievement*. Rolling Meadows, IL: Riverside.

Schrank, F. A., Mather, N., & McGrew, K. S. (2014b). *Woodcock-Johnson IV Tests of Oral Language*. Rolling Meadows, IL: Riverside.

Schrank, F. A., McGrew, K. S., & Mather, N. (2014c). *Woodcock-Johnson IV Tests of Cognitive Abilities*. Rolling Meadows, IL: Riverside.

Schumaker, J. B., & Deshler, D. D. (2009). Adolescents with learning disabilities as writers: Are we selling them short? *Learning Disabilities Research and Practice, 24,* 81–92.

Sebag, R. (2010). Behavior management through self-advocacy: A strategy for secondary students with learning disabilities. *Teaching Exceptional Children, 42*(6), 22–29.

Semrud-Clikeman, M., Walkowiak, J., Wilkinson, A., & Minne, E. (2010). Direct and indirect measures of social perception, behavior, and emotional functioning in children with Asperger's disorder, nonverbal learning disability, or ADHD. *Journal of Abnormal Child Psychology, 38,* 509–519.

Sharabi, A., & Margalit, M. (2011). The mediating role of Internet connection, virtual friends, and mood in predicting loneliness among students with and without learning disabilities in different educational environments. *Journal of Learning Disabilities, 44,* 215–227.

Shaw, S. F., Dukes, L. L., & Madaus, J. W. (2012). Beyond compliance: Using the summary of performance to enhance transition planning. *Teaching Exceptional Children, 44*(5), 6–12.

Shifrer, D. (2013). Stigma of a label: Educational expectations for high school students labeled with learning disabilities. *Journal of Health and Social Behavior, 54,* 462–480.

Siegel, L. S., & Smythe, I. S. (2005). Reflections on research on reading disability with special attention to gender issues. *Journal of Learning Disabilities, 38,* 473–477.

Silver, L. B. (2004). *Reading and learning disabilities* [Briefing paper 17]. Washington, DC: National Dissemination Center for Children with Disabilities. Retrieved from www.nichcy.org/pubs/factshe/fs17txt.htm

Silver, L. B., & Silver, D. L. (2014). Guide to learning disabilities for primary care: How to screen, identify, manage, and advocate for children with learning disabilities. Elk Grove Village, IL: American Academy of Pediatrics.

Skiba, R. J., Simmons, A. B., Ritter, S., Gibb, A. C., Rausch, M. K., Cuadrado, J., & Chung, C. G. (2008). Achieving equity in special education: History, status, and current challenges. *Exceptional Children, 74,* 264–288.

Smith, C. R. (1998). History, definitions, and prevalence. In *Learning disabilities: The interaction of learner, task, and setting* (4th ed., pp. 1–51). Boston, MA: Allyn & Bacon.

Smith, C. R. (2004). *Learning disabilities: The interaction of learner, task, and setting* (5th ed.). Boston, MA: Allyn & Bacon.

Smith, T. J., & Wallace, S. (2011). Social skills of children in the U.S. with comorbid learning disabilities and AD/HD. *International Journal of Special Education, 26,* 238–247.

Snowling, M. J., & Hulme, C. (2012). Annual research review: The nature and classification of reading disorders–a commentary on proposals for DSM-5. *Journal of Child Psychology and Psychiatry, 53,* 593–607.

Snowling, M. J., & Melby-Lervåg, M. (2016). Oral language deficits in familial dyslexia: A meta-analysis and review. *Psychological Bulletin,* doi:10.1037/bul0000037.

Solis, M., Ciullo, S., Vaughn, S., Pyle, N., Hassaram, B., & Leroux, A. (2012). Reading comprehension interventions for middle school students with learning disabilities: A synthesis of 30 years of research. *Journal of Learning Disabilities, 45,* 327–340.

Spear-Swerling, L., & Cheesman, E. (2012). Teachers' knowledge base for implementing response-to-intervention models in reading. *Reading and Writing: An Interdisciplinary Journal, 25,* 1691–1723.

Starr, E. M., Foy, J. B., Cramer, K. M., & Singh, H. (2006). How are schools doing? Parental perceptions of children with autism spectrum disorders, Down syndrome, and learning disabilities: A comparative analysis. *Education and Training in Developmental Disabilities, 41,* 315–332.

Stecker, P. M., Lembke, E. S., & Foegen, A. (2008). Using progress-monitoring data to improve instructional decision making. *Preventing School Failure, 52*(2), 48–58.

Strauss, A., & Lehtinen, L. (1947). *Psychopathology and education of the brain-injured child.* New York, NY: Grune & Stratton.

Strauss, S. L., Goodman, K. S., & Paulson, E. J. (2009). Brain research and reading: How emerging concepts in neuroscience support a meaning construction view of the reading process. *Educational Research and Review, 4*(2), 21–33.

Stuebing, K. K., Fletcher, J. M., Branum-Martin, L., & Francis, D. J. (2012). Evaluation of the technical adequacy of three methods for identifying specific learning disabilities based on cognitive discrepancies. *School Psychology Review, 41,* 3–22.

Suggate, S. P. (2016). A meta-analysis of the long-term effects of phonemic awareness, phonics, fluency, and reading comprehension interventions. *Journal of Learning Disabilities, 49,* 77–96.

Sullivan, A. L. (2011). Disproportionality in special education identification and placement of English language learners. *Exceptional Children, 77,* 317–334.

Swanson, E. A., & Vaughn, S. (2010). An observation study of reading instruction provided to elementary students with learning disabilities in the resource room. *Psychology in the Schools, 47,* 481–492.

Swanson, H. L., Zheng, X., & Jerman, O. (2009). Working memory, short-term memory, and reading disabilities: A selective meta-analysis of the literature. *Journal of Learning Disabilities, 42,* 260–287.

Tanaka, H., Black, J. M., Hulme, C., Stanley, L. M., Kesler, S. R., Whitfield-Gabrieli, S., . . . Hoeft, F. (2011). The brain basis of the phonological deficit in dyslexia is independent of IQ. *Psychological Science, 22,* 1442–1451.

Toll, S. M., Van der Ven, S. G., Kroesbergen, E. H., & Van Luit, J. H. (2011). Executive functions as predictors of math learning disabilities. *Journal of Learning Disabilities, 44,* 521–532.

Torgesen, J. K., Foorman, B. R., & Wagner, R. K. (n.d.). *Dyslexia: A brief for educators, parents, and legislators in Florida.* Tallahassee: Florida Center for Reading Research. Retrieved from http://www.fcrr.org/TechnicalReports/Dyslexia_Technical_Assistance_Paper-Final.pdf

Tran, L., Sanchez, T., Arellano, B., & Swanson, H. L. (2011). A meta-analysis of the RTI literature for children at risk for reading disabilities. *Journal of Learning Disabilities, 44,* 283–295.

Tremaine Foundation. (2010, September). *Measuring progress in public & parental understanding of learning disabilities.* Retrieved from http://www.tremainefoundation.org/images/customer-files/TremaineReportofFindingsSeptember2010.pdf

Tremblay, P. (2013). Comparative outcomes of two instructional models for students with learning disabilities: Inclusion with co-teaching and solo-taught special education. *Journal of Research in Special Educational Needs, 13,* 251–258.

U.S. Department of Education. (1993). *Fifteenth annual report to Congress on the implementation of IDEA.* Washington, DC: Author.

U. S. Department of Education. (2004). *Twenty-sixth annual report to Congress on the implementation of the Individuals with Disabilities Education Act.* Washington, DC: Author.

U.S. Department of Education. (2011, July). *OMB #1820-0043: Children with disabilities receiving special education under part B of the Individuals with Disabilities Education Act, 2010.* Washington, DC: Office of Special Education Programs, Data Analysis System (DANS).

U.S. Department of Education. (2015). *37th annual report to Congress on the implementation of the Individuals with Disabilities Education Act, 2015.* Washington, DC: Office of Special Education and Rehabilitative Services, Office of Special Education Programs. Retrieved from http://www.ed.gov/about/reports/annual/osep.

Van der Molen, M. J., Henry, L. A., & Van Luit, J. E. H. (2014). Working memory development in children with mild to borderline intellectual disabilities. *Journal of Intellectual Disability Research, 58*(7), 637–650.

Vellutino, F. R., Scanlon, D. M., Small, S., & Faneule, D. P. (2006). Response to intervention as a vehicle for distinguishing between children with and without reading disabilities: Evidence for the role of kindergarten and first-grade interventions. *Journal of Learning Disabilities, 39,* 157–169.

Volonino, V., & Zigmond, N. (2007). Promoting research-based practices through inclusion. *Theory into Practice, 46,* 291–300.

Vujnovic, R. K., Fabiano, G. A., Morris, K. L., Norman, K., Hallmark, C., & Hartley, C. (2014). Examining school psychologists' and teachers' application of approaches within a response to intervention framework. *Exceptionality, 22,* 129–140.

Wadlington, E., & Wadlington, P. L. (2008). Helping students with mathematical disabilities to succeed. *Preventing School Failure, 53,* 2–7.

Walker, A. R., & Test, D. W. (2011). Using a self-advocacy intervention on African American college students' ability to request academic accommodations. *Learning Disabilities Research & Practice, 26,* 134–144.

Wechsler, D. (2003). *Wechsler intelligence scale for children–IV.* San Antonio, TX: Psychological Corporation.

Wechsler, D. (2014). *Wechsler Intelligence Scale for Children* (5th ed.) (WISC-V). Bloomington, MN: Psych Corp/Pearson.

Wehmeyer, M. L., Palmer, S. B., Shogren, K., Williams-Diehm, K., & Soukup, J. H. (2013). Establishing a causal relationship between intervention to promote self-determination and enhanced student self-determination. *Journal of Special Education, 46,* 195–210.

Wei, X., Yu, J. W., & Shaver, D. (2014). Longitudinal effects of ADHD in children with learning disabilities or emotional disturbances. *Exceptional Children, 80,* 205–219.

Wheldall, K., & Limbrick, L. (2010). Do more boys than girls have reading problems? *Journal of Learning Disabilities, 43,* 418–429.

Wilkinson, C. Y., Ortiz, A. A., Robertson, P. M., & Kushner, M. I. (2006). English language learners with reading related LD: Linking data from multiple sources to make eligibility decisions. *Journal of Learning Disabilities, 39,* 129–141.

Woodcock, R. W., McGrew, K. S., Schrank, F. A., & Mather, N. (2007). *Woodcock-Johnson III-Normative Update*. Rolling Meadows, IL: Riverside.

Zera, D. A., & Lucian, D. G. (2001). Self-organization and learning disabilities: A theoretical perspective for the interpretation and understanding of dysfunction. *Learning Disability Quarterly, 24*, 107–118.

Zirkel, P. A. (2011a). RTI confusion in the case law and the legal commentary. *Learning Disability Quarterly, 34*, 242–247.

Zirkel, P. A. (2011b). What does the law say? *Teaching Exceptional Children, 43*(3), 65–67.

Zumeta, R. O., Zirkel, P. A., & Danielson, L. (2014). Identifying specific learning disabilities: Legislation, regulation, and court decisions. *Topics in Language Disorders, 34*, 8–24.

Chapter 6

Achenbach, T. M. (1991). *Child behavior checklist, teacher's report form*. Burlington, VT: Author.

Achenbach, T. M., & Rescorla, L. A. (2007). *Manual for ASEBA school-age forms & profiles*. Burlington: University of Vermont, Research Center for Children, Youth, & Families.

Adler, L. A., Spencer, T., & McGough, J. J. (2009). Long-term effectiveness and safety of dexmethylphenidate extended-release capsules in adult ADHD. *Journal of Attention Disorders, 12*, 449–459.

Advokat, C. (2009). What exactly are the benefits of stimulants for ADHD? *Journal of Attention Disorders, 12*, 495–498.

Agency for Toxic Substances and Disease Registry (ATSDR). (2007, August). *Case studies in environmental medicine (CSEM): Lead toxicity—What are the physiologic effects of lead exposure?* Atlanta, GA: Centers for Disease Control and Prevention. Retrieved from http://www.atsdr.cdc.gov/csem/lead/pbphysiologic_effects2.html#child

Akutagava-Martins, G. C., Rohde, L. A., & Hutz, M. H. (2016). Genetics of attention-deficit/hyperactivity disorder: An update. *Expert Review of Neurotherapeutics, 16*, 145–156.

Al-Yagon, M. (2016). Perceived close relationships with parents, teachers, and peers predictors of social, emotional, and behavioral features in adolescents with LD or comorbid LD and ADHD. *Journal of Learning Disabilities, 49*, 597–615.

American Academy of Pediatrics. (2000). Clinical practice guideline: Diagnosis and evaluation of the child with attention-deficit/hyperactivity disorder. *Pediatrics, 105*, 1158–1170.

American Academy of Pediatrics. (2011). ADHD: Clinical practice guideline for the diagnosis, evaluation, and treatment of attention-deficit/hyperactivity disorder in children and adolescents. *Pediatrics, 128*, 1007–1022.

American Psychiatric Association. (1980). *Diagnostic and statistical manual of mental disorders* (3rd edition). Washington, DC: Author.

American Psychiatric Association. (1994). *Diagnostic and statistical manual of mental disorders* (4th ed.). Washington, DC: Author.

American Psychiatric Association. (2000). *Diagnostic and statistical manual of mental disorders* (4th ed., Text revision). Washington, DC: Author.

American Psychiatric Association. (2013). *Diagnostic and statistical manual of mental disorders* (5th ed.). Washington, DC: Author.

Arnold, L. (1995). ADHD sex differences. *Journal of Abnormal Child Psychology, 23*, 555–569.

Arnsten, A. F., & Berridge, C. W. (2015). Catecholamine influences on prefrontal cortex circuits and function. In L. A. Adler, T. J. Spencer, & T. E. Wilens (Eds.), *Attention-deficit hyperactivity disorder in adults and children* (pp. 161–173). New York, NY: Cambridge University Press.

Assouline, S. G., & Whiteman, C. S. (2011). Twice-exceptionality: Implications for school psychologists in the post–IDEA 2004 era. *Journal of Applied School Psychology, 27*, 380–402.

Babinski, D. E., Pelham, W. R., Molina, B. G., Gnagy, E. M., Waschbusch, D. A., Yu, J., . . . Karch, K. M. (2011). Late adolescent and young adult outcomes of girls diagnosed with ADHD in childhood: An exploratory investigation. *Journal of Attention Disorders, 15*, 204–214.

Baldwin, L., Omdal, S. N., & Pereles, D. (2015). Beyond stereotypes: Understanding, recognizing, and working with twice-exceptional learners. *Teaching Exceptional Children, 47*(4), 216–225.

Barkley, R. A. (2006). ADHD in adults: Developmental course and outcome of children with ADHD, and ADHD in clinic-referred adults. In R. A. Barkley (Ed.), *Attention-deficit hyperactivity disorder: A handbook for diagnosis and treatment* (pp. 248–296). New York, NY: Guilford Press.

Barkley, R. A. (2012). *Executive functions: What they are, how they work, and why they evolved*. New York, NY: Guilford Press.

Barkley, R. A. (2015). History of ADHD. In R. A. Barkley (Ed.), *Attention-deficit hyperactivity disorder: A handbook for diagnosis and treatment* (4th ed.) (pp. 1–2). New York, NY: Guilford Press.

Barkley, R. A., et al. (2002). International consensus statement on ADHD. *Clinical Child and Family Psychology Review, 5*, 89–111.

Barnett, B., Corkum, P., & Elik, N. (2012). A web-based intervention for elementary school teachers of students with attention-deficit/hyperactivity disorder (ADHD). *Psychological Services, 9*, 227–230.

Basch, C. E. (2011). Inattention and hyperactivity and the achievement gap among urban minority youth. *Journal of School Health, 81*, 641–649.

Bauermeister, J. J., Canino, G., Polanczyk, G., & Rohde, L. A. (2010). ADHD across cultures: Is there evidence for a bidimensional organization of symptoms? *Journal of Clinical Child and Adolescent Psychology, 39*, 362–372.

Baumeister, A. A., Henderson, K., Pow, J., & Advokat, C. (2012). The early history of the neuroscience of attention-deficit/hyperactivity disorder. *Journal of the History of the Neurosciences, 21*, 263–279.

Berridge, C. W., & Arnsten, A. F. (2015). Catecholamine mechanisms in the prefrontal cortex: proven strategies for enhancing higher cognitive function. *Current Opinion in Behavioral Sciences, 4*, 33–40.

Biederman, J. (2003). Pharmacotherapy for attention-deficit/hyperactivity disorder (ADHD) decreases the risk for substance abuse: Findings from a longitudinal follow-up of youths with and without ADHD. *Journal of Clinical Psychiatry, 64*, 3–8.

Biederman, J., Ball, S. W., & Monuteaux, M. C. (2008). New insights into the comorbidity between ADHD and major depression in adolescent and young adult females. *Journal of the American Academy of Child & Adolescent Psychiatry, 47*, 426–434.

Biederman, J., Wilens, T., Mick, E., Spencer, T., & Faraone, S. V. (1999b). Pharmacotherapy of attention-deficit/hyperactivity disorder reduces risk for substance use disorder. *Pediatrics, 104*(2), 20.

Birchwood, J., & Daley, D. (2012). Brief report: The impact of attention deficit hyperactivity disorder (ADHD) symptoms on academic performance in an adolescent community sample. *Journal of Adolescence, 35*, 225–231.

Bramham, J., Young, S., Bickerdike, A., Spain, D., McCartan, D., & Xenitidis, K. (2009). Evaluation of group cognitive behavioral therapy for adults with ADHD. *Journal of Attention Disorders, 12*, 434–441.

Brennan, A. R., & Arnsten, F. T. (2008). Neuronal mechanisms underlying attention deficit hyperactivity disorder: The influence of arousal on prefrontal cortical function. *Annals of the New York Academy of Science, 1129*, 236–245.

Brieber, S., Neufang, S., Bruning, N., Kamp-Becker, I., Remschmidt, H., Herpertz-Dahlmann, B., Fink, G. R., . . . Konrad, K. (2007). Structural brain abnormalities in adolescents with autism spectrum disorder and patients with attention deficit/hyperactivity disorder. *Journal of Child Psychology and Psychiatry, 48*, 1251–1258.

Bubnik, M. G., Hawk, L. J., Pelham, W. J., Waxmonsky, J. G., & Rosch, K. S. (2015). Reinforcement enhances vigilance among children with ADHD: Comparisons to typically developing children and to the effects of methylphenidate. *Journal of Abnormal Child Psychology, 43*, 149–161.

Buitelaar, J. K. (2012). Adolescence as a turning point: For better and worse. *European Child & Adolescent Psychiatry, 21*, 357–359.

Buoli, M., Serati, M., & Cahn, W. (2016). Alternative pharmacological strategies for adult ADHD treatment: A systematic review. *Expert Review of Neurotherapeutics, 16*, 131–144.

Burke, J. D., & Loeber, R. (2015). The effectiveness of the Stop Now and Plan (SNAP) Program for boys at risk for violence and delinquency. *Prevention Science, 16*, 242–253.

Bussing, R., Koro-Ljungberg, M., Gurnani, T., Garvan, C. W., Mason, D., Noguchi, K., & Albarracin, D. (2015). Willingness to use ADHD self-management: Mixed methods study of perceptions by adolescents and parents. *Journal of Child and Family Studies, 25*, 562–573.

Bussing, R., Koro-Ljungberg, M., Noguchi, K., Mason, D., Mayerson, G., & Garvan, C. W. (2012a). Willingness to use ADHD treatments: A mixed methods study of perceptions by adolescents, parents, health professionals and teachers. *Social Science & Medicine, 74*, 92–100.

Bussing, R., Meyer, J., Zima, B. T., Mason, D. M., Gary, F. A., & Garvan, C. W. (2015). Childhood ADHD symptoms: Association with parental social networks and mental health service use during adolescence. *International Journal of Environmental Research and Public Health, 12*, 11893–11909.

Bussing, R., Zima, B. T., Mason, D. M., Meyer, J. M., White, K., & Garvan, C. W. (2012). ADHD knowledge, perceptions, and information sources: Perspectives from a community sample of adolescents and their parents. *Journal of Adolescent Health.* doi:10.1016/j.jadohealth.2012.03.004

Bussing, R., Zima, B. T., Mason, D. M., Meyer, J. M., White, K., & Garvan, C. W. (2012b). ADHD knowledge, perceptions, and information sources: Perspectives from a community sample of adolescents and their parents. *Journal of Adolescent Health.* doi:10.1016/j.jadohealth.2012.03.004

Canu, W. H., & Mancil, E. B. (2012). An examination of teacher trainees' knowledge of attention-deficit/hyperactivity disorder. *School Mental Health, 4*, 105–114.

Capelatto, I. V., de Lima, R. F., Ciasca, S. M., & Salgado-Azoni, C. A. (2014). Cognitive functions, self-esteem and self-concept of children with attention deficit and hyperactivity disorder. *Psicologia: Reflexão E Crítica, 27*, 331–340.

Cardoos, S. L., & Hinshaw, S. P. (2011). Friendship as protection from peer victimization for girls with and without ADHD. *Journal of Abnormal Child Psychology, 39*, 1035–1045.

Casey, B. J., & Durston, S. (2014). The impact of stimulants on cognition and the brain in attention-deficit/hyperactivity disorder: What does age have to do with it? *Biological Psychiatry, 76*, 596–598.

Centers for Disease Control and Prevention. (2011). *Attention-deficit/hyperactivity disorder (ADHD): Data and statistics.* Atlanta, GA: Author. Retrieved from http://www.cdc.gov/ncbddd/adhd/data.html

Centers for Disease Control and Prevention. (2011, July 1). QuickStats: Percentage of children aged 5–17 years ever receiving a diagnosis of learning disability, by race/ethnicity and family income group—National Health Interview Survey, United States, 2007–2009. *Morbidity and Mortality Weekly Report.* Atlanta, GA: Author. Retrieved from http://www.cdc.gov/mmwr/preview/mmwrhtml/mm6025a6.htm?s_cid=mm6025a6_w

Centers for Disease Control and Prevention. (2011, June). *Developmental disabilities increasing in US.* Atlanta, GA: Author. Retrieved from http://www.cdc.gov/Features/dsDev_Disabilities/index.html

Centers for Disease Control and Prevention. (2011a). *Attention-deficit/hyperactivity disorder (ADHD): Data and statistics.* Atlanta, GA: Author. Retrieved from http://www.cdc.gov/ncbddd/adhd/data.html

Centers for Disease Control and Prevention. (2016, February). *Faststats: Attention deficit hyperactivity disorder (ADHD).* Atlanta, GA: U.S. Department of Health and Human Services. Retrieved from http://www.cdc.gov/nchs/fastats/adhd.htm

Centers for Disease Control and Prevention. (2016, January). *Facts about ADHD.* Atlanta, GA: U.S. Department of Health and Human Services. Retrieved from http://www.cdc.gov/ncbddd/adhd/facts.html

Chako, A., Wymbs, B. T., & Flammer-Rivera, L. M. (2008). A pilot study of the feasibility and efficacy of the strategies to enhance positive parenting (STEPP) program for single mothers of children with ADHD. *Journal of Attention Disorders, 12*, 270–280.

Chromik, L. C., Quintin, E. M., Lepage, J. F., Hustyi, K. M., Lightbody, A. A., & Reiss, A. L. (2015). The influence of hyperactivity, impulsivity, and attention problems on social functioning in adolescents and young adults with fragile X syndrome. *Journal of Attention Disorders.* DOI: 10.1177/1087054715571739

Coletti, D. J., Pappadopulos, E., Katsiotas, N. J., Berest, A., Jensen, P. S., & Vivian, K. (2012). Parent perspectives on the decision to initiate medication treatment of attention-deficit/hyperactivity disorder. *Journal of Child and Adolescent Psychopharmacology, 22*, 226–237.

Colson, S. E., & Brandt, M. D. (2000). Working with families of children with attention-deficit/hyperactivity disorder. In M. J. Fine & R. L. Simpson (Eds.), *Collaboration with parents and families of children and youth with exceptionalities* (2nd ed., pp. 347–367). Austin, TX: Pro-Ed.

Conners, C. K. (1997a). *Conners' Teacher Rating Scale—Revised (CTRS-R).* North Tonawanda, NY: Multi-Health Systems.

Conners, C. K. (1997b). *Conners' Parent Rating Scale—Revised (CPRS-R).* North Tonawanda, NY: Multi-Health Systems.

Conners, C. K. (2004). *Conners' continuous performance test II* (version 5). San Antonio, TX: Psychological Corporation.

Conners, C. K. (2014). *Conners Continuous Performance Test* (3rd ed.).

Connor, D. F. (2011, August). Problems of overdiagnosis and overprescribing in ADHD. *Psychiatric Times.* Retrieved from http://www.psychiatrictimes.com/adhd/problems-overdiagnosis-and-overprescribing-adhd/page/0/1

Craparo, G., Magnano, P., Gori, A., Passanisi, A., Lo Piccolo, A., & Pace, W. (2015). ADD symptoms, self-image and emotional intelligence in early adolescence. *Life Span and Disability 18*, 167–188.

Cukrowicz, K., Taylor, J., Schatschneider, C., & Iacono, W. (2006). Personality differences in children and adolescents with attention-deficit/hyperactivity disorder, conduct disorder, and controls. *Journal of Child Psychology and Psychiatry, 47*, 151–159.

Daley, D., Jacobsen, R. H., Lange, A. M., Soprensen, A., & Walldorf, J. (2015). *Costing adult attention deficit hyperactivity disorder: Impact on the individual and society.* Oxford, U.K.: Oxford University Press.

Davidson, M. A. (2008). ADHD in adults–A review of the literature. *Journal of Attention Disorders, 11*, 628–641.

de Luis-García, R., Cabús-Piñol, G., Imaz-Roncero, C., Argibay-Quiñones, D., Barrio-Arranz, G., Aja-Fernández, S., & Alberola-López, C. (2015). Attention deficit/hyperactivity disorder and medication with stimulants in young children: A DTI study. *Progress in Neuro-Psychopharmacology & Biological Psychiatry, 57*, 176–184.

de Zeeuw, P., Schnack, H. G., van Belle, J., Weusten, J., van Dijk, S., Langen, M., . . . Durston, S. (2012). Differential brain development with low and high IQ in attention-deficit/hyperactivity disorder. *Public Library of Science ONE, 7*(4).

Dipeolu, A., Hargrave, S., & Storlie, C. A. (2015). Enhancing ADHD and LD diagnostic accuracy using career instruments. *Journal of Career Development, 42*, 19–32.

Duerden, E. G., Tannock, R., & Dockstader, C. (2012). Altered cortical morphology in sensorimotor processing regions in adolescents and adults with attention-deficit/hyperactivity disorder. *Brain Research, 1445*, 82–91.

DuPaul, G. J., & Jimerson, S. R. (2014). Assessing, understanding, and supporting students with ADHD at school: Contemporary science, practice, and policy. *School Psychology Quarterly, 29*, 379–384.

DuPaul, G. J., & Kern, L. (2011). *Young children with ADHD: Early identification and intervention.* Washington, DC: American Psychological Association Books.

DuPaul, G. J., Kern, L., Gormley, M. J., & Volpe, R. J. (2011). Early intervention for young children with ADHD: Academic outcomes for responders to behavioral treatment. *School Mental Health, 3*, 117–126.

Eiraldi, R. B., Mautone, J. A., & Power, T. J. (2012). Strategies for implementing evidence-based psychosocial interventions for children with attention-deficit/hyperactivity disorder. *Child and Adolescent Psychiatric Clinics of North America, 21*, 145–159.

Eisenberg, D., & Schneider, H. (2007). Perceptions of academic skills of children diagnosed with ADHD. *Journal of Attention Disorders, 10*, 390–397.

Ekstein, S., Glick, B., Weill, M., Kay, B., & Berger, I. (2011). Down syndrome and attention-deficit/hyperactivity disorder (ADHD). *Journal of Child Neurology, 26*, 1290–1295.

Eli Lilly. (2003). *The history of ADHD.* Retrieved from www.strattera.com/1_3_childhood_adhd/1_3_1_1_2_history.jsp

Evans, S. W., Langberg, J. M., Schultz, B. K., Vaughn, A., Altaye, M., Marshall, S. A., & Zoromski, A. K. (2016). Evaluation of a school-based treatment program for young adolescents with ADHD. *Journal of Consulting and Clinical Psychology, 84*, 15–30.

Evans, S. W., Sibley, M., & Serpell, Z. N. (2009). Changes in caregiver strain over time in young adolescents with ADHD: The role of oppositional and delinquent behavior. *Journal of Attention Disorders, 12*, 516–524.

Fabiano, G. A., Vujnovic, R. K., Pelham, W. E., Waschbusch, D. A., Massetti, G. M., Pariseau, M. E., . . . Volker, M. (2010). Enhancing the effectiveness of special education programming for children with attention deficit hyperactivity disorder using a daily report card. *School Psychology Review, 39*, 219–239.

Fad, K. M. (1998). Success through collaboration. In C. A. Dowdy, J. R. Patton, T. E. C. Smith, & E. A. Polloway (Eds.), *Attention-deficit/hyperactivity disorder in the classroom: A practical guide for teachers* (pp. 173–194). Austin, TX: Pro-Ed.

Fletcher, J. M. (2014). The effects of childhood ADHD on adult labor market outcomes. *Health Economics, 23*, 159–181.

Foley-Nicpon, M., Assouline, S. G., & Fosenburg, S. (2015). The relationship between self-concept, ability, and academic programming among twice-exceptional youth. *Journal of Advanced Academics, 26*, 256–273.

Forness, S. R., & Kavale, K. A. (2001a). ADHD and a return to the medical model of special education. *Education and Treatment of Children, 24*, 224–247.

Fredriksen, M., & Peleikis, D. E. (2016). ADHD in older adults. *Neuropsychiatric Disease and Treatment, 118*, 23–31.

Friend, M., & Bursuck, W. (2009). *Including students with special needs: A practical guide for classroom teachers* (5th ed., pp. 447–449). Upper Saddle River, NJ: Pearson/Merrill.

Gerdes, A. C., Haack, L. M., & Schneider, B. W. (2012). Parental functioning in families of children with ADHD: Evidence for behavioral parent training and importance of clinically meaningful change. *Journal of Attention Disorders, 16*, 147–156.

Gilsbach, S., Neufang, S., Scherag, S., Vloet, T. D., Fink, G. R., Herpertz-Dahlmann, B., & Konrad, K. (2012). Effects of the DRD4 genotype on neural networks associated with executive functions in children and adolescents. *Developmental Cognitive Neuroscience, 2*, 417–427.

Graves, S. J., & Serpell, Z. (2013). Racial differences in medication use in a national sample of children with ADHD enrolled in special education. *School Mental Health, 5*, 175–182.

Greenhill, L., Kollins, S., Abikoff, H., McCracken, J., Riddle, M., Swanson, J., . . . Cooper, T. (2006). Efficacy and safety of immediate-release methylphenidate treatment for preschoolers with ADHD. *Journal of the American Academy of Child and Adolescent Psychiatry, 45*, 1284–1293.

Greenhill, L., Kollins, S., Abikoff, H., McCracken, J., Riddle, M., Swanson, J., . . . Cooper, T. (2006). Efficacy and safety of immediate-release emthylphenidate treatment for preschoolers with ADHD. *Journal of the American Academy of Child and Adolescent Psychiatry, 45*, 1284–1293.

Greven, C. U., Rijsdijk, F. V., & Plomin, R. (2011). A twin study of ADHD symptoms in early adolescence: Hyperactivity-impulsivity and inattentiveness show substantial genetic overlap but also genetic specificity. *Journal of Abnormal Child Psychology, 39*, 265–275.

Hall, C. L., Valentine, A. Z., Groom, M. J., Walker, G. M., Sayal, K., Daley, D., & Hollis, C. (2015). The clinical utility of the continuous performance test and objective measures of activity for diagnosing and monitoring ADHD in children: A systematic review. *European Child & Adolescent Psychiatry*, doi:10.1007/s00787-015-0798-x

Harty, S., Miller, C., Newcorn, J., & Halperin, J. (2009). Adolescents with childhood ADHD and comorbid disruptive behavior disorders: Aggression, anger, and hostility. *Child Psychiatry & Human Development, 40*, 85–97.

Harvey, E. A., Youngwirth, S. D., & Thakar, D. A. (2009). Predicting attention- deficit/hyperactivity disorder and oppositional defiant disorder from preschool diagnostic assessments. *Journal of Consulting and Clinical Psychology, 77*, 349–354.

Harzke, A., Baillargeon, J., Baillargeon, G., Henry, J., Olvera, R. L., Torrealday, O., & Parikh, R. (2012). Prevalence of psychiatric disorders in the Texas juvenile correctional system. *Journal of Correctional Health Care, 18*, 143–157.

Healthyplace.com. (2002, November). *Atomoxetine HCl.* Retrieved from http://healthyplace.com/medications/strattera.htm

Hinshaw, S. P., Owens, E. B., Zalecki, C., Huggins, S., Montenegro-Nevado, A. J., Schrodek, E., & Swanson, E. N. (2012). Prospective follow-up of girls with attention-deficit/hyperactivity disorder into early adulthood: Continuing impairment includes elevated risk for suicide attempts and self-injury. *Journal of Consulting and Clinical Psychology.* doi:10.1037/a0029451

Hosterman, S., DuPaul, G., & Jitendra, A. (2008). Teacher ratings of ADHD symptoms in ethnic minority students: Bias or behavioral difference? *School Psychology Quarterly, 23*, 418–435.

Howard, A. L., Strickland, N. J., Murray, D. W., Tamm, L., Swanson, J. M., Hinshaw, S. P., . . . Molina, B. G. (2016). Progression of impairment in adolescents with attention-deficit/hyperactivity disorder through the transition out of high school: Contributions of parent involvement and college attendance. *Journal of Abnormal Psychology, 125*, 233–247.

Huang-Pollock, C. L., Karalunas, S. L., Tam, H., & Moore, A. N. (2012). Evaluating vigilance deficits in ADHD: A meta-analysis of CPT performance. *Journal of Abnormal Psychology, 121*, 360–371.

Jacobson, L., & Reid, R. (2010). Improving the persuasive essay writing of high school students with ADHD. *Exceptional Children, 76*, 157–174.

Jarrett, M. A. (2016). Attention-deficit/hyperactivity disorder (ADHD) symptoms, anxiety symptoms, and executive functioning in emerging adults. *Psychological Assessment, 28*, 245–250.

Johnson, J. W., Reid, R., & Mason, L. H. (2012). Improving the reading recall of high school students with ADHD. *Remedial and Special Education, 33*, 258–268.

Jones, H., & Chronis-Tuscano, A. (2008). Efficacy of teacher in-service training for attention-deficit/hyper-activity disorder. *Psychology in the Schools, 45*, 918–929.

Karpouzis, F., & Bonello, R. (2012). Nutritional complementary and alternative medicine for pediatric attention-deficit/hyperactivity disorder. *Ethical Human Psychology and Psychiatry: An International Journal of Critical Inquiry, 14*(1), 41–60.

Pliszka, S. R. (2015). Comorbid psychiatric disorders in children with ADHD. In R. A. Barkley (Eds.), *Attention-deficit hyperactivity disorder: A handbook for diagnosis and treatment* (4th ed.) (pp. 314–342). New York, NY: Guilford Press.

Polanczyk, G. V., Salum, G. A., Sugaya, L. S., Caye, A., & Rohde, L. A. (2015). Annual research review: A meta-analysis of the worldwide prevalence of mental disorders in children and adolescents. *Journal of Child Psychology and Psychiatry, 56,* 345–365.

Powell, S. G., Frydenberg, M., & Thomsen, P. H. (2015). The effects of long-term medication on growth in children and adolescents with ADHD: An observational study of a large cohort of real-life patients. *Child and Adolescent Psychiatry and Mental Health, 9,* doi: 10.186/s13034-015-0082-3.

Power, T. J., Mautone, J. A., Marshall, S. A., Jones, H. A., Cacia, J., Tresco, K., ... Blum, N. J. (2014). Feasibility and potential effectiveness of integrated services for children with ADHD in urban primary care practices. *Clinical Practice in Pediatric Psychology, 2,* 412–426.

Rafalovich, A. (2001). The conceptual history of attention-deficit hyperactivity disorder: Idiocy, imbecility, encephalitis and the child deviant, 1877–1929. *Deviant Behavior: An Interdisciplinary Journal, 22,* 93–115.

Rafferty, L. A. (2010). Step-by-step: Teaching students to self-monitor. *Teaching Exceptional Children, 43*(2), 50–58.

Rajwan, E., Chacko, A., & Moeller, M. (2012). Nonpharmacological interventions for preschool ADHD: State of the evidence and implications for practice. *Professional Psychology: Research and Practice.* doi:10.1037/a0028812

Ramsay, J. R., & Rostain, A. L. (2016). Adult attention-deficit/hyperactivity disorder as an implementation problem: Clinical significance, underlying mechanisms, and psychosocial treatment. *Practice Innovations, 1*(1), 36–52.

Reis, E. M. (2002). Attention deficit hyperactivity disorder: Implications for the classroom teacher. *Journal of Instructional Psychology, 29,* 175–178.

Reitman, V. (2003, February 10). Attention deficit disorder in adults: A new drug could help people who have trouble focusing. But it's likely to sharpen the debate on the prevalence of the disorder and how it's diagnosed. *Los Angeles Times,* part 6, p. 1. Retrieved from www.latimes.com/features/health/la-he-srattera10feb10001516,1,5387828.story

Renshaw, D. C. (1974). *The hyperactive child.* Chicago, IL: Nelson-Hall.

Retz, W., Rösler, M., Ose, C., Scherag, A., Alm, B., Philipsen, A., ... Ammer, R. (2012). Multiscale assessment of treatment efficacy in adults with ADHD: A randomized placebo-controlled, multi-centre study with extended-release methylphenidate. *World Journal of Biological Psychiatry, 13*(1), 48–59.

Rinn, A. N., & Reynolds, M. J. (2012). Overexcitabilities and ADHD in the gifted: An examination. *Roeper Review, 34*(1), 38–45.

Roberts, G., Rane, S., Fall, A., Denton, C. A., Fletcher, J. M., & Vaughn, S. (2015). The impact of intensive reading intervention on level of attention in middle school students. *Journal of Clinical Child and Adolescent Psychology, 44,* 942–953.

Rogers, M. A., Wiener, J., Marton, I., & Tannock, R. (2009). Parental involvement in children's learning: Comparing parents of children with and without attention-deficit/hyperactivity disorder (ADHD). *Journal of School Psychology, 47,* 167–185.

Rubin, R. (2009, June 15). Sudden death in kids, ADHD drugs linked. *USA Today* [Online]. Retrieved from http://www.usatoday.com/news/health/2009-06-15-fda-adhd_N.htm

Sanford, J. A., & Turner, A. (2006). *Integrated Visual and Auditory Continuous Performance Test_PLUS.* Richmond, VA: BrainTrain.

Saul, R. (2014). *ADHD does not exist.* New York, NY: Harper Wave.

Schmitz, M. F., & Velez, M. (2003). Latino cultural differences in maternal assessments of attention deficit/hyperactivity symptoms in children. *Hispanic Journal of Behavioral Sciences, 25,* 110–122.

Schneider, H. E., Lam, J. C., & Mahone, E. M. (2016). Sleep disturbance and neuropsychological function in young children with ADHD. *Child Neuropsychology, 22,* 493–506.

Schuck, S. E. B., & Crinella, F. M. (2005). Why children with ADHD do not have low IQs. *Journal of Learning Disabilities, 38,* 262–280.

Sciutto, M. J., Terjesen, M. D., Kučerová, A., Michalová, Z., Schmiedeler, S., Antonopoulou, K., ... Rossouw, J. (2016). Cross-national comparisons of teachers' knowledge and misconceptions of ADHD. *International Perspectives in Psychology: Research, Practice, Consultation, 5,* 34–50.

Scudder, L. E., Lipkin, P. H., & Finding, R. L. (2015, March). ADHD: 2015's most important research. *Medscape: News and Perspectives.* Retrieved from http://www.medscape.com/viewarticle/848240

Serra-Pinheiro, M. A., Coutinho, E. F., Souza, I. S., Pinna, C., Fortes, D., Araujo, C., ... Mattos, P. (2013). Is ADHD a risk factor independent of conduct disorder for illicit substance use? A meta-analysis and meta-regression investigation. *Journal of Attention Disorders, 17,* 459–469.

Smith, B. H., & Shapiro, C. J. (2015). Combined treatments for ADHD. In R. A. Barkley (Eds.), *Attention-deficit hyperactivity disorder: A handbook for diagnosis and treatment* (4th ed.) (pp. 666–704). New York, NY: Guilford Press.

Smith, M. (2012). *Hyperactive: The controversial history of ADHD.* London, England: Rasktion Books.

Stolzer, J. M. (2012). The risks associated with stimulant medication use in child and adolescent populations diagnosed with attention-deficit hyperactivity disorder. *Ethical Human Psychology and Psychiatry: An International Journal of Critical Inquiry, 14*(1), 5–14.

Stormont, M., & Stebbins, M. (2005). Preschool teachers' knowledge, opinions and educational experiences with attention deficit/hyperactivity disorder. *Teacher Education and Special Education, 28,* 52–61.

Stringaris, A., & Goodman, R. (2009). Three dimensions of oppositionality in youth. *Journal of Child Psychology and Psychiatry, 50,* 216–223.

Swanson, J., Arnold, L. E., Kraemer, H., Hechtman, L., Molina, B., Hinshaw, S., ... Wigal, T. (2008). Evidence, interpretation, and qualification from multiple reports of long-term outcomes in the multimodal treatment study of children with ADHD (MTA): Part I–executive summary. *Journal of Attention Disorders, 12,* 4–14.

Tamm, L., & Juranek, J. (2012). Fluid reasoning deficits in children with ADHD: Evidence from fMRI. *Brain Research, 1465,* 48–56.

Toplak, M. E., Sorge, G. B., Flora, D. B., Chen, W., Banaschewski, T., Buitelaar, J., ... Faraone, S. V. (2012). The hierarchical factor model of ADHD: Invariant across age and national groupings? *Journal of Child Psychology and Psychiatry, 53,* 292–303.

U.S. Department of Education. (2008). *Teaching children with attention deficit hyperactivity disorder: Instructional strategies and practices.* Washington, DC: Office of Special Education and Rehabilitative Services, Office of Special Education Programs. Retrieved from https://www2.ed.gov/rschstat/research/pubs/adhd/adhd-teaching-2008.pdf

U.S. Department of Education. (2011, July). *OMB #1820-0043: Children with disabilities receiving special education under part B of the Individuals with Disabilities Education Act, 2010.* Washington, DC: Office of Special Education Programs, Data Analysis System (DANS).

U.S. Department of Education. (2015). *37th annual report to Congress on the implementation of the Individuals with Disabilities Education Act, 2015.* Washington, DC: Office of Special Education and Rehabilitative Services, Office of Special Education Programs. Retrieved from http://www.ed.gov/about/reports/annual/osep

Varley, C. K. (2011). Perspectives of adolescents with attention-deficit hyperactivity disorder do matter. *Journal of Adolescent Health, 49*(1), 1–2.

Vaughan, B. S., March, J. S., & Kratochvil, C. J. (2012). The evidence-based pharmacological treatment of paediatric ADHD. *International Journal of Neuropsychopharmacology, 15,* 27–39.

Visser S.N., Zablotsky B., Holbrook J.R., Danielson, M. L., & Bitsko, R. H. (2015, September). Diagnostic experiences of children with attention-deficit/hyperactivity disorder. *National Health Statistics Reports* [No. 81]. Hyattsville, MD: National Center for Health Statistics. 2015. Retrieved from http://www.cdc.gov/nchs/data/nhsr/nhsr081.pdf

Wasserstein, J., Wasserstein, A., & Wolf, L. E. (2001). *Adults with attention deficit hyperactivity disorder* (ERIC Digest). (ERIC Document Reproduction Service No. ED461959) Retrieved from http://libproxy.uncg.edu:2101/Webstore/Download.cfm?ID_689824&CFID_5160408&CFTOKEN_44519503

Wells, K. C., Pelham, Jr., W. E., Kotkin, R. A., Hoza, B., Abikoff, H. B., Abramowitz, A. A., et al. (2000). Psychosocial treatment strategies in the MTA study: Rationale, methods, and critical issues in design and implementation. *Journal of Abnormal Child Psychology, 28*, 483–505.

West, J., Taylor, M., Houghton, S., & Hudyma, S. (2005). A comparison of teachers' and parents' knowledge and beliefs about attention-deficit/ hyperactivity disorder (ADHD). *School Psychology International, 26*, 192–208.

Weyandt, L. L. (2006). Disorders of childhood origin. In *The physiological bases of cognitive and behavioral disorders* (pp. 231–266). Mahwah, NJ: Lawrence Erlbaum.

Weyandt, L. L., & Gudmundsdottir, B. G. (2015). Developmental and neuropsychological deficits in children with ADHD. In R. A. Barkley (Ed.), *Attention-deficit hyperactivity disorder: A handbook for diagnosis and treatment* (4th ed.) (pp. 81–115). New York, NY: Guilford Press.

Wiener, J., & Mak, M. (2009). Peer victimization in children with attention-deficit/ hyperactivity disorder. *Psychology in the Schools, 46*, 116–131.

Wiggs, K., Elmore, A. L., Nigg, J. T., & Nikolas, M. A. (2016). Pre- and perinatal risk for attention-deficit hyperactivity disorder: Does neuropsychological weakness explain the link? *Journal of Abnormal Child Psychology.* doi:10.1007/s10802-016-0142-z

Wills, H. P., & Mason, B. A. (2014). Implementation of a self-monitoring application to improve on-task behavior: A high-school pilot study. *Journal of Behavioral Education, 23*, 421–434.

Young, S., Gray, K., & Bramham, J. (2009). A phenomenological analysis of the experience of receiving a diagnosis and treatment of ADHD in adulthood: A partner's perspective. *Journal of Attention Disorders, 12*, 299–307.

Zachor, D. A., Roberts, A. W., Hodgens, J. B., Isaacs, J. S., & Merrick, J. (2006). Effects of long-term psychostimulant medication on growth of children with ADHD. *Research in Developmental Disabilities: A Multidisciplinary Journal, 27*, 162–174.

Zambo, D. (2008). Looking at ADHD through multiple lenses: Identifying girls with the inattentive type. *Intervention in School and Clinic, 44*(1), 34–40.

Zentall, S. S., Moon, S. M., Hall, A. M., & Grskovic, J. A. (2001). Learning and motivational characteristics of boys with AD/HD and/or giftedness. *Exceptional Children, 67*, 499–519.

Chapter 7

Abelev, M. S. (2009). Advancing out of poverty: Social class worldview and its relation to resilience. *Journal of Adolescent Research, 24*, 114–141.

Allday, R., Hinkson-Lee, K., Hudson, T., Neilsen-Gatti, S., Kleinke, A., & Russel, C. S. (2012). Training general educators to increase behavior-specific praise: Effects on students with EBD. *Behavioral Disorders, 37*, 87–98.

American Academy of Child and Adolescent Psychiatry. (2009, March). *Child and Adolescent Mental Illness Statistics.* Retrieved from http://www.aacap.org/cs/root/resources_for_families/child_and_adolescent_mental_illness_statistics

American Academy of Family Physicians. (2015, September). *Violence in the media and entertainment* (position paper). Leawood, KS: Author. Retrieved from http://www.aafp.org/about/policies/all/violence-media.html

American Academy of Pediatrics. (2006). *The 7 C's of resilience.* Retrieved from http://www2.aap.org/stress/childcopehome.htm

American Academy of Pediatrics. (2016, April). *Promoting children's mental health.* Elk Grove Village, IL: Author. Retrieved from https://www.aap.org/en-us/advocacy-and-policy/federal-advocacy/pages/mentalhealth.aspx

American Psychiatric Association. (2000). *Diagnostic and statistical manual of mental disorders* (4th ed., Text revision). Washington, DC: Author.

American Psychiatric Association. (2013). *Diagnostic and statistical manual of mental disorders* (5th ed.). Washington, DC: Author.

Anderson, C. M., Rodriguez, B. J., & Campbell, A. (2015). Functional behavior assessment in schools: Current status and future directions. *Journal of Behavioral Education, 24*, 338–371.

Avenevoli, S., Swendsen, J., He, J. P., Burstein, M., & Merikangas, K. R. (2015). Major depression in the National Comorbidity Survey—Adolescent Supplement: Prevalence, correlates, and treatment. *Journal of the American Academy of Child & Adolescent Psychiatry, 54*, 37–44.

Bagner, D. M., Coxe, S., Hungerford, G. M., Garcia, D., Barroso, N. E., Hernandez, J., & Rosa-Olivares, J. (2015). Behavioral parent training in infancy: A window of opportunity for high-risk families. *Journal of Abnormal Child Psychology.* doi:10.1007/s10802-015-0089-5

Bagner, D. M., Garcia, D., & Hill, R. (2016). Direct and indirect effects of behavioral parent training on infant language production. *Behavior Therapy, 47*, 184–197.

Bagner, D. M., Rodriguez, G. M., Blake, C. A., Linares, D., & Carter, A. S. (2012). Assessment of behavioral and emotional problems in infancy: A systematic review. *Clinical Child and Family Psychology Review, 15*, 113–128.

Balcazar, F. E., Taylor-Ritzler, T., Dimpfl, S., Portillo-Pena, N., Guzman, A., Schiff, R., & Murvay, M. (2012). Improving the transition outcomes of low-income minority youth with disabilities. *Exceptionality, 20*, 114–132.

Barbosa-Leiker, C., Fleming, S., Hollins Martin, C. J., & Martin, C. R. (2015). Psychometric properties of the Birth Satisfaction Scale-Revised (BSS-R) for U.S. mothers. *Journal of Reproductive and Infant Psychology, 33*, 504–511.

Bartels, M., van de Aa, N., van Beijsterveldt, C. M., Middeldorp, C. M., & Boomsma, D. I. (2011). Adolescent self-report of emotional and behavioral problems: Interactions of genetic factors with sex and age. *Journal of the Canadian Academy of Child and Adolescent Psychiatry/Journal de L'académie Canadienne de Psychiatrie de L'enfant et de L'adolescent, 20*, 35–52.

Basten, M., Tiemeier, H., Althoff, R. R., van de Schoot, R., Jaddoe, V. V., Hofman, A., ... van der Ende, J. (2016). The stability of problem behavior across the preschool years: An empirical approach in the general population. *Journal of Abnormal Child Psychology, 44*, 393–404.

Beauchaine, T. P. (2015). Future directions in emotion dysregulation and youth psychopathology. *Journal of Clinical Child & Adolescent Psychology, 44*, 875–896.

Beauchaine, T. P., Hinshaw, S. P., & Gatzke-Kopp, L. (2008). Genetic and environmental influences on behavior. In T. P. Beauchaine & S. P. Hinshaw (Eds.), *Child and adolescent psychopathology* (pp. 58–90). Hoboken, NJ: Wiley.

Beauchaine, T. P., Neuhaus, E., Brenner, S. L., & Gatzke-Kopp, L. (2008). Ten good reasons to consider biological processes in prevention and intervention research. *Development and Psychopathology, 20*, 745–774.

Benner, G. J., Kutash, K., Nelson, J. R., & Fisher, M. B. (2013). Closing the achievement gap of youth with emotional and behavioral disorders through multi-tiered systems of support. *Education and Treatment of Children, 36*(3), 15–29.

Benner, G. J., Nelson, J., Sanders, E. A., & Ralston, N. C. (2012). Behavior intervention for students with externalizing behavior problems: Primary-level standard protocol. *Exceptional Children, 78*, 181–198.

Benningfield, M. M., & Stephan, S. H. (2015). Integrating mental health into schools to support student success. *Child and Adolescent Psychiatric Clinics of North America, 24*(2), xv–xvii. doi:10.1016/j.chc.2014.12.005

Blood, E., Johnson, J. W., Ridenour, L., Simmons, K., & Crouch, S. (2011). Using an iPod Touch to teach social and self-management skills to an elementary student with emotional/behavioral disorders. *Education and Treatment of Children, 34*, 299–321.

Bountress, K., Chassin, L., & Lemery-Chalfant, K. (2016). Parent and peer influences on emerging adult substance use disorder: A genetically informed study. *Development and Psychopathology.* doi:10.1017/S095457941500125X

Bowman-Perrott, L. (2009). Classwide peer tutoring: An effective strategy for students with emotional and behavioral disorders. *Intervention in School and Clinic, 44*, 259–267.

Bradshaw, C. P., Waasdorp, T. E., & Leaf, P. J. (2015). Examining variation in the impact of SWPBS: Findings from a randomized controlled effectiveness trial. *Journal of Educational Psychology, 107*, 546–557.

Brauner, C. B., & Stephens, C. B. (2006). Estimating the prevalence of early childhood serious emotional/behavioral disorders: Challenges and recommendations. *Public Health Report, 121*, 303–310.

Brown, L., & Hammill, D. R. (1990). *Behavior rating profile.* Austin, TX: Pro-Ed.

Bruhn, A. L., Woods-Groves, S., & Huddle, S. (2014). A preliminary investigation of emotional and behavioral screening practices in K–12 schools. *Education and Treatment of Children, 37*, 611–634.

Burke, M. D., Davis, J. L., Lee, Y., Hagan-Burke, S., Kwok, O., & Sugai, G. (2012). Universal screening for behavioral risk in elementary schools using SWPBS expectations. *Journal of Emotional and Behavioral Disorders, 20*, 38–54.

Butler, J. (2015, July). *How safe is the schoolhouse? An analysis of state seclusion and restraint laws and policies.* Retrieved from http://www.autcom.org/pdf/HowSafeSchoolhouse.pdf

Castro-Olivo, S. M., Preciado, J. A., Sanford, A. K., & Perry, V. (2011). The academic and social-emotional needs of secondary Latino English learners: Implications for screening, identification, and instructional planning. *Exceptionality, 19*, 160–174.

Centers for Disease Control and Prevention. (2010, June). *CDC survey finds that 1 in 5 U.S. high school students have abused prescription drugs* [press release]. Retrieved from http://www.cdc.gov/media/pressrel/2010/r100603.htm

Centers for Disease Control and Prevention. (2012, August). *Violence prevention.* Atlanta, GA: Author. Retrieved from http://www.cdc.gov/ViolencePrevention/index.html

Children's Bureau. (2012). *Child maltreatment 2010.* Washington, DC: Department of Health and Human Services. Retrieved from http://www.acf.hhs.gov/programs/cb/stats_research/index.htm#can

Children's Bureau. (2016). *Child maltreatment 2014.* Washington, DC: U.S. Department of Health & Human Services, Administration for Children and Families, Administration on Children, Youth and Families. Available from http://www.acf.hhs.gov/programs/cb/research-data-technology/statistics-research/child-maltreatment

Chin, J. K., Dowdy, E., Jimerson, S. R., & Rime, W. (2012). Alternatives to suspensions: Rationale and recommendations. *Journal of School Violence, 11*, 156–173.

Chitiyo, M., May, M. E., & Chitiyo, G. (2012). An assessment of the evidence-base for school-wide positive behavior support. *Education and Treatment of Children, 35*, 1–24.

Clay, R. A. (2009, July). Coordinating care for children with serious mental health challenges: Positive outcomes for families, children, youth. *SAMHSA News, 17*(4). Retrieved from http://www.samhsa.gov/samhsanewsletter/Volume_17_Number_4/CoordinatingCare.aspx

Coffey, J. H., & Horner, R. H. (2012). The sustainability of schoolwide positive behavior interventions and supports. *Exceptional Children, 78*, 407–422.

Cohen, R. (2013, December). Families forced to relinquish child custody to get mental health services. *Nonprofit Quarterly.* Retrieved from https://nonprofitquarterly.org/2013/12/19/families-forced-to-relinquish-child-custody-to-get-mental-health-services/

Coleman, M. C., & Webber, J. (2002). *Emotional and behavioral disorders: Theory and practice* (4th ed., pp. 1–19). Boston, MD: Allyn & Bacon.

Collins, S. (2003, July 17). Mentally ill children face life without necessary services. *USA Today*, p. 13A.

Conderman, G., & Hedin, L. (2015). Differentiating instruction in co-taught classrooms for students with emotional/behaviour difficulties. *Emotional & Behavioural Difficulties, 20*, 349–361.

Conroy, M., Sutherland, K. S., Algina, J. J., Wilson, R. E., Martinez, J. R., & Whalon, K. J. (2015). Measuring teacher implementation of the BEST in CLASS intervention program and corollary child outcomes. *Journal of Emotional & Behavioral Disorders, 23*, 144–155.

Conroy, M., Sutherland, K., Haydon, T., Stormont, M., & Harmon, J. (2009). Preventing and ameliorating young children's chronic problem behaviors: An ecological classroom-based approach. *Psychology in the Schools, 46*, 3–17.

Constantine, R. J., Andel, R., Robst, J., & Givens, E. M. (2013). The impact of emotional disturbances on the arrest trajectories of youth as they transition into young adulthood. *Journal of Youth and Adolescence, 42*, 1286–1298.

Cook, B. G., Tankersley, M., & Landrum, T. J. (Eds.). (2014). *Special education past, present, and future: Perspectives from the field* (Vol. 27). London, England: Emerald Group Publishing.

Cook, C. R., Mayer, G., Wright, D., Kraemer, B., Wallace, M. D., Dart, E., . . . Restori, A. (2012). Exploring the link among behavior intervention plans, treatment integrity, and student outcomes under natural educational conditions. *Journal of Special Education, 46*, 3–16.

Copeland, W., Shanahan, L., Costello, E. J., & Angold, A. (2009). Configurations of common childhood psychosocial risk factors. *Journal of Child Psychology and Psychiatry, 50*, 451–459.

Copp, H. L., Bordnick, P. S., Traylor, A. C., & Thyer, B. A. (2007). Evaluating wraparound services for seriously emotionally disturbed youth: Pilot study outcomes in Georgia. *Adolescence, 42*, 723–732.

Council for Children with Behavioral Disorders. (2009a, May). *CCBD position summary: The use of physical restraints procedures in school settings.* Arlington, VA: Council for Exceptional Children.

Council for Children with Behavioral Disorders. (2009b, May). *CCBD position summary: The use of seclusion in school settings.* Arlington, VA: Council for Exceptional Children.

Crone, D. A., Hawken, L. S., & Horner, R. H. (2015). *Building positive behavior support systems in schools: Functional behavioral assessment* (2nd ed.). New York, NY: Guilford.

Cuenca-Sanchez, Y., Mastropieri, M. A., Scruggs, T. E., & Kidd, J. K. (2012). Teaching students with emotional and behavioral disorders to self-advocate through persuasive writing. *Exceptionality, 20*, 71–93.

De Graaf, I., Speetjens, P., Smit, F., de Wolff, M., & Tavecchio, L. (2008). Effectiveness of the Triple P Positive Parenting Program on behavioral problems in children: A meta-analysis. *Behavior Modification, 32*, 714–735.

Dikel, W. (2014). *The teacher's guide to student mental health.* New York, NY: W. W. Norton.

Dube, S. R., & Orpinas, P. (2009). Understanding excessive school absenteeism as school refusal behavior. *Children & Schools, 31*, 87–95.

Duchnowski, A. J., & Kutash, K. K. (2011). School reform and mental health services for students with emotional disturbances educated in urban schools. *Education and Treatment of Children, 34*, 323–346.

Duchnowski, A. J., Kutash, K., Green, A. L., Ferron, J. M., Wagner, M., & Vengrofski, B. (2012). Parent support services for families of children with emotional disturbances served in elementary school special education settings: Examination of data from the Special Education Elementary Longitudinal Study. *Journal of Disability Policy Studies, 24*, 36–52.

Effland, V., Walton, B. A., & McIntyre, J. S. (2011). Connecting the dots: Stages of implementation, wraparound fidelity and youth outcomes. *Journal of Child and Family Studies, 20,* 736–746.

Epstein, M. H. (2004). *Behavioral and Emotional Rating Scale: A Strength-Based Approach to Assessment* (2nd ed.). Austin, TX: Pro-Ed.

Epstein, M. H., & Cullinan, D. (2010). *Scales for Assessing Emotional Disturbance— Second Edition (SAED-2).* Austin, TX: Pro-Ed.

Evans, C., Weiss, S. L., & Cullinan, D. (2012). Teacher perceptions and behavioral strategies for students with emotional disturbance across educational environments. *Preventing School Failure, 56,* 82–90.

Evans, M. E., Armstrong, M. I., Beckstead, J. W., & Lee, J. (2007). Examining the impact of policy on collaboration in systems of care. *Journal of Child and Family Studies, 16,* 567–576.

Fitzpatrick, M., & Knowlton, E. (2009). Bringing evidence-based self-directed intervention practices to the trenches for students with emotional and behavioral disorders. *Preventing School Failure, 53,* 253–266.

Fleming, M. P., & Martin, C. R. (2011). Genes and schizophrenia: A pseudoscientific disenfranchisement of the individual. *Journal of Psychiatric and Mental Health Nursing, 18,* 469–478.

Flower, A., McDaniel, S. C., & Jolivette, K. (2011). A literature review of research quality and effective practices in alternative education settings. *Education and Treatment of Children, 34,* 489–510.

Fogt, J. B., George, M. P., Kern, L., White, G. P., & George, N. L. (2008). Physical restraint of students with behavior disorders in day treatment and residential settings. *Behavioral Disorders, 34,* 4–13.

Forness, S. R., & Knitzer, J. (1992). A new proposed definition and terminology to replace "serious emotional disturbance." *School Psychology Review, 21,* 12–20.

Freeman, J., Simonsen, B., McCoach, D. B., Sugai, G., Lombardi, A., & Horner, R. (2016). Relationship between school-wide positive behavior interventions and supports and academic, attendance, and behavior outcomes in high schools. *Journal of Positive Behavior Interventions, 18,* 41–51.

Frey, L. M., & Wilhite, K. (2005). Our five basic needs: Application for under standing the function of behavior. *Intervention in School and Clinic, 40,* 156–160.

Fries, D., Carney, K. J., Blackman-Urteaga, L., & Savas, S. (2012). Wraparound services: Infusion into secondary schools as a dropout prevention strategy. *NASSP Bulletin, 96,* 119–136.

Friesen, B. J., Giliberti, M., Katz-Leavy, J., Osher, T., & Pullmann, M. D. (2003). Research in the service of policy change: The "custody problem." *Journal of Emotional and Behavioral Disorders, 11,* 39–47.

Gable, R. A., Tonelson, S. W., Sheth, M., Wilson, C., & Park, K. L. (2012). Importance, usage, and preparedness to implement evidence-based practices for students with emotional disabilities: A comparison of knowledge and skills of special education and general education teachers. *Education and Treatment of Children, 35,* 499–519.

Gage, N. A., Lewis, T. J., & Stichter, J. P. (2012). Functional behavioral assessment- based interventions for students with or at risk for emotional and/or behavioral disorders in school: A hierarchical linear modeling meta-analysis. *Behavioral Disorders, 37,* 55–77.

Ghuman, H.S., & Sarles, R. M. (Eds.). (2013). *Handbook of child and adolescent outpatient, day treatment, and community psychiatry.* Philadelphia, PA: Taylor & Francis.

Gruttadaro, D. (2008, Fall). Capitol Hill watch: The federal government focuses on young adults with serious mental illnesses. *NAMI Beginnings* [Issue 1], pp. 2–3. Retrieved from http://www.nami.org/Template.cfm?Section[1]Your_Local_Nami&template[1]/ContentManagement/ContentDisplay.cfm&ContentID[1]81640

Gudino, O., Lau, A., Yeh, M., McCabe, K., & Hough, R. (2009). Understanding racial/ethnic disparities in youth mental health services: Do disparities vary by problem type?. *Journal of Emotional and Behavioral Disorders, 17,* 3–16.

Gulchak, D. J. (2008). Using a mobile handheld computer to teach a student with an emotional and behavioral disorder to self-monitor attention. *Education and Treatment of Children, 31,* 567–581.

Hardy, C., Hackett, E., Murphy, E., Cooper, B., Ford, T., & Conroy, S. (2015). Mental health screening and early intervention: Clinical research study for under 5-year-old children in care in an inner London borough. *Clinical Child Psychology and Psychiatry, 20,* 261–275.

Harrison, J. R., Vannest, K., Davis, J., & Reynolds, C. (2012). Common problem behaviors of children and adolescents in general education classrooms in the United States. *Journal of Emotional and Behavioral Disorders, 20,* 55–64.

Hauth, C., Mastropieri, M., Scruggs, T., & Regan, K. (2013). Can students with emotional and/or behavioral disabilities improve on planning and writing in the content areas of civics and mathematics? *Behavioral Disorders, 38,* 154–170.

Healthy Children. (2015, December). *Building resilience in children.* Elk Grove Village, IL: American Academy of Pediatrics. Retrieved from https://www.healthychildren.org/English/healthy-living/emotional-wellness/Building-Resilience/Pages/Building-Resilience-in-Children.aspx

Horwitz, S., Hurlburt, M. S., Heneghan, A., Zhang, J., Rolls-Reutz, J., Fisher, E., . . . Stein, R. K. (2012). Mental health problems in young children investigated by U.S. child welfare agencies. *Journal of the American Academy of Child & Adolescent Psychiatry, 51,* 572–581.

Hosp, J. L. (2008). A correlated constraints model of risk and resilience for Latino students with emotional/behavioral disorders. *Behavioral Disorders, 33,* 246–254.

Hosp, J. L., Huddle, S., Ford, J. W., & Hensley, K. (2016). Learning disabilities/special education. In S. R. Jimerson, M. K. Burns, & A. M. VanDerHeyden (Eds.), *Handbook of response to intervention* (pp. 43–58). New York, NY: Springer.

Hunter, W., & Haydon, T. (2013). Examining the effectiveness of Numbered Heads Together for students with emotional and behavioral disorders. *Beyond Behavior, 22,* 40–45.

Jennings, P. A., Frank, J. L., Snowberg, K. E., Coccia, M. A., & Greenberg, M. T. (2013). Improving classroom learning environments by Cultivating Awareness and Resilience in Education (CARE): Results of a randomized controlled trial. *School Psychology Quarterly, 28,* 374–390.

Jones, V., Dohrn, E., & Dunn, C. (2004). *Creating effective programs for students with emotional and behavior disorders: Interdisciplinary approaches for adding meaning and hope to behavior change interventions.* Boston, MA: Allyn & Bacon.

Kaff, M., Teagarden, J., & Zabel, R. (2014). Advocating for children with emotional and behavioral disorders: An interview with Eleanor Guetzloe. *Intervention in School and Clinic, 49,* 317–321.

Kalke, T., Glanton, A., & Cristalli, M. (2007). Positive behavioral interventions and supports: Using strength-based approaches to enhance the culture of care in residential and day treatment education. *Child Welfare, 86,* 151–174.

Kauffman, J. M. (2014). Past, present, and future in EBD and special education. In B. G. Cook, M. Tankersley, & T. J. Landrum (Eds.), *Special education past, present, and future: Perspectives from the field* (Vol. 27) (pp. 62–88). London, England: Emerald Group Publishing.

Kauffman, J. M., & Landrum, T. J. (2006). *Children and youth with emotional and behavioral disorders: A history of their education.* Austin, TX: Pro-Ed.

Kauffman, J. M., & Landrum, T. J. (2009). Politics, civil rights, and disproportional identification of students with emotional and behavioral disorders. *Exceptionality, 17,* 177–188.

Kelch-Oliver, K. (2011). African American grandchildren raised in grandparent-headed families: An exploratory study. *Family Journal: Counseling and Therapy for Couples and Families, 19,* 396–406.

Kellner, M. H., Bry, B. H., & Salvador, D. S. (2008). Anger management effects on middle school students with emotional behavioral disorders: Anger log use, aggressive and prosocial behavior. *Child & Family Behavior Therapy, 30,* 215–230.

Kelly, J. R., & Shogren, K. A. (2014). The impact of teaching self-determination skills on the on-task and off-task behaviors of students with emotional and behavioral disorders. *Journal of Emotional and Behavioral Disorders, 22,* 27–40.

Kentucky Department of Education and Department of Special Education and Rehabilitation Counseling at the University of Kentucky. (1999, December). *Behavioral examples.* Retrieved from www.state.ky.us/agencies/behave/EBD%20TA%20Manual/beexaman.html

Kern, L., Evans, S. W., Lewis, T. J., State, T. M., Weist, M. D., & Wills, H. P. (2015). CARS comprehensive intervention for secondary students with emotional and behavioral problems: Conceptualization and development. *Journal of Emotional and Behavioral Disorders, 23,* 195–205.

Killu, K. (2008). Developing effective behavior intervention plans: Suggestions for school personnel. *Intervention in School and Clinic, 43,* 140–149.

Knitzer, J. (2005). Advocacy for children's mental health: A personal journey. *Journal of Clinical Child and Adolescent Psychology, 34,* 612–618.

Komro, K. A., Flay, B. R., & Biglan, A. (2011). Creating nurturing environments: A science-based framework for promoting child health and development within high-poverty neighborhoods. *Clinical Child and Family Psychology Review, 14,* 111–134.

Kratochwill, T. R., McDonald, L., Levin, J. R., Scalia, P. A., & Coover, G. (2009). Families and schools together: An experimental study of multifamily support groups for children at risk. *Journal of School Psychology, 47,* 245–265.

Kroeger, S. D., Burton, C., & Preston, C. (2009). Integrating evidence-based practices in middle science reading. *Teaching Exceptional Children, 41*(3), 6–15.

Kutz, G. D. (2009). *Seclusion and restraints: Selected cases of death and abuse at public and private schools and treatment centers* [testimony before the Committee on Education and Labor, House of Representatives; GAO-09-719T]. Washington, DC: U.S. General Accountability Office.

Lassen, S. R., Steele, M. M., & Sailor, W. (2006). The relationship of schoolwide positive behavior supports to academic achievement in an urban middle. *Psychology in the Schools, 43,* 701–712.

LeBel, J., Nunno, M. A., Mohr, W. K., & O'Halloran, R. (2012). Restraint and seclusion use in U.S. school settings: Recommendations from allied treatment disciplines. *American Journal of Orthopsychiatry, 82,* 75–86.

Lee, I. H., Rojewski, J. W., Gregg, N., & Jeong, S. O. (2014). Postsecondary education persistence of adolescents with specific learning disabilities or emotional/behavioral disorders. *Journal of Special Education, 49,* 77–88.

Leyfer, O., Gallo, K. P., Cooper-Vince, C., & Pincus, D. B. (2013). Patterns and predictors of comorbidity of DSM-IV anxiety disorders in a clinical sample of children and adolescents. *Journal of Anxiety Disorders, 27,* 306–311.

Liaupsin, C. J. (2015). Improving treatment integrity through a functional approach to intervention support. *Behavioral Disorders, 41,* 67–76.

Liljequist, L., & Renk, K. (2007). The relationships among teachers' perceptions of student behavior, teachers' characteristics, and ratings of students' emotional and behavioural problems. *Educational Psychology, 27,* 557–571.

Lo, Y., Mustian, A. L., Brophy, A., & White, R. B. (2011). Peer-mediated social skill instruction for African American males with or at risk for mild disabilities. *Exceptionality, 19,* 191–209.

Longenecker, R., Zink, T., & Florence, J. (2012). Teaching and learning resilience—Building adaptive capacity for rural practice: A report and subsequent analysis of a workshop conducted at the Rural Medical Educators Conference, Savannah, Georgia, May 18, 2010. *Journal of Rural Health, 28,* 122–127.

Losinski, M., Maag, J. W., & Katsiyannis, A. (2015). Characteristics and attitudes of pre-service teachers toward individuals with mental illness. *Journal of Education and Practice, 6*(3), 11–16.

Maheady, L., Harper, G. F., & Mallette, B. (2001). Peer-mediated instruction and interventions and students with mild disabilities. *Remedial and Special Education, 22,* 4–14.

Mann, A. K., & Heflinger, C. A. (2016). Community setting-specific and service-seeking stigma toward children with emotional and behavioral disorders and their families. *Journal of Community Psychology, 44,* 199–213.

Mantymaa, M., Puura, K., Luoma, I., Latva, R., Salmelin, R. K., & Tamminen, T. (2012). Predicting internalizing and externalizing problems at five years by child and parental factors in infancy and toddlerhood. *Child Psychiatry and Human Development, 43,* 153–170.

Martinez-Torteya, C., Bogat, G. A., von Eye, A., & Levendosky, A. A. (2009). Resilience among children exposed to domestic violence: The role of risk and protective factors. *Child Development, 80,* 562–577.

Mattison, R. E. (2011). Comparison of students classified ED in self-contained classrooms and a self-contained school. *Education and Treatment of Children, 34,* 15–33.

Mattison, R. E., & Blader, J. C. (2013). What affects academic functioning in secondary special education students with serious emotional and/or behavioral problems?. *Behavioral Disorders, 38,* 201–211.

McDuffie, K. A., Landrum, T. J., & Gelman, J. A. (2008). Co-teaching and students with emotional and behavioral disorders. *Beyond Behavior, 17*(2), 11–16.

McIntosh, K., Kim, J., Mercer, S. H., Strickland-Cohen, K. M., Horner, R. H. (2015). Variables associated with enhanced sustainability of schoolwide positive behavioral interventions and supports. *Assessment for Effective intervention, 40,* 184–191.

Mendenhall, A. N., Arnold, L. E., & Fristad, M. A. (2016). Parent counseling, psychoeducation, and parent support groups. In M. K. Dulcan, M. K. Dulcan (Eds.) *Dulcan's textbook of child and adolescent psychiatry* (2nd ed.) (pp. 875–899). Arlington, VA: American Psychiatric Publishing.

Merikangas, K. R., He, J. P., Brody, D., Fisher, P. W., Bourdon, K., & Koretz, D. S. (2010). Prevalence and treatment of mental disorders among U.S. children in the 2001–2004 NHANES. *Pediatrics, 125,* 75–81.

Mihalas, S., Morse, W. C., Allsopp, D. H., & McHatton, P. A. (2009). Cultivating caring relationships between teachers and secondary students with emotional and behavioral disorders: Implications for research and practice. *Remedial and Special Education, 30,* 108–125.

Moodi, M., Alizadeh, H., Bonab, B. G., & Soleimani, M. (2015). Effectiveness of cognitive behavior therapy on anger management in children with attention deficit/hyperactivity disorder. *Psychological Research, 17,* 112–127.

Mundschenk, N. A., & Foley, R. M. (2000). Building blocks to effective partnerships: Meeting the needs of students with emotional or behavioral disorders and their families. In M. J. Fine & R. L. Simpson (Eds.), *Collaboration with parents and families of children and youth with exceptionalities* (2nd ed., pp. 369–387). Austin, TX: Pro-Ed.

Murray, C., & Zvoch, K. (2011). Teacher-student relationships among behaviorally at-risk African American youth from low-income backgrounds: Student perceptions, teacher perceptions, and socioemotional adjustment correlates. *Journal of Emotional and Behavioral Disorders, 19,* 41–54.

Murray, F. R. (2005). Effective advocacy for students with emotional/behavioral disorders: How high the cost? *Education and Treatment of Children, 28,* 414–429.

National Alliance on Mental Illness. (2010). *Mental illness: Facts and numbers.* Retrieved from http://www.nami.org/Template.cfm?Section=About_Mental_Illness&Template=/ContentManagement/ContentDisplay.cfm&ContentID=53155

National Alliance on Mental Illness. (2013). *Mental health by the numbers.* Arlington, VA: Author. Retrieved from http://www.nami.org/Learn-More/Mental-Health-By-the-Numbers.

National Center for Child Traumatic Stress. (2016). Understanding child traumatic stress. Durham, NC: Author. Retrieved from http://www.nctsnet.org/sites/default/files/assets/pdfs/understanding_child_traumatic_stress_brochure_9-29-05.pdf

National Dissemination Center for Children with Disabilities. (2010, June). *Emotional disturbance* [Disability fact sheet #5]. Retrieved from http://nichcy.org/wp-content/uploads/docs/fs5.pdf

National Institute of Mental Health. (2009). *Treatment of children with mental illness: Frequently asked questions about the treatment of mental illness in children.* Bethesda, MD: Author. Retrieved from https://www.nimh.nih.gov/health/publications/treatment-of-children-with-mental-illness-fact-sheet/nimh-treatment-children-mental-illness-faq_34669.pdf

National Institute of Mental Health. (2010). *Suicide in the U.S.: Statistics and prevention.* Retrieved from http://www.nimh.nih.gov/health/publications/suicide-in-the-us-statistics-and-prevention/index.shtml

National Institute of Mental Health. (2011, July). *What are the different forms of depression?* Retrieved from http://www.nimh.nih.gov/health/publications/depression/what-are-the-different-forms-of-depression.shtml

National Institute of Mental Health. (2012, September). *Treatment of children with mental illness* [NIH Publication No. 09-4702]. Retrieved from http://www.nimh.nih.gov/health/publications/treatment-of-children-with-mental-illness-fact-sheet/index.shtml

National Institute of Mentla Health. (2015). *Suicide in America: Frequently asked questions.* Bethesda, MD: Author. Retrieved from https://www.nimh.nih.gov/health/publications/suicide-faq/index.shtml

Nelson, J. R., Stage, S., Duppong-Hurley, K., Synhorst, L., & Epstein, M. H. (2007). Risk factors predictive of the problem behavior of children at risk for emotional and behavioral disorders. *Exceptional Children, 73,* 367–379.

Nelson, T. D., Smith, T. R., Hurley, K. D., Epstein, M. H., Thompson, R. W., & Tonniges, T. F. (2013). Association between psychopathology and physical health problems among youth in residential treatment. *Journal of Emotional and Behavioral Disorders, 21,* 150–160.

Niarchou, M., Zammit, S., & Lewis, G. (2015). The Avon Longitudinal Study of Parents and Children (ALSPAC) birth cohort as a resource for studying psychopathology in childhood and adolescence: A summary of findings for depression and psychosis. *Social Psychiatry and Psychiatric Epidemiology, 50,* 1017–1027.

Nikolaros, J. (2014). High school teachers with significant teaching experience support the effectiveness of direct instructional strategies. *Contemporary Issues in Education Research, 7,* 189–194.

O'Neill, R. E., Albin, R. W., Storey, K., Horner, R. H., & Sprague, J. R. (2015). *Functional assessment and program development for problem behavior: A practical handbook.* Stamford, CT: Cengage.

Olfson, M., Blanco, C., Wang, S., Laje, G., & Correll, C. U. (2014). National trends in the mental health care of children, adolescents, and adults by office-based physicians. *JAMA Psychiatry, 71,* 81–90.

Otero, T. L., & Haut, J. M. (2016). Differential effects of reinforcement on the self-monitoring of on-task behavior. *School Psychology Quarterly, 31,* 91–103.

Overstreet, S., & Mathews, T. (2011). Challenges associated with exposure to chronic trauma: Using a public health framework to foster resilient outcomes among youth. *Psychology in the Schools, 48,* 738–754.

Painter, K. (2012). Outcomes for youth with severe emotional disturbance: A repeated measures longitudinal study of a wraparound approach of service delivery in systems of care. *Child & Youth Care Forum, 41,* 407–425.

Pfuntner, A., Wier, L. M., & Stocks, C. (2013, September). Most frequent conditions in U.S. hospitals, 2011 [Healthcare Cost and Utilization Project Statistical Brief #62]. Retrieved from http://www.hcup-us.ahrq.gov/reports/statbriefs/sb162.pdf

Poncin, Y., & Woolston, J. (2016). Systems of care, wraparound services, and home-based services. In M. K. Dulcan, M. K. Dulcan (Eds.), *Dulcan's textbook of child and adolescent psychiatry* (2nd ed.) (pp. 1007–1026). Arlington, VA: American Psychiatric Publishing.

Povenmire-Kirk, T., Diegelmann, K., Crump, K., Schnorr, C., Test, D., Flowers, C., & Aspel, N. (2015). Implementing CIRCLES: A new model for interagency collaboration in transition planning. *Journal of Vocational Rehabilitation, 42,* 51–65.

Puzzanchera, C., & Adams, B. (2011). Juvenile arrests 2009. *OJJDP Bulletin.* Washington, DC: Office of Juvenile Justice and Delinquency Prevention. Retrieved from http://www.ojjdp.gov/pubs/236477.pdf

Rüsch, N., Heekeren, K., Theodoridou, A., Müller, M., Corrigan, P. W., Mayer, B., & … Rössler, W. (2015). Stigma as a stressor and transition to schizophrenia after one year among young people at risk of psychosis. *Schizophrenia Research, 166,* 43–48.

Reddy, L. A., Newman, E., De Thomas, C. A., & Chun, V. (2009). Effectiveness of school-based prevention and intervention programs for children and adolescents with emotional disturbance: A meta-analysis. *Journal of School Psychology, 47,* 77–99.

Regan, K. S. (2009). Improving the way we think about students with emotional and/or behavioral disorders. *Teaching Exceptional Children, 41*(5), 60–65.

Regan, K. S., & Michaud, K. M. (2011). Best practices to support student behavior. *Beyond Behavior, 20*(2), 40–47.

Reynolds, C. R., & Kamphaus, R. W. (2004). *Behavior assessment system for children: Manual* (BASC-2). Circle Pines, MN: American Guidance.

Riney, S., & Bullock, L. M. (2012). Teachers' perspectives on student problematic behavior and social skills. *Emotional & Behavioural Difficulties, 17,* 195–211.

Ritzman, M. J., & Sanger, D. (2007). Principals' opinions on the role of speech-language pathologists serving students with communication disorders involved in violence. *Language, Speech, and Hearing Services in Schools, 38,* 365–377.

Ryan, A. L., Halsey, H. N., & Matthews, W. J. (2003). Using functional assessment to promote desirable student behavior in schools. *Teaching Exceptional Children, 35*(5), 8–15.

Sabornie, E. J., Evans, C., & Cullinan, D. (2006). Comparing characteristics of high-incidence disability groups: A descriptive review. *Remedial and Special Education, 27,* 95–104.

Sachs, J. (1999). The hidden conspiracy in our nation's schools. *Behavioral Disorders, 25,* 80–82.

Sadler, C., & Sugai, G. (2009). Effective behavior and instructional support: A district model for early identification and prevention of reading and behavior problems. *Journal of Positive Behavior Interventions, 11,* 35–46.

Samuels, C. A. (2008, September 12). Behavior disorders in teens are focus of new R & D effort. *Education Week, 28*(2), pp. 1–2.

Sauder, C. L., Beauchaine, T. P., Gatzke-Kopp, L. M., Shannon, K. E., & Aylward, E. (2012). Neuroanatomical correlates of heterotypic comorbidity in externalizing male adolescents. *Journal of Clinical Child and Adolescent Psychology, 41,* 346–352.

Schrank, F. A., Mather, N., & McGrew, K. S. (2014). *Woodcock-Johnson IV Tests of Achievement.* Rolling Meadows, IL: Riverside.

Scott, T. M., Anderson, C. M., & Spaulding, S. A. (2008). Strategies for developing and carrying out functional assessment and behavior intervention planning. *Preventing School Failure, 52*(3), 39–49.

Simpson, R., & Mundschenk, N. A. (2012). Inclusion and students with emotional and behavioral disorders. In F. E. Obiakor & J. P. Bakken (Eds.), *Advances In Special Education (Behavior disorders: Practice concerns and students with EBD)(Volume 23)* (pp. 1–22). Bingley, West Yorkshire, England: Emerald Group Publishing.

Skerbetz, M. D., & Kostewicz, D. E. (2015). Consequence choice and students with emotional and behavioral disabilities: Effects on academic engagement. *Exceptionality, 23,* 14–33.

Skowron, E. A., Cipriano-Essel, E., Gatzke-Kopp, L. M., Teti, D. M., & Ammerman, R. T. (2014). Early adversity, RSA, and inhibitory control: Evidence of children's neurobiological sensitivity to social context. *Developmental Psychobiology, 56,* 964–978.

Slomski, A. (2012). Chronic mental health issues in children now loom larger than physical problems. *JAMA: Journal of the American Medical Association, 308,* 223–225.

Smith, C. R., Katsiyannis, A., & Ryan, J. B. (2011). Challenges of serving students with emotional and behavioral disorders: Legal and policy considerations. *Behavioral Disorders, 36,* 185–194.

Smith, C. R., Katsiyannis, A., Losinski, M., & Ryan, J. B. (2014). Eligibility for students with emotional or behavioral disorders: The social maladjustment dilemma continues. *Journal of Disability Policy Studies, 25,* 252–259.

Stroul, B. A. (1996). *Children's mental health: Creating systems of care in a changing society.* Baltimore, MD: Paul H. Brookes.

Suicide Awareness Voices of Education. (2003, August). *Suicide: Identifying high risk children and adolescents.* Retrieved from www.save.org/Identify.shtml

Sukhera, J., Fisman, S., & Davidson, S. (2015). Mind the gap: A review of mental health service delivery for transition age youth. *Vulnerable Children and Youth Studies, 10,* 271–280.

Sullivan, T. N., Sutherland, K. S., Lotze, G. M., Helms, S. W., Wright, S. A., & Ulmer, L. J. (2015). Problem situations experienced by urban middle school students with high incidence disabilities that impact emotional and behavioral adjustment. *Journal of Emotional and Behavioral Disorders, 23,* 101–114.

Tahhan, J., St. Pierre, J., Stewart, S. L., Leschied, A. W., & Cook, S. (2010). Families of children with serious emotional disorder: Maternal reports on the decision and impact of their child's placement in residential treatment. *Residential Treatment for Children & Youth, 27,* 191–213.

Taylor, S. (2011). Educational and vocational exploration in vulnerable youth. *Child & Youth Services, 32,* 355–379.

Taylor-Richardson, K. D., Heflinger, C. A., & Brown, T. N. (2006). Experience of strain among types of caregivers responsible for children with serious emotional and behavioral disorders. *Journal of Emotional and Behavioral Disorders, 14,* 157–168.

Test, D. W., Fowler, C. H., White, J., Richter, S., & Walker, A. (2009). Evidence based secondary transition practices for enhancing school completion. *Exceptionality, 17*(1), 16–29.

Trosper, S. E., Whitton, S. W., Brown, T. A., & Pincus, D. B. (2012). Understanding the latent structure of the emotional disorders in children and adolescents. *Journal of Abnormal Child Psychology, 40,* 621–632.

U.S. Department of Education, Office of Special Education Programs. (2011a, July). *Children with disabilities receiving special education under Part B of the Individuals with Disabilities Education Act, 2010* [Data Analysis Systems (DANS), OMB #1820-0043]. Washington, DC: Author.

U.S. Department of Education. (2012). *Restraint and seclusion: Resource document.* Washington, DC: Author. Retrieved from www.ed.gov/policy/restraintseclusion

U.S. Department of Education. (2015). *37th annual report to Congress on the implementation of the Individuals with Disabilities Education Act.* Washington, DC: Author, Office of Special Education Programs. Retrieved from http://www2.ed.gov/about/reports/annual/osep/2015/parts-b-c/37th-arc-for-idea.pdf

U.S. Department of Education. (2015). *37th annual report to Congress on the implementation of the Individuals with Disabilities Education Act.* Washington, DC: Author, Office of Special Education Programs. Retrieved from http://www2.ed.gov/about/reports/annual/osep/2013/parts-b-c/35th-idea-arc.pdf

U.S. Department of Health and Human Services. (2003, August). *Blamed and ashamed: The treatment experiences of youth with co-occurring substance abuse and mental health disorders and their families.* Retrieved from www.mentalhealth.org/publications/allpubs/KEN02-0129/execsumm.asp

U.S. Senate. Committee on Health, Education, Labor and Pensions. (2014, February). *Dangerous use of seclusion and restraints in schools remains widespread and difficult to remedy: A review of ten cases.* Washington, DC: Author. [ERIC Document Reproduction No. ED544755]. Retrieved from http://eric.ed.gov/?id=ED544755

Van Acker, R., Boreson, L., Gable, R. A., & Potterton, T. (2005). Are we on the right course? Lessons learned about current FBA/BIP practices in schools. *Journal of Behavioral Education, 14,* 35–56.

van Beijsterveldt, C. E., Groen-Blokhuis, M., Hottenga, J. J., Franić, S., Hudziak, J. J., Lamb, D., ... Swagerman, S. (2013). The Young Netherlands Twin Register (YNTR): Longitudinal twin and family studies in over 70,000 children. *Twin Research and Human Genetics, 16,* 252–267.

Van Haren, N. M., Rijsdijk, F., Schnack, H. G., Picchioni, M. M., Toulopoulou, T., Weisbrod, M., . . . Kahn, R. S. (2012). The genetic and environmental determinants of the association between brain abnormalities and schizophrenia: The schizophrenia twins and relatives consortium. *Biological Psychiatry, 71,* 915–921.

Vannest, K. J., Harrison, J. R., Temple-Harvey, K., Ramsey, L., & Parker, R. I. (2011). Improvement rate differences of academic interventions for students with emotional and behavioral disorders. *Remedial and Special Education, 32,* 521–534.

Vannest, K. J., Temple-Harvey, K. K., & Mason, B. A. (2009). Adequate yearly progress for students with emotional and behavioral disorders through research-based practices. *Preventing School Failure, 53*(2), 73–84.

Villani, V., Parsons, A. E., Church, R. P., & Beetar, J. T. (2012). A descriptive study of the use of restraint and seclusion in a special education school. *Child & Youth Care Forum, 41,* 295–309.

Villarreal, V. (2015). State-level variability of educational outcomes of students with emotional disturbance. *Exceptionality, 23,* 1–13.

Wagner, M. (2014). Longitudinal outcomes and post-high school status of students with emotional or behavioral disorders. In H. M. Walker & F. M. Gresham (Eds.), *Handbook of evidence-based practices for emotional and behavioral disorders: Applications in schools* (pp. 86–103). New York, NY: Guilford.

Wagner, M. M., Sumi, W. C., Woodbridge, M. W., Javitz, H. S., & Thornton, S. P. (2009). The National Behavior Research Coordination Center: Coordinating research and implementation of evidence-based school interventions for children with serious behavior problems. *Journal of Emotional and Behavioral Disorders, 17,* 244–249.

Wagner, M., Kutash, K., Duchnowski, A. J., Epstein, M. H., & Sumi, W. C. (2005). The children and youth we serve: A national picture of the characteristics of students with emotional disturbances receiving special education. *Journal of Emotional and Behavioral disorders, 13,* 79–96.

Walsh, M. P. (2010). Employers' perceptions of transition programming for students with emotional disturbances. *Journal of Employment Counseling, 47,* 123–133.

Wechsler, D. (2003). *Wechsler intelligence scale for children–IV.* San Antonio, TX: Psychological Corporation.

Wechsler, D. (2014). *Wechsler Intelligence Scale for Children* (5th ed.). Bloomington, MN: Psych Corp.

Wexler, J., Reed, D. K., Pyle, N., Mitchell, M., & Barton, E. E. (2015). A synthesis of peer-mediated academic interventions for secondary struggling learners. *Journal of Learning Disabilities, 48,* 451–470.

What Works Clearinghouse. (2007). *Intervention: Classwide peer tutoring (CWPT).* Retrieved from http://ies.ed.gov/ncee/wwc/reports/beginning_reading/cwpt/index.asp

What Works Clearinghouse. (2012). *First step to success* [What Works Clearinghouse Intervention Report]. Washington, DC: Author.

Wiley, A. L., Siperstein, G. N., & Forness, S. R. (2011). School context and the academic and behavioral progress of students with emotional disturbance. *Behavioral Disorders, 36,* 172–184.

Wiley, A. L., Siperstein, G. N., Bountress, K. E., Forness, S. R., & Brigham, F. J. (2008). School context and the academic achievement of students with emotional disturbance. *Behavioral Disorders, 33,* 198–210.

Wilhite, S., & Bullock, L. M. (2012). Effects of the Why Try Social Skills program on students with emotional and/or behavioral problems in an alternative school. *Emotional & Behavioural Difficulties, 17,* 175–194.

Winzer, M. A. (1993). *The history of special education: From isolation to integration.* Washington, DC: Gallaudet University Press.

Woodcock, R. W., McGrew, K. S., & Mather, N. (2001). *Woodcock–Johnson Psychoeducational Battery–III* (tests of achievement). Allen, TX: DLM.

Woodier, D. (2011). Building resilience in looked after young people: A moral values approach. *British Journal of Guidance & Counselling, 39,* 259–282.

Worcester, J. A., Nesman, T. M., Raffaele Mendez, L. M., & Keller, H. R. (2008). Giving voice to parents of young children with challenging behavior. *Exceptional Children, 74,* 509–525.

Wu, G., Feder, A., Cohen, H., Kim, J. J., Calderon, S., Charney, D. S., & Mathé, A. A. (2013). Understanding resilience. *Frontiers in behavioral neuroscience, 7.* doi:10.3389/fnbeh.2013.00010.

Zammit, S., Thomas, K., Thompson, A., Horwood, J., Menezes, P., Gunnell, D., . . . Harrison, G. (2009). Maternal tobacco, cannabis and alcohol use during pregnancy and risk of adolescent psychotic symptoms in offspring. *British Journal of Psychiatry, 195,* 294–300.

Zigmond, N. (2006). Twenty-four months after high school: Paths taken by youth diagnosed with severe emotional and behavioral disorders. *Journal of Emotional and Behavioral Disorders, 14,* 99–107.

Zirkel, P. A. (2009c). What does the law say? *Teaching Exceptional Children, 41*(5), 73–75.

Zolkoski, S. M., & Bullock, L. M. (2012). Resilience in children and youth: A review. *Children and Youth Services Review, 34,* 2295–2303.

Chapter 8

Allor, J. H., Gifford, D. B., Al Otaiba, S., Miller, S. J., & Cheatham, J. P. (2013). Teaching students with intellectual disability to integrate reading skills: Effects of text and text-based lessons. *Remedial and Special Education, 34,* 346–356.

American Association on Intellectual and Developmental Disabilities (AAIDD), American Network of Community Options and Resources (ANCOR), National Association of Councils on Developmental Disabilities (NCDD), The Arc, & United Cerebral Palsy (UCP). (2015). *Public policy agenda for the 114th congress (2015–2016).* Washington, DC: Author. Retrieved from http://www.thearc.org/document.doc?id=5075

Angell, M., Bailey, R., & Larson, L. (2008). Systematic instruction for social-pragmatic language skills in lunchroom settings. *Education and Training in Developmental Disabilities, 43,* 342–359.

Ault, M. J., Collins, B. C., & Carter, E. W. (2013). Congregational participation and supports for children and adults with disabilities: Parent perceptions. *Intellectual and Developmental Disabilities, 51,* 48–61.

Ayres, K. M., Lowrey, K., Douglas, K. H., & Sievers, C. (2011). I can identify Saturn but I can't brush my teeth: What happens when the curricular focus for students with severe disabilities shifts. *Education and Training in Autism and Developmental Disabilities, 46,* 11–21.

Ayres, K. M., Mechling, L., & Sansosti, F. J. (2013). The use of mobile technologies to assist with life skills/independence of students with moderate/severe intellectual disability and/or autism spectrum disorders: Considerations for the future of school psychology. *Psychology in the Schools, 50,* 259–271.

Baer, R. M., Daviso, A., Flexer, R. W., Queen, R., & Meindl, R. S. (2011). Students with intellectual disabilities: Predictors of transition outcomes. *Career Development for Exceptional Individuals, 34,* 132–141.

Bayat, M. (2007). Evidence of resilience in families of children with autism. *Journal of Intellectual Disability Research, 51,* 702–714.

Beers, M. H., & Berkow, R. (2003). *Mental retardation* (Sec. 19, Chap. 262). *Merck manual of diagnosis and therapy* (17th ed.). Retrieved on from www.merck.com/pubs/mmanual/section19/chapter262/262e.htm

Behrman, R. E., & Butler, A. S. (Eds.). (2007). Causes, consequences, and prevention. In *Neurodevelopmental, health, and family outcomes for infants born preterm.* Washington, DC: National Academies Press/U.S. Committee on Understanding Premature Birth and Assuring Healthy Outcomes. Retrieved from http://www.ncbi.nlm.nih.gov/books/NBK11356/

Beirne-Smith, M., Ittenbach, R. F., & Patton, J. R. (2002). *Mental retardation* (6th ed., pp. 312–357). Upper Saddle River, NJ: Pearson.

Bergeron, R., & Floyd, R. (2006). Broad cognitive abilities of children with mental retardation: An analysis of group and individual profiles. *American Journal on Mental Retardation, 111,* 417–432.

Berglund, E., Eriksson, M., & Johansson, I. (2001). Parental reports of spoken language skills in children with Down syndrome. *Journal of Speech, Language, and Hearing Research, 44,* 179–191.

Berry-Kravis, E., Raspa, M., Loggin-Hester, L., Bishop, E., Holiday, D., & Bailey, D. B. (2010). Seizures in fragile X syndrome: Characteristics and comorbid diagnoses. *American Journal on Intellectual and Developmental Disabilities, 115,* 461–472.

Black, R. S., & Rojewski, J. W. (1998). The role of social awareness in the employment success of adolescents with mild mental retardation. *Education and Training in Mental Retardation and Developmental Disabilities, 33,* 144–161.

Blanks, A. B., & Smith, J. D. (2009). Multiculturalism, religion, and disability: Implications for special education practitioners. *Education and Training in Developmental Disabilities, 44,* 295–303.

Bouck, E. C. (2008). Factors impacting the enactment of a functional curriculum in self-contained cross-categorical programs. *Education and Training in Developmental Disabilities, 43,* 294–310.

Bouck, E. C. (2009). No Child Left Behind, the Individuals with Disabilities Education Act and functional curricula: A conflict of interest? *Education and Training in Developmental Disabilities, 44,* 3–13.

Bouck, E. C. (2014). The postschool outcomes of students with mild intellectual disability: Does it get better with time? *Journal of Intellectual Disability Research, 5,* 534–548.

Bouck, E. C., & Satsangi, R. (2014). Evidence-base of a functional curriculum for secondary students with mild intellectual disability: A historical perspective. *Education and Training in Autism and Developmental Disabilities, 49,* 478–486.

Bouck, E. C., & Satsangi, R. (2015). Is there really a difference? Distinguishing mild intellectual disability from similar disability categories. *Education and Training in Autism and Developmental Disabilities, 50,* 186–198.

Calefati, J. (February 13, 2009). College is possible for students with intellectual disabilities: New support programs and federal funds can help students with intellectual disabilities. *U.S. New and World Report.* Retrieved from http://www.usnews.com/education/articles/2009/02/13/college-is-possible-for-students-with-intellectual-disabilities?page=2

Carter, E. W., Lane, K. L., Cooney, M., Weir, K., Moss, C. K., & Machalicek, W. (2013). Parent assessments of self-determination importance and performance for students with autism or intellectual disability. *American Journal on Intellectual and Developmental Disabilities, 118,* 16–31.

Carter, E. W., Lane, K. L., Pierson, M. R., & Stang, K. K. (2008). Promoting self-determination for transition-age youth: Views of high school general and special educators. *Exceptional Children, 75,* 55–70.

Carter, E. W., Moss, C. K., Hoffman, A., Chung, Y., & Sisco, L. (2011). Efficacy and social validity of peer support arrangements for adolescents with disabilities. *Exceptional Children, 78*, 107–125.

Carter, E. W., Sisco, L. G., Brown, L., Brickham, D., & Al-Khabbaz, Z. A. (2008). Peer interactions and academic engagement of youth with developmental disabilities in inclusive middle and high school classrooms. *American Journal on Mental Retardation, 113*, 479–494.

Centers for Disease Control and Prevention. (2011). *Attention-deficit/hyperactivity disorder (ADHD): Data and statistics*. Atlanta, GA: Author. Retrieved from http://www.cdc.gov/ncbddd/adhd/data.html

Centers for Disease Control and Prevention. (2011, June). *Developmental disabilities increasing in US*. Atlanta, GA: Author. Retrieved from http://www.cdc.gov/Features/dsDev_Disabilities/index.html

Centers for Disease Control and Prevention. (2012). *Facts about cerebral palsy*. Atlanta, GA: author. Retrieved from http://www.cdc.gov/ncbddd/cp/facts.html

Centers for Disease Control and Prevention. (2012, February). *Toxoplasmosis (Toxoplasma infection)*. Atlanta, GA: Author. http://www.cdc.gov/parasites/toxoplasmosis/

Centers for Disease Control and Prevention. (2012a, August). *Fetal alcohol spectrum disorders (FASDs)*. Atlanta, GA: Author. Retrieved from http://www.cdc.gov/ncbddd/fasd/data.html

Centers for Disease Control and Prevention. (2012b, August). *Lead*. Atlanta, GA: Author. Retrieved from http://www.cdc.gov/nceh/lead/

Centers for Disease Control and Prevention. (2013, January). *Toxoplasmosis*. Atlanta, GA: Author. Retrieved from http://www.cdc.gov/parasites/toxoplasmosis/

Centers for Disease Control and Prevention. (2015, September). *Metropolitan Atlanta developmental disabilities surveillance program* (MADDSP). Atlanta, GA: Author. Retrieved from http://www.cdc.gov/ncbddd/developmentaldisabilities/MADDSP.html

Centers for Disease Control and Prevention. (2016a, January). *Lead*. Atlanta, GA: Author. Retrieved from http://www.cdc.gov/nceh/lead/

Centers for Disease Control and Prevention. (2016b, March). *Fetal alcohol syndrome disorders (FASDs): Data and statistics*. Atlanta, GA: Author. Retrieved from http://www.cdc.gov/ncbddd/fasd/data.html#ref

Chevalère, J., Postal, V., Jauregui, J., Copet, P., Laurier, V., & Thuilleaux, D. (2015). Executive functions and Prader-Willi syndrome: Global deficit linked with intellectual level and syndrome-specific associations. *American Journal on Intellectual and Developmental Disabilities, 120*, 215–229.

Cho, H., & Kingston, N. (2011). Capturing implicit policy from NCLB test type assignments of students with disabilities. *Exceptional Children, 78*, 58–72.

Cihak, D. F., Wright, R., McMahon, D., Smith, C. C., & Kraiss, K. (2015). Incorporating functional digital literacy skills as part of the curriculum for high school students with intellectual disability. *Education and Training in Autism and Developmental Disabilities, 50*, 155–171.

Clarke, L. S., Haydon, T., Bauer, A., & Epperly, A. C. (2016). Inclusion of students with an intellectual disability in the general education classroom with the use of response cards. *Preventing School Failure, 60*, 35–42.

Clegg, J., Murphy, E., Almack, K., & Harvey, A. (2008). Tensions around inclusion: Reframing the moral horizon. *Journal of Applied Research in Intellectual Disabilities, 21*(1), 81–94.

Cooper R. (2014). Shifting boundaries between the normal and the pathological: The case of mild intellectual disability. *History of Psychiatry* [serial online], *25*, 171–186.

Copeland, S. R., McCall, J., Williams, C. R., Guth, C., Presley, J. A., . . . Hughes, C. (2002). High school peer buddies: A win-win situation. *Teaching Exceptional Children, 35*(1), 16–21.

Cramm, J. M., & Nieboer, A. P. (2012). Longitudinal study of parents' impact on quality of life of children and young adults with intellectual disabilities. *Journal of Applied Research in Intellectual Disabilities, 25*, 20–28.

de Boer, A., Pijl, S. J., Minnaert, A., & Post, W. (2014). Evaluating the effectiveness of an intervention program to influence attitudes of students towards peers with disabilities. *Journal of Autism and Developmental Disorders, 44*, 572–583.

de Graaf, G., Buckley, F., & Skotko, B.G. (2015). Estimates of the live births, natural losses, and elective terminations with Down syndrome in the United States. *American Journal of Medical Genetics (Part A), 167A*, 756–767.

de Souza, M. A., McAllister, C., Suttie, M., Perrotta, C., Mattina, T., Faravelli, F., ... Hammond, P. (2013). Growth hormone, gender and face shape in Prader-Willi syndrome. *American Journal of Medical Genetics (Part A), 161*, 2453–2463.

Delgado, C. E. F., Vagi, S. J., & Scott, K. G. (2006). Tracking preschool children with developmental delay: Third grade outcomes. *American Journal on Mental Retardation, 111*, 299–306.

Dempsey, I., Keen D., Pennell, D. J., O'Reilly, L., & Neilands, J. (2009). Parent stress, parenting competence and family-centered support to young children with an intellectual or developmental disability. *Research in Developmental Disabilities: A Multidisciplinary Journal, 30*, 558–566.

Dessemontet, R., Bless, G. G., & Morin, D. D. (2012). Effects of inclusion on the academic achievement and adaptive behaviour of children with intellectual disabilities. *Journal of Intellectual Disability Research, 56*, 579–587.

Dimitropoulos, A., Ho, A. Y., Klaiman, C., Koenig, K., & Schultz, R. T. (2009). A comparison of behavioral and emotional characteristics in children with autism, Prader-Willi syndrome, and Williams syndrome. *Journal of Mental Health Research in Intellectual Disabilities, 2*, 220–243.

Douglas, K. H., Ayres, K. M., & Langone, J. (2015). Comparing self-management strategies delivered via an iPhone to promote grocery shopping and literacy. *Education and Training in Autism and Developmental Disabilities, 50*, 446–465.

Doyle, M. B., & Giangreco, M. F. (2009). Making presentation software accessible to high school students with intellectual disabilities. *Teaching Exceptional Children, 41*(3), 24–31.

Dunst, C. J., & Bruder, M. B. (2002). Valued outcomes of service coordination, early intervention, and natural environments. *Exceptional Children, 68*, 361–375.

Dybdahl, C. S., & Ryan, S. (2009). Inclusion for students with fetal alcohol syndrome: Classroom teachers talk about practice. *Preventing School Failure, 53*, 185–196.

Edmonds, K., & Crichton, S. (2008). Finding ways to teach to students with FASD: A research study. *International Journal of Special Education, 23*(1), 54–73.

Eidelman, S. M. (2013). Special Olympics, sports, and the path to social inclusion for students with intellectual disabilities. *State Education Standard, 13*(1), 34–37.

Elliot, T. R., Patnaik, A., Naiser, E., Fournier, C. J., McMaughan, D. K., Dyer, J. A., & Phillips, C. D. (2014). Medicaid personal care services for children with intellectual disabilities: What assistance is provided? When is assistance provided? *Intellectual and Developmental Disabilities, 52*, 24–31.

Fast, D. (2003, April). *What is the molecular cause of Fragile X syndrome?* Retrieved from http://fragilex.org/html/molecular.htm

Fey, M. E., Yoder, P. J., Warren, S. F., & Bredin-Oja, S. L. (2013). Is more better? Milieu communication teaching in toddlers with intellectual disabilities. *Journal of Speech, Language, and Hearing Research, 56*(2), 679–693.

Ford, D. Y. (2012). Culturally different students in special education: Looking backward to move forward. *Exceptional Children, 78*, 391–405.

Forts, A. M., & Luckasson, R. (2011). Reading, writing, and friendship: Adult implications of effective literacy instruction for students with intellectual disability. *Research and Practice for Persons with Severe Disabilities (RPSD), 36*, 121–125.

Fulk, B. M., & King, K. (2001). Classwide peer tutoring at work. *Teaching Exceptional Children, 34*(2), 49–53.

Genetics Home Reference. (2012a, April). *Fragile X syndrome*. Retrieved from http://ghr.nlm.nih.gov/condition/fragile-x-syndrome

Genetics Home Reference. (2012b, February). *Phenylketonuria*. Retrieved from http://ghr.nlm.nih.gov/condition/phenylketonuria

Genetics Home Reference. (2016a, May). *Fragile X syndrome*. Bethesda, MD: National Institutes of Health. Retrieved from https://ghr.nlm.nih.gov/condition/fragile-x-syndrome

Genetics Home Reference. (2016b, May). *Phenylketonuria*. Bethesda, MD: National Institutes of Health. Retrieved from https://ghr.nlm.nih.gov/condition/phenylketonuria#statistics

Giangreco, M. F. (2010). One-to-one paraprofessionals for students with disabilities in inclusive classrooms: Is conventional wisdom wrong? *Intellectual and Developmental Disabilities, 48*, 1–13.

Gillette, Y., & DePompei, R. (2008). Do PDAs enhance the organization and memory skills of students with cognitive disabilities? *Psychology in the Schools, 45*, 665–677.

Gilmore, L., & Cuskelly, M. (2014). Vulnerability to loneliness in people with intellectual disability: An explanatory model. *Journal of Policy and Practice in Intellectual Disabilities, 11*, 192–199.

Gold, M. E., & Richards, H. (2012). To label or not to label: The special education question for African Americans. *Educational Foundations, 26*, 143–156.

Golubovic, S., Maksimovic, J., Golubovic, B., & Glumbic, N. (2012). Effects of exercise on physical fitness in children with intellectual disability. *Research in Developmental Disabilities: A Multidisciplinary Journal, 33*, 608–614.

Grondhuis, S. N., & Aman, M. G. (2014). Overweight and obesity in youth with developmental disabilities: A call to action. *Journal of Intellectual Disability Research, 58*, 787–799.

Gross, B., & Hahn, H. (2004). Developing issues in the classification of mental and physical disabilities. *Journal of Disability Policy Studies, 15*, 130–134.

Grossberg, M. (2011). From feeble-minded to mentally retarded: Child protection and the changing place of disabled children in the mid-twentieth century United States. *Paedagogica Historica: International Journal of the History of Education, 47*, 729–747.

Guralnick, M. J. (2007). The system of early intervention for children with developmental disabilities: Current status and challenges for the future. In J. W. Jacobson, J. A. Mulick, J. Rojahn, J. W. Jacobson, J. A. Mulick, J. Rojahn (Eds.), *Handbook of intellectual and developmental disabilities* (pp. 465–480). New York, NY: Springer.

Guralnick, M. J. (2016). Early intervention for children with intellectual disabilities: An update. *Journal of Applied Research in Intellectual Disabilities*, doi:10.1111/jar.12233

Hall v. Florida 2014 134 S. Ct. 1986 (2014).

Hannah, M., & Midlarsky, E. (2005). Helping by siblings of children with mental retardation. *American Journal on Mental Retardation, 110*, 87–99.

Harries, J., Guscia, R., Kirby, N., Nettelbeck, T., & Taplin, J. (2005). Support needs and adaptive behaviors. *American Journal on Mental Retardation, 110*, 393–404.

Harris, K., & Meltzer, L. (Eds.). (2015). *The power of peers in the classroom: Enhancing learning and social skills*. New York, NY: Guilford Press.

Harry, B. (2008). Collaboration with culturally and linguistically diverse families: Ideal versus reality. *Exceptional Children, 74*, 372–388.

Hart, D., Grigal, M., & Weir, C. (2010). Expanding the paradigm: Postsecondary education options for individuals with autism spectrum disorder and intellectual disabilities. *Focus on Autism and Other Developmental Disabilities, 25*, 134–150.

Hawks, D. E. (2009). Thinking ahead: A special kind of planning. *Exceptional Parent, 39*(4), 64–65.

Hickson, L., Blackman, L. S., & Reis, E. M. (1995). *Mental retardation: Foundations of educational programming* (pp. 1–37). Boston, MA: Allyn & Bacon.

Hieneman, M., Dunlap, G., & Kincaid, D. (2005). Positive support strategies for students with behavioral disorders in general education settings. *Psychology in the Schools, 42*, 779–794.

Howell, A., Hauser-Cram, P., & Kersh, J. E. (2007). Setting the stage: Early child and family characteristics as predictors of later loneliness in children with developmental disabilities. *American Journal on Mental Retardation, 112*, 18–30.

Hughes, C., & Carter, E. (2008). *Peer buddy programs for successful secondary school inclusion*. Baltimore, MD: Brookes.

Hughes, C., Golas, M., Cosgriff, J., Brigham, N., Edwards, C., & Cashen, K. (2011). Effects of a social skills intervention among high school students with intellectual disabilities and autism and their general education peers. *Research and Practice for Persons with Severe Disabilities (RPSD), 36*, 46–61.

Hughes, C., Kaplan, L., Bernstein, R., Boykin, M., Reilly, C., Brigham, N., ... Harvey, M. (2012). Increasing social interaction skills of secondary school students with autism and/or intellectual disability: A review of interventions. *Research and Practice for Persons with Severe Disabilities, 37*, 288–307.

Hughes, M. T., Schumm, J. S., & Vaughn, S. (1999). Home literacy activities: Perceptions and practices of Hispanic parents of children with learning disabilities. *Learning Disability Quarterly, 22*, 224–235.

Hughes, R. S. (1999). An investigation of coping skills of parents of children with disabilities: Implications for service providers. *Education and Training in Mental Retardation and Developmental Disabilities, 34*, 271–280.

International Association for the Scientific Study of Intellectual and Developmental Disabilities, Families Special Interest Research Group. (2014). Families supporting a child with intellectual or developmental disabilities: The current state of knowledge. *Journal of Applied Research in Intellectual Disabilities, 27*, 420–430.

Jimenez, B. A., Browder, D. M., Spooner, F., & Dibiase, W. (2012). Inclusive inquiry science using peer-mediated embedded instruction for students with moderate intellectual disability. *Exceptional Children, 78*, 301–317.

Johnson, D. R., & Johnson, F. P. (2009). *Joining together: Group theory and group skills* (10th ed.). Boston, MA: Allyn & Bacon.

Johnson, J. R., & McIntosh, A. S. (2009). Toward a cultural perspective and understanding of the disability and deaf experience in special and multicultural education. *Remedial and Special Education, 30*, 67–83.

Kaehne, A., & Beyer, S. (2014). Person-centered reviews as a mechanism for planning the post-school transition of young people with intellectual disability. *Journal of Intellectual Disability Research, 58*, 603–613.

Kamps, D. M., Greenwood, C., Arreaga-Mayer, C., Veerkamp, M. B., Utley, C., Tapia, Y., Bowman-Perrott, L., . . . Bannister, H. (2008). The efficacy of classwide peer tutoring in middle schools. *Education and Treatment of Children, 31*, 119–152.

Kanner, L. (1964). *A history of the care and study of the mentally retarded* (pp. 9–44). Springfield, IL: Charles C. Thomas.

King-Sears, M. E. (2008). Facts and fallacies: Differentiation and the general education curriculum for students with special education needs. *Support for Learning, 23*(2), 55–62.

Kingsley, E. P. (1987). *Down syndrome web page*. Retrieved from www.nas.com/downsyn/holland.html

Koenig, K., & Tsatsanis, K. (2005). Pervasive developmental disorders in girls. In D. J. Bell, S. L. Foster, & E. J. Mash (Eds.), *Handbook of behavioral and emotional problems in girls* (pp. 211–238). New York, NY: Kluwer.

Kok, L., van der Waa, A., Klip, H., & Staal, W. (2016). The effectiveness of psychosocial interventions for children with a psychiatric disorder and mild intellectual disability to borderline intellectual functioning: A systematic literature review and meta-analysis. *Clinical Child Psychology and Psychiatry, 21*, 156–171.

Krajewski, J. J., & Hyde, M. S. (2000). Comparison of teen attitudes toward individuals with mental retardation between 1987 and 1998: Has inclusion made a difference? *Education and Training in Mental Retardation and Developmental Disabilities, 35,* 284–293.

Krajewski, J. J., Hyde, M. S., & O'Keefe, M. K. (2002). Teen attitudes toward individuals with mental retardation from 1987 to 1998: Impact of respondent gender and school variables. *Education and Training in Mental Retardation and Developmental Disabilities, 37,* 27–39.

Kundert, D. K. (2008). Prader-Willi syndrome. *School Psychology Quarterly, 23,* 246–257.

Lambert, N. M., Nihira, K., & Leland, H. (1993). *AAMR Adaptive Behavior Scale-School* (2nd edition) (ABS-S:2). Austin, TX: Pro-Ed.

Landmark, L., Ju, S., & Zhang, D. (2010). Substantiated best practices in transition: Fifteen plus years later. *Career Development for Exceptional Individuals, 33,* 165–176.

Langthorne, P., & McGill, P. (2012). An indirect examination of the function of problem behavior associated with Fragile X syndrome and Smith-Magenis syndrome. *Journal of Autism and Developmental Disorders, 42,* 201–209.

Lee, S., Palmer, S., Turnbull, A., & Wehmeyer, M. (2006). A model for parent-teacher collaboration to promote self-determination in young children with disabilities. *Teaching Exceptional Children, 38*(3), 36–41.

Lobato, D., Kao, B., Plante, W., Seifer, R., Grullon, E., Cheas, L., & Canino, G. (2011). Psychological and school functioning of Latino siblings of children with intellectual disability. *Journal of Child Psychology and Psychiatry, 52,* 696–703.

Lorenzi, D. G., Horvat, M., & Pellegrini, A. D. (2000). Physical activity of children with and without mental retardation in inclusive recess settings. *Education and Training in Mental Retardation and Developmental Disabilities, 35,* 160–167.

Luckasson, R., & Schalock, R. L. (2013). Defining and applying a functionality approach to intellectual disability. *Journal of Intellectual Disability Research, 57,* 657–668.

Luckasson, R., Borthwick-Duffy, S., Buntinx, W. H. E., Coulter, D. L., Craig, E. M., Reeve, A., et al. (2002). *Mental retardation: Definition, classification, and systems of supports* (10th edition). Washington, DC: AAMR (now the American Association on Intellectual and Developmental Disabilities [AAIDD]).

Ly, T. M. (2008). Asian American parents' attributions of children with Down syndrome: Connections with child characteristics and culture. *Intellectual and Developmental Disabilities, 46,* 129–140.

Lyle, M. L., & Simplican, S. C. (2015). Elite repudiation of the r-word and public opinion about intellectual disability. *Intellectual and Developmental Disabilities, 53,* 211–227.

Maheady, L., & Gard, J. (2010). Classwide peer tutoring: Practice, theory, research, and personal narrative. *Intervention in School and Clinic, 46,* 71–78.

Maheady, L., Mallette, B., & Harper, G. E. (2006). Four classwide peer tutoring models: Similarities, differences, and implications for research and practice. *Reading and Writing Quarterly, 22,* 65–89.

Manning, K. E., McAllister, C. J., Ring, H. A., Finer, N., Kelly, C. L., Sylvester, K. P., ... Holland, A. J. (2016). Novel insights into maladaptive behaviors in Prader-Willi syndrome: Serendipitous findings from an open trial of vagus nerve stimulation. *Journal of Intellectual Disability Research, 60,* 149–155.

March of Dimes. (2012). *Birth defects: Down syndrome.* Retrieved from http://www.marchofdimes.com/baby/birthdefects_downsyndrome.html

Martin, J. E., Van Dycke, J. L., Christensen, W. R., Greene, B. A., Gardner, J. E., & Lovett, D. L. (2006). Increasing student participation in IEP meetings: Establishing the self-directed IEP as an evidence-based practice. *Exceptional Children, 72,* 299–316.

Matheson, C., Olsen, R. J., & Weisner, T. (2007). A good friend is hard to find: Friendship among adolescents with disabilities. *American Journal on Mental Retardation, 112,* 319–329.

May, P. A., & Gossage, J. P. (2016). *Estimating the prevalence of fetal alcohol syndrome: A summary.* Bethesda, MD: National Institutes of Health, National Institute on Alcohol Abuse and Alcoholism. Retrieved from http://pubs.niaaa.nih.gov/publications/arh25-3/159-167.htm

May, P. A., Baete, A., Russo, J., Elliott, A. J., Blankenship, J., Kalberg, W. O., ... Hoyme, E. (2014). Prevalence and characteristics of fetal alcohol spectrum disorders. *Pediatrics, 134,* 854–866.

McIntyre, T. (2003). *Sociograms.* Retrieved from www.behavioradvisor.com

McVilly, K. R., Stancliffe, R. J., Parmenter, T. R., & Burton-Smith, R. M. (2006). "I get by with a little help from my friend": Adults with intellectual disability discuss loneliness. *Journal of Applied Research in Intellectual Disabilities, 19,* 191–203.

Mechling, L. C., Ayres, K. M., Bryant, K. J., & Foster, A. L. (2014). Continuous video modeling to assist with completion of multi-step home living tasks by young adults with moderate intellectual disability. *Education and Training in Autism and Developmental Disabilities, 49,* 368–380.

Miller, B., Doughty, T., & Krockover, G. (2015). Using science inquiry methods to promote self-determination and problem-solving skills for students with moderate intellectual disability. *Education and Training in Autism and Developmental Disabilities, 50,* 356–368.

Mitchell, W. (2008). The role played by grandparents in family support and learning: Considerations for mainstream and special schools. *Support for Learning, 23,* 126–135.

Mogharreban, C. C., & Bruns, D. A. (2009). Moving to inclusive prekindergarten classrooms: Lessons from the field. *Early Childhood Education Journal, 36,* 407–414.

Moyson, T. T., & Roeyers, H. H. (2012). "The overall quality of my life as a sibling is all right, but of course, it could always be better." Quality of life of siblings of children with intellectual disability: The siblings' perspectives. *Journal of Intellectual Disability Research, 56,* 87–101.

Nasr, M., Cranston-Gingras, A., & Jang, S. (2015). Friendship experiences of participants in a university based transition program. *International Journal of Whole Schooling, 11*(2), 1–15.

National Center for Education Statistics. (2015). Percentage distribution of students 6 to 21 years old served under Individuals with Disabilities Education Act (IDEA), Part B, by educational environment and type of disability: Selected years, fall 1989 through fall 2012 [Table 204.60]. In *Digest of Education Statistics.* Washington, DC: U.S. Department of Education. Retrieved from http://nces.ed.gov/programs/digest/d14/tables/dt14_204.60.asp

National Down Syndrome Society. (2012). *What is Down syndrome?* Retrieved from http://www.ndss.org/Down-Syndrome/What-Is-Down-Syndrome/

National Down Syndrome Society. (2016, April). *Facts about Down syndrome.* Retrieved from http://www.nads.org/resources/facts-about-down-syndrome/

National Fragile X Foundation. (2016, May). *Genetics and inheritance.* Washington, DC: Author. Retrieved from https://fragilex.org/fragile-x/genetics-and-inheritance/

National Institute of Child Health and Human Development. (2008, September). *National Institutes of Health research plan on Fragile X syndrome and associated disorders.* Washington, DC: National Institutes of Health. Retrieved from http://www.nichd.nih.gov/search.cfm?search_string_fragile_x_syndrome_prevalence&submitbtn_Search

National Institute of Child Health and Human Development. (2012, February). *Down Syndrome.* Retrieved September 22, 2012, from http://www.nichd.nih.gov/health/topics/Down_Syndrome.cfm

National Institute of Child Health and Human Development. (2013, October). *How many people are affected by Fragile X syndrome?* Bethesda, MD: National Institutes of Health. Retrieved from https://www.nichd.nih.gov/health/topics/fragilex/conditioninfo/Pages/howmanyaffected.aspx

National Institute of Child Health and Human Development. (2014, January). *How many people are affected by or at risk for Down syndrome?* Bethesda, MD: National Institutes of Health. Retrieved from https://www.nichd.nih.gov/health/topics/ down/conditioninfo/Pages/risk.aspx

National Institutes of Health. (2012, September). *Phenylketonuria.* Retrieved from http://www.nlm.nih.gov/medlineplus/phenylketonuria.html

Patel, D. R., Greydanus, D. E., & Merrick, J. (2014). Intellectual and developmental disability. In J. Merrick, D. E. Greydanus, D. R. Patel, J. Merrick, D. E. Greydanus, & D. R. Patel (Eds.), *Intellectual disability: Some current issues* (pp. 3–13). Hauppauge, NY: Nova Science.

Peer, J. W., & Hillman, S. B. (2014). Stress and resilience for parents of children with intellectual and developmental disabilities: A review of key factors and recommendations for practitioners. *Journal of Policy and Practice in Intellectual Disabilities, 11*, 92–98.

Plotner, A. J., & Marshall, K. J. (2015). Postsecondary education programs for students with an intellectual disability: Facilitators and barriers to implementation. *Intellectual and Developmental Disabilities, 53*, 58–69.

Prader-Willi Association. (2009, July). What is Prader-Willi syndrome? Retrieved from http://www.pwsausa.org/syndrome/index.htm

Prader-Willi Syndrome Association. (2015). *PWS basic facts.* Sarasota, FL: Author. Retrieved from http://www.pwsausa.org/basic-facts/

Pretis, M. (2011). Meeting the needs of parents in early childhood intervention: The educational partnership with parents–good practice and challenges. *Journal of Policy and Practice in Intellectual Disabilities, 8*(2), 73–76.

Prince, A. T., Katsiyannis, A., & Farmer, J. (2013). Postsecondary transition under IDEA 2004: A legal update. *Intervention in School and Clinic, 48*, 286–293.

Prout, H. T., & Prout, S. M. (2000). The family with a child with mental retardation. In M. J. Fine & R. L. Simpson (Eds.), *Collaboration with parents and families of children and youth with exceptionalities* (2nd ed., pp. 217–235). Austin, TX: Pro-Ed.

Reilly, C., & Holland, N. (2011). Symptoms of attention deficit hyperactivity disorder in children and adults with intellectual disability: A review. *Journal of Applied Research in Intellectual Disabilities, 24*, 291–309.

Roberts, J. E., Hatton, D. D., & Bailey, D. B. (2001). Development and behavior of male toddlers with Fragile X syndrome. *Journal of Early Intervention, 24*, 207–223.

Roberts, J., Schaaf, J., Skinner, M., Wheeler, A., Hooper, D., Hatton, D., & Bailey, D. (2005). Academic skills of boys with fragile X syndrome: Profiles and predictors. *American Journal on Mental Retardation, 110*, 107–120.

Roid, G. (2003). *Stanford-Binet Intelligence Scales* (5th ed.). Rolling Meadows, IL: Riverside.

Rosa's Law, P.L. 111-256, S. 2781–111th Congress. (2009). [GovTrack.us (database of federal legislation)]. Retrieved from http://www.govtrack.us/congress/bills/111/s2781

Rossetti, Z. (2015). Descriptors of friendship between secondary students with and without autism or intellectual and developmental disability. *Remedial and Special Education, 36*, 181–192.

Schalock, R. A., Borthwick-Duffy, S. A., Bradley, V. J., Buntinx, W. H. E., Coulter, D. L., Craig, E. M., . . . Yeager, M. H. (2010). *Intellectual disability: Definition, classification, and systems of support* (11th ed.). Washington, DC: American Association on Intellectual and Developmental Disabilities.

Schalock, R. A., Borthwick-Duffy, S. A., Bradley, V. J., Buntinx, W. H. E., Coulter, D. L., Craig, E. M., . . . Yeager, M. H. (2010). *Intellectual disability: Definition, classification, and systems of support* (11th ed.). Washington, DC: American Association on Intellectual and Developmental Disabilities.

Schalock, R. R., & Luckasson, R. (2013). What's at stake in the lives of people with intellectual disability? Part I: The power of naming, defining, diagnosing, classifying, and planning supports. *Intellectual and Developmental Disabilities, 51*, 86–93.

Schwarte, A. (2008). Fragile X Syndrome. *School Psychology Quarterly, 23*, 290–300.

Seligman, M., & Darling, R. B. (2007). *Ordinary families, special children: A systems approach to childhood disability* (3rd ed.). New York, NY: Guilford Publications.

Sharabi, A. (2015). Coping with loneliness in children with disabilities. In A. Sha'ked, A. Rokach, A. Sha'ked, & A. Rokach (Eds.), *Addressing loneliness: Coping, prevention and clinical interventions* (pp. 88–101). New York, NY: Routledge/Taylor & Francis.

Shepherd, A., Hoban, G., & Dixon, R. (2014). Using slowmation to develop the social skills of primary school students with mild intellectual disabilities: Four case studies. *Australasian Journal of Special Education, 38*, 150–168.

Sheppard-Jones, K., Kleinert, H. L., Druckemiller, W., & Ray, M. K. (2015). Students with intellectual disability in higher education: Adult service provider perspectives. *Intellectual and Developmental Disabilities, 53*, 120–128.

Shogren, K. A., Luckasson, R., & Schalock, R. L. (2014). The definition of "context" and its application in the field of intellectual disability. *Journal of Policy and Practice in Intellectual Disabilities, 11*, 109–116.

Singh, D. K. (2000, October). *Families of children with mental retardation: Effective collaboration.* Paper presented at the Biennial Meeting of the Division on Mental Retardation and Developmental Disabilities, Baltimore, MD. (ERIC Document Reproduction Service No. ED455636)

Skiba, R. J., Simmons, A. B., Ritter, S., Gibb, A. C., Rausch, M. K., Cuadrado, J., & Chung, C. G. (2008). Achieving equity in special education: History, status, and current challenges. *Exceptional Children, 74*, 264–288.

Smith, K. A., Ayres, K. M., Mechling, L. C., Alexander, J. L., Mataras, T. K., & Shepley, S. B. (2015). Evaluating the effects of a video prompt in a system of least prompts procedure. *Career Development and Transition for Exceptional Individuals, 38*, 39–49.

Sparrow, S. S., Cicchetti, D. V., & Saulnier, C. A. (2016). *Vineland Adaptive Behavior Scales* (3rd ed.) (Vineland-3). San Antonio, TX: Pearson/Psych Corp.

Sparrow, S., Balla, D., & Cicchetti, D. (2005). *Vineland adaptive behavior scales* (2nd ed.). Bloomington, MN: American Guidance Services.

Spencer, V. G., & Balboni, G. (2003). Can students with mental retardation teach their peers? *Education and Training in Mental Retardation and Developmental Disabilities, 38*, 32–61.

Stockall, N. S. (2014). When an aide really becomes an aid: Providing professional development for special education paraprofessionals. *Teaching Exceptional Children, 46*(6), 197–205.

Stoneman, Z., & Gavidia-Payne, S. (2006). Marital adjustment in families of young children with disabilities: Associations with daily hassles and problem-focused coping. *American Journal on Mental Retardation. 3*, 1–14.

Substance Abuse and Mental Health Services Administration. (2012, July). *Fetal alcohol spectrum disorders (FASD).* Rockville, MD: Author. Retrieved from http://fasdcenter.samhsa.gov/

Switsky, H. N., & Greenspan, S. (Eds.). (2006). *What is mental retardation? Ideas for an evolving disability in the 21st century.* Washington, D.C.: American Association on Mental Retardation.

Tassé, M. J., Schalock, R. L., Balboni, G., Bersani, H., Borthwick-Duffy, S. A., Spreat, S., . . . Navas, P. (2014). *Diagnostic adaptive behavior scale* (DABS). Washington, DC: American Association on Intellectual and Developmental Disabilities.

Tassé, M. J., Schalock, R. L., Balboni, G., Spreat, S., & Navas, P. (2016). Validity and reliability of the diagnostic adaptive behavior scale. *Journal of Intellectual Disabilities Research, 60*, 80–88.

Test, D. W., Fowler, C. H., White, J., Richter, S., & Walker, A. (2009). Evidence-based secondary transition practices for enhancing school completion. *Exceptionality, 17*(1), 16–29. Thousand Oaks, CA: Corwin Press.

Think College!. (2016, May). *Find a college.* Retrieved from http://www.thinkcollege.net/component/programsdatabase/

Thoma, C. A., Lakin, K., Carlson, D., Domzal, C., Austin, K., & Boyd, K. (2011). Participation in postsecondary education for students with intellectual disabilities: A review of the literature 2001–2010. *Journal of Postsecondary Education and Disability, 24,* 175–191.

Totsika, V., Hastings, R. P., Vagenas, D., & Emerson, E. (2014). Parenting and the Behavior Problems of Young Children with an Intellectual Disability: Concurrent and Longitudinal Relationships in a Population-Based Study. *American Journal on Intellectual and Developmental Disabilities, 119*(5), 422–435.

U.S. Department of Education, Office of Special Education Programs. (2011b, July). *Infants and toddlers receiving early intervention services in accordance with Part C of the Individuals with Disabilities Education Act, 2010* [Data Analysis Systems (DANS), OMB #1820-0557]. Washington, DC: Author.

U.S. Department of Education. (2009). *28th annual report to Congress on the implementation of the Individuals with Disabilities Education Act.* Washington, DC: Author.

U.S. Department of Education. (2011a). *Thirtieth annual report to Congress on the implementation of the Individuals with Disabilities Education Act, 2008.* Washington, DC: Author.

U.S. Department of Education. (2011b). *The digest of education statistics 2010* [NCES 2011-015, Table 46]. Washington, DC: Author, National Center for Education Statistics. Retrieved from http://nces.ed.gov/fastfacts/display.asp?id=59

U.S. Department of Education. (2015). *37th annual report to Congress on the implementation of the Individuals with Disabilities Education Act.* Washington, DC: Author, Office of Special Education Programs. Retrieved from http://www2.ed.gov/about/reports/annual/osep/2015/parts-b-c/37th-arc-for-idea.pdf

U.S. Department of Education. (2016, February). Racial and ethnic disparities in special education: A multi-year disproportionality analysis by state, analysis category, and race/ethnicity. Washington, DC: Office of Special Education and Rehabilitative Services. Retrieved from https://www2.ed.gov/programs/osepidea/618-data/LEA-racial-ethnic-disparities-tables/disproportionality-analysis-by-state-analysis-category.pdf

U.S. Department of Health and Human Services. (2001, November). *Emotional and behavioral health in persons with mental retardation/developmental disabilities: Research challenges and opportunities.* Retrieved from http://ohrp.osophs.dhhs.gov/nhrpac/mtg07-02/nhrpac11.pdf

Van Naarden Braun, K., Christensen, D., Doernberg, N., Schieve, L., Rice, C., Wiggins, L., ... Yeargin-Allsopp, M. . . . (2015). Trends in the prevalence of autism spectrum disorder, cerebral palsy, hearing loss, intellectual disability, and vision impairment, metropolitan Atlanta, 1991–2010. *PLoS ONE, 10*(4). doi:10.1371/journal.pone.0124120

Van Norman, R. K. (2007). "Who's on first?" Using sports trivia peer tutoring to increase conversational language. *Intervention in School and Clinic, 43,* 88–100.

Vekeman, F. F., Gauthier-Loiselle, M., Faust, E., Lefebvre, P., Lahoz, R., Duh, M. S., & Sacco, P. (2015). Patient and caregiver burden associated with fragile x syndrome in the United States. *American Journal on Intellectual and Developmental Disabilities, 120,* 444–459.

Wadsworth, J. P., Hansen, B. D., & Wills, S. B. (2015). increasing compliance in students with intellectual disabilities using functional behavioral assessment and self-monitoring. *Remedial and Special Education, 36,* 195–207.

Washington, B. H., Hughes, C., & Cosgriff, J. C. (2012). High-poverty youth: Self-determination and involvement in educational planning. *Career Development for Exceptional Individuals, 35,* 14–28.

Watson, A., & McCathren, R. (2009). Including children with special needs: Are you and your early childhood program ready? *Young Children, 64*(2), 20–26.

Wechsler, D. (2003). *Wechsler intelligence scale for children—IV.* San Antonio, TX: Psychological Corporation.

Wechsler, D. (2014). *Wechsler Intelligence Scale for Children* (5th ed.) (WISC-V). Bloomington, MN: Psych Corp/Pearson.

Wehmeyer, M. L., & Patton, J. R. (2000). Mental retardation in the twenty-first century: Introduction to the special issue. *Focus on Autism and Other Developmental Disabilities, 15,* 66–67, 79.

Wei, X., Blackorby, J., & Schiller, E. (2011). Growth in reading achievement of students with disabilities, ages 7 to 17. *Exceptional Children, 78,* 89–106.

Whittington, J. J., Holland, A. A., & Webb, T. T. (2009). Relationship between the IQ of people with Prader-Willi syndrome and that of their siblings: Evidence for imprinted gene effects. *Journal of Intellectual Disability Research, 53,* 411–418.

Winzer, M. A. (1993). *The history of special education: From isolation to integration.* Washington, DC: Gallaudet University Press.

Winzer, M. A. (2009). From integration to inclusion: A history of special education in the 20th century. Washington, DC: Gallaudet University Press.

Wulffaert, J., Scholte, E. M., & Van Berckelaer-Onnes, I. A. (2010). Maternal parenting stress in families with a child with Angelman syndrome or Prader-Willi syndrome. *Journal of Intellectual & Developmental Disability, 35,* 165–174.

Yakubova, G., & Bouck, E. C. (2014). Not all created equally: Exploring calculator use by students with mild intellectual disability. *Education and Training in Autism and Developmental Disabilities, 49,* 111–126.

Yoong, A. A., & Koritsas, S. S. (2012). The impact of caring for adults with intellectual disability on the quality of life of parents. *Journal of Intellectual Disability Research, 56,* 609–619.

Yu, J., Newman, L., & Wagner, M. (2009, July). *Secondary school experiences and academic performance of student with mental retardation* [Facts from NLTS2]. Washington, DC: Institute of Education Sciences National Center for Special Education Research. Retrieved from http://ies.ed.gov/ncser/pubs/20093020.asp

Zhang, D. D., Katsiyannis, A. A., Ju, S., & Roberts, E. (2014). Minority representation in special education: 5-year trends. *Journal of Child & Family Studies, 23,* 118–127.

Chapter 9

Akbari, M. (2014). A multidimensional review of bilingual aphasia as a language disorder. *Advances in Language and Literary Studies, 5,* 73–86.

Al Otaiba, S., & Smartt, S. M. (2003). Summer sound camp: Involving parents in early literacy intervention for children with speech and language delays. *Teaching Exceptional Children, 35*(1), 30–34.

American Speech-Language-Hearing Association. (2007). *Childhood apraxia of speech* [Position Statement]. Retrieved from www.asha.org/policy

American Speech-Language-Hearing Association. (2016). *Speech-language pathologists: Language experts and literacy resource.* Rockville MD: Author. Retrieved from http://www.asha.org/topics/literacy/

Anderson, R. A. (2010). *How many languages are there in the world?* [brochure]. Washington, DC: Linguistic Society of America. Retrieved from http://www.linguisticsociety.org/files/how-many-languages.pdf

Apel, K., & Henbest, V. S. (2016). Affix meaning knowledge in first through third grade students. *Language, Speech, and Hearing Services in Schools, 47,* 148–156.

Apel, K., Wilson-Fowler, E. B., Brimo, D., & Perrin, N. A. (2012). Metalinguistic contributions to reading and spelling in second and third grade students. *Reading and Writing, 25,* 1283–1305.

Archibald, L. M. D., Joanisse, M., & Edmunds, A. (2011). Specific language or working memory impairments: A small-scale observational study. *Child Language Teaching and Therapy, 27,* 294–312.

Armstrong, J. (2011, August 30). Serving children with emotional-behavioral and language disorders: A collaborative approach. *The ASHA Leader.* Retrieved from http://www.asha.org/Publications/leader/2011/110830/Serving-Children-With-Emotional-Behavioral-and-Language-Disorders-A-Collaborative-Approach.htm

Badcock, N. A., Bishop, D. V. M., Hardiman, M. J., Barry, J. G., & Watkins, K. E. (2012). Co-localisation of abnormal brain structure and function in specific language impairment. *Brain and Language, 120,* 310–320.

Baird, A. S., Kibler, A., & Palacios, N. (2015). "Yo te estoy ayudando; Estoy aprendiendo también/I am helping you; I am learning too:" A bilingual family's community of practice during home literacy events. *Journal of Early Childhood Literacy, 15,* 147–176.

Baker, E., & McLeod, S. (2011a). Evidence-based practice for children with speech sound disorders: Part 1 Narrative review. *Language, Speech, and Hearing Services in Schools, 42,* 102–139.

Baker, E., & McLeod, S. (2011b). Evidence-based practice for children with speech sound disorders: Part 2 Application to clinical practice. *Language, Speech, and Hearing Services in Schools, 42,* 140–151.

Ballard, K. J., Wambaugh, J. L., Duffy, J. R., Layfield, C., Maas, E., Mauszycki, S., & McNeil, M. R. (2015). Treatment for acquired apraxia of speech: A systematic review of intervention research between 2004 and 2012. *American Journal of Speech-Langauge Pathology, 24,* 316–337.

Bauer, K. L., Iyer, S., Boon, R. T., & Fore, C. (2010). 20 ways for classroom teachers to collaborate with speech-language pathologists. *Intervention in School and Clinic, 45,* 333–337.

Bedore, L. M., Pena, E. D., Summers, C. L., Boerger, K. M., Resendiz, M. D., Greene, K., . . . Gillam, R. B. (2012). The measure matters: Language dominance profiles across measures in Spanish-English bilingual children. *Bilingualism: Language and Cognition, 15,* 616–629.

Bellis, T. J. (2012). *Understanding auditory processing disorders in children.* Washington, DC: American Speech-Language-Hearing Association. Retrieved from http://www.asha.org/public/hearing/disorders/understand-apd-child.htm

Beneke, M., & Cheatham, G. A. (2015). Speaking up for African American English: Equity and inclusion in early childhood settings. *Early Childhood Education Journal, 43,* 127–134.

Benner, G. J., Nelson, J. R., & Epstein, M. H. (2002). Language skills of children with EBD: A literature review. *Journal of Emotional and Behavioral Disorders, 10,* 43–59.

Benner, G. J., Ralston, N. C., & Feuerborn, L. (2012). The effect of the Language for Thinking program on the cognitive processing and social adjustment of students with emotional and behavioral disorders. *Preventing School Failure, 56*(1), 47–54.

Blood, G. W., Blood, I., Kreiger, J., O'Connor, S., & Qualls, C. (2009). Double jeopardy for children who stutter: Race and coexisting disorders. *Communication Disorders Quarterly, 30,* 131–141.

Bond, M. A., & Wasik, B. A. (2009). "Conversations stations": Promoting language development in young children. *Early Childhood Education Journal, 36,* 467–473.

Brackenbury, T., Burroughs, E., & Hewitt, L. E. (2008). A qualitative examination of current guidelines for evidence-based practice in child language intervention. *Language, Speech, and Hearing Services in Schools, 39,* 78–88.

Brady, N. C., Bruce, S., Goldman, A., Erickson, K., Mineo, B., Ogletree, B. T., ... Wilkinson, K. (2016). Communication services and supports for individuals with severe disabilities: Guidance for assessment and intervention. *American Journal on Intellectual and Developmental Disabilities, 121,* 121–138.

Brice, A. E., Franklin, E., & Ratusnik, D. L. (2008). *Hola, shalom, hello: Adolescent pragmatics from a cross-cultural perspective.* (ERIC Document Reproduction Service No. ED503417). Retrieved from http://www.eric .ed.gov/ERICWebPortal/contentdelivery/servlet/ERICServlet?accno_ED503417

Byrd, C. T., Logan, K. J., & Gillam, R. B. (2012). Speech disfluency in school-age children's conversational and narrative discourse. *Language, Speech, and Hearing Services in Schools, 43,* 153–163.

Cacace, A. T., & McFarland, D. J. (Eds.) (2009). *Controversies in central auditory processing disorder.* San Diego, CA: Plural Publishing.

Carrow-Woolfolk, E. (1999). *Comprehensive Assessment of Spoken Language (CASL).* Circle Pines, MN: AGS.

Castrogiovanni, A. (2002). *Prison population communicative disorders information.* Rockville, MD: American Speech-Language-Hearing Association. Retrieved from www.audiologyonline.com/audiology/newroot/'associations/userpages/digicare/news/newsdisp.asp?newsid_126

Castrogiovanni, A. (2008). *Incidence and prevalence of speech, voice, and language disorders in adults in the United States: 2008 edition.* Rockville (MD): American Speech-Language-Hearing Association.

Centers for Disease Control and Prevention. (2016, February). *National estimates for 21 selected major birth defects, 2004–2006.* Atlanta, GA: National Center of Birth Defects and Developmental Disabilities. Retrieved from http://www.cdc.gov/ncbddd/birthdefects/data.html

Clarke, M., Newton, C., Petrides, K., Griffiths, T., Lysley, A., & Price, K. (2012). An examination of relations between participation, communication and age in children with complex communication needs. *AAC: Augmentative and Alternative Communication, 28,* 44–51.

Cohen-Mimran, R., Reznik-Nevet, L., & Korona-Gaon, S. (2016). An activity-based language intervention program for kindergarten children: A retrospective evaluation. *Early Childhood Education Journal, 44,* 69–78.

Conti-Ramsden, G., Botting, N., & Durkin, K. (2008). Parental perspectives during the transition to adulthood of adolescents with a history of specific language impairment (SLI). *Journal of Speech, Language, and Hearing Research, 51,* 84–96.

Cordewener, K. A. H., Bosman, A. M. T., & Verhoeven, L. (2012). Specific language impairment affects the early spelling process quantitatively but not qualitatively. *Research in Developmental Disabilities: A Multidisciplinary Journal, 33,* 1041–1047.

Culatta, B., & Wiig, E. H. (2002). Language disabilities in school-age children and youth. In G. H. Shames & N. B. Anderson (Eds.), *Human communication disorders: An introduction* (6th ed., pp. 218–257). Boston, MA: Allyn & Bacon.

da Cruz, A. D., Silvério, K. C. A., Da Costa, A. R. A., Moret, A. L. M., Lauris, J. R. P., & de Souza Jacob, R. T. (2016). Evaluating effectiveness of dynamic soundfield system in the classroom. *Noise and Health, 18*(80), 42.

DeBonis, D. A. (2015). It is time to rethink central auditory processing disorder protocols for school-aged children. *American Journal of Audiology, 24,* 124–136.

DeThorne, L. S., Petrill, S. A., Hayiou-Thomas, M. E., & Plomin, R. (2005). Low expressive vocabulary: Higher heritability as a function of more severe cases. *Journal of Speech, Language, and Hearing Research, 48,* 792–804.

Dockrell, J. E., & Shield, B. (2012). The impact of sound-field systems on learning and attention in elementary school classrooms. *Journal of Speech, Language, and Hearing Research, 55,* 1163–1176.

Drager, K. R., Reichle, J., & Pinkoski, C. (2010). Synthesized speech output and children: A scoping review. *American Journal of Speech-Language Pathology, 19,* 259–273.

Duchan, J. (2011). *Getting here: A short history of speech-pathology in America.* Retrieved from http://www.acsu.buffalo.edu/~duchan/new_history/overview.html

Duchan, J. F. (2010). The early years of language, speech, and hearing services in U.S. schools. *Language, Speech & Hearing Services in Schools, 41,* 152–160.

Duffy, J. R., Strand, E. A., & Josephs, K. A. (2014). Motor speech disorders associated with primary progressive aphasia. *Aphasiology, 28,* 1004–1017.

Durkin, K., Conti-Ramsden, G., & Simkin, Z. (2012). Functional outcomes of adolescents with a history of specific language impairment (SLI) with and without autistic symptomatology. *Journal of Autism and Developmental Disorders, 42,* 123–138.

Fisher, D., & Lapp, D. (2013). Learning to talk like the test: Guiding speakers of African American Vernacular English. *Journal of Adolescent & Adult Literacy, 56*, 634–648.

Fisher, H., & Logemann, J. A. (1971). *Fisher–Logemann Test of Articulation Competence*. Oceanside, CA: Academic Communication Associates.

Games, F., Curran, A., & Porter, S. (2012). A small-scale pilot study into language difficulties in children who offend. *Educational Psychology in Practice, 28*, 127–140.

Gerber, S., Brice, A., Capone, N., Fujiki, M., & Timler, G. (2012). Language use in social interactions of school-age children with language impairments: An evidence-based systematic review of treatment. *Language, Speech, and Hearing Services in Schools, 43*, 235–249.

Glazer, S. M. (2001). Communication disorders: How to identify when students are having difficulty connecting. *Teaching PreK–8, 31*(5), 86–87.

Goldman, R., & Fristoe, M. (2000). *Goldman–Fristoe Test of Articulation 2*. Circle Pines, MN: AGS.

Goldman, R., & Fristoe, M. (2015). *Goldman-Fristoe Test of Articulation 3*. Bloomington, MN: Pearson Clinical.

Gottardo, A., & Meuller, J. (2009). Are first- and second-language factors related in predicting second-language reading comprehension? A study of Spanish-speaking children acquiring English as a second language from first to second grade. *Journal of Educational Psychology, 101*, 330–344.

Gregory, J., & Bryan, K. (2015). Speech and language therapy intervention with a group of persistent and prolific young offenders in a non-custodial setting with previously undiagnosed speech, language and communication difficulties. *International Journal of Language and Communication Disorders, 46*, 202–215.

Guiberson, M., & Atkins, J. (2012). Speech-language pathologists' preparation, practices, and perspectives on serving culturally and linguistically diverse children. *Communication Disorders Quarterly, 33*, 169–180.

Hammill, D. D., Brown, V. L., Larsen, S. C., & Wiederholt, J. L. (2007). *Test of Adolescent and Adult Language* (4th edition) (TOAL-4). Austin, TX: Proed.

Harris, S. F., Prater, M. A., Dyches, T. T., & Heath, M. A. (2009). Job stress of school-based speech-language pathologists. *Communication Disorders Quarterly, 30*, 103–111.

Havstam, C., Laakso, K., & Ringsberg, K. C. (2011). Making sense of the cleft: Young adults' accounts of growing up with a cleft and deviant speech. *Journal of Health Psychology, 16*, 22–30.

Helenius, P., Parviainen, T., Paetau, R., & Salmelin, R. (2009). Neural processing of spoken words in specific language impairment and dyslexia. *Brain, 132*, 1918–1927.

Hoff, E., & Shatz, M. (Eds.). (2007). *Blackwell handbook of language development*. Malden, MA: Blackwell.

Hopkins, T., Clegg, J., & Stackhouse, J. (2016). Young offenders' perspectives on their literacy and communication skills. *International Journal of Language & Communication Disorders, 51*, 95–109.

Houwen, S., Visser, L., van der Putten, A., & Vlaskamp, C. (2016). The interrelationships between motor, cognitive, and language development in children with and without intellectual and developmental disabilities. *Research in Developmental Disabilities, 53–54*, 19–31.

Jackson, C. W., Wahlquist, J., & Marquis, C. (2011). Visual supports for shared reading with young children: The effect of static overlay design. *AAC: Augmentative and Alternative Communication, 27*, 91–102.

Kaiser, A. P., & Roberts, M. Y. (2011). Advances in early communication and language intervention. *Journal of Early Intervention, 33*, 298–309.

Kamhi, A. G. (2003). *The role of the SLP in improving reading fluency*. Retrieved from www.asha.org/about/publications/leader-online/archives/2003/q2/030415f.htm

King, A. M., & Fahsl, A. J. (2012). Supporting social competence in children who use augmentative and alternative communication. *Teaching Exceptional Children, 45*(1), 42–49.

Kohnert, K., Windsor, J., & Yim, D. (2006). Do language-based processing tasks separate children with language impairment from typical bilinguals? *Learning Disabilities Research and Practice, 21*, 19–29.

Kojima, T., Mimura, M., Auchi, K., Yoshino, F., & Kato, M. (2011). Long-term recovery from acquired childhood aphasia and changes of cerebral blood flow. *Journal of Neurolinguistics, 24*, 96–112.

Koutsoftas, A. D., Harmon, M. T., & Gray, S. (2009). The effect of tier 2 intervention for phonemic awareness in a response-to-intervention model in low-income preschool classrooms. *Language, Speech, and Hearing Services in Schools, 40*, 116–130.

Kummer, A. W. (2011). Disorders of resonance and air flow secondary to cleft palate and/or velopharyngeal dysfunction. *Seminars in Speech & Language, 32*, 141–149.

Kummerer, S. E., Lopez-Reyna, N. A., & Hughes, M. T. (2007). Immigrant mothers' perceptions of their children's communication disabilities, emergent literacy development, and speech-language therapy programs. *American Journal of Speech-Language Pathology, 16*, 271–282.

Language Varieties Network. (2004). *Pidgins, creoles, and other stigmatized varieties*. Retrieved from www2.hawaii.edu/gavinm/home.htm

LaSalle, L. R., & Wolk, L. (2011). Stuttering, cluttering, and phonological complexity: Case studies. *Journal of Fluency Disorders, 36*, 285–289.

Law, J., Plunkett, C. C., & Stringer, H. (2012). Communication interventions and their impact on behaviour in the young child: A systematic review. *Child Language Teaching and Therapy, 28*, 7–23.

Lederberg, A. R., Schick, B., & Spencer, P. E. (2012). Language and literacy development of deaf and hard-of-hearing children: Successes and challenges. *Developmental Psychology*. doi:10.1037/a0029558

Lee, A., Gibbon, F. E., & Spivey, K. (2016, March). Children's attitudes toward peers with unintelligible speech associated with cleft lip and/or palate. *The Cleft Palate-Craniofacial Journal*. doi: 10.1597/15-088

Lewis, B. A., Avrich, A. A., Freebairn, L. A., Hansen, A. J., Sucheston, L. E., Kuo, I., . . . Steina, C. M. (2011). Literacy outcomes of children with early childhood speech sound disorders: Impact of endophenotypes. *Journal of Speech, Language, and Hearing Research, 54*, 1628–1643.

Light, J., & McNaughton, D. (2008). Making a difference: A celebration of the 25th anniversary of the International Society for Augmentative and Alternative Communication. *Augmentative and Alternative Communication, 24*, 175–193.

Lindeman, K. W., & Magiera, K. (2014). A co-teaching model: Committed professionals, high expectations, and the inclusive classroom. *Odyssey: New Directions in Deaf Education, 15*, 40–45.

Long, C. E., Gurka, M. J., & Blackman, J. A. (2008). Family stress and children's language and behavior problems: Results from the National Survey of Children's Health. *Topics in Early Childhood Special Education, 28*, 148–157.

Lue, M. S. (2001). *A survey of communication disorders for the classroom teacher*. Boston, MA: Allyn & Bacon.

Lukács, Á., Ladányi, E., Fazekas, K., & Kemény, F. (2016). Executive functions and the contribution of short-term memory span in children with specific language impairment. *Neuropsychology, 30*, 296–303.

Lyons, R., O'Malley, M., O'Connor, P., & Monaghan, U. (2010). "It's just so lovely to hear him talking": Exploring the early-intervention expectations and experiences of parents. *Child Language Teaching and Therapy, 26*, 61–76.

Matson, G., & Cline, T. (2012). The impact of specific language impairment on performance in science and suggested implications for pedagogy. *Child Language Teaching and Therapy, 28,* 25–37.

McLeod, A. N., & Apel, K. (2015). Morphological awareness intervention study of a child with a history of speech and language impairment. *Communication Disorders Quarterly, 36,* 208–218.

Miron, C. (2012). The parent experience: When a child is diagnosed with childhood apraxia of speech. *Communication Disorders Quarterly, 33,* 96–110.

Mock, J., Zadina, J. N., Corey, D. M., Cohen, J. D., Lemen, L. C., & Foundas, A. L. (2012). Atypical brain torque in boys with developmental stuttering. *Developmental Neuropsychology, 37,* 434–452.

Mok, P. H., Pickles, A., Durkin, K., & Conti-Ramsden, G. (2014). Longitudinal trajectories of peer relations in children with specific language impairment. *Journal of Child Psychology and Psychiatry, 55,* 516–527.

Moore, L., Koger, D., Blomberg, S., Legg, L., McConahy, R., Wit, S., & Gatmaitman, M. (2012). Making best practice our practice: Reflections on our journey into natural environments. *Infants and Young Children, 25,* 95–105.

Nail-Chiwetalu, B. J., & Ratner, N. B. (2006). Information literacy for speech-language pathologists: A key to evidence-based practice. *Language, Speech, and Hearing Services in Schools, 37,* 157–167.

National Institute of Dental and Craniofacial Research. (2011). *Prevalence (number of cases) of cleft lip and cleft palate.* Bethesda, MD: Author, National Institutes of Health. Retrieved from http://www.nidcr.nih.gov/DataStatistics/FindDataByTopic/CraniofacialBirthDefects/PrevalenceCleft+LipCleftPalate.htm

National Institute on Deafness and Other Communication Disorders [NIDCD]. (2009, June). *Statistics on voice, speech, and language.* Washington, DC: National Institutes of Health. Retrieved from http://www.nidcd.nih.gov/health/statistics/vsl.asp

National Institute on Deafness and Other Communication Disorders [NIDCD]. (2015, June). *About 1 in 12 children has a disorder related to voice, speech, language, or swallowing.* Bethesda, MD: National Institutes of Health. Retrieved from https://www.nidcd.nih.gov/news/2015/about-1-12-children-has-disorder-related-voice-speech-language-or-swallowing

National Institute on Deafness and Other Communication Disorders [NIDCD]. (2016, April). *Quick statistics about voice, speech, and language.* Bethesda, MD: National Institutes of Health. Retrieved from https://www.nidcd.nih.gov/health/statistics/quick-statistics-voice-speech-language

National Institute on Deafness and Other Communication Disorders. (2006). *Ear infections: Facts for parents about otitis media.* Retrieved from www.nidcd.nih.gov/health/hearing/otitismedia.htm

National Institute on Deafness and Other Communication Disorders. (2009, June). *Statistics on voice, speech, and language.* Washington, DC: National Institutes of Health. Retrieved from http://www.nidcd.nih.gov/health/statistics/vsl.asp

Nellis, L. M., Sickman, L. S., Newman, D. S., & Harman, D. R. (2014). Schoolwide collaboration to prevent and address reading difficulties: Opportunities for school psychologists and speech-language pathologists. *Journal of Educational & Psychological Consultation, 24,* 110–127.

Newman, M. (2006). Definitions of literacy and their consequences. In H. Luria, D. M. Seymour, & T. Smoke (Eds.), *Language and linguistics in context: Readings and applications for teachers* (pp. 243–255). Mahwah, NJ: Lawrence Erlbaum.

Newton, D. W. (2004). *The reality of dialects.* Retrieved from www.wetga.edu/~dnewton/eng12000/dialects.html

Nielsen, D., & Friesen, L. (2012). A study of the effectiveness of a small-group intervention on the vocabulary and narrative development of at-risk kindergarten children. *Reading Psychology, 33,* 269–299.

Nippold, M. (2012). Different service delivery models for different communication disorders. *Language, Speech, and Hearing Services in Schools, 43,* 117–120.

Norbury, C. F. (2014). Practitioner review: Social (pragmatic) communication disorder conceptualization, evidence and clinical implications. *Journal of Child Psychology & Psychiatry, 55,* 204–216.

Olswang, L. B., & Prelock, P. A. (2015). Bridging the gap between research and practice: Implementation science. *Journal of Speech, Language, and Hearing Research, 58,* S1818-S1826.

Overby, M., Carrell, T., & Bernthal, J. (2007). Teachers' perceptions of students with speech sound disorders: A quantitative and qualitative analysis. *Language, Speech, and Hearing Services in Schools, 38,* 327–341.

Owens, R. E., Metz, D. E., & Haas, A. (2003). *Introduction to communication disorders: A life span perspective* (2nd ed.). Boston, MA: Allyn & Bacon.

Paradis, J., Schneider, P., & Duncan, T. S. (2013). Discriminating children with language impairment among English-language learners from diverse first-language backgrounds. *Journal of Speech, Language, and Hearing Research, 56,* 971–981.

Parette, P., & Huer, M. B. (2002). Working with Asian American families whose children have augmentative and alternative communication needs. *Journal of Special Education Technology, 17*(4), 5–13.

Paul, D., & Roth, F. P. (2011). Guiding principles and clinical applications for speech-language pathology practice in early intervention. *Language, Speech, and Hearing Services in Schools, 42,* 320–330.

Peña, E. D., Gillam, R. B., & Bedore, L. M. (2014). Dynamic assessment of narrative ability in English accurately identifies language impairment in English language learners. *Journal of Speech, Language, and Hearing Research, 57,* 2208–2220.

Peets, K. (2009). The effects of context on the classroom discourse skills of children with language impairment. *Language, Speech, and Hearing Services in Schools, 40,* 5–16.

Perkins, S. C., Finegood, E. D., & Swain, J. E. (2013). Poverty and language development: Roles of parenting and stress. *Innovations in Clinical Neuroscience, 10*(4), 10–19.

Peter, B., Wijsman, E. M., Nato Jr, A. Q., Matsushita, M. M., Chapman, K. L., Stanaway, I. B., ... Raskin, W. H. (2016, April). Genetic candidate variants in two multigenerational families with childhood apraxia of speech. *PloS One, 11*(4). doi: 10.1371/journal.pone.0153864

Pickl, G. (2011). Communication intervention in children with severe disabilities and multilingual backgrounds: Perceptions of pedagogues and parents. *AAC: Augmentative and Alternative Communication, 27,* 229–244.

Pickles, A., Simonoff, E., Conti-Ramsden, G., Falcaro, M., Simkin, Z., Charman, T., . . . Baird, G. (2009). Loss of language in early development of autism and specific language impairment. *Journal of Child Psychology and Psychiatry, 50,* 843–852.

Pratt, C., Dotting, N., & Conti-Ramsden, G. (2006). The characteristics and concerns of mothers of adolescents with a history of SLI. *Child Language Teaching and Therapy, 22,* 177–196.

Prins, D., & Ingham, R. J. (2009). Evidence-based treatment and stuttering-historical perspective. *Journal of Speech, Language, and Hearing Research, 52,* 254–263.

Pufpaff, L. A. (2008). Barriers to participation in kindergarten literacy instruction for a student with augmentative and alternative communication needs. *Psychology in the Schools, 45,* 582–599.

Quattlebaum, P. D., Grier, B. C., & Klubnik, C. (2012). Bipolar disorder in children: Implications for speech-language pathologists. *Communication Disorders Quarterly, 33,* 181–192.

Racanello, A., & McCabe, P. C. (2010). Role of otitis media in hearing loss and language deficits. In P. C. McCabe, S. R. Shaw (Eds.), *Pediatric disorders* (pp. 22–31). Thousand Oaks, CA: Corwin.

Raghavendra, P., Olsson, C., Sampson, J., Mcinerney, R., & Connell, T. (2012). School participation and social networks of children with complex communication needs, physical disabilities, and typically developing peers. *AAC: Augmentative and Alternative Communication, 28,* 33–43.

Rescorla, L., Ross, G. S., & McClure, S. (2007). Language delay and behavioral/ emotional problems in toddlers: Findings from two developmental clinics. *Journal of Speech, Language, and Hearing Research, 50,* 1063–1078.

Research and Scientific Affairs Committee, American Speech-Language-Hearing Association. (2004). *Evidence-based practice in communication disorders: An introduction* [Technical report]. Retrieved from www.asha.org/members/deskref-journals/deskref/default

Roberts, M. Y., & Kaiser, A. P. (2012). Assessing the effects of a parent-implemented language intervention for children with language impairments using empirical benchmarks: A pilot study. *Journal of Speech, Language, and Hearing Research, 55,* 1655–1670.

Romski, M., Sevcik, R. A., Adamson, L. B., Smith, A., Cheslock, M., & Bakeman, R. (2011). Parent perceptions of the language development of toddlers with developmental delays before and after participation in parent-coached language interventions. *American Journal of Speech-Language Pathology, 20,* 111–118.

Ryan, A., Gibbon, F. E., & O'shea, A. (2016). Expressive and receptive language skills in preschool children from a socially disadvantaged area. *International Journal of Speech-Language Pathology, 18,* 41–52.

Sayer, P. (2008). Demystifying language mixing: Spanglish in school. *Journal of Latinos and Education, 7,* 94–112.

Schmitt, M. B., Justice, L. M., & O'Connell, A. (2014). Vocabulary gain among children with language disorders: Contributions of children's behavior regulation and emotionally supportive environments. *American Journal of Speech-Language Pathology, 23,* 373–384.

Scott, C. M. (2014). One size does not fit all: Improving clinical practice in older children and adolescents with language and learning disorders. *Language, Speech, and Hearing Services in Schools, 45,* 145–152.

Scott, L., & Guitar, C. (2008). *Stuttering: Straight talk for teachers* (3rd ed.) [Publication No. 0125]. Memphis, TN: The Stuttering Foundation. Retrieved from www.stutteringhelp.org

Shames, G. H., & Anderson, N. B. (2006). *Human communication disorders: An introduction* (7th ed.). Boston, MA: Allyn & Bacon.

Shapiro, L. R., Hurry, J., Masterson, J., Wydell, T. N., & Doctor, E. (2009). Classroom implications of recent research into literacy development: From predictors to assessment. *Dyslexia, 15,* 1–22.

Shive, T., & Bellis, T. (2011). (Central) auditory processing disorders: Current conceptualizations. In J. Guendouzi, F. Loncke, M. J. Williams (Eds.), *The handbook of psycholinguistic and cognitive processes: Perspectives in communication disorders* (pp. 347–360). New York, NY: Psychology Press.

Skwerer, D. P., Jordan, S. E., Brukilacchio, B. H., & Tager-Flusberg, H. (2015). Comparing methods for assessing receptive language skills in minimally verbal children and adolescents with autism spectrum disorders. *Autism.* doi:10.1177/1362361315600146

Smith, M. M. (2015). Adolescence and AAC: Intervention challenges and possible solutions. *Communication Disorders Quarterly, 36,* 112–118.

Snell, M. E., Brady, N., McLean, L., Ogletree, B. T., Siegel, E., Sylvester, L., & Sevcik, R. (2010). Twenty years of communication intervention research with individuals who have severe intellectual and developmental disabilities. *American Journal on Intellectual and Developmental Disabilities, 115,* 364–380.

Snowling, M. J., & Melby-Lervåg, M. (2016). Oral language deficits in familial dyslexia: A meta-analysis and review. *Psychological Bulletin, 142,* 498–545.

Stiles, M. (2013). "Do we make ourselves clear?" Developing a social, emotional and behavioural difficulties (SEBD) support service's effectiveness in detecting and supporting children experiencing speech, language and communication difficulties (SLCD). *Emotional & Behavioural Difficulties, 18,* 213–232.

Suarez, S. C., & Daniels, K. J. (2009). Listening for competence through documentation: Assess children with language delays using digital video. *Remedial and Special Education, 30,* 177–190.

Swanson, T. J., Hodson, B. W., & Schommer-Aikins, M. (2005). An examination of phonological awareness treatment outcomes for seventh-grade poor readers from a bilingual community. *Language, Speech, and Hearing Services in Schools, 36,* 336–345.

Tommerdahl, J. (2009). What teachers of students with SEBD need to know about speech and language difficulties. *Emotional & Behavioural Difficulties, 14,* 19–31.

Turner, K. H. (2009). Flipping the switch: Code-switching from text speak to standard English. *English Journal, 98*(5), 60–65.

U.S. Department of Education, Office of Special Education Programs. (2011b, July). *Infants and toddlers receiving early intervention services in accordance with Part C of the Individuals with Disabilities Education Act, 2010* [Data Analysis Systems (DANS), OMB #1820-0557]. Washington, DC: Author.

U.S. Department of Education. (2009). *28th annual report to Congress on the implementation of the Individuals with Disabilities Education Act.* Washington, DC: Author.

U.S. Department of Education. (2011b). *The digest of education statistics 2010* [NCES 2011-015, Table 46]. Washington, DC: Author, National Center for Education Statistics. Retrieved from http://nces.ed.gov/fastfacts/display.asp?id=59

U.S. Department of Education. (2012). *Data tables for OSEP state reported data: Number of children ages 3 through 5 served under IDEA, Part B, by disability category and state, Fall 2011* [Table B11-2]. Retrieved from https://www.ideadata.org/arc_toc13.asp#partbCC

U.S. Department of Education. (2012, July). *Children with disabilities receiving special education under Part B of the Individuals with Disabilities Education Act 2011* [OMB #1820-0043]. Washington, DC: U.S. Department of Education, Office of Special Education Programs, Data Analysis System (DANS).

U.S. Department of Education. (2015). *37th annual report to Congress on the implementation of the Individuals with Disabilities Education Act.* Washington, DC: Author, Office of Special Education Programs. Retrieved from http://www2.ed.gov/about/reports/annual/osep/2015/parts-b-c/37th-arc-for-idea.pdf

Ukrainetz, T. A., & Gillam, R. B. (2009). The expressive elaboration of imaginative narratives by children with specific language impairment. *Journal of Speech, Language, and Hearing Research, 52,* 883–898.

Vandewalle, E., Boets, B., Ghesquiere, P., & Zink, I. (2012). Auditory processing and speech perception in children with specific language impairment: Relations with oral language and literacy skills. *Research in Developmental Disabilities: A Multidisciplinary Journal, 33,* 635–644.

Venker, C. E., Bolt, D. M., Meyer, A., Sindberg, H., Weismer, S. E., & Tager-Flusberg, H. (2015). Parent telegraphic speech use and spoken language in preschoolers with ASD. *Journal of Speech, Language, and Hearing Research, 58,* 1733–1746.

Verdon, S., McLeod, S., & Wong, S. (2015). Reconceptualizing practice with multilingual children with speech sound disorders: People, practicalities and policy. *International Journal of Language & Communication Disorders, 50,* 48–62.

Vicker, B. (2009). The 21st-century speech language pathologist and integrated services in classrooms. *Indiana Resource Center for Autism Reporter 14*(2), 1–5, 17.

Volden, J., Coolican, J., & Garon, N. (2009). Brief report: Pragmatic language in autism spectrum disorder–Relationships to measures of ability and disability. *Journal of Autism and Developmental Disorders, 39,* 388–393.

Vouloumanos, A., & Waxman, S. R. (2014). Listen up! Speech is for thinking during infancy. *Trends in Cognitive Sciences, 18,* 642–646.

Wankoff, L. S. (2011). Warning signs in the development of speech, language, and communication: When to refer to a speech-language pathologist. *Journal of Child and Adolescent Psychiatric Nursing, 24,* 175–184.

Watson, G. D., & Bellon-Harn, M. L. (2014). Speech-language pathologist and general educator collaboration: A model for tier 2 service delivery. *Intervention in School and Clinic, 49*, 237–243.

Weil, M. (2011). Listen Up! *T.H.E. Journal, 38*(7), 16.

Wheeler, R. S. (2008). Becoming adept at code-switching. *Educational Leadership, 65*(7), 54–58.

Wheeler, R., Cartwright, K. B., & Swords, R. (2012). Factoring AAVE into reading assessment and instruction. *Reading Teacher, 65*, 416–425.

Wickenden, M. (2011). Talking to teenagers: Using anthropological methods to explore identity and the lifeworlds of young people who use AAC. *Communication Disorders Quarterly, 32*, 151–163.

Wilcox, M., & Woods, J. (2011). Participation as a basis for developing early intervention outcomes. *Language, Speech, and Hearing Services in Schools, 42*, 365–378.

Wilson, L., McNeill, B., & Gillon, G. T. (2015). The knowledge and perceptions of prospective teachers and speech language therapists in collaborative language and literacy instruction. *Child Language Teaching and Therapy, 31*, 347–362.

Wolk, L., & LaSalle, L. R. (2015). Phonological complexity in school-aged children who stutter and exhibit a language disorder. *Journal of Fluency Disorders, 43*, 40–53.

Wolter, J. A., Wood, A., & D'Zatko, K. W. (2009). The influence of morphological awareness on the literacy development of first-grade children. *Language, Speech, and Hearing Services in Schools, 40*, 286–298.

Woods, J. J., Wilcox, M. J., Friedman, M., & Murch, T. (2011). Collaborative consultation in natural environments: Strategies to enhance family-centered supports and services. *Language, Speech, and Hearing Services in Schools, 42*, 379–392.

Xin, J. F., & Leonard, D. A. (2015). Using iPads to teach communication skills of students with autism. *Journal of Autism and Developmental Disorders, 45*, 4154–4164.

Zebron, S., Mhute, I., & Musingafi, M. C. (2015). Classroom challenges: Working with pupils with communication disorders. *Journal of Education and Practice, 6*(9), 18–22.

Chapter 10

Alderson-Day, B. (2011). Verbal problem solving in autism spectrum disorders: A problem of plan construction? *Autism Research, 4*, 401–411.

Ali, S., & Frederickson, N. (2006). Investigating the evidence base of social stories. *Educational Psychology in Practice, 22*, 355–377.

American Academy of Pediatrics. (2010). *Vaccine studies: Examine the evidence.* Elk Grove, IL: Author. Retrieved from http://www.aap.org/en-us/advocacy-and-policy/Documents/vaccinestudies.pdf

American Academy of Pediatrics. (2013, April). Vaccine safety: Examine the evidence. Elk Grove, IL: Author. Retrieved from https://www.aap.org/en-us/Documents/immunization_vaccine_studies.pdf

American Psychiatric Association. (2000). *Diagnostic and statistical manual of mental disorders* (4th ed., Text revision). Washington, DC: Author.

American Psychiatric Association. (2011, January). *DSM-V development: A 05 Autism Spectrum Disorder.* Retrieved from http://www.dsm5.org/ proposedrevisions/pages/proposedrevision.aspx?rid=94

American Psychiatric Association. (2013). *Diagnostic and statistical manual of mental disorders* (5th ed.). Washington, DC: Author.

Asaro-Saddler, K. (2016). Using evidence-based practices to teach writing to children with autism spectrum disorders. *Preventing School Failure, 60*, 79–85.

Ashby, C. E., & Causton-Theoharis, J. (2012). "Moving quietly through the door of opportunity": Perspectives of college students who type to communicate. *Equity & Excellence in Education, 45*, 261–282.

Aspy, R., & Grossman, B. (2006). *The Ziggurat Model: A framework for designing comprehensive interventions for individuals with high-functioning autism and Asperger syndrome.* Shawnee Mission, KS: Autism Asperger Publishing.

Axe, J. B., & Evans, C. J. (2012). Using video modeling to teach children with PDD-NOS to respond to facial expressions. *Research in Autism Spectrum Disorders, 6*, 1176–1185.

Baghdadli, A., Assouline, B., Sonie, S., Pernon, E., Darrou, C., Michelon, C., . . . Pry, R. (2012). Developmental trajectories of adaptive behaviors from early childhood to adolescence in a cohort of 152 children with autism spectrum disorders. *Journal of Autism and Developmental Disorders, 42*, 1314–1325.

Baio, J. (2012, March). Prevalence of autism spectrum disorders–Autism and developmental disabilities monitoring network, 14 Sites, United States, 2008 [surveillance summaries]. *Morbidity and Mortality Weekly Report, 61*, 1–19. Retrieved from http://www.cdc.gov/mmwr/preview/mmwrhtml/ss6103a1.htm?s_cid=ss6103a1_w

Baker, S., Lang, R., & O'Reilly, M. (2009). Review of video modeling with students with emotional and behavioral disorders. *Education and Treatment of Children, 32*, 403–420.

Banda, D. R. (2015). Review of sibling interventions with children with autism. *Education and Training in Autism and Developmental Disabilities, 50*, 303–315.

Barnhill, G. P. (2016). Supporting students with Asperger syndrome on college campuses. *Focus on Autism & Other Developmental Disabilities, 31*, 3–15.

Barnhill, G., Cook, K., Tebbenkamp, K., & Myles, B. (2002). The effectiveness of social skills intervention: Targeting nonverbal communication for adolescents with Asperger Syndrome and related pervasive developmental delays. *Focus on Autism and Other Developmental Disabilities, 17*, 112–118.

Baron-Cohen, S. (2015). Leo Kanner, Hans Asperger, and the discovery of autism. *The Lancet, 386*, 1329–1330.

Barton, M., Robins, D., & Fein, D. (1999). *Modified Checklist for Autism in Toddlers* (M-CHAT). Retrieved from http://www.dbpeds.org/articles/detail.cfm?TextID=466

Bazzano, A., Zeldin, A., Schuster, E., Barrett, C., & Lehrer, D. (2012). Vaccine-related beliefs and practices of parents of children with autism spectrum disorders. *American Journal on Intellectual and Developmental Disabilities, 117*, 233–242.

Ben-Itzchak, E., Zukerman, G., & Zachor, D. A. (2016). Having older siblings is associated with less severe social communication symptoms in young children with autism spectrum disorder. *Journal of Abnormal Child Psychology.* doi:10.1007/s10802-016-0133-0

Bergbaum, A., & Ogilvie, C. M. (2016). Autism and chromosome abnormalities—A review. *Clinical Anatomy.* doi: 10.1002/ca.22719

Biederman, G., & Freedman, B. (2007). Modeling skills, signs and lettering for children with Down syndrome, autism and other severe developmental delays by video instruction in classroom setting. *Journal of Early and Intensive Behavior Intervention, 4*, 736–743.

Bleach, F. (2001). *Everybody is different: A book for young people who have brothers and sisters with autism.* Shawnee Mission, KS: Autism Asperger Publishing.

Bondy, A., & Weiss, M. J. (2013). Teaching social skills to people with autism: Best practices in individualizing interventions. Bethesda, MD: Woodbine House.

Boucher, J. (2012). Putting theory of mind in its place: Psychological explanations of the socio-emotional-communicative impairments in autistic spectrum disorder. *Autism: The International Journal of Research and Practice, 16*, 226–246.

Braida, D., Guerini, F. R., Ponzoni, I., Corradini, I., DeAstis, S., Pattini, L., ... Sala, M. (2015). Association between SNAP-25 gene polymorphisms and cognition in autism: Functional consequences and potential therapeutic strategies. *Translational Psychiatry, 5.* doi:10.1038/tp.2014.136

Braun, K. V. N., Christensen, D., Doernberg, N., Schieve, L., Rice, C., Wiggins, L., ... Yeargin-Allsopp, M. (2015). Trends in the prevalence of autism spectrum disorder, cerebral palsy, hearing loss, intellectual disability, and vision impairment, metropolitan Atlanta, 1991–2010. *PLoS One, 10*(4), e0124120. doi: 10.1371/journal.pone.0124120

Brewton, C. M., Nowell, K. P., Lasala, M. W., & Goin-Kochel, R. P. (2012). Relationship between the social functioning of children with autism spectrum disorders and their siblings' competencies/problem behaviors. *Research in Autism Spectrum Disorders, 6*, 646–653.

Burrell, T., & Borrego, J. R. (2012). Parents' involvement in ASD treatment: What is their role? *Cognitive and Behavioral Practice, 19*, 423–432.

Cardon, T. A. (2016). Do as I'm doing: Video modeling and autism. In T. A. Cardon, T. A. Cardon (Eds.), *Technology and the treatment of children with autism spectrum disorder* (pp. 87–96). Cham, Switzerland: Springer International.

Carmack, H. J. (2014). Social and tertiary health identities as argument in the DSM-V Asperger's/autism debate. *Western Journal of Communication, 78*, 462–479.

Carnahan, C., Musti-Rao, S., & Bailey, J. (2009). Promoting active engagement in small group learning experiences for students with autism and significant learning needs. *Education and Treatment of Children, 32*(1), 37–61.

Carpenter, L. (2001). Travel card. In B. S. Myles & D. Adreon (Eds.), *Asperger syndrome and adolescence: Practical solutions for school success* (pp. 92–96). Shawnee Mission, KS: Autism Asperger Publishing.

Centers for Disease Control and Prevention. (2012, March). *Autism spectrum disorders: Data and statistics/prevalence.* Atlanta, GA: Author. Retrieved from http://www.cdc.gov/NCBDDD/autism/data.html

Centers for Disease Control and Prevention. (2015a, August). Autism: Signs and symptoms. Atlanta, GA: Author. Retrieved from http://www.cdc.gov/ncbddd/autism/signs.html

Centers for Disease Control and Prevention. (2015b, November). Vaccine safety: Vaccines do not cause autism. Atlanta, GA: Author. Retrieved from http://www.cdc.gov/vaccinesafety/concerns/autism.html

Centers for Disease Control and Prevention. (2016, August). Autism: Data and Statistics. Atlanta, GA: Author. Retrieved from http://www.cdc.gov/ncbddd/autism/data.html

Chan, J., & O'Reilly, M. (2008). A "Social Stories" intervention package with students with autism in inclusive classroom settings. *Journal of Applied Behavior Analysis, 41*, 405–409.

Channon, S., Collins, R., Swain, E., Young, M., & Fitzpatrick, S. (2012). The use of skilled strategies in social interactions by groups high and low in self-reported social skill. *Journal of Autism and Developmental Disorders, 42*, 1425–1434.

Chevallier, C., Noveck, I., Happe, F., & Wilson, D. (2009). From acoustics to grammar: Perceiving and interpreting grammatical prosody in adolescents with Asperger syndrome. *Research in Autism Spectrum Disorders, 3*, 502–516.

Christensen, D. L., Baio, J., Van Naarden, B.M., Bilder, D., Charles, J., Constantine, J. N., Daniels, J., ... Yeargin-Allsopp, M. (2016). Prevalence and characteristics of autism spectrum disorder among children aged 8 years—Autism and Developmental Disabilities Monitoring Network, 11 Sites, United States, 2012. *Morbidity and Mortality Weekly Report, 65*(3), 1–23. Retrieved from http://www.cdc.gov/mmwr/volumes/65/ss/ss6503a1.htm

Christensen, D. L., Bilder, D. A., Zahorodny, W., Pettygrove, S., Durkin, M. S., Fitzgerald, R. T., ... Yeargin-Allsopp, M. (2016). Prevalence and characteristics of autism spectrum disorder among 4-year-old children in the Autism and Developmental Disabilities Monitoring Network. *Journal of Developmental & Behavioral Pediatrics, 37*, 1–8.

Chung, W., Edgar-Smith, S., Palmer, R. B., Chung, S., DeLambo, D., & Huang, W. (2015). An examination of in-service teacher attitudes toward students with autism spectrum disorder: Implications for professional practice. *Current Issues in Education, 18*(2), 1–10.

Cihak, D. F., Smith, C. C., Cornett, A., & Coleman, M. (2012). The use of video modeling with the Picture Exchange Communication System to increase independent communicative initiations in preschoolers with autism and developmental delays. *Focus on Autism and Other Developmental Disabilities, 27*, 3–11.

Crosland, K., & Dunlap, G. (2012). Effective strategies for the inclusion of children with autism in general education classrooms. *Behavior Modification, 36*, 251–269.

Daniels, A. M., & Mandell, D. S. (2014). Explaining differences in age at autism spectrum disorder diagnosis: A critical review. *Autism, 18*, 583–597.

Daubert, A., Hornstein, S., & Tincani, M. (2015). Effects of a modified Power Card strategy on turn taking and social commenting of children with autism spectrum disorder playing board games. *Journal of Developmental and Physical Disabilities, 27*, 93–110.

De la Marche, W., Noens, I., Luts, J., Scholte, E., Van Huffel, S., & Steyaert, J. (2012). Quantitative autism traits in first degree relatives: Evidence for the broader autism phenotype in fathers, but not in mothers and siblings. *Autism: The International Journal of Research and Practice, 16*, 247–260.

Delano, M. E. (2007). Video modeling interventions for individuals with autism. *Remedial and Special Education, 28*, 33–42.

Delmolino, L., & Harris, S. L. (2012). Matching children on the autism spectrum to classrooms: A guide for parents and professionals. *Journal of Autism and Developmental Disorders, 42*, 1197–1204.

Delmolino, L., Hansford, A. P., Bamond, M. J., Fiske, K. E., & LaRue, R. H. (2013). The use of instruction feedback for teaching language skills to children with autism. *Research in Autism Spectrum Disorders, 7*, 648–661.

DiStefano, C., Shih, W., Kaiser, A., Landa, R., & Kasari, C. (2016). Communication growth in minimally verbal children with ASD: The importance of interaction. *Autism Research.* doi:10.1002/aur.1594

Domire, S. C., & Wolfe, P. (2014). Effects of video prompting techniques on teaching daily living skills to children with autism spectrum disorders: A review. *Research and Practice for Persons with Severe Disabilities, 39*, 211–226.

Dougherty C, Evans D, Myers S, Moore G, Michael A. (2016). A comparison of structural brain imaging findings in autism spectrum disorder and attention-deficit hyperactivity disorder. *Neuropsychology Review* [serial online], *26*(1), 25–43.

Dunn, W. (1999). *Sensory profile.* San Antonio, TX: Psychological Corporation.

Dunn, W. (2014). *Sensory Profile-2.* San Antonio, TX: Psychological Corporation.

Ekas, N. V., & Whitman, T. L. (2011). Adaptation to daily stress among mothers of children with an autism spectrum disorder: The role of daily positive affect. *Journal of Autism and Developmental Disorders, 41*, 1202–1213.

Elamin, N.E., & AL-Ayadhi, L.Y. (2015). Genetic markers association in autism spectrum disorder. *Journal of Clinical and Medical Genomics, 3*(2), 1–5.

Ellis, J. (2016). Researching the social worlds of autistic children: An exploration of how an understanding of autistic children's social worlds is best achieved. *Children & Society.* doi: 10.1111/chso.12160

Epstein, G. G. (2014). Refrigerator mothers and sick little boys: Bruno Bettelheim, eugenics and the de-pathologization of Jewish identity. *Disability Studies Quarterly, 34*, (3). doi: http://dx.doi.org/10.18061/dsq.v34i3.3312

Ferraioli, S. J., Hansford, A., & Harris, S. L. (2012). Benefits of including siblings in the treatment of autism spectrum disorders. *Cognitive and Behavioral Practice, 19*, 413–422.

Fiske, K. E., Isenhower, R. W., Bamond, M. J., Delmolino, L., Sloman, K. N., & LaRue, R. H. (2015). Assessing the value of token reinforcement for individuals with autism. *Journal of Applied Behavior Analysis, 48*, 448–453.

Frazier, T. W., Thompson, L., Youngstrom, E. A., Law, P., Hardan, A. Y., Eng, C., & Morris, N. (2014). A twin study of heritable and shared environmental contributions to autism. *Journal of Autism and Developmental Disorders, 44,* 2013-2025.

Frey, A. J., Small, J. W., Feil, E. G., Seeley, J. R., Walker, H. M., & Forness, S. (2015). First Step to Success: Applications to preschoolers at risk of developing autism spectrum disorders. *Education and Training in Autism and Developmental Disabilities, 50,* 397-407.

Gabig, C. (2008). Verbal working memory and story retelling in school-age children with autism. *Language, Speech, and Hearing Services in Schools, 39,* 498-511.

Gagnon, E. (2001). *The power card strategy: Using special interests to motivate children and youth with Asperger syndrome.* Shawnee Mission, KS: Autism Asperger Publishing.

Gengoux, G. W. (2015). Priming for social activities: Effects on interactions between children with autism and typically developing peers. *Journal of Positive Behavior Interventions, 17,* 181-192.

Gerhardt, P. (2001, April). Transition and life after school. *PDD Network, 31,* 2-9.

Ghezzi, P. (2007). Discrete trials teaching. *Psychology in the Schools, 44,* 667-679.

Gillberg, C., & Coleman, M. (2000). *The biology of the autistic syndromes* (3rd ed.). London, England: Mac Keith Press.

Gillberg, I. C., Helles, A., Billstedt, E., & Gillberg, C. (2016). Boys with Asperger syndrome grow up: Psychiatric and neurodevelopmental disorders 20 years after initial diagnosis. *Journal of Autism and Developmental Disorders, 46,* 74-82.

Gillis, J. M., & Beights, R. (2012). New and familiar roles for clinical psychologists in the effective treatment for children with an autism spectrum disorder. *Cognitive and Behavioral Practice, 19,* 392-400.

Goddard, L., Howlin, P., Dritschel, B., & Patel, T. (2007). Autobiographical memory and social problem-solving in Asperger syndrome. *Journal of Autism and Developmental Disorders, 37,* 291-300.

Gong, L., Yan, Y., Xie, J., Liu, H., & Sun, X. (2012). Prediction of autism susceptibility genes based on association rules. *Journal of Neuroscience Research, 90,* 1119-1125.

Gongola, L., & Sweeney, J. (2012). Discrete trial teaching: Getting started. *Intervention in School and Clinic, 47,* 183-190.

Guinchat, V., Chamak, B., Bonniau, B., Bodeau, N., Perisse, D., Cohen, D., & Danion, A. (2012). Very early signs of autism reported by parents include many concerns not specific to autism criteria. *Research in Autism Spectrum Disorders, 6,* 589-601.

Gupta, B. (2015). Theory of mind in autism: A case study. *Psychological Studies, 60,* 339-345.

Gutierrez, A., Jr., Hale, M. N., O'Brien, H. A., Fischer, A., Durocher, J., & Alessandri, M. (2009). Evaluating the effectiveness of two commonly used discrete trial procedures for teaching receptive discrimination to young children with autism spectrum disorders. *Research in Autism Spectrum Disorders, 3,* 630-638.

Gutstein, S., & Whitney, T. (2002). Asperger syndrome and the development of social competence. *Focus on Autism and Other Developmental Disabilities, 17,* 161-171.

Höher Camargo, S. P., Rispoli, M., Ganz, J., Hong, E. R., Davis, H., & Mason, R. (2016). Behaviorally based interventions for teaching social interaction skills to children with ASD in inclusive settings: A meta-analysis. *Journal of Behavioral Education, 25,* 223-248.

Hallmayer, J., Cleveland, S., Torres, A., Phillips, J., Cohen, B., Torigoe, T., . . . Risch, N. (2011). Genetic heritability and shared environmental factors among twin pairs with autism. *Archives of General Psychiatry, 68,* 1095-1102.

Harfterkamp, M., van de Loo-Neus, G., Minderaa, R. B., van der Gaag, R., Escobar, R., Schacht, A., . . . Hoekstra, P. J. (2012). A randomized double-blind study of atomoxetine versus placebo for attention-deficit/hyperactivity disorder symptoms in children with autism spectrum disorder. *Journal of the American Academy of Child & Adolescent Psychiatry, 51,* 733-741.

Hastings, R. P. (2003). Behavioral adjustment of siblings of children with autism engaged in applied behavior analysis early intervention programs: The moderating role of social support. *Journal of Autism and Developmental Disorders, 33,* 141-150.

Hendricks, D., & Wehman, P. (2009). Transition from school to adulthood for youth with autism spectrum disorders: Review and recommendations. *Focus on Autism and Other Developmental Disabilities, 24,* 77-88.

Hess, H. L., Morrier, M. J., Heflin, L. J., & Ivey, M. L. (2008). Autism treatment survey: Services received by children with autism spectrum disorders in public school classrooms. *Journal of Autism and Developmental Disorders, 38,* 961-971.

Houwen, S., Visser, L., van der Putten, A., & Vlaskamp, C. (2016). The interrelationships between motor, cognitive, and language development in children with and without intellectual and developmental disabilities. *Research in Developmental Disabilities, 53–54,* 19-31.

Howlin, P. (2011). Which ASC treatments are ineffective or lack a sound evidence base?. In S. Bölte, J. Hallmayer, S. Bölte, J. Hallmayer (Eds.), *Autism spectrum conditions: FAQs on autism, Asperger syndrome, and atypical autism answered by international experts* (pp. 162-163). Cambridge, MA: Hogrefe.

Howlin, P., & Moss, P. (2012). Adults with autism spectrum disorders. *The Canadian Journal of Psychiatry / La Revue Canadienne De Psychiatrie, 57,* 275-283.

Howlin, P., & Taylor, J. L. (2015). Addressing the need for high quality research on autism in adulthood. *Autism, 19,* 771-773.

Howlin, P., Magiati, I., & Charman, T. (2009). Systematic review of early intensive behavioral interventions for children with autism. *American Journal on Intellectual and Developmental Disabilities, 114,* 23-41.

Hubl, D., Bölte, S., Feineis-Matthews, S., Lanfermann, H., Federspiel, A., Strik, W., . . . Dierks, T. (2003). Functional imbalance of visual pathways indicates alternative face processing strategies in autism. *Neurology, 61,* 1232-1237.

Hutchins, T. L., Prelock, P. A., Morris, H., Benner, J., LaVigne, T., & Hoza, B. (2016). Explicit vs. applied theory of mind competence: A comparison of typically developing males, males with ASD, and males with ADHD. *Research in Autism Spectrum Disorders, 21,* 94-108.

Iadarola, S., Hetherington, S., Clinton, C., Dean, M., Reisinger, E., Huynh, L., ... Kasari, C. (2015). Services for children with autism spectrum disorder in three, large urban school districts: Perspectives of parents and educators. *Autism: The International Journal of Research and Practice, 19,* 694-703.

Insel, T. (2012, March). *Autism prevalence: More affected or more detected?* Washington, DC: National Institute of Mental Health. Retrieved from http://www.nimh.nih.gov/about/director/2012/autism-prevalence-more-affected-or-more-detected.shtml

Institute of Medicine. (2012). *Adverse effects of vaccines: Evidence and causality.* Washington, DC: National Academies Press. Retrieved from http://www.nap.edu/catalog.php?record_id=13164

Ipser, J. C., Syal, S., Bentley, J., Adnams, C. M., Steyn, B., & Stein, D. J. (2012). 1H-MRS in autism spectrum disorders: A systematic meta-analysis. *Metabolic Brain Disease, 27,* 275-287.

Irvin, D. W., McBee, M., Boyd, B. A., Hume, K., & Odom, S. L. (2012). Child and family factors associated with the use of services for preschoolers with autism spectrum disorder. *Research in Autism Spectrum Disorders, 6,* 565-572.

Itier, R., & Taylor, M. (2004). N170 or N1? Spatiotemporal differences between object and face processing using ERps. *Cerebral Cortex, 14*, 132–142.

Janzen, J. (2003). *Understanding the nature of autism: A guide to the autism spectrum disorders* (2nd ed.). San Antonio, TX: Therapy Skill Builders.

Johnson, N. L., Burkett, K., Reinhold, J., & Bultas, M. W. (2016). Translating research to practice for children with autism spectrum disorder: Part I: Definition, associated behaviors, prevalence, diagnostic process, and interventions. *Journal of Pediatric Health Care, 30*, 15–26.

Kaldy, Z., Giserman, I., Carter, A. S., & Blaser, E. (2016). The mechanisms underlying the ASD advantage in visual search. *Journal of Autism and Developmental Disorders, 46*, 1513–1527.

Kanner, L. (1943). Autistic disturbances of affective content. *The Nervous Child, 2*, 217–250.

Kleinert, H., Towles-Reeves, E., Quenemoen, R., Thurlow, M., Fluegge, L., Weseman, L., & Kerbel, A. (2015). Where students with the most significant cognitive disabilities are taught: Implications for general curriculum access. *Exceptional Children, 81*, 312–328.

Klin, A., Jones, W., Schultz, R., & Volkmar, F. (2003). The enactive mind, or from actions to cognition: Lessons from autism. *Philosophical Transactions of the Royal Society of London, Series B, 358*, 345–360.

Kluth, P. (2010). *You're going to love this kid! Teaching students with autism in the inclusion classroom* (2nd ed.). Baltimore, MD: Brookes.

Kocovska, E., Fernell, E., Billstedt, E., Minnis, H., & Gillberg, C. (2012). Vitamin D and autism: Clinical review. *Research in Developmental Disabilities: A Multidisciplinary Journal, 33*, 1541–1550.

Koegel, L., Matos-Freden, R., Lang, R., & Koegel, R. (2012). Interventions for children with autism spectrum disorders in inclusive school settings. *Cognitive and Behavioral Practice, 19*, 401–412.

Kogan, M. D., Blumberg, S. J., Schieve, L. A., Boyle, C. A., Perrin, J. M., Ghandour, R. M., . . . van Dyck, P. C. (2009, October 5 on-line publication). Prevalence of parent-reported diagnosis of autism spectrum disorder among children in the US, 2007. *Pediatrics*. doi:10.1542/peds.2009-1522

Kurth, J. A. (2015). Educational placement of students with autism: The impact of state of residence. *Focus on Autism and Other Developmental Disabilities, 30*, 249–256.

Lainhart, J. E. (2015). Brain imaging research in autism spectrum disorders: In search of neuropathology and health across the lifespan. *Current Opinion in Psychiatry, 28*, 76–82.

Landrigan, P. J. (2011). Environment and autism. In E. Hollander, A. Kolevzon, & J. T. Coyle (Eds.), *Textbook of autism spectrum disorders* (pp. 247–264). Arlington, VA: American Psychiatric Association.

Lane, J. D., Lieberman-Betz, R., & Gast, D. L. (2016). An analysis of naturalistic interventions for increasing spontaneous expressive language in children with autism spectrum disorder. *Journal of Special Education, 50*, 49–61.

Langan, M. (2011). Parental voices and controversies in autism. *Disability & Society, 26*, 193–205.

Lazenby, D. C., Sideridis, G. D., Huntington, N., Prante, M., Dale, P. S., Curtin, S., ... Tager-Flusberg, H. (2016). Language differences at 12 months in infants who develop autism spectrum disorder. *Journal of Autism and Developmental Disorders, 46*, 899–909.

Le Couteur, A., Lord, C., & Rutter, M. (2003). *Autism Diagnostic Interview-Revised (ADI-R)*. Los Angeles, CA: Western Psychological Services.

Leader, G., & Mannion, A. (2016). Challenging behaviors. In J. L. Matson, J. L. Matson (Eds.), *Handbook of assessment and diagnosis of autism spectrum disorder* (pp. 209–232). Cham, Switzerland: Springer International.

Leaf, J. B., Oppenheim-Leaf, M. L., Leaf, R. B., Taubman, M., McEachin, J., Parker, T., ... Mountjoy, T. (2015). What is the proof? A methodological review of studies that have utilized social stories. *Education and Training in Autism and Developmental Disabilities, 50*, 127–141.

Leaf, J. B., Tsuji, K. H., Griggs, B., Edwards, A., Taubman, M., McEachin, J., . . . Oppenheim-Leaf, M. L. (2012). Teaching social skills to children with autism using the cool versus not cool procedure. *Education and Training in Autism and Developmental Disabilities, 47*, 165–175.

Lee, S., Odom, S. L., Loftin, R. (2007). Social engagement with peers and stereotypic behavior of children with autism. *Journal of Positive Behavior Interventions. 9*, 67–79.

Li, X., Zou, H., & Brown, W. T. (2012). Genes associated with autism spectrum disorder. *Brain Research Bulletin, 88*, 543–552.

Lo-Castro, A., & Curatolo, P. (2014). Epilepsy associated with autism and attention deficit hyperactivity disorder: Is there a genetic link? *Brain and Development, 36*, 185–193.

Lo-Castro, A., Benvenuto, A., Galasso, C., Porfirio, C., & Curatolo, P. (2010). Autism spectrum disorders associated with chromosomal abnormalities. *Research in Autism Spectrum Disorders, 4*, 319–327.

Longtin, S. E., & Principe, G. (2016). The relationship between poverty level and urban African American parents' awareness of evidence-based interventions for children with autism spectrum disorders: Preliminary data. *Focus on Autism & Other Developmental Disabilities, 31*, 83–91.

Lovaas, O. I. (1987). *Teaching developmentally disabled children: The ME book*. Austin, TX: Pro-Ed.

Lubas, M., Mitchell, J., & De Leo, G. (2016). Evidence-based practice for teachers of children with autism: A dynamic approach. *Intervention in School and Clinic, 51*, 188–193.

Ludlow, A., Skelly, C., & Rohleder, P. (2012). Challenges faced by parents of children diagnosed with autism spectrum disorder. *Journal of Health Psychology, 17*, 702–711.

Macpherson, K., Charlop, M. H., & Miltenberger, C. A. (2015). Using portable video modeling technology to increase the compliment behaviors of children with autism during athletic group play. *Journal of Autism and Developmental Disorders, 45*, 3836–3845.

Maenner, M. J., Rice, C. E., Arneson, C. L., Cunniff, C., Schieve, L. A., Carpenter, L. A., ... Durkin, M. S. (2014). Potential impact of DSM-5 criteria on autism spectrum disorder prevalence estimates. *JAMA Psychiatry, 71*, 292–300.

Magaña, S., Parish, S. L., & Son, E. (2015). Have racial and ethnic disparities in the quality of health care relationships changed for children with developmental disabilities and ASD? *American Journal on Intellectual and Developmental Disabilities, 120*, 504–513.

Majoko, T. (2016). Inclusion of children with autism spectrum disorders: Listening and hearing to voices form the grassroots. *Journal of Autism and Developmental Disorders, 46*, 1429–1440.

Mandy, W., & Lai, M. (2016). Annual research review: The role of the environment in the developmental psychopathology of autism spectrum condition. *Journal of Child Psychology and Psychiatry, 57*, 271–292.

Mason, R. A., Davis, H. S., Ayres, K. M., Davis, J. L., & Mason, B. A. (2016). Video self-modeling for individuals with disabilities: A best-evidence, single case meta-analysis. *Journal of Developmental and Physical Disabilities*. doi:10.1007/s10882-016-9484-2

Matson, J. L., & LoVullo, S. V. (2009). Trends and topics in autism spectrum disorders research. *Research in Autism Spectrum Disorders, 3*, 252–257.

Matson, J. L., & Goldin, R. L. (2013). Comorbidity and autism: Trends, topics and future directions. *Research in Autism Spectrum Disorders, 7*, 1228–1233.

Matson, J. L., Beighley, J., & Turygin, N. (2012). Autism diagnosis and screening: Factors to consider in differential diagnosis. *Research in Autism Spectrum Disorders, 6*, 19–24.

Matson, J. L., Hattier, M. A., & Williams, L. W. (2012). How does relaxing the algorithm for autism affect DSM-V prevalence rates? *Journal of Autism and Developmental Disorders, 42*, 1549–1556.

Matson, J. L., Hattier, M. A., & Belva, B. (2012). Treating adaptive living skills of persons with autism using applied behavior analysis: A review. *Research in Autism Spectrum Disorders, 6*, 271–276.

Mayes, S., & Calhoun, S. (2008). WISC-IV and WIAT-II profiles in children with high-functioning autism. *Journal of Autism and Developmental Disorders, 38*, 428–439.

Mays, N. M., Beal-Alvarez, J., & Jolivette, K. (2011). Using movement-based sensory interventions to address self-stimulatory behaviors in students with autism. *Teaching Exceptional Children, 43*(6), 46–52.

Mazurek, M. O., Shattuck, P. T., Wagner, M., & Cooper, B. P. (2012). Prevalence and correlates of screen-based media use among youths with autism spectrum disorders. *Journal of Autism and Developmental Disorders, 42*, 1757–1767.

McCormick, C., Hepburn, S., Young, G. S., & Rogers, S. J. (2015). Sensory symptoms in children with autism spectrum disorder, other developmental disorders and typical development: A longitudinal study. *Autism, 20*, 572–579.

McCoy, K., & Hermansen, E. (2007). Video modeling for individuals with autism: A review of model types and effects. *Education and Treatment of Children, 30*, 183–213.

McHale, S. M., Updegraff, K. A., & Feinberg, M. E. (2016). Siblings of youth with autism spectrum disorders: Theoretical perspectives on sibling relationships and individual adjustment. *Journal of Autism and Developmental Disorders, 46*, 589–602.

McPartland, J. C., Bernier, R., & South, M. (2015). Realizing the translational promise of psychophysiological research in ASD. *Journal of Autism and Developmental Disorders, 45*, 277–282.

Meadan, H., Halle, J. W., & Kelly, S. M. (2012). Intentional communication of young children with autism spectrum disorder: Judgments of different communication partners. *Journal of Developmental and Physical Disabilities, 24*, 437–450.

Meadan, H., Ostrosky, M. M., Triplett, B., Michna, A., & Fettig, A. (2011). Using visual supports with young children with autism spectrum disorder. *Teaching Exceptional Children, 43*(6), 28–35.

Mesibov, G., Howley, M., & Naftel, S. (2016). *Accessing the curriculum for learners with autism spectrum disorders: Using the TEACCH programme to help inclusion* 2nd edition). New York, NY: Routledge.

Miller, S. A. (2012). *Theory of mind: Beyond the preschool years*. New York, NY: Psychology Press.

Moore, S. T. (2002). *Asperger syndrome and the elementary school experience: Practical solutions for academic and social difficulties*. Shawnee Mission, KS: Autism Asperger Publishing.

Morlock, L., Reynolds, J. L., Fisher, S., & Comer, R. J. (2015). Video modeling and word identification in adolescents with autism spectrum disorders. *Child Language Teaching and Therapy, 31*, 101–111.

Morrier, M. J., & Hess, K. L. (2012). Ethnic differences in autism eligibility in the United States public schools. *Journal of Special Education, 46*, 49–63.

Morrier, M. J., Hess, K. L., & Heflin, L. J. (2008). Ethnic disproportionality in students with autism spectrum disorders. *Multicultural Education, 16*(1), 31–38.

Moulton, E., Barton, M., Robins, D. L., Abrams, D. N., & Fein, D. (2016). Early characteristics of children with ASD who demonstrate optimal progress between age two and four. *Journal of Autism and Developmental Disorders, 46*, 2160–2173.

Myers, B. J., Mackintosh, V. H., & Goin-Kochel, R. P. (2009). "My greatest joy and my greatest heart ache": Parents' own words on how having a child in the autism spectrum has affected their lives and their families' lives. *Research in Autism Spectrum Disorders, 3*, 670–684.

Myles, B. S., & Adreon, D. (2001). *Asperger syndrome and adolescence: Practical solutions for school success*. Shawnee Mission, KS: Autism Asperger Publishing.

Myles, B. S., & Southwick, J. (2005). *Asperger syndrome and difficult moments: Practical solutions for tantrums, rage, and meltdowns*. Shawnee Mission, KS: Autism Asperger Publishing.

Myles, B. S., Bock, S. J., & Simpson, R. L. (2001). *Asperger Syndrome Diagnostic Scale*. Austin, TX: Pro-Ed.

National Institute of Child Health and Human Development. (2005, May). *Autism overview: What we know*. Retrieved from http://www.eric.ed.gov/ERICWebPortal/contentdelivery/servlet/ERICServlet?accno[1]ED485723

National Institute of Mental Health. (2012, September). *The numbers count: Mental disorders in America*. Retrieved from http://www.nimh.nih.gov/health/publications/the-numbers-count-mental-disorders-in-america/index.shtml

National Institute of Neurological Disorders and Stroke. (2009, September). *Autism fact sheet*. Washington, DC: National Institutes of Health. Retrieved from http://www.ninds.nih.gov/disorders/autism/detail_autism.htm

National Research Council. (2001). *Educating children with autism*. Washington, DC: National Academy Press.

O'Handley, R. D., Radley, K. C., & Whipple, H. M. (2015). The relative effects of social stories and video modeling toward increasing eye contact of adolescents with autism spectrum disorder. *Research in Autism Spectrum Disorders, 11*, 101–111.

Odom, S., & Wong, C. (2015). Connecting the dots: Supporting students with autism spectrum disorder. *American Educator, 6*(7), 12–19, 44.

Ooi, K. L., Ong, Y. S., Jacob, S. A., & Khan, T. M. (2016). A meta-synthesis on parenting a child with autism. *Neuropsychiatric Disease and Treatment, 12*, 745–762.

Orsmond, G., Kuo, H., & Seltzer, M. (2009). Siblings of individuals with an autism spectrum disorder: Sibling relationships and well-being in adolescence and adulthood. *Autism: The International Journal of Research and Practice, 13*(1), 59–80.

Palmen, A., Didden, R., & Lang, R. (2012). A systematic review of behavioral intervention research on adaptive skill building in high-functioning young adults with autism spectrum disorder. *Research in Autism Spectrum Disorders, 6*, 602–617.

Papageorgiou, V., & Kalyva, E. (2010). Self-reported needs and expectations of parents of children with autism spectrum disorders who participate in support groups. *Research in Autism Spectrum Disorders, 4*, 653–660.

Park, S., Cho, S., Cho, I., Kim, B., Kim, J., Shin, M., . . . Yoo, H. (2012). Sleep problems and their correlates and comorbid psychopathology of children with autism spectrum disorders. *Research in Autism Spectrum Disorders, 6*, 1068–1072.

Parsloe, S. M., & Babrow, A. S. (2016). Removal of Asperger's syndrome from the DSM V: Community response to uncertainty. *Health Communication, 31*, 485–494.

Pasco, G., & Tohill, C. (2015). Predicting progress in Picture Exchange Communication System (PECS) use by children with autism. *International Journal of Language & Communication Disorders, 46*, 120–125.

Passarotti, A., Paul, B., Bussiere, J., Buxton, R., Wong, E., & Stiles, J. (2003). The development of face and location processing: An fMRI study. *Developmental Science, 6*, 100–117.

Pennington, R. C., Stenhoff, D. M., Gibson, J., & Ballou, K. (2012). Using simultaneous prompting to teach computer-based story writing to a student with autism. *Education & Treatment of Children, 35*, 389–406.

Peterson, C., & Slaughter, V. (2009). Theory of mind in children with autism or typical development: Links between eye-reading and false belief understanding. *Research in Autism Spectrum Disorders, 3*, 462–473.

Pierce, K., & Courchesne, E. (2001). Evidence for a cerebellar role in reduced exploration and stereotyped behavior in autism. *Biological Psychiatry, 49*, 655–664.

Plaisance, L., Lerman, D. C., Laudont, C., & Wu, W. (2016). Inserting mastered targets during error correction when teaching skills to children with autism. *Journal of Applied Behavior Analysis*. doi:10.1002/jaba.292

Plavnick, J. B., & Ferreri, S. J. (2011). Establishing verbal repertoires in children with autism using function-based video modeling. *Journal of Applied Behavior Analysis, 44,* 747–766.

Porter, N. (2012). Promotion of pretend play for children with high-functioning autism through the use of circumscribed interests. *Early Childhood Education Journal,* 40, 161–167.

Posar, A., Resca, F., & Visconti, P. (2015). Autism according to Diagnostic and Statistical Manual of Mental Disorders, 5th edition: The need for further improvements. *Journal of Pediatric Neurosciences, 10,* 146–148.

Radley, K. C., Dart, E. H., Furlow, C. M., & Ness, E. J. (2015). Peer-mediated discrete trial training within a school setting. *Research in Autism Spectrum Disorders, 9,* 53–67.

Rahko, J. S., Vuontela, V. A., Carlson, S., Nikkinen, J., Hurtig, T. M., Kuusikko-Gauffin, S., ... Kiviniemi, V. J. (2016). Attention and working memory in adolescents with autism spectrum disorder: A functional MRI study. *Child Psychiatry and Human Development, 47,* 503–517.

Rayner, C. (2015). Video-based intervention for children with autism: Towards improved assessment of pre-requisite imitation skills. *Developmental Neurorehabilitation, 18,* 113–121.

Rayner, C., Denholm, C., & Sigafoos, J. (2009). Video-based intervention for individuals with autism: Key questions that remain unanswered. *Research in Autism Spectrum Disorders, 3,* 291–303.

Reynhout, G., & Carter, M. (2009). The use of social stories by teachers and their perceived efficacy. *Research in Autism Spectrum Disorders, 3,* 232–251.

Rhodes, C. (2014). Do social stories help to decrease disruptive behaviour in children with autistic spectrum disorders? A review of the published literature. *Journal of Intellectual Disabilities, 18,* 35–50.

Robins, D. L., & Dumont-Mathieu, T. (2006). The Modified Checklist for Autism in Toddler (M-CHAT): A review of current findings and future directions. *Journal of Developmental and Behavioral Pediatrics, 27* (Supplement 2), S111–S119.

Robins, T. M., Fein, D., & Barton, M. (2009). Modified Checklist for Autism in Toddlers, Revised with Follow-Up (M-CHAT-R/F). Retrieved from https://m-chat.org/_references/mchatDOTorg.pdf

Rodgers, J., Riby, D. M., Janes, E., Connolly, B., & McConachie, H. (2012). Anxiety and repetitive behaviours in autism spectrum disorders and Williams syndrome: A cross-syndrome comparison. *Journal of Autism and Developmental Disorders, 42,* 175–180.

Rodriguez, D. (2009). Culturally and linguistically diverse students with autism. *Childhood Education.* 85, 313–317.

Rollins, P. R., Campbell, M., Hoffman, R. T., & Self, K. (2016). A community-based early intervention program for toddlers with autism spectrum disorders. *Autism: The International Journal of Research and Practice, 20,* 219–232.

Roosa, J. B. (1995). *Men on the move: Competence and cooperation—Conflict resolution and beyond.* Kansas City, MO: Author.

Rotheram-Fuller, E., & Hoda, R. (2015). Using CBT to assist children with autism spectrum disorders/pervasive developmental disorders in the school setting. In R. Flanagan, K. Allen, & E. Levine (Eds.), *Cognitive and behavioral interventions in the schools* (pp. 181–197). New York, NY: Springer.

Rowley, E., Chandler, S., Baird, G., Simonoff, E., Pickles, A., Loucas, T., & Charman, T. (2012). The experience of friendship, victimization and bullying in children with an autism spectrum disorder: Associations with child characteristics and school placement. *Research in Autism Spectrum Disorders, 6,* 1126–1134.

Rubenstein, L. D., Schelling, N., Wilczynski, S. M., & Hooks, E. N. (2015). Lived experiences of parents of gifted students with autism spectrum disorder: The struggle to find appropriate educational experiences. *Gifted Child Quarterly, 59,* 283–298.

Rutter, M. (2000). Genetic studies of autism: From the 1970s into the millennium. *Journal of Abnormal Child Psychology, 28,* 3–14.

Saalasti, S., Lepisto, T., Toppila, E., Kujala, T., Laakso, M., Nieminen-von Wendt, T., . . . Jansson-Verkasalo, E. (2008). Language abilities of children with Asperger syndrome. *Journal of Autism and Developmental Disorders, 38,* 1574–1580.

Sainato, D. M., Morrison, R. S., Jung, S., Axe, J., & Nixon, P. A. (2015). A Comprehensive inclusion program for kindergarten children with autism spectrum disorder. *Journal of Early Intervention, 37,* 208–225.

Salazar, F., Baird, G., Chandler, S., Tseng, E., O'sullivan, T., Howlin, P., ... Simonoff, E. (2015). Co-occurring psychiatric disorders in preschool and elementary school-aged children with autism spectrum disorder. *Journal of Autism and Developmental Disorders, 45,* 2283–2294.

Scattone, D. (2008). Enhancing the conversation skills of a boy with Asperger's disorder through "Social Stories" and video modeling. *Journal of Autism and Developmental Disorders, 38,* 395–400.

Schectman M. (2007). Scientifically unsupported therapies in the treatment of young children with autism spectrum disorders. *Pediatric Annals, 36,* 497–505.

Schelvan, R., Swanson, T. C., & Smith, S. M. (2005). Making each year successful: Issues in transition. In B. S. Myles (Ed.), *Children and youth with Asperger syndrome: Strategies for success in inclusive settings.* Thousand Oaks, CA: Corwin.

Schertz, H. H., Odom, S. L., Baggett, K. M., & Sideris, J. H. (2012). Effects of joint attention mediated learning for toddlers with autism spectrum disorders: An initial randomized controlled study. *Early Childhood Research Quarterly.* doi:10.1016/j.ecresq.2012.06.006

Scheuermann, B., & Webber, J. (2002a). Autism: Teaching DOES make a difference. *Education and Treatment of Children, 25,* 370–372.

Scheuermann, B., & Webber, J. (2002b). *Autism: Teaching does make a difference.* Stamford, CT: Wadsworth.

Schopler, E., Lansing, M. D., Reichler, M. D., & Marcus, L. M. (2005). *Psychoeducational Profile* (3rd edition) (PEP-3). Torrance, CA: WPS.

Seaman, R. L., & Cannella-Malone, H. I. (2016). Vocational skills interventions for adults with autism spectrum disorder: A review of the literature. *Journal of Developmental and Physical Disabilities, 28,* 479–494.

Shyman, E. (2012). Teacher education in autism spectrum disorders: A potential blueprint. *Education and Training in Autism and Developmental Disabilities, 47,* 187–197.

Simpson, R. L., & Myles, B. S. (1998). Understanding and responding to the needs of students with autism. In R. L. Simpson & B. S. Myles (Eds.), *Educating children and youth with autism: Strategies for effective practice* (pp. 1–24). Austin, TX: Pro-Ed.

Simpson, R. L., de Boer-Ott, S. R., & Smith-Myles, B. (2003). Inclusion of learners with autism spectrum disorders in general education settings. *Topics in Language Disorders, 23,* 116–33.

Simpson, R. L., McKee, M., Teeter, D., & Beytien, A. (2007). Evidence-based methods for children and youth with autism spectrum disorders: Stakeholder issues and perspectives. *Exceptionality, 15,* 203–217.

Siu, W., Lam, C., Gao, W., Vincent Tang, H., Jin, D., & Mak, C. M. (2016). Unmasking a novel disease gene NEO1 associated with autism spectrum disorders by a hemizygous deletion on chromosome 15 and a functional polymorphism. *Behavioural Brain Research, 300,* 135–142.

Skuse, D. H. (2012). DSM-5's conceptualization of autistic disorders. *Journal of the American Academy of Child & Adolescent Psychiatry, 51,* 344–346.

Smith, C. J., Lang, C. M., Kryzak, L., Reichenberg, A., Hollander, E., & Silverman, J. M. (2009). Familial associations of intense preoccupations, an empirical factor of the restricted, repetitive behaviors and interests domain of autism. *Journal of Child Psychology and Psychiatry, 50,* 982–990.

Smith, K. A., Ayres, K. A., Alexander, J., Ledford, J. R., Shepley, C., & Shepley, S. B. (2016). Initiation and generalization of self-instructional skills in adolescents with autism and intellectual disability. *Journal of Autism and Developmental Disorders, 46,* 1196–1209.

Solomon, O. (2008). Language, autism, and childhood: An ethnographic perspective. *Annual Review of Applied Linguistics, 28,* 150–169.

Stewart, R. (2001). Essential components of community living: A life span approach. *Indiana Resource Center for Autism Reporter, 5*(1), 18–27.

Stoner, J. B., & Stoner, C. R. (2016). Career disruption: The impact of transitioning from a full-time career professional to the primary caregiver of a child with autism spectrum disorder. *Focus on Autism and Other Developmental Disabilities, 31,* 104–114.

Tager-Flusberg, H., Rogers, S., Cooper, J., Landa, R., Lord, C., & Paul, R. (2009). Defining spoken language benchmarks and selecting measures of expressive language development for young children with autism spectrum disorders. *Journal of Speech, Language, and Hearing Research, 52,* 643–652.

Teffs, E. E., & Whitbread, K. M. (2009). Level of preparation of general education teachers to include students with autism spectrum disorders. *Current Issues in Education, 12*(10). Retrieved from http://cie.asu.edu.lib-proxy.uncg.edu/ojs/index.php/cieatasu/article/viewFile/172/4

U.S. Department of Education. (2011a). *Thirtieth annual report to Congress on the implementation of the Individuals with Disabilities Education Act, 2008.* Washington, DC: Author.

U.S. Department of Education. (2012). *Part B child count.* Retrieved from https://www.ideadata.org/arc_toc13.asp#partbCC

U.S. Department of Education. (2015). *37th annual report to Congress on the implementation of the Individuals with Disabilities Education Act.* Washington, DC: Author, Office of Special Education Programs. Retrieved from http://www2.ed.gov/about/reports/annual/osep/2015/parts-b-c/37th-arc-for-idea.pdf

Veness, C., Prior, M., Bavin, E., Eadie, P., Cini, E., & Reilly, S. (2012). Early indicators of autism spectrum disorders at 12 and 24 months of age: A prospective, longitudinal comparative study. *Autism: The International Journal of Research and Practice, 16,* 163–177.

Vijayakumar, N. T., & Judy, M. V. (2016). Autism spectrum disorders: Integration of the genome, transcriptome and the environment. *Journal of the Neurological Sciences, 364,* 167–176.

Virues-Ortega, J., Rodríguez, V., & Yu, C. T. (2013). Prediction of treatment outcomes and longitudinal analysis in children with autism undergoing intensive behavioral intervention. *International Journal of Clinical and Health Psychology, 13,* 91–100.

Vismara, L., & Lyons, G. (2007). Using perseverative interests to elicit joint attention behaviors in young children with autism: Theoretical and clinical implications for understanding motivation. *Journal of Positive Behavior Interventions, 9,* 214–228.

White, S., & Roberson-Nay, R. (2009). Anxiety, social deficits, and loneliness in youth with autism spectrum disorders. *Journal of Autism and Developmental Disorders, 39,* 1006–1013.

Wiggins, L., Robins, D., Bakeman, R., & Adamson, L. (2009). Brief report: Sensory abnormalities as distinguishing symptoms of autism spectrum disorders in young children. *Journal of Autism and Developmental Disorders, 39,* 1087–1091.

Wilde, L. D., Koegel, L. K., & Koegel, R. L. (1992). *Increasing success in school through priming: A training manual.* Santa Barbara: University of California Press.

Williams, D. (2008). What neuroscience has taught us about autism: Implications for early intervention. *Zero to Three, 28*(4), 11–17.

Williams, M., Atkins, M., & Soles, T. (2009). Assessment of autism in community settings: Discrepancies in classification. *Journal of Autism and Developmental Disorders, 39,* 660–669.

Wing, L. (1981). Asperger syndrome: A clinical account. *Psychological Medicine, 11,* 115–129.

Wing, L. (1991). The relationship between Asperger's syndrome and Kanner's autism. In U. Frith (Ed.), *Autism and Asperger syndrome* (pp. 93–121). Cambridge, UK: Cambridge University Press.

Wing, L., & Gould, J. (1979). Severe impairments of social interaction and associated abnormalities in children: Epidemiology and classification. *Journal of Autism and Developmental Disorders, 9,* 11–29.

Woodard, C. R., Goodwin, M. S., Zelazo, P. R., Aube, D., Scrimgeour, M., Ostholthoff, T., & Brickley, M. (2012). A comparison of autonomic, behavioral, and parent-report measures of sensory sensitivity in young children with autism. *Research in Autism Spectrum Disorders, 6,* 1234–1246.

Wynkoop, K. S. (2016). Watch this! A guide to implementing video modeling in the classroom. *Intervention in School and Clinic, 51,* 178–183.

Yakubova, G., Hughes, E. M., & Hornberger, E. (2015). Video-based intervention in teaching fraction problem-solving to students with autism spectrum disorder. *Journal of Autism and Developmental Disorders, 45,* 2865–2875.

Yirmiya, N., Shaked, M., & Erel, O. (2001). Comparison of siblings of individuals with autism and siblings of individuals with other diagnoses: An empirical summary. In E. Schoper, N. Yirmiya, & C. Shulman (Eds.), *The research basis for autism intervention* (pp. 59–73). New York, NY: Kluwer Academic/Plenum Publishers.

Yoo, H. (2015). Genetics of autism spectrum disorder: Current status and possible clinical applications. *Experimental Neurobiology, 24,* 257–272.

Zwaigenbaum, L., Bauman, M. L., Stone, W. L., Yirmiya, N., Estes, A., Hansen, R. L., ... Smith Roley, S. (2015). Early identification of autism spectrum disorder: Recommendations for practice and research. *Pediatrics, 136,* S10-S40.

Chapter 11

Ahearn, E. M. (2011, September). *Children who are deaf/hard of hearing: State of the educational practices [inForum policy brief].* Alexandria, VA: Project Forum, National Association of State Directors or Special Education. Retrieved from http://www.projectforum.org/docs/ChildrenWhoare-Deaf-HOH-StateoftheEducationalPractice.pdf

American Speech-Language-Hearing Association. (2004). *Cochlear implants* [Technical Report]. Retrieved from http://www.asha.org/policy/TR2004-00041/

Antia, S. D., Jones, P., Luckner, J., Kreimeyer, K. H., & Reed, S. (2011). Social outcomes of students who are deaf and hard of hearing in general education classrooms. *Exceptional Children, 77,* 489–504.

Antia, S., Jones, P., Reed, S., & Kreimeyer, K. (2009). Academic status and progress of deaf and hard-of-hearing students in general education classrooms. *Journal of Deaf Studies and Deaf Education, 14,* 293–311.

Antia, S., Kreimeyer, K., & Eldredge, N. (1994). Promoting social interaction between young children with hearing impairments and their peers. *Exceptional Children, 60,* 262–275.

Antia, S., Sabers, D., & Stinson, M. (2007). Validity and reliability of the Classroom Participation Questionnaire with deaf and hard of hearing students in public schools. *Journal of Deaf Studies and Deaf Education, 12,* 158–171.

Aram, D., Most, T., & Simon, A. B. (2008). Early literacy of kindergartners with hearing impairment: The role of mother-child collaborative writing. *Topics in Early Childhood Special Education, 28,* 31–41.

Arfé, B. (2015). Oral and written discourse skills in deaf and hard of hearing children. *Topics in Language Disorders, 35,* 180–197.

Ayantoye, C. A., & Luckner, J. L. (2016). Successful students who are deaf or hard of hearing and culturally and/or linguistically diverse in inclusive settings. *American Annals of the Deaf, 160,* 453–466.

Bat-Chava, Y., Martin, D., & Imperatore, L. (2014). Long-term improvements in oral communication skills and quality of peer relations in children with cochlear implants: Parental testimony. *Child: Care, Health & Development, 40,* 870–881.

Berndsen, M., & Luckner, J. (2012). Supporting students who are deaf or hard of hearing in general education classrooms: A Washington state case study. *Communication Disorders Quarterly, 33,* 111–118.

Borich, G. D., & Tombari, M. L. (1997). *Educational psychology: A contemporary approach* (2nd ed.). New York, NY: Longman.

Boys Town National Research Hospital. (n.d.). *Getting started with early intervention.* Retrieved from www.babyhearing.org/LanguageLearning/ EarlyIntervention/howhelps.asp

Brasel, K., & Qugiley, S. (1977). The influence of certain language and communication environments in early childhood on the development of language in deaf individuals. *Journal of Speech and Hearing Research, 20,* 95–107.

Bromley, K., Irwin-De Vitis, L., & Modlo, M. (1995). *Graphic organizers: Visual strategies for active learning.* New York, NY: Scholastic Professional Books.

Bruner, J. S., Oliver, R., & Greenfield, P. (1966). *Studies in cognitive growth.* New York, NY: Wiley.

Cannon, J. E., Fredrick, L. D., & Easterbrooks, S. R. (2010). Vocabulary instruction through books read in American sign language for English-language learners with hearing loss. *Communication Disorders Quarterly, 31,* 98–112.

Carroll, C., & Mather, S. M. (1997). *Movers and shakers: Deaf people who changed the world.* San Diego, CA: Dawn Sign Press.

Centers for Disease Control and Prevention. (December, 2016). *Hearing loss in children: Data and statistics.* Atlanta, GA: Author. Retrieved from http://www.cdc.gov/ncbddd/hearingloss/data.html

Collins, J., Goyne, T. R., & McCabe, P. C. (2013). Deafness and hard of hearing in childhood: Identification and intervention through modern listening technologies and other accommodations. *Communique, 41*(6), 4, 6, 8.

Communication Services for the Deaf (CSD). (2001). *Video relay service info.* Retrieved from www.covrs.com/VRS2Index.asp

Compton, M. V., Appenzeller, M., Kemmery, M., & Gardiner-Walsh, S. (2015). Itinerant teachers' perspectives of using collaborative practices in serving students who are deaf or hard of hearing. *American Annals of the Deaf, 160,* 255–272.

Convertino, C. M., Marschark, M., Sapere, P., Sarchet, T., & Zupan, M. (2009). Predicting academic success among deaf college students. *Journal of Deaf Studies and Deaf Education, 14,* 324–343.

Coyner, L. (1993). Academic success, self-concept, social acceptance and perceived social acceptance for hearing, hard of hearing and deaf students in a mainstream setting. *Journal of the American Deafness and Rehabilitation Association, 27*(2), 13–20.

Crow, K. L. (2008). Four types of disabilities: Their impact on online learning. *TechTrends: Linking Research and Practice to Improve Learning, 5,* 51–55.

Curtis, C., & Norgate, R. (2007). An evaluation of the Promoting Alternative Thinking Strategies curriculum at key stage. *Educational Psychology in Practice: Theory, Research and Practice in Educational Psychology, 23,* 33–44.

Danek, M. M., & Busby, H. (1999). *Transition planning and programming: Empowerment through partnership.* Washington, DC: Gallaudet University.

Desai, P., & Patel, D. R. (2014). Unilateral versus sequential cochlear implants: A mini-review. *International Journal of Child Health and Human Development, 7*(1), 7–10.

DesJardin, J. L. (2006). Family empowerment: Supporting language development in young children who are deaf or hard of hearing. *The Volta Review, 106*(3), 275–298.

DesJardin, J. L., Doll, E. R., Stika, C. J., Eisenberg, L. S., Johnson, K. J., Ganguly, D. H., … Henning, S. C. (2014). Parental support for language development during joint book reading for young children with hearing loss. *Communication Disorders Quarterly, 35,* 167–181.

Diamond, M., & Hopson, J. (1998). *Magic trees of the mind.* New York, NY: Penguin Putnam.

Donne, V. J., & Zigmond, N. (2008). An observational study of reading instruction for students who are deaf or hard of hearing in public schools. *Communication Disorders Quarterly, 29,* 219–235.

Dostal, H. M., & Wolbers, K. A. (2014). Developing language and writing skills of deaf and hard of hearing students: A simultaneous approach. *Literacy Research and Instruction, 53,* 245–268.

Easterbrooks, S. (2010). Educational practices and literacy development during the school years. In M. Marschark & P. Spencer (Eds.). *Oxford handbook of deaf studies, language, and education, Vol. 2* (pp. 11–126). New York, NY: Oxford University Press.

Easterbrooks, S. R., & Beal-Alvarez, J. S. (2012). States' reading outcomes of students who are d/Deaf and hard of hearing. *American Annals of the Deaf, 157,* 27–40.

Easterbrooks, S. R., Lederberg, A. R., Antia, S., Schick, B., Kushalnagar, P., Webb, M. Y., …Connor, C. M. (2015). Reading among diverse DHH learners: What, how, and for whom? *American Annals of the Deaf, 159,* 419–432.

Eckert, R. (2010). Toward a theory of deaf ethnos: Deafnicity ≈ D/deaf. *Journal of Deaf Studies and Deaf Education, 15,* 317–333.

Eckert, R. C., & Rowley, A. J. (2013). Audism: A theory and practice of audiocentric privilege. *Humanity & Society, 37,* 101–130.

Edwards, R. A. R. (2012). *Words made flesh: Nineteenth-century deaf education and the growth of Deaf culture.* New York: New York University Press.

Elliot, L. B., Stinson, M. S., McKee, B. G., Everhart, V. S., & Francis, P. J. (2001). College students' perceptions of the C-print speech-to-text transcription system. *Journal of Deaf Studies and Deaf Education, 6*(4), 285–298.

English, K. M. (1997). *Self advocacy for students who are deaf or hard of hearing.* Austin, TX: Pro-Ed.

Eriks-Brophy, A., & Whittingham, J. (2013). Teachers' perceptions of the inclusion of children with hearing loss in general education settings. *American Annals of the Deaf, 158,* 63–97.

Fitzpatrick, E. M., & Olds, J. (2015). Practitioners' perspectives on the functioning of school-age children with cochlear implants. *Cochlear Implants International, 16*(1), 9–23.

Foster, S., & Cue, K. (2009). Roles and responsibilities of itinerant specialist teachers of deaf and hard of hearing students. *American Annals of the Deaf, 153,* 435–449

Frangulov, A., Rehm, H., & Kenna, M. (2004). *Common causes of hearing loss: For parents and families.* Cambridge, MA: Harvard Medical School Center on Heredity Deafness. Retrieved from http://hearing.harvard.edu/info/common-causes-of-hearingloss.pdf

Freebody, P., & Power, D. (2001). Interviewing deaf adults in postsecondary educational settings: Stories, cultures, and life histories. *Journal of Deaf Studies and Deaf Education, 6,* 130–142.

Gallaudet Research Institute (2011). *Regional and national summary report of data from the 2009–2010 annual survey of deaf or hard of hearing children and youth.* Washington, DC: Gallaudet University.

Gallaudet Research Institute. (November 2008). *Regional and national summary report of data from the 2007–08 annual survey of deaf and hard of hearing children and youth.* Washington, DC: Gallaudet Research Institute, Gallaudet University.

Gallimore, L., & Woodruff, S. (1996). The bilingual-bicultural (Bi–Bi) approach: A professional point of view. In S. Schwartz (Ed.), *Choices in deafness: A parents' guide to communication options* (2nd ed., pp. 89–115). Bethesda, MD: Woodbine House.

Geers, A., & Moog, J. (1989). Factors predictive of the development of literacy in profoundly hearing-impaired adolescents. *The Volta Review, 91,* 69–86.

Goldin-Meadow, S., & Mayberry, R. I. (2001). How do profoundly deaf children learn to read. *Learning Disabilities Research and Practice, 16*(4), 222–229.

Greenberg, M. T., & Kusché, C. A. (1993). Promoting social and emotional development in deaf children: *The PATHS project.* Seattle: University of Washington Press.

Guardino, C. A. (2008). Identification and placement for deaf students with multiple disabilities: Choosing the path less followed. *American Annals of the Deaf, 153*, 55–64.

Guardino, C., & Cannon, J. E. (2015). Theory, research, and practice for students who are deaf and hard of hearing with disabilities: Addressing the challenges from birth to postsecondary education. *American Annals of the Deaf, 160*, 347–355.

Hamill, A. C., & Stein, C. H. (2011). Culture and empowerment in the Deaf community: An analysis of Internet weblogs. *Journal of Community & Applied Social Psychology, 21*, 388–406.

Harris, M. (2010). Early communication in sign and speech. In M. Marschark, P. E. Spencer, M. Marschark, & P. E. Spencer (Eds.), *The Oxford handbook of deaf studies, language, and education* (Vol. 2) (2nd ed.) (pp. 316–330). New York, NY: Oxford University Press.

Harris, M. (2015). The impact of new technologies on the literacy attainment of deaf children. *Topics in Language Disorders, 35*, 120–132.

Hart, B., & Risley, T. R. (1999). *The social world of children learning to talk.* Baltimore, MD: Paul H. Brookes.

Higgins, M., & Lieberman, A. M. (2016). Deaf students as a linguistic and cultural minority: Shifting perspectives and implications for teaching and learning. *Journal of Education, 196*, 9–18.

Hinsliff, G., & McKie, R. (2008, March 9). This couple want a deaf child. Should we try to stop them? *The Guardian.* Retrieved from https://www.theguardian.com/science/2008/mar/09/genetics.medicalresearch

Hrastinski, I., & Wilbur, R. B. (2016). Academic achievement of deaf and hard-of-hearing students in an ASL/English bilingual program. *Journal of Deaf Studies & Deaf Education, 21*, 156–170.

Jackson, C. W., Wegner, J. R., & Turnbull, A. P. (2010). Family quality of life following early identification of deafness. *Language, Speech, and Hearing Services in Schools, 41*, 194–205.

Johnson, C. D., & Seaton, J. B. (2012). *Educational audiology handbook* (2nd ed.). Clifton Park, NY: Delmar, Cengage Learning.

Jones, D. D. (2004). Relative earnings of deaf and hard-of-hearing individuals. *Journal of Deaf Studies and Deaf Education, 9*, 459–461.

Jones, T. W., Jones, J. K., & Ewing, K. M. (2006). Students with multiple disabilities. In D. F. Moores & D. S. Martin (Eds.), *Deaf learners: Developments in curriculum and instruction* (pp. 127–144). Washington, DC: Gallaudet University Press.

Kelly, R. R. (2014). Beyond high school. *Hands & Voices.* Retrieved from http://www.handsandvoices.org/articles/education/ed/V13-1_beyondHS.htm

Kisor, H. (1990). *What's that pig outdoors? A memoir of deafness.* New York, NY: Penguin.

Kritzer, K. L. (2009). Barely started and already left behind: A descriptive analysis of the mathematics ability demonstrated by young deaf children. *Journal of Deaf Studies & Deaf Education, 14*, 409–421.

Kusché, C. A., & Greenberg, M. T. (1993). *The PATHS Curriculum.* Seattle, WA: Developmental Research and Programs.

Lane, H., Hoffmeister, R., & Bahan, B. (1996). *A journey into the deaf-world.* San Diego, CA: Dawn Sign Press.

Laurent Clerc National Deaf Education Center. (2015). *Frequently asked questions: Considerations for using an ASL and spoken English bilingual approach with young children who are deaf and hard of hearing.* Retrieved from https://www.gallaudet.edu/clerc-center/info-to-go/language/faq-asl-spoken-english.html

Lederberg, A. R., Miller, E. M., Easterbrooks, S. R., & Connor, C. M. (2014). "Foundations for Literacy": An early literacy intervention for deaf and hard-of-hearing children. *Journal of Deaf Studies and Deaf Education, 19*, 438–455.

Lindeman, K. W., & Magiera, K. (2014). A co-teaching model: Committed professionals, high expectations, and the inclusive classroom. *Odyssey: New Directions in Deaf Education, 15*, 40–45.

Lu, J., Jones, A., & Morgan, G. (2016). The impact of input quality on early sign development in native and non-native language learners. *Journal of Child Language, 43*, 537–552.

Luckner, J. L. (2002). *Facilitating the transition of students who are deaf or hard of hearing.* Austin, TX: Pro-Ed.

Luckner, J. L., & Bowen, S. K. (2010). Teachers' use and perceptions of progress monitoring. *American Annals of the Deaf, 155*, 397–406.

Luckner, J. L., & Muir, S. (2001). Successful students who are deaf in general education settings. *American Annals of the Deaf, 146*, 450–461.

Luckner, J. L., & Sebald, A. M. (2013). Promoting self-determination of students who are deaf or hard of hearing. *American Annals of the Deaf, 158*, 377–386.

Luckner, J. L., & Urbach, J. (2012). Reading fluency and students who are deaf or hard of hearing: Synthesis of the research. *Communication Disorders Quarterly, 33*, 230–241.

Luckner, J. L., Bruce, S. M., & Ferrell, K. A. (2015). A summary of the communication and literacy evidence-based practices for students who are deaf or hard of hearing, visually impaired, and deafblind. *Communication Disorders Quarterly.* doi: 1525740115597507.

Luckner, J. L., Slike, S. B., & Johnson, H. (2012). Helping students who are deaf or hard of hearing succeed. *Teaching Exceptional Children, 44*(4), 58–67.

Luckner, J., Bowen, S., & Carter, K. (2001). Visual teaching strategies for students who are deaf or hard of hearing. *Teaching Exceptional Children, 33*(3), 38–44.

Macleod-Gallinger, J. (1992). Employment attainments of deaf adults one and ten years after graduation from high school. *Journal of the American Deafness and Rehabilitation Association, 25*(4), 1–10.

Maller, S. J., & Braden, J. P. (2011). Intellectual assessment of deaf people: A critical review of core concepts and issues. In M. Marschark, P. E. Spencer, M. Marschark, & P. E. Spencer (Eds.), *The Oxford handbook of deaf studies, language, and education* (Vol. 1) (2nd ed.) (pp. 473–485). New York, NY: Oxford University Press.

Manchaiah, V., Stein, G., Danermark, B., & Germundsson, P. (2015). Positive, neutral, and negative connotations associated with social representation of "hearing loss" and "hearing aids." *Journal of Audiology & Otology, 19*, 132–137.

Marchbank, A. (2011). Early detection of hearing loss: The case for listening to mothers. *Deafness and Education International, 13*, 199–219.

Marschark, M. (2007). *Raising and educating a deaf child* (2nd ed.). New York, NY: Oxford University Press.

Marschark, M., Convertino, C., & LaRock, D. (2006). Optimizing academic performance of deaf students: Access, opportunities, and outcomes. In D. F. Moores & D. S. Martin, (Eds.), *Deaf learners: Developments in curriculum and instruction* (pp. 179–200). Washington, DC: Gallaudet University Press.

Martin, D., Bat-Chava, Y., Lalwani, A., & Waltzman, S. B. (2011). Peer relationships of deaf children with cochlear implants: Predictors of peer entry and peer interaction success. *Journal of Deaf Studies and Deaf Education, 16*(1), 108–120.

Mascia-Reed, C. (2010). Partners with a purpose: The consultant teacher model in educating deaf and hard of hearing students. *Odyssey: New Directions in Deaf Education, 11*(1), 25–29.

Maxon, A. B., Brackett, D., & van den Berg, S. A. (1991). Self perception of socialization: The effects of hearing status, age, and gender. *The Volta Review, 93*, 7–17.

Mayberry, R. I. (2010). Early language acquisition and adult language ability: What sign language reveals about the critical period for language. In M. Marschark & P. E. Spencer (Eds.). *Oxford handbook of deaf studies, language, and education—Volume 2* (pp. 281–291). New York, NY: Oxford University Press.

Mayne, A. M., Yoshinaga-Itano, C., Sedey, A. L., & Carey, A. (2000). Expressive vocabulary development of infants and toddlers who are deaf or hard of hearing. *Volta Review, 100*(5), 1–28.

McClatchie, A., & Therres, M. (2003). *AuSpLan: A manual for professionals working with children who have cochlear implants or amplification.* Oakland, CA: Children's Hospital & Research Center at Oakland.

McConkey Robbins, A. (2001). A sign of the times. *Loud and Clear Newsletter, 4*(2), 1–4.

McGowan, R. S., Nittrouer, S., Chenausky, K. (2008). Speech production in 12-month-old children with and without hearing loss. *Journal of Speech, Language, and Hearing Research, 51*, 879–888.

Meinzen-Derr, J., Wiley, S., & Choo, D. I. (2011). Impact of early intervention on expressive and receptive language development among young children with permanent hearing loss. *American Annals of the Deaf, 155*, 580–591.

Michael, R., Most, T., & Cinamon, R. G. (2013). The contribution of perceived parental support to the career self-efficacy of deaf, hard-of-hearing, and hearing adolescents. *Journal of deaf studies and deaf education, 18*(3), 329–343.

Miller, K. J. (2015). Thinking anew: Trends in the education of students who are deaf or hard of hearing and their implications. *SIG 9 Perspectives on Hearing and Hearing Disorders in Childhood, 25*(1), 37–44.

Mitchell, R. E., & Karchmer, M. A. (2004). Chasing the mythical ten percent: Parental hearing status of deaf and hard of hearing students in the United States. *Sign Language Studies, 4*, 138–163.

Moeller, M. P. (2000). Early intervention and language development in children who are deaf and hard of hearing. *Pediatrics, 106*(3), 43. Retrieved from www.pediatrics.org/cgi/content/full/106/3/e43

Moeller, M. P., Carr, G., Seaver, L., Stredler-Brown, A., & Holzinger, D. (2013). Best practices in family-centered early intervention for children who are deaf or hard of hearing: An international consensus statement. *Journal of Deaf Studies and Deaf Education, 18*, 429–445.

Moore, M. S., & Levitan, L. (1993). *For hearing people only: Answers to some of the most commonly asked questions about the deaf community, its culture and the "deaf reality."* Rochester, NY: Deaf Life Press.

Moore, M. S., & Panara, R. F. (1996). *Great Deaf Americans* (2nd ed.). Rochester, NY: MSM Productions, Ltd.

Moores, D. (2001). *Educating the deaf: Psychology, principles, and practices* (5th ed.). Boston, MA: Houghton Mifflin.

Moores, D. F. (2009). Cochlear failures. *American Annals of the Deaf, 153*, 423–424.

Morton, C., & Nance, W. (2006, May). Newborn hearing screening: A silent revolution. *New England Journal of Medicine* [serial online], *354*, 2151–2164.

Muse, C., Harrison, J., Yoshinaga-Itano, C., Grimes, A., Brookhouser, P. E., Epstein, S., ... Martin, P. (2013). Supplement to the JCIH 2007 position statement: Principles and guidelines for early intervention after confirmation that a child is deaf or hard of hearing. *Pediatrics, 131*, e1324–e1349.

Musyoka, M. M., Gentry, M. A., & Bartlett, J. J. (2016). Voices from the classroom: Experiences of teachers of deaf students with additional disabilities. *Journal of Education and Training Studies, 4*, 85–96.

National Association of State Directors of Special Education. (2006). *Meeting the needs of students who are deaf or hard of hearing: Educational service guidelines.* Alexandria, VA: Author.

National Center for Education Statistics. (2000). *Pursuing excellence: Comparisons of international eighth grade mathematics and science achievement from a U.S. perspective, 1995 and 1999.* Washington, DC: U.S. Department of Education.

National Center for Education Statistics. (2015). *Percentage distribution of students 6 to 21 years old served under Individuals with Disabilities Education Act (IDEA), Part B, by educational environment and type of disability: Selected years, fall 1989 through fall 2013* [Table 204.60]. Washington, DC: Author.

Retrieved from http://nces.ed.gov/programs/digest/d15/tables/dt15_204.60.asp?current=yes.

National Center for Health Statistics. (n.d.). *Disabilities/impairments.* Retrieved from www.cdc.gov/nchs/fastats/disable.htm

National Center for Hearing Assessment and Management. (2011). *Early hearing detection and intervention components.* Retrieved from: http://www.infanthearing.org/components/

National Institute on Deafness and Other Communication Disorders (NIDCD). (2016, May). *Quick statistics about hearing.* Bethesda, MD: National Institutes of Health. Retrieved from https://www.nidcd.nih.gov/health/statistics/quick-statistics-hearing

National Technical Institute for the Deaf. (2013, October). *What is C-print?* Retrieved from https://www.rit.edu/ntid/cprint/

Nover, S. M., & Andrews, J. F. (1998). *Critical pedagogy in deaf education: Bilingual methodology and staff development.* Santa Fe: New Mexico School for the Deaf.

Nowell, R., & Innes, J. (1997). *Educating children who are deaf or hard of hearing: Inclusion* (ERIC Digest #E557). (ERIC Document Reproduction Service No. ED414675). Retrieved from www.edrs.com/members/sp.cfm?AN-ED414675

Nussbaum, D. B., Scott, S., & Simms, L. E. (2012). The "why" and "how" of an ASL/English bimodal bilingual program. *Odyssey, 13*, 14–19.

O'Brien, C. A., & Placier, P. (2015). Deaf culture and competing discourses in a residential school for the Deaf: "Can do" versus "can't do." *Equity & Excellence in Education, 48*, 320–338.

Obasi, C. (2008). Seeing the Deaf in "Deafness." *Journal of Deaf Studies and Deaf Education, 13*, 455–65.

Obasi, C. (2014). Negotiating the insider/outsider continua: A Black female hearing perspective on research with Deaf women and Black women. *Qualitative Research, 14*, 61–78.

Padden, C., & Humphries, T. (1988). *Deaf in America: Voices from a culture.* Cambridge, MA: Harvard University Press.

Pagliaro, C. M. (2006). Mathematics education and the deaf learner. In D. F. Moores & D. S. Martin (Eds.), *Deaf learners: Developments in curriculum and instruction* (pp. 29–40). Washington, DC: Gallaudet University Press.

Patterson, T. (2015, November 23). A hearing son in deaf family: "I'd rather be deaf." *Cable News Network.* Retrieved from http://www.cnn.com/2015/11/23/living/deaf-culture-all-american-family-cnn-digital-short/

Paul, P. V. (1998). *Literacy and deafness: The development of reading, writing, and literate thought.* Boston, MA: Allyn & Bacon.

Podmore, R. (1995). *Signs in success: Profiles of deaf Americans.* Hillsboro, OR: Butte Publications.

Poeppelmeyer, D., & Reichert, L. (2015). Pioneering program teaches families sign language through tele-intervention. *Odyssey: New Directions in Deaf Education, 16*, 46–50.

Powers, S. (2003). Influences of student and family factors on academic outcomes of mainstream secondary school deaf students. *Journal of Deaf Studies and Deaf Education, 8*, 57–78.

Pray, J. L., & Jordan, I. K. (2010). The Deaf community and culture at a crossroads: Issues and challenges. *Journal of Social Work in Disability & Rehabilitation, 9*, 168–193.

Pray, J. L., & Jordan, I. K. (2012). The Deaf community and culture at a crossroads: Issues and challenges. In R. Meinert & F. Yuen (Eds.), *Controversies and disputes in disability and rehabilitation* (pp. 100–125). New York, NY: Routledge.

Qi, S., & Mitchell, R. E. (2012). Large-scale academic achievement testing of deaf and hard-of-hearing students: Past, present, and future. *Journal of Deaf Studies and Deaf Education, 17*(1), 1–18.

Reed, S., Antia, S. D., & Kreimeyer, K. H. (2008). Academic status of deaf and hard-of-hearing students in public schools: Student, home, and service facilitators and detractors. *Journal of Deaf Studies and Deaf Education, 13*, 485–502.

Reeves, J. B., Wollenhaupt, P., & Caccamise, F. (1995). *Deaf students as visual learners: Power for improving literacy and communication.* Paper presented at the 18th International Congress on Education of the Deaf, Tel Aviv, Israel. (ERIC Document Reproduction Service No. ED390209). Retrieved from www.edrs.com/Webstore/Download2.cfm?ID-405624

Robertson, L. (2014). *Literacy and deafness: Listening and spoken language* (2nd edition). San Diego, CA: Plural Publishing.

Robinette, D. (1990). *Hometown heroes: Successful deaf youth in America.* Washington, DC: Gallaudet University Press.

Ryndak, D. L., & Alper, S. (1996). *Curriculum content for students with moderate and severe disabilities in inclusive settings.* Boston, MA: Allyn & Bacon.

Salend, S. J. (1998). *Effective mainstreaming: Creating inclusive classrooms* (3rd ed.). Upper Saddle River, NJ: Merrill.

Sarchet, T., Marschark, M., Borgna, G., Convertino, C., Sapere, P., & Dirmyer, R. (2014). Vocabulary knowledge of deaf and hearing postsecondary students. *Journal of Postsecondary Education and Disability, 27,* 161–178.

Scheetz, N. A. (2001). *Orientation to deafness* (2nd ed.). Boston, MA: Allyn & Bacon.

Schick, B., Williams, K., & Bolster, L. (1999). Skill levels of educational interpreters working in public schools. *Journal of Deaf Studies and Deaf Education, 4,* 144–155.

Schirmer, B. R. (2001). *Psychological, social, and educational dimensions of deafness.* Boston, MA: Allyn & Bacon.

Schirmer, B. R., Bailey, J., & Fitzgerald, S. M. (1999). Using a writing assessment rubric or writing development of children who are deaf. *Exceptional Children, 65,* 383–397.

Schorr, E., Roth, F., & Fox, N. (2009). Quality of life for children with cochlear implants: Perceived benefits and problems and the perception of single words and emotional sounds. *Journal of Speech, Language, and Hearing Research, 52,* 141–152.

Schroedel, J. G., & Geyer, P. D. (2000). Long-term career attainments of deaf and hard of hearing college graduates: Results of a fifteen-year follow-up survey. *American Annals of the Deaf, 145*(4), 303–313.

Schroedel, J. G., & Watson, D. (1991). *Enhancing opportunities in postsecondary education for deaf students.* Little Rock: University of Arkansas Rehabilitation Research and Training Center on Deafness and Hearing Impairment.

Schwartz, S. (2007). *Choices in deafness: A parent's guide to communication options* (3rd ed.). Bethseda, MD: Woodbine House.

Scott, G. A. (2011). *Deaf and hard of hearing children: Federal support for developing language and literacy* [Report to Congressional Requesters, GAO-11-357]. Washington, DC: U.S. Government Accountability Office. Retrieved from http://www.gao.gov/assets/320/318707.pdf

Shea, G. (2013, February). *Song without words: Discovering my deafness halfway through life.* Jackson, TN: De Capo Press.

Shearer, A. E., Hildebrand, M. S., Sloan, C. M., & Smith, R. H. (2011). Deafness in the genomics era. *Hearing Research, 282,* 1–9.

Siegel, L. (2000). *The educational and communication needs of deaf and hard of hearing children: A statement of principle regarding fundamental systematic educational changes.* Greenbrae, CA: National Deaf Education Project.

Social Security Administration. (2011). *Annual statistical report on the social security disability insurance program.* Washington, DC: Author.

Spencer, P. E., & Marschark, M. (2010). *Evidence-based practice in educating deaf and hard-of-hearing students.* New York, NY: Oxford University Press.

Stewart, D., & Kluwin, T. N. (2001). *Teaching deaf and hard of hearing students: Content, strategies, and curriculum.* Boston, MA: Allyn & Bacon.

Stika, C. J., Eisenberg, L. S., Johnson, K. C., Henning, S. C., Colson, B. G., Ganguly, D. H., & DesJardin, J. L. (2015). Developmental outcomes of early-identified children who are hard of hearing at 12 to 18 months of age. *Early Human Development, 91,* 47–55.

Stinson, M. S., & Kluwin, T. N. (2011). Educational consequences of alternative school placements. In M. Marschark & P. E. Spencer (Eds.). *Oxford handbook of deaf studies, language, and education–Volume 2* (pp. 47–62). New York, NY: Oxford University Press.

Stinson, M. S., & Liu, Y. (1999). Participation of deaf and hard-of-hearing students in classes with hearing students. *Journal of Deaf Studies and Deaf Education, 4*(3), 191–202.

Stinson, M. S., & McKee, B. (Eds.). (2000). *Development and evaluation of a computer-aided speech-to-print transcription system.* Rochester, NY: National Technical Institute for the Deaf.

Swanwick, R., & Marschark, M. (2011). Enhancing education for deaf children: Research into practice and back again. *Deafness & Education International, 12,* 217–235.

Tarquin, P., & Walker, S. (1997). *Creating success in the classroom: Visual organizers and how to use them.* Englewood, CO: Teacher Ideas Press.

Traci, M., & Koester, L. S. (2011). Parent–infant interactions: A transactional approach to understanding the development of deaf infants. In M. Marschark, P. E. Spencer, M. Marschark, & P. E. Spencer (Eds.), *The Oxford handbook of deaf studies, language, and education* (Vol. 1) (2nd ed.) (pp. 200–213). New York, NY: Oxford University Press.

Traxler, C. B. (2000). The Stanford Achievement Test, ninth edition: National norming and performance standards for deaf and hard-of-hearing students. *Journal of Deaf Studies and Deaf Education, 5*(4), 337–348.

Tye-Murray, N. (1994). *Let's converse: A "how-to" guide to develop and expand conversational skills of children and teenagers who are hearing impaired.* Washington, DC: Alexander Graham Bell Association for the Deaf.

Tyler, R. S. (1993). *Cochlear implants: Audiological foundations.* San Diego, CA: Singular.

U.S. Department of Education. (1992). Deaf students education services: Policy guidance. *Federal Register, 57*(211), October 30, 1992, 49274–49276.

U.S. Department of Education. (2011). *The digest of education statistics 2010* [NCES 2011-015, Table 46]. Washington, DC: Author, National Center for Education Statistics. Retrieved from http://nces.ed.gov/fastfacts/display.asp?id=59

U.S. Department of Education. (2011). *Thirtieth Annual report to Congress on the implementation of the Individuals with Disabilities Education Act, 2008.* Washington, DC: Author.

U.S. Department of Education. (2016). *IDEA Section 618 data products: State level data files, child count.* Washington DC: Author. Retrieved from http://www2.ed.gov/programs/osepidea/618-data/state-level-data-files/index.html#bcc

U.S. Food and Drug Administration. (2006). *Cochlear implants: Benefits/risks.* Retrieved from www.fda.gov/cdrh/cochlear/riskbenefit.html

U.S. Food and Drug Administration. (2014). *Benefits and risks of cochlear implants.* Silver Spring, MD: Author. Retrieved from http://www.fda.gov/MedicalDevices/ProductsandMedicalProcedures/Implantsand-Prosthetics/CochlearImplants/ucm062843.htm

van Staden, A. (2013). An evaluation of an intervention using sign language and multi-sensory coding to support word learning and reading comprehension of deaf signing children. *Child Language Teaching and Therapy, 29,* 305–318.

Vernon, M., & Rhodes, A. (2009). Deafness and autism spectrum disorders. *American Annals of the Deaf, 154,* 5–14.

Wagner, M., Newman, L., Cameto, R., & Levine, P. (2005). *Changes over time in the early postschool outcomes of youth with disabilities. A report of findings from the National Longitudinal Transition Study (NLTS) and the National Longitudinal Transition Study-2 (NLTS2).* Menlo Park, CA: SRI International. Retrieved from www.nlts2.org/pdfs/str6completereport.pdf

Wakil, N., Fitzpatrick, E. M., Olds, J., Schramm, D., & Whittingham, J. (2014). Long-term outcome after cochlear implantation in children with additional developmental disabilities. *International Journal of Audiology, 53,* 587–594.

Walker, L. A. (2001, May 13). They're breaking the sound barrier. *Parade Magazine*, pp. 4–5.

Walsh, M. M., & Gluck, K. A. (2015). Mechanisms for robust cognition. *Cognitive Science, 39*, 1131–1171.

Walter, G. G., Foster, S. B., & Elliot, L. (1987, July). *Attrition and accommodation of hearing-impaired college students in the U.S.* Paper presented at the tenth national conference of the Association of Handicapped Student Service Programs in Postsecondary Education. Washington, DC.

Webb, M., Lederberg, A. R., Branum-Martin, L., & Connor, C. M. (2015). Evaluating the structure of early English literacy skills in deaf and hard-of-hearing children. *Journal of Deaf Studies and Deaf Education, 20*, 343–355.

Weinberg, J. (2011). Picturing time: Visual techniques for teaching the concepts of yesterday, today, and tomorrow. *Odyssey: New Directions in Deaf Education, 12*, 52–56.

Wells, G. (1986). *The meaning makers: Children learning language and using language to learn.* Portsmouth, NH: Heinemann.

Wiefferink, C. H., Rieffe, C., Ketelaar, L., De Raeve, L., & Frijns, J. M. (2013). Emotion understanding in deaf children with a cochlear implant. *Journal of Deaf Studies and Deaf Education, 18*, 175–186.

Williams, C., & Mayer, C. (2015). Writing in young deaf children. *Review of Educational Research, 85*, 630–666.

Winzer, M. A. (1993). *The history of special education: From isolation to integration.* Washington, DC: Gallaudet University Press.

Woblers, K. A. (2008). Using balanced and interactive writing instruction to improve the higher order and lower order writing skills of deaf students. *Journal of Deaf Studies and Deaf Education, 13*, 257–277.

Wolbers, K. A., Dostal, H. M., & Bowers, L. M. (2012). "I was born full deaf." Written language outcomes after 1 year of strategic and interactive writing instruction. *Journal of Deaf Studies & Deaf Education, 17*, 19–38.

Wolters, N., Knoors, H. T., Cillessen, A. N., & Verhoeven, L. (2011). Predicting acceptance and popularity in early adolescence as a function of hearing status, gender, and educational setting. *Research in Developmental Disabilities: A Multidisciplinary Journal, 32*, 2553–2565.

Wood, D., & Wood, H. (1997). Communicating with children who are deaf: Pitfalls and possibilities. *Language, Speech, and Hearing Services in Schools, 28*, 348–354.

Xie, Y., Potmešil, M., & Peters, B. (2014). Children who are deaf or hard of hearing in inclusive educational settings: A literature review on interactions with peers. *Journal of Deaf Studies and Deaf Education, 19*, 423–437.

Yoshinaga-Itano, C., & Downey, D. M. (1996). The psychoeducational characteristics of school-aged students in Colorado with significant hearing losses. *Volta Review, 98*(1), 65–96.

Yoshinaga-Itano, C., Sedey, A. L., Coulter, D. K., & Mehl, A. L. (1998). The language of early- and later-identified children with hearing loss. *Pediatrics, 102*, 1161–1171.

Zapien, C. (1998, July). *Options in deaf education—History, methodologies, and strategies for surviving the system.* Retrieved from www.listen-up.org/edu/options1.htm

Chapter 12

Ajuwon, P. M., & Craig, C. J. (2007). Distance education in the preparation of teachers of the visually impaired and orientation and mobility specialists: Profile of a new training paradigm. *RE:view: Rehabilitation Education for Blindness and Visual Impairment, 39*, 3–14.

Ajuwon, P. M., & Oyinlade, A. O. (2008). Educational placement of children who are blind or have low vision in residential and public schools: A national study of parents' perspectives. *Journal of Visual Impairment & Blindness, 102*, 325–339.

Ali, E., MacFarland, S. Z., & Umbreit, J. (2011). Effectiveness of combining tangible symbols with the picture exchange communication system to teach requesting skills to children with multiple disabilities including visual impairment. *Education and Training in Autism and Developmental Disabilities, 46*, 425–435.

Alimovic, S. (2013). Emotional and behavioural problems in children with visual impairment, intellectual and multiple disabilities. *Journal of Intellectual Disability Research, 57*, 153–160.

Allman, C. B., & Lewis, S. (Eds.). (2014). *ECC essentials: Teaching the expanded core curriculum to students with visual impairments.* New York, NY: AFB Press.

American Foundation for the Blind. (2009, May). *Estimates of severely visually impaired children.* New York, NY: Author. Retrieved from http://www.afb.org/section.aspx?FolderID=3&SectionID=3&TopicID=138&DocumentID=3350

American Foundation for the Blind. (2012a, August). *Educating students with visual impairments for inclusion in society: A paper on the inclusion of students with visual impairments.* Retrieved from http://www.afb.org/section.aspx?FolderID=3&SectionID=44&TopicID=189&DocumentID=1344

American Foundation for the Blind. (2012b, August). *Estimates of severely visually impaired children.* New York, NY: Author. Retrieved from http://www.afb.org/section.aspx?FolderID=3&SectionID=3&TopicID=138&DocumentID=3350

American Foundation for the Blind. (2016a). *Accommodations and modifications at a glance: Educational accommodations for students who are blind or visually impaired.* New York, NY: Author. Retrieved from http://www.afb.org/info/programs-and-services/professional-development/experts-guide/accommodations-and-modifications-at-a-glance/1235

American Foundation for the Blind. (2016b). *Low vision and legal blindness: Terms and descriptions.* New York, NY: Author. Retrieved from http://www.visionaware.org/info/your-eye-condition/eye-health/low-vision/low-vision-terms-and-descriptions/1235

American Foundation for the Blind. (2016c). *Assessment considerations for students who are blind and visually impaired.* New York, NY: Author. Retrieved from http://www.afb.org/info/assessment-considerations-for-students-who-are-blind-and-visually-impaired/5

American Printing House for the Blind. (2010). *Annual report 2010.* Louisville, KY: Author. Retrieved from http://www.aph.org/about/ar2010.html

American Printing House for the Blind. (2014). *Annual Report 2014: Distribution of eligible students based on the federal quota census of January 7, 2013.* Louisville, KY: Author. Retrieved from http://www.aph.org/federal-quota/distribution-2014

Ashcroft, S. C., Halliday, C., & Barraga, N. C. (1965). *Study II: Effects of experimental teaching on the visual behavior of children educated as though they had no vision.* Nashville, TN: George Peabody College for Teachers.

Barclay, L., Herlich, S. A., & Sacks, S. Z. (2010). Effective teaching strategies: Case studies from the alphabetic braille and contracted braille study. *Journal of Visual Impairment & Blindness, 104*, 753–764.

Bardin, J. A., & Lewis, S. (2008). A survey of the academic engagement of students with visual impairments in general education classes. *Journal of Visual Impairment & Blindness, 102*, 472–483.

Barraga, N. C. (1964). *Increased visual behavior in low vision children.* New York, NY: American Foundation for the Blind Press.

Barton, M. (2011). Vision screening for children 1 to 5 years of age: U.S. Preventive Services Task Force recommendation statement. *Pediatrics, 127*, 340–346.

Bell, E. (2010). U.S. national certification in literary braille: History and current administration. *Journal of Visual Impairment & Blindness, 104*, 489–498.

Bishop, V. E. (2004). *Teaching visually impaired children* (3rd ed.). Springfield, IL: Charles C. Thomas.

Bosman, A. M. T., Gompel, M., Vervloed, M. P. J., & van Bon, W. H. J. (2006). Low vision affects the reading process quantitatively but not qualitatively. *Journal of Special Education, 39*, 208–219.

Braille Authority of North America. (2013, March). *Overview of changes from current literary braille to UEB*. Baltimore, MD: National Federation of the Blind. Retrieved from http://www.brailleauthority.org/ueb/overview_changes_ebae_ueb.html

Brambring, M. (2007). Divergent development of verbal skills in children who are blind or sighted. *Journal of Visual Impairment & Blindness, 101*, 749–762.

Brambring, M., & Asbrock, D. (2010). Validity of false belief tasks in blind children. *Journal of Autism and Developmental Disorders, 40*, 1471–1484.

Cameto, R., & Nagle, K. (2007). *Orientation and mobility skills of secondary school students with visual impairments: Facts from NLTS2* [NCSER 2008-3007]. Washington, DC: National Center for Special Education Research.

Celeste, M. (2007). Social skills intervention for a child who is blind. *Journal of Visual Impairment & Blindness, 101*, 521–533.

Cho, H. J., & Palmer, S. B. (2008). Fostering self-determination in infants and toddlers with visual impairments or blindness. *Young Exceptional Children, 11*(4), 26–34.

Clark, C., & McDonnell, A. P. (2008). Teaching choice making to children with visual impairments and multiple disabilities in preschool and kindergarten classrooms. *Journal of Visual Impairment & Blindness, 102*, 397–409.

Conroy, P. W. (2005). English language learners with visual impairments: Strategies to enhance learning. *RE:view, 37*, 101–108.

Conroy, P. W. (2006). Hmong culture and visual impairment: Strategies for culturally sensitive practices. *RE:view: Rehabilitation Education for Blindness and Visual Impairment, 38*, 55–64.

Conroy, P. W. (2008). Paraprofessionals and students with visual impairments: Potential pitfalls and solutions. *RE:view: Rehabilitation Education for Blindness and Visual Impairment, 39*, 43–55.

Corn, A. L., & Koenig, A. J. (2002). Literacy for students with low vision: A framework for delivering instruction. *Journal of Visual Impairment and Blindness, 95*, 305–321.

Corn, A. L., & Spungin, S. J. (2003). *Free and appropriate public education and the personnel crisis for students with visual impairments and blindness*. Gainesville: University of Florida, Center on Personnel Studies in Special Education. Retrieved from www.coe.ufl.edu/copsse/docs/IB-10/1/IB-10.pdf#search=%22visual%20impairment%20personnel%20crisis%20corn%22

Correa, V. I., Fazzi, D. L., & Pogrund, R. L. (2002). Team focus: Current trends, service delivery, and advocacy. In R. L. Pogrund & D. L. Fazzi (Eds.), *Early focus: Working with young children who are blind or visually impaired and their families* (pp. 405–441). New York, NY: American Foundation for the Blind Press.

Correa-Torres, S. M. (2008). The nature of the social experiences of students with deaf-blindness who are educated in inclusive settings. *Journal of Visual Impairment & Blindness, 102*, 272–283.

Correa-Torres, S. M., & Durando, J. (2011). Perceived training needs of teachers of students with visual impairments who work with students from culturally and linguistically diverse backgrounds. *Journal of Visual Impairment & Blindness, 105*, 521–532.

Correa-Torres, S. M., & Johnson, J. (2004). Facing the challenges of itinerant teaching: Perspectives and suggestions from the field. *Journal of Visual Impairment and Blindness, 98*, 420–433.

Crawford, S., & Elliott, R. T. (2007). Analysis of phonemes, graphemes, onsetrimes, and words with Braille-learning children. *Journal of Visual Impairment & Blindness, 101*, 534–544.

Dammeyer, J. (2013). Symptoms of autism among children with congenital deafblindness. *Journal of Autism and Developmental Disorders, 44*, 1095–1102.

Day, J. N., McDonnell, A. P., & O'Neill, R. (2008). Teaching beginning Braille reading using an alphabet or uncontracted Braille approach. *Journal of Behavioral Education, 17*, 253–277.

de Klerk, H., & Greeff, A. P. (2011). Resilience in parents of young adults with visual impairments. *Journal of Visual Impairment & Blindness, 105*, 414–424.

Dell, A. G., Newton, D. A., & Petroff, J. G. (2016). *Assistive technology in the classroom: Enhancing the school experiences of students with disabilities*. Boston, MA: Pearson.

Desrochers, M. N., Oshlag, R., & Kennelly, A. M. (2014). Using background music to reduce problem behavior during assessment with an adolescent who is blind with multiple disabilities. *Journal of Visual Impairment & Blindness, 108*, 61–66.

Douglas, G., McLinden, M., McCall, S., Pavey, S., Ware, J., & Farrell, A. M. (2011). Access to print literacy for children and young people with visual impairment: Findings from a review of literature. *European Journal of Special Needs Education, 26*, 25–38.

Durando, J. (2008). A survey on literacy instruction for students with multiple disabilities. *Journal of Visual Impairment & Blindness, 102*, 40–45.

Eisenbraun, K., Johnstone, C., Lazarus, S., Liu, K., Matchett, D., Moen, R., . . . Thurlow, M. (2009). *Reading and students with visual impairments or blindness*. Minneapolis: Partnership for Accessible Reading Assessment, University of Minnesota. Retrieved from http://www.readingassessment.info/resources/publications/visualimpairment.htm

Ely, R., Emerson, R. W., Maggiore, T., Rothberg, M., O'Connell, T., & Hudson, L. (2006). Increased content knowledge of students with visual impairments as a result of extended descriptions. *Journal of Special Education Technology, 21*(3), 31–43.

Emerson, R. W., Corn, A., & Siller, M. A. (2006). Trends in braille and large-print production in the United States: 2000–2004. *Journal of Visual Impairment and Blindness, 100*, 137–151.

Erickson, S., Lee, C., & von Schrader, S. (2015, September). *Disability statistics from the 2013 American Community Survey (ACS)*. Ithaca, NY: Cornell University Employment and Disability Institute (EDI). Retrieved from www.disabilitystatistics.org

Erin, J. N., Fazzi, D. L., Gordon, R. L., Isenberg, S. J., & Paysse, E. A. (2002). Vision focus: Understanding the medical and functional implications of vision loss. In R. L. Pogrund & D. L. Fazzi (Eds.), *Early focus: Working with young children who are blind or visually impaired and their families* (pp. 52–106). New York, NY: American Foundation for the Blind Press.

Farnsworth, C. R., & Luckner, J. L. (2008). The impact of assistive technology on curriculum accommodations for a Braille-reading student. *RE:view: Rehabilitation Education for Blindness and Visual Impairment, 39*, 171–187.

Ferrell, K. A. (2000). Growth and development of young children. In M. C. Holbrook & A. J. Koenig (Eds.), *Foundations of education: History and theory of teaching children and youths with visual impairments* (2nd ed., pp. 111–134). New York, NY: American Foundation for the Blind Press.

Ferrell, K. A. (2005). The effects of NCLB. *Journal of Visual Impairment and Blindness, 99*, 681–683.

Gale, E., Trief, E., & Lengel, J. (2010). The use of video analysis in a personnel preparation program for teachers of students who are visually impaired. *Journal of Visual Impairment & Blindness, 104*, 700–704.

George, A. L., & Duquette, C. (2006). The psychosocial experiences of a student with low vision. *Journal of Visual Impairment and Blindness, 100*, 152–163.

Green, N. E. (2010). Teaching (dis)abled: Reflections on teaching, learning, power, and classroom community. *English Journal, 100*, 86–92.

Griffin-Shirley, N., Layton, C. A., Koenig, A. J., Robinson, M. C., Siew, L. K., & Davidson, R. C. (2003). *A survey of teachers of students with visual impairments: Responsibilities, satisfactions, and needs*. Manuscript submitted for publication.

Guerette, A. R., Lewis, S., & Mattingly, C. (2011). Students with low vision describe their visual impairments and visual functioning. *Journal of Visual Impairment & Blindness, 105*, 287–298.

Gulati, S., Andrews, C. A., Apkarian, A. O., Musch, D. C., Lee, P. P., & Stein, J. D. (2014). Effect of gestational age and birth weight on the risk of strabismus among premature infants. *JAMA Pediatrics, 168*, 850–856.

Hall, E. M. (2012). *Dr. Samuel Gridley Howe*. Bloomington: *Learning to Give* and the Center on Philanthropy at Indiana University. Retrieved from http://learningtogive.org/papers/paper105.html

Harris, B. A. (2011). Effects of the proximity of paraeducators on the interactions of braille readers in inclusive settings. *Journal of Visual Impairment & Blindness, 105*, 467–478.

Hatlen, P. (2000). Historical perspectives. In M. C. Holbrook & A. J. Koenig (Eds.), *Foundations of education: History and theory of teaching children and youths with visual impairments* (pp. 1–54). New York, NY: American Foundation for the Blind Press.

Hatlen, P., & Spungin, J. (2008). The nature and future of literacy: Point and counterpoint. *Journal of Visual Impairment & Blindness, 102*, 389–396.

Hewett, R., Douglas, G., Ramli, A., & Keil, S. (2012, February). *Post-14 transitions: A survey of the social activity and social networking of blind and partially sighted young people* [technical report]. Birmingham, England: Visual Impairment Centre for Teaching and Research, Department of Disability Inclusion and Special Needs. Retrieved from https://www.rnib.org.uk/sites/default/files/social_networking_report.doc

Holbrook, M. C. (2015). Renewing and refreshing the knowledge base of the field of visual impairment: A call to action. *Journal of Visual Impairment & Blindness, 109*(2), 159–162.

Holbrook, M. C., & Koenig, A. J. (2000). Basic techniques for modifying instruction. In A. J. Koenig & M. C. Holbrook (Eds.), *Foundations of education: Instructional strategies for teaching children and youths with visual impairments* (2nd ed., pp. 173–195). New York, NY: AFB Press.

Holmes, R. B. (1967). *Training residual vision in adolescents educated previously as nonvisual*. Unpublished master's thesis, Illinois State University, Normal, Illinois.

Houwen, S., Visscher, C., Lemmick, L. A. P. M., & Hartman, E. (2009). Motor skill performance of children and adolescents with visual impairments: A review. *Exceptional Children, 75*, 464–492.

Huebner, K. M. (2000). Visual impairment. In M. C. Holbrook & A. J. Koenig (Eds.), *Foundations of education: History and theory of teaching children and youths with visual impairments* (2nd ed., pp. 55–76). New York, NY: American Foundation for the Blind Press.

Jones, B. A., & Hensley-Maloney, L. (2015). Meeting the needs of students with coexisting visual impairments and learning disabilities. *Intervention in School and Clinic, 50*, 226–233.

Jones, B. A., Smith, H. H., Hensley-Maloney, L., & Gansle, K. A. (2015). Applying response to intervention to identify learning disabilities in students with visual impairments. *Intervention in School and Clinic, 51*, 28–36.

Kamei-Hannan, C., Holbrook, M. C., & Ricci, L. A. (2012). Applying a response-to-intervention model to literacy instruction for students who are blind or have low vision. *Journal of Visual Impairment & Blindness, 106*, 69–80.

Kelly, S. M., & Smith, D. W. (2011). The impact of assistive technology on the educational performance of students with visual impairments: A synthesis of the research. *Journal of Visual Impairment & Blindness, 105*, 73–83.

Kelly, S. M., & Smith, T. J. (2008). The digital social interactions of students with visual impairments: Findings from two national surveys. *Journal of Visual Impairment & Blindness, 102*, 528–539.

KNFB Reading Technology. (2010). *Kurzweil-National Federation for the Blind readers*. Retrieved from http://www.knfbreader.com/faq.php

KNFB. (2016). *Introducing the KNFB Reader*. Retrieved from http://www.knfbreader.com/#welcome.

Koenig, A. J., & Holbrook, M. C. (1995). *Learning media assessment of students with visual impairments: A resource guide for teachers* (2nd ed.). Austin: TX School for the Blind and Visually Impaired.

Koenig, A. J., & Holbrook, M. C. (2000). Planning instruction in unique skills. In A. J. Koenig & M. C. Holbrook (Eds.), *Foundations of education: Instructional strategies for teaching children and youths with visual impairments* (2nd ed., pp.196–221). New York, NY: American Foundation for the Blind Press.

Koestler, F. A. (1976). *The unseen minority: A social history of blindness in the United States*. New York, NY: David McKay.

Krebs, C. (2006). Using a dialogue journal to build responsibility and self-reliance: A case study. *RE:view, 37*, 173–176.

Learning Ally. (2016). *Search our library of over 80,000 audiobooks!* Retrieved from http://www.learningally.org/BrowseAudiobooks.aspx

Lewis, S., & Allman, C. B. (2000). Educational programming. In M. C. Holbrook & A. J. Koenig (Eds.), *Foundations of education: History and theory of teaching children and youths with visual impairments* (2nd ed., pp. 218–259). New York, NY: American Foundation for the Blind Press.

Lewis, S., & McKenzie, A. R. (2010). The competencies, roles, supervision, and training needs of paraeducators working with students with visual impairments in local and residential schools. *Journal of Visual Impairment & Blindness, 104*, 464–477.

Leyser, Y., & Heinze, T. (2001). Perspectives of parents of children who are visually impaired: Implications for the field. *RE:view, 33*, 37–48.

Lieberman, L. J., Haegele, J. A., Columna, L., & Conroy, P. (2014). How students with visual impairments can learn components of the expanded core curriculum through physical education. *Journal of Visual Impairment & Blindness, 108*, 239–247.

Lighthouse International. (2012). *Prevalence of vision impairment*. New York, NY: Author. Retrieved from http://www.lighthouse.org/research/statistics-on-vision-impairment/prevalence-of-vision-impairment/

Lohmeier, K., Blankenship, K., & Hatlen, P. (2009). Expanded core curriculum: 12 years later. *Journal of Visual Impairment & Blindness, 103*, 102–112.

Lohmeier, L. L. (2009). Aligning state standards and the expanded core curriculum: Balancing the impact of the No Child Left Behind Act. *Journal of Visual Impairment & Blindness, 103*, 44–47.

Louisville, KY: Author. Retrieved from http://www.afb.org/info/blindness-statistics/children-and-youth/children-and-youth-with-vision-loss/235

Lowenfeld, B. (1973). Psychological considerations. In B. Lowenfeld (Ed.), *The visually handicapped child in school*. New York, NY: The John Day Company.

Luckner, J. L., Bruce, S. M., & Ferrell, K. A. (2015). A summary of the communication and literacy evidence-based practices for students who are deaf or hard of hearing, visually impaired, and deafblind. *Communication Disorders Quarterly*. doi: 10.1177/1525740115597507

Lueck, A. H. (2010). Cortical or cerebral visual impairment in children: A brief overview. *Journal of Visual Impairment & Blindness, 104*, 585–592.

Lussenhop, K., & Corn, A. L. (2002). Comparative studies of the reading performance of students with low vision. *RE:view, 34*, 57–69.

Mason, C., Davidson, R., & McNerney, C. (2000). *National plan for training personnel to serve children with blindness and low vision*. Reston, VA: Council for Exceptional Children.

McAllister, R., & Gray, C. (2007). Low vision: Mobility and independence training for the early years child. *Early Child Development and Care, 177*, 839–852.

McDonnall, M. (2011). Predictors of employment for youths with visual impairments: Findings from the Second National Longitudinal Transition Study. *Journal of Visual Impairment & Blindness, 105*, 453–466.

McDonnall, M. C., & O'Mally, J. (2012). Characteristics of early work experiences and their association with future employment. *Journal of Visual Impairment & Blindness, 106*, 133–144.

McKenzie, A. R. (2007). The use of learning media assessments with students who are deaf-blind. *Journal of Visual Impairment & Blindness, 101*, 587–600.

McLinden, M., & Douglas, G. (2014). Education of children with sensory needs: Reducing barriers to learning for children with visual impairment. In A. J. Holliman, A. J. Holliman (Eds.), *The Routledge international companion to educational psychology* (pp. 246–255). New York, NY: Routledge/Taylor & Francis.

Muhlenhaupt, M. (2002). Family and school partnerships for IEP development. *Journal of Visual Impairment and Blindness, 96*, 175–178.

National Association of Blind Teachers. (2012). *Colleges and universities offering programs in the education of the visually impaired.* Retrieved from http://www.blindteachers.net/degree-college.html

National Eye Institute, National Institutes of Health. (2003, October). *Eye diagram.* Retrieved from www.nei.nih.gov/photo/eyean/index.asp

National Eye Institute. (2009, May). *Retinopathy of prematurity.* Washington, DC: National Institutes of Health. Retrieved from http://www.nei.nih.gov/health/ropindex.asp

National Eye Institute. (2012). *About sports eye injury and protective eyewear.* Bethesda, MD: National Institutes of Health. Retrieved from http://www.nei.nih.gov/sports/index.asp

National Eye Institute. (2014, June). *Facts about retinopathy of prematurity (ROP).* Bethesda, MD: National Institutes of Health. Retrieved from https://nei.nih.gov/health/rop/rop

O'Connor, A. R., Wilson, C. M., & Fielder, A. R. (2007). Ophthalmological problems associated with preterm birth. *Eye, 21*, 1254–1260.

Ophir-Cohen, M., Ashkenazy, E., Cohen, A., & Tirosh, E. (2005). Emotional status and development in children who are visually impaired. *Journal of Visual Impairment and Blindness, 99*, 478–485.

Ozkubat, U., & Ozdemir, S. (2014). A comparison of social skills in Turkish children with visual impairments, children with intellectual impairments and typically developing children. *International Journal of Inclusive Education, 18*, 500–514.

Pevsner, D., Sanspree, M. J., & Allison, C. (2012). Teaching strategies for learning styles of students with visual impairments. *Insight: Research & Practice in Visual Impairment & Blindness, 5*(2), 59–69.

Piscitello, J. (2007, January). *Braille reading rates.* Retrieved from http://lists.aerbvi.org/pipermail/aernet_lists.aerbvi.org/2007-January/005992.html

Pogrund, R. L., & Fazzi, D. L. (Eds.). (2002). *Early focus: Working with young children who are blind or visually impaired and their families* (pp. 405–441). New York, NY: American Foundation for the Blind Press.

Pogrund, R. L., Darst, S., & Boland, T. (2013). Evaluation study of short-term programs at a residential school for students who are blind and visually impaired. *Journal of Visual Impairment & Blindness, 107*, 30–42.

Rainey, L., Elsman, E. M., Nispen, R. A., Leeuwen, L. M., & Rens, G. B. (2016). Comprehending the impact of low vision on the lives of children and adolescents: A qualitative approach. *Quality of Life Research: An International Journal of Quality of Life Aspects of Treatment, Care & Rehabilitation.* doi:10.1007/s11136-016-1292-8

Reed, M., & Curtis, K. (2011). High school teachers' perspectives on supporting students with visual impairments toward higher education: Access, barriers, and success. *Journal of Visual Impairment & Blindness, 105*, 548–559.

Roberts, F. K. (1986). Education for the visually handicapped: A social and educational history. In G. School (Ed.), *Foundations of education for blind and visually handicapped children and youth: Theory and practice* (pp. 1–18). New York, NY: American Foundation for the Blind Press.

Roe, J., Rogers, S., Donaldson, M., Gordon, C., & Meager, N. (2014). Teaching literacy through braille in mainstream settings whilst promoting inclusion: Reflections on our practice. *International Journal of Disability, Development and Education, 61*, 165–177.

Runyan, M. (2013). Seeing is believing! *Learning & Leading with Technology, 40*(5), 12–17.

Sacks, S. Z., & Silberman, R. K. (2000). Social skills. In A. J. Koenig & M. C. Holbrook (Eds.), *Foundations of education: Instructional strategies for teaching children and youths with visual impairments* (2nd ed., pp. 616–652). New York, NY: American Foundation for the Blind Press.

Sapp, W. (2011). Somebody's jumping on the floor: Incorporating music into orientation and mobility for preschoolers with visual impairments. *Journal of Visual Impairment & Blindness, 105*, 715–719.

Sapp, W., & Hatlen, P. (2010). The expanded core curriculum: Where we have been, where we are going, and how we can get there. *Journal of Visual Impairment & Blindness, 104*, 338–348.

Savaiano, M. E., & Hatton, D. D. (2013). Using repeated reading to improve reading speed and comprehension in students with visual impairments. *Journal of Visual Impairment & Blindness, 107*, 93–106.

Shapiro, D. R., Moffett, A., Lieberman, L., & Dummer, G. M. (2005). Perceived competence of children with visual impairments. *Journal of Visual Impairment and Blindness, 99*, 15–25.

Sharma, U., Moore, D., & Furlonger, B. (2010). Forming effective partnerships to facilitate inclusion of students with vision impairments: Perceptions of a regular classroom teacher and an itinerant teacher. *British Journal of Visual Impairment, 28*, 57–67.

Silberman, R. K. (2000). Children and youth with visual impairments and other exceptionalities. In M. C. Holbrook & A. J. Koenig (Eds.), *Foundations of education: History and theory of teaching children and youths with visual impairments* (2nd ed., pp. 173–196). New York, NY: American Foundation for the Blind Press.

Smith, D. W., & Kelly, P. (2007). A survey of assistive technology and teacher preparation programs for individuals with visual impairments. *Journal of Visual Impairment and Blindness, 101*, 429–433.

Smyth, C. A., Spicer, C. L., & Morgese, Z. L. (2014). Family voices at mealtime: Experiences with young children with visual impairment. *Topics in Early Childhood Special Education, 34*, 175–185.

Spungin, S. J., & Ferrell, K. A. (1999). The role and function of the teacher of students with visual handicaps. In G. S. Pugh & J. Erin (Eds.), *Blind and visually impaired students: Educational service guidelines.* Watertown, MA: Perkins School for the Blind.

Steinman, B. A., LeJeune, B. J., & Kimbrough, B. T. (2006). Developmental stages of reading processes in children who are blind and sighted. *Journal of Visual Impairment and Blindness, 100*, 36–46.

Summers, S., Leigh, L., & Arnold, J. (2006). Personnel shortage and caseload management of students with visual impairments. *Journal of Visual Impairment & Blindness, 100*, 593.

Swenson, A. M. (2008). Reflections on teaching reading in braille. *Journal of Visual Impairment & Blindness, 102*, 206–209.

Swenson, A. M. (2011). *The ABC braille study: Results and implications for teachers.* Retrieved from http://www.pathstoliteracy.org/braille/content/research/abc-braille-study-results-and-implications-teachers

Swenson, A. M. (2012). Learning to listen/listening to learn: Teaching listening skills to students with visual impairments. *Journal of Visual Impairment & Blindness, 106*, 185–187.

Swift, S. H., Davidson, R. C., & Weems, L. J. (2008). Cortical visual impairment in children: Presentation intervention, and prognosis in educational settings. *Teaching Exceptional Children Plus, 4*(5). Retrieved from http://www.eric.ed.gov/PDFS/EJ967486.pdf

Trief, E., Bruce, S. M., & Cascella, P. W. (2010). The selection of tangible symbols by educators of students with visual impairments and additional disabilities. *Journal of Visual Impairment & Blindness, 104*, 499–504.

U.S. Department of Education (2012, July). *Children with disabilities receiving special education under Part B of the Individuals with Disabilities Education Act 2011* [OMB #1820-0043]. Washington, DC: U.S. Department of Education, Office of Special Education Programs, Data Analysis System (DANS).

U.S. Department of Education, Office of Special Education and Rehabilitative Services, Office of Special Education Programs. (2015). *Thirty-seventh Annual Report to Congress on the implementation of the Individuals with Disabilities Education Act.* Washington, DC: Author.

U.S. Department of Education. (2011). *Thirty-eighth annual report to Congress on the implementation of the Individuals with Disabilities Education Act.* Washington, DC: Author.

U.S. Department of Education. (2015, March). *Teacher shortage areas nationwide listing 1990–1991 through 2015–2016.* Washington, DC: U.S. Department of Education, Office of Postsecondary Education. Retrieved from https://www2.ed.gov/about/offices/list/ope/pol/tsa.pdf

Ulster, A. A., & Antle, B. J. (2005). In the darkness there can be light: A family's adaptation to a child's blindness. *Journal of Visual Impairment and Blindness, 99,* 209–218.

Vermont Association for the Blind and Visually Impaired. (2016). *Five leading causes of visual impairments in children in the USA.* South Burlington, VT: Author. Retrieved from http://www.vabvi.org/five-leading-causes-of-visual-impairments-in-children-in-the-usa/

VisionAware. (2012). *What is the individualized plan for employment?* Retrieved from http://www.visionaware.org/section.aspx?FolderID=9&SectionID=131&DocumentID=5902

Vitale, S., Cotch, M. F., & Sperduto, R. D. (2006). Prevalence of visual impairment in the United States. *JAMA, 295,* 2158–2163.

Ward, M. E. (2000). The visual system. In M. C. Holbrook & A. J. Koenig (Eds.), *Foundations of education: History and theory of teaching children and youths with visual impairments* (2nd ed., pp. 77–110). New York, NY: American Foundation for the Blind Press.

Watson, A., & McCathren, R. (2009). Including children with special needs: Are you and your early childhood program ready? *Young Children, 64*(2), 20–26.

Wei, X., Blackorby, J., & Schiller, E. (2011). Growth in reading achievement of students with disabilities, ages 7 to 17. *Exceptional Children, 78,* 89–106.

West, J. E. (2005). An opportunity slipping away? *Journal of Visual Impairment and Blindness, 99,* 677–679.

Wolffe, K. E. (2000). Career education. In A. J. Koenig & M. C. Holbrook (Eds.), *Foundations of education: Instructional strategies for teaching children and youths with visual impairments* (2nd ed., pp. 679–719). New York, NY: American Foundation for the Blind Press.

Wolffe, K. E., & Spungin, S. J. (2002). A glance at worldwide employment of people with visual impairments. *Journal of Visual Impairment and Blindness, 96,* 246–253.

Zabala, J. S., & Carl, D. (2010, October). *What educators and families need to know about accessible instructional materials—Part One: Introduction and legal context* [The AIMing for Achievement series]. Retrieved from http://aim.cast.org/sites/aim.cast.org/files/ClosingtheGap1.pdf

Zebehazy, K. T., & Smith, T. J. (2011). An examination of characteristics related to the social skills of youths with visual impairments. *Journal of Visual Impairment & Blindness, 105,* 84–95.

Zebehazy, K. T., & Wilton, A. P. (2014). Charting success: The experience of teachers of students with visual impairments in promoting student use of graphics. *Journal of Visual Impairment & Blindness, 108,* 263–274.

Zebehazy, K., & Whitten, E. (2003). Collaboration between special schools and local education agencies: A progress report. *Journal of Visual Impairment and Blindness, 97,* 73–84.

Zhou, L., Smith, D. W., Parker, A. T., & Griffin-Shirley, N. (2011). Assistive technology competencies of teachers of students with visual impairments: A comparison of perceptions. *Journal of Visual Impairment and Blindness, 105,* 533–547.

Chapter 13

Abbott, C., Brown, D., Evett, L., & Standen, P. (2014). Emerging issues and current trends in assistive technology use 2007–2010: Practising, assisting and enabling learning for all. *Disability and Rehabilitation: Assistive Technology, 9,* 453–462.

Adams-Chapman, I. (2009). Insults to the developing brain and impact on neurodevelopmental outcome. *Journal of Communication Disorders, 42,* 256–242.

Akinbami, L. J., Simon, A. E., & Rossen, L. M. (2016). Changing trends in asthma prevalence among children. *Pediatrics, 137*(1). doi:10.1542/peds.2015-2354

Aldrich, E. M., & Obrzut, J. E. (2012). Assisting students with a traumatic brain injury in school interventions. *Canadian Journal of School Psychology, 27,* 291–301.

Allen, D. B. (2012). Today—A stark glimpse of tomorrow. *New England Journal of Medicine, 366,* 2315–2316.

Alsem, M. W., Verhoef, M., Gorter, J. W., Langezaal, L. M., Visser-Meily, J. A., & Ketelaar, M. (2016). Parents' perceptions of the services provided to children with cerebral palsy in the transition from preschool rehabilitation to school-based services. *Child: Care, Health and Development, 42,* 455–463.

American Obesity Association. (2005). *AOA fact sheet: Obesity in youth.* Retrieved from www.obesity.org/subs/fastfacts/obesityyouth.shtml

Anderson, J. D., Newby, R., Kehm, R., Barland, P., & Hearst, M. O. (2015). Taking steps together: A family- and community-based obesity intervention for urban, multiethnic children. *Health Education & Behavior, 42,* 194–201.

Arbogast, K. B., Curry, A. E., Pfeiffer, M. R., Zonfrillo, M. R., Haarbauer-Krupa, J., Breiding, M. J., Coronado, V. G., & Master, C. L. (2016, May). Point of health care entry for youth with concussion within a large pediatric care. *JAMA Pediatrics.* doi:10.1001/jamapediatrics.2016.0294

Baldwin, J. L. (2007). Standards for teachers of students with physical and health disabilities. *Physical Disabilities: Education and Related Services, 26,* 1–7.

Barnes, S. B., & Whinnery, K. W. (2002). Effects of functional mobility skills training for young students with physical disabilities. *Exceptional Children, 68,* 313–324.

Berliner, D. C. (2009). *Poverty and potential: Out-of-school factors and school success.* Tucson, AZ: Education Policy Research Unit. [ERIC Document Reproduction Service No. ED507359]

Best, S. J., Heller, K. W., & Bigge, J. L. (2010). *Teaching individuals with physical or multiple disabilities* (6th edition). Upper Saddle River, NJ: Merrill/Prentice Hall.

Bigge, J. L., Best, S. J., & Heller, K. W. (2000). *Teaching individuals with physical, health, or multiple disabilities* (4th ed.). Upper Saddle River, NJ: Merrill.

[The] Body. (2011). *HIV/AIDS in the United States: 2008–2010.* Retrieved from http://www.thebody.com/content/66501/hivaids-in-the-united-states-2008-2010.html

Bowe, F. (2000). *Physical, sensory, and health disabilities: An introduction.* Upper Saddle River, NJ: Merrill.

Boyer, C. (2011). Stay aHEAD of the game: Get the facts about concussion in sports. *Exceptional Parent, 41*(3), 22–23.

Brain Injury Association of America. (2009). *Living with brain injury.* Retrieved from http://www.biausa.org/education.htm

Brain Injury Association of America. (2015). *Fact sheet: About brain injury.* Vienna, VA: Author. Retrieved from http://www.biausa.org/glossary.htm

Brent, R. L., & Oakley, G. P. (2006). Triumph or tragedy: The present Food and Drug Administration program of enriching grains with folic acid. *Pediatrics, 117*, 930–932.

Brier, M. J., Schwartz, L. A., & Kazak, A. E. (2015). Psychosocial, health-promotion, and neurocognitive interventions for survivors of childhood cancer: A systematic review. *Health Psychology, 34*, 130–148.

Brown, P., Stephenson, J., & Carter, M. (2014). Multicomponent training of teachers of students with severe disabilities. *Teacher Education and Special Education, 37*, 347–362.

Brown, R. T., & Madan-Swain, A. (1993). Cognitive, neuropsychological, and academic sequelae in children with leukemia. *Journal of Learning Disabilities, 26*, 74–90.

Burbank, A. J., Lewis, S. D., Hewes, M., Schellhase, D. E., Rettiganti, M., Hall-Barrow, J., ... Perry, T. T. (2015). Mobile-based asthma action plans for adolescents. *Journal of Asthma, 52*, 583–586.

Burwell, N. R., Wessel, R. D., & Mulvihill, T. (2015). Attendant care for college students with physical disabilities using wheelchairs: Transition issues and experiences. *Journal of Postsecondary Education and Disability, 28*, 293–307.

Canter, K. S., & Roberts, M. C. (2012). A systematic and quantitative review of interventions to facilitate school reentry for children with chronic health conditions. *Journal of Pediatric Psychology, 37*, 1065–1075.

Canto, A. I., Chesire, D. J., & Buckley, V. A. (2011). On impact: Students with head injuries. *Communique, 40*(1), 1.

Capio, C. M., Sit, C. P., Abernethy, B., & Masters, R. W. (2012). Fundamental movement skills and physical activity among children with and without cerebral palsy. *Research in Developmental Disabilities: A Multidisciplinary Journal, 33*, 1235–1241.

Cates, C. (2009). Using education to improve control of asthma in children. *Canadian Medical Association Journal, 181*, 248–249.

Centers for Disease Control and Prevention. (2006, September). *Traumatic brain injury: Overview.* Atlanta, GA: Department of Health and Human Services. Retrieved from http://www.cdc.gov/ncipc/tbi/Overview.htm

Centers for Disease Control and Prevention. (2009). *Cancer in children.* Retrieved from http://www.cdc.gov/Features/dsCancerInChildren/index.html

Centers for Disease Control and Prevention. (2011a). *HIV/AIDS basic facts.* Retrieved from http://www.cdc.gov/hiv/topics/surveillance/basic.htm

Centers for Disease Control and Prevention. (2011b). *National diabetes fact sheet.* Retrieved from http://www.cdc.gov/diabetes/pubs/estimates11.htm#3

Centers for Disease Control and Prevention. (2011c). *Nonfatal traumatic brain injuries related to sports and recreation activities among persons aged ≤19 years–United States, 2001–2009.* Atlanta, GA: Author. Retrieved from http://www.cdc.gov/mmwr/preview/mmwrhtml/mm6039a1.htm?s_cid= mm6039a1_w

Centers for Disease Control and Prevention. (2011d). *Sickle cell disease: Data and statistics.* Retrieved from http://www.cdc.gov/NCBDDD/sicklecell/data.html

Centers for Disease Control and Prevention. (2011e). *Sickle cell disease: Facts about sickle cell disease.* Retrieved from http://www.cdc.gov/ncbddd/-sicklecell/facts.html

Centers for Disease Control and Prevention. (2012). *Facts about cerebral palsy.* Atlanta, GA: Author. Retrieved from http://www.cdc.gov/ncbddd/cp/facts.html

Centers for Disease Control and Prevention. (2014). *National diabetes statistics report: Estimates of diabetes and its burden in the United States, 2014.* Atlanta, GA: U.S. Department of Health and Human Services. Retrieved from http://www.cdc.gov/diabetes/pubs/statsreport14/national-diabetes-report-web.pdf

Centers for Disease Control and Prevention. (2015a, August). *Childhood obesity facts.* Atlanta, GA: Author. Retrieved from https://www.cdc.gov/healthyschools/obesity/facts.htm

Centers for Disease Control and Prevention. (2015b). *Spina bifida data and statistics.* Atlanta, GA: Author. Retrieved from http://www.cdc.gov/ncbddd/spinabifida/data.html

Centers for Disease Control and Prevention. (2015c, December). *HIV transmission.* Atlanta, GA: Author. Retrieved from http://www.cdc.gov/hiv/basics/transmission.html

Centers for Disease Control and Prevention. (2015d, March). *Basics about diabetes.* Atlanta, GA: Author. Retrieved from http://www.cdc.gov/diabetes/basics/diabetes.html

Centers for Disease Control and Prevention. (2015e, October). *Childhood arthritis.* Atlanta, GA: Author. Retrieved from http://www.cdc.gov/arthritis/basics/childhood.htm

Centers for Disease Control and Prevention. (2016a, April). *Asthma: Most recent asthma data-national data.* Atlanta, GA: Author. Retrieved from http://www.cdc.gov/asthma/most_recent_data.htm

Centers for Disease Control and Prevention. (2016b, April). *HIV among youth.* Atlanta, GA: Author. Retrieved from http://www.cdc.gov/hiv/group/age/youth/

Centers for Disease Control and Prevention. (2016c, April). *Muscular dystrophy data and statistics.* Atlanta, GA: Author. Retrieved from http://www.cdc.gov/ncbddd/musculardystrophy/data.html

Centers for Disease Control and Prevention. (2016d, February). *Injury prevention & control: Traumatic brain injury & concussion.* Atlanta, GA: Author. Retrieved from http://www.cdc.gov/traumaticbraininjury/

Centers for Disease Control and Prevention. (2016e, February). *Sickle cell disease: Data & statistics.* Atlanta, GA: Author. Retrieved from http://www.cdc.gov/ncbddd/sicklecell/data.html

Centers for Disease Control and Prevention. (2016f, May). *Data and statistics about cerebral palsy.* Atlanta, GA: Author. Retrieved from http://www.cdc.gov/ncbddd/cp/data.html

Centers for Disease Control and Prevention. (2016g, May). *Cerebral palsy: Facts about cerebral palsy.* Atlanta, GA: Author. Retrieved from https://www.cdc.gov/ncbddd/cp/facts.html

Cheong, S. K., Lang, C. P., Hemphill, S. A., & Johnston, L. M. (2016). What constitutes self-concept for children with CP? A Delphi consensus survey. *Journal of Developmental and Physical Disabilities, 28*, 333–346.

Cherng, R. J., Liu, C. F., Lau, T. W., & Hong, R. B. (2007). Effect of treadmill training with body weight support on gait and gross motor function in children with spastic cerebral palsy. *American Journal of Physical Medicine & Rehabilitation, 86*, 548–555.

Chesire, D. J., Buckley, V. A., & Canto, A. I. (2011). Assessment of students with traumatic brain injury. *Communique, 40*(2), 8–9.

Chrisler, A., & Child, T. (2012). *What works for asthma education programs: Lessons from experimental evaluations of social programs and interventions for children* [Fact Sheet; Publication #2012-01]. Washington, DC: Child Trends. Retrieved from http://www.childtrends.org/listAllPubs.cfm?LID=14856219-D5D2-4547-AC3203F6C3726495

Closs, A. (2000). Issues for the effectiveness of children's school education. In A. Closs (Ed.), *The education of children with medical conditions* (pp. 93–106). London, England: David Fulton.

Coleman, M. (2011). Successful implementation of assistive technology to promote access to curriculum and instruction for students with physical disabilities. *Physical Disabilities: Education and Related Services, 30*(2), 2–22.

Coleman, M. B., & Cramer, E. S. (2015). Creating meaningful art experiences with assistive technology for students with physical, visual, severe, and multiple disabilities. *Art Education, 68*(2), 6–13.

Crosby, L. E., Joffe, N. E., Irwin, M. K., Strong, H., Peugh, J., Shook, L., ... Mitchell, M. J. (2015). School performance and disease interference in adolescents with sickle cell disease. *Physical Disabilities: Education and Related Services, 34*(1), 14–30.

Crow, R., Kohler, P. A., Cooper, M., & Atkins, K. (2010). I. A.C.C.E.P.T. M.E.: Strategies for developing self-acceptance when parenting children who challenge. *Exceptional Parent, 40*(12), 14–15.

Dale, J., Cochran, C. J., Roy, L., Jernigan, E., & Buchanan, G. R. (2011). Health-related quality of life in children and adolescents with sickle cell disease. *Journal of Pediatric Health Care, 25,* 208–215.

Daly, B. P., Kral, M. C., & Brown, R. T. (2008). Cognitive and academic problems associated with childhood cancers and sickle cell disease. *School Psychology Quarterly, 23,* 230–242.

Darcy, L., Knutsson, S., Huus, K., & Enskar, K. (2014). The everyday life of the young child shortly after receiving a cancer diagnosis, from both children's and parent's perspectives. *Cancer Nursing, 37,* 445–456.

Davies, S. C., Jones, K. M., & Rafoth, M. A. (2010). Effects of a self-monitoring intervention on children with traumatic brain injury. *Journal of Applied School Psychology, 26,* 308–326.

Davis, E., Shelly, A., Waters, E., MacKinnon, A., Reddihough, D., Boyd, R., & Graham, H. K. (2009). Quality of life of adolescents with cerebral palsy: Perspectives of adolescents and parents. *Developmental Medicine & Child Neurology, 51,* 193–199.

Deidrick, K. K. M., & Farmer, J. E. (2005). School reentry following traumatic brain injury. *Preventing School Failure, 49*(4), 23–33.

Delaney, L., & Smith, J. P. (2012). Childhood health: Trends and consequences over the life course. *Future of Children, 22*(1), 43–63.

DePaepe, P., Garrison-Kane, L., & Doelling, J. (2002). Supporting students with health needs in schools: An overview of selected health conditions. *Focus on Exceptional Children, 35*(1), 1–24.

Dew, A., Balandin, S., & Llewellyn, G. (2008). The psychosocial impact on siblings of people with lifelong physical disability: A review of the literature. *Journal of Developmental & Physical Disabilities, 20,* 485–507.

Edens, R., Murdick, N., & Gartin, B. (2003) Preventing infection in the classroom: The use of universal precautions. *Teaching Exceptional Children, 35*(4), 62–65.

Epilepsy Foundation of America. (2009). *Epilepsy and seizure statistics.* Retrieved from http://www.epilepsyfoundation.org/about/statistics.cfm

Epilepsy Foundation of America. (2014a, March). *Absence seizures.* Retrieved from http://www.epilepsy.com/learn/treating-seizures-and-epilepsy/first-aid/absence-seizures

Epilepsy Foundation. (2012). *First aid.* Retrieved from http://www.epilepsyfoundation.org/aboutepilepsy/firstaid/index.cfm

Epilepsy Foundation. (2014b, March). *About kids.* Landover, MD: Author. Retrieved from http://www.epilepsy.com/dare-defy-seizures/contact-us

Epilepsy Foundation. (2014c, March). *Basics on tonic-clonic seizures.* Landover, MD: Author. Retrieved from http://www.epilepsy.com/learn/treating-seizures-and-epilepsy/first-aid/tonic-clonic-seizures

Finnanger, T. G., Olsen, A., Skandsen, T., Lydersen, S., Vik, A., Evensen, K. I., ... Indredavik, M. S. (2015). Life after adolescent and adult moderate and severe traumatic brain injury: Self-reported executive, emotional, and behavioural function 2–5 years after injury (article id. 329241). *Behavioural Neurology, 2015.* http://dx.doi.org/10.1155/2015/329241

Gabe, J., Bury, M., & Ramsay, R. (2002). Living with asthma: The experiences of young people at home and at school. *Social Science and Medicine, 55,* 1619–1633.

Gabis, L. V., Tsubary, N. M., Leon, O., Ashkenasi, A., & Shefer, S. (2015). Assessment of abilities and comorbidities in children with cerebral palsy. *Journal of Child Neurology, 30,* 1640–1645.

Garfinkle, J., Wintermark, P., Shevell, M. I., & Oskoui, M. (2016). Cerebral palsy after neonatal encephalopathy: Do neonates with suspected asphyxia have worse outcomes? *Developmental Medicine & Child Neurology, 58,* 189–194.

Gartin, B. C., & Murdick, N. L. (2009). Children with cancer: School related issues. *Physical Disabilities: Education and Related Services, 27*(2), 19–36.

Gilette Children's Specialty Healthcare. (2007). *Returning to school after a traumatic brain injury: A guide for teachers.* St. Paul, MN: Author. Retrieved from http://www.gillettechildrens.org/fileUpload%5CReturning%20to%20School%20After%20a%20Traumatic%20Brain%20Injury.pdf

Gorman, S., Barnes, M. A., Swank, P. R., Prasad, M., Cox, C. J., & Ewing-Cobbs, L. (2016). Does processing speed mediate the effect of pediatric traumatic brain injury on working memory? *Neuropsychology, 30,* 263–273.

Greiling, A. K., Boss, L. P., & Wheeler, L. S. (2005). A preliminary investigation of asthma mortality in schools. *Journal of School Health, 75,* 286–290.

Halfon, N., Houtrow, A., Larson, K., & Newacheck, P. W. (2012). The changing landscape of disability in childhood. *Future of Children, 22,* 13–42.

Harold, C. (Ed.). (2009). *Professional guide to diseases* (9th edition). Philadelphia, PA: Lippincott, Williams, & Williams.

Harris, M. S. (2009). School reintegration for children and adolescents with cancer: The role of school psychologists. *Psychology in the Schools, 46,* 579–592.

Harrison, M. M. (2007, Fall). "Does this child have a friend?" *Teaching Tolerance, 32,* 26–31.

Hart Barnett, J. E., & Gay, C. (2015). Accommodating students with epilepsy or seizure disorders: Effective strategies for teachers. *Physical Disabilities: Education and Related Services, 34*(1), 1–13.

Hay, G. H., Nabors, M. L., Sullivan, A., & Zygmund, A. (2015). Students with pediatric cancer: A prescription for school success. *Physical Disabilities: Education and Related Services, 34*(2), 1–13.

Heller, K. W., & Swinehart-Jones, D. (2003). Supporting the educational needs of students with orthopedic impairments. *Physical Disabilities: Education and Related Services, 22*(1), 3–24.

Huang, Y., Kellett, U. M., & St John, W. (2010). Cerebral palsy: Experiences of mothers after learning their child's diagnosis. *Journal of Advanced Nursing, 66,* 1213–1221.

Kao, B. B., Romero-Bosch, L. L., Plante, W. W., & Lobato, D. D. (2012). The experiences of Latino siblings of children with developmental disabilities. *Child: Care, Health and Development, 38,* 545–552.

Katsiyannis, A., & Yell, M. L. (1999). Education and the law: School health services: Cedar Rapids Community School District v. Garrett F. *Preventing School Failure, 44*(1), 37–38.

Kay, T., Spaulding, J., & Smerdon, L. (2004). *Behavioral challenges in children: Linking school and home.* Redmond, WA: Brain Injury Association of Washington. Retrieved from www.biawa.orgpax/children/Behavioral%20Challenges%20in%20Children.doc

Kenardy, J., Le Brocque, R., Hendrikz, J., Iselin, G., Anderson, V., & McKinlay, L. (2012). Impact of posttraumatic stress disorder and injury severity on recovery in children with traumatic brain injury. *Journal of Clinical Child and Adolescent Psychology, 41,* 5–14.

Kennedy, M. R. T. (2008). Assessment, treatment, and service issues for students with traumatic brain injury. *NeuroRehabilitation, 23,* 455–456.

Kennedy, M. T. (2011). Parenting: From the perspective of a child with a disability. *Exceptional Parent, 41*(12), 24–25.

Kilincaslan, A., & Mukaddes, N. M. (2009). Pervasive developmental disorders in individuals with cerebral palsy. *Developmental Medicine & Child Neurology, 51,* 289–294.

Knight-Madden, J. M., Lewis, N., Tyson, E., Reid, M. E., & MooSang, M. (2011). The possible impact of teachers and school nurses on the lives of children living with sickle cell disease. *Journal of School Health, 81,* 219–222.

Kraska, M., Zinner, B., & Abebe, A. (2007). Employment status of individuals with disabilities. *Journal for Vocational Special Needs Education, 29*(3), 22–29.

Kroshus, E., Garnett, B., Hawrilenko, M., Baugh, C. M., & Calzo, J. P. (2015). Concussion under-reporting and pressure from coaches, teammates, fans, and parents. *Social Science & Medicine, 134,* 66–75.

Kurtzweil, P. (1999). How folate can help prevent birth defects. *FDA Consumer.* Retrieved from www.cfsan.fda.gov/~dms/fdafolic.html

LaFee, S. (2005). Another weighty burden: How much responsibility do schools bear for addressing the obesity of their students? *School Administrator, 62*(9), 10–16.

LeBovidge, J. S., Lavigne, J. V., Donenberg, G. R., & Miller, M. L. (2003). Psychological adjustment of children and adolescents with chronic arthritis: A meta-analytic review. *Journal of Pediatric Psychology, 228*, 29–39.

Lee, S. W., & Guck, T. P. (2000). Parents and families with a chronically ill child. In M. J. Fine and R. L. Simpson (Eds.), *Collaboration with parents of exceptional children* (pp. 257–276). Brandon, VT: Clinical Psychology Publishing.

Lehmkuhl, H. D., Merlo, L. J., Storch, E. A., Heidgerken, A., Silverstein, J. H., & Geffken, G. R. (2008). Cognitive abilities in a sample of youth with multiple episodes of diabetic ketoacidosis. *Journal of Developmental & Physical Disabilities, 21*, 1–8.

Lemanek, K. L. (2004). Adherence. In R. T. Brown (Ed.), *Handbook of pediatric psychology in school settings* (pp. 129–148). Mahwah, NJ: Erlbaum.

Lemanek, K. L., & Hood, C. (1999). Asthma. In R. T. Brown (Ed.), *Cognitive aspects of chronic illness in children* (pp. 78–104). New York, NY: Guilford Press.

Lemkuhl, H., & Nabors, L. (2008). Children with diabetes: Satisfaction with school support, illness perceptions, and HbA1c levels. *Journal of Developmental & Physical Disabilities, 20*, 101–114.

Lim, J., Wood, B., & Cheah, P. (2009). Understanding children with asthma: Trouble and triggers. *Childhood Education, 85*, 307–313.

Lindsay, S. (2016). Child and youth experiences and perspectives of cerebral palsy: A qualitative systematic review. *Child: Care, Health and Development, 42*, 153–175.

Longmore, P. K., & Umansky, L. (Eds.). (2001). *The new disability history: -American perspectives.* New York: New York University Press.

Marlin, A. E. (2004). Management of hydrocephalus in the patient with myelomeningocele: An argument against third ventriculostomy. *Neurosurgical Focus, 16*(2), 1–3.

Mathews, T. J. (2009, April). *Trends in spina bifida and anencephalus in the United States, 1991–2006* [Health e-stats]. Atlanta, GA: Centers for Disease Control and Prevention. Retrieved from http://www.cdc.gov/nchs/products/hestats.htm

Moore, J. B., Kaffenberger, C., Oh, K. M., Goldberg, P., & Hudspeth, R. (2009). School reentry for children with cancer: Perceptions of nurses, school personnel, and parents. *Journal of Pediatric Oncology Nursing, 26*, 86–99.

Mukherjee, S., & Lightfoot, J. (2000). The inclusion of pupils with a chronic health condition in mainstream school: What does it mean? *Educational Research, 42*, 59–72.

Muscular Dystrophy Association. (2000). *Facts about Duchenne and Becker muscular dystrophies.* Tucson, AZ: Author. Retrieved from www.mdausa.org/publications/fa-dmdbmd-what.html

Muscular Dystrophy Association. (2011). *Facts about Duchenne & Becker muscular dystrophies.* Chicago, IL: Author. Retrieved from https://www.mda.org/sites/default/files/publications/Facts_DMD-BMD_P-211_0.pdf

Myers, C. (2007). "Please listen, it's my turn": Instructional approaches, curricula and contexts for supporting communication and increasing access to inclusion. *Journal of Intellectual & Developmental Disability, 32*, 263–278.

Nabors, L. A., Iobst, E. A., Weisman, J., Precht, B., Chiu, P., & Brunner, H. (2007). School support and functioning for children with juvenile rheumatic diseases. *Journal of Developmental & Physical Disabilities, 19*, 81–89.

National Cancer Institute. (2005). *National Cancer Institute research on childhood cancers.* Retrieved from www.nci.nih.gov/cancertopics/factsheet/Sites-Types/childhood

National Cancer Institute. (2008). *Childhood cancers* [fact sheet]. Retrieved from http://www.cancer.gov/cancertopics/factsheet/Sites-Types/childhood

National Cancer Institute. (2014, February). *Common cancer myths and misconceptions.* Bethesda, MD: Author. Retrieved from http://www.cancer.gov/about-cancer/causes-prevention/risk/myths

National Center for Biotechnology Information. (2011). *Juvenile rheumatoid arthritis.* Retrieved from http://www.ncbi.nlm.nih.gov/pubmedhealth/PMH0001487/

National Center for Biotechnology Information. (2012). *Duchenne muscular dystrophy.* Retrieved from http://www.ncbi.nlm.nih.gov/pubmedhealth/PMH0001724/

National Center on Birth Defects and Developmental Disabilities (NCBDDD). (2015, May). *Sickle cell disease.* Atlanta, GA: Author. Retrieved from http://www.cdc.gov/ncbddd/sicklecell/index.html

National Heart, Lung, and Blood Institute. (2014, August). *What is asthma?.* Bethesda, MD: National Institutes of Health. Retrieved from http://www.nhlbi.nih.gov/health/health-topics/topics/asthma

National Institute of Neurological Disorders and Stroke (NINDS). (2016a, March). *NINDS muscular dystrophy information page.* Bethesda, MD: National Institutes of Health. Retrieved from http://www.ninds.nih.gov/disorders/md/md.htm

National Institute of Neurological Disorders and Stroke (NINDS). (2016b, February). *The epilepsies and seizures: Hope through research.* Bethesda, MD: Author. Retrieved from http://www.ninds.nih.gov/disorders/epilepsy/detail_epilepsy.htm#3109_4

National Institute of Neurological Disorders and Stroke. (2009, June). *Muscular dystrophy: Hope through research.* Washington, DC: National Institutes of Health. Retrieved from http://www.ninds.nih.gov/disorders/md/detail_md.htm#110183171

National Institute of Neurological Disorders and Stroke. (2012). *Traumatic brain injury: Hope through research.* Retrieved from http://www.ninds.nih.gov/disorders/tbi/detail_tbi.htm#193633218

National Institutes of Health. (2011). *Myelomeningocele Spina bifida; Cleft spine.* Rockville, MD: National Center for Biotechnology Information. Retrieved from http://www.ncbi.nlm.nih.gov/pubmedhealth/PMH0002525/

National Institutes of Health. (2012a). *Cancer in children.* Retrieved from http://www.nlm.nih.gov/medlineplus/cancerinchildren.html

National Institutes of Health. (2012b). *Sickle cell disease.* Retrieved from http://ghr.nlm.nih.gov/condition/sickle-cell-disease

National Institutes of Health. (2012c). *Spina bifida fact sheet.* Retrieved from http://www.ninds.nih.gov/-disorders/spina_bifida/detail_spina_bifida.htm#203473258

National Institutes of Health. (2015, May). *Childhood cancers.* Bethesda, MD: Author. Retrieved from http://www.cancer.gov/types/childhood-cancers

National Spinal Cord Injury Statistical Center. (2009). *Spinal cord injury: Facts and figures at a glance.* Birmingham, AL: Author. Retrieved from http://www.spinalcord.uab.edu/show.asp?durki=119513

National Spinal Cord Injury Statistical Center. (2016). *Facts and figures at a glance.* Birmingham, AL: University of Alabama at Birmingham. Retrieved from https://www.nscisc.uab.edu/Public/Facts%202016.pdf

Osgood, D., Foster, E., & Courtney, M. E. (2010). Vulnerable populations and the transition to adulthood. *Future of Children, 20*, 209–229.

Pfeifer, L. I., Pacciulio, A. M., dos Santos, C. A., dos Santos, J. L., & Stagnitti, K. E. (2011). Pretend play of children with cerebral palsy. *Physical & Occupational Therapy in Pediatrics, 31*, 390–402.

Popp, J. M., Conway, M., & Pantaleao, A. (2015). Parents' experience with their child's cancer diagnosis: Do hopefulness, family functioning, and perceptions of care matter? *Journal of Pediatric Oncology Nursing, 32*, 253–260.

Postma, J. M., Evans-Agnew, R., & Capouya, J. (2015). Mexican-American caregivers' perceptions about asthma management: A photovoice study. *Journal of Asthma, 52*, 593–599.

Ransom, D. M., Vaughan, C. G., Pratson, L., Sady, M. D., McGill, C. A., & Gioia, G. A. (2015). Academic effects of concussion in children and adolescents. *Pediatrics, 135*, 1043–1050.

Reilly, C., & Ballantine, R. (2011). Epilepsy in school-aged children: More than just seizures? *Support for Learning, 26*, 144–151.

Roberts, J., & Whiting, C. (2011). Caregivers of school children with epilepsy: Findings of a phenomenological study. *British Journal of Special Education, 38*, 169–177.

Ruppar, A., Roberts, C., & Olson, A. J. (2015). Faculty perceptions of expertise among teachers of students with severe disabilities. *Teacher Education and Special Education, 38*, 240–253.

Schanzenbach, D. W. (2009). Do school lunches contribute to childhood obesity? *Journal of Human Resources, 44*, 684–709.

Schinkel, A. (2010). Pragmatic communication deficits in children with epilepsy. *International Journal of Language & Communication Disorders, 45*, 608–616.

Shin, M., Besser, L. M., Siffer, C., Kucik, J. E., Shaw, G. M., Lu, C., & Correa, A. (2010). Prevalence of spina bifida among children and adolescents in 10 regions in the United States. *Pediatrics, 126*, 274–279.

Sileo, N. M. (2005). Design HIV/AIDS prevention education: What are the roles and responsibilities of classroom teachers? *Intervention in School and Clinic, 40*, 177–181.

Singh, D. K. (2003). Families of children with spina bifida: A review. *Journal of Developmental and Physical Disabilities, 15*(1), 37–55.

Sneed, R. C., May, W. L., & Stencel, C. S. (2000). Training of pediatricians in care of physical disabilities in children with special health needs: Results of a two-state survey of practicing pediatricians and national resident training programs. *Pediatrics, 105*(3), 554.

Spina Bifida Association of America. (2012). *Folic acid supplementation before conception reduces the risk of spina bifida*. Retrieved from http://www.spinabifidaassociation.org/atf/cf/%7B85F88192-26E1-421E-9E30-4C0EA744A7F0%7D/Folic%20Acid.pdf

Stewart, D. A., Lawless, J. J., Shimmell, L. J., Palisano, R. J., Freeman, M., Rosenbaum, P. L., & Russell, D. J. (2012). Social participation of adolescents with cerebral palsy: Trade-offs and choices. *Physical & Occupational Therapy in Pediatrics, 32*, 167–179.

Strickland, B. B., Jones, J. R., Newacheck, P. W., Bethell, C. D., Blumberg, S. J., & Kogan, M. D. (2015). Assessing systems quality in a changing health care environment: The 2009–10 National Survey of Children with Special Health Care Needs. *Maternal and Child Health Journal, 19*, 353–361.

Stumbo, N. J., Martin, J. K., & Hedrick, B. N. (2009). Personal assistance for students with severe physical disabilities in post-secondary education: Is it the deal breaker? *Journal of Vocational Rehabilitation, 30*, 11–20.

Taras, H., & Potts-Datema, W. (2005). Childhood asthma and student performance at school. *Journal of School Health, 75*, 296–312.

Titus, J. B., & Thio, L. (2009). The effects of antiepileptic drugs on classroom performance. *Psychology in the Schools, 46*, 885–891.

Trask, C. L., & Peterson, C. C. (2016). Educational issues: The impact of cancer in the classroom. In A. N. Abrams, A. C. Muriel, L. Wiener, A. N. Abrams, A. C. Muriel, L. Wiener (Eds.), *Pediatric psychosocial oncology: Textbook for multidisciplinary care* (pp. 175–198). Cham, Switzerland: Springer International Publishing.

Tucker, S., & Lanningham-Foster, L. M. (2015). Nurse-led school-based child obesity prevention. *Journal of School Nursing, 31*, 450–466.

Turkstra, L. S., Williams, W. H., Tonks, J., & Frampton, I. (2008). Measuring social cognition in adolescents: Implications for students with TBI returning to school. *NeuroRehabilitation, 23*, 501–509.

U.S. Department of Education. (1997). *Nineteenth annual report to Congress on the implementation of the Individuals with Disabilities Education Act*. Washington, DC: Author.

U.S. Department of Education. (2011). *The digest of education statistics 2010* [NCES 2011-015, Table 46]. Washington, DC: Author, National Center for Education Statistics. Retrieved from http://nces.ed.gov/fastfacts/display.asp?id=59

U.S. Department of Education. (2015). *37th annual report to Congress on the implementation of the Individuals with Disabilities Education Act*. Washington, DC: Author, Office of Special Education Programs. Retrieved from http://www2.ed.gov/about/reports/annual/osep/2015/parts-b-c/37th-arc-for-idea.pdf

United States Bone and Joint Initiative (2014). *The burden of musculoskeletal diseases in the United States* (BMUS) (3rd ed.). Rosemont, IL: Author. Retrieved from http://www.boneandjointburden.org

Van Laarhoven, T., & Conderman, G. (2011). Integrating assistive technology into special education teacher preparation programs. *Journal of Technology and Teacher Education, 19*, 473–497.

van Rooijen, M., Verhoeven, L., Smits, D., Ketelaar, M., Becher, J. G., & Steenbergen, B. (2012). Arithmetic performance of children with cerebral palsy: The influence of cognitive and motor factors. *Research in Developmental Disabilities: A Multidisciplinary Journal, 33*, 530–537.

van Schie, P. M., Siebes, R. C., Dallmeijer, A. J., Schuengel, C., Smits, D., Gorter, J. W., & Becher, J. G. (2013). Development of social functioning and communication in school-aged (5–9 years) children with cerebral palsy. *Research in Developmental Disabilities, 34*, 4485–4494.

Vaz, S., Cordier, R., Falkmer, M., Ciccarelli, M., Parsons, R., McAuliffe, T., & Falkmer, T. (2015). Should schools expect poor physical and mental health, social adjustment, and participation outcomes in students with disability? *Plos ONE, 10*(5). doi:10.1371/journal.pone.0126630

Vitello, S. J. (1986). The Tatro case: Who gets what and why. *Exceptional Children, 52*, 353–356.

Vu, J. A., Babikian, T., & Asarnow, R. (2011). Academic and language outcomes in children after traumatic brain injury: A meta-analysis. *Exceptional Children, 77*, 263–281.

Wehman, P., & Targett, P. (2010). *Returning to school after traumatic brain injury*. Washington, DC: Model Systems Knowledge Translation Center (MSKTC), American Institutes for Research. Retrieved from http://www.msktc.org/lib/docs/Factsheets/TBI_School_after_TBI.pdf

Weinstein, S. (2002). Epilepsy. In M. L. Batshaw (Ed.), *Children with disabilities* (5th edition) (pp. 493–524). Baltimore, MD: Paul H. Brookes.

Wiart, L. (2011). Exploring mobility options for children with physical disabilities: A focus on powered mobility. *Physical & Occupational Therapy in Pediatrics, 31*, 16–18.

Williams, J., Mai, C. T., Mulinare, J., Isenburg, J., Flood, T. J., Ethen, M., ... Kirby, R. S. (2015, January). Updated estimates of neural tube defects prevented by mandatory folic acid fortification—United States, 1995–2011. *Morbidity and Mortality Weekly Report, 64*(1), 1–5. Retrieved from http://www.cdc.gov/mmwr/preview/mmwrhtml/mm6401a2.htm

Winter, S. M. (2009). Childhood obesity in the testing era: What teachers and schools can do! *Childhood Education, 85*, 283–288.

Winzer, M. A. (1993). *The history of special education: From isolation to integration*. Washington, DC: Gallaudet University Press.

Yeates, K. O., Bigler, E. D., Dennis, M., Gerhardt, C. A., Rubin, K. H., Stancin, T., . . . Vannatta, K. (2007). Social outcomes in childhood brain disorder: A heuristic integration of social neuroscience and developmental psychology. *Psychological Bulletin, 133*, 535–556.

Zegaczewski, T., Chang, K., Coddington, J., & Berg, A. (2016). Factors related to healthy siblings' psychosocial adjustment to children with cancer: An integrative review. *Journal of Pediatric Oncology Nursing, 33*, 218–227.

Ziviani, J., Feeney, R. B., & Khan, A. (2011). Early intervention services for children with physical disability: Parents' perceptions of family-centeredness and service satisfaction. *Infants and Young Children, 24*, 364–382.

Chapter 14

Al Khateeb, J. M., Al Hadidi, M. S., & Al Khatib, A. J. (2015). Addressing the unique needs of Arab American children with disabilities. *Journal of Child and Family Studies, 24*, 2432-2440.

Anderson, D., Farley, D., & Tindal, G. (2013). Test design considerations for students with significant cognitive disabilities. *Journal of Special Education, 49*, 209-220.

Anderson, D., Farley, D., & Tindal, G. (2015). Test design considerations for students with significant cognitive disabilities. *Journal of Special Education, 49*, 3-15.

Barned, N. E., Knapp, N., & Neuharth-Pritchett, S. (2011). Knowledge and attitudes of early childhood preservice teachers regarding the inclusion of children with autism spectrum disorder. *Journal of Early Childhood Teacher Education, 32*, 302-321.

Batshaw, M. L., Pellegrino, L., & Roizen, N. J. (Eds.). (2007). *Children with disabilities* (6th ed.). Baltimore, MD: Paul H. Brookes Publishing Co.

Bethune, K. S., & Wood, C. L. (2013). Effects of coaching on teachers' use of function-based interventions for students with severe disabilities. *Teacher Education and Special Education, 36*, 97-114.

Beukelman, D. R., & Mirenda, P. (2005). *Augmentative and alternative communication: Management of severe communication disorders in children and adults* (3rd ed.). Baltimore, MD: Paul H. Brookes.

Bezdek, J., Summers, J., & Turnbull, A. (2010). Professionals' attitudes on partnering with families of children and youth with disabilities. *Education and Training in Autism and Developmental Disabilities, 45*, 356-365.

Bilder, D. A., Pinborough-Zimmerman, J., Bakian, A. V., Miller, J. S., Dorius, J. T., Nangle, B., & McMahon, W. M. (2013). Prenatal and perinatal factors associated with intellectual disability. *American Journal on Intellectual and Developmental Disabilities, 118*, 156-176.

Bottcher, L. (2012). Culture and the learning and cognitive development of children with severe disabilities–continuities and discontinuities with children without disabilities. *Mind, Culture, and Activity, 19*, 89-106.

Brock, M. E., & Carter, E. W. (2013). A systematic review of paraprofessional-delivered educational practices to improve outcomes for students with intellectual and developmental disabilities. *Research and Practice for Persons with Severe Disabilities, 38*, 211-221.

Brock, M. E., Biggs, E. E., Carter, E. W., Cattey, G. N., & Raley, K. S. (2016). Implementation and generalization of peer support arrangements for students with severe disabilities in inclusive classrooms. *Journal of Special Education, 49*, 221-232.

Browder, D. M. (2012). Finding the balance: A response to Hunt and McDonnell. *Research and Practice for Persons with Severe Disabilities, 37*, 157-159.

Browder, D. M., & Spooner, F. (2011). *Teaching students with moderate and severe disabilities*. New York, NY: Guilford.

Browder, D. M., Lee, A., & Mims, P. (2011). Using shared stories and individual response modes to promote comprehension and engagement in literacy for students with multiple, severe disabilities. *Education and Training in Autism and Developmental Disabilities, 46*, 339-351.

Browder, D. M., Mims, P. J., Spooner, F., Ahlgrim-Delzell, L., & Lee, A. (2008). Teaching elementary students with multiple disabilities to participate in shared stories. *Research and Practice for Persons with Severe Disabilities, 33*(1-2), 3-12.

Browder, D. M., Trela, K., Courtade, G. R., Jimenez, B. A., Knight, V., & Flowers, C. (2012). Teaching mathematics and science standards to students with moderate and severe developmental disabilities. *Journal of Special Education, 46*, 26-35.

Browder, D. M., Wakeman, S. Y., Spooner, F., Ahlgrim-Delzell, L., & Algozzine, B. (2006). Research on reading instruction for individuals with significant cognitive disabilities. *Exceptional Children, 72*, 392-408.

Browder, D., Flowers, C., Ahlgrim-Delzell, L., Karvonen, M., Spooner, F., & Algozzine, R. (2004). The alignment of alternate assessment content with academic and functional curricula. *Journal of Special Education, 37*, 211-223.

Brown, F., Snell, M., & Lehr, D. (2006). Meaningful assessment. In M. E. Snell & F. Brown (Eds.), *Instruction of students with severe disabilities* (pp. 67-114). Upper Saddle River, NJ: Merrill.

Cameron, D. L., & Cook, B. G. (2013). General education teachers' goals and expectations for their included students with mild and severe disabilities. *Education and Training in Autism and Developmental Disabilities, 48*, 18-30.

Campbell, D. J., Reilly, A., & Henley, J. (2008). Comparison of assessment results of children with low incidence disabilities. *Education and Training in Developmental Disabilities, 43*, 217-25.

Carr, E. G., Dunlap, G., Horner, R. H., Koegel, R. J., Turnbull, A. P., Sailor, W., . . . Fox, L., (2002). Positive behavior support: Evolution of an applied science. *Journal of Positive Behavior Interventions, 4*, 1-16, 20.

Carroll, S. Z., Blumberg, E. R., & Petroff, J. G. (2008). The promise of liberal learning: Creating a challenging postsecondary curriculum for youth with intellectual disabilities. *Focus on Exceptional Children, 40*(9), 1-12.

Carter, E. W., & Kennedy, C. H. (2006). Promoting access to the general curriculum using peer support strategies. *Research and Practice for Persons with Severe Disabilities, 31*, 284-292.

Carter, E. W., Asmus, J., Moss, C. K., Biggs, E. E., Bolt, D. M., Born, T. L., ... Weir, K. (2016). Randomized evaluation of peer support arrangements to support the inclusion of high school students with severe disabilities. *Exceptional Children, 82*, 209-233.

Carter, E. W., Austin, D., & Trainor, A. A. (2011). Factors associated with the early work experiences of adolescents with severe disabilities. *Intellectual and Developmental Disabilities, 49*, 233-247.

Carter, E. W., Austin, D., & Trainor, A. A. (2012). Predictors of postschool employment outcomes for young adults with severe disabilities. *Journal of Disability Policy Studies, 23*, 50-63.

Carter, E. W., Hughes, C., Guth, C. B., & Copeland, S. R. (2005). Factors influencing social interaction among high school students with intellectual disabilities and their general education peers. *American Journal of Mental Retardation, 110*, 366-377.

Carter, E. W., Moss, C. K., Asmus, J., Fesperman, E., Cooney, M., Brock, M. E., ... Vincent, L. B. (2015). Promoting inclusion, social connections, and learning through peer support arrangements. *Teaching Exceptional Children, 48*(1), 9-18.

Carter, E. W., Moss, C. K., Hoffman, A., Chung, Y., & Sisco, L. (2011). Efficacy and social validity of peer support arrangements for adolescents with disabilities. *Exceptional Children, 78*, 107-125.

Carter, E. W., Sisco, L. G., Melekoglu, M. A., & Kurkowski, C. (2007). Peer supports as an alternative to individually assigned paraprofessionals in inclusive high school classrooms. *Research and Practice for Persons with Severe Disabilities, 32*, 213-227.

Carter, E. W., Trainor, A. A., Ditchman, N., Swedeen, B., & Owens, L. (2009). Evaluation of a multicomponent intervention package to increase summer work experiences for transition-age youth with severe disabilities. *Research and Practice for Persons with Severe Disabilities* (RPSD), 34, 1-12.

Cartledge, G. (2011). Introduction to the special issue: Cultural diversity and special education. *Exceptionality, 19*, 137-139.

Casebolt, K. M., & Hodge, S. R. (2010). High school physical education teachers' beliefs about teaching students with mild to severe disabilities. *Physical Educator, 67*, 140-155.

Causton-Theoharis, J. N., Giangreco, M. F., Doyle, M., & Vadasy, P. F. (2007). Paraprofessionals: The "sous-chefs" of literacy instruction. *Teaching Exceptional Children, 40*(1), 56-62.

Chen, D., Downing, J. E., & Peckham-Hardin, K. D. (2002). Working with families of diverse cultural and linguistic backgrounds: Considerations for culturally responsive positive behavior support. In J. M. Lucyshyn, G. Dunlap, & R. W. Albin (Eds.), *Families and positive behavior support: Addressing problem behavior in family contexts* (pp. 133–154). Baltimore, MD: Paul H. Brookes Publishing Co.

Cimera, R. (2007). Utilizing natural supports to lower the cost of supported employment. *Research and Practice for Persons with Severe Disabilities* (RPSD), *32*, 184–189.

Cole, C. M., Waldron, N., & Majd, M. (2004). Academic progress of students across inclusive and traditional settings. *Mental Retardation, 42*, 136–144.

Collins, B. C., Karl, J., Riggs, L., Galloway, C. C., & Hager, K. D. (2010). Teaching core content with real-life applications to secondary students with moderate and severe disabilities. *Teaching Exceptional Children, 43*(1), 52–59.

Collins, B. C., Kleinert, H. L., & Land, L. E. (2006). Addressing math standards and functional math. In D. M. Browder & F. Spooner (Eds.), *Teaching language arts, math, & science to students with significant cognitive disabilities* (pp. 197–228). Baltimore, MD: Paul H. Brookes Publishing Co.

Cologon, K. (2013). Debunking myths: Reading development in children with Down syndrome. *Australian Journal of Teacher Education, 38*, 130–151.

Darrow, A. A. (2009). Barriers to effective inclusion and strategies to overcome them. *General Music Today, 22*(3), 29–31.

Davis, D. H., Fredrick, L. D., Alberto, P. A., & Gama, R. (2012). Functional communication training without extinction using concurrent schedules of differing magnitudes of reinforcement in classrooms. *Journal of Positive Behavior Interventions, 14*, 162–172.

De Bortoli, T., Balandin, S., Foreman, P., Arthur-Kelly, M., & Mathisen, B. (2012). Mainstream teachers' experiences of communicating with students with multiple and severe disabilities. *Education and Training in Autism and Developmental Disabilities, 47*, 236–252.

Downing, J. E. (2005a). *Teaching communication skills to students with severe disabilities.* Baltimore, MD: Paul H. Brookes Publishing Co.

Downing, J. E. (2005b). *Teaching literacy skills to students with significant disabilities.* Corwin Press.

Downing, J. E. (2008). *Including students with severe and multiple disabilities in typical classrooms: Practical strategies for teachers.* (3rd ed.). Baltimore, MD: Paul H. Brookes Publishing Co.

Downing, J. E., & Demchak, M. A. (2008). First steps: Determining individual abilities and how best to support students. In J. E. Downing (Ed.), *Including students with severe and multiple disabilities in typical classrooms: Practical strategies for teachers* (3rd ed., pp. 49–90). Baltimore, MD: Paul H. Brookes Publishing Co.

Downing, J. E., & Peckham-Hardin, K. D. (2007). Inclusive education: What makes it a good education for students with moderate to severe disabilities? *Research and Practice for Persons with Severe Disabilities, 32*, 16–30.

Downing, J. E., Spencer, S., & Cavallaro, C. (2004). The development of an inclusive elementary school: Perceptions from stakeholders. *Research and Practice for Persons with Severe Disabilities, 29*, 11–24.

Downing, J., & Eichinger, J. (2011). Instructional strategies for learners with dual sensory impairments in integrated settings. *Research and Practice for Persons with Severe Disabilities* (RPSD), *36*, 150–157.

Dunst, C., & Trivette, C. M. (2009). Using research evidence to inform and evaluate early childhood intervention practices. *Topics in Early Childhood Special Education, 29*, 40–52.

Erwin, E. J., Maude, S. P., Palmer, S. B., Summers, J. A., Brotherson, M. J., Haines, S. J., ... Peck, N. F. (2016). Fostering the foundations of self-determination in early childhood: A process for enhancing child outcomes across home and school. *Early Childhood Education Journal, 44*, 325–333.

Etscheidt, S. (2006). Least restrictive and natural environments for young children with disabilities: A legal analysis of issues. *Topics in Early Childhood Special Education, 26*, 167–178.

Feldman, R., Carter, E. W., Asmus, J., & Brock, M. E. (2016). Presence, proximity, and peer interactions of adolescents with severe disabilities in general education classrooms. *Exceptional Children, 82*, 192–208.

Ferm, U., Ahlsen, E., & Bjorck-Akesson, E. (2012). Patterns of communicative interaction between a child with severe speech and physical impairments and her caregiver during a mealtime activity. *Journal of Intellectual & Developmental Disability, 37*, 11–26.

Fisher, M., & Meyer, L. H. (2002). Development and social competence after two years for students enrolled in inclusive and self-contained educational programs. *Research and Practice for Persons with Severe Disabilities, 27*, 165–174.

Foreman, P., Arthur-Kelly, M., Bennett, D., Neilands, J., & Colyvas, K. (2014). Observed changes in the alertness and communicative involvement of students with multiple and severe disability following in-class mentor modelling for staff in segregated and general education classrooms. *Journal of Intellectual Disability Research, 58*, 704–720.

Frattura, E., & Capper, C. A. (2006). Segregated programs versus integrated comprehensive service delivery for all learners: Assessing the differences. *Remedial and Special Education, 27*, 355–364.

Friend, M., & Cook, L. (2013). *Interactions: Collaboration skills for school professionals* (7th ed.). Upper Saddle River, NJ: Pearson/Merrill.

Friend, M., & Cook, L. (2017). *Interactions: Collaboration skills for school professionals* (8th ed.). Boston: Pearson.

Gardner, H. (1993). *Multiple intelligences: The theory in practice.* New York, NY: Basic Books.

Giangreco, M. F. (2010). One-to-one paraprofessionals for students with disabilities in inclusive classrooms: Is conventional wisdom wrong? *Intellectual and Developmental Disabilities, 48*, 1–13.

Giangreco, M. F., Doyle, M. B., & Suter, J. C. (2012). Constructively responding to requests for paraprofessionals: We keep asking the wrong questions. *Remedial and Special Education, 33*, 362–373.

Giangreco, M. F., Suter, J. C., & Doyle, M. (2010). Paraprofessionals in inclusive schools: A review of recent research. *Journal of Educational & Psychological Consultation, 20*, 41–57.

Goldstein, J., & Behuniak, P. (2011). Assumptions in alternate assessment: An argument-based approach to validation. *Assessment for Effective Intervention, 36*, 179–191.

Grossman, H. J. (1983). *Classification in mental retardation.* Washington, DC: American Association on Mental Deficiency.

Guon, J., Wilfond, B. S., Farlow, B., Brazg, T., & Janvier, A. (2014). Our children are not a diagnosis: The experience of parents who continue their pregnancy after a prenatal diagnosis of trisomy 13 or 18. *American Journal of Medical Genetics Part A, 164*, 308–318.

Hanline, M. F., & Correa-Torres, S. M. (2012). Experiences of preschoolers with severe disabilities in an inclusive early education setting: A qualitative study. *Education and Training in Autism and Developmental Disabilities, 47*, 109–121.

Hanline, M., & Correa-Torres, S. M. (2012). Experiences of Preschoolers with severe disabilities in an inclusive early education setting: A qualitative study. *Education and Training in Autism and Developmental Disabilities, 47*, 109–121.

Hartman, M. A. (2009). Step by Step: Creating a community-based transition program for students with intellectual disabilities. *Teaching Exceptional Children, 41*(6), 6–11.

Hartmann, E. (2011). *Universal design for learning. Practice perspectives— highlighting information on deaf-blindness* [No. 8]. Monmouth, OR: National Consortium on Deaf-Blindness. Retrieved from http://www.nationaldb.org/SearchNetwork.php?q=UDL

Hartmann, E. (2015). Universal design for learning (UDL) and learners with severe support needs. *International Journal of Whole Schooling, 11*(1), 54–67.

Heward, W. L. (2006). *Exceptional children* (8th ed.). Upper Saddle River, NJ: Merrill/Pearson.

Horrocks, E. L., & Morgan, R. L. (2011). Effects of inservice teacher training on correct implementation of assessment and instructional procedures for teachers of students with profound multiple disabilities. *Teacher Education and Special Education, 34*, 283–319.

Hubert, J. (2011). "My heart is always where he is." Perspectives of mothers of young people with severe intellectual disabilities and challenging behaviour living at home. *British Journal of Learning Disabilities, 39*, 216–224.

Hudson, M. E., Browder, D. M., & Wood, L. A. (2013). Review of experimental research on academic learning by students with moderate and severe intellectual disability in general education. *Research and Practice for Persons with Severe Disabilities, 38*, 17–29.

Hughes, C., Golas, M., Cosgriff, J., Brigham, N., Edwards, C., & Cashen, K. (2011). Effects of a social skills intervention among high school students with intellectual disabilities and autism and their general education peers. *Research and Practice for Persons with Severe Disabilities* (RPSD), *36*, 46–61.

Hunt, P., Soto, G., Maier, J., & Doering, K. (2003). Collaborative teaming to support students at risk and students with severe disabilities in general education classrooms. *Exceptional Children, 69*, 315–332.

Jackson, J. B., & Roper, S. O. (2014). Parental adaptation to out-of-home placement of a child with severe or profound developmental disabilities. *American Journal on Intellectual and Developmental Disabilities, 119*, 203–219.

Jaeger, P. (2012). We don't live in a multiple-choice world: Inquiry and the common core. *Library Media Connection, 30*(4), 10–12.

Jimenez, B. A., Mims, P. J., & Browder, D. M. (2012). Data-based decisions guidelines for teachers of students with severe intellectual and developmental disabilities. *Education and Training in Autism and Developmental Disabilities, 47*, 407–413.

Jones, J. L. (2012). Factors associated with self-concept: Adolescents with intellectual and development disabilities share their perspectives. *Intellectual and Developmental Disabilities, 50*, 31–40.

Kearns, J., Burdge, M. D., Clayton, J., Denham, A. P., & Kleinert, H. L. (2006). How students demonstrate academic performance in Portfolio Assessment. In D. M. Browder & F. Spooner (Eds.), *Teaching language arts, math and science to students with significant disabilities* (pp. 277–293). Baltimore, MD: Paul H. Brookes.

Kim, K. H., Lee, Y., & Morningstar, M. E. (2007). An unheard voice: Korean American parents' expectations, hopes, and experiences concerning their adolescent child's future. *Research and Practice for Persons with Severe Disabilities, 32*, 253–264.

Kim, M., Blair, K. C., & Lim, K. (2014). Using tablet assisted Social Stories™ to improve classroom behavior for adolescents with intellectual disabilities. *Research in Developmental Disabilities, 35*, 2241–2251.

Kleinert, H. L., & Kearns, J. F. (2001). *Alternate assessment: Measuring outcomes and supports for students with disabilities.* Baltimore, MD: Paul H. Brookes Publishing Co.

Kleinert, H., Towles-Reeves, E., Quenemoen, R., Thurlow, M., Fluegge, L., Weseman, L., & Kerbel, A. (2015). Where students with the most significant cognitive disabilities are taught: Implications for general curriculum access. *Exceptional Children, 81*, 312–328.

Kleinert, J. O. R., Harrison, E., Mills, K. R., Dueppen, B. M., & Trailor, A. M. (2014). Self-determined goal selection and planning by students with disabilities across grade bands and disability categories. *Education and Training in Autism and Developmental Disabilities, 49*, 464–477.

Kliewer, C., & Biklen, D. (2001). "School's not really a place for reading": A research synthesis of the literate lives of students with severe disabilities. *Journal of the Association for Persons with Severe Handicaps, 26*, 1–12.

Kliewer, C., Biklen, D., & Petersen, A. (2015). At the end of intellectual disability. *Harvard Educational Review, 85*(1), 1–28.

Koegel, R. L., Openden, D., Fredeen, R., & Koegel, L. K. (2006). The basics of pivotal response treatment. In R. L. Koegel & L. K. Koegel (Eds.), *Pivotal response treatments for autism: Communicative, social, and academic development* (pp. 4–30). Baltimore, MD: Paul H. Brookes.

Kozleski, E. B., Yu, T., Satter, A. L., Francis, G. L., & Haines, S. J. (2015). A never ending journey: Inclusive education is a principle of practice, not an end game. *Research and Practice for Persons with Severe Disabilities, 40*, 211–226.

Kurth, J. A., Lyon, K. J., & Shogren, K. A. (2015). Supporting students with severe disabilities in inclusive schools: A descriptive account from schools implementing inclusive practices. *Research and Practice for Persons with Severe Disabilities, 40*, 261–274.

La Paro, K. M., Olsen, K., & Pianta, R. C. (2002). Special education eligibility: Developmental precursors over the first three years of life. *Exceptional Children, 69*, 55–66.

Lewis, S., & Tolla, J. (2003). Creating and using tactile experience books for young children with vision impairments. *TEACHING Exceptional Children, 35*(3), 22–29.

Light, J., & McNaughton, D. (2012). Supporting the communication, language, and literacy development of children with complex communication needs: State of the science and future research priorities. *Assistive Technology, 24*(1), 34–44.

Light, J., & McNaughton, D. (2014). Communicative competence for individuals who require augmentative and alternative communication: A new definition for a new era of communication? *Augmentative and Alternative Communication, 30*, 1–18.

Logan, K., Jacobs, H. A., Gast, D. A., Murray, A. S., Daino, K., & Skala, C. (1998). The impact of typical peers on the perceived happiness of students with profound multiple disabilities. *Journal of the Association for Persons with Severe Handicaps, 23*, 309–318.

Long, K. A., Kao, B., Plante, W., Seifer, R., & Lobato, D. (2015). Cultural and child-related predictors of distress among Latina caregivers of children with intellectual disabilities. *American Journal on Intellectual and Developmental Disabilities, 120*, 145–165.

MacLean, W. E., & Dornbush, K. (2012). Self-injury in a statewide sample of young children with developmental disabilities. *Journal of Mental Health Research in Intellectual Disabilities, 5*, 236–245.

Mansell, J., & Beadle-Brown, J. (2010). Deinstitutionalization and community living: Position statement of the Comparative Policy and Practice Special Interest Research Group of the International Association for the Scientific Study of Intellectual Disabilities. *Journal of Intellectual Disability Research, 54*, 104–112.

Matzen, K., Ryndak, D., & Nakao, T. (2010). Middle school teams increasing access to general education for students with significant disabilities: Issues encountered and activities observed across contexts. *Remedial and Special Education, 31*, 287–304.

Mautz, D., Storey, K., & Certo, N. (2001). Increasing integrated work place social interactions: The effects of job modification, natural supports, adaptive communication instruction, and job coach training. *Journal of the Association for Persons with Severe Handicaps, 26*, 257–269.

McCabe, H. (2008). Autism and family in the People's Republic of China: Learning from parents' perspectives. *Research and Practice for Persons with Severe Disabilities, 33*(1–2), 37–47.

McDonnell, J. J., Hardman, M. L., & McDonnell, A. P. (2003). *An introduction to persons with moderate and severe disabilities: Educational and social issues* (2nd ed.). Boston, MA: Allyn & Bacon.

McNaughton, D., & Light, J. (2013). The iPad and mobile technology revolution: Benefits and challenges for individuals who require augmentative and alternative communication. *Augmentative and Alternative Communication, 29*, 107–116.

McVay, P. (2000). Paraprofessionals in the classroom: What role do they play? *T/TAC Bulletin, 8*(3), 1–2. Retrieved from https://ttac.vt.edu/newsletters/newsletterv8n3.pdf

Mechling, L. C., & Bishop, V. A. (2011). Assessment of computer-based preferences of students with profound multiple disabilities. *Journal of Special Education, 45*, 15–27.

Moes, D. R., & Frea, W. D. (2002). Contextualized behavioral support in early interventions for children with autism and their families. *Journal of Autism and Developmental Disorders, 32*(6), 519–533.

Mueller, M. M., Nkosi, A., & Hine, J. F. (2011). Functional analysis in public schools: A summary of 90 functional analyses. *Journal of Applied Behavior Analysis, 44*, 807–818.

Naraian, S. (2010). "Why not have fun?": Peers make sense of an inclusive high school program. *Intellectual and Developmental Disabilities, 48*, 14–30.

New York State Education Department. (2009). *2009–10 New York State alternate assessment administration manual and supplemental materials.* Retrieved from http://www.emsc.nysed.gov/osa/nysaa/nysaa-manual-0910.html

Ogletree, B. T., Bruce, S. M., Finch, A., Fahey, R., & McLean, L. (2011). Recommended communication-based interventions for individuals with severe intellectual disabilities. *Communication Disorders Quarterly, 32*, 164–175.

Oliver, C., Petty, J., Ruddick, L., & Bacarese-Hamilton, M. (2012). The association between repetitive, self-injurious and aggressive behavior in children with severe intellectual disability. *Journal of Autism and Developmental Disorders, 42*, 910–919.

Olson, A., Leko, M. M., & Roberts, C. A. (2016). Providing students with severe disabilities access to the general education curriculum. *Research and Practice for Persons with Severe Disabilities.* doi: 10.1177/1540796916651975

Orelove, F. P. (1991). Educating all students: The future is now. In L. Meyer, C. A. Peck, & L. Brown (Eds.), *Critical issues in the lives of people with severe disabilities* (pp. 67–92). Baltimore, MD: Paul H. Brookes Publishing Co.

Parsons, M. B., Reid, D. H., Green, C. W., & Browning, L. B. (1999). Reducing individualized job coach assistance provided to persons with multiple severe disabilities in supported work. *Journal of the Association for Persons with Severe Handicaps, 24*, 292–297.

Peck, C. A., Staub, D., Gallucci, C., & Schwartz, I. (2004). Parent perception of the impact of inclusion on their nondisabled child. *Research and Practice for Persons with Severe Disabilities, 29*, 135–143.

Pickens, J. L., & Dymond, S. K. (2014). Special education directors' views of community-based vocational instruction. *Research and Practice for Persons with Severe Disabilities, 39*, 290–304.

Polloway, E. A., Smith, J. D., & Patton, J. R. (2015). Charles Dickens and intellectual disability. *Journal of Intellectual Disability-Diagnosis and Treatment, 3*(1), 1–6.

Purcell, M. G., Horn, E., & Palmer, S. (2007). A qualitative study of the initiation and continuation of preschool inclusion programs. *Exceptional Children, 74*, 85–100.

Purvis, B., Malloy, P., Schalock, M., McNulty, K., Davies, S., Thomas, K. S., & Udell, T. (2014). *Early identification and referral of infants who are deaf-blind.* Monmouth, OR: National Center on Deaf-Blindness. Retrieved from http://eric.ed.gov/?id=ED548232

Purvis, B., Malloy, P., Schalock, M., McNulty, K., Davies, S., Thomas, K. S., & Udell, T. (2014). *Early identification and referral of infants who are deaf-blind.* Monmouth, OR: National Center on Deaf-Blindness. Retrieved from http://eric.ed.gov/?id=ED548232

Ravindran, N., & Myers, B. J. (2012). Cultural influences on perceptions of health, illness, and disability: A review and focus on autism. *Journal of Child and Family Studies, 21*, 311–319.

Rogers-Adkinson, D. L., Ochoa, T. A., & Delgado, B. (2003). Developing crosscultural competence: Serving families of children with significant developmental needs. *Focus on Autism and Developmental Disabilities, 18*(1), 4–8.

Rossetti, Z. S. (2011). "That's how we do it": Friendship work between high school students with and without autism or developmental disability. *Research and Practice for Persons with Severe Disabilities (RPSD), 36*, 23–33.

Ruppar, A. L., & Gaffney, J. S. (2011). Individualized education program team decisions: A preliminary study of conversations, negotiations, and power. *Research and Practice for Persons with Severe Disabilities (RPSD), 36*, 11–22.

Rusch, F. R., & Wolfe, P. (2008). When will our values finally result in the creation of new pathways for change—change that we can believe in? *Research and Practice for Persons with Severe Disabilities (RPSD), 33*, 96–97.

Russel, C. S., Allday, R. A., & Duhon, G. J. (2015). Effects of increasing distance of a one-on-one paraprofessional on student engagement. *Education and Treatment of Children, 38*, 193–210.

Ryndak, D. L., & Alper, S. (2003). *Curriculum and instruction for students with significant disabilities in inclusive settings* (2nd ed.). Boston, MA: Allyn & Bacon.

Ryndak, D. L., Taub, D., Jorgensen, C. M., Gonsier-Gerdin, J., Arndt, K., Sauer, J., ... Allcock, H. (2014). Policy and the impact on placement, involvement, and progress in general education critical issues that require rectification. *Research and Practice for Persons with Severe Disabilities, 39*, 65–74.

Ryndak, D., Jackson, L. B., & White, J. M. (2013). Involvement and progress in the general curriculum for students with extensive support needs: K–12 inclusive-education research and implications for the future. *Inclusion, 1*(1), 28–49.

Salisbury, C. L., & Copeland, C. G. (2013). Progress of infants/toddlers with severe disabilities: Perceived and measured change. *Topics in Early Childhood Special Education, 33*, 68–77.

Sarkar, T. (2015). Intellectual and developmental disability: Transition to adulthood and decision making process. *International Journal of Child Health and Human Development, 8*, 517–527.

Saunders, A. F., Bethune, K. S., Spooner, F., & Browder, D. (2013). Solving the Common Core equation: Teaching mathematics CCSS to students with moderate and severe disabilities. *Teaching Exceptional Children, 45*(3), 24–33.

Schafer, W. D., & Lissitz, R. W. (2009). *Alternate assessments based on alternate achievement standards: Policy, practice, and potential.* Baltimore, MD: Brookes.

Shokoohi-Yekta, M., & Hendrickson, J. M. (2010). Friendships with peers with severe disabilities: American and Iranian secondary students' ideas about being a friend. *Education and Training in Autism and Developmental Disabilities, 45*, 23–37.

Siegel-Causey, E., & Allinder, R. M. (2005). Review of assessment procedures for students with moderate and severe disabilities. *Education and Training in Developmental Disabilities, 40*, 343–351.

Smith, A. (2006). Access, participation, and progress in the general education curriculum in the least restrictive environment for students with significant cognitive disabilities. *Research and Practice for Persons with Severe Disabilities, 31*, 331–337.

Smith, J. D., & Polloway, E. A. (2008). Defining disability up and down: The problem of "normality." *Intellectual and Developmental Disabilities, 46*, 234–238.

Spooner, F., & Browder, D. M. (2015). Raising the bar: Significant advances and future needs for promoting learning for students with severe disabilities. *Remedial and Special Education, 36*, 28–32.

Stewart, D. (2011). Take time to listen: A first step toward collaborative transition planning. *Physical & Occupational Therapy in Pediatrics, 31*, 359–361.

TASH. (2000). *TASH resolution on the people for whom TASH advocates.* Retrieved from www.tash.org/resolutions/res02advocate.htm

Taylor, M. A., & Pastor, D. A. (2013). An application of generalizability theory to evaluate the technical quality of an alternate assessment. *Applied Measurement in Education, 26*, 279–297.

Tindal, G., Yovanoff, P., & Geller, J. P. (2010). Generalizability theory applied to reading assessments for students with significant cognitive disabilities. *Journal of Special Education, 44,* 3–17.

Tullis, C. A., Cannella-Malone, H. I., & Payne, D. O. (2015). Literature review of interventions for between-task transitioning for individuals with intellectual and developmental disabilities including autism spectrum disorders. *Review Journal of Autism and Developmental Disorders, 2,* 91–102.

Tullis, C. A., Cannella-Malone, H. I., Basbigill, A. R., Yeager, A., Fleming, C. V., Payne, D., & Pei-Fang, W. (2011). Review of the choice and preference assessment literature for individuals with severe to profound disabilities. *Education and Training in Autism and Developmental Disabilities, 46,* 576–595.

Turnbull, A. P., Turnbull, H. R., Erwin, E., & Soodak, L. (2006). *Families, professionals, and exceptionality: Positive outcomes through partnerships and trust* (5th ed.). Upper Saddle River, NJ: Pearson.

U.S. Department of Education. (1993a). *Fifteenth annual report to Congress on the implementation of IDEA.* Washington, DC: Author.

U.S. Department of Education. (2003). *Twenty-fifth annual report to Congress on the implementation of the Individuals with Disabilities Education Act.* Washington, DC: Author.

U.S. Department of Education. (2015). *Thirty-seventh annual report to Congress on the implementation of the Individuals with Disabilities Education Act.* Washington, DC: Author, Office of Special Education Programs. Retrieved from http://www2.ed.gov/about/reports/annual/osep/2015/parts-b-c/37th-arc-for-idea.pdf

Van Laarhoven-Myers, T. E., Van Laarhoven, T. R., Smith, T. J., Johnson, H., & Olson, J. (2016). Promoting self-determination and transition planning using technology: Student and parent perspectives. *Career Development and Transition for Exceptional Individuals, 39,* 99–110.

Ward, T. (2009). Voice, Vision, and the Journey Ahead: Redefining access to the general curriculum and outcomes for learners with significant support needs. *Research and Practice for Persons with Severe Disabilities (RPSD), 33–34,* 241–248.

Wehman, P., Chan, F., Ditchman, N., & Kang, H. (2014). Effect of supported employment on vocational rehabilitation outcomes of transition-age youth with intellectual and developmental disabilities: A case control study. *Intellectual and Developmental Disabilities, 52,* 296–310.

Wehmeyer, M. L. (2002). *Teaching students with mental retardation: Providing access to the general curriculum.* Baltimore, MD: Paul H. Brookes.

Wells, J. C., & Sheehey, P. H. (2012). Person-centered planning: Strategies to encourage participation and facilitate communication. *Teaching Exceptional Children, 44*(3), 32–39.

Werner, G. A., Vismara, L. A., Koegel, R. L., & Koegel, L. K. (2006). Play dates, social interactions, and friendships. In R. L. Koegel & L. K. Koegel (Eds.), *Pivotal response treatments for autism: Communication, social, and academic development* (pp. 200–213). Baltimore, MD: Paul H. Brookes.

Westling, D. L. (2015). *Evidence-based practices for improving challenging behaviors of students with severe disabilities* (Document No. IC-14). Gainesville, FL: Collaboration for Effective Educator, Development, Accountability, and Reform (CEEDAR) Center. Retrieved from http://ceedar.education.ufl.edu/tools/innovation-configurations/

Westling, D. L., & Fox, L. (2009). *Teaching students with severe disabilities* (4th ed.). Upper Saddle River, NJ: Merrill.

Westling, D. L., Salzberg, C., Collins, B. C., Morgan, R., & Knight, V. (2014). Research on the preparation of teachers of students with severe disabilities. In P. T. Sindelar, E. D. McCray, M. T. Brownell, & B. Lignugaris/Kraft (Eds.), *Handbook of research on special education teacher preparation* (pp. 305–319). New York, NY: Routledge.

Zambo, D. M. (2010). Strategies to enhance the social identities and social networks of adolescent students with disabilities. *Teaching Exceptional Children, 43*(2), 28–35.

Zheng, Y., Maude, S. P., Brotherson, M. J., Summers, J. A., Palmer, S. B., & Erwin, E. J. (2015). Foundations for self-determination perceived and promoted by families of young children with disabilities in China. *Education and Training in Autism and Developmental Disabilities, 50,* 109–122.

Zionts, L. T., Zionts, P., Harrison, S., & Bellinger, O. (2003). Urban African American families' perceptions of cultural sensitivity within the special education system. *Focus on Autism and Other Developmental Disabilities, 18,* 41–50.

Zuniga, M. A. (1998). Families with Latino roots. In E. W. Lynch & M. J. Hanson (Eds.), *Developing cross-cultural competence: A guide for working with children and their families* (2nd ed., pp. 209–250). Baltimore, MD: Paul H. Brookes Publishing Co.

Chapter 15

Amend, E. R., & Peters, D. (2015). The role of clinical psychologist: Building a comprehensive understanding of 2e students. *Gifted Child Today, 38,* 243–245.

Assouline, S. G., & Whiteman, C. S. (2011). Twice-exceptionality: Implications for school psychologists in the post-IDEA 2004 era. *Journal of Applied School Psychology, 27,* 380–402.

Bélanger, J., & Gagné, F. (2006). Examining the size of the gifted/talented population from multiple identification criteria. *Journal for the Education of the Gifted, 30,* 131–163.

Bailey, C. L. (2011). An examination of the relationships between ego development, Dabrowski's theory of positive disintegration, and the behavioral characteristics of gifted adolescents. *Gifted Child Quarterly, 55,* 208–222.

Benbow, C. P., & Stanley, J. C. (1996). Inequity in equity. How "equity" can lead to inequity for high-potential students. *Psychology, Public Policy and Policy, 2,* 249–292.

Bergen, D. (2009). Gifted children's humor preferences, sense of humor, and comprehension of riddles. *Humor: International Journal of Humor Research, 22,* 419–436.

Besnov, K. D., Manning, S., & Karnes, F. A. (2006). Screening students with visual impairments for intellectual giftedness. *RE:view, 37,* 134–140.

Bianco, M., & Harris, B. (2014). Strength-based RTI: Developing gifted potential in Spanish-speaking English language learners. *Gifted Child Today, 37,* 169–176.

Bianco, M., Harris, B., Garrison-Wade, D., & Leech, N. (2011). Gifted girls: Gender bias in gifted referrals. *Roeper Review: A Journal on Gifted Education, 33,* 170–181.

Bracken, B. A., & Brown, E. F. (2006). Behavioral identification and assessment of gifted and talented students. *Journal of Psychoeducational Assessment, 24,* 112–122.

Bracken, B. A., & McCallum, R. S. (1998). *Universal Nonverbal Intelligence Test.* Itasca, IL: Riverside.

Bracken, B. A., & McCallum, R. S. (2016). *Universal Nonverbal Intelligence Test* (2nd ed.) (UNIT2). Rolling Meadows, IL: Riverside.

Brown, E. F., & Abernethy, S. H. (2009). Policy implications at the state and district level with RtI for gifted students. *Gifted Child Today, 32*(3), 52–57.

Brown, S. W., Renzulli, J. S., Gubbins, E. J., Siegle, D., Zhang, W., & Chen, C. (2016). Assumptions underlying the identification of gifted and talented students. In S. M. Reis & S. M. Reis (Eds.), *Reflections on gifted education: Critical works by Joseph S. Renzulli and colleagues* (pp. 151–169). Waco, TX: Prufrock Press.

Brulles, D., & Winebrenner, S. (2012). Clustered for success. *Educational Leadership, 69*(5), 41–45.

Brulles, D., Castellano, J. A., & Laing, P. C. (2010). Identifying and enfranchising gifted English language learners. In J. Castellano & A. D. Frazier (Eds.) *Special populations in gifted education: Understanding our most able students from diverse backgrounds* (pp. 305–313). Waco, TX: Prufrock Press.

Buerk, S. (2016). Inquiry learning models and gifted education: A curriculum of innovation and possibility. In T. Kettler & T. Kettler (Eds.), *Modern curriculum for gifted and advanced academic students* (pp. 129–170). Waco, TX: Prufrock Press.

Buescher, T. M., & Higham, S. (2001). *Helping adolescents adjust to giftedness.* (ERIC Digest #E489). Retrieved from www.kidsource.com/kidsource/content/adjust_to_giftedness.html

Callahan, C. M., & Miller, E. M. (2005). A child-responsive model of giftedness. In R. J. Sternberg & J. E. Davidson (Eds.), *Conceptions of giftedness* (2nd ed.) (pp. 120–146). New York, NY: Cambridge University Press.

Callahan, C. M., Moon, T. R., & Oh, S. (2014). National surveys of gifted programs [Executive summary]. Charlottesville, VA: National Research Center on the Gifted and Talented. Retrieved from http://www.nagc.org/sites/default/files/key%20reports/2014%20Survey%20of%20GT%20programs%20Exec%20Summ.pdf

Callahan, C. M., Moon, T. R., Oh, S., Azano, A. P., & Hailey, E. P. (2014). What works in gifted education: Documenting the effects of an integrated curricular/instructional model for gifted students. *American Educational Research Journal, 52,* 137–167.

Callard-Szulgit, R. (2005). *Teaching the gifted in an inclusion classroom: Activities that work.* Lanham, MD: Scarecrow Education.

Carman, C. A. (2013). Comparing apples and oranges: Fifteen years of definitions of giftedness in research. *Journal of Advanced Academics, 24,* 52–70.

Castellano, J. A., & Díaz, E. (Eds.). (2002). *Reaching new horizons: Gifted and talented education for culturally and linguistically diverse students.* Boston, MA: Allyn & Bacon.

Castellano, J. A., & Frazier, A. (2011). *Special populations in gifted education: Understanding our most able students from diverse backgrounds.* Waco, TX: Prufrock Press.

Cavilla, D. (2014). Thoughts on access, differentiation, and implementation of a multicultural curriculum. *Gifted Education International, 30,* 281–287.

Chamberlin, S. A., Buchanan, M., & Vercimak, D. (2007). Serving twice exceptional preschoolers: Blending gifted education and early childhood special education practices in assessment and program planning. *Journal for the Education of the Gifted, 30,* 372–394.

Coleman, M. R., & Gallagher, S. (2015). Meeting the needs of students with 2e: It takes a team. *Gifted Child Today, 38,* 252–254.

Coleman, M. R., & Shah-Coltrane, S. (2015). Children of promise: Dr. James Gallagher's thoughts on underrepresentation within gifted education. *Journal for the Education of the Gifted, 38,* 70–76.

Colorado Department of Education. (2009). *Twice-exceptional students: Gifted students with disabilities, an introductory resource book* (2nd ed.). Denver, CO: Author. Retrieved from http://www.cde.state.co.us/gt/download/pdf/twiceexceptionalresourcehandbook.pdf

Council of State Directors of Programs for the Gifted & National Association for Gifted Children. (2009). *The state of the states in gifted education (2008–2009): National policy and practice data.* Washington, DC: Author.

Cross, T. L., & Frazier, A. (2010). Guiding the psychosocial development of gifted students attending specialized residential STEM schools. *Roeper Review, 32*(1), 32–41.

Dai, D., Swanson, J., & Cheng, H. (2011). State of research on giftedness and gifted education: A survey of empirical studies published during 1998-2010 (April). *Gifted Child Quarterly, 55,* 126–138.

Donovan, M. S., & Cross, C. T. (Eds.). (2002a). *Minority students in special and gifted education.* Retrieved from www.edrs.com/members/sp.cfm?ANED469543

Eckstein, M. (2009). Enrichment 2.0: Gifted and talented education for the 21st century. *Gifted Child Today, 32,* 59–63.

Education Program for Gifted Youth (EPGY). (2016). *About Stanford's Education Program for Gifted Youth (EPGY).* Stanford, CA: Author. Retrieved from https://giftedandtalented.com/how-it-works/research-results

Erwin, J. O., & Worrell, F. C. (2012). Assessment practices and the underrepresentation of minority students in gifted and talented education. *Journal of Psychoeducational Assessment, 30,* 74–87.

Esquierdo, J., & Arreguin-Anderson, M. (2012). The "invisible" gifted and talented bilingual students: A current report on enrollment in GT programs. *Journal for the Education of the Gifted, 35,* 35–47.

Feng, A. X., & Van Tassel-Baska, J. (2008). Identifying low-income and minority students for gifted programs: Academic and affective impact of performance-based assessment. In J. L. Van Tassel-Baska (Ed.), *Alternative assessments with gifted and talented students* (129–146). Waco, TX: Prufrock.

Fiebig, J., & Beauregard, E. (2010). Longitudinal change and maternal influence on occupational aspirations of gifted female American and German adolescents. *Journal for the Education of the Gifted, 34,* 45–67.

Figg, S. D., Rogers, K. B., McCormick, J., & Low, R. (2012). Differentiating low performance of the gifted learner: Achieving, underachieving, and selective consuming students. *Journal of Advanced Academics, 23,* 53–71.

Fletcher, K. L. & Neumeister, K. L. (2012). Research on perfectionism and achievement motivation: Implications for gifted students. *Psychology in the Schools, 49,* 668–677.

Foley-Nicpon, M., Assouline, S. G., & Fosenburg, S. (2015). The relationship between self-concept, ability, and academic programming among twice-exceptional youth. *Journal of Advanced Academics, 26,* 256–273.

Fonseca, C. (2016). *Emotional intensity in gifted students: Helping kids cope with explosive feelings* (2nd ed.). Waco, TX: Prufrock Press.

Ford D. (2015). Multicultural issues: Recruiting and retaining Black and Hispanic students in gifted education: Equality versus equity schools. *Gifted Child Today 38,* 187–191.

Ford, D. Y., Grantham, T. C., & Whiting, G. W. (2008). Culturally and linguistically diverse students in gifted education: Recruitment and retention issues. *Exceptional Children, 74,* 289–306.

Ford, D. Y., Moore, J., & Scott, M. (2011). Key theories and frameworks for improving the recruitment and retention of African American students in gifted education. *Journal of Negro Education, 80,* 239–253.

Fowler, S., Ogston, K., Roberts-Fiati, G., & Swenson, A. (1995). Patterns of giftedness and high competence in high school students educationally enriched during infancy: Variation across educational racial/ethnic backgrounds. *Gifted and Talented International, 10*(1), 31–36.

Gallagher, J. J. (2015). Education of gifted students: A civil rights issue? *Journal for the Education of the Gifted, 38,* 64–69.

Gardner, H. (1993). *Multiple intelligences: The theory in practice.* New York, NY: Basic Books.

Garn, A. C., Matthews, M. S., & Jolly, J. L. (2012). Parents' role in the academic motivation of students with gifts and talents. *Psychology in the Schools, 49,* 656–667.

Garrett, T., Antrop-Gonzalez, R., & Velez, W. (2010). Examining the success factors of high-achieving Puerto Rican male high-school students. *Roeper Review, 32,* 106–115.

Gentry, M., & Fugate, C. (2012). Gifted Native American students: Underperforming, under-identified, and overlooked. *Psychology in the Schools, 49,* 631–646.

Goodwin, C. B., & Gustavson, M. (2012). Education outside of the box: Homeschooling your gifted or twice-exceptional child. *Understanding Our Gifted, 24*(4), 8–11.

Grantham, T. C., & Henfield, M. S. (2011). Black father involvement in gifted education: Thoughts from Black fathers on increasing/improving Black father-gifted teacher partnerships. *Gifted Child Today, 34*(4), 47–53.

Gregory, G. H., & Chapman, C. (2002). *Differentiated instructional strategies* (pp. 126–130). Thousand Oaks, CA: Corwin.

Gubbins, E. J., Callahan, C. M., & Renzulli, J. S. (2014). Contributions to the impact of the Javits Act by The National Research Center on the Gifted and Talented. *Journal of Advanced Academics, 25*, 422-444.

Hargrove, K. (2012). From the classroom: Advocating acceleration. *Gifted Child Today, 35*, 72-73.

Havighurst, R. J., Stivers, E., & DeHaan, R. F. (1955). *A survey of education of gifted children.* Chicago, IL: University of Chicago Press.

Heacox, D. (2002). *Differentiating instruction in the regular classroom.* Minneapolis, MN: Free Spirit.

Heilbronner, N. (2009). Jumpstarting Jill: Strategies to nurture talented girls in your science classroom. *Gifted Child Today, 32*, 46-54.

Hertberg-Davis, H. (2009). Myth 7: Differentiation in the regular classroom is equivalent to gifted programs and is sufficient—Classroom teachers have the time, the skill, and the will to differentiate adequately. *Gifted Child Quarterly, 53*, 251-253.

Hollingworth, L. S. (1926). *Gifted children: Their nature and nurture.* New York, NY: Macmillan.

Hollingworth, L. S. (1942). *Children above 180 IQ.* New York, NY: World Book.

Housand, A. M. (2016a). In context: Gifted characteristics and the implications for curriculum. In K. R. Stephens, F. A. Karnes, K. R. Stephens, & F. A. Karnes (Eds.), *Introduction to curriculum design in gifted education* (pp. 3-22). Waco, TX: Prufrock Press.

Housand, B. C. (2016b). The role of technology in curriculum for the gifted: From little acorns grow mighty oaks. In K. R. Stephens, F. A. Karnes, K. R. Stephens, & F. A. Karnes (Eds.), *Introduction to curriculum design in gifted education* (pp. 261-279). Waco, TX: Prufrock Press.

Housand, B. C., & Housand, A. M. (2012). The role of technology in gifted students' motivation. *Psychology in the Schools, 49*, 706-715.

Howley, A., Rhodes, M., & Beall, J. (2009). Challenges facing rural schools: Implications for gifted students. *Journal for the Education of the Gifted, 32*, 515-536.

Johnsen, S. K. (2009). Best practices for identifying gifted students. *Principal, 88*(5), 8-14.

Johnsen, S. K., Parker, S. L., & Farah, Y. N. (2015). Providing services for students with gifts and talents within a response-to-intervention framework. *Teaching Exceptional Children, 47*, 226-233.

Jolly, J. L. (2005). Foundations of the field of gifted education. *Gifted Child Today, 28*(2), 14-18, 65.

Jolly, J. L. (2008). Lew Terman: Genetic study of genius—Elementary school students. *Gifted Child Today, 31*(1), 27-33.

Jolly, J. L., & Kettler, T. (2008). Gifted education research 1993-2003: A disconnect between priorities and practice. *Journal for the Education of the Gifted, 31*, 427-446.

Jolly, J. L., Matthews, M. S., & Nester, J. (2013). Homeschooling the gifted: A parent's perspective. *Gifted Child Quarterly, 57*, 121-134.

Jones, B. M. (2011). The Texas Academy of Mathematics and Science: A 20-year perspective. *Journal for the Education of the Gifted, 34, 513-543.*

Kalbfleisch, M. L., & Gillmarten, C. (2013). Left brain vs. right brain: Findings on visual spatial capacities and the functional neurology of giftedness. *Roeper Review, 35*, 265-275.

Kanevsky, L. (2011). Deferential differentiation: What types of differentiation do students want? *Gifted Child Quarterly, 55*, 279-299.

Kaplan, S. N. (2011). Developing membership in the gifted culture for gifted students in urban schools. *Gifted Child Today, 34*, 63-65.

Kaufman, J. C., Plucker, J. A., & Russell, C. M. (2012). Identifying and assessing creativity as a component of giftedness. *Journal of Psychoeducational Assessment, 30*, 60-73.

Kaul, C. R., Johnsen, S. K., Saxon, T. F., & Witte, M. M. (2016). Project promise: A long-term follow-up of low-income gifted students who participated in a summer enrichment program. *Journal for the Education of the Gifted, 39*, 83-102.

Kerr, B. A., Vuyk, M., & Rea, C. (2012). Gendered practices in the education of gifted girls and boys. *Psychology in the Schools, 49*, 647-655.

Kim, M. (2016). A meta-analysis of the effects of enrichment programs on gifted students. *Gifted Child Quarterly, 60*, 102-116.

King, K. A., Kozleski, E. B., & Landsdowne, K. (2009). Where are all the students of color in gifted education? *Principal, 88*(5), 16-20.

Kornilov, S. A., Tan, M., Elliott, J. G., Sternberg, R. J., & Grigorenko, E. L. (2012). Gifted identification with Aurora: Widening the spotlight. *Journal of Psychoeducational Assessment, 30*, 117-133.

Kuo, Y., & Lohman, D. F. (2011). The timing of grade skipping. *Journal for the Education of the Gifted, 34*, 731-741.

Lakin, J. M. (2016). Universal screening and the representation of historically underrepresented minority students in gifted education: Minding the gaps in Card and Giuliano's research. *Journal of Advanced Academics, 27*, 139-149.

Lawrence, B. K. (2009). Rural gifted education: A comprehensive literature review. *Journal for the Education of the Gifted, 32*, 461-494.

Lee, S., Olszewski-Kubilius, P., & Peternel, G. (2010). The efficacy of academic acceleration for gifted minority students. *Gifted Child Quarterly, 54*, 189-208.

Lee, S., Olszewski-Kubilius, P., & Thomson, D. (2012). Academically gifted students' perceived interpersonal competence and peer relationships. *Gifted Child Quarterly, 56*, 90-104.

Liem, G. D., & Chua, C. S. (2016). Motivation in talent development of high-ability students: Research trends, practical implications, and future directions. In M. Neihart, S. I. Pfeiffer, T. L. Cross, M. Neihart, S. I. Pfeiffer, & T. L. Cross (Eds.), *The social and emotional development of gifted children: What do we know?* (2nd ed.) (pp. 173-189). Waco, TX: Prufrock Press.

Meier, E., Vogl, K., & Preckel, F. (2014). Motivational characteristics of students in gifted classes: The pivotal role of need for cognition. *Learning and Individual Differences, 33*, 39-46.

Missett, T. C., & Brunner, M. C. (2013). The use of traditional assessment tools for identifying gifted students. In C. M. Callahan, H. L. Hertberg-Davis, C. M. Callahan, & H. L. Hertberg-Davis (Eds.), *Fundamentals of gifted education: Considering multiple perspectives* (pp. 105-111). New York, NY: Routledge/Taylor & Francis.

Mofield, E. L., & Peters, M. P. (2015). Multidimensional perfectionism within gifted suburban adolescents: An exploration of typology and comparison of samples. *Roeper Review, 37*, 97-109.

Mokher, C. G. ,& McLendon, M. K. (2009). Uniting secondary and postsecondary education: An event history analysis of state adoption of dual enrollment policies. *American Journal of Education, 115*, 249-277.

Montana Department of Education (2015). *Serving Montana's high ability/ high potential students.* Helena, MT: Author. Retrieved from http://opi. mt.gov/pdf/Gifted/GTPlanningGuideStrategies.pdf

Montana Office of Public Instruction (OPI). (2009). *Response to intervention (RTI) and gifted and talented education.* Retrieved from http://opi.mt.gov/ pub/RTI/Resources/RTI_Gifted_Talented.pdf

Moon, T. R. (2009). Myth 16: High-stakes tests are synonymous with rigor and difficulty. *Gifted Child Quarterly, 53*, 277-279.

Moore, J. L., Ford, D. Y., & Milner, H. R. (2005). Underachievement among gifted students of color: Implications for educators. *Theory into Practice, 44*, 167-177.

Mourgues, C., Tan, M., Hein, S., Elliott, J. G., & Grigorenko, E. L. (2016). Using creativity to predict future academic performance: An application of Aurora's five subtests for creativity. *Learning and Individual Differences.* doi:10.1016/j.lindif.2016.02.001

Muratori, M., & Brody, L. (2012). Schools and talent search centers: Meeting the needs of academically talented students. *Parenting for High Potential, 1*(6), 16-19.

National Association for Gifted Children (NAGC) & The Council of State Directors of Programs for the Gifted. (2015, November). 2014-2015 state of the states in gifted education policy and practice data. Washington, DC: NAGC. Retrieved from http://www.nagc.org/sites/default/files/key%20 reports/2014-2015%20State%20of%20the%20States%20%28final%29.pdf

Name Index

A

Abbott, C., 416
Abebe, A., 407
Abernethy, B., 390
Abrams, D. N., 295
Adams-Chapman, I., 390
Addai-Davis, J., 86
Adebisi, R. O., 158
Adreon, D., 310, 312
Aganza, J. S., 78
Agran, M., 151
Aguilar, J., 85
Ahearn, E. M., 157
Ahlgrim-Delzell, L., 427, 446
Ahlsen, E., 428
Akinbami, L. J., 395
Al-Ayadhi, L.Y., 318
Alberto, P. A., 430
Albin, R. W., 218
Albrecht, S. F., 62, 76
Alderson-Day, B., 297
Aldrich, E. M., 401
Alexander, J., 293, 299
Alexander, J. L., 241
Alexander Graham Bell Association for the Deaf and Hard of Hearing, 330
Alfonso, V., 127, 129
Algina, J. J., 209
Algozzine, B., 71, 427
Algozzine, K. M., 103
Algozzine, R., 446
Algozzine, R. F., 103
Al Hadidi, M. S., 445
Alhumam, I., 68
Ali, E., 364
Alimovic, S., 358
Alizadeh, H., 213
Al Khateeb, J. M., 445
Al Khatib, A. J., 445
Allcock, H., 427
Allday, R., 212
Allday, R. A., 427
Allen, E., 386, 400
Allinder, R. M., 433
Allison, C, 375
Allman, C. B., 377
Allor, J. H., 242
Al Otaiba, S., 242
Alsem, M. W., 405
Althoff, R. R., 213
Alvarez-McHatton, P., 70, 71, 89
Aman, M. G., 244
Amend, E. R., 480
American Academy of Family Physicians, 200
American Academy of Pediatrics, 201, 225
American Association on Intellectual and Developmental Disabilities (AAIDD), 232, 240

American Foundation for the Blind, 358, 360, 369, 370, 374, 375
American Network of Community Options and Resources, 232
American Printing House for the Blind, 360
American Psychiatric Association, 128–129, 290, 291, 300–301
American Speech-Language-Hearing Association, 350
Ames, D., 100
Ammerman, R. T., 199, 200
Andel, R., 212
Anderson, A. L., 79, 140
Anderson, B., 74
Anderson, C., 35
Anderson, C. M., 217
Anderson, D., 158, 434, 446
Anderson, J. A., 88, 132
Anderson, J. D., 400
Andrews, C. A., 358
Andrews, S. W., 87
Angelou, M., 460
Angold, A., 223
Antia, S., 344, 347
Apkarian, A. O., 358
Appenzeller, M., 340
Aram, D., 334
Arbogast, K. B., 394
The Arc, 18, 232
Arfé, B., 335
Armer, B., 95
Arndt, K., 34, 427
Arneson, C. L., 291, 293
Arnold, J., 381
Arnold, L. E., 224
Aro, M. T., 145
Arreguin-Anderson, M., 459
Arthur-Kelly, M., 428
Artiles, A. J., 18
Artiles, A.J., 66, 74
Artiles, A. J., 75, 157
Asarnow, R., 400
Asaro-Saddler, K., 311
Asbrock, D., 369
Ashbaker, B., 119
Ashby, C. E., 307
Ashcroft, S. C., 358
Ashkenasi, A., 390
Ashkenazy, E., 368
Ashton, T. M., 80
Asmus, J., 428, 430, 431, 437, 439
Aspel, N., 215
Asperger, H., 7, 290
Association for Retarded Citizens, 18
Assouline, S. G., 480
Aston, C., 35
Athanases, S. Z., 69

Atkins, K., 414
Aube, D., 299
Aud, S., 69
Ault, M. J., 254
Austin, D., 439
Autism Network International, 291
Autism Research Institute (ARI), 290, 294
Avenevoli, S., 198
Axe, J., 304
Axe, J. B., 311
Ayantoye, C. A., 336
Ayres, K. A., 293, 299
Ayres, K. M., 241, 257, 311

B

Babikian, T., 400
Babrow, A. S., 291
Bacarese-Hamilton, M., 431
Badar, J., 106
Baggett, K. M., 303
Bagner, D. M., 209
Bailey, C. L., 473
Bailey, D. B., 236
Bain, S. K., 464
Baio, J., 292
Baird, G., 290, 294
Baker, T. L., 76, 132, 157
Bakian, A. V., 424
Bakken, J. P., 8, 46
Bal, A., 69, 73, 75, 77, 78, 157
Balandin, S., 428
Balboni, G., 246
Bales, B. L., 89
Ballantine, R., 396
Balu, R., 156
Bamond, M. J., 290, 299
Banda, D. R., 317
Banks, C. A. M., 70, 80
Banks, J. A., 70, 80
Banks, T., 71, 470
Barbosa-Leiker, C., 199
Barclay, L., 364
Bardin, J. A., 374
Barland, P., 400
Barnard-Brak, L., 17
Barned, N. E., 436
Barnes, M. A., 394
Barnhill, G. P., 307
Baron-Cohen, S., 289
Barraga, N. C., 358
Barrett, C., 295
Barrio, B. L., 105
Barroso, N. E., 209
Bartlett, J. J., 327
Barton, E. E., 220
Barton, M., 295, 301, 369
Barton-Arwood, S. M., 105–106
Basham, J. D., 80
Bassett, D., & Dunn, C., 158
Basten, M., 213
Bat-Chava, Y., 350

Bateman, B., 4
Bateman, D., 59
Bauer, A., 250
Bauer, A. M., 87
Baugh, C. M., 394
Bauman, M. L., 318
Baumer, P., 95, 105
Bavin, E., 297
Baxter, C. M., 12, 53
Bazzano, A., 295
Beadle-Brown, J., 421
Beal-Alvarez, J., 299
Beal-Alvarez, J. S., 334
Beall, J., 474
Beauchaine, T. P., 199, 200
Beauregard, E., 479
Becher, J. G., 402, 411
Becht, K., 80
Beck, L., 116
Beebe, S. A., 100, 101
Beebe, S. J., 101
Behrman, R. E., 238
Behuniak, P., 446
Beighley, J., 301
Beisse, K., 35
Beller, E., 17
Belva, B., 305
Benbow, C. P., 467
Bender, W. N., 16, 79
Ben-Itzchak, E., 317
Ben-Naim, S., 138
Benner, G. J., 212
Benner, J., 296
Bennett, A., 8
Bennett, D., 428
Bennett, K. D., 28
Bennett, L. H, 69
Bennett, S. V., 69
Benningfield, M. M., 213
Berg, A., 414
Bergbaum, A., 289, 290
Bergen, D., 464
Bergeron, R., 240
Bergmann, S., 18
Berkeley, S., 16
Berliner, D. C., 417
Berndsen, M., 324, 340
Bernier, R., 299
Berninger, V., 127, 129, 133
Berninger, V. W., 135
Bernstein, R., 242
Bernstein, R. R., 479
Berry-Kravis, E., 236
Berry Kuchle, L., 139
Bersani, H., 246
Besser, L. M., 391
Best, S. J., 389, 410
Bethell, C. D., 388
Bethune, K. S., 429, 431, 443
Bettelheim, B., 290
Bettini, E. A., 61
Beukelman, D. R., 429

Subject Index